THE OXFORD HANDBOOK OF
CHARLES S. PEIRCE

THE OXFORD HANDBOOK OF

CHARLES S. PEIRCE

Edited by
CORNELIS DE WAAL

OXFORD
UNIVERSITY PRESS

Oxford University Press is a department of the University of Oxford. It furthers the University's objective of excellence in research, scholarship, and education by publishing worldwide. Oxford is a registered trade mark of Oxford University Press in the UK and certain other countries.

Published in the United States of America by Oxford University Press
198 Madison Avenue, New York, NY 10016, United States of America.

© Oxford University Press 2024

All rights reserved. No part of this publication may be reproduced, stored in a retrieval system, or transmitted, in any form or by any means, without the prior permission in writing of Oxford University Press, or as expressly permitted by law, by license, or under terms agreed with the appropriate reproduction rights organization. Inquiries concerning reproduction outside the scope of the above should be sent to the Rights Department, Oxford University Press, at the address above.

You must not circulate this work in any other form
and you must impose this same condition on any acquirer.

Library of Congress Cataloging-in-Publication Data
Names: De Waal, Cornelis, editor.
Title: The Oxford handbook of Charles S. Peirce / [edited by] Cornelis de Waal.
Description: New York, NY : Oxford University Press, [2024] |
Includes bibliographical references and index. |
Identifiers: LCCN 2023040365 (print) | LCCN 2023040366 (ebook) |
ISBN 9780197548561 (hardback) | ISBN 9780197548592 |
ISBN 9780197548585 (epub)
Subjects: LCSH: Peirce, Charles S. (Charles Sanders), 1839–1914.
Classification: LCC B945.P44 O94 2024 (print) | LCC B945.P44 (ebook) |
DDC 191—dc23/eng/20231213
LC record available at https://lccn.loc.gov/2023040365
LC ebook record available at https://lccn.loc.gov/2023040366

DOI: 10.1093/oxfordhb/9780197548561.001.0001

Printed by Integrated Books International, United States of America

Contents

Preface	ix
List of Contributors	xi
The Significance of Charles Sanders Peirce for the Twenty-First Century	xvii
Cornelis de Waal	
Note on the Primary Literature	xxxi

PART I. LIFE AND CAREER

1. Peirce's Journey to the End of Inquiry: The Tenure of the Soul Daniel L. Everett	3
2. The Cosmopolitan Peirce: His Five Visits to Europe Jaime Nubiola and Sara Barrena	26
3. Peirce's Thwarted Career Cheryl Misak	43

PART II. PHENOMENOLOGY AND THE NORMATIVE SCIENCES

4. Peirce's Formal and Material Categories in Phenomenology Richard Kenneth Atkins	61
5. The Vicissitudes of Experience Nathan Houser	77
6. Charles S. Peirce on the Inquiry into the Discovery of Ideals, Norms, and Values Tiago da Costa e Silva	94
7. The Aesthetic Imperative: From Normative Science and Self-Control to Somaesthetics Richard Shusterman	111

8. Morality and Ethics in the Work of Charles Peirce 129
   James Jakób Liszka

9. Love and the Growth of Justice 148
   Juliana Acosta López de Mesa and Daniel G. Campos

PART III. LOGIC AND MATHEMATICS

10. Why Study Logic? 167
    Mark Migotti

11. Peirce's Philosophy of Logic 193
    Leila Haaparanta

12. Peirce's Abduction and Its Interpretations 208
    Ilkka Niiniluoto

13. Peirce's Theories of Generalized Propositions 226
    Frederik Stjernfelt

14. Existential Graphs: History and Interpretation 240
    Francesco Bellucci and Ahti-Veikko Pietarinen

15. Diagrammatic Thinking, Diagrammatic Representations, and the Moral Economy of Nineteenth-Century Science 261
    Chiara Ambrosio

16. The Logic and Mathematics of Charles Sanders Peirce 278
    Louis H. Kauffman

17. Advances in Peirce's Mathematics: A Short Survey (1960–2020) 299
    Fernando Zalamea

PART IV. PRAGMATISM

18. Pragmatisms? 315
    Philip Kitcher

19. Why Philosophers Must Be Pragmatists: Taking Cues from Peirce 335
    Cornelis de Waal

20. Theory, Practice, and Deliberation: Peirce's Pragmatism Comprehensively Conceived   350
    VINCENT COLAPIETRO

21. Pragmatic Clarification: Contexts and Purposes   367
    MATS BERGMAN

22. Peirce, Perception, and Empiricism   384
    AARON BRUCE WILSON

PART V. METAPHYSICS

23. Peirce on Reality and Existence   409
    ROBERT LANE

24. Scientific Pride and Metaphysical Prejudice: *Ens Quantum Ens*, Quantum Theory, and Peirce   423
    ROSA MAYORGA

25. Peirce on Kant's Refutation of Idealism   442
    GABRIELE GAVA

26. Peirce on Truth   458
    ANDREW HOWAT

27. Peirce and Religion   479
    GARY SLATER

PART VI. SCIENCE AND SEMIOTICS

28. A Science Like Any Other: A Peircean Philosophy of Sex?   499
    SHANNON DEA

29. Charles S. Peirce and the Feeling of Understanding: The Power and Limit of Science from a Pragmatist Perspective   514
    HERMAN C. D. G. DE REGT

30. Peirce's Views on Education and Learning   531
    TORJUS MIDTGARDEN

31. The Philosophical Relevance of Peirce's Historical Studies   550
    TULLIO VIOLA

32. Diagrams, Semiosis, and Peirce's Metaphor   567
    TONY JAPPY

33. Peirce on Biology: A Critical Review   585
    KALEVI KULL

34. Peirce's Universal Grammar: Some Implications for
    Modern Linguistics   601
    DANIEL L. EVERETT

Index   641

Preface

The *Oxford Handbook of Charles S. Peirce* brings together about three dozen essays that can be considered representative of current research on Peirce, as well as applications of his thought to present-day questions both within and outside philosophy. Naturally, a book like this can only scratch the surface. Much excellent work is being done that could not make it into a volume this size. The hope is that this handbook provides at least a helpful springboard that enables readers to find their way through the existing literature or that provides enough of an understanding of Peirce's thought to envision how it can be applied to one's own field. I would like to thank Peter Ohlin for being a wise, encouraging, and above all patient editor, as well as the contributors to this volume for their commitment to carrying the project to completion despite significant challenges caused by the COVID-19 pandemic. Finally, the editing of this volume received generous and most welcome support from the Stephen J. Kern Programmatic Fund for Philosophy at Indiana University Indianapolis.

List of Contributors

Juliana Acosta López de Mesa is professor of philosophy at Universidad de Antioquia, Medellín, Colombia. Her main fields of academic interests are ethics, justice, and Peirce's pragmaticism. She has published articles on pragmatism such as "Peirce and Aesthetic Education" (2018) and, in coauthorship, "A New Approach to the Problem of the Order of the Ten Trichotomies and the Classification of Sixty-Six Types of Signs in Peirce's Late Speculative Grammar" (2021) and "Peirce's Open Community in Light of Sentimentalism and Normative Sciences" (2022).

Chiara Ambrosio is associate professor in history and philosophy of science at the Department of Science and Technology Studies, University College London. Her research focuses on representations across art and science, nineteenth- and twentieth-century visual culture, and the relations between classical pragmatism and science, with a particular focus on Charles S. Peirce.

Richard Kenneth Atkins is associate professor of philosophy at Boston College. He is the author of *Peirce on Inference* (2024), *Charles S. Peirce's Phenomenology* (2018), and *Peirce and the Conduct of Life* (2016). His articles have appeared in *Transactions of the Charles S. Peirce Society*, *Synthese*, *Journal of the American Philosophical Association*, and *European Journal of Philosophy*, among other venues.

Sara Barrena is director of the Grupo de Estudios Peirceanos at the University of Navarra, Spain. She has written extensively on Charles S. Peirce and American pragmatism, and she has translated numerous Peirce texts into Spanish. Her publications include *La razón creativa* (2007), *La belleza en Charles S. Peirce* (2015), and *Pragmatismo y educación: Charles S. Peirce y John Dewey en las aulas* (2015). In 2022 she coauthored with Jaime Nubiola a volume on *Los viajes europeos de Charles S. Peirce, 1870–1883*. She combines her dedication to philosophy with creative writing.

Francesco Bellucci is associate professor of semiotics at the University of Bologna. He is the author of *Peirce's Speculative Grammar* (2017), editor of *Charles S. Peirce: Selected Writings on Semiotics* (2020), and coauthor (with C. Marmo) of *Signs and Demonstrations from Aristotle to Radulphus Brito* (2023).

Mats Bergman is associate professor of communication at the Swedish School of Social Science of the University of Helsinki. In addition to Peirce studies, his research interests include communication theory and the philosophy of communication, media, and communication ethics; pragmatistic philosophy and social theory; and propaganda studies. Bergman is the author of *Peirce's Philosophy of Communication: The Rhetorical Underpinnings of the Theory of Signs* (2009) and *Moral Agency in Communication Ethics: A Pragmatist Approach* (forthcoming).

Daniel G. Campos is professor and chairperson in the philosophy department, Brooklyn College of the City University of New York. He is the author of *Loving Immigrants in America: An Experiential Philosophy of Personal Interaction* (2017), structured by Peircean phenomenology and ethics of love, and of several articles on Peirce's logic of mathematical and scientific inquiry.

Vincent Colapietro is Liberal Arts Research Professor Emeritus at Pennsylvania State University and Adjunct Professor of Humanities at University of Rhode Island. Colapietro is the author of *Peirce's Approach to the Self* (1988), *A Glossary of Semiotics* (1993), and *Fateful Shapes of Human Freedom* (2003), as well as numerous journal articles. His areas of specialization include American pragmatism, dominant intellectual traditions in the United States, and philosophical naturalism.

Tiago da Costa e Silva studied industrial design and semiotics. He resides in Germany, where he worked at the Universität der Künste–Berlin and at the Cluster of Excellence "Image Knowledge Gestaltung: An Interdisciplinary Laboratory" of the Humboldt Universität zu Berlin. A specialist in semiotics, he received the Charles S. Peirce Young Scholar Award in 2017. Further research interests include design, engineering, art, cultural techniques, and pragmatism. He currently works as an independent researcher and writer.

Shannon Dea is professor of philosophy and dean of arts at the University of Regina in Canada. She is the author of *Beyond the Binary: Thinking About Sex and Gender* (2016) and numerous articles and book chapters on pragmatism, history of philosophy, social philosophy, and gender studies. Shannon lives and works on Treaty 4, the territory of the nêhiyawak, Anihšināpēk, Dakota, Lakota, and Nakoda, and the homeland of the Métis/Michif nation.

Herman C. D. G. de Regt is associate professor of epistemology and philosophy of science at Tilburg University, the Netherlands, and currently the director of TiLIA, the Tilburg Center of Philosophy and Society. He was a visiting professor in Cambridge (UK) and Princeton (US). With two colleagues, he published the handbook *Exploring Humans: Philosophy of Science for the Social Sciences—A Historical Introduction* (9th rev. ed., 2023). His most recent research project deals with the role of the feeling of understanding in science.

Cornelis de Waal is professor of philosophy at Indiana University Indianapolis, and editor-in-chief of the *Transactions of the Charles S. Peirce Society*. Previously, he was one of the editors of *The Writings of Charles S. Peirce: A Chronological Edition*. De Waal edited several books, including *American New Realism 1910–1920* (3 vols., 2001), *Charles Peirce's Illustrations of the Logic of Science* (2014), and *Susan Haack: A Lady of Distinctions* (2007). His own books include *Introducing Pragmatism: A Tool for Rethinking Philosophy* (2022) and *Charles S. Peirce: A Guide for the Perplexed* (2013).

Daniel L. Everett is Trustee Professor of Cognitive Sciences at Bentley University in Waltham, Massachusetts. He has also held appointments at the State University of Campinas, the University of Pittsburgh, and the University of Manchester. He has published extensively on Indigenous languages of the Americas, as well as all subfields of theoretical linguistics. His book, *Charles Peirce and the Philosophy of Linguistics*, will be appearing from Oxford University Press in 2024 and his biography of Peirce, *American Aristotle*, is in currently in progress for Princeton University Press.

Gabriele Gava is associate professor of theoretical philosophy at the University of Turin. He has published articles in leading philosophical journals on Peirce, pragmatism, Kant, and epistemology. He is the author of *Peirce's Account of Purposefulness: A Kantian Perspective* (2014) and *Kant's* Critique of Pure Reason *and the Method of Metaphysics* (2023).

Leila Haaparanta is professor of philosophy (emerita) at Tampere University and docent of theoretical philosophy at the University of Helsinki. She has published on the history of logic, early-twentieth-century analytic philosophy and phenomenology, epistemology, philosophy of mind and language, philosophy of religion, and pragmatism. Currently, she focuses on theories of judgment and assertion, epistemology of testimony, and early-twentieth-century philosophy. Her edited works include *The Development of Modern Logic* (2009) and *Categories of Being* (with H. J. Koskinen, 2012).

Nathan Houser is professor emeritus of philosophy at Indiana University in Indianapolis. He has served as director of the Peirce Edition Project and the Institute for American Thought and as president of the Charles S. Peirce Society. From 1993 to 2009 he was general editor for the Indianapolis critical edition of Peirce's *Writings* and he co-edited the two-volume *Essential Peirce* and *Studies in the Logic of Charles Sanders Peirce* (1997). He is the author of many articles on Peirce's pragmatic and semiotic philosophy.

Andrew Howat is professor of philosophy at California State University, Fullerton, in Orange County, California. His research focuses on Peirce, pragmatism, theories of truth, metaphysics, philosophy of language, and philosophical methods. He has published articles in journals such as *Philosophical Studies*, *Erkenntnis*, *Synthese* and *Transactions of the Charles Sanders Peirce Society*.

Tony Jappy is *professeur honoraire* at the University of Perpignan Via Domitia, France. He has published numerous articles on linguistics, semiotics, and visual semiotics. His research is devoted primarily to C. S. Peirce's post-1904 six-correlate system of semiotics, which is the subject of the monographs *Introduction to Peircean Visual Semiotics* (2013) and *Peirce's Twenty-Eight Classes of Signs and the Philosophy of Representation* (2016), as well as a forthcoming monograph *Developing a Neo-Peircean Approach to Signs*. Jappy also is the general editor of *The Bloomsbury Companion to Contemporary Peircean Semiotics* (2019).

Louis H. Kauffman is a mathematician, topologist, and professor of mathematics emeritus at the University of Illinois at Chicago. His work is primarily in knot theory, connecting it with statistical mechanics, quantum theory, algebra, combinatorics, and foundations of mathematics and physics. Kauffman is known for his discovery of the bracket state sum model of the Jones polynomial and for his discovery of a generalization of the Jones polynomial called the Kauffman polynomial, for his discovery of virtual knot theory and other topological structures. His books include *On Knots* (1987), *Quantum Topology* (with Randy A. Baadhio, 1993), *Formal Knot Theory* (2006), and *Knots and Physics* (4th ed., 2012).

Philip Kitcher is John Dewey Professor of Philosophy Emeritus at Columbia University and has written books on a wide range of philosophical topics. *Moral Progress* (2021) and *The Main Enterprise of the World: Rethinking Education* (2021) form the first two parts of an envisaged "pragmatism trilogy."

Kalevi Kull is professor of biosemiotics at the Department of Semiotics, University of Tartu, Estonia. His research focuses on semiotic phenomena of life, processes responsible for diversity, umwelt, subjective time and space, semiotic approaches in biology, theory of general semiotics, history of biosemiotics, and ecosemiotics. Since 2015, he is the president of the International Society for Biosemiotic Studies. He is a co-editor of the journal *Sign Systems Studies* and of three book series (*Biosemiotics*; *Semiotics, Communication and Cognition*; and *Tartu Semiotics Library*), all specializing in semiotics.

Robert Lane is professor of philosophy at the University of West Georgia. He is the author of *Peirce on Realism and Idealism* (2018), editor for Peirce submissions to the *Transactions of the Charles S. Peirce Society*, and associate editor of Susan Haack (ed.), *Pragmatism, Old and New* (2006).

James Jakób Liszka is senior scholar at the Institute for Ethics in Public Life and professor of philosophy at the State University of New York, University at Plattsburgh. He is professor emeritus at the University of Alaska, Anchorage. He is the author of *Charles Peirce on Ethics, Esthetics and the Normative Sciences* (2021), *Pragmatist Ethics: A Problem-Based Approach to What Matters* (2021), *A General Introduction to the Semeiotic of Charles S. Peirce* (1996), *Moral Competence* (1999), *The Semiotic of Myth* (1989), and *The Philosopher's Alaska* (2023).

Rosa Mayorga is chairperson of arts and philosophy at Miami Dade College, Wolfson Campus. The author of *From Realism to Realicism: On the Metaphysics of Charles Sanders Peirce* (2007), her work has appeared in *The Normative Thought of Charles Sanders Peirce* (2012), *Pragmatism and Objectivity* (2016), and *Charles S. Peirce Ciencia, filosofia y verdad* (2017) and in *Transactions of the Charles S. Peirce Society, European Journal of Pragmatism and American Philosophy, Cognitio*, and *Contemporary Pragmatism*, to name a few. She served as president of the Charles S. Peirce Society in 2022.

Torjus Midtgarden is professor at the Centre for the Study of the Sciences and the Humanities at the University of Bergen. His research interests are social and political philosophy, philosophy of science, and American pragmatism—in particular, the philosophy of Charles S. Peirce and John Dewey. He has contributed to several book projects and published articles on pragmatism and its relevance for contemporary philosophy in journals such as *Transactions of the Charles S. Peirce Society*, *Journal of the History of Philosophy*, *Contemporary Pragmatism*, *European Journal of Social Theory*, *Philosophy and Social Criticism*, *Semiotica*, and *Revue Internationale de Philosophie*.

Mark Migotti is professor of philosophy at the University of Calgary. He works in the history of philosophy, focusing on ancient philosophy, nineteenth-century German philosophy, classical American pragmatism, epistemology, ethics, and philosophy of history. Migotti is the author of *Ethics and the Life of the Mind: Nietzsche's Critique of Modern Morality* (2009), as well as numerous papers.

Cheryl Misak is university professor and professor of philosophy at the University of Toronto. Her books include *Frank Ramsey: A Sheer Excess of Powers* (2020), *Cambridge Pragmatism: From Peirce and James to Ramsey and Wittgenstein* (2016), *The American Pragmatists* (2013), *Truth and the End of Inquiry: A Peircean Account of Truth* (1991), *Truth, Politics, Morality: Pragmatism and Deliberation* (1999), and edited volumes such as *The Cambridge Companion to C. S. Peirce* (2004), *The Oxford Handbook of American Philosophy* (2008), and *The Practical Turn: Pragmatism in Britain in the Long Twentieth Century* (with Huw Price, 2017).

Ilkka Niiniluoto is professor emeritus of theoretical philosophy at the University of Helsinki, Finland, where he also served as rector (2003–2008) and chancellor (2008–2013). In 2017 he received the title Academician of Science. Niiniluoto's defense of scientific realism, inspired by Charles S. Peirce, employs his original explication of the notion of truthlikeness or verisimilitude. Niiniluoto's main works in philosophy of science include *Is Science Progressive?* (1984), *Truthlikeness* (1987), *Critical Scientific Realism* (1999), *Truth-Seeking by Abduction* (2018), and *Beauty, Truth, and Justice* (2022).

Jaime Nubiola is professor of philosophy at the University of Navarra, Spain. He is the author of 16 books and 150 papers on philosophy of language, history of analytic philosophy, American philosophy, C. S. Peirce, and pragmatism. In 1994 he launched in Navarre the Grupo de Estudios Peirceanos to promote the study of C. S. Peirce and pragmatism, especially in the Spanish-speaking countries (http://www.unav.es/gep/). He was president of the Charles S. Peirce Society (2008). In 2022 he coauthored with Sara Barrena a volume on *Los viajes europeos de Charles S. Peirce, 1870–1883*.

Ahti-Veikko Pietarinen is professor at the Department of Religion and Philosophy, Hong Kong Baptist University, and at its Transdisciplinary Theoretical and Ethical Artificial Intelligence Lab. Pietarinen's research on the human and artificial minds and their complexities has been published in over one hundred Web of Science journal articles. His work addresses emerging human and machine reasoning competences, capabilities, and defects; diverse and creative aspects of cognitions; signs, meanings, and notations; and history and philosophy of logic, pragmatism, and scientific method; as well as Charles Peirce's manuscripts.

Richard Shusterman is the Dorothy F. Schmidt Eminent Scholar in the Humanities at Florida Atlantic University and director of its Center for Body, Mind, and Culture. His

Pragmatist Aesthetics is published in fifteen languages. His books on philosophy and somaesthetics include *Body Consciousness* (2008), *Thinking through the Body* (2012), *Ars Erotica* (2021), and *Philosophy and the Art of Writing* (2022). The French government awarded him the title of Chevalier dans l'ordre des palmes académiques for his philosophical and cultural work.

Gary Slater is a research associate at the Institute for Christian Social Sciences at the University of Münster. He leads a grant-funded research project, "Borders: Religious, Political, and Planetary," funded by the German Research Council (DFG). His most recent monograph is *Our Common, Bordered Home: Laudato si' and the Promise of an Integrated Migration-Ecological Ethics* (2023). Trained in Christian theology and the pragmatic philosophical tradition, particularly C. S. Peirce, he writes on religious ethics: research topics include migration, ecological devastation, interreligious dialogue, and international borders. He also edits the *American Journal of Theology and Philosophy*.

Frederik Stjernfelt is a Danish writer and professor of philosophy at Aalborg University, Copenhagen, where he co-directs the Humanomics Center. His research interests cover cognitive semiotics, philosophy of science, intellectual history, theory of literature, and political philosophy. Stjernfelt's books include *Diagrammatology: An Investigation on the Borderlines of Phenomenology, Ontology, and Semiotics* (2007), *Natural Propositions: The Actuality of Peirce's Doctrine of Dicisigns* (2014), and *The Democratic Contradictions of Multiculturalism* (with Jens-Martin Eriksen, 2012).

Tullio Viola is assistant professor of philosophy of art and culture at Maastricht University in the Netherlands. His research focuses on historical epistemology and the philosophy of culture. He is the author of *Peirce on the Uses of History* (2020). In addition to his work on Peirce and pragmatism, he has written on French and German thought and the interplay between philosophy and the sociocultural sciences in the nineteenth century.

Aaron Bruce Wilson is associate professor of philosophy at South Texas College, in McAllen, Texas. He is currently executive director of the Charles S. Peirce Society. He is also the author of *Peirce's Empiricism: Its Roots and Originality* (2016) and about a dozen other articles related to Peirce.

Fernando Zalamea is professor of mathematics at Universidad Nacional de Colombia. After earning a PhD in category theory and recursion theory, Zalamea has been working in alternative logics, Peirce and Lautman studies, and the philosophy of modern (1830–1950) and contemporary (post-1950) mathematics. His recent *Grothendieck: Una guía a la obra matemática y filosófica* (2019) is the first complete guide to Grothendieck's work. He is the author of thirty books around cultural studies, philosophy, and mathematics. He has been included as one of *100 Global Minds. The Most Daring Cross-Disciplinary Thinkers in the World* (Roads 2015).

The Significance of Charles Sanders Peirce for the Twenty-First Century

CORNELIS DE WAAL

CHARLES Sanders Peirce (pronounced *purse*, not *pierce*) was born on September 10, 1839, in Cambridge, Massachusetts, as the second child of the renowned Harvard astronomer and mathematician Benjamin Peirce.[1] In addition to his professorship at Harvard, Peirce's father was involved in the creation of the National Academy of Sciences and the Smithsonian Institution, and from 1867 to 1874 he oversaw the US Coast Survey as its third superintendent. The Coast Survey was at the time America's premier scientific institution. Benjamin also played an active role in his son's education, mostly by giving him interesting problems and seeing how he would solve them. As Peirce later reminiscences, "he very seldom could be entrapped into disclosing to me any theorem or rule of arithmetic. He would give an example; but the rest I must think out for myself" (R619:5, 1909). In this way Peirce acquired at a young age the habit of thinking things out for himself, a habit that no doubt added to his originality as a thinker.[2]

Peirce's father was not the only influence. When Peirce was twelve, his uncle, Charles Henry Peirce, helped him set up a chemistry laboratory at home. Charles Henry had been introduced to Justus von Liebig's experimental method for teaching chemistry. Rejecting the overly theoretical way that chemistry was being taught, Liebig gave each student a series of bottles marked with letters of the alphabet. The student was then asked to analyze the contents of each bottle, guided only by an introductory textbook in qualitative analysis. In brief, Peirce was already deeply immersing himself in the experimental method at the age of twelve, and again, working out problems by himself. Moreover, as the Liebig method is a very hands-on way of learning chemical analysis—one where the content of each bottle had to be determined by observing the practical consequences of the operations performed on it—it helped steer Peirce in the direction of pragmatism.

It was also at the age of twelve that Peirce was introduced to logic. It happened sort of by accident. As Peirce narrates it, he stumbled on a copy of Whately's *Elements of Logic* in his older brother's room, and he promptly devoured it. Later, he repeatedly wrote that from then on logic was his strongest passion. In fact, his general approach both in philosophy and in science was that of trying to penetrate the logic of things. Peirce quickly learned, however, that logic itself needed significant improvement, as it was not well adapted to scientific inquiry. Logic had narrowly concerned itself with deduction, whereas science had come to rely heavily on induction as well as a third mode of inference that Peirce called abduction. In fact, one may look at Peirce's philosophical work as a lifelong attempt at writing a logic book, or, more precisely, a book on the logic of inquiry.

At sixteen, Peirce attended Harvard University, graduating with an AB in 1859. Following his graduation, he joined the US Coast Survey as a temporary aide. It proved the beginning of a highly successful scientific career, one that was greatly facilitated by his powerful father. On July 1, 1861, he was appointed a regular aide, which exempted him from military service and kept him out of the war (the American Civil War had begun less than three months earlier and lasted until 1865). Also in 1861, Peirce entered Harvard's Lawrence Scientific School, taking the ScB, summa cum laude, in 1863. He finished his MA the year before.

In 1867, Peirce's father reluctantly accepted the position of chief administrative officer, or superintendent, of a rather troubled Coast Survey, a position he held until 1874. During his brief tenure as superintendent, Benjamin transformed the Coast Survey into an internationally recognized scientific institution. A central pillar of the new Coast Survey was gravitation research. On November 30, 1872, he put his son in charge of this, which required giving him the proper administrative clout. To make this happen, Charles Peirce was promoted to assistant to the superintendent, the second highest rank in the Coast Survey. During the same period, Peirce continued astronomical research he had started a few years earlier at the Harvard College Observatory, which led to the publication, in 1878, of *Photometric Researches*—the only book he authored that was published during his lifetime.

Between 1870 and 1883, Peirce traveled five times to Europe on Coast Survey business.[3] The first trip, which culminated with the 1870 solar eclipse, involved extensive travel through Europe. The purpose of the second trip, which lasted from April 1875 till August of the following year, was to connect American and European gravitation research. Peirce learned to use the new convertible pendulum and compare it with the invariable pendulums he had been using. In the process, he discovered a mistake in the European measurements caused by flexure in their pendulum stand. Based in part on his European experience, Peirce also invented a new pendulum, which became known as the Peirce pendulum. Other notable scientific work of this period includes determining the length of the meter from a wavelength of light, rather than using a prototype meter bar of platinum and iridium, and the quincuncial world map. The latter showcases Peirce's acumen in mathematics, which throughout his life continued to be an area of focus. Peirce expanded on his father's work in linear associative algebra. He developed criteria for distinguishing finite from infinite collections and between different types of infinite collections. The latter led him to the concept of a supermultitudinous collection in which the elements become so tightly "welded together" that they come to form a true continuum. Peirce further worked on topology, knot theory, and linkage problems. Much of this mathematical work he carried into his philosophy, including logic, cosmology, the theory of the categories, and the logical graphs. In many ways, what we have in Peirce is a mathematician and scientist who delved into philosophical questions often from the vantage point of logic conceived as a theory of inquiry.

It was on one of his travels, while crossing the ocean on a steamer, that publisher William Henry Appleton asked Peirce to write something for the *Popular Science Monthly*. This became Peirce's "Illustrations of the Logic of Science," a series of six papers, which, among other things, introduced pragmatism—a school in philosophy for which Peirce was later crowned the founder. Peirce had already made his mark with a series of technical papers, mostly on logic, in the *Proceedings of the American Academy of Arts and Sciences*, as well as three strongly anti-Cartesian papers for the *Journal of Speculative Philosophy*. Observing that "most modern philosophers have been, in effect, Cartesians," Peirce concluded that "modern science and modern logic require us to stand upon a very different platform from this" (W2:212)—a platform that he subsequently set forth to develop. The American Academy series includes Peirce's pivotal "On a New List of Categories," whereas the *Journal of Speculative Philosophy* series is considered by some the starting point of postmodernism.

In 1879, shortly after publishing the *Popular Science Monthly* papers, Peirce was appointed lecturer in logic at Johns Hopkins University, while continuing his work for the Coast Survey. Johns Hopkins had opened its doors only a few years earlier as the first research university in the US. Though successful in academic terms, Peirce's tenure at John Hopkins did not last long. The divorce from his first wife, Zina Fay, followed two days later by the marriage to his French mistress, Juliette Froissy, is thought to have played a considerable role in his dismissal from Johns Hopkins in 1884.[4] After his dismissal, Peirce and Juliette moved first to Washington, DC, and then to New York City, to finally settle down in a farmhouse near Milford, Pennsylvania, situated at the road to Port Jervis, which had a direct connection by train to New York City. At the time, Peirce was still employed by the Coast Survey, until his dismissal there as well, at the end of 1891. Peirce spent the next twenty-three years in Milford in relative isolation as an independent scholar, spending most of his time writing. During this period, he wrote numerous book reviews, published important papers for *The Monist*, gave influential lecture series—including the 1898 Cambridge Conference Lectures, the 1903 Lowell Lectures, and the 1903 Harvard Lectures—and kept a lively intellectual correspondence with Paul Carus, Francis Russell, William James, Josiah Royce, Victoria Lady Welby, and many others.[5] It is also during this period that James began to promote pragmatism while crediting Peirce for it. What Peirce lacked, though, was an active academic setting, one where his ideas could directly influence students who would then form the next generation of scholars. It is generally believed that had Peirce been able to continue teaching at Johns Hopkins, or elsewhere, philosophy in America would have looked very different. Due to a lack of regular income starting at age fifty-two, Juliette's expensive health issues, and poor financial management, Peirce died in abject poverty on April 19, 1914.

This raises the question, one that is taken up in the opening chapter of this handbook, whether Peirce was essentially a failure, even if a brilliant one. Insofar as Peirce entered the minds of philosophers in the early parts of the twentieth century, this seems to have been the general sentiment. This view was further reinforced by vivid tales about his personal life—tales that portrayed him as an immoral and undisciplined person with a knack for turning people against him. The worst offender is no doubt Mina Samuels, who, in *The Queen of Cups*, a fictional account of Juliette's life, describes Peirce as a brilliant but difficult man, prone to violence and unable to keep a job, whose drug addiction made him all but dysfunctional.[6] It was further reinforced by how the *Collected Papers* were edited, as they left the impression of a brilliant but undisciplined mind by combining comments written decades apart as if they were written conjointly. Stories about the vast trove of unpublished manuscripts also led to the misapprehension that he must not have published much during his life—a view that is easily refuted by the roughly twelve thousand pages that *did* make it into print. A discussion of the unpublished manuscripts with the various posthumous editions that came out of it (and that are still coming out of it) can be found in the "Note on the Primary Literature" that follows this introduction. From where we are now standing, however, it is safe to say that Peirce survived the twentieth century with flying colors and is likely to be a permanent fixture in the history of philosophy. The chapters that follow most certainly confirm this.

Peirce's Life and Career

The question whether Peirce's life was truly a failure is taken up by Daniel L. Everett in the opening chapter of this handbook. Everett seeks to debunk the still-common notion that Peirce led a miserable life and that he could have done so much better intellectually had he been less self-destructive. The standard story is that after he was fired from Johns Hopkins and the US Coast Survey—having already been declared persona non grata at Harvard—Peirce spent the final decades of his life isolated in the small town of Milford, Pennsylvania, while unsuccessfully trying to make ends meet. Everett's account provides a great anodyne to the trope of the unhappy Peirce who brought poverty and ostracism onto himself and Juliette, and whose legacy would have been destroyed had Josiah Royce not saved his manuscripts by having them brought to Harvard. Everett argues that there is no evidence that Peirce was any more difficult (or eccentric) than other successful thinkers, that despite all hardship Peirce and Juliette lived a happy life overall, and that Peirce, far from an intellectual failure, truly embodied what Ralph Waldo Emerson had termed the self-reliance of the true American scholar: free to develop his ideas unburdened by the weight of God, religion, and society. Though no university would grant him tenure (or even a job), Everett argues that "Peirce created his own tenure in all of his life's circumstances and arguably this independence was much greater and led to more significant results than any other way of life for him might have" and that, on a personal level, the Peirces lived a life that can be considered happy and fulfilling.

In the next chapter, the focus is on the years that Peirce was perhaps most successful when considered in traditional terms. In "The Cosmopolitan Peirce," Jaime Nubiola and

Sara Barrena discuss a period during which Peirce was deeply engaged with the scientific community. They focus specifically on his five voyages to Europe (briefly touched upon also by Everett), all on behest of the US Coast Survey. According to Nubiola and Barrena, Peirce's travels greatly affected his outlook on scientific inquiry and on life and culture more generally. They made him a true cosmopolitan thinker for the remainder of his life. Particularly, his first trip was instrumental to the development of his pragmatism and his continued insistence that science is the product of a community of investigators, rather than of solitary geniuses. It also pointed him, Nubiola and Barrena explain, toward the importance of esthetics and the challenges of trying to give expression to one's experience—something he experimented with when writing his fictional tale "Embroidered Thessaly" (W8, sel. 51, 1892 and *c.* 1897) and that came to play a central role after the turn of the century when he was seeking to connect phenomenology to metaphysics through esthetics, ethics, and logic.

The third and final biographical chapter, "Peirce's Thwarted Career," by Cheryl Misak, discusses Peirce's problematic relation with academia, especially Harvard and Johns Hopkins, but also the US Coast Survey. Like Everett, Misak recognizes in Peirce the embodiment of the American scholar that Emerson had called for, but she also emphasizes Zina Fay's description of her husband as a brilliant but erratic genius, one who proved to be too erratic for university and governmental administrators to handle, even though his contributions to logic and philosophy were well recognized, as was the tremendous impact he had on his students. The consequences, Misak argues, were disastrous, not just for Peirce personally but also for the state of knowledge within the US in general. According to Misak, had Peirce been allowed to continue to educate students (recall that Johns Hopkins was a graduate research university), the course of philosophy in the US would have been very different, and much for the better. Misak thus concludes that in dismissing this most brilliant mind the presidents of Harvard and Johns Hopkins not only failed Peirce, but also failed America.

The remainder of the handbook follows, very roughly and not without some violence, Peirce's division of the sciences of discovery. It begins with phenomenology; runs through the normative sciences of esthetics, ethics, and logic; touches upon mathematics; and then moves on to pragmatism, metaphysics, and semiotics. The handbook concludes with a few examples of Peirce's influence, actual or potential, in various disciplines.

Phenomenology and the Normative Sciences

In Chapter 4, "Peirce's Formal and Material Categories in Phenomenology," Richard Atkins discusses Peirce's phenomenology, or phaneroscopy, as Peirce himself liked to call it. Phenomenology, the most basic of the positive sciences of discovery is, for Peirce, primarily an observational and classificatory science. Its main purpose is to identify the basic constituents, or categories, that apply to "anything that can come before the mind in any sense whatsoever" (R336:2, 1904). For that reason, Peirce also called this discipline categorics. In this fourth chapter, Atkins explains what phaneroscopy is and why it is important and discusses Peirce's work on the formal and material categories. Peirce spent most of his efforts on the former, leaving only hints regarding the latter. According to Atkins, Peirce believed that it was possible to construe something like Mendeleev's periodic table for phaneroscopy, albeit that this remained clearly an unfinished project and one for which the prospects are quite uncertain.

In the next chapter, "The Vicissitudes of Experience," Nathan Houser takes a closer look at experience. Proceeding from Peirce's conception of experience as framed by his doctrine of categories, Houser seeks to develop a more integrated general Peircean theory of experience by drawing on such notions as consciousness, perception, and semiosis and by making connections with current philosophers, such as Daniel Dennett. Rejecting a nominalist empiricism, Peirce's theory of perception gives us, Houser argues, a unified world of experience, one where general conceptions and abstract objects are not impotent abstractions but can really influence events and help shape the world to come.

With Tiago da Costa e Silva's "Charles S. Peirce on the Inquiry into the Discovery of Ideals, Norms, and Values," we enter the domain of the normative sciences. Peirce's interest in ethics and later esthetics was primarily motivated by his desire to give an account of logic (at times identifying it with semiotics), which he came to realize was a normative science. Da Costa e Silva confines himself largely to the first two normative sciences Peirce distinguished, esthetics and ethics, and how they feature within what Peirce called heuretic sciences, or sciences of discovery.

A quite different avenue into Peirce's esthetics is found in Richard Shusterman's "The Aesthetic Imperative: From Normative Science and Self-Control to Somaesthetics." According to Shusterman, Peirce's views on aesthetics not only contributed to the development of a pragmatist aesthetics but also are pertinent for the pragmatist projects of somaesthetics—an approach to aesthetics that foregrounds bodily experience—and of the art of living.

James Jacób Liszka's "Morality and Ethics in the Work of Charles Peirce" brings us into the domain of ethics. Though Peirce never completed a systematic account of ethics, Liszka argues that we can find in his work the outline of an ethics grammar, critic, and rhetoric—a threefold division that emerges in a more developed form in Peirce's logic. Conceiving of ethics in this manner, Liszka argues, provides us with interesting insights that are relevant to current debates.

In "Love and the Growth of Justice," Juliana Acosta López de Mesa and Daniel G. Campos take Peirce's notion of agape as he developed it in his cosmology as a sentiment that nourishes and sustains human ethical life in a way that furthers the growth of concrete reasonableness in human communities—especially as it manifests itself in the ideal of justice. With concrete reasonableness, Peirce meant reason insofar as it has become embodied in the universe, which, given his evolutionary take on the universe, is always incipient, always in a state of growth (EP2:255). Connecting justice with the ideal of human flourishing, Acosta López de Mesa and Campos conclude that agapastic love encourages the development of just communities wherein such flourishing is possible.

Logic and Mathematics

The next section of the handbook discusses Peirce's work in logic and semeiotic (or semiotics), two terms Peirce occasionally used interchangeably. The first chapter in this section, Mark Migotti's "Why Study Logic?," details Peirce's work on *The Minute Logic*, one of Peirce's more significant attempts at writing a logic book. Migotti is specifically interested in exploring how this question—which is also the title of one of the book's original chapters—informs Peirce's own conception of logic. As Migotti shows, to properly grasp what logic is, we must pay serious attention to why it is worth studying. This because the answer to the question of why we should study logic will shape the answer to the question of what logic is.

In line with the previous chapter, Leila Haaparanta argues in "Peirce's Philosophy of Logic" that what informs Peirce's conception of logic is the idea of the primacy of the practical. Haaparanta examines a variety of issues, ranging from Peirce's fallibilism to his ideas of a three-valued logic. She concludes the chapter with a discussion of the relation between logic and psychology, arguing that Peirce's emphasis on practical reason is not reconcilable with a logical psychologism.

Peirce is perhaps most famous for having distinguished, besides deduction and induction, a third form of inference, which he called abduction, though he used other terms for it as well. In "Peirce's Abduction and Its Interpretations," Ilkka Niiniluoto discusses Peirce's views on abduction—which he concisely describes as reasoning from effects to causes, or from surprising observations to explanatory theories—and he puts them within the context of contemporary debates, especially within philosophy of science.

The following chapter, "Peirce's Theories of Generalized Propositions," by Frederik Stjernfelt, discusses Peirce's theories of propositions, especially his mature theories. Stjernfelt does so with a special focus on how the notion of proposition becomes increasingly generalized such as to encompass all truth-claiming signs. Stjernfelt further details how propositions relate to terms and feature within arguments, as well as how they relate to notions such as truth, reference, facts, and states of things. Finally, Stjernfelt discerns in Peirce the beginnings of a speech act theory.

Partly inspired by how chemists depict the combining capacity, or affinity, of atoms, as well as his work in mathematics, Peirce long experimented with graphical renderings of logic, effectively aiming for a geometric rather than an algebraic approach to mathematical logic. The next four chapters discuss a variety of issues related to the graphs.

In "Existential Graphs: History and Interpretation," by Francesco Bellucci and Ahti-Veikko Pietarinen, we find a survey of the evolution of Peirce's graphical experiments, running from the early 1880s, through the discovery of the existential graphs in 1896, to Peirce's later work after the turn of the century.

In "Diagrammatic Thinking, Diagrammatic Representations, and the Moral Economy of Nineteenth-Century Science," Chiara Ambrosio takes a broader and more historiographic approach to Peirce's use of diagrams, or graphs, arguing that the nineteenth century was a period during which the graphical representation of knowledge truly burgeoned. Ambrosio connects this interest in graphs not only with the need for the presentation and evaluation of rapidly increasing amounts of data, but also with the professionalization of science and how scientists came to understand themselves as scientists. In her chapter, Ambrosio identifies a relatively wide variety of influences on the development of graphical logic in Peirce.

In "The Logic and Mathematics of Charles S. Peirce," mathematician Louis H. Kauffman discusses several aspects of Peirce's views on mathematics and mathematical logic while drawing connections with Gottlob Frege (1848–1925) and George Spencer-Brown (1923–2016). Kauffman begins by discussing a system of logic devised by Peirce that is based on a single sign for inference, which he called the sign of illation—a sign that casts implication in terms of the logical operators for disjunction and negation. Kauffman next turns to Peirce's graphical logic and its relationship to both his ideas about infinity and infinitesimals and his theory that we are not just sign users, but that we too are a sign—that is, Peirce's doctrine of the man-sign.

In the concluding chapter of this section, Fernando Zalamea provides us with a short survey of advances in Peirce's mathematics over the past sixty years. In part, what Zalamea aims to do is to show how more contemporary developments help us better understand Peirce's original contributions. While doing so, Zalamea concentrates on four central themes: topology and combinatorics, the continuum, existential graphs, and the pragmatic maxim. We already encountered the graphs, and we return to the pragmatic maxim, and pragmatism more generally, next.

Pragmatism

Peirce is best known as the father of pragmatism, which, like analytic philosophy or phenomenology, can be seen as a distinctive approach to doing philosophy. The official birthplace of pragmatism lies in meetings of the Metaphysical Club, a group of young men who met periodically in Cambridge, Massachusetts, during the early 1870s. One of these young men was Peirce. Though his presentation to the club has not been recovered, his take on pragmatism resurfaced, albeit without mentioning the term, as the third way of making our ideas clear in the second of his *Popular Science Monthly* papers. It was William James who later popularized the idea, crediting Peirce for it.

In "Pragmatisms?" Philip Kitcher compares the pragmatisms of Peirce, James, and Dewey. Concentrating on Peirce's *Popular Science* papers of the late 1870s, Kitcher argues that there is no single "pragmatism" that is shared by all three thinkers. Examining their takes (and use) of Peirce's pragmatic maxim, their (pragmatic) conceptions of truth, and the doubt–belief model of inquiry that originally inspired Peirce's pragmatism, Kitcher argues that we are not justified in claiming that what James and Dewey are doing is simply extending the work started by Peirce, or that they can all three be seen as part of some reasonably well-defined movement. From this Kitcher concludes that "if Peirce was the first pragmatist, it seems he was also the last."

In "Why Philosophers Must Be Pragmatists: Taking Cues from Peirce," Cornelis de Waal follows Peirce's conception of philosophy as a science of discovery and uses it to argue that philosophers must be pragmatists. De Waal examines what this pragmatism comes down to, how it features within inquiry, and what its limits are. In the process, he discusses what Peirce meant by philosophy and how it relates to science and inquiry more generally. Proceeding from the idea that doing philosophy is to be engaged in deliberate, purpose-directed activity, de Waal argues that doing philosophy entails having some idea of what the outcome is likely to be and how to obtain it (even if only in principle), and that naturally leads to pragmatism.

In "Theory, Practice, and Deliberation: Peirce's Pragmatism Comprehensively Conceived," Vincent Colapietro looks at Peirce's seemingly extreme separation between theory and practice as can be found, for instance, in the often discussed first Cambridge Conference Lecture of 1898. Colapietro observes that there are other passages where Peirce seems to imply that theory is rather an instance of practice, as he tends to look at theory in terms of inquiry and inquiry in terms of communal deliberative action. With that in mind, Colapietro seeks to disambiguate Peirce's use of *theory* in his writings, highlighting two different but compatible senses. A larger part of his purpose is to show how human rationality is at bottom a *deliberative* capacity. While the form of deliberation in an urgently practical context is dramatically different from that in a strictly theoretical context, both practical agents and theoretical inquirers are engaged in deliberative practices. Accordingly, deliberation allows us to see both the unity and the differences between practical and theoretical reason.

In "Pragmatic Clarification: Contexts and Purposes," Mats Bergman asks what he calls a deceptively simple question: What purpose is Peirce's pragmatism meant to serve? The answer seems obvious: to make our ideas clear. But, Bergman argues, this is too crude of an answer. When we look more closely, we get a far more nuanced picture, one that allows us to distinguish between at least three different aims for conceptual clarification. This plays into the largely neglected question whether Peirce's pragmatism is best understood as a form of "Socratic midwifery," a tool for clearing the way for inquiry proper, or the kind of investigation that, fueled by genuine doubt, aims at settlement of belief or habit change. Bergman concludes by arguing that at least some uses of the pragmatic maxim can plausibly be construed as forms of melioristic inquiry.

The section is concluded with a chapter by Aaron Bruce Wilson titled "Peirce, Perception, and Empiricism." While Peirce confesses to a form of empiricism, Wilson observes, he does not consider perception as the incorrigible foundation for knowledge that empiricists traditionally have taken it to be. For Peirce, all reasoning and inquiry rest on perceptual judgments, and we cannot reach beyond them. The best we can do is try to explain how, or why, we reach the perceptual judgments we do. In his chapter, Wilson traces the development of Peirce's theory of perception from 1868 to 1906, paying special attention to the 1903 Harvard Lectures, while explaining how Peirce's views on perception address *what* we perceive, how perception represents the world, and how this affects science and inquiry.

Metaphysics

The opening chapter of this section, by Robert Lane, examines Peirce's take on two key metaphysical concepts: reality and existence. Lane first shows how our concept of what is real differs from other metaphysical concepts such as our concepts of external, internal, and fictional. Lane next uses the interconnection of these concepts to explicate Peirce's attempt at a pragmatic clarification of the concept of reality, one that relies on Peirce's idea that a true belief is one that would be permanently fixed as a result of investigation. Lane then describes how Peirce's concept of *existence* gradually emerged out of this concept of reality, and he ends with a discussion of whether, when understood in Peircean terms, the reality of something can be a matter of degree.

In "Scientific Pride and Metaphysical Prejudice," Rosa Mayorga examines how quantum theory has led to a concept of reality that is dramatically at odds with our most rooted metaphysical convictions. According to Mayorga, Peirce, who was well versed in physics as well as metaphysics, was well positioned to identify some of the metaphysical prejudices that quantum theory would later expose as such. In her chapter, Mayorga traces how Peirce's realism, inspired by the thirteenth-century Franciscan monk John Duns Scotus and adapted for a reconceived scientific metaphysics, presages some of the familiar enigmas posed by quantum physics.

The next chapter, by Gabriele Gava, analyzes two short texts where Peirce sketches out an anti-skeptical argument inspired by Kant's famous refutation of idealism. Gava begins by considering what attracted Peirce to Kant's refutation, given that the refutation is often considered problematic and unsuccessful. He then briefly reconstructs Kant's refutation while highlighting its most problematic passages. Moreover, since Peirce's own version of the argument relies on Kant's views regarding the temporal structure of consciousness, Gava connects it with how Peirce tackles this issue in "The Law of Mind." Finally, he looks at Peirce's anti-skeptical argument and examines whether and how it can be seen as appropriating Kant's strategy.

In "Peirce on Truth," Andrew Howat gives a brief introduction to Peirce's conception of truth. It includes a guide to the most relevant primary sources; brief summaries of three recent, influential interpretations of those sources; and discussion of several ongoing controversies regarding these interpretations and common objections to Peirce's view.

In the last chapter of this section, Gary Slater brings us to Peirce's views on religion. Slater discusses the content, reception, and applications of Peirce's writings on religion.

After discussing the central texts on religion in Peirce's corpus—the *Monist* series of the early 1890s, the Cambridge Conference Lectures, and the "Neglected Argument for the Reality of God"—Slater traces the reception of Peirce's thought, from Josiah Royce, through John E. Smith, to the more recent work of Robert Neville, Peter Ochs, Robert Corrington, and Michael Raposa. The chapter concludes with some excursions into the current landscape of scholarship on Peirce and religion and speculates on potential developments.

SCIENCE AND SEMIOTICS

The final section of the handbook brings together several essays broadly related to science and semiotics. In "A Science Like Any Other: A Peircean Philosophy of Sex?," Shannon Dea argues that a Peircean philosophy of sex offers a nonreductionist approach to sex as a biological category. She starts off with a survey of traditional biological accounts of sex categories and of several social constructivist accounts of sex, followed by an overview of Peirce's scholastic realism and his ethics of inquiry. Though Peirce regarded the distinction between the sexes as a rare "polar distinction," Dea develops the nuanced view of sex that she believes Peirce ought to have adopted had he extended his scholastic realism to reproductive biology. The chapter concludes by illustrating some applications of this Peircean philosophy of sex and by gesturing to others that we can yet barely imagine.

In "Charles S. Peirce and the Feeling of Understanding," Herman C. D. G. de Regt looks at two early papers of Peirce that have become classics: "The Fixation of Belief" and "How to Make Our Ideas Clear." In these papers, Peirce draws attention to how our feelings—the irritation of doubt and the serenity of belief—relate to the results of inquiry even when that inquiry is scientific. De Regt next uses Peirce's pragmatism to show that mathematically expressed natural laws do scientifically explain also when they do not result in something like a feeling of understanding, whether because of their complexity or because of their remoteness from everyday experience. Quantum theory would be a good example of this. The result is a disconnect between what science tells us and a feeling of understanding—a disconnect that plays into the hands of pseudoscience and science denial. Revisiting Peirce, de Regt argues, gives us a fruitful framework for thinking about science in a society that struggles with near apocalyptic issues while being overwhelmed by information and disinformation.

In "Peirce's Views on Education and Learning," Torjus Midtgarden examines how Peirce's semiotic work suggests perspectives on learning and education. Midtgarden focuses mainly on Peirce's outlines of a speculative grammar that go back to the mid-1890s, but also considers earlier and later phases of Peirce's philosophical development. Midtgarden shows how Peirce's analysis may shed further light on learning through a comparison with Jürgen Habermas's theory of communicative action. Finally, he considers how Peirce's analysis can be complemented by perspectives on learning and education that philosophers of education recently developed from his post-1900 semiotic work.

In the subsequent chapter, "The Philosophical Relevance of Peirce's Historical Studies," Tullio Viola explores the different uses of history that emerge from Peirce's writings and asks to what extent history, from a Peircean perspective, is relevant to philosophy. Viola begins by looking at the emergence of Peirce's interest in history as part and parcel of his polymathic profile. He goes on to analyze the role of history in his evolutionary account of the mind. Finally, Viola looks at the relationship between history and logic. Peirce was interested not only in exploring history's bearing on the investigation of logical questions, but also in employing his logical theories to develop a methodology of historical inquiry.

Tony Jappy, in "Diagrams, Semiosis, and Peirce's Metaphor," uses Peirce's concept of the icon to provide an innovative theoretical background to our understanding of metaphor, the media it is communicated through, and the intentionalities that determine it. As Jappy explains, changes in Peirce's conception of the sign threatened the abandonment of his very insightful 1903 definition of metaphor as one of three hypoicons. Jappy first contextualizes and illustrates this 1903 definition and then reviews significant developments in the semiotics over the 1905–1906 period to propose a form of mediatization as a way to reconcile two seemingly distinct conceptions of the sign.

In the next chapter, Kalevi Kull examines Peirce's views on biology, especially in his Guess at the Riddle and in his *Monist* papers of the early 1990s. When we look purely at Peirce's biological statements, we see a more emergentist take on biology than we get from canonical readings of Peirce. Kull further looks at how semiotic biologists have used Peirce, both before and after 1990, and at various criticisms of the application of some of Peirce's concepts in biosemiotics.

Finally, in "Peirce's Universal Grammar," American linguist Daniel L. Everett discusses several ideas of Peirce's philosophy that bear on modern linguistics. Utilizing Peirce's conception of universal grammar, which he describes as running in terms of semiotic (that is, logical) constraints on grammars, Everett opposes the Chomskyan theory, which casts universal grammar in terms of a biological capacity for language. Observing that Chomsky was familiar with some of Peirce's work, and even identified with Peirce, Everett further draws out various ways in which Chomsky misunderstood Peirce and why a truly Peirce-inspired linguistics is preferable.

Notes

1. A full biography is found in Joseph Brent, *Charles Sanders Peirce*, 2nd ed. (Bloomington: Indiana University Press, 1998).
2. Cornelis de Waal, *Charles S. Peirce: A Guide for the Perplexed* (London: Continuum, 2014).
3. For a detailed account of Peirce's European travels, see Chapter 2 of the current handbook, written by Jaime Nubiola and Sara Barrena. See also Jaime Nubiola, "The Cosmopolitan Peirce: His European Travels," *Transactions of the Charles S. Peirce Society* 56.2 (2020): 190–198.

4. Zina left Peirce in 1876, and later that same year he first met Juliette (W4:xxii). A detailed account of Peirce at Johns Hopkins is found in Chapter 3 of the current handbook, written by Cheryl Misak. See also Brent, *Charles Sanders Peirce*, 141–160.
5. The Cambridge Conference Lectures and the 1903 Harvard Lectures have been published in stand-alone volumes, as has the correspondence with Victoria Lady Welby. The 1903 Lowell Lectures are included in *Logic of the Future* as Volume 2.2. For bibliographic details, see "Note on the Primary Literature in the handbook."
6. Mina Samuels, *The Queen of Cups—A Novel* (Bloomington, IN: Unlimited Publishing, 2006). For a discussion, see Cornelis de Waal's review in *Transactions of the Charles S. Peirce Society* 44.1 (2008): 164–172.

Note on the Primary Literature

Since much of Peirce's work is still unpublished, many scholars rely at least to some extent on unpublished manuscripts, the largest holding of which is found at Harvard's Houghton Library. The majority of the Harvard manuscripts are fairly readily available on microfilm and increasingly so in digital form on the web. For the years covered by *The Writings of Charles S. Peirce, A Chronological Edition*, most of the surviving manuscripts, both at Harvard and elsewhere, have been published. However, even though the *Writings* are quite comprehensive, they are still selective. Moreover, especially since the *Writings* seem to have run out of steam with Volume 8, the situation is quite different for Peirce's later work. A complicating factor is that with Peirce devoting pretty much all his time to writing with little incentive to throw anything away (as he spent the last decades of his life in a sizable house), the amount of surviving manuscript material for the later period is significantly greater. Over the years, some targeted editions have appeared, and digitized copies of manuscripts are increasingly put online. However, there is still material that is available only by archival visit.

The manuscripts ended up at Harvard shortly following Peirce's death, as his widow, Juliette Peirce, sold them to Harvard together with his library. Peirce thought with his pen, and it is estimated that the collection at Harvard alone comprises an estimated eighty thousand pages. It seems that not everything was sold, however, and that the manuscripts were in a state of relative disarray even before they were picked up. Unfortunately, this got quite a bit worse after the manuscripts arrived at Harvard.[1] Josiah Royce, who was the driving force in getting the manuscripts to Harvard, died the next year, and with nobody to take over the helm, the disarray increased significantly. In the late 1920s, Charles Hartshorne, whom Harvard hired to edit a collection of Peirce's papers, was given eleven piles of stacked manuscripts on a large table to work with, together with fifty-two empty but carefully labeled boxes, suggesting that at some point the contents on the table had been sorted. The *Collected Papers* that Hartshorne and Weiss edited in the 1930s, supplemented by two additional volumes edited by Arthur Burks in the late 1950s, was the first large-scale edition of Peirce's work that tried to grapple with the manuscripts and their disorganized state. The eight-volume edition that came out of it was set up thematically with little attention to how Peirce's thought developed during the more than five decades he was writing. One consequence of publishing texts on the same topic together, without identifying that they were composed decades apart, is that it gave Peirce's thought an air of inconsistency rather than showing that his thought matured over time. This had a negative effect on the early reception of Peirce's ideas. Aiming to remedy this, references to the *Collected Papers* are often accompanied by a date.

A capstone volume was meant to contain an intellectual biography of Peirce, written by Max H. Fisch. This volume, however, was never written.[2] Fisch quickly discovered that such a biography required a chronological understanding of Peirce's thought, and hence of his manuscripts. This led to a large-scale attempt at reorganizing the manuscripts that began in the 1950s and is ongoing. The results that came out of this include Richard Robin's catalog, a thirty-two-reel microfilm, and the *Writings of Charles S. Peirce*—a projected thirty-volume chronological edition published by the Peirce Edition Project. The first volume of this edition appeared in 1982.

One consequence of the rather tortured history of the surviving manuscripts is that different editions may contain different renderings of the same manuscript depending on where the reorganization of the manuscripts stood at the time and how well the editors were informed about it. At times these differences are significant enough to affect one's understanding of the text. The *Writings* were meant to be as final an edition of Peirce's work as is humanly possible, while also including a detailed record of how the text had been generated and what source material was used, down to the individual sheets. Dating undated manuscripts can be especially challenging. The primary sources published in the Peirceana series, such as *Logic of the Future*, edited by Ahti-Veikko Pietarinen, and the *Selected Writings on Semiotics 1894–1912*, edited by Francesco Bellucci, also follow this practice.

The Harvard collection is not the sole deposit of Peirce manuscripts. Because of Peirce's thirty-year involvement with the US Coast Survey, there is quite a bit of material preserved also in the National Archives in Washington, DC.[3] And because of his two decades of collaboration with Paul Carus of the Open Court Publishing Company, there is quite a bit too in the Open Court Collection at Southern Illinois University, Carbondale.[4] There are other, smaller holdings too,[5] and there is still the faint hope that additional collections might come to the surface, such as the material Peirce sent to the Century Company and to James Mark Baldwin for their respective dictionaries.[6]

Because there are several holdings of manuscripts, the Harvard manuscripts, which have been cataloged by Richard Robin, are typically referred to by the letter *R*. The manuscripts on the microfilm are also ordered by their Robin number. The ordering of manuscripts by their Robin number, however, represents a relatively early stage in the reorganization process. Even though it had progressed significantly—from eleven piles to 1,644 folders (not including correspondence)—still much remained misplaced or out of order. In the early 1970s, to further facilitate the continued reordering of the manuscripts, a full photocopy was made of the microfilm and each sheet was given a unique identifier. These identifiers are called ISP numbers after the Institute for Studies in Pragmaticism at Texas Tech University, which spearheaded the effort. The ISP numbers solved the problem that folders designated by Robin Catalog numbers often contain unnumbered pages or, when they are numbered, multiple sheets with the same page number (as well as single sheets with multiple page numbers). This is because Peirce kept revising what he had written, sometimes even pulling sheets from work he had done years before. Though Peirce occasionally used notebooks, he most often wrote on loose sheets, as this offered him far more flexibility. Consequently, the benefits of having such a unique ID number cannot be overestimated. The ISP numbers follow the sequence of the pages as they are found on the microfilm. A major drawback of the ISP numbers is that there exist only two complete sets of photocopied manuscripts that have them, one at the Institute for Studies in Pragmaticism in Texas and one at the Peirce Edition Project in Indiana. Because of all of this, when scholars cite manuscript pages by Robin and page number, it is not always clear whether they are using an ISP number or an original page number (and if the latter, it is not always clear which one). Except for large and unwieldy fragments folders, however, this problem is in most cases not too difficult to resolve by consulting the microfilm.

The *Collected Papers* is for the most part an edition of Peirce's philosophical work, supplemented with some of his contributions to mathematics and mathematical logic. In the mid-1970s Carolyn Eisele, a mathematician and historian of mathematics, published a four-volume edition of Peirce's mathematical work titled *The New Elements of Mathematics*. Eisele had taken an interest in Peirce after discovering a handwritten letter by Peirce stuck in Fibonacci's *Liber Abaci* held at the Plimpton collection at Columbia University.[7] Eisele's *New Elements* relies heavily on the manuscripts as they appear on the microfilm. (Eisele had herself participated in the reorganization effort that preceded it.) The volumes include Peirce's work on arithmetic, algebra, and geometry as well as work on mathematical logic and philosophy of mathematics. Less than a decade later, we see the appearance of the first volume of the *Writings*, which also cover Peirce's scientific writings, including the reports he wrote for the US Coast Survey.

The *Essential Peirce*, volume 2, edited by the Peirce Edition Project; the three-volume *Logic of the Future*, edited by Ahti-Veikko Pietarinen; and *Selected Writings on Semiotics, 1894–1912*, edited by Francesco Bellucci, all focus on Peirce's later work. The *Essential Peirce* concentrates on Peirce's philosophical work, the *Logic of the Future* addresses his writings in logic (starting from 1895 and including his graphical logic), and the *Selected Writings on Semiotics* makes available a number of important texts related to semiotics that had not yet been published. Peirce's extensive correspondence with Victoria Lady Welby, who played a central role introducing Peirce's later work in Britain in the early twentieth century, is covered in *Semiotic and Significs*, edited by Charles Hardwick. Peirce's unsigned book reviews for *The Nation* are identified and collected in the four-volume *Charles Sanders Peirce: Contributions to The Nation*, edited by Kenneth Ketner and James Cook. In addition to these broader editions there is an increasing number of more targeted collections.

Though Peirce left behind an enormous amount of unpublished material, he also published a staggering twelve thousand pages. He authored one book (*Photometric Researches*) and edited one volume of work mostly by his students (*Studies in Logic*), in addition to numerous papers—scientific as well as philosophical—and countless book reviews. A bibliography of Peirce's published work is found in Kenneth Laine Ketner et al. (eds.), *A Comprehensive Bibliography of the Published Works of Charles Sanders Peirce* with a Bibliography of Secondary Studies, 2nd ed. (Bowling Green, OH: Philosophy Documentation Center, 1988).

There is a long-standing tradition within Peirce scholarship of abbreviating primary sources when giving in-line references. This convention is used also in the current handbook and is detailed in the references for each chapter, as well as in the list below.[8]

HARVARD MANUSCRIPTS

Charles S. Peirce Papers. Microfilm, 39 reels, 35mm. Cambridge, MA: Houghton Library, Harvard University, 1966–1970.

Reels 1–30, Papers as cataloged in Robin 1967 and referred to by R;
Reels 31–32, Supplement as cataloged in Robin 1971 and referred to by RS;
Reels L1–L6, Professional correspondence as cataloged in Robin 1967 and referred to by RL.
Robin, Richard. *Annotated Catalogue of the Papers of Charles S. Peirce*. Amherst: University of Massachusetts Press, 1967.
Robin, Richard. "The Peirce Papers: A Supplementary Catalogue." *Transactions of the Charles S. Peirce Society* 7, no. 1 (1971): 37–57.

PUBLISHED EDITIONS

CN[volume#]:[page#]. *Charles Sanders Peirce: Contributions to The Nation*. 4 vols. Edited by Kenneth L. Ketner and James E. Cook. Lubbock: Texas Tech University Press, 1975–1987.
CP[volume#].[paragraph#]. *The Collected Papers of Charles Sanders Peirce*. 8 vols. Vols. 1–6 edited by Charles Hartshorne and Paul Weiss; vols. 7–8 edited by Arthur W. Burks. Cambridge, MA: Harvard University Press, 1931–1958.
EP[volume#]:[page#]. *The Essential Peirce: Selected Philosophical Writings*. 2 vols. Vol. 1 edited by Nathan Houser and Christian Kloesel; vol. 2 edited by the Peirce Edition Project. Bloomington: Indiana University Press, 1992–1998.
HPPLS[volume#]:[page#]. *Historical Perspectives on Peirce's Logic of Science*. 2 vols. Edited by Carolyn Eisele. The Hague: Mouton, 1985.
ILS:[page#]. *Illustrations of the Logic of Science*. Edited by Cornelis de Waal. Chicago: Open Court, 2014.
LI:[page#]. *The Logic of Interdisciplinarity*. Edited by Elize Bisanz. Berlin: Akademie Verlag, 2009.
LoF[volume#]:[page#]. *Logic of the Future*. 4 vols. in 3. Edited by Ahti-Veikko Pietarinen. Berlin: De Gruyter Mouton, 2019– .
NEM[volume#]:[page#]. *The New Elements of Mathematics*, 4 vols. in 5. Edited by Carolyn Eisele. The Hague: Mouton, 1976.

PM:[page#]. *Philosophy of Mathematics: Selected Writings*. Edited by Matthew Moore. Bloomington: Indiana University Press, 2010.

PPM:[page#]. *Pragmatism as a Principle and Method of Right Thinking: The 1903 Harvard Lectures on Pragmatism*. Edited by Patricia Turrisi. Albany: State University of New York Press, 1997.

RLT:[page#]. *Reasoning and the Logic of Things: The Cambridge Conferences Lectures of 1898*. Edited by Kenneth L. Ketner. Cambridge, MA: Harvard University Press, 1992.

SS:[page#]. *Semiotic and Significs: The Correspondence between Charles S. Peirce and Victoria Lady Welby*. Edited by Charles S. Hardwick. Bloomington: Indiana University Press, 1977.

SWS[volume#]:[page#]. *Selected Writings on Semiotics, 1894–1912*. Edited by Francesco Bellucci. Berlin: De Gruyter Mouton, 2020.

W[volume#]:[page#]. *The Writings of Charles S. Peirce: A Chronological Edition*. 7 vols. to date. Edited by the Peirce Edition Project. Bloomington: Indiana University Press, 1982– .

Notes

1. For a brief history of Peirce's Nachlass, see Nathan Houser, "The Fortunes and Misfortunes of the Peirce Papers," in Gérard Deledalle et al., eds., *Signs of Humanity*, 3 vols. (Berlin: Mouton de Gruyter, 1992), 3:1259–1268.
2. In the decades that followed, Fisch conducted an enormous amount of research for the biography—research that survives in two large sets of small notecards, referred to as "Fisch slips," which are kept at the Peirce Edition Project. One set is alphabetical by keyword; the other is chronological and traces Peirce's life almost day by day. In addition to the challenge caused by the disorder of the manuscripts, Fisch found his attempt at writing a biography severely hampered by not knowing anything about Juliette Peirce (d. 1934), Peirce's companion for over thirty years. Juliette's background was, and still is, totally mysterious (there is no certainty even about her name), and she and this mystery significantly affected Peirce's life and career.
3. Most of Peirce's work related to the US Coast Survey is included in the *Writings*, including his final and never-before-published "Report on Gravity," which is in many ways the culmination of his gravitational research (W6, sel. 36, 1889). The archival holdings can be found in National Archives Record Group 23/22.
4. Southern Illinois University, Carbondale, Morris Library, Special Collections, MSS 027, Open Court Publishing Company Records.
5. An example is the Cuddeback Letter Book, held at the Pike County Historical Society in Milford, Pennsylvania, which contains approximately two hundred letters sent to Charles Peirce between 1859 and 1861. See Charles Seibert, "Cuddeback Letter Book Is Available for Scholarly Use," *Transactions of the Charles S. Peirce Society* 42.3 (2006): 431–437.
6. Peirce's heavily annotated interleaved copy of the twenty-four-volume *Century Dictionary* is preserved at Harvard (R1597) and included on the microfilm. A list of the entries that Peirce wrote or worked on is found in Kenneth Ketner et al., eds., *A Comprehensive Bibliography of the Published Works of Charles Sanders Peirce with a Bibliography of Secondary Studies* (Bowling Green, OH: Philosophy Documentation Center, Bowling Green State University, 1986). Whereas work for the *Century Dictionary* was anonymous, contributions to Baldwin's dictionary are written under the author's name.
7. The letter, addressed to George Arthur Plimpton, describes what the content of the manuscript must be if it were to be Fibonacci's famed *Liber Abaci*.
8. Foreign-language editions are not listed.

PART I

LIFE AND CAREER

CHAPTER 1

PEIRCE'S JOURNEY TO THE END OF INQUIRY
The Tenure of the Soul

DANIEL L. EVERETT

1. Peirce's History

1.1. Family Background

THE Peirce family (pronounced "purse," originally spelled Pers, cognate with Pierce and Peter, meaning 'rock') originated most likely in Belgium, but came to have deep roots in Massachusetts. Below I constructed an iconic representation of the prose accounts of both sides of his family from Massachusetts, many associated with the fishing industry in Salem:

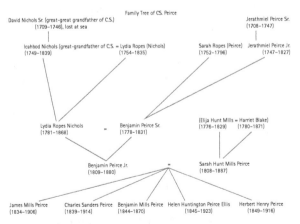

Charles Sanders Peirce was born into this illustrious family on September 10, 1839, in Cambridge, Massachusetts, dying seventy-four years later on April 19, 1914, in

Milford, Pennsylvania. Among his most notable contemporaries were General George Armstrong Custer, John D. Rockefeller, Samuel L. Clemens, Andrew Carnegie, Thomas Edison, Frederick Douglass, Clara Barton, Nikola Tesla, George Washington Carver, Alfred North Whitehead, Louis Agassiz, Leo Szilard, Edwin Hubble, Katharine Blodgett, Gerty Cori, Maria Mitchell, and Annie Jump Cannon. International contemporaries included Renoir and the impressionists, Charles Darwin, and Michael Faraday. Important thinkers and other figures of historical significance were abundant during Peirce's life.

Peirce was born at 3 Phillips Lane, the very same house now serving as the home of Lesley University's Graduate School of Arts and Social Studies. He was the second child of Benjamin Peirce Jr. and Sarah Hunt Mills Peirce. Benjamin was a professor of mathematics and astronomy at Harvard for over fifty years. Ben's own father, Benjamin Sr., was for five years the librarian of Harvard (1826–1831). Charles's first wife, Harriet Melusina ("Zina") Fay, was an early feminist leader and writer. His older brother, James Mills Peirce, also became a professor of mathematics and astronomy at Harvard and served for a few years as dean of the college of arts and sciences there. Another of Peirce's brothers, Benjamin Mills Peirce, died alone at twenty-five years after struggling with finding his way in the world. Charles's youngest sibling, Herbert Henry Peirce, served in the US diplomatic corps and represented the US government at the coronation of Tzar Nicholas II of Russia. The sister of these four men was Helen Huntington Peirce Ellis, a constant source of support in letters, in person, and with her pocketbook for "Charley" until the end of his life. The family was very close and there is extensive, always warm and caring, correspondence between them all.

Beyond his nuclear family, Peirce's maternal and paternal families formed a well-to-do, prominent clade of senators, businessmen, and mathematicians. Benjamin Peirce Jr. was considered the greatest US mathematician of his generation and a pioneer in the organization and stimulation of the formation of science as a profession in the US. Charles Peirce's life began just as Benjamin and others were establishing the legal and cultural bases of US scientific research and culture. In 1839, the year Charles was born, his father Benjamin aided in the establishment of the first American astronomical observatory in Philadelphia. In 1848, Benjamin helped found the American Association for the Advancement of Science. And in 1863, when Charles was twenty-four, Benjamin was a leader in the foundation of the National Academy of Sciences. The law creating it was signed by Abraham Lincoln.

Benjamin's work in astronomy and his book, *Linear Associative Algebra* (Peirce 1882), put American science on the world intellectual map as no other American, except perhaps another Ben, Benjamin Franklin, had done. Benjamin helped found a group that was significant in Charles's formative thinking, the Lazzaroni, most of whom went on to founding memberships in the National Academy of Sciences.

Charles's mother, Sarah, was likewise born into a prominent family that included politicians and successful businesspeople in Massachusetts. Her own father, Elijah Hunt Mills (1776–1829), was elected to the Massachusetts State Legislature, where he became Speaker of the House. He was later elected to the US House of Representatives and then to the US Senate. Others descending from Elijah were US senators John Davis Lodge and Henry Cabot Lodge Jr. (defeated eventually in a bid for re-election to the Senate by John F. Kennedy).

The Peirces were rooted in Salem, Massachusetts (where Benjamin Sr. and Benjamin Jr. were born), establishing a successful shipping business. Benjamin Sr. came along as that business was fading, thus moving to Cambridge to accept the post of the librarian of Harvard, after working briefly in the family shipping business in Salem.

Charles's family was committed to science, logic, and the life of the mind. They were loving and financially successful. But there were also severe shortcomings in their worldview. These should not be overlooked. In spite of all his brilliance, Charles's father believed that slavery was a good thing, freeing up the better (i.e., white) people for intellectual life, business, the arts, and so on. Several of Benjamin's friends reinforced his biases against Blacks. Of special note are Louis Agassiz and the pro-slavery Confederate physicist and chemist at the University of Georgia (formerly a New England physician), John LeConte. As Raposa (2021 34ff.) says of Agassiz, he "defended polygenism, for example, a theory that rejected Darwinian evolution and argued that the races were created separately." LeConte (1818–1891) became the first (acting) president of the University of California, in spite of his enthusiastic support for slavery and the Confederacy.

Unfortunately, Charles seems to have shared his father's opinions and believed that the average person should serve the "higher" classes. Charles's own bias is displayed in the following syllogism, which he created to demonstrate that syllogistic reasoning can fail if given a wrong (in this case the minor) premise:

> All men are equal in their political rights.
> Negroes are men.
> Therefore, negroes are equal in political rights to whites. (W1:444, 1866)

But it is hardly news that privileged white people of the nineteenth century, with many ties to friends in the slaveholding states, were racist. This racism, despicable as it is in the hard light of the twenty-first century, does not cancel out the importance of the Peirce family's contributions to science. Their racism means that, like all families, they had serious faults, typical of their age (though not for that reason excusable).

During Charles's life, the Peirce family lived within walking distance of the homes of William James, Henry Wadsworth Longfellow, Louis Agassiz, and many other prominent intellectuals of the nineteenth century. Agassiz would show up at the Peirce home in the morning and shout "Ben!," and as Ben joined him, they would walk to their offices together, a custom that continued even after Harvard built homes for both of them in Harvard Yard and their walk was much shorter (the Peirce house stood where Sever Hall is now).

1.2. Peirce's Educational Background

Peirce learned largely on his own, by reading and discussions and argumentation exercises with his father. Because he was primarily homeschooled, he had fewer peers and opportunities for socialization with those of his own age than most children might. Peirce's obvious precociousness delighted his father and he received not only material but also emotional and intellectual indulgence and stimulation that few others, including his own siblings, received. From an early age Charles had the freedom to pursue and discuss and write about his intellectual interests, experiencing a form of tenure from childhood on, if tenure is understood as security to freely pursue one's own questions. He completed his undergraduate studies at Harvard in 1859, not a standout student at that time, though later he graduated from the Lawrence Scientific School, receiving the very first summa cum laude degree in chemistry in Harvard history.

Charles Peirce was arguably the most fecund thinker to have ever lived in the US, among the best the world has known. The range of his work is unparalleled, as is its creativity and quality. Although my purpose in this chapter is to defend the thesis that he lived a successful, fulfilling life in spite of many outward defeats, it is important to offer a brief survey of his work and the American intellectual tradition behind this work, to understand what it is that brought him that inner and outer purpose and achievement.

In spite of his rare brilliance, Peirce was but the primus inter pares of many individuals of a golden age of US literature and science, led primarily from three Massachusetts towns, Amherst (where Emily Dickinson revolutionized American poetry), Concord (where Ralph Waldo Emerson, Henry David Thoreau, Louisa May Alcott, Branson Alcott, Margaret Fuller, and Nathaniel Hawthorne, inter alia, produced literary works unequaled in quality and quantity anyplace in the world, rivaling the Athens of Euripides and Socrates), and Cambridge (Benjamin Peirce, Henry Wadsworth Longfellow, Louis Agassiz, Chauncey Wright, and Henry James Sr.). Charles was the heir to a great intellectual fortune uniquely rooted in New England.

2. Transcendentalist New England and Peirce's Intellectual Roots

Peirce's enveloping intellectual world was richer even than his profoundly cerebral home life. New England was bringing America to academic and artistic equality with Europe, becoming a literary and scientific world leader. Of the three leading cities of the Commonwealth mentioned already, the initial intellectual engine of the US in the nineteenth century was found in Concord, Massachusetts. There, Emerson innovated approaches to thinking and knowing whose influence has only strengthened in the nearly two centuries that followed it. The intellectual influences behind this birth of American philosophy, literature, and science were many, though one intellect outshines the rest. German philosopher Immanuel Kant's work altered the thinking of American and world philosophers, authors, and scientists alike. Not only did Emerson pay homage to Kant in many places, but also Charles said that he "drank at the udders of Kant" for his primary intellectual development (for the interconnection of Emerson, Peirce, and, indirectly, Kant, see Kaag [2013]).

The influences of Kant and Emerson are important because Peirce's intellectual development always included their ideas as touchstones (though not the only ones). Peirce's intellectual life parallels that of Emerson's American scholar. One can in fact make a plausible case that Peirce was the finest example of "the American scholar" of the nineteenth and subsequent centuries. Peirce helped shape American thought, with his ideas more widely studied in the early twenty-first century than ever. Peirce's thought enjoys a very long pedigree. But to understand Peirce's *life* as success, contra the common idea that it was a tragic failure, we need to grasp his place and role in American intellectual history, in particular as he exemplified Emerson's concepts of self-reliance (avoidance of conformity being central to that idea), grit, and action. His success was not merely a subjective feeling but also an objective fact, the apex of the American tradition as it had formed itself. So, what is that tradition and how did it begin? And how does it provide evidence that Peirce's life was not tragic but successful?

To understand Peirce in his cultural Zeitgeist, we must return to Emerson and the roots of his philosophy. Emerson frequently acknowledged that his philosophy was inspired by Immanuel Kant. Kant's influence crossed many national and intellectual boundaries. In New England his influence was felt especially in his view of transcendental idealism, the idea that the spatial and temporal characteristics we attribute to the world are simply ideas within ourselves. It isn't raw sensory experience that shapes our minds as Locke had it, but our minds preform our experiences so that we perceive them not as they are, but as our minds represent/shape them to/for us. By the time of Emerson's youth transcendentalism had traveled the world, from Prussia to the still-youthful American Commonwealth of Massachusetts.

Inspired by Kant and his own thinking about nature and the divine, Emerson founded what became known as New England transcendentalism. Eventually, with money from his popular and frequent lectures and his first, deceased wife's inheritance, he began to gather the cream of American letters around his home—the Alcott family, Henry David Thoreau, Nathaniel Hawthorne, Edgar Allan Poe, Margaret Fuller, and others, all within sight of the old North Bridge where the American War of Independence from the tyranny of the Old World began.

As Emerson continued to expound his ideas, he wrote, "All that you call the world is the shadow of that substance which you are, the perpetual creation of the powers of thought" (Emerson 1866, 2:281). The mind is not limited to one individual, but it is produced through the efforts of a society of serious minds working together, "Man as Thinker," to put it in Emersonian terms, rather than merely men thinking (Emerson 1866, 2:175). These non-empiricist ideas all reappear in one form or another in Charles Peirce's work, either as the objects of criticism or as input to his own philosophy.

At the same time when Emerson was gathering intellectual partners in Concord, fifteen miles to the east, a group of scientists and others was forming in Cambridge: Benjamin Peirce, Louis Agassiz, Annie Jump Cannon, William Bond, and John Whipple, inter alia, including the poet Henry Wadsworth Longfellow. Both groups saw themselves as students of nature. Emerson's most important book is in fact simply titled *Nature*. But whereas the Concord group contemplated nature to understand its importance for the transcendental mind and soul of humans, the Cambridge group studied nature scientifically, to understand it as an end in itself. In addition to the Cambridge and Concord groups, another contemporary Massachusetts-born creator of the American mind was working in Amherst, within the four walls of her bedroom. Creating visions and pondering truths through her art, Emily Dickinson, one of the founders of modern American poetry, surpassed even Longfellow as a pioneer of American letters. She is recognized in the early twenty-first century as a leader in American art, thought, and reflection, a non-empiricist and to a degree a transcendentalist, without being explicitly labeled as such.

All these people working individually, though in some cases collectively, established the foundations of an American scholarship that was to eventually become the equal of European science and literature. And there were connections among them. Thoreau took math classes from Benjamin Peirce at Harvard. Emerson was an acquaintance of the Peirce family. Charles Peirce remembered Margaret Fuller visiting his home when he was small.

Although the Concord experiment ended years before Emerson's death in 1882, the second Cambridge generation of truly American scholars—in particular the James brothers (William and Henry) and the Peirce brothers (Charles and James)—absorbed the intellectual values and ideas of their parents' generation. From the later teachings and writings of William James and Charles Peirce, many other scholars emerged as the third wave of American scholars (in Emerson's sense): Christine Ladd-Franklin, John Dewey, Josiah Royce, Edwin Holt, Ralph Barton Perry, and many others. Though they were younger than Peirce, many had ideas that influenced Peirce profoundly.[1]

Emerson recognized the intellectual transformation that was occurring in the US, especially in Massachusetts. He saw the day arriving when "the sluggard intellect of this continent will look from under its iron lids and fill the postponed expectations of the world" (Emerson 1866, 2:174). He further asserted the duty of America to independently learn and write, not merely follow: "Each age ... must write its own books ... each generation for the next succeeding.... The books of an older period will not fit this" (Emerson 1866, 2:177). Or, to put it another way, we need to be our own scholars rather than simply learn at the feet of the scholars of the Old World because "love of the hero corrupts into worship of his statue" (Emerson 1866, 2:177). For Emerson, the way to learn, to innovate, to create new knowledge was through *action*—doing rather than merely contemplating. Emerson here anticipates the movement that Peirce was to found some decades later, namely, American pragmatism (or, as Peirce came eventually to call it, pragmaticism). For Emerson, action, including working on one's own theories and applications, enhanced comprehension: "When the mind is braced by labor and invention, the page of whatever book we read becomes luminous with manifold allusion" (Emerson 1866, 2:179).

Emerson was a Romanticist, as well as a transcendentalist. And Romanticism was a vital component of this era of the American mind, indirectly influencing Peirce. The former component of his philosophy led (according to Frye 1968, 5) to rejection of the "encyclopedic myth" of God as the origin of all creation and all knowledge. "In the new Romantic myth, human creativity assumes a central place" (5). As Isaiah Berlin says of Romanticism (Berlin [1999] 2000, 119), "The heart of the entire process [of Romanticism] is invention, creation, making, out of literally nothing, or out of any materials that may be to hand." Berlin was not speaking of Emerson directly, but he nonetheless captures Emerson's viewpoint well. As Emerson worded it, "the 'fountain of all good' is in oneself" (Emerson 1866, 2:193). Thus the American scholar had self-reliance, free to develop their ideas unburdened by the weight of god and religion. Emerson's philosophical work came to dominate a great deal of thinking in the US. As the *Stanford Encyclopedia of Philosophy* puts it, "He influenced generations of Americans, from his friend Henry David Thoreau to John Dewey, and in Europe, Friedrich Nietzsche." Emerson's transcendentalism also inspired American scholars to consider Kant more thoughtfully. Peirce, our exemplar of Emerson's American scholar, combined all these characteristics and lived, even if unknowingly, guided by these Emersonian values.

So, as Emerson helped bring Kant to American scholarship and the American transcendentalist movement, he did this as part of a project to install the Romanticist view in the US. Emerson urged his audiences not to look for wisdom only in old books of the past (such as the Bible) but in new books, as well as in one's own thinking and interactions with nature. The pragmatists inherited the Kantian idealism and transcendentalism—we are all part of the creative force of the world that is immanent in and around us—in part from Emerson and his Concord band. They also applied to it the rigor of their new pragmatist standards—if you cannot test something, if you cannot say how to apply something, then it means nothing.

In sum, an understanding of Peirce's trajectory and thought requires an appreciation of the Emersonian revolution. Peirce looked at nature independent of doctrinal pressure. Although he believed in God, his inquiry was not shaped by the church, but by the spirit of the Romanticism sketched above. Although Benjamin Peirce and Louis Agassiz set the scientific standards of their time, the next generation of New England thinkers was deeply influenced also by the values of the Concordian Romanticists that undergirded their quest for knowledge, their self-reliance, and their intellectual independence from religion. Peirce, of course, rejected what was so important to Emerson, intuitionism as the foundation of intellectual work, replacing it with inferential reasoning. But it was Emerson as much as any other who freed American thinkers from the severe constraints of religion, a freedom that Peirce pursued his entire adult life. Peirce's life was thus a preeminently American life, imbued from start to finish with the concerns of the Concord and Cambridge of his father's generation. His success should therefore be judged to some degree on how well he achieved the objectives of the agenda set originally by Benjamin Peirce and Ralph Waldo Emerson.

3. From Ease to Hardship: The Price of Focus

3.1. Introduction

Charles Peirce never held a long-term academic appointment, largely because he came to be despised by the presidents of Harvard (Charles Eliot; where Peirce studied) and Johns Hopkins University (Daniel Coit Gilman; where Peirce initially taught).[2] Eliot and Gilman, among others, came to actively oppose Peirce's employment at any US institution of higher education, successfully keeping him in penury for the latter years of his life. They accused him of immorality and underestimated his brilliance due to input from jealous rivals, such as Simon Newcomb (Brent 1998,152ff.). From 1861 to 1892, Peirce earned his living as a geophysicist with the US Coast Survey (the National Oceanic and Atmospheric Administration in the early twenty-first century). In 1892, due in part to politics, Peirce's uncompromising attitude, and the machinations of Newcomb, Peirce was fired from the US Coast Survey. Though Peirce's accumulated difficulties were slow in coming, the warning signs came often and early. But Peirce persisted in doing his work according to his own sense of what was best. Much of Peirce's difficulty resulted from his behavior being in advance of the state of his culture. Faculty members today routinely behave as Peirce did.

3.2. The Halcyon Days

Peirce began his academic career with the support of one of the then most powerful academics in the US, his father. Benjamin had helped found the US Coast Survey and was one of its early directors. Charles, at Benjamin's urging, was hired as an assistant director. As Brent puts it, "On April 8, 1872, Benjamin Peirce appointed his son, over the heads of the more experienced assistants, to the position of acting assistant in charge of the Coast Survey office in Washington . . . [next] his father appointed him assistant in charge of gravimetric experiments" (Brent 1998, 89). There is no question that Charles was qualified for these positions. Nor is there much doubt that he was superior to all other candidates. But what came back to haunt him after his father's death about eight years later was the resentment that this nepotism engendered in his colleagues at the Coast Survey.

But regardless of how he came to be appointed, Peirce was energetic, original, and brilliant as a geophysicist with the Coast Survey. Up until this appointment Peirce had held the assistant position at the Harvard observatory (also due to his father). Assistantships in those days were positions of high responsibility and generous remuneration. Charles was riding high and doing scientific work of world-class caliber. As a rather typical academic, Peirce was slow to clear his accounts at the Coast Survey and resentment began to build. His work was of the highest quality. But his accounting and sense of financial responsibility were adolescent, though his privileges continued.

3.3. International Travel

One of the great perks of academe is international travel. Peirce certainly enjoyed this part of his profession and made five important and very enjoyable trips to Europe.[3]

3.3.1. *First European Trip: June 18, 1870–March 7, 1871*

The purpose of the first trip to Europe was to identify locations "suitable for establishing observatories in order to study the total solar eclipse that was to take place at noon on December 22nd, 1870 over the Mediterranean Sea" (Nubiola 2020, 191). His father also "wanted to introduce his son to several prominent European mathematicians (De Morgan, Jevons, Clifford, etc.)" (191). After the eclipse Peirce and Zina traveled through Italy, Switzerland, Germany, and England. They sailed back to Boston on February 21 from Liverpool, arriving March 7, 1871.

3.3.2. *Second European Journey: April 3, 1875–August 20, 1876*

In 1875 Peirce traveled to conduct extensive work on gravimetric pendulums, at the stations of Berlin, Geneva, Paris, and Kew. Peirce was expected to spend at least a year in Europe to "improve the American Geodesy" (Nubiola 2020, 192). "In England, Peirce spoke of geodesy with several British instrument makers and scientists, including James Clerk Maxwell at the Cavendish Laboratory in Cambridge, who agreed with his views on the characteristics of the resistance that affects pendulums" (Nubiola 2020, 193). Peirce and Zina sailed back to the US on August 8, just about two weeks after the defeat of Custer's 7th Calvary at Little Big Horn.

3.3.3. *Third European Journey: September 13, 1877–November 18, 1877*

The third trip was Peirce's shortest trip, "but is extremely important for his scientific profile as Peirce defended his views on design flaws in the stand of the European pendulum and their effects on the accuracy of the measurement of gravity" (Nubiola 2020, 194). "From Berlin he goes to Paris where he arranges with Théodule Ribot the publication in the *Revue Philosophique* of the articles prepared during his trip" (Nubiola 2020, 194). During his voyage back to the US, he wrote "How to Make Our Ideas Clear."

3.3.4. *Fourth European Visit: April 28, 1880–August 4, 1880*

This trip was primarily a stay in Paris with an excursion to London (Nubiola 2020, 195). He cut his trip short due to his father's illness, arriving August 4, 1880. Benjamin died on October 6, roughly eight weeks after Charles's return.

3.3.5. *Peirce's Final European Trip: May 2, 1883–September 18, 1883*

Just before leaving for this final trip to Europe, Charles obtained his legal divorce from Zina, on April 24, 1883. On April 26, he married Juliette Annette Froissy (the name she used on their marriage certificate, though she was also known as Pourtalai). This visit seems to have been mainly so that Peirce and Juliette could honeymoon in Europe, though there were important discussions with other scientists in Paris and London. In the latter location he also compared the American yard with the London version.

These trips were fairly luxurious, and as photos of Peirce at the time show, he was enjoying himself a great deal, living the high life of one of the most successful US academics. It is not surprising that during these trips he had no inkling of the difficulties to come or that this standard of living could ever end for one as talented and respected as he was. What strikes one who is familiar with the entire course of Peirce's life, seeing it at a distance, which of course Peirce could not do, is that even though the joy of these trips stands in stark contrast to his later financial difficulties, Peirce's work never slowed, never stopped, during all the vicissitudes of his life until just before his death.

3.4. Johns Hopkins University

In March 1878, again in part because of his father's efforts, Peirce received the offer of a lectureship at Johns Hopkins from its inaugural president, Daniel Coit Gilman. Peirce was still an employee of the Coast Survey and gave thought to switching full-time to university life; however, Gilman's offer was not for a professorship but for the lower-ranked, less stable position of lecturer. In 1883, though he had been promised a professorship by Gilman, Peirce was fired from Johns Hopkins and was left only with his relatively low income from the Coast Survey. Peirce was fired because of his extramarital affair with Juliette (though he had been separated from Zina for years), who was to be his wife for more than three decades, and because he was prickly and critical, self-indulgent, and demanding—that is, he was like most academics, in my experience. But unlike modern academics, tenure was not well established yet in US universities (it began in the late 1800s but was not officialized until 1915) and Peirce lacked any such protection. And even if there had been secure tenure in the US at the time, Peirce had been appointed as a lecturer, not a professor, and so would not have had this protection in any case. As mentioned, Harvard's president, Eliot, already disliked Peirce and he, Newcomb, and Gilman subsequently worked to keep Peirce out of US academe altogether. They were quite successful. Moreover, since Gilman went on to control the academic grants of the Carnegie Foundation, that rich source of funding was also to be forever denied to Peirce.

3.5. Lowell and Harvard Lecture Series

Peirce was able to make money with occasional lectures, such as his Lowell Lectures of 1866 and 1903, his Cambridge Conference Lectures of 1898, and his Harvard Lectures of 1869 and 1903. The 1903 Lowell and Harvard Lectures are among the most important lecture series ever given in America. The Harvard Lectures were on his pragmatism and the Lowell Lectures on his existential graphs and modes of reasoning. The latter are often ignored although they include some of the most important innovations ever in semiotic and linguistic theories. If there had not been so much bias against Peirce, these lectures would almost certainly have led to other lecture offers from universities, perhaps even job offers, in spite of his age of sixty-three. But in addition to the bias, Peirce's lectures did not achieve the popularity they deserved because they were so innovative and technical that even James referred to them as largely "Cimmerian darkness."

3.6. The Dream of Arisbe

In 1882, when Juliette and Charles purchased their two-thousand-acre estate and large home in Milford, Pennsylvania, they were doing all right financially, even though their income was largely limited to Charles's salary as a geophysicist with the US Coast Survey and occasional income that Juliette received from murky sources in Europe and from renting out fancy clothes she owned. They were, in fact, optimistic about their future finances. Peirce believed that as an inventor, teacher, and logician, along with his many other polymathic skills, he would be a sought-after teacher and intellectual leader, sure to eventually make his fortune through one endeavor or another. (He created on paper the first workable design for an electronic computer and drew up workable plans for acetylene lighting of homes, among several other potentially lucrative innovations that never came to pass. His lighting system, for example, was superseded by Edison's near-simultaneous invention of electric lights.) The purchased home, which Peirce named Arisbe, was not far from New York City. Peirce believed that this home would become the center of a salon culture of wealthy New York summer vacationers, among his other aspirations for it.[4] Indeed, soon after their move to Milford, he and Juliette became good friends of the James W. Pinchot family and their two boys, Amos and Gifford, both of whom Charles influenced intellectually. Amos became a wealthy New York attorney (and the father of Mary Pinchot, who had an affair with John F. Kennedy and was murdered under mysterious circumstances not long after Kennedy's death, having claimed that she possessed evidence that the CIA killed Kennedy). Gifford became, under Theodore Roosevelt, the first director of the US Forestry Service and eventually governor of Pennsylvania. The Peirces were close friends of all the Pinchots and frequent dinner guests. Gifford continued to support Peirce and then Juliette until her death in 1934.[5] In fact, even in the early twenty-first century, the Pinchots of Milford, Tony Pinchot's daughters in particular, include Charles and Juliette in their family lore (Nancy Pinchot, pers. comm.).

Adding to their optimism no doubt was a letter Peirce received in 1890 from Paul Carus, who had recently become the editor of two important journals that Peirce was to publish in regularly, *The Monist* and *The Open Court* (named after the publishing house), both financed by wealthy German-born zinc manufacturer and father-in-law of Carus, Edward C. Hegeler. In this July 1890 letter, Carus invited Peirce to contribute to *Open Court*. Peirce was already writing for *The Nation* (currently the oldest continuously published weekly magazine in the US). These writing opportunities gave a nonnegligible boost to Peirce's income and fame. Peirce was also fortunate that Carus was so keen to have him write for *Open Court* that he often paid him for unwritten articles merely suggested by Peirce, providing financial advances to help Peirce in what later became his precarious poverty.

But ever faithful to his inner principles, and consistent with the thesis that Peirce possessed an inner tenure of the soul, Charles refused to write the easy-to-understand "popular science" that Carus requested, always writing rigorously argued material that would stand up to professional scrutiny. This frustrated Carus, as he expressed in many letters to Peirce. He wanted articles that the average citizen would want to read and buy. But although Peirce wrote difficult material, he did write well. In 1891, commenting in the *American Journal of Psychology* (3, 591), G. Stanley Hall wrote in his review of William James's *Psychology* that James's writing contrasts strongly with that of "Charles Peirce, who burns his own smoke and shoots with a rifle rather than with the shot gun or water hose." Therefore, even though Peirce had been let go from Johns Hopkins, his financial state and professional prospects in Arisbe were still reasonably positive. He had his writing income and the income from the Coast Survey.

However, just nine years after moving to Arisbe, Peirce's financial status was shattered by his dismissal from the US Coast Survey. On September 21, 1891, Peirce received a handwritten letter from the director of the US Coast and Geodetic Survey (the new name for the US Coast Survey), Thomas Corwin Mendenhall. Mendenhall had come into the directorship in 1889 and had heard complaints that Peirce took too long to submit his reports and often failed to justify his spending. The new director had also received a very negative review of the scientific value of Peirce's reports from, who else, Simon Newcomb. These facts contributed to Mendenhall's decision to fire Peirce. He began his letter as follows: "Dear Professor Peirce: Returning to my desk a few days ago after an absence in the West of several months, I was somewhat surprised to learn that nothing had come from you in the way of a report upon the unfinished pendulum work on which you have been so long engaged, or anything showing that you were making any progress towards completing it." From this, the letter proceeds to Mendenhall's statement that "I therefore deem it my duty to inform you by this personal communication that I shall ask that your services be discontinued after the 31st of December next."

In letters subsequent to his dismissal, Charles wrote to James and others of his thoughts of suicide and his feelings of worthlessness in the eyes of the scientific and philosophical communities. James offered emotional encouragement and aided him financially. He did this by arranging lectures for Peirce, such as the Harvard Lectures mentioned earlier, and by recruiting several people to contribute monthly to a fund controlled by James that would guarantee a minimal annual income for Charles and Juliette. Peirce's income therefore now depended entirely on his freelance writing, paid lectures, contributions from those recruited by James, and any entrepreneurial success he might have (though there were many ideas, there were no notable successes). The combined income from all of Peirce's sources was relatively small (often roughly $25,000 annually in twenty-first-century dollars, well below the poverty line now and then). In fact, the Peirces were often unable to buy food or clothes or even heat their home, suffering intense hardship.

It is frequently claimed that Peirce brought these hardships on himself because of quirks, perhaps genetic abnormalities, in his personality. And yet the evidence suggests that his hardships were primarily the result of his refusal to compromise, his utter rejection of the philosophy that guides many, namely, that one should "go along to get along." But because of the widespread view that Peirce's neurodiversity brought about his ruin, it is worth considering this possibility in more detail.

3.7. Neurodiversity?

According to contemporary accounts, Peirce could be unintentionally rude, fail to sense what other people were thinking, lose track of time and social appropriateness, and so on. Taken individually, however, no particular incident in my opinion makes him stand out from any number of academics. I have myself long thought that social awkwardness is common among academics because so many of us spend a disproportionate amount of our time alone, focused on narrow problems that only a handful of people will understand and even fewer care about. It never occurred to me in my study of Peirce that he was particularly abnormal, either neurally or emotionally. Of course, on the ever-rarer occasions when Charles did have an opportunity to give a public lecture and be taken seriously by his fellow academics, he sometimes drank a bit too much or went on for too long. These faux pas seemed to result from Peirce's pleasure in having an audience and being taken seriously. Again, this is not likely different from how many academics would feel and behave after years of ostracism.

As an example of this type of behavior, there is a report by then Harvard philosopher George Santayana: "I heard one of [Peirce's] Harvard lectures. He had been dining at the James's and his evening shirt kept coming out of his evening waistcoat. He looked red-nosed and disheveled, and a part of his lecture seemed to be *ex-tempore* and whimsical. But I remember and have often used in my own thoughts, if not in actual writing, a classification he made that evening of signs into indexes and symbols and images [icons]: possibly there was still another distinct category which I don't remember."[6] Santayana describes the state of a happy man, following a few glasses of wine with his best friend, yet still capable of impressing with new ideas that were clearly of deep significance. From my perspective, Peirce's "disheveled" appearance and red nose are unremarkable. I have had professors in college, including some who were later colleagues, who came to class with their blazer tucked into their pants, their flies unzipped, toilet paper stuck to their shoes, laughing quite alone at their own jokes, and so on. Such oddities seem to be a hazard of the profession of scholarship and at least partially an effect of the constant focus on research.

Of course, it is possible that Peirce fell somewhere along the continuum (he did like continua, so this would not have likely bothered him to discover) of autism spectrum disorder. Temple Grandin, someone who learned to function in society in spite of her autism, joked that autism often accompanies/facilitates creativity, getting laughs for remarking in an address in Silicon Valley that this portion of California is a world center of autism—because autistic people often are able to concentrate and focus more effectively than others. Peirce might have had a degree of autism. We cannot be sure. But I see nothing particularly noteworthy in Peirce's psychology except toughness and focus and, yes, self-centeredness (prerequisites perhaps for being a successful academic). However, some Peirce scholars argue that he did in fact experience a more pronounced form of neurodiversity.

David Pfeifer (2013, 203), for example, says:

> Charles Peirce regularly stated and complained that his thinking processes were not like those of other people. Peirce accounted for his mental difficulty with the notion that he was left-handed. Neurologists consulted in this study note that one in seven people is left-handed and that the thought processes of left-handed people are not noticeably different from right-handed people. Joseph Brent in his biography of Charles Peirce accounts for Peirce's mental anomalies with the claim that Peirce suffered from a manic–depressive disorder or what today is called bipolar disorder.

This article challenges that conclusion. The argument is that Peirce suffered from Asperger's Syndrome.

Pfeifer's conclusions seem moderately supported by more recent research, such as that of Atkin, Richardson, and Blackmore (2007, 1141), though the data on Peirce are to my mind far too sketchy to draw any firm conclusion. With or without some form of neurodiversity, Peirce was an intellectual living in isolation and exercising greater mental focus than the vast majority of other researchers and thinkers, more than the average person of any profession or work.

Of course, as I described earlier, Peirce was banned from Harvard by President Eliot and fired from Johns Hopkins by President Gilman. What can account for this? In the Harvard case, Eliot's feelings against Peirce went back a long time. The first event that Eliot held against Peirce was that Peirce vandalized his classroom when Eliot was a professor of chemistry at Harvard. But much more important (though one cannot say what long-term effect Peirce's youthful pranks might have had), it was known, including to Eliot, that both Charles and Benjamin Peirce held rather low opinions of Eliot as a scholar and as a potential intellectual leader. Benjamin had voted against Eliot's tenure case at Harvard and was chagrined when Eliot eventually returned to Harvard as its president. Later, Eliot added to his reasons for disliking Peirce the claims of immorality raised by Gilman, as well as the claims of professional inadequacy raised (falsely) by Newcomb.

Gilman found Peirce difficult to deal with because, among other reasons, Peirce already had a full-time job with the US Coast Survey, and he wouldn't give it up without assurance that the Johns Hopkins position would become permanent. Gilman, as first president of Johns Hopkins, considered offering a permanent appointment to Peirce (Peirce felt one had been promised), but his budget was severely constrained and the trustees had priorities other than philosophy, which was the department Peirce was in (though he could have just as easily have been assigned to the physics, chemistry, math, psychology, or other departments). But, fatally for Peirce's professorial career, when a Johns Hopkins trustee saw Peirce emerging from a hotel with Juliette, who was not then his wife, the "immorality" and scandal potential for Johns Hopkins University led Gilman not only to fire Peirce, but also to work against him for the remainder of both their lives. He even refused to enter the home of a friend on one occasion when he discovered that Peirce was there. There was deep animosity and disgust, however unfair, in Gilman and Eliot toward Charles.

The same Simon Newcomb also wrote ignorant and falsely accusatory reviews of Peirce's Coast Survey work to Peirce's superiors. These letters were particularly effective because Peirce had already earned the resentment of several Coast Survey colleagues and superiors, who felt that Peirce did not respect his superiors because his father had once been the director. Some thought he acted with a strong sense of entitlement.

Many who knew him at the Coast Survey also believed that he was dilatory in his work and that he failed to follow some regulations because of his father's former power and nepotism in appointing his own son. Peirce was often perceived as acting as though he were superior to others (he likely *did* think he was intellectually and socially superior).

Moreover, as discontent built toward Charles, the Coast Survey's budget was being threatened by Congress. As we saw earlier, his "perfect storm" eventually led to Peirce's dismissal and subsequent poverty, after thirty-one years of brilliant work for the US government. No retirement. No severance.

There are many theories as to why Peirce fell into disfavor, but none of them really requires him being mentally different from anyone else, other than his arrogance from confidence in his superior intelligence.[7] So did Peirce have Asperger's or bipolar disorder? Perhaps. But I see no convincing evidence.

3.8. Recalling Charles Peirce

The various blows to his financial security might have devasted Peirce, as near financial ruin has psychologically hobbled many throughout history. But how did Peirce respond? Tragically? As a failure, hunkered down in eremitic seclusion? No. He responded with hard work and vigorous research. And even as he worked hard, even though he was eccentric from, at least in part, long years of focus on his work, he was a well-liked neighbor by many of the children who knew him, as well as their parents.

Evidence for this comes from some of those very children. On September 17, 1977, ten people who had known Charles or Juliette Peirce as young people gathered in the Peirces' former home of Arisbe, in Milford, Pennsylvania, to answer questions put to them by philosopher Preston Tuttle, along with the director of the interviews, George Stoney. The interviewees, most in their eighties, one in his nineties (Walter Gassmann), remembered Peirce and carried on a lively and entertaining discussion about him.[8]

From 1898 on, the Peirces' closest neighbors in Milford were the Gassmanns. There were three brothers and one sister, Walter, Charles, Ralph, and Hazel, all of whom knew the Peirces well. In the interviews it became clear that Ralph, the youngest brother, held a negative opinion of Charles, owing to his being a small boy when the events being recalled occurred, somewhat put off by the long white beard and strange (to him at least) mannerisms of then a very old Charles Peirce. His older brother, Walter, however, knew Peirce longer, from childhood till his teen years, and had a much more positive view of Peirce as a kind, helpful, down-to-earth yet brilliant man who made him a gift of what Walter called the most useful book he ever owned, as he prepared to leave Milford to train and work as an engineer. The book was *The Mechanical Engineer's Reference Book*, by Henry Harrison Suplee.

The Gassmanns recalled Peirce eating with them frequently when Juliette would go out of town, usually on a visit to Europe. The meal that he seemed to love the first time he had dinner with them was "pigs in a blanket," sausages wrapped in pancakes with sweet syrup. After dinner, the brothers recalled, Charles performed card tricks for them. They were impressed both by how many card tricks he knew and by how well he performed them.

Hazel, with Ralph nodding affirmatively and commenting with her, talked about how Charles would have their mother boil down coffee until it was a jelly, which he would then take home to eat by the spoonful to keep him going as he worked late at night, which he also said soothed the pain caused by the cancer in his intestines.

Several of them mentioned that in their youth Indians still lived in the area and that many times they saw Peirce talking to them on his property. They recalled Charles standing on his front porch from time to time, calling his dog, Zola: "Zola, Zola, Zola," they repeated. Everyone laughed with the memory. And they warmly remembered how Peirce loved his horse, Cora. And Juliette loved her small dog, Fifi. (One recollected that she kept Fifi on a short leash and that he seemed much happier after she died, when he was adopted by a neighbor who let him roam free.)

Walter's memories of Peirce were still vivid and warm, about seventy years later (Walter left the area years before Peirce died):

> The first memories of him was when I used to come over here and was making a French rose garden for his wife.... I don't know just exactly how I got into his study ... he knew that I liked that ... what'll I say, research work, to create something that isn't. He knew that, and that's when I used to sit in his study and talk to him.... And, of course, I could tell that he was a very brilliant man, when you talked to him ... he stands out just vividly right in front of ... I can see him just as plain right now as I did then. Yeah, I can see him ... standing there with his long white beard ... he was sharp. His eyes was sharp. Sometimes when he'd look at you, he'd look right through you.

Caroline Depuy, one who remembered the couple from when she was a young girl, spoke of their relationship: "If ever a woman adored her husband, Madame Peirce adored him. And I believe it was mutual because they sort of lived for each other.... He was devoted." Fellow interviewee Robert Blood added to this, "There was no one ever more in love with her husband than Madame Peirce. To me that made an impression as a small boy even then. Everything was Papa (Juliette's term for Charles)." Most of the interviewees also remembered Charles as very fond of children and very kind to them.

Charles Gassmann, the middle brother, was no longer living at the time of the interviews. But Walter and Ralph described vividly how Charles, checking one sad day in April to see how Charles and Juliette were coping with the cold, found Juliette alone, bundled, and shivering in her room. She immediately asked him to check on "Papa." Charles entered Peirce's upstairs study to find him dying, also shaking from the cold. He had arrived just in time to hold Peirce in his arms as he expired in discomfort and pain, in his large, dark house without heat.

Depuy (former honorary chairman of the Pike County Historical Society, whose farmer father knew Charles well) then offers perhaps the most striking image of Charles Peirce:

> I often think of Professor Peirce and liken him to [George] DeForest [Grush], the famous artist who did so many of the finest Indian paintings in the Metropolitan. He spent his last days in the Middletown Sanitarium. He used his own blood to paint the reds, and a nurse that I knew brought him from the asylum down to the Metropolitan, and he selected each one of his pictures. Professor Peirce spent

so many years dying of cancer, so I feel that everything he has left to posterity now that means so much he wrote with his own blood, as he was really dying during all that time. And thank goodness, thank goodness, the time has come when he is being recognized.

3.9. The End of Dreams

A few years after moving to their beloved Arisbe, when their financial situation had declined steeply, with fears of destitution plaguing Charles, the Peirces variously tried to sell the home or turn it into a profit-generating hotel, both unsuccessfully. Peirce realized that as a man in his sixties, with no income, with bleak prospects for his future, he was going to remain poor, outcast from the intellectual culture that he was raised in and that he so enjoyed. He knew he was unlikely to hold another job of any prestige. He also knew that his problems were by and large of his own making. This, unsurprisingly, often depressed him. Still, until the end of his life he drew plans for expanding Arisbe and invested what little money he had, money that could have been better used elsewhere, in preparing his home for guests and students who never came. His vision of teaching, of an intellectual salon, and of his research motivated him to the end.

Brent (1998, 319), as he discusses these hard years, concludes that "with a distant grief, I muse about this tragic life." But to this the appropriate reply is, "What tragedy? The tragedy of poverty? Of isolation? The tragedy of a lack of professional position?" These were unpleasant realities, of course. But there was no tragic life. Peirce did live a hard, challenging existence that his own choices brought him. But these are choices that he would not have changed and that were consequences of his inner values and perception of his role in the world, a man committed to inquiry. Yes, of course, Peirce died in discomfort from a painful cancer that had been killing him slowly for many years (already in 1901, thirteen years before Peirce's death, Doctor Otto Sommer sent him an article he published in *The Medical Times* in the July–August 1901 edition, "The Abdomino-Sacral and Other New Methods for the Extirpation of Rectal Cancer," indirect evidence that Peirce was already feeling the onset of his cancer). But it is equally true that all of us will die, most likely in sickness and pain. This is the universal end of all life. Death and hardship are hardly tragedies unique to Peirce.

To understand and evaluate Peirce's life as a success or as a failure, we must analyze him *pragmatically*: What were his *actions* during this time? What was he *doing* and what was he *saying* as he watched his body age and his strength and health depart?

As an example of his grit and focus, one reads in his diary entry of March 30, 1914, just under three weeks before he died, suffering the worst agonies of the intestinal cancer that killed him. Peirce wrote, "Had taken Castor oil last night and on waking 'Salts' (Probably Epsom). This mornight good washing out with hot water [referring to his ever-doubtful and painful bowel movements]. Of course a good deal of pain. But was grateful to Dickens for allowing the book to end as he makes it." In his pain and agony, we see that Peirce did not stop reading until the last days of his life. He wasn't writing much by this time and stopped altogether soon after this. But here he was reading Charles Dickens and thinking simultaneously about the endings of life in reality and in novels. His diary rarely, if ever, displays bitterness. He complains occasionally (especially when trying to get money from others, such as Carus and James). But his complaints are remarkable for their scarcity given his many disappointments and difficulties. One is reminded of another important American who died of cancer, twenty-nine years before Charles, Ulysses S. Grant, who also wrote and thought until the very end, having also lost his earlier wealth and also dying of an excruciatingly painful cancer. Yet who would say General Grant died a failure?[9]

Charles writes of a full life, one that, according to his diaries, tended to begin at 7:30 am and end around 1:30 am. His days were full of writing, reading, thinking, some beer drinking, much cigar smoking, occasional shopping, daily correspondence with brilliant friends, and drawing out plans for future projects and research. He played with his dog Zola. He rode to town in his wagon, pulled by his beloved horse Cora. He enjoyed relationships with many neighborhood children, relationships that marked them positively for the rest of their lives. There is no evidence of unusual tragedy or any all-consuming despair. There is certainly little evidence whatsoever of the "moral blindness" that Joseph Brent accuses him of in his biography (Brent 1998, 119).

Intellectually Peirce was active to the end, especially in his active correspondence during his final years. He corresponded with Lady Welby, with James, with Royce, and with a multitude of other philosophers, geologists, physicists, mathematicians, biologists, authors, artists, and others. He also wrote plays in French and English, acted in plays, and was engaged in an amazing range of polymathic endeavors (Everett in progress). He did not live the life of a recluse, except as forced upon him by finances. Instead, he lived in an intellectual universe of his own creation, in which he was the center. And from this creation and his own choices emerged the work that has brought so many into that universe, with Charles still at the center.

3.10. The End of Inquiry

Peirce avoided painkillers and faced the pain of cancer bravely, purposely, and purposefully until he died in young Charles Gassmann's arms. He faced his pain in order to write and think more clearly. He worked at problem-solving until just a few days before he died. Most intellectuals I know would consider this both a good life and a good death.

4. Peirce's Influence and the Trope of Tragedy

Most modern intellectuals have failed to recognize Peirce's importance in world philosophy, though his indirect influence is widespread. This neglect of his legacy leads many philosophers who neglect his work to conclude that Peirce was a minor figure and thus largely a failure. This cycle of neglect, negative opinion, and then more neglect, leading to more negativity, is sustained by the erroneous but common assumption in academics that if someone were really important, they would also be famous. One example of the neglect of Peirce's legacy that reinforces the bias that Peirce is of little significance can be found in Scott Soames's book *The World Philosophy Made: From Plato to the Digital Age*, wherein we find just one note about Peirce (spelled incorrectly in the index as Pierce) mentioning (incorrectly) that Peirce's logic "did not have the historical impact that Frege's did" (Soames 2019, 413). This ignores the fact that in *Principia Mathematica* Bertrand Russell and Alfred North Whitehead used Peirce's notation, not Gottlob Frege's, and that it was Giuseppe Peano's adaptation of Peirce, not Frege, that led to modern mathematical logic. This neglect cycle is a form of what one might call in the early twenty-first century the "canceling" of Peirce. In some ways it is still the legacy of his dismissal from Johns Hopkins, which deprived him of students and a more standard forum for his ideas and work.

We might have excused Soames's book had it been written in the 1970s, as at that time Peirce's writings were harder to access. But this is not true any longer and certainly it was not the case when Soames wrote his book. The effect is that Soames's book arguably omits any discussion of the most important philosopher in American history and arguably the most important system-builder since Aristotle, contributing to the false idea that Peirce never achieved the importance he aspired to, typical of many tragic features, reinforcing the myth of the "tragic Peirce" that is so widespread.

Peirce set out to create a philosophy and build a system that would "rival Aristotle's." And one can make the case that he did just that. The importance and range of Peirce's contributions to science, mathematics, and philosophy can be appreciated again by recognizing that many of the most important advances in philosophy and science during the twentieth century originated with him: the development of mathematical logic (independent of Gottlob Frege and with a clearer notational system that led many to adopt Peirce's logical system over Frege's, contra Soames), the development of semiotics (before and in more detail than Ferdinand de Saussure's work), the philosophical school of pragmatism (before William James), the modern development of phenomenology (independent of Edmund Husserl), and the invention of universal grammar with the property of interpretational recursion (before Noam Chomsky; though, for Peirce, universal grammar, a term Peirce seems to have been the first American to use, in 1865, was subordinate to speculative grammar, in part a set of constraints on signs and their expression).

In another recent survey, A. C. Grayling's 2019 *The History of Philosophy*, Peirce is just as inexplicably overlooked. In Grayling's work, the discussion of Peirce is slightly better than that in Soames's, but it is still marred by the myopia typical of overly ambitious intellectual histories, with their focus on the familiar and avoidance of more difficult and less well-known ideas and people, again suggesting that Peirce was but a minor figure and, thus, in Peirce's own values, a failure.

Such omissions as we find in Soames, Grayling, and others not only are detrimental to the value of these works, but also simply propagate popular and widely accepted "official" histories. What passes for intellectual history is often not all that different from a great deal of modern journalism, which tends to repeat twice-told stories, use the same experts, frame debates in the same terms, regurgitate opinions and information from popular works, and repeat standard views uncritically. This can be harmful no matter how deeply thoughtful these views might otherwise be. In the case of Peirce, this too frequent way of surveying history is particularly unfortunate because of his significance and because it reinforces the trope of the "tragic Peirce."[10]

It is undeniable that Peirce struck many of his contemporaries as eccentric, sometimes just weird. But was he really so eccentric? As discussed above, the eccentricity we have evidence for is most easily explained as the oddness that comes with the job of a lifetime of intellectual focus. However, being odd is not tragedy. Some might still argue that Peirce's life was tragic simply because he died in obscurity and poverty. But this facile view of success and failure also seems misguided.

5. Writing in His Own Blood

Although those who knew him as children talk extensively about his poverty, about how Arisbe fell into disrepair, about Peirce's painful suffering from cancer, and about how desperately cold Arisbe was, the conclusion that the evidence of his life forces upon us is that he would rather have lived conducting his research freely as he did than to lead a wealthy or at least more secure life without his research. His uncompromising faithfulness to his research and his faith in its quality, in spite of criticism, are ultimately what led to Newcomb's corrosive jealousy and the dislike of his cocksureness (arrogance to many) among many colleagues and administrators. That is how his poverty is reconciled with the idea that Peirce lived a good and successful life. Nearly everyone who wrote about his life has talked about how he ruined it by failure to conform and weird behavior. But few have argued that he did always what he thought was right and what he felt he had to do. His was a life of free inquiry. And it was a deeply ethical life: he lived and died by his own values. Peirce created his own tenure in all of his life's circumstances and arguably this independence was much greater and led to more significant results that any other way of life for him might have.[11]

Moreover, if we examine standard ideas of happiness and success, to me there is much evidence for the conclusion that Peirce *was* a happy man. He had fulfilling work that he knew was important. He had friends of the highest intellectual caliber. He had a loving marital relationship and always enjoyed the love and respect of his siblings and many friends. His home, in spite of all its problems, was large, usually comfortable (it was not always winter, after all), housed his books, and offered him a wonderful place to work in one of the most beautiful parts of the US.

Of course, he lost several opportunities and jobs. He was denied grants. People called him a crackpot. But he was also widely respected. This kind of mixed reaction is the lot of most academics. And the more prominent the academic, the more mixed the reaction from their peers. Why was this the case with Peirce? Because he refused to compromise. He told people they were wrong openly, publicly or not, often to their face, and no matter whether they were friend or foe. He was a serious pursuer of truth, and it is in that pursuit that his fulfillment is found.

Tenure is defined in Wikipedia as "a means of defending the principle of academic freedom, which holds that it is beneficial for society in the long run if scholars are free to hold and examine a variety of views." This is a fair definition. But in this wider sense, tenure can be a basis for living and fulfillment. One greater than happiness. Not a professional tenure, but a "tenure of the soul."

The great British phonetician, Peter Ladefoged of the University of California at Los Angeles, a resident of Los Angeles for more than five decades, told me once during fieldwork in the Amazon that he had not yet naturalized as a US citizen because he did not want to belong to a country that placed "the pursuit of happiness" in its founding documents. "There are more important things than happiness." Of course, much depends on how one defines happiness. If what is meant is giddy emotion, then no thanks. But one can make purpose, love, respect, sense of achievement, fulfillment in relationships and work, and other components part of a combined concept of happiness and success. For this reason, it has been argued here that Peirce lived a successful life, even a happy life. As we saw, people who knew him personally remarked that they could not imagine a couple who loved each other more. They talked about his love for his horse and his dog. And they talked about his brilliance, his love of his work, and his dedication to that work in a home that provided room for his books and was a lovely place outside the winter months. We must reconsider the ideas of happiness and success if we think Peirce was unhappy, or if we believe that happiness is found in typical academic achievement—position, salary, awards, citations, and so on.

Peirce worked until his own end of inquiry, writing for years in his own blood, as Caroline Depuy had put it. But defeated? Tragic? A failure? I would like to be such a failure.

Notes

1. Many other famous, innovative Americans were born or active around this time. In fact, Henry and William James were not even the most famous James brothers. Frank and Jesse were innovating ways of robbing banks and trains while their less well-known contemporaries, William and Henry, were creating literature and psychological science.
2. See also Cheryl Misak's "Peirce's Thwarted Career," which appears as Chapter 3 of this handbook.
3. For a more detailed discussion of Peirce's European travels, see the next chapter in this handbook, by Jaime Nubiola and Sara Barrena.
4. The name Arisbe, according to Fisch, comes from Peirce's knowledge of and interest in Greek history and philosophy: "Arisbe was a colony of Miletus, the home of the first philosophers of Greece—Thales, Anaximander, and Anaximenes—who first had sought the *Archê* the Principle, the First of things (R905:22–26, 1907). Of Peirce's three categories, it was Firstness that had given him the greatest difficulties, and it was only when Epicurus had helped him to a partial solution of them that he was ready to join the Greek cosmologists, and that his Arisbe too became a colony of Miletus" (Fisch 1986, 244).

5. Due to their poverty, the Peirces were buried together in a plot owned by the Pinchot family in the Milford cemetery.
6. Letter from George Santayana to Justus Buchler, October 15, 1937, *The Letters of George Santayana: Book Six, 1937–1940* (Cambridge, MA: MIT Press, 2004).
7. But this is another common ailment of the academic profession. As I have often heard, an academic audience is one in which every person in the audience likely believes they are the smartest person in the room.
8. Thanks to the Columns Museum of the Pike County Historical Society in Milford, Pennsylvania, for providing me with a digital copy of the video recording of these discussions and reminiscences.
9. And one can hardly say that Grant's life ended better than Peirce's because Grant left his widow financially well-off by finishing his autobiography, marketed successfully by his friend and publisher Mark Twain, after his death.
10. As Max Fisch put it,

    Who is the most original and the most versatile intellect that the Americas have so far produced? The answer "Charles S. Peirce" is uncontested, because any second would be so far behind as not to be worth nominating. Mathematician, astronomer, chemist, geodesist, surveyor, cartographer, metrologist, spectroscopist, engineer, inventor; psychologist, philologist, lexicographer, historian of science, mathematical economist, lifelong student of medicine; book reviewer, dramatist, actor, short-story writer; phenomenologist, semiotician, logician, rhetorician [and] metaphysician. . . . He was, for a few examples, . . . the first metrologist to use a wavelength of light as a unit of measure, the inventor of the quincuncial projection of the sphere, the first known conceiver of the design and theory of an electric switching-circuit computer, and the founder of "the economy of research." He is the only system-building philosopher in the Americas who has been both competent and productive in logic, in mathematics, and in a wide range of sciences. If he has had any equals in that respect in the entire history of philosophy, they do not number more than two. (Fisch 1981, 17)

11. Camus's great work, *The Myth of Sisyphus* (1942), talks about the so-called tragedy of a man (Sisyphus) who is condemned by the gods to push a boulder to the top of a hill during the day only to see it roll back down the hill and have to begin again the next day. Though this is originally intended as a horrible example of divine punishment, Camus argues that this work gave the man purpose and measurable goals and that his life was therefore not tragic. There is a sense in which we are all personifications of Sisyphus. Thus, even in the worst possible interpretation, as in the Greek myth, purposeful work that faces us every day is not a tragedy, but a blessing, according to Camus. It is a blessing that all laborers enjoy and one that motivated Peirce throughout his life.

Bibliography

Atkin, Albert, J. E. Richardson, and C. Blackmore. 2007. "Arguing with Asperger Syndrome," In Frans H. van Eemeren (ed.), *Proceedings of the International Society for the Study of Argumentation (ISSA)*. Amsterdam: SIC SAT, 1141–1146.
Berlin, Isaiah. [1999] 2000. *The Roots of Romanticism*. Princeton: Princeton University Press.
Brent, Joseph. 1998. *Charles Sanders Peirce: A Life*. Bloomington: Indiana University Press.

Camus, Albert. 1942. *Le Mythe de Sisyphe*. Paris: Editions Gallimard.

Emerson, Ralph W. 1866. *The Complete Works of Ralph Waldo Emerson, Comprising His Essays, Lectures, Poems and Orations*, 2 Vols. London: Bell and Daldy.

Everett, Daniel L. Forthcoming. *American Aristotle: The Life of Charles Sanders Peirce*. Princeton: Princeton University Press.

Fisch, Max H. 1981. Introduction to Thomas Sebeok, & Jean U. Sebeok: "You Know My Method." In Thomas Sebeok (ed.), *The Play of Musement*. Bloomington: Indiana University Press, 1–16.

Fisch, Max H. 1986. *Peirce, Semeiotic, and Pragmatism*. Bloomington: Indiana University Press.

Frye, Northrop. 1968. *Anatomy of Criticism*. New York: Atheneum.

Goodman, Nelson. 1983. *Fact, Fiction, and Forecast*. Cambridge, Massachusetts: Harvard University Press.

Grayling, Anthony C. 2019. *The History of Philosophy*. New York: Penguin Press.

Houser, Nathan. 2009. Santayana's Peirce. *Transactions of the Charles S. Peirce Society* 45, no. 4 (Fall): 516–531.

Kaag, John. 2013. "Returning to the Unformed: Emerson and Peirce on the 'Law of Mind.'" *Cognitio* 14: 189–202.

Nubiola, Jaime. 2020. "The Cosmopolitan Peirce: His European Travels." *Transactions of the Charles S. Peirce Society* 56, no. 2 (Spring): 190–198.

Peirce, Benjamin. 1882. *Linear Associative Algebra, with Notes and Addenda by C. S. Peirce, Son of the Author*. Van Nostrand.

Peirce, Charles S. 1931–1958. *The Collected Papers of Charles Sanders Peirce*. 8 vols. Vols. 1–6 edited by Charles Hartshorne and Paul Weiss; vols. 7–8 edited by Arthur W. Burks. Cambridge, Massachusetts: Harvard University Press. (Referred to as CP.)

Pfeifer, David E. 2013. Charles Peirce: "... My Brain Must Be Different..." *Cognitio*, 14, 203–220.

Pfeifer, David E. 2015. "A Singular Love Affair—Charles and Juliette Peirce." *Cognitio*, 16, 137–152.

Raposa, Michael L. 2021. "Peirce and Racism: Biographical and Philosophical Considerations." *Transactions of the Charles S. Peirce Society* 57, no. 1 (Winter): 32–44.

Soames, Scott. 2019. *The World Philosophy Made: From Plato to the Digital World*. Princeton: Princeton University Press.

Tuttle, Preston. 1977. *Transcript of TV Taped Group Interview of the Friends and Neighbors of Charles and Juliette Peirce*. Manuscript. Princeton, NJ.

CHAPTER 2

THE COSMOPOLITAN PEIRCE

His Five Visits to Europe

JAIME NUBIOLA AND SARA BARRENA

> Philosophy is a study which needs a very protracted concentrated study before one so much as begins to be at all expert in the handling of it, if one is to be precise, systematic, and scientific. I gave ten years [1855–1865] to it before I ventured to offer half a dozen brief contributions of my own. Three years later, when I had produced something more elaborated I went abroad and in England, Germany, Italy, Spain, learned from their own mouths what certain students at once of science and of philosophy were turning in their minds.
>
> C. S. Peirce, draft of a letter to the editor of *The Sun*, R325:4–5, *c.* 1907

CHARLES Peirce traveled to Europe on five occasions.[1] The five trips took place between 1870 and 1883, all of them in the service of the Coast and Geodetic Survey, at the time the chief scientific agency of the United States. Those trips—which covered a total of thirty-eight months—were a rich mixture of scientific research and tourism, communication with other scientists, and enjoyment of the artistic treasures of Europe. The impact of this extensive traveling was so important in Peirce's life and thought that it makes perfect sense to identify this period of time as his "cosmopolitan period"—to use Max Fisch's expression.[2]

Our contribution describes Peirce's five European trips and highlights some of the main relevant points related to those journeys. The common image of Peirce as an isolated thinker writing in Arisbe without any contact with the world not only is historically inaccurate, but also makes it difficult to understand some key elements of his philosophy. Peirce's experiences of his European trips are reflected in his broad correspondence (professional and family letters), which until now has been unduly neglected by the scholarship. We are convinced that the feelings that Peirce experienced in Europe were seeds that bore fruit in later years. A close study of Peirce's letters and other documents of those years helps to avoid a number of misunderstandings about his thought and its evolution, highlighting his active participation in the first line of cooperative scientific research (astronomy, geodesy, metrology, etc.).

THE COSMOPOLITAN PEIRCE

The great scholar Max Fisch identified three periods in Peirce's philosophic activity: his Cambridge period, covering his formative years from 1851 to 1870; the cosmopolitan period from 1870 to 1887, in which he traveled extensively and did his most important scientific work; and the Arisbe period from 1887 until his death, "the longest of the three, and the most productive philosophically."[3] This chronological division of Peirce's development is, according to Houser, "convenient and well-considered,"[4] but it seems to us that this middle period is the less commonly studied, although it is essential to get a faithful understanding of Peirce's life and thought.

The word "cosmopolitan" in the title of the chapter refers to this specific middle period of Peirce's life, but also aspires to reflect the double meaning of the term according to the *Merriam-Webster Dictionary*: on the one hand, a cosmopolitan person has "wide international sophistication," and on the other hand, someone is identified as cosmopolitan when he or she has "worldwide rather than limited or provincial scope or bearing." In both senses the adjective "cosmopolitan" can be applied to Peirce in this period of his life. He not only used to stay in the best hotels in the main cities of Europe and enjoyed all the luxuries of the touristic places he visited, but also invested rigorous and extenuating blocks of time in serious activities in the laboratories of Kew, near London, and in Paris, Berlin, Geneva, and several other places. He was on the front line of science, particularly in geodesy, astronomy, and metrology.

We can illustrate the latter by Peirce's efforts to improve the scientific instruments available for research in order to refine his experimental observations. Let us quote, for instance, from a letter his wife Zina wrote to his mother on June 25, 1876, from Richmond, near London, at the end of his second European journey (the quotation also gives insight into Peirce's character)[5]: "His experiments seem to have been entirely satisfactory. 'They are as good as in the present state of the science could have been expected, and will be creditable to him & to the Survey. More than that,' he says [CSP], 'I do not claim.' But he says that 'Science is in a bad way because there are no instrument makers who want to make instruments suited for research. They only want to make things that will pay, like school apparatus.'"

The main point we want to higlight, however, is that pragmatism—born in the meetings of the Metaphysical Club in Cambridge in the early 1870s and expressed for the first time in print in Peirce's "How to Make Our Ideas Clear" of 1878—was based at least in part in the experiences of Peirce during the three European journeys that preceded it. As we like to say, the seeds planted in his mind and in his heart during these European travels bore their best fruit in the pragmatist approach to some traditional problems of knowledge typical of modern philosophy. In fact, when Peirce was trying to explain the birth of pragmatism ("Pragmatism Made Easy") in his letter to the editor of *The Sun* of the year 1907, this was precisely what he asserted. Just following the epigraph we opened our chapter with, in which Peirce briefly described his biographical training and his first journey through Europe in 1870–1871, Peirce wrote:

> After my return, a knot of us, Chauncey Wright, Nicholas St. John Green, William James, and others, including occasionally Francis Ellingwood Abbot and John Fiske, used frequently to meet to discuss fundamental questions. Green was especially impressed with the doctrines of Bain, and impressed the rest of us with them; and finally the writer of this brought forward what we called the principle of pragmatism. Several years later, this was set forth in two articles printed in the *Popular Science Monthly* (Nov. 1877 and Jan. 1878) and subsequently in the *Revue Philosophique*.
>
> The particular point that had been made by Bain and that had most struck Green, and through him, the rest of us, was the insistence that what a man really believes is what he would be ready to act upon, and to risk much upon. The writer endeavoured to weave that truth in *with others which he had made out for himself*, so as to make a consistent doctrine of cognition [our italics]. (R325:4–6)

Alexander Bain (1818–1903) was a Scottish philosopher, the founder of *Mind*, who tried to apply the scientific method to psychology. Peirce did not meet him personally, but he and William James were well versed in Bain's books *The Senses and the Intellect* (1855), *The Emotions and the Will* (1859), and *Mental and Moral Science* (1868). Max Fisch meticulously studied all the data available about the links between Bain and the members of the Metaphysical Club to clarify his role in the genealogy of pragmatism.[6] We want also to highlight the relevance of the scientific and the artistic experiences gained by Peirce in his European journeys to develop his pragmatism. As Houser suggested, "Peirce's sense of the existential impact of his European experiences and the need to somehow link the qualitative firstness of experience with its existential secondness to form a conception of it may have helped him draw together some of the early ideas drawing him to pragmatism."[7] In this sense, it is important to acknowledge that Peirce's travels through Europe were instrumental in the genealogy of pragmatism and in the development of his later aesthetics; they are also instrumental to contemporary readers of Peirce in order to fully understand him.

1. First European Journey: June 18, 1870–March 7, 1871

The main goal of Peirce's first trip to Europe was to identify suitable locations for establishing observatories in order to study the total solar eclipse that was to take place at noon on December 22, 1870, over the Mediterranean Sea. Moreover, his father, Benjamin Peirce, wanted to introduce him to several prominent European mathematicians (Augustus De Morgan, W. Stanley Jevons, William K. Clifford, etc.). On June 18, Peirce sailed for London in the company of his brother Jem, on the steamer SS *Deutschland*. The brothers separated in London, and Charles crossed to the continent. In the fall, Charles was joined by his father, his wife Zina, and the rest of the team of observers in charge of the observation of the solar eclipse.

Charles Peirce's itinerary led him from London to Berlin, Dresden, Prague, Vienna, Pest, the Danube River, Varna (Bulgaria), the Black Sea, and, finally, Constantinople. From Constantinople, Peirce traced the path of totality, that is to say, the path of the locations where the total eclipse would be visible, scouting for the most suitable locations for scientific observation. Thus, he scouted out locations in Greece, Italy, and Spain and thereby contributed to the success of the scientific expedition under the command of his father Benjamin. On the way, he also visited his sister-in-law Amy Fay in Berlin, who accompanied him during what appears to have been a delightful visit to Dresden. In Vienna he was kindly received by Edmund Weiss and Karl L. Littrow, director of the observatory, and in Constantinople he enjoyed the guidance of the British orientalist Edward H. Palmer and his friend Charles Drake. All in all, Peirce traveled extensively through the part of Europe that since July of 1870 had been involved in the Franco-Prussian War before he joined the American team that observed the eclipse in the vicinity of Catania, in Sicily. In spite of some bad weather, the results of the American expedition were fully successful. As Joseph Brent wrote in his biography of Peirce, "this expedition was Charles's first experience of large-scale international scientific cooperation, and it illustrated for him the importance of the community of science in reevaluating and validating its hypotheses."[8]

After the eclipse, the American group returned to Rome via Naples, and Charles and Zina began an extensive trip through Italy, Switzerland, Germany, and England, recorded in quite a bit of detail in a notebook that Peirce bought in Geneva on January 13, 1871. Peirce registered in that notebook his most relevant activities of the first six weeks of the year 1871. Charles and Zina embarked on the *Aleppo* steamer, which left Liverpool on February 21 and arrived in Boston on March 7.

This journey constituted an important experience for the young Peirce. His letters are full of accounts of the impressions that the various places made upon him, and they also show the human side of Peirce, as when he worries about being robbed or getting ill, or when he is subject to mood swings and changing sentiments. As a cosmopolitan traveler, Peirce wrote pages and pages with comments about the climate and the weather, the dirt of the cities and places where he stayed, wines and food, prices and bargaining, clothes, means of transportation, and the customs and curiosities of the many places he was visiting.[9] It can be said, however, that Peirce was not a typical tourist, or at least that he did not pay attention to the things that attract attention at first sight. He was not impressed at all by grandeur or magnificence. On the contrary, in several letters he wrote disparagingly of important monuments and paid attention to lesser-known works of art or anodyne details.

His views about some places are somewhat peculiar. For instance, he obviously enjoyed London ("I am pleased with England, the air is so mild and moist and one can walk and eat so much. The country is very picturesque and the city is too in another way"), but not Berlin, and he complained in several letters of its awful smell (Letters of June 30 and August 11 to his brother Jem and Letter to his wife Zina of September 4). Peirce advised against visiting Berlin, unless you go there to visit someone you know, and he wrote that its architecture and sculpture did not express anything: "The architecture and sculpture have a very artificial and made up look, generally imitations of classic style and fail altogether of any real effect even when you must acknowledge them to be fine. The finest thing is the Victory over the Brandenburg Thor and that has the effect of a small bronze. The artist has taken no advantage at the large size to produce any particular effect of greatness or sublimity" (Letter of July 30 to his brother Jem, RL339).

He describes Pest as "a rather pleasant place to stay" (Letter of August 25 to his brother Jem) and Constantinople as "by all odds the most beautiful & fascinating place I have been in yet" (Letter of September 2 to his wife Zina, RL337). Constantinople seems to him a completely different city: "There is such a flood of complete novelty before my eyes everywhere that I have not time to get used to it at all even enough to describe it. What shall I begin with?" (Letter of August 28 to his wife Zina, RL337). Peirce seems to be most comfortable in the most picturesque places he visited, which include Cavalla, the first walled city he had ever seen (Letter of September 5); Volo, an "odd looking town," which will appear later in his fictional story, "Topographical Sketches in Thessaly with Fictional Embroideries," in which he intended to convey his fascination with Greece; Bern, where he liked the fountains and the cathedral; Dresden, where he noted with surprise that none of his acquaintances who had been there had spoken of the beauty of the city; and Narbonne, where he visited the cathedral and an interesting local museum.

The references from his letters could be multiplied indefinitely. However, the point that we want to underline is that Peirce in his first trip not only "discovered" Europe, but also learned the great importance of the sensations that things produce in us, and thus the importance of the aesthetic experience. Throughout all his life Peirce, through his scientific methodology, tried to combine sensations with the imagination and rational elaboration of those sensations. For Peirce, science—and also art—had to be derived from experience and observation. In this sense it can be said that his European voyages certainly belonged to the process that Peirce described in 1903, a process that would become essential for his notion of art and science: "I have gone through a systematic course of training in recognizing my feelings. I have worked with intensity for so many hours a day every day for long years to train myself to this; and it is a training which I would recommend to all of you. The artist has such a training" (CP5.112).

2. Second European Journey: April 3, 1875–August 20, 1876

In 1872, Charles Peirce had been promoted by his father Benjamin to the rank of assistant in the Coast Survey, the rank just below that of superintendent. (Although 'assistant' may sound nowadays to be a low-level position, it was quite the opposite: probably the assistants of the superintendent would be called today 'senior scientists' or something analogous.) In November 1872, Peirce was "directed to take charge of the Pendulum experiments of the Coast Survey, and to direct and inspect all the parties engaged in such experiments."[10] Consequently, his primary field of scientific endeavor became geodesy: "The two main aims of Peirce's geodetic operations were to determine the force of gravity at various locations in the United States and abroad and, from these results, determine the figure of the earth."[11]

Peirce's second assignment to Europe (April 1875–August 1876)—the longest one—was particularly relevant for his extensive work with pendulums: gravimetric determinations in what were called the 'initial stations' (Geneva, Paris, Berlin, and Kew, near London) were to be compared with the determinations of the gravity in Hoboken, New Jersey. In the spring of 1874, Benjamin Peirce resigned from his position as superintendent of the Coast Survey and became a 'consulting geometer,' maintaining his influence in the institution but freeing himself from the administrative burden. Benjamin and Carlile P. Patterson, the new superintendent, decided at the end of 1874 that Charles Peirce should spend at least one year in Europe to improve American geodesy and to try to put it at the European level. According to this decision, Charles and his wife Zina, together with Peirce's assistant Henry Farquhar, left for Europe in April 1875 on the steamer *Adriatic*. Here Peirce met William H. Appleton, editor of the *Popular Science Monthly*, who offered him a good price for some articles for the magazine.

The main places visited on this second journey were London, the Kew Observatory, Hamburg, Berlin, Geneva, and Paris, and the main purpose was to collect the reversible Bessel pendulum in Hamburg—from the instrument makers Repsold & Sohne—that Peirce had ordered for the Coast Survey three years before to be used in absolute determinations of gravity in Berlin, Geneva, Paris, London, and New York. This second trip was also relevant for the development of Peirce's aesthetic sense, as it is reflected in his beautiful touristic letters from England, in April 1875, or in his extensive report from Paris of the theaters and operas in that city (Letter to his brother Jem of December 10, 1875, RL339). In these letters Peirce provides a rich account of his impressions and experiences, such as those produced by the worship service he attended in the cathedral of Chester, which he said was "beautifully intoned & spiritually refreshing" (Letter to his family of April 14, 1875, RL341), or his impression of London: "Of course the first thing which strikes one in approaching London is the darkening of the light from the smoke. Everywhere in England on the brightest days there seems to be a veil over the sun which is by no means disagreeable but London is decidedly too dark. [. . .] The next thing which strikes one is the immensity of the city and the enormous throng of vehicles and especially of handsome equipages extending for miles and miles" (Letter to his family of April 14, 1875, RL341).

He states that everything English seemed to him to be well-made, complete, and properly taken care of, excepting the smoke that poured from factories, forges, and coal pits, although he also was impressed by the hellish aspect that it gave to the "black country" in Wales (Letter to his family of April 18, 1875, RL341).

In England, Peirce spoke with several British instrument makers (Casella, Browning) and scientists, including James Clerk Maxwell at the new Cavendish Laboratory in Cambridge, who agreed with his views on the characteristics of the resistance affecting pendulums. He also met again with the mathematician William K. Clifford—who had observed the solar eclipse in Sicily in 1870—and they talked about the logic of relatives and Peirce's proposed book on the subject.[12]

After receiving the pendulum in Hamburg, Charles and Zina moved to Berlin, where the new American pendulum was compared with the Prussian standard. Zina visited again her sister Amy, who studied music there, and both went to visit Liszt in Weimar. For his part, Peirce had several meetings with General Johann Jacob Baeyer, founder and president of the Royal Prussian Geodetic Institute. Baeyer "informed me that he had become dissatisfied with the reversible pendulum and wished to adopt the plan of swinging an invariable pendulum *in vacuo* [...] He was so decided in his condemnation of the instrument & of all that had been done with it that it will somewhat modify the immediate value of my swings here" (Letter of June 4, 1875, from Berlin to Superintendent Carlile P. Patterson).[13] The problem was concentrated in the vibrations of the stand of the pendulum, which very likely distorted the results.

On July 16, Peirce visited Leipzig to study the publication of his *Photometric Researches* with Engelmann, "the greatest publisher of such things in the world," as Peirce wrote to his colleague in the Harvard observatory, Arthur Searle (Letter of July 17, 1875). At the end of July, Peirce proceeded alone—without Zina, who stayed with her sister and in September traveled back to Cambridge—to Geneva, where he met Émile Plantamour, director of the observatory, to test the Repsold pendulum and also to measure the flexure of the support suspected by Baeyer. In September, Peirce traveled to Paris, where the Permanent Commission of the International Association of Geodesy met for ten days, chaired by the Spaniard Carlos Ibáñez de Ibero, and here the issue of the pendulum raised by Baeyer was considered. As Peirce wrote to Superintendent Patterson: "The subject of the pendulum was minutely discussed. The preference was given to the reversible over the invariable pendulum, quite rightly I do not doubt. It was at the same time admitted that there were various defects in the apparatus. These were not precisely specified in the resolution adopted except that it was recognized as desirable to ascertain whether the axis of rotation of the pendulum coincided with the knife-edge" (Letter of September 23, 1875). As Max Fisch writes, with Peirce's exposition of the report of his Geneva findings, "he thus became the first invited American participant in the committee meetings of an international association."[14]

During his long stay in Paris that winter, Peirce outlined the ideas for the "Illustrations of the Logic of Science,"[15] the series of articles that would appear two years later (1877–1878) in the *Popular Science Monthly*.[16] Despite his work and his interest in French life and culture, that period was marked for Peirce by a deep depression due to the departure of his wife, economic difficulties, the breakage of some instruments during travel, and the reluctance of the Paris Observatory to allow him to use the necessary laboratory instruments to continue his pendular investigations.[17] In October, he was considering returning to the United States early, with the job unfinished. However, Peirce remained in Paris, where he enjoyed, among other things, the support of the writer Henry James, brother of William James. During this stay, Peirce was able also to examine in depth medieval and Renaissance manuscripts from Ptolemy's star catalog at the National Library of Paris that were useful for his *Photometric Researches*, which would be printed in 1878 by Engelmann and distributed to the main astronomers of Europe and America.[18]

In March 1876, Peirce traveled to Berlin in order to make determinations of gravity with the reversible pendulum. In May he suffered a serious nervous breakdown, the main symptom of which was a temporary but complete paralysis.[19] In mid-June, already recovered, Peirce returned to London to make similar gravimetric determinations at the Kew observatory. On June 20, Zina arrived in England to take care of him and they returned together in the steamer *Marathon*, which left Liverpool on August 8 and arrived in Boston on August 20.

3. Third European Journey: September 13, 1877–November 18, 1877

This was Peirce's shortest European trip—but extremely important for his scientific profile—occasioned by the meeting of the International Geodetic Association in Stuttgart, Germany, from September 27 to October 2, in which Peirce defended his views on the bending of the stand of the pendulum and its influence on the accuracy of the measurement of gravity. It was, therefore, a trip mainly focused on his professional activity in which, in addition to Stuttgart, he traveled to Leipzig, Berlin, and Paris.

Peirce left on September 13, 1877, to Europe in the steamer *Suevia*. He traveled by himself this time. During the sailing Peirce took the opportunity to write most of the second article, "How to Make Our Ideas Clear," of the series that would be published in the *Popular Science Monthly* the following year, as well as the French translation of the first one, "The Fixation of Belief."[20] Upon arrival in Plymouth on Monday, September 24, Peirce passed through London and continued his evening trip through Dover and Ostend to Brussels, where he took the night train to Stuttgart. As he describes in his letters, there he met old friends who gave him a great welcome, among them Theodor von Oppolzer and the old General Baeyer. Let us transcribe Peirce's description forty years later of his great success:

> I met Genl. Baeyer and his daughter in the corridor of the hotel as I was being shown to my room and the old General who had been fighting for me all day but really did not *know* much about the subject was so delighted to see me that he threw his arms round me and kissed me on both cheeks! The next morning I went into the meeting which was a particularly distinguished gathering, several men who were not regular geodesists being among them, as Henri St. Claire Deville—M. Faye—etc. I began with the mathematical theory which I had, in coming across, succeeded in putting into a form in which every man of them could see the correctness of it. Then

I described the instrument by which I had automatically registered the instants of the passage of the pendulum over the vertical, while it was swinging on the brass tripod and when it was on a properly stiff support. I had the chronograph sheets with me, and the whole demonstration was complete, and when I sat down each of my three antagonists at Brussels [the previous meeting where Peirce's proposal had been criticized in his absence] got up one after another and very handsomely admitted that I was entirely right. And from that time I was acknowledged as the head of that small branch or twig of science.[21]

After the success of Stuttgart, Peirce went to Leipzig and to Berlin, where he made comparisons in the observatory between the North American and the Prussian pendulums. From Berlin he went to Paris, where he arranged with Théodule Ribot the publication in the *Revue Philosophique* of the articles prepared during his trip and visited the observatory and some builders of instruments. On November 1 he traveled to Rouen, where he admired its cathedral, and on November 2 he returned from Le Havre to the United States on the steamer *Herder*. He arrived on November 18 and soon after suffered a new nervous breakdown, perhaps caused by the excessive work and activity of the previous months.

The *Coast Survey Report* for the year 1876 included the long study of Peirce—signed on December 13, 1878—"Measurements of Gravity at Initial Stations in America and Europe," covering 135 pages (pp. 202–337 of the Appendix No. 15). As Max Fisch notes,[22] on the second page of this study Peirce wrote: "The value of gravity-determinations depends upon their being bound together, each with all the others which have been made anywhere upon the earth. [...] Geodesy is the one science the successful prosecution of which absolutely depends upon international solidarity" (W 4:81).

Peirce's traveling through Europe and his exhausting work in gravity determinations in the different initial stations made him an acknowledged scientist in the field of geodesy. For this reason, it seems completely true to say—as Fisch wrote—that "Peirce was not merely a philosopher or a logician who had read up on science. He was a full-fledged professional scientist, who carried into all his work the concerns of the philosopher and logician."[23]

4. Fourth European Journey: April 28, 1880–August 4, 1880

The fourth trip of Charles S. Peirce is given the least attention by Brent in his biography[24] and by Houser in his introduction to volume 4 of the *Writings*, where only one paragraph is dedicated to it.[25] But it is nonetheless interesting and worthy of attention. It consists primarily of a long stay in Paris with a short trip to London.

In Paris, Peirce dedicated himself to measurements of gravity in the observatory of Paris, then directed by Admiral Ernest Mouchez. The determinations that had been made there during his previous two trips had varied significantly with respect to the measurements established by Jean-Charles de Borda (1733–1799) and Jean-Baptiste Biot (1774–1862) decades earlier, but Peirce managed to show that by correcting some errors of which Borda and Biot were unaware, the results of their work were very similar. The text "On the Value of Gravity at Paris" (W4:148–151) is a translation of "Sur la valeur de la pesanteur à Paris," which Peirce presented at the French Academy of Sciences and published in *Comptes Rendus des Séances of l'Académie des Sciences* (1880, vol. 90, 1401–1403).

We know from the Paris Observatory diary that on May 21, 1880, Peirce requested authorization to install and use the Biot and François Arago instruments to determine the length of the pendulum of seconds, which were finally installed on May 22 by the instrument maker Émile Brunner and disassembled on May 27. Apart from this, on May 26, 1880, Peirce requested permission from the director of the French National Library, Leopold Delisle, to work in the manuscript room for a study he was preparing on "the history of the physical sciences for which the treasures of the National Library contain precious materials."[26]

On this fourth trip to Europe, Peirce met frequently with Hervé Faye, president of the Bureau des longitudes in Paris, about the gravity determinations with the pendulum that he carried out at the observatory. The minutes of the weekly meetings of the bureau are preserved. Specifically, in the May 26 session, Faye gave news of Peirce's work at the observatory with the Repsold pendulum. In the session of June 9, Mouchez reported on the data obtained by Peirce in his observations and their comparison with those of Borda and Biot. At the time, Hervé Faye was the leading scientist in France dealing with the questions of gravity. As president of the French Academy of Sciences, he decided to make new determinations of the value of gravity in Paris, as Peirce explained to Superintendent Patterson in his letter of June 21, 1880. On his fifth trip in the spring of 1883, to which we turn next, Peirce reviewed those experiments. On May 31, 1883, in a letter to Julius E. Hilgard—superintendent of the Coast Survey after Patterson's death in 1881—Peirce further explained that the "Bureau of Longitudes began their pendulum work in 1880, when I was last here. (Probably my presence determined them to begin at that particular time)."

Peirce expected to travel to Munich in September, where he wanted to present the results of his experiments with the pendulum at a new meeting of the International Geodetical Association, but he was forced to return to the United States because his father got seriously ill. He sent an abbreviated report in the form of a letter to Hervé Faye, which was published in the proceedings of the meeting of the association.[27] In fact, Charles Anthony Schott in his review of the volume of conference proceedings was to write: "In connection with the pendulum of reversion, Hirsch refers to the observations of Mr. C. S. Peirce of the U.S. Coast and Geodetic Survey, at Geneva, Berlin, and Hoboken in America, which prove experimentally the theoretical conclusion of the complete elimination of the resistance of the air by the use of the Bessel's pendulum of reversion."[28]

Peirce probably returned aboard the French steamer *St. Laurent* that departed from Le Havre on July 24 and arrived in New York on August 4 after a voyage "in which there were strong winds from the west and fog most of the time."[29] Peirce remained near Cambridge, Massachusetts, until his father's death on October 6, 1880. Benjamin's death was to affect him greatly, as there is no doubt that Benjamin had more influence than anyone else on Charles's intellectual development. In the fall of 1880, Peirce resumed his teaching in Baltimore at the Johns Hopkins University, where he had been appointed lecturer of logic in June 1879.

5. Fifth European Journey: May 2, 1883–September 18, 1883

Peirce's last European journey had a scientific side, but also a relevant personal side. On April 24, 1883, Peirce obtained a legal divorce from Zina, and on April 26 he married Juliette in New York City. Apparently Juliette had told Peirce that she would not marry him unless they traveled to Europe, and they repeated the ceremony there.[30] In his letter of April 15, 1883, to Superintendent Hilgard, Peirce explained his six "serious matters" for going back to Europe: (1) yard comparison in London; (2) kilogram comparison in the Bureau des longitudes; (3) the construction of a new pendulum by Brunner in Paris; (4) to make new determinations of gravity in Kew and Geneva; (5) to attend a geodesic conference in Rome in September; and (6) to check the progress in France into the methods of determining gravity. Peirce adds a personal reason for this trip: "I will now privately state to you my personal reasons for wishing to go abroad. I wish to marry a French lady, Madame Pourtalai, who has been in this country for a good while being detained here by the bad state of her health. Her condition of health has now become almost desperate, her financial affairs are going wrong and demand her presence, she will not consent to being married here unless I will go to France to have the ceremony repeated, and for all these imperative reasons she must go and I must go with her."

In fact, six days after the marriage, the couple made the trip on the ship *Labrador* that left New York on May 2 and arrived in Le Havre on Saturday, May 12, at night. They stayed there at the Grand Hotel & Bains Frascati. Juliette immediately left for Paris with some friends and Peirce stayed at Le Havre for the disembarkation of the boxes of scientific material he had brought and their passage through customs.

On Thursday, May 17, Peirce left for Paris, where he stayed with Juliette at the Hotel Louvois. He was in Paris until June 6. In these three weeks he went to the National Library, where he transcribed the *Petrus Peregrinus* manuscript; visited the instrument makers Émile Brunner, Antoine Breguet, and Paul Gautier; talked with Théodule Ribot, the editor of the *Revue Philosophique*; and went to the Bureau des longitudes. In his letter to Hilgard of May 31 he described in detail the scientific work conducted during these weeks.

On June 7 the couple left for London, stopping probably in Boulogne-sur-Mer to pay a visit to the Scottish mathematician Hugh MacColl. In London, Peirce devoted two weeks to a careful comparison of the Coast Survey yard with the British one in the British Standards Office with the help of Henry J. Chaney. At the beginning of July, Peirce and Juliette moved to Richmond, Surrey, where the Kew observatory is located. On July 25, they left for Brussels, Liege, and Cologne. On August 1, they were already in Brühl, Prussia, near Cologne, from where Peirce wrote an extensive letter to Hilgard about his scientific activities during the month of July. After that, every trace of the couple is lost. Probably at some point during the month of August they had their second marriage ceremony somewhere in France—perhaps in Nancy—where Juliette had her family background.

There are some traces of them passing through Bremen and Prague, and probably they also visited Vienna. Finally, they went to Geneva, where Peirce measured the flexion of the support he had used as the stand of the pendulum, and to Basel, as indicated by Hilgard in his instructions of April 24, 1883. Back in Paris, Peirce supervised the new pendulum he had ordered from Gautier. On September 8, both embarked in Le Havre on the steamer *France*, which arrived in New York on September 18, without going to Rome to attend the seventh international geodesic conference, which was held in October as was initially planned.

Peirce's fifth and final trip to Europe gave him the opportunity to spend a four-month honeymoon with his wife Juliette, while working diligently to carry out his duties as a researcher for the Coast Survey. Julius E. Hilgard, superintendent of the US Coast Survey, in his official report of December 15, 1884, described with detail how much scientific work had been done by Peirce during this last stay in Europe.

6. The Impact of Traveling

As we reported, Peirce traveled intensively to Europe during what can be called the cosmopolitan period of his life. During this same period, however, he also visited different places in the United States and went to Montreal, Canada, following the instructions or duties of his job at the US Coast Survey. It is not unfair to say that Peirce loved traveling. On August 6, 1870, Amy Fay, after Peirce had visited her, described his attitude marvelously to Zina, in Cambridge: "You ought to see Charlie with all his contrivances—his guide books, his pedometer, his new umbrella, his new trunk, his new opera-glass, his new bag, his new cane. He sits down & enumerates one after the other the places he is going to. Can't you hear him saying 'from Berlin to Dresden, from Dresden to Vienna, from Vienna to Prague, from Prague to Pest,' etc.?"[31]

Also, we can conclude that traveling by himself was a good experience for him. In his long first European trip, Peirce wrote his mother from Chambéry, Savoie, four days before joining his wife and his father in Munich: "This travelling about alone is good to teach a man the gift of silence. You won't find me such a rattle pate when I return" (Letter of November 16, 1870, RL341).

Some particular experience of fruitful traveling is linked with the sea. Not only did he much enjoy his trip over the Mediterranean, but also he loved the experience of crossing the Atlantic Ocean. For instance, in a paper about science and immortality Peirce wrote: "I should feel as I do when I find myself on an ocean steamer and know that for ten days no business can turn up, and nothing can happen" (CP6.550, 1887). In particular, during his first passage on the Aegean Sea he wrote long letters to his wife that constitute almost a delightful diary. There are letters written on other trips, but in particular it should be highlighted—as it was mentioned above—that Peirce wrote 'the best part' of his seminal paper "How to Make Our Ideas Clear" on the steamer *Suevia* of the Hamburg–American Line from Hoboken, New Jersey, to Plymouth, England, which it reached on September 24, 1877 (de Waal 2014, 14). This paper is usually considered the birthplace of pragmatism, because it includes the first appearance in print of the "rule for attaining the third grade of clearness of apprehension": "Consider what effects, which might conceivably have practical bearings, we conceive the object of our conception to have. Then, our conception of these effects is the whole of our conception of the object" (CP5.402, 1878). For this reason, it might be said that the principle of pragmatism (or the pragmatic maxim) took shape while Peirce was traveling by himself on a steamer to Europe.

Another very relevant impact of his European journeys is Peirce's firsthand experience participating in an international scientific community, constituted by the cooperation of researchers from different countries and fields. This experience was to provide a solid ground for Peirce's belief in science as a real and effective community: "I do not call the solitary studies of a single man a science. It is only when a group of men, more or less in intercommunication, are aiding and stimulating one another by their understanding of a particular group of studies as outsiders cannot understand them, that I call their life a science" (R1334, 1905). It may be considered anecdotical, but it seems significant that when in the spring of 1878 Peirce's *Photometric Researches* finally appeared in print, he urged Edward C. Pickering, director of the Harvard College Observatory, to send a copy of the volume to thirty-five European astronomers and scientists with whom Peirce had come into contact during his European travels. The list included people from Leipzig, Berlin, Hamburg, London, Paris, Geneva, Neuchâtel, Bonn, Munich, Vienna, Brussels, Stuttgart, Madrid, and Florence.[32] In this sense we want to highlight that the image of Peirce as a lonely thinker confined in Arisbe does not apply to his cosmopolitan years; stating otherwise would make it difficult to understand Peirce's thought, especially his conception of science as communal. Moreover, Peirce's insistence on bringing the laboratory method into philosophy, his focus on practical consequences in his maxim, his choice of examples that follow it, and his effort to make philosophy a positive science are all connected and undoubtedly influenced by his participation in the European scientific community, which was a relatively new phenomenon not yet equaled in the United States.

Finally, it seems clear that his trips through Europe and the contemplation of so many works of art and historic places left in his memory the impressions that are at the basis of the importance that he would later assign to art and aesthetics. Although we would undoubtedly have liked to find a further development of these issues, the elements identified are more than enough to sketch a Peircean or "pragmaticist" aesthetics that comes to occupy an important place in his thought, especially since his European travels.[33] Certain paintings, sculptures, and buildings powerfully drew Peirce's attention over the course of his journeys. Years later, he would affirm that art consists precisely in capturing certain sensations, in being able to express them, and in producing an effect on the one who contemplates the artwork. On various occasions during his voyages, Peirce had already remarked on the expressive dimension of the artistic phenomenon, and indeed the expressive capacity of a work became for him a criterion of its artistic quality.

The capacity of artists to listen to what surrounds them and to have new sensations, of being impressed by the world around them, to be impacted by impressions that they later seek to express, is something essential to the artistic phenomenon, as Peirce already made clear in his letters from Europe. Those who are unable to perceive the qualities of things are not artists, since they will have nothing to express. Neither are artists those persons who are not impressionable and observant to an above-average degree. Rather, those people are artists who are able to capture the uncapturable and to make it understandable, to trap and express that which otherwise would remain hidden, unrealized, as a mere potentiality. The effort of the artist, for Peirce, is directed to reproduce, in one way or another, that which he or she sees, hears, perceives, or feels, "which is in every art a very complicated trade" (CP5.112, 1903).

Thus, his European experience could be at the origin of his idea that the artist is the one who is able to rationalize the inexpressible, to express the admiration that something provokes in us. He himself would later attempt to do so writing a story, "Topographical Sketches in Thessaly, with Fictional Embroideries" (R1561, 1892), which is the only fictional work that we have of Peirce, and which seeks to bring together the impressions and sentiments that he had experienced in his trip through Greece in the fall of 1870.

The European voyages of Peirce were without a doubt tremendously important for his formation as a person, as a scientist, and as a philosopher. They also involved an intense contact with art and with a cultural world that provided a fertile field for his later developments in these areas. Peirce the traveler is revealed as someone who is human, alive, and subject to the force of his experiences and the impressions that his journeys provoked in him. The sensations he received in Europe would last, and with time would bear fruit in new ways of viewing science as well as art and beauty.

As Nathan Houser has noted,[34] his European letters show that much of what Peirce saw overwhelmed him and, without a doubt, had a long-lasting impact on his sense and appreciation of beauty. Prior to his voyages, his opinions on aesthetics were based more on intellectual considerations than on aesthetic experiences. Europe changed this and gave the force of lived experience to his opinions. The same happened with science, which thanks to his European experience Peirce came to consider as a living activity carried out within a community. In this sense, we want to conclude that Peirce is not so much an American philosopher, but more a *cosmopolitan philosopher* with strong European influences.

Notes

1. We are very grateful to Cornelis de Waal for his kind invitation to take part in this volume and for his corrections and suggestions. Our contribution is based in what we have been working on during the past two decades about Peirce's visits to Europe and we have published extensively on our website: https://www.unav.es/gep/CorrespondenciaEuropea CSP.html.

    We are extremely indebted to the Peirce Edition Project, in particular to its directors, Nathan Houser and André de Tienne, who made possible our work thanks to the trove of documents collected by Max Fisch and kept in Indianapolis. We are also grateful to all the information available in the volumes of the *Writings* and in Brent (1998). The exposition relies upon our previous publications: Barrena (2014); Nubiola (2014); and Nubiola (2020).
2. Fisch, *Peirce, Semeiotic, and Pragmatism* (1986, 227).
3. Ibid., 227.
4. Houser (2014).
5. All letters quoted in the text have been digitized by the Grupo de Estudios Peirceanos at the University of Navarra, Spain, and can be accessed at https://www.unav.es/gep/Corres pondenciaEuropeaCSP.html. The original of this letter is kept in the Houghton Library with the Benjamin Peirce Papers: bMS Am 2368 Box 10.
6. Fisch, *Peirce, Semeiotic, and Pragmatism* (1986, 79–109).
7. Houser (2014, 431–432).
8. Brent (1998, 80); W2:xxxiv.
9. Barrena (2014), and Nubiola (2014).
10. Letter of the Superintendent Benjamin Peirce to Charles S. Peirce, November 30, 1872; Max H. Fisch, "Introduction" (1986, W3:xxiv).
11. Houser (1989, W4:xxii).
12. Brent (1998, 96).
13. The letters from Peirce to the superintendents of the US Coast Survey are kept in the National Archives, Record Group 23, Assistants P. They have been digitized by the Grupo de Estudios Peirceanos at the University of Navarra, Spain: https://www.unav.es/gep/ CorrespondenciaEuropeaCSP.html.
14. Fisch, "Introduction" (1986, W3:xxv).
15. Brent (1998, 99).
16. de Waal (2014, ILS:10).
17. Brent (1998, 101).
18. *Photometric Researches by C. S. Peirce. Made in the Years 1872–1875* is available online at https://archive.org/stream/photometricreseoopeirgoog#page/n10/mode/1up. As a curiosity, some of the manuscripts that Peirce consulted in the French National Library are now available online.
19. Brent (1998, 105).
20. De Waal (2014, ILS:10–15).
21. Draft letter from Peirce to J. H. Kehler, Milford, 22.06.1911, RL231. http://www.unav.es/ gep/Milford22.06.1911.html.
22. Fisch, "Introduction" (1986, W3:xxvi).
23. Fisch, "Introduction" (1986, W3:xxviii–xxix).
24. Brent (1998, 132).
25. Houser (1989, W4:xxx).

26. Both findings of our group can be seen at http://www.unav.es/gep/DiarioObservatorioPa ris.html and http://www.unav.es/gep/Paris26.05.1880B.html.
27. Adolphe Hirsch and Theodor von Oppolzer, eds., *Verhandlungen der Europäischen Gradmessung* (Berlin: Georg Reimer, 1881), 30–32 and 84–86; https://www.unav.es/gep/Paris23.07.1880.html.
28. Schott (1883).
29. Victor Lenzen to Max Fisch, March 3, 1963, W 4:xx.
30. Brent (1998, 143).
31. Letter from Amy Fay to her sister Zina Fay Peirce, Fay Family Papers, Schlesinger Library; available at http://www.unav.es/gep/Milford22.06.1911.html.
32. The complete list may be consulted at https://www.unav.es/gep/DistribucionEuropeaPh otometricResearches.html.
33. Barrena (2014, 440–442); Barrena (2015).
34. Houser (2014, 431–432).

Bibliographic References

Barrena, Sara. 2015. *La belleza en Charles S. Peirce: Origen y alcance de sus ideas estéticas.* Pamplona, Spain: Ediciones Universidad de Navarra.
Barrena, Sara. 2014. "Charles S. Peirce in Europe: The 'Aesthetic Letters.'" *Transactions of the Charles S. Peirce Society* 50, no. 3 (Summer): 435–442.
Brent, Joseph. 1998. *Charles S. Peirce: A Life.* 2nd ed. Bloomington: Indiana University Press.
De Waal, Cornelis. 2014. "Introduction." In Charles S. Peirce, *Illustrations of the Logic of Science*, 1–42. Chicago: Open Court.
Fisch, Max H. 1986. "Introduction." In *Writings of Charles S Peirce. A Chronological Edition*, vol. 3, edited by Christian J. W. Kloesel et al., xxi–xxxvii. Bloomington: Indiana University Press.
Fisch, Max H. 1986. *Peirce, Semeiotic, and Pragmatism.* Edited by Kenneth L. Ketner and Christian J. W. Kloesel. Bloomington: Indiana University Press.
Grupo de Estudios Peirceanos, Universidad de Navarra. 2008. "Correspondencia europea de C. S. Peirce: creatividad y cooperación científica." https://www.unav.es/gep/Correspondenci aEuropeaCSP.html.
Houser, Nathan. 1989. "Introduction." In *Writings of Charles S Peirce. A Chronological Edition*, vol. 4, edited by Christian J. W. Kloesel et al., xix–lxx. Bloomington: Indiana University Press.
Houser, Nathan. 2014. "Peirce's Cosmopolitan Thought." *Transactions of the Charles S. Peirce Society* 50, no. 3 (Fall): 428–433.
Nubiola, Jaime. 2020. "The Cosmopolitan Peirce: His European Travels." *Transactions of the Charles S. Peirce Society* 56, no. 2 (Summer): 190–198.
Nubiola, Jaime. 2014. "Scientific Community and Cooperation in Peirce's European Letters." *Transactions of the Charles S. Peirce Society* 50, no. 3 (Summer): 444–452.
Peirce, Charles S. 1857–1914. Manuscripts held at the Houghton Library of Harvard University, as identified in Richard Robin. 1967. *Annotated Catalogue of the Papers of Charles S. Peirce.* Amherst: University of Massachusetts Press. (Referred to as R[catalog#]:[sheet#]; with RL for letters.)
Peirce, Charles S. 1931–1958. *The Collected Papers of Charles Sanders Peirce.* 8 vols. Vols. 1–6 edited by Charles Hartshorne and Paul Weiss. Vols. 7–8 edited by Arthur W. Burks. Cambridge, MA: Harvard University Press. (Referred to as CP.)

Peirce, Charles S. 2014. *Illustrations of the Logic of Science*. Edited by Cornelis de Waal. Chicago: Open Court. (Referred to as ILS.)

Peirce, Charles S. 1982–2010. *The Writings of Charles S. Peirce: A Chronological Edition*. 7 vols. to date. Edited by the Peirce Edition Project. Bloomington: Indiana University Press. (Referred to as W.)

Schott, Charles A. 1883. "Review of *Verhandlungen der vom 11 bis zum 15 September 1882, im Haag Vereinigten Permanenten Kommission der Europäischen Gradmessung*." *Science* 2.41: 656–658.

CHAPTER 3

PEIRCE'S THWARTED CAREER

CHERYL MISAK

CHARLES S. Peirce is the most original and important philosopher and logician America has ever produced. He is the founder of the philosophical system of pragmatism (along with William James and Chauncey Wright). He is the founder of semiotics and of modern quantified logic, designing a diagrammatic proof system at the same time Gottlob Frege was designing his own algebraic system. He made major contributions to logic of scientific method and statistical inference and named a new kind of inference—abduction or inference to the best explanation. He also made important scientific advances in gravity, geodesy (measuring the precise figure of the earth), and spectroscopy (the interaction of matter with electromagnetic radiation). His pragmatist theory of truth is still one of the main contenders in truth theory. The depth and breadth of his thought are astonishing. But he could not find secure employment as an academic in the America of the turn of the twentieth century and lived the long last part of his life in abject poverty (he died at the age of seventy-four in 1914).

At one point in his career, Peirce's trajectory was promising. He had jobs at the US Coast Survey, where he was doing important measurement research, and as an instructor in logic and metaphysics at Johns Hopkins University, which had just started the first PhD program in the United States. He was well known and highly respected by European logicians, such as Ernst Schröder, and by American philosophers, such as William James and Josiah Royce. But his career soon disintegrated, and he struggled for economic security and professional recognition. He entertained suicidal thoughts and died penurious and lonely, feeling that his work was destined for obscurity. His name was frequently misspelled—even in journal proofs of his own papers and in the American Philosophical Association's minutes recording his death.

A question that has dogged the reputation of America's first universities—especially Harvard and Johns Hopkins—is how they failed to recognize and support their country's most brilliant thinker. In 1837 Ralph Waldo Emerson had called for an "American scholar" to free his country's thought from the dominance of the Europeans. He looked forward to a time "when the sluggard intellect of this continent will look up from under its iron lids and fill the postponed expectation of the world with something better than the exertions of mechanical skill" (Emerson 1940, 45). His call was answered by William James and Charles Sanders Peirce, one of whom became rightly famous, while the other languished in desperate isolation.

I will attempt some answers in this chapter, arguing that, while Peirce was a major contributor to his own misfortune, America's institutions carry a large burden of blame. In doing so, I draw on the fine biographical work of Nathan Houser in his introductions to volumes 4 and 6 of the *Writings of Charles S. Peirce* and Joseph Brent's 1993 biography of Peirce, as well as a close examination of the archival materials.

1. A Fitful Start

Peirce's early days in the academy were rocky. As a schoolboy he was precocious and lauded as a budding genius, but his Harvard undergraduate degree was decidedly underwhelming. He graduated in 1959, a lazy student ranked seventy-ninth of ninety in his senior year, reprimanded for intoxication and making penknife cuts in his laboratory benches. After graduation, his father, Benjamin Peirce, professor of mathematics at Harvard and a powerful force in the US Coast and Geodetic Survey, secured a job for his son at the Harvard observatory.

The observatory job did not go well. There were disputes and misunderstandings about how much compensation Peirce was to receive for various projects. For instance, in 1870, he was part of a scientific team sent by the Coast Survey to Europe to observe the solar eclipse. The president of Harvard, Charles Eliot, suspended Peirce's salary at the observatory while he took on this project, adding to Peirce's growing store of grievances. There were political issues lingering in the background about Peirce being lobbed into the job by his father. They were not unrelated to political issues in the foreground about whether the observatory was a Harvard entity, under the direction of Eliot, or a branch of the Coast Survey, under the direction of Benjamin Peirce. As James, the great psychologist and reader of human beings, said of this period in Peirce's life, he "dished himself at Harvard by inspiring dislike in Eliot" (CWJ 7:498, 1874). And Eliot was not someone to be on the wrong side of. He was perfectly happy to convey his low opinion of Peirce whenever he was asked for informal references.

In his spare time, Peirce was getting deep into the study of logic and philosophy, publishing and giving occasional series of lectures. When in Europe for the observatory, he saw the great logician Augustus de Morgan in London, introducing himself with a letter from his father and copies of some of his own papers in logic. He also made contact with W. Stanley Jevons, the economist and logician, who formed the opinion that Peirce was one of the most important logicians writing in the English language. A decade after graduating from Harvard, Peirce was starting a career in academic logic and philosophy. But in 1869, James already saw trouble on the rise: "The poor cuss sees no chance of getting a professorship anywhere.... It seems a great pity that as original a man as he is, who is willing and able to devote the powers of his life to logic and metaphysics, should be starved out of a career, when there are lots of professorships ... to be given ... to 'safe,' orthodox men" (James 1920, 149). Eliot definitely wanted safe men for Harvard.

The observatory proving difficult and no professorships coming his way, Peirce's father arranged for a full-time position at the Coast Survey. It paid well and was supposed to leave time for logic, which was now fully registered as Peirce's passion. The nepotism of the appointment again did not sit right with Peirce's new colleagues and there were problems from the start. The first patch of fieldwork in which he was in charge saw a number of subordinates quit and Peirce testified against in Congress.[1]

In 1875, Peirce was sent to Europe for a year to bring the Coast Survey up to higher standards. His wife Zina—a highly educated, independent-minded feminist and social reformer—accompanied him. During the trip Peirce made a mess of his accounts, spent the money the Coast Survey had advanced to him on extravagant living (including by hiring a sommelier to give him a course in French wine), and failed to provide the Coast Survey with addresses at which he might be reached. Louis Menand surmises that he also had "some sort of sexual escapade" while in Paris (Menand 2001, 274). His marriage was stormy even before they embarked and Zina's response to Peirce's behavior was to return home early. Peirce, lonely, depressed, and anxious, suffered a breakdown, complete with physical paralysis. His father ordered Zina back to London. Peirce was under the care of a physician who blamed overwork, but he saw that the cause was "mental distress" and "nervous attacks" (Brent 1993, 105). When they returned home, the marriage was in effect over. But Zina nonetheless wrote to the superintendent of the Coast Survey, asking him to write "a few cheering words to poor Charley":

> I do not know how far you may have noticed it, but I have known for a long time that he has been going on in a way that could not but end in wretchedness if not in humiliation. His parents and brother are utterly incapable of seeing that anything is amiss in one of their children and so he has never had a word of advice or warning from any one but me.... It has been peculiarly unfortunate for his temperament that his father's position on the Survey has always been so influential that he had not ... been held strictly to account as other officers in similar positions are. All his life from babyhood it seems as though everything had conspired to spoil him with indulgence.... Charley is now at a great crisis of his life, and if the good in him is encouraged, disciplined, and called to the front, he will rise as a man to the level of his wonderful intellectual gifts, and be a shining ornament in the future to his country. I hope and trust, dear sire, that you will act a noble, wise and paternal part to this brilliant but erratic genius who is now, as it were in your charge. (Brent 1993, 100)

She harbored no bitterness toward Peirce, but could not go on living with him.

The European year was another excellent opportunity for building connections. In England, Peirce met the physicist James Clerk Maxwell to discuss pendulum research and the important philosopher and mathematician W. K. Clifford, who would later engage in a famous disagreement with James about the will to believe. Henry James did what he could to help him in Paris, prompting advice from his brother:

> "I am bemused that you should have fallen into the arms of C. S. Peirce, whom I imagine you find a rather uncomfortable bedfellow, thorny and spinous, but the way to treat him is after the fabled 'nettle' receipt: grasp firmly, contradict, push hard, make fun of him, and he is as pleasant as anyone." (CWJ1:246, 1875)

Henry thought that although "one must appreciate his mental ability," "he has too little social talent, too little art of making himself agreeable" (CWJ1:255, 1876). William again put his finger on the problem, saying that Peirce

> "hates to make connexion with anyone he is with. With all this curious misanthropy, he has a genuine vein of sentiment and softness running through him, but so narrow a vein that it always surprises me when I meet it. Anyhow, he's a genius, and I look forward with avidity to his work." (CWJ 7:498, 1874)

I suspect James had Peirce in mind when he said in *The Varieties of Religious Experience* that crankiness and loss of mental balance, when combined with a superior intellect, are often a mark of genius (James [1902] 1985, 27).

That crankiness manifested itself often. Disputes about how much money was owed for various tasks, in which Peirce always seems in the wrong, litter his correspondence.[2] His judgment was nearly always poor. Here is the editor of *The Nation*, refusing to let Peirce hurl insults in print: "I need not enumerate the liberties I have taken with your text. I cut some anti-English remarks, for I desire to do nothing unnecessarily to foster antipathy between us & our British cousins.... At the end I forbore to call Sidgwick a dunce."[3]

Peirce's work in logic and philosophy, in contrast, was going extremely well. He and James (along with Oliver Wendell Holmes Jr., Chauncey Wright, and others) started the Metaphysical Club in 1872—a discussion group in which the philosophical tradition of pragmatism was born. Peirce, still a youngish man in midlife, was an internationally recognized figure in logic, philosophy, and the science of measurement. Both his logic and his pendulum work had attracted the attention of excellent Europeans working in these areas, something he was proud of. Despite his tendency toward nervous breakdown and the trouble he kept getting into, he felt optimistic about his future.

2. A Job at Hopkins

Founded in 1876, Johns Hopkins in Baltimore had an excellent endowment, stemming from what was at the time the largest private gift in America. Unlike Harvard, Hopkins was designed not for undergraduate education, but for research and doctoral studies.

The first president was Daniel Coit Gilman, who aggressively pursued the top scientists and scholars for his incoming fleet of professors. He tried to poach William James and Benjamin Peirce from Harvard. James was tempted and vacillated, as was his wont, for six years, eventually disappointing Gilman. Benjamin Peirce also turned him down but recommended his son to be the chair of physics.

Charles Peirce wrote to Gilman on January 13, 1878, that, while he would very much like to be called to Johns Hopkins, it was in logic, not physics, that he would make his most important mark. He also said he needed to mention two things. The first was that he couldn't give up his pendulum experiments with the Coast Survey. The second was "a very painful personal matter":

> "I have been for a number of years in disagreement with my wife, not having lived with her for a long time, & not having even seen her for over a year, and the reasons for this on the one side and on the other will, I hope, never be known. It is however certain that we shall never live together again. This is a fact to which you will naturally give a weight, should you seriously consider inviting me to Baltimore." (DCG: Peirce to Gilman, January 13, 1878)

James had been advising Gilman on how to build a philosophy department. In January 1879, his counsel was that it wouldn't be straightforward:

> "If you want original work done by your first-appointed philosopher I hardly know who to recommend. . . . If you want a philosophic scholar and expert who would guide students through the history of the subject, I suppose Morris would be an excellent man. . . . In the psychological line proper the only workers I know of are Peirce and Hall. Peirce's drawbacks you know. Hall, although a thoroughly original and able worker is perhaps deficient in the practical and organizing qualities which the J.H.U. especially needs now in its professors." (CWJ5:35–36)

James had in the past been more enthusiastic in his recommendations of Peirce to Gilman, saying of Peirce: "I don't think it extravagant praise to say that of late years there has been no intellect in Cambridge of such a general power & originality as his" (CWJ 4:525). If further recommendations were needed, James said that Jevons and Clifford, England's two great logicians and philosophers, would vouch for Peirce (along with a host of American philosophers and scientists).

The pros and cons were weighed and in the end Peirce was offered a half-time lectureship. George Sylvester Morris and G. Stanley Hall also took part-time appointments.

If there was concern about Peirce's morals—the fact that Peirce and his wife had separated—it did not carry the day. The half-time idea was Peirce's, as it would enable him to continue his work for the Coast Survey. Nonetheless, he agonized over whether it was indeed possible to split his attention along those lines and commute between Washington, New York, and Baltimore. He communicated that anxiety to Gilman.

The lectureship idea, however, didn't sit well with Peirce and when he wrote to Gilman to accept the position, he asserted that "I should require . . . that there be an intention of ultimately making a full Professorship for it" (Peirce to Gilman, June 6, 1879).[4] Peirce would bank on that condition, although there is no evidence that Gilman committed to it. He began at Hopkins in the autumn of 1879.

3. Success at Hopkins

Peirce seems at first to have been conscientious in his new job. He resurrected the Metaphysical Club that he and James had run in Cambridge. One of his students, the logician Christine Ladd-Franklin, described that as follows: "So devious and unpredictable was his [Peirce's] course that he once, to the delight of his students, proposed at the end of his lecture, that we should form (for greater freedom of discussion) a Metaphysical Club, though he had begun the lecture by defining metaphysics to be the 'science of unclear thinking'" (Ladd-Franklin 1916, 716–717). Peirce served as its president and went to its meetings whenever he was in Baltimore. Morris and Hall were regular participants and the philosophy and logic students attended. They covered a broad range of topics—philosophical, psychological, and biological. Peirce presented his important paper "Design and Chance." He invited Royce, then at Berkeley, to read a paper in the spring of 1880. Royce delivered "On Purpose in Thought," which was fully engaged with the pragmatist account of belief, inquiry, and truth that Peirce was now actively promoting. It was a superb discussion group, rivaling those in England and Europe, which was precisely Peirce's intention.

Peirce taught a wide array of courses at Hopkins, including a full-year course on logic. It wasn't nearly as technical as it might have been. Peirce announced in the first lecture that "no brilliant talent for mathematics is at all necessary" (W5:381, 1877). He started the course with two papers he had recently published in the *Popular Science Monthly*: "The Fixation of Belief" and "How to Make Our Ideas Clear," which set out the essentials of pragmatism: a theory of meaning that holds that part of the meaning of an expression is its effects on action and a theory of truth that holds that truth is what would survive all inquiry. He went on to teach about probability, the method of least squares, inductive reasoning, and the theory of gases.

Peirce seems to have been an excellent teacher. He attracted, on top of his philosophy students, several mathematics students from the stable of J. J. Sylvester, the English mathematician who had been recruited by Hopkins in 1876 to be the inaugural professor of mathematics. Ladd-Franklin thought Peirce "created the impression that we had before us a profound, original, dispassionate and impassioned seeker of the truth" (Ladd-Franklin 1916, 716–717). Another student, Joseph Jastrow, said that Peirce gave him his "first real experience of intellectual muscle" and described him as the leader of "a select band of disciples (Jastrow 1916, 724–725). Peirce treated his students well, with an eye out for their careers. In 1883, he gathered together some of their papers, along with his own work, in a volume titled *Studies in Logic by Members of the Johns Hopkins University*. It was reviewed positively in *Mind*.

John Dewey was also one of Peirce's students, less enamored of Peirce's teaching than the others, as he couldn't cope with the technical parts of Peirce's courses. Hence Dewey only discovered (and adopted) Peirce's account of inquiry and truth well after he left Hopkins. The economist Thorstein Veblen was also a student and seems to have picked up Peirce's view of scientific inquiry (Dyer 1986). Peirce was having a tremendous impact on his students, who would go on to intellectual renown. There was a buzz around him that would have been noticeable to an alert administrator.

The other members of the philosophy department would have no such impact. Morris was a Hegelian who moved to Michigan in 1881 and left no real philosophical legacy. Hall had turned his back against Hegel and toward the new experimental psychology that was being taught by William James. Peirce too had a fondness for experimental psychology (he coauthored papers with Hall) and he knew his Hegel. But Peirce alone stood out for his originality and brilliance. John Venn, the great English probability theorist, in his review of *Studies in Logic* made that clear: "Mr. C. S. Peirce's name is so well known to those who take an interest in the development of Boolean or symbolic treatment of Logic that the knowledge that he was engaged in lecturing upon the subject to advance classes at the Johns Hopkins University will have been an assurance that some interesting contributions to the subject might soon be looked for" (Venn 1883, 594).

4. Failure at Hopkins

Alas, Peirce's time at Hopkins was marred by his usual quarrels. He was choosy about the time slots for his lectures. He fought with the library, demanding they purchase second copies of books, wanting to keep items beyond their return date, and borrowing more books than the rules allowed. These squabbles made their way up to President Gilman's office. At the end of one of them, Peirce apologized to Gilman: "I deeply regret having said anything which seems to offend you," before going on to complain about the "jailer" librarian (Brent 1993, 150).

Peirce often missed lectures, due to a painful facial neuralgia, headaches, respiratory infections, and nervous breakdowns. He suffered another breakdown during the Christmas vacation of 1880 and wrote to Gilman from New York, where he was staying at the University Club on 5th Avenue, listing symptoms which included rheumatism, neuralgia, and severe diarrhea and expressing his regret that he would have to miss yet another week of lectures. In the spring of 1893, Peirce wrote to Gilman to say that something had gone wrong at the Coast Survey and he had to go to Washington so that he couldn't make his 5:00 p.m. lecture that very day. Since he then had to go on to New York, he thought he "had better bring my course to a close" (DCG: Peirce to Gilman, April 24, 1883). Three weeks later, he sent his syllabi for the following year from the Grand Hotel & Bains in Frascati, on the hills outside Rome, having gone there with his new wife Juliette. After apologizing for what would become a seven-week absence, he asked: "Will you have the goodness to have the cheque which is payable to me on Monday sent to me at the above address?" (DCG, Peirce to Gilman, February 28, 1880). The following summer, he was apologizing (from Paris) for his poor performance and promising to be more present on campus the next year, adding that he had an "ambition & an expectation of making my lectures the coming year a great improvement everyway on last year's" (DCG: Peirce to Gilman, August 19, 1880).

Peirce had started taking cocaine and other opiates in an effort to cope with the facial neuralgia and perhaps with his psychological difficulties. That couldn't have helped his already erratic behavior. Neither could his father's illness and death in 1880. Peirce lost not only someone who was dear to him, but also his promoter and protector at the Coast Survey.

Four months after his father's death, Peirce wrote to Gilman to say that, while no life was more enjoyable for him than that at Hopkins, he feared that in the spring, his connection with the university must cease: "I could not arrange to be here another season without modifying my connection with the Coast Survey, which I do not certainly care to do for the sake of the subordinate position which I hold here" (DCG: Peirce to Gilman, December 18, 1880). This resignation, or threat of one, was designed as a pitch for a less subordinate position and a raise in salary. A couple of months later, he wrote to Gilman again, saying that he was "unwilling to remain" on the current terms. He felt that he had been of use to his students; and acquitted himself well; and that he was "entitled" to an expression of satisfaction from the university, evidenced by "a distinct proposal" for better terms. The issue was "a pure question of price for my services" (GCG: Peirce to Gilman, February 4, 1881).

Gilman simply accepted his resignation. He communicated to the board of trustees that "Mr. C. S. Peirce, Lecturer in Logic, was unwilling to continue his present relations to the University another year." The board communicated their thanks for Peirce's "enthusiasm and ability" over the last two years and regretted that his "other engagements" prevented him from continuing as a lecturer. Gilman conveyed the board's sentiments to Peirce, who replied in kind:

> "I shall never cease to be profited and comforted by my memories of this University and its noble ideals. If I have sometimes suspected that your discernment was here and there at fault, I have never wavered in my fervid approbation of the conception of the University nor in my conviction of its destined success in the main. It has been a great thing to me in many ways to be here, and I heartily wish you may secure somebody whose real merits may surpass all my self-conceit." (DCG: Peirce to Gilman, February 9, 1881)

But almost immediately, Sylvester convinced Gilman to offer Peirce a better salary and on June 23, 1881, Peirce accepted another appointment as a lecturer of logic. Having sold his books to Hopkins upon his resignation, he tried to get them back. But the deed was done, as he could not afford to purchase them at the price he had sold them. He then suspended one of his classes because, absurdly, he didn't have the books he needed.

Alas, his relationship with Sylvester, never great on the personal level, disintegrated further over the next two years. The story is one of typical Peircean arrogance and skill for self-harm. He discovered that a paper he had written titled the *Algebra of Relatives* had been anticipated by Sylvester and another English mathematician, Arthur Cayley. Peirce was convinced that his own work was broader and, as was his habit, he elevated the matter immediately to Gilman, asking him to intervene and see whether their claim to originality might be a "just" one or merely "the systematic arrogance of these Britishers" (DCG: Peirce to Gilman, February 7, 1883). After much to and fro, Peirce withheld publication of his own paper, which reproduced the Sylvester/Cayley results. Then, a year later, Peirce made an astonishing error of judgment. Sylvester asked him to check the proofs for a paper of his. Peirce slipped a sentence into Sylvester's abstract that said that a part of Sylvester's work had been anticipated by Peirce. That quite rightly enraged Sylvester and a long and vicious dispute was again played out in Gilman's office and that of the board of trustees. A letter from the chairman of the executive committee of the board about "this annoying matter" sums up the feeling. He proposed a solution and asserted, "This however should be the last of it and would it not be well to say so both in advance" (DCG: Hand to Gilman, April 17, 1883). But it wasn't the last of it. Peirce was never inclined to let a matter rest and Sylvester wouldn't do so in this instance either. Perhaps all this added up in Gilman's mind and when yet another problem about Peirce landed on his desk the following year, he acted in a devastating manner.

Peirce's divorce was finally finalized on April 24, 1883, and he wrote to Gilman a week later to announce his marriage to one Madame Juliette Pourtalai. She was a much younger Frenchwoman he had met at a ball, in 1876, at the lavish Brevoort Hotel in New York, where he often stayed. (His tastes always ran expensive.) The couple moved to Baltimore after their wedding, a sign that Peirce was indeed going to be more present on campus and less often held up in New York. But the happy future was almost immediately derailed. A colleague at the Coast Survey, who knew that Juliette traveled with Peirce on Coast Survey expeditions before they were married, made that fact known to the Hopkins astronomer Simon Newcomb. Newcomb marshaled all his moral outrage and communicated it to a Hopkins trustee and to Gilman, later confirming his accusation by letter to Gilman after confirming it with his own "informant" (DCG: Newcomb to Gilman, December 22, 1883). As Newcomb put it to his wife, the marriage had "made no change in the relations of the parties." Peirce and Juliette had intimate relations before they were wed. Newcomb remarked, "It is sad to think of the weaknesses which may accompany genius" (Brent 1993, 151).

Gilman and the trustees then did something that can only be seen as a plot to get rid of Peirce. On January 6, 1884, the trustees issued a statement that the contracts of all those who were part-time or on some other kind of nonpermanent contract in the Department of Philosophy and Psychology would not be renewed at the end of the academic year. Financial exigencies were cited. Then everyone but Peirce was straightaway renewed. He was in effect fired.

Peirce sent a volley of bewildered letters. Some were to Gilman, demanding to know the reason. Some were to the trustees, asking if he might appear in person to make his case and complaining that Gilman had made him assurances about the future, on which he had acted—for instance, renting a house in Baltimore for two years. These letters suggest that the reasons for his dismissal were not made clear to him. Indeed, the responses to his letters suggest that the reasons for getting rid of Peirce were not even clear in the minds of Gilman and the trustees. For one thing, there seem to have been no hard feelings swirling around, as one would expect from a morally outraged president and board. A month after being dismissed, Peirce wrote to Gilman to ask if he could express his gratitude to him in the dedication of a book he was writing and "associate his name" with it. Gilman wrote back with warmth, affection, and a positive answer (DCG: Gilman to Peirce, February 6, 1894). In one of his letters, Peirce had said that Juliette had had a collapse on hearing the news about his job and that he was "advised to throw up everything and take her abroad." He asked for the balance of his salary to be paid out, despite ending his lectures early. One of the trustees wrote to Gilman that while Peirce's letter "furnishes the new proof of the desirableness of making a change," he was content to pay out the salary (and indeed, eventually the two years' rent for the house) in order to see the back of Peirce. But he also expressed a concern about Peirce's future:

> "What is to become of him and his wife in Europe unless they have money and friends? The plan seems to be too wild even for him to attempt to put into execution. If we could part on friendly terms by paying him the rest of his year's salary and seeing him transferred elsewhere I should be glad" (DCG: Brown to Gilman, February 18, 1884).

The sense of sadness and futility suggest that the revelation about premarital sex was merely the final irritation for Gilman and the board of trustees.

Peirce soon saw that the European plan was indeed wild and abandoned it. He then wrote long letters asking for another year of work in which he would show Gilman and the trustees that they ought to keep him on permanently. Gilman's reply was considerate, if negative:

> "It is better for the university that your engagement should be terminated. . . . It gives me great pain to say this so plainly because I appreciate your high intellectual powers & your lofty conception of the Science and Art of Logic, but I am forced to believe that you are adapted to the work of an investigator than to that of a university professor." (DCG: Gilman to Peirce, April 12, 1884)

The crossed-out words seem to suggest some uncertainty in Gilman's mind about the status of the morality issue as part of his reasoning. Peirce would later say, at least once, that Juliette was to blame for him losing his jobs, and his family certainly blamed Juliette. But they were not referring to sex before marriage. One of Peirce's brothers wrote to their sister:

> "Juliette had so prejudiced the then head of the Institution, Pres. Gilman, that I saw he would do nothing favorable to Charley. You remember he was president of Johns

Hopkins when Charley was there and Juliette accused him of the vilest conduct and took her nasty stories to Gilman. In the same way she ruined his career on the Coast Survey coming to Washington and destroying his prestige with the authorities."[5]

Theirs was a complex and tumultuous relationship.

Sylvester, who had returned to England to take up the Savilian Professorship of Mathematics in Oxford, had been shocked at the news that Peirce was no longer at Hopkins and wrote to Gilman: "What was the cause of C. Peirce's leaving? I am truly sorry on his account. I regret the differences which sprang up between him and me for which I was primarily to blame. I fear that he may not have acted with entire prudence in some personal matters" (Brent 1993, 141). Sylvester thought it obvious that Peirce's abilities should outweigh the difficulties of his personality. His intervention made no difference. Peirce's five years at Hopkins and his academic career were over.

5. POST-HOPKINS

The Peirces moved to Washington in order for Charles to fully re-engage his work for the Coast Survey. That had been going well, with his extensive fieldwork and pendulum experiments putting him on the cusp of important work in determining gravity and the shape of the earth. But here, too, he would be drummed out.

Grover Cleveland had been sworn in as president of the United States in 1885, with the express intention of reforming the civil service. The Coast Survey was the first to fall under scrutiny and in 1885 there was an investigation of it, after which the superintendent was fired and replaced by a crony of Cleveland's. Part of the reform was a shift to applied science, rather than the pure science that most interested Peirce. Disheartened with the "men of Red Tape," he moved back to New York City (Houser 2000, xxvi).

Peirce had always been late in writing up his reports, often sitting on a treasure trove of data, infuriating his colleagues and the superintendent of the Coast Survey. He was, as always, quick to offer reasons (often excuses) for the delays. Sometimes it was because the mathematics involved was genuinely difficult, but other times he said he was distracted by, for instance, the false accusations of his colleagues. In the margins of this particular letter, one of those colleagues, B. A. Colonna, wrote: "What about other people's distractions of mind? Also what distracted his mind at all except the last 3 stations?" (xxxvii). The whiff of scandal about Juliette accompanying Peirce when he was at his field stations remained in the air. But the excuses for the lateness of his reports hung heavier in it. Colonna echoed the feelings of Gilman and the Hopkins trustees when he sent this note to the new superintendent in July 1887: "Charles Peirce about crazes me. He has no system, no idea of order or business & with all his talent is a deadweight. I wish he could get a larger salary somewhere else and leave us. We could spare his talent for the sake of a better order" (Houser 2000, xxxvii).

The end came when Peirce's nemesis, Simon Newcomb, was asked to review Peirce's long-awaited (and long) report on pendulum research. Newcomb trashed it. In 1891, Peirce was told by the Coast Survey that his services were no longer required. His thirty-one years there, while certainly a second best as far as his own ambitions went, had been hugely productive. He made significant advances in pendulum studies to determine the shape of the earth, in photometric research on stars, and in chromatics. But again, his personality defects were weighed more than his intellectual abilities.

In 1892, Peirce was shortlisted for a job at Chicago, but his former student John Dewey got it instead. James had recommended Peirce, but the Harvard philosopher George Palmer wrote the decisive letter to the president of the university: "I know, too, very well his eminence as a logician. But from so many sources I have heard of his broken and dissolute character that I should advise you to make most careful inquiries before engaging him" (Brent 1993, 152). James tried everything in his considerable power to secure him some teaching or a lecture—any academic crumb.

But it was a downward slide. Charles and Juliette moved to Milford, Pennsylvania, less costly than city living. Not only was money a major problem, but also Juliette was fragile and Peirce's family disliked her. Debt mounted and, with it, desperation and erratic behavior. Peirce forged and cashed checks in the names of his admirers at the Century Club (Pfeifer 2014, 55–56). In more legal attempts at securing funds, he thought that he might be able to turn the Milford property, which they had named Arisbe, into a resort and summer school for philosophy. Considerable money went into these fruitless ideas. He tried to write logic and mathematics textbooks, which he thought would earn him money, but for one reason or another, they came to naught. He tried to set up a correspondence course titled *The Art of Reasoning* and wrote a staggering number of fee-paying reviews for the *Nation* and entries for the *Century Dictionary*, for which he was well paid. He applied for grants that would have enabled him to write a book. He even had brief stints as a chemical consultant; worked on boilers, electricity, and a suspension bridge; and tried to make Arisbe into a testing site for airplanes. He applied for jobs at other universities. But mostly the Peirces lived on family handouts and a fund from friends, set up by James.

Peirce continued working away at his logic and philosophy, often in the middle of the night, in isolation from any academic community. He was desperately trying to write a book titled *The Minute Logic*, which would be his magnum opus. While he had the respect of logicians and mathematicians worldwide, his interactions with them faded. His correspondence with Schröder ended with Schröder's death in 1902. After that, he was almost alone intellectually. His main philosophical interlocutor in the early 1900s, aside from William James and Josiah Royce, was the independent English scholar, Lady Victoria Welby, whose book on signs Peirce had reviewed for the *Nation*.

The fact that Peirce's work didn't die with him was almost an accident. Yes, Dewey eventually discovered Peirce's work and built his theory of inquiry upon it. But no one would call Dewey a Peircean pragmatist. Peirce's two most impressive direct successors, C. I. Lewis at Harvard and Frank Ramsey in the other Cambridge (England), had to discover Peirce through unusual means. For his writings were not in prominent journals and they were undisciplined, given the absence of structure and colleagues in Peirce's life. He didn't manage to write his book. Harvard struggled to find someone to edit his papers after his death, the first selection finally coming out only in 1922.

Harvard's struggle with Peirce's papers was the conduit for Lewis's discovery of Peirce. When he joined the Harvard philosophy department as a junior faculty member in 1920, he "practically lived with" the massive "manuscript remains" of Peirce for two years (Lewis 1968, 16). The chair of the philosophy department hoped that by housing Lewis there, he would start to put the papers into order. Lewis declined to do that, but he read them carefully and developed his own version of Peircean pragmatism, which ties truth to human inquiry without giving up on objectivity.

Ramsey discovered Peirce through Lady Welby, who circulated copies of Peirce's letters to the likes of Bertrand Russell and John Cook Wilson, in an effort to get others to take an interest in Peirce. She was unsuccessful, with one exception. The publisher and jack of all academic trades C. K. Ogden became a fan. He happened to be a family friend of the Ramseys and placed Peirce's work in the young Frank Ramsey's hands. Ramsey then developed his own version of Peircean pragmatism, showing how to think of partial belief in terms of action. Ramsey's pragmatism, before his tragic death at the age of twenty-six in 1930, had a major effect, including on Ludwig Wittgenstein.[6] It is ironic that it was on the supposedly hostile British territory that the views of the founder of American pragmatism thrived.

6. A Stain on Harvard and Hopkins

History is unforgiving. It judges actions by their effects, not by the intentions of the actors. Indeed, this idea lies at the heart of Peirce's theory of meaning, belief, and truth. He argued that we "must look to the upshot of our concepts in order to rightly apprehend them" (CP5.4, 1901). "By their fruits ye shall know them" (EP2:401).

The consequences of the actions of Eliot and Gilman were calamitous. Of course, they were disastrous for Peirce's health and well-being, but that is not the judgment with which history concerns itself. They were disastrous for the state of knowledge in America. Eliot and Gilman failed in one of their primary duties as presidents of prestigious and well-endowed universities: to identify and nurture exceptional talent. Eliot is somewhat shielded from this judgment by the fact that a major part of Harvard's mission at the time was to educate young men. One can understand why Peirce would be thought not well suited for that. But Gilman was building a research university. He dismissed one of the most brilliant minds in the country, leaving the research mission of Hopkins unfulfilled in logic and philosophy and depriving a generation of graduate students of Peirce's instruction. His decision changed the trajectory of American thought, not in a good way.

Perhaps this judgment might be mitigated by noting that America was a young country and it didn't have the maturity or self-assurance or ability to recognize a self-destructive genius in its midst. But Peirce's importance was pointed out to Eliot and Gilman again and again. The lawyer and philosopher Francis Russell at one point wrote to Gilman to ask what was wrong with the country for failing to recognize and employ "the extraordinary genius" of Peirce (DCG: Russell to Gilman, April 11, 1896). We have seen that the British mathematician Sylvester, who disliked Peirce for good reason, told Gilman that it was shocking that Peirce was ousted from Johns Hopkins. America's two other great philosophers of the time, William James and Josiah Royce (latter had arrived as a student at Hopkins the year after Peirce had left), thought so too. James did what he could to get America's institutions to support Peirce, so much so that Peirce adopted "Santiago" (St. James) as his middle name.[7] James had to deal with Peirce on a regular basis and was under no illusions about his character. Peirce knew that he and his friend William had completely different natures: "He so concrete, so living; I a mere table of contents, so abstract, a very snarl of twine" (CP6.184, 1911).

Yes, collegiality is important, and Peirce was a very difficult colleague who soaked up an inordinate amount of administrative labor. But as Nathaniel Southgate Shaler, the Harvard professor of paleontology and geology and dean of the Lawrence Scientific School, put it in a 1902 letter of recommendation for Peirce: "The trouble is that he is as irresponsible as he is able."[8] History's verdict has to be that the great universities of early America, Harvard and especially Johns Hopkins, failed to accurately weigh those two sides of the scale.

In 1895, one of Peirce's brothers wrote to James:

> It is certainly amazing that with all Charlie's power of doing work of high ability, scientific, literary, philosophic, & his devotion to work, he commands no public & offers his wares in vain. Admitting all that is erratic in his judgment & temperament, all that is rebellious against the commonplace in his personality, I must think it a glaring proof of the want in our country of the sincere love of intellectual truth, & even of the ordinarily current respect for intellectual standards that we see in Europe, that nobody cares even to render a formal encouragement to one who shows intellectual originality without popular gifts. (CWJ 8:17, 1895)

Peirce said that one motto "deserves to be inscribed upon every wall of the city of philosophy: Do not block the way of inquiry." Harvard and Hopkins, despite being committed to the pursuit of truth, blocked it. They were unwilling to do as Zina had pleaded: encourage what was good in him, provide the required discipline—"act a noble, wise and paternal part to this brilliant but erratic genius."

Acknowledgements and Reference Policy

The research for this paper was conducted during the pandemic when university libraries and archives were closed. I thank the archivists at Johns Hopkins University, who kindly sent me digitized copies of what I needed from their collections. I also thank Kees de Waal for his excellent comments on an earlier draft. My reference policy is to cite a passage in a published volume if it appears in one and, if not, to cite the archival source.

Notes

1. See Brent (1993, 93) for an account of the debacle.
2. See, for instance, Pfeifer (2014, 57).
3. William P. Garrison to Charles S. Peirce, October 14, 1892 (Pfeifer 2014, 55).
4. Johns Hopkins University Special Collections: *Daniel Coit Gilman Papers*, folder 3, MS 1. Subsequently referred to as DCG.
5. Herbert Peirce to Helen Peirce Ellis, January 22, 1907 (Pfeifer 2014, 91).
6. See Misak (2020).
7. That didn't prevent him from, at an especially low point, including James in a paranoid rant about his friends: "Prof. Wm. James always thinks of his own ambitions, and ready to shove another man down if tempted in that way" (Pfeifer 2014, 67).
8. Nathaniel Southgate Shaler in his letter for recommendation on Charles S. Peirce, January 2, 1902 (Pfeifer 2014, 76).

References

Brent, Joseph. 1993. *Charles Sanders Peirce: A Life*. Bloomington: Indiana University Press.
Dyer, Alan. 1986. "Veblen on Scientific Creativity: The Influence of Charles S. Peirce," *Journal of Economic Issues* 20, no. 1: 21–41.
Houser, Nathan. 2000. "Introduction," in *The Writings of Charles S. Peirce: A Chronological Edition*. Vol. 6. (7 vols. to date.), general editor Nathan Houser. Bloomington: Indiana University Press, xxv–lxxxiv.
James, William. [1902] 1985. *The Varieties of Religious Experience*, in *The Works of William James*, edited by F. H. Burkhard, F. Bowers, and I. K. Skrupskelis. 18 vols. Cambridge MA: Harvard University Press (1975–1988), vol. 15.
James, William. 1920. *The Letters of William James*. Vol. 1. Edited by Henry James. Boston: Atlantic Monthly Press.
James, William. 1992–2004. *The Correspondence of William James*. Vols. 1–12. Edited by Ignas K. Skrupskelis and E. M. Berkeley. Charlottesville: University Press of Virginia. (Referred to as CWJ.)
Jastrow, Joseph. 1916. "Charles Sanders Peirce as Teacher," *The Journal of Philosophy, Psychology and Scientific Methods* 13: 723–725.
Ladd-Franklin, Christine. 1916. "Charles S. Peirce at the Johns Hopkins," *The Journal of Philosophy, Psychology, and Scientific Methods* 13: 716–717.
Lewis, Clarence Irving. 1968. "Autobiography," in *The Philosophy of C. I. Lewis*, ed. P. A. Schlipp. La Salle, IL: Open Court, 1–21.
Menand, Louis. 2001. *The Metaphysical Club: A Story of Ideas in America*. New York: Farrar, Straus and Giroux.
Misak, Cheryl. 2013. *The American Pragmatists*, Oxford: Oxford University Press.
Misak, Cheryl. 2020. *Frank Ramsey: A Sheer Excess of Powers*. Oxford: Oxford University Press.

Peirce, Charles S. 1931–1958. *The Collected Papers of Charles Sanders Peirce*. 8 vols. Vols. 1–6, edited by Charles Hartshorne and Paul Weiss. Vols. 7–8. edited by Arthur W. Burks. Cambridge, MA: Harvard University Press. (Referred to as CP).

Peirce, Charles Sanders. 1982–2010. *The Writings of Charles S. Peirce: A Chronological Edition*. 7 vols. to date, edited by the Peirce Edition Project. Bloomington: Indiana University Press. (Referred to as W.)

Peirce, Charles Sanders. 1992–1998. *The Essential Peirce: Selected Philosophical Writings*. 2 vols. Vol. 1. edited by Nathan Houser and Christian Kloesel. Vol. 2 edited by the Peirce Edition Project. Bloomington: Indiana University Press. (Referred to as EP.)

Pfeifer, David. 2014. "CSP Medical History Excerpts," www.unav.es/gep/CSPMedicalHistoryExcerpts.pdf.

Venn, John. 1883. "Review of Studies in Logic," *Mind* 8: 594–603.

PART II

PHENOMENOLOGY AND THE NORMATIVE SCIENCES

CHAPTER 4

PEIRCE'S FORMAL AND MATERIAL CATEGORIES IN PHENOMENOLOGY

RICHARD KENNETH ATKINS

PHANEROSCOPY, Peirce's preferred name for what we typically call phenomenology, is primarily an observational and classificatory science. To get an initial grasp, it is helpful to consider other *-scopic* sciences, such as spectroscopy and microscopy. Spectroscopy classifies chemical elements based on observation of their spectra. It is used in other fields, such as in astronomy to discover the chemical composition of stars. Microscopy classifies cells, bacteria, and other objects not within resolution range of the human eye. It is used in other fields, such as in oncology to ascertain what kind of cancer a patient has.

Phaneroscopy differs from spectroscopy and microscopy in at least two noteworthy ways. First, phaneroscopy is a philosophical domain of inquiry. Peirce borrows Jeremy Bentham's distinction between cenoscopic and idioscopic sciences. Idioscopic sciences require special instruments or travel to study their objects. Cenoscopic sciences study objects that are open to common observation without the need of special instruments or travel. Peirce regards all philosophical sciences to be cenoscopic, including phaneroscopy. Hence, unlike spectroscopy and microscopy, phaneroscopy uses no special instruments, though it does use techniques of observation.

Second, the object of phaneroscopic inquiry is the phaneron. "Phaneron" is Greek for "manifest" or "evident." Peirce offers many (sometimes inconsistent) characterizations of the phaneron. Roughly, the phaneron is whatsoever could come before the mind howsoever, whether it be real or not. Peirce writes, "Let us call the collective whole of all that could ever be present to the mind in any way or in any sense, the *Phaneron*. Then the substance of every Thought (and much beside Thought proper) will be a Consistituent [*sic*] of the Phaneron" (NEM4:320, 1906). A person's stream of consciousness is an instantiation of the phaneron. A cross-section of that stream is a synthetic unity such that considered prior to analysis we do not distinguish even between the act of consciousness and its contents (see EP2:472, 1913). Nonetheless, it is a collection, and we are able to distinguish among constituents of it. Analyzing the phaneron, we sort out the most general categories into which the phaneron's constituents fall. By studying what does come before the mind, we can ascertain whatsoever could come before the mind howsoever. Analyzing instantiations of the phaneron and classifying its most basic constituents is the phaneroscopist's primary task.

It may seem that no one is a phaneroscopist. If the sciences are "so many businesses of groups of living men" (EP2:258, 1903) and yet no one is engaged in the business of phaneroscopy, then there is no science of phaneroscopy. But it does not follow from the fact that one does not describe herself as a phaneroscopist that she is not engaging in the business of phaneroscopy. To the contrary, the general practice of phaneroscopy is perfectly familiar to all of us.

Phaneroscopic observation consists in analyzing the phaneron in ways tractable to classification. We all do this, and our classifications are reflected in our ordinary language and folk psychological conceptions. We distinguish between the cognitive act and the object of cognition, and among various cognitive acts (imagining, perceiving, believing, etc.) and various objects of cognition. For instance, if one perceives that a car is driving by, we distinguish between the perception and the judgment, between the sense contents and the propositional contents. In some respects, we are all phaneroscopists; it is part of the mastery of language to learn to distinguish among different constituents of the phaneron.

Nonetheless, some of the distinctions we make among the phaneron's different constituents are learned through more advanced training. Just as one can be a better or worse spectroscopist or microscopist, one can be a better or worse phaneroscopist. For example, ancient astronomers were trained to classify stars by their magnitudes and colors (see CP7.258, c. 1900; CN3:191, 1904; Short 2008). Sommeliers train to distinguish among different aspects of wine. Visual artists are trained to make fine-grained distinctions among qualities of color. Musicians are trained to distinguish among different qualities of sounds. Educational courses enable us to make more precise observations. Generally, there is a difference between skilled and unskilled observation of the phaneron. Plainly, those who are more skilled observers of the phaneron will have richer and more accurate classifications of its constituents. Their more skilled perceptions will be evident in the more detailed and careful descriptions they give of their experiences.

At this juncture, one may wonder whether most of the work of phaneroscopy is done, for we already have rich vocabularies to describe our experiences. Yet it is one thing to identify the phaneron's various constituents and quite another to show that they admit of systematic classification. An aggregation of distinctions is not a classification until there is some principle that informs how we draw the distinctions. Peirce often likens phaneroscopy to chemistry, and the analogy is especially illustrative on this point. Prior to the work of Dmitri Mendeleev, chemists had identified numerous elements, developed techniques to distinguish among them, and proposed various classifications of them.[1] However, not until Mendeleev's discovery of the periodic law did chemists have a satisfactory classification of the elements, one that exhibited the relations among them and predicted elements yet to be discovered. The phaneroscopist aims at the same: a way of systematically classifying the phaneron's constituents that exhibits the relations among the constituents known and predicts other constituents yet to be distinguished.

Why should we want a classification of the phaneron's constituents? One benefit to be derived from phaneroscopic inquiry is an increased sensitivity to how we describe the phaneron, for we will have a more technical vocabulary, a better classification of its constituents, and better training in distinguishing among those constituents. A vocabulary that conflates two distinct properties (e.g., weight and mass in physics) is liable to lead investigators astray. Similarly, a confusion between qualitative intensity and vividness in experience may lead inquirers astray. Furthermore, much research in the cognitive sciences relies on first-person reports. The better the reporters, the more reliable will be the reports. Better reports give us better data. Better data give us better results. Daniel Dennett remarks, "Subjects often fail to tell the whole truth because some of the psychological things that happen in them are unsuspected by them, and hence go unreported, and subjects often fail to tell nothing but the truth because they are tempted into theorizing that goes beyond what we can demonstrate to be the limit of their experience" (Dennett 2005, 39). On the Peircean view, better training in phaneroscopy would ameliorate both problems in reporting.

A second benefit is that in focusing on the categories into which the phaneron's constituents fall, phaneroscopy aims to examine the structure of experience. If there is a structural isomorphism between (for example) seeing a scarlet red and hearing a trumpet's blare, then an accurate and adequate classification of the phaneron's constituents ought to enable us to describe what that isomorphism is. The prospects of developing an objective phenomenological vocabulary lie with phaneroscopy.

We care to develop an objective phenomenological vocabulary for two reasons. First, some scholars suggest that the prospects for closing the explanatory gap between conscious experience and brain activity depend strongly on our ability to develop just such a vocabulary (e.g., Nagel 1974, 449). Second, understanding the structural isomorphism between experiences may aid our understanding of such phenomena as synesthesia and neural reorganization following sensory loss by helping us identify rules or structures that bear on the phenomena.

Granted the preceding, by what principle shall we classify the phaneron's constituents? Presumably there are multiple ways of classifying them, just as there are multiple ways of classifying people (height, weight, etc.). Peirce hypothesizes there are at least two different kinds of categories by which we may classify the phaneron's constituents. These are the formal (quantitative) and material (qualitative) categories. He avers both classifications are "quite true" but regards the former as "the most important" (CP1.288, 1906). In what follows, I take up each in turn.

1. The Formal Categories

Peirce's presentations of the formal categories often implicitly assume his theory of inquiry. I shall follow suit and exposit his account in that context. According to Peirce, scientific inquiry involves three different (not always linear) stages of investigation. In the abductive stage, the inquirer forms hypotheses and ranks them by pursuitworthiness. In the deductive stage, the inquirer makes the hypothesis she is pursuing more definite and ascertains its testable consequences. In the inductive stage, she undertakes the investigation, gathering data and determining how well those data fit the hypothesis.

For the formal categories, Peirce pursues the hypothesis that the phaneron's constituents can be classified according to the basic adicities of predicate terms (i.e., whether a predicate is monadic, dyadic, triadic, etc.). Second, having ascertained what are the irreducible adicities of predicates, Peirce endeavors to make this hypothesis more definite as it should apply to phaneroscopic inquiry. Third, Peirce investigates the phaneron in an attempt to determine whether the phaneron's constituents can in fact be so classified.

1.1. The Abductive Stage

Peirce pursues the hypothesis that the phaneron's constituents can be categorized in a manner corresponding to the adicities of predicates. Peirce calls these the formal, quantitative categories. I refer to this hypothesis as the modified Kantian insight (MKI), that "the phenomenological categories somehow are based on ... or otherwise correspond to the logical forms of propositions as discovered in formal logic" (Atkins 2018, 9). As Kant endeavored to base a set of metaphysical categories on the logical forms of judgments, Peirce endeavors to base a set of phaneroscopic categories on the most basic elements that are used to form propositions, namely, predicates.

Why is this a pursuitworthy hypothesis? Four considerations support pursuing MKI. First, by drawing on the formal science of mathematics, we avoid smuggling in prejudices that might affect how we categorize the phaneron's constituents (Short 2015, 17–18). But this is not a strong reason for favoring MKI. At most, it supports classifying the phaneron's constituents in accordance with some formal structure but not specifically the adicities of predicates.

Second, Peirce holds mental action is inferential. Inference works on propositions. Therefore, mental states can be modeled on the structure of propositions (Atkins 2018, 26). Neither is this argument a strong reason to favor MKI. That we model a structure on something else does not imply we model the constituents of that structure on the constituents of that other thing. Modeling molecular interactions on billiard balls striking one another does not favor modeling molecules on billiard balls.

A third reason to favor MKI is that some of the greatest minds have found it fruitful to construct models based on logical forms. For examples, Aristotle's *Categories* and Kant's *Critique of Pure Reason* have been a tremendous source of insight in spite of their shortcomings. Similarly, even if MKI should prove false, there is reason to suspect that pursuing the hypothesis will be fruitful (see LI:296, c. 1905).

Fourth, sensations, while not conceptual predicates, are predicate-like. The sensation of red "sense-predicates" red of the object that is sensed. "Sense predicates" are akin to conceptual predicates, a claim supported by two considerations. One, there is no sharp line of demarcation between the immediate deliverances of the "stimulations of the peripheral nerve-terminals" and "the quasi-inferential interpolations of sense" (R831:2, n.d.). "Modern psychology," Peirce writes, "shows us that there is no such thing as pure observation free from reasoning nor as pure reasoning without any observational element" (W4:400–401, 1883). Two, all sensations are general and so are concept-like; the same sensation of red can be produced by different objects. Peirce claims, "That perceptions are not absolutely determinate and singular is obvious from the fact that each sense is an abstracting mechanism" (W2:236, 1868).

1.2. The Deductive Stage

I turn to consider what classifying the phaneron's constituents according to the adicities of predicates involves. There are two issues to be resolved at this stage. The first is that we need to ascertain what the most basic adicities of predicates are. These will be the formal categories. The second issue is that we need to make these mathematical conceptions more definite so that we can identify constituents of the phaneron that fall under each of the categories.

1.2.1. The Adicities of Predicates

Fully appreciating Peirce's hypothesis requires treading into minutiae related to his logical notation the existential graphs (EGs). As such an exposition is outside the scope of this chapter, I must content myself with the barest of details.[2] The beta segment of the EGs is roughly equivalent to first-order quantified predicate logic. Predicate terms may come in any number of adicities: monadic (e.g., ___ is red); dyadic (e.g., ___ loves . . .); triadic (e.g., ___ gives . . . to***); tetradic (e.g., ___ gives . . . to*** for###); etc. In these examples, "___," ". . .", etc., are blanks. These blanks are the subject of the proposition, akin to the existential quantifier "there is." The word (together with its prepositions) is the predicate. These predicates become complete propositions when their blanks are connected. For instance, the monadic predicates ___ *is a man* and . . . *is a woman* and the dyadic predicate ___ *loves* . . . can be combined by connecting the two "___" blanks and the two ". . ." blanks to get the complete proposition *a man loves a woman*, that is, *there is something that is a man and that thing loves something that is a woman*.[3]

If we abstract from the meanings of the predicate terms, what are the most basic predicate forms we need to construct an *n*-adic predicate, where *n* is any positive integer greater than zero? Let n be the number of blanks a predicate has. If two predicates are combined by connecting just one blank of each predicate, then the total number of blanks resulting from the combination of predicate a with n blanks and predicate b with n blanks will be: $n_a + n_b - 2$. For example, combining a monad with a dyad results in one blank, a monad. Patently, the combination of monads and dyads cannot give us adicities greater than two. Yet there are triadic predicates. Hence, there must be at least monadic, dyadic, and triadic basic predicate forms.

Are tetrads a basic predicate form? A triad and monad combined is a dyad. A triad combined with a dyad is a triad. A triad combined with a triad is a tetrad. But then combining an additional triad with that tetrad gives us a pentad, an additional triad with the pentad gives us a hexad, and so on. Let x be a number of triads greater than zero. If x triads are combined with each other by connecting just one blank of each to just one blank of another, the resulting combination gives us a predicate form with $3x - 2(x - 1)$ blanks. Accordingly, the total number of blanks increases by one with each triad added. Consequently, there is no need to postulate any more basic predicate forms than monads, dyads, and triads since greater adicities can be constructed from triads but triads cannot be constructed from monads and dyads alone.

So far as the previous argument goes, we have only considered cases wherein the blanks of distinct predicates are joined one by one. However, if we consider triads alone, it is possible to construct monads and dyads from these. Suppose that we have just one triad and we connect two of its blanks. If we do so, we are left with one blank, a monad. Moreover, combining two triads by combining two each of their blanks results in a dyad. It seems to follow there is no need to posit monads or dyads as basic predicate forms since we can construct these from triads. Consequently, the objection goes, there is only one basic predicate form, the triad.

Peirce responds that monads and dyads are nevertheless "logical ingredients" of triads (EP2:364–365, 1905). For example, the proposition *the wealthy give money to charities* is comprised of ___ *wealthy*, . . . *money*, ***charities, and ___ *give* . . . *to****. But we can ignore one or more of the monadic predicates to obtain *the wealthy give to charities* or *the wealthy give*. The former treats the triad ___ *give* . . . *to**** as the dyad ___ *give to****, whereas the latter treats it as the monad ___ *give*. In this way, monadic and dyadic predicates are nevertheless "logical ingredients" of triads.

The preceding is a thumbnail sketch of Peirce's argument for the thesis that there are three basic predicate forms, namely, monads, dyads, and triads. Based on these considerations, Peirce posits that there are three formal categories of firstness, secondness, and thirdness.

1.2.2. *Making the Hypothesis More Definite*

How are we to connect the mathematical insight that the basic predicate forms are firstness, secondness, and thirdness to the classification of the phaneron's constituents? In accordance with Peirce's theory of inquiry, we must make the hypothesis more definite.

Peirce admits it is hard to make these ideas definite, sometimes referring to them as mere "tones" of thought rather than definite conceptions (W6:169, 1887). Plainly, the phaneron's constituents must not be exactly like predicates, for our experience involves more than just words or concepts: "These divisions are not exactly like the corresponding divisions of Existential Graphs" (CP1.292, 1906). Moreover, Peirce must tread cautiously. He developed a theory of the categories long before he recognized phaneroscopy as a distinctive area of inquiry. Making his hypothesis more definite runs the risk of biasing his characterization of the categories as applied to phaneroscopy in ways that confirm his prior suspicions. He claimed as early as 1867 that the three categories are quality, relation (or reaction), and representation, but he only recognized phaneroscopy as a distinct science in 1902. Peirce does think qualities are instances of firstness (mutatis mutandis for reactions and representations). However, to make the hypothesis definite in reference to these features of the phaneron would be sham reasoning: reasoning with a view to the conclusion one already accepts. Instead, Peirce must initially characterize what a phaneral first should be like, and only then may he determine whether qualities are firsts.

Peirce typically hews as close to the mathematical characterization of the phaneron's constituents as he can. He describes a first as a constituent "which, except that it is thought as applying to some subject, has no other characters than those which are complete in it without any reference to anything else" (CP1.292, 1906). A dyadic constituent will be "of something that would possess such characters as it does possess relatively to something else but regardless of any third object of any category" (CP1.292, 1906). Finally, a triadic constituent will be "an elementary idea of something which should be such as it were relatively to two others in different ways, but regardless of any fourth" (CP1.292, 1906). The next task is to turn to the phaneron to ascertain whether we can in fact isolate constituents of it that fall under each of these categories.

1.3. The Inductive Stage

Having (1) given reasons for adopting the hypothesis that the phaneron's constituents can be classified by the basic predicate forms and (2) determined (a) what those forms are and (b) for what we should be looking in the phaneron, Peirce turns to an investigation of the phaneron itself. At the inductive stage, it is (3) requisite (a) to provide some account of the techniques of observation, (b) to observe the phaneron and ascertain whether its constituents can be categorized as firsts, seconds, and thirds, and (c) to endeavor to disprove the hypothesis, including to consider whether it suffices to classify all of the phaneron's constituents.

1.3.1. *Techniques of Observation*

Earlier I noted that the phaneroscopist does not use special instruments but only those resources at everyone's disposal. If she is a good observer, then she may discover facts about her experience that surprise even her. For instance, she may discover there is a blind spot in her field of vision, though she may not know this is where the optical nerve meets the eye (for this last fact would require special observation of the eye's anatomy). Similarly, she may discover that though it seems her visual experience is rich and detailed even in the periphery of her vision, she cannot in fact distinguish colors of objects held in the far periphery of her vision. She will not know by phaneroscopic observation alone that this is to be explained by the anatomy of the eye, but she will be able to discover it by astute observation of her own visual field.

Peirce provides no comprehensive, detailed account of what techniques of observation are used in phaneroscopy. His only explicit overview of the varieties of analysis is one page from his *Logic Notebook*, dated August 21, 1908. There, he distinguishes among organic analysis, attentional analysis, comparational analysis, and experimental analysis. Each of these kinds of analysis is illustrated in reference to the analysis of feelings.

Organic analysis involves distinguishing among different sense modalities and parts of sense modalities. Peirce notes, "We do directly distinguish in our feelings a visible part an audible part, etc." (R339:291r, 1908). To illustrate, suppose someone perceives people playing basketball. This is a synthetic unity capable of analysis. She closes her eyes and hears the ball bouncing but does not see it. She opens her eyes, plugs her ears, and sees the ball bouncing but does not hear it. She thereby performs an organic analysis of the experience and discovers that there is a distinction between the visual and the auditory features of the experience. Furthermore, Peirce states, "We separate the sensations of different parts of the retina" (R339:291r, 1908). We discover, for instance, that the visual sense organ is an extended surface, since it is possible to occlude part of one's visual field without occluding it entirely. Similarly, we can affect auditory experiences by turning our heads or by gently pushing on the tragus.

Attentional analysis is accomplished by attending to some constituent of the phaneron and ignoring others. Across sense modalities, we may attend to what we hear rather than what we see. Within a sense modality, we may attend to some features of what we hear. For example, when listening to a piece of music, one may attend to the bass line while ignoring the trumpet's sounds. Peirce states, "We hear harmonies in musical notes, by simply listening for them" (R339:291r, 1908).

Comparational analysis of a feeling is accomplished by comparing different feelings. It is that sort of analysis "by which we perceive likenesses of different feelings. As between different vowels & consonants, whence the triangle of vowels. Also in colors where we recognize likenesses in hue, in chroma, and in luminosity" (R339:291r, 1908). Comparational analysis is most familiar from comparing sensations within a sense modality. One can distinguish between the timbres of a trumpet and a violin, even when they are playing a note at the same pitch. One can also distinguish among differences in pitch, loudness, etc. Furthermore, we perform comparational analysis across sense modalities. The qualitative intensity of a seen dim star is much less than the qualitative intensity of a heard trumpet blaring.

Finally, Peirce briefly describes experimental analysis as "color box & color wheel analysis" (R339:291r, 1908). Presumably Peirce would include other sorts of analysis, such as by using tuning forks, as experimental analysis.

Although Peirce mentions each of organic, attentional, comparational, and experimental analysis, it is not clear which he regards as appropriate to phaneroscopic inquiry. What is clear is that Peirce thinks analysis of the phaneron should be restricted to direct (i.e., without the aid of instruments) inspective analysis. Accordingly, he would exclude experimental analysis as appropriate to phaneroscopic inquiry, since it involves the use of observational aids. This is not surprising since phaneroscopy is a cenoscopic rather than idioscopic science. None of organic, attentional, or comparational analysis can be excluded from phaneroscopy on the same grounds. However, in some passages Peirce excludes comparational analysis from phaneroscopy. In such passages, he asks the reader to imagine that a universe consists only of some feeling, and only ever of that feeling: "Suppose I begin by inquiring of you, Reader, in what particulars a feeling of redness or of purple . . . that should constitute the entire universe, would differ from a substance? I suppose you will tell me that no such thing could be alone in the universe because . . . each would have a quality . . . the color in hue, luminosity, chroma, and vividness. . . . But I point out to you that these things are only known to us by extraneous experience" (CP1.305, 1907). In such a universe, it would not be possible to perform comparational analyses because there would be no other sensation to which we could compare the first. Presumably, we should have to exclude organic analysis on similar grounds: We would have no hands to occlude the visual field, no tragus on which to press, etc. Why should Peirce restrict phaneroscopic analysis in this way? To answer that question, we must turn to the results of Peirce's phaneroscopic inquiries.

1.3.2. *Peirce's Phaneroscopic Inquiries*

Although Peirce only recognized phaneroscopy as a distinct science in 1902, many of his earlier writings anticipate some of his key claims. In fact, in several passages Peirce mentions an early essay of his, "On a New List of Categories" from 1867, as anticipating his later work. A brief survey of some of the ideas from that essay helps to put his later work—and some of the problems raised therein—into greater focus.

In "On a New List," Peirce identifies three categories, namely, quality, relation, and representation. These categories are derived from the different functions of the copula. In the first case, the copula merely applies some predicate to a subject, as in *the stove is black*. In the second case, it applies a predicate to a subject in a way such that the subject and predicate can be switched, as in *scarlet is like burgundy*. In the third case, the subject and another term can be switched in place and we are provided some way to interpret their relation, as in b *is like p by way of turning on a horizontal axis*. Beginning in the 1880s and continuing into the 1900s, Peirce associated these three categories with those of being a first, a second, and a third. He also experimented with different names for them, for example, replacing "relation" with "reaction" or "representation" with "mediation." And he developed different ways of extending these categories, recognizing degenerate and genuine cases of secondness and thirdness (e.g., *Cicero is Tully* is degenerate secondness whereas *Daniel Webster was like Cicero* is genuine secondness). Peirce applies these logical considerations to his metaphysical investigations.

Once Peirce identified phaneroscopy as a distinctive field of inquiry, he imported many of the insights he developed over the preceding decades into his results. This is not surprising or even of doubtful legitimacy, since within metaphysics he had included psychical metaphysics as distinct from psychology. Accordingly, Peirce wondered whether among the phaneron's constituents may be found qualities, reactions, and representations. He had no difficulty in identifying such constituents. Among the constituents of our experiences are qualities, such as the scarlet red of a stick of courthouse sealing wax. Brute reactions (reactions that do not involve a mediating third) are harder to identify because they are often accompanied with qualities. Peirce gives as an example of a reactive constituent of the phaneron being unexpectedly poked in the back of the head (EP2:150, 1903). Finally, among representations are all sorts of signs, which represent objects to us (whether veridically or not the phaneroscopist does not care).

However, Peirce's writings from 1903 reveal a tension. On the one hand, he holds that colors and sounds are qualities. They are instances of firstness in the phaneron because they are what they are independent of aught else. On the other hand, colors and sounds are themselves composed of other qualities. A color is composed of its hue, its chroma, and its luminosity. A sound has its timbre, pitch, and loudness. Consequently, qualities are not what they are independent of aught else. To the contrary, they are constituted of other qualities, what Peirce calls qualities of qualities.

Peirce resolves the problem by regarding phaneroscopic investigation as concerned with universes of experience. He asks us to imagine a universe that consists of nothing but an unvarying sound, such as the sound of a train whistle. Note that the sound is unvarying. There are no changes in pitch, in loudness, etc. Supposing that this were all anyone ever experienced, Peirce claims, no one could ever discern that the quality (the sound) is further analyzable into other qualities (timbre, pitch, loudness, etc.). Peirce claims that these qualities of qualities are known to us only because we are able to perform comparational or experimental analyses. But since there is nothing with which to compare the sound and no instruments (since ex hypothesi the universe consists only of the sound), it is not possible to perform such analyses. Presumably organic analysis is also ruled out in this case, since the universe consists of a sound only and so no sense organ. In fact, it must not even consist of a substance (e.g., air) through which the sound travels!

This borders on the absurd, and Peirce was fully aware of these problems. His "The First Part of an Apology for Pragmaticism" presents a series of objections to supposing an unvarying sound to be alone in the universe: "firstly, because it would suppose a mind to feel it . . .; secondly because colors and sounds . . . are due to vibrations or alternations of impulses and cannot exist without them. . . . Thirdly, no feeling could last forever without a flow of Time. . . . Fourthly, the color, the sound . . . would each have its peculiar character which would be a compound of several elements . . .; and fifthly because every feeling supposes, in addition to a pneumatic substratum a physical substratum" (LI:372–373, 1907). Peirce replies, "It will suffice to point out that each of them is known to us only by experience, and can therefore be logically supposed to be absent" (LI:373, 1907). Even if from a physical or metaphysical point of view colors, sounds, etc., require these concomitants or substrates, from a logical point of view we can consider the qualities independent of them.

Recognizing a tension between regarding qualities as instances of firstness in the phaneron and yet qualities not being what they are independent of aught else, Peirce restricts the sort of analysis appropriate to phaneroscopy to direct attentional inspective analysis. For firstness, we conceive of a universe constituted of just one unvarying quality. But there is a question of whether this is a good or even plausible solution to the problem. One might suspect that Peirce's resolution of the problem is partly motivated by his earlier pre-phaneroscopic subsumption of qualities under the category of firstness. At the very least, it is worthwhile to consider other possible solutions to the problem that Peirce faces.

I have proposed an alternate solution—and adduced passages to show that on occasion Peirce entertains it—on which we should regard qualities of qualities as instances of firstness in the phaneron (see Atkins 2018, 136–139). These are still qualities, albeit they are not immediately apprehended by us but known to us by comparison with other qualities. This solution requires little modification to the rest of Peirce's phaneroscopy and has the benefit of permitting organic and comparational analysis as phaneroscopic techniques. (Experimental analysis is still excluded, as it involves the use of special instruments.) One consideration in favor of this solution, not elsewhere mentioned, is that Peirce's account of colors as firsts may be prejudiced toward human perceptual capacities. Consider that we have complex eyes, which are responsive to a number of different qualities of qualities of color. Other creatures, however, have simple eyes, and a simple eye may perceive only one quality of a quality (e.g., the brightness of the color). Supposing a creature with simple eyes to be endowed with conscious experience, it would perceive qualities of qualities merely and not the colors that we perceive. These qualities of qualities would be instances of firstness independent of the complex color qualities of our perceptions.

However such matters may be decided, the previous comments only concern instances of firstness in the phaneron. Also of note are Peirce's comments on the category of secondness. Peirce takes considerable interest in vividness as an instance of secondness in the phaneron. He is careful to distinguish vividness from qualitative intensity. Scarlet red is a more intense color than pink, though both are shades of red. However, the perception of a pink carnation is more vivid than the mere imagining of a scarlet rose mallow. He also draws a distinction between vividness as the force of the object of thought upon one's mind and vividness as a feeling of that force.[4] For instance, one's perceptual experiences upon just awaking may feel less vivid than perceptual experiences after a strong cup of coffee. There is much more to be said about secondness, but space prevents a more detailed consideration of it.

Turning now to a few brief comments on thirdness, Peirce regards signs as instances of thirdness in the phaneron. At this juncture, there is a close connection between Peirce's phaneroscopy and his semiotics. Peirce endeavors to classify all sorts of signs and sign relations, and his reflections on the matter have received significant scholarly attention.[5] There is, though, a question of how closely Peirce's semiotics is tied to his phaneroscopy. For Peirce thinks that every sign has some material quality as well as some denotative or demonstrative application. These might be thought of as the firstness of thirdness and the secondness of thirdness, respectively (recall here the logical ingredient thesis mentioned earlier: monads and dyads are nevertheless logical ingredients of triads). However, it is hasty to conclude from this that Peirce thinks every quality is the material quality of a sign. If Peirce were of that opinion, it would follow that there are no genuine firsts; they are all the firsts of thirds. Yet there are evidently qualities that are not the material qualities of signs, such as a ringing in one's ears. If this is a sign, what does it signify? Moreover, there may be signs that do not produce qualitative experiences. Bacteria, for instance, may respond to gradient changes in sucrose without having experiences that involve qualities. One could view such a response semiotically without committing oneself to the claim that bacteria have conscious experiences of qualities. However, these are difficult questions and want of space prohibits me from pursuing them.

1.3.3. *Endeavoring to Disprove the Hypothesis*

Peirce's hypothesis is that the phaneron's constituents fall into three broad categories correlative with firstness, secondness, and thirdness. Qualities are firsts, reactions are seconds, and representations are thirds. Peirce thought, however, that we should not only seek to confirm our hypotheses but also to disprove them. Are there good reasons for doubting his hypothesis?

Disproving the hypothesis would require identifying a constituent of the phaneron that is neither a first, nor a second, nor a third. Peirce mentions no such constituents, and I know of no counterexamples. Nevertheless, Peirce frequently expresses doubts about the categories both explicitly and implicitly. In 1903, he remarked, "If I were asked today which of the two propositions, that the categories are Quality, Relation, and Representation . . . or that the three forms of inference are Hypothesis, Induction, and Deduction, which of those two seemed today to be most fully supported by evidence, I should say the latter" (PPM:276fn3, 1903). Lest one surmise that Peirce thinks both are strongly supported by the evidence, only the latter more so, he proceeds to record doubts about his classification of inferences. He also claims, "In saying that the three, Firstness, Secondness, and Thirdness, complete the list, I by no means deny that there are other categories. On the contrary, at every step of every analysis, conceptions are met with which presumably do not belong to this series of ideas" (CP1.525, 1903).

Peirce ultimately holds that while firstness, secondness, and thirdness complete the list of the formal, quantitative categories, there are also material, qualitative categories. Every constituent of the phaneron is a first, second, or third, but the constituents are not merely firsts, seconds, and thirds. The phaneron's constituents are not adequately categorized by the formal categories alone.

2. THE MATERIAL CATEGORIES

Peirce wrote very little on the material categories. In fact, there is no passage where Peirce explicitly states what he takes the material categories to be. Typically, he backs away from presenting them, with comments like this: "The two most passionately laborious years of my life were exclusively devoted to trying to ascertain something for certain about the [material categories]; but I abandoned the attempt as beyond my powers, or, at any rate, unsuited to my genius" (CP1.288, 1906).

Nevertheless, there are some indications throughout Peirce's writings as to what the material categories are. Here, I will mention just three (see Atkins 2018, 180–203, for a fuller discussion). One hint is the names "quantitative" and "qualitative." Taking these in the Kantian sense, quantitative categories are extensive magnitudes that can be aggregated, much as predicates can be aggregated by connecting them. Qualitative categories, in contrast, are intensive magnitudes on a continuous scale. These come in degrees. As such, we might expect the material categories to be the extremes of a continuum.

Second, Peirce wanted his phaneroscopic categories to be based on his unique logical notation, the EGs. Earlier, I explained how the formal categories are related to predicate forms. But there are two other features of the graphs: the line of identity (which represents an individual) and the sheet of assertions (which is that on which the statements are written). In one passage, immediately after describing how the "really scientific research into the Phaneron must be" related to the basic predicate forms, he proceeds to note that nonetheless there are two features of the graphs that are "remarkable for being truly *continuous* both in their Matter and in their corresponding Signification" (NEM4:324, 1906). Peirce's reference to matter in a context in which he has emphasized the "precedence of Form over Matter" in a "Classification of Elements of the Phaneron" (NEM4:322, 1906) suggests he conceives of the material categories as a continuum.

A third and final passage is one page from a draft for "The Basis of Pragmatism" (R284:10v, 1905). There, Peirce distinguishes among the priman, secundan, and tertian (first, second, and third) and then between the logical form and matter of each. With respect to the logical matter of the priman, Peirce distinguishes between its "Positive Suchness" and its "Negative Absence of Matter," suggesting that a negative first is an uninstantiated quality whereas a positive first is an instantiated quality. With respect to the secundan, he describes the logical matter as "Positive. Existence" and as "Negative," with no description. Similarly, for the tertian the logical matter is "Positive Rationality," and there is no additional description of "Negative." This is perhaps the strongest piece of evidence that Peirce thinks of the material categories as being a continuum the extremes of which are positiveness and negativeness, and that these are somehow related to existence and rationality.

Developing these ideas in reference to Peirce's writings, I have argued that once we examine Peirce's manuscripts with these categories in mind, we find them put to use in many different ways. With respect to firstness, qualities such as colors and sounds have degrees of intensity, and so do qualities of qualities. With respect to secondness, vividness comes in degrees, as I earlier indicated that perceptions are typically more vivid than mere imaginings. Albeit grudgingly, Peirce states he "is obliged, for the present, to admit degrees of reality" since it is hard to draw a sharp line between the inner and outer worlds and between "direct willing and willing to bring about through the accomplishment of other volitions" (R1041:15, c. 1906). With respect to thirdness, Peirce acknowledges that there are "qualitative differences" in how clear our ideas are (R649:1–2, 1910). Also, rationality comes in degrees, as does the strength of our arguments. For these reasons, I have proposed that Peirce's material categories are positiveness and negativeness, which are the extremes of a continuum.

3. Conclusion

Peirce explores two different hypotheses with respect to classifying the phaneron's constituents. The first is that they may be classified according to the three basic predicate forms of firstness, secondness, and thirdness. This is the formal classification and the one to which Peirce devotes the most energy. The second is that the phaneron's constituents may be classified on a continuum between positiveness and negativeness. There are only hints throughout Peirce's manuscripts as to how such a classification is to work. Nonetheless, Peirce evidently holds that the formal and material categories can be combined to construct a sort of "phanerochemical" table of constituents. Much as the chemical elements are classified by their periodicity and atomic weight, a phanerochemical table of constituents would have (I) as its columns (A) firstness, secondness, and thirdness, including these in (B) their logical ingredient relations (the firstness of secondness, the secondness of thirdness, etc.) and (C) their degenerate and genuine forms and (II) as its rows degrees of intensity between positiveness and negativeness. Yet it must be admitted that Peirce's project remains largely unfinished and its prospects remain uncertain.

Notes

1. Among these chemists is Peirce. His table bears a striking resemblance to contemporary tables (see W2:282–84, 1869). The resemblance is most notable if the table is turned upside down. Read upside down, the first two columns of Peirce's table mix together elements found in columns 8–13. The remaining correspond well with rows 14, 16, 2, 11, 1, 17, 15, and 13. But his table does not exhibit well the periodic law.
2. See Ketner (1986) and Atkins (2018, ch. 3) for more graphical presentations.
3. I am here glossing over complications related to Peirce's graphical logic. To be a well-formed graph in the EGs, every n-adic predicate will have n pegs to which must be attached some line of identity, which functions like the existential quantifier. Consequently, the predicates and blanks I refer to here are propositional forms in the context of the EGs.
4. This distinction correlates with his distinction between secondness and firstness as a logical ingredient of secondness.
5. For examples, see Short (2007) and Bellucci (2018).

Bibliography

Atkins, Richard Kenneth. 2018. *Charles S. Peirce's Phenomenology*. New York: Oxford University Press.

Bellucci, Francesco. 2018. *Peirce's Speculative Grammar: Logic as Semiotics*. New York: Routledge.

Dennett, Daniel C. 2005. *Sweet Dreams: Philosophical Obstacles to a Science of Consciousness* Cambridge, MA: MIT Press.

Ketner, Kenneth Laine. 1986. "Peirce's Most Interesting and Lucid Paper." *International Philosophical Quarterly* 26, no. 4: 375–392.

Nagel, Thomas. 1974. "What Is It Like to Be a Bat?" *The Philosophical Review* 83, no. 4: 435–450.

Peirce, Charles S. 1857–1914. Manuscripts held at the Houghton Library of Harvard University, as identified in Richard Robin, *Annotated Catalogue of the Papers of Charles S. Peirce*. Amherst: University of Massachusetts Press, 1967. And in Richard Robin, "The Peirce Papers: A Supplementary Catalogue." *Transactions of the Charles S. Peirce Society* 7, no. 1 (Winter 1971): 37–57. (Referred to as R[catalogue#]:[sheet#]; with RL for letters and RS for supplement.)

Peirce, Charles S. 1931–1958. *The Collected Papers of Charles Sanders Peirce*. 8 vols. Vols. 1–6 edited by Charles Hartshorne and Paul Weiss. Vols. 7–8 edited by Arthur W. Burks. Cambridge, MA: Harvard University Press. (Referred to as CP.)

Peirce, Charles S. 1975–1987. *Charles Sanders Peirce: Contributions to The Nation*. 4 vols. Edited by Kenneth L. Ketner and James E. Cook. Lubbock: Texas Tech University Press. (Referred to as CN.)

Peirce, Charles S. 1976. *The New Elements of Mathematics*, 4 vols. in 5. Edited by Carolyn Eisele. The Hague: Mouton. (Referred to as NEM.)

Peirce, Charles S. 1977. *Semiotic and Significs: The Correspondence between Charles S. Peirce and Victoria Lady Welby*. Edited by Charles S. Hardwick. Bloomington: Indiana University Press. (Referred to as SS.)

Peirce, Charles S. 1982–2010. *The Writings of Charles S. Peirce: A Chronological Edition*. 7 vols. to date. Edited by the Peirce Edition Project. Bloomington: Indiana University Press. (Referred to as W.)

Peirce, Charles S. 1922–1998. *The Essential Peirce: Selected Philosophical Writings*. 2 vols. Vol. 1 edited by Nathan Houser and Christian Kloesel. Vol. 2 edited by the Peirce Edition Project. Bloomington, Indiana University Press. (Referred to as EP.)

Peirce, Charles S. 1997. *Pragmatism as a Principle and Method of Right Reasoning: The 1903 Harvard Lectures on Pragmatism*. Edited by Patricia Ann Turrisi. Albany: State University of New York Press. (Referred to as PPM.)

Peirce, Charles S. 2009. *The Logic of Interdisciplinarity: The Monist Series*. Edited by Elize Bisanz. Berlin: Akademie Verlag. (Referred to as LI.)

Short, T. L. 2007. *Peirce's Theory of Signs*. New York: Cambridge University Press.

Short, T. L. 2008. "Measurement and Philosophy." *Cognitio* 9, no. 1: 111–124.

Short, T. L. 2015. "Empiricism Expanded." *Transactions of the Charles S. Peirce Society* 51, no. 1 (Winter): 1–33.

Further Reading

Atkins, Richard Kenneth. 2019. "Semiotics and Phenomenality." *Journal of Mind and Behavior* 40, no. 1: 67–82.

Bellucci, Francesco. 2015. "Peirce on Phaneroscopical Analysis." *Journal Phänomenologie* 44: 56–72.

Champagne, Marc. 2018. *Consciousness and the Philosophy of Signs: How Peircean Semiotics Combines Phenomenal Qualia and Practical Effects*. Cham, Switzerland: Springer.

Colapietro, Vincent. 2015. "C. S. Peirce's Phenomenological Categories: Their Basic Form, Recursive Elaboration, and Heuristic Purpose." *Journal Phänomenologie* 44: 10–20.

De Tienne, André. 1993. "Peirce's Definitions of the Phaneron." In *Charles S. Peirce and the Philosophy of Science*, edited by Edward C. Moore, 279–288. Tuscaloosa: University of Alabama Press.

De Tienne, André. 1996. *L'Analytique de la représentation chez Peirce: La genése de la théorie des categories*. Brussels: Facultés universitaires Sant-Louis.

De Tienne, André. 2004. "Is Phaneroscopy as a Pre-semiotic Science Possible?" *Semiotiche* 2: 15–30.

Dougherty, Charles J. 1980. "The Common Root of Husserl's and Peirce's Phenomenologies." *New Scholaticism* 54, no. 3: 305–325.

Downard, Jeffrey Brian. 2015. "The Main Questions and Aims Guiding Peirce's Phenomenology." *Cognitio* 16, no. 1: 87–102.

Fuhrman, Gary. 2013. "Peirce's Retrospectives on His Phenomenological Quest." *Transactions of the Charles S. Peirce Society* 49, no. 4 (Fall): 490–508.

Houser, Nathan. 1983. "Peirce's General Taxonomy of Consciousness." *Transactions of the Charles S. Peirce Society* 19, no. 4 (Fall): 331–359.

Houser, Nathan. 1989. "La structure formelle de l'experience selon Peirce." *Etudes Phénoménologiques* 5, no. 9–10: 77–111.

Kruse, Felicia E. 1991. "Genuineness and Degeneracy in Peirce's Categories." *Transactions of the Charles S. Peirce Society* 27, no. 3 (Summer): 267–298.

Ransdell, Joseph. 1989. "Is Peirce a Phenomenologist?" Arisbe: The Peirce Gateway, https://arisbe.sitehost.iu.edu/menu/library/aboutcsp/ransdell/PHENOM.HTM. Published as "Peirce est-il un phénoménologue?" *Études Phénoménologiques*, 9–10: 51–75.

Rosensohn, William L. 1974. *The Phenomenology of Charles S. Peirce: From the Doctrine of Categories to Phaneroscopy*. Amsterdam: B. R. Grüner.

Shafiei, Mohammad, and Pietarinen, Ahti-Veikko, eds. 2019. *Peirce and Husserl: Mutual Insights on Logic, Mathematics, and Cognition*. Cham, Switzerland: Springer.

Spiegelberg, Herbert. 1956. "Husserl's and Peirce's Phenomenologies: Coincidence or Interaction?" *Philosophy and Phenomenological Research* 17, no. 2: 164–185.

Stern, Robert. 2013. "An Hegelian in a Strange Costume? On Peirce's Relation to Hegel I." *Philosophy Compass* 8, no. 1: 53–62.

Stern, Robert. 2013. "An Hegelian in a Strange Costume? On Peirce's Relation to Hegel II." *Philosophy Compass* 8, no. 1: 63–72.

CHAPTER 5

THE VICISSITUDES OF EXPERIENCE

NATHAN HOUSER

On September 28, 1904, Charles Peirce wrote to William James to ask what he meant by saying that consciousness is often regarded as an entity. James had said this in his paper "Does 'Consciousness' Exist?" (James 1904), which Peirce had just started to read. Peirce told James that he didn't believe "anybody has any such opinions" (CP8.279). He continued with a brief account of his own conception of consciousness as encompassing three distinct kinds corresponding to his categories: firstness, secondness, thirdness. James replied on September 30, saying, "I don't understand a word of your letter..." (CP8.285n31). Three days later Peirce responded with equal candor, as was commonplace in the epistolary exchanges between these two old friends: "It is very vexatious to be told at every turn that I am utterly incomprehensible, notwithstanding my careful study of language" (CP8.287). In fairness to James, it must be admitted that Peirce's thought is often more difficult to fully grasp than he believed it to be. That is the case with the subject of this chapter: experience according to Peirce. In fairness to Peirce, the difficulty with grasping his thought is often due to its depth and originality.

Clear and distinct conceptions of experience adequate for technical philosophy are uncommon even though there is general agreement that experience is pivotal for acquiring knowledge. Given such an important function, it would seem requisite that such a key conception should have a precise philosophical definition. Writing for Baldwin's *Dictionary of Philosophy and Psychology* in 1901, George F. Stout remarked that "the word ['experience'] is used so vaguely and ambiguously by writers on philosophy that definition is difficult" (Stout, 360). Four years later, in a discussion paper for *The Monist*, James B. Peterson remarked that philosophers and psychologists regard experience as a primary source of knowledge "as if its meaning was perfectly well known" and asked if "some of the knowing ones" would clarify its meaning (Peterson 1905). Peirce, who had long been an advocate of reforming philosophical terminology,[1] responded with a note on the meaning of 'experience' (CP5.610–614, 1906).

Few could have been more qualified than Peirce to answer Peterson's call. A decade earlier Peirce had contributed or given approval for over fifteen thousand definitions, including 'experience,' for the *Century Dictionary and Cyclopedia*, America's single greatest contribution to lexicography.[2] In defining 'experience' for the *Century* he gave six variant definitions of its meaning as a noun and provided exemplary quotations. The definition Peirce gave for 'experience' in its philosophical usage was "knowledge acquired through external or internal perception; also, the totality of the cognitions given by perception, taken in their connection; all that is perceived, understood, and remembered." He continued with John Locke's definition: "our observation, employed either about external sensible objects or about the internal operations of our minds, perceived and reflected upon by ourselves."[3] On the face of it, Peirce's definition and Locke's are comparable.

In his response to Peterson, Peirce privileged Locke's definition of 'experience' as authoritative for philosophy because he believed Locke to have been the first philosopher to explicitly and adequately define it. It was Peirce's view that for philosophy to become a successful science it was requisite to adopt an ethics of terminology, one rule of which is to adopt technical terms as defined by the first specialist to formally define them.[4] Peirce acknowledged that Locke's definition of 'experience' is vague but it is a good definition of the idea Locke meant to express: "The idea of the word 'experience,' was to refer to that which is forced upon a man's recognition, will-he nill-he, and shapes his thoughts to something quite different from what they naturally would have been" (CP5.613, 1906). It was Locke's view that nature provides us with a blank slate at birth to be written upon by our perceptions, external and internal. But Peirce believed that "the philosophers of experience" forget that "we are all of us natural products, naturally partaking of the characteristics that are found everywhere" and that it is "in some measure nonsensical to talk of a man's nature as opposed to what perceptions force him to think" (CP5.613, 1906). If, as Peirce supposed, nature provides us with minds that are not blank slates but that come supplied with innate knowledge (as other animals and even insects are supplied with instinctive knowledge), then the perceptual and reflective observations that define experience for Locke are not the exclusive springs of knowledge and understanding.[5] Moreover, in Locke's thinking, perception and sense-experience were near synonyms, whereas, for Peirce, a lot of cognitive processing is necessary to get from sensations to perceptual judgments. But whether we are born with a Lockean blank slate ready to receive and store information gleaned from sensory intake or are minded at birth with some instinctual or innate programming in place, it is experience that awakens the intellect and prompts us to form perceptual judgments. In this sense, Peirce could say that "experience is our only teacher" (EP2:153, 1903).

Contemporary discussions of experience exhibit much of the vagueness and ambiguity Stout pointed to in 1901. Nearly everyone agrees with Locke that experience is key to learning about the world we inhabit and are part of, but there continues to be disagreement, and perhaps confusion, about what should count as experience and how it furnishes information to intellects. To some extent this may be due to regarding experience as "the upshot of the workings of many cognitive sub-systems" or, as Kant held, a synthesis of "various active operations of the mind" (Blackburn 1994, 130). But it is also differing metaphysical commitments that foster differing conceptions of experience and its role in funding the intellect. Peirce tended to bifurcate conceptions and theories of experience as either nominalistic (Locke's) or realistic (his own, with roots in the philosophy of Duns Scotus), but as Cornelis de Waal has shown, this bifurcation is not definitive (de Waal 1998). Nevertheless, the modern nominalist tradition that began with the empiricists (Thomas Hobbes, John Locke, David Hume, etc.),[6] together with the rise of experimental science, abetted a physicalist and particularist outlook dismissive of universals and abstract objects and committed to a causal closure principle that precludes teleology and that established the program for and gave momentum to the mighty stream of philosophical thought culminating in analytical philosophy. Concerns about the epistemological and ontological ground of mathematics along with developments in psychology, neuroscience, and, more generally, cognitive science have given rise to a less unyielding nominalism among contemporary analytic and postanalytic philosophers, arguably substituting a commitment to evolutionary naturalism for a more unyielding physicalism. Willard Van Orman Quine, for example, came to accept the reality of mathematical entities but his naturalism did not go far beyond traditional Lockean empiricism, adhering as he did to the empiricist manifesto, *nihil in mente quod non prius in sensu*, where "in sensu" was understood as "our meager contacts" with the physical world, that is, "the mere impacts of rays and particles on our surfaces and a few odds and ends such as the strain of walking uphill" (Quine 1995, 16).

Another interesting example is Daniel Dennett, who in his recent book, *From Bacteria to Bach and Back*, claims that, after fifty years of intellectual struggle, he has "found a path that takes us all the way to a satisfactory—and satisfying—account of how the 'magic' or our minds is accomplished without any magic" (Dennett 2017, 4). Dennett adopts Wilfrid Sellars's idea of the *manifest image*, "the world according to us," to characterize the world of everyday experience. This is the world of minds and consciousness that anchors "our interactions and conversations" (Dennett 2017, 61). But this world, with its own ontology, an ontology quite distinct from the ontology of the scientific world, is a world of user-illusion.

Dennett is far from dismissive of this manifest image world as a useless artifact of human imagination. This manifest image world that "has been cobbled together by genetic evolutionary processes over billions of years, and by cultural evolutionary processes [meme infections] over thousands of years, is an extremely sophisticated system of helpful metaphorical renderings of the underlying reality" (Dennett 2017, 366). But even though Dennett maintains that the ontology of our manifest image, our world of user-illusion, is a product of evolution that we shouldn't want to live without, he vacillates on that point. There is a constant tension in Dennett between the usefulness of such constituents of the manifest image world as mind, consciousness, qualia, and so on and the nonillusory underlying causal processes that belong to the world of science. Dennett has never endorsed a strong eliminativist approach, yet he looks forward to "a completely materialistic account of consciousness" and he maintains that "we won't have a complete science of consciousness until we can align our manifest-image identifications of mental states by their contents with scientific-image identifications of the subpersonal information structures and events that are causally responsible for generating the details of the user-illusion we take ourselves to operate in" (Dennett 2017, 367).

Arguably, it is Dennett's nominalist faith that requires him to insist that the lived world is illusory, lacking the reality necessary for scientific relevance. He wisely does not dismiss the lived world as not worthy of investigation on its own terms and has constructed a quite elaborate theory to explain how it evolved and why it is important. He argues that "human consciousness is unlike all other varieties of animal consciousness in that it is a product in large part of cultural evolution, which installs a bounty of words and many other thinking tools in our brains, thus creating a cognitive architecture unlike the 'bottom-up' minds of animals. By supplying our minds with systems of representations, this architecture furnishes each of us with a perspective—a user-illusion—from which we have a limited, biased access to the workings of our brains" (Dennett 2017, 370). So Dennett has found a way to account for the rich ontology of our lived world, a world of mental events and conscious awareness, and he even associates minds with "systems of representation," a very Peircean approach to mind. In fact, Dennett has finally admitted Peirce's type–token distinction into his philosophy and described types as "like a species" of words (Dennett 2017, 189)—but he can't help worrying about the underlying metaphysics: the "whiff of essentialism" (Dennett 2017, 187).[7] What seems pretty consistent with Dennett is that his anchor for our lived world and all its constituents is the workings of our brains.

Although there is sometimes a whiff of pragmatism about Dennett's work, even bringing to mind the motivations of Peirce and his early Metaphysical Club friends, he has never yielded to what Peirce believes to be the obvious causal power of words as types and of general ideas. Dennett will not accept any kind of causation other than efficient physical causation—not really. He talks of the "sin of teleology" and quotes Karl Marx's praise of Charles Darwin for having dealt teleology a death blow (Dennett 2017, 33). But he then shifts to his "design stance," which allows for reasons and purposes in our manifest image world, and he credits Darwin not with having dealt teleology a death blow, but with having naturalized it, and he says that "a vague squeamishness" about teleology "leads some scientists to go overboard avoiding design talk and reason talk" (Dennett 2017, 51). Dennett seems always to be looking for a way to admit at least some of the fruits of a Peircean-style metaphysical realism into his ontology, albeit by a sort of sleight of hand—by finding a stance that will allow for them as legitimate interpretations or patternings of the underlying physical reality. But when push comes to shove, Dennett relegates the fruits of a more expansive Peircean ontology to the narrative of our illusory lived world, maintaining, for example, that qualia, "so beloved by philosophers of consciousness who yearn to reinstate dualism as a serious theory of mind," are just "artifacts of imagination" (Dennett 2017, 354). So Dennett, for all his attention to the ontology of the human manifest image lived world, like Quine, has not moved far beyond traditional Lockean empiricism.

Locke's views on experience, and those of the nominalist empiricists who have followed him, are consistent with Peirce's in many respects. As noted above, Peirce held that "experience is our only teacher," though he was quick to add: "Far be it from me to enunciate any doctrine of a *tabula rasa*" (EP2:153, 1903). Peirce stood on different metaphysical ground, rejecting the view that general and abstract entities can at most have a conceptual existence (in name only) and accepting that although they might not exist in the concrete (in time and space), they might nonetheless be real. Peirce espoused a nuanced metaphysical realism that distinguished reality from existence and that admitted general and abstract entities as reals without attributing to them direct causal powers, although he held that nonexistent reals can influence the course of events by means of final causation.[8] Moreover, nonexistent reals (generals and abstract entities) can be experienced, if not directly then indirectly, through the mediation of other experience (CP5.539, c. 1902).

Peirce may also appear to be in agreement with nominalist empiricists in espousing the peripatetic maxim (EP2:226, 1903): *Nihil est in intellectu quod non prius fuerit in sensu* (nothing is in the intellect that was not first in the senses).[9] But after putting forward this maxim as a useful whetstone for sharpening the conception of pragmatism, he explained that in his view the intellect consists of cognitions of all kinds including general symbols: "Berkeley and nominalists of his stripe deny that we have any idea at all of a triangle in general, which is neither equilateral, isosceles, nor scalene. But he cannot deny that there are propositions about triangles in general, which propositions are either true or false; and as long as that is the case, whether we have an *idea* of a triangle in some psychological sense or not, I do not, as a logician, care. We have an *intellectus*, a meaning, of which the triangle in general is an element" (EP2:227, 1903). Peirce then explained that by "*in sensu*" he meant "in a perceptual judgment," which brings the idea of a triangle in general within the scope of what can be experienced. It is key to generality that it is not tied to specific sensory experiences or otherwise it would not be possible for a blind man and a deaf man to witness the same murder (W2:468/EP1:89, 1871).

Insofar as experience is supposed to be fundamental to learning about our world, it is usually assumed that sensation and perception are the principal cognitive functions at issue. For Locke and subsequent nominalist epistemologists, sense experience and perceptual experience are much the same, but for Peirce, who held that we can perceive generals, and even processes, an empiricism based on perceptual experience as he conceived of it accounts for a richer harvest of knowledge. To consider more deeply what Peirce means by experience it is necessary to briefly review his theory of perception.

Perception begins with sensation. It is rooted in sensory impingements (proximal stimuli) that are unconsciously synthesized into percepts. According to Peirce, sensation initiates "a state of feeling" or "sensation *minus* the attribution of it to any particular subject" (CP1.332, c.1905). This state of feeling is the percept. Presumably the process by which percepts are formed involves nonconceptual cognitive operations at a qualitative or pattern recognition level under the influence of cognitive habits. The noted psychologist Irvin Rock submits that the perceptual processing triggered by proximal stimuli, though in effect an "effort after meaning," is not a consciously goal-oriented process but that "the motivation for it must be the result of evolutionary adaptation" (Rock 1983, 16).

The percept is the empirical given—"an image or moving picture or other exhibition" (EP2:191, 1903)—and is neither conceptual nor propositional and thus is distinct from the "cognitive given" of the logical empiricists (Bernstein 1964, 167). Sometimes Peirce characterizes the formation of the percept as an uncriticizable psychological operation of little importance for logic (EP2:155, 1903), yet he also tells us that "we have to set out on our intellectual travels from the home where we already find ourselves" and that home "is the parish of percepts" (EP2:62, 1901). "The percept," Peirce says, "is absolutely dumb. It acts upon us, it forces itself upon us; but it does not address the reason, nor appeal to anything for support" (CP7.622, 1903).

If percepts are "absolutely dumb" without any intellectual content, how can they serve as starting points for reasoning and the growth of knowledge? According to Carl Hausman, percepts present us with compelling qualitative experience, which sets the interpretative process in motion and prompts interpreters to form perceptual judgments (Hausman 2006, 237). According to Peirce, "we know nothing about the percept otherwise than by testimony of the perceptual judgment, excepting that we feel the blow of it, the reaction of it against us, and we see the contents of it arranged into an object, in its totality" (CP7.643, 1903). If we think of perception as a process involving three stages, the formation of the percept, the impact or forcefulness of the percept, and the perceptual judgment, the first two stages are the preconceptual antecedents crucial for the formation of the perceptual judgment. But what accounts for this leap from the preconceptual to the conceptual?[10]

What seems to be required is an inference that draws a conceptual conclusion; but how can a conceptual conclusion be logically drawn from a nonconceptual percept? Only abduction in its most primitive form can plausibly make this leap. Instead of dealing with what logically follows from premises, perceptual abduction is concerned with identifying something that is surprising or unexpected—a form of conceptual labeling or tagging. Peirce recognized that perceptual judgments are the result of a process that is too uncontrolled to be regarded as fully rational, so one cannot say unequivocally that perceptual judgments arise from percepts by an act of abductive inference, but Peirce insisted that "abductive inference shades into perceptual judgment without any sharp line of demarcation between them" and that "our first premisses, the perceptual judgments, are to be regarded as an extreme case of abductive inferences" (EP2:227, 1903). It is by reasoning from our perceptual judgments that we can draw distant conclusions to be tested and revised over the course of continuing experience.

The preceding four paragraphs, in utmost brevity, give Peirce's account of perception.[11] But as was typical with Peirce, he kept digging to deeper levels of analysis. In recognition of the distinction between the percept in itself and as it is conceived of in a perceptual judgment, Peirce named the latter the *percipuum*. To account for a sense of temporality in perceptual experience, he introduced the *antecept*, a near anticipation of the percept, and the *ponecept*, a recent memory, and to distinguish between antecepts and ponecepts in themselves and as conceived of in perceptual judgments he introduced the *antecipuum* and the *ponecipuum* to name their "direct and uncontrollable interpretations" (CP7.648, 1903). Peirce did not fully develop this deeper level of analysis.[12]

Peirce's views on perception were not simply armchair ruminations. For much of his life he carried on a dialogue on questions pertinent to consciousness and perception with William James, who is usually recognized as America's first experimental psychologist, although Peirce is sometimes accorded that designation (Cadwallader 1974). Peirce was an experienced observer of qualitative sensations, having been trained as a chemist and astronomer, and he began early in life to make a systematic study of conscious experience. By his mid-twenties he had concluded that there are three distinct elements of consciousness: "1st, *Feelings* or Elements of comprehension; 2nd, *Efforts* or Elements of extension; and 3rd, *Notions* or Elements of information" (W1:491, 1866). Throughout the rest of his life Peirce carried forward his study of experience gravitating to systematic phenomenological investigations, which he called "phaneroscopy." The object of study for phaneroscopy is the phaneron (taken from the Greek word φανερον, meaning manifest) by which Peirce meant "all that is present to the mind in any sense or in any way whatever, regardless of whether it be fact or figment" (CP8.213, c. 1905).[13] What Peirce sought from phaneroscopy was a set of fundamental elements of phenomenal experience distilled from the phaneron by a method of abstraction he called *prescission* (EP2:270, 1903). This method, which depends neither on the meanings of terms nor on the actual separability of the elements of our experience, but simply on their supposed separability (EP1:2, 1868), provides the chief tool for phenomenology in its pursuit of objective universal categories. But in addition, the phaneroscopist imports from mathematics the technique of hypostatic abstraction, by which we derive substantive abstract singular terms from predicate expressions or from numerical expressions used adjectivally, to provide a means for ascending to the generality necessary for a list of universal categories.

Peirce's phaneroscopic investigations, which were carried out over many years, led him to conclude that there are three general classes of elements (or, as Peirce sometimes said, ingredients) in every phaneron: elements of feeling, "the unanalyzed total impression made by any manifold not thought of as actual fact, but simply as a quality" (CP8.329, 1904); elements of reaction or compulsion (the shock of experience); and elements of habituation or learning (Peirce sometimes calls this element thought). These three general classes of elements of the phaneron "form a sort of system.... Feeling, or *primisense*, is the consciousness of firstness; altersense is [the] consciousness of otherness or secondness; medisense is the consciousness of means or thirdness" (CP7.551, n.d.). So in Peirce's view, the three distinct elements or ingredients of experience (quality, reaction, thought) are experienced as three forms of consciousness, feeling (monadic experiences), altersense (dyadic experiences), and medisense (triadic experiences), from which Peirce abstracted to his universal categories: firstness, secondness, and thirdness. Thus we see that the universal categories of experience correspond to the universal categories of relation that Peirce derived in his logic of relations (a branch of mathematics according to Peirce). At the most basic level, *firstness* is that which is as it is independent of anything else, *secondness* is that which is as it is in relation to something else, and *thirdness* is that which is as it is as mediate between two others.[14] As abstract categories of experience they provide the key to the structure of the phaneron (and, thus, of experience). Considering the three stages of perception, the percept in itself as a state of feeling (primisense) is experience in its firstness; the compulsion or insistence of the percept (altersense) is experience in its brute secondness, and the perceptual judgment (medisense) is experience in its thirdness.

During the final decade of his life Peirce embarked on an intensive development of the deep structure of his formal semiotic theory. Early on Peirce had adopted a semiotic approach to philosophy, encouraged, perhaps, by Locke's recommendation to regard semiotics as a general science of logic.[15] In the mid-1860s Peirce began working out the fundamentals of a theory of signs, including the irreducibility of the triadic relation linking signs with their objects and interpretants, and he concluded that there are three kinds of signs distinguished by how they stand for or connect with their objects: icons, indices, and symbols. In his 1877–1878 cognition series in the *Journal of Speculative Philosophy*, which Richard Bernstein argues gave birth to pragmatism,[16] Peirce made his famous declaration that all thought is in signs (EP1:24). This postulate, together with the icon/index/symbol trichotomy, is the base on which Peirce's philosophy of signs took shape over the following three and a half decades. It was not until 1903 when Peirce took up his theory of signs with renewed vigor.

It is a matter of speculation why Peirce returned to sign theory with such intensity but it may have been an indirect consequence of William James having ignited international interest in pragmatism following his famous August 26, 1898, lecture to the Berkeley Philosophical Union in which he introduced pragmatism by name for the first time and acknowledged Charles Peirce as its father. Peirce followed the ensuing developments and soon realized that his original conception of pragmatism as a maxim of logic, rather than "a sublime principle of speculative philosophy," was being supplanted (EP2:134, 1903). Peirce believed that his initial pragmatism had the advantage of being provable and set about drawing together the necessary fundamentals. In his 1903 Harvard Lectures he built a case for pragmatism based on his theory of perception and his early semiotic theory. He argued that pragmatism is a thesis concerning the meaning of a particular kind of symbol, the proposition, and explained that propositions are signs that must refer to their objects in two ways: indexically, by means of subjects, and iconically, by means of predicates. The crucial element of Peirce's argument involved the connection between propositional thought and perception. He distinguished percepts, which are not propositional, from perceptual judgments, which are, and which are, furthermore, the first premisses of all our reasonings.[17]

Six months after delivering his Harvard Lectures, Peirce gave a series of lectures at the Lowell Institute in Boston where he continued building his argument for pragmatism, drawing on his growing focus on the normative sciences: aesthetics, ethics, and logic. He had come to equate normative logic with semiotics, which he insisted must avoid any tendency to be descriptive of mental operations as psychology must be. In conjunction with his Lowell Lectures, Peirce composed a "Syllabus of Certain Topics of Logic" (EP2:258–299, 1903) in which he began a systematic in-depth recasting of his theory of signs as the normative logic of mental operations. To his early analysis of signs into icons, indices, and symbols, based on the relation of signs to objects, Peirce added a qualisign/sinsign/legisign trichotomy dividing signs by whether, in themselves, they are qualities, existents, or laws, and a rheme/dicent/argument trichotomy dividing signs by whether they are interpreted as signs of possibility, fact, or reason. Based on these three divisions, Peirce's derived ten classes of signs, his most widely known extended classification.[18]

In the years that followed, Peirce's letters to Victoria Lady Welby and the pages of his Logic Notebook, in which he explored and developed new ideas, are replete with increasingly complex elaborations of the basic sign/object/interpretant sign relation.[19] By 1904 Peirce had distinguished two objects and three interpretants as fundamental components of all signs: "a sign has two objects, its object as it is represented and its object in itself. It has also three interpretants, its interpretant as represented or meant to be understood, its interpretant as it is produced, and its interpretant in itself" (SS:32). Writing to James some years later, he identified the two objects as an immediate object, "the Object as cognized in the Sign, and therefore an Idea," and a dynamical object, "the Object as it is regardless of any particular aspect of it, . . . the Object that Dynamical Science . . . can investigate." He identified three interpretants: the immediate interpretant "consists in the Quality of the Impression that a sign is fit to produce, not to any actual reaction," the dynamical interpretant "is whatever interpretation any mind actually makes of a sign," and the final interpretant "is that which would finally be decided to be the true interpretation if consideration of the matter were carried so far that an ultimate opinion were reached" (EP2:495–500, 1909). Two years previously, in 1907, as he painstakingly constructed his proof of pragmatism based on his extended theory of signs, Peirce had identified the three kinds of interpretants as emotional, energetic, and logical (EP2:409). There is some disagreement over whether he intended to distinguish between final and logical interpretants or whether he was only trying different names for essentially the same thing.[20] However, in the 1907 paper Peirce stated clearly that an interpretant is the "total proper effect of the sign" (EP2:429) and that this effect may be emotional, energetic, or logical, but it is the logical interpretant alone that constitutes "the intellectual apprehension of the meaning of a sign" (EP2:430). The logical interpretant is forward-looking, what Peirce called a would-be: "general in its possibilities of reference" (EP2:412). He pointed out that concepts, propositions, or arguments can all be logical interpretants but they are, themselves, signs calling for further interpretation. Thus they cannot be final, or ultimate, logical interpretants. Only habits, which exhaust the function of the sign and call only for action, can be final logical interpretants (EP2:418). From these considerations it seems that it is logical interpretants that correspond to thirdness in semiosis and that energetic and emotional interpretants correspond, respectively, to secondness and firstness. Whether there are final energetic and emotional interpretants, as well as final logical interpretants, was not made clear although it is plausible that there are.

So Peirce's understanding of the sign relation had evolved from one involving three components to one involving six components: a dynamic object, an immediate object, the sign itself, an immediate interpretant, a dynamic interpretant, and a logical interpretant.[21] Taking into account that signs are not static things but are mental operations or, as Peirce once said, "vehicles of psychic influence" (R675, 1911), the aim of his theory of signs is not to produce a mere catalog of sign types but to distinguish and investigate the "essential nature and fundamental varieties of possible semiosis" (EP2:413, 1907). Peirce's emphasis on semiosis shifts the focus of his sign classification labors from sign architecture and taxonomy to critical analysis of sign functionality.

Given this deeper analysis involving six sign components, Peirce expanded his inventory of distinguishing features fundamental to all signs and by 1906 had arrived at a list of ten triadic divisions that, in turn, led Peirce to identify sixty-six distinct types of signs, or more revealingly, sixty-six distinct types of semiosis, or sign action.[22] Peirce never supposed that his findings were unassailable, and though he could give a compelling rationale for ten divisions (EP2:482, 1908) and sixty-six classes, and clearly believed what he was developing was a fundamental framework for semiotic analysis, he readily conceded that his results were provisional.

Although it may be that Peirce's turn to the deep structure of signs after 1903 was related to his desire to prove pragmatism, it seems likely that his transition from a proof based on perception to one based on signs revealed important relational isomorphisms that enabled him to see that, in a way, his formal semiotics amounted, at least in part, to a logic of perception. Even though Peirce took seriously the neurophysical ground of sensory experience and recognized its causal role in the formation of percepts, he understood perception to be a mental operation directed more by purpose (bearing in mind that purpose is inherent in habits) than by efficient causation. From Peirce's long-held tenet that all thought is in signs, it followed that mental operations are operations on signs, that cognition in all its forms is semiosis, which is to say inference from signs. Although Peirce tended to equate inference with reasoning and thus limit it to argument types, he gradually generalized his conception to be more expansive, recognizing that three forms of association function in cognition: association by resemblance, association by contiguity, and association involving "intellectual operations" (CP2.306, 1901). These forms of association correspond to associative mental operations based on feeling, effort, or thought, the first two of which are inference-like but are not strictly rational (corresponding to argument forms). These operations correspond to the realms of emotional, energetic, and intellectual semiosis. It is revealing that fewer than half of Peirce's sixty-six sign types are intellectual (symbolic) signs, the rest being either emotional or energetic sign types.

Although, as noted above, the percept is the empirical given and is "absolutely dumb" (without any conceptual content), the perceptual process leading from the percept to the perceptual judgment is a mental operation and is, therefore, an operation on signs. Perception is semiosis. Consequently, Peirce's formal theory of perception should line up with his formal theory of signs (the logic of mental operations) and, conversely, Peirce's semiotic theory should provide guidance for working through the complexities of perception. Perception is the ongoing process by which information is gleaned from experience[23] and the cognitive operations that implement this process are possible types of semiosis. Ultimately one hopes that Peirce's sixty-six sign types, or a significant subset or them, will be aligned with the kinds of inferences and quasi-inferences involved in perception.

It is well beyond the scope of this chapter to undertake a detailed semiotic analysis of perception, but a few points of comparison may help illustrate the potential utility of Peirce's semiotics for the study of perception and, ultimately, given present purposes, for shedding light on Peirce's conception of experience. Consider the elements of perceptual experience that correspond to the three kinds of being that signs can have in themselves. Signs as such are either qualities (qualisigns), existing individuals or actual events (sinsigns), or laws or general types (legisigns). Presumably, qualisigns correspond to nonconceptual feelings in perception, namely, the percept as an empirical given (primisense). Sinsigns must correspond to the insistency of the percept (altersense). And legisigns must correspond to conceptual thought in perception (medisense). We know that every sign is related, presumably by a complex of linked triadic relations, to two objects (immediate and dynamic) and three interpretants (immediate, dynamic, and logical). Probably dynamic objects in perception are percepts and immediate objects are percipua (percepts as represented in perceptual judgments). How the three kinds of interpretants line up with elements of perception is less clear but perhaps dynamic interpretants correspond to perceptual judgments and immediate interpretants with facts of immediate perception (prescissions from precepts). Logical interpretants may correspond to the conceptual content of the perceptual judgment not as an act of judgment, but as a belief consequent to that judgment, but this is quite speculative. Even more speculative is the guess that final logical interpretants correspond to habits of perceptual interpretation that virtually eliminate the need for intellectual processing.

These remarks toward a semiotic analysis of perception are obviously preliminary. This is a relatively undeveloped area of research but a promising one.[24] But why is this important, anyway, for working out details of Peirce's theory of experience? As noted above, for Peirce, as it had been for Locke, experience was understood generally as the process and outcome of perception. If perception, as a cognitive process (a mental operation), is semiosis, as is here maintained, then Peirce's theory of signs (as the logic of mental operations) is directly relevant to understanding the inferential and quasi-inferential structures and operations underlying and supporting the possibilities of experience. Moreover, if Peirce's classification of signs (provisionally into sixty-six distinct types) is, at the same time, a classification of sixty-six types of possible semiotic (mental) operations, then his classification includes the possible types of experience. That is what is here being supposed.

But isn't something missing from the foregoing account of experience? Lived experience doesn't seem to be captured by phaneroscopic or semiotic analysis. When we consider the elements of experience piecemeal as abstracted (prescinded) from occasions of lived experience, we are dealing with conceptualizations of those elements. As Peirce pointed out, "experience is not what analysis discovers but the raw material upon which analysis works" (CP7.535, c. 1899). Although experience involves feeling and thought as well as reaction, it is reaction or insistency that is most characteristic of lived experience and, as Peirce maintained, "a reaction may be experienced, but it cannot be conceived in its character of a reaction; for that element evaporates from every general idea" (CP3.613, 1901). It is one thing to *have* an experience, to actually undergo it, and quite another thing to think about it.

Having an experience is what Peirce described as a direct experience. Although feeling is essential for direct experience and thought may be experienced directly as a mediating event, it is altersense, dyadic experience, which is the anchor for experiencing directly, and the key factor is secondness, the compulsive or reactive element. Dyadic, or reactive, experience must have a temporal dimension, however brief. As Peirce noted, although we "perceive objects brought before us," what "we especially experience—the kind of thing to which the word 'experience' is more particularly applied—is an event ... more particularly to changes and contrasts of perception.... We experience vicissitudes, especially. We cannot experience the vicissitude without experiencing the perception which undergoes the change; but the concept of *experience* is broader than that of *perception*, and includes much that is not, strictly speaking, an object of perception" (CP1.336, c. 1905).

Our lived experience runs continuously throughout our lives in a symphony of unfolding experiential phenomena and interactions. Percepts are the direct perceptual experiences that add both phenomenal content and vitality to our life of experience. They are the empirical givens; they confront us and demand attention: "We know nothing about the percept otherwise than by testimony of the perceptual judgment, excepting that we feel the blow of it, the reaction of it against us, and we see the contents of it arranged into an object, in its totality" (CP7.643, 1903). Even though we cannot reason *from* percepts, for they have no conceptual content, we can, so to speak, reason *to* them by our abductive guesses about what is before us, and we can reason from our guesses in predictive ways that can be tested and refined in light of future experiences. Peirce conceived of the content of one's informed mind metaphorically as a bottomless lake filled with ideas (interpretants) "suspended at different depths." The surface of this lake is covered with percepts. "We must imagine that there is a continual fall of rain upon the lake; which images the constant inflow of percepts in experience" (CP7.553, n.d.). This rain of percepts is the inflow of phenomenal content from our direct experiences of all kinds. The content at the deeper levels of our bottomless lake of conscious and subconscious mind consists mainly of conceptual, or intellectual, content based on our perceptual judgments.

Our experience is what connects us both vitally and conceptually with the world we live in and are part of. Our direct experiences engender percepts that confront us with fresh phenomenal content. We perceive generals (thirdness) in our perceptual judgments. It is not clear whether Peirce regarded the perception of generals to be direct or indirect experiences. Around 1899, after asserting that all experience involves the flow of time that is conceived of as continuous, Peirce claimed, "No matter whether this continuity is a datum of sense, or a quasi-hypothesis imported by the mind into experience, or even an illusion; in any case it remains a direct experience" (CP7.535). But about three years later he agreed with an imagined interlocutor that "one can have no direct experience of the general," though he quickly added that "generality, Thirdness, pours in upon us in our very perceptual judgments" (EP2:207). So even though general and abstract entities may be "imported by the mind into experience," they are fundamental for harnessing the content of our direct perceptual experience and amplifying it into a general knowledge base. Not only do generals and abstract entities enable us to understand what we experience, they also have a nonexistent reality that can influence the course of future events. Peirce elaborated on his understanding of abstract entities in drafting his second Lowell Lecture of 1903:

> All *entia rationis* have their birth in the consideration of general signs, . . . not the replicas but the types. It is true that these types are not singulars; that is, exert no brute force, . . . [b]ut they govern replicas which can be perceived; and by a process of thought . . . the mind is led to a perceptual judgment that the type, or rule, governs the replicas. The mind then goes on to create a new universe,—a universe which may be fictitious, until the fiction turns out to be fact,—a collection of singulars each of which is an abstraction, like "truth," "right," "inclusion," this or that collection, an orbit, a solid, "matter," and the like. These are properly enough, although in a secondary way, singulars; for though the force they exert is, in one sense, not blind, yet it is always mysterious; and the blindness of force in all cases really consists in our inability to fathom its reasonableness. Guided by these abstract ideas, the mind hazards a conjecture as to a law as defining the hidden mode of intelligibility of certain phenomena. If, then, experimental induction verifies that conjecture, the abstractions involved in the strict expression of the law as such need no longer any indulgent sufferance: they have proved their reality. (LoF2:172)

Obviously Peirce was not an empiricist in the traditional sense—not as he defined "empiricist" for the *Century Dictionary*: "one who regards sensuous experience as the sole source of all ideas and knowledge." Nevertheless, he regarded himself as an empiricist in a broader sense: "I myself happen, in common with a small but select circle, to be a pragmatist, or 'radical empiricist,' and as such, do not believe in anything that I do not (as I think) perceive: and I am far from believing in the whole of that" (CP7.617, 1903).[25] But how does Peirce's experienced world compare to that, say, of Dennett? How distinct is Peirce's new universe of abstractions, of *entia rationis*, from Dennett's manifest image world of mental events and conscious awarenesses? It seems that Dennett has succeeded quite remarkably in fitting up his world in a way that matches up with Peirce's realist world. But in denying the reality of his manifest image world by limiting it to metaphorical renderings of an underlying reality, Dennett has severed it from the nonillusory world of science. Peirce's world is a unified world of experience where general conceptions and abstract objects can really influence events and help shape the world to come.

Notes

1. In a printed "syllabus" that was distributed to the auditors of his 1903 Lowell Lectures, Peirce included a section on "The Ethics of Terminology" in which he explained the advantages of a scientific vocabulary and proposed seven rules to achieve it (EP2:263–266).
2. The *Century Dictionary*, hailed as the "most conspicuous literary monument of the nineteenth century" (Henshaw, *American Anthropologist*, Apr. 1892, 184–185), was not only a dictionary of historical and common English usage but also distinguished by its comprehensive inclusion of scientific terms and was said to embody "the scientific spirit and work" of its time (*Science*, February 8, 1889, 103). Peirce was recruited for the dictionary project while teaching at Johns Hopkins and began drafting definitions as early as 1883. The first edition of the *Century* was published from 1889 to 1891 and a supplement, to which Peirce also contributed, was published in 1909.
3. Locke's definition is found in his *Essay Concerning Human Understanding*, Book 2, Chapter 1, Section 2.
4. This is the fifth rule of Peirce's "Ethics of Terminology": "for precise philosophical conceptions introduced into philosophy since the Middle Ages, to use the anglicized form of the original expression, if not positively unsuitable, but only in its precise original sense" (EP2:266, 1903).
5. This innate knowledge may be best thought of as inborn programming rather than as propositional content.
6. This is the nominalism propagated in what is typically known as the modern period of the history of philosophy. Its roots extend back at least to William of Ockham. The origin of contemporary nominalism is sometimes supposed to have begun later, in the early twentieth century with the Warsaw school logicians, and to have become anchored with Goodman and Quine's (1947) "Steps toward a Constructive Nominalism."
7. Dennett quotes David Kaplan here (Kaplan 1990).
8. For an in-depth treatment of Peirce's conception of final causation, see Short (2007, chs. 4 and 5, especially).
9. Although there are other peripatetic maxims, this is the one Quine recognized as the watchword of epistemology (Quine 1990, 19). He, however, replaced "*intellectu*" with "*mente*."
10. The leap that is required is over what Catherine Legg calls the experience–truth gap: see her discussion in "Idealism Operationalized" (Legg 2017).
11. For a more detailed elaboration of Peirce's account of perception, see Bernstein (1964), Rosenthal (2004), Hausman (2006), Wilson (2016, ch. 6), and the papers by Aaron Wilson, Evelyn Vargas, Richard Atkins, and Catherine Legg in Hull and Atkins (2019).
12. For some recent discussions of this deeper level of perceptual analysis, see Hausman (2012); Wilson (2016, 200–204); and Legg (2017).
13. See De Tienne (1993) for a discussion of Peirce's differing views on the phaneron.
14. With respect to the ontology of thirdness, Peirce said that its being "consists in its bringing about a secondness" (EP2:267, 1903).
15. Locke made this recommendation at the end of Book 4 (Ch. 20, p. 361, in the first edition) of his famous *Essay Concerning Human Understanding* (Locke 1690). In later editions it came at the end of Chapter 21.
16. See Bernstein (2010), especially chapter 1, for an excellent account of Peirce's anti-Cartesian program that laid the groundwork for his pragmatism. Peirce's *Journal of Speculative Philosophy* cognition series is published in EP1, selections 2–4.

17. See the introduction to EP2, pp. xxv–xxvi and xxxiv–xxxv, for some further discussion of the Lowell Lectures proof.
18. For a convenient account of Peirce's theory of signs, see Albert Atkin's article: "Peirce's Theory of Signs," in *The Stanford Encyclopedia of Philosophy*, edited by Edward N. Zalta. For more in-depth accounts see Liszka (1996) and Short (2007).
19. The Logic Notebook (R339) was a working notebook in which Peirce recorded, over a period of forty-four years (1865–1909), emerging ideas in logic and semiotics. The notebook consists of approximately 530 written pages and is an invaluable window into Peirce's developing thought. R339 is available in digital form at https://pds.lib.harvard.edu/pds/view/15255301. For an excellent description and discussion of the Logic Notebook, see Zalamea (2013).
20. For differing views on this question, see Liszka (1996, 120–123n12), and Short (2007, ch. 7).
21. For the remainder of this paper, I will continue to use the designations "immediate" and "dynamic" interpretants instead of Peirce's "emotional" and "energetic" interpretants, although perhaps the latter are a bit more revealing when considered with respect to perception. But I will use "logical interpretant" instead of "final interpretant" for the general class of intellectual or conceptual interpretants and will use "final logical interpretant" to mean that habit which concludes, or which would conclude, a sequence of intellectual semiosis.
22. The 1906 list of ten divisions is found in the Logic Notebook (R339: 285r; see also 1908, EP2:483–490). For the first study of Peirce's sixty-six-sign typology, see Weiss and Burks (1945). For some later studies see Jappy (1989), Farias and Queiroz (2003), Romanini (2006), and Borges (2010). Consult the references in these papers for other contributors to this issue.
23. Evolution is of course a more basic process by which we can be said to have been shaped by information gleaned from experience.
24. See Wilson (2016, ch. 6), Hausman (2006, 2012), Romanini (2006), and Santaella (1998) for some initial work in this area.
25. Radical empiricism is the name William James gave to the "philosophic attitude" characteristic of his pragmatic philosophy (James 1897, vii.); see the preface to James (1909) for a more complete explanation. A succinct description of radical empiricism from Wikipedia is the following: "It asserts that experience includes both particulars and relations between those particulars, and that therefore both deserve a place in our explanations. In concrete terms: Any philosophical worldview is flawed if it stops at the physical level and fails to explain how meaning, values and intentionality can arise from that." For an excellent discussion of Peirce's radical empiricism in relation to that of William James, see Anderson (2012).

References

Anderson, Douglas. 2012. "Another Radical Empiricism, Peirce 1903." In *Conversations on Peirce: Reals and Ideals*, edited by Douglas R. Anderson and Carl R. Hausman, 100–113. New York: Fordham University Press.
Bernstein, Richard J. 1964. "Peirce's Theory of Perception." In *Studies in the Philosophy of Charles Sanders Peirce; Second Series*, edited by Edward C. Moore and Richard S. Robin, 165–189. Amherst: University of Massachusetts Press.
Bernstein, Richard J. 2010. *The Pragmatic Turn*. Malden, MA: Polity Press.

Blackburn, Simon. 1994. *The Oxford Dictionary of Philosophy.* Oxford: Oxford University Press.

Borges, Priscila Monteiro. 2010. "A Visual Model of Peirce's 66 Classes of Signs Unravels His Late Proposal of Enlarging Semiotic Theory." In *Model-Based Reasoning in Science and Technology,* edited by Lorenzo Magnani, Walter Carnielli, and Claudio Pizzi, 221–237. Berlin: Springer-Verlag.

Cadwallader, Thomas C. 1974. "Charles S. Peirce (1839–1914): The First American Experimental Psychologist." *Journal of the History of the Behavioral Sciences* 10: 291–298.

Dennett, Daniel C. 2017. *From Bacteria to Bach and Back: The Evolution of Minds.* New York: Norton.

De Tienne, André. 1993. "Peirce's Definitions of the Phaneron." In *Charles S. Peirce and the Philosophy of Science,* edited by Edward C. Moore, 279–288. Tuscaloosa: University of Alabama Press.

De Waal, Cornelis. 1998. "Peirce's Nominalist–Realist Distinction, an Untenable Dualism." *Transactions of the Charles S. Peirce Society* 34, no. 1 (Winter): 183–202.

Farias, Priscila, and João Queiroz. 2003. "On Diagrams for Peirce's 10, 28, and 66 Classes of Signs." *Semiotica* 147, no. 1/4: 165–184.

Goodman, Nelson, and Willard Van Orman Quine. 1947. "Steps toward a Constructive Nominalism." *Journal of Symbolic Logic* 12: 105–122.

Hausman, Carl. 2006. "Peirce's Semeiotic Applied to Perception: The Role of Dynamic Objects and Percepts in Perceptual Interpretation." *Cognitio; Revista de Filosofia* 7, no. 2: 231–246.

Hausman, Carl. 2012. "Peirce on Interpretation." In *Conversations on Peirce: Reals and Ideals,* edited by Douglas R. Anderson and Carl R. Hausman, 114–131. New York: Fordham University Press.

Hull, Kathleen A., and Richard Kenneth Atkins, eds. 2019. *Peirce on Perception and Reasoning: From Icons to Logic.* London: Routledge.

James, William. 1897. *The Will to Believe and Other Essays in Popular Philosophy.* New York: Longmans, Green.

James, William. 1904. "Does 'Consciousness' Exist?" *Journal of Philosophy, Psychology, and Scientific Methods* 1, no. 18: 477–91.

James, William. 1909. *The Meaning of Truth.* New York: Longmans.

Jappy, Tony. 1989. "Peirce's Sixty-six Signs Revisited." In *Semiotics and Pragmatics: Proceedings of the Perpignan Symposium, 1983,* edited by Gérard Deledalle, 143–154. Amsterdam: John Benjamins.

Kaplan, David. 1990. "Words." In *Proceedings of the Aristotelian Society, Supplementary Volumes* 64: 93–119.

Legg, Catherine. 2017. "Idealism Operationalized: How Peirce's Pragmatism Can Help Explicate and Motivate the Possibly Surprising Idea of Reality as Representational." In *Peirce on Perception and Reasoning: From Icons to Logic,* edited by Kathleen A. Hull and Richard Kenneth Atkins, 40–53. London: Routledge.

Liszka, James J. 1966. *A General Introduction to the Semeiotic of Charles Sanders Peirce.* Bloomington, IN: Indiana University Press.

Locke, John. 1690. *An Essay Concerning Humane Understanding.* London: Printed by Eliz. Holt, for Thomas Basset.

Peirce, Charles S. 1857–1914. Manuscripts held at the Houghton Library of Harvard University, as identified in Richard Robin, *Annotated Catalogue of the Papers of Charles S. Peirce.* Amherst: University of Massachusetts Press, 1967. And in Richard Robin, "The Peirce Papers: A Supplementary Catalogue." *Transactions of the Charles S. Peirce Society* 7, no. 1

(Winter 1971): 37–57. (Referred to as R[catalogue#]:[sheet#]; with RL for letters and RS for supplement.)

Peirce, Charles S. 1031–1958. *The Collected Papers of Charles Sanders Peirce*. 8 vols. Vols. 1–6 edited by Charles Hartshorne and Paul Weiss. Vols. 7–8 edited by Arthur W. Burks. Cambridge, MA: Harvard University Press. (Referred to as CP.)

Peirce, Charles S. 1977. *Semiotic and Significs: The Correspondence between Charles S. Peirce and Victoria Lady Welby*. Edited by Charles S. Hardwick. Bloomington: Indiana University Press. (Referred to as SS.)

Peirce, Charles S. 1982– . *The Writings of Charles S. Peirce: A Chronological Edition*. 7 vols. to date. Edited by the Peirce Edition Project. Bloomington: Indiana University Press. (Referred to as W.)

Peirce, Charles S. 1992–1998. *The Essential Peirce: Selected Philosophical Writings*. 2 vols. Vol. 1 edited by Nathan Houser and Christian Kloesel. Vol. 2 edited by the Peirce Edition Project. Bloomington, Indiana University Press. (Referred to as EP.)

Peirce, Charles S. 2019– . *Logic of the Future. Writings on Existential Graphs*. 3 vols in 4. Edited by A.-V. Pietarinen. Berlin: De Gruyter. (Referred to as LoF.)

Peterson, James B. 1905. "Some Philosophical Terms." *The Monist* 15, no. 4: 629–633.

Quine, Willard Van Orman. 1990. *Pursuit of Truth*. Cambridge, MA: Harvard University Press.

Quine, Willard Van Orman. 1995. *From Stimulus to Science*. Cambridge, MA: Harvard University Press.

Rock, Irvin. 1983. *The Logic of Perception*. Cambridge, MA: MIT Press.

Romanini, Anderson Vinícius. 2006. "Minute Semiotic: Speculations on the Grammar of Signs and Communication in C. S. Peirce." PhD diss., University of São Paulo. See in elaborated form http://www.minutesemeiotic.org/.

Rosenthal, Sandra. 2004. "Peirce's Pragmatic Account of Perception: Issues and Implications." In *The Cambridge Companion to Peirce*, edited by Cheryl Misak, 193–240. Cambridge: Cambridge University Press.

Santaella, Lucia. 1998. *A Percepção: uma Teoria Semiótica*. São Paulo: Experimento.

Short, Thomas L. 2007. *Peirce's Theory of Signs*. New York: Cambridge University Press.

Stout, George Frederick. 1901. "Experience." In *Dictionary of Philosophy and Psychology*, vol. 1, edited by James Mark Baldwin, 360–362. New York: Macmillan.

Weiss, Paul, and Arthur Burks. 1945. "Peirce's Sixty-Six Signs." *Journal of Philosophy* 42: 383–388.

Wilson, Aaron Bruce. 2016. *Peirce's Empiricism: Its Roots and Its Originality*. Lanham, MD: Lexington Books.

Zalamea, Fernando. 2013. "Plasticity and Creativity in the Logic Notebook." *European Journal of Pragmatism and American Philosophy* 1, online publication. http://journals.openedition.org/ejpap/593.

CHAPTER 6

CHARLES S. PEIRCE ON THE INQUIRY INTO THE DISCOVERY OF IDEALS, NORMS, AND VALUES

TIAGO DA COSTA E SILVA

1. INTRODUCTION

ONE of the most important contributions for the general theory of inquiry as well as for the development of the *heuretic sciences*, that is, sciences of discovery, is the concept of *normative science*. Normative science lies at the heart of the heuretic sciences and bears the utmost important task of providing the theory of inquiry with guidance in the form of ideals, norms, values, and principles.

As Peirce has established it, normative science is comprised by three distinct but systematically connected sciences: *esthetics*, *ethics*, and *logic*, the latter conceived as *semiotics*. They are normative, for they are tasked with the study of the universal and necessary laws of relation of the phenomena to *ends* involving the development and the active, deliberate application of self-control. The three normative sciences set up norms implying ideals, ends, purposes, and values in general, which work by attraction and guidance rather than by compulsion, coercion, or any deterministic means; and these norms and rules should be followed, not because it is necessary, but because they recommend themselves as manifestations of powerful *ideals* that *ought to be* adopted, understood, pursued, and applied. Generally stated, the inquiry of the normative sciences of esthetics, ethics, and logic, as Peirce affirms, consists, respectively, in the study and pursuit of *the admirable*, of *ideals of conduct*, and of *the advancement of knowledge toward truth*.

The primary objective of the present chapter is to inquire into the two first normative sciences, esthetics and ethics, focusing upon the exposition of their systemic structure, their function within the ladder of the sciences, and their mode of operation in relation to other sciences of discovery. Moreover, the chapter will define the specific objects of inquiry of esthetics and ethics, as well as the results they arrive at and provide to other, less abstract, sciences. Of great importance for the present undertaking is the close relationship between the studies performed by phaneroscopy and the specific inquiries of the normative sciences. Therefore, the chapter makes recourse to important passages from Peirce's manuscripts[1] mostly written between 1902 and 1911, in which he specifically discusses these two first normative sciences.

From this trio of the normative sciences, logic, or semiotics,[2] is by far the most developed by Peirce, as he spent most of his energy developing it. Along with the maxim of pragmatism, or *pragmaticism*,[3] logic inquires into the conditions of the advancement of knowledge and attainment of truth, as well as into the necessary laws of thought, studying the general conditions of signs as signs—for thought always takes place by employing signs and the necessary conditions of the transmission of meaning from mind to mind and from one state of mind to another by means of signs. However, by realizing that the normative sciences are systemically connected, Peirce concluded that logic depends upon the principles furnished to it by ethics, for logic is a special determination of the inquiry of ethics whose object of inquiry is the formation of deliberate habits of conduct in relation to an ideal of conduct previously discovered and determined. And, by the same principle, ethics is a special determination of esthetics, which is responsible for the discovery of a "state of things that *reasonably* recommends *itself in itself* aside from any ulterior determination," being, therefore, an "*admirable ideal* having the only kind of goodness that such an ideal *can* have namely esthetic goodness" (EP2:201, 1903). As Peirce considers it, "the morally good," as generally referred to the object of inquiry of ethics, "appears as a particular species of the esthetic good" (EP2:201). "It astonishes me now that none of us seem to have been ready, until 1903, to plant himself upon the position that logic ought to be founded upon ethics, when I, for one, had been making ethics one of my particular studies for twenty years. I infer that the doctrine will not be much liked, and still less its companion that ethics ought to be founded upon esthetics. The truth is that they do not recommend themselves until both ethics and esthetics are conceived differently from the traditional notions of them" (R288:23, 1905).

It is clear from the outset that Peirce's conception of esthetics and ethics as normative sciences and as philosophical disciplines differs radically from the more traditional views of these philosophical disciplines. Ethics is often regarded, from a more traditional perspective, either as a discipline within the realm of practical philosophy, occupying itself with practical questions of morality, or, in its more inflated manifestations, as a discipline solely occupied with the definition of the *summum bonum*, while esthetics is traditionally viewed as either a philosophical study of the fine arts, involving the critical reading of a certain particular artistic movement or work, or the judgment of sentiments of good taste. Peirce adopts the three normative sciences, acknowledging hereby the necessity of restructuring these sciences according to the current developments in scientific and philosophical inquiries: "It is especially the normative sciences, esthetics, ethics, and logic, that men are in dire need of having severely criticized in their relation to the new world created by science. Unfortunately, this need is unconscious as it is great. The evils are in some superficial way recognized; but it never occurs to anybody that the study of esthetics, ethics, and logic, [is as of now hampered] because these sciences are thought of in their old forms. It only concerns my present purpose to glance at this state of things. The needed new criticism must know where it stands" (R288:20, 1905, remarks in brackets added).

And yet, despite this courageous recognition of establishing esthetics and ethics as normative sciences bearing the utmost importance for the development of the theory of inquiry, Peirce himself was not sure about either their structural positioning or their legitimacy as such. This is accentuated by a grave problem. At first glance, Peirce's writings on esthetics and ethics are proportionally scarce in comparison to other philosophical and scientific subjects in his thought. However, esthetics and ethics as high-ranking normative sciences became of paramount importance for the whole theory of inquiry in Peirce's later and more mature thought.

This problem can be expressed in a more synthetic manner: Regarding the development of an all-encompassing theory of inquiry and the structure of the sciences of discovery, *what are normative esthetics and ethics for?* Attached to this is a more concrete, but equally important question: How is it possible to conceive a powerful theory of inquiry, and, furthermore, to develop a maxim of logic underlying all manners of scientific inquiries based upon a set of normative sciences that remain in a project state?

According to the hypothesis guiding this work, it is possible, by thoroughly searching the later manuscripts from Peirce, to *reconstruct* the normative sciences of esthetics and ethics, as well as their objects of inquiry, their operational principles as normative sciences, and their overall mode of operation, only, however, insofar as Peirce was able to formulate them. This should be the departing point for the further development of these normative sciences along with his philosophy, which, as Peirce himself affirmed, should be carried out by future communities of inquirers. Every further development in esthetics and ethics, in relation to Peirce's thought, will be, then, a joint effort by future communities of inquirers toward the *construction* of esthetics and ethics as normative sciences.

It is the intention of the author to enable the reader, regardless of any previous knowledge concerning the normative sciences, to understand the idiosyncrasies and the mode of operation of esthetics and ethics in this specific context as normative sciences, their relative positioning in Peirce's architectonic of sciences, and their relation to the philosophical inquiry into norms, values, and principles involving the formation of habits of feeling, of conduct, and of thought. The present exposition shows how Peirce conceived of his version of esthetics and ethics and how he discovered their overall functioning and their inalienable leading role for the sciences of discovery.

Moreover, it should be clear that the fact that the two first normative sciences have not been as thoroughly developed as other areas of his thought does not pose a hindrance to the theoretical premises of interdependence of the sciences functioning within a system. This difference of stages of development of the sciences, though not an ideal situation for such high-ranking sciences within the sciences of discovery, does not block the development of the architectonic system of philosophy. In fact, the systematic development of areas such as logic, of the maxim of pragmaticism, of the existential graphs, of mathematics, of phaneroscopy, have often and simultaneously contributed to the enrichment of the general principles, functioning, and forms of operation of esthetics and ethics.

The chapter is divided into sections. The second section localizes the place and operation of normative sciences within heuretic sciences as Peirce conceived them. The third section presents esthetics, delineates its object of inquiry, and also investigates its mode of operation in discovering and putting forth its results. The fourth section focuses on ethics and on its object of inquiry as it searches for the ideals of conduct according to the esthetic ideals just disclosed. We conclude with an overview of the operation of esthetics and ethics as theories of values in a relative perspective concerning their pragmatistic adequacy.

2. The Place of Normative Sciences within Heuretic Sciences

To grasp the intricate relationships between the sciences and their specific inquiries, it is necessary to elaborate in more detail the role of the normative sciences within Peirce's conceptions of systemic sciences and his more mature philosophical system. Esthetics, ethics, and logic study the norms of how phenomena interact with a perceiver and how the perceiver should interact with these phenomena. They are, as normative sciences, highly theoretical, and as such have no *direct* practical application, although their applied results *may* lead to deliberate actions and growth. Furthermore, as Peirce has affirmed, the three normative sciences are infused by an inherent form of duality most akin to self-control. As he contends: "the Normative Sciences, Esthetics, Ethics, and Logic, which are confined respectively to ascertaining [to] how Feeling, Conduct, and Thought ought to be controlled supposing them to be subject *in a measure*, and only in a measure, to self-control exercised by means of self-criticism, and the purposive formation of habit, as common sense tells us they are in a measure controllable" (R655:24, 1910).

Moreover, the normative sciences, as all of the sciences in Peirce's system, are classified and organized according to the *categories of experience*. For instance, as he affirms, the normative sciences study phenomena of experience in the aspect of the *second category*. But what does this mean exactly? In order to better comprehend these characteristics of Peirce' thought, the normative sciences, as well as of his system in general, it is necessary to observe the scientific and philosophical contexts in which they ought to function.

For Peirce, all sciences within his architectonic are systemically connected, constantly providing other sciences with principles and data according to their specific inquiry.

This characteristic dynamic of Peirce's philosophical architecture is known as the precept of *principle and data-dependency*. That is to say, Peirce sought, with this principle, to enable his system to function according to the degree of abstractness of the sciences implied according to the level of abstraction of their objects of inquiry, as well as according to their intrinsic systemic interdependence (cf. Kent 1987, 93). The more abstracted sciences provide the less abstract sciences with principles and regulations. Reciprocally, the less abstract and more specialized sciences provide the more abstract sciences with results, data, and problems.

Peirce conceived of a ladder of sciences involving three major segments: (1) sciences of discovery, (2) sciences of review, and (3) practical sciences. Of these, Peirce was most concerned with the operational development of the very first segment of science, the sciences of discovery, which he often called *heuretic science*:[4]

1. Sciences of discovery (or *heuretic sciences*) consisting in:
   I. Mathematics
   II. Philosophy or *cenoscopy*, embracing:
      (a) *Phaneroscopy* (or *phenomenology*)
      (b) *Normative sciences*, embracing:
         i. Esthetics
         ii. Ethics
         iii. Logic or semiotics
      (c) *Metaphysics*
   III. Idioscopy (or special sciences)

In accordance with the classification as presented in his more perennial ladder of sciences, this first branch of the sciences of discovery makes up the core of his *theory of inquiry*—considered in this context in the broadest sense of *Erkenntnistheorie*.[5] Briefly stated, the systemic structure of this architectonic begins with *mathematics* (I) as the first science within the sciences of discovery. It is a highly theoretical and abstract science functioning independently from positive experience. Therefore, mathematics does not depend on any other science but furnishes all other sciences in the system with principles. The second branch of the heuretic sciences is occupied by *philosophy*, or *cenoscopy* (II), which is the first positive section of the heuretic sciences; that is, they depend upon positive experience. The operation of cenoscopy is hallmarked by its ability to inquire both into actual existence and into the reality of potential being utilizing, however, no special instruments or specialized skills to perform observations that can eventually lead to discoveries, only the openness of common experience available to all.

Cenoscopy[6] comprises three major subdivisions: *phaneroscopy*, or *phenomenology* (a), the first positive science of the system, is the study of *phanera*, or *phenomena* as perceived. It is a science that collects from experience the universal categories that present themselves in every phenomenon. Peirce uses the term phenomenon, derived from the ancient Greek φαινόμενον (*phainómenon*), but also *phaneron*, from the ancient Greek φανερός (*phanerós*), which means "manifestation," "visible," or "perceivable through the senses," to represent that element which appears in an interpretative mind in any form.

These observations describe three indecomposable categories, under which every element of experience can be ordered. The first category, *firstness*, as Peirce affirms, "is the Idea of that which is such as it is regardless of anything else. That is to say, it is a *Quality of Feeling*" (cf. EP2:160, 1903).

The second category, *secondness*, is the "Idea of that which is such as it is as being Second to some First, regardless of anything else and in particular regardless of any law [...]. That is to say, it is a *Reaction* as an element of the Phenomenon" (cf. EP2:160, 1903).

The third category, *thirdness*, is the "Idea of that which is such as it is as being a Third, or Medium, between a Second and a First. That is to say, it is *Representation* as an element of the Phenomenon" (cf. EP2:161, 1903).

The *normative sciences* (b), in their turn, inquire into possible responses to phaneroscopic study and interactions with the positive experience drawn from phaneroscopy. Thus, they prescribe guides to feelings, conduct, and thoughts based on that experience and provide the next science, *metaphysics* (c), with principles to inquire into the general features of reality accessible to all, as well as into whatever may possess individual reality. Reality is here understood as regularity, as active law. And the last department of the heuretic sciences is occupied by the *idioscopy*, or *special sciences* (III). Idioscopy refers to the common activity of a myriad of actual or soon-to-be established sciences of inquiring into phanera using special observations, special and definite skills, and specialized instrumentation to achieve very specific forms of knowledge and thereby enable the advancement of knowledge (cf. Kent 1987, 181–184).

Hence, the three normative sciences, esthetics, ethics, and logic, form a distinctly separate department of *heuretic science*. The main objective of this branch is the discovery of leading principles that will guide the search for the truth. Within the sciences of discovery, which is the chief and most important part of Peirce's theory of inquiry, the normative sciences play a systemic and fundamental role. As Peirce affirms, esthetics relates to feeling, ethics to action, and logic to thought (R283:44–45, 1906). However, it is the interconnection between feeling, conduct, and thought as relating to *ends* that grants the normative sciences their leading role in this realm of discovery. Moreover, and more important for the exposition of the present chapter, Peirce's recognition of esthetics as a high-ranking normative science is responsible for the functioning of his theory of inquiry, which ethics, logic, pragmaticism, metaphysics, and the special sciences subsequently depend upon.

> Logic regarded from one instructive, though practical and narrow, point of view, is the theory of deliberate thinking. To say that anything is deliberate is to imply that it is controlled with a view to making it conform to a purpose or ideal. Thinking is universally acknowledged to be an active operation. Consequently, the control of thinking with a view to its conformity to a standard or ideal is a special case of the control of action to make it conform to a standard; and the theory of the former must be a special determination of the latter. Now special theories should always be made

to rest upon the general theories of which they are amplifications. The present writer takes the theory of the control of the conduct, and the action in general, so as to conform to an ideal, as being the mid-normative science; that is, as the second of the trio, one and as that one of the three sciences in which the distinctive characters of normative science are most strongly marked. (R283:36–38, 1906)

In accordance with the system's precept of principle and data-dependency, the normative science of esthetics receives principles from the more abstract sciences and provides, in its turn, principles to the next normative science, ethics, which is the normative science tasked with, first, the formulation of a theory of the formation of habits of conduct according to an esthetic ideal, and second, how these newly found habits of conduct must be consistent with the ethical ideal, the latter being a special designation of the esthetic ideal (R693:86, 1904; R478:35, 1903). Ethics, moreover, drawing on the ideals discovered by esthetics, inquires how the esthetic ideal should be pursued, and in doing so determines what should be deliberately avoided as nonesthetic and nonethic.

A genuine secondness of the nature of volition characterizes the struggle of *action-reaction*, or of *approval* or *disapproval*, this being the main characteristic of self-control. Self-control presupposes both a discovered and a deliberately adopted ideal and the volitional effort to deliberately avoid what is not in conformity with that chosen ideal. For, as Peirce contends, all forms of inhibition of action, and, iteratively, inhibition of action upon action, must involve a reaction and thus duality. All forms of self-control involve, necessarily, inhibition. And since the main characteristic of the normative sciences is that of guiding inquiry toward ends and ideals, these sciences are, in their respective domains, thoroughly infused with this form of duality (R283:82–84, 1906). It is in this light that Peirce affirms that the normative sciences study positive experience in its secondness. Self-control and inhibition are strictly connected with the idea of volition, the strongest form of secondness characterizing the normative sciences. Furthermore, the interplay of esthetics and ethics provides semiotics with its main characteristic, normative logic, which ultimately inquires into how knowledge is advanced, making use of its character of differentiating correct from incorrect thinking in order to arrive at the truth (R655:25–26, 1910).

3. Esthetics, the Admirable, and the Deliberate Formations of Habits of Feeling

Peirce initially followed the original consideration of *aesthetics*, at least from its beginnings; and even if he had diligently studied Friedrich Schiller's work *Über die Ästhetische Erziehung des Menschen in einer Reihe von Briefen* in his youth, only much later in his career did he eventually come to consider esthetics as a legitimate normative science. As he vehemently contends: "instead of a silly science of Esthetics, that tries to bring our enjoyment of sensuous beauty,—by which I mean all beauty that appeals to our five senses,—that which ought to be fostered is *meditation, ponderings, day-dreams* (under due control), *concerning ideals*—oh, no, no, no! "ideals" is far too cold a word! I mean rather passionate admiring aspirations after an inward state that anybody may hope to attain or to approach, but whatever more specific completion may enchant the dreamer" (R675:15–16, 1911, emphasis added).

And he did so with the utmost care of restructuring this philosophical discipline as a normative inquiry of the heuretic sciences. As stated in the previous section, a normative science studies the laws of relation of the phenomena to *ends*. What is the *end*, or *good* of esthetics, as Peirce conceives of? He responds: "I would throw the study of the *summum bonum* over to esthetics, of which it would become the chief problem in the form, *What quality of anything is it that is fine [admirable][7] in itself without any ulterior reason?*" (R288:23–25, 1905, emphasis and brackets added).

Esthetics is, accordingly, tasked with discovering two important philosophical components. First, esthetics must discover the most ideal state of things, something ideal and highly attractive as such, *lovely in itself* regardless of aught else—something very *fine*, κᾶλός (*kalós*), or *admirable*, as Peirce called it, which could possibly, by an overwhelming force of attraction and affectability, have practical bearings on a perceiver's sensibility as quality of feeling. Esthetics is, thus, *the science of ideals*, or of that which is *objectively admirable* without any ulterior reason (R478:8, 1903, emphasis added). Second, esthetics develops a theory of the deliberate formation of habits of feeling through a series of self-criticisms and heterocriticisms. This iteration of esthetic experiences prompts the perceiver to re-evaluate and systematically reformulate what should be sought and pursued as one's highest ideal through the cultivation of "passionate admiring aspirations after an inward state that anybody may hope to attain or to approach, but whatever more specific completion may enchant the dreamer" (R675:15–16, 1911). How does this ideal become perceivable? Is it an apparition of a mere exercise of the "World-spirit's Spieltrieb," mere *amusement*?[8] It is much more than that. The ideal, as identified by the inquiry of esthetics, makes itself present, in its suchness, that is, in its *presentness, such as it is*, as an attractive ideal, something so admirable that tends to modify the very formation of future habits of feeling. It appears as an unanalyzed quality possessing a great potential of being unfolded and rendering admirable results. This ideal appears as a quality in its firstness, but a firstness ready to be envisaged, pursued, and applied, for it enables inquirers to esthetically grasp higher perceptions, possibilities, and aims by simply appearing to the mind as a quality of feeling. As Peirce defines it, albeit in the form of an analogy, the esthetic ideal

> must be a dream of extreme variety and must seem to embrace an eventful history extending through millions of years. It shall be a drama in which numberless living caprices shall jostle and work themselves out in larger and stronger harmonies and antagonisms, and ultimately execute intelligent reasonableness of existence more and more intellectually stupendous and bring forth new designs still more admirable

and prolific. [...] Let my intelligence in the dream develop powers infinitely beyond what I can now conceive and let me at least find that boundless reason [is] utterly helpless to comprehend the glories of the thoughts that are to become materialized in the future, and that will be *denouement* enough for me. It may then return to the total unanalyzable impression of it. (R310:8–9, 1903, brackets added)

Esthetics is, thus, the normative science that inquires into the conditions for a perceptive form to be admirable, that is, a form that is pervaded by so powerful an attractive loveliness and admirableness that it can infuse the perceiving mind with these admiring aspirations. Stated differently, the perceiving mind becomes infused with *esthetic* qualities of feelings, that is, inward qualities engendered by feelings set off by the perception and qualitative consideration of the admirable. Therefore, esthetics studies phanera very close to the phaneroscopic inquiry and has prime access to the passage of the continual inflow of phanera through perception into the scrutiny of phaneroscopy. Although esthetics receives the results of the inventory of phaneroscopy, esthetics can access the myriad of selections of phanera as well as it can glimpse, mediately though, at the continuity of phanera as it pervades the perceptive senses in a continual motion. Hence, esthetics not only accesses the firstness available in the results of the inventory of phaneroscopy but also captures the very selectivity and sensible openness of perception itself. This is what Peirce means when he posits that esthetics inquires into the firstness of the data provided by phaneroscopy, for esthetics ought to repose on this science (R478:8, 1903).

Esthetics discovers, defines, and renders the admirable in itself more precise, as well as its character as an *ideal* in terms of the universal elements of experience that have been studied and inventoried by phaneroscopy (R693:127–128, 1904). This rather difficult task of the discovery and definition of the admirable is of paramount importance for the establishment of the inquiry of esthetics, and consequently for the whole theory of inquiry. Peirce contends that "unless this can be done, and it can be shown that there are certain conditions which would make a form *beautiful*[9] in any world, whether it contained beings who would be pleased with such forms or not, there is no true normative science of *esthetics*" (R693:128, 1904; emphasis added).

Peirce had effectively granted esthetics the highest philosophical importance within his philosophical architectonic, acknowledging esthetics not only as the first of the normative sciences, but also as *the normative* science per se: "For it is evident that it is in esthetics that we ought to seek for the *deepest characteristics of normative science*, since esthetics, in dealing with the very ideal itself, whose mere materialization engrosses the attention of practics[10] [ethics] and of logic, must contain the heart, soul, and spirit of normative science" (R283:49–50, 1906; italics and remarks in brackets are added).

With this realization, Peirce arrived at a more mature formulation about the normative science of esthetics, its definite object of inquiry, its difficult task of determining the highest ideal that could be perceived and strived at and pursued by human conduct, and its relation to the other sciences within the sciences of discovery. It becomes clear, therefore, that Peirce's proposal for a normative esthetics consists of a very general, abstract, and highly *prescissive*,[11] processual study. This study presupposes an inquiry that shifts both the focus of attention from a concrete, actual, and finite set of goals and, at the same time, the positioning of the inquirers from a particularized, utilitarian perspective by promoting the individual ability of the inquirers to contribute actively, deliberately, and in a self-controlled manner—that is to say, *reasonably*—to something higher and more developed, being guided by general esthetic ideals that foster the welding of separated *individuals* into esthetically devised communities.

Peirce's esthetics thus contains key elements that will come into play as an important base for his theory of inquiry. These are, first, the perceptive sensibility regarding phanera in their appearance; second, enabling an esthetic receptiveness toward that which is admirable in itself as a quality of feeling; and third, the ability to reasonably interact with these appearing forms and simultaneously conform to them, thereby engendering and translating these newly constituted forms into esthetic realities through deliberate habits of feeling. Then, as Peirce affirms: "If conduct is to be thoroughly deliberate, the ideal must be a habit of feeling which has grown up under the influence of a course of self-criticisms and heterocriticisms; *and the theory of the deliberate formation of habits of feeling is what ought to be meant by esthetics*" (R283:41–43, 1906, emphasis added).

The esthetic qualities of those feelings engendered by the admirable or ideal prompt an analysis and reorganization of the perceiver's conduct. In endeavoring to conform one's actions to an ideal, it becomes necessary to develop a form of self-control that conforms to that ideal. In brief, a sort of sensibility accompanies the esthetic experience; a further attendant factor is the reorganization of inner emotions, habits of feeling and the sensibility toward this or that goal. The perceiving mind identifies this process of self-modification as an asymptotic approach to an ideal, that is, as a habit of feeling modification.

The constant sensibility toward perception, ideals, conduct, and thought set in motion by an initial normative inquiry promotes the modification of the habits of feeling, conduct, and thought, for they will be pervaded by a higher degree of reasonableness, which, in its turn, is fostered by the discovery of and attraction to higher dimensions of the esthetic ideal. The more a perceiving mind nourishes sensibility and the growth of reasonableness by the replication of self-control upon self-control, the clearer and the more developed will the esthetic ideal present itself to the perceiving mind. And thus, it will continue influencing the formation of the perceiver's habits, for the esthetic ideal also presupposes the modification of the rules of self-control, action and, consequently, experience (R290:36–37, 1905).

Therefore, the admirable, from which the esthetic ideal is discovered and determined, *esthetically* modifies both the inquirer's and others' perceptive sensibility, habits of feeling, conduct, and thoughts, and "this centrifugal movement thus rebounds in a new centripetal movement" (R290:36–37, 1905). That is to say, the esthetic ideal tends to spread continuously through the growth of habits of feelings—thus also influencing habits of perceptive sensibility and consequently modifying conduct and thought—and fosters what Peirce called *the growth of the idea-potentiality*.

Thus, it is in this sense that the word *ideal* is understood by Peirce in relation to his conception of esthetic inquiry: it is not a crystallized aim itself, but rather a developmental process, a *living principle*. The perceived ideal must be realized and developed so as to form a theory of the deliberate formation of habits of feeling. This requires specific self-control at the level of qualities of feeling. This self-control is formed by an interpolation of sensibility toward feelings and sensibility toward perceptions, which implies the ability to seek different approaches and interfaces with inner and outer perceived qualities of feeling. The results of the esthetic inquiry directly influence how phaneral experience will be perceived and how the newly formed habits of feeling will tend to perceive a newer manifestation of the admirable. Moreover, the more the sensibility toward the admirable and highest ideals becomes cultivated, the higher the apprehension of manifested form of the admirable will be captured and strived for. The growth of esthetic perceptiveness allows an ever-increasing modification of the habits of perception, which constantly establish new perceptive habits related to *dimensions of feeling*. That is to say, once a new perceptive dimension is trained, a particular feature of an esthetic ideal is selected and the deliberation upon this habitualization begins. The effort of striving toward a definition of habit formation calls for self-control. Self-control at this level of qualities of feelings and of the continua of phaneral experience is not an *imposed* control, for it does not *dominate* feeling but makes these conform to newly discovered elements that lead to the formation of new habits of feeling regarding ideals, perception, and, consequently, as a result of this inquiry into esthetics, the future pursuit of the embodiment of the *reasonableness*. Moreover, these constituted forms are the results from the inquiry of esthetics, which, in their turn, will be applied in the study of ethics as translated, newly constituted forms into reality through *concrete* conduct.

To feel more sensibility in light of a mature ideal, to act in accordance with a purpose grown from this ideal, to think and act in a self-controlled way in accordance with this purpose—seeking to embody the highest ideals not for individual purposes, but to be part of the general embodiment of reasonableness—is what Peirce conceives as the inquiry of esthetics and ethics, which characterizes the very quality of reasonableness. "Under this conception," affirms Peirce, "the ideal of conduct will be to execute our little function in the operation of the creation by giving a hand toward rendering the world more *reasonable* whenever, as the slang is, it is 'up to us,' to do so" (R449:49, 1903, emphasis added).

4. Ethics, Ideals, and the Formation of Deliberate Habits of Conduct

Ethics receives the results of the inquiry of esthetics into the admirable, into the highest attainable ideal, the *summum bonum*, which could be embodied through deliberate conduct. As Peirce states, the problem of ethics is now to inquire into the general conditions for making this admirable, this newly discovered ideal *concrete, existent* (R288:25, 1905).

Peirce describes three ways in which ideals may recommend themselves to inquirers—or, for that matter, to a perceiving mind or more perceivers acting as *one mind* (R448:13–19, 1903). He also analyzes in detail how one can interact with these appearing ideals and how to study them in order to reflect upon their formation and development, in the sense of forming new habits of feeling, and, from this study, to inquire into the general conditions for embodying the esthetic ideal, now a problem of ethics.

After the deliberate adoption of an esthetic ideal, one engages in the revision of the habits of formation of conduct according to ideals, and into how to gauge the conduct against the ideals with the specific aim of devising rules of conduct as to deliberately embody these determined ideals. And this process occurs in a form of *iconoscopy*, that is to say, it takes the diagrammatic form of a systematic gauging of past formed habits of conduct with the newly acquired habits of feeling as determined from the inquiry of esthetics. In order to understand these relations, it is necessary to analyze the three kinds of recommendations that Peirce mentions. First, certain kinds of ideals of conduct that are present to the inquirers' minds have an esthetic quality attached to them. And this esthetic quality of feeling is present in the very moment when one contemplates the ideals and concludes that the type of conduct guided by these ideals is acceptable or recommendable. If this is the case, inquirers tend to reflect upon these ideals and to bring them progressively into harmony with their nature. Second, inquirers endeavor to bring those ideals that recommend themselves into consistency with their nature by shaping them accordingly. Third, inquirers will mentally extract the consequences of carrying out these ideals by projecting how these ideals would be if they were to be performed. Furthermore, they tend also to ask what *would be* the esthetic feeling attached to the projected consequences.

Peirce proposes, moreover, that one's ideals are imbibed during one's childhood and that they continue to develop, gradually being shaped to one's personal nature as well as to the ideas of one's social environment, by a continuous process of growth. Within this growth and maturation process, one will tend to conform, either partially or completely, one's own conduct to these ideals, at least to the ideals in which one *totally believes*. According to Peirce: "When I speak of a man's Real Self, or True Self, I mean the Very Springs of Action in him, which I mean how he would act, not when in haste, but after due consideration; and by 'due consideration,' I mean such deliberation as shall give him time to develop, to grow up to his proper Manhood, which many a man never does actually attain in this world, scarce any of us, fully" (R649:26–27, 1910).

In doing so, inquirers tend to formulate, however vaguely, their rules of conduct. The subsequent reflection upon these newly formed rules of conduct, and also upon the general ideals guiding these rules, evokes an effect on the inquirer's disposition to act in a certain way. Therefore, what inquirers are inclined to do is also modified. This reflection upon the ideals and rules of conduct also activates a mental projection in which these rules of conduct might be applicable, should a specific occasion arise. This reflecting upon and projecting the rules of conduct catalyzes the gathering of active forces and drives the reflection toward the possibility of an occasion arising in which the rules would command certain actual forms of conduct to be carried out. This causes the inquirer to consider how they would act according to their disposition. The catalyzation process produces a *resolution* as to how to act in that projected occasion. It follows that this resolution eventually takes the shape of a *plan* or, as Peirce puts it, a *diagram*. According to him, this plan or diagram has the nature of a general mental formula against which future conduct within the framework of a possible occasion will be gauged. This formed resolution *will not necessarily* or directly influence the inquirer's conduct.

However, if inquirers engage with a sort of learning process, a process similar to that of imprinting a lesson upon their memory (cf. R448:15, 1903), this process results in the conversion of the previously formed resolution, as a mental plan, into a *determination*, that is to say, into something not anymore of the nature of a mental plan, but of the nature of an *efficient agency* to act in a certain way, should the specific occasion *actually* arise. One resynthesizes, enacts, and tries the proposed line of conduct before the imagination. Upon the selection of a newly chosen line of conduct, one rehearses it in a sort of imagined future performance again and anew, as an imprint of it in one's *qualitative* mental memory. This form of self-control, for it is the development of a deliberate habit of conduct, becomes affected by this readiness to act according to a devised ideal of conduct should the occasion for it arise. The essential parts of this self-preparation are, first, the review of the past conduct; second, esthetic valuation and re-evaluation of that conduct, as well as the constant gauging between the achieved esthetic ideal and the past conduct; third, analytic criticism regarding the faulty parts of past conducts, discarded ideals of conduct, and how they should be mended; and fourth, *synthesis* and imaginative rehearsal of the proposed future conduct, which tends to generate a new habit of so behaving (cf. R288:29, 1905).

An accompanying quality of feeling appears along with the process of the formation of this determination, even if the determination is not totally defined. Even a poorly defined determination will have the power to produce some kind of *disposition*. According to Peirce, by reflecting upon and formulating the dispositions growing out of the ideals of conduct, inquirers must ask themselves

> whether my conduct accorded with my resolution. That resolution, as we agreed, was a mental formula. The memory of my action may be roughly described as an image. I contemplate that image and put the question to myself. Shall I say that that image satisfies the stipulations of my resolution, or not? The answer to this question, like the answer to any mental question, is necessarily of the nature of a mental formula. It is accompanied, however, by a certain quality of feeling which is related to the formula itself very much as the color of the ink in which anything is printed is related to the sense of what is printed. (R448:18, 1903)

This being the case, inquirers should investigate afterward whether they could identify, or be aware of, a certain quality of feeling in the very moment of the formulation of the disposition. Was this accompanying quality of feeling somewhat *"pleasurable"*? To do this, they must inquire deeper into their conduct and gauge it against their general intentions. Upon doing this, a judgment will be produced, along with a new accompanying quality of feeling. Immediately after this there will be the recognition that this quality of feeling is either something of a *"pleasurable"* feeling or a *"painful"* one, and that it possesses a *deeper* character.

If inquirers then ask themselves anew how this proposed mental plan accords with their ideals, rules, and conduct, a new judgment is produced, followed by another newly produced quality of feeling—also either pleasurable or painful. This is exactly the characteristic point that qualifies the normativity of the inquiries performed by esthetics, as well as by ethics and semiotics, that is, the characteristic of possessing an active *volition:* "Perhaps one says to oneself (all meditation being in dialogue,) Why did I not behave as I intended to behave, and how am I to make sure of doing so next time? Or perhaps one says: I acted as I had resolved to act. How did I ever come to suppose such conduct would meet my approbation?" (R288:27, 1905).

These qualities of feeling accompanying the judgment of the act of gauging the mental plan with the ideals, rules, and actual conduct then elicit a feeling of either *approval* or *disapproval* regarding the ideals involved in the normative inquiry.

However, independent of the particular outcome of the gathered experience of gauging the mental plan with the ideals, rules, and actual conduct, as well as with the subsequent judgment produced, the very experience will provide inquirers with fruitful lessons that, upon being instilled, will set the parameters for the next revision of ideals, rules, actual conduct, and the judgments produced.

The resolution and the meditation upon the ideals of conduct proceed to agitate a mass of tendencies and allow these to more readily conform to the inquirer's nature. And, although the inquiry upon ideals can prompt the formation of resolutions and is able to catalyze determinations that actually will regulate *future* courses of action guided by newly discovered and adopted ideals in a self-controlled manner, the normative inquiry into ideals and purposes is a purely theoretical study entirely distinct, as Peirce reinforces, "from the business of *shaping* one's own conduct" (R448:21, 1903, emphasis added). "For there are different orders of self-control, without counting the simple inhibition of an impulse by a habit as self-control at all. The first order of self-control simply prepares one's conduct by creating a habit in advance. In the second order, the manner in which the process of preparation shall be conducted has itself been prepared in advance; and this must have been the case when one deliberately sets oneself to the task of *impressing a line of conduct upon oneself by iterations of the lesson*" (R288:29–31, 1905, emphasis added).

Consequently, the process of habit formation proposed by the inquiry of the normative sciences prompts inquirers to repeat over and over the processes of perceiving ideals, drawing resolutions from these ideals, and from these resolutions drawing determinations, so as to *habitually* acquire more elaborate forms of self-controlled conduct based upon experience and reflection in an integrated and reciprocal way. "One has to go on trying one mode of effort after another, while closely watching the efforts one makes, until at last one comes upon one that is remarkably successful. Then one must make an endeavour to repeat the same kind of effort, and often *one will find that he has suddenly acquired a new power*" (R649:15 1910, emphasis added).

5. Closing Notes on the Normative Inquiry

As we have shown, the concatenation of the normative sciences implies that logic, or semiotics, responsible for the inquiry into the conditions for the attainment of truth and self-control applied to thought (R655:25–26,1910) is a special determination of ethics. Ethics, on its turn, as the theory of the deliberate formation of habits of conduct, is a special determination of esthetics. And esthetics—the theory of the deliberate formation of habits of feeling—the normative science par excellence according to Peirce, is directly responsible for the discovery and determination of the highest ideal, which, upon perception, should be pursued. This is, according to him, the highest attainable ideal—as abstract as it may be—the *summum bonum* guiding human conduct and, consequently, inquiry.

The interplay of the normative sciences suggests that it is through attraction and affectability by a powerful esthetic ideal that the adoption of a conduct leading to the continual increase of variation of esthetic forms, of innovations, of the embodiment of what Peirce calls the *increase of idea-potentiality*, takes place (R283:101–104, 1906). This guidance is noticeably carried out by the disclosure of the normativity guiding the *pragmatistic adequacy*, that is, "what *ought to be* the substance, or meaning of the concept or other symbol in question, in order that its true usefulness may be fulfilled" (R649:2, 1910). For it is by the continuous iteration of self-control upon self-control that inquirers cultivate and constantly develop their esthetic ideal. And accordingly, to the degree of the development of the esthetic sensibility and perceptive openness, inquirers become endowed with higher ideals for the attainment of general and collective purposes, which should be put forth for the beneficial effects of communities. The attainment of the esthetic ideal enables, thus, the modification of the specific rules of self-control regarding the formations of habits of feeling and, consequently, through the application of the results of the inquiry of esthetics into the ethical inquiry, modifies the rules of the formation of habits of conduct. Experience, too, becomes herewith modified and the continual embodiment of these potentialities, that is, of the disclosed ideals of conduct, which become existent, influence in the form of irradiating waves individuals, communities of inquiry, and any perceptive mind opened to these experiences.

These irradiations, by proposing the increase of the embodiment of the idea potentiality—for the constant embodiment of new habits of conduct based upon esthetic ideals promotes the increase of idea potentiality—enables the growth of concrete reasonableness in the world, in the form of possible modifications of habit based upon the discoveries performed by esthetics, implemented by the inquiry of ethics, and by the careful articulation of logic, especially characterized by the living inferential metaboly of signs, especially symbols, whose purport lies in conditional resolutions to act (R290:36, 1905). As an answer to the initial question, *What is normative esthetics and ethics for?*: it is their work, along with logic, in the long run, to provide all other sciences involved in the work of discovery with the adaptation of admirable final causes, *ends*, related to possibilities of actualization that recommend themselves to the *attention* of inquiry.

Notes

1. All references to Peirce's manuscripts refer to the Charles S. Peirce Papers microfilm edition (Harvard University Library, Photographic Service, 1966). References employ the numbering system for manuscripts developed by Richard S. Robin in his *Annotated Catalogue of the Papers of Charles S. Peirce* (Amherst: University of Massachusetts Press, 1967) and as supplemented by Richard S. Robin in "The Peirce Papers: A Supplementary Catalogue," *Transactions of the Charles S. Peirce Society* 7(1), 1971, 37–57. Manuscripts are henceforth referenced as R (Robin's reference system) or RS (for Robin's supplement, if applicable), followed by the number of the manuscript and page number, followed then by the year of the manuscript.
2. We consider Peirce's logic as synonymous to semiotics. Peirce makes this consideration quite explicit in his writings, one of the most characteristic of which being the 1904 manuscript R693 entitled "Reason's Conscience: A Practical Treatise on Discovery wherein Logic Is Conceived as Semeiotic."
3. Peirce introduces this denomination, *pragmaticism*, in his 1905 article "What Pragmatism Is" for the journal *The Monist* (EP2:334–335). In accordance with Peirce's later developments, we consider in the present chapter both terms as synonyms for the specific meaning Peirce conveyed to his maxim.
4. Peirce uses the term *heuretic science* to denominate a highly theoretical science that operates within the context of the sciences of discovery, the first echelon of his philosophical architectonic. In order to designate his sciences of discovery, Peirce coined the term *heuretic* as a direct derivation from the Greek verb εὑρίσκω (*heurískō*), meaning 'to find', 'to discover', and also 'to happen upon by chance'. The ancient Greek adjective εὑρετικός (*heuretikós*), which means 'inventive', 'ingenious', is usually attributed to any creative operation, accounting thus for processes by which novelty is achieved in a certain context.
5. The German concept of *Erkenntnislehre*, or, as it is nowadays more commonly used, *Erkenntnistheorie*, embraces the philosophical and scientific area of the general inquiry into the conditions through which knowledge can advance. Peirce's concept of theory of inquiry, in this light, consists in "the result of inquiry by different men, though they may start with preconceptions ever so varied [. . .], and may build upon experiences (or irresistible results of outward influences) as diverse and unlike as they may, is to loving them, in spite of their original resolves, to one common opinion. It may be in the long run, if they were to persist long enough in their inquiries, there would be no limit to their result of their coming to agreement at last" (R655:25–26, 1910). Furthermore, Peirce states that translating *Erkenntnistheorie* as "epistemology" is *atrocious* (cf. EP2:420, 1907).

6. Peirce adopts the denomination of *cenoscopy* to denote his philosophy from the philosopher, jurist, and reformist Jeremy Bentham (1748–1832). As Peirce states: "Beside [the] idioscopic sciences [i.e., special sciences], there are others which analyze and reason from phenomena that are perfectly familiar to all mankind. Because these are founded on common observation, Bentham gave them the collective designation *Cenoscopy*, which I adopt as expressive of my own opinion of the basis on which these sciences, which are otherwise called Philosophy, rest" (R601:20, 1906; brackets added).
7. In this manuscript, Peirce wrote *admirable*, but then deleted it and wrote *fine* instead.
8. Peirce criticizes the traditional aspect of the relativistic notion of *taste* imparted to the main predicate of esthetic. He affirms: "It is true that the Germans, who invented the word, and have done the most toward developing the science, limit it to *taste*, that is, to action of the *Spieltrieb*, from which deep and earnest emotion would seem to be excluded. But in the writer's opinion, the theory is the same whether it be a question of forming a taste in bonnets or of a preference between electrocution and decapitation, or between supporting one's family by agriculture or by highway robbery. The difference of earnestness is of vast practical moment; but it has nothing to do with heuretic science" (R283:43–44, 1906).
9. In the several manuscripts written between 1902 and 1911, Peirce tries to define the highest category of esthetics, that is, that which recommends itself for itself, regardless of aught else. Among these formulations are *summum bonum*, *highest ideal*, *beautiful*, *fine*, *kalós*, and *admirable*. The constant change of concepts denotes Peirce's continual search for a more accurate characterization of the object of esthetics.
10. In this manuscript, Peirce coins a different concept, *practics*, to denote his version of ethics. However, in subsequent writings, he reverts back to *ethics*.
11. As Peirce explains, the term prescission consists in "supposing a state of things in which one element is present without the other, the one being logically possible without the other. Thus, we cannot imagine a sensuous quality without some degree of vividness. But we usually suppose that redness, as it is in red things, has no vividness; and it would certainly be impossible to demonstrate that everything red must have a degree of vividness. [...] It is usually called 'abstraction,' but since the other name for it, 'prescission' or 'precision,' is in good use, while the term 'abstraction' is indispensable for another purpose, that of designating the passage from 'good' to 'goodness,' and the like, it is better to restrict it to meaning either this act or its result. Prescission may be termed 'precisive abstraction,' but that phrase is needlessly long" (R478:34, 1903).

Bibliography

Kent, Beverley. 1987. *Charles S. Peirce. Logic and the Classification of the Sciences*. Kingston, Montreal: McGill–Queen's University Press.

Peirce, Charles S. 1998. *The Essential Peirce. Selected Philosophical Writings*. Vol. 2, edited by Nathan Houser et al. Bloomington: Indiana University Press.

Peirce, Charles S. 1966. *The Charles S. Peirce Papers Microfilm Edition*. Cambridge, MA: Harvard University Library, Photographic Service.

CHAPTER 7

THE AESTHETIC IMPERATIVE

From Normative Science and Self-Control to Somaesthetics

RICHARD SHUSTERMAN

1. PEIRCE AND PRAGMATIST AESTHETICS

C. S. Peirce's writings on aesthetics are quite limited, and he confessed to knowing too little about the field to be very confident in his views about it. While recognizing Peirce's lack of expertise in aesthetic theory, this chapter will argue that his views on aesthetics not only contributed to the development of pragmatist aesthetics but also are surprisingly pertinent for the pragmatist projects of somaesthetics and the ethical art of living. These two projects, however, lie outside the realm of Peirce's definition of aesthetics as a normative science. They involve the conduct of life, which Peirce insistently sought to separate from the fields of pure science, which he understood as "theoretical sciences," including the normative sciences he identified as logic, ethics, and aesthetics (CP1.239, c. 1902; EP2:200, 1903). Peirce, however, recognized that alongside the field of theoretical science there is a wide realm of practical science, including a bewildering variety of specific disciplines that serve the conduct of life. After examining Peirce's views on aesthetics as normative science, this chapter shows how these views, together with his views on consciousness and attention and his crucial notion of self-control, clearly point to the project of somaesthetics. We could best characterize somaesthetics (in Peircean terms) as a practical normative science because it is essentially concerned with practice that serves the ethical art of living, but also incorporates the findings of theoretical science in order better to serve the uses of life.[1]

Aesthetics was the first philosophical field to which Peirce devoted attention as a young student, exploring Schiller's *Letters on the Aesthetic Education of Man* with his friend Horatio Paine.[2] However, having soon abandoned such study to make logic his prime philosophical pursuit, Peirce repeatedly describes himself as an "ignoramus in esthetics" and "ignorant . . . of Art" and thus "incompetent [for] . . . defining the esthetically good" (EP2:189–190, 1903; EP2:201, 1903). This was not false modesty. Peirce wrongly assumes that aesthetics has previously been entirely devoted to matters of taste for sensuous beauty. He ignores that Alexander Baumgarten founded aesthetics as an essentially scientific discipline of sensory cognition that provides "good foundations for all contemplative activity and the liberal arts" and that Georg Wilhelm Friedrich Hegel famously repudiated identifying aesthetics with the theory of taste and limiting it to sensuous beauty.[3]

Lacking expertise in the history of aesthetics and inspired by his "true scientific *Eros*" (CP1.620, 1898), Peirce creatively rethought the aesthetic dimension of experience in ways that served his theoretical projects of pragmatism and the architectonics of classifying the sciences, while suggesting productive new paths for future pragmatist thinking. Before examining the value of his ideas for the new field of somaesthetics (which emerged from pragmatist aesthetics), we briefly note how Peircean views inform the founding masterpiece of pragmatist aesthetics, John Dewey's *Art as Experience*. Three key points should suffice.

1. First is the Peircean notion of "firstness" and its intrinsic connection with the aesthetic, an idea that translates into the key Deweyan notion of the immediacy of aesthetic experience. Proceeding from his phenomenology, Peirce defines "firstness" as "presentness" in the most concrete sense of immediacy (CP5.44,71, 1903), without any conceptual or relational overlay, such as we experience in immediate "quality of feeling" (CP1.304, c. 1904). To explain firstness, Peirce invokes the idea of "the poetic mood which approaches the state in which the present appears as it is present" in itself, "regardless of the absent, regardless of past and future," and without reflective judgment (CP5.44, 1903). In explaining aesthetic enjoyment Peirce writes: "Ignorant as I am of Art, I have a fair share of capacity for esthetic enjoyment; and it seems to me that while in esthetic enjoyment we attend to the totality of Feeling—and especially to the total resultant Quality of Feeling presented in the work of art we are contemplating—yet it is a sort of intellectual sympathy, a sense that here is a Feeling that one can comprehend, a reasonable Feeling" (EP2:190, 1903). But, Peirce continues, in its immediacy of firstness, one does not achieve a clear comprehension of that quality, so "I do not succeed in saying exactly *what* it is" (EP2:190, 1903).

Dewey makes such immediate qualitative feeling of "poetic" mood the foundation not only of his aesthetics but also of his entire theory of experience and coherent thought. Such immediate quality of feeling is like a Peircean firstness that is experienced or *had* but is too immediate to be *known*. Yet it provides the felt quality that unifies the diversity of our sensory input into a coherent experiential whole by selecting what fits that mood, just as it provides the directional tendency, focus, and energy for thought's progress toward its conclusion.[4] Dewey emphasizes how such immediate quality of feeling provides the unity necessary for coherent thought and for fulfilling experience, a unity whose paradigmatic expression is in the enriching wholeness of works of art. The "artist and perceiver alike begin with what may be called a total seizure, an inclusive qualitative whole" that precedes "the poetical idea" and its articulation into the concrete parts of the poem. Not only does the mood or qualitative feeling "come first, but it persists as the substratum after distinctions [of the parts] emerge; in fact, they emerge as *its* distinctions," emerging from the felt quality of firstness (AE 195–196).

2. The principle of continuity or synechism is a second key Peircean notion central to Dewey's aesthetics. Whether we take this as a metaphysical "doctrine that all that exists is continuous" (CP1.172, c. 1897) or more prudently (as Peirce later redefined it) as simply the logical "tendency to regard everything as continuous" (EP2:1, 1893), synechism speaks decisively against our conventional dualistic distinctions that ignore the continuities between the dualities and thus leaves them as "unrelated chunks of being" (EP2:2, 1893).[5] Perhaps the most pervasive theme of Dewey's aesthetics is undermining entrenched dualisms by revealing the continuities and relations between the opposed or compartmentalized binaries. Dewey's somatic naturalism, aimed at "recovering the continuity of esthetic experience with normal processes of living," is part of his rejection of the dualism that opposed art to real life (AE 16). He further insists on the fundamental continuity of a host of traditional binary notions whose long-assumed oppositional contrast has structured so much of philosophical aesthetics. These include the fine versus the applied or practical arts (AE 11–12, 87, 181), the high versus the popular arts (AE 191), the spatial versus the temporal arts (AE 187), the aesthetic versus the cognitive (AE 45, 52, 80, 126, 154, 202), the aesthetic versus the practical (AE 45–47, 203), and artists versus the "ordinary" people who constitute their audience (AE 54, 60, 80). To secure continuity in aesthetic theory, Dewey extends his synechistic assault on other dualisms that underlie and reinforce the compartmentalization of art and aesthetic experience. Foremost among these are the dichotomies of body and mind, material and ideal, thought and feeling, form and substance, man and nature, self and world, subject and object, and means and ends.[6]

3. Synechism suggests a third Peircean idea that informs pragmatist aesthetics in Dewey and beyond: that aesthetics is more than a theory of art and taste because it concerns values that ground the conduct of thought and action, and therefore there is a deep continuity between ethics and aesthetics. Indeed, for Peirce they tend to merge into the ideal of beautifully admirable conduct whose attraction and merit are simultaneously aesthetic and ethical. Most post-Kantian philosophers regard ethics and aesthetics as designating two divergent domains within the general realm of value and governed by very different goals, methods, and criteria, and even embodied in rival, conflicting stereotypes: the amoral aesthete and the philistine moralist who has no aesthetic taste. Whereas the ethical attitude is concerned with action, the aesthetic attitude eschews it, but instead involves disinterested or purposeless contemplation. Although Peirce repeatedly lists ethics and aesthetics as two different normative sciences (along with logic as a third), he also acknowledges the difficulties of sharply distinguishing the two. Before considering in detail the relations between ethics and aesthetics within Peirce's normative science, I now simply highlight his advocacy of their union in the Greek notion of "*kalos k'agathos*" (the beautiful and good). Peirce employs this term to characterize "a

definite ideal" that is more admirable and attractive than what we normally understand by the English word "beautiful" (CP1.586, *c*. 1903). He elsewhere simply uses the term *kalos* or the French word *beau* to describe this aesthetic yet ethical ideal, envisioning it as the "adorably admirable" *summum bonum* that serves as the ultimate ideal for determining norms of conduct (CP2.199, *c*. 1902).[7]

This same Greek notion serves in Dewey's aesthetics to challenge the Kantian tradition of contrasting the aesthetic and the moral. "The Greek identification of good conduct with conduct having proportion, grace, and harmony, the *kalon-agathon*, is a more obvious example of distinctive aesthetic quality in moral action. One great defect in what passes as morality is its anesthetic quality. Instead of exemplifying wholehearted action, it takes the form of grudging piecemeal concessions to the demands of duty" (AE 46). This Peircean–Deweyan mingling of ethics and aesthetics is salient in some neopragmatists, notably Richard Rorty and myself.[8]

2. Aesthetics as Philosophy and Normative Science

Peirce reconceived aesthetics to make it fit more effectively into his global project of ensuring philosophy's scientific status and place among the most important theoretical sciences, the sciences of discovery. Peirce first distinguishes between "theoretical science" ("whose purpose is simply and solely knowledge of God's truth") and the "motley crowd" of "practical sciences" whose concern with knowledge is not purely for truth but "for the uses of life" (CP1.239, 243, *c*. 1902). Theoretical science includes sciences of discovery and sciences of review, the latter being concerned "with arranging the results of discovery," to classify and "sum up the results [of discovery] ... and to study them as forming one system" (CP1.182, 1903; CP1.256, *c*. 1902). "Science of discovery is either I. Mathematics; II. Philosophy; or III. Idioscopy"; this last "embraces all the special sciences, which are principally occupied with the accumulation of new facts" and which "has two wings: . . . the Physical Sciences . . . and the Psychical or Human Sciences" (CP1.183, 184, 187, *c*. 1903). For Peirce, "philosophy is divided into a. Phenomenology; b. Normative Science; c. Metaphysics"; and "normative science divides into esthetics, ethics, and logic" (CP1.186, CP5.129; cf. CP1.191, all 1903).

Normative science "investigates the universal and necessary laws of the relation of phenomena to Ends" and therefore "ought to be guided by the facts of phenomenology," though its fields of logic, ethics, and aesthetics go beyond phenomenal data in considering such ends as "Truth, Right, and Beauty" (CP5.121, 126, 1903). As belonging to philosophy, hence to sciences of discovery, these normative sciences are "purely theoretical" and not aimed at practical purposes or "the production of skill' (CP1.125, *c*. 1896). In its purely theoretical character as a science of discovery, Peircean ethics is altogether different from the standard notion of ethics as a "science of morality, virtuous conduct, right living," which could not "claim a place among the heuristic sciences," that is, sciences of discovery (EP2:377, 1906). The moral knowledge guiding actual conduct is just "a composite ... of the conscience of the members of the community" intuited through feelings (EP2:377, 1906), but it is no less useful and accurate for being so. Similarly, Peircean aesthetics is different from the field's conventional conception as philosophy of art, beauty, and taste.

If Peircean normative science "in general [is] the science of the laws of the conformity of things to ends, [then] esthetics considers those things whose ends are to embody qualities of feeling, ethics those things whose ends lie in action, and logic those things whose end is to represent something" in thought (CP5.129, 1903). Constituting the second branch of philosophy, the normative sciences share an aspect of Peircean secondness, "the essentially Dualistic distinction of Good and Bad," of approval versus disapproval (EP2:189, 1903). In distinguishing "good and bad[,] . . . Logic [does so] in regard to representations of truth, Ethics in regard to efforts of will, and Esthetics in objects considered simply in their presentation" (CP5.36, 1903). "But that dualism which is so much marked in the True and the False, logic's object of study, and in the Useful and Pernicious ... of practics [or ethics], is softened almost to obliteration in esthetics. Nevertheless, it would be the height of stupidity to say that esthetics knows no good and no bad" (EP2:379, 1906).

Peirce offers two different accounts of aesthetic goodness. One account (which he describes as merely a "suggestion" that "may be worth ... very little") is essentially formalistic. "I should say that an object, to be esthetically good, must have a multitude of parts so related to one another as to impart a positive simple immediate quality to their totality; and whatever does this is, in so far, esthetically good, no matter what the particular quality of the total may be" (CP5.132, 1903). Even if "that quality be such as to nauseate us, to scare us, or otherwise to disturb us to the point of throwing us out of the mood of esthetic enjoyment, out of the mood of simply contemplating the embodiment of the quality[,] ... then the object remains none the less esthetically good, although people in our condition are incapacitated from a calm esthetic contemplation of it" (CP5.132, 1903). This, however, paradoxically suggests "that there is no such thing as positive esthetic badness; and since by goodness we chiefly in this discussion mean merely the absence of badness, or faultlessness, there will be no such thing as esthetic goodness ... [but only] various esthetic qualities; that is, simple qualities of totalities not capable of full embodiment in the parts, which qualities may be more decided and strong in one case than in another" (CP5.132, 1903).

Peirce's second account of aesthetic goodness concerns his notion of an aesthetic ideal. Such "an esthetic ideal of what is fine" constitutes "an ultimate end of action" that deliberately and rationally guides our behavior by the attraction of its fineness or *kalos* quality (CP5.133, 1903; CP5.533, c. 1905). As "an ultimate end of action *deliberately* adopted—that is to say, *reasonably* adopted—[it] must be a state of things that *reasonably recommends itself in itself* aside from any ulterior consideration. It must be an *admirable ideal*, having the only kind of goodness that such an ideal *can* have; namely, esthetic goodness. From this point of view the morally good appears as a particular species of the esthetically good" (CP5.130, 1903). Indeed, given the deep continuity (merging on fusion) between the aesthetic and ethical, the aesthetic ideal "as in itself {*kalos k'agathos*}" is adorably admirable or "universally and absolutely desirable" in itself (with no ulterior motive), constituting or "determining the *summum bonum* . . . [to which] the theory of self-controlled, or deliberate, conduct" (i.e., ethics) is directed (CP1.191, 1903; CP.586, *c.* 1903). "Esthetics is the science of ideals, of that which is objectively admirable without any ulterior reason . . . but it ought to repose on phenomenology" because aesthetics is concerned with "qualities of feeling" (CP1.191, 1903; CP5.129, 1903).

In treating "the laws of conformity of things to ends" through "voluntary acts" or "deliberate conduct," Peirce's three normative sciences involve a hierarchy of ends and require self-control to pursue them (CP5.129–130, 1903; CP5.441, 1905). "A logical reasoner is a reasoner who exercises great self-control in his intellectual operations; and therefore the logically good is simply a particular species of the morally good" (CP5.130, 1903). "Logic is the theory of self-controlled, or deliberate, thought; and as such, must appeal to ethics for its principles" (CP1.191, 1903). Ethics, in turn, as "the theory of self-controlled, or deliberate, conduct" or "the science of right and wrong, must appeal to Esthetics for aid in determining the *summum bonum*" or the ideal to which ethics should aspire (CP1.191, 1903). For "esthetics is the science of ideals, or of that which is objectively admirable without any ulterior reason" (CP1.191, 1903). "Its problem is to determine by analysis what it is that one ought deliberately to admire *per se* in itself regardless of what it may lead to and regardless of its bearings upon human conduct" (CP5.36, 1903).

Peirce explains this lack of regard for practical real-life results and actual action as essential to the purely theoretic character of normative science. Although "these sciences do study what ought to be, i.e., ideals, they are the very most purely theoretical of purely theoretical sciences" (CP1.281, *c.* 1902). Nonetheless, Peirce is willing to accommodate in some way our common understandings of logic, ethics, and aesthetics as deeply concerned with actual practices and their real-life consequences. Alongside and "closely related to" the theoretical normative sciences, he recognizes "three corresponding arts or practical sciences," namely, "the arts of reasoning, of the conduct of life, and of fine art" (CP1.281, *c.* 1902). In what follows, I consider somaesthetics as a Peircean practical science while suggesting how Peircean ideas inform some of its central themes.[9]

3. Practical Science, Somaesthetics, and Self-Control

Peirce hardly discusses the practical sciences, which he sometimes calls "Applied Sciences or Arts" (EP2.37). They did not appeal to his "scientific Eros," which preferred the purely theoretical, precise, and well structured; and he confessed to "being utterly bewildered by [their] motley crowd" (CP1.243, *c.* 1902). He is willing to "mention a few of them, just to give an idea of what [he means] . . . under that name," and his list includes "all such well-recognized sciences now in *actu*, as pedagogics, gold-beating, etiquette, pigeon-fancying, vulgar arithmetic, horology, surveying, navigation, telegraphy, printing, bookbinding, paper-making, deciphering, ink-making, librarian's work, engraving, etc." (CP1.243, *c*. 1902).[10] Peirce meant his list to be indicative rather than "exhaustive," so he would have no problem recognizing new practical sciences. Somaesthetics could be such a science, as he certainly affirms practical scientific analogs for philosophy's normative sciences of logic, ethics, and aesthetics.

Affirming practical counterparts for philosophical sciences deemed purely theoretical rescues Peirce from the notoriously controversial position of his 1898 essay "Philosophy and the Conduct of Life," which boldly denies the whole Greek tradition of seeing philosophy as a guide to the practice of living or to "vital" matters.[11] In "condemning with the whole strength of conviction the Hellenic tendency to mingle Philosophy and Practice," Peirce says he does so as "a scientific man" concerned with "Philosophical Science," which he sees as a purely theoretical science of discovery, and such "pure theoretical knowledge, or science, has nothing directly to say concerning practical matters" (EP2:29, 33,1898). This does not preclude the existence of practical philosophical sciences that do serve the conduct of life, and the essay indeed mentions "Applied Sciences or Arts," among which he includes "ethics" (EP2:37, 1898). Indeed, late in life, recognizing how his wrong decisions and inadequately controlled behavior resulted in poverty and professional ruin, Peirce clearly speaks of self-control guided by ethics and aesthetics (perhaps in their *practical* analogs) as necessary for proper training in directing the conduct of life.

> If I had a son, I should instill into him this view of morality, (that is, that Ethics is the science of the method of bringing Self-Control to bear to gain satisfaction) and force him to see that there is but one thing that raises one individual animal above another,—Self-Mastery; and should teach him that the Will is Free only in the sense that, by employing the proper appliances, he can make himself behave in the way he really desires to behave. As to what one ought to desire, it is, I should show him, what he will desire if he sufficiently considers it, and that will be to make his life beautiful, admirable. Now the science of the Admirable is *true* Esthetics.[12]

This "ought" to desire to make one's life beautiful (which functions as the ultimate, overarching, or subsuming aim of the normative sciences of logic, ethics, and aesthetics) is what I call "the aesthetic imperative" in Peirce. He does not use the term, but his language suggests it when this "esthetic ideal is proposed as an ultimate end of action" and is compared to Immanuel Kant's "categorical imperative" (CP5.133, 1903). However, we find traces of this aesthetic imperative to live a beautiful, admirable life in Peirce's own practice of the art of living, not only in his refined tastes in clothes, food, wines, and furnishings, but also in his tenacious ambition for admirable scientific achievement. It is not surprising that biographer Joseph Brent describes him as a dandy, though one lacking sufficient self-control to attain his desired aims of action and to achieve beautiful, admirable living.

Somaesthetics devotes considerable attention to studying the somatic "appliances" or body–mind methods for controlling one's action as one freely and consciously wills to perform it instead of ineffectively performing the action (or a related action) through entrenched habits without one's conscious control. A key principle of somaesthetics is that to ensure properly performing the action one wishes to do, it is often necessary to know what one's body is actually doing. For example, many golfers make a poor swing because they have a bad habit of lifting their head and thus taking their eyes off the ball. They do not even realize this because this way of swinging has become so habitual. Given this habit, to ensure the desired action of swinging while keeping one's head down and eyes on the ball, one must develop better body awareness to notice when and how the head lifting occurs. This need for improved body awareness is relevant for the body mechanics of all sorts of somatic actions. But such heightened somatic perception is not part of our ordinary consciousness, and it requires disciplined efforts and training in attentive awareness through somaesthetic perception and reflection. In other words, self-mastery requires self-knowledge, and the requisite self-knowledge includes improved awareness and consequent control of the somatic "appliances" that guide action and shape our feelings.

Recognizing that feelings powerfully shape actions, somaesthetics insists that self-control in action involves self-control of feelings. Consider a matter far more important than golf. Enmity toward certain races, ethnicities, or gender identities typically has a deep, though often unnoticed, visceral quality, which is why rational arguments for multicultural tolerance alone fail to solve the problem because such prejudice relies on somatic feelings that, although unpleasant, are often only distractedly or implicitly felt. As long as we do not attend to these visceral feelings through improved somaesthetic consciousness, we can neither control nor transform them to become more tolerant and reasonable. Such feelings are transformable because they are the product not of innate instinct but of unconscious habit formation. Retraining habits of feeling is commonplace in gastronomy, athletics, and somatic therapies, but modern philosophical ethics and political theory have not given it enough attention. Peirce, however, recognizes the importance of training habits of feeling as central to self-control and the pursuit of ideals through reasonable, deliberate action. "If conduct is to be thoroughly deliberate, the ideal must be a habit of feeling which has grown up under the influence of a course of self-criticisms and of heterocriticisms; and the theory of the deliberate formulation of such habits of feeling is what ought to be meant by *esthetics*" (EP2:377–378, 1906). Somaesthetics includes both theory and practical methods for better perception, critique, and reform of our habits of feeling and action.

As practical science, somaesthetics is a field of inquiry devoted to the critical study and meliorative cultivation of the experience and use of the living body (or soma) as a site of sensory perception (aesthesis), performance, and creative self-fashioning. Such self-fashioning relates to the Peircean aim of shaping, through self-control, an admirable character with "that special variety of esthetic goodness . . . , namely, expressiveness" (CP5.137, 1903). An ameliorative discipline of both theory and practice, somaesthetics seeks to enrich not only our discursive knowledge of the body but also our somatic self-mastery, lived experience, and performance; it aims to improve the meaning, understanding, efficacy, and beauty of our movements and of the environments to which our actions contribute and from which they derive their energies and significance. To pursue these aims, somaesthetics is concerned with a wide diversity of knowledge forms, discourses, social practices and institutions, cultural traditions and values, and practical body disciplines that structure (or could improve) somatic understanding and cultivation. Therefore, although rooted in pragmatist philosophy, somaesthetics is an interdisciplinary field, in which theory and practice reciprocally nourish each other. It provides a framework for more fruitful interaction between the diverse forms of somatic knowledge provided by different disciplines focused on embodiment.

Somaesthetics shares Peirce's interest in triads and synechism. It consists of three branches and three dimensions that interconnect and somewhat overlap. *Analytic somaesthetics*, an essentially descriptive and theoretical field of inquiry, is devoted to explaining the nature of somatic perceptions and practices and their role in our world of experience. It includes not only issues relating to embodied consciousness and action but also genealogical, sociological, and cultural analyses of somatic norms or ideals. It thus incorporates some Peircean theoretical sciences. *Pragmatic somaesthetics* has a distinctly normative character, as it involves proposing specific methods for somatic improvement and their comparative critique. Moreover, because the notion of improvement implies norms or values, this study of methods of improvement includes the comparative critique of the values that those methods imply. Since any method for improvement will depend on facts about the body, this pragmatic dimension presupposes or incorporates the facts and findings of the analytic or theoretical branch, but successful methods can conversely change some facts. *Practical somaesthetics*, which involves the actual practice of somatic disciplines aimed at improving somatic experience and performance, obviously relies on the methods of pragmatic somaesthetics but can lead to their modification.

The three dimensions of somaesthetics (present in all three branches) are, respectively, *representational, experiential,* and *performative*; they too have clear interconnections and overlap. *Representational somaesthetics* (e.g., cosmetics or bodybuilding) deals with the body's surface forms, while *experiential somaesthetics* (e.g., yoga) aims more at making the quality of our somatic experience more satisfying and acutely perceptive. Yet yoga also has representational benefits, just as bodybuilding has experiential benefits. Many somatic disciplines involve both dimensions because inner experience and outer appearance are often related; how we feel influences how we look and vice versa. The third dimension, *performative somaesthetics*, focuses primarily on building strength, health, or performative skill (e.g., in athletics or martial arts). Insofar as these performative disciplines aim at the external exhibition of performance or at one's inner feeling of power and skill, they might be associated with or assimilated into the representational or experiential categories.[13]

4. Consciousness, Reflection, and Somaesthetic Training

If improving self-control requires somaesthetic self-knowledge, this in turn requires heightened capacities of self-perception through somaesthetic training. Affirming the value of such training, Peirce claims: "I have gone through a systematic course of training in recognizing my feelings. I have worked with intensity for so many hours a day every day for long years to train myself to do this; and it is a training which I would recommend to all of you" (EP 2:190). This confession comes in the context of noting the variety of pain, in which he had an agonizingly rigorous training. Beginning in his senior year at Harvard and continuing throughout his life, Peirce suffered from an excruciatingly painful neurological disease called "trigeminal neuralgia—then medically termed *facial neuralgia*," which worsens with age and whose pain is "debilitating" to normal functioning, let alone intense mental labor.[14] His training in discriminating sensory feelings also included the more pleasurable study of the olfactory and gustatory discrimination of fine wines. In Paris he hired "the tutelage of a sommelier [and] became a connoisseur of wines."[15] In his twenties Peirce rigorously trained in weightlifting and later wrote how it both increased his muscular strength and boosted his spirits, making him "wonderfully exhilarated and refreshed." He further claimed such "exercise which systematically [builds strength by] . . . overcoming successively increased weights or resistances, produces a definite increase of steadiness of the nerves." Indeed, the felt resistance of his "state of consciousness while weightlifting" inspired his notion of secondness as resistance, as all his "muscles were . . . under such tension as almost to abolish all sensation."[16]

To control one's feelings one must be aware of them, and we wrongly assume that we readily know them because we believe that consciousness is transparent to immediate introspection. Somaesthetics follows Peirce in denying this, recognizing that many of our feelings escape our awareness because they fall beneath the scope of our attention. Somaesthetics identifies four levels of somatic consciousness. We could paradoxically describe the most basic form of body intentionality as unconscious consciousness. This is the sort of limited, obscure consciousness we exhibit in our sleep, when, for example, we intentionally (though unconsciously) move a pillow that is disturbing our breathing. Above this level is that of being awake and conscious of the object we perceive but not explicitly aware of it as a distinct object of consciousness. We typically pay no attention to the position of our feet when we are walking, yet we walk with no difficulty. This level of unreflective, unthematized perception is what Maurice Merleau-Ponty hails as "primary consciousness" and the fundamental, unappreciated key to the mystery of our successful perception and action.[17] However, sometimes we raise our consciousness of our feet to the level of explicit awareness, for example, when we are crossing difficult terrain, when we have problems of balance, or when our feet are hurting. Similarly, we sometimes move from inexplicit consciousness of breathing to situations where our breathing becomes an explicit object of our somatic consciousness, as when we notice that we are short of breath or have difficulty breathing. We reach a fourth, higher level of reflective consciousness when we are not only explicitly aware that we are breathing but also clearly conscious of our conscious awareness of breathing and of how that reflexive consciousness affects our breathing and other dimensions of somatic experience. These explicit and reflective levels of consciousness, which can blend or overlap into each other (in synechistic fashion), I describe, respectively, as somaesthetic perception and somaesthetic reflection.[18]

A pioneer in experimental psychology's exploration of conscious sensations (while at Johns Hopkins University), Peirce recognized the multiple levels of consciousness and showed that there exist sensations or feelings in consciousness that aid performance but exist beneath explicit awareness. If consciousness contains feelings that guide our choices yet remain "so faint that we are not fairly aware of having them," then Peirce concludes, "such faint sensations ought to be fully studied by the psychologist and assiduously cultivated by every man" (CP7.35, 1884). Such inquiry involves learning how to bring those sensations into clearer conscious awareness. Peirce strikingly describes consciousness as "a bottomless lake, whose waters seem transparent, yet into which we can clearly see but a little way. But in this water there are countless objects at different depths," many of which are "sunk" too deep ("in a great depth of dimness") for us to be aware that they are even in our consciousness (CP7.547, n.d.).

Various influences can give those deeply hidden feelings "an upward impulse which may be intense enough and continue long enough to bring them into the upper visible layer" or "level of easy discernment" in which they can emerge into clear, explicit awareness (CP7.547, 554, n.d.). Other factors drive things down into the "deeper" and "dimmer" levels of consciousness beneath awareness. These factors of upward and downward influence include momentum, associations with vivid ideas, relationship to our purposes, and the momentum of temporal succession "so that the idea originally dimmer becomes move vivid than the one that brought it up" (CP7.554, n.d.). Most important for conduct, however, is the critical attention, reflection, and "control which we exercise over our thoughts," which have the capacity of calling up ideas from deeper levels and holding them up in explicit consciousness "where they may be scrutinized" (CP7.554, n.d.). This capacity for attentive and reflective discipline has practical consequences for monitoring, regulating, and transforming habits of thought and behavior.

Convergent with the different levels of consciousness, Peirce notes "different degrees of vividness" of the "ideas in [one's] consciousness": "How vivid the most vivid of them are depends upon how wide awake I am." There is only room in one's "consciousness for a few at [the] highest level of vividness." Thus, if other ideas "force themselves up, some of those that were at the surface must subside. Below these vivid surface ideas there are others less vivid, and still deeper others that are so dim that only by intense effort, perhaps by no effort that I can possibly exert, can I assure myself of their presence" (CP7.497, 1898). Yet, his experiments "proved indirectly" that such ideas "are really there" in consciousness because they enable a percentage of correct sensory judgments significantly higher than what mere probability would yield (CP7.497, 1898).[19] Faint feelings with "light subjective intensity" nonetheless "affect the emotions and the voluntary actions" and "are much less under control than ... more [subjectively] intense" feelings. This is because to control a feeling (or "to affect its transformations"), we need to direct our attention to it, and it is hard to attend to that which "is scarcely perceptible" in faint consciousness (CP7.555, c. 1893). Consequently, if we wish to increase our control of feelings and thus better control the actions that feelings affect, then we should devote efforts to improving our recognition and discrimination of feelings (including the very faint ones) by improving our skills of attentive consciousness. This is the central perceptual goal of somaesthetics, crucial to its further aims of improved performance, better critical self-study, and enhanced self-control in fashioning an admirable character reflecting the aesthetic ideal of *kalos k'agathos*.

Among the very faint feelings that influence us without our awareness, Peirce highlights as "specially interesting ... those which tend toward a reaction between mind and body, whether in sense, in the action of the glands, in contractions of involuntary muscles, in coordinated voluntary deeds," and so on (CP7.555, c. 1893). The improved perception of such mind–body feelings is central to the project of somaesthetics, which, however, rejects ontological mind–body dualism. In affirming the notion of soma as comprising both mental and physical functions under different aspects, somaesthetics recalls Spinoza's views: not only "that mind and body are one and the same thing, conceived first under the attribute of thought, secondly, under the attribute of [spatial] extension," but also "that the mind is not at all times equally fit for thinking ... but according as the body is more or less fitted for ... this."[20] Peirce argues we can render faint sensations more vivid and present to explicit awareness by augmenting our efforts of attention—by increasing either the "intensity of attention" or "the period of attention" (CP7.546, n.d.). Somaesthetics would add a further option: increasing one's skills of attention.[21]

Besides the various levels of vividness in consciousness, the different degrees of objective and subjective intensity, and the diverse degrees of attentive effort, Peirce distinguishes between mere consciousness of feelings, explicit awareness of feelings, and "reflex consciousness" of feelings. There are imperceptibly faint feelings in consciousness that "a greater effort of attention would detect" and bring into vivid awareness, but such awareness is not the highest level of consciousness. Insisting, "It is one thing to feel a thing [even if it is felt vividly] and it is another thing to have a reflex feeling that there is a feeling," Peirce claims his "experiments conclusively show that consciousness must reach a considerable vividness before the least reflex feeling of it is produced" (CP7.547, n.d.). This higher, more reflective level of consciousness—that somaesthetics describes as somaesthetic reflection—involves not only vivid, explicit awareness of a feeling but also a reflective awareness of our conscious attention to that feeling and how that attention affects the experience of that feeling. As Peirce puts it, it is only at the "upper layer of consciousness" whose elements have high "degrees of vividness" that we find our "reflex consciousness, or self-consciousness, is attached" (CP7.547, n.d.). His psychological research suggests the somaesthetic project of cultivating skills of disciplined attention to render imperceptibly faint feelings more vivid, discernable, and consequently more manageable. As such feelings often determine our choices and actions without our knowing it, improved awareness of them is essential to Peirce's goal of self-control: serving "the formation or modification thereby of habits or dispositions of the occult something behind [explicit] consciousness" that shapes our attitudes and actions (R939, 1905).[22]

Peirce recognizes the dangers of reflective feelings and self-consciousness. "Everybody knows how self-consciousness makes one awkward and may even quite paralyze the mind . . . and that those things that I have done spontaneously were the best done" (CP7.45, c. 1907). Because of such dangers William James rejected somaesthetic reflection in practical life, although advocating it in psychological research.[23] If spontaneity usually serves us best in everyday functioning, then self-conscious reflection has practical importance in stages of learning sensorimotor skills but also in stages of correcting habits (where spontaneity simply reinforces the habit), and in self-control. Many cases where we blame reflective consciousness of one's bodily movements in performing an action as the cause of awkward or failed performance are instead cases resulting from being distracted from the proper bodily movements (and their attendant feelings). We are distracted, for example, by overriding feelings of desire or of anxious worry regarding the success of the action and how one's performance will be judged. The problem, then, is not that of reflective awareness of what one is actually doing but, rather, distraction from one's actual actions by thoughts about one's success in achieving the ends of those actions.[24] Peirce makes an analogous point. "Perhaps it is because in trying very hard we are thinking about our effort instead of about the problem in hand" (CP7.45, c. 1907).

The somaesthetic solution is not abandoning reflective consciousness and self-control and instead embracing pure uncritical spontaneity. It is rather to develop greater skills of self-conscious attention and self-control that one can focus more precisely on the right targets at the right times. Such skills of reflective conscious control include knowing when and when not to let spontaneous feelings, choices, and actions direct our conduct. Synechism connects spontaneity and reflective control. Actions that once required critical consciousness and careful choice (such as writing in a new language) become spontaneous once the relevant skills are acquired. Ethical action is spontaneous once conscious efforts of reflective self-control have established the relevant moral habit. Wisdom lies in properly coordinating the two factors of spontaneity and reflection, so that skilled reflection tells us when to stop reflecting, while spontaneity recognizes when it needs to pause for reflection.

5. Rationality, Sentiment, and the Aesthetic Ideal

Peirce's key factors of rationality and sentiment display a similar dialectical coordination, which takes three (somewhat overlapping) forms. One is division of labor. In contexts of pure science (including scientific philosophy), "right reasoning ... is absolutely essential" (CP1.623, 1898), while sentiment should not "receive any weight whatsoever in theoretical matters" (CP1.634, 1898). "But in practical affairs, in matters of vital importance, it is very easy to exaggerate the importance of ratiocination," and we should instead rely on "sentiment or instinct." Peirce continues, "If I allow the supremacy of sentiment in human affairs, I do so at the dictation of reason itself; and equally at the dictation of sentiment, in theoretical matters I refuse to allow sentiment any weight whatever" (CP1.634, 1898). This suggests a second form of coordination: a balance of power through a system of checks and balances. As pure theoretical reasoning will follow its logic no matter where it leads, even into the most radically dangerous ideas (such as experimenting on humans in ways that kill or gravely injure them), so sentiment will check that line of reasoning with feelings of outrage or horror and thus prevent it from further exploration or from being put into practice. If "Do not block the way of inquiry" comes from the scientific "rule of reason" that has no "dread of consequences" (CP1.135, c. 1899; CP.148, c. 1897), then sentiment as a conservative force is there to check inquiries that too radically offend our moral feelings and threaten the conduct of life. Conversely, if our feelings about how we conduct our lives too often clash with the facts of experience, we will eventually learn to revise our feelings. Sentiment can develop, and "the development of sentiment ... chiefly takes place through the instrumentality of cognition" (CP1.648, 1898).

A third form of coordination involves guidance. Here sentiment seems especially important. As rational inquiry begins with the "irritation of doubt," a discomforting feeling (EP1:114), so "Reason," claims Peirce, "appeals to sentiment in the last resort" (CP1.623, 1898). Even in theoretical matters, Peirce sometimes seems willing to give sentiment some weight, claiming "strong feeling is in itself, I think, an argument of some weight in favor of the agapastic theory of evolution" (EP1:357). Moreover, though distrusting the individual's "feeling of logicality" as proof of valid reasoning, he maintains the whole enterprise of logic relies on three sentiments. These "three sentiments, namely interest in an indefinite community, recognition of the possibility of this interest being made supreme, and the hope in the unlimited continuance of intellectual activity, [are] indispensable requirements of logic" (EP1:150). As feelings are the distinctive material of aesthetics, we see again the imperative importance of this field.

What then, is Peirce's aesthetic ideal, this "ultimate end" or "admirable ideal" that is valued for its own sake "aside from any ulterior consideration," which "is admirable without any reason for being admirable beyond its inherent character" (CP5.130, 1903; CP1.612, 1903)? The only thing seemingly close to meeting that criterion is pleasure, because it "is the only conceivable result that is satisfied with itself" (CP1.614, 1903). Although Peirce admits that this "is a respectable argument," his sentiments of outrage that pleasure would be the supreme ideal compel him to suggest another ideal, relying on future "progress and growth" (CP1.614, 1903). This is an ideal of reasonableness through "the development of Reason," a faculty beyond individual humans but to whose development and "embodiment" humans contribute through their lives "of feeling, including pleasure in its proper place" (CP1.615, 1903). Peirce concludes, "I do not see how one can have a more satisfying ideal of the admirable than the development of Reason so understood. The one thing whose admirableness is not due to an ulterior reason is Reason itself comprehended in all its fullness, so far as we can comprehend it" (CP1.615, 1903). His ultimate aesthetic imperative as an "ideal of conduct will be ... giving a hand toward rendering the world more reasonable whenever, as the slang is, it is 'up to us' to do so" (CP1.615, 1903).

If this seems a one-sidedly rationalistic ideal for an aesthetic imperative to govern our conduct, we can defend Peirce by arguing that being reasonable in human life includes allowing for the enjoyment of things or states that are not in themselves rational. Sleeping is not a rational state nor is the intensity of sexual passion. Yet, in the proper contexts, it is eminently reasonable to sleep and to engage in sexual activity, and indeed unreasonable to refrain from them. Somaesthetics, as a Peircean practical science that incorporates improving our powers of perception, self-control, and performance for the conduct of life, could help us better determine the proper balance of reason and sentiment in life's diverse and changing contexts.

Notes

1. For detailed accounts of somaesthetics and its relationship to the ethical art of living, see Shusterman (2008, 2012, 2021).
2. See Brent (1993, 53–54a).
3. Baumgarten begins with this definition: "Aesthetics (as the theory of the liberal arts, science of lower cognition, the art of beautiful thinking, and art of analogical rationality) is the science of sensory cognition." My citations from Baumgarten are from the Latin–German abridged edition of this work, Baumgarten (1988, §§1, 3; pp. 2–3). The English translations are mine. For Hegel, aesthetics as "the philosophy of fine art" has as "its true task to bring to consciousness the highest interests of the mind" through art's expression of "the deepest interests of humanity, and the most comprehensive truths of mankind." Hegel (1993, 9, 15).
4. Dewey writes: "Any predominant mood automatically excludes all that is uncongenial with it.... It reaches out tentacles for that which is cognate, for things which feed it and carry it to completion." Dewey (1987, 73); hereafter AE.
5. Peirce notes, "The synechist will not admit that physical and psychical phenomena are entirely distinct" (EP2.2). He elsewhere explicitly describes synechism (in 1902) as "not an ultimate and absolute metaphysical doctrine but "a regulative principle of logic, prescribing what sort of hypothesis is fit to be entertained and examined" (CP6.173).
6. For elaboration of these points, see Shusterman (1992, ch. 1).
7. See Peirce's "Lecture I to the Adirondack Summer School 1905," R1334. https://fromthepage.com/jeffdown1/c-s-peirce-manuscripts/ms-1334-1905-adirondack-summer-school-lectures?page=1.
8. For a comparative analysis of these two neopragmatist approaches, see Shusterman (2012).
9. The field of somaesthetics emerged at the end of the 1990s as a field of theory and practice, defined provisionally as "the critical, meliorative study of the experience and use of one's body as a locus of sensory–aesthetic appreciation (*aisthesis*) and creative self-fashioning." See Shusterman (1999, quotation 302). In considering somaesthetics here as Peircean practical science, we should recognize its engagement with inquiries belonging to Peirce's

category of theoretical sciences. Certainly, its branch of analytic aesthetics includes inquiries concerning metaphysics (e.g., the nature of embodied selves and embodied thought) as well as physiology (e.g., somatic functioning) and sociology (e.g., norms of beauty, health, and behavior). Nonetheless, because of somaesthetics' distinctive pragmatic and practical branches and its overarching, generative pragmatic motivation as service "for the uses of life" rather than for "simply and solely knowledge of God's truth" (CP1.239, c. 1902), it seems better, in terms of Peirce's categories, to consider somaesthetics as a practical science rather than a theoretical science. However, one might prefer to take somaesthetics as a hybrid that challenges any rigid dichotomy between theoretical and practical sciences. Peirce himself recognizes significant transactions between these different categories of science (or between pure science and practical arts). This is not surprising, given his insistence that "science is a pursuit of living men, and . . . is in an incessant state of metabolism and growth" and thus "a living thing," which should make classifications provisional because of the complex possibilities of "transformation" (CP1.232, 234, c. 1902). He notes, for example, how the "art of medicine grew from . . . Egyptian physiology. The study of the steam engine gave birth to modern thermodynamics" (EP2:38). Moreover, a scientist's better practical use of himself through somaesthetics could enhance his perception and endurance in pursuit of pure theoretical science.

10. Peirce's original list "of upwards of three hundred" applied sciences (EP2:37) is so long that the editors of Peirce's *Collected Papers* decided to truncate it, declaring, "The editors have abbreviated a very long list" (CP1.243, c. 1902). The original list is in R427 (65–66, c. 1902).
11. For extensive discussion of such controversy, see Atkins (2016).
12. From Peirce's (April 14, 1909) letter to Lady Welby, cited in Brent, *Charles Sanders Peirce*, 49.
13. For a more detailed account of the different branches and dimensions of somaesthetics, see Shusterman, *Body Consciousness*, ch. 1.
14. See Brent, *Charles Sanders Peirce*, 14. Peirce's father also suffered from this ailment, and they both took strong drugs (such as opium) to deal with it. There is thus poignancy in Peirce's remark that among artists there "are extremely few who are artists in pain" (EP2:190).
15. See Weiss (1934, 398).
16. Remark from October 1913, cited in Ketner (1998, 230–233).
17. Merleau-Ponty (1962, xv–xvi).
18. For discussion of these levels of body consciousness and their application in critique of the limits of Merleau-Ponty's somatic philosophy, see Richard Shusterman, *Body Consciousness*, ch. 2. Roughly parallel to somaesthetics' three higher levels of consciousness, Peirce identifies three "forms of consciousness," which he calls "Feeling, Altersense, and Medisense" (CP7.551, n.d.). "Feeling is . . . consciousness taken in its pristine simplicity," which implies lack of explicit objectification. "Altersense is the consciousness of a directly present other or second, withstanding us," which suggests the explicit attention of somaesthetic perception; while "Medisense is the consciousness of a thirdness, . . . the consciousness of a process of bringing to mind," which seems analogous to the level of somaesthetic reflection (CP7.551, n.d.).
19. Recognizing that "feeling is subject to degrees" of consciousness, Peirce distinguishes between objective and subjective intensity. There is "objective intensity which distinguishes a loud sound from a faint sound" and "subjective intensity which distinguishes a lively

consciousness of a sound, from a dull consciousness of it." Although "the two kinds of intensity are apt to go together, yet it is possible for a person at the same time to recall the tick of a watch and the sound of a neighboring canon, and to have a livelier consciousness of the former than of the latter, without however remembering the latter [as] a fainter sound than the former" (CP7.555, c. 1893). Peirce's examples here unfortunately jumble together the sensations of present experiences of loudness with one's very different retrospective consciousness of those sensations, which are, by necessity, different as remembered feelings. A different example that avoids this confusion is contrasting the loud noise of a radio to the soft tap on one's door from an eagerly awaited guest. The sound of the tap may be objectively lower in intensity, but it has greater subjective intensity since attention is more intently directed toward it. This greater subjective, attentive intensity in the present can also explain how, later, the recalled idea of the tapping sound is clearer and more subjectively intense than the remembered radio noise.
20. Spinoza (1884, 131–132).
21. Peirce's experiments deployed two levels of "effort of attention" ("vigorous" and "very light effort") and demonstrated that "sensations that differed less, no matter how little, could still be discriminated just as well as sensations that differed more, if the effort of attention were greater, or if it were longer continued" (CP7.546, c. 1908).
22. The citation is from Robin 939. Peirce also speaks about achieving self-control through better mastery of habit formation and modification through attention both to consciousness and to an unconscious region of the occult in nature, mind, soul, or physiological basis that Peirce sees as ultimately continuous with consciousness (CP5.440, 1905).
23. For detailed study of this tension in James, see Shusterman (2008, 158–179).
24. For more detailed argument on this point, see Shusterman (2012, ch. 9).

References

Atkins, Richard Kenneth. 2016. *Peirce and the Conduct of Life*. Cambridge: Cambridge University Press.
Baumgarten, Alexander. 1988. *Theoretische Ästhetik: Die grundlengenden Abschnitte aus der "Aesthetica" (1750/58)*, trans. Hans Rudolf Schweizer. Hamburg, Germany: Meiner.
Brent, Joseph. 1993. *Charles Sanders Peirce: A Life*. Bloomington: Indiana University Press.
Dewey, John. 1987. *Art as Experience*. Carbondale: Southern Illinois University Press.
Hegel, Georg Wilhelm Friedrich. 1993. *Introductory Lectures on Aesthetics*, trans. Bernard Bosanquet. London: Penguin.
Ketner, Kenneth. 1998. *His Glassy Essence*. Nashville, TN: Vanderbilt University Press.
Merleau-Ponty, Maurice. 1962. *The Phenomenology of Perception*, trans. Colin Smith. London: Routledge.
Peirce, Charles S. 1931–1958. *The Collected Papers of Charles Sanders Peirce*. 8 vols. Vols. 1–6 edited by Charles Hartshorne and Paul Weiss. Vols. 7–8 edited by Arthur W. Burks. Cambridge, MA: Harvard University Press. (Referred to as CP.)
Peirce, Charles S. 1867. Manuscripts held at the Houghton Library of Harvard University, as identified in Richard Robin. *Annotated Catalogue of the Papers of Charles S. Peirce*. Amherst: University of Massachusetts Press. And in Richard Robin. 1971. "The Peirce Papers: A Supplementary Catalogue." *Transactions of the Charles S. Peirce Society* 7, no. 1 (Winter): 37–57. (Referred to as R.)

Peirce, Charles S. 1992–1998. *The Essential Peirce: Selected Philosophical Writings*. 2 vols. Vol. 1 edited by Nathan Houser and Christian Kloesel. Vol. 2 edited by the Peirce Edition Project. Bloomington, IN: Indiana University Press. (Referred to as EP.)

Shusterman, Richard. 1992. *Pragmatist Aesthetics: Living Beauty, Rethinking Art*. Oxford: Blackwell.

Shusterman, Richard. 1999. "Somaesthetics: A Disciplinary Proposal." *Journal of Aesthetics and Art Criticism* 57: 299–313.

Shusterman, Richard. 2008. *Body Consciousness: A Philosophy of Mindfulness and Somaesthetics*. Cambridge: Cambridge University Press.

Shusterman, Richard. 2012. *Thinking through the Body: Essays in Somaesthetics*. Cambridge: Cambridge University Press.

Shusterman, Richard. 2021. *Ars Erotica: Sex and Somaesthetics in the Classical Arts of Love*. Cambridge: Cambridge University Press.

Spinoza, Baruch. 1884. *Ethics*, in *The Chief Works of Benedict de Spinoza*, trans. Robert Harvey Monro Elwes, vol. 2. London: George Bell.

Weiss, Paul. 1934. *Dictionary of American Biography*. New York: Scribner.

CHAPTER 8

MORALITY AND ETHICS IN THE WORK OF CHARLES PEIRCE

JAMES JAKÓB LISZKA

1. INTRODUCTION

PEIRCE was a practicing scientist whose philosophical work was mostly on logic and scientific method. He came late to the study of ethics once he realized that it was essential for comprehending reasoning in its entirety. As he writes to William James: "It was not until after that [the Cambridge Lectures in 1898] that I obtained the proof that logic must be founded on ethics, of which it is a higher development. Even then, I was for some time so stupid as not to see that ethics rests in the same manner on a foundation of esthetics" (CP8.255, 1902). Logic is normative since it claims how people *ought to think*. It was then beholden to ethics, which studies what people *ought to do*. "Under the guidance of ethics," logic "is now a comparatively brilliant lens, showing much that was not discernible before" (CP2.198, 1902).

Peirce also seemed motivated to study ethics because of his worry about the instrumental use of science in the Gilded Age that threatened its purpose—the search for truth. By the late nineteenth century, science had allied with business and industry, especially in Peirce's own fields of chemistry and physics. He expresses this fear in a review of Karl Pearson's *The Grammar of Science*: "The worst feature of the present state of things is that the great majority of the members of many scientific societies, and a large part of others, are men whose chief interest in science is as a means of gaining money, and who have a contempt, or half-contempt, for pure science" (CP8.142, 1901). Peirce defends "pure science" in his spirited Cambridge Lectures from a few years earlier (RLT:105–122, 1898). In "The Century's Great Men in Science," for *The New York Evening Post* in 1900, Peirce praises them for their "devotion to the pursuit of truth for truth's sake" (VC:267) and is hopeful that the earlier age in which "knowledge was power" had become one where knowledge was pursued for its own sake (VC:274).

Peirce was also worried about the use of scientific theories to promote unsavory ethical theories such as social Darwinism. In "Evolutionary Love" in 1893, Peirce railed against this doctrine in favor of an intergenerational altruism—to do one's part for the sake of those to come, to fix what is broken now, improve it, while passing on what is best (CP6.289, 1893; CP7.87, 1902). Even earlier, Peirce saw science as an intergenerational, altruistic endeavor. "Logic is rooted in the social principle," connected to an "unlimited community of inquiry" (CP2.653, 1878). By the turn of the century, he amplified the importance of ethics in inquiry: "The most vital factors in the method of modern science have not been the following of this or that logical prescription—although these have had their value too," but "moral factors" (CP7.87, 1902).

The challenge in interpreting Peirce's ethical thought is its fragmentary nature. His effort at a systematic account in *The Minute Logic* in 1902 was never completed, and his presentation of the normative sciences in his Harvard Lectures of 1903 is rather enigmatic in parts. But a careful reading of his works can reveal a more coherent picture of his ethical thinking.

Based on the model of his more developed normative science of logic or semiotic, with its division of grammar, critic, and rhetoric, there is the basis for a parallel organization in the normative science of ethics—an ethics grammar, critic, and rhetoric. Just as semiotic grammar analyzes the nature of signs and sign agency, an ethics grammar analyzes the elements of ethical agency and conduct. Just as critic is concerned with the proper use of reasoning, so critical ethics would be concerned with ethical reasoning. Finally, just as semiotic rhetoric is about a proper community of inquiry, an ethical rhetoric would establish a basis for ethical communities (Liszka 2012, 51; 2019, 70–71).

2. Peirce's Moral Sentimentalism

For Peirce, morality is the development of habits under the direction of a culture that form through associations with negative feelings, manifested in conscience, in response to doing or not doing certain things (R892:1, n.d.). "Morality consists in the folklore of right conduct" (CP1.50, c. 1896).

Although Peirce thought a science of ethics and aesthetics was critical to his scholarly enterprise, he believed that these disciplines as they stood in his time were ill-suited to serve as a guide for the "conduct of life" or to be trusted in "vital matters"; nor were they up to disclosing a *summum bonum* (R602:10–11, 1906). Here, Peirce echoed the British moral sentimentalists, particularly Francis Hutcheson and Thomas Reid, that moral sentiments and moral sense were better guides for practical life than ethical theory (EP2:71, 1901).

In his Cambridge Lecture of 1898, "Philosophy and the Conduct of Life," he promotes a version that might be called conservative sentimentalism. He gave a preview five years earlier in "Evolutionary Love." There he defines it as "the doctrine that great respect should be paid to the natural judgments of the sensible heart" (CP6.292, 1893). By *conservatism*, Peirce means "to believe in thinking as you have been brought up to think" (CP1.666, 1898). By *sentimentalism*, Peirce means reliance on emotion and instinct.

The influence of Reid in his Cambridge Lectures is patent. Peirce later adopted his common-sense philosophy, flavored with his fallibilism, in what he called *critical common sense* (CP5.439, 1905). For Reid, reason was too nascent of a human ability to be trusted ([1788] 1969, 138–139). The moral instincts and sentiments are more reliable guides (145–161). Ethical theory is in a sorry state of disagreements (376–377). Whenever ethical theories and moral sentiments conflict, it is safer to stick with sentiments (387). Peirce echoes these same themes. In vital matters, reason should defer to sentiment and instinct (CP1.630, 1898; R436:34, 1898). Not only is the science of ethics useless for the conduct of life, it's downright dangerous. People should conduct their lives by their sentiments and instincts, not ethical theory (CP1.666–667, 1898).

Many scholars find the lecture perplexing since it apparently contradicts his pragmatism (Misak 2004, 164; Hookway 2002, 23, 224). The pragmatic maxim argues for a link between theory and practice (CP5.18, 1903). It's also inconsistent with themes in "The Fixation of Belief," where Peirce argues that science can play a social function in securing belief better than alternatives, particularly methods of authority—which his conservative sentimentalism seems to invoke (CP5.387, 1877). The lecture seems to fly in the face of his evolutionism, synechism, and agapism, all of which advocate progressive change for the better (CP6.303, 1893). For these reasons, some scholars think Peirce was being sarcastic or ironic here. However, he supports conservative sentimentalism in later years (CP8.158, 1901).

This apparent conflict between his moral sentimentalism and pragmatism is reconciled once his evolutionism, synechism, and fallibilism are considered (Liszka 2021, 43–45). Unlike the British moral sentimentalists, Peirce did not believe in a once-for-all set of moral instincts or common-sense beliefs (Atkins 2018, 76). Peirce argued that "instinct is capable of development and growth—though by a movement which is slow in the proportion in which it is vital." Sentiment arises from experience (CP1.648, 1898). Peirce thinks "sentiment lays no claim to infallibility" (CP1.661, 1898). He insists that "we are by no means to think that the utterances of this faculty [our heart and conscience] are infallible" (R434:15, 1902).

With this consideration, Peirce makes a distinction between good and bad conservatism. Bad conservatives tend to be infallibilists (CP1.151, c. 1897). "But morality, doctrinaire conservatist that it is, destroys its own vitality by resisting change, and positively insisting, This is eternally right: That is eternally wrong" (CP2.197, 1902). "Common sense corrects itself, improves its conclusions," and if "common sense improves; it does not, then, attain infallibility" (CP6.574, c. 1905). Just as Peirce called his version of Reid's common-sense philosophy *critical* common sense, he would have been better served by calling his sentimentalism *critical* sentimentalism.

Although the moral sentiments and common-sense prescriptions were wrought through evolution, Peirce argued that a Lamarckian type—based on the capacity to learn and pass on that learning—could accelerate Darwinian-type evolution (CP6.296–300, 1893). Peirce thought, then, that there were at least two paths through which evolution works itself out: through natural selection and through learning by inquiry. Inquiry can accelerate evolution. It will bring about truth and knowledge "most speedily" (CP1.615, 1903). There was certainly hope, then, that an ethical science, pursued with the right methodologies, could accelerate moral evolution.

3. The Normative Science of Ethics

Peirce's complaint was not that ethics could never become useful for the conduct of life, but that it did not employ genuine scientific methodology. It was the product of "seminarians" who often rationalized the dominant norms of their culture, engaging in "sham" reasoning (RLT:107–108, 1898; R893:2, n.d.; CP1.57, c. 1896; Houser 2010, 3). It needed to forego its "old ways" in favor of "the new world created by science" (CP5.513, c. 1905). Cornelis de Waal notes that if the science of ethics is useless for the conduct of life, then the normative science of ethics was useless for logic (2012, 87).

Peirce directly contradicts his claims in the Cambridge Lectures later on. He thinks "the study [of theoretical ethics] is more or less favorable to right living" (CP1.600, 1903). He bemoans the fact that ethics is not more widely used in "law, jurisprudence and sociology," "diplomacy and economics" (CP1.251, 1902). In his Lowell Lectures, he thinks that the science of ethics "has been a deep study from the dawn of history" and that "there is no more encouraging chapter of history than that one recounts the gradual improvement of the science of ethics," although he cautions that the "fully satisfactory solution of the problem is still hidden from us" (R453:14, 1903).

With this attitude, Peirce set about to develop a science of ethics. His evolving classifications of the sciences show him moving from thinking of ethics as just a practical science, to part of psychology, to a normative science (Kent 1987, 94, 109–110). This culminates with logic, understood as a normative science, the study of how people ought to reason, and dependent on ethics as a study of how people ought to conduct themselves (CP8.255, 1902). Ethics, in turn, is dependent on aesthetics, concerned with what makes an end admirable and worthy of pursuit (PPM:118, 1903). In a draft of his Harvard Lectures of 1903, he gives one of his most cogent accounts of these studies: "Normative science ought to examine all questions relating to the possible consistent ends of phenomena. Not merely what the ends are and what are the conditions of conformity to those ends, or their mere quantity of goodness and badness, but also, the diversity in the different paths by which such ends may be pursued, and the different stadia in those paths; as well as the different ways in which the ends may be missed" (R311:9, 1903). In other words, the normative sciences are engaged in practical reasoning, standardly expressed as the logic of means and ends (Audi 2006).

In the drafts of both *The Minute Logic* and the Harvard Lectures of 1903, Peirce sorts out the differences in the roles of ethics and aesthetics. Both are concerned with the ends, but from different aspects. In *The Minute Logic*, ethics is subdivided into *pure ethics*, as "the science of aims" (Feibleman 1943, 100; Potter 1967, 35). It is a "theatre of discussion" for "the gradual development of a distinct recognition of a satisfactory aim" (CP4.243, 1902). It answers the question "What is good?" (CP1.577, 1902). Whereas ethics is concerned with what ends people *ought to* pursue, aesthetics is concerned with what ends people would admire and *want to* pursue (CP2.199, 1902).

For this reason, Peirce adopts Plato's and Aristotle's notion of *to kalon*, as an alternative to 'beauty' as the subject of aesthetics. For the Greeks, *to kalon* connoted the nobility of design of things. The sum of Plato's dialogs characterize *to kalon* as a well-ordered form designed to fulfill a beneficial purpose (1961a, 64e–65a; 1961b, 506e; Barney 2010, 364–365; Grube 1927, 273–274; Hoerber 1964). Thus, Peirce envisions a different role for aesthetics than a study of beauty and art (R602:11, 1906).

In the Harvard Lectures, Peirce refines the function of ethics in terms of not only what ends ought to be pursued, but also the right way to attain them (PPM:212, 1903). Thus, ethics has at least two functions: to determine what ends ought to be pursued and the righteous means to attain them. In 1906, he makes a similar distinction between ethics proper, as the study of ends, and *practics* as the study of standards of conduct that will conform to those ends and distinguish the "useful" from the "pernicious" (EP2:379).

4. The Grammar of Ethics

Just as semiotic grammar is concerned with the elements of signs and sign agency, Peirce addresses some of the elements of moral agency and ethical conduct. He assumes moral agents have some degree of voluntariness, self-control (CP1.592, 1903). Without it, blaming or praising is "not less ridiculous than it would be to pronounce the growth of your hair to be morally good or bad" (CP5.109, 1903). Peirce also assumes that voluntary conduct is generally goal-seeking and purposive, and self-control is necessary for it. "All direction toward an end or good supposes self-control" (R283:84, 1905). Thus, self-control "is precisely that that gives room for an ought-to-be of conduct, I mean Morality" (CP4.540, *c.* 1902).

The normative sciences are concerned with normativity—what people *ought* to do. Logic is concerned with how people ought to reason; ethics, how they should act; and aesthetics with what ends are admirable to pursue (CP1.186, 1903; CP1.191, 1903). Normativity is tied to ends or purposes: "the word "ought" has no meaning except relatively to an end" (CP5.594, 1898; CP7.186, 1901). Without an end there is no way to measure what is done, compared with what ought to be. As Thomas Short argues, alternatives such as better or worse, good or bad apply whenever there is a purpose, since it can be determined whether some action has met it or not (2007, 154).

Self-control is the ability to correct conduct toward an end. It distinguishes purposive from mechanical action. The latter is a causal relation between action and result, but purposive action is rational or *reasonable* in the sense that such agents will adjust means to attain ends. "The essence of rationality lies in the fact that the rational being will act so, as to attain certain ends. Prevent his doing so in one way, and he will act in some utterly different way which will produce the same result" (CP2.66, 1902). The possibility of self-correction, reasonableness, allows for change, growth, and adaptation.

Peirce argues that purposive conduct is a triadic relation among three basic elements, *desire for an end, deliberation about the means* to that end, and the *intention to act* on what is deliberated: "The execution of a purpose has at least three very distinct parts. . . . the first is the working out of the desire itself; the second is the devising of a course of procedure by which the means . . . can be applied to the attainment of the desire; and the third is the energetic performance of the acts that this scheme requires" (R602:9, 1906).

In one example, opening a window in order to cool the room is the result of a triadic relation among the desire for an end (cooling the room), a belief that opening the window will likely do so, and an intention to open the window for that reason (NEM4:254, 1904). The owner believes that commanding the dog to fetch a book will attain the owner's end and intentionally commands the dog so, but the intention of the dog is to fetch the book in order to please the owner (CP2.86, 1902). If a man believes that anthracite coal is the best fuel to heat his house, then that man will on the right occasion, with right circumstances, intentionally act on that belief (CP5.538, c. 1902). These actions are the result of a triadic relation among the three elements of purposive action, proven by the fact that such actions cannot be fully explained with the absence of one or more of these elements (Liszka 2021, 75).

Desire, practical belief, and intention are each analyzed in detail by Peirce. Desires for ends are indeterminate in three aspects (CP1.205, 1902). They are *general* in that people initially desire "some kind of thing or event" (CP1.205, 1902; CP1.341, 1894). Typically, the end desired is ill-defined but becomes more specified in the process of deliberation about its means (CP1.205, 1902). Specification reduces the *vagueness* of the end (CP1.206, 1902). The third source of indeterminacy is its *longitude*. Further specification of an end is constrained by other desirable ends. A larger, attractive, and powerful lamp might be perfect for reading, but the cost would be excessive (CP1.207, 1902).

Peirce's account of desire conflicts with David Hume's thesis that desires can have no representational content, a claim key to moral internalism ([1739] 1978, 415). Desire for an indeterminate end may influence, but specification of ends modulates motivation. This is consonant with Thomas Nagel's distinction between motivated and unmotivated desires. The latter, like hunger or thirst, happen without much cognitive mediation. But to the extent that desires are influenced or changed by the deliberation about ends and means, then they are motivated (Nagel 1978, 29).

The second element of purposive action is a belief about what is likely to attain the desired end. Peirce thought pragmatism "scarce more than a corollary" to Alexander Bain's theory of belief (CP5.12, 1906). Bain claimed, "Belief is preparedness to act, for a given end, in a given way" (1889, 508). This "practical belief" is the result of deliberation about means to the desired end. "A practical belief is what a man proposes to go upon. A decision is more or less pressing. What ought it to be? That must depend upon what the purpose of his action is" (CP7.185, 1901). A practical belief engenders "a habit of deliberate behavior," directed "to one's present purpose" (CP5.538, *c.* 1902; CP5.491, *c.* 1906).

Practical beliefs are the outcome of a pragmatic maxim. His earliest formulation in "How to Make Our Ideas Clear" commands thinkers to "consider what effects, that might conceivably have practical bearings, we conceive the object of our conception to have. Then, our conception of these effects is the whole of our conception of the object" (CP5.402, 1878). In his standard example, the meaning of scratch-hard is clarified best by outlaying its observable, practical effects. If a diamond is scratch-hard, then it should scratch rather than be scratched by other materials. Peirce soon realized that the pragmatic maxim had implications not only about meaning but also about truth and its relation to human purposes: "Every proposition has its practical aspect. If it means anything it will, on some possible occasion, determine the conduct of the person who accepts it" (NEM4:291, 1902).

The pragmatic maxim has two important implications. It showed, first, that theoretical claims are transposable into practical ones. If diamonds are scratch-hard, then they would be expected to scratch glass and other materials. If so, it is transposable to a practical claim: If one desires to cut glass, then use a diamond cutter. As Peirce says, "every theoretical belief is, at least indirectly, a practical belief" and will "have some possible bearing upon practice" (CP5.539, *c.* 1902). Second, the pragmatic maxim showed that the truth of the practical claim depended on the truth of the corresponding empirical or theoretical claim.

If Peirce follows Bain, then he would be committed to a more externalist account of moral motivation, against Hume's internalist claim that beliefs cannot influence desires and desires are the only motivators (Hume [1739] 1978, 413, 415, 458). Although desires for an end must be present, beliefs about the means or the end may modulate motivation. Bain (1865) argues, for example, that the desire to quench thirst does not motivate a person to drink a cup of water. It is the belief that this action would satisfy one's thirst that motivates people to act so (Bain 1865, 525), an argument similar to Nagel's (1970, 33).

The third element of purposive conduct is the intention to act on practical beliefs. Aristotle argues that intention is neither part of deliberation nor should it be confused with desire for an end (1984, 1111b5–30). Intention, for Peirce, is wrapped up in self-control. Intentions can be "strengthened" as beliefs about "rules of conduct" are more rigidly "adopted" (R1132:11, n.d.). This leads to the formation of a resolve" when an "occasion is going to arise" (CP8.320, 1906; R1132:11, n.d.). A resolution "is of the nature of a plan." It is an "act of stamping with approval, "endorsing" as one's own, an imaginary line of conduct so that it shall give a general shape to our actual future conduct" (CP5.538, *c.* 1902). Because it is "more or less general ... it does not necessarily influence ... conduct" (R1132:12, n.d.) It is at this point there is a further process whereby the plan "is converted into a *determination*, by which I mean a really efficient agency, such that if one knows what its special character is one can forecast the man's conduct on the anticipated occasion" (R1132:12, n.d.).

In general, "this operation of self-control is a process in which logical sequence is converted into mechanical sequence or something of the sort" (CP8.320, 1906).

Peirce argues similarly to Michael Bratman. Although desires can influence conduct, intentions are conduct-controlling (Bratman 1999, 16). Intentions are mental states distinct from desires and beliefs (20). Internalist models of human motivation attempt to reduce intention to some combination of beliefs and desires, but Bratman argues intention is an irreducible element of human conduct (18).

All in all, Peirce advocates a triadic belief–desire–intention model of human conduct that falls somewhere between internalism and externalism. The triadic interrelation of all three is needed in order to fully explain purposive conduct. With internalism, desires for the end are necessary but, with externalism, desires can be modulated by deliberation about ends and means. Desires are influencers in motivation but intentions are the controlling aspects of conduct, the core of self-control.

5. Ethical Reasoning, Moral Realism, and Moral Truth

If there is a parallel to the organization of the science of ethics with the normative science of logic or semiotic, then the second branch should be about ethical reasoning. Indeed, Peirce thinks that the parallel between logical reasoning as "the theory of the conditions of truth" (CP2.93, 1902) and ethical reasoning about *moral* truth is "almost exact" (CP1.608, 1903).

The core of ethical reasoning for Peirce is what is standardly called practical reasoning. It falls out of Peirce's triadic desire–belief–intention model of purposive conduct and the pragmatic maxim (CP5.538, 1902). Practical reasoning is about the means by which ends are likely to be attained (CP5.491, c. 1906). But practical reasoning is also guided by an implicit norm, which, in Peirce's language, is to do "what is most conducive to an end" (CP5.594, 1898), the core of reasonableness. People ought to do what is likely to attain their ends. "Belief," Peirce claims, "consists mainly in being deliberately prepared to adopt the formula believed in as the guide to action." As such, "the proposition believed in can itself be nothing but a maxim of conduct" (CP5.27, 1903).

In a later formulation of the pragmatic maxim, Peirce articulates it as essentially what Kant called a hypothetical or "pragmatic" maxim ([1785] 1959, 31–32n4): "Pragmatism is the principle that every theoretical judgment expressible in a sentence in the indicative mood is a confused form of thought whose only meaning, if it has any, lies in its tendency to enforce a corresponding practical maxim expressible as a conditional sentence having its apodosis in the imperative mood" (CP5.18, 1903). In *The Foundations of the Metaphysics of Morals*, "pragmatic" or hypothetical imperatives are essentially prudential rules of how best to attain ends (Kant [1785] 1959, 31–32n4)—in other words, practical reasoning. Kant defines it as a form of prudence that "instructs the world how it could provide for its interest better than . . . as has been done in the past" ([1785] 1959, 34n6), a similar account in Kant's *Anthropology from a Pragmatic Point of View* ([1798]

1978, 3–4). This is why Peirce is careful to distinguish the "pragmatic" from the "practical" in Kant's sense of the terms: "For one who had learned philosophy out of Kant … *praktisch* and *pragmatisch* were as far apart as the two poles, the former belonging in a region of thought where no mind of the experimentalist type can ever make sure of solid ground under his feet, the latter expressing relation to some definite human purpose" (CP5.412, 1905). For Kant, *praktisch* has to do with practical reason as an aspect of the more ethereal realm of moral law. "The most striking feature of the new theory [of pragmatism]," Peirce notes, "was its recognition of an inseparable connection between rational cognition and rational purpose; and that consideration it was which determined the preference for the name *pragmatism*" (CP5.412, 1905).

However, Peirce had to realize that if hypothetical imperatives and practical reasoning were the basis of ethical reasoning, this led to a subjectivism and amoral instrumentalism. The pragmatic maxim connected theory and practice to the ends of conduct, but it did not specify which ends are good or the righteous means to attain them. He was aware that without the guidance of ethics, reasoning could be used for any purpose, good or ill. "A man," Peirce says, "might be ever so great a rogue without being the worse reasoner for that" (R432:6, 1902).

Kant thought he had solved the moral instrumentalism of hypothetical or pragmatic imperatives by arguing for categorical imperatives. These demonstrated duties that were inherently right to do independent of the consideration of any ends or consequences. However, Peirce was doubtful about the validity of the categorical imperative. He did not think the truth of moral claims could be established by a formal contradiction or reductio ad absurdum, nor did he have much faith in transcendental arguments (CP5.4, 1902; CP2.114, c. 1902). Instead, Peirce favored a "synthetical" process of testing rooted in experience, evolving from experiments of life that set constraints on norms and ideals (CP5.4, 1902).

Peirce had to find a way to avoid the moral pitfalls of practical reasoning without resorting to the formalism and transcendentalism of Kant. He thought a science of ends might do the trick. An ultimate end might be the key. Rather than a Kantian approach to ethics, Peirce seemed to adopt an Aristotelian one. For Aristotle, all human activity aimed at the end of flourishing (*eudaimonia*), something which ordered all other ends. Although he did not agree with Aristotle's candidate for the highest end, Peirce appears to have adopted the same strategy.

Practical reasoning, if it is to become ethical, must come closer to what Aristotle called *phronesis*, "the disposition with true reason and ability for actions concerning human goods" (1984, 1140b20–21). Such reasoning implicitly appeals to three norms; truth, righteousness, and goodness. What ends are good to pursue? What are the right means to attain them? Which among righteous means will likely attain them? "Ethics," Peirce says is "right action" that is in "conformity" to ends that people are "prepared deliberately to adopt as *ultimate*" (CP5.130, 1903).

The normative sciences would each take up these tasks: aesthetics with identifying those ends that can be counted as ultimate and inherently admirable; ethics with which among admirable ends are good to pursue, and the righteous constraints on their means; logic, understood as truth-apt methodology, with what will likely achieve those ends (CP1.573, 1906; CP1.191, 1903). "It is only after the moralist has shown us what is our ultimate aim, that the logician can tell how we ought to think in order to conform to that end" (CP8.158n3, 1901). This, in design, transforms practical reasoning from amoral instrumentalism to something more like a scientific version of *phronesis*. It entails an ethical project—the pursuit of good ends by righteous means. Like Aristotle, the crucial matter for Peirce was to determine an ultimate end, a *summum bonum*, something that would be an ordering principle for all worthy ends. Ends that serve the ultimate end ought to be pursued and those that do not, ought not.

If this is Peirce's ethical project, then how is it known which norms are morally true and which ends good? Peirce is a realist, and it can be assumed a moral realist (Mayorga 2012). A central thesis of moral realism is that there are moral truths that can be determined objectively, independent of what people may happen to believe or what cultures happen to adopt. Peirce certainly objects to moral subjectivism: "It is true that the majority of writers on ethics in the past have made the root of morals subjective: but the best opinion is very plainly moving in the opposite direction" (CP2.156, 1902; R451:3–4, 1903). He certainly recognizes that there is ethical truth (CP5.570, 1906) and that "the same definitions [of positive scientific truth] equally hold in the normative sciences" (CP5.566, 1901). Peirce also adheres to the stance-independence of all types of truth claims (CP5.384, 1877). "The real is that which is not whatever we happen to think it, but is unaffected by what we may think of it" (CP8.12, 1871).

Peirce argues for a rather novel, so-called convergence theory of truth. True claims would be those that were the result of inquiries rightly done, sufficiently long, so that further inquiries find little or no reason to doubt such claims. A true claim is one toward which inquiries over time tend to converge (CP5.407, 1878; CP2.781, 1902). This would also apply to moral truths: "conduct controlled by ethical reason tends toward fixing certain habits of conduct" (CP5.430, 1905), so that "good morals" would "come to be approved if studies of right behavior were carried sufficiently far" (R673:12, c. 1911).

There are ways to extrapolate Peirce's three senses of convergence as progressive approximation over time, convergence of opinion, and independent discovery, to the moral sphere (Liszka 2019, 2021, 112–123). However, both David Wiggins and Philip Kitcher adopt versions of the convergence theory of truth to moral truths that capture some of this. Wiggins claims as one mark of moral truth that if x is true, then, "if conditions are fully hospitable to inquiry, those who understand x will tend to converge upon x, and the best explanation of this convergence will be inconsistent with the denial of x" (2006, 360). Kitcher argues that "descriptive counterparts of ethical rules count as true just in case those rules would be adopted in ethical codes as the result of progressive transitions and would be retained through an indefinite sequence of further progressive transitions" (2011, 246). A true norm would be one that approximates the limits of its improvability. Changes would only be regressive.

In general, Peirce argues, "if . . . the future development of man's moral nature will only lead to a firmer satisfaction with the described ideal, the doctrine is true" (CP5.566, 1906). Convergence would demonstrate what is *generalizable* in the way of belief, conduct, and sentiment (CP7.187, 1901). It shows which norms of conduct can have widespread adherence and consistently work with the constraints of lived experience. Unlike the formal, universalizability test of the categorical imperative, Peirce argues for a test of generalizability in the course of experiments of living over time (CP5.133, 1903; PPM:214).

6. Ethical Communities

If moral truths are the result of inquiries, then they depend on proper inquiry, a matter for ethical rhetoric. Peirce recognized early on that inquiries not only need a good method, but also require an intergenerational, cooperative effort—a *community* of inquiry bound by certain norms, virtues, and sentiments (CP7.87, 1902). Moreover, as Peirce argues in "The Fixation of Belief," the norms of inquiry can serve as a model for the norms of a community that aims at truth, moral or otherwise.

As to sentiments, inquirers must be fueled by an intergenerational altruism—an "evolutionary love"—to do one's part for those to come, to correct errors while passing on what is better (CP6.289, 1893; CP7.87, 1902). Good inquirers have certain virtues, honesty above all, fair-mindedness in considering evidence, the courage to advocate for claims against received views, and the humility to change beliefs when warranted (CP8.136, 1901; CP2.82, 1902; CP1.49, 1903). These sentiments and virtues are the hallmark of reasonable people and make it more likely for inquirers to self-correct.

Communities of inquiry also have implicit norms of conduct (Robin 1964, 273–274). In "The Fixation of Belief," true beliefs are thwarted if people hold them tenaciously despite evidence; or if imposed by authority, coercion or force; or if people believe merely from popular opinion (CP5.378; CP5.380; CP5.383, all 1877).

Thomas Short (2012) thinks there is a circularity here. Inquiry requires certain norms to attain its end of truth, so a normative science must presuppose these norms in its inquiry about norms (Short 2012, 311). Thinkers sympathetic to Peirce have attempted to resolve this circularity in three different ways. Karl-Otto Apel (1980) and the early Jürgen Habermas (1990) take a Kantian approach and argue that these norms are necessary presuppositions for any inquiry. As their discourse ethics argues, inquirers who seek consensus about what is true and right, versus those who aim at strategic manipulation, must presuppose certain norms. These include openness to inquiry, equality of roles in the give and take of debate, lack of coercion or force to press a claim, or capricious exclusion of inquirers. However, as noted, Peirce does not endorse transcendental approaches, a position that Cheryl Misak also takes (CP2.113, 1902; Misak 2000, 35ff.).

Misak suggests a second strategy employing a hypothetical imperative. Since adopting these norms of inquiry are more likely to lead to truth, then to the extent that one wants "beliefs which will withstand the force of experience," then one should adopt these norms (Misak 2000, 106–107). However, hypothetical imperatives are conditional on whether the end is desired and do not have the normative force that would be needed to break the circularity Short notes.

There is a third approach, embryonic in Peirce, also championed by Misak (2000), and explicit in Robert Brandom's (1994) theory of normative pragmatics. Speech practices, such as making assertions, involve commitments to the norms concerning how it is correct to use speech and what consequences such performances entail (Brandom 1994, xiii). Brandom argues: "The attitude of taking-true is just that of acknowledging an assertional commitment" (1994, 202). Peirce has a similar claim: "But to assert a proposition is to make oneself responsible for its truth" (CP5.543, *c*. 1902), and likens it to taking a binding oath (CP2.252, *c*. 1897; CP5.30, 1903; Boyd 2016).

There is a fourth strategy based on the convergence theory of truth. The better practices of inquiry have converged precisely toward these norms over time. In other words, inquiry itself has worked out the norms needed to successfully seek true claims, empirical or moral. The practice of science is an exemplary form of inquiry that has in fact come to be the master science, successful in delivering the epistemological goods, in part, due to the adherence of these norms. Violation of these norms only retards scientific progress.

7. ENDS

Peirce's ethical project requires a reckoning of good ends, especially a *summum bonum*, a division of labor between the normative science of ethics and aesthetics: A worthy end must be both aesthetically and ethically good. Peirce aligned himself with Friedrich Schiller, who disagreed with Kant that goodness is pursued out of the command and respect of a reasoned moral law alone. Morality is a matter of a "living shape," a balance of sentiment and reason (Schiller [1795] 1965, 48, 76).

Peirce's tentative account of aesthetic goodness in the Harvard Lectures suggests it has to do with design, the arrangement of parts, such that its totality produces a certain quality (PPM:213, 1903). But, he notes, this would be just as true of base and disgusting designs as of those that are noble and admirable. Peirce realizes that such an account of aesthetic goodness makes it indifferent to the goodness of an end (PPM:213–214).

Assuming Peirce reads Plato and Aristotle reasonably, adopting the Greek notion of *to kalon* instead of *beauty* would suggest their solution to this problem. Plato and Aristotle argue that whatever is *kalos* is also morally good (Aristotle 1941b, 1366a34–35; Hoerber 1964, 151–152). Generally, Plato characterizes it as something that is well ordered to fit a beneficial end (1961a, 64e–65a; 1961b, 506e; 1961c, 296c; Barney 2010, 364–65; Grube 1927, 272). A well-designed soup spoon is as *kalos* as a well-ordered republic (Barney 2010, 365). For example, Plato argues in *The Republic* that all the known musical modes are *harmonia* and well designed to produce certain emotions, but the Ionian and Lydian produce ones not befitting the guardians of his republic (1961d, 398d–e). Aristotle argues in *The Politics* that the end of government is the common good or justice

(1941a, 1282b15). Monarchies, aristocracies, and constitutional republics are designed to produce this end but by different means. In contrast, tyrannies, oligarchies, and democracies are "perversions" of this end and serve the end of power for the governors instead (1279a30). The virtues, on the one hand, are well designed for their end, flourishing. They hit the golden mean. Vices, on the other hand, are excessive or defective in this regard (Aristotle 1984, 1106a14–b35). For Aristotle, someone *kalos k'agathos* is admirable and noble because that person has virtuous character and aims at higher goods (1941b, 1367b35–39). If Peirce follows the lead of Aristotle and Plato, he must show that an end is both aesthetically and ethically good. As Peirce writes in his application to the Carnegie Endowment, aesthetics answers the question of "what it is that we would deliberately pronounce to be *kalon k'agathon*" (RL75:232draftD, 1902).

In *The Minute Logic*, Peirce devotes a chapter on ethics and proposes another on aesthetics (CP2.197, 1902). He intends to analyze twenty-eight different candidates for the *summum bonum*, the job he assigns to pure ethics (CP1.581, 1902; R434:28draftB, 1902). He never completes the task. The twenty-eight ends were developed earlier, prompted by reviews of books by Frank Thilly and Karl Pearson (CN2:249–250, 1900; R1429, 1900; CP8.132, 1901; R1434, 1901).

Peirce develops a classification of ends based on the history of such efforts. There are three broad categories so proposed: hedonistic, as represented by the Epicurean and utilitarian traditions; contractualist, which focus on the stability of society, exemplified by Thomas Hobbes, John Locke, and the British sentimentalists; and in terms of "law," "general ideal," or "rationalization of the universe," in the Stoic, natural law, and Kantian traditions (R1429:7, 1900).

Based on his phenomenological categories of firstness (qualities of feeling), secondness (experiential fact), and thirdness (generalized patterns), these can be combined such that seconds can determine firsts, and thirds can determine seconds and firsts. For example, the firstness of hedonism would be the end of pursuing immediate pleasures—satisfactions of the moment (CP1.582, 1902). The thirdness of the end of pleasure would be some generalizable rule, like utilitarianism—the greatest pleasure for the greatest number (R1429:14, 1900). These can be combined further, for example, a third of the second of the first, until one reaches the twenty-eight ends (Liszka 2021, 216–217). Peirce then fills in the content of these formally derived ends.

The twenty-eight ends are organized in diagrams in drafts of the Pearson review (R1434draftC, after7, 1901). For example, one category of organization is the degree of objectivity in the end. Subjectively determined ends, like immediate pleasures, are at one end of the spectrum; intersubjectively determined ends, such as social norms, in the middle; and reason-determined ends at the other end. The categories are too sketchy to understand completely, but it does show that Peirce had some organizing principles in mind (Liszka 2021, 213–216).

Peirce lists these ends in the Pearson review, but they are not well explained (CP8.138, 1901). The earlier 1900 classifications are more understandable. They suggest three general ends: the greatest pleasure for the greatest number, peaceable and prosperous communities, and a third, interesting general end: "to further the realization of an ideal not definable in advance ... to realize itself in the long run" (R1429:14, 1900). These are certainly admirable ends that would be hard-pressed to gainsay: A stable, peaceable society that maximizes pleasures of its members and minimizes conflict, so designed as to press on inquiries into what ought to be its highest ends. It's clear that Peirce considers the last the highest end, but he says nothing that precludes thinking of these hierarchically. After all inquiries would do best in a community that is prosperous and at peace and where its members live relatively comfortable lives.

The last of the three general ends, the pursuit of a final end not known in advance, is further elaborated in the classifications associated with the Pearson review. There Peirce clarified that the third ideal is a "process," presumably one that leads to growth and improvement (CP8.138, 1901). It's nicely expressed in his Lowell Lectures: "When these ideas of progress and growth have themselves grown up ... how can we be expected to allow the assumption pass that the admirable in itself is any stationary result? ... Reason always looks forward to an endless future and expects endlessly to improve its results" (CP1.614, 1903). As Beverly Kent comments, Peirce "can now adopt an end that will always anticipate an improvement in its results" (1976, 270). Peirce expresses here the essentials of a meliorist ethic: the highest end is to improve on what is (Bergman 2012). Peirce subdivides these processes into the development of sentiments, the evolution of the world of experience, and the development of the reasonable itself (R1434:6, 1901; CP8.138, 1901). This suggests a melioristic ethic that comprehends all three: a community designed to improve sentiment, the experience of living together—sociality and solidarity—and increasing reasonableness in the search for ultimate ends.

However, Peirce makes it clear that end of reasonableness is the highest end: "the only desirable object which is quite satisfactory in itself without any ulterior reason for desiring it, is the reasonable itself" (CP8.140, 1901). He had declared it so earlier in 1899 (CN2:220–221), and continues to do so afterward (CP5.3, 1902; CP1.615, 1903; CP5.433, 1905).

This requires a better understanding of reasonableness. Peirce defines it sparingly, describing it as an evolutionary process that tends toward what is generalizable in experience: "Almost everybody will now agree that the ultimate good lies in the evolutionary process in some way." It is something that is "general or continuous," related to his synechism. It is "founded on the notion that the coalescence, the becoming continuous, the becoming governed by laws, the becoming instinct with general ideas, are but phases of one and the same process of the growth of reasonableness" (CP5.4, 1902). "Evolution," as Peirce writes, "means nothing but growth in the widest sense of the word" (CP1.174, c. 1987). Here, Peirce comes close to John Dewey's claim that "growth itself is the only moral 'end'" (Dewey, 2008; MW12, 180–181). A critical feature of growth is "diversification" (CP1.174, c. 1897); another aspect is the design of diversity into a "rationalized variety" (CP6.101, 1903). This is certainly true of the tree of life but is also exemplified in the architectonic of the sciences, diagrammed by Peirce's various classifications. As knowledge grows, there is more diversification of disciplines but, at the same time, they become organized into a coherent system that progresses knowledge. It recalls Peirce's definition of the aesthetic, understood as a certain design of parts in a whole conducive to its end that engenders a certain quality.

This suggests that that which can become generalizable is a mark of reasonableness. "Generalization," Peirce writes, is "the spilling out of continuous systems, in thought, in sentiment, in deed." It is "the true end of life" (NEM4:346, 1898). Something is generalizable that binds together parts into a whole and makes an order of them that continues its growth (Parker 1998, 132). As Peirce expresses it: "to bind together ideas, to bind together facts, to bind together knowledge, to bind together sentiment, to bind together the purposes of men, to bind together industry, to bind together great works, to bind together power, to bind together nations into great natural, living, and enduring systems" (NEM4:346, 1898). It is a matter of "trying to make our arbitrariness conform" to an "order of things" (NEM4:346, 1898). As Kelly Parker interprets it, "the arbitrary, irrational, destructive aspects of the individual components are 'ground off' in the evolution of reasonableness, while healthy growth, evolution toward greater harmony and rationality, are promoted" (1998, 132). That which cannot be generalized in experience languishes, falls apart; that which can be persists and grows, just as erroneous beliefs eventually fall out of the practice of inquiry. Despite the "perversity" that can happen for generations (CP5.408, 1878), Peirce thought progress inevitable. Despite the troubled nineteenth century, Peirce believed this binding of thought, sentiment, and purpose, initiated by earlier generations, now passed "into a second and more advanced stage of achievement" (NEM4:346, 1898).

If processes tend toward a growth that weeds out that which is not capable of generalization, then self-correction would be a second feature of reasonableness. This is certainly exemplified in science that adheres to norms and efficient methods of self-correction and advances knowledge by means of rejecting erroneous hypotheses (CP5.575, 1898; CP5.591, 1898; CP2.769, c. 1905). Peirce also connects learning with growth, a process by which new information is acquired and false beliefs are discarded (CP6.301, 1893).

The end is to make reasonableness "concrete" (CP5.3, 1902), to have it "actually governing events" (CP1.615, 1903; Parker 1998, 132). "The *summum bonum*" does not "consist in action," but consists "in that process of evolution whereby the existent comes more and more to embody those generals which were just now said to be *destined*, which is what we strive to express in calling them *reasonable*" (CP5.433, 1905; Parker 1998, 132).

8. Conclusion

Around the turn of the twentieth century, having witnessed the effects of the marriage of science and industry, Peirce realized that logic and scientific reasoning needed the guidance of ethics. Peirce also realized that his pragmatic maxim was in fact a formula that encouraged this transposition of scientific theory to practice. Peirce recognized it essentially as a version of Kant's hypothetical or pragmatic imperative. As a consequence, he had to resolve its rather instrumental and amoral character. Rather than employing

Kant's strategy to use categorical imperatives as a moral test of hypothetical ones, he adopted Aristotle's approach—to identify a highest end so that any means or ends conducive to that highest end would serve such a function.

As Peirce's grammar of ethics makes clear, human beings are purposive agents and have the self-control to direct their conduct toward ends and correct that conduct when those ends are not attained (R448:22, 1903; CP5.160, 1903). To be reasonable is to self-correct toward an end (CP2.66, 1902). But it must also mean correcting means and ends. Self-correction, as the core of reasonableness, makes progress possible and is key to his melioristic ethic. To be *unreasonable*, as his well-known article, "The Fixation of Belief," argues is to refuse to change, alter, or correct beliefs when the weight of experience and evidence dictates, or to rely unreflectively on authority (CP5.377–384, 1877). Reasonableness is an ultimate end because it is the process itself of correcting toward something better.

Understanding reasonableness in this way solves two anomalies. If the highest end is characterized by Peirce as "the realization of an ideal not definable in advance" and "in the long run" (R1429:14, 1900), then how can he declare reasonableness to be the highest end ahead of such a process of inquiry? Since inquiry is needed to disclose such an ideal and inquiry is a process of self-correction, and since reasonableness is, in the main, self-correction, then it is implicit in the highest end.

However, this creates a second anomaly. Typically, it is the result of the process that would be counted as the end rather than the process itself as a means to that end. But if improvement is understood as an ongoing process, then this might resolve the anomaly.

One additional boon is that if the process is primarily a process of inquiry then inquiry, in its best form, already has implicit sentiments, virtues, and norms that can, in the very least, guide the process of self-correction provisionally. Reasonableness is not only a feature of inquirers but also of the practice of inquiry as well.

If Peirce is influenced by Schiller, then it can be speculated that concrete reasonableness is something akin to his notion of "living shape." It is the way in which people and practices settle into a way of working in the world, a design to things that is loved, admired, continued, and reproduced for the very reason that it makes things better. If reasonableness is the end, then communities, practices, and institutions must have a design conducive to self-correction and geared toward improvement.

References

Apel, Karl-Otto. 1980. "The a Priori of the Communication Community and the Foundation of Ethics." In *Towards a Transformation of Philosophy*, translated by Glyn Adey and David Frisby, 225–300. London: Routledge & Kegan Paul.

Aristotle. 1941a. *Politics*. In *The Basic Works of Aristotle*, edited by R. McKeon, translated by W. Roberts, 1127–1324. New York: Random House.

Aristotle. 1941b. *Rhetoric*. In *The Basic Works of Aristotle*, edited by R. McKeon, translated by W. Roberts, 1325–1454. New York: Random House.

Aristotle. 1984. *Nicomachean Ethics*. Translated by Hippocrates Apostle. Grinnell, IA: Peripatetic Press.

Atkins, Richard. 2018. *Peirce and the Conduct of Life*. Cambridge: Cambridge University Press.
Audi, Robert. 2006. *Practical Reasoning and Ethical Decision*. New York: Routledge.
Bain, Alexander. 1865. *The Emotions and the Will* (2nd ed.). London: Longmans, Green.
Bain, Alexander. 1889. *Logic: Deductive and Inductive*. London: Appleton.
Barney, Rachel. 2010. "Notes on Plato on *To Kalon* and the Good." *Classical Philology* 105, no. 4: 363–377.
Bergman, Mats. 2012. "Improving Our Habits: Peirce and Meliorism." In *The Normative Thought of Charles S. Peirce*, edited by Cornelis de Waal and Piotr Skowronski, 125–148. New York: Fordham University Press.
Boyd, Kenneth. 2016. "Peirce on Assertion, Speech Acts, and Taking Responsibility." *Transactions of the Charles S. Peirce Society* 52, no. 1 (Winter): 21–46.
Brandom, Robert. 1994. *Making It Explicit: Reasoning, Representing, and Discursive Commitment*. Cambridge, MA: Harvard University Press.
Bratman, Michael. 1999. *Intention, Plans and Practical Reason*. Stanford, CA: CSLI Publications.
De Waal, Cornelis. 2012. "Who's Afraid of Charles Sanders Peirce? Knocking Some Critical Common Sense into Moral Philosophy." In *The Normative Thought of Charles S. Peirce*, edited by Cornelis de Waal and Krzysztof Skowronski, 83–100. New York: Fordham University Press.
Dewey, John. 2008. *John Dewey: The Middle Works, 1899–1924*, edited by Jo Ann Boydson. 15 vols. Carbondale: Southern Illinois University Press.
Feibleman, James. 1943. "A Systematic Presentation of Peirce's Ethics." *Ethics* 53, no. 2: 98–109.
Grube, Hans. 1927. "Plato's Theory of Beauty." *The Monist* 37, no. 2: 269–288.
Habermas, Jürgen. 1990. "Discourse Ethics: Notes on a Program of Philosophical Justification." In *Moral Consciousness and Communicative Action*, edited by Thomas McCarthy, 43–115. Translated by Christian Lenhardt and Shierry Nicholsen. Cambridge, MA: MIT Press.
Hoerber, Robert. 1964. "Plato's Greater Hippias." *Phronesis* 9, no. 2: 143–155.
Hookway, Christopher. 2002. *Truth, Rationality and Pragmatism*. Oxford: Clarendon Press.
Houser, Nathan. 2010. "Reconsidering Peirce's Relevance." In *Ideas in Action: Proceedings of the Applying Peirce Conference*, edited by M. Bergman, S. Paavola, A. Pietarinen, and H. Rydenfelt, 1–15. Helsinki: Nordic Studies in Pragmatism.
Hume, David. [1739] 1978. *Treatise of Human Nature* (L. A. Selby-Rigge and P. H. Nidditch, eds.). Oxford: Clarendon Press.
Kant, Immanuel. [1785] 1959. *Foundations of the Metaphysics of Morals*. Translated by Lewis White Beck. Indianapolis: Bobbs-Merrill Press,.
Kant, Immanuel. [1798] 1978. *Anthropology from a Pragmatic Point of View*. Translated by Victor Lyle Dowdell. Carbondale: Southern Illinois University Press.
Kent, Beverley. 1976. "Peirce's Esthetics: A New Look." *Transactions of the Charles S. Peirce Society* 12, no. 3 (Summer): 263–283.
Kent, Beverley. 1987. *Charles S. Peirce: Logic and the Classification of the Sciences*. Montreal: McGill-Queens University Press.
Kitcher, Philip. 2011. *The Ethical Project*. Cambridge, MA: Harvard University Press.
Liszka, James Jakób. 2012. "Charles Peirce on Ethics." In *The Normative Thought of Charles S. Peirce*, edited by Cornelis de Waal and Krzysztof Skowronski, 44–82. New York: Fordham University Press.
Liszka, James Jakób. 2019. "Peirce's Convergence Theory of Truth Redux." *Cognitio* 20, no. 1: 91–112.

Liszka, James Jakób. 2021. *Charles Peirce on Ethics, Esthetics and the Normative Sciences.* New York: Routledge.
Mayorga, Rosa. 2012. "Peirce's Moral Realism." In *The Normative Thought of Charles S. Peirce*, edited by Cornelis de Waal and Piotr Skowronski, 101–124. New York: Fordham University Press.
Mill, John Stuart. 1957. *Utilitarianism.* Indianapolis, IN: Bobbs-Merrill.
Misak, Cheryl. 2000. *Truth, Politics, Morality: Pragmatism and Deliberation.* New York: Routledge.
Misak, Cheryl. 2004. "C. S. Peirce on Vital Matters." In *The Cambridge Companion to Peirce*, edited by Cheryl Misak, 150–174. Cambridge: Cambridge University Press.
Nagel, Thomas. 1978. *The Possibility of Altruism.* Princeton, NJ: Princeton University Press.
Parker, Kelly. 1998. *The Continuity of Peirce's Thought.* Nashville, TN: Vanderbilt University Press.
Peirce, Charles S. Manuscripts from 1857 to 1914 held at the Houghton Library of Harvard University, as identified in Richard Robin. *Annotated Catalogue of the Papers of Charles S. Peirce.* Amherst: University of Massachusetts Press, 1967. And in Richard Robin. "The Peirce Papers: A Supplementary Catalogue." *Transactions of the Charles S. Peirce Society* 7, no. 1 (Winter 1971): 37–57. (Referred to as R[catalogue#]:[sheet#]; with RL for letters and RS for supplement.)
Peirce, Charles S. 1931–1958. *The Collected Papers of Charles Sanders Peirce.* 8 vols. Vols. 1–6 edited by Charles Hartshorne and Paul Weiss. Vols. 7–8 edited by Arthur W. Burks. Cambridge, MA: Harvard University Press. (Referred to as CP.)
Peirce, Charles. 1958. *Values in a Universe of Chance: Selected Writings of Charles S. Peirce.* Edited by Philip Wiener. New York: Doubleday. (Referred to as VC.)
Peirce, Charles S. 1975–1987. *Charles Sanders Peirce: Contributions to The Nation.* 4 vols. Edited by Kenneth L. Ketner and James E. Cook. Lubbock: Texas Tech University Press. (Referred to as CN.)
Peirce, Charles S. 1976. *The New Elements of Mathematics*, 4 vols. in 5. Edited by Carolyn Eisele. The Hague: Mouton. (Referred to as NEM.)
Peirce, Charles S. 1992. *Reasoning and the Logic of Things: The Cambridge Conferences Lectures of 1898.* Edited by Kenneth L. Ketner. Cambridge, MA: Harvard University Press. (Referred to as RLT.)
Peirce, Charles S. 1992–1998. *The Essential Peirce: Selected Philosophical Writings.* 2 vols. Vol. 1 edited by Nathan Houser and Christian Kloesel. Vol. 2 edited by the Peirce Edition Project. Bloomington: Indiana University Press. (Referred to as EP.)
Peirce, Charles S. 1997. *Pragmatism as a Principle and Method of Right Reasoning: The 1903 Harvard Lectures on Pragmatism.* Edited by Patricia Ann Turrisi. Albany: State University of New York Press. (Referred to as PPM.)
Plato. 1961a. *The Philebus.* In *The Collected Dialogues of Plato*, edited by Edith Hamilton and Huntington Cairns, translated by R. Hackforth, 1086–1050. Princeton, NJ: Princeton University Press.
Plato. 1961b. *Gorgias.* In *The Collected Dialogues of Plato*, edited by Edith Hamilton and Huntington Cairns, translated by W. D. Woodhead, 229–307. Princeton, NJ: Princeton University Press.
Plato. 1961c. *Greater Hippias.* In *The Collected Dialogues of Plato*, edited by Edith Hamilton and Huntington Cairns, translated by Benjamin Jowett, 1534–1559. Princeton, NJ: Princeton University Press.

Plato. 1961d. *The Republic*. In *The Collected Dialogues of Plato*, edited by Edith Hamilton and Huntington Cairns, translated by Paul Shorey, 575–844. Princeton, NJ: Princeton University Press.

Potter, Vincent. 1967. *Charles S. Peirce: On Norms and Ideals*. Amherst: University of Massachusetts Press.

Reid, Thomas. [1788] 1969. *Essays on the Active Powers of the Mind*. Cambridge, MA: MIT Press.

Robin, Richard. 1964. "Peirce's Doctrine of the Normative Sciences." In *Studies in the Philosophy of Charles Peirce*, edited by Edward Moore and Richard Robin, 271–289 (2nd ed.). Amherst: University of Massachusetts Press.

Schiller, Friedrich. [1795] 1965. *The Aesthetic Education of Man*. Translated by Reginald Snell. New York: Frederick Ungar.

Short, Thomas. *Peirce's Theory of Signs*. Cambridge, MA: Cambridge University Press, 2007.

Short, Thomas. 2012. "Normative Science?" *Transactions of the Charles S. Peirce Society* 48, no. 3 (Summer): 310–334.

Wiggins, David. 2006. *Ethics: Twelve Lectures on the Philosophy of Morality*. Cambridge, MA: Harvard University Press.

CHAPTER 9

LOVE AND THE GROWTH OF JUSTICE

JULIANA ACOSTA LÓPEZ DE MESA AND
DANIEL G. CAMPOS

THIS chapter focuses on agape or cherishing-love as a sentiment that nourishes and sustains human ethical life in such a way that it fosters the growth of concrete reasonableness—especially the ideal of justice—in human communities. After introducing agape as a cosmological power of development and evolution, the chapter will argue that, in the case of human agency, it is a sentiment that propels and guides ethical life. This sentiment allows creative, loving agents (1) to cherish the freedom of their beloved to choose their own ends and (2) to help their beloved grow toward those ends. The chapter will also explain the relationship between eros and agape, the role of self-control in loving activity, the communal environment in which it takes place, and creative love's contribution to the growth of concrete reasonableness in human communities, focusing primarily on the ideal of justice as harmony.[1]

The first section—introducing agape as a cosmological power—is descriptive and exegetical. It relates agape to Peirce's evolutionary cosmology and, within the constraints of a short text, to his philosophical system. The following two sections interpret agape as a human ethical sentiment that enables the creative agent to nurture the personal growth of neighbors and the progress of justice in communities. They foreground and develop important strands of reasoning that bloom from Peirce's philosophy, as if they were flowers from his garden, and demonstrate its relevance to contemporary world affairs where the ideal of justice is at stake.

1. AGAPE: CREATIVE LOVE IN EVOLUTIONARY TELEOLOGY

Toward the end of the nineteenth century, Charles Peirce deliberately set out to develop an architectonic philosophy. The categories that he had discovered since his early logical studies (W2:49–59, 1867) structured this architectonic. As he claimed in "The Architecture of Theories" (W8:98–110, 1890), he aimed for his philosophy to be responsive to the main scientific theories at the time. Accordingly, he aimed for an evolutionary philosophy.

As part of his overall architectonic project, in the early 1890s Peirce published a series of articles in *The Monist* that established the main conceptual strands of his cosmology. Developing the views that he had preliminarily sketched in "A Guess at the Riddle" (W6:165–202, 1887–1888), Peirce provided an open systematic account of his cosmological principles. In his view, the dominant philosophies of his time suffered from a mechanistic, nominalistic, and individualistic conception of the universe. He had ardently attacked this perspective since his early writings, seeking to refute the main tenets of Cartesianism and of modern deterministic philosophy (W2:193–211, 1868; W2:211–242, 1868). Peirce proposed, instead, an architectonic in which freedom, spontaneity, and chance, as well as mediation, growth, and diversification, are understood as inextricable features of the universe, alongside the necessary action of mechanical forces.

In such a context, Peirce claimed that "philosophy requires thorough-going evolutionism or none" (W8:102, 1890). Thus, in "Evolutionary Love" (W8:184–205, 1892), Peirce introduced love, or *agape*, as an evolutionary impulse that permeates the cosmos in all its aspects. In broad outline, Peirce argued that cosmological growth leads to increasing diversity and complexity. Chance and necessity are part of an evolutionary development in which agape nurtures diversifying growth. Thus, chance, mechanical necessity, and creative love—all three together—are the powers at work in the evolution of the universe, and it is not possible to provide a full account of this process when taking only one of these categories into account. His argument proceeds by looking at three different evolutionary philosophies and what features of the universe each of them explains. The correct theory must account for chance, necessary mechanical action, and diversifying growth. The details of these three evolutionary theories are as follows.

First, evolution by chance or spontaneity can produce order from a primal state of potency, through the emergence of relations among primal cosmic components, but, Peirce argues, it cannot explain diversity and growth (W8:190–191, 1892). This theory allows for a certain freedom within which creativity can take place, but as it relies solely on chance and habit-taking as the principles at work in the universe its result is death or the final crystallization of habits after the right reaction (effect) to a certain stimulus (cause) has been established. Peirce illustrates this crystallization process of habit acquisition through an example with cards in "A Guess at the Riddle" as follows. Each suit of the deck of cards exemplifies different ways in which a cell may react. Spades stand for the kind of reaction that successfully removes an external stimulus. In order to represent the original state of the cell, one picks two cards of each suit and shuffles them thoroughly. Then, one turns a card from the top, one by one, until a spade is reached. Once the reaction of the cell has taken place, one adds one card of each of the suits that has been used in the process, representing habit, and removes one card from the suits one has not used, representing forgetfulness. If one repeats this process until spades have been exhausted, at the end, one will have the hands full of spades with no further possibilities for growth or diversity, since it has achieved a definite goal through action and reaction (W6:190–193, 1887–1888).[2] Peirce called this type of evolution by sporting or fortuitous variation "tychasm" (W8:194, 1894) and emphasized its aspects related to the category of firstness, that is, of freshness, originality, spontaneity, and freedom (W6:211, 1887–1888).

Second, evolution by necessity is the carrying out of mechanical development toward a fixed end, with no place for freedom, creativity, diversification, and growth in the process (W8:191–192, 1894). It has two modes, one internal and one external to the evolving process itself. According to the internal one, which Peirce exemplifies with Georg Wilhelm Friedrich Hegel's system, there is a final, preestablished aim to cosmic evolution. A certain growth happens, but only in the way in which a seed becomes a tree. After the seed achieves its final form nothing else can come out of it but that tree: there is no place for creativity and diversification. In the external mode of necessary evolution, which may be exemplified by Karl Marx's dialectical materialism, material forces act to determine evolution along a fixed, inescapable path. There is no freedom or creativity on the side of individuals, but only reaction to external forces that lead to a determinate result. Peirce called this type of evolution by mechanical necessity "anancasm" (W8:194, 1892) and emphasized its aspects related to the category of secondness, that is, of determination, correlation, force, and reaction (W6:211, 1888).

Third, in evolution through agapic love, there is freedom, interaction, habit, diversification, and creative growth toward an open-ended purpose (W8:192–195, 1892). This evolutionary development is twofold: the cosmos and all its creatures develop toward an end, but the end itself also changes and evolves; in other words, the end is not static but dynamic and ever-developing. Creatures themselves have an active role in bringing about cosmic evolution. On the contrary, in evolution by necessity or by chance, creatures have no role in helping cosmic evolution either because the cosmos is entirely mechanical or because evolution occurs by chance alone and creatures merely adapt to evolving circumstances. For Peirce, the mode of evolution by love is the genuine one since it comprehends all the main traits of natural evolution, namely, fortuitous variation, tendency toward order, growing diversity, and creative agency. These are all real features of the cosmos. Peirce called this type of evolution by love "agapasm" (W8:194, 1892) and emphasized its aspects related to the category of thirdness, that is, of creating, mediating, developing, becoming, and bringing about (W6:211, 1888).[3]

Peirce, in sum, conceives of agape as the source of evolution that permeates all aspects of the universe. Since agapic love is at work at *all* levels of cosmic evolution, then it can be at work in human living—in the course of history, the practice of science, legislation, and the development of moral character, to name a few areas of human endeavor.[4] According to Peirce, everything that evolves and grows does so by virtue of applying some form or expression of evolutionary love. In his words: "It is not by dealing out cold justice to the circle of my ideas that I can make them grow, but by cherishing and tending them as I would the flowers in my garden" (W8:185, 1892). This is why agape is called cherishing-love.

In what follows, we will focus our discussion of agape on its ethical and political manifestations. We will deepen its characterization as a vital impulse that enables the growth of loving reasonableness in personal and social endeavors and in achieving warm justice in a loving community. Although it is possible to show how human agape follows deductively from Peirce's overall system,[5] our approach will highlight Peirce's own abductive reasoning in "Evolutionary Love." Peirce came to the idea of cosmic agape from the idea of humanly experienced agape. In formulating his hypothesis of evolution by cherishing-love, his reasoning was abductive:

P1. There isn't only spontaneity or only order and growth in the evolving cosmos, but also increasing diversity.

P2. If, beyond spontaneity and force, a cosmic agapastic power—analogous to humanly experienced agape—were at work in the universe, then increasing diversity, alongside chance, order, and growth, would be explained.

C. Therefore, plausibly a cosmic agapastic power is at work in the evolving cosmos.[6]

In the course of this reasoning, Peirce articulated his concept of agape by characterizing it in terms of human experience. The following section, then, reads very closely Peirce's discussion of agape in the first part of "Evolutionary Love." It foregrounds and develops some of the key characteristics of humanly experienced agape as Peirce presents it. The upshot is a partial pragmatist clarification of agape: What would be the conceivable practical consequences if agape were at work in interpersonal relations and in the creation of just societies?[7]

2. AGAPE AS ETHICAL SENTIMENT

What, then, is agape? According to Peirce, agape is a creative impulse that can be characterized in analogy to circular motion: "The movement of love is circular, at one and the same impulse projecting creations into independency and drawing them into harmony" (W8:185, 1892). According to this image, love allows creatures to flourish on their own terms, with freedom and independence, but also as part of a whole that draws them back into community. This means that creatures are whole not merely as individuals but also to the degree that they creatively harmonize their own interests and goals with the cosmos. There are at least two reasons for this. If a creature only pursues its own goals at the expense of the cosmos, its individualist goal might not be attainable, or else the creature may work as a blind egoistic force against others, a force that will be extinguished by the reaction against it.

With specific regard to the evolution of organic species, Peirce explained evolution by the "force of habit" in terms of this "circular" action of love (agapasm):

> Now it is energetic projaculation . . . by which in the typical instances of Lamarckian evolution the new elements of form are first created. Habit, however, forces them to take practical shapes, compatible with the structures they affect, and, in the form of heredity and otherwise, gradually replaces the spontaneous energy that sustains them. Thus, habit plays a double part; it serves to establish the new features, and also

to bring them into harmony with the general morphology and function of the animals and plants to which they belong.... This account of Lamarckian evolution coincides with the general description of the action of love. (W8:192–193, 1892)

This is, in effect, a pragmatist clarification of what agape, as a creative and harmonizing impulse, means in the context of the evolution of organic species.

This image of the circular movement of evolutionary love seems to be inspired by Friedrich Schelling's metaphor in his *Philosophical Investigations into the Essence of Human Freedom*, which Peirce acknowledged as an important influence (CP6.605, 1893; W8:135, 1892; W8:391, 1892; R958:203, c. 1891; W8:410, 1892; R890:2–3, n.d.). Schelling (2006) explains the path of creation and freedom using the image of the rotary and centrifugal movement of a body in circular motion. From Peirce's perspective, the impulse promoting the independence of creatures is analogous to the centrifugal movement, while the impulse fostering harmony among creatures is analogous to the rotary movement. We suggest, however, that the image of a spiral trajectory is more apt. A spiral curve emanates from a point and moves farther away as it revolves around that central point. Whether the spiral is arithmetic, logarithmic, or otherwise, movement along the curve always revolves around the original point and maintains a pattern (harmony), but there is also growth away from that center (independence).

Another possibility to visualize love in terms of this circular or spiral motion can be through the coordinated action of agape and eros, not literally as opposing forces but rather metaphorically as coordinated impulses. Carl Hausman provides an insightful way to understand self-controlled growth in terms of erotic and agapic love that reflects Peirce's metaphor. Hausman notes that growth works according to a developmental teleology, which means "a growth of purposes, not a growth of ideas in accord with purposes" (1974). This highlights the vagueness of the goal that allows growth and its gradual development. Moreover, the coordinated action of eros and agape explains the way in which the cosmos grows through creativity or, in Peirce's words, through diversity and complexity. He explains the difference between eros and agape as follows: "If eros were the exclusive dynamic principle of a process, that process would not be creative.... The subject would appropriate what it lacks, but it would have no way of varying its growth against the background of established goals and patterns of development." However, "if a process is creative, then, the subject contributes out of itself to the evolution of its process. Its spontaneity is given direction not because the subject is concerned for itself exclusively or for a predetermined goal which lures it, but because it is concerned for a creature to be in the future" (1974). In terms of the foregoing metaphor, eros is a power that expresses the way in which normative ideals as *telos* may lure us in a centrifugal movement; however, in order to grow harmoniously with the cosmos, following the rotary movement, we need the creative power of agape.

Seen from Douglas Anderson's angle, humans need erotic motivation in order to create, but "because it is such a powerful 'drug,' [eros] comes with some limitations as well" (2021). Eros is passionate-love that desires possession of (beauty in) the beloved person or thing. Every work of art starts with erotic love, which passionately calls us, but it can work as a drug that aims at its goal in an egotistic way. Our lives can reflect such works of art. We can lead controlling lives inspired by eros or we can lead creative, self-controlled, agapastic ones attracted to beauty. Anderson makes an analogous claim about the erotic and agapastic impulses in scientific practice when he writes that "other-directedness is an agapistic trait of Peircean inquiry. Thus, while eros as a drive to inquire is useful, it is not sufficient for inquiry precisely because it runs the risk of becoming egotistic. . . . Inquiry is not *for me*, nor even *for us*; it is *for achieving the ideal of truth*" (2012, 161). The erotic drive to inquire must become the agapastic impulse to learn and share the truth in community.

Eros, as a centrifugal impulse, attracts us toward something we desire; agape, as a rotary impulse, leads eros to transcend its egotistic interests in others and transforms these interests into cherishing care. While eros arises as a natural tendency to love passionately, cultivating agape requires an ethical choice and self-control to care for creatures. We grow in enabling others to grow as well; we grow in the measure that we allow ourselves to interact creatively with others. But since eros works as a blind power, a purely erotic life will reflect such a power in the form of an egotistic purpose. In sum, eros and agape are complementary, eros functioning as the starting impulse that agape then guides in a coordinated motion toward independence and harmony.

Agape's two impulses can be expressed in human action. Human beings have the natural capacity to enact cherishing-love, but doing so depends on a primordial ethical choice. It requires the cultivation of habits that respond to the dual agapic impulse to respect the liberty of the beloved to pursue their own ends and to nourish the beloved's growth toward those ends in harmony with normative ideals that guide and enrich communal life.

In fact, in spite of the cosmological import of "Evolutionary Love," Peirce introduced agape, first, in terms of human ethical living. He presented it as a form of interpersonal love: "Love is not directed to abstractions but to persons; not to persons we do not know, nor to numbers of people, but to our own dear ones, our family and neighbors. 'Our neighbor,' we remember, is one whom we live near, not locally perhaps but in life and feeling" (W8:185, 1892). Agape respects and nurtures persons; it cultivates affective, vital relations among loving people. This does not mean, however, that vital, affective proximity is the starting point of agape. Following Henry James Sr., Peirce states that the agapastic impulse to cherish the intrinsic worth and freedom of the beloved is directed most genuinely at what is most radically opposed to the lover (W8:185, 1892). But creative love cultivates harmony by recognizing first the independence and intrinsic worth of what is initially hostile to the lover: "Love, recognizing germs of loveliness in the hateful, gradually warms it into life, and makes it lovely" (W8:186, 1892). In such action we can see both loving impulses—to value independence and to foster harmony—working in unison.

Peirce describes the nurturing practice of love in other explicitly human, ethical ways. Secularizing the message of the Christian gospel of Saint John, he writes that the golden rule "does not, of course, say, Do everything possible to gratify the egoistic impulses of others, but it says, Sacrifice your own perfection to the perfectionment of your neighbor" (W8:185, 1892). He re-emphasizes this way of promoting the growth of the beloved when he adds that the golden rule is "the formula of an evolutionary philosophy, which teaches that growth comes only from love, from I will not say self-*sacrifice*, but from the ardent impulse to fulfill another's highest impulse" (W8:185, 1892). Agape commits to effective cooperation and solidarity with others for their sake.

This ethical ideal is not achieved without commitment to a loving practice. As stated above, this way of living and acting requires a primordial ethical choice to develop the affective dispositions that enable a person to act lovingly. The coordinated habits that allow an ethical agent to cherish the freedom and nourish the growth of a beloved person constitute a sentiment. Persons become disposed toward loving action when they deliberately cultivate their potential for nurturing others. Thus, agapastic love is not an emotion. It rather requires us to cultivate our emotions according to the normative ideals of truth, goodness, and admirableness. A better depiction would be to understand sentiments as "enduring systems of emotions" (Savan 1981, 331) that are coordinated by self-control toward those normative ideals, and then to class agape as a sentiment.

Lara Trout's conception of Peircean affectivity is enlightening in this regard. By affectivity she means "the on-going body-minded communication between the human organism and its individual, social, and external environments, for the promotion of survival and growth. This communication is shaped by biological, individual, semiotic, social, and other factors.... Peircean affectivity includes feelings, emotion, instinct, interest, sympathy, and agapic love, as well as belief, doubt, and habit" (Trout 2010, 9). Importantly, she emphasizes Peirce's view of the human being as an animal organism that must live in community to survive and thrive in natural, social, political, and other environments (10). In such environments, "sympathy, the term Peirce uses to describe the law of mind as it functions in human communities," must ideally develop into agapic sympathy, since "in its ideal agapic form, sympathy embraces as sources of growth the creative bursts of spontaneity that arise within the existing habit systems of a community" (195).[8] In the terms we are using here, then, a sentiment is a coordinated web of affective habits, and the important role of love as a sentiment is that it allows and fosters the growth of beloved individuals and communities. For Peirce, we have seen, everything that evolves and grows does so by the transformative action of love.

As a human sentiment, moreover, agape requires self-control. For example, an attentive reading of Peirce's writings shows that our limits in logic, and by extension in science, are related to our moral character, primarily to our own egotistical hindrances at the moment of opening our hearts to experience and to other people's genuine criticism or perspectives (W3:284–285, 1878). In other words, our failures in science are primarily related to our incapacity to acknowledge, through self-control, our own fallibility. Scientific inquiry, as well as a mature moral character, is an expression of self-control. Highlighting the close relationship between love and self-control, Peirce defines the latter as "the capacity for rising to an extended view of a practical subject instead of seeing only temporary urgency. This is the only freedom of which man has any reason to be proud; and it is because love of what is good for all on the whole [not merely what is good for me here and now], which is the widest possible consideration, is the essence of Christianity, that it is said that the service of Christ is perfect freedom" (W2:261n6, 1869). Accordingly, self-control over our own egotistical impulses is necessary for engaging in true scientific research as part of a community of inquiry.

In general, beyond the example of science, caring self-control implies more than fallibilist self-regulation. It is also self-mastery for the sake of creatively fostering growth. Genuine agape requires the development of one's potential for acting as creative lovers in order to promote the growth of beloved persons and of loving reasonableness in the community—a growth that can only be achieved in cultivating our relationships with others and in helping to build a beloved community. As Douglas Anderson (2012) discusses, "the community of a nontheological church of love" provides a second model for community in Peirce's corpus (162). Like the community of inquiry, this loving community is "shot through with agapastic features," especially its "other-directedness" or primary engagement with the well-being of others (162–163). The upshot is that "this community must be ameliorative and inclusive" (163). As Peirce wrote, the "*raison d'etre* of a church [or loving community] is to confer upon men a life broader than their narrow personalities, a life rooted in the very truth of being" (CP6.451, n.d.). Consequently, Anderson writes: "Just as inquiry is directed outward toward the ideal of truth, the practical community aims to liberate and thus to ameliorate" (2012, 163). That is, the loving community is committed in practice to improving the well-being of all of its members, and especially to promoting their freedom to choose and pursue their own ends in harmony with the higher ideals of the community. Moreover, the community must be inclusive in its membership, allowing not only all persons, but also all voices and perspectives to be considered in its pursuit of its highest ideals (163). In short, this loving community is characterized by its openness and inclusivity, its active engagement with the well-being of all community members, and the effective progress of the community toward achieving its highest ideals.

Normative ideals as agapastic ends guide the actions of the loving agent and of the overall community in promoting such growth. In 1905, Peirce argued that normative ideals as human purposes are not only real generals but also physically efficient; that is, they do cause human action (EP2:343, 1905). He concluded that general ideas such as justice and truth were not only real but also "notwithstanding the iniquity of the world, the mightiest of the forces that move it" (EP2:343, 1905). He meant that our vague conceptions of truth and justice—of logical and ethical goodness and ultimately of aesthetic admirableness—can give direction to our individual and communal lives and cause us to act for the sake of those ideals as worthy purposes.

Adopting and pursuing these ideals as purposes requires love. Peirce has a particular way to understand what an ideal is. According to him, we all have motives, but not all of us have ideals. He writes: "Every action has a motive; but an ideal only belongs to a line [of] conduct which is deliberate. To say that conduct is deliberate implies that each action, or each important action, is reviewed by the actor and that his judgment is passed upon it, as to whether he wishes his future conduct to be like that or not. His ideal is the kind of conduct which attracts him upon review" (EP2:377, 1906).[9] Notice that the attractiveness of the ideal is important. It must lure us. It must be lovable and propel us to loving action.

Agapic love is the main impulse for acting toward those ideals—for adopting them as our ends and working toward their concrete actualization. This is an aspect of what Peirce termed the growth of loving reasonableness in the cosmos, as expressed in the world of human communities (EP2:343–344, 1905). In what follows, we will focus on our interpretation of the theory of justice for human communities that can be gleaned from Peirce's conception of agape in relation to ethical living. Justice is a manifestation of the good in human living guided by love.

3. Loving Reasonableness in Human Community: Warm Justice as Harmony

In *Democracy and Education* John Dewey, one of the most perceptive readers of Charles Peirce's philosophy in the early twentieth century, wrote in a fallibilistic spirit about principles. He did not view them as necessary inward rules that absolutely determine a course of action, but as the continuity—or synechistic nature, in Peircean terms—of fallible, experimental, creative practice: "The principle is not what justifies an activity, for the principle is but another name for the continuity of the activity. If the activity as manifested in its consequences is undesirable, to act upon principle is to accentuate its evil. And a man who prides himself upon acting upon principle is likely to be a man who insists upon having his own way without learning from experience what is the better way" (Dewey 2012, 372). Retrojecting this view into Peirce's principle of agape—in the sense of the continuity of fallibilistic, experimental, creative practice, nourished by love and oriented toward the growth of goodness in human communities—leads us to re-think the way in which we talk today about justice.

The Western philosophical tradition started with a notion of justice related to virtue. Plato (2008) thought of it as a way of harmonizing the elements in a polis in his *Republic*, while Aristotle defended justice not only as a virtue but also as the most complete one "because he who possesses it can exercise his virtue not only in himself but towards his neighbour also; for many men can exercise virtue in their own affairs, but not in their relations to their neighbour" (2014, 1129b25ff).

However, later developments of the idea of justice, mostly based on a limited conception of the one originally proposed by Aristotle, and mainly focused on two of its subspecies, namely, distributive and rectificatory justice, neglected its more general understanding as a virtue and transformed it, with the aid of Thomas Hobbes, Immanuel Kant, and John Stuart Mill, into a dogmatic principle, and later on into a good in the hands of John Rawls.

From a Peircean stance, the exercise of justice should not be based on fixed universal principles but rather on critical commonsense beliefs[10] and should be guided by general, developmental normative ideals open to growth.[11] This new perspective proposes that justice is a developmental ideal that grows through history and aims to harmonize human beings and their environment, as in the metaphor of a rotary movement that harmonizes a centrifugal impulse. Accordingly, justice is not a universal principle that determines the course toward a preestablished goal that can be reached following one single, simple path. Justice cannot be merely applied as a principle in order to take place; rather, in order to become actual, justice has to be embodied in actions that are guided by its normative ideal.

As a contemporary example, we could ponder what human rights are, perhaps the theoretical and practical achievement of which humanity feels most proud. From a Peircean perspective, these rights should be understood as commonsense beliefs that we have achieved in the history of humanity and, as such, they should and have grown—from first, to second, to third generation of rights—following new social achievements. This explains, for instance, why we have third-generation human rights that not only reach the human species but also consider the protection of the environment and the diversity of the planet.

The main problem in thinking of justice as a universal principle or as something applied through a universal principle—in the form of a categorical imperative of duty or a utilitarian rule, for example—is that it imposes a hegemonic rule upon a diversity of perspectives on what might be conceived as just. This is one way to understand Peirce's admonition, quoted earlier, not to deal "cold justice" to an idea, if our aim is to make it grow (W8:185, 1892). Justice is not a universal principle to be applied in particular cases, but an ideal that develops and grows, if we nourish it agapastically by opening it to critical conversation (logical and critical-commonsensist inquiry) with a diversity of perspectives and experiences. Dewey articulated the upshot in claiming that acting by principles or "blind" habits may cause greater evils when circumstances show us a need for a better receptivity to experience. Following this idea, human rights should be open for discussion to all cultures and societies, and we should be ready to acknowledge different ways to put them into practice, or even to readjust them, if different cultural and social experiences show us that it should be done.[12]

Let us explain, then, what Peirce understands by critical commonsensism and what a normative ideal is. These concepts will support the idea of warm justice that we develop from Peirce's thought. By warm justice we mean the creation and cultivation of social and political conditions for the flourishing of all community members, respecting their freedom to choose and pursue their own purposes in harmony with normative ideals. This sense of community is open and inclusive; it is vague and general enough to embrace all beings with whom we can reach some kind of mediate or immediate sensible and reasonable relation (W3:284, 1878). This concept of justice, if well understood, should be general enough to embrace other ideas of justice as one of its expressions, without such expressions exhausting the general ideal, since they become a particular manifestation of it.

According to Peirce, all inquiry starts from our preconceived ideas and the cultural heritage we carry with us. Our instincts are constituted by the body of background beliefs that we do not doubt. These include beliefs learned through education, personal and communal experiences, and culture, as well as nonconscious naturally inherited habits (EP2:346–359, 1905). They are not immutable but flexible, since they may change following both the demands of our aspirations as persons, communities, and species and the exigencies of the evolving environment. These cultural and communal habits or social instincts correspond to our commonsense beliefs that help us to get around in life. However, for Peirce they should be open to criticism once the course of experience puts them into question (EP2:346–359, 1905).

A good example of this, in the political context of our contemporary world, can be provided by the recent movements of people from marginalized and minority groups who—as an act of anti-racist resistance—tore down the monument of the slave trader Edward Colston in Bristol, United Kingdom; a form of protest replicated in Colombia, South America, where a group of originary peoples, mostly Misak, pulled down the monument of the Spanish conquistador Sebastián de Belalcázar in Popayán and Cali as a protest against the extermination of Indigenous peoples and state negligence. Their protests aimed to bear witness, before society at large, to the ongoing sociopolitical violence against them.

As history testifies, the dominant ideas of justice have not embraced all types of life, not even all of humankind. But all human beings do start from some background idea—a commonsense belief about justice—that has to be questioned, criticized, and enriched through these acts of resistance. Such resistance is necessary because hegemonic peoples, sociopolitical institutions, and laws sometimes thwart or silence the voices of the oppressed from the articulation of an inclusive and encompassing idea of justice. For example, Lara Trout discusses the problem that in the United States even well-meaning white people, who identify themselves as nonracist, can display racist acts and ideas. Following Peirce's ideas, Trout explains that this happens because such acts are the expression of nonconscious beliefs that are part of their commonsense. Nonetheless, she claims that there can be ways to recuperate ourselves from our own blindness and provides tools for such endeavors that involve the coordinated work of critical commonsensism and agapastic sympathy (Trout 2010, 4–5).

It is important for people in hegemonic positions to be lovingly open and receptive to testimony and evidence about sociopolitical obstacles and violence directed at specific groups of people (Trout 2010, 12). Following the example of the protests in Colombia, the reactions of *la gente de bien*—the well-to-do people who speak Spanish, have a traditional family and work, and pay their taxes—have been, mainly, of political blindness. When Minga, the organized political group that represents most Colombian Indigenous peoples, arrived in Cali in the midst of the popular protests, renowned politicians, public workers, and ordinary citizens made public racist comments against Minga's participation in the protests. *La Silla Vacía*'s article, "The Racist Wall," exhibits these racist narratives against originary peoples, such as the idea, meant to undermine the historical debt of Hispanic American society toward Native American peoples, that they are persons "kept" by the state; or that they belong to another place (referred to as their "natural habitat") and must stay away from the cities; or that they are not citizens; or that they are vandals or barbarians, unlike the civilized *gente de bien* (Arbeláez-Jaramillo and Chavarriaga-Garzón, 2021).

If we take Lara Trout's proposal as a guide for interpreting such events, these widespread racist beliefs should be taken as signs that the political idea of justice is not working for an important part of the people who should be included, in Colombia and in the world. For Trout, minorities are best situated to identify what is not rightly functioning in a political community (2010, 57–60). While hegemonic groups live their lives without social or political obstacles to their talents and desires in order to have a meaningful life, minorities do find such obstacles in the way of social stereotypes— as expressed in the "racist wall"—or even laws. In fact, laws are prone to display our deepest social stereotypes and biased commonsense beliefs.

Thus, as noted above, in order to achieve a more inclusive idea of justice it is necessary to be receptive to criticism of our commonsense beliefs. For that, we have to be able to empathize with those who do not belong to our narrow group or share our own perspective. Self-control plays a key role here. As Trout argues, self-control is both purposeful and inhibitory; agapastic sympathy aids the inhibitory function of self-control by keeping us from rejecting testimony—for example, about various forms of discrimination—and remaining open to conversation out of loving regard for others (2010, 36–38). Trout writes: "When Peirce says that 'Self-control seems to be the capacity for rising to an extended view of a practical subject instead of seeing only temporary urgency,' the inhibitory dimension of self-control is prominent alongside the purposeful dimension (W2:261n6). To achieve goals . . . we often must say 'no' to the 'temporary urgency' of existing habits that resist growth. . . . Within the sociopolitical context, those in hegemonic groups may need to inhibit the 'temporary urgency' of dismissing negative feedback about discrimination from someone in a nonhegemonic group" (2010, 36). This loving openness to testimony and criticism would be required for the ideal of justice to grow in the Colombian example. In general, improvement of social conditions can only be achieved by acknowledging the special place that marginalized communities have in experiencing and pointing out what is not functioning well in a society and by seeing these manifestations as an opportunity to listen empathically and respond with care.

Agapastic empathy is thus at the core of a Peircean conception of warm justice, as opposed to cold justice understood as the application of universal principles, or a universal *rational* principle, to particular cases. Recall that, according to Peirce, love "warms" the hateful into loveliness and makes it grow (W8:185–186, 1892). Agape should be understood, following this approach, as a sentiment that grows from a coordinated web of self-controlled habits with the aim of bringing about reasonability or harmony (Acosta-López de Mesa 2020). Love grows by including what is other, not by contemplating what is already loved.

Some contemporary scholars have already pointed out the importance of the feeling of compassion for the implementation of justice (e.g., Nussbaum 2007 and 2010). Nonetheless, the idea of warm justice gleaned from Peirce's philosophy goes further in claiming that without the cultivation of the sentiment of love, or agape, one faces important limitations for the flourishing of justice as such. In this sense, aesthetic education is more than a means for cultivating empathy and enabling justice from an ethical point of view; it is necessary for its very possibility (Acosta-López de Mesa, 2018).

Accordingly, the defense of an aesthetic, sentimental education—in the sense of an education that cultivates imagination, fosters the capacity for empathy, and teaches us self-control in our actions and emotions—is not a question of taste, but a matter of justice. Persons who do not cultivate agapastic love as an important part of their lives will have limitations in understanding what justice is. Even though we may have social norms or laws to guide us, these become empty without the right sentiments to lead the norms back into the actual world. Without loving sentiments, other persons become merely the object of an empty formal law for the agent.

In the fifth book of the *Nicomachean Ethics*, dedicated precisely to the virtue of justice, Aristotle maintained that if we don't know "what is fitting" (*epieikos*), we also risk committing injustice. This shows that to follow the law and to know about merits and proportions is not enough to make things right. Aristotle compares the *epieíkeia* with the Lesbian rule used for construction that adapts to the surface of the rocks (2014, 1137b30). Following this metaphor, we may conclude that, in order to implement justice, our judgments and actions should adapt to our particular circumstances. We can do it best by engaging lovingly with the lives of the people involved in the situation and by creatively searching for the best solution so that all people are included in the ideal of a life worth living, or *eudaimonia*.

This view shows the role of love as a transformative power based on our capacity to imagine and engage with other people's lives. It leads us to pose creative solutions to social challenges, while being guided by the agapastic purpose of the flourishing of all people. This goes beyond the aim of "making things even," a limited and cold interpretation of the role of justice. Contrary to this, warm justice should be understood in a twofold sense as the communal conditions that make people's flourishing possible and as the normative ideal that guides the creation of those conditions.

We come, then, to the consideration of the normative ideals that guide agapastic love toward worthy aims such as the creation of warm justice.[13] According to Peirce, there are three normative ideals (truth, goodness, and beauty or admirableness) and three normative sciences that study what *ought to be* true (logic or semiotics), what *ought to be* good (ethics), and what *ought to be* admirable per se (aesthetics) (EP2:197–207, 1903). These ideals are interdependent. As a result, logic may establish what is true having a purpose in mind, namely, what ought to be good. In turn, something is good insofar as it follows an idea of the admirable per se or what is beautiful. Peirce named this ultimate ideal loving reasonableness—in human living, the generation of the conditions for the harmonious flourishing of all persons. This is, or should be, the main function of justice broadly understood also as a normative ideal closely related to what is good.

A normative ideal is an idea that lures us due to its admirableness per se but that also grows according to a developmental teleology—that is, that changes and is enriched in a continuum with history and that has no preestablished goal. It evolves in a similar way to how our own idea of a life worth living may grow with our own development through life. Agape is the creative power that actualizes and harmonizes our fallible attempts to achieve the ideal.

In *Politics of Survival*, for instance, Lara Trout describes the creation of social justice in terms of the circular motion of agape, as involving two movements: "First, a creative projection of newness, and second, an embracing and stabilizing of this spontaneous novelty. When human sympathy is agapic, it completes the circle by allowing for both movements" (2010, 203). This is another partial pragmatist clarification of the meaning of agape. The creative projection can consist in the experiential feedback of insightful individuals to the community about its habits. It can also consist in expressions of creative resistance by oppressed peoples, such as the symbolic destruction by the Colombian Indigenous peoples of a Spanish conqueror's monument. The harmonizing embrace would then consist in evaluating this feedback with an attitude of care for the individual or marginalized group and in revising communal habits or norms to address injustice. As Trout emphasizes, such transformation requires societal inquiry into the truth and critical commonsensist deactivation of prejudicial, oppressing belief-habits in favor of cultivating caring, nurturing ones (2010, 229–272). Love energizes both the inquiry and the critical commonsensist endeavors.

In Peirce's own words about the person who is agapastically committed to inquiring into truth and goodness and diffusing false or pernicious belief-habits through critical commonsense: "What he adores, if he is a good pragmaticist, is *power*; not the sham power of brute force, which, even in its own specialty of spoiling things, secures such slight results; but the creative power of reasonableness, which subdues all other powers, and rules over them with its scepter, knowledge, and its globe, love" (CP5.520, 1905). As Vincent Colapietro puts it, "the ideal of reasonableness requires overcoming . . . hatred; stated positively, there is a vital connection between concrete reasonableness and creative love. The higher developments of human reason [and, we would add, of humans in general] can only be agapastic" (1989, 93; see CP6.289, 1891).

Justice, as a normative ideal, is an appealing idea that grows through the history of humankind. Its growth is possible through the criticism of our commonsense ideas of what is just and right by vulnerable groups who are especially situated to experience injustice, although enriching perspectives are not limited to them. Moreover, as a warm idea, justice is nourished by agape since the limits of our capability to empathize with others will show the limits of our own capability to act justly, that is, to understand other persons' situations and to conceive and execute those actions that will help them flourish and grow accordingly.

In sum, justice, understood as the ideal of human flourishing, lures us by our aspiration to goodness and consists in the conditions that a community provides in order to make people's harmonious growth possible. Agapastic love nurtures the creation of those conditions. If the conception of a life worth living is related to the idea of flourishing, cold justice is too limited to allow it. Love provides our best choice for the creation of warm justice. More generally, agape underwrites the pursuit of a life worth living in which individuals and communities act for the sake of the growth of loving reasonableness, as guided by evolving normative ideals. Warm justice is an expression of how we can aspire to embody these ideals in open, inclusive communities.

Notes

1. We will focus on the main sentiment that enlivens ethical practice according to Peirce's thought, rather than on what he called the normative science of ethics. For a detailed overview of the development of this science in Peirce's philosophy, see Boero (2014). For another systematic account, see Herdy (2014). Liszka (2012) and de Waal (2012) both aim to bridge the alleged divide between normative and practical ethics in Peirce's thought.
2. This example indicates how growth through action and reaction toward a definite aim ends up at a dead end. The point is to show that Peirce was aware of this issue following his writings on probabilities starting in 1878. For a further analysis on this subject see Acosta-López de Mesa (2014).
3. All three modes of evolution manifest mediation, development, and bringing about (thirdness), but in tychasm spontaneity and chance (firstness) are foremost, while in anancasm reaction, force, and mechanical necessity (secondness) predominate. For a systematic, logical discussion see de Waal (2013, 144–148).
4. Love "can" rather than "must be" at work in human living since, as we will see, responsibility, choice, and creative self-control have a role to play in helping to bring about reasonability in the cosmos, if we choose to do so.
5. The chapter thus aims for a didactic approach, leading the reader through Peirce's reasoning as it progressed on the basis of phenomenal observation of evolutionary processes and abductive inference, rather than presenting a systematic, retrospective exegesis, in the style of a deduction. For an approach that shows how the three modes of evolution fit within Peirce's system, including its logical categories, see de Waal (2013, 144–148).
6. For Peirce's discussion of the logic of abduction in terms of this form of inference, see "Pragmatism as the Logic of Abduction" (EP2:226–241, especially 231).
7. For previous pragmatist clarifications of agape as a power at work in human interpersonal relations, see Campos (2017, 2019).
8. See "The Law of Mind" (W8:135-157). For another proposal that connects agape's cultural and scientific role to the law of mind, see Pape (1997). For a critical examination of how sympathy as the law of mind can go awry and become a source of marginalizing prejudice and bias, unless its creations are approached as experiments and criticized in fallibilistic attitude, see Staab (1999). Staab's article is a precursor to Trout's more thorough treatment of the coordinated functions of scientific inquiry, critical commonsensism, and agapic love in propelling communities toward the growth of social justice.
9. For a detailed discussion of the role of logical, diagrammatic reasoning and ethical deliberation, see Campos (2015).
10. See Peirce's 1905 article "Issues of Pragmaticism" (EP2:346–359).
11. See Peirce's 1903 lecture "The Three Normative Sciences" (EP2:197–207).
12. Our proposal about justice has points in common with de Waal's (2012) proposal for a Peircean experimental ethics. De Waal proposes an ethics in which theory and practice inform and influence each other, and what matters most is not the reification of rational moral principles but the resolution of genuine moral problems in a community. His proposal emphasizes the role of critical commonsensism for the sake of eliminating

homogeneity of perspective and unchecked biases on the part of inquirers into moral problems. Our proposal here, akin to Trout (2010), emphasizes the necessary and complementary role of an agapastic sentiment by inquirers toward all persons and their perspectives in order to progress toward the fallibilist realization of an evolving ideal of justice.

13. The question of what normative ideals are arises naturally at this point. If agape is the creative, harmonizing impulse that promotes cosmic and thus human growth, now it makes sense to ask: Growth toward what end or ideal? In this case, we focus on justice as part of loving reasonableness. For a systematic treatment of agapastic love in relation to normative ideals, see Potter (1997, 171–190).

References

Acosta-López de Mesa, Juliana. 2014. "Peirce's Philosophical Project from Chance to Evolutionary Love." *Discusiones Filosóficas* 15, no. 20: 31–41.

Acosta-López de Mesa, Juliana. 2018. "Peirce and the Aesthetic Education." *Journal of Philosophy of Education* 52, no. 2: 246–261. https://doi.org/10.1111/1467-9752.12296.

Acosta-López de Mesa, Juliana. 2020. "A Semiotic Theory of Self-Control." *Cognitio Revista de Filosofia* 20, no. 2: 217–229. https://doi.org/10.23925/2316-5278.2019v20i2p217-229.

Anderson, Douglas R. 2012. "The Pragmatic Importance of Peirce's Religious Writings." In *Conversations on Peirce: Reals and Ideals*, by Douglas R. Anderson and Carl Hausman, 149–165. New York: Fordham University Press.

Anderson, Douglas R. 2021. "Creativity: What's Love Got to Do with It." *Philosophy Americana*, February 21. https://philosophyamericana.wordpress.com/2021/02/21/creativity-whats-love-got-to-do-with-it/.

Arbeláez-Jaramillo, Natalia, and Santiago Chavarriaga-Garzón. 2021. "El muro del racismo contra la Minga indígena en Cali." *La Silla Vacía*, May 14. https://www.lasillavacia.com/historias/historia-academica/el-muro-del-racismo-contra-la-minga-ind%c3%adgena-en-cali.

Aristotle. 2014. *Aristotle's Ethics: Writings from the Complete Works*, edited by Jonathan Barnes and Anthony Kenny. Princeton, NJ: Princeton University Press.

Boero, Hedy. 2014. *Charles S. Peirce: claves para una ética pragmaticista*. Barañáin, Navarra, Spain: EUNSA.

Campos, Daniel G. 2015. "The Role of Diagrammatic Reasoning in Ethical Deliberation." *Transactions of the Charles S. Peirce Society* 51, no. 3 (Summer): 338–357.

Campos, Daniel G. 2017. *Loving Immigrants in America: An Experiential Philosophy of Personal Interaction*. Lanham, MD: Lexington Books.

Campos, Daniel G. 2019. "Eros and Agape in Interpersonal Relations: Plato, Emerson, and Peirce." In *The Routledge Handbook on Love in Philosophy*, edited by Adrienne Martin, 116–127. New York: Routledge.

Colapietro, Vincent. 1989. *Peirce's Approach to the Self: A Semiotic Perspective on Human Subjectivity*. Albany: State University of New York Press.

de Waal, Cornelis. 2012. "Who's Afraid of Charles Sanders Peirce? Knocking Some Critical Common Sense into Moral Philosophy." In *The Normative Thought of Charles Peirce*, edited by Cornelis de Waal and Krzysztof Piotr Skowronski, 83–100. New York: Fordham University Press.

de Waal, Cornelis. 2013. *Peirce: A Guide for the Perplexed*. London: Bloomsbury.

Dewey, John. 2012. *Democracy and Education*. Lexington, KY: Simon & Brown.

Hausman, Carl. 1974. "Eros and Agape in Creative Evolution: A Peircean Insight." *Process Studies* 4, no. 1: 11–25. Available without original pagination in *Religion Online*. https://www.religion-online.org/article/eros-and-agape-in-creative-evolution-a-peircean-insight/.

Herdy, Rachel. 2014. "The Origin and Growth of Peirce's Ethics: A Categorical Analysis." *European Journal of Pragmatism and American Philosophy* 6, no. 2: 264–286.

Liszka, James. 2012. "Charles Peirce on Ethics." In *The Normative Thought of Charles Peirce*, edited by Cornelis de Waal and Krzysztof Piotr Skowronski, 44–82. New York: Fordham University Press.

Nussbaum, Martha C. 2007. *Frontiers of Justice: Disability, Nationality, Species Membership*. Cambridge, MA: Harvard University Press.

Nussbaum, Martha C. 2010. *Not For Profit*. Princeton, NJ: Princeton University Press.

Pape, Helmut. 1997. "Love's Power and the Causality of Mind: C. S. Peirce on the Place of Mind and Culture in Evolution." *Transactions of the Charles S. Peirce Society* 33, no. 1 (Winter): 59–90.

Peirce, Charles S. 1931–1958. *The Collected Papers of Charles Sanders Peirce*. 8 vols. Vols. 1–6 edited by Charles Hartshorne and Paul Weiss. Vols. 7–8 edited by Arthur W. Burks. Cambridge, MA: Harvard University Press. Referred to as CP.

Peirce, Charles S. 1867. Manuscripts held at the Houghton Library of Harvard University, as identified in Richard Robin. *Annotated Catalogue of the Papers of Charles S. Peirce*. Amherst: University of Massachusetts Press. And in Richard Robin. 1971. "The Peirce Papers: A Supplementary Catalogue." *Transactions of the Charles S. Peirce Society* 7, no. 1 (Winter): 37–57. (Referred to as R.)

Peirce, Charles S. 1982–2010. *The Writings of Charles S. Peirce: A Chronological Edition*. 7 vols. to date. Edited by the Peirce Edition Project. Bloomington: Indiana University Press. (Referred to as W.)

Peirce, Charles S. 1992–1998. *The Essential Peirce: Selected Philosophical Writings*. 2 vols. Vol. 1 edited by Nathan Houser and Christian Kloesel. Vol. 2 edited by the Peirce Edition Project. Bloomington, Indiana University Press. (Referred to as EP.)

Plato. 2008. *Republic*. Translated by Robin Waterfield. Oxford: Oxford University Press.

Potter, Vincent G. 1997. *Charles S. Peirce on Norms and Ideals*. New York: Fordham University Press.

Savan, David. 1981. "Peirce's Semiotic Theory of Emotions." In *Proceedings of the C. S. Peirce Bicentennial International Congress*, edited by Kenneth L. Ketner, Joseph M. Ransdell, Carolyn Eisele, Max H. Fisch, and Charles S. Hardwick, 319–333. Lubbock: Texas Tech University Press.

Schelling, Friedrich. 2006. *Philosophical Investigations into the Essence of Human Freedom*. Translated by Jeff Love and Johannes Schmidt. Albany: State University of New York Press.

Staab, Janice M. 1999. "Questions Concerning Peirce's Agapic Continuity." *Transactions of the Charles S. Peirce Society* 35, no. 1: 157–176.

Trout, Lara. 2010. *The Politics of Survival: Peirce, Affectivity, and Social Criticism*. New York: Fordham University Press.

PART III

LOGIC AND MATHEMATICS

CHAPTER 10

WHY STUDY LOGIC?

MARK MIGOTTI

This chapter is about a question and a book—the question that gives me my title, and the *Minute Logic* (ML), a book Peirce began to write in the summer of 1901, but abandoned four chapters in, by the end of the following year.[1] He concludes the second chapter of this work with a dialogue in ten questions between author and reader entitled "Why Study Logic?" I aim, first, to explain how this question informs the conception of logic that animates ML and outline what the resulting conception is; and, second, to draw attention to certain of its signal merits.

According to Peirce, a due appreciation of why logic is worth studying is indispensable for arriving at a sound understanding of what it is—and vice versa. Writing a century after his death, I would say "all but" indispensable, not *absolutely* indispensable, on the grounds that advances in logic *can* undoubtedly be made without concern for why it's worth studying—or, for that matter, what it fundamentally is. Most of the progress in the subject of the past century and more attests to this. But to make this qualification is not to weaken the Peircean contention but to strengthen it: where mainstream work in logic has long taken the value of the enterprise more or less for granted, Peirce placed its point and purpose at the very center of his thinking, and is the better for it. Peirce's pragmaticist understanding of logic, philosophy, mathematics, and their interrelations alerts us to ways in which ingrained assumptions and categories of more familiar approaches can hinder more than help; and this is especially and pointedly true of his distinctive way of connecting the neglected question Why *study* logic? with the venerable question What *is* logic?

Thematically, the first half of my paper deals mainly with the relationship between logic and experience and the second half mainly with that between logic and mathematics. Textually, the first half is devoted mainly to the first two sections of ML's first chapter and the second half to select portions of the chapter's third section.[2]

1. Theory and Utility

"Begin, if you will," Peirce begins, "by calling logic the theory of the conditions which determine reasonings to be secure. A conception at once more exact and extended may be looked for in the sequel" (CP2.1, 1902). Twenty-five years earlier, in "The Fixation of Belief," he had observed that, because "the object of reasoning is to find out, from the consideration of what we already know, something else which we do not know [, . . .] reasoning is good if it be such as to give a true conclusion from true premises, and not otherwise" (CP5.365). In expressing himself thus, Peirce might naturally be read as offering a cautious—if not vague or ambiguous—variant of the familiar textbook definition of validity in argument: an argument is valid, students are told on the first day of logic class, just in case it is impossible for its premises to be true and its conclusion false. On the hard-to-question assumption that an ironclad guarantee of the preservation of truth from premises to conclusion bestows a remarkable pitch of security on stretches of reasoning, we may think that ML's opening description of the book's subject amounts to a third version of the same basic idea: logic is about moving from true premises to true conclusions without slippage . . . or something like that. But this would be either banal or specious.

Before neophytes can be taught the conditions under which an argument is valid, they must be introduced to the very idea of an argument, in the technical sense required to get their field of study off the ground. So the first difference between Peirce and the textbooks is that, whereas the latter set their sights on abstract, structural objects—purpose-built sets of sentences or well-formed formulae, the final member(s) of which is/are designated CONCLUSION(s),[3] the others PREMISES—the former proposes to inquire into an *activity* in which we all engage throughout our waking lives: reasoning; more precisely stretches or instances of such activity, reasonings. A second difference concerns the degree of security in inference aspired to: a deductively valid argument *guarantees* successful transmission of truth from premises to conclusion, and while ratiocinative security in such abundance may in some sense be "as good as it gets," it may fairly be thought—and Peirce does think—that reasonings not as supremely secure as that can still be of logical interest. If it is indeed *impossible* for these premises to be true if that conclusion is false, reasoning from the truth of the premises to the truth of the conclusion is mightily secure; but premises may support conclusions to lesser degrees in manifold ways, and Peirce thinks of logic as "the theory of *all* reasoning,"[4] anything and everything that may materially bear on whether a sort or instance of reasoning is in some measure good. Third, and for present purposes most important, whereas "logic" as a term of current academic art denotes an inherently formal enterprise, Peirce holds that "formal logic is by no means the whole of logic, or even its principal part."[5]

To recapitulate: we have three contrasts between Peirce's understanding of logic and the conception that has become familiar to us, one in respect of the *objects* studied, one in respect of the *strength* of inference examined, and one in respect of the *scope* of the undertaking. Regarding objects studied, we have reasonings in which we engage on the one side and arguments we formulate on the other; regarding strength of inference, the difference between deductive necessitation and weaker forms of support for beliefs arrived at by means of reasoning; and regarding the scope of the science, the contrast between formal logic and logic tout court.

Writing some seventy years after the composition of ML in the preface to his *Philosophy of Logic*, Quine, apropos the fact that "precedent could be cited for applying the word ["logic"] to two dissimilar studies: deductive and inductive logic," opined that, since "the philosophy of inductive logic would be in no way distinguishable from philosophy's main stem, the theory of knowledge, [what] calls for a distinctive bit of philosophy is deductive logic" (1970, vii). In claiming a virtual equivalence between the *philosophy* of inductive logic and epistemology, Quine chooses his words carefully; to assert flatly that *inductive logic* itself (as distinct from the philosophy thereof) would be in no way distinguishable from the theory of knowledge would be rash, not least because it would immediately draw awkward attention to the thorny question, What is inductive logic anyway? The logic of inductive inference or argument? And which inferences and arguments are these? Any that aspire to a form or degree of validity other than the deductive? In this case inductive logic would be the logic of all "ampliative reasoning," and we would have a contrast between the logic of necessary preservation of truth and the logic of everything else. But conceiving inductive logic as broadly as this would ignore important distinctions.

When Hume raised his notorious "problem of induction," and Goodman proposed a New Riddle thereof, the focus of attention was on the difference between well and ill-founded expectations about the future. Reasoning from evidence drawn from the past (every day so far the sun has risen) to a conclusion about the future (the sun will rise tomorrow) is distinct from what Peirce calls abductive inference, and what is in the early twenty-first century often, misleadingly enough, referred to as "inference to the best explanation."[6] As Peirce conceives it, induction properly so called is employed when we draw conclusions about collections on the basis of facts about samples thereof. Because the sun has risen at dawn *every* day so far, we infer that the collection of days on which it rises includes days that have not yet arrived—just as if, having drawn nothing but shiny yellow balls from a capacious bag over a long period of time, we concluded that the bag contained yellow balls only.[7]

In abduction, we seek not to establish relative frequencies in populations, but to explain something in need of explanation.[8] And whereas inductive reasoning in one or another narrow sense has given rise to formal systems of inductive logic, the prospects for fruitful formal treatments of abductive reasoning are dim. More to the point, that there is a notable gap in formal achievements between the study of deductive argument and the study of all other kinds, however characterized, can hardly be denied: deductive logic has long been well entrenched in the curriculum and is eminently respectable; inductive logic either belongs to the intellectual demimonde of the critical thinking racket[9] or is a bone of contention among specialists, a subject of debate between Bayesian epistemologists and their opponents, or among defenders of different versions of confirmation theory, for example.[10] Hence, presumably, Quine's breezy contention that deductive and inductive logic are "dissimilar studies," another bit of disciplinary lore that is either true but trivial, or simply not true (or not simply true).[11]

Returning to ML's opening paragraph, Peirce follows his initial demarcation of logic, not with the more exact and extended conception of the enterprise that was promised "in the sequel"—that doesn't arrive for another two hundred pages[12]—but by fastening on the idea that logic is a theory. "The end of any theory [being] to furnish a rational account of its object," Peirce writes, "[a] theory aims directly at nothing but knowing," so that "fairness forbids our making utility the criterion of excellence of the theory" (CP2.1). At the very outset readers of ML are warned against misapprehension: since, qua theory, logic is concerned only and exactly to further an improved understanding of its subject matter, it isn't immediately concerned to enhance anyone's ability to *do* anything. Works of theory are not manuals of practical art. Just as "criteria for judging whether a meal is nutritious differ from directions for cooking or menu-planning" (Haack [1993] 2009, 264), so the theory of the conditions that determine reasonings to be secure differs from the provision of guidelines for the achievement of secure reasoning.[13]

"For the most part," Peirce continues, "theories do little or nothing for every-day business. Nobody fit to be at large would recommend a carpenter who had to put up a pigsty or an ordinary cottage to make an engineer's statical diagram[14] of the structure" (§3).[15] And as a trained carpenter can put up a pigsty without the aid of statical diagrams, we can all of us trained masters of the art of getting through the day manage the reasoning needed for our familiar routines without studying logic.[16] We have, Peirce claims, "a natural instinct for right reasoning, which, within the special business of each of us, has received a severe training by its conclusions being constantly brought into comparison with experiential results" (§3). "Nay", he goes on, "we not only have a reasoning instinct, but ... we have an instinctive *theory* of reasoning which gets corrected in the course of our experience" (§3). Further on (in "Why Study Logic?") he puts the point this way: "Every reasoner ... has some general idea of what good reasoning is. This constitutes a theory of logic: the scholastics called it the reasoner's *logica utens* [logic in use]" (§186). In light of the fact that anyone who decides to *study* logic is already in possession of a well-tested *logica utens*, arrived at without explicit reflection, "it would be most unreasonable to demand that the study of logic should supply an artificial method of doing the thinking that his regular business requires a man daily to do" (§3).

At their worst, classes in critical reasoning require their instructors to shill for, precisely, an artificial method of doing the thinking that, by their very presence in the classroom, their students have proven already to do sufficiently well. By contrast, one might think, introductions to formal logic should be in a different case, and so they should. But at *their* worst, teachers of such courses do little to discourage their students from thinking that first-order logic differs from the quasi-formal diagramming and evaluating of "real-life" arguments chiefly in being more recondite and formidable. Often enough, students in introductory logic courses can be forgiven the misimpression that the predicate calculus is a curious kind of intellectual Rube Goldberg machine for checking and underwriting the most humdrum of reasonings. In effect, such students come away with the idea that the difference between formal logic and informal logic is akin to that between formal dress and loungewear—basically a contrast between the loose and comfortable and the stiff and ceremonial. Where run-of-the-mill classroom and textbook pay only lip service to the idea that the study of logic is well served by serious reflection on its point and value, Peirce begins ML with a frank statement of what *not* to expect from logic and what it would be silly to hope for from it. Approaching his subject obliquely, he shifts smoothly from a preliminary description of what logic is to a penetrating account of circumstances that render the study of it entirely otiose. Having entitled the first section of this opening chapter "Logic's Promises," Peirce spends most of his time warding off false promises.

But if the theory of reasoning can't "with any semblance of fairness" be considered helpful "in questions closely concerning a man's business," where can it be helpful? What *is* the point of studying logic? Logic, Peirce answers, is needed when it comes to "extraordinary and unusual problems—especially . . . those of a speculative character, whose conclusions are not readily checked by experience, and where our instinctive reasoning power begins to lose its self-confidence; as when we question what we ought to think about psychical research, about the Gospels, about difficult questions of political economy, about the constitution of matter, or when we inquire by what methods we can most speedily advance our knowledge of such matters" (§4). Beyond this, logic may be useful "apart from any direct application, by supplying us with modes of conception which are useful" (§5). In the final reckoning, however, the "highest and greatest value" of the study "is that it affords us an understanding of the processes of reasoning" (§6): in this "the Platos are thoroughly right" (§6), by which, I think, Peirce means to say that a just appreciation of the value and importance of logic requires a firm grip on the difference between the true value of something and its usefulness, in the sense of aptitude to further predesignated, practical aims.[17] If your chief concern is your daily business, and that business is not of a speculative, theoretical nature, logic has little to offer you. But if you are a philosopher, things are entirely otherwise, as they are if you are a mathematician of a philosophical cast of mind, especially in the decades spanning the turn of the twentieth century.

2. Loose Reasoning and Minute Study

"When I was beginning my philosophical reading," Peirce relates, "my father, Benjamin Peirce, forced me to recognize the extremely loose reasoning common to philosophers. It was a matter open to the remark of every mathematician even before Weierstrass, when mathematical reasoning was far less strict than it has since become" (CP2.9, 1902). In citing Weierstrass in this connection, Peirce may have in mind his definition of real number, which played a crucial role in "arithmetical proofs of the basic theorems on continuous functions" (Stillwell 2019, 38–39); and it is certainly true that loose reasoning and loose definition can reinforce one another to baleful effect. But Peirce isn't remarking on Weierstrass as opposed to other pioneering nineteenth-century mathematicians; he is remarking on a characteristic defect in the reasonings of philosophers, one he alleges to have been evident to mathematicians even before Weierstrass. While philosophers of recent times may have become somewhat stricter in their reasonings, so too has "logical criticism ... grown more searching." In any case, "you may search the whole library of modern metaphysics from Descartes to the most accurate metaphysical reasoners of today and hardly find a vital argument of an elaborate and apodictical kind that does not leave room to drive a coach and four through it" (CP2.9).

As Peirce was writing ML, logical criticism was growing more searching by the day.[18] It was in the decades spanning the turn of the twentieth century that modern mathematical logic took shape, and the shape it took owes much to "the development of modern mathematics in the direction of abstractness" (Putnam 1982 294), a development that was already clear to Peirce, who avers in ML's third chapter that "it is only within the last half century that mathematicians have come to have a perfectly clear recognition of what is mathematical soil and what foreign to mathematics" (CP4.243, c. 1902).[19] The point of this chapter, entitled "The Simplest Mathematics," is to introduce readers to "certain extremely simple branches of mathematics which, owing to their utility in logic have to be treated in considerable detail, although to the mathematician they are hardly worth consideration."[20] The utility of mathematics for logic, Peirce holds, is in part a consequence of the fact that "*every* science ... has a mathematical branch," so that "there is a mathematical logic, just as there is a mathematical optics and a mathematical economics" (§240; emphasis added). But logic has a distinctive need of mathematics, as it stands in a more intimate relationship to that science, than do other fields of inquiry: for "all formal logic is merely mathematics applied to logic [...;] formal logic, however developed, is mathematics" (§228, §240).

The branches of mathematics developed in ML chapter 3 are not "simple" in the sense of easy—as single-digit additions are easier to do in your head than divisions by fractions, because they're simpler. The mathematical studies that Peirce equates with formal logic are simple in respect of their assumptions and postulates.[21] The very simplest of them rests only on "the simplest possible hypothesis," namely, "that there are two objects, which we denote by v and f" (§250). In due course, these values—as we would now call them[22]—will be ascribed to propositions, and "when dichotomous algebra comes to be applied to logic, it will be found necessary to call one of them verity and the other falsity; and the letters v and f were chosen with a view to that" (§259). To do what they need to do mathematically, however, "v" and "f" may be given any number of outré interpretations. Peirce allows that "to ... make v represent, let us say, Julius Caesar, and f, Pompey, since they may represent any subjects that are individual and definite, and thereupon further to propose to make every proposition either v or f, shocks the lower order of formal logicians," but replies that such "stickling for usage bars the progress of mathematical thought" (§263). Not that anyone could take v and f to refer to actual Roman generals; *that*, Peirce grants, "nobody could mean to do" (§263). The point, rather, is that "the conception of Caesar may be [generalized] so as to make it include those propositions which are destined to triumph over the others" (§263), and mutatis mutandis for the conception of Pompey and propositions destined to go down to defeat.

Writing in review of CP volume 4 in 1935, Quine describes Peirce's concerns in his simplest mathematics as resembling those of "the Polish logicians of the present day," the common focus being "the propositional calculus in its structural aspect as the simplest of all non-trivial calculi" (551).[23] It will be observed that Quine describes Peirce's enterprise in terms natural to him, but not available to the author he's reviewing; Peirce's dichotomous algebra has become the propositional calculus. Quine's terminology, and a battery of assumptions that come with it, has remained standard. Students beginning the study of the formal conditions of deductive validity for arguments that turn only on the role of sentential connectives are told that they are learning elementary logic, beginning with the propositional calculus. They aren't told that they are being introduced to a mathematically negligible but logically important branch of mathematics, beginning with a formal system based on the simplest possible hypothesis.

Against this background, and in light of the importance of mathematics in Peirce's thought and the scale and abundance of his contributions to mathematical logic, his taking pains to insist that formal logic is not only by no means the whole of logic, but also *not even its principal part* takes us aback. Why not say the very opposite? Why not hold that although there may be *more* to logic than what is formally tractable, it is exactly here that logic comes into its own? Why, more pointedly, should Peirce be especially concerned to insist that, while "it is generally understood that I hold logical algebra to be the most important part of logic," that is "quite a mistake. I am in but not of the world of formal logic" (R1334, 1905)?

When Peirce derided metaphysical arguments that leave room to drive a coach and four through them, he carefully restricted his target to arguments of an elaborate *and apodictical* kind, arguments that set out to be decisive. And mathematics, in Peirce's view, is the home of truly decisive argumentation. In mathematics in general, and in deductive logic specifically, we aim to *prove* things, not merely render them plausible. But what, exactly, is required in order to prove that something is true? If a proposition C is proven only if it is established beyond any rational doubt or prospect of refutation by further evidence, proof becomes an infallibilist notion by definition, requiring epistemological fallibilists to deny that *anything* is ever really *proven* to be true. But if a series of premises $P_1 \ldots P_n$ entails a conclusion C, it is natural to regard the premises as proving the conclusion. Formal rigor, formal proof, and formal proof theory work together and are at the center of the welter of advances in mathematical logic already alluded to more than once. Nevertheless, as Timothy Smiley reminds us, "most deductions aren't proofs" (1995, 729), for the simple reason that valid chains of inference may rest on false premises. Having been taught what it is for an argument to be valid, students of logic are informed that a *sound* argument is valid with true premises, so that only if an argument is sound can it be safely taken to have a true conclusion.

Just as reasonings may be secure to a degree that falls short of deductive validity, so may they be rigorous in a sense that transcends the realm of formal provability. Predictably, in the opening pages of ML, Peirce focuses on this broader notion, which he calls "minuteness": "How shall the theory of right reasoning be investigated? The nature of the subject must be an important factor in determining the method. Before touching on that, however, suppose we ask how, in the roughest sense, any theory ought to be investigated. Am I wrong in thinking I catch a whisper of good sense that, for one item of the reply, a theory should be investigated *carefully and minutely*?" (CP2.8,[24] emphasis Peirce's). The "minuteness" of the *Minute Logic*, we see, is a matter not of smallness in bulk (far from it!), but of close accuracy in design and execution. And rigorous reasoning and minute study being required of theoretical work across the board, it's as distressing as it is predictable that a penchant for loose reasoning is so often accompanied by a disdain for "piddling minuteness" in the examination of logical principles—an aversion that, notably, is not typically carried over to questions of empirical science or engineering, for example.[25] Accordingly, Peirce warns readers that they "will often think that the writer makes far too much of microscopic distinctions" and offers in his defense the fact that "in this science errors become enormously magnified in their effects, and stricter accuracy is for that reason rendered obligatory" (§16).[26] In any case, he continues, "no distinction—the reader may assure himself—will here be insisted upon without an adequate motive, even if it be a mistaken one" (§16).

Peirce ends the second section of ML chapter 1 with a paragraph that deserves quotation in full:

> The reader may find the matter so dry, husky, and innutritious to the spirit that he cannot believe there is any human good in it. Stuff which offers no images more enlivening than that "Socrates is a man and therefore mortal" or that of "a person who stands to some woman in the relation of a lover of every benefactor of hers," may be too desperately inhuman to be accounted by him anything but diabolic idiocy, the product of hell's bedlam. But the fault is his. It shall not be more tedious than the multiplication table, that may be promised; and as the multiplication table is worth the pains of learning, unless one is a prince, so shall this be, even if one be a prince. (§17)

"Socrates is a man and therefore mortal" is a staple of Aristotelian syllogistic logic; "a person who stands to some woman in the relation of a lover of every benefactor of hers" cannot be represented within that traditional formalism: the logical import of nested quantifiers—as indeed of quantification itself[27]—can be grasped only in the wake of the deepening and clarifying of basic logical concepts achieved by the likes of Weierstrass, Dedekind, Frege, . . . and the author of ML.[28] At one stroke, Peirce invokes a venerable criticism of formal logic as such,[29] Aristotelian or modern, and makes a sly allusion to a pathbreaking achievement of modern logic, one for which he himself deserves a goodly share of credit.

3. Logic and Experience

Why study logic? Because you want to pursue philosophical questions and don't want to be taken in by those arguments through which you could drive a coach and four: that is the burden of the first two sections of ML chapter 1.

Fair enough, you may say, but mustn't we be careful not to get bogged down in matters of terminology and usage rather than philosophical substance? Evidently, many inquiries that Peirce would regard as belonging to the field of logic would in the early twenty-first century be classified as something else, epistemology, for example, or philosophy of language, or philosophy of science, or cognitive psychology, or etc.; and would not have stood out from contemporaries such as John Stuart Mill in this respect. In light of this, there is tempting to blunt the force of Peirce's challenge to familiar ways of thinking about logic by suggesting that our present division of intellectual labor has something to be said for it. To be sure, we must be on our guard against verbal quibbling of course; and current academic fashion may in many areas be more than mere fashion. But the difference between construing logic narrowly, as we have become accustomed to do, so that it is virtually synonymous with "formal, mathematical logic," and construing it broadly, as Peirce does, so that it covers the full gamut of considerations pertinent to the security and fruitfulness of patterns and habits of reasoning,[30] has serious theoretical consequences. Nomenclature simply isn't to the point.

Why are philosophers so prone to acquiesce in unconvincing argumentation? Largely because their conclusions are so little able to be "checked by experience"; and this is also the reason that mathematical training can be helpful in detecting outsized holes in philosophical arguments. Philosophical positions being stubbornly resistant to outright refutation by recalcitrant experience and congenitally insusceptible to decisive test by "crucial experiment,"[31] bold imagination and subtle ingenuity can be needed to detect flaws and make plain why the premises from which a large, weighty conclusion is said ineluctably to follow are too slender and fragile to provide the requisite support.[32] Since the question how, if at all, logic and experience bear upon each other is substantial, not verbal, it follows that the question how best to understand the scope of logical inquiry isn't to be settled by an appeal to idiom and usage. And studying Peirce helps us appreciate this point, since in his philosophy, the mutual bearing of logic and experience is at the top of the agenda.[33]

When we begin studying logic, we have been reasoning for a long time, and, if Peirce is right, have also developed an instinctive theory of reasoning that has ensured that we reason well enough to meet our everyday needs. Now that we have, ex hypothesi, become interested in questions outside the scope of those everyday needs, we must subject our inchoate, instinctive conception of what makes for security in reasoning, our *logica utens*, to scientific scrutiny. We require what the medieval called a *logica docens*, a theory of the conditions that make reasonings secure that is not "antecedent to any systematic study of the subject," but rather "the result of [a] scientific study [of it]" (CP2.204). And indispensable to scientific reasoning and its logic is an appreciation of the fact that, although immediate utility is emphatically not the measure of the excellence of a theory, nevertheless "a theory cannot be sound unless it be susceptible of applications, immediate or remote" (CP2.7).

Readers of "How to Make Our Ideas Clear," or of the definitions of "Pragmatic and Pragmatism" in J. M. Baldwin's *Dictionary of Philosophy and Psychology*, will recognize in the claim that a sound theory must be susceptible of application—somehow, somewhere, somewhen[34]—a veiled allusion to what has come to be called the pragmatic maxim of meaning: the principle that (in Peirce's 1902 formulation from Baldwin's dictionary) "in order to ascertain the meaning of an intellectual conception one should consider what practical consequences might conceivably result by necessity from the truth of that conception; and the sum of these consequences will constitute the entire meaning of the conception" (CP5.9). A conception is intellectual when it is such that "reasonings may turn on it" (CP5.8); and since a concern to understand the conditions that determine reasonings to be secure betokens a desire to understand "what reasoning *ought* to be, not . . . what it is" (CP2.7, emphasis added), it is of cardinal importance that the conceptions with which we reason be clear: "The very first lesson that we have a right to demand that logic shall teach us is, how to make our ideas clear[35]; and a most important one it is, deprecated only by minds who stand in need of it" (CP5.393, 1877).[36] As reasonings can be secure enough for everyday purposes without passing scientific muster, so ideas may be clear enough for ordinary life without being really clear. If we are to study logic seriously—and if we're not prepared to do that we may as well spare ourselves the bother[37]—we must take this deceptively unprepossessing truism to heart, which is to say that we must entertain serious doubts about the soundness of our present theory of reasoning.

"Why is it [O Reader]," Peirce asks, "that you have undertaken the study of logic? . . . Presuming that, aside from personal reasons, you desire in singleness of heart to examine the theory of reasoning under the guidance of an older student, I remark that this very fact is evidence that you are already a much better logician than the mass of mankind, who are thoroughly persuaded that they reason well enough already" (CP2.123). As we've seen, Peirce holds, emphatically, that the run of humanity *does* reason "well enough" . . . to get through the day. But for precisely this reason few of them care to study logic.[38] To think that reasoning well enough for immediately practical purposes is tantamount to reasoning well enough full stop is to "trust to common sense as affording all the security that could be desired for reasoning" (CP2.123), and while it is a dictum of common sense that people can reason badly, nevertheless, the mass of mankind is "majestically unanimous [in their adhesion] to the proposition that of all the race there is but one single individual who never falls into fallacy; and their only point of difference is that each is quite sure that he himself is that man" (CP2.123). So, for all that you do reason well enough to handle familiar circumstances and questions, unless you want to study logic, or at least see the point of doing so— which is to say, unless you desire in singleness of heart to improve your philosophy— you are not a good reasoner. For "to be cocksure that one is an infallible reasoner is to furnish conclusive evidence either that one does not reason at all, or that one reasons very badly, since that deluded state of mind prevents the constant self-criticism which is . . . the very life of reasoning" (CP2.123).

The suggestion that most of us take ourselves to be infallible reasoners may seem farfetched. But the context makes it clear that Peirce isn't denying that we can be made aware of our mistakes (painful consequences of error being a notoriously effective teacher), or claiming that most of us think that we are incapable of drawing mistaken conclusions. His point is that insofar as one sees no reason to examine and criticize one's habitual *theory* of reasoning, that theory is in effect taken to be impeccable: and *that* it most definitely is not!³⁹

4. Justification and the Categories

As well as, and integrally connected to, its connection to the nature of the subject inquired into, logic, the question Why study logic? functions in ML as a kind of synecdoche for the question Why *study* at all? For if you have "in singleness of heart" committed yourself to scrutinizing your habitual theory of good reasoning and finding out what scientific logic might have to offer you, your reason for doing so can't lie in an extraneous, extraintellectual goal. By the same token, if your motivation for studying something is entirely parasitic on some other, nonintellectual end, the value of study as such is beside the point. Simple structures such as pig sties may be put together with no study at all; advanced fruits of technology such as rocket ships need a great deal of it. But insofar as you are learning what needs to be learned to build a rocket that can get you to the moon solely and entirely because you wish to get to the moon, the value of study and understanding as such has nothing to do with it.

Because the fledgling logician Peirce addresses throughout ML genuinely wants better to understand what it is truly to understand things, he (or of course she) can be expected to ask hard questions at the very outset; he may wonder how in logic genuine advances in theoretical understanding are to be distinguished from fruitless diversions.⁴⁰ In the third section of ML chapter 1, Peirce canvases "a swarm" of competing answers to this question, a "conspectus" of thirteen distinct "methods of establishing the truths of logic" (CP2.18).⁴¹

On first reading it's hard to discern a principle of organization in the approaches to grounding logic that Peirce considers, but on closer inspection, patterns emerge. In respect of length, for example, the methods fall into two groups: nine of them—methods one, two, four through eight, and thirteen—are dealt with in two or three pages each. Method three stands out in taking up ten pages, while methods nine through twelve are crammed into not quite two pages combined. In the present chapter, only the first three methods and the last will be examined, beginning with the opening trio, which are presented in order of Peirce's three universal categories.

Being concerned with reasoning, logic by nature deals with a species of thirdness, the category of law, intelligibility, semiosis, argument, etc. But since the categories can be nested within one another, so that there can be a firstness of a kind of third, and a secondness of it and a thirdness of it,⁴² one might try to establish the truths of logic by reference to any one of the three categories. To attempt to ground logic in a species of firstness, the category of feeling, is to hold that "the goodness and badness of reasonings is not merely indicated by but is constituted and composed of the satisfaction and dissatisfaction respectively, of a certain logical feeling or taste, within us" (CP2.19). As Quine remarks in his review of CP2—the volume that contains ML's first chapter and the portion of its second chapter that contains "Why Study Logic?"—this is "a point of view which [Peirce] most vehemently opposes" (1933, 221). To hold that the ultimate justification of logical principles consists in certain feelings of approbation is to make "gratify[ing] a sense of rationality analogous to taste or conscience" to be the ultimate aim of reasoning, whereas the fact of the matter is that "the sole purpose of reasoning ... is to ascertain the Truth in the sense of that which is SO no matter what be thought about it" (CP2.153). As Peirce had put it in "Fixation," the question of validity in inference "is purely one of fact and not of thinking: A being the facts stated in the premisses and B being that concluded, the question is, whether these facts are really so related that if A were B would generally be" (CP5.365, 1877).

To put it mildly, Quine (1993) conceives of the doctrine that "the validity of logical principles [is based] upon an ultimate subjective *Rechtsgefühl*" (221) broadly and loosely. For he regards this view as in essence the same as "the Euclidean basis of self-evidence," and "the criterion of clearness and distinctness emphasized by Descartes and Leibniz," and also "the criterion of the inconceivability of the denial, as adopted by Spencer and others" (221). But Peirce discusses this latter suite of ideas in the course of examining the third method he canvases, "the opinion ... that logical principles are known by an inward light of reason, called the 'light of nature' to distinguish it from the 'light of grace'" (CP2.23), not the first; so nothing in Peirce's text supports amalgamating his first method with his third, and a great deal speaks against it, for example, the fact that the third method is discussed at such disproportionate length. Attention to the method Peirce interposes between the *Rechtsgefühl* idea and the light of nature idea brings the point into sharp relief.

"Since it must be nearly forty years since I read *La Logique* of the Abbé Gratry, a writer of subtlety and exactitude of thought as well as of elevation of reason," Peirce allows, "my account of his doctrine may not be accurate in its details. I insert it here because after feeling it seems natural to place any proposed method of basing logical principles upon direct individual experience" (CP2.21). Readers of the later Peirce will understand why it seems natural to him to proceed in this way: after logical firstness, a pure feeling of validity, comes logical secondness in the guise of an experiential interaction with something *other*. "Now," Peirce notes, without skipping a beat, "since [logical] principles are general, only a mystical experience could give them" (CP2.21); and while Abbé Gratry may not have put the point quite this way, he does (as best Peirce can remember) "consider[] every act of inductive reasoning in which one passes from the finite to the infinite—particularly every inference which from observation concludes that there is in certain objects of observation a true continuity which cannot be directly observed—to be due to a direct inspiration of the Holy Spirit" (CP2.21).

In the "Fixation," Peirce had maintained that the manifest failure of tenacity, authority, or agreeableness to reason to function as a satisfactory method of fixing belief leads ineluctably to the conclusion that "to satisfy our doubts ... it is necessary that a method should be found by which our beliefs may be determined by nothing human, but by some external permanency—by something upon which our thinking has no effect"; and had followed this by remarking that "some mystics imagine that they have such a method in a private inspiration from on high" (CP5.384, 1877). But, he had declared summarily in response, "that is only a form of the method of tenacity, in which the conception of truth as something public is not yet developed" (CP5.384). In light of this brisk riposte, ML's discussion of Gratry's theologically oriented grounding of logic is striking for its respectful, serious tone. Our surprise at the contrasting treatments of claims of mystical communication in logical inquiry is mitigated when we highlight the crucial qualification "*private* inspiration" in the passage from "Fixation." What Peirce finds worthy of dismissive mention only, not serious discussion, is the idea that the on high might convey vitally important information about the nature of things to certain singularly favored individuals for no particular reason.

The mystics of the "Fixation" are outside the ambit of scientific inquiry. Their claim to have access to an esoteric nonhuman external permanancy in a self-vouchsafed supernal realm from which they receive special deliverances betrays their inability to understand what it is to have a conception of truth as something essentially public. By contrast, the Abbé Gratry is a fellow worker in the field of logic, a theorist with, by secular standards, an unorthodox doctrine. If he is right, we all of us regularly and unwittingly rely on supernatural inspiration for the tight web of conclusions that forms the ingrained "common sense" that guides our everyday activities. This contention may not survive criticism, but it deserves consideration. In the event, and unsurprisingly, Peirce thinks that the mystical experience justification of logic fares no better than the aesthetic feeling view. If Gratry were right, Peirce argues, "every inductive reasoning which passes from observation of the finite and the discrete to belief in the infinite or continuous ought to be accompanied by the sense that that belief was forced upon me, whether I will or not" (§22).[43] But it can be *seen* that this is wrong, the contention "is contradicted by observation."[44] When he reasons inductively, Peirce reports (and, he takes it, when any of us do, including the Abbé Gratry), "instead of experiencing any ... compulsion," such as, for example, he experiences when he sees a snake on the barn floor as he is putting his mare back into her stable, "I feel rather a sort of sympathy with nature which makes me sure that the continuity or the generality is there, somewhat as I felt sure I understood the particular state of mind of my mare at the time I was putting her up" (§22).

This inward sympathy with nature is, Peirce will go on to say, another name for the "inward light of reason." From logical secondness we turn to logical thirdness, which explains immediately why his examination of the credentials of the light of nature to ground logic is so much more thoroughgoing than those of the aesthetic taste view or the communication from on high theory. For reasoning, the activity of which logic seeks a sound theory, already and as such belongs to the province of thirdness, the realm of law and intelligibility, as opposed to that of surd feeling or brute resistance. The idea that logic rests on the deliverances of the "light of reason" is, therefore, from the outset in better shape than the feeling of validity view or the grace-of-the-Holy Spirit view.

"The phrase 'light of reason,' or its near equivalent," writes Peirce, ""may probably be found in every literature" (§24); and "the reasonings of the present treatise will, I expect, make it appear that the history of science, as well as other facts, prove that there is a natural light of reason" (§25). Nevertheless, "the same facts [that support the existence of a light of nature] equally prove that this light is extremely uncertain and deceptive, and consequently unfit to strengthen the principles of logic in any sensible degree" (§25). If we weren't endowed with a natural light of reason, we couldn't justify logic; indeed, if we weren't equipped with a natural light of reason we wouldn't *have* logic! But, says Peirce, the mere possession of an inherent tendency to understand things correctly, in the main and sooner than a chance sampling of explanatory hypotheses would predict—a built-in prophylactic against theoretical wild goose chases so to speak—isn't sufficient in and of itself and without further ado to underwrite the validity of valid logical principles. While the natural light of reason will invariably be part of the correct account of the ultimate source of logical truth and has as more to offer than a sui generis *Rechtsgefühl* or a mystical communion with the infinite, it is too indiscerning and fallible to ground logical truth without further aid.

5. Mathematics and Logic

Peirce concludes his conspectus of methods of establishing the truths of logic with the view that seems to him most promising: "The chief source of logical truth," he writes, "though never recognized by logicians, always has been and always must be the same as the source of mathematical truth" (CP2.76). Inquiry into the grounds of logical truth thus requires inquiry into the source of mathematical truth, "one of the most vexed of questions" (CP2.77). In Peirce's opinion, "mathematical truth is derived from observation of creations of our own visual imagination, which we may set down on paper in form of diagrams" (CP2.77), a hypothesis that, he declares, has been effectively substantiated by Friedrich Albert Lange, in "a little book ... [that] I can recommend ... as one of the very few works on logic that I have found too short" (CP2.76).[45]

Lange ([1877] 2010) takes logical truth to be verified by "imagin[ing] something like an Euler's diagram" and "holds up as a model Aristotle's proof of the conversion of the universal negative proposition" (2.77), the fact that if no A is B, no B can be A. To represent Aristotle's reasoning by means of an Euler diagram, or a Venn diagram as they are more commonly called,[46] you draw two overlapping circles, naming the leftmost, say, A and the rightmost B. The premise No A is B is depicted by blackening out all of the A circle that overlaps with the B circle. This done, it can be seen at a glance that all of the B circle that overlaps with the A circle has necessarily also been blackened. Reflection on this fact reveals that the verbal difference between No A is B and No B is A vanishes when the common logical import of the distinct English sentences is rendered in the form of a single diagram. To see this is to see that universal negatives convert, to *observe* that if no A is B, it is quite impossible for any B to be A.[47]

Today, students of logic may be taught that No A is B can be expressed as (x) (IF Ax THEN NOT-Bx) and may also be told that the conversion of negative universals is a special case of the contraposition of the material conditional thus embedded in a universal quantification.[48] Moreover, when logical equivalence—for example, of a material conditional and its contrapositive—is demonstrated by means of truth tables, the basic iconic principle is the same as in an Euler–Venn demonstration of valid syllogistic reasoning.[49] In the one case, you begin by seeing that shading the overlap between an A circle and a B circle is the same thing as shading the overlap between the B circle and the A circle. Then, given the relevant conventions, you can see that this precludes the possibility of overlap between potential occupants of the circles, the A's and B's themselves. Consequently, you see that under these circumstances no A's can be B's and no B's can be A's, that you have made the set of A's disjoint from the set of B's, etc. etc. In the other case, you begin by learning how to calculate a truth table; once you can do this, you can see that, given the relevant conventions, the result of such a calculation for a conditional statement is exactly the same as that for its contrapositive.

The idea that logical-cum-mathematical truth is rooted in a kind of observation undertaken by the mind's eye, the objects of which can then be set down on paper for convenient (re)examination, is clearly very different from the logicist view that mathematics has its foundations in "general logical laws and . . . definitions," (Frege 1980 [1884], 4) and it should not be confused with the intuitionist idea that logic and mathematics both need to be provided with a secure constructivist footing. In effect, Peirce, before the fact, refuses the terms of the familiar debate between logicism and intuitionism; and he is in consequence ripe for misinterpretation by reviewers in the grip of the reigning paradigm. In his 1933 review mentioned above, Quine compounds his confusions about logical firstness and logical thirdness with something more egregious, and also more revealing: a mixing together of his self-fabricated aesthetic feeling-cum-light of nature foundation for logical truth with the contention that mathematical and logical truth have a common source.

According to Peirce, "true mathematical reasoning is so much more evident than it is possible to render any doctrine of logic proper—without just such reasoning—that an appeal in mathematics to logic would only embroil a situation" (CP4.243, c. 1902). Quine (1933) paraphrases this line of thought as follows: "Prior to all logic, Peirce holds, we are aware of 'mathematical' necessities" (221), whereby the inverted commas around "mathematical" deserve mention. They are there because Quine takes himself to know better than Peirce, so much so that he is quite incapable of finding Peirce's position on the nature of mathematics and logic and their interrelations to be anything other than utterly perverse.

On the one, creditable, hand, Peirce "does not seek to found the validity of mathematical reasoning upon any metaphysical basis of pure intuition, . . . but contemns rather all false philosophical pretense of doubt and declares that mathematical reasoning, self-evident as it is, demands neither faith nor substantiation" (Quine 1933, 221). Moreover, unlike "the German subjectivism," he maintains that "truth does not consist in momentary acceptance by reason, or a present inconceivability of falsity, but rather in 'a final unshakable compulsion' preventing one ever to imagine the falsity of the proposition" (221–222). But on the other, discreditable, hand, "at the level of the so-called mathematical reasoning" German subjectivist doctrines are frankly embraced, so that "in the matter of a criterion of logical validity, . . . it is difficult to detect any fundamental difference between Peirce's view and the German or Cartesian doctrines which he opposes: self-evidence, instinctive common sense or *Rechtsgefühl* is retained in full force as the final touchstone of logical truth" (221).

On Quine's (1933) showing, Peirce's first method of establishing logical truth and his thirteenth end up in flat contradiction to one another: "for a criterion of the validity of a reasoning process Peirce is ultimately driven, with his self-justificatory 'mathematical' reasoning, to a basis not unlike the *Rechtsgefühl* he condemns" (222). As J. L. Austin ([1962] 1990) said, in philosophy there's the bit where you say it and the bit where you take it back.[50] Indeed Peirce says it: logical validity can't be based on either a surd *Rechtsgefühl* or the natural light of reason; but then he takers it back: mathematics is the foundation of logic, and *it* rests on an apprehension of necessities—for example, the impossibility of two contradictory propositions both being true—which derives from something not fundamentally different from a *Rechtsgefühl* or a light of reason.

Quine's attempted *tu quoque* is a serious muddle, born of a double conflation, the first of which has been noted—of the distinctively nineteenth-century German view that goodness and badness of reasonings *is not merely indicated by but is constituted and composed of* the satisfaction and dissatisfaction, respectively, of a certain logical feeling or taste with the age-old view that logical principles are known by an inward light of reason—and the second of which is the confusion of the mishmash produced by the first conflation with the idea that Peirce thinks is on the right track, that mathematical and logical truth spring from the same source. And there's more to it than just this. For part of what explains Quine's egregious sloppiness and virtual refusal to so much as try to understand what Peirce is up to may be that he is inchoately aware that Peirce had already articulated views for which he, Quine, would become celebrated many decades later.[51]

In explanation of his disagreement with the view of "the philosophical mathematician, Dr. Richard Dedekind," that "mathematics [is] a branch of logic" (CP4.239, *c.* 1902) Peirce touches on why it is (in his view) that the mathematics most pertinent to logic can be so inconsiderable to mathematicians. Dedekind's position, he observes, "would not result from my father's definition [of mathematics], which runs, not that mathematics is the science of *drawing* necessary conclusions—which would be deductive logic—but that it is the science which *draws* necessary conclusions." If you are chiefly concerned to unearth new and interesting necessary conclusions, you show yourself to be a mathematician by intellectual temperament. As such, you will be "intensely interested in efficient methods of reasoning, with a view to their possible extension to new problems" (CP4.239). By the same token, however, you will not "trouble [yourself] minutely to dissect those parts of this method whose correctness is a matter of course" (CP4.239); but it is exactly those parts that interest the logician. So, of a given "algebra of logic . . . the mathematician asks what value [it] has as a calculus. Can it be applied to unravelling a complicated question? Will it, at one stroke, produce a remote consequence?" (CP4.239). The logician, by contrast, "does not wish the algebra to have that character" (CP4.239). For his purposes, "the greater number of distinct logical steps into which the algebra breaks up an inference, will for him constitute a superiority of it over another which moves more swiftly to its conclusions" (CP4.239).

When Quine turned Peirce's dichotomous algebra into the propositional calculus, there was more to it than appeared on the surface, an initial indication of which is the repeated use of scare quotation marks around "mathematical" in his rehearsal of Peirce's views on the role of mathematical reasoning in the justification of logical principles. As we saw above, Peirce's broad conception of logic invites inquiry into the boundaries between logic and epistemology, logic and cognitive science, etc.; and we see now that his understanding of formal logic in particular invites inquiry into the boundaries between logic and mathematics; and that subject, of course, has long been dominated by the long shadow of logicism.

When we ask what makes a given mathematical formalism a system of logic, as distinct from a set theory, or an algebra of a nonlogical kind, or whatever, from within the mainstream, Fregean tradition of thinking about these matters, we are soon led to the question, What is logical about the logical constants? What makes propositional conjunction logical while numerical addition is arithmetical? According to Ian Hacking, the problem of defining logical constants (as opposed to simply enumerating them) "would be unimportant were it not for the [logicist] analytic program" (1979, 287). For apart from "that profound speculation about the nature and origin of necessary truth," there is "no point in trying to separate logic from other science" (287, emphasis mine). It doesn't take much to find fault with this remarkable contention, which surely fails on either of the two most natural readings of the crucial notion of "separating" one science from others.

If separating logic from "other science" means singling it out as the sole keeper of unimpeachable, infallible truth, Peirce—and, I think, good philosophical sense—takes this to be a bad idea full stop. Fallibilism holds true in logic and mathematics every bit as robustly as it does in empirical science and garden-variety knowledge.[52] So on this interpretation there is less than no point to trying to separate logic from other science, and the futility of any such undertaking is independent of the Fregean-analytic program. But if separating out the sciences one from the other means assigning to each its proper place in the overall ambit of scientific inquiry, then separating logic from other science is a matter of establishing what distinguishes it as the science that it is; and on this interpretation, there is every point to the project of "separating" logic from the rest of science; and the truth of this is, again, not beholden to a Fregean-analytic approach to the foundations of mathematics.[53]

Why study logic? Because you want to know more about the conditions that determine reasonings to be secure, especially where the nature of the subject matter makes reasonings notoriously *in*secure. To Peirce's examples of psychical research, the Gospels, and the rest, I offer, by way of ending with an eye to future work, the following handful of pertinent issues in the philosophy of logic: logical form,[54] quantification,[55] deviant logic,[56] formalism.[57] There is ample reason to believe that the more thoroughly and rigorously Peircean ideas are brought to bear on these topics, the clearer it will become that he was right: understanding what logic *is* goes hand in hand with understanding why it's worth studying.

Acknowledgments

For helpful comments on early versions of this chapter and fruitful discussion of its contents, I would like to thank Francesco Belluci, Patricia Blanchette, Frank Jankunis, Noa Latham, Brent Odlund, Nicole Wyatt, Richard Zach, and audiences at the University of Calgary Department of Philosophy, the Charles S. Peirce International Centennial Congress, World Logic Day (Southern Alberta), and the History and Philosophy of Math Reading Group at Exeter. I thank Susan Haack for a host of pertinent suggestions and for paving the way. Diana Heney, Vincent Colapietro, Kees de Waal, and Gillman Payette offered valuable insights and observations on later drafts.

6. Appendix

Minute Logic

In *Collected Papers*[58]

Table of Contents

Chapter 1: **Intended Characters of This Treatise** (CP2.1–118, 66 pages)
1. Logic's Promise, CP2.1–8, 3 pages
2. Of Minute Accuracy, CP2.9–17, 4 pages
3. Different Methods in Logic, CP2.18–78, 21 pages
4. [The Categories as such], CP2.79–94, 10 pages
5. [The Categories in semiotic form, applied to Argument(s)], CP2.95–97, 3 pages
6. Clearness of Ideas, CP2.98–99, half a page
7. [Deduction, Chance/Induction, Abduction], CP2.100–104, 3 pages
8. [Methodeutic, or Speculative Rhetoric; "a method of discovering methods"], CP2.105–110, 3 pages
9. [Objective, Hegelian logic; a life history of symbols/signs; modes of Being], CP2.111–118, 4 pages

Chapter 2: ("Pre-logical Notions"; title provided in a Hartshorne and Weiss footnote to "Why Study Logic"; 120 pages)
  CP 1.203–283, 54 pages;
  CP 7.362–387, c. 14 pages;
  CP 2.119–202, 52 pages.
1. [classifying sciences, natural classes], CP1.203–223, 16 pages
2. [higher order classes], CP1.224–231, 4 pages
3. [defining science, the life of science], CP1.232–237, 4 pages

4. [branches of science], CP1.238–272, 20 pages
5. [divisions of philosophy], CP1.273–282, 7 pages
6. [divisions of mathematics and psychology], CP1.283 & CP7.362–387, 15 pages
7. **Why Study Logic?** CP2.119–202, 52 pages

Chapter 3: The Simplest Mathematics (CP4.227–323, 73 pages)
1. [historico-philosophical orienting remarks], CP4.227–244, 15 pages
2. Division of Pure Mathematics, CP4.245–249, 2 pages
3. The Simplest Branch of Mathematics, CP4.250–323, 56 pages

Chapter 4: [no Peirce title given]
CP1.575–584, 8 pages;
CP6.349–352, *c.* 6 pages.

Hartshorne and Weiss's comment at the end of the material in CP1, which deals with logic as a normative science, and the nature of ultimate ends, reads: "There are about five pages missing at this point. The manuscript then continues by repeating some of the foregoing, goes on to list a number of ultimate 'ends' proposed by the early Greeks and concludes with a one-hundred-and-twenty-five-page discussion on the order, history, and contents of the Platonic Dialogues. Except for a short digression which will appear as §7–§8, ch. 11, bk. I, vol. 6, the rest of the manuscript will not be published."

Their comments on the "digression," in CP6, which concerns "reality and existence" and "truth, being, nothing," reads: "§§7 and 8 form a digression in ch. 4 of the Minute Logic (1902-3). The Velian is the stranger of Plato's Sophist, a dialogue which Peirce characterizes in the preceding, unpublished portion of the manuscript (see 1.584n) as being 'purely a logical dialogue' with 'all Hegel's faults and more than a glimmer of Hegel's merit.' The present section is part of an attempt to give the Velian stranger 'a little dose of his own cathartic.'"

Notes

1. See R1579, dated July 10, 1901.
2. A textual overview of the *Minute Logic* as its contents appear in CP is provided in an appendix.
3. Not that introductory courses and textbooks often mention multiple conclusion logic, for reasons that would likely well repay examination.
4. Emphasis added; the quotation, taken from the undated R83, is found in Roberts (1973, 16).
5. CP4.240, from ML, chapter 3.
6. The inaptness of the name "inference to the *best* explanation" lies in the adventitious superlative adjective. A better description (owing to Diana Heney) would be inference to a proximate explanation, or simply to *an* explanation. For an account of the development of Peirce's thinking about abduction (which he sometimes called "hypothesis" or "retroduction"), see Anderson (1986).

7. In fact, our knowledge that sunrises occur every twenty-four hours is based on nothing remotely like this cartoon rendering of the textbook way of conceiving it. Although we didn't used to, we now know that when a sunrise occurs nothing actually *rises*, since (remarkably enough) it's the spinning of the earth that accounts for the appearance of that red disk ascending above the horizon at dawn. Our belief that there will be a sunrise tomorrow (which is not really very aptly termed a prediction) is supported by scientific reasoning, which invariably interweaves and integrates the abductive, the deductive, and the inductive.
8. In consequence, as Cheryl Misak observes, Goodman's challenge to explain why green is a projectible predicate while grue isn't is "not a matter for induction, but for abduction" (2013, 212).
9. No, thankfully it isn't all a racket, but enough of it is to warrant the rude expression. My Peircean reasons for this opinion are found in the next paragraph but two.
10. In line with his title, John Norton, in *The Material Theory of Induction*, presents an account of inductive inference (construed quite broadly) that restricts the scope of formal treatments severely: while formal treatments of specific local domains may be useful, he writes, "a formal approach is the wrong one for understanding inductive inference overall" (2021, vi). As Susan Haack had observed much earlier, the idea that "there is such a thing as favorable-but-not-conclusive evidence" is quite independent of a commitment to there being "such a thing as 'inductive implication' or 'inductive logic,'" especially if "'inductive logic' is taken to indicate relations susceptible of a purely syntactic characterization" ([1993] 2009, 129).
11. The claim is true but trivial if "dissimilar" means not identical; simply not true if it means somehow radically different; and not simply true if it is taken to gesture at the important question of the unity of logical inquiry.
12. In this account, presented in a single, very long sentence that makes up almost all of CP2.200, Peirce identifies the business of logic as that of "ascertaining methods of sound reasoning" and details what this amounts to in the deductive, inductive, and abductive cases. This passage occurs at the tail end of "Why Study Logic?," immediately before the concluding paragraph of ML chapter 2. These closing remarks are preceded by a discussion of aesthetics and ethics, construed as the normative science of firstness and of secondness, respectively—leaving logic as the normative science of thirdness, a point that will come up for discussion below—which has been the textual focus of much work on Peirce's views on these subjects. See Potter ([1967] 1996) and Legg (2014).
13. Or, to add a pertinent example from Haack and offer one of my own: the conditions that determine how good a subject's evidence is are not the same as rules for the conduct of inquiry; and the conditions that determine human memory to be veridical are not the same as techniques for improving one's memory.
14. That is, a diagram of the equilibria of forces acting on the components of a structure.
15. From here until the end of this section of the chapter, all quotations in the main text are taken from ML and identified by paragraph number to CP2.
16. As Peirce had put it in 1893: "The ordinary business of life is . . . best conducted without too much self-criticism. Respiration, circulation, and digestion are, depend upon it, better carried on as they are, without any meddling by Reason; and the countless little inferences we are continually making,—be they ever so defective,—are, at any rate, less ill performed unconsciously than they would be under the regimen of a captious and hypochondriac logic" (CP7.448, 1893). I am grateful to Vincent Colapietro for drawing my attention to this passage.
17. "In order to enjoy it [logic], it will be needful to have one's heart set on something remote from enjoyment" (CP2.15). In "Why Study Logic?," Peirce aligns himself with those

who "abhor" the doctrine that "action [is] the ultimate end of man" (CP2.151). In "What Is Pragmatism?," from 1905, he writes that "if pragmaticism ... made Doing to be the Be-all and the End-all of life, that would be its death. For to say that we live for the mere sake of action as action, regardless of the thought it carries out, would be to say that there is no such thing as rational purport" (CP5.429). If action were the ultimate end, utility would be the highest value, and the Platos would be wrong; and if the Platos were wrong (on this point), the pragmatic maxim would be pointless, as the phenomenon it seeks to explicate and illuminate, rational purport, would not exist.

18. The year after Peirce worked on ML, Russell published *The Principles of Mathematics*; two years after that Hilbert delivered lectures on "The Logical Principles of Mathematical Thought."

19. From here until the end of the next paragraph all quotations in the main text are taken from ML chapter 3 and identified by paragraph number to CP4.

20. Cf. Paul Bernays on his 1918 *Habilitationschrift*, in which "seminal early results on propositional and first order logic" are presented: "It certainly had a mathematical character, but the prevailing opinion at the time didn't take these foundational investigations that connected to mathematical logic in full seriousness; sure that's all very pretty, half playful if you know what I mean" (Zach 1999, 332, emphasis deleted, and 355, translation mine).

21. Cf. CP3.173, 1880, footnote: "The term *simpler* has an exact meaning in logic; it means that whose logical depth is smaller; that is, if one conception implies another, but not the reverse, then the latter is said to be the simpler."

22. As Peirce's willingness to countenance curious interpretations of his two objects makes clear, it is not anachronistic to couch his point in the terms long since familiar to us.

23. Quine says nothing further about what would make a calculus trivial, but Peirce's rejection of the idea that the simplest possible hypothesis might require only one object on the grounds that it "would not [allow] a possibility of a question, since only one answer would be possible" (CP4.250), suggests the idea that a one-valued calculus, in which all well-formed formulae received one and the same value, would be no real *calculus* at all, or at best a singularly useless one.

24. From here until the end of the present section all quotations in the main text are taken from ML chapter 1 and identified by paragraph number to CP2.

25. When a grinding error led to an aberration in the Hubble space telescope's mirror one-fiftieth the thickness of a human hair, the results were patent to all: the images that first came back from the multi-million-dollar instrument were grainy and hard to use. See "Hubble's Mirror Flaw" at https://www.nasa.gov/content/hubbles-mirror-flaw (accessed November 8, 2022).

26. In an illuminating paper on models in geometry and logic (2017), Patricia Blanchette observes that "the questions we can ... raise and answer, ... [are] shaped significantly by the tools we have developed [to answer them]" (2), and in elaborating the point she provides a nice illustration of the idea that minute distinctions in logic can function as a kind of conceptual microscope. In the case with which she is concerned, the history of attempts to prove the independence of the parallel postulate from the rest of Euclid's axioms, what is magnified by increasing strictness of reasoning is not error but difference. Upon investigation, she concludes, "the gap between ... independence claims clearly demonstrable via ... modern methods and the independence claims that motivated much geometric work prior to the end of the 19th century ... is sufficiently large that we cannot take the newer methods to be merely cleaned-up ways of answering the old questions" (21).

27. And as various authors have pointed out, the question of what quantification is closely bound up with questions of quantifier dependence. See Hintikka (1988) and Goldfarb (1979).
28. And his students at Johns Hopkins, especially O. H. Mitchell.
29. For example, by Goethe, in Mephistopheles's parody of the logic portion of the traditional university *trivium*: "So, Friend (my views to briefly sum), / First, the *collegium logicum*. / There will your mind be drilled and braced, / As if in Spanish boots 'twere laced, / And thus, to graver paces brought, / 'Twill plod along the path of thought, / Instead of shooting here and there, / A will-o'-the-wisp in murky air," *Faust* I (1911–1918).
30. By 1909 we find Peirce distinguishing two "principal aims" for logicians, the first being (as per ML) "to bring out the amount and kind of security (approach to certainty) of each kind of reasoning, and the second (designated by a typically recondite Peircean appellation) "to bring out the possible and esperable uberty, or value in productiveness, of each kind" (CP8.384).
31. As Peirce memorably puts it: "To make laboratory experiments to ascertain, for example, whether there be any uniformity in nature or no, would vie with adding a teaspoonful of saccharine to the ocean to sweeten it" (CP5.522, 1905).
32. Being used to thinking that "*all* pertinent facts [that may bear on a hypothesis are] within the beck and call of the imagination" (CP4.232; emphasis added), mathematicians are used to recognizing that *any* fact so summonable may be pertinent to their investigations. Students of the actual world, of experiential fact, can more easily overlook unusual possibilities that would render, say, a universal generalization more dubious than it seems at first to be.
33. No one fit to be at large would contend that inductive logic, understood to include everything not included in deductive logic, can float superbly free of the vagaries of experience; but exactly such a pristine status has, for good or ill, frequently been ascribed to the "sheer logic" (Quine) that Peirce would count as a branch of mathematics, that is, the formal study of deductive, syntactically tractable argument.
34. To echo William James (in his presentation of the pragmatic maxim, or "principle of Peirce," in his *Lectures on Pragmatism* from 1906).
35. It is the point and purpose of the pragmatic maxim to replace the antiquated doctrine of clear and distinct ideas with something "better adapted to modern uses" (CP5.392, 1877).
36. In the terms of the subtitle to the article that gave rise to the much-bruited Dunning-Kruger effect, "difficulties in recognizing one's incompetence" in something are strongly correlated with an "inflated self-assessment" as to one's competence in the area (from the title of Kruger and Dunning 1999, 1121).
37. "A reader who is not disposed to work upon logic as slowly, as minutely, as laboriously as he would upon any other subject whatsoever—at the very least—simply will have to go without learning much about the theory of reasoning from any source" (CP2.14).
38. The main clause of this sentence is taken verbatim from the opening sentence of "The Fixation of Belief" (CP5.358, 1877).
39. In recent decades psychologists have begun systematically to investigate a host of "cognitive and motivational biases that compromise lay inference and judgment" (Pronin, Lin and Ross 2002, 369). One such tendency, the so-called bias blind spot, is pertinent here. Whereas we are quick to register disabling biases in the reasonings of others, we are systematically and stubbornly resistant to recognizing our own reasonings as similarly vulnerable to partisan error. Part of the explanation for this, it is widely held, lies in a "naive

realism," according to which "people think, or simply assume *without giving the matter any thought at all,* that their own take on the world . . . will be shared by other . . . perceivers and seekers of truth" (369, emphasis added), which is pretty much Peirce's point exactly.

40. Apropos the need for a theory to be answerable to possible application if it is to be taken seriously, Peirce had remarked that "it would be easy enough—much too easy—to marshal a goodly squadron of treatises on logic, each of them swelled out with matter foreign to any conceivable applicability until, like a corpulent man, it can no longer see on what it is standing, and the reader loses all clear view of the true problems of the science" (CP2.7).

41. In a draft version of ML chapter 1, Peirce wrote that "the main reason logic is unsettled is that thirteen different opinions are current opinions as to the *true aim* of the science" and had remarked that "this is not a logical difficulty, but an ethical difficulty, for ethics is the science of aims" (R429, emphasis added). Evidently the true aim of a science isn't the same thing as a method for establishing its truths, and the latter formulation fits what Peirce does in ML chapter 1, section 3, better than the former. But the fact that the two issues are closely connected in Peirce's mind is a signal instance of the deep connection he sees between the subject matter of logic and the point and value of studying it.

42. As in one of Peirce's most famous trichotomies, of icon, index, and symbol, three grounds of signification. A sign is already a third, but it may signify iconically, in respect of sheer resemblance, a firstness, or of causation of the sign by the signified, a secondness, or by means of a system of symbolic conventions, a thirdness.

43. From here until the end of this section of the chapter, all quotations in the main text are taken from ML and identified by paragraph number to CP2.

44. In 1879 Peirce had objected to Gratry's view on the different, no less telling, grounds that "to assert a perpetual miracle seems to be an abandonment of all hope of doing that, without sufficient justification" (CP2.690, 1878).

45. The book is Lange's posthumously published *Logische Studien. Ein Beitrag zur Neubegründung der formalen Logik und der Erkenntnisstheorie* (1877). Belluci (2013) (to whom I owe the reference to R1579, 1901, in Note 2) provides an overview of Pierce's remarks about Lange, together with helpful observations about what Peirce took from Lange and where he disagreed and apt discussion of the Kantian origin of both men's views. Thiel (1994) contains the most thorough account of Lange's work on logic known to me.

46. In his *Symbolic Logic*, Venn (1881) informed readers that "when the substance of this [first] chapter was written out for *Mind* I was unable to ascertain that any attempt had been made to reconstruct the syllogistic figures upon this propositional scheme. I have since found that almost exactly the same results as are given here had been already obtained by F. A. Lange, in his admirable *Logische Studien*, though from a somewhat different point of view" (17n1). In 1903 Peirce devoted several pages to a discussion of Euler's method of rendering syllogistic reasoning by means of the spatial relations between circles. Crediting Venn with "a distinct improvement" on Euler's system (CP4.353), he goes on to make further advances of his own.

47. In fact, the conversion of negative universals can be represented by simply drawing the A circle and the B circle at a distance from each other, with no overlap at all. As Venn remarks in his 1880 article in *Mind* (alluded to above in the quotation from *Symbolic Logic*), this result doesn't generalize; and as Peirce emphasizes (in the piece just mentioned and elsewhere), fruitful generalizability is a cardinal virtue of a formal system of logic. Venn (1880) counts it "a great merit" of his system that it enables us "to *intuite* [*sic*] . . . proposition[s]" (349). For recent work on iconic proof and reasoning, see Chapman et al. (2018) (especially

the pieces by Legris and Terra Rodrigues, Baimagambetov et al., and Lampert, those gathered in the sections devoted to Euler and Venn diagrams, and to Peirce and existential graphs) and Lampert (2021).

48. Aristotelian negative universals may also be represented as the negation of an existential quantification over a conjunction, in which case the point can be made by way of the commutativity of conjunction. Thanks to Gillman Payette for alerting me to this.

49. Cf. Lampert 2018 (in Chapman et al. 2018). I owe my acquaintance with Lampert's work to Kirsten Walsh.

50. *Sense and Sensibilia*, 2.

51. See Haack (1993, 50) on the clear echoes of Peircean themes to be found in Quine's settled "verdict on logicism."

52. In the present context, Susan Haack's attempts, in the years leading up to her formulation of foundherentism, to make precise one of that doctrine's vital epistemological underpinnings, fallibilism, bear mentioning. If fallibilism is coherent, it must occupy territory in between dogmatism (some knowledge is infallible) and skepticism (no knowledge is possible). But Haack discovered that if you begin with the plausible-enough-sounding idea that fallibilism holds that we could be mistaken in any of our beliefs and attempt to spell this idea out in terms of a universal quantification over propositions, to the effect that they are all able to be believed even though false, you in fact rule fallibilism out of court. For if you construe the relationship between knowing subjects and the objects of their beliefs in terms of predicates applied to those objects, propositions, the resulting theses will collapse into either a denial of necessary truth or an endorsement of skepticism. Haack takes this result to be a *reductio* of that way of construing the relationship between knowing subjects and the objects of their beliefs, and I agree with her. What we learn from the exercise is that fallibilism is a thesis about us, to the effect that we are invariably liable to make mistakes; it applies to subject matters only incidentally, insofar as it is always we who inquire into them. See Haack (1979a, 1979b) and Migotti (2018).

53. In reference to the logic of what we would now call restricted domains, Peirce puts the point with characteristic force: "Some logicians treat [this] subject as 'extra-logical'; but that only means it is outside the scope of their own studies. If a mathematician should choose to characterize the differential calculus as 'extra-mathematical,' he would exhibit the same determination to keep his science small and simple that animates many of the logicians" (2.453, 1893).

54. Cf. Oliver (2010): "It is a curious fact that although there is plenty of (rather inconsequential) debate about the constituents of arguments—whether sentences, statements, or propositions—it is rare to find a proper discussion of form. Yet form is what logic is all about. What limited discussion there now is often displays all the hallmarks of primitive inchoate conceptualization. It is riddled with toxic ambiguity, and shrouded with dark sayings and oppositions" (165).

55. Cf. Goldfarb (1979): "[A] 'full' analysis of the nature of the quantifier . . . includes the questions of what we can and cannot do with first-order logic, as well as the question of finding new notions to explain the deep facts lying behind seemingly transparent uses of quantification. Much of contemporary model theory, proof theory, and work on decision problems aims at contributing to our understanding of these questions" (366).

56. Cf. Haack ([1974] 1996), "Rosser and Turquette suggested ([1952], p.20 that discussion of the motivation and interpretation of non-standard systems [of logic] was premature; it should have waited upon comprehensive examination of the formal characteristics of

these systems. But, as I shall argue, it is still unclear, for instance, what formal distinction there might be between non-standard systems which are rivals, and those which are merely supplements of classical logic; or between systems embodying the assumption that there are truth-value gaps, and systems embodying the assumption that there are intermediate truth values. And so in advance of some philosophical work, it is sometimes uncertain what formal investigations are likely to be fruitful" (xxvi).

57. Cf. Smiley (1982): "If it were really true that to formalize logic is to eliminate everything that gives meaning and application to it, the student could well ask why anyone should be expected to learn such a subject or be paid to teach it. In fact, however, formalization and formalism are rivals, not allies. Historically they can be seen as embodying rival methods of achieving rigour. Formalism tries to avoid the danger of unconscious assumptions by replacing contentful terms by 'bare symbols,' for there is obviously no risk of exploiting the meaning of symbols that do not have any meaning. Formalization takes a completely different tack, asking that every step in a proof should indisputably (i.e. decidably) conform to some one or other of a fixed battery of explicitly stated rules" (12).

58. For a description of the manuscripts found on the microfilm that are related to the *Minute Logic*, see Robin (1967), R425–434.

Bibliography

Anderson, Douglas. 1986. "The Evolution of Peirce's Concept of Abduction." *Transactions of the Charles S. Peirce Society* 22, no. 2 (Spring): 145–164.

Austin, John L. [1962] 1990. *Sense and Sensibilia*. Revised edition. Oxford: Oxford University Press.

Belluci, Francesco. 2013. "Diagrammatic Reasoning: Some Notes on Charles S. Peirce and Friedrich A. Lange." *History and Philosophy of Logic* 34 no. 4: 293–305.

Blanchette, Patricia. 2017. "Models in Geometry and Logic." In *Logic, Methodology, and Philosophy of Science: Proceedings of the 15th International Congress*, edited by Hannes Leitgeb, Ilkka Niniluoto, and Paivi Seppala, 41–61. Suwanee, GA: College Publications.

Chapman, Peter, Gem Stapleton, Amirouche Moktefi, and Francesco Belluci, eds. 2018. *Diagrammatic Representation and Inference: Proceedings of the 10th International Conference on Diagrams*. Berlin: Springer Verlag.

Frege, Gottlob. 1980 (1884). *The Foundations of Arithmetic: A Logico-Mathematical Enquiry into the Foundations of Number*. Translated by John L. Austin. Evanston IL: Northwestern University Press.

Goldfarb, Warren. 1979. "Logic in the Twenties: The Nature of the Quantifier." *Journal of Symbolic Logic* 44, no. 3 (September): 351–368.

Haack, Susan. [1974] 1996. *Deviant Logic, Fuzzy Logic: Beyond the Formalism*. Chicago: University of Chicago Press.

Haack, Susan. 1979a. "Epistemology *with* a Knowing Subject." *Review of Metaphysics* 33, no. 2 (December): 309–335.

Haack, Susan. 1979b. "Fallibilism and Necessity." *Synthese* 41, no. 1: 37–63.

Haack, Susan. 1993. "Peirce and Logicism: Notes towards an Exposition." *Transactions of the Charles S. Peirce Society* 29, no. 1 (Winter): 33–56.

Haack, Susan. [1993] 2009. *Evidence and Inquiry: A Pragmatist Reconstruction of Epistemology*. Buffalo, NY: Prometheus Books.

Hacking, Ian. 1979. "What Is Logic?" *Journal of Philosophy* 76 no. 6 (June): 285–319.

Hintikka, Jaakko. 1988. "On the Development of the Model-Theoretic Viewpoint in Logical Theory." *Synthese* 77, no. 1: 1–36.

Hintikka, Jaakko, and Gabriel Sandu. 1994. "What Is a Quantifier?" *Synthese* 98, no. 1: 113–129.

James, William. [1906] 1978. *Pragmatism and the Meaning of Truth*. Cambridge, MA: Harvard University Press.

Kruger, Justin, and David Dunning. 1999. "Unskilled and Unaware of It: How Difficulties in Recognizing One's Own Incompetence Lead to Inflated Self-Assessments." *Journal of Personality and Social Psychology* 77, no. 6 (December): 1121–1134.

Lampert, Timm. 2021. "Newton's Experimental Proofs." *Theoria: An International Journal for Theory, History, and Foundations of Science* 36, no. 2: 261–283.

Lange, Friedrich Albert [1877] 2010. *Logische Studien. Ein Beitrag zur Neubegründung der formalen Logik und der Erkenntnisstheorie*. Whitefish, MT: Kessinger Publishing.

Legg, Catherine. 2014, "Logic, Ethics and the Ethics of Logic," in *Charles Sanders Peirce in His Own Words*, edited by Torkild Thellefesen and Brent Sorensen, 271–278. Berlin: De Gruyter.

Migotti, Mark. 2018. "From Fallibilism to Foundherentism: A Genealogy of Susan Haack's Reconstruction of Epistemology." *Estudios Filosoficós* 67, no. 167: 503–515.

Misak, Cheryl. 2013. *The American Pragmatists*. Oxford: Oxford University Press.

Norton, John. 2021. *The Material Theory of Induction*. Calgary: University of Calgary Press.

Oliver, Alex. 2010. "The Matter of Form: Logic's Beginnings," in *The Force of Argument: Essays in Honour of Timothy Smiley*, edited by Jonathan Lear and Alex Oliver. London: Routledge Press, 165–185.

Peirce, Charles S. 1931–1958. *The Collected Papers of Charles Sanders Peirce*. 8 vols. Vols. 1–6 edited by Charles Hartshorne and Paul Weiss, vols. 7–8 edited by Arthur W. Burks. Cambridge, MA: Harvard University Press. Cited as CP[volume#].[paragraph#].

Potter, Vincent. [1967] 1996. *Charles S. Peirce on Norms and Ideals*. New York: Fordham University Press.

Pronin, Emily, Daniel Y. Lin, and Lee Ross. 2002. "The Bias Blind Spot: Perceptions of Bias in Self versus Others." *Personality and Social Psychology Bulletin* 28, no. 3: 369–381.

Putnam, Hilary 1982. "Peirce the Logician." *Historia Mathematica* 9, no. 3 (August): 290–301.

Quine, Willard Van Orman 1933. Review of CP 2. *Isis* 19, no. 1: 220–229.

Quine, Willard Van Orman 1935. Review of CP 4. *Isis* 22, no. 2: 551–553.

Quine, Willard Van Orman 1970. *Philosophy of Logic*. Englewood Cliffs, NJ: Prentice Hall.

Robin, Richard. 1967. *Annotated Catalogue of the Papers of Charles S. Peirce*. Amherst: University of Massachusetts Press. Cited as R.

Roberts, Don. 1973. *The Existential Graphs of Charles S. Peirce*. The Hague: Mouton.

Smiley, Timothy. 1982. "The Schematic Fallacy." *Proceedings of the Aristotelian Society* 83: 1–17.

Smiley, Timothy. 1995. "A Tale of Two Tortoises." *Mind* 105, no. 416 (October): 725–736.

Stillwell, John. 2019. *A Concise History of Mathematics for Philosophers*. Cambridge: Cambridge University Press.

Thiel, Christian. 1994. "Friedrich Albert Langes bewundernswerte Logische Studien." *History and Philosophy of Logic* 15, no. 1: 105–126.

Venn, John. 1880. "On the Forms of Logical Proposition." *Mind* 5, no. 19 (July): 336–349.

Venn, John. 1881. *Symbolic Logic*. London: MacMillan.

Zach, Richard. 1999. "Completeness before Post: Bernays, Hilbert, and the Development of Propositional Logic." *Bulletin of Symbolic Logic* 5, no. 3: 331–366.

CHAPTER 11

PEIRCE'S PHILOSOPHY OF LOGIC

LEILA HAAPARANTA

1. INTRODUCTION

THE word "logic" is ambiguous.[1] It may mean the art of reasoning, a set of rules of valid reasoning, or the science that studies valid reasoning. In contemporary terminology, it also means a language that is specified by giving a vocabulary and syntactic rules, and a field that studies such languages. Charles Peirce relied on those various meanings in his logical studies. Besides being a mixture of themes in ancient and medieval logic and modern developments, his logic was intertwined with his epistemology, philosophy of science, and philosophy of language, and he even regarded logic and semiotic as identical. Therefore, it is not easy to distinguish between his achievements in logic and his contributions to other fields of philosophy. One who wishes to study his logic can either scrutinize the rich textual material and draw a map of his multifaceted logical views and theories or go in for asking his texts those questions which are discussed in what is nowadays called logic. Gottlob Frege's book entitled *Begriffsschrift: eine der arithmetischen nachgebildete Formelsprache des reinen Denkens* (1879) is usually regarded as the starting point of modern logic, although the rise of a few modern formal developments in logic can be dated back to the seventeenth century, and philosophical ideas emphasized by medieval logicians, such as the distinction between individuals and concepts, already anticipated modern formal logic. Peirce discovered the logic of relatives in the 1870s, which was inspired by George Boole's algebra of logic and Augustus de Morgan's theory of relations. Boole's algebra of logic had been restricted to unary predicates and could thus serve as a formalization of Aristotelian syllogistic reasoning. Peirce's logic of relatives was an extension of Boole's method to reasoning which involved relations. In the articles "The Logic of Relatives" (1883) and "On the Algebra of Logic: A Contribution to the Philosophy of Notation" (1885) he formulated his general algebra of logic, which introduced the theory of quantification, independent of Frege's discovery. It is very likely that Peirce was not familiar with Frege's achievements, even if Frege's book appears in the bibliography of a paper by Christine Ladd (1883), who was Peirce's student.

Besides the term "logic," the term "philosophy of logic" carries several meanings. In this chapter, philosophy of logic is understood as a subfield of philosophy that studies philosophical themes related to logic, such as the epistemological foundations of logic and relations between logic and other fields of philosophy; problems concerning the various features of logical formal systems, such as its basic vocabulary; and questions about modal notions and the possibility of alternatives to classical logic. The present chapter focuses on five themes. First, in Section 2, it analyzes Peirce's notion of logic and discusses the place of logic in his classification of the sciences. Then, in Section 3, it seeks the philosophical background and content of his logical discoveries in his evaluation of Immanuel Kant's philosophy and ancient geometry. Section 4 considers his philosophy of logic from the contemporary perspective and pays special attention to the much-discussed distinction between the ideas of logic as calculus and logic as universal language. It also makes a few remarks on his views of modalities and on his introduction of three-valued logic. Section 5 discusses fallibilism and its relevance to Peirce's view of logic. The chapter concludes with an effort to find out Peirce's position in the debate between psychologism and antipsychologism of his time. It seeks to show by means of a few examples that the emphasis on normative sciences that focus on practice is a prominent feature in Peirce's philosophy of logic. One might also suggest that Peirce follows Kant, who defended the thesis concerning the primacy of practical reason.[2] This chapter does not participate in scholarly debates concerning the interpretation of Kant's thesis, nor does it argue that Peirce followed Kant at this point. Instead, it focuses on Peirce's ways of considering logic via the model of overt action and pays attention to Peirce's view that logic depends on ethical principles.

2. Peirce's Notion of Logic

In his paper "Of Reasoning in General" (EP2 sel. 3, 1895), Peirce describes logic as the art of reasoning. He remarks that in the history there were "endless disputes as to whether logic was an art or a science" (EP2:11). In his classification of the sciences, logic appears as the science that studies valid reasoning, or the discipline concerning the art of reasoning. Peirce notes that the "facts upon which logic is based come mostly within ordinary knowledge," and the "science is largely, not wholly, one of rearrangement" (EP2:11). He also concludes that as all thought is performed by means of signs, logic may be regarded as semiotic or the science of the general laws of signs (CP1.191, 1903). Peirce construes an inference as an act or a series of acts that starts from beliefs and leads to a belief, that is, to a conclusion. By a belief, he means "a state of mind of the nature of a habit, of which the person is aware, and which, if he acts deliberately on a suitable occasion, would induce him to act in a way different from what he might act in the absence of such a habit" (EP2:12). He thus maintains that the word "belief" does not apply to occasions of action that are not guided by deliberation. On his view, a belief is "an intelligent habit" (EP2:19). In a paper written in about 1898, Peirce puts forward a rule, his "first rule of reason," which demands that in order to learn we must desire to learn and not to be satisfied with what we already incline to think. He provides his rule with a corollary, which says that you must not block the way of inquiry (EP2:48; CP1.135, c. 1899).[3] Hence, on his view, logic helps us in forming beliefs, which are outcomes of deliberation. Peirce distinguishes between a proposition and an assertion, which he regards as "the deliberate exercise ... of a force tending to determine a belief in it in the mind of the interpreter" (NEM4:249, 1904). For him, judging, doubting, denying, expressing, and asserting a proposition are acts. He notes that the judgment is more than a mental replica of a proposition, because it also accepts the proposition (NEM4:248-249, 1904). He construes asserting a proposition as making oneself responsible for it (CP5.543, c. 1902). A proof of a proposition in logic can thus be understood as signalizing that the asserter has taken the required responsibility.

In Peirce's classification, mathematics is independent of the rest of the sciences, and it studies what is and what is not logically possible. Peirce calls one of its branches the mathematics of logic. He regards philosophy as a positive science, which is divided into three branches; they are phenomenology, normative science—or normative sciences—and metaphysics. Normative science, whose task it is to distinguish what ought to be from what ought not to be, is dependent on mathematics and phenomenology, while metaphysics rests on phenomenology and normative science. Peirce divides normative science into three different sciences, which are aesthetics, ethics, and logic (CP1.183-186, 1903). Besides characterizing normative sciences by means of "oughts," he also notes that they are interested in the distinction between what is good and what is bad. Logic concerns the realm of cognition, ethics is related to the realm of action, and aesthetics works in the realm of feeling. Peirce regards phenomenology as the initial part of philosophy, which seeks to find out the elements of appearance that are present to us "every hour and every minute whether we are pursuing earnest investigations, or are undergoing the strangest vicissitudes of experience, or are dreamily listening to the tales of Scheherazade" (EP2:146-147, 1903). Hence, in his division, logic rests on mathematics and on the study of the elements of what appears to us. Peirce describes aesthetics as the science of ideals, or the science of what is objectively admirable, and construes it as the primary normative science. In his classification, ethics, which is the science of right and wrong, appeals to aesthetics. For Peirce, logic is the theory of self-controlled and deliberate thought, and its principles are based on ethics, which Peirce calls the theory of self-controlled or deliberate conduct. His model for thought is overt action, which means that he gives priority to practical over theoretical reason in the order of understanding what thought is like and what makes it rational.

On Peirce's view, it is the task philosophy to "furnish a *Weltanschauung*, or conception of the universe," which would serve as a basis of the special sciences. That task is preserved for metaphysics, which is the final branch of philosophy and which rests on the three branches of normative science (EP2:146–147, 1903). As a normative science, logic is theoretical, even if it is connected to practice. Peirce characterizes it as a positive science, although he describes its reasoning as mostly mathematical. His statements about mathematics and logic are not very helpful if one wishes to understand his construal of the relations between the two fields. Peirce discerns three branches in logic. They are speculative grammar, or the general theory of the nature and meanings of signs; critic, which serves in classifying arguments and determining their validity and force; and methodeutic, which works on the methods that ought to be "pursued in the investigation, in the exposition, and in the application of truth" (CP1.191, 1903). He also notes in his "Minute Logic" in 1902–1903 that the goal which the reasoner tries to reach is truth, and the logician seeks to analyze its conditions; moreover, the truth itself is "nothing but a phase of the *summum bonum* which forms the subject of pure ethics" (CP1.575, *c.* 1902). The branch of logic that he calls critic corresponds to the description of logic that he gives in several contexts. He thus seems to have a wide and a narrow notion of logic, and he also points to several connections between logic and mathematics.

3. The Philosophical Background of Peirce's Logical Discoveries

Peirce's logical discoveries in the 1880s were not just contributions to the mathematical and logical developments of his time. Besides taking part in those discussions, Peirce motivated his logical ideas by means of philosophical doctrines and arguments. Three important themes will be discussed in this section. They are Peirce's evaluation and elaboration of Kant's doctrine of categories; his views on terms, assertions, and inferences; and his interest in visual thinking and ancient geometry.

In his early thought, Peirce relied on Kant's transcendental logic. He later confessed that he "believed more implicitly in the two tables of the Functions of Judgment and the Categories than if they had been brought down from Sinai" (CP4.2, 1898). Murray Murphey has remarked that it was the manner in which Kant discovered his categories that interested Peirce most of all. However, careful consideration revealed problems and insufficiencies in Kant's transcendental analytic. In 1867, Peirce suggested a new list of categories, because he had reached the conclusion that Kant's examination, as he would later put it, was "hasty, superficial, trivial, and even trifling" (CP1.560, *c.* 1905).[4] Peirce thought that Kant's way of dividing judgments was not warranted.

The numerous changes in Peirce's theory of categories and the roles of different types of signs in the logic of relations and quantification theory have been discussed in great detail in the literature.[5] Murphey has shown that the discovery of the logic of relations and the theory of quantification led to changes in Peirce's theory of the three categories since the 1880s. Monadic, dyadic, and triadic relations turned out to be equally abstract and simply the three kinds of predicate in propositions. The same observation is also made by Christopher Hookway, who points out that Peirce's categories were present in his new logical notation as incomplete expressions of valences one, two, and three. Murphey notes, for example, that after introducing quantifiers and indices, which referred directly to individuals or haecceities, Peirce rehabilitated Kant's view that existence can only be given in intuition.[6] A similar view is supported by Jeffrey DiLeo, who argues that around 1890 Peirce started to support haecceitism, which was similar to Duns Scotus's view of haecceitas. Peirce's first use of the term "haecceity" can be found in his paper entitled "A Guess at the Riddle," on which Peirce worked between 1886 and 1890, but it was during Peirce's *Monist* period (1891–1914) that haecceitism was clearly articulated. DiLeo argues that an implicit acceptance of that doctrine can be found in Peirce's writings as early as 1885. In 1911 Peirce wrote that an individual is something that reacts, and existence is the totality of that which is actual, and "whatever exists is individual, since existence (not reality) and individuality are essentially the same thing" (CP3.613, 1901).[7]

On Peirce's own testimony, his general algebra of logic was inspired by O. H. Mitchell's, his student's, ideas (CP3.363, 393, 1885).[8] Peirce added indices to relations and introduced quantifiers "some" and "every." In his article in *The Monist* (1897), he writes that in his algebra every proposition consists of two parts, namely, its quantifiers and its Boolean part. The Boolean part consists of relatives, which are united by multiplication and aggregation, and each elementary relative has indices, which denote haecceities. According to Peirce, haecceities are fit to receive proper names or to be indicated by "this" or "that," and they fill the blanks of relatives (CP3.460, 500, 1897).

When introducing indices and quantifiers, Peirce referred to Mitchell's article "On a New Algebra of Logic" (1883).[9] In his "Lecture on Propositions" (1883) he praises Christine Ladd's paper, in which Ladd introduces her idea of the constitution of the universe. Ladd starts with the law of the excluded middle and forms descriptions of the universe with predicates and their negations. Peirce regards her idea as a development of the law of the excluded middle. A contemporary reader may see Ladd's descriptions as anticipators of normal forms introduced in the twentieth century. Peirce adds quantifiers to Ladd's descriptions of the universe and thus modifies her ideas along the same lines as those of Mitchell (W4:490–491, 1883).[10] He thinks that quantifiers indicate an object or objects, and the predicates say something about those objects. At this point, Peirce's construal comes close to medieval logicians' ideas of such syncategorematic terms as "all" and "some" (CP2.357–358, 1902).[11]

In his manuscript "On Existential Graphs as an Instrument of Logical Research" (R498, 1896), Peirce notes that all thinking proper takes the form of a dialogue. He contrasts his conception with the view that thinking proceeds from premises to conclusions via routine transformations. He criticizes Boole for the assumption that the great problem for one who tries to invent an algebra or other system of logical representation is to create something like a calculating engine. As early as in his "Grounds of Validity of the Laws of Logic: Further Consequences of Four Capacities" (1869), he points out that every judgment results from inference (W2:242). In his manuscript

"On Existential Graphs as an Instrument of Logical Research," he also remarks that the most important question that has troubled logicians for a decade has been the nature of judgments or propositions. He puts forth two alternative answers; a proposition is either built up of subject and predicate or it is an act called "assertion." He detects problems in the former view, because it makes one ask how two concepts can be combined and how a component that one may choose to combine the two concepts can itself be combined to the concepts. In his manuscript "On the System of Existential Graphs Considered as an Instrument for the Investigation of Logic" (R499, n.d.), he states that "the essence of the proposition does not lie in its being compound, but on the contrary upon its being asserted or at least conceived to be asserted." He also points out that assertion does not add any new element to thought, as it is a deed. Contrary to the order of priorities of Aristotelian logic, Peirce thus claims that concepts are embedded in judgments and judgments are embedded in inferential chains. His emphasis that assertions are deeds testifies to his position that the mind and its thoughts should be modeled on human action and its ethical principles.

On Peirce's characterization, thinking is dialogue, and the human mind draws figures. In his writings after 1885, for example, in the middle of the 1890s, Peirce emphasizes the distinction between corollarial and theorematic reasoning. As he describes, in corollarial deduction it is only necessary to imagine any case in which the premises are true in order to realize that the conclusion is true; instead, in theorematic deduction it is necessary to "experiment in the imagination upon the image of the premise in order from the result of such experiment to make corollarial deductions to the truth of the conclusion" (NEM4:38, 1902). Peirce states that a corollary, that is, the conclusion of corollarial deduction, is a proposition that is deduced directly from propositions already established "without the use of any other construction than one necessarily suggested in apprehending the enunciation of the proposition" (NEM4:288, c. 1903). In his terminology, a theorem, that is, the conclusion of theorematic deduction, is a proposition that can be deduced from previously established propositions only by imagining something more than is supposed in the conditions.

In his Carnegie application in 1902, Peirce remarks that the distinction between corollarial and theorematic reasoning was his first real discovery about mathematical procedure. He seems to connect his insight with his logical discoveries, as he remarks that Kant was unaware of theorematic reasoning, because he had not studied the logic of relatives (NEM4:49, 59, 1902). In his paper "Explanation of Curiosity the First," published in *The Monist* in 1908, Peirce describes Euclid's procedure in proving theorems: Euclid first presents his theorem in general terms, which is called *protasis* or proposition. He then translates it into singular terms, hence, replaces each general subject by a Greek letter that is the proper name for one of those objects that the general subject denotes. However, the generality of the statement is not lost by that move. The new singular statement is called *ekthesis* or exposition. Peirce adds that *ekthesis* is always carried out. The next step is "preparation" for the demonstration, or construction. This is "the principal theoric step" of the demonstration. That step is followed by demonstration, which contains mere corollarial reasoning. After this, the *ergo*-sentence repeats *protasis*. This is called the conclusion (CP4.616, 1908).[12] The importance of the logic of relatives is also visible in Peirce's writings in 1911, when Peirce remarks that deductive logic can only be understood by means of the logic of relatives. In Peirce's view, one misunderstanding is that demonstrative reasoning is something completely different from observation (CP3.641, 1902). For Peirce, mathematics and logic are observational sciences, that is, they experiment upon diagrams. As Peirce writes to William James in 1909, it is essential that "every Deduction involves the observation of a Diagram" (NEM3:869). In his paper "On the Algebra of Logic" (1885) he already labels the formulas of his general algebra of logic as icons (CP3.363). In his "Minute Logic," (1902) he states "Thinking in general terms is not enough. It is necessary that something should be DONE" (CP4.233). Peirce thus emphasizes the role of constructing activities in mathematicians' and logicians' practice.

Peirce formulates his view of the role of diagrams in his Carnegie application as follows: "The first things I found out were that all mathematical reasoning is diagrammatic and that all necessary reasoning is mathematical reasoning, how simple it may be" (NEM4:47–48, 1902). On his view, the only difference between mathematical and philosophical necessary deduction is that philosophical deduction is so simple that the construction is overlooked (CP3.560, 1898). He argues that even a simple syllogism contains a construction, which is to say that logic depends on observing facts about mental products (NEM4:267, *c*. 1895). He even goes so far as to claim that when a student has once read the first book of Euclid's *Elements*, he will have an idea of how philosophy must be read (NEM4:72, 1902). Moreover, he proposes that philosophers ought to make experiments on diagrams in order to avoid errors (CP6.204, 1898). He must direct that piece of advice to logicians as well, because logic is part of philosophy.

4. Peirce's Calculus, Analysis of Modalities, and Three-Valued Logic

Many scholars, most notably Jean van Heijenoort (1967), Jaakko Hintikka (1979), and Warren Goldfarb (1979), have emphasized that Peirce and Frege were philosophically far apart as to their views of the nature of their logical systems. Frege is said to belong to a tradition in which logic is seen as a universal language, while Peirce is a member of a tradition in which logic is regarded as a calculus. The distinction between the two traditions has been made from the perspective of twentieth-century developments in logic; however, the beginning of the division has been located in nineteenth-century logic. According to van Heijenoort's seminal article, those who stressed the idea of logic as language were committed to the view that logic speaks about one single world. Those who supported the view that logic is a calculus gave various interpretations or models for their formal systems.

Hintikka describes Peirce's view in various ways.[13] Peirce did not think, like Frege, that logic or language is an intermediary between I and my world and that I cannot step beyond its limits. If one thinks that it is not possible to step outside logic, one must also be committed to the view that it is not possible to meaningfully express its semantic relations to the world. As the supporter of the calculus view, Peirce is ready to give various models for the propositions of logic. To argue that logic is re-interpretable is not to argue that it is empty or only a tool for inferences that are understood as calculations. Peirce states that his system of graphs is not like Guiseppe Peano's system, which he describes as a universal language (CP4.424, c. 1903). In his conception of logic, Peirce was a follower of Boole, and Ernst Schröder was one of those who was influenced by Peirce and belonged to the calculus tradition.[14]

Peirce regards modal propositions as quantified propositions. For him, necessary and impossible propositions are universal, and possible propositions are particular. Peirce follows the traditional view whose conception of modalities has been called "temporal" or "statistical"; on that view, necessity corresponds to the word "always," possibility to the word "sometimes," and impossibility to the word "never." Peirce also distinguishes between subjective and objective modality. His subjective concept of modality links modal concepts to what a person knows. He writes that if a person does not know that a proposition is false, he takes it to be possible. He also states that if there is more than one state of things such that no knowledge excludes, then each of these is possible (CP2.382, 1902; CP5.454, 1905).[15] Peirce regards conditional or hypothetical propositions as implicitly modal. On his characterization, a hypothetical proposition is not confined to stating what actually happens; instead, it states what is invariably true throughout a universe of possibility. Peirce refers to Diodorus and Philo in his discussion of those propositions. It has been shown that his theory of existential graphs was also influenced by the two ancient philosophers' analysis of conditional propositions (CP2.347, c. 1895; CP3.366, 1885).[16]

Peirce also defines logical operators for a many-valued system of logic.[17] Max Fisch and Atwell Turquette (1966) pay attention to three pages in Peirce's manuscripts, which were written in February 1909 (R339).[18] There Peirce outlines a system of triadic logic, in which he uses values "V," "F," and "L" and interprets "V" as "verum" ("true"), "F" "falsum" ("false"), and the third value, "L," as "the limit." Robert Lane notes that Peirce was motivated by the desire to accommodate within formal logic propositions that are neither true nor false. He thus rejected the principle of bivalence, according to which any proposition is either true or false. There are several interpretations on what Peirce means by his value "L." Lane convincingly argues that Peirce intends "L" to value propositions that are boundary propositions. For example, the boundary between the black and the nonblack areas of the paper is a continuity breach; it is a line in an otherwise uninterrupted surface. Lane argues that in rejecting bivalence with regard to a proposition "S is P," Peirce comes to give up the hope that, "if inquiry with regard to whether S is P were pursued as far as it could go," it would result in consensus whether S is P. As Lane notes, it thus seems that here Peirce blocks the "way of inquiry" for a certain type of propositions.

5. Peirce's Logic and Fallibilism

The question naturally arises whether Peirce thought that we may be fallible agents in the art and in the science of reasoning. In order to outline an answer, we have to look at the content of Peirce's fallibilism. Fallibilism is not the same as skepticism, even if it may occasionally be difficult to see where the difference lies. Sextus Empiricus, the Pyrrhonist sceptic, distinguished between three possible attitudes: some people think that they have discovered the truth, others think that the truth cannot be apprehended, and still others continue searching (PH1:1–10). Sextus held the third view. On Sextus's view, academic skeptics, who held the second view, maintain that knowledge cannot be attained; still, they have preferences concerning propositions, because they search for plausible opinions (PH1:228–230). Peirce's fallibilism is the doctrine that we cannot attain absolute certainty concerning questions of fact. Still, he argues that we should not block the way of inquiry and that a bar that "philosophers often set up across the roadway of inquiry" is the view that there are things that cannot be known. That statement is clearly a rejection of skepticism. Peirce considers it most likely that we hold true beliefs in numberless cases; however, he maintains that we can never be absolutely certain that we have knowledge in any special case; hence, that we cannot have conclusive justification for any of our beliefs. He also argues that our beliefs can never be perfectly precise or universal (CP1.135–40, c. 1899; CP1.141–149, c. 1897; CP5.311, 1868).[19]

Peirce scholars have discussed tensions between Peirce's fallibilism and his philosophy of mathematics.[20] In some of his texts, Peirce extends fallibilism to mathematics; in others, he argues that mathematical truths are necessary. There need not be any contradiction between these two views; we as human beings are fallible, but mathematical truths may still be necessary. However, Peirce seems to seek for explanation for the fact that our mathematical beliefs occasionally turn out to be false. In the last years of the nineteenth century, he wrote that the doctrine of fallibilism does not apply to mathematics, because it only applies to questions of fact, not to our knowledge of creations of our minds (CP1.149, c. 1897). His view of mathematical practice is that "the necessary reasoning of mathematics is performed by means of observation and experiment, and its necessary character is due simply to the circumstance that the subject of this observation and experiment is a diagram of our own creation, the conditions of whose being we know all about" (CP3.560, 1898). Peirce wavers between various ways of understanding the relation between fallibilism and mathematics, between mathematics and logic, and hence also between fallibilism and logic. He argues in 1892 that we do not know anything with absolute certainty (CP7.108). Later, in 1897 and in 1902, he points out that if we think of practical infallibility, then the truths of mathematics are infallible (CP1.149, CP1.248).

As already noted above, Peirce's construal of the relations between mathematics and logic is quite complex. Some of Peirce's early views come close to logicism; for example, in 1867 Peirce states that some propositions may be regarded as definitions of mathematical objects, from which the truths of mathematics follow "syllogistically" (CP3.20). In his later philosophical texts, he seems to take a step away from logicism and approach intuitionism, because he argues that mathematics is about creations of our minds, and as mentioned above, it also precedes logic in his classification of the sciences. Those views suggest that he rejects logicism. Susan Haack distinguishes between two theses of logicism. One of them states that arithmetic, or the whole field of mathematics, is reducible to logic. The other thesis, which can be called epistemological, states that the epistemological foundations of arithmetic, or of the whole field of mathematics, lie in logic. According to Haack, Peirce has sympathies with the reducibility thesis, but he does not approve of the epistemological thesis.[21] Although it is difficult to label Peirce as a firm logicist or as a firm intuitionist, it is worth noting that he detects similarities between mathematical and philosophical reasoning, because he claims that all necessary reasoning proceeds by constructions. He pays attention to common features of logical and mathematical practice and the comparisons that arise from his view of how the human mind works. For Peirce, the human mind is not a calculating engine; instead, he sees it as a mind that draws figures. As concluded above, that view testifies to his basic attitude that both mathematics and philosophy, including logic, ought to be modeled on overt action.

Phenomenology, which is the basic positive science, precedes logic, on Peirce's view, and its categories firstness, secondness, and thirdness are essential to logic. One might suggest that logic also inherits other features of phenomenology, say, its fallibility or infallibility. Peirce does not argue that phenomenology is fallible. However, he appears to think that phenomenology has made progress; hence, that his phenomenology overcomes the phenomenologies that have been proposed earlier in the history of philosophy (EP2:148–151, 1903). As Joseph Margolis points out, Peirce is not clear as to whether he, besides offering the three categories, also believes that phenomenology could reveal universal regularities on which a further positive science, such as logic, for example, could build.[22]

Peirce certainly admits the obvious fact that we as reasoners are fallible, even if he naturally accepts that what formal systems of logic bring about as their theorems are necessary within those systems. Still, because he also proposes an alternative system such as his triadic logic, he is likely to think that we are fallible also in the sense that we may be mistaken about what system applies to a given area. As one who seeks to improve logic with his discoveries, he must also think that we may be mistaken about what formal system is the correct one.

6. Peirce on the Relation between Logic and Psychology

In the late nineteenth century, the relations between logic and psychology were actively discussed. Most, if not all, philosophers thought that logic is normative in relation to our thought, hence, that logic tells us how we ought to think. Some philosophers added to this shared view that logic describes our thought and the epistemological foundations of logic are to be found in psychology. It is not obvious that anyone really maintained any strong version of a doctrine that became to be called psychologism.[23] What can be stated, however, is that logicians who were regarded as antipsychologists, Frege, for example, heavily criticized the view that logic describes actual human thought and that psychology could offer any foundation for logic (GGA I, xiv–xv). The doctrine that antipsychologists opposed was either a version of transcendentalism that regarded the transcendental conditions of experience as the conditions determined by the structure of the factual human mind or a version of empiricism that attempted to base all knowledge on experience.[24]

Peirce states in several writings that logic has nothing to do with psychology. Even if he emphasizes the importance of mental constructions in logical practice, he denies that logic would have something to do with acts of the mind (W1:164, 1865) and that questions of psychology would be relevant to logic (W2:349, 1869–1870; CP5.157, 1903). Interpreters agree that Peirce cannot be called a psychologist in any strong sense of the term. Claudine Tiercelin adds the reservation that Peirce's antipsychologism never denied the relevance of facts of psychology. She argues that since logic is a positive science, it may, or even must, take into account certain facts, for example, doubts and beliefs or indubitable observations concerning the mind.[25] Even if Peirce does not wish to cut off the connection between logic and the human mind, he holds the opinion that the science called psychology is not a useful source of information for logical research.

It goes without saying that Peirce regards logic as normative and thus agrees with Frege. Frege maintains that laws of logic prescribe universally how one ought to think if one is to think at all. In the preface of the *Grundgesetze der Arithmetik I* he notes that the expression "law of thought" leads us astray: it tempts us to think that the laws of logic govern thinking in the same way as the laws of nature govern events in the external world, and further to hold the view that they are psychological laws, because thinking is a mental process. On Frege's view, that is a serious mistake; logical laws are not psychological laws of holding as true, but laws of being true (GGA I, xv–xvi). Peirce, for his part, writes that logic is "the theory of right reasoning, of what reasoning ought to be, not of what it is" (CP2.7, c. 1902). In order to explain where the normative power of these laws on our minds comes from, Peirce needs to bring forth his conception of human beings as truth-seeking agents, who are capable of reflection. He emphasizes the role of logical study in our efforts to advance knowledge and our ability to evaluate the capacity of those laws in their task (EP2:256, 1903). Unlike Frege, Peirce does not argue that an objective realm of thoughts ought to be acknowledged as the realm that logic studies. Instead, he regards the principles of logic both as based on ethics and as tools in searching for truth. That view is a sign of Peirce's willingness to give priority to the science of practical reason over the science of theoretical reason and to see an essential connection between human epistemic endeavors and the demands of morality. Besides his explicit antipsychologistic statements, his emphasis on normativity and ethics excludes the interpretation that he supports logical psychologism.

Jonathan Dancy opens up the idea of the primacy of the practical in a number of ways. One version says that believing is not merely a state that happens to a subject, but that it is something that the subject does. On his construal, the thesis also implies that the notion of judgment ought to be understood as something that agent does, not as something that a person receives.[26] If the thesis concerning the primacy of the practical is understood along these lines, several aspects of Peirce's philosophy of logic are true to this basic conviction.

Notes

1. This chapter contains excerpts from Leila Haaparanta, "Peirce and the Logic of Logical Discovery," published in *Charles S. Peirce and the Philosophy of Science: Papers from the Harvard Sesquicentennial Congress*, ed. C. Moore (Tuscaloosa and London: University of Alabama Press, 1993), 105–118, Copyright © 1993 by The University of Alabama Press, which appear here with the kind permission of The University of Alabama Press. It also contains excerpts from Leila Haaparanta, "On Peirce's Methodology of Logic and Philosophy," which was first published in *Cognitio: Revista de Filosofia* 3 (2002): 32–45. The reprint was duly authorized by *Cognitio* editors.
2. Kant, *Kritik der praktischen Vernunft* (1788), Kant 1908, 1–167, 119–121. Cf. Williams (2018).
3. See Haack (1997).
4. See Murphey (1961, 33).
5. See, for example, Murphey (1961), Esposito (1980), Hookway (1985), Tursman (1987).
6. See Murphey (1961, 4, 137–138, 153, 298–300, 309–310) and Hookway (1985, 87).
7. See DiLeo (1991, 79, 91, 97).
8. See Mitchell (1883). For Peirce's place in the history of modern logic, see Putnam (1982).
9. For the similarities and the differences between Mitchell's and Peirce's interpretations of formulas, as well as the methods of Peirce's discovery of the new logic, see Haaparanta (1993, 2009, 250–252). In his letter to Christine Ladd-Franklin, December 1903, Peirce mentions that Mitchell's article has greatly helped him, although he regards the positive words about Mitchell that Christine Ladd-Franklin has written as somewhat exaggerated (RL237).
10. See Ladd (1883, 61).
11. See Hilpinen (1992, 472–478). On Peirce and medieval philosophy, see Boler (2006). Also see Pietarinen (2006, 182–186), Bellucci (2016), and Dipert (2006).
12. Cf. Hintikka (1980, 306). Hintikka argues that Peirce generalized this geometrical distinction to all deductive reasoning. See Haaparanta (2002).
13. Hintikka (1997, 14–16).
14. See Peckhaus (2004, 2009).
15. See Hilpinen (2009, 552, 555).
16. Ibid., 551. Also Zeman (1997).
17. See Shin and Hammer (2016). Also Lane (n.d.).
18. Fisch and Turquette (1966).
19. Cf. Niiniluoto (2000, 150–154) for the distinction between strong and weak fallibilism. Niiniluoto argues that Peirce supports the weak version of fallibilism. Also see Hookway (2012, 20–38).

20. For Peirce's views on mathematics and fallibilism, see, for example, Haack (1979), Margolis (1998, 2007), Hookway (2012, 20–38); cf. Haack (1993, 37).
21. See Haack (1993, 35, 38–42).
22. See Margolis (2007, 248).
23. See Ziehen (1920) and Kusch (1995).
24. See Haaparanta (2009, 235–236).
25. See, for example, J. Kasser (1999, 501, 508–509) and Tiercelin (2017). Cf. Hookway (2012, 83).
26. See Dancy (2018, 175).

References

Primary sources

Peirce, Charles S. 1857–1914. Manuscripts held at the Houghton Library of Harvard University, as identified in Richard Robin. *Annotated Catalogue of the Papers of Charles S. Peirce.* Amherst: University of Massachusetts Press, 1967, and in Richard Robin, "The Peirce Papers: A Supplementary Catalogue." *Transactions of the Charles S. Peirce Society* 7, 1971, no. 1 (Winter): 37–57. (Referred to as R, with RL for letters and RS for supplement.)

Peirce, Charles S. 1931–1958. *The Collected Papers of Charles Sanders Peirce.* 8 vols. Vols. 1–6 edited by Charles Hartshorne and Paul Weiss. Vols. 7–8 edited by Arthur W. Burks. Cambridge, MA: Harvard University Press. (Referred to as CP.)

Peirce, Charles S. 1976. *The New Elements of Mathematics*, 4 vols. in 5. Edited by Carolyn Eisele. The Hague: Mouton. (Referred to as NEM.)

Peirce, Charles S. 1982–2010. *The Writings of Charles S. Peirce: A Chronological Edition.* 7 vols. to date. Edited by the Peirce Edition Project. Bloomington: Indiana University Press. (Referred to as W.)

Peirce, Charles S. 1992–1998. *The Essential Peirce: Selected Philosophical Writings.* 2 vols. Vol. 1 edited by Nathan Houser and Christian Kloesel. Vol. 2 edited by the Peirce Edition Project. Bloomington: Indiana University Press. (Referred to as EP.)

Secondary literature

Bellucci, Francesco. 2016. "Charles S. Peirce and the Medieval Doctrine of *consequentiae*." *History and Philosophy of Logic* 37: 244–268.

Boler, John. 2006. "Peirce and Medieval Thought." In Misak (2006): 58–86.

Brunning, Jacqueline, and Paul Forster (eds.). 1997. *The Rule of Reason: The Philosophy of C. S. Peirce.* Toronto: University of Toronto Press.

Dancy, Jonathan. 2018. *Practical Shape: A Theory of Practical Reasoning.* Oxford: Oxford University Press.

DiLeo, Jeffrey R. 1991. "Peirce's Haecceitism." *Transactions of the Charles S. Peirce Society* 27, no. 1 (Winter): 79–109.

Dipert, Randall. 2006. "Peirce's Deductive Logic: Its Development, Influence, and Philosophical Significance." In Misak (2006): 287–324.

Esposito, Joseph L. 1980. *Evolutionary Metaphysics: The Development of Peirce's Theory of Categories.* Athens, OH: Ohio University Press.

Fisch, Max, and Atwell Turquette. 1966. "Peirce's Triadic Logic." *Transactions of the Charles S. Society* 2, no. 2 (Spring): 71–75.

Frege, Gottlob. 1964. *Begriffsschrift, eine der arithmetischen nachgebildete Formelsprache des reinen Denkens* (1879). In Gottlob Frege, *Begriffsschrift und andere Aufsätze*, hrsg. Ignacio Angelelli. Hildesheim, Germany: Georg Olms. (Referred to as BS.)

Frege, Gottlob. 1893. *Grundgesetze der Arithmetik, begriffsschriftlich abgeleitet, I. Band*. Jena, Germany: Verlag von H. Pohle. (Referred to as GGA I.)

Goldfarb, Warren D. 1979. "Logic in the Twenties: The Nature of the Quantifier." *The Journal of Symbolic Logic* 44: 351–368.

Haack, Susan. 1979. "Fallibilism and Necessity." *Synthese* 41: 37–63.

Haack, Susan. 1993. "Peirce and Logicism: Notes towards an Exposition." *Transactions of the Charles S. Peirce Society* 29, no. 1 (Winter): 33–56.

Haack, Susan. 1997. "The First Rule of Reason." In Brunning and Forster (1997): 241–261.

Haaparanta, Leila. 1993. "Peirce and the Logic of Logical Discovery." In *Charles S. Peirce and the Philosophy of Science: Papers from the Harvard Sesquicentennial Congress*, edited by Edward C. Moore, 105–118. Tuscaloosa: University of Alabama Press.

Haaparanta, Leila. 2002. "On Peirce's Methodology of Logic and Philosophy." *Cognitio* 3: 32–45.

Haaparanta, Leila. 2009. "The Relations between Logic and Philosophy, 1874–1931." In Haaparanta (2009): 222–262.

Haaparanta, Leila (ed.). 2009. *The Development of Modern Logic*. New York: Oxford University Press.

Hilpinen, Risto. 1992. "On Peirce's Philosophical Logic: Propositions and Their Objects." *Transactions of the Charles S. Peirce Society* 28 no. 3 (Summer): 467–488.

Hilpinen, Risto. 2009. "Appendix to Chapter 12: Conditionals and Possible Worlds: On C. S. Peirce's Conception of Conditionals and Modalities." In Haaparanta (2009): 551–561.

Hintikka, Jaakko. 1979. "Frege's Hidden Semantics." *Revue Internationale de Philosophie* 33: 716–722.

Hintikka, Jaakko. 1980. "C. S. Peirce's 'First Real Discovery' and Its Contemporary Relevance." *The Monist* 63: 304–315.

Hintikka, Jaakko. 1997. "The Place of C. S. Peirce in the History of Logical Theory." In Brunning and Forster (1997): 13–33.

Hookway, Christopher. 1985. *Peirce*. London: Routledge & Kegan Paul.

Hookway, Christopher. 2012. *The Pragmatic Maxim: Essays on Peirce and Pragmatism*. Oxford: Oxford University Press.

Kant, Immanuel. [1788] 1908. *Kritik der praktischen Vernunft*. In *Kant's gesammelte Schriften, Band V*, 1–167. Berlin: Reimer.

Kasser, Jeff. 1999. "Peirce's Supposed Psychologism." *Transactions of the Charles S. Peirce Society* 35, no. 3 (Summer): 501–526.

Kusch, Martin. 1995. *Psychologism: A Case Study in the Sociology of Philosophical Knowledge*. London: Routledge & Kegan Paul.

Ladd, Christine. 1883. "On the Algebra of Logic." In Peirce (1883): 17–71.

Lane, Robert. 2001. "Triadic Logic." In *The Commens Encyclopedia: The Digital Encyclopedia of Peirce Studies. New Edition*, edited by Mats Bergman and João Queiroz. Pub. 140917-1304a. Retrieved from http://www.commens.org/encyclopedia/article/lane-robert-triadic-logic. on 21.01.2022.

Margolis, Joseph. 1998. "Peirce's Fallibilism." *Transactions of the Charles S. Peirce Society* 34, no. 2 (Spring): 535–569.

Margolis, Joseph. 2007. "Rethinking Peirce's Fallibilism." *Transactions of the Charles S. Peirce Society* 43, no. 2 (Spring): 229–249.

Misak, Cheryl (ed.). 2006. *Cambridge Companion to Peirce*. Cambridge: Cambridge University Press.

Mitchell, O. H. 1883. "On a New Algebra of Logic." In Peirce (1883): 72–106.

Murphey, Murray G. 1961. *The Development of Peirce's Philosophy*. Cambridge, MA: Harvard University Press.

Niiniluoto, Ilkka. 2000. "Scepticism, Fallibilism, and Verisimilitude." In *"Ancient Scepticism and the Sceptical Tradition,"* edited by Juha Sihvola, special issue, *Acta Philosophica Fennica* 66: 145–169.

Peckhaus, Volker. 2004. "Calculus Ratiocinator versus Characteristica Universalis? The Two Traditions in Logic, Revisited." *History and Philosophy of Logic* 25: 3–14.

Peckhaus, Volker. 2009. "The Mathematical Origins of Nineteenth-Century Algebra of Logic." In Haaparanta (2009): 159–195.

Peirce, Charles S. (ed.). 1883. *Studies in Logic*. By Members of the Johns Hopkins University, Boston: Little, Brown,.

Pietarinen, Ahti-Veikko. 2006. *Signs of Logic: Peircean Themes on the Philosophy of Language, Games, and Communication*. Dordrecht, The Netherlands: Springer.

Putnam, Hilary. 1982. "Peirce the Logician." *Historia Mathematica* 9: 290–301.

Sextus, Empiricus. 2000. *Outlines of Scepticism*, edited by Julia Annas and Jonathan Barnes. Cambridge: Cambridge University Press. (Referred to as PH.)

Shin, Sun-Joo, and Eric Hammer. 2016. "Peirce's Deductive Logic." In *The Stanford Encyclopedia of Philosophy*, edited by Edward N. Zalta. https://plato.stanford.edu/archives/win2016/entries/peirce-logic/.

Tiercelin, Claudine. 2017. "Was Peirce a Genuine Anti-Psychologist in Logic?" *European Journal of Pragmatism and American Philosophy* 9, no. 1 (July 22, 2017). http://journals.openedition.org/ejpap/1003.

Tursman, Richard. 1987. *Peirce's Theory of Scientific Discovery: A System of Logic Conceived as Semiotic*. Bloomington: Indiana University Press.

van Heijenoort, Jean. 1967. "Logic as Calculus and Logic as Language." *Synthese* 17: 324–330.

Williams, Garrath. 2018. "Kant's Account of Reason." *The Stanford Encyclopedia of Philosophy* (Summer 2018 Edition), Edward N. Zalta (ed.), https://plato.stanford.edu/archives/sum2018/entries/kant-reason/

Zeman, Jay. 1997. "Peirce and Philo." In *Studies in the Logic of Charles Sanders Peirce*, edited by Nathan Houser, Don D. Roberts, and James Van Evra, 402–417. Bloomington: Indiana University Press.

Ziehen, Theodor. 1920. *Lehrbuch der Logik* auf positivistischer Grundlage mit Berücksichtigung der Geschichte der Logik. Bonn: A. Marcus & E. Webers Verlag.

CHAPTER 12

PEIRCE'S ABDUCTION AND ITS INTERPRETATIONS

ILKKA NIINILUOTO

1. Peirce's Classification of Inferences

CHARLES S. Peirce made a distinction between three modes of scientific reasoning already in his Harvard Lectures during the spring of 1865. Starting from Aristotle's doctrine of induction as the inference of the major premise of a syllogism (of the first figure), Peirce observed that there is "a large class of reasonings" that are neither deductive nor inductive: reasoning a posteriori to a physical hypothesis, or inference of a cause from its effect (W1:180). This reasoning, which Peirce called hypothesis, can be represented as the inference of the minor premise of a syllogism. Besides Aristotle, Peirce's inspiration and the term "hypothesis" came from the 1800 edition of Immanuel Kant's *Logic*, which defined hypothesis as "holding-to-be-true of a judgment of the truth of a ground, for the sake of its sufficiency for consequences" (W1:451). This classification of inferences was elaborated in Peirce's Lowell Lectures in the fall of 1866 and published in the next year. In Peirce's series for *Popular Scientific Monthly* in 1878, this distinction was presented in the article "Deduction, Induction, and Hypothesis" (CP2.619–644), and later in 1883 he treated it in detail in "A Theory of Probable Inference" (CP2.694–754).

Peirce illustrated the two ways of inverting deductive arguments by the following example with a Barbara syllogism (in the first figure). *Deduction* is an inference of a result from a rule and a case:

(1) Rule.   All the beans from this bag are white.
     Case.   These beans are from this bag.
     ∴ Result. These beans are white.

Induction is the inference of the rule from the case and result:

(2) These beans are from this bag.
These beans are white.
∴ All the beans from this bag are white.

Hypothesis is the inference of the case from the rule and result:

(3) All the beans from this bag are white.
These beans are white.
∴ These beans are from this bag. (W3:325; CP2.623)

With singular cases, induction infers the general law $\forall x(Fx \to Gx)$ from its instances $Fa\&Ga$. A typical example of hypothesis in the sense of (3) has the following logical form:

(4) Given the law $\forall x(Fx \to Gx)$,
from Ga infer Fa.

Hypothetical reasoning (4) proceeds backward from effects to causes, while a typical deduction proceeds from causes to effects.

Already in the Harvard Lectures 1865, Peirce made it perfectly clear that hypothesis is an *inference to an explanation*: "We find that light gives certain peculiar fringes. Required an explanation of the fact. We reflect that ether waves would give the same fringes. We have therefore only to suppose that light is ether waves and the marvel is explained" (W1:267). In the Lowell Lectures of 1866, Peirce said that hypothesis is the inversion of the corresponding *explaining syllogism*, which typically has the structure (1) (W1:428, 425, 440, 452). Here Peirce formulated the subsumption theory of explanation for singular facts and general laws, earlier sketched by John Stuart Mill in the 1840s and later made precise by Carl G. Hempel's deductive-nomological model in the 1940s.

Inspired by John Venn's frequency theory of probability in *The Logic of Chance* (1866), Peirce formulated deduction, induction, and hypothesis as probable arguments in 1867, where probability is interpreted as a *truth-frequency*, that is, the proportion of cases in which an argument "carries truth with it." In 1878, he formulated probabilistic versions of the Barbara syllogism (1) and its inversions by replacing the universal rule "All the beans from this bag are white" with a statistical generalization, "Most of the beans in this bag are white" (CP2.627, 1878; CP2.508–516, 1867).

The 1883 article gives several models of *probable* and *statistical deduction* from a quantitative statistical premise, "The proportion r of F's are G." Here "deduction" means inference from a population to a sample and is not necessarily truth-preserving. The inversion of statistical deduction forms the model of "quantitative induction" from a sample to a population:

(5) b', b'', b''', etc. are a numerous set, taken at random from among the F's,
the proportion r of the b's are G;
Hence, probably and approximately the proportion r of the F's are G.

When the sample b', b'', b''', etc., is collected, the property G has to be predesignated. This schema (5) reduces to inductive generalization (2) when $r = 1$. The hypothetical inversion might be characterized as an inference from an effect to its probabilistic or statistical cause. Peirce was again explicit in reasserting his earlier view that inductions and hypotheses, as the two forms of "ampliative reasoning," are "inferences from the conclusion and one premiss of a statistical syllogism to the other premiss," and in the case of hypothesis, "this syllogism is called the *explanation*." Indeed, Peirce repeated, "we commonly say that the hypothesis is adopted *for the sake of* the explanation," and a statistical syllogism "may be conveniently termed the explanatory syllogism" (CP2.716–717, 1883). Here Peirce anticipated Hempel's 1962 model of inductive-probabilistic explanation of particular facts, but his treatment was even richer as it included probabilistic explanations of statistical facts.[1]

To keep the number of different kinds of inferences as three, in his early papers Peirce treated what traditional logicians like Kant called *analogy* as a kind of hypothetical inference: "We find that in certain respects two objects have a strong resemblance, and infer that they resemble one another strongly in other respects" (CP2.624, 1878). In 1883, he formulated a probabilistic argument that clearly involves analogical reasoning (CP2.706):

(6) a has the numerous marks G, G', G'', etc.
b has the proportion r of the marks G, G', G'', etc.
Hence, probably and approximately, b has an r-likeness to a.

Here a has an *r-likeness* to b if the proportion of the shared properties of a and b is r; hence, by Leibniz's law, $r = 1$ if and only if a and b are completely similar. Peirce classified this inference as being a hypothesis, but noted that it is in fact "an induction of characters" or "induction respecting qualities instead of respecting things," since G, G', G'', etc., constitutes a random sample of the characters of a, and the probability of the argument increases when the positive analogy r increases.[2] If $r = 1$, so that b is found to share all these properties with a, (6) reduces to the case where a hypothetical proposition is believed because its consequences agree with experience (CP2.707, 1883).[3]

In his 1878 paper, Peirce gave three examples of hypothetical inference (CP2.625). In meeting a Turkish man surrounded by four horsemen holding a canopy over his head, Peirce inferred that this man was the governor of the province. In finding fish-like fossils far in the interior of the country, we suppose that the sea once washed over this land. Countless documents and monuments refer to a conqueror called Napoleon Bonaparte, and we explain them by supposing that Napoleon really existed.

The example of Napoleon shows that past events can be known only by hypothetical reasoning by the traces or effects of their historical causes. Ordinary perception is an extreme case of such causal (but largely unconscious) inference (CP5.181, 1903; EP2:227, 1903). But in addition to historical studies, perception, and many everyday inferences, hypothetical reasoning is needed in theoretical sciences, since it "infers very frequently a fact not capable of direct observation" (CP2.641, 1878): "The great difference between induction and hypothesis is, that the former infers the existence of phenomena such as we have observed in cases which are similar, while hypothesis supposes something of a different kind from what we have directly observed, and frequently something which it would be impossible for us to observe directly" (CP2.640, 1878). Therefore, Peirce concluded in the spirit of scientific realism against Auguste Comte's positivism, science should not be restricted to hypotheses "verifiable by direct observation" (EP2:225, 1903).

2. New Treatment of Induction and Abduction

In his manuscript "Lessons from the History of Science," Peirce introduced the term *retroduction* for "the provisional adoption of a hypothesis" (CP1.68, c. 1896). In his Cambridge Lectures of 1898, Peirce said that, on the one hand, induction, what Aristotle called *epagoge* (RLT:139), was translated as *inductio* ("a leading in") by Cicero. Hypothesis or retroduction, on the other hand, is what Aristotle called *apagoge* ("a leading out"). The general form of such retroductive inference is:

(7) If μ were true, π, π', π'' would follow as miscellaneous consequences.
But π, π', π'' are in fact true.
∴ Provisionally, we may suppose that μ is true.
(RLT:140)

Already in his unfinished "Dictionary of Logic" in 1867 Peirce had noted that modern logicians have translated Aristotle's account of *apagoge* in *Prior Analytics*, II, Chapter 25 (69a20-36) into Latin as *abductio* (W2:108), so that *abduction* is the English counterpart of the term used by Julius Pacius (Guilio Pacio) in 1597. This notion is sometimes translated as "reduction," but Peirce denied that it has any connection to indirect or "apagogical proof." Rather, Aristotle's example refers to a syllogism where the major premise is evident but the minor only probable. In this early stage, Peirce did not associate "abduction" to his account of hypothetical inference. But later he came to think that Aristotle's text here is corrupted (CP1.65, c. 1896), and what Aristotle really meant was the inversion given by his own schema of hypothesis (3) (cf. CP5.144, 1903; CP7.249, c. 1901; EP2:527-528, 1903). For this reason he was ready in 1898 to use this "otherwise useless term" *abduction* for his new account of hypothesis.

In his 1903 Harvard Lectures, Peirce expressed the general form of the "operation of adopting an explanatory hypothesis" as follows (CP5.189, EP2:231):

(8) The surprising fact C is observed;
But if A were true, C would be a matter of course.
Hence, there is reason to suspect that A is true.

This schema, which has become Peirce's best known or canonical formulation of abduction, indicates how a hypothesis can be "abductively conjectured" if it accounts "for the facts or some of them." Peirce added that the conclusion is not A itself, but the assertion that "there is reason to suspect that A is true." In this sense, abduction "only infers a *maybe*" from an actual fact (CP8.238, *c.* 1910).

In spite of terminological novelty, and the wish to get rid of the restricted framework of Aristotle's syllogisms, there is a lot of continuity in Peirce's account of abduction. Schema (8) is obviously a generalization of the original patterns (3) and (4) of hypothetical inference: the emphasis that the fact C is surprising (and therefore in need of explanation) has been added, and there are no restrictions on the logical complexity of A. As here A may be a general theory, it might be said to express *theoretical abduction*, in contrast to *singular abduction* (4).[4] The idea of explanation is maintained in the second premise, but this is not any more associated with the relation of cause and effect.

Schema (8) also shows that Peirce's formulation (7) of retroduction is slightly misleading, since as an abduction it should start from the second premise (i.e., the surprising observation about the truth of π, π', π''), and then conclude with the potential explanation μ of this fact. When Peirce complained in his later work that before the twentieth century he "more or less mixed up Hypothesis and Induction" (CP8.227, *c.* 1910), his somewhat cryptic remark is explained in the same letter to Paul Carus: he had failed to sharply distinguish cases where (i) a hypothesis is tested by deriving from it miscellaneous observable consequences and then comparing these consequences to phenomena (cf. (7)) and (ii) the hypothesis (first adopted by retroduction) is further found to explain some already known facts (CP8.231–232, *c.* 1910). As Peirce's remarks in 1905 make clear, he became aware that some historically important theories have received their strongest support from the surprising finding that they are able to explain some already well-known phenomenon (CP2.759). In the early twenty-first century, this is known as the "problem of old evidence."

Already in 1878 Peirce argued that hypotheses have to be put into "fair and unbiased" tests by comparing their predictions with observations (CP2.634). In his papers and lectures in 1901–1903, Peirce defined induction in a new way as "the operation of testing a hypothesis by experiment" (CP6.526, *c.* 1901), which is quite different from the account of "crude" inductive generalization in (2) or its probabilistic versions. Indeed, Peirce's new treatment of induction resembles the hypothetico-deductive model of science, but he also allowed for cases where the test evidence is only a probabilistic consequence of the hypothesis. Abduction is methodologically characterized as an "inferential step," which is "the first starting of a hypothesis and the entertaining of it, whether as a simple interrogation or with any degree of confidence" (CP6.525, c. 1901). Thus, abduction and induction are successive steps in scientific inquiry: abduction is "the first step of scientific reasoning, as induction is the concluding step." "Abduction seeks a theory. Induction seeks for facts" (EP2:106, 1901).

> Abduction is the process of forming an explanatory hypothesis. It is the only logical operation which introduces any new idea; for induction does nothing but determine a value and deduction merely evolves the necessary consequences of a pure hypothesis.
> Deduction proves that something *must* be, Induction shows that something *actually is* operative, Abduction merely suggests that something *may be*. Its only justification is that from its suggestion deduction can draw a prediction which can be tested by induction and that, if we are ever to learn anything or to understand phenomena at all, it must be by abduction that this is to be brought about. (EP2:216, 1903)

3. Interpretations of Abduction

Like many other aspects of Peirce's contributions to logic and philosophy, his work on abduction gained attention only slowly after his death in 1914. Even after the first six volumes of Peirce's *Collected Papers* in 1931–1935 and the two additional volumes in 1958, leading philosophers were inclined to think that the idea of abductive reasoning as a combination of creativity and inference is in some way confused. Following Karl Popper's and Hans Reichenbach's distinction between the context of discovery and the context of justification, the mainstream view in the 1930s and the 1940s claimed that only the latter belongs to the province of logical reconstruction, so that the conception of a "logic of discovery" appeared to be some kind of oxymoron. But gradually Peirce's views were taken seriously, when new material on his works became available, his output was better organized, and scholars like K. T. Fann (1970) published expositions of the development of his approach to abductive reasoning. Still, Peirce's formulations are open to various and even conflicting interpretations, so that at least three alternatives are subjects of ongoing debate: abduction as (i) discovery, (ii) pursuit, and (iii) justification.

3.1. Abduction as Discovery

An important step in the re-evaluation of abduction came from Norwood Russell Hanson, who argued in *Patterns of Discovery* (1958) that Peirce's abduction gives a basis for studying the logic of discovery. Hanson thought that logical empiricists have given a too-static picture of scientific theories as "finished research reports": the focus should be in theory finding instead of theory testing. He was impressed by Peirce's reconstruction of "the greatest piece of retroductive reasoning ever performed" (CP1.71–74, c. 1896), namely, Kepler's discovery of the elliptic orbit of Mars. Hanson concluded that Peirce's canonical schema (8) describes the "logic of scientific discovery." In a later paper, Hanson (1961) argued that (8) gives reasons for *suggesting* a hypothesis, instead of reasons for *accepting* a hypothesis. In this way Hanson was able to encourage Thomas Nickles (1980) and other "friends of discovery" to analyze the heuristic role of abduction in the discovery of new scientific theories. Soon abduction became a hot topic also in philosophical logic and artificial intelligence, which started to develop formal and computational systems, capable of generating conclusions from data with nondeductive rules of inference like

(9) $A \to B$
B
$\therefore A$

(cf. Peirce's hypothetical schema (4)).[5] Even though the schema (9) is not generally valid in deductive logic, since it is an instance of the well-known fallacy of affirming the consequent, as a rule of discovery it may lead to interesting new results.

Peirce himself stated in 1883 that the scientific task of "discovering laws" is accomplished by induction and "discovering causes" by hypothetic inference (CP2.713, 1893). He repeatedly insisted that "all the ideas of science come to it by way of abduction" (CP5.145, 1903). In creative abduction, the relevant hypotheses are not selected from a ready-made list (e.g., causes of death), but use new theoretical concepts.[6] This gives support to the Hansonian way of looking at Peirce's work.[7] But there is still the standard objection that in the canonical schema (8) the hypothesis A occurs already in one of the premises, so that (8) cannot tell how A was discovered in the first place. As a possible solution, the specific hypothesis A in (8) can be replaced by a type (or class) K of hypotheses:

(10) The surprising fact C is observed;
there is reason to suspect that some hypothesis of kind K explains C,
hence, there is reason to suspect that some hypothesis of kind K is true.

When the conclusion of (10) leads a scientists to think about a particular hypothesis A of kind K, then this schema succeeds to describe the process of discovery of A. Schema (10) is clearly related to many later accounts of discovery in artificial intelligence, which involve a space of search K from which the desired solution is to be found. In heuristic search, the class K is effectively narrowed down to relevant hypotheses or "abducibles," which have explanatory power with respect to the initial problem.[8] Schema (10) is also related to the historically most significant model of heuristic reasoning, geometrical analysis, which proceeds backward from a supposed solution to its conditions, or from a theorem to the axioms. The applications of this kind of retroductive method, where the class of potential suspects is narrowed with appropriate questions and forensic evidence, can be found in classical detective stories: the logical moves of Edgar Allan Poe's hero C. Auguste Dupin and Arthur Conan Doyle's Sherlock Holmes are typically abductive.[9]

Detective stories gave inspiration to Jaakko Hintikka's interrogative model of inquiry, where abduction has an important role in truth-seeking. Hintikka (1998) argued that Peirce did not fully see that the success of abduction should be assessed from the strategic perspective. But in his own model, all inferential steps are deductive, the role of induction is downplayed, and "abductive moves" are questions put to nature or oracles.[10] The power of Hintikka's "Socratic" model of truth-seeking would be increased if it allowed fallible ampliative inferences (induction and abduction).

3.2. Abduction as Pursuit

Larry Laudan (1980) challenged Hanson's logic of discovery by suggesting that abduction tells instead "when an idea is worthy of pursuit." Martin Curd's (1980) "logic of pursuit" asks "which hypothesis should we bother taking seriously enough to test." He argues that Peirce's schema (8) for abductive inference should be interpreted as the logic of pursuit:

(11)   The surprising fact C is observed;
       The hypothesis H is capable of explaining C.
       Hence, there are prima facie grounds for *pursuing* H.

Schema (11) belongs to a stage of inquiry where we try to identify which hypotheses are plausible enough to be *testworthy*. The ability of a hypothesis to give at least a potentially correct answer to a why question, or to give a potential explanation of the facts known so far, is an important part of the *before-trial evaluation* of a hypothesis. According to this conception, abduction is at best a route for finding worthwhile hypotheses, but does not lend any support or justification to a hypothesis. To confirm a hypothesis or to make it acceptable, we have to put it into trials or tests by deriving observable predictions from it. This stage of testing was called "induction" by Peirce in his later work after 1901.

Daniel McKaughan (2008) contrasts the generative and justificatory interpretations with the *pursuitworthiness* interpretation, which takes Peirce's abductive reasoning "to lead to judgments about the relative pursuitworthiness of hypotheses," and such conclusions "can be thoroughly disconnected from assessments of truth-value." This agrees with the schema (11) and with Tomas Kapitan's (1997) thesis that the conclusions of abduction are practical directives of the form "it is recommended to further examine hypothesis H," based upon considerations of economy.

Peirce distinguished before-trial and after-trial criteria in 1903 by asking, "What is good abduction?" His reply that "of course it must explain the facts" indicates that the schema (8) expresses only the minimum condition of abductive reasoning. The hypothesis must also "be capable of experimental verification" (EP2:235). But Peirce discussed additional criteria for hypotheses beyond explanatory power and testability. His most detailed account of the criteria for the choice of good hypotheses in 1901 includes again the explanation of "the surprising facts we have before us" and experimental testability by new predictions, but also economic factors like cost (testability "with very little expense of any kind"), caution (breaking a hypothesis up "into its smallest logical components" for investigation), breadth (finding one cause for different phenomena "saves repetitious work"), and incomplexity (we may start with simple hypotheses even though by complicating them they could be "brought nearer the truth") (see CP7.220–221, *c*. 1901; EP2:106–114, 1901). Peirce needed these criteria, as he was well aware that "the possible explanations of our facts may be strictly innumerable" (EP2:107). Davies and Coltheart (2020) defend the pursuit interpretation by arguing that the application of these criteria for good hypotheses belong only to the before-trial stage, so that they only help to pick out the most testworthy hypothesis to be "further evaluated as a candidate-for-belief" by deduction and induction. This could be supported by Peirce's remark that "as soon as a hypothesis has been settled upon as preferable to others," the next business is to deduce from it predictions in order to subject them to the test of experiment (CP7.182, *c*. 1901).

The so-called GW model of abduction, developed by Dov Gabbay and John Woods (2005), can be included in the pursuit approach. In their framework, abduction is *ignorance-preserving*, since the presumptive solution H of a cognitive problem does not secure us knowledge or warrant belief at all. Still, in "partial" abduction H is presented as a conjecture, and in "full" abduction H is used as a basis of new action.[11]

As an interpretation of Peirce, the pursuit account is based on the ambiguity of the conclusion of the canonical schema (8). What does it mean to say that "there is reason to suspect that A is true"? In Kant's logic, hypothesis is a species of "holding-to-be-true," and a fallibilist might read Peirce as speaking here about tentative acceptance, that is, cautious approval with readiness to revise the claim on further evidence.[12] In Peirce's early work, hypothesis (4) was an ampliative argument, whose probability (i.e., truth-frequency between 0 and 1) depends on the proportion of F's in the class of G's. But in his later writings, Peirce stated that abduction is "nothing but guessing" (EP2.107, 1901) and "probability proper has nothing to do with the validity of Abduction" (CP2.102, *c*. 1902). The problem here seems to be that Peirce's logic lacked sufficiently rich distinctions between a proposition and its assertion. In the "Sundry Logical Conceptions" manuscript for the 1903 *Syllabus*, Peirce stated that the conclusion of abduction is "not accepted as shown to be *true*, nor even *probable* in the technical sense, ... but is shown to be *likely*, in the sense of being some sort of approach to the truth, in an indefinite sense"; thus, the conclusion is drawn in "the interrogative mood" (EP2:287). Bellucci and Pietarinen (2020) have found, in an unpublished 1905 letter to Lady Welby (RL463), an interesting attempt by Peirce to characterize "the interrogative mood" as "the investigand mood." Here Peirce formulated the conclusion of abduction, or "Reasoning from Surprise to Inquiry," as the recommendation to investigate the hypothetical explanation:

(12) It is to be inquired whether A is not true.

This textual evidence seems to reconfirm the pursuit interpretation of abduction.

In spite of these arguments, it is not quite clear that pursuit and acceptance can always be sharply separated from each other.[13] In his 1910 reflections on "The Doctrine of Chances," Peirce defined the *plausibility* of a theory in the following way: "By Plausible, I mean that a theory that has not yet been subjected to any test, although more or less surprising phenomena have occurred which it would explain if it were true, is in itself of such a character as to recommend it for further examination or, if it be *highly* plausible, justify us in seriously inclining toward belief in it, as long as the phenomena be inexplicable otherwise" (CP2.662, 1910). McKaughan (2008, 454) quotes the first part, which supports his case for pursuitworthiness, but omits the last part, which is related to justification. Elsewhere in 1908 Peirce stated that holding a hypothesis to be plausible ranges "from a mere expression of it in the interrogative mood, as a question meriting attention and reply, up through all appraisals of Plausibility, to uncontrollable inclination to believe" (CP6.469, 1908; EP2:441). The "first stage of inquiry," with a characteristic formula of retroduction, that is, reasoning from consequent to antecedent, covers "the whole series of mental performances between the notice of the wonderful phenomenon and the acceptance of the hypothesis" (EP2:441, 1908). But he immediately added that "retroduction does not afford security," so that "the hypothesis must be tested."

Davies and Coltheart (2020, 417–418) also quote the definition of high plausibility, concluding that sometimes Peirce allowed a "short-cutting" from a pursuitworthy hypothesis to its adoption as a belief without the deductive and inductive steps of experimental testing. They suggest that this is motivated by "an intrinsic rather than a comparative property of the hypothesis," but they overlook Peirce's condition that serious inclination to belief arises "as long as the phenomena be inexplicable otherwise."

3.3. Abduction as Justification

While discovery and pursuit belong to the generation of hypotheses for further investigation, a broader view allows that abduction has a function in the selection and evaluation of explanatory hypotheses that belongs to the context of *justification*, where the role of abduction in justification can be understood in the weak sense as confirmation and in the strong sense as acceptance.[14]

In spite of the fallibility and uncertainty of hypothetical reasoning, Peirce was aware that in some cases inference from effect to cause may be irresistible or "compelling": the abductive suggestion may come to us "like a flash." According to Peirce, this happens in *perceptual judgments*, which are "an extreme case of abductive inferences" (CP5.181–185, 1903; EP2:229–230). Another important area of human knowledge that is based upon abduction is *history*. For example, the fact that Napoleon Bonaparte once lived is not any more "suspectible of direct observation," but we believe it because "its effects (such as the histories, the monuments, etc.) are observed" (CP2.714, 1883). This inference is "perfectly certain," and it "would surely be downright insanity" to entertain doubt about Napoleon's existence (EP2:54, 1898).[15]

Inspired by Hempel's work on the *qualitative* concept of *confirmation*, Howard Smokler (1968) suggested that abductive inference satisfies the following conditions:

(CE) (Converse Entailment) If H entails E, then E confirms H.
(CC) (Converse Consequence) If E confirms H and K entails H, then E confirms K.

We come even closer to Peirce's "explanationist" views if abduction is characterized by conditions CE* and CC*, which are obtained from CE and CC by replacing the notion of entailment by the stronger notion of deductive explanation (cf. the difference between (7) and (8)). For example, CE* can exclude cases where the entailment is too trivial or ad hoc. In contrast, Smokler argued that enumerative and eliminative induction, where a generalization receives support from its instances, satisfy the condition

(E)   (Entailment) If E logically entails H, then E confirms H.
(SC) (Special Consequence) If E confirms H, and K is entailed by H, then E confirms K.

It is known that SC cannot be satisfied at the same time as CE or CC, which supports Peirce's original thesis that abduction and inductive generalization are two different kinds of ampliative inference.

In the *Bayesian* school, Bayes's theorem has traditionally been used for the calculation of "inverse probabilities," that is, the probabilities of causes given effects. For a personalist Bayesian, such probabilities express credences or degrees of belief in the truth of a hypothesis given evidence. Bayesian confirmation theory (Stanley Jevons, J. M. Keynes) was conceived as an account of induction as converse deduction. As a frequentist, Peirce was sharply critical about such applications (EP2:215, 1903), so that a quantitative notion of confirmation in terms of probabilities was not available to him. If confirmation is defined by *high probability* (the posterior probability $P(H/E)$ of hypothesis H given evidence E is sufficiently large), then the enumerative conditions (E) and (SC) are satisfied. But if confirmation is defined by *positive relevance* or increase of probability ($P(H/E) > P(H)$), then the abductive principles CE and CE* are satisfied:

(13) Assuming that $P(H) > 0$ and $P(E) < 1$, if H entails E, then $P(H/E) > P(H)$.

(14) If H and E are contingent statements, and H deductively explains E, then E confirms H in the positive relevance sense.

As positive relevance is a symmetric relation, even a weaker premise is sufficient in (14):[16]

(15) If H is a positively relevant inductive explanation of E, then E confirms H.

The Bayesian approach thus immediately justifies the idea that explanatory success is confirmatory: abduction is not ignorance-preserving but credence-increasing.[17]

Results about positive confirmation do not yet guarantee that H would be *acceptable* on evidence E. It may happen that no one of the rival hypotheses is clearly superior to others, so that suspension of judgment is the most rational conclusion. To improve the situation, new evidence may be needed (cf. EP2:114, 1901), or alternatively the problem set has to be expanded by the introduction of new concepts. The extended cognitive problem contains then new rival hypotheses, which may be evaluated by their explanatory value. This kind of proposal was given by Gilbert Harman (1965) with his notion of *inference to the best explanation*:

(IBE)   A hypothesis H may be inferred from evidence E when H is a better explanation of E than any other rival hypothesis.

As an interpretation of abductive reasoning, Harman's IBE claims that the best of rival explanations of given evidence is inductively acceptable on E. Harman also tried to reduce all inductive inference to IBE.

The notion of IBE has been a powerful stimulus for studies in artificial intelligence,[18] logic,[19] argumentation theory,[20] and philosophy of science.[21] Some philosophers like Schurz (2008) and Psillos (2011) regard IBE as an independent principle of scientific rationality, while some others like Niiniluoto (1999) have proposed Bayesian analyses where the "best explanation" is the explanation that maximizes a probabilistic measure of explanatory power. For example, Schurz (2008) proposes as a special case of IBE the principle of common cause abduction:

(16)   Accept C as the hypothetical common cause, if C is able explain many intercorrelated but analytically independent phenomena.

For example, Newton showed that gravitation is the common cause of the planetary orbits (Kepler) and free fall (Galileo).[22]

Bas van Fraassen (1989) has presented technical objections to the Bayesian treatment of abduction. As IBE is always restricted to a set of historically given or formulated hypotheses, it may lead to "the best of a bad lot." How could we know that the true hypothesis is among the so far proposed? In the Bayesian framework such worries have a straightforward technical answer: in order to apply Bayes's theorem, the cognitive problem has to be treated in terms of a set of mutually exclusive and jointly exhaustive hypotheses—usually one of them is the "catchall hypothesis." In the simplest case, this set contains only two elements, a hypothesis H and its negation ~H. So trivially one and only one element of this set is true. Still, the catchall hypothesis need not be an interesting one, so that in many cases investigation has to be continued in order to find a relevant interesting explanation. Peirce himself repeatedly appealed to Galileo's notion of *il lume naturale*, our natural disposition to light upon the correct hypothesis in a finite number of guesses (CP7.223, c. 1901).

Van Fraassen (1989) also points out that result (13) is blocked if the prior probability P(H) is zero, but this kind of assignment leads him to aprioristic theoretical skepticism.

An alternative approach is to replace the strict notion of truth with the graded concept of *truthlikeness* and to reformulate Peirce's abductive schema with the conclusion that the best explanatory theory is closest to the truth or most truthlike of the available alternatives.[23]

4. Concluding Remarks: Abduction versus IBE

Some philosophers use the terms "abduction" and "inference to the best explanation" as synonyms—among them Thagard (1978), van Fraassen (1989), Walton (2004), Lipton (2004), Psillos (2011), and Kuipers (2019). They usually appeal to criteria that are similar to Peirce's own 1901 conditions for good explanations: testability by novel predictions, unifying power, and simplicity. But, as Douven (2011) observes, Peirce's canonical schema (8) is different from IBE, since it does not include any reference to alternative explanations. Indeed, unlike the main twentieth-century theories of statistical inference, the Neyman–Pearson tests of significance and Bayesian testing, Peirce's account of theory evaluation is not comparative in any explicit way. But, at least occasionally, Peirce appealed to the comparative perspective. In 1878, he pointed out that successful explanation is not alone sufficient for the adoption of a hypothesis, but it is also needed that "the contrary hypothesis would probably lead to results contrary to the observed" (CP2.628). And we have seen that, in his definition of "high plausibility" in 1910, "serious inclining toward belief" in a theory is justified "as long as the phenomena be inexplicable otherwise" (CP2.662).

Many Peirce scholars have been concerned that abduction should not be "confused" with IBE. The term "confusion" appears in the titles of Minnameier (2004) and Mcauliffe (2015); Yu and Zenker (2018) even claim that "Peirce knew why abduction isn't IBE." While we have already acknowledged that it would not be correct to identify abduction and IBE, one should not draw an absolute or strict separation between them. This is the theme of the concluding remarks in this section.

Mcauliffe (2015, 310–311) appeals to Peirce's condemnation in "the ethics of terminology": "whoever deliberately uses a word or other symbol in any other sense than that which was conferred upon it by its sole rightful creator commits a shameful offence" (CP2.224, 1903). It is, indeed, highly important that Peirce scholars should study the intended meaning(s) of his original term "abduction," but this cannot fix all of its future uses forever. Peirce also praised "mental freedom": "every symbol is a living thing," so that "the body of the symbol changes slowly, . . . its meaning inevitably grows, incorporates new elements and throws off old ones" (CP2.219–221, 1903). When Peirce still required that "the essence of every scientific term" should be kept unchanged and exact (EP2:264, 1903), it seems fair to suggest that the "essence" of abduction is the employment of explanatory considerations in the selection of hypotheses. In this respect, the contemporary logicians and philosophers of science who extend the application of the term "abduction" for comparative inferential patterns like IBE are celebrating Peirce's original insights without going too far from them.

Daniel Campos (2011) argues that abduction should be restricted to the generation of explanatory hypotheses, while IBE involves both the generation and the evaluation of hypotheses. He disagrees with Fann (1970), who thought that Peirce did not wish to make a clear distinction between the construction and selection of hypotheses. Yu and Zenker (2018) concur with Campos. But they do not mention the fact that Peirce associated some forms or cases of abduction to justification. The sharp dichotomy between discovery and justification can also be questioned, since one can find examples of backward reasoning from effects to causes (e.g., applications of tomography to find tumors in medical diagnosis), where the unique solution of an inverse problem gives at the same time a discovery and its justification.[24]

Gerhard Minnameier (2004) argues that the confusion between abduction and IBE would violate Peirce's distinction between abduction and induction. It is true that some advocates of IBE, like Lipton (2004), regard it as a species of induction, but still there are types of IBE that allow for the introduction of new explanatory concepts and therefore cannot be formulated as Peircean induction. It is not evident that Peirce really "mixed up" hypothetical reasoning and induction, as he claimed (CP8.227, c. 1910). After all, the logical structure of arguments (2) and (3) is clearly different, and Peirce's methodological requirements for quantitative induction—random sampling and predesignation of the character sampled (CP2.736–739, 1883)—are not satisfied by hypothetical inference. If the best hypothesis is required, besides explanatory power and independent testability, to pass some severe tests,[25] then IBE includes what Peirce later called the second "inductive" stage. But most formulations of IBE allow that sometimes purely explanatory considerations are sufficient to warrant the tentative acceptance of a hypothesis (e.g., the dark matter theory in contemporary physics).

William Mcauliffe (2015) traces the "distortion" of Peirce's abduction to Paul Thagard's (1978) study on the criteria of "best hypotheses" and his influence to van Fraassen (1989) and Lipton (1991). He draws attention to Thagard's discussion of Peirce's 1901 example about a Catholic priest. Thagard's description can be understood as a common cause abduction (16) from the premises that a man speaks Latin, dresses like a priest, and abstains from sex to the explanation that he is a Catholic priest. Thereby it is a precursor of IBE, as no other explanation of the combination of these characters is available. But in Peirce's own formulation, the hypothesis that a man is a Catholic priest is tested by checking that he understands Latin in the Italian pronunciation. By Peirce's new terminology, this kind of test is qualitative induction, and it gives "weak confirmation" to the hypothesis. But as it involves some guesswork and sampling about the characters of priests, Peirce suggested to call it "abductory induction" (CP6.525–526, c. 1901). This is clearly a new name to what Peirce had earlier called "induction from qualities." It resembles Peirce's schema (8), but it is not abduction in the sense of (9), since there is no surprise that is explained by the priest hypothesis.

We have already seen in Section 3.2 that there is no absolute division between pursuit and acceptance. As a thoroughgoing fallibilist, Peirce urged that "any scientific proposition whatever is always liable to be refuted and dropped at short notice" (CP1.120, c. 1896). All temporary results of inquiry can be questioned and corrected by further inquiry: what are called "established truths" in science are "propositions into which the economy of endeavor prescribes that for the time being further inquiry shall cease" (EP2:56, 1898). Thus, even the strongest results of inquiry are some kind of recommendations for further investigation. When the most readily falsifiable hypotheses are refuted, the field is left free for "the main struggle" (CP1.120, c. 1896). Therefore, Peirce's later view of abduction, deduction, and induction as successive steps in inquiry should be understood in a dynamic way: after testing abductive conjectures, the cycle starts again.[26] Abduction is an essential element of self-corrective science that recursively moves back and forth between observations and generalizations: abduction is a creative inferential process producing theoretical hypotheses on the basis of surprising evidence, and for such hypotheses we find new observations by deduction and induction, which again give rise to new corrected theoretical interpretations.[27] In this sense, abduction plays an important *strategic* role in truth-seeking or the approximation to the truth.[28]

For Mcauliffe (2015, 311), "the gravest danger in the confusion of abduction with IBE" is that "it results in Peirce's notion of abduction being ignored." This worry seems to be exaggerated: a philosopher may very well be a *pluralist* about the functions of abduction. Peirce maintained that abduction is a form—albeit a weak one—of inference. He still assumed that abduction has a definite logical form given by (9), which is a natural generalization of his earlier account of hypothetical reasoning. Even though IBE is not identical to abduction, it is *abductive* in the sense that hypotheses are considered from the perspective of their explanatory virtues. This means that IBE is a natural extension of Peirce's work. The real power of Peirce's ideas about truth-seeking inference is that the same logical pattern (or its close variations) can serve discovery, pursuit, confirmation, and justification in different contexts.

Notes

1. See Niiniluoto (1993).
2. Peirce remarked that "hypothesis has been called an induction of characters" already in 1878 (CP2.632), but it is misleading to state with Yu and Zenker (2018) that he classified abduction (hypothesis) as "a special case of induction." The relation of analogy and enumerative induction goes back to John Stuart Mill's treatment of the probability of analogical reasoning (Niiniluoto 1988).
3. Peirce also formulated an analogical argument (CP2.733, 1883), which he thought to be a combination of retroduction, induction, and deduction (CP2.513, 1867; CP7.98, c. 1910). See Misiewicz (2020).
4. For a classification of different cases of abduction, see Schurz (2008).
5. For a survey with references, see Niiniluoto (2018, ch. 3).
6. See Magnani (2001, 20).
7. See Paavola (2006).

8. See Niiniluoto (2018, 76–79).
9. See Niiniluoto (2018, ch. 2).
10. Peirce was familiar with the idea that good experiments are "questions put to nature" (see EP2:215); that is, they have to be designed so that they give answers to our requests of important information.
11. For the GW model, see also Magnani and Bertolotti (2017). It has inspired Lorenzo Magnani's (2017) studies in "manipulative abduction," but a conception of "non-explanationist abduction" already leads quite far beyond Peirce's original ideas.
12. Such fallibilist reading applies to Peirce's conception of belief in "The Fixation of Belief" (CP5.358–387, 1877), whose dynamic development is described by the schema (→ belief → habit → action → surprise → doubt → inquiry → belief →) (CP5.12, c. 1907).
13. Niiniluoto (2018, 84–85).
14. See Niiniluoto (1999), Schurz (2008).
15. However, in the case of mythological or legendary figures such historical claims may be mistaken.
16. For these results, see Niiniluoto (1999).
17. For this argument against the GW model, see Niiniluoto (2018, 85, 96).
18. See Josephson and Josephson (1994) and Flach and Kakas (2000).
19. See Aliseda (2006) for a link between abduction and belief revision.
20. See Walton (2004).
21. See Lipton (2004), Niiniluoto (1999), Schurz (2008), Psillos (2011), and Kuipers (2019).
22. See the treatment of theoretical unification in Niiniluoto (2018, 101–107).
23. See Niiniluoto (2018, ch. 8), and Kuipers (2019, chs. 10 and 11).
24. For inverse problems, a branch of applied mathematics created after Peirce's career, see Niiniluoto (2018, ch. 4).
25. See, for example, Popper (1963, 242–243).
26. See Minnameier (2004), Mcauliffe (2015), Niiniluoto (2018), and Davies and Coltheart (2020).
27. Tavory and Timmermans (2014) call this whole process "abductive analysis."
28. See Hintikka (1998), Paavola (2006), Schurz (2008), and Niiniluoto (2018).

Bibliography

Aliseda, Atocha. 2006. *Abductive Reasoning: Logical Investigations into Discovery and Explanation*. Dordrecht, The Netherlands: Springer.

Bellucci, Francesco, and Ahti-Veikko Pietarinen. 2020. "Icons, Interrogations, and Graphs: On Peirce's Integrated Notion of Abduction." *Transactions of the Charles S. Peirce Society* 56, no. 1 (Winter): 43–61.

Campos, Daniel. 2011. "On the Distinction between Peirce's Abduction and Lipton's Inference to the Best Explanation." *Synthese* 180: 419–442.

Curd, Martin. 1980. "The Logic of Discovery: An Analysis of Three Approaches." In Thomas Nickles, editor, *Scientific Discovery, Logic, and Rationality*, 201–219. Dordrecht, The Netherlands: Reidel.

Davies, Martin, and Max Coltheart. 2020. "A Peircean Pathway from Surprising Facts to New Beliefs." *Transactions of the Charles S. Peirce Society* 56, no. 3 (Summer): 400–426.

Douven, Igor. 2011. "Abduction." In Edward N. Zalta, editor, *Stanford Encyclopedia of Philosophy*. Stanford, CA: Stanford University. http://plato.stanford.edu/archives/spr2011/entries/abduction/.

Fann, K. T. 1970. *Peirce's Theory of Abduction*. The Hague: Martinus Nijhoff.

Flach, P. A., and A. C. Kakas, editors. 2000. *Abduction and Induction: Essays on Their Relation and Integration*. Dordrecht, The Netherlands: Kluwer.

Gabbay, Dov M., and John Woods. 2005. *The Reach of Abduction: Insight and Trial*. Amsterdam: Elsevier.

Hanson, Norwood R. 1958. *Patterns of Discovery*. Cambridge: Cambridge University Press.

Hanson, Norwood R. 1961. "Is There a Logic of Discovery?" In *Current Issues in the Philosophy of Science*, edited by Herbert Feigl and Growell Maxwell, 20–35. New York: Holt, Rinehart, & Winston.

Harman, Gilbert. 1965. "Inference to the Best Explanation." *The Philosophical Review* 74: 88–95.

Hintikka, Jaakko. 1998. "What Is Abduction? The Fundamental Problem of Contemporary Epistemology." *Transactions of the Charles S. Peirce Society* 34, no. 3 (Summer): 503–533.

Josephson, John, and Susan Josephson, editors. 1994. *Abductive Inference*. Cambridge: Cambridge University Press.

Kapitan, Tomas. 1997. "Peirce and the Structure of Abductive Inference." In *Studies in the Logic of Charles Peirce*, edited by Nathan Houser, D. D. Roberts, and J. van Evra, 477–496. Bloomington: Indiana University Press.

Kuipers, Theo. 2019. *Nomic Truth Approximation Revisited*. Cham, Switzerland: Springer.

Laudan, Larry. 1980. "Why Was the Logic of Discovery Abandoned?" In Thomas Nickles, editor, *Scientific Discovery, Logic, and Rationality*, 173–183. Dordrecht, The Netherlands: Reidel.

Lipton, Peter. 2004. *Inference to the Best Explanation*. London: Routledge. (First edition in 1991)

Magnani, Lorenzo. 2001. *Abduction, Reason, and Science: Processes of Discovery and Explanation*. New York: Kluwer.

Magnani, Lorenzo. 2017. *The Abductive Structure of Scientific Creativity: An Essay on the Ecology of Cognition*. Cham, Switzerland: Springer.

Magnani, Lorenzo, and Tommaso Bertolotti, editors. 2017. *Springer Handbook of Model-Based Science*. Dordrecht, The Netherlands: Springer.

Mcauliffe, William. 2015. "How Did Abduction Get Confused with Inference to the Best Explanation?" *Transactions of the Charles S. Peirce Society* 51, no. 3 (Summer): 300–319.

McKaughan, Daniel. 2008. "From Ugly Duckling to Swan: C. S. Peirce, Abduction, and the Pursuit of Scientific Theories." *Transactions of the Charles S. Peirce Society* 44, no. 3 (Summer): 446–468.

Minnameier, Gerhard. 2004. "Peirce-Suit of Truth: Why Inference to the Best Explanation and Abduction Ought Not to Be Confused." *Erkenntnis* 60: 75–105.

Misiewicz, Rory. 2020. "Peirce on Analogy." *Transactions of the Charles S. Peirce Society* 56, no. 4 (Fall): 299–325.

Nickles, Thomas, editor. 1980. *Scientific Discovery, Logic, and Rationality*. Dordrecht, The Netherlands: Reidel.

Niiniluoto, Ilkka. 1988. "Analogy and Similarity in Scientific Reasoning." In *Analogical Reasoning*, edited by David Helman, 271–298. Dordrecht: Kluwer.

Niiniluoto, Ilkka. 1993. "Peirce's Theory of Statistical Explanation." In *Charles S. Peirce and Philosophy of Science*, edited by Edward C. Moore, 186–207. Tuscaloosa: The University of Alabama Press.

Niiniluoto, Ilkka. 1999. "Defending Abduction." *Philosophy of Science (Proceedings)* 66: S436–S451.

Niiniluoto, Ilkka. 2018. *Truth-Seeking by Abduction*. Cham, Switzerland: Springer.

Paavola, Sami. 2006. "Hansonian and Harmanian Abduction as Models of Discovery." *International Studies in the Philosophy of Science* 20: 91–106.

Peirce, Charles S. 1931–1935, 1958. *Collected Papers*. Vols. 1–6 edited by Charles Hartshorne and Paul Weiss; vols. 7–8 edited by Arthur Burks. Cambridge, MA: Harvard University Press. (Referred to as CP.)

Peirce, Charles S. 1982—2010. *Writings of Charles S. Peirce: A Chronological Edition*. Vols. 1–6, edited by Max Fisch et al. Bloomington, IN: Indiana University Press. (Referred to as W.)

Peirce, Charles S. 1992. *Reasoning and the Logic of Things: The Cambridge Conferences Lectures of 1898* (edited by K. L. Ketner). Cambridge, MA: Harvard University Press. (Referred to as RLT.)

Peirce, Charles S. 1998. *The Essential Peirce vol. 2 (1893–1913)*, edited by the Peirce Edition Project. Bloomington: Indiana University Press. (Referred to as EP2.)

Popper, Karl R. 1963. *Conjectures and Refutations*. London: Routledge & Kegan Paul.

Psillos, Stathis. 2011. "An Explorer upon Untrodden Ground: Peirce on Abduction." In *Handbook of the History of Logic. vol. 10: Inductive Logic*, edited by Dov Gabbay, Stephan Hartmann, and John Woods, 117–151. Amsterdam: North-Holland.

Schurz, Gerhard. 2008. "Patterns of Abduction." *Synthese* 164: 201–234.

Smokler, Howard. 1968. "Conflicting Conceptions of Confirmation." *The Journal of Philosophy* 65: 300–312.

Tavory, Iddo, and Stefan Timmermans. 2014. *Abductive Analysis: Theorizing Qualitative Research*. Chicago: University of Chicago Press.

Thagard, Paul. 1978. "The Best Explanation: Criteria for Theory Choice." *The Journal of Philosophy* 75: 76–92.

van Fraassen, Bas. 1989. *Laws and Symmetry*. Oxford: Oxford University Press.

Venn, John. 1866. *The Logic of Chance*. London: Macmillan and Co.

Walton, Douglas. 2004. *Abductive Reasoning*. Tuscaloosa: University of Alabama Press.

Yu, Shiyang, and Frank Zenker. 2018. "Peirce Knew Why Abduction Isn't IBE—A Scheme and Critical Questions for Abductive Argument." *Argumentation* 32: 529–587.

CHAPTER 13

PEIRCE'S THEORIES OF GENERALIZED PROPOSITIONS

FREDERIK STJERNFELT

An important achievement of Peirce's logic and semiotics is an original and wide-ranging theory of propositions. Propositions are truth-claiming signs, and understanding the condition of such signs would tie together logic, semiotics, and the philosophy of science in Peirce. This issue, central to the philosophy of logic, occupied Peirce for most of his career, but it only found its final shape in his strong theoretical push of the 1900s. After a brief sketch of the development of Peirce's notion of proposition, we shall present his overall, mature theory, covering the extension of propositions, the unity and inner structure of propositions, their systematic relation to terms and arguments, and their relation to notions such as truth, reference, facts, and states-of-things. We will finish with their place in Peirce's germ-like outline of a speech act theory.

1. PROPOSITIONS, 1860S–1900S

Propositions were already central to the young Peirce's first results of the mid-1860s, and his famous category table of three was derived from his conception of propositions. The triad of *quality, relation, and representation* of his 1867 paper "On a New List of Categories," later *first-, second-, and thirdness*, was abstracted from the predicate, reference, and copula of propositions, respectively (W2:54–55). In these early efforts, Peirce unproblematically took over the *term–proposition–argument* distinction from the Aristotelian tradition, and its simple relation to semiotics was assumed to consist in the fact that this conceptual triad formed a distinction between three subtypes of symbols from the *icon–index–symbol* trichotomy:[1]

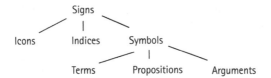

Using the standard Port-Royal logical terminology of extension and comprehension (or breadth and depth), Peirce argued that unlike the case of single terms, the extension and comprehension of propositions varied independently. Extension is the scope of a sign's object reference, while the intension is the scope of the signification ascribed to those objects. This gave rise to the idea that the approximate product of the two, E × C, gave a measure of the *information* of a proposition.[2] The central role of propositions in Peirce's emerging version of realism is clear in his idea that what is real is that which must exist to make true propositions true. "A realist is simply one who knows no more recondite reality than that which is represented in a true representation."[3]

An early, decisive development is the generalization of predicates from simple, one-place predicates to polyadic, relational predicates in Peirce's "Logic of Relations" of 1870, antedating Gottlob Frege's 1879 *Begriffsschrift*.[4] As to the analysis of the structure of propositions, Peirce's "Algebra of Logic" papers of 1880 and 1885 present the first linear formalizations of propositional logic and predicate logic, respectively.[5] The latter provides Peirce's formal analysis of quantified propositions, distinguishing between quantifications, gathered in the left end of the expression, and the predicate claim, placed in the right end of the expression—corresponding to the modern distinction between a prenex and a matrix part of the proposition. Thus, "$\Pi_x \Sigma_y l_{x,y}$" in Peirce's 1885 formalism, means "for all x, there exists a y, so that x loves y"—that is, everybody loves somebody.[6] The syntax is identical to modern logic usage, only the notation of single signs has changed. This analysis was undertaken by Peirce and some of his Johns Hopkins students, most notably O. H. Mitchell, and it formalized a central idea of Peirce, namely, that propositions involve two simpler signs, one that indicates the objects spoken about (here, the quantification part) and another describing those objects (here the "x loves y" claim). This, of course, generalizes the age-old notions of subject and predicate, respectively. The former function, reference, is undertaken by some sort of *index* able to point out the objects to which the proposition refers, while the latter function, signification, is undertaken by some sort of *icon* describing properties or relations of those objects. An important corollary of this formalism, then, is that all three sign types (icons, indices, and symbols) are involved in propositions.

The *subject–predicate* doubleness of propositions would go on to inform Peirce's mature conception of propositions, subjected, however, to ongoing generalization. In the large revolutions of Peirce's sign theory around 1902–1903, the place as well as extension of propositions in his system fundamentally changed. Now, an additional trichotomy was added as the first one, *qualisign–sinsign–legisign*, while *icon–index–symbol* and *term–proposition–argument* became numbers two and three, respectively. Simultaneously, these triads ceased to refer directly to sign types. Now, they rather referred to types of *aspects* or properties of signs, and for this reason, the three trichotomies would combine in order to form ten sign types.[7] This gave rise to the famous sign taxonomy of the 1903 *Syllabus*:[8]

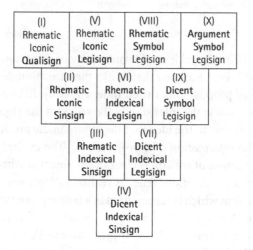

This innovation involved new terminology. Propositions would be renamed "dicents" or "dicisigns" (from Lat. "Dico," I say), from the idea that they say something about something, and the whole of the *term–proposition–argument* triad was renamed *rheme–dicisign–argument*. This terminological change was made for an important reason, namely, that in order to be combinable, the three trichotomies had to range over the same set of objects. So, now the idea became that each of the three trichotomies referred to *all signs*. With respect to propositions in particular, this implied that all signs are either a rheme, a dicisign, or an argument. This involved a vast generalization of the three that were earlier subtypes of symbols, not of all signs. As to rhemes, they no longer only comprise terms, that is, unsaturated predicates, but also unsaturated subject terms, so that they generalize to all nonpropositional signs. Such signs, isolated icons or indices, may also be seen as abbreviated propositions, their main purpose being to participate in propositions. This doctrine may also be expressed in characterizing rheme–dicisigns–arguments as single, double, and triple signs, respectively;[9] Dicisigns involve at least two rhemes; arguments involve at least two propositions.

As to propositions in particular, this implied that their generalized version, dicisigns, would now comprise *all signs able to take a truth value*—not only those truth-claiming signs that are symbols or articulated linguistically. Now, of the three dicisigns of the ten combined signs, only one would be symbolic (no. IX), while the two others were indexical legi- and sinsigns, respectively (nos. VII and IV). This paved the way for seeing natural signs like fossils and weathercocks as quasi-propositions, just like it introduced the multimodal character of Peirce's mature philosophy of propositions, so that *A painting with a legend* might even become a standard Peircean example of a dicisign. This step had long been underway, ever since the first clear articulation of Peirce's idea of diagrammatic reasoning in 1885, implying that propositions may be expressed diagrammatically, but now, it became enshrined in a far-reaching, explicit multimodality covering propositions involving nonlinguistic means of expression like diagrams, images, and gesture.

This mature theory of dicisigns involves the most elaborated—and also the most interesting—philosophy of proposition in Peirce, and it is the contours of this theory that shall be drawn in the following.

2. The Extension of Propositions in the 1900s Dicisigns Theory

The overall analysis is now that propositions are double signs, claiming that each of their two constituent signs is involved with the same object. The *subjects* of a proposition will refer, by different means, to the objects of the proposition, while the *predicate* of a proposition will describe, by different means, properties or relations of those objects.[10] It is a *functional* definition because subjects and predicates are no longer defined by means of, for example, word classes, but are defined by the functions they enact, reference and description, respectively. Those two functions are enacted by indices and icons, respectively, so a short version of the theory says that propositions consist of an index part and an icon part and that the overall proposition sign claims that both of those two signs are involved with the same set of objects.

This simple formula covers a series of complicated issues, however. The indexical function may be satisfied not only by simple indices like pointing to the relevant objects, foregrounding them in an image, indicating them by a gaze, adding the predicate directly onto the surface of the object, etc., but also by means of symbolic indices like dots on a map, arrows, and distance indications, including linguistic symbols like proper names, pronouns, demonstratives, time-and-place adverbs, etc. Correlatively, the iconic function may be satisfied not only by means of simple images like paintings, photographs, drawings, and object or property samples, but also by more or less symbolic icons like diagrams, involving maps, algebras, graphs, etc., and by linguistic symbols like common nouns, adjectives, verbs, adverbs, etc. All of these lists remain open because of the functional definition: any semiotic means that may prove to satisfy one of the two functions are relevant. Moreover, their combination may be cross-modal, as Peirce's recurring proposition example of a painting with a label shows: one function may be linguistic, the other not so.[11] There is even the possibility that none of the two functions is undertaken by language, as hinted at by one brief proposition definition: *an image with a pointer*.[12] So on this account, a vast amount of different types of empirical signs in the wild will count as dicisigns: illustrations with text, diagrams with a legend, newsreel with voiceover speech, gestures combined with text or picture, and much more. The two functions may even be performed, simultaneously, by one single sign vehicle such as a photograph where the causal connection of the shapes on the photographic plate with the objects depicted there plays the index role, while the similarity of those shapes with those of the objects depicted plays the icon role. So, on this theory of proposition as dicisigns, a single photograph may function as a proposition.[13] This involves some requirements, however, to which we shall return below. So, the generalization of propositions to dicisigns in the 1903 theory opens a vista of a much-enlarged array of truth-claiming signs in the wild.

As mentioned, the 1903 ten-signs theory distinguishes three types among the new category of dicisigns: *dicent symbolical legisigns, dicent indexical legisigns*, and *dicent indexical sinsigns*. They differ in the following way. The first, dicent symbols for short, are general signs in two senses: they are general signs in the sense of repeatable and existing in replicas, but they are also general signs in the sense of having a general meaning. Next, dicent indexical legisigns are not symbols as they have no general meaning, but they are general signs as existing in replicas. Finally, the dicent indexical sinsigns are not general in any of the senses mentioned and thus constitute one-shot signs (like the weathercock or the painting-with-a-legend). This latter category, however, holds a special subcategory, namely, the concrete replicas of the former two categories. Such replicas are also sinsigns or tokens, but with the specific function of forming access to the general signs of which they are replicas. Thus "The sky is blue" and "His name is John" are concrete single signs and thus function as sinsign replicas of a dicent symbol and a dicent indexical legisign, respectively.

3. The Unity of Propositions

A complicated issue in Peirce's mature theory is how to account for the *unity* of the proposition. This is connected to the equally important issue of how to account for the fact that propositions are not only signs that may take a truth value, but also signs able to *claim* that value in assertions. Earlier, Peirce had been content with logical tradition saying that the latter function is undertaken by the copula of propositions, but he increasingly grew weary of this idea because of his chemical take on the subject–predicate combination. Unlike Frege, who saw predicates (propositional functions) as unsaturated elements to be potentially saturated by subjects (arguments), Peirce took *both* relata to be unsaturated, after the halogen–alkali metals analogy in inorganic chemistry.[14] But if the proposition components form a saturated proposition merely through their own combination, there is no need for a copula, and Peirce increasingly began to see the assertive possibility of propositions as inhering in its predicate part. But while the possibility of expressing truths could simply be accounted for by a picture theory of the proposition, such that the subject–predicate distinction is an image of the object–property distinction of reality, that picture theory does not account for the proposition's *claim* about its truth.[15] This was further confirmed by his observation, in his new existential graph formalism for propositional and predicate logic beginning around 1896, that merely drawing the sinsign of a proposition graph on a sheet was equivalent to claiming its truth, without the addition of any specific copula sign. Thus, asserting the proposition "Everybody Loves Someone" in this formalism was expressed by writing this token on a sheet:[16]

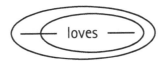

The idea that thus uttering a token of the proposition was equal to asserting it took Peirce into a very complicated argument in the 1903 *Syllabus*, the "deduction of the Dicisign."[17] Already in the 1890s, he had the idea that the claim aspect of a proposition lay in the proposition saying that its two constituent signs referred to the same object. So, the claiming ability of propositions would inhere in a special self-reference of the proposition saying something like "this sign is true because its icon part correctly describes the objects indicated by its index part." This idea lays behind Peirce's claim that the syntax of the dicisign is provided by the *fact* that it represents.[18] So, the fact that the color blue is connected to the sky forms the reason why the subject "sky" and the predicate "blue" are similarly syntactically connected in the corresponding proposition "The sky is blue."

In the deduction of the dicisign, this self-reference idea of the claim is generalized to the idea that the proposition claims about itself that it is indeed indexically connected to its objects, which is why it is authorized to claim that its predicate holds for those objects. This more complicated self-reference is assumed to inhere in the predicate part of the proposition, so that the predicate now really has two levels: (1) a general, implicit level, self-referentially claiming an indexical connection of the sign to its objects; and (2) a particular, explicit level, involving the standard predicate that is claimed to apply to the objects. This implies to Peirce that this general level of the predicate, claiming the sign–object connection, must *also* be described iconically by the sign. This iconic description is undertaken and presented via the putting together of the predicate and the subject in the sign token. So, the fact that the subject and the particular-level predicate are juxtaposed or co-localized in the sign token is the iconic way of claiming that the objects and the dicisign are connected.

This complicated maneuver, now, simultaneously accounts for the *syntax* of propositions. As long as propositions were assumed to be symbols, typically linguistically expressed, the issue of the syntax of propositions would refer to linguistic syntax taking care of putting together subject and predicate, typically using the copula "is" as a glue. With the multimodal generalization of propositions to dicisigns, however, linguistic syntax would no longer be the sole means of syntactically fusing the two parts of the dicisign. This is now undertaken by the co-localization of the predicate and the subject—a simple case being the subject title being put onto the frame of the portrait painting in the "painting with a legend" example. The two must co-localize in a propositional field granting that they will actually be fused into one dicisign by the interpreter of the sign. Peirce's simultaneous coining of a "sheet of assertion" in the context of the existential graphs formalism presents a specific version of such a propositional field, adding the particular notation device of "identity lines" to co-localize subjects and predicate of propositions. In dicisigns encountered in the empirical world, you find many particular versions of how to co-localize subjects and predicates so as to fuse into propositions, some much conventionalized (like the painter's name in the lower corner of a painting), others less so (like the packaging of a product giving information about the goods inside it). Given Peirce's dicisign analyses, there is room for a whole study of different rhetorical means to realize this coupling of multimodal subjects and predicate to synthesize into dicisigns.

The chemical bond metaphor for the combination of predicate and subjects in a proposition is investigated further in Peirce's idea that all predicates possess a "continuous predicate" at their core.[19] To see this, he invents a sort of cleaning procedure whereby all semantic content of the predicate may be bracketed: "Cain kills Abel" may be translated into "Cain stands in the relation of Killing to Abel." When this procedure does not reach further results by repetition, in this case with "Cain stands in the relation of a relation of Killing to Abel," which means the same thing, this final structure is the "continuous predicate." In this case, it is "x stands in the relation of y to z." The small but indefinite list of such continuous predicates with open slots—*identity, coexistence, predication, relation, existence, class subsumption, implication*—is so to speak the predicate atom, potentially binding to it as many objects as it has empty slots, some of them semantic, making more precise the predicate in endowing it with regional ontology (like "killing"); others of them are standard subject indices referring to objects (like "Cain" and "Abel").

A particular type of propositions must be mentioned: those directly involving a diagram as its predicate.[20] In propositions directly using diagrams as predicates—such as maps—the geometrical structures furnish the predicate while the subjects connecting these structures to objects are the indices, proper nouns, arrows, etc., attached to parts of the diagram. But also more generally, propositions with no explicit diagrams indirectly involve diagrams because linguistic predicates, for example, are assumed to be interpretable only by means of diagrams in the sense of schematic mental representations. In diagrammatic reasoning, a diagram proposition is manipulated after rules pertaining to the diagram type, and the result forms another diagram proposition.

4. False and Mendacious Propositions: Propositional Realism

It appeared as a central problem for competing early proposition theories, for example, like Russell's, to account for false and mendacious propositions. Peirce's plastic theory evades those difficulties. Taking object reference and property description as the two main functions of a proposition, Peirce merely generalized the Aristotelian subject–predicate structure. But he added to that a theory of the *fact* represented by true propositions, taking care to distinguish this from the notion of reference. A proposition may succeed in pointing out an object by means of its subject indices—like the sky—but still fail to describe that object correctly, for example, claiming it is blue while it is, in reality, gray. So, the corresponding object is there, but the corresponding fact is not there. This ontology of states-of-things shares many similarities with the famous, contemporary notion of *Sachverhalt* or states-of-affairs developed by Austrian philosophers and popularized by Edmund Husserl and Ludwig Wittgenstein. Peirce may define a state-of-things as so much of reality as is represented in a true proposition.[21] This clear distinction between reference and state-of-things, then, easily accounts for false propositions that succeed in referring to objects pointed out but fail to describe correctly the fact they co-constitute. This, however, implies that Russell's famous example of "The present king of France is bald" would, on a Peircean analysis, be meaningless rather than false: it does not represent a fact, but it also doesn't succeed in pointing out any existing object. Facts or states-of-things are not, however, supposed to form an elementary (e.g., physical) bottom level of reality; rather such states-of-things and the corresponding propositions addressing them may be found on all levels of reality and theories, fantasies, and fictions developing in that reality.

Similarly, Peirce's investigation of the role of the proposition in different act types makes space for understanding lies. A false proposition may be expressed innocently, in good faith, in which case it is not a lie, but if it is asserted while the asserter does not assent to its truth and thus does not believe in it, it will be a lie; more on this below.

Peirce's analysis of propositions is very closely related to his metaphysical realism.[22] Already in the 1860s, he said that reality is simply that which is presupposed by a true proposition. This idea of reality as the truth-maker of true propositions is, of course, related to Kant's idea of beginning his investigation with the truth of science and then going on to find the conditions of that truth. In Peirce, however, the result is a much more robust realism than is found in the Kantian tradition. In a certain sense, the structure of propositions gives rise to three different aspects of realism in Peirce. The indexical aspect of true propositions gives the idea that reality is that which exists independent of any particular description of it—in short, scientific realism. The iconic aspect of a true proposition implies, to Peirce, that the predicate utilized in that proposition must be instantiated in the world, taking him to assume the reality of (some) general concepts, in short, realism as to universals, or "Scotist" realism, as he would often call it. Finally, the unity of the proposition gives rise to his idea of the reality of facts, or states-of-things, combining independence realism and universals realism. Realism of facts involves ideas such as that causes do not connect objects; they rather connect facts, so that one fact can be the cause of another. So, the structure of propositions is the main source of Peirce's metaphysical realism.

5. Two Objects, Three Interpretants

In the further development of Peirce's theory of propositions after 1903, the most important one goes into further detail regarding the objects and interpretants (meanings) of propositions. As to the former, a new distinction between immediate objects and dynamic objects is introduced. The latter is the standard, eventual, real object, independent of the sign, to which the proposition claims to refer. The former, "immediate object," has often been misunderstood as a sort of first description of that object. But it is a notion of reference, not a notion of description. Peirce often says that the immediate object is the way the sign represents the dynamic object, sometimes adding that it does so by means of a hint, and that it regards the identity of the object, not its description.[23] So, the "immediate object" is related to the analysis of the dicisign as claiming to be an index of its object. The immediate object, in short, is the object as it appears in that indexical relation. Louis XIV may be referred to by means of indices like pointing gestures, gazes, or expressions like "he," "the king," "the king of France," "the son of Louis XIII," "that guy over there," "the person who wore this wig"—different indexical ways of picking out and identifying one and the same dynamical object. No sign is able to address the totality of its object, so it necessarily must select some way among many of indexically identifying it. What may have led to the confusion is that many such indices also contain descriptive material, and oftentimes such description aids in the identification of an object. Peirce, however, insists that no amount of description may suffice to pick out an individual object, so descriptive support to identifying is added to a function that is elementarily referential, indexical.

Peirce's original idea in closely connecting semiotics and logic, already in the 1860s, was his inferentialist theory of meaning. Taking inference as the central object of logic, he saw the interpretation of signs as identical to drawing inferences from them. Now, in his theory of three interpretants, three meanings of a proposition, he distinguishes three different sets of inferences drawn from a proposition: immediate, dynamic, and final interpretants, respectively.[24] The former are the "obvious" inferences, that is, immediate corollaries, easily drawn from a proposition, often supported by common habits, so that the immediate interpretant of a proposition is close to combining dictionary explications of its constituting terms, in case of linguistically represented propositions. The second are the inferences that are *actually* made in every single interpretation act of the proposition, differing potentially highly from one interpretation to the next and subject to the ongoing negotiation between communication dialogue partners. The third is every possible inference from the proposition, that is, the contribution it may add to the ongoing process of research and its convergence toward truth in the limit—an ideal concept that may never be completely determined and exhausted in the present now.

6. Collateral Observation, Universes of Discourse, Reinterpretability of Propositions

On a number of central issues, Peirce's theory of propositions connects to a wider context of interpretation, of habits, of research. An important way of situating propositions in a real-world context is Peirce's notion of *collateral observation*: "By collateral observation, I mean previous acquaintance with what the sign denotes" (Review of Lady Welby, CP8.179, 1903). This refers to the idea that the indexical object-referring function of propositions is not sufficient to ground reference. The interpreter of the sign must possess some degree of former information about those objects, independent of the proposition. A recurrent example in Peirce is two persons meeting, the one of them exclaiming: "There's a house on fire!" The other will immediately begin to look around, assuming that the reference of that proposition would be a house in the well-known vicinity of the place of conversation, and not some house on some other planet. This idea does not, of course, imply that no new objects may ever enter propositions, but in that case the relation of those new objects to already-known objects or reference frames must be indicated. "Collateral observation" is a precondition, for instance, to Peirce's insistence that a single photograph may function as a proposition: If the interpreter is able to recognize, for example, a person in the photograph from facial features, the photo will function as a proposition that this person has actually been involved in the situation depicted (such indexicality may be falsified, the result of Photoshop manipulation, etc., so that the photo proposition is false, but that is another issue).

This idea of collateral observation forms an insistence that all propositions require some knowledge of acquaintance grounding the proposition. That ground Peirce refers to as the relevant "Universe of Discourse," a notion borrowed and generalized from Augustus de Morgan and George Boole.[25] That universe is the subset of reality to which a proposition refers, more or less implicitly agreed upon by the communicating parties, and truth and falsity of propositions are relative to that universe of discourse. That universe might be the immediate pragmatic surroundings, could be a field of scientific investigation, a particular topic—or, in some cases, all of reality. This differs from simpler assumptions immediately taking all propositions to refer to reality tout court. Thus, in the closed, fictive universe of discourse, the Duckburg world of Disney comics, it is true that Donald Duck wears a sailor's shirt, while in other such universes it might be meaningless.

This relatedness of propositions to universes of discourse implies that there is no single correct interpretation of propositions. They are reinterpretable, relative to the universe of discourse to which they pertain. This also implies that the very same proposition expression may be parsed differently with respect to its S–P indexical–iconical functions, in different contexts. Some version of the distinction must prevail, however, otherwise the sign would cease to function as a proposition and shrink to a mere rheme. It may, for instance, be different aspects of a proposition that function as indexical cues to object identification for different observers: some might identify Louis XIV in a painting without a title on his facial expression, others by his crown, others by his attire, others by the hall in which he sits—because different interpreters have different collateral observations. So, each picks out the relevant feature as an object-identifying index, leaving the other features as parts of the iconic predicate giving further descriptive information of the object thus identified.

7. Assertions and Other Proposition Acts

As mentioned, during his work with the existential graphs logic system around 1900, Peirce realized that it requires the writing of a token graph on the sheet to claim the truth of that graph. That gave him the idea of the introduction of the new trichotomy quali-sin-legisign (later: tone-token-type) to distinguish the individual sign vehicle (token) from the general type it instantiates. This also made him realize that the self-reference involved in the proposition truth claim is not sufficient to actually *assert* the truth of that proposition. It must be uttered, producing a concrete token of the general proposition sign in a specific situation.

This feeds into his mature theory of assertion.[26] Until the 1890s, Peirce had used "assertion" and "proposition" interchangeably, assuming that a proposition was able to assert itself, but now he made a distinction sketching a speech act theory for propositions. Now, a proposition would be a general type, requiring an additional act in order to be asserted. Assertion now has two levels: the first is that to assert something is to try to persuade some interlocutor of (1) the fact that the utterer assents to the proposition; and (2) the truth of the proposition. The second is that by asserting a proposition, the utterer deliberately assumes responsibility for the truth of it, so that the utterer willingly faces some social retribution or penalty in case it proves not to be true. Given the three different interpretants above, it is an open question which of them the utterer is responsible for, and indeed how many of the possible consequences of a given proposition are covered by the utterer's responsibility when uttering it. In any case, this theory of assertion refers to public utterance of a proposition, analyzed differently from *assent*, the utterer's own belief in the truth of the proposition. To lie, then, is to assert a proposition without assenting to it. In general, Peirce now saw that the naked, unasserted proposition might be the core of an open series of proposition acts: "One and the same proposition may be affirmed, denied, judged, doubted, inwardly inquired into, put as a question, wished, asked for, effectively commanded, taught, or merely expressed, and does not thereby become a different proposition" (*Kaina Stoicheia*, EP2:312, 1904). Accordingly, he further generalized the third trichotomy of *rheme-dicisign-argument*, which now became the core of the more general *seme-pheme-delome* triad.[27] Phemes would now cover propositional acts of all the types mentioned: dicisigns, questions, wishes, imperatives, etc.

In the further development of Peirce's semiotics after the 1903 three-trichotomies, ten-signs theory, much effort is spent to extend this theory to six or even ten trichotomies, many of them pertaining to different act types and their effects. In a certain sense, these unfinished sketches, aiming at twenty-eight or even sixty-six combined signs, are the ruins of a vast theory of proposition acts.[28]

8. Perspectives

Peirce's general philosophy of propositions constitutes a rich alternative to the standard line from Frege-Russell-Wittgenstein-positivists-analytical philosophy. In particular, it is a multimodal theory finding propositions expressed in many different modes and their combination. Propositions are not limited to the linguistic form or to human beings, immediately allowing us to categorize much animal behavior as using propositions in an extended sense. This also gives the theory a strong interest in trying to establish which empirical signs are actually apt to express propositions. In particular, this pertains to the philosophy of science and the widespread use of diagrams of many different types to express scientific truth claims. Finally, Peirce's conception of propositions is closely related to his hard and ambitious version of scientific realism.

Notes

1. Then, "copies–signs–symbols" (W1:467, 1866)—the settling on the terminological choice of "icons–indices–symbols"—emerges later.
2. In "Upon Logical Comprehension and Extension" (W2:70–86, 1870). For the Port-Royal school, comprehension and extension were inversely proportional in terms: more objects falling under a term would correspond to a decrease in meaning, and vice versa.
3. "Some Consequences of Four Incapacities" (EP1:53, 1868).
4. "Description of a Notation for the Logic of Relatives, Resulting from an Amplification of the Conceptions of Boole's Calculus" (CP3.45–148, 1870).
5. "On the Algebra of Logic" (W4:169–204, 1880); "On the Algebra of Logic: A Contribution to the Philosophy of Notation" (W5:162–90, 1885). As to predicate logic, Frege was first with his 1879 graphical formalization, but in the long run, it was Peirce's 1885 notation that won out, via Ernst Schröder, Guiseppe Peano, and Bertrand Russell, and provided the syntax of modern formal logic.
6. Cf. Stjernfelt (2015).
7. The step from triadic distinctions of signs to distinctions of combinable sign aspects occurred in the 1902 *Minute Logic* and is referred to as the First Revolution of Peirce's semiotics by Bellucci (2017, ch. 6). The Second Revolution, then, is the step of adding a further trichotomy, resulting in the ten-sign theory of the 1903 *Syllabus*, in particular its final version of "Nomenclature" (Bellucci 2017, ch. 7). The latter simultaneously made clear the combination principle reducing the $3 \times 3 \times 3 = 27$ immediate combined signs to ten. The three trichotomies are numbered sequentially: (1) qualisign–sinsign–legisign; (2) icon–index–symbol; (3) rheme–dicisign–argument; now, a higher member of a higher category does not combine with a lower member of a lower category, ruling out seventeen of the possible combinations.
8. EP2:296, *c.* 1903.
9. *Syllabus* 1903 (EP2:275, *c.* 1902).
10. Here, I speak of the subjects in plural and the predicate in the singular. With the introduction of polyadic predicates, many predicates may take more than one subject. So, a proposition with one predicate may have several subjects referring to several objects, cf. the "x loves y" example.
11. "A Portrait with a Legend"—Peirce exemplifying dicent sinsigns, Letter to Lady Welby (CP8.341, 1904).
12. "An Image with a Label or Pointer Attached to It," "Reason's Rules" (CP5.543, 1902).
13. "A better example is a photograph. The mere print does not, in itself, convey any information. But the fact that it is virtually a section of rays projected from an object *otherwise known*, renders it a *Dicisign*." *Syllabus* (EP2:282, *c.* 1902).
14. "Logic of Relatives" (CP3.470, 1897); cf. Stjernfelt (2014, 57); Bellucci (2017, ch. 7).

15. Peirce's theory of propositions is obviously a picture theory, the structure of the proposition mirroring a state-of-things structure of reality. This was also an elementary idea of Ludwig Wittgenstein's *Tractatus*. The differences between these two picture theories, however, are important. To Wittgenstein, the logical structure of propositions was ineffable; to Peirce, not so. To Wittgenstein, propositions ultimately referred to a rock bottom of logical atoms; to Peirce, propositions might refer to facts on all levels of reality. To Wittgenstein, propositions referred directly to states-of-affairs of reality; to Peirce, they referred to some selected universe of discourse, more or less explicitly. To Wittgenstein, propositions were supposed to admit of one correct analysis; to Peirce, they were reinterpretable. To Wittgenstein, they were linguistic, to Peirce, multimodal.
16. The ovals are negations, and their nested combination is implication. The two line segments are "identity lines" symbolizing simultaneously existential quantification, identity, and predication. For Peirce's writings on existential graphs, see LoF.
17. The notion is Bellucci's (2014); the deduction takes place in the "Sundry Logical Conceptions" version of the *Syllabus* (EP2:275ff, 1903).
18. "Every informational sign thus involves a fact, which is its Syntax." *Syllabus* (EP2:282, 1903).
19. In a letter to Lady Welby, 14 December 1908, SS:66–86; cf. Bellucci (2013); Stjernfelt (2016).
20. Cf. 'PAP' (NEM4:313–330, 1906). Cf. also Stjernfelt (2007, ch. 4); Stjernfelt (2019).
21. "A *state of things* is an abstract constituent part of reality, of such a nature that a proposition is needed to represent it. There is but one *individual*, or completely determinate, state of things, namely, the all of reality. A *fact* is so highly a prescissively abstract state of things, that it can be wholly represented in a simple proposition, and the term 'simple,' here, has no absolute meaning, but is merely a comparative expression" ("The Basis of Pragmaticism," EP2:378, 1906).
22. Cf. Stjernfelt (2021a).
23. "It is usual and proper to distinguish two Objects of a Sign, the Mediate without, and the Immediate within the Sign. Its Interpretant is all that the Sign conveys: acquaintance with its Object must be gained by collateral experience. The Mediate Object is the Object outside of the Sign; I call it the Dynamoid Object. The Sign must indicate it by a hint; and this hint, or its substance, is the Immediate Object" (Letter to Lady Welby, SS:83, 1908).
24. "In regard to the Interpretant we have [...] to distinguish, in the first place, the Immediate Interpretant, which is the interpretant as it is revealed in the right understanding of the Sign itself, and is ordinarily called the *meaning* of the sign; while in the second place, we have to take note of the Dynamical Interpretant which is the actual effect which the Sign, as a Sign, really determines. Finally there is what I provisionally term the Final Interpretant, which refers to the manner in which the Sign tends to represent itself to be related to its Object. I confess that my own conception of this third interpretant is not yet quite free from mist" ("Prolegomena to an Apology for Pragmaticism," CP4.536, 1906).
25. Cf. "Universe of Discourse" (CP2.536, 1902).
26. Stjernfelt (2021b).
27. As argued by Bellucci (2017, ch. 8); cf. "Prolegomena to an Apology for Pragmaticism" (CP4.538, 1906).
28. They are unfinished for two reasons. In the three-trichotomy theory, the three triads pertained to the sign itself, its object, and its interpretant. With the differentiation of object and interpretant types, new trichotomies related to them would be added, with one more object and two more interpretants giving six trichotomies. With the idea that higher such types admit for subtypes, this grew to ten trichotomies. One unsolved problem was how to precisely characterize those ten triads semantically. Another problem, more challenging,

is that these ten trichotomies now form a tree structure. But they must be sequentially linearized in order to subject them to the combination rules of 1903, and no such canonical linearization has been reached.

Literature

Bellucci, Francesco. 2013 "Peirce's Continuous Predicates," *Transactions of the Charles S. Peirce Society* 49, no. 2 (Spring): 178–202.

Bellucci, Francesco. 2014 "Peirce and the Unity of the Proposition," *Transactions of the Charles S. Peirce Society* 50, no. 2 (Spring): 201–219.

Bellucci, Francesco. 2017 *Peirce's Speculative Grammar. Logic as Semiotics*, New York: Routledge.

Peirce, Charles S.1967–1971 Manuscripts held at the Houghton Library of Harvard University (Cambridge, MA: Harvard University Library Photographic Service), as identified in Richard Robin. *Annotated Catalogue of the Papers of Charles S. Peirce*. Amherst: University of Massachusetts Press, 1967. And in Richard Robin. "The Peirce Papers: A Supplementary Catalogue." *Transactions of the Charles S. Peirce Society* 7, no. 1 (1971): 37–57. (Referred to as R.)

Peirce, Charles S. 1931–1958 *The Collected Papers of Charles Sanders Peirce*. 8 vols. Vols. 1–6, edited by Charles Hartshorne and Paul Weiss, vols. 7–8, edited by Arthur W. Burks. Cambridge, MA, Harvard University Press. (Referred to as CP.)

Peirce, Charles S. 1976 *The New Elements of Mathematics*. 4 vols. in 5. Edited by Carolyn Eisele. The Hague: Mouton. (Referred to as NEM.)

Peirce, Charles S. 1977 *Semiotic & Significs: The Correspondence between Charles S. Peirce & Victoria Lady Welby*. Edited by Charles S. Hardwick and James Cook. Bloomington: Indiana University Press. (Referred to as SS.)

Peirce, Charles S. 1982– *Writings of Charles S. Peirce: A Chronological Edition*. 7 vols. completed. Bloomington: Indiana University Press. (Referred to as W.)

Peirce, Charles S. 1992 *The Essential Peirce*, vol. I (1867–1893). Edited by Nathan Houser and Christian Kloesel), Bloomington: Indiana University Press. (Referred to as EP1.)

Peirce, Charles S. 1998 *The Essential Peirce*, vol. II (1893–1913). Edited by The Peirce Edition Project. Bloomington: Indiana University Press. (Referred to as EP2.)

Peirce, Charles S. 2020–2022 *Logic of the Future: Writings on Existential Graphs*. 3 vols. in 5. Edited by Ahti Pietarinen. Berlin: De Gruyter. (Referred to as LoF.)

Stjernfelt, Frederik. 2007 *Diagrammatology. An Investigation on the Borderlines of Phenomenology, Ontology, and Semiotics*, Dordrecht, The Netherlands: Springer Verlag.

Stjernfelt, Frederik. 2014 *Natural Propositions: The Actuality of Peirce's Doctrine of Dicisigns*, Boston: Docent Press.

Stjernfelt, Frederik. 2015 "Iconicity of Logic—and the Roots of the "Iconicity" Concept," in *Iconicity: East Meets West* (Iconicity in Language and Literature). Edited by Masako K. Hiraga, William J. Herlofsky, Kazuko Shinohara, and Kimi Akita, 35–56 Amsterdam: John Benjamins.

Stjernfelt, Frederik. 2016 "Blocking Evil Infinites: A Note on a Note on a Peircean Strategy," *Sign Systems Studies* 42, no. 4: 518–522.

Stjernfelt, Frederik. 2019 "Dimensions of Peircean Diagrammaticality," *Semiotica* 228: 301–331.

Stjernfelt, Frederik. 2021a "'Peirce as a Truthmaker Realist: Propositional Realism as Backbone of Peircean Metaphysics," *Blityri. Studi di storia delle idee sui segni e le lingue* 9, no. 2: 123–136.

Stjernfelt F. 2021b "Peirce's Theories of Assertion," *Transactions of the Charles S. Peirce Society* 57, no. 2 (Spring): 248–269.

CHAPTER 14

EXISTENTIAL GRAPHS

History and Interpretation

FRANCESCO BELLUCCI AND
AHTI-VEIKKO PIETARINEN

1. INTRODUCTION

CHARLES S. Peirce thought that the graphical notation invented in summer 1896 and later termed the "existential graphs" was his chef d'œuvre in logic (R482; LoF1). This chapter surveys the history of the evolution of the theory and the language of existential graphs, from Peirce's experiments with graphical notations in the early 1880s up to the later developments, expansions, and refinements of the theory in 1896 and beyond.

2. PROTOGRAPHS

"Logic of relatives" is Peirce's name for what we nowadays call quantificational polyadic logic. In the 1880 "Algebra of Logic" a relative is defined as "a term whose definition describes what sort of a system of objects that is whose first member (which is termed the relate) is denoted by the term; and names for the other members of the system (which are termed the correlates) are usually appended to limit the denotation still further" (W4:195). Peirce would soon abandon the nominal characterization of relatives that he had been using ("lover of __," "benefactor of __") in favor of the verbal one ("__ loves __," "__ benefits __"). Relatives can have different "valences": there are monadic relatives (nominal: "man"; verbal: "__ is a man"), dyadic relatives (nominal: "lover of __"; verbal: "__ loves __"), triadic relatives (nominal: "giver of __ to __"; verbal: "__ gives __ to __"), and so on. By 1882 Peirce was in possession of two powerful methods for expressing the logic of relatives, both of which he presents in "Note B" of the 1883

Studies in Logic (W4:453–466) and which he would later call the algebra of dual relatives (ADR) and the general algebra of logic (GAL). He develops and generalizes the GAL in the 1885 paper "On the Algebra of Logic" (W5:162–190).

The ADR is based on the nominal forms of relatives; it can only express dyadic relatives and has four operations, two of which are relative operations (nonrelative sum and product, relative sum and product). The GAL is based on the verbal forms of relatives; it can represent triadic relatives and is based on two operations only (nonrelative sum and product). The reason for this is the following. The difference between a relative and a nonrelative operation is that the former applies only to monadic relatives while the latter applies to relatives of any valence. Now Peirce understands that a relative of any valence can be transformed into a relative of higher valence by combining it with a triadic relative.[1] Hence, triadic relatives dispense with the distinction between relative and nonrelative operations. Since it can express triadic relatives, the GAL is more expressive than the ADR. But since triadic relatives render the distinction between relative and nonrelative operations superfluous, the GAL can do everything that the ADR does with only two operations and is thus more "economic" or "analytic" than the ADR.

In the ADR a dyadic relative is the representation of an ordered pair. Take the ordered pair $(I:J)$ and the dyadic relative "l," signifying "lover of __"; then, the equation "$\Sigma_i \Sigma_j l_{ij} (I:J)$" gives the meaning of "$l$." Peirce explains: "$l_{ij}$ is a numerical coefficient, whose value is 1 in case I is a lover of J, and 0 in the opposite case, and where the sums are to be taken for all individuals in the universe" (W4:454, 1883). Each relative has its *negative*, symbolized by the relative letter with a vinculum over it, and its *converse*, symbolized by the relative letter with a curved vinculum over it. Relatives may be summed (disjunctively combined, symbolized by "+") and multiplied (conjunctively combined, symbolized by the comma) according to the following equations:

$$(l+b)_{ij} = (l)_{ij} + (b)_{ij}$$
$$(l,b)_{ij} = (l)_{ij} \cdot (b)_{ij}$$

These are the standard nonrelative operations of sum and product, respectively. Peirce then introduces relative sum (symbolized by "†") and product (symbolized by simple concatenation), which contain an implicit quantification (W4:455). These are defined by the equations

$$(l \dagger b)_{ij} = \Sigma_x (l)_{ix} + (b)_{xj}$$
$$(lb)_{ij} = \Sigma_x (l)_{ix} (b)_{xj}$$

Toward the end of "Note B" Peirce proposes a unifying method, which in fact constitutes a version of the GAL: "Any proposition whatever is equivalent to saying that some complexus of aggregates and products of such numerical coefficients is greater than zero. Thus, $\Sigma_i \Sigma_j l_{ij} > 0$ means that something is a lover of something; and $\Pi_i \Sigma_j l_{ij} > 0$ means that everything is a lover of something" (W4:464). In this notation, the variables occur explicitly in the subscripts of the relative letters and are "bounded" by the corresponding quantifier. In fact, Peirce suggests that these formulas may be written, omitting the inequality to zero, as

$\Sigma_i \Sigma_j (l_{ij})$ for "something is a lover of something";
$\Pi_i \Sigma_j (l_{ij})$ for "everything is a lover of something."

Peirce has thus found the means for expressing the general notion of prenex formula.[2] While the ADR uses implicitly quantified relatives and operations on relatives, the GAL distinctly separates the quantifying part from the "Boolean" or relative part and gets rid of implicit quantification. In the 1885 paper, this method is further developed.

We now come to the graphical method. In a fragment written in fall/winter 1882 (R747 = W4:391–393) and in a coeval letter to his Johns Hopkins student Oscar H. Mitchell dated December 21, 1882 (RL294 = W4:394–399), Peirce explores and regiments a two-dimensional notation capable of expressing the logic of relatives. Roberts wrote that the 1882 notation was "the first attempt by anyone to apply diagrams to the logic of relatives in general."[3] The notation, Roberts suggested, is in a very important sense an anticipation of the later existential graphs. We call this 1882 notation Peirce's "protographs."

Peirce now explains a relative as a fragment of an entire expression (i.e., a proposition) with a certain number of "fractures"; for example, a dyadic relative can be regarded as a fragment of a proposition having two fractures, "or points where it has been broken off and where it can again be joined to other fragments to make up a new entire expression" (W4:391). Likewise, a monadic relative may be considered as a fragment with one fracture, a triadic relative as a fragment with three fractures, and so on. He then introduces a chemical analogy:[4] "Chemistry here offers us two suggestions. First, it suggests that instead of subscript numbers, lines extending from one symbol to another should be used to distinguish arrangement of the junctions; and second, it suggests that to constitute an entire expression, all that is necessary is that there should be no fracture unfilled, whether univalent fragments enter into its composition or not" (W4:391). The second suggestion amounts to the idea that an entire expression (i.e., a proposition) is obtained by "saturating" all the fractures of a fractured expression. It is the idea of having verbal rather than nominal relatives: a relative is a fragment of a proposition, and a proposition must contain a verb. The first suggestion concerns the notation that represents the fractures. A dyadic relative "l_{ij}" has two fractures, one for its relate, "i," and one for its correlate, "j." Peirce imagines the relative letter to be enclosed within a circle divided in as many parts as it has fractures, with one line attached to each fracture. Thus "l_{ij}" is represented in the protographs as in Figure 14.1:

FIG. 14.1.

EXISTENTIAL GRAPHS: HISTORY AND INTERPRETATION   243

These expressions, Peirce says, are to be interpreted clockwise; the line on the left represents the first member of the ordered pair, the line on the right the second. He also suggests that the oval drawn around the letter can be omitted, as in Figure 14.2, which means "Something loves something" or "$\Sigma_i \Sigma_j (l_{ij})$" in the GAL:

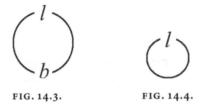

FIG. 14.2.

Figure 14.3 means "Something loves something whose benefactor he is," that is, "Something is a lover and benefactor of something," or "$\Sigma_i \Sigma_j (l_{ij}) (b_{ij})$" in GAL; Figure 14.4 means "Something is a lover of itself," or "$\Sigma_i (l_{ii})$" in the GAL.

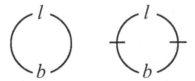

FIG. 14.3.   FIG. 14.4.

In the protographs, the lines are both individual variables (corresponding to the "i's" and the "j's" of the GAL) and signs of (quantified) operations. The plain lines occurring in Figures 14.1–14.4 represent (existentially quantified) relative product; Peirce also employs lines crossed by short marks to represent (universally quantified) relative sum. The parallel is best illustrated by means of the examples contained in the 1882 letter to Mitchell:

FIG. 14.5.

The left-hand formula in Figure 14.5 represents "Something is a lover and a benefactor of something." Each line represents an existentially quantified multiplication, "$\Sigma_x \Sigma_y (l_{xy}) (b_{xy})$" in the GAL. The right-hand formula represents "Anything is either a lover or a benefactor of everything." Each crossed line represents a universally quantified sum, "$\Pi_x \Pi_y (l_{xy}) + (b_{xy})$" in the GAL. These graphs and formulas are duals of each other.

Negation is represented in the protographs by means of a vinculum above the relative to be negated, a notation that we find in Boole and that Peirce used in many of his algebraic papers. In the protographs, the rule for negating an entire formula "is to negative every letter and every junction in it" (W4:392).

As Roberts correctly emphasized, the 1882 protographs are the historical antecedent of Peirce's later "logical graphs." These protographs, as the later logical graphs, differ from Peirce's earlier algebraical versions of the logic of relatives in two important respects. In the first place, the protographs are nonlinear. A linear notation is a notation in which symbols are combined by linear concatenation. Linear concatenation is an antisymmetric mode of syntactical combination. A consequence of the antisymmetric character of linear concatenation is that when we express a symmetric relation or operation (like conjunction "&") by linear concatenation (as in "A & B"), we need to introduce axioms or theorems of commutativity and associativity to "restore" the symmetric character of the relation expressed ("A & B = B & A"). Conversely, the advantage of operating in a linear system is that whenever we need to express an antisymmetric relation (for example, a dyadic antisymmetric predicate like "__ loves __," or material implication, or quantificational dependencies) we can exploit the basic antisymmetry of the language without introducing further conventions. Linear concatenation expresses antisymmetric relations by default. If one abandons linear concatenation, then in order to express dependencies one has to resort to some other convention.

The 1882 protographs only have symmetric operators (conjunction and disjunction) and negation. The only antisymmetric relations that have to be represented are the ordering of the correlates of a relative and the relations of dependence in quantification. As to the first problem, we noticed that Peirce intends his protographs to be read clockwise; similar conventions are sometimes referred to and employed in his later works on the existential graphs. As to the second problem, in 1882 Peirce made a couple of attempts to solve it, first by using numerical indices and second by using the length of the lines as a sign of priority. Neither method seems to have satisfied him, and this is perhaps one of the reasons why his graphical experiments, begun in 1882, came to a halt and were resumed in earnest only fourteen years later, when a new method for expressing dependent quantification was found, as we shall see in the next section.[5]

In the second place, the protographs differ from Peirce's algebraical versions of relative logic in the way individual variables are represented. In the GAL formula "$\Sigma_x (l_{xx})$" the fact that both "x's" refer to the same individual is determined by the fact that they are two occurrences of the same variable type. Likewise, in the GAL formula "$\Pi_x \Pi_y (l_{xy}) + (b_{xy})$" the fact that "$x$" and "$y$" may (though they need not) refer to distinct individuals is determined by the fact that they are occurrences of distinct variable types. Following a suggestion by John Etchemendy to Keith Stenning,[6] we call "type-referential" a language in which sameness of variable type determines sameness of reference, while distinctness of variable type may (though it need not) determine distinctness of reference. We call "occurrence-referential" a language in which sameness of variable occurrence determines sameness of reference, while distinctness of variable occurrence may (though it need not) determine distinctness of reference. The ADR, the GAL, and the ordinary notation of first-order logic are type-referential. Peirce's graphs are occurrence-referential. Consider the protograph in Figure 14.2. Here, the two correlates of the relation, the "lover" and the "beloved," are both represented by lines; they are distinguished by the fact that each is represented by a distinct occurrence of the line; in fact, there is just one variable type, the line, and the sameness and distinctness of individuals is represented by sameness and distinctness of the occurrence of the type, and not, as in type-referential languages, by the sameness and distinctness of the type itself.[7]

Nonlinearity and occurrence-referentiality determine what may count as distinct formulas or as the same formula. In the linear GAL, the formulas "$\Pi_x \Pi_y\, l_{xy} + b_{xy}$" and "$\Pi_x \Pi_y\, b_{xy} + l_{xy}$," though perfectly equivalent from the logical point of view, are two distinct formulas; they are syntactically distinct. But in the nonlinear protographs, there is just one graph for each pair of logically equivalent GAL formulas obtained by permutation. Likewise, in the type-referential GAL, the formulas "$\Sigma_x\, l_{xx}$" and "$\Sigma_x \Sigma_y\, l_{xy}\, 1_{xy}$" (where "$1_{xy}$" means that "$x = y$"), though perfectly equivalent from the logical point of view, are two distinct formulas; they are syntactically distinct. But in the occurrence-referential protographs, there is just one graph corresponding to any pair of formulas of this sort and to infinitely many other formulas that can be constructed with as many distinct variables.

Occurrence-referentiality is no hindrance in expressivity.[8] Nonlinearity, by contrast, renders more difficult both the representation of the ordering of the correlates of a relative and quantificational dependencies. The second of these problems was solved in 1896 with the discovery of the logical graphs.

3. ENTITATIVE GRAPHS

Roberts claimed that the 1882 "protographs" lacked a sign of negation.[9] Taken literally, the claim is false, as the vinculum is used in this system to express the negative of a relative. What the protographs lacked was a sign of negation that would also function as a collectional sign, that is, as a sign that expresses the order of application of the operations and thus the nesting structure of formulas.[10] A more correct claim is that the protographs lacked a sign fulfilling both the office of a logical connective and that of a collectional sign. It is thanks to this "fusion" that in 1896 Peirce solved the problem, which he left unresolved in 1882, of representing quantificational dependencies.

This happened with the first of the two parallel systems of logical graphs that he discovered in 1896, that is, the system that he later called "entitative graphs." The most important European admirer and follower of Peirce's work in logic was Ernst Schröder, who between 1890 and 1895 published the three volumes of the monumental *Vorlesungen über die Algebra der Logik*.[11] The first two volumes of the *Vorlesungen* were devoted to nonrelative logic. Peirce wrote a review of them for Paul Carus's *The Monist* that was published in May 1896 (CP3.425–455). The third volume of the *Vorlesungen* contained Schröder's "Algebra der Relative," which in substance was a development and systematization of Peirce's the ADR. During summer 1896 Peirce wrote a review of the third volume for Carus's journal, which appeared in January 1897 (CP3.456–552). It was in this second review, and in particular in the context of a criticism of Schröder's "Algebra der Relative" (which, in view of the fact that Schröder's algebra was based on the ADR, was in fact a self-criticism, too), that Peirce proposed a system of logical graphs for the logic of relatives. And it was while working on this first system in summer 1896 that he also discovered some "simplifications" of it that would constitute the beginning of his work on "existential graphs," as we shall see in the next section.

Building again on the chemical analogy, Peirce conceived a relative as a "logical atom" with a certain number of loose ends or unsaturated bonds (the 1882 "fractures") and a proposition as what we get by joining all the bonds of a logical atom with the bonds of another logical atom: "A chemical atom is quite like a relative in having a definite number of loose ends or 'unsaturated bonds,' corresponding to the blanks of the relative. In a chemical molecule, each loose end of one atom is joined to a loose end, which it is assumed must belong to some other atom. [. . .] Thus the chemical molecule is a *medad*, like a complete proposition" (CP3.469). This chemical analogy idea was already at the basis of the 1882 protographs. The novelty of the new system was that now Peirce conceived a medad or proposition as composed of a negative and of a positive component: "In logic, the medad must always be composed of one part having a negative, or antecedental, character, and another part of a positive, or consequential, character; and if either of these parts is compound its constituents are similarly related to one another. Yet this does not, at all, interfere with the doctrine that each relative has a definite number of blanks or loose ends" (CP3.470).

In the protographs there were two basic operations: existentially quantified multiplication, represented by plain lines, and universally quantified sum, represented by crossed lines. Consider again the first protograph in Figure 14.5. Provided that the "fractures" or "bonds" are properly identified and ordered (we mentioned that Peirce considered the bonds to be ordered clockwise around the relative), there is no other special ordering about it; it can be translated into the GAL both as "$\Sigma_x \Sigma_y (l_{xy}) (b_{xy})$" and as "$\Sigma_x \Sigma_y (b_{xy}) (l_{xy})$"; the protographs are nonlinear and the GAL is linear, so that the relation between the relatives "*b*" and "*l*," once the bonds have been properly ordered, is symmetric. In the 1896 system, on the contrary, the medad (the "entire expression" of 1882, i.e., the proposition) is conceived as having a negative antecedent character and a positive consequential character. In other words, the medad is conceived as a conditional proposition; and since the most basic form of the conditional proposition is the material conditional or conditional *de inesse*, which can always be expressed as "either not the antecedent or the consequent," the analysis of the medad that Peirce placed at the basis of his logical graphs is in terms of the conditional form. Now the conditional form is based on the antisymmetric relation of implication; since he abandoned linearity, he had to find another way to indicate which of the two components of his graphical medads is the antecedent and which is the consequent. This is where his new device for negation entered the picture.[12]

There is a further complication, however. We saw that in the protographs, just like in the ADR, the operations bear an implicit quantification. The 1896 logical graphs inherit this feature. However, if the line that connects the bonds of two relatives, that is, the two components of the graphical medad, is implicitly quantified, the medad cannot be a material conditional. It must be a *quantified* conditional. Thus, the graphical medad that Peirce is seeking has to express not the simple "Either not A or C" (i.e., "If A then C"), but the more complex "For every x, either x is not A or x is C" (i.e., "For every x, if x is A then x is C," or "All A's are C").

Peirce must therefore find a way to represent in graphs (i.e., in a nonlinear and occurrence-referential language) a quantified conditional proposition. Let us assume that "h" symbolizes the monadic relative "__ is a man" and "d" the monadic relative "__ dies." In the 1882 notation these relatives are represented as letters having fractures or bonds to which lines can be attached. In order to have a complete proposition or medad, we need to join the bonds of each by a line, as in Figure 14.6:

$$h\text{———}d$$

FIGURE 14.6.

However, since every medad is or can be regarded as being composed of antecedent and consequent, to mark the difference between antecedent and consequent we need to introduce one further convention. Peirce draws the line joining the two relatives so as to encircle the antecedent, as in Figure 14.7:

FIGURE 14.7. (from Peirce 1986)

This graph thus expresses the proposition that "For every x, either x is not a man or x dies," that is, "For every x, if x is a man then x dies," or "All men die"; in modern notation "$\forall x(\sim Hx \lor Dx)$" or "$\forall x(Hx \to Dx)$." The real innovation over the 1882 protographs is that Peirce now has an instrument to express order in a nonlinear language. The oval that encircles the antecedent of the graphical medad is a sign fulfilling both the office of a logical connective (negation) and that of a collectional sign, that is, of a sign that indicates the order of application of the operations. In the 1882 protographs, the graph in Figure 14.7 would be represented as in Figure 14.8:

$$\overline{h}\mathrel{+\!\!\!+}d$$

FIGURE 14.8.

where the vinculum signifies negation and the crossed line disjunction. But it is impossible to represent the more complex proposition "Whoever loves only the virtuous is wise" (in contemporary notation, "$\forall x \forall y \,[(Lxy \to Vy) \to Wx]$") with the protographs. This is equivalent to "$\forall x \forall y \,[\sim(\sim Lxy \vee Vy) \vee Wx]$." The reason for this impossibility is that in the protographs it is possible to negate a relative (by the vinculum), but it is not possible to negate a complex subcomponent of a formula. In order to do so, one should introduce "collectional signs" or some other device to indicate the scope of the application of an operation (and thus the ordering of operations). The oval of the 1896 logical graphs is precisely such a sign: it is both a sign of negation (like the vinculum) and a collectional sign. The sentence "$\forall x \forall y \,[\sim(\sim Lxy \vee Vy) \vee Wx]$" is represented in this language as in Figure 14.9:

FIGURE 14.9. (from Peirce 1896)

The outer oval of Figure 14.9 corresponds to the outer negation, the inner oval to the inner negation. Truth-function (negation) and collectional function are "fused" in one single notational device. Peirce was acutely aware of the importance of this innovation. He wrote in 1911 regarding existential graphs: "While the syntax of existential graphs thus needs both a sign of negation and an endless series of collectional signs, there is no reason why a single sign should not perfectly fulfill both these purposes" (R670:14 = LoF1:570). And it is precisely by fulfilling both the truth-functional and the collectional purpose that the oval, first introduced in the logical graphs of 1896, was able to overcome the shortcomings in expressivity of the 1882 protographs.

If we transform the vinculum of Figure 14.8 into an oval and remove the cross from the line, Figure 14.8 becomes Figure 14.10:

FIGURE 14.10.

This is not the manner Peirce explicitly presents his oval, since in the first, published version of the 1896 logical graphs he does not explicitly regard the oval as an evolution of the vinculum that allows representing nested conditionals. On the contrary, in that context he tends to think of the oval *plus* the line as one single sign, and rather presents the oval as a modification of the line connecting the two relatives: "It is necessary to use, as the sign of the relative copula, some symbol which shall distinguish the antecedent from the consequent" (CP3.475). The oval *plus* the line is the "relative copula": it connects antecedent and consequent relatives by joining their bonds by a standard line, and in addition it completely encircles the antecedent in order to distinguish it from the consequent and to allow more complex structures with nested conditionals. However, if the oval and the line are considered two distinct signs, then the oval realizes only the "fusion" of truth-function and collectional function that we expounded above. In that case, the line expresses a universally quantified disjunction. As we now proceed to show, in existential graphs oval and line are regarded as two distinct signs: the signification of the oval remains the same (negation plus collectional function), while the line expresses existential quantification.

4. EXISTENTIAL GRAPHS

Peirce spent much of the rest of his life experimenting with alternative notations to serve the theory of logic and to advance scientific inquiry. The outcome of his notational researches was a system of logical graphs, which he in December 1896 termed "the system of existential graphs." Existential graphs are the graphical method of logic for which he in the 1903 Lowell Lectures coined the now-customary terminology that divides the method into the alpha, beta, and gamma parts. The logic of the alpha part is a propositional (sentential) logic and agrees with the two-element Boolean algebra. Peirce often began his presentation of existential graphs with the second, beta part of the method that corresponds to a fragment of first-order predicate logic with identity. The main ideas of the gamma part had to do with modal logics, among others.

How do existential graphs, and especially the alpha and beta parts, relate to Peirce's earlier notational experiments and how did they develop from their immediate predecessor system, the entitative graphs? This story is still to be told in full, but here are some elements for a rational reconstruction. In R280 (*c.* 1904; LoF3/1) Peirce recounts how the "ink was hardly dry on the sheets" when he discovered that existential graphs "are merely entitative graphs turned inside out." While working on "The Logic of Relatives" in the summer of 1896 Peirce discovered that entitative graphs could be so modified as to obtain another system. He proposed to publish this new system instead of the old one, but the *Monist*'s editor Paul Carus refused it.[13]

The new system is just the old one "turned inside out." This substantially means that existential graphs are obtained from entitative graphs by, first, separating the two components of the "relative copula," that is, the line and the oval (this is one of the "simplifications" alluded to above), and, second, by changing the signification of the line. When the line is considered as a separate and autonomous sign, it must express a universally quantified disjunction. Now, since no presentation of the sentential fragment of entitative graphs was included in "The Logic of Relatives," it is difficult to make a direct comparison with existential graphs.[14] In existential graphs, the line expresses existential quantification, while conjunction is represented by means of juxtaposition on the "sheet of assertion." There's no sheet of assertion in entitative graphs. If there had been one, it would have expressed disjunction (which was instead "loaded" on the line). Take the graph in Figure 14.6. Interpreted entitatively, it means "For every *x*, either *x* is a man or *x* dies"; interpreted existentially, it means "For some *x*, *x* is a man and *x* dies." The line expresses existential, not universal, quantification, and juxtaposition of two graphs means conjunction, not disjunction. Again, take the graph in Figure 14.7. Interpreted entitatively, it means "For every *x*, if *x* is a man then *x* dies"; interpreted existentially, it means "For some *x*, *x* is not a man and *x* dies." In both entitative and existential graphs the oval represents both negation and the collectional function. One may thus describe the existential system by saying that like Peirce's earlier systems of logical graphs (the 1882 protographs and the 1896 entitative graphs), it is a nonlinear, occurrence-referential language in which (i) juxtaposition of the graphs on the sheet of assertion expresses conjunction; (ii) any occurrence of the line expresses an existentially quantified variable; and (iii) the oval represents negation and the collectional function.

In R145 (*c.* 1905) the existential system is succinctly presented as follows:

> In existential graphs, we have the following signs: First, a sheet upon which every proposition scribed (so I say, since the symbols used may not be written rather than drawn), is understood to be asserted; second, two states of things expressed by propositions scribed simultaneously on the sheet are understood to be coexistent; third, a heavy dot scribed upon the sheet, whether alone, or as a part of a heavy line, or attached to a relative term, is understood to assert "something exists"; fourth, a heavy line, however long or short, is understood to assert the identity of the individuals represented by its points, and that of the corresponding subjects of the propositions upon which it abuts. [...] Fifthly, a finely drawn oval on the sheet of assertion denies the truth of what is scribed upon its enclosed area, as a whole. (LoF1:510)

More often than not, the first sign (the sheet of assertion) and the second (juxtaposition on the sheet) were presented as one and the same "convention" of the system. The reason for this has to do with another "fusion": the sheet of assertion, that is, the blank space on which the graphs are scribed, is both a sign of assertion and a sign of conjunction; it has both an illocutionary force and a locutionary, truth-functional content. Take the three alpha graphs in Figure 14.11:

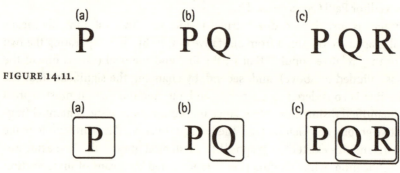

FIGURE 14.11.

FIGURE 14.12.

The graph in Figure 14.11a represents the assertion of "P," which in standard language is expressed by "P" alone, and in a language that uses some ad hoc sign of assertion is expressed as "⊢ P." The graph in Figure 14.11b then should express "⊢ (P & Q)"; but this is the same as "(⊢ P) & (⊢ Q)," because assertion distributes over conjunction. The same applies to the graph in Figure 14.11c: "⊢ (P & Q & R)" = "(⊢ P) & (⊢ Q) & (⊢ R)." The fusion of illocutionary and locutionary function is possible because assertion distributes over conjunction. In a language in which no such merging is effected, there will always be the possibility of expressing the logical equivalence of the syntactically distinct sentences "⊢ (P & Q)" and "(⊢ P) & (⊢ Q)." In alpha graphs no such difference can be expressed.

Assertion distributes over conjunction but not over disjunction: "⊢ (P ∨ Q)" ≠ "(⊢ P) ∨ (⊢ Q)." This is one of the reasons why it was not possible to separate the disjunctive meaning of the line from its quantificational meaning in entitative graphs: the result would have made it explicit that entitative graphs are based upon a potential systematic ambiguity. For does Figure 14.11b express, in (the sentential fragment of) entitative graphs, "⊢ (P ∨ Q)" or "(⊢ P) ∨ (⊢ Q)"?

Topologically, the sheet of assertion is an isotropic space, unordered and without direction. A partial ordering is introduced in it by the ovals. This is possible because the oval is both a sign of negation and a sign of collectional function. The ovals divide the sheet of assertion into "areas." In Figure 14.12b the sheet is divided into two areas, the area outside the oval and the area inside; in Figure 14.12c there are three areas: the area outside the outer oval, the area inside the outer oval and outside the inner oval, and the area inside the inner oval. Existential graphs are not interpreted linearly from left to right or from right to left, but "endoporeutically": "the interpretation of existential graphs is *endoporeutic*, that is proceeds inwardly; so that a nest sucks the meaning from without inwards unto its center, as a sponge absorbs water" (R650 = LoF1:168). The endoporeutic interpretation prescribes that we consider the outermost area first, systematically proceeding inward into any area enclosed in whatever oval is placed on the first area, and so on. Thus, any enclosed area depends, or is in the scope of, the area on which the enclosing oval lies. Graphs in the same area are "endoporeutically neutral," and graphs in distinct areas are "endoporeutically (i.e., partially) ordered." The endoporeutic structure is inherited from the entitative graphs of 1896: the crucial step of having a sign that is both a sign of a truth-function (negation) and of a collectional function is made in 1896.

Let us go back to the succinct presentation in R145. The third sign (the dot) and the fourth (the line) were sometimes considered as one and the same sign by Peirce and were often introduced under one and the same convention (e.g., R478 = LoF2/2:368). The sign of the variable is at the same time the sign of identity. This must be so in every occurrence-referential language, that is, in any language in which it is the *occurrence* and not the *type* of the variable that determines sameness and distinctness of reference. Indeed, the standard sign of identity "=" is used to express that two *distinct* variable occurrences have the same reference "$x = y$"; but in an occurrence-referential language two distinct variable occurrences must become *the same* variable occurrence in order to express identity; and this is nothing more than the "fusion" of variable and identity signs that we have in existential graphs. So, in Figure 14.13a there are two disconnected occurrences of the line of identity, which thus refer to two possibly distinct individuals. When the two lines are joined, as in Figure 14.13b, they become one occurrence of the line of identity, which thus refers to one single individual. There is no way in existential graphs to say of two distinct variables that they refer to the same individual without turning their distinctness (i.e., the distinctness of their separate occurrences) into sameness (i.e., the sameness of one single occurrence).

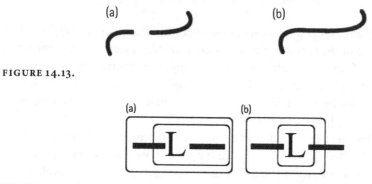

FIGURE 14.13.

FIGURE 14.14.

Not only that: in a system that employs two distinct quantifiers (universal and existential) there must be a sign that distinguishes the one from the other. By contrast, in a system that only employs either the universal or the existential quantifier as primary, the variable itself is the sign of quantification. Of course, relations of quantificational dependence must be determined. Now existential graphs are nonlinear, because the sheet on which the graphs are scribed is unordered and without direction. A partial ordering is introduced in the sheet by the ovals (endoporeutic reading or nestedness of structure). Quantificational dependence is represented in beta graphs by means of the interaction of the lines with the endoporeutic structure determined by the ovals: the nesting of an already existing sign, the oval, suffices to determine the recursive structure of the graphs and thus the relations of dependence between the quantifiers. In the beta graph of Figure 14.14a, the line occurrence to the left of the spot "L" is less enclosed than the one to the right of it. Hence its corresponding quantifier has wider scope. In Figure 14.14b, the dependence relation is reversed, because the line occurrence to the right of the spot "L" is less enclosed than that to the left of it, and thus its quantifier has wider scope. By means of the endoporeutic structure, which Peirce is now able to express by the nesting of the ovals, beta graphs determine how sentences are constructed in stages corresponding to the quantifiers occurring in them.

Thus, the line is the sign of the variable, the sign of quantification, and the sign of identity, all in one. It combines the sign of the variable and the sign of identity because of its occurrence-referential character; it combines these two functions with the third, the quantificational function, because in a system with only one type of quantifier, the sign of the variable is ipso facto the sign of the quantifier, provided that quantificational dependencies are adequately expressed; and it is sufficient for the expression of quantificational dependencies because of its interaction with the endoporeutic structure created by the ovals. All of this was already contained *in nuce* in the entitative graphs of 1896, which are an occurrence-referential language in which the sign of the variable is also the sign of the quantifier and which adequately expresses quantificational dependence. The existential version changes the meaning of the quantifier (from the universal to the existential) along with a parallel change in the meaning of the sheet of assertion (from disjunction to conjunction).

5. ANALYSIS OF INFERENCE

Peirce claimed that the principal business of a logical notation is to aid logical analysis and that existential graphs are the best instrument for that purpose that had been devised: "The system of Existential Graphs alone enables us to carry the logical analysis of terms, propositions, and arguments to the furthest point possible in the nature of things" (R296:7–8 = LoF3/1:329); "there is no organ of definition and logical analysis that is at all equal to [existential graphs]" (Peirce to Carus, 18 September 1908). Existential graphs are an "analytical" notation because they are "economic"; there are two primitives in the sentential fragment (negation and conjunction) and one quantifier in the quantificational fragment (existential quantifier); in addition, negation is fused with the collectional function, and the quantifier is fused with the sign of the variable and the sign of identity.

The analytic power of the system is not limited to its syntax, however. The system is also analytic in the way it represents deduction. It speaks to the superiority of existential graphs over the algebraic systems that in it deduction, as follows from Mitchell's work,[15] is reduced to a minimum number of permissive operations. Peirce termed these operations "(illative) rules of transformation," and they are of two classes: "insertions" (that is, permissions to draw a graph-instance on the sheet of assertion) and "erasures" (that is, permissions to erase a graph-instance from the sheet). More precisely, the "oddly enclosed" areas of graphs (areas within a non-even number of ovals) permit inserting any graph in that area, while "evenly enclosed" areas permit erasing any graph from that area. Furthermore, a copy of a graph-instance can be pasted on that same area or any area deeper within the same nest of ovals. This is the rule of "iteration." A copy thus iterated can be erased by the converse rule termed "deiteration." An interpretational corollary is that a double oval with no intervening graphs (other than the blank graph) in the middle area can be inserted and erased at will. A more detailed exposition of these illative rules of transformation would need to show their application to quantificational expressions, namely, applying insertions and erasures to ligatures.[16]

Roberts demonstrated that the transformation rules Peirce had reached by 1903 form a semantically complete system of deduction. Roberts did not mention, however, that Peirce had demonstrated their soundness in 1898 and again in 1903 and that he had an inkling of how to argue for their completeness in a couple of places, including in unpublished parts of his Lowell Lectures (LoF2/2).

6. Gamma Graphs

What Peirce in 1903 termed the gamma part consists of a number of developments, including various modalities (metaphysical, epistemic, and temporal modalities), as well as extensions of modal graphs with ligatures (a "ligature" is a combination of lines of identity). In Peirce's repositories one finds numerous proposals regarding how to develop graphical systems for second-order logic and abstraction in the logic of "potentials," logics of collections, as well as metagraphs in which the language of graphs is used to talk about notions and properties of the graphs themselves ("graphs of graphs"). He even proposed this idea to serve as the method of logical analysis of assertions and meta-assertions. In connection to one of his last remarks on existential graphs in a letter to Allan Douglas Risteen (RL376/R500, 1911), Peirce mentioned that one would also need to add a "delta" component to the system: "The better exposition of 1903 divided the system into three parts, distinguished as the Alpha, the Beta, and the Gamma, parts; a division I shall here adhere to, although I shall now have to add a *Delta* part in order to deal with modals. A cross division of the description which here, as in that of 1903, is given precedence over the other is into the *Conventions*, the *Rules*, and the *working* of the System." While no direct evidence remains of the details of what the projected delta could have been, most likely Peirce thought that a new compartment was needed to accommodate the ever-expanding number of graphical systems that had been mushrooming in the gamma part. On the one hand, perhaps he planned the delta part to capture quantificational multimodal logics in ways similar to those that can be discerned in how he desired his theory of tinctured graphs to look like as it was fledgling in late 1905 and later. On the other hand, the term "modals" suggests that Peirce had prospected to work on a new kind of logic that could analyze the realizations of "*would-bes*," "*could-bes*," and "*may-bes*"—indeed the central concepts of his pragmaticism and extreme scholastic realism—with the resources of this new instrument of logical analysis provided by graphical modal logic and its interpretation of habits of action "in intension," as realities of general facts (R671, 1911).

Be this as it may, Peirce's graphical systems of modal logic included suggestions for defining several types of multimodal logics in terms of tinctures of areas of graphs. Tinctures enable one to assert, among other things, necessities and metaphysical possibilities, and so call for changes in the nature of how the corresponding logics behave, including the identification of individuals in the presence of multiple universes of discourses. Peirce defined epistemic operators in terms of subjective possibilities, which, as in contemporary epistemic logic, are epistemic possibilities defined as the duals of knowledge operators.

Peirce analyzed the meaning of identities between actual and possible objects in quantified multimodal logics. As an example, the two graphs given in Figures 14.15 and 14.16 that he presented in a 1906 draft of the "Prolegomena" paper (R292a = LoF3/1) illustrate the nature of the interplay between epistemic modalities and quantification. The graph in Figure 14.15 is read "There is a man who is loved by one woman and loves a woman known by the Graphist to be another." The reason is that in the equivalent graph depicted in Figure 14.16, the loving woman is denoted by the name "A," and the beloved woman is denoted by the name "B." (Figure 14.16 is how Peirce scribed the graph on the manuscript leaf—it misses the lines connecting the two instances of "loves" and one occurrence of "man" as shown in the graph of Figure 14.15.) The shaded area is a tincture (argent in colors) that refers to the modality of subjective possibility. Thus, the graph in Figure 14.16 means that it is subjectively impossible, by which Peirce means "is contrary to what is known by the Graphist" (i.e., the modeler of the graph), that A should be B. In other words, the woman who loves and the woman who is loved (whom the graph does not assert to be otherwise known to the Graphist) are known by the Graphist not to be the same person.

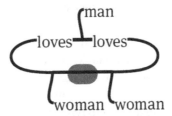

FIG. 14.15.

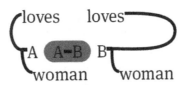

FIG. 14.16.

Peirce's work on such topics highlights the importance of underlying ideas that were rediscovered significantly later, often in different guises. In his largely unpublished works one finds topics later rediscovered as, for example, multimodal logics, possible-worlds semantics, game-theoretic semantics, quantification into modal contexts, cross-world identities (in R490 he termed these special relations connecting objects in different possible worlds "references"[17]), and what is termed "Peirce's puzzle" in formal semantics and pragmatics, that is, the problem of representing the meaning of indefinites in conditional sentences.[18] Peirce himself proposed to analyze these sentences in quantified modal extensions of existential graphs of his own devising.

7. Legacy

In Peirce's lifetime, only some sketchy presentations of existential graphs appeared in print, in 1902 in the *Dictionary of Philosophy and Psychology* edited by James Mark Baldwin (entry "Symbolic Logic," 2:640–651), in *A Syllabus of Certain Topics of Logic*, a twenty-three-page printed pamphlet circulated in one hundred copies that Peirce wrote to accompany his Lowell Lectures of 1903 (R478 = LoF2/2), and in the 1906 *Monist* article "Prolegomena to an Apology for Pragmaticism" (CP4.530–584). Nearly all of his prolific writings on existential graphs remained unpublished in his lifetime and even a century later. Peirce recorded extensive notes on existential graphs in his 1903 Lowell Lectures (LoF2/1, 2/2), letters and correspondences (LoF3/2), and elsewhere in his *Nachlass* (LoF1, 3/1). Only a few references to existential graphs exist in Peirce's other published papers, such as in the 1905–1908 "Some Amazing Mazes" series (CP4.585–593, 4.594–642, 4.643–646). Yet he continued working on the theory of logical graphs for the rest of his life. On Christmas Day of 1909 Peirce began writing a long letter to William James in which he claimed that this graphical method "ought to be the logic of the future" (Peirce to William James, December 25–31, 1909; RL224 = LoF3/2).[19]

As far as the twentieth century is concerned, existential graphs have not been its logic. The Frege–Russell philosophical paradigm dominated analytic philosophy and the Peano–Russell linear, type-referential sort of notation constituted the language of that paradigm. Ironically, the "Begriffsschrift," the logical notation created by Gottlob Frege, the father of analytic philosophy, was nonlinear (though it was type-referential). Frege thought that linearity hampers the perspicuous representation of logical relations. Of course, a nonlinear notation is much more difficult to typeset and print than a linear one. The correspondence between Peirce and Carus in summer/autumn 1896 reveals how hard Peirce had to press in order to have his graphs correctly typeset and printed in the *Monist*. The existential graphs contained in the "Symbolic Logic" entry in Baldwin's dictionary are a linearization of the nonlinear, standard version, and recourse to such linearized version was largely dictated by the need to control the costs that the setting of nonlinear types would incur.[20] Linearity is a feature of the notations of natural languages and of many formalized languages alike, but while in the case of natural languages linearity is a direct consequence of its reproducing oral speech, in the case of formalized languages linearity is only a consequence of their routinely unquestioned imitation of natural languages. This point was clearly made by Herbert Enderton: "Natural languages are spoken. We speak in real time, and real time progresses linearly. Consequently formal languages were constructed with linear expressions. But formal languages are not spoken (at least not easily). So there is no reason to be influenced by the linearity of time into being narrow minded about formulas. And linearity is the ultimate in narrowness."[21] Frege put the point thus: "The convenience of the typesetter is certainly not the *summum bonum*."[22]

Occurrence-referentiality did not help. In his review of CP4, where a selection of Peirce's work on the graphs had been published, Willard Quine judged the basic machinery of existential graphs to be "too complex" for the purposes of logical analysis.[23] Here arises another irony. In his 1940 *Mathematical Logic*, in order to make the point that variables "serve merely to indicate cross-references to various positions of quantification," Quine proposed a notation in which such cross-references are represented by "curved lines or bonds," that is, by lines of identity. Such "quantificational diagrams," as he called them, constitute the beginnings of a linear, occurrence-referential notation, which Quine immediately dismissed as too "cumbersome" and "unpractical."[24] Like Quine's 1940 quantificational diagrams, Peirce's linearized graphs in Baldwin's dictionary were occurrence-referential, and this, too, created no small problems in typesetting.

Frege's nonlinear, type-referential language and Quine's linear, occurrence-referential language are two small exceptions to the large predominance of linearity and type-referentiality in twentieth-century logic and philosophy. The last quarter of the century, however, saw a renewed interest in Peirce's graphical logic, not only on the part of Peirce's specialists,[25] but also in other fields like computer science and artificial intelligence,[26] diagrammatic logic,[27] and synthetic and cognitive mathematics.[28] More than a century after Peirce's death, we are perhaps beginning to appreciate the philosophical richness of his logical graphs and their genuine, radical difference from other languages, even when equivalently expressive. The "future" to which reference was made in the Christmas letter to James had to wait, but there is growing evidence that the time is beginning to be ripe for Peirce's logical graphs to become the twenty-first century's model for new kinds of logics.

Notes

1. This is the positive part of Peirce's "reduction thesis." See Burch (1991).
2. Cf. Brady (2000, 106).
3. Roberts (1973, 18).
4. On the role of the chemical analogy in the development of the logical graphs, see Roberts (1973, 17–25); and Abeles (2015).
5. See the detailed story in Bellucci and Pietarinen (2016), and Pietarinen (2019) in LoF1:14–134. We say "in earnest" because there were interim and not insignificant transitory explorations in Peirce's studies on the algebra of logic between 1886 ("Qualitative Logic") and 1894 (*How to Reason*), which combine algebraic notation with what featured later in his graphical logics after 1896, such as the rule of iteration and deiteration.
6. Stenning (2000, 134).
7. See Bellucci and Pietarinen (2021, 7705–7726).
8. But see Pietarinen (2015a).
9. Roberts (1973, 20).
10. Peirce considered that of "collectional signs" to be the most important class of algebraical signs; cf. R430:53 63 (1902); R253:8–9 (1905); R646:19 (1910); R670:13–14 (1911).
11. Schröder (1890–1895).
12. Peirce had been using some antisymmetrical operation since his first works in relative logic. The binary connective, "—⟨," called "copula of inclusion," is first introduced in the

1870 "Description of a Notation for the Logic of Relatives" (W2:360) and remains his preferred symbol for material implication (and logical consequence: see Dipert 1981) until about 1886, when it is substituted by the "sign of consequence" (W5:341–343, 361–378). The sign of consequence, which Peirce heavily uses also in his monumental *How to Reason: The Critick of Arguments* (R411, R559, 1894), is a direct anticipation of the graphical "relative copula" of 1896. It is formed by a horizontal line (the vinculum) extending over the antecedent and by a cross that separates antecedent and consequent; it expresses the conditional *de inesse* or material conditional (W5:341); see Bellucci and Pietarinen (2016, 559–562).
13. Peirce recounts much later in 1911 that existential graphs were "suggested to me in reading the proof sheets of an article by me that was published in *The Monist* of January 1897; and I at once wrote a full account of it for the same journal. But Dr. Carus would not print it. I gave an oral account of it, soon after, to the National Academy of Sciences" (CSP to Risteen, December 6, 1911, RL376 = LoF3/2). The whole story is found in LoF1:69–75.
14. But see Roberts (1973, 25–27).
15. Mitchell (1883, 72–106).
16. For the beta rules, see Roberts (1973, 56–60).
17. See Pietarinen (2006).
18. See Dekker (2001); Hintikka (2011); Pietarinen (2015b).
19. See the "General Introduction" in LoF1.
20. On linear existential graphs see Bellucci, Xinwen, and Pietarinen (2020).
21. Enderton (1970, 393–397, at 393).
22. Frege (1984, 236).
23. *Isis* XXII, no. 2 (1934): 551–553; see also Bellucci and Pietarinen (2020).
24. Quine (1940, 70).
25. Besides Roberts's classic monograph and Jay J. Zeman's unpublished dissertation (1964), valuable work on Peirce's existential graphs is in Houser, Roberts, and Evra (1997) and in Hilpinen (2004, 611–658).
26. Sowa (1984).
27. Shin (2002).
28. Zalamea (2012). Pietarinen (2022, 1243–1279).

References

Abeles, Francine. 2015. "The Influence of Arthur Cayley and Alfred Kempe on Charles Peirce's Diagrammatic Logic." In *Research in History and Philosophy of Mathematics*, edited by M. Zackand and E. Landry. 139–148. Dordrecht, The Netherlands: Birkhäuser.

Bellucci, Francesco, and Ahti-Veikko Pietarinen. 2016. "From Mitchell to Carus. Fourteen Years of Logical Graphs in the Making." *Transactions of the Charles S. Peirce Society* 52, no. 3 (Summer): 539–575.

Bellucci, Francesco, and Ahti-Veikko Pietarinen. 2020. "Notational Differences." *Acta Analytica* 35: 289–314.

Bellucci, Francesco, and Ahti-Veikko Pietarinen. 2021. "An Analysis of Existential Graphs. Part 2: Beta." *Synthese* 199: 7705–7726.

Bellucci, Francesco, Liu, Xinwen, and Ahti-Veikko Pietarinen. 2020. "On Linear Existential Graphs." *Logique & Analyse* 251: 261–296.

Brady, Geraldine. 2000. *From Peirce to Skolem: A Neglected Chapter in the History of Logic.* Amsterdam: Elsevier.

Burch, Robert W. 1991. *A Peircean Reduction Thesis.* Lubbock: Texas Tech University Press.

Dekker, Paul. 2001. "Dynamics and Pragmatics of 'Peirce's Puzzle.'" *Journal of Semantics* 18: 211–241.

Dipert, Randall R. 1981. "Peirce's Propositional Logic." *Review of Metaphysics* 34: 569–595.

Enderton, Herbert B. 1970. "Finite Partially Ordered Quantifiers." *Zeitschrift für Mathematische Logik und Grundlagen der Mathematik* 16: 393–397.

Frege, Gottlob. 1984. *Collected Papers on Mathematics, Logic, and Philosophy.* Edited by Brian McGuinness. Oxford: Blackwell.

Hilpinen, Risto. 2004. "Peirce's Logic." In *Handbook of the History of Logic. Vol. 3*, edited by Dov M. Gabbay and John Woods, 611–658. Amsterdam: Elsevier.

Hintikka, Jaakko. 2011. "What the Bald Man Can Tell Us." In *Hues of Philosophy: Essays in Memory of Ruth Manor*, edited by A. Biletzky. London: College Publications.

Houser, Nathan, Don D. Roberts, and James Van Evra, eds. 1997. *Studies in the Logic of Charles S. Peirce.* Bloomington: Indiana University Press.

Mitchell, Oscar Howard. 1883. "On a New Algebra of Logic." In *Studies in Logic*, edited by Charles S. Peirce, 72–106. Boston: Little, Brown.

Peirce, Charles S. 1857–1914. Manuscripts held at the Houghton Library of Harvard University, as identified in Richard Robin. *Annotated Catalogue of the Papers of Charles S. Peirce.* Amherst: University of Massachusetts Press, 1967. And in Richard Robin. "The Peirce Papers: A Supplementary Catalogue." *Transactions of the Charles S. Peirce Society* 7, no. 1 (1971): 37–57. (Referred to as R[catalogue#]:[sheet#]; with RL for letters and RS for supplement.)

Peirce, Charles S. 1896. "The Logic of Relatives." *The Monist* 7: 161-217; in CP 3.456–552.

Peirce, Charles S. 1931–1958. *The Collected Papers of Charles Sanders Peirce.* 8 vols. Vols. 1–6 edited by Charles Hartshorne and Paul Weiss. Vols. 7–8 edited by Arthur W. Burks. Cambridge, MA: Harvard University Press. (Referred to as CP[volume#].[paragraph#]).

Peirce, Charles S. 2019- . *Logic of the Future. Writings on Existential Graphs.* 3 vols in 5. Edited by A.-V. Pietarinen. Vol. 1: *History and Applications.* Vol. 2/1: *The Logical Tracts.* Vol. 2/2: *The 1903 Lowell Lectures.* Vol. 3/1: *Pragmaticism.* Vol. 3/2: *Correspondence.* Berlin: De Gruyter. (Referred to as LoF [volume#]:[page#])

Peirce, Charles S. 1982–2010. *The Writings of Charles S. Peirce: A Chronological Edition.* 7 vols. to date. Edited by the Peirce Edition Project. Bloomington: Indiana University Press. (Referred to as W [volume#]:[page#])

Pietarinen, Ahti-Veikko. 2006. "Peirce's Contributions to Possible-Worlds Semantics." *Studia Logica* 82, no. 3: 345–369.

Pietarinen, Ahti-Veikko. 2015a. "Exploring the Beta Quadrant." *Synthese* 192, no. 4: 941–970.

Pietarinen, Ahti-Veikko. 2015b. "Two Papers on Existential Graphs by Charles S. Peirce." *Synthese* 192, no. 4: 881–922.

Pietarinen, Ahti-Veikko. 2019. "Introduction to the Theory of Existential Graphs and Vol 1." In *Logic of the Future. Writings on Existential Graphs*, vol. 1, *History and Applications*, by Charles S. Peirce, edited by A.-V. Pietarinen, 14–134. Berlin: De Gruyter.

Pietarinen, Ahti-Veikko. 2022. "Pragmaticism as a Philosophy of Cognitive Mathematics." In *Handbook of Cognitive Mathematics*, edited by Marcelo Danesi, 1243–1279. Cham: Springer.

Quine, Willard V. 1940. *Mathematical Logic.* Cambridge, MA: Harvard University Press.

Quine, Willard V. 1934. Review of *Charles S. Peirce.* Collected Papers Vol. 4. *Isis* XII, no. 2: 551–553.

Roberts, Don D. 1973. *The Existential Graphs of Charles S. Peirce*. The Hague: Mouton.
Schröder, Ernst. 1890–1895. *Vorlesungen über die Algebra der Logik*. 3 vols. Leipzig: Teubner.
Shin, Sun-Joo. 2002. *The Iconic Logic of Peirce's Graphs*. Cambridge, MA: MIT Press.
Sowa, John F. 1984. *Conceptual Structures: Information Processing in Mind and Machine*. Reading, MA: Addison–Wesley.
Stenning, Keith K. 2000. "Distinctions with Differences: Comparing Criteria for Distinguishing Diagrammatic from Sentential Systems." In *Theory and Application of Diagrams*, edited by M. Anderson, P. Cheng, and V. Haarslev, 132–148. Dordrecht, The Netherlands: Springer..
Zalamea, Fernando. 2012. *Peirce's Logic of Continuity: A Mathematical and Conceptual Approach*. New York: Docent Press.
Zeman, Jay J. 1964. "The Graphical Logic of Charles S. Peirce." PhD diss., University of Chicago.

CHAPTER 15

DIAGRAMMATIC THINKING, DIAGRAMMATIC REPRESENTATIONS, AND THE MORAL ECONOMY OF NINETEENTH-CENTURY SCIENCE

CHIARA AMBROSIO

1. INTRODUCTION

"I do not think I ever reflect in words," Charles S. Peirce famously reminisced in 1909; "I employ visual diagrams firstly because this way of thinking is my natural language of self-communion, and secondly because I am convinced that it is the best system for the purpose" (R619:8). This passage, contained in a manuscript titled "Studies in Meaning," is well known to Peirce scholars.[1] Regularly featuring in the literature that examines Peirce's approach to diagrams,[2] it has offered precious evidence in support of a characterization of Peirce as a distinctively and uniquely diagrammatic thinker, lending further validation to the broader role that diagrammatic representations and diagrammatic reasoning played in his philosophical, logical, and scientific works.[3]

But a closer look at the passage also reveals an apparent tension in Peirce's attitude toward diagrams. On the one hand, Peirce seems to be making a somewhat psychological, or at least descriptive, statement: diagrams are his "natural language of self-communion." This descriptive statement is immediately followed by the normative consideration that they are also "the best system for the purpose."[4] Recent studies of Peirce's diagrammatic system of logic, the existential graphs, stress how this tension dissolves when one considers the logical sense in which Peirce uses the term "thinking" in relation to diagrams. Thus, in his introduction to *Logic of the Future* (vol. 1), Ahti Pietarinen points out that, for Peirce, "thinking as a logical operation is not a description of what goes on in our minds but the matter of logical analysis that translates a thought into another thought" (LoF:39). Within this logical conception of thinking, Pietarinen continues, "the significance of diagrams . . . lies in great measure in their capacity to render the contents of thought transparent and rigorous" (LoF:45).

Without underplaying this purely logical line of interpretation, in this chapter I want to argue that a bigger story lurks in the background of Peirce's twofold statement about thinking with diagrams—a story that goes beyond adjudicating between normative and descriptive levels, or logic and psychology. Drawing on current research at the interface of the history and epistemology of science, I aim to show that the scientific context in which Peirce's approach to diagrammatic representations emerged matters a great deal for the subsequent form and direction of his arguments about diagrammatic representations and diagrammatic thinking. In particular, I aim to locate Peirce's work on diagrams within what historians and philosophers of science have described as the "moral economy" of nineteenth-century science: the system of epistemic virtues that allowed scientists to approach and use diagrams as "working objects," around which they negotiated their identities and commitments (Daston 1995; Daston and Galison 2007).[5] This contextualization has, in turn, both a methodological and a historiographical aim. Studies of Peirce's philosophy often tend to leverage the exceptionality of his character to substantiate the exceptionality of his philosophical genius. In this chapter, I draw on contemporary historiographies of science as well as on recent scholarship on Peirce to show that—however original as an approach in its own right—Peirce's work on and with diagrams was not the isolated pursuit of a solitary genius. It was instead deeply embedded in a much broader array of diagrammatic practices and graphical methods, which were in turn woven into debates over the professionalization of science, the presentation and evaluation of scientific data, and more broadly the formation of a distinctive kind of "scientific self" (Daston and Galison, 2007) in the nineteenth century. I will argue that diagrams and diagrammatic practices, as they emerged and consolidated throughout Peirce's lifetime, were the shared common ground over which an ever-expanding community of scientists negotiated their reasonings, and that debates over validity, rigor, perspicuity, and communicability were as much about issues of reliable representation as they were about the reliability and standing of scientists themselves.

2. Peirce and the "Diagrammatic Moment" in Nineteenth-Century Science

The nineteenth century was a century of diagrams. Diagrammatic methods, of course, had existed for a long time,[6] but the nineteenth century saw a genuine explosion and systematic use of a whole new repertoire of graphical and diagrammatic methods in the sciences. In an "age of methods," as Peirce himself described his lifetime in his introductory lecture on logic at Johns Hopkins University in 1882 (W 4:379; Cowles 2016, 2020, ch. 1), diagrams were part of the scientist's arsenal to control and coordinate the ever-expanding quantity of data and information that characterized the second half of the century. Lorraine Daston and Peter Galison (2009) describe the scientific community of this period as converging into "a many-headed knower," which captured the kind of scientific identity emerging from the realization of the distinctively collective nature of the scientific enterprise. In its growing complexity and specialization, staged in newly founded institutions across the world as well as on the pages of an ever-increasing number of specialized periodicals (Csiszar 2010), nineteenth-century science posed "a problem of the division of labour and the multiplication of knowers," Daston and Galison claim, "akin to any other such problem in the organisation of work: how to analyse a complex inquiry into modular parts, finding willing and able hands to undertake each part, and efficiently integrate the results" (Daston and Galison 2009, 297). Among the examples of this impulse toward coordination they refer to the Internationale Grandmessung, an attempt at a complete measurement of the shape and dimensions of the Earth—a grandiose international project to which Peirce himself contributed while employed at the US Coast and Geodetic Survey. And alongside hours and days spent calculating and measuring, the US Coast and Geodetic Survey also gave Peirce the opportunity to experiment with types of diagrams that were progressively becoming the distinctive tools of the empirical sciences of his time.

As Thomas Hankins (1999) has shown, the kind of representations nowadays referred to as "graphs" in the empirical sciences began to appear in the 1770s and became widespread only from the 1830s. Variously defined as "lineal arithmetic" by William Playfair, "the Method of Curves" by William Whewell, or simply "diagrams" by John Herschel and James Watt (Hankins 1999; see also Hankins and Silverman 1995), these graphical methods aimed precisely to solve the problem of handling complex data by relating two measured quantities and their respective changes by means of a curve. While the term "graph" (in the sense later used by Peirce to refer to his logical diagrams) is also of nineteenth-century coinage, Hankins (1999, 52) carefully points out that it initially indicated a very different kind of representation—and in doing so he explicitly refers to Peirce. Indeed, Peirce was a witness and a staunch defender of its original coinage by the mathematician (and soon to be Peirce's colleague at Johns Hopkins) James Joseph Sylvester, who used it in 1878 to describe the similarity that graphical representations of invariants and covariants of binary quantics exhibited with chemical bonds in molecules (Sylvester 1878; Hankins 1999; Hankins and Silverman 1995; Parshall 1997, 2006).[7] As Peirce scholars very well know, Peirce adopted the meaning Sylvester and his lifelong friend, the mathematician William Kingdon Clifford, originally intended for the term in his later usage of "graph" in logic. In "Prolegomena to an Apology of Pragmaticism" (1906), for example, he famously stated: "By a graph (a word overworked of late years), I, for my part, following my friends Clifford and Sylvester, the introducers of the term, understand in general a diagram composed principally of spots and of lines connecting certain of the spots" (CP4.535). Peirce's complaint that the term was becoming "overworked" signals that by 1906 it might have been stretching beyond its initial algebraic use, to cover the use of graphical representations in the experimental sciences, which is still in use (Hankins and Silverman 1995, 141). Or perhaps this is yet another indication that the nineteenth century had genuinely brought about a "diagrammatic moment," in logic as well as in the empirical sciences, and Peirce had been part of it all along.

The relationship between the logical (and originally chemical/algebraic) sense of "graphs," adopted by Peirce for his system of existential graphs, and the broader use of graphical representations across the experimental sciences has been surprisingly poorly investigated by Peirce scholars. This is a missed opportunity, as Peirce clearly worked across both domains. One exception is a recent study by Claudia Cristalli and Ahti Pietarinen (2021), whose investigation of abstraction and generalization in Peirce's logic of science insightfully brings together his experimental and logical works with diagrammatic representations.[8] Particularly important for the purposes of this chapter is the lineage Cristalli and Pietarinen draw from the British astronomer John Herschel's (and, via Herschel, William Whewell's) characterization of the graphical method to Peirce's own scientific practice, especially in experimental areas at the interface between psychology and astronomy.[9] They convincingly show how the experimental tradition of graphical representation, which substantively underpinned Peirce's work during his years at the US Coast and Geodetic Survey, was crucial in directing Peirce's attention to the process of abstraction: "In both capacities—geodetic scientist and astronomer—Peirce would come across problems for which the graphical method constituted at the time the only possible solution," Cristalli and Pietarinen argue. "Moreover, Peirce utilised graphical methods to abstract patterns from a large amount of data and design new objects of inquiry" (Cristalli and Pietarinen 2021, 107). This process, they argue, is analogous to what Peirce would later define, in a logical context, as *hypostatic abstraction*: "the operation by which we seem to create *entia rationis* . . . [and which] furnishes us the means of turning predicates from being signs that we think or think through, into being subjects *thought of*" (CP4.549, 1906). Hypostatic abstraction isolates the qualitative element of thought, so that we can consider it as an object of inquiry in itself.

Comparing Peirce's use of experimental graphical methods in a Geodetic Survey report produced in 1873 and his (later) logical system of gamma graphs,[10] Cristalli and Pietarinen (2021) highlight how in both cases Peirce deploys a "technology of abstraction" which crucially hinges on judgment in bringing about new objects of inquiry. The experimental curves of the graphical method introduce, "by the mere judgment of the eye" (Herschel 1833, 179), a new object that is partly determined by the data points connected by the curve, but is also more informative and more reliable than each data point on its own. In an analogous manner, Peirce's gamma graphs introduce, via hypostatic abstraction, the idea of "substantive possibility," turning the graphs themselves and the qualities and relations they express into new objects of inquiry in their own right (Cristalli and Pietarinen 2021, 107–112, 118). This connection between experimental and logical methods is of crucial methodological importance for Peirce studies. For one thing, it fills in, with new empirical evidence, the argument that Peirce's system of diagrammatic logic did not exist in a void and demands to be placed in dialogue with his practice as a scientist. This is in line with what Kenneth Ketner (1982, 328) identified as "what ought to be called Eisele's law": the idea, to which the indefatigable Peirce scholar Caroline Eisele devoted most of her scholarly work, that Peirce's philosophy cannot be properly understood independently of his mathematics and science. In what follows, I want to add to this line of investigation and show that, alongside disclosing new aspects of Peirce's own philosophy and scientific work, connecting Peirce to the broader history of nineteenth-century diagrammatic practices also has a distinctive historiographical import—both in terms of how we regard his place in the history of science and (perhaps more importantly) in terms of how the historiography of science can help us revisit the dilemma opened by Peirce's statement, introduced at the beginning of this chapter, that diagrams were at the same time his "language of self-communion" and "the best system for the purpose" of analyzing the process of thinking.

3. The Method of Curves and the Moral Economy of Science

In their study of Peirce's use of the graphical method, Cristalli and Pietarinen (2021, 107) highlight that Herschel's account of judgment was part of a broader inductive argument, which he developed in dialogue with—and partly in response to—another key figure in British science: William Whewell. I will return to Whewell below, first because he was profoundly influential on Peirce, and secondly because his philosophy allows us to appreciate in finer detail how the "diagrammatic moment" of the nineteenth century was part and parcel of a broader "moral economy" of science. In a straightforward sense, both Whewell and Herschel's involvement in the methods and logic of science had a moral aim: both theorized induction—crafting the graphical method as a material expression of it—as part of a systematic project of reform, which they envisaged should extend from science to society as a whole (Snyder 2006). But I want to add that there is a subtler sense in which Whewell's epistemology and his approach to the method of curves had a distinctive moral dimension, which nicely complements Cristalli and Pietarinen's emphasis on the role of judgment in Herschel and Peirce. Here I borrow the definition of moral economy of science introduced by Lorraine Daston, who uses it to indicate "a web of affect-saturated values that stand and function in well-defined relationship with each other" (Daston 1995, 4). Moral economies are contingent constellations of epistemic virtues, which "derive both their forms and their emotional force from the cultures in which they are embedded," and once internalized, Daston argues, they become naturalized: "they reassert rather than dissolve, the boundaries that separate the mentalities and sensibilities of scientists from those of ambient societies" (Daston 1995, 24). Importantly, moral economies are not just abstract and disembodied systems of values and virtues: they have a material life in scientists' "working objects" (Daston and Galison 2007, 19–20); they arise from, and in turn inform, the practices that lead to the construction and standardization of common objects of inquiry, and they fuel the conversations and controversies that arise around them. Diagrammatic representations—in their experimental as well as in their logical and mathematical form—count as "working objects" in this sense.

Peirce's quote about thinking with diagrams as his "natural language of self-communion" and at the same time as "the best system for the purpose" is an excellent illustration of how moral economies at once source their emotional force from ambient cultures (what I have called the nineteenth-century "diagrammatic moment"—the historically contingent ways in which diagrams *came to be* Peirce's language of self-communion), but also acquire normative import, precisely by naturalizing the values from which they derive. The historical context I have briefly sketched in the previous section should suffice to show that there was no inevitability to the development of Peirce's views and uses of diagrams across logic and the experimental sciences, and that the contingent crossover between these two fields and their respective methods discloses ways in which we might want to reconsider the moral economy of his logical diagrams in analogy with the moral economy of the experimental context he operated in.

Connecting Peirce's approach to diagrams with Whewell's views of how the graphical method—or, as he called it, "the Method of Curves"—served as a "special method of induction" allows just this. Whewell articulated the method of curves with Herschel's graphs in mind in his *Philosophy of the Inductive Sciences* (1840) and used it to show how general laws in the sciences could be obtained from observations. The most concise description of the method is presented in the second edition (1847) of volume 2 of the *Philosophy of the Inductive Sciences*, where he states: "The Method of Curves consists in drawing a curve, of which the observed quantities are the Ordinates, the quantity on which the change of these quantities depends being the Abscissa. The efficacy of this Method depends upon the faculty which the eye possesses of readily detecting regularity and irregularity in forms. The Method may be used to detect the Laws which the observed quantities follow; and also, when the Observations are inexact, it may be used to correct these Observations, so as to obtain data more true than the observed facts themselves" (Whewell 1847, vol. 2, 475; 1858a 202).

Whewell highlighted how graphs allow scientists to grasp the relationship between observational data, in a way that numerical tables could not afford. Referencing his own tidal researches, he gave a vivid description of how the scientist's eye discovered order by following the line of a graph: "If these Numbers [i.e., on tide tables] are expressed by the magnitude of Lines, and if these Lines are arranged in regular order, *the eye discovers the rule of their changes*: it follows the curve which runs along their extremities and takes note of the order in which the convexities and concavities succeed each other, if any order be readily discoverable" (Whewell 1840, vol 2, 543–44; 1858a, 205; emphasis added).

Hankins (2006, 618) notes that the method of curves is in line with Whewell's account of the crucial role of ideas in induction. Indeed, inductive inference for Whewell is not exhausted by the simple enumeration, juxtaposition, or combination of observed facts. Instead, it involves an active contribution by the mind: "There is a New Element added to the combination by the very act of thought by which they are combined. There is a Conception of the mind introduced in the general proposition which did not exist in any of the observed facts" (Whewell 1840, 213). Thus, a great advantage of the method of curves is that it makes the process of introducing a new idea visible. As Hankins notes: "A graph allowed the mind to 'see' the general idea in a set of data and impose the necessary mental superinduction to arrive at a scientific law" (Hankins 2006, 618).

Whewell's characterization of ideas was deeply influential on Peirce, and we will see in a moment how he responded to it. Ideas were indeed part of a broader argument Whewell put forward to demonstrate that inductive reasoning reconciled the "fundamental antithesis" of philosophy: he thought that ideas were as indispensable as sensations in the production of knowledge. But in articulating his argument about knowledge being at the same time ideal and empirical, Whewell also presented ideas as *innate*: he claimed that they were "not a consequence of experience, but a result of the particular constitution and activity of the mind, which is independent of all experience in its origin, though constantly combined with experience in its exercise" (1858b, 91).[11] That ideas were innate, however, for Whewell did not mean that they remained *private*. Quite the contrary: a less obvious but fundamental point emerging from Whewell's account of the method of curves is that graphs make ideas and their role in inductive inferences more than just visible to the individual scientist: they make them *public* and *communicable* within an entire community. This aspect of Whewell's work has been noticed especially in accounts of the influence of the method of curves beyond the natural sciences. As Harro Maas and Mary Morgan (2002) have noticed, Whewell's defense of the graphical method was crucial in setting the premises and methodological context for the use of graphs in support of inductive arguments in economics and the social sciences in the second half of the nineteenth century. What Whewell offered was an articulation of how the graphical method prompted external (as opposed to introspective) reflection: as Maas and Morgan explain, "for Whewell ... induction had nothing to do with internal reflection and everything to do with external reflection, the reflection of observations made over time 'in the clear mirror space' of the graph" (2002, 111).

The method of curves was among the innovations that allowed Whewell to gain a central position in methodological debates around scientific identity and scientific and social reform in the second half of the nineteenth century. He famously introduced the term "scientist" for the first time in print in the *Quarterly Review* in 1834, posing it as a remedy to the state of British science, which he saw as "a great empire falling to pieces" (Anon [Whewell] 1834, 59).[12] An indefatigable advocate of the necessity of a renewed and expanded space for science in society, Whewell presented his account of ideas as defining the very identity of scientific practitioners. Baconian "facts" were no longer enough, in the reformed world of nineteenth-century science: ideas sanctioned the reliability of the inductions performed by scientific practitioners, being precisely what connected observations, making them intelligible. But in order to bind the scientific community, alongside connecting "facts," ideas needed to connect scientists:

they needed to be communicable. The method of curves allowed precisely that. Communicability for Whewell had thus both a methodological and at the same time a moral import: it was an essential epistemic virtue, underpinning the reformed philosophy that was functional to Whewell's proposal of reforming science.

4. Peirce's Diagrams and the Moral Economy of Science

Given the inferential nature of Peirce's semiotics and processual philosophy, it is rather unsurprising to see that he disagreed with Whewell on the innate nature of ideas. While firmly positioning himself as continuing Whewell's project in his historical works of the 1890s (HPPLS1; Viola 2020, 18–21, 46–47), for example, Peirce vocally complained about Whewell's ambiguity on the origin and mode of growth of ideas. "We want to know just how these ideas came to be implemented in the nature of the mind," Peirce complains. "Besides, these ideas have most of them grown up during the course of scientific history, and we want to know just how they have grown up and under what general agency" (R1274a:5, *c.* 1892). But while any account of innate knowledge would have hardly found a friendly reception in Peirce's philosophical thought, there is an aspect of Whewell's application of the method of curves that shares some important epistemic virtues with Peirce's own account of logical diagrams. Whewell's insight that the graphical method serves the important purpose of making ideas public and communicable has a counterpart in Peirce's broader approach to the very purpose of constructing a system of *diagrammatic* logic. Here I am not arguing that there is a direct influence of Whewell's method of curves on Peirce's existential graphs. What I want to argue, instead, is that while Whewell's experimental and Peirce's logical systems are very different in aims and application, their motivations for pursuing a diagrammatic method share an analogous sentiment: just like graphical methods make ideas public, so Peirce's graphs trace the movement of thought in reasoning in a way that renders reasoning shareable and amenable to the scrutiny of a community.

Peirce scholars have stressed how Peirce framed his logical program for the existential graphs as providing the best method to "perform the needed logical analyses of intellectual thought" (LoF1:41). Pietarinen (LoF1, introduction), for example, frames this explicitly in contrast with a psychologistic account of thinking. As we saw at the beginning of this chapter, he is adamant in clarifying that for Peirce "thinking as a logical operation is not a description of what goes on in our minds but the matter of logical analysis that translates a thought into another thought" (LoF1:39). Indeed, his interpretation of the second part of Peirce's famous quote about reflecting with diagrams as "his natural language of self communion" is that they are also "the best method for the purpose [*of logical analysis*]" (LoF1:47, insertion in the original, emphasis added). But while logical analysis is undoubtedly one of the chief aims of Peirce's program for a diagrammatic logic, approaching it from the viewpoint of historical epistemology allows us to ask the question of under what conditions it came to be so, what epistemic virtues informed his logical program, and how they related to his commitment to the methodology of science.

Even without venturing into historical epistemology, Pietarinen accounts for the fact that the relationship between logic and the sciences was of crucial importance for Peirce. "This is not to claim," he explains in his introduction to volume 1 of *Logic of the Future*, "that the relevant [logical] studies have nothing to do with experimental issues" (LoF1:41). In order to show this connection, he turns to a well-known passage in "Prolegomena to an Apology for Pragmaticism" (1906), where Peirce draws a parallel between experimenting with logical diagrams and the kind of experimentation that takes place in chemistry. "Chemists have ... described experimentation as the putting of questions to Nature. Just so, experiments upon diagrams are questions put to the Nature of the Relations concerned" (CP4.530). One might object, Peirce preempts in the passage, that there may be "a good deal of difference between experiments like the chemist's, which are trials made upon the very substance whose behaviour is in question, and experiments made upon diagrams, these latter having no physical connection with the things they represent" (CP4.530). But this criticism misses the point, in that it assumes that chemists merely manipulate individual samples "which could very well be thrown away, as having no further interest" beyond the experiment itself (CP4.530). Instead, Peirce claims, the chemist's quest is a quest for generality: "for it was not the particular sample that the chemist was investigating," Peirce reiterates: "it was the molecular structure" (CP4.530).

Pietarinen (LoF1:42) notes that commentators have usually interpreted this quote by Peirce as a kind of mathematical structuralism or through a structural realist lens (see, for example, Hookway 2012). In contrast, he reads Peirce's quote in a way that reconciles logic and the empirical sciences on far more promising grounds:

> Experiments aim at answering questions that the formulation of research hypotheses allows the experimenter to put forth. The experimenters ultimately want to have their information states updated concerning general phenomena and general laws as answers to a question, in the sense that whenever the same sort of an experiment is made, the same sort of result would follow. But general laws are not directly available in experiments. They have to be inferred from observational phenomena. Forms of relations concern such *inferred generalities of the structures*. Their nature has to be inferred from the representations of those structures by certain peculiar means of reasoning best fitted to the task at hand. (LoF1:42, emphasis in original)

Here Pietarinen reads the "Form of a Relation" of Peirce's passage not as static metaphysical structure, but as concerning *inferred generalities*: reasoning on a chemical sample or on an instance of logical diagram prompts inferences on what general laws may be operating in each of these cases, and the study of diagrams is precisely the study and evaluation of how those inferences come to be. Specifically, when it comes to diagrams, it is the emphasis on the *process* of inferring and on the perspicuous character of diagrams in disclosing generalities—not just about structures, but about reasoning itself—that matters: whatever approach one might take to what counts as "structure," the important point is that diagrams make that process transparent and therefore *communicable* across a community of inquirers.

Here the analogy with Whewell's method of curves comes into sharper focus. In claiming, with reference to his own researches in tidology, that through the graphical method "the eye *discovers the rule* of [the curves'] changes," Whewell was wrestling precisely with the quest for a method that would transparently convey how "the images of laws and phenomena" can be made "manifest" so that the scientist's eye could detect their regularity and order (Whewell 1840, vol 2, 544; 1858a, 205; emphasis added). For Whewell, however, this was a method of making the action of ultimately innate ideas public. Peirce's logical program in a sense started where Whewell's philosophical and methodological reform of science stopped: recall that in his historical writings Peirce found Whewell wanting precisely for his lack of an explanation of how ideas *grow* "in the course of scientific history" (R1274a:5). As "a veritable moving picture of the mind in reasoning" (R905, 1907), the existential graphs aspired to capture the process that allows reasoning to be fruitful, by making evident how generality—about laws, structures, and ultimately reasoning itself—could be inferred. In this sense, Peirce's grand project to reform logic was analogous, and indeed a necessary complement, to Whewell's ambitions of reforming philosophy and the sciences.

But precisely for this reason, and again in analogy with Whewell's aspirations, diagrams for Peirce should not simply make the process of reasoning transparent and rigorous. They had to make it *communicable* and *publicly ascertainable*. A forceful—albeit dense—formulation of this combination of perspicuity and communicability is invoked by Peirce in a manuscript (R293 [*c*. 1906–1907]) that is clearly related to the "Prolegomena" of 1906 but might have been written after the completion of the published version of that article.[13] A diagram here is defined as "an Icon of a set of rationally related objects." Peirce's definition here points to a semiotic category—iconicity—that has become a standard point of reference in the literature on diagrams. Icons exhibit qualities of the objects they stand for, qualities they would possess "whether any such Object existed or not" (EP2:291). By reasoning on the diagram's significant parts we can observe, manipulate, and discover new logical relations. But the definition of diagrams as icons of "rationally related objects" goes even further than this. By "rationally related" Peirce means "that there is between them, not merely one of those relations which we know by experience, but know not how to comprehend, but one of those relations which *anybody who reasons* must have an inward acquaintance with" (R293:10–11; emphasis added). This is in line with Peirce's dictum that all necessary reasoning is ultimately diagrammatic (R293:6), and in particular with his idea that necessary reasoning makes (or should make) its conclusions *evident*. Reasoning upon diagrams, Peirce explains, allows for the truth of the conclusion to be "*perceived*, in all its generality; and in the generality the how and why of the truth is perceived" (R293:11; emphasis in original). He further elaborates: "It is, therefore, a very extraordinary feature of diagrams that they show—as literally *show* as a Percept shows the Perceptual Judgment to be true,—that a consequence does follow, and more marvellous yet, that it would follow under all varieties of circumstances accompanying the premises" (R293:13; emphasis in original).[14] Here the emphasis for Peirce is on how diagrams, in the case of necessary reasoning, compel us to *perceive* the truth of a certain conclusion. Peirce's choice of words is not accidental, nor is his reference to the distinction between percept and perceptual judgment, which is in fact a cornerstone of his mature theory of perception. Just like the percept's insistency serves as a *trigger* for general habits (perceptual judgments) that can then be put to the scrutiny of the community of inquirers (Legg 2017, 45–46), so necessity—which Cathy Legg (2012) has redefined in Peircean terms as "the hardness of the *iconic must*"— is made *evident* when diagrams are manipulated through their rules of use. Legg's argument is technical and addresses foundational issues in mathematics that I have not covered in this chapter. But the insight that, in this interpretation, necessity is made 'observable' (as Legg shows, in a way that overcomes Humean skeptical stances on this issue) is an important one, as it feeds precisely in the view of communicability that Peirce built in his entire philosophy, from his theory of perception to his semiotics, and in the very account of perspicuity that he built into his diagrammatic system of logic.

In their history of scientific objectivity, Daston and Galison (2007) discuss Peirce's approach to logic and philosophy under the epistemic virtue of "structural objectivity": the attitude, which began in the nineteenth century but spilled into the twentieth and twenty-first, of "giving up one's own sensations and ideas in favour of formal structures accessible to all human beings" (Daston and Galison 2007, 257). Peirce's cosmic community of inquirers was modeled, they argue, precisely in response to the demands of an ever-expanding and international scientific community, whose primary epistemic concerns were the threats of subjectivity, solipsism, and mutual incomprehension suggested by the recent rise of disciplines such as psychology and sensory physiology. Supporters of structural objectivity appealed to logical formalisms and mathematical invariants in their attempts at breaking away from the contingency of private experience and individual sensations: "Objectivity, according to the structuralists, was not about sensation or even about things; it had nothing to do with images, made or mental. It was about enduring structural relationships that survived mathematical transformations, scientific revolutions, shifts of linguistic perspective, cultural diversity, psychological evolution, the vagaries of history, and the quirks of individual physiology" (Daston and Galison 2007, 259). Daston and Galison's account of the shaping and emergence of the quest for invariant structures and logical formalisms offers a reasonable ground to understand and problematize the very notion of objectivity, by demonstrating how it was itself part and parcel of the moral economy of science. Their inclusion of Peirce under the category of structural objectivity is, however, less convincing. For one thing, Peirce himself had participated in—and substantively contributed to—the rise of the very tradition of empirical psychology and psychophysiology that Daston and Galison identify as one of the possible motivations behind the rise of structural objectivity, and yet his epistemology is continuous with, rather than opposed to, his works and findings in those fields.[15] And as I showed above, even in the case of his most technical logical works, appealing to structure is only part of the story: in the best case, Peirce approached it dynamically and was far more interested in the inferential practices through which the generality of structures can be established, evaluated, and communicated than in metaphysical structures in themselves. Where Peirce fits in Daston and Galison's story is in his emphasis on communicability—not because of a fear of the subjective or variable aspects of experience and sensation, but because communicability was part and parcel of the philosophical, semiotic, and logical program he had developed in tandem with his science, and in dialogue with the very demands and tensions of the science of his time. The moral economy of Peirce's logic and science, encoded in his approach to diagrams, is thus less about the restraint imposed by mathematical and logical structures and more about the freedoms deriving from establishing that logic is itself subject to the same moral codes as the sciences.

5. Conclusions

Drawing on a quote from a letter Peirce wrote in 1909 to William James, the new and much-awaited edition of Peirce's logical works is titled *Logic of the Future* (LoF1:viii). There could be no more apt title for a series of volumes of this kind, for Peirce's logic is indeed an extraordinary future-oriented program aimed at advancing inquiry, in logic as well as in the sciences. In this chapter, I hope to have shown that the construction of Peirce's vision for logic, including the futures it may open, was also firmly grounded in the science of his time, and particularly in its moral economy. Far from the pursuits of an isolated genius, Peirce's works could stand as a revolutionary program to reform logic precisely because they emerged from, and in dialogue with, the scientific and diagrammatic practices of his time.

Peirce operated both as a scientist and as a logician in an exciting time for the sciences, which I have described as the "diagrammatic moment" of nineteenth-century science. That diagrams were ubiquitous in Peirce's time does not detract from the originality of his approach: on the contrary, the "diagrammatic moment" helps establish contextual connections that can only enrich Peirce scholarship with insights from the histories and historiographies of the science of his time. This is precisely what I have tried to do, inevitably partially, in this chapter, by bringing to the fore analogies between Peirce's logical approach to diagrams and William Whewell's approach to the graphical method in the experimental sciences. Despite their differences in aims and applications, Peirce and Whewell's respective approaches were animated by a common pursuit of reforming science, by making the reasonings of scientists transparent and communicable. But I hope to have also shown how transparency, rigor, and communicability emerged as part of broader discussions about the identity of a distinctive kind of "scientific self" in an age of increasing scientific specialization and of intense debates on the nature of science and its methods.

Lastly, I have tried show that a systematic contextualization of Peirce's diagrams within the history and historiography of science can disclose novel and fruitful vistas on the ambitious project of reform that Peirce envisioned for his logic of the future and on the commitments and epistemic virtues that motivated that project. The study of Peirce's diagrams has still much to offer, and the historical pathways I hope to have opened with this chapter show that the histories and historiographies of nineteenth-century science should be part of it.

Notes

1. R619 was part of Peirce's reworking, upon Paul Carus's request, of his 1877–1878 *Illustrations of the Logic of Science* series into a prospective book with Open Court. Alas, the book did not appear in Peirce's own lifetime, but see ILS for an edition of selected revisions to the original texts, complete with an introduction outlining the vicissitudes of Peirce's later amendments. On R619 in particular, see ILS 18–19 and 24–25.
2. See, for example, Leja (2000, 97); Pietarinen (2006, 103); Engel, Viola, and Queisner (2012, 15); Ambrosio and Campbell (2017, 101); and Ambrosio (2020, 348); LoF, 47.
3. Whether "diagrammatic" here is to be identified with "visual" is a matter of debate among Peirce scholars. Pietarinen and Bellucci (2017) criticize this identification as one of the "dogmas" of diagrammatic reasoning. Stjernfelt (2014) proposes a scale of diagrammaticity, based on a distinction between "operational" and "optimal" iconicity. Shin (2002) places diagrammatic representation within the broader class of "multimodal" and "heterogeneous" representations. Legg (2008, 2012) appeals to perspicuity (a concept to which I will return in section 4).
4. Benoit Gaultier (2017, 380) notices this discrepancy but uses it as an indication that Peirce might be exclusively referring to necessary reasoning, and not as a statement that all thinking is necessarily diagrammatic.
5. Daston (1995, 3n1) points out that her articulation of "moral economy" is different from how the expression has been used in an economic context, particularly as a critique of classical economic theory, following Edward P. Thompson's (1971) influential study of class struggle in eighteenth-century Britain. For an overview of the longer conceptual history of "moral economy" and how it traveled beyond economics, see Götz (2015). Daston notes that her usage of the expression retains deliberately the eighteenth- and nineteenth-century combination of psychological *and* normative connotations of the adjective "moral." Her usage of "economy," however, does not refer to money, class struggle, or distribution of material resources. Instead, it aims more broadly to investigate science as "an organised system that displays certain regularities . . . that are explicable but not predictable in detail. A moral economy is a balanced system of emotional forces, with equilibrium points and constraints" (Daston 1995, 4). With reference to Thompson's classic study, she acknowledges a connection insofar as both usages appeal to a broader sense of "legitimising notion" (Datson 1995, 3n1).
6. See, for example, Netz (1999) on the use of diagrams in Greek mathematics, Chemla (2020) on the diagrammatic form of ancient Chinese texts, Bray (2020) on the uses of diagrammatic thinking in the transmission of ancient Chinese agricultural knowledge, Raphael (2013) on the pedagogical uses of diagrams in Galileo's texts; Kusukawa and Maclean

(2006) and Jardine and Fay (2013) on diagrams in the Early Modern period, Müller-Wille (2021) on the role of diagrams in the history of race and race relations; Eddy (2014) on diagrams in eighteenth-century chemistry, and Eddy (2022, esp. ch. 9) on the role of diagrams in the context of university teaching in the Scottish Enlightenment. This list is of course not exhaustive—the role of diagrammatic practices and diagrammatic thinking is undergoing a genuine revival in current history of science, well beyond the suggestions I could outline here. But these examples should give a clear sense that there is a large body of literature on the history of diagrammatic practices prior to the explosion of the graphical method I discuss below.

7. Indeed, at least since the days of his degree at the Lawrence Scientific School, Peirce had become very well versed in another application of the diagrammatic method in chemistry—notably via the teachings in crystallography of his teacher Josiah Parsons Cooke. See Campbell (2017) and Ambrosio and Campbell (2017).

8. For obvious reasons of space and focus, Cristalli and Pietarinen (2021) do not explicitly refer to Sylvester, but it is worthwhile noting that, while the relationship between Sylvester and Peirce's mathematics has been investigated—particularly by historians of mathematics (see, for example, Parshall 2006, Abeles 2016; see also Fisch 1986, 54–62)—the specific influence of Sylvester's chemical/algebraic notation on Peirce's existential graphs, particularly in their "topological" reading, still awaits systematic investigation.

9. This is especially important as the nineteenth century saw heated debates on what became known as the "personal equation": the realization that astronomical observations were subject to errors that came to be seen as inextricably related to observers' different reaction times (see Schaffer 1988; Canales 2009). The report used as a case study by Cristalli and Pietarinen (2021) is a classic example of how psychological and astronomical measurements were systematically combined in assessing and attempting to predict observational errors, precisely in response to widespread concerns about the personal equation.

10. Peirce subdivided his existential graphs into three systems: the alpha system dealt with propositional calculus, the beta system covered predicate logic, and the (unfinished) gamma system covered modal and higher-order notions, including abstraction and reasoning upon the graphs themselves.

11. Incidentally, this was a ground of disagreement between Whewell and Herschel, who in his 1841 essay-long review of Whewell's volumes on the history and philosophy of the inductive sciences positioned himself firmly in the empiricist camp: sound inductions do introduce new objects of inquiry in the form of general propositions that are more than the sum of individual observations, but this, according to Herschel, had nothing to do with innate knowledge. Instead, "the course of a general proposition is ... dotted out before the mind" (Herschel 1841, 193): the task of scientific judgment for him was to intervene to connect the dots.

12. Whewell introduced the term in a discourse presented at the 1833 meeting of the British Association. See Yeo (1993, 110–111), but alas it took almost another century (and a trip to America and back) for the term to be adopted in Britain.

13. Pietarinen dates it after the completion of the published version of the "Prolegomena." See LoF1:39.

14. In a brilliant technical article, Cathy Legg (2012) shows that the notion of iconicity involved in Peirce's existential graphs should prompt us to revisit the very foundational question of how we come to know mathematical necessity, for which she provides a phenomenological argument grounded in "the hardness of the iconic must." Albeit Legg does

not cite this specific passage, I believe her account illuminates precisely (among other things) the sense of "necessity" here invoked by Peirce.

15. For an exceptional, historically rigorous, and philosophically original study of the relation between Peirce's works in psychology and his philosophy, see Cristalli (2020).

Bibliography

Abeles, Francine. 2016. "Clifford and Sylvester on the Development of Peirce's Matrix Formulation of the Algebra of Relations, 1870–1882," *Research in History and Philosophy of Mathematics*, edited by Maria Zack and Dirk Schlimm, 83–91. Dordrecht, The Netherlands: Springer.

Ambrosio, Chiara. 2020. "Toward an integrated History and Philosophy of Diagrammatic Practices," *East Asian Science, Technology and Society* 14, no. 2: 347–376.

Ambrosio, Chiara, and Chris Campbell. 2017. "The Chemistry of Relations: Peirce, Perspicuous Representations, and Experiments with Diagrams," in *Peirce on Perception and Reasoning: From Icons to Logic*, edited by Kathleen A. Hull and Richard Kenneth Atkins, 86–106. New York: Routledge.

Anon [John Herschel].1841. "History of the Inductive Sciences" and "Philosophy of the Inductive Sciences, Founded upon Their History," *Quarterly Review* 68: 177–238.

Anon [William Whewell]. 1834. "On the Connexion of the Sciences," *Quarterly Review* 51: 54–168.

Bray, Francesca. 2020. "Thinking with Diagrams: The *Chaîne Opératoire* and the Transmission of Technical Knowledge in Chinese Agricultural Texts," *East Asian Science, Technology and Society* 14, no. 2: 199–223.

Campbell, Chris. 2017. "The Chemistry of Relations: The Periodic Table Examined through the Lens of C.S. Peirce's Philosophy." PhD Diss., University College London.

Canales, Jimena. 2009. *A Tenth of a Second*. Chicago: University of Chicago Press.

Chemla, Karine. 2020. "On the Diagrammaticity of Ancient Texts and Its Importance for the History of Science: Based on the Example of the Early Chinese Mathematical Text *The Gnomon of the Zhou*," *East Asian Science, Technology and Society* 14, no. 2: 279–308.

Cowles, Henry. 2016. "The Age of Methods: William Whewell, Charles Peirce, and Scientific Kinds," *ISIS* 107, no. 4: 722–737.

Cowles, Henry. 2020. *The Scientific Method*. Cambridge, MA: Harvard University Press.

Cristalli, Claudia. 2020. "The Philosophical Psychology of Charles S. Peirce." PhD Diss., University College London.

Cristalli, Claudia, and Ahti Pietarinen. 2021. "Abstraction and Generalisation in the Logic of Science: Cases from Nineteenth-Century Scientific Practice," *HOPOS* 11: 93–121.

Csiszar, Alex. 2010. "Seriality and the Search for Order: Scientific Print and Its Problems during the Late Nineteenth Century," *History of Science* 48: 399–434.

Daston, Lorraine. 1995. "The Moral Economy of Science." *Osiris* 10: 2–124.

Daston, Lorraine, and Peter Galison. 2007. *Objectivity*. New York: Zone Books.

Daston, Lorraine, and Peter Galison. 2009. "Scientific Coordination as Ethos and Epistemology," in *Instruments in Art and Science*, edited by Helmar Schramm, Ludger Schwarte, and Jan Lazardzig, 296–333. Berlin: De Gruyter.

Eddy, Matthew. 2014. "How to See a Diagram: A Visual Anthropology of Chemical Affinity," *Osiris* 29: 178–196.

Eddy, Matthew. 2022. *Media and the Mind. Art, Science, and Notebooks as Paper Machines, 1700–1830*. Chicago: University of Chicago Press.

Engel, Franz, Tullio Viola, and Moritz Queisner (Eds.). 2012. *Das bildnerische Denken: Charles S. Peirce*. Berlin: Akademie Verlag.

Fisch, Max. 1986. "Peirce at the Johns Hopkins," in *Peirce, Semeiotic and Pragmatism*, edited by Kenneth Laine Ketner and Christian J. W. Kloesel, 35–178. Bloomington: Indiana University Press.

Gautier, Benoit. 2017. "The Iconicity of Thought and Its Moving Pictures: Following the Sinuosities of Peirce's Path," *Transactions of the Charles S. Peirce Society* 53, no. 3 (Summer): 374–399.

Götz, Norbert. 2015. "Moral Economy: Its Conceptual History and Analytic Prospects," *Journal of Global Ethics* 11, no. 2: 147–162.

Hankins, Thomas. 1999. "Blood, Dirt, and Nomograms," *ISIS* 90, no. 1: 50–80.

Hankins, Thomas. 2006. "'A Large and Graceful Sinuosity': John Herschel's Graphical Method," *ISIS* 97, no. 4: 605–633.

Hankins, Thomas, and Silverman, Robert J. 1995. *Instruments and the Imagination*. Princeton, NJ: Princeton University Press.

Herschel, John F. W. 1833. "On the Investigation of the Orbits of Revolving Double Stars: Being a Supplement to a Paper Entitled "Micrometrical Measures of 364 Double Stars &c. &c.," *Memoirs of the Royal Astronomical Society* 5: 171–222.

Hookway, Christopher. 2012. *The Pragmatic Maxim: Essays on Peirce and Pragmatism*. Oxford: Oxford University Press.

Jardine, Nicholas, and Isla Fay (Eds.). 2013. *Observing the World through Images: Diagrams and Figures in the Early-Modern Arts and Sciences*. Leiden: Brill.

Ketner, Kenneth L. 1982. "Carolyn Eisele's Place in Peirce's Studies," *Historia Mathematica* 9: 326–332.

Kusukawa, Sachiko, and Ian Maclean (eds.). 2006. *Transmitting Knowledge: Words, Images, and Instruments in Early Modern Europe*. Oxford: Oxford University Press.

Legg, Catherine. 2008. "The Problem of the Essential Icon." *American Philosophical Quarterly* 45, no. 3: 207–232.

Legg, Catherine. 2012. "The Hardness of the Iconic Must: Can Peirce's Existential Graphs Assist Modal Epistemology?" *Philosophia Mathematica* (III) 20: 1–24.

Legg, Catherine. 2017. "Idealism Operationalised: How Peirce's Pragmatism Can Help Explicate and Motivate the Possibly Surprising Idea of Reality as Representational," in *Peirce on Perception and Reasoning: From Icons to Logic*, edited by Kathleen A. Hull and Richard Kenneth Atkins, 40–53. New York: Routledge.

Leja, Michael, 2000. "Peirce, Visuality and Art," *Representations* 72: 97–122.

Maas, Harro, and Mary S. Morgan. 2002. "Timing History: The Introduction of Graphical Analysis in 19th Century British Economics." *Revue d'histoire des sciences humaines* 7: 97–127.

Müller-Wille, Staffan. 2021. "Corners, Tables, Lines. Towards a Diagrammatics of Race," *Nuncius* 36, no. 3: 517–531.

Netz, Reviel. 1999. *The Shaping of Deduction in Greek Mathematics. A Study in Cognitive History*. Cambridge: Cambridge University Press.

Parshall, Karen. 1997. "Chemistry through Invariant Theory? James Joseph Sylvester's Mathematization of the Atomic Theory," in *Experiencing Nature*, edited by Paul H. Theerman and Karen Parshall, 81–111. Dordrecht, The Netherlands: Kluwer.

Parshall, Karen. 2006. *James Joseph Sylvester: Jewish Mathematician in a Victorian World* Baltimore: Johns Hopkins University Press.

Peirce, Charles S. 1857–1914. Manuscripts held at the Houghton Library of Harvard University, as identified in Richard Robin. 1967. *Annotated Catalogue of the Papers of Charles S. Peirce.* Amherst: University of Massachusetts Press. And in Richard Robin. 1971. "The Peirce Papers: A Supplementary Catalogue." *Transactions of the Charles S. Peirce Society* 7, no. 1 (Winter): 37–57. (Referred to as R.)

Peirce, Charles S. 1931–1958. *The Collected Papers of Charles Sanders Peirce.* 8 vols. Vols. 1–6 edited by Charles Hartshorne and Paul Weiss. Vols. 7–8 edited by Arthur W. Burks. Cambridge, MA: Harvard University Press. (Referred to as CP.)

Peirce, Charles S. 1982–. *The Writings of Charles S. Peirce: A Chronological Edition.* 7 vols. to date. Edited by the Peirce Edition Project. Bloomington: Indiana University Press. (Referred to as W.)

Peirce, Charles S. 1985. *Historical Perspectives on Peirce's Logic of Science.* 2 vols. Edited by Carolyn Eisele. The Hague: Mouton. (Referred to as HPPLS.)

Peirce, Charles S. 1992–98. *The Essential Peirce: Selected Philosophical Writings.* 2 vols. Vol. 1 edited by Nathan Houser and Christian Kloesel. Vol. 2 edited by the Peirce Edition Project. Bloomington: Indiana University Press. (Referred to as EP.)

Peirce, Charles S. 2014. *Illustrations of the Logic of Science.* Edited by Cornelis de Waal. Chicago: Open Court. (Referred to as ILS.)

Peirce, Charles S. 2019– . *Logic of the Future. Writings on Existential Graphs.* 3 vols in 4. Edited by A.-V. Pietarinen. Berlin: De Gruyter. (Referred to as LoF.)

Pietarinen, Ahti-Veikko. 2006. *Signs of Logic.* Dordrecht, The Netherlands: Springer.

Pietarinen, Ahti-Veikko, and Bellucci, Francesco. 2017. "Two Dogmas of Diagrammatic Reasoning," in *Peirce on Perception and Reasoning: From Icons to Logic*, edited by Kathleen A. Hull and Richard Kenneth Atkins, 86–106. New York: Routledge.

Raphael, Renée. 2013. "Teaching through Diagrams: Galileo's *Dialogo* and *Discorsi* and His Pisan Readers," *Early Science and Medicine* 18, no. 1–2: 201–230.

Schaffer, Simon. 1988. "Astronomers Mark Time: Discipline and the Personal Equation," *Science in Context* 2, no. 1: 115–145.

Shin, Sun-Joo. 2002. *The Iconic Logic of Peirce's Graphs.* Cambridge, MA: MIT Press.

Snyder, Laura. 2006. *Reforming Philosophy.* Chicago: University of Chicago Press.

Stjernfelt, Frederik. 2014. *Natural Propositions: The Actuality of Peirce's Doctrine of Dicisigns.* Boston: Docent Press.

Sylvester, Joseph J. 1878. "On the Application of the New Atomic Theory to the Graphical Representations of the Invariants and Covariants of Binary Quantics, with Three Appendices," *American Journal of Mathematics* 1, no. 1: 64–128.

Thompson, Edward P. 1971. "The Moral Economy of the English Crowd in the Eighteenth Century," *Past and Present* 50: 76–136.

Viola, Tullio. 2020. *Peirce on the Uses of History.* Berlin: De Gruyter.

Whewell, William. 1840. *Philosophy of the Inductive Sciences, Founded upon their History.* 2 Vols. London: J. W. Parker.

Whewell, William. 1847. *Philosophy of the Inductive Sciences: Founded upon their History.* Vol. 2 (2nd ed.). London: J. W. Parker.

Whewell, William. 1858a. *Novum Organon Renovatum.* London: J. W. Parker.

Whewell, William. 1858b. *The History of Scientific Ideas*, in 2 vols. London: J. W. Parker.

Yeo Richard. 1993. *Defining Science. William Whewell, Natural Knowledge and Public Debate in Victorian Britain.* Cambridge: Cambridge University Press.

CHAPTER 16

THE LOGIC AND MATHEMATICS OF CHARLES SANDERS PEIRCE

LOUIS H. KAUFFMAN

1. INTRODUCTION

THIS chapter explores the mathematics and logic of Charles Sanders Peirce. We concentrate on his notational approaches to basic logic and his general ideas about symbol and diagrammatic thought. (This chapter was preceded by Kauffman and Varela 1980, Foerster 1981, Kauffman 1987a–b, 1990, 1995, 2001a–c), and expands on material in these previous papers.

We study a system of logic devised by Peirce based on a single sign for inference that he calls his "sign of illation." We then turn to Peirce's existential and beta graphs. Peirce's ideas about the existential graphs are related to his ideas about infinity and infinitesimals and with his more general philosophy that regards a human being as a sign. We bring forth these themes in both their generality and their particularity.

2. THE SIGN OF ILLATION

Peirce wrote a remarkable essay, "The Logical Algebra of Boole," (NEM4:106–115; compare also with Nicod [1916]) on the Boolean mathematics of a sign that combines the properties of addition and negation. It is a portmanteau sign in the sense of Lewis

Carroll (see below). We do not have the capabilities to typeset the Peirce sign of illation, but see below for a rendition of it.

Instead, I shall use the following version in this text: [A]B. When you see [A]B in the text you are to imagine that a horizontal bar has been placed over the top of the letter A and a vertical bar, crossed with a horizontal bar (very like a plus sign), has been placed just to the right of the A in such a way that the vertical bar and the horizontal overbar share a corner. In this way [A]B forms the Peirce sign of illation, and we see that this sign has been created by fusing a horizontal bar with a plus sign. The horizontal bar can be interpreted as negating the sign beneath it.

$$A \mathbin{\overline{+}} B = \overline{A} + B$$

$$\overline{A} = \text{not } A$$

Peirce went on to write an essay on the formal properties of his sign of illation and how it could be used in symbolic logic.

The sign of illation enables a number of notational conveniences, not the least of which is that the implication "A implies B," usually written as "A → B" is expressed as "[A]B" using the sign of illation.

The sign of illation is a portmanteau sign in the sense of Lewis Carroll (Carroll 1960, 1988), who created that concept in his poem "Jabberwocky," where one encounters a bestiary of words like "slithy"—a combination of "lithe" and "slimy." A portmanteau is literally a coat and hat rack (also a suitcase), an object designed to hold a multiplicity of objects. Just so, a portmanteau word is a holder of two or more words, each justly truncated to fit with the truncate of the other. A modern version to contemplate is the word "smog," a combination of "smoke" and "fog."

In Peirce's case of his portmanteau sign of illation there is a perfect fit at the corner of the horizontal overbar as sign of negation and the vertical plus sign as sign of "logical or." The two fit into one sign that can then hold neatly yet another meaning as a sign of implication.

It is the meaning of the sign of illation as implication that Peirce takes as primary. In his essay, he begins with this interpretation, deduces many properties of the sign from this interpretation, and only in the last paragraph reveals that his sign can be taken apart into a plus sign and overbar (interpreted as a negation).

One of the charming features of the essay is that he deduces many formal properties of this symbolism wholly conceptually, based on this interpretation of the sign of illation as implication.

3. Peirce's Existential Graphs

We now turn to a development of Peirce for logic that is closely related to the sign of illation. These are his existential graphs (CP4.397–4.417, NEM3:406–446, Ketner 1990). The first stage of the existential graphs is called the "alpha" graphs. These alpha graphs are concerned with the logic of implication, and we shall concentrate on their structure.

Here is a quick description of the context for the existential graphs.

We are given a plane on which to make inscriptions. If we place a graph or symbol on the plane, then the proposition corresponding to this symbol is asserted. If we place two disjoint complexes of symbols on the plane, call them A and B, then we are asserting the conjunction "A and B."

$$A \; B$$

A circle (or simple closed curve) drawn around a symbol changes the assertion to the negative. Thus, a circle around A asserts the negation of A.

$$(A) = \text{not } A$$

For ease of notation, we shall make an algebraic version of the existential graphs where AB denotes "A and B" and (A) denotes a circle around A. Hence (A) denotes "not A."

Since "A implies B" is logically equivalent to "not (A and not B)," we see that "A implies B" has existential graph consisting of a big circle that contains both A and a circle around B. Algebraically, this is (A(B)) for "A implies B."

$$\underset{}{\boxed{A\ (B)}} = A\ \text{implies}\ B$$

Peirce worked out a number of rules for manipulating these graphs by different patterns of substitution and replacement. With such rules in place, the graphs become an arena for analyzing basic arguments and tautologies in logic. Note that the idea behind the existential graphs and the sign of illation is essentially the same, although the underlying model for implication is "(not A) or B" in the case of the sign of illation.

Extra decorations on the existential graphs allow for the inclusion of quantifiers and modal logic as well. What is quite fascinating in reading Peirce on these developments is his maintenance of a clear conceptual line connecting spoken and written language on the one hand and diagrammatic and written formalisms on the other. Just so, a minimal formalism may not be the most effective interface with speech and word, and yet the mathematician must continue to search for these least structures. Peirce walks the creative middle road.

4. Existential Graphs and Laws of Form

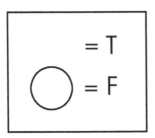

We now make a descent into the internal structure of the existential graphs in a direction that Peirce apparently did not take to its full conclusion. What is the truth value of the empty existential plane? In that plane nothing is asserted to exist. By convention, the truth value of the empty plane is True, T. An empty circle encloses empty space and so negates it, giving rise to the value False, F.

With this convention, we can evaluate patterns of adjacent and nested circles in the plane.

0. "nothing" = T
1. () = F

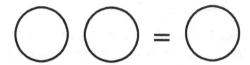

2. False and False = False. Thus () () = ().
3. (()) = (F) = not F = T. Thus (()) = "nothing."

More complex expressions can be simplified uniquely by the successive application of these rules.

The arithmetic of circles handles the evaluation and properties for the existential graphs in an automatic fashion. This arithmetic provides a direct decision procedure for determining the equivalence of any two existential graphs. The two graphs are equivalent exactly when they have the same circle evaluations for all possible substitutions of circles or blanks into the variables in the two graphs.

Remarkably, this arithmetic of circles, implicit in C. S. Peirce's existential graphs, is isomorphic with the primary arithmetic (calculus of indications) discovered by George Spencer-Brown in his lucid book *Laws of Form* (1969).

The basic symbol in *Laws of Form* is a right angle bracket, rather than a circle, but its use is just the same (as an enclosure) and the primary algebra of Spencer-Brown is also isomorphic with the existential graphs themselves. In the usual interpretation for logic in *Laws of Form*, one takes juxtaposition of forms to be "or" rather than "and," thus getting a dual calculus where (A)B stands for "A implies B" and () stands for "True." Access to this primary arithmetic adds an extra dimension to the structure of the existential graphs.

Remark on Notation. We remark that in Spencer-Brown's *Laws of Form* (1969), the notation for an enclosure is not a circle, but a right angle bracket.

Thus the laws of calling and crossing as we have drawn them in circles become the following patterns in the right angle bracket.

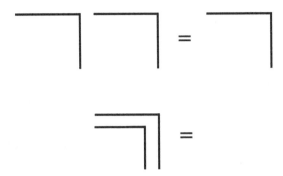

As we go from arithmetic to algebra and logic, Spencer-Brown makes the choice that AB (A juxtaposed with B) represents "A or B" rather than "A and B" as we have seen in the existential graphs and with the sign of illation. However, with the marked state interpreted as "True" and the unmarked state interpreted as "False," implication in the Spencer-Brown algebra is given by the form shown below.

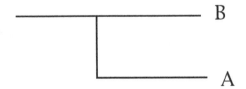

This puts implication in *Laws of Form* in exactly the same pattern as in Peirce's sign of illation.

5. Gottlob Frege, George Spencer-Brown, and Peirce's Existential and Beta Graphs

We start with Gottlob Frege's implication diagram (Frege 1967) for "A implies B."

```
─────────────── B
           ┬
           └───── A
```

Now place closed curves on the diagram as shown below.

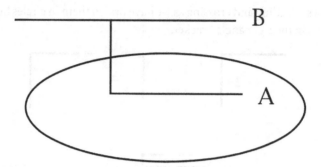

We now see that this implication form is essentially the same as the circle-diagram form of the Spencer-Brown implication [A]B.

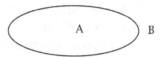

Note that crossing the circle negates the value of A. Again, we have the precise agreement with the interpretation of the ninety-degree turn as negation and the crossing of the boundary as negation in the form.

Frege's tree is the tree naturally associated to the (nested) circles.

The next diagrams illustrates this situation for

"A implies (B implies C),"

which, in Spencer-Brown form, is [A][B]C.

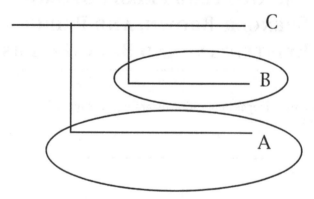

The previous diagram contrasts with

"(A implies B) implies C,"

which in Spencer-Brown form is [[A]B]C.

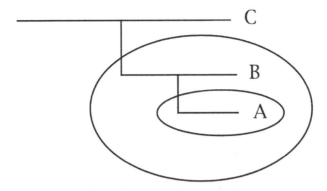

All this can be illustrated dually for Peirce's existential graphs.

These graphs, as we have noted earlier, invert the use of the circles but are otherwise equivalent to the Spencer-Brown expressions.

Thus, we can translate between Frege and Peirce and Spencer-Brown by this method of adding circles to Frege's trees.

For the reader of Frege who is familiar with either Peirce or Spencer-Brown, such a nested-circles transcription of the conceptual notation of Frege is surely the most efficient way to handle Frege and to translate him into an algebraic format.

5.1. Quantifiers in Frege and in Existential Graphs

We first recall how Frege introduced quantifiers into the syntax of his conceptual notation. View the diagram below.

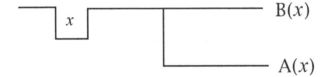

Here is the form of Frege's rendering of

"For all x, $A(x)$ implies $B(x)$."

The placement of x in the small depression in the line indicates "for all x." Frege then achieves the statement

"There exists an x such that $A(x)$ implies $B(x)$"

by the following diagram.

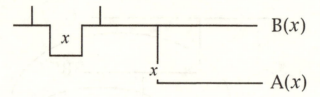

Here we see that Frege uses the equivalence of "There exists an x such that $P(x)$" with "It is not the case that for all x it is the case that not $P(x)$."

It is clear from this version of quantification that one can adopt a similar strategy to quantify the Peirce or Spencer-Brown versions of existential graphs. Note how the quantified implication appears when we impose the circle.

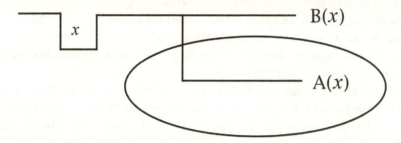

We can translate this as follows to a diagrammatic syntax in the circles form.

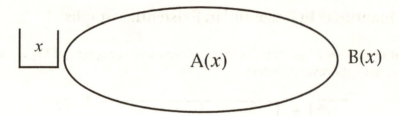

In this form, the partially boxed x stands for the quantifier "for all x." If we used $<x>$ to mean "for all x" in a linear notation, then the statement "For all x, $A(x)$ implies $B(x)$" would be rendered as

$$< x > [A(x)]B(x)]$$

in the Spencer-Brown diagrammatic.

Existence via two negatives becomes the following rendition of "There exists an x such that $A(x)$ implies $B(x)$."

$$[< x > [[A(x)]B(x)]]].$$

THE LOGIC AND MATHEMATICS OF CHARLES SANDERS PEIRCE 287

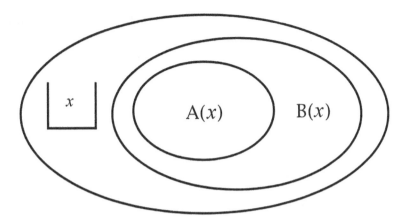

With this experiment in notational design we see that it is quite easy to add quantification to the existential graphs. Peirce added quantification via his beta graphs as we now show.

5.2. From Frege to Peirce's Beta Graphs

First recall that in Peirce's graphs, AB stands for A and B. Just as in Spencer-Brown, a circle around A is the negation of A. With this we have, as previously discussed,

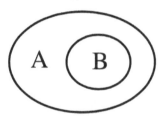

which is the Peirce existential graph for A implies B. How does this compare with Frege? Let us take a superposition once more.

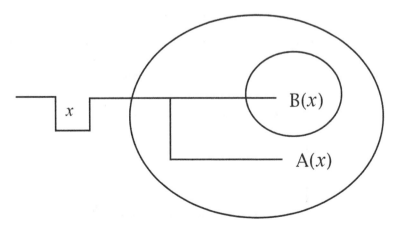

Here we have superimposed the Peircean existential graph with Frege's quantified implication. This graph should mean "For all x, $A(x)$ implies $B(x)$," or, more simply, "All A are B." We can now abbreviate this graph to the following one.

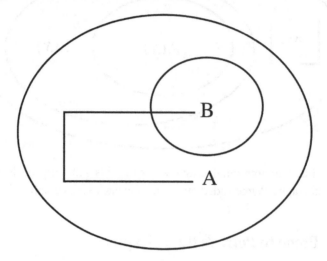

We would take this decorated existential graph to mean "All A are B." This is exactly the Peirce beta-graph for this statement (see Ketner 1990). From here it is not hard to construct the rest of Peirce's beta graphs. To summarize, one can now say that the following graph stands for "No A is a B."

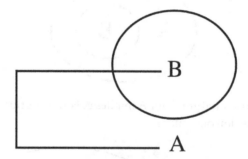

The graph below stands for "There exists an A that is a B." Note that this is symmetrical. If there is an A that is a B, then there is a B that is an A, and indeed the graph makes the simple assertion of the existence of a nonempty intersection of A and B.

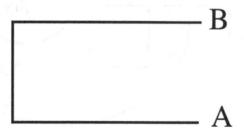

6. Infinity and Infinitesimals

Peirce was an advocate of the notion that infinitesimal numbers were as natural as the concepts of infinity and infinite numbers.

That there was a controversy over this point is a consequence of the history of the calculus where, at first, Newton and Leibniz both used infinitesimals freely. Later, as a critical period set in, mathematicians decided to keep track of all approximations as precisely as possible and the concept of limits was born. With this, a direct need for infinitesimals vanished and the machinery of mathematical scholarship kept these "ghosts of departed quantities" in the background. Peirce was one of the few mathematical people who still advocated infinitesimals in the early part of the twentieth century.

The situation did not begin to clear up until the 1970s when the logician Abraham Robinson published his beautiful work (Robinson 1966) showing how to work with infinitesimals in their full subtlety. Later developments produced different models of numbers that included infinitesimals with less formal machinery than the Robinson theory. For example, there are the surreal numbers of John Conway (Conway 1976), the square zero infinitesimals of Lawvere and Bell (Bell 1998), the sequence infinitesimals of Henle (Henle 1999). It will help this discussion to consider the concept of infinitesimal in an informal way and then to compare with what Peirce said about them.

We imagine a new sort of positive number d that is not zero and that is nevertheless "smaller" than any ordinary positive number that you can name. This infinitesimal d is in itself a generator of other infinitesimals. Thus $d + d = 2d$ is also infinitesimal and larger than d, while $d \times d = d^2$ is smaller than d. If we take the reciprocal $1/d$, we obtain a number that is larger than any standard number. This means that $1/d$ is a kind of infinite number, but $1/d$ is not the same as the reciprocal of 0 (and we do not allow $1/0$ in our calculations since it leads to contradictions). The addition of d and its powers and reciprocals to the number system actually does not, if handled correctly, lead to any contradictions. Adding d to the numbers is quite analogous to extending the number system to include the square root of -1 (to create the complex numbers). The extension of numbers to include infinitesimals can be accomplished, and once it is done one can do calculus without using limits at the fundamental level. The basic idea is that with an infinitesimal one can study how a function changes instantaneously. That is, we can form the ratio $(f(x + d) - f(x))/d$ and call the standard part (the noninfinitesimal part) of this quotient the derivative of the function f at the point x, df/dx.

For example, if $f(x) = x^2$ (the product of x with itself), then

$$(f(x+d) - f(x))/d = ((x+d)(x+d) - x^2)/d = (2xd - dd)/d = 2x - d.$$

Since $2x$ is the noninfinitesimal part of this difference quotient, we conclude that the derivative of x^2 is $2x$.

The concept of infinitesimal is closely tied with the concept of continuity. Infinitesimals form a glue that holds the points of the line together. These sorts of intuitions were at the core of Peirce's discussion of infinitesimals. Here is his voice:

> It is singular that nobody objects to $\sqrt{-1}$ as involving any contradiction, nor, since Cantor, are infinitely great quantities much objected to, but still the antique prejudice against infinitesimally small quantities remains. (NEM3:123)

> It is difficult to explain the fact of memory and our apparently perceiving the flow of time, unless we suppose immediate consciousness to extend beyond a single instant. Yet if we make such a supposition we fall into grave difficulties, unless we suppose the time of which we are immediately conscious to be strictly infinitesimal. (NEM3:124)

> We are conscious only of the present time, which is an instant, if there be any such thing as an instant. But in the present we are conscious of the flow of time. There is no flow in an instant. Hence, the present is not an instant. (NEM3:126)

Along with this notion that the perception of the present is not a point but rather an infinitesimal, Peirce takes the stance that the continuum of the line is not made of points and that any attempt to analyze the line into points will lead to higher and higher orders of infinity for the number of points on that line. This idea is precisely borne out in the surreal numbers of John Conway (Conway 1976).

Here is another quote from Peirce:

> Now if we are to accept the common sense idea of continuity (after correcting its vagueness and fixing it to mean something) we must either say that a continuous line contains no points or we must say that that the principle of excluded middle does not hold of these points. The principle of excluded middle applies only to an individual. . . . But places being mere possibles without actual existence are not individuals. (CP6.168, 1903)

Here Peirce comes to the notion that *a denial of the law of the excluded middle must be related to the connectivity/continuity of the line.* This concept has found its place in the structure of topological spaces and also in the structure of infinitesimals. We briefly explain each of these in turn.

It is of interest to compare this notion of the infinitesimal as the glue of the present moment with the point of view of J. L. Bell (Bell 1998). To see Bell's point of view, consider the following neighborhood of zero:

$$NZ = \{x \mid x^2 = 0\}.$$

We have in mind the usual real numbers with an extra number @ such that $@^2 = 0$ *and we stipulate that @ is indistinguishable from 0*. Then @ is in the neighborhood NZ. How does our logic hold up under such conditions? We are not allowed to say that @ is not equal to 0, since @ is only indistinguishable from 0. We would like to say

P: "It is not the case that every x in NZ is equal to zero."

If our logic is standard logic, then it follows from P, by the law of the excluded middle, that

Q: "There exists an x in NZ so that x is not equal to zero."

Thus, in order to have the @ as indistinguishable from 0, we need to abandon the law of the excluded middle. Then we can assert

"It is not the case that @ is equal to 0."

and

"@ is indistinguishable from 0."

This also appears to reject Leibniz's law of the identity of indiscernibles, which, like the law of excluded middle, seems to hinge on it applying only to individuals. This suggests that numbers need not necessarily be treated as individuals and perhaps should not be looked upon as individuals at all.

Infinitesimals like @ form the glue that holds the line together and force, as Peirce saw, a relinquishment of the law of the excluded middle for the sake of continuity.

Twenty-first-century mathematicians do not unanimously relinquish that mathematical law, and they nevertheless have notions for the continuity of the real line.

Let me explain the topological point of view, common to many mathematicians, and you will see how Peirce's idea emerges in a different way.

A *topological space* S is a set S with a special collection T of subsets of S called a *topology on S*. We say that the subsets in T are the *open sets in S*. The open sets satisfy the following properties:

1. The empty set {} is in T.
2. The space S itself is in T.
3. If U and V are in T, then their intersection U∧V is also in T.
4. Any union of open sets in T is an open set in T.

In point set topology, the collection of open sets T provides the glue to give S a topological or continuous structure. A mapping $f:S \to S'$ of topological spaces is said to be continuous if it satisfies that the inverse image of an open set in S' is an open set in S. The motivations for these definitions are very well explained in many books on topology. I will explain how nonstandard logic features in this apparently classical set theoretic approach to continuity.

The key to the relation with nonstandard logic is in an operation on subsets X of S, denoted *Interior(X)*.

$$\text{Interior}(X) = \{p \text{ in } X \text{ such that there is an open set } U \text{ with } p \text{ in } U \text{ and } U \text{ is contained in } X.\}$$

The interior of any subset X is by its very definition an open set. For example, the standard topology on the plane is generated by open discs, discs that do not include their boundary points. An example of such an open set is the collection of points at distance less than one from the origin of the plane. If D is a closed disc such as

D = {p in the plane with distance of p from the origin less than or equal to 1}, then Interior(D) = {points p in the disk of distance less than one from the origin}. The boundary of the disk D is the unit circle C = {p at exactly unit distance from the origin}. We see that D − Interior(D) = C, the boundary of D. Topological concepts let us talk about interior and boundary of sets.

The collection of open sets has a logical structure (a Heyting algebra [Vickers 1989]) that is not Boolean and that does not satisfy the law of the excluded middle. We define the "negation" ~U of an open set U by the formula (where S is the topological space in which U is an open set)

$$\sim U = \text{Interior}(S - U).$$

The complement of an open set U is denoted S-U and is the set of all points p in S that are not in U. We define the negation ~U as the interior of this complement.

When U is open, so is ~U, but the union of U and ~U is not necessarily equal to all of S. Generally, we have U v ~U is not equal to S. This is a failure of the law of the excluded middle for this logic of open subsets of a topological space. The reason that U v ~U is not all of S is because we have not included the boundary of S-U. A good example to contemplate is S = the plane, and U = Interior(D) above. Then we have that U v ~U = S − C. The boundary that we have eliminated is the circle C, but the complement of this circle is an open set. The set S-C is very close to being all of S. In fact, if we let V = S-C, then we have ~V = Interior(C), which is empty! That is, we have ~V = {} and so ~~V = S. Thus ~~V is not equal to V, and we see that the law of double negation is no longer satisfied in the Heyting algebra of open sets on S.

This failure of double negation and of the law of the excluded middle is due to the connectivity of the plane. You could say the open disk U = Interior(D) and its negation ~U are "held together" by the infinitely thin circle C. It is this circle that makes the Heyting structure happen. Whenever we have a connected topological space, there is a nonstandard double negation occurring in the Heyting algebra of the open sets and a failure of the law of the excluded middle. In this way, nonstandard logics are occurring just beneath the classical surface and these ideas are clearly connected with the intuitions of Peirce.

We may compare the Heyting algebra with the adjustment needed for speaking about infinitesimals @ that are indistinguishable from 0. In the Heyting algebra we can say that S-C and S are indistinguishable from one another in the sense that their Heyting complements are equal: ~(S-C) = ~S = {}. In this language we can say that open sets U and V are indistinguishable if ~U = ~V. Then we have provided, in terms of the nonstandard Heyting negation, *a definition of indistinguishability*, and it is possible for U and V to be distinct and yet indistinguishable. The distinction between them is available because the open sets are included in all the subsets of the topological space, and this larger collection of sets has a classical logic. One can wonder what Peirce would have thought about these relationships between classical and nonclassical logics that evolved in relation to his work.

Let us return to the matter of how o is glued into the rest of the real number line. If it were possible to say of any real number that it is equal to o or it is not equal to o, then we could define a function F: R → {0,1} where F(r) = 0 if F is equal to o and F(r) = 1 if r is not equal to o. This function is discontinuous at the origin. Failure of the law of the excluded middle is directly correlated with the possibility of discontinuity. When Peirce asserts the fundamental continuity of the line and that it cannot be composed of only individual points, he is using the essentials of this argument. Note also that if we give {0,1} the discrete topology where the sets {0} and {1} are both open, then the inverse image under F (above) of the set {0} is {0} and is not an open subset of the real line. This illustrates how the topological descriptions are related to the concepts via continuity. In a topological space we have the option to "glue" two points together by choosing a topology so that every open set containing one of them must contain the other. A variation on this is the fact that in the real line R, any neighborhood of o contains infinitely many points not equal to o. It is in this way that o is glued to the rest of the line from the classical topological point of view.

The infinitesimal point of view of the set of x with $x^2 = 0$, where all such x are indistinguishable from o gives another intuitive gluing. In fact, we can see how with o indistinguishable from these infinitesimals we can write the calculus via

$$F(x + @) = F(x) + F'(x)@$$

where $@^2 = 0$. This serves to define the derivative. For example, $(x + @)^2 = x^2 + 2x@$ implies that the derivative of x^2 is $2x$. Here it is the indistinguishability of @ from o that makes @ the conceptually correct infinitesimal step away from o.

6.1. Zero Is Subject to Two Interpretations

Zero can stand for a very tiny number. Then we can interpret the equation $o^2 = 0$ as Tiny^2 = Vanishingly Tiny. The second o in the equation stands for *actual vanishment*. That vanishment is the second meaning for o. In the second meaning o stands for absolute nothingness, not a quantity at all, but the absence of quantity. When we write $o^2 = 0$ we are affirming the relationship that makes something nearly vanishing actually vanish when applied to itself. We can interpret o as "very tiny" and then it becomes the glue that holds the number line together. We can interpret o as no quantity and then it becomes the starting point for counting. Remarkably, the number o fits comfortably into this multiplicity of roles.

We may speculate whether Peirce took these ideas of infinitesimals, continuity, and infinity into the arena of his existential graphs. If so, he might have considered infinite graphs such as the one shown below. And he might also have thought of the circles in his graphs as precursors for zero and for indistinguishables.

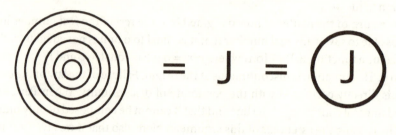

Peirce's view of an inexhaustible infinity is closely related conceptually with the reflexivity embodied in the self-containing form J depicted above. If we say that J is identical to J with a circle around it, then this identification is really the step of adding one more circle to the pattern. It is a conceptual recognition of the potential endlessness of the series of nested circles. (See Varela 1979, Kauffman and Varela 1980, Maturana and Varela 1987, Kauffman 1995).

7. A Sign of Itself

There is clearly much more to be done in this arena of investigation and speculation into the nature and structure of the mathematics of Charles Peirce. A clue for a deeper foray into these matters may come from Peirce himself in speaking about "a Sign of itself":

> But in order that anything should be a Sign it must "represent," as we say, something else called its *Object*, although the condition that a Sign must be other than its Object is perhaps arbitrary, since, if we insist upon it we must at least make an exception in the case of a Sign that is part of a Sign. Thus nothing prevents an actor who acts a character in a an historical drama from carrying as a theatrical "property" the very relic that that article is supposed merely to represent, such as the crucifix that Bulwer's Richelieu holds up with such an effort in his defiance. On a map of an island laid down upon the soil of that island there must, under all ordinary circumstances, be some position, some point, marked or not, that represents *qua* place on the map the very same point *qua* place on the island. . . .
>
> If a Sign is other than its Object, there must exist, either in thought or in expression, some explanation or argument or other context, showing how—upon what system or for what reason the Sign represents the Object or set of Objects that it does. Now the Sign and the Explanation together make up another Sign, and since

the explanation will be a Sign, it will probably require an additional explanation, which taken together with the already enlarged Sign will make up a still larger Sign; and proceeding in the same way, we shall, or should, ultimately reach a Sign of itself, containing its own explanation and those of all its significant parts; and according to this explanation each such part has some other part as its Object. (CP2.230, 1910)

In this passage Peirce speaks as a topologist. He tells us that if we overlay or in any (continuous) way place the map of a territory upon that territory then there must be a point on the map that coincides with the corresponding point on the territory. At first this statement might seem quite astonishing, but it is indeed true, and it is the content of the famous Brouwer fixed-point theorem (Courant and Robbins 1969). If F is any continuous mapping of a disk D to itself, then there exists a point p in the disk D that is left fixed by the mapping: $F(p) = p$.

Presumably Peirce is assuming that his territory is in the topological shape of a disk. Otherwise the result is false. Imagine a world in the shape of a donut and a map of that world just the size of the world itself. Rotate the map a small amount in both of the turns available on a donut and every point of the map will move away from itself.

When Peirce says of the place of coincidence of map and territory "we shall reach, or should, ultimately reach a Sign of itself, containing its own explanation and those of all its significant parts: and according to this explanation each such part has some other part as its Object," he is describing a sign that refers to a significant part of itself and through that to itself. The sign should "contain its own explanation." This is the reflexive or recursive nature of the re-entrant or self-referential form.

Compare this discussion with the re-entrant J of the previous section. The equation

$$J = \boxed{J}$$

asserts the re-entry of J into its own indicational space, and it exhibits J as a "part of itself." The equation is the explanation of the nature of J as re-entrant and can be taken as a description of the recursive process that generates an infinite nest of circles. It is only J as an equation that yields J as a sign of itself. If we wish to embody the equation in the sign itself, then we need to allow the sign to indicate its own re-entry with the symbol shown below.

This symbol does "contain its own explanation" in the sense that we interpret the arrow as an instruction to re-enter the form inside the circle (ad infinitum). Self-reference is infinity in finite guise.

Peirce, in speaking of the necessary occurrence of a "sign for itself" in the relation of map and territory, is referring, through a topological metaphor, to the reflexive nature of the domain of human discourse. Each person is both an object/sign in the discourse and an actor/participant in that discourse. Signs may refer to other signs, or, as is the case with persons, they may refer to themselves. The position of a person in the social discourse depends on this duality of roles and upon that person's ability to recognize this duality in each of the others. Social systems in this sense necessarily are composed of observers, of signs for themselves. This is an attitude toward systems that has been called second-order cybernetics, particularly by Heinz von Foerster (Foerster 1981).

In the last part of the passage quoted above Peirce speaks of a hierarchy of signs and explanations leading eventually to the sign of itself "containing its own explanation and those of all its significant parts." The hierarchy occurs each time one looks into the context for the explanation of the given sign. Sign and explanation form a new sign to be explained ad infinitum (or in a circular network of explanations of explanations).

Continuing the previous quotation, Peirce goes on to say,

> According to this, every Sign has a *Precept* of explanation according to which it is understood to be a sort of emanation, so to speak, of its Object. (If the Sign be an Icon, a scholastic might say that the "*species*" of the Object emanating from it found its matter in the Icon. If the Sign be an Index, we may think of it as a fragment torn away from the Object, the two in their Existence being one whole or a part of such a whole. If the Sign is a Symbol, we may think of it as embodying the "*ratio*" or reason, of the Object that has emanated from it. These, of course, are mere figures of speech; but that does not render them useless.) (CP2.230, 1910)

Here Peirce speaks of the interlocking relationship of sign and object. An example of the use of this concept in mathematics is the notion of Gödel numbering where the sign for a text is a code number assigned to that text (by a definite procedure specified beforehand). The text is the object and its indexical sign is the Gödelian code number. It is through this interlock of sign and object that Gödel constructs a text that asserts its own unprovability in the given formal system. (See Kauffman 2001, Barendregt 1981, Nagel and Newman 1960.)

The interlocking relationship of sign and object was already well understood by Peirce. The mathematical ingredient for Gödel is the careful use of a restricted context (the given formal system).

The Gödelian result is the ultimate inability of such restricted formal systems to express the full range of mathematical truth. The full sign of itself lies beyond such restrictions.

As we saw in descending from Peirce's existential graphs to the calculus of indications, the circle lives in a language where it is a sign of itself as a maker of distinctions. As a sign of itself, the circle has only itself as a part. That part, equal to the whole, makes the distinction that is the referent of the sign. If the circle represents a first distinction, then we, its observers, cannot be distinct from it, the observed, and so, in the first place, the sign, the signifier, and the interpretant are identical in the form.

References

Barendregt, Hendrik Pieter. 1981. *The Lambda Calculus Its Syntax and Semantics*, Amsterdam: North-Holland Publishing Co.

Bell, John L. 1998. *A Primer of Infinitesimal Analysis*, Cambridge: Cambridge University Press.

Carroll, Lewis. 1960. *The Annotated Alice—Alice's Adventures in Wonderland & through the Looking Glass*, with notes by Martin Gardner. New York: New American Library.

Carroll, Lewis. [1865] 1988. *Alice's Adventures in Wonderland & through the Looking Glass*. New York: Bantam Books.

Conway, John Horton. 1976. *On Numbers and Games*. New York: Academic Press.

Courant, Richard, and Herbert Robbins. [1941] 1969. *What Is Mathematics?* Oxford: Oxford University Press.

Frege, Gottlob. 1967. *The Basic Laws of Arithmetic—Exposition of the System*, translated by Montgomery Furth. Berkeley, CA: University of California Press.

Henle, James M. 1999. "Non-nonstandard Analysis: Real Infinitesimals." *Mathematical Intelligencer* 21, no. 1: 67–73.

Kauffman, Louis Hirsch. 1987a. "Imaginary Values in Mathematical Logic." In *Proceedings of the Seventeenth International Conference on Multiple Valued Logic*, May 26–28 1987. Boston, MA: IEEE Computer Society Press, 282–289.

Kauffman, Louis Hirsch. 1987b. "Self-Reference and Recursive Forms." *Journal of Social and Biological Structures*, 10, no. 1: 53–72.

Kauffman, Louis Hirsch. 1990. "Robbins Algebra. *Proceedings of the Twentieth International Symposium on Multiple Valued Logic*. Boston, MA: IEEE Computer Society Press, 54–60.

Kauffman, Louis Hirsch. 1995. "Knot Logic." In *Knots and Applications*, edited by Louis H. Kauffman. Singapore: World Scientific, 1–110.

Kauffman, Louis Hirsch. 2001a. "The Mathematics of Charles Sanders Peirce." *Cybernetics and Human Knowing* 8, no. 1/2: 79–110.

Kauffman, Louis Hirsch. 2001b. "The Robbins Problem—Computer Proofs and Human Proofs," *Kybernetes—The International Journal of Systems and Cybernetics* 30, no. 5/6: 726–751.

Kauffman, Louis Hirsch. 2001c. "Virtual Logic—The Key to Frege," *Cybernetics and Human Knowing* 8, no. 4: 75–86.

Kauffman, Louis Hirsch, and Franscisco Javier Varela. 1980. "Form Dynamics." *Journal of Social and Biological Structures* 3: 171–206.

Ketner, Kenneth Laine. 1990. *Elements of Logic—An Introduction to Peirce's Existential Graphs*. Lubbock: Texas Tech University Press.

Maturana, Humberto Romesin, and Francisco Javier Varela. 1987. *The Tree of Knowledge—The Biological Roots of Human Understanding*, Boston, MA: New Science Library.

Nagel, Ernst, and James Roy Newman. 1960. *Gödel's Proof*. New York: New York University Press.

Nicod, Jean George Pierre. 1916. "A Reduction in the Number of Primitive Propositions of Logic." *Proceedings of the Cambridge Philosophical Society* 19: 32–40.

Peirce, Charles S. 1931–1958. *The Collected Papers of Charles Sanders Peirce*. 8 vols. Vols. 1–6 edited by Charles Hartshorne and Paul Weiss. Vols. 7–8 edited by Arthur W. Burks. Cambridge, MA: Harvard University Press. (Referred to as CP.)

Peirce, Charles Sanders. 1976. *The New Elements of Mathematics*. 4 vols. in 5. Edited by Carolyn Eisele. The Hague: Mouton. (Referred to as NEM.)

Robinson, Abraham. 1966. *Non-standard Analysis*, Amsterdam: North-Holland Publishing Co.

Spencer-Brown, George. 1969. *Laws of Form*, New York: Julian Press.

Varela, Francisco Javier. 1979. *Foundations of Biological Autonomy*. North-Holland: North Holland Publishing Co.

von Foerster, Heinz. 1981. *Observing Systems*. Seaside, CA: Intersystems Publications, 274–285.

Vickers, Steven. 1989. *Topology via Logic*. Cambridge: Cambridge University Press.

CHAPTER 17

ADVANCES IN PEIRCE'S MATHEMATICS

A Short Survey (1960–2020)

FERNANDO ZALAMEA

1. INTRODUCTION

PEIRCE's most appreciated work, either philosophical or semiotical, as forcefully expressed in this handbook, is deeply connected to his studies in mathematics and logic. The continuity of his system, interconnecting each of its parts, is an application of his more general synechistic standpoints: continuity, operative in nature and culture, turns out to be also operative along Peirce's own architectonics. A back and forth between global general (philosophical) concepts and local particular (mathematical) techniques is one of the main forces of Peirce's approach. In particular, Peirce was able to introduce very precise ideas to support his main conjectures, around (1) the pragmaticist maxim, (2) topology and combinatorics, (3) the continuum, and (4) the existential graphs. In this chapter we will not deal with Peirce's original contributions—which we assume and are surveyed extensively in other chapters of this handbook—but rather describe and assess some of the main contributions offered by Peirce scholars on themes (1) through (4) in the past sixty years (1960–2020), which use in their perspectives explicit modern mathematical tools not available to Peirce.

Section 2 recalls Peirce's pragmatic maxim (in actual realms) and its *pragmaticist* extension (in modal contexts) and summarizes some attempts to prove the maxim, using modal logics, gamma existential graphs, and category-theoretic tools. Section 3 describes some Peircean views on *topology* and gauges some advances to systematize both the combinatorial and the set-point topology laid out by Peirce, using diverse tools in algebraic topology and diagrammatic formalization. Section 4 circumscribes the originality of Peirce's *continuum*, describes its main logical and mathematical characteristics, and sketches some partial models for the continuum, until the emergence of a full ZFC inverse ordinal model (where ZFC stands for Zermelo–Fraenkel set theory with the axiom of choice included). Section 5 surveys some of the main proofs for logical equivalences around the *existential graphs*, using many algebraic, geometric, analytical, and logical tools, and explores extensions of the graphs to intuitionistic, modal, and higher-dimension spatial environments. We must emphasize that in this chapter attention is mainly drawn to mathematics. For complementary perspectives around Peirce's logic, we refer to other chapters of this handbook.

Connections between Sections 2–5 are drawn in the following full symmetrical Hasse diagram, showing the strong interdependence of Peirce's architectonics:

2. The Pragmaticist Maxim

The pragmatic maxim appears formulated several times throughout Peirce's intellectual development. The better-known statement is from 1878, but more precise expressions appear (among others) in 1903 and 1905:

> Consider what effects which might conceivably have practical bearings we conceive the object of our conception to have. Then, our conception of these effects is the whole of our conception of the object. (CP5.402, 1878; "How to Make Our Ideas Clear")

> Pragmatism is the principle that every theoretical judgement expressible in a sentence in the indicative mood is a confused form of thought whose only meaning, if it has any, lies in its tendency to enforce a corresponding practical maxim expressible as a conditional sentence having its apodosis in the imperative mood. (CP5.18, 1903; "Harvard Lectures on Pragmatism")

> The entire intellectual purport of any symbol consists in the total of all general modes of rational conduct which, conditionally upon all the possible different circumstances, would ensue upon the acceptance of the symbol. (CP 5.438, 1905; "Issues of Pragmaticism")

The *pragmaticist maxim* (PM) (1903–1905, *possible* effects) is a modal extension of the pragmatic maxim (1878, *actual* effects) and signals that knowledge, seen as a semiotic-logical process, is preeminently contextual (versus absolute), relational (versus substantial), modal (versus determined), and synthetic (versus analytic). PM serves as a sophisticated *sheaf of filters* to decant reality. According to Peirce's thought, we can only know through signs, and, according to the maxim, we can only know those signs through diverse correlations of its conceivable effects in interpretation contexts. The PM "filters" the world by means of three complex webs, which can "differentiate" the one into the many and, conversely, can "integrate" the many into the one: a *representational* web, a *relational* web, a *modal* web. Even if the twentieth century has clearly retrieved the importance of representations and has emphasized (since cubism, for example) a privileged role for interpretations, both the relational and the modal web seem to have been much less understood (or made good use of) through the century.

For Peirce, the understanding of an arbitrary *actual* sign is obtained contrasting all *necessary* reactions between the interpretations (subdeterminations) of the sign, going over all *possible* interpretative contexts. The pragmatic(ist) dimension emphasizes the correlation of all possible contexts: even if PM detects the fundamental importance of local interpretations, it also urges the reconstruction of global approaches, by means of appropriate relational and modal glueings of localities. A diagrammatic scheme of the PM—which follows closely the 1903 and 1905 enunciations above stated—is the following (Zalamea 2001, 22; 2012, 55):

Figure 17.1 emphasizes how an actual sign (S) should be equivalent to its pragmatic modalized meaning (PMS), after differentiation and reintegration of its interpretations. The back and forth between differentiation and integration is one of the main strengths of the PM, capable to capture both postmodernist (local, differential, relative) forces and modernist (global, integral, universal) tensions.

In 1903, in his Harvard Lectures, Peirce thought he had guessed a "proof of pragmaticism" (PPM; EP2:398–433, 1907). Since then, the problem of a "proof of pragmaticism" has been one of the crucial open problems in Peircean scholarship (see, e.g., Robin 1997). Many philosophical and methodological strategies have been offered to approach the problem (see, e.g., Zalamea 2001, 109–121; 2012, 93–103). Nevertheless, in order to really obtain, at least partially, such a proof, some bounded mathematical definitions were needed to proceed. Using gamma modal graphs to represent modalities, and based on modal systems in which $\Diamond \Box p \to p$, Zalamea (2001, 105–108; 2012, 89–92) obtained half a proof of pragmaticism, as represented in Figure 17.1: (S) ⇒ (PMS). Nevertheless, the other implication (PMS) ⇒ (S), arguably the hardest part of the proof, could not be achieved at that time.

Going well beyond that rough initial try and working with much richer and global category theory concepts instead of local existential graphs, Arengas (2019) has now fully mathematized PM, as sketched in Figure 17.1, yielding a vast array of particular theorems in completely formalized contexts. Using the basic tools of category theory (synthetic morphisms composition, instead of analytic elements decomposition), Arengas's PhD dissertation studies the contextual, pragmatic understanding

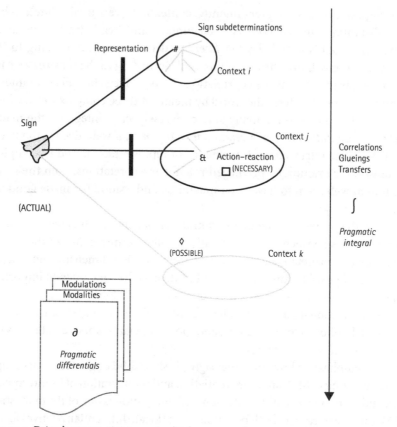

FIGURE 17.1 Peirce's pragmaticist maxim (Zalamea 2001).

of a given sign (S) through its visible interpretation arrows (from the sign to its subdeterminations, see Figure 17.1), hoping afterward to capture back (S) thanks to the category-theoretic limit (L) of those arrows. This produces in a natural way an arrow $s: S \to L$, and the PM can be expressed by the simple property: PM *s is an isomorphism* (Arengas 2019, 13). Thanks to the duality capabilities of category theory, the situation can be inverted, and a *co-pragmaticist* maxim (co-PM) expresses how a hidden sign (S) can emerge from its residual interpretations (Arengas 2019, 14). The main bulk of Arengas's technical definitions, lemmas, and theorems consists then in obtaining nice conditions in categories (generators, reflections, adjointness, separation, glueing, filtering, projectivity) in order to prove either PM (Proposition 1.2.17: Arengas 2019, 35) or co-PM (Theorem 1.2.9: Arengas 2019, 29). Applying those general theorems to the particular category of bi-Heyting algebras, Arengas obtains deep PM representations in terms of orders and iterated modal operators (Theorem 2.2.4: Arengas 2019, 59). Further, the general (category-theoretic) and particular (order) results are studied through the lens of Voevodsky's homotopy type theory (Chapter 3: Arengas 2019, 97–147), providing bounded, *computable* proofs. In this way, Peirce's "proof of pragmaticism" turns out to be fully mathematized, and conclusively proved, at least in the very broad context of category theory.

3. Topology and Combinatorics

Murray Murphey's *The Development of Peirce's Philosophy* (1961) remains, after sixty years, the best general guide to understand Peirce's research in topology (and, beyond that, stands still today as the best global survey of Peirce's entire work). Part three of the monograph (Murphey 1961, 183–288)—devoted to topology, geometry, number, and the classification of continua following Listing—offers a full panorama of Peirce's combinatorial topology wanderings, in particular around cyclosis, that is, the study of the genus of a surface (number of cuts, minus one, which disconnects the surface). Assessing in further detail Peirce's topological writings, Jérôme Havenel's PhD dissertation (2006) extends Murphey's first readings and offers the most precise particular guide to date of Peirce's ideas on topology. Havenel's "Peirce's Topological Concepts" (Havenel 2010) sums up his main findings around Peirce's definition of topology (Havenel 2010, 284–286), Peirce's reading of listing and his extension of the census theorem $V - E + F - S = 0$ (for a given figure, V stands for its vertices, E for edges, F for faces, and S for the disjoint spaces that conform the figure) (Havenel 2010, 287–293, 306–313), Peirce's work on the problem of map-coloring (Havenel 2010, 299–300), and Peirce's explorations around dimensions, motions, singularities, and defects of continuity (Havenel 2010, 300–305). Havenel concludes that Peirce's main topological insights were his understanding "that one could classify spatial complexes according to the value of their census number," his attention to "continuous structures useful for analysis (like lines, circles, disks, spheres, toruses, etc.)," and his combinatorial calibration of associated "topological singularities" (Havenel 2010, 314).

The work of William James McCurdy has fostered the most original contemporary developments around Peirce's combinatorial topology. His "Peirce's Composability-of-Relations Theorem: A Proof in the Combinatorial Topology of the Logic of Relations" (McCurdy 2016), introduces Peircean relational graph theory (PRGT), a new branch of topology that studies the mathematics of relational graphs with exactly three kinds of relational vertices (see, e.g., Figure 17.2), motivated by ideas to model Peirce's topological logic, Peirce's semiotic systems, and certain results in quantum physics (McCurdy 2016, 165). Two main operations—relative multiplication and autorelative multiplication (McCurdy 2016, 167–169)—help to develop PRGT, yielding some strong generalizations of Euler's formulas in classical graph theory (McCurdy 2016, 170) and, especially, an extended version of Listing's census theorem (McCurdy 2016, 171–172). McCurdy's major result ("Peirce's Composability-of-Relations Theorem") states that to de/construct any kind of relational network in PRGT, it is necessary and sufficient to compose monadic, dyadic, and triadic vertices (McCurdy 2016, 173–180). This can be seen as an extension, and simplification, of Burch's proof of Peirce's reduction thesis (Burch 1991), which

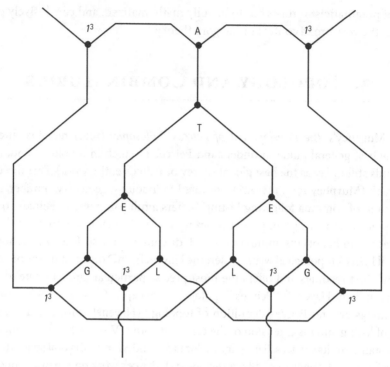

FIGURE 17.2 An example of relational graphs (McCurdy 2016).

states that thirdness is required in the continuous combinatorics of existential graphs (see Section 5) and cannot be reduced to a discrete combinatorics of units and couples, as happens in set theory (via Kuratowski's ordered pairs).

On another line, Downard (2015) presents a simple graphical system based on Peirce's account of elementary relations (Downard 2015, 65) and proceeds to study its combinatorial core (Downard 2015, 65–70, 80–84), before applying it to a diagrammatic classification of relations (Downard 2015, 70–76). In these efforts to formalize Peirce's ideas through well-defined combinatorial definitions, Peirce's spirit is enhanced thanks to added mathematical precision.

On the one hand, building on his own mathematical expertise in imagining knot theory, Louis Kauffman's "The Mathematics of Charles Sanders Peirce" (Kauffman 2001) emphasizes Peirce's diagrammatic thinking and describes some notational approaches in the twentieth century (Jean Nicod and George Spencer-Brown) (Kauffman 2001, 83–84, 90–93), which lead to a simple and natural classification of binary connectives (Zellweger's "Logical Garnet") (Kauffman 2001, 94–99). On the other hand, Kauffman proceeds to synthesize Peirce's rich ideas around infinity and infinitesimals (Kauffman 2001, 100–101), before extrapolating them to recursive definitions (Kauffman [2001], 101–102], including a brilliant idea on infinite graphs, yet to be worked out), fixed point theorems (Kauffman 2001, 103–105), and second-order cybernetics (Kauffman 2001, 106–109). For a thorough vision, see Kauffman's chapter in this handbook.

4. The Continuum

Peirce's continuum is one of his most original mathematical and logical contributions (the other one certainly being the existential graphs; see Section 5). At the center of his philosophical, methodological, and semiotical edifice, the continuum pervades completely Peirce's architecture. Far from being "a castle in the air" (Murphey 1961, 407), Peirce had very precise views on how to handle the continuum. Going well beyond Georg Cantor's real numbers system, accepting infinitesimals, introducing strong reflexive and supermultitudinousness properties, and delving into modalities, Peirce opened a vast field of inquiry to probe a generic continuum, of which Cantor's construction was to become just "a first embryo of continuity" (for a thorough view of the situation, see Zalamea [2001, 2012]). The genesis of Peirce's continuum is better understood when Peirce's ideas are contrasted with Cantor's (Moore 2010, 2015; Maddalena 2012). On the one hand, comparing Cantor's definitional experiment, ordinals, and well-ordered stratifications with Peirce's real abstraction, multitudes, and a welded continuum, Moore (2010) shows how the two views can be seen as almost "orthogonal." On the other hand, comparing Cantor's logico-analytical approach, logical surgery, and theological idealism against Peirce's mathematico-synthetical perspectives, diagrammatic gestures, and metaphysical realism, Maddalena (2012) emphasizes the power of "orthogonality" inscribed in the alternative continuum.

Going further, and exploring in detail some sort of "orthogonal projections," many *local* mathematical formalizations help to understand Peirce's continuum. Lane's "Peirce Triadic Logic Revisited" (Lane 1999) studies the emergence of "boundary propositions" related to breaches of continuity and views Peirce's *triadic logic* as a natural logic concerning the "ink blot," mediating triadicity and continuity. Herron's "C. S. Peirce's Theories of Infinitesimals" (Herron 1997) compares Peirce infinitesimals with Abraham Robinson's infinitesimals in nonstandard analysis, Edward Nelson's model in set theory, and Anders Kock's model in synthetic differential geometry. On another level, Ehrlich's "The Absolute Arithmetic Continuum and Its Peircean Counterpart" (Ehrlich 2010) shows how, through John Conway's surreals in von Neumann–Bernays–Gödel set theory, an *absolute arithmetic continuum* can be constructed, which unifies reals and ordinals and which partially models Peirce's continuum. In fact, Conway's surreal numbers No, containing "all numbers great and small," restricted to the substructure No_P of finite and infinitesimal numbers, captures well the big size (supermultitudinousness) of Peirce's continuum.

Nevertheless, a *full global* model for Peirce's continuum, which encompassed all of its generic/supermultitudinous, reflexive/inextensible, and modal/plastic characteristics (Zalamea 2001, 53; 2012, 9) was still to be imagined, against all cutting prejudices of the "experts" involved (including this writer). As often happens in mathematics, the solution turned out to be as simple, as deep. Francisco Vargas (2015) combined two powerful ideas to produce a straightforward ZFC model for Peirce's continuum, something that

Definition 1.1 *For $\alpha \in \text{Ord} \smallsetminus \{0\}$ let $\langle \mathcal{C}_\alpha, <_\alpha \rangle$ be defined as the set of α-real sequences with the lexicographical order.*

Definition 1.3 *Let $\langle \mathcal{C}_{Ord}, <_{Ord} \rangle$ be defined as*

- $\mathcal{C}_{Ord} = \bigcup_{\alpha \in Ord} \mathcal{C}_\alpha$
- *For any $x, y \in \mathcal{C}_{Ord}$ we define $x <_{Ord} y$ iff, for $\alpha = \min(\text{dom}(x), \text{dom}(y))$, $x \restriction \alpha <_\alpha y \restriction \alpha$*

Definition 1.4 *For $x, y \in \mathcal{C}_{Ord}$ we have that xEy iff $\text{dom}(y) < \text{dom}(x)$ and $x \restriction \text{dom}(y) = y$.*

Definition 1.5 *For $x \in \mathcal{C}_{Ord}$ let $\mathcal{M}_x$, the monad associated to x, be defined as the class of elements $y \in \mathcal{C}_{Ord}$ such that yEx.*

Theorem 1.6 *For any $x \in \mathcal{C}_{Ord}$*

$$\langle \mathcal{M}_x, <_{Ord}, E \rangle \simeq \langle \mathcal{C}_{Ord}, <_{Ord}, E \rangle$$

FIGURE 17.3 A full model for Peirce's continuum (Vargas and Moore 2021).

seemed in principle very difficult, or almost impossible: (1) first, a sheaf of copies of the real line (see Definition 1.1) is iterated along the class of all ordinals (Definition 1.3) (for an English version, see Vargas and Moore 2021, 334–335); (2) second, the lexicographic order relation obtained in the iterated model is inverted ("Order E," Definition 1.4) (Vargas and Moore 2021, 335). The result produces an infinitely ordinal-iterated tree of real lines, with its branches looking down (via E). Through that extremely simple characteristic, any local, partial cut in the tree ("Monad," Definition 1.5) (Vargas and Moore 2021, 336) turns out to be isomorphic to the global, whole tree (Theorem 1.6, six lines in the proof!) (Vargas and Moore 2021, 336).

From there, the main generic/supermultitudinous, reflexive/inextensible properties of Peirce's continuum are obtained at once, and with some more detail, modalities can be defined and developed through ordinal levels and ramifications. There are no more points whatsoever, only extended parts, and a continuous weldedness governs the model, as predicted by Peirce (Vargas and Moore 2021, 337–340).

5. The Existential Graphs

Last, but not least, we turn to the existential graphs (EG), in Peirce's words, his chef-d'oeuvre (Letter to Jourdain, 1908, cfr. Roberts 1973, 110). For the first exhaustive presentation of EG, see Pietarinen (2020–2021), and for a survey, see Bellucci and Pietarinen's chapter in this handbook. Peirce invented his EG (*c.* 1896) to cover diagrammatically a wide diversity of logics, ranging from classical propositional calculus (alpha graphs), to classical first-order logic (beta graphs), to modal calculi (gamma graphs I) and second-order logic (gamma graphs II). Over a blank sheet of assertion (representing truth), cuts are made (representing negation, via an alpha language, and representing possibilities, via a gamma language), which divide the sheet in nested cut regions. Following precise control rules, one can introduce, eliminate, and transmit information around those nets (in particular, via a beta language, one can extend, or restrict, a line of identity along the cuts, representing the existential quantifier: this is the reason for the generic name "existential graphs"). The simultaneous axiomatization of classical propositional calculus and purely relational first-order logic, with five uniform generic rules (double alpha cuts, insertion, erasure, iteration, and deiteration), renders explicit technical common roots for both calculi, which have been entirely ignored in all other available presentations of classical logic. The same rules detect, in the context of alpha language, the handling of classical negation and conjunction and, in the context of beta language, the handling of the existential quantifier: something just unimaginable for any logic student raised into Hilbert-type logic systems. The calculi show thus that there exists a kernel, a "real general" for classical thought, a kernel that, in some representational contexts, gives rise to the classical modes of connection and that, in other contexts, gives rise to the classical modes of quantification. For a general discussion of the mathematical, methodological, and philosophical aspects of EG, see Zalamea (2010b, 2012), and for the strong connections of EG with Peirce's overall architecture, see Zalamea (2010a).

EG remained ignored for sixty years—in good part due to Willard Quine's infamous review, where he qualified EG as some sort of "good entertainment" (Quine 1934, 553)—until a remarkable situation emerged at the beginning of the 1960s, when two independent PhD dissertations in Illinois delved duly into EG. On the one hand, Don Roberts's "The Existential Graphs of Charles S. Peirce" (Roberts 1963) offered a thorough description of the genesis of the EG, its diagrammatic achievements, and its philosophical bottoms. On the other hand, Jay Zeman's "The Graphical Logic of C. S. Peirce" (Zeman 1964) provided the first complete technical proofs of the deep logical equivalences associated to EG: alpha graphs equivalent to classical propositional logic (chapter 1 of the thesis), beta graphs equivalent to first-order logic (chapter 2), and a variety of gamma graphs equivalent to C. I. Lewis's modal logic systems S4, S4.2, and S5 (chapter 3).

Nevertheless, after these exceptional achievements, only appreciated by some scattered Peirce scholars and not truly valued by logicians, mathematicians, or philosophers alike, another thirty years went by without new important contributions in the field. Robert Burch's *A Peircean Reduction Thesis: The Foundations of Topological Logic* (Burch 1991) introduced a new combinatorial reading of composition (PAL for "Peircean algebraic logic"), related to beta combining valences in EG, and proved in a definitive way that ternary relations cannot be reduced to binary and unary relations *over a language of continuous operators (junctions)* on relations. Burch naturally captured thus Peirce's *topological logic*, going beyond the discrete operations usually employed in set theory (relations via ordered pairs). Opening entire new perspectives, and introducing category theory techniques to model the graphs, Geraldine Brady and Todd Trimble's "A Categorical Interpretation of C. S. Peirce's Propositional Logic Alpha" (Brady and Trimble 2000a) showed that (i) every (classical) alpha graph gives rise to an algebraic operation in a *Lawvere algebraic theory* (particular case of a monoidal category), and (ii) the (classical) alpha deduction rules are factorized through Maxwell Kelly's "functorial forces." Brady and Trimble discovered thus the existence of an *universal algebraic bottom* (semantics) behind the pragmatics of the existential graphs: (i) association of operations to graphs, and (ii) association of forces to rules (for a complementary approach, see Prada (2012). Further, Brady and Trimble (2000b) began to explore some category theory modeling (Joyal–Street diagrams, relational allegories) for beta graphs, a road still to be fully cleared.

Many mathematical perspectives have been offered to understand EG: combinatorial topology, topological logic, algebraic logic, nonstandard logics, category theory, graph theory, game theory, computer science, artificial intelligence, complex variables, etc. Pietarinen's current mastery of the graphs (Pietarinen 2020–2021) was preceded by many works dedicated to EG (see, e.g., Pietarinen 2006, 2016), where a blend of semiotic, informational, logical, and graph-theoretic tools offered a strong basis to capture the entanglements between EG and Peirce's pragmaticist architecture. Further, Ma and Pietarinen (2018) have offered a thorough study of Peirce's gamma graphs, proving completeness theorems for fifteen modal logics associated to diverse rules for the broken cut. In a similar vein, exploring EG with alternative tools, Atarashi painstakingly dissects the compositional construction (Atarashi 2016) and the transformational behavior (Atarashi 2020) of the beta graphs. In contrast, building on his expertise in computer science, John Sowa has been presenting an alternative graphical system (conceptual graphs, Sowa 2008) closely related to EG, and has studied the bridges (Sowa 2013) between Peirce's graphs, his own conceptual graphs, and common logic (EGIF, for "existential graph interchange format," Sowa 2016).

Finally, special mention is due to what has certainly become the center of the mathematical study of EG in the world. Arnold Oostra's school, situated in Ibagué, Colombia, a far distant, abandoned academic place that reminds us of the isolation of Peirce's Arisbe, has produced in the past twenty years some twenty first-rate undergraduate and master's dissertations on Peirce's logical work, from modern mathematical perspectives. The completeness proofs for alpha, beta, and gamma systems (as well as an alpha decision method, Oostra 2016) have acquired a fully rigorous technical support through Oostra's school, something not entirely accomplished in Roberts's (1963) or Zeman's (1964) dissertations (for a final presentation of these results, see Oostra (2021). Oostra was the first to extend Peirce's graphs to a nonclassical realm, constructing new diagrams for *intuitionistic logic* (IEG), adapting the inference rules, and proving completeness (Oostra 2010, 2011). One of his main results shows that an intuitionistic IEG implication yields a classical EG implication (Oostra 2010, 49–50), but not conversely, revealing that the true topological difference between those logics consists, in diagrammatic terms, in allowing some sort of separation, but not glueing (see Figure 17.4). The importance of IEG must be emphasized, since it provides the first deep, underlying, intrinsic natural connection between Peirce's topo/logical ideas and topology (the natural models for intuitionism being topological spaces, according to Alfred Tarski).

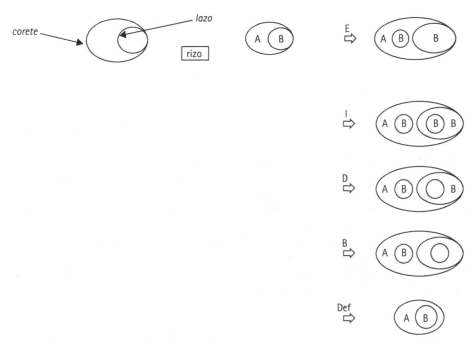

FIGURE 17.4 Intuitionistic existential graphs and a proof that intuitionistic implication forces classical implication (Oostra 2010).

Going beyond, Oostra has lately begun to explore *spatial* extensions of the EG, in nonplanar elementary surfaces, such as the cylinder, the sphere, or the torus (Oostra 2019a, 2019b), showing a yet mysterious interdependence between the different shapes of the sheet of assertion and the different logics therein inscribed. The developments of EG in these two-dimensional Riemann surfaces, nonisomorphic to the plane (by their compactness or their genus > 1) (for a complex variable anticipation, see Zalamea 2010c), may be one of the most intriguing and potentially fruitful developments of the *Logic of the Future* (Pietarinen 2020–2021).

References

Arengas, Gustavo. 2019. "La máxima pragmática peirceana: modelos categóricos, dualización, aproximaciones algebraicas y modalizaciones lógicas." PhD diss., Universidad Nacional de Colombia.

Atarashi, Shigeyuki. 2016. "The Dot Reading of Graphs in Peirce's Existential Graphs." *Cuadernos de Sistemática Peirceana* 8:119–135.

Atarashi, Shigeyuki. 2020. "An Alternative Reformulation of the Transformation Rules in the Beta Part of Peirce's Existential Graphs." In *Diagrammatic Representation and Inference. Diagrams 2020*, edited by Ahti-Veikko Pietarinen, Peter Chapman, Leonie Bosveld-de Smet, Valeria Giardino, James Corter, and Sven Linker, 187–201. New York: Springer.

Brady, Geraldine, and Todd Trimble. 2000a. "A Categorical Interpretation of C. S. Peirce's Propositional Logic Alpha." *Journal of Pure and Applied Algebra* 149: 213–239.

Brady, Geraldine, and Todd Trimble. 2000b. "A String Diagram Calculus for Predicate Logic and C. S. Peirce's System Beta." Preprint.

Burch, Robert. 1991. *A Peircean Reduction Thesis. The Foundations of Topological Logic*. Lubbock: Texas Tech University Press.

Downard, Jeffrey. 2015. "On the Hypotheses That Lie at the Bases of Discrete Systems of Mathematics: Drawing on Peirce's Phenomenology." *Cuadernos de Sistemática Peirceana* 7: 41–100.

Ehrlich, Philip. 2010. "The Absolute Arithmetic Continuum and Its Peircean Counterpart." In *New Essays on Peirce's Mathematical Philosophy*, edited by Matthew Moore, 235–281. Chicago: Open Court.

Havenel, Jérôme. 2006. "Logique et mathématique du Continu chez Charles Sanders Peirce." PhD diss., École des hautes études en sciences sociales.

Havenel, Jérôme. 2010. "Peirce's Topological Concepts." In *New Essays on Peirce's Mathematical Philosophy*, edited by Matthew Moore, 283–322. Chicago: Open Court.

Herron, Timothy. 1997. "C. S. Peirce's Theories of Infinitesimals." *Transactions of the Charles S. Peirce Society* 33, no. 3 (Summer): 590–645.

Kauffman, Louis. 2001. "The Mathematics of Charles Sanders Peirce." *Cybernetics & Human Knowing* 8 (1–2): 79–110.

Lane, Robert. 1999. "Peirce's Triadic Logic Revisited." *Transactions of the Charles S. Peirce Society* 35, no. 2 (Spring): 284–311.

Ma, Minghui, and Ahti-Veikko Pietarinen. 2018. "Gamma Graph Calculi for Modal Logics." *Synthese* 195: 3621–3650.

Maddalena, Giovanni. 2012. "Peirce's Incomplete Synthetic Turn." *The Review of Metaphysics* 65 (3): 613–640.

McCurdy, William James. 2016. "Peirce's Composability-of-Relations Theorem: A Proof in the Combinatorial Topology of the Logic of Relations." *Cuadernos de Sistemática Peirceana* 8: 163–189.

Moore, Matthew. 2010. "Peirce's Cantor." In *New Essays on Peirce's Mathematical Philosophy*, edited by Matthew Moore, 323–362. Chicago: Open Court.

Moore, Matthew. 2015. "Peirce's Prepunctual Continuum." *Cuadernos de Sistemática Peirceana* 7: 128–139.

Murphey, Murray. 1961. *The Development of Peirce's Philosophy*. New York: Harvard University Press.

Oostra, Arnold. 2010. "Los gráficos Alfa de Peirce aplicados a la lógica intuicionista." *Cuadernos de Sistemática Peirceana* 2: 25–60.

Oostra, Arnold. 2011. "Gráficos existenciales Beta intuicionistas." *Cuadernos de Sistemática Peirceana* 3: 53–78.

Oostra, Arnold. 2016. "Peirce's Decision Method for Alpha Graphs Revisited." *Cuadernos de Sistemática Peirceana* 8: 119–135.

Oostra, Arnold. 2019a. "Existential Graphs on Nonplanar Surfaces." *Revista Colombiana de Matemáticas* 53(2): 205–219.

Oostra, Arnold. 2019b. "Representación compleja de los gráficos Alfa para la lógica implicativa con conjunción". *Boletín de Matemáticas* 26(1): 31–50.

Oostra, Arnold. 2021. *Notas de lógica matemática*. Ibagué, Colombia: Universidad del Tolima.

Peirce, Charles Sanders. 1931–1958. *Collected Papers* (8 vols.) (eds. Charles Hartshorne, Paul Weiss, Arthur Burks). New York: Harvard University Press. (Referred to as CP.)

Peirce, Charles Sanders. 1992–1998. *The Essential Peirce* (2 vols.). Volume 1 edited by Christian Kloesel and Nathan Houser. Volume 2 edited by the Peirce Edition Project. Bloomington: Indiana University Press. (Referred to as EP.)

Peirce, Charles Sanders. 1997. *Pragmatism as a Principle and Method of Right Thinking* (Harvard Lectures 1903) (ed. Patricia Turrisi). Albany: State University of New York Press. (Referred to as PPM.)

Pietarinen, Ahti-Veikko. 2006. *Signs of Logic. Peircean Themes on the Philosophy of Languages, Games, and Communication.* New York: Springer.

Pietarinen, Ahti-Veikko. 2016. "On the Supreme Beauty of Logical Graphs." *Cuadernos de Sistemática Peirceana* 8: 5–40.

Pietarinen, Ahti-Veikko. 2019–2021. *Charles S. Peirce. The Logic of the Future. Writings on Existential Graphs.* 3 vols. in 4. Berlin: De Gruyter.

Prada, Juan Ricardo. 2012. "Gráficos existenciales Alfa y teoría de categorías." Undergraduate diss., Universidad del Tolima.

Quine, Willard Van Orman. 1934. "Review—*Collected Papers* of Charles Sanders Peirce—Volume IV." *Isis* XXII: 551–553.

Roberts, Don. 1963. "The Existential Graphs of Charles S. Peirce." PhD diss., University of Illinois.

Roberts, Don. 1973. *The Existential Graphs of Charles S. Peirce.* The Hague: Mouton.

Robin, Richard. 1997. "Classical Pragmatism and Pragmatism's Proof." In *The Rule of Reason. The Philosophy of Charles Sanders Peirce*, edited by Jacqueline Brunning and Paul Forster, 145–146. Toronto: University of Toronto Press.

Sowa, John. 2008. "Conceptual Graphs." In *Handbook of Knowledge Representation*, edited by Frank van Harmelen, Vladimir Lifschitz, and Bruce Porter, 213–237. Amsterdam: Elsevier.

Sowa, John. 2013. "From Existential Graphs to Conceptual Graphs." *International Journal of Conceptual Structures* 1: 39–72.

Sowa, John. 2016. "Diagrammatic Reasoning with EGs and EGIF." *Cuadernos de Sistemática Peirceana* 8: 41–76.

Vargas, Francisco. 2015. "Modelos y variaciones sobre las ideas peirceanas del continuo." *Cuadernos de Sistemática Peirceana* 7: 139–156.

Vargas, Francisco, and Matthew Moore. 2021. "The Peircean Continuum." In *The History of Continua: Philosophical and Mathematical Perspectives*, edited by Stewart Shapiro and Geoffrey Hellman, 328–346. Oxford: Oxford University Press.

Zalamea, Fernando. 2001. *El continuo peirceano.* Bogotá: Universidad Nacional de Colombia.

Zalamea, Fernando. 2010a. "A Category-Theoretic Reading of Peirce's System: Pragmaticism, Continuity, and the Existential Graphs." In *New Essays on Peirce's Mathematical Philosophy*, edited by Matthew Moore, 203–233. Chicago: Open Court.

Zalamea, Fernando. 2010b. *Los gráficos existenciales peirceanos.* Bogotá: Universidad Nacional de Colombia.

Zalamea, Fernando. 2010c. "Towards a Complex Variable Interpretation of Peirce's Existential Graphs." In *Ideas in Action. Proceedings of the Applying Peirce Conference*, edited by Matts Bergman, Sami Paavola, Ahti Pietarinen, and Henrik Rydenfelt, 254–264. Helsinki: Nordic Pragmatism Network.

Zalamea, Fernando. 2012. *Peirce's Logic of Continuity.* Boston: Docent Press. (Extended translation of *El continuo peirceano*, Bogotá: Universidad Nacional de Colombia, 2001, and *Los gráficos existenciales peirceanos*, Bogotá: Universidad Nacional de Colombia, 2010).

Zeman, Jay. 1964. "The Graphical Logic of C. S. Peirce." PhD diss., University of Chicago.

PART IV

PRAGMATISM

CHAPTER 18

PRAGMATISMS?

PHILIP KITCHER

1.

Like siblings in children's stories, participants in major philosophical movements tend to come in threes. Three classical rationalists (Descartes, Spinoza, and Leibniz) correspond to three British empiricists (Locke, Berkeley, and Hume.) Inevitably, then, there must be three American pragmatists—Peirce, James, and Dewey.

The habit of choosing trios brings unfortunate consequences, relegating important thinkers to subordinate status. But that is not my complaint in what follows. I am concerned with a common characterization of Charles Sanders Peirce. Unfortunately, many supposedly well-read philosophers are entirely ignorant of Peirce's writings. Almost everyone "knows," however, that Peirce founded a movement—pragmatism—and that his "principal successors" in this venture were William James and John Dewey.

Is that correct? Is there a single species of philosophy uniting these three intellectual giants?

2.

Peirce himself was clear that the idea of a philosophical stance embracing the three "classical pragmatists" required at least some qualification. In 1905, long after he had written the seminal articles on which "pragmatism was founded," he introduced a new term—'pragmaticism'—to mark out his own distinctive approach, not, as is sometimes claimed, to repudiate the figures identified as his companions-in-arms. To be sure, from 1905 on, he distinguished his own position from that endorsed by James, while acknowledging their intellectual kinship. His main purpose, however, was to distance himself from an increasing usage of 'pragmatism' to cover views he utterly rejected. Peirce regarded both James and James's Oxford ally, F. C. S. Schiller, as card-carrying members of a generic pragmatist party. Indeed, each of the pair had used new terms to distinguish his own species of pragmatism—"radical empiricism" in James's case, "humanism" in Schiller's. Peirce proposed to follow the trend, coining a neologism for his own views. "So then, the writer, finding his bantling 'pragmatism' so promoted, feels that it is time to kiss his child goodbye and relinquish it to its higher destiny; while to serve the precise purpose of expressing the original definition, he begs to announce the birth of the word 'pragmaticism,' which is ugly enough to be safe from kidnappers" (CP5.414, 1905).[1] As we shall discover, there are nuances in this sentence, and in the context that surrounds it, to illuminate the question whether pragmatism is a single philosophical movement.

Who were these kidnappers? Neither James nor Schiller, the former credited with "seeing" that radical empiricism "sufficiently answered" to Peirce's conception, "albeit with a certain difference in the point of view," the latter praised as "admirably clear and brilliant." The culprits, apparently, are writers for "the literary journals, where it [the word 'pragmatism': PK] gets abused in the merciless way that words have to expect when they fall into literary clutches" (CP5.414, 1905).

Peirce published these passages two years before James's widely read and influential *Pragmatism* appeared. The two had long been friends, exchanging ideas for decades, and Peirce had probably seen drafts of the lecture James had given in 1898 at the University of California. Many of the formulations of the lecture—"The Pragmatic Method"—occur in crucial sections of *Pragmatism*. So, even in advance of James's more systematic account of pragmatism, Peirce is likely to have known the lines along which James would present the central ideas of the novel approach to philosophy. I conjecture that his judgment in 1905 was well informed. He probably understood what James had in mind when he spoke of pragmatism and of radical empiricism. If so, nothing in *Pragmatism* should have changed his evaluation of James as an ally.[2]

Yet James clearly didn't share Peirce's anxieties about the lax usage of 'pragmatism.' Apparently he was not bothered by the alleged contamination to which the literary journals had subjected Peirce's "bantling." Although James had long presented himself as a radical empiricist—as well as a pragmatist—he didn't find it necessary to opt for the former label, and thus to give the famous lectures a different title. For the rest of his life, both 'pragmatism' and 'radical empiricism' remained options for James in presenting his ideas. Why was Peirce so linguistically sensitive, where James was not?[3]

Let's take a look at how James understood pragmatism, not only in the systematic introduction he published in 1907, or in the lecture that preceded it almost a decade earlier, but also in the place where he was most concerned to be precise (and concise.)

3.

In 1902, James wrote an entry under "pragmatism" for Baldwin's *Dictionary* (a work devoted to explaining psychological vocabulary.) It is hardly surprising that James was invited to provide this entry, given the enthusiasm with which his *Principles* of Psychology (published in 1890) had been greeted. Nor should anyone, including Peirce, have been any less enthusiastic about the dictionary entry. Pragmatism is "the doctrine that the whole 'meaning' of a conception expresses itself in practical consequences, consequences either in the shape of conduct to be recommended, or in that of experiences to be expected if the conception be true; which consequences would be different if it were untrue, and must be different from the consequences by which the meaning of other conceptions is in turn expressed" (James 1978, 94). A second sentence points to the moral that conceptions don't differ unless they have different consequences, and a third remarks on the methodological gains stemming from tracing differences in consequences. After that, James the lexicographer is done.

Peirce ought to have approved. James offers a friendly amendment to the cloudier version presented in the original formulation of the pragmatic maxim (in "How to Make Our Ideas Clear"; CP5.401–402, 1878) and in the presentation in the 1905 article: "the theory that a *conception*, that is, the rational purport of a word or other expression, lies exclusively in its conceivable bearing upon the conduct of life; so that obviously nothing that might not result from experiment can have any direct bearing upon conduct, if one can define accurately all the conceivable experimental phenomena which the affirmation or denial of a concept could imply, one will have a complete definition of the concept, and *there is absolutely nothing more in it*. For this doctrine [I] invented the name *pragmatism*" (CP5.412, 1905). This view is more tortuous and tangled than James's three sentences, but substantially in agreement with them. Peirce and James both identify pragmatism with a central doctrine, the *pragmatic maxim*: to understand an expression, look for its potential consequences in action and experience.

Commentators have probed the status of the maxim, wondering, for example, if tracing consequences *replaces* the definition a dictionary provides, or whether attention to consequences *supplements* the definition, by providing an *exposition* or *development*, enabling the expression to be used (I incline to the latter option; Christopher Hookway [2012] provides a lucid and thorough treatment of many related issues in his chapter 9.) Those discussions are not pertinent to our present purposes. On the face of it, as we have seen, Peirce and James appear to use the same expressions in characterizing pragmatism.

But, mindful of the maxim, perhaps we should attend to the effects their acceptance of it has on their conduct.

4.

What does Peirce do with the tool he has offered? In his original presentation, immediately after telling readers that we attain "clearness of apprehension" by considering "what effects, that might conceivably have practical bearings, we conceive the object of our conception to have" (CP5.402, 1878), he turns to examples that illustrate his counsel. The first few concern concepts from physics. The examples of *hardness*[4] and *weight* offer an easy entry, before he considers *force* (a concept that, as he surely knew, often causes problems for students, who struggle to grasp it.) Here, then, Peirce is concerned with reforming the language used in a branch of science (indeed, the branch he regards as epitomizing proper scientific inquiry.) Famously, the article concludes with applying the maxim to two well-entrenched—and problematic—philosophical notions, the twin concepts of *reality* and *truth*. Does Peirce think that what is needed (in a relatively mild vein) to clarify high-status sciences is required far more urgently in philosophical discussions?

Apparently so. When we turn to the 1905 article, that thought pervades the entire discussion. Peirce begins by suggesting that philosophy has been led astray because many of those who attempt to philosophize lack the experience, and consequently the mental habits, of the laboratory scientist. Occasionally, in the most fruitful writings of the most fruitful philosophers, he has found "strains of thought that recalled the ways of the laboratory," and in these instances he has "felt he might trust to them" (CP5.412, 1905). No surprise why: these rare passages reveal something like the pragmatic maxim at work.

Because the maxim is so rarely applied by philosophers, even by the great figures of the past, philosophy needs reform. Philosophical discussions should come to resemble those scientists have with one another. Peirce offers a very specific plan for realizing the goal. Those who "deplore the present state of that study [philosophy]" and "who are intent upon rescuing it . . . and bringing it to a condition like that of the natural sciences" ought to give up "contemning each the work of most others" and instead "cooperate, stand on one another's shoulders, and multiply incontestible results" (CP5.413, 1905). To achieve this goal, they must reconstruct the language they employ. Peirce envisages a new "philosophical nomenclature," a vocabulary whose terms have fixed meanings, in accordance with the pragmatic maxim, formed so that the meanings are transparent (at least to people with a grasp of "prefixes and suffixes," and, perhaps, other root morphemes.) Once the linguistic reforms have taken place, and been absorbed by the philosophical community, its members can return to their traditional work, re-posing the central questions of philosophy and, no longer wandering in the fogs of the past, collaborating productively, without misunderstandings and the acrimony they generate, and thus building patiently toward answers, just as their colleagues in the mature sciences do.

If the ambition to reform philosophy in this way is viewed as the center of Peirce's philosophical stance, regarded as his conception of the consequences of following the pragmatic maxim in philosophy, many apparently puzzling features of his work fall into place. His taste for metaphysical questions becomes explicable. Inquiries into the order of nature, or the nature of time, or "the reality of generals" are not debarred as misguided ventures. What is needed is to cut away the imprecision of traditional philosophical language, discard the rubbish of the opaque formulations of them, and use the new nomenclature to pursue them scientifically. Peirce's lifelong interest in refining logic expresses his wish for clear methods to carry out the work of reform. The attention he gives to drawing distinctions among various types of signs and the apparently obsessive interest in finding a transparent label for a particular conception are no longer mysterious. Guided by the pragmatic maxim, philosophy's task is first to bring order to the language it will deploy, then to reformulate the traditional questions that gave birth to the philosophical enterprise, and to resolve them. The queen of the sciences is to exhibit the virtues of her subjects.

James, as we shall now see, heads off in a very different direction.

5.

As anyone who reads James's writings, and who reflects on Peirce's disdain for "literary writers" might already anticipate. For James is an elegant stylist, one of the most literary of philosophers, ready to quote poetry at the drop of a hat, to illustrate his points with vivid examples and well-told tales, often concerned, in the interests of style, to phrase the same idea in different (and questionably equivalent) ways. James was scientifically trained, able to teach scientific subjects at Harvard, and appreciated as a towering figure among scientists. (It is worth recalling that Harvard's psychology department inhabits William James Hall, while the philosophers' home is named for Emerson.) Nevertheless, not only are James's sciences strikingly different from those of interest to Peirce—who sometimes characterizes his friend as someone to whom the exact sciences, logic, mathematics and physics, are alien[5]—but also, as we shall soon discover, at the heart of James's philosophical preoccupations is a worry about remaking all human thought and culture in the images of the sciences.

Chapter (Lecture) 2 of *Pragmatism* contains a pivotal paragraph, consisting of three sentences (including one—the middle one—that is almost invariably quoted by people seeking to characterize either pragmatism or James's version of it.) Those sentences occur in a longer, equally pivotal, paragraph in the California lecture of 1898. They follow a passage in which James has appealed to "the principle of Peirce, the principle of pragmatism" to resolve the issue declared in the chapter's title: "What Pragmatism Means." In fact, James's formulation strays a little further from Peirce than the 1902 definition did, in that James treats the practical consequences that provide "clearness" in our conceptions to include expected sensations as well as prepared reactions. That allows him to illustrate the principle by quoting the "illustrious Leipzig chemist" Wilhelm Ostwald. In considering scientific debates, Ostwald suggests looking for whatever "experimental facts" would be different under the rival hypotheses. In cases where there were none, "the quarrel was as unreal as if, theorizing in primitive times about the raising of dough by yeast, one party should have invoked a 'brownie,' while another insisted on an 'elf' as the true cause of the phenomenon" (James 1975a, 29, 30).

At this point, James makes a transition to discussing philosophy, with his three-sentence paragraph.

> It is astonishing to see how many philosophical disputes collapse into insignificance the moment you subject them to this simple test of tracing a concrete consequence.

> There can *be* no difference anywhere that doesn't *make* a difference elsewhere—no difference in abstract truth that doesn't express itself in a difference in concrete fact and in conduct consequent upon that fact, imposed on somebody, somehow, somewhere, and somewhen. The whole function of philosophy ought to be to find out what definite difference it will make to you and me, at definite instants of our life, if this world-formula or that world-formula be the true one. (James 1975a, 30)

Peirce might be happy with the first sentence, reading 'insignificance' to point to the lack of difference in semantic meaning between the positions taken by the disputants in question, a lack that renders the supposed conflict empty. And, *perhaps*, that is what James had in mind in writing that sentence. By the time he has arrived at the third sentence, however, he is invoking a general idea of what philosophers should be doing, one entirely different from Peirce's picture of the community of scientific philosophers patiently revising their language and then constructively exchanging their transparently formulated ideas. *World-formulas??*—I fancy I hear Peirce's angry snort.[6]

As I've already noted, Peirce and James differed in their scientific roots and in their views about the relations between various sciences and philosophical practice. For Peirce, the physical sciences, especially those in which exactitude reigns, take precedence. James cleaves to the long-standing philosophical tradition in which philosophy and psychology are closely allied. Hence he starts *Pragmatism* with a chapter that Peirce probably viewed as unnecessary, if not misguided. (I wonder how many modern readers of *Pragmatism* agree that the philosophical action starts with Chapter 2.) That chapter starts by affirming the importance of the general view of the universe that a person has, that individual human being's "philosophy," a "world-formula"—"our individual way of just seeing and feeling the total push and pressure of the cosmos" (James 1975a, 9). It advances a psychological hypothesis. There are two major types of human temperaments. Some people are tough-minded, concerned with facts and impatient with abstract speculations; others are idealistic, believing, with Hamlet, that there are more things in heaven and earth than in their tough-minded friends' philosophies. Reflective people understand that there are virtues and vices on both sides of the divide. But they have trouble in understanding how to frame a "philosophy" that combines all the themes they find correct, or inspiring, or important, or attractive. As James had remarked in an earlier essay ("The Sentiment of Rationality," originally published in 1879; James 1979, 57–89), their efforts to do so typically fall short. Philosophy must step in to assist them.

The sentence about "the whole function of philosophy" develops the account of philosophy James had presented in that article, published almost thirty years before *Pragmatism* appeared. "What is the task which philosophers set themselves to perform; and why do they philosophize at all? Almost everyone will immediately reply: They desire to attain a conception of the frame of things which shall on the whole be more rational than that somewhat chaotic view which everyone by nature carries about with him under his hat" (James 1979, 57). Philosophers bring order to chaos. The chaos arises from the difficulties of balancing the competing claims of tough- and tender-mindedness.

Pragmatism is a strategy for addressing the problem. It succeeds by making particular parts of the formulations of our tough-minded or tender-minded tendencies concrete, linking them to action and experience. But, as James took pains to point out to his Californian audience, the task of philosophy must always remain unfinished, for there are always facets of the inarticulate positions toward which our temperaments are drawn to require further work in linking them to concrete particularities.

> It is true that a certain shrinkage of values often seems to occur in our general formulas when we measure their meaning in this prosaic and practical way. They diminish. But the vastness that is merely based on vagueness is a false appearance of importance, and not a vastness worth retaining. The x's, y's and z's always do shrivel, as I have heard a learned friend say, whenever at the end of your algebraic computation they change into so many plain a's, b's and c's, but the whole function of algebra is, after all, to get them into that more definite shape; and the whole function of philosophy ought to be to find out what definite difference it will make to you and me, at definite instants of our life, if this world-formula or that world-formula be the one which is true. (James 1978, 125)

So the philosophical task is to begin with admittedly vague conceptions, drawn up in inadequate efforts to capture features of the world celebrated by one or the other of the two species of temperament, and connect these to aspects of human life and conduct, so as to facilitate the ordering of the chaos, bubbling away under all those hats.

A philosopher who views the discipline as James does will pursue rather different projects from those favored by Peirce. Peirce starts with the existing disputes of philosophers and aims to clear them up through linguistic reform, inspiring a cooperative effort to solve them. For James, the Peircean project seems far too close to the ambitions of the "Rocky Mountain tough"—to what, today, is often called "scientism." The transparent language Peirce envisages emerges, term by term, without regard for whether some larger inchoate whole is diminished. Indeed, James appears—not only in *Pragmatism*, but throughout his whole corpus, as quite uninterested in *linguistic* reform. What moves him is the need to redirect philosophy to what he conceives as its central mission: to appraise the questions philosophers discuss, and to change the agenda.

So, when he worries about the insignificance of many philosophical disputes, he may not be claiming that the bone of contention is semantically deficient, "meaningless." What is on his mind likely reflects a different sense of the ambiguous word "significant." Reading the first sentence in light of the third, I suggest that he is seeing the disputes as unimportant, as distractions from the proper work of philosophy.

For the questions Peirce wants to regiment and resolve in his linguistic reforms are not always—or even often—connected with James's "whole function." James wants to address the confusions of ordinary folk, not any esoteric metaphysical conundrums. Indeed, as so much of his work, early and late, reveals, his main impetus is the felt need to resist the imperialism of the physical sciences, their claim to be able to account for everything, with the consequent elimination of value from the world. The tough-minded philosopher emerges in his pages as intent on viewing the sciences as supplying the answers to any question it is proper to pose—and thereby ruling out the religious and ethical issues James is so anxious to retain, to clarify, and to resolve. His task is to *reconcile* the legitimate claims and insights of the sciences with the insights of the tender-minded—not to dismiss the latter as muddled failures to accept a comprehensive ("disenchanted") world-picture.

Both Peirce and James want to apply the pragmatic maxim to philosophy. When they do so they draw radically different—and *opposed*—consequences for conduct. Thus, as Peirce interpreted the maxim, and as James defined it for Baldwin's dictionary, their conceptions of the maxim must be distinct. Consequently, despite linguistic agreement on the supposedly characteristic feature of pragmatism, their "pragmatisms" diverge at the root. Pragmaticism is far less closely related to Jamesian pragmatism than Peirce took it to be.

6.

Moreover, if the pragmatic maxim is taken to be the central commitment of any pragmatist, Dewey should no longer be counted as part of the movement. To be sure, like both Peirce and James, he aims to reform philosophy, but the application of the maxim plays a negligible role in his envisaged program. The ills of philosophy, as he diagnoses them, largely proceed from the tendency of philosophical discussions to drift away from the problems arising in human experience. Questions once introduced to respond to live issues in people's lives, arising at a particular stage of human history and typically generated by the social conditions of the age, fade in importance as human culture evolves. Philosophers who continue to debate them in their traditionally approved forms fail to see how they are no longer relevant—not because they have been solved, but simply because the root difficulties have been overcome in other ways. At best, the allegedly "timeless questions" require very different formulations to cope with the exigencies of the age. So, for example, Dewey would view continued epistemological inquiries into the proper definition of "S knows that p" or further discussion of ancient forms of skepticism as entirely insignificant in a world where people need to navigate the Internet to find trustworthy sources of information. What kinds of characteristics should they use to select sites where they can avoid being misled and can discover what they need to know?

For Dewey, as for James, revising the philosophical agenda to enable philosophers to perform their proper task is the core of pragmatism. Holding that a faulty conception of experience prompts "all the questions of epistemology with which the technical student of philosophy is so familiar, and which have made modern philosophy in especial so remote from the understanding of the everyday person and from the results and processes of science" (Dewey 1982, 150), he lambasts "vain metaphysics and idle epistemology" (Dewey 1982, 151). Insofar as the pragmatic maxim occurs here, it is conceived as demanding a connection between the issues philosophers investigate and the problems of human life—in the current social setting. One of his most provocative suggestions for delimiting the province of philosophy characterizes the subject "*as the general theory of education*" (Dewey 1980, 338). This proposal is supported by an oblique appeal to the pragmatic maxim in the only version in which he uses it: "If a theory makes no difference in educational endeavor, it must be artificial. The educational point of view enables one to envisage the philosophic problems where they arise and thrive, where they are at home, and where acceptance or rejection makes a difference in practice" (Dewey 1980, 338). Without that tie, philosophy becomes "a sentimental indulgence for the few" (Dewey 1980, 338).

In his call for "reconstruction in philosophy," the point is developed through a critique of those who see themselves as pursuing "truth for its own sake" (Dewey 1982, 164). Theory and knowledge, he tells us, are "ends in themselves for some persons. But these persons represent a social division of labor; and their specialization can be trusted only when such persons are in unobstructed cooperation with other social occupations, sensitive to others' problems and transmitting results to them for wider application in action. When this social relationship of persons particularly engaged in carrying on the enterprise of knowing is forgotten and the class becomes isolated, inquiry loses stimulus and purpose. It degenerates into sterile speculation, a kind of intellectual busy work carried on by socially absent-minded men" (Dewey 1982, 164). The kinship with James's concerns about the "collapse into insignificance" of many philosophical discussions should be evident.

Yet, although James and Dewey are closer than either is to Peirce, there are large differences between their conceptions of how pragmatism brings philosophy back to its proper task. James sees one enduring problem: that of reconciling science and values, or integrating the insights of the tough- and tender-minded, so as to display the implications of a world-formula for experience, and thus ordering some of the chaos of people's conceptions of "the frame of things." For Dewey, however, who sometimes characterizes his position as "instrumentalism," philosophical problems arise in many areas of human life. James's big issue is one of them, possibly reduced in scale, and viewed not as "timeless" but tied to the circumstances of a specific age. Dewey sees it as one of recognizing values in a world of facts, and of preserving what is valuable in religion without falling into superstition. But there are many other topics requiring philosophical treatment: understanding how existing educational practices distort young people's growth, diagnosing the limitations of democratic institutions, trying to discover ways of bringing art back into people's everyday lives, and resolving tensions between cultivating individuality and fostering community and fellow-citizenship. In Isaiah Berlin's famous comparison, with respect to philosophical investigations, Dewey is a fox and James a hedgehog.

Peirce undoubtedly influenced both James and Dewey. Yet, if adherence to some univocal pragmatic maxim is to be the criterion for being a pragmatist, there is no single "pragmatism" shared by all three. If Peirce was the first pragmatist, it seems he was also the last.

7.

That conclusion may well seem absurd. To resist it, we might attend to the points at which James and Dewey appear to develop prominent Peircean themes. Two of these are especially evident: the approach to the concept of truth and Peirce's "belief–doubt" model of inquiry. So let's abandon the pragmatic maxim as the gold standard for pragmatism and explore whether we can find closer kinship elsewhere.

Like Peirce before him, James finds popular accounts of truth defective, not because they are wrong but because they are unhelpful. Peirce preserves the idea that true statements "correspond to" (or "agree with," or "represent") reality in accepting the duality of the two concepts. The famous exposition reads: "The opinion which is fated to be ultimately agreed to by all who investigate, is what we mean by the truth, and the object represented in this opinion is the real. That is the way I would explain reality" (CP5.407, 1878). The final sentence, rarely quoted in discussions of "Peirce's account of truth," is a reminder of where this phase of the discussion began: in an effort to "consider a conception which particularly concerns [logic], that of *reality*" (CP5.405, 1878). His aim is to clarify the notion of reality, and the road to the goal runs through the concept of truth. Of course, if that concept were completely clear, if we understood the formula given by defenders of the correspondence theory, there would be no need to consider how people come to make judgments about truth. Clarity with respect to truth would yield clarity about reality. Since the formula is empty, work must be done to show how the notion of truth can be used. After that work is complete, the idea of representation can be reduced to licensing a particular kind of inference: we are allowed to move, for example, from

>'Snow is white' is true

to

>Snow is white (or even: Snow is white. Really!)

James makes the point more explicitly. The preface to *The Meaning of Truth*, a work devoted to defending the approach to the concept of truth he views himself as deriving from Peirce, opens by identifying the discussion of truth offered in *Pragmatism* as "pivotal." He recalls his agreement with defenders of the correspondence theory.

> "Truth," I there say, "is a property of certain of our ideas. It means their 'agreement' as falsity means their disagreement, with 'reality.' Pragmatists and intellectualists [correspondence theorists] both accept this definition as a matter of course...."
>
> "Where our ideas [do] not copy definitely their object, what does agreement with the object mean? Pragmatism asks its usual question. 'Grant an idea or belief to be true,' it says, 'what concrete difference will its being true make in anyone's actual life?'" (James 1975b, 3; cf. James 1975a, 96, 97)

The trouble with the agreed-upon definition is that we can't use it to answer this question. Instead, James supplies an exposition that does make connections to human conduct. When people are prepared to attach the label 'true' to a sentence, they are prepared to rely on that sentence, as they understand it, in their efforts to reach their goals. Hence, James arrives at his famous (notorious?) explanation of truth. "'*The true*,' to put it very briefly, is only the expedient in the way of our thinking, just as 'the right' is only the expedient in our way of behaving. Expedient in almost any fashion; and expedient in the long run and on the whole of course; for what meets expediently all the experience in sight won't necessarily meet all farther experiences equally satisfactorily. Experience, as we know, has ways of *boiling over*, and making us correct our present formulas" (James 1975a, 106; quoted in James 1975b, 4). The focus on the long run suggests a kinship with Peirce's exposition, offered three decades earlier. Yet, we might wonder, are they equivalent?

Formally, yes. Peirce's test for truth envisages a process of inquiry that attains (or potentially attains) a limit when all the relevant phenomena have been taken into account. James focuses on a person who adjusts beliefs in response to further experiences and finds that the sizes of the required adjustments grow smaller and smaller as the total corpus of phenomena grows ever larger. Viewed in this way, an important result from nineteenth-century mathematics yields the equivalence.

Cauchy resolved some of the confusions of real analysis by offering a precise definition of 'limit.' An infinite sequence of real numbers converges to a limit, just in case, for any number (however small but greater than zero), you can find a place in the sequence, beyond which all the following terms diverge from the limit by less than that number. Cauchy also provided a criterion for testing whether a particular sequence will converge to a limit: for any number (however small but greater than zero) you can find a place in the sequence, beyond which all the following terms differ from one another by less than that number. He then proved that the test picks out all and only the sequences counting as convergent by his definition.

James's exposition depends on an analog of the Cauchy test. When people find that the changes in belief they are forced to make become smaller and smaller as experiences pile up, they are entitled to think that they will continue to diminish in the future—and thus that there would be convergence in the ideal limit of inquiry. In fact, James improves on Peirce, offering an experiential basis for judging what will happen as inquiry proceeds indefinitely. I conjecture that Peirce, mathematician that he was, recognized the mathematical analogy and saw James as offering a friendly amendment.

So far, so good.

8.

Yet, as we probe more deeply, differences emerge. The most obvious of these lies in the conception of inquiry. James, on the one hand, envisages an *individual*, adjusting beliefs in the interests of achieving goals, possibly out of detached curiosity, but surely very often in practical activities oriented toward what the person singles out as most valuable. For Peirce, on the other hand, inquiry is a collective affair. Different members of a community start out with divergent beliefs. In their investigations, they "are animated by a cheerful hope that the processes of investigation, if only pushed far enough, will give one certain solution to each question to which they apply it" (CP5.407, 1878). It's no accident that Peirce gives this community a definite aim: they consist of "the followers of science" (CP5.407, 1878). Indeed, he tells us that convergence is typical of "all scientific research": "Different minds may set out with the most antagonistic force, but the process of investigation carries them by a force outside of themselves to one and the same conclusion" (CP5.407, 1878).

This idea of inexorability in inquiry surfaces in a Peircean footnote. His exposition contains a word he recognized as having, at least for some readers, disconcerting overtones: *fated* to be ultimately agreed to? The footnote is designed to reassure. "Fate means merely that which is sure to come true, and can nohow be avoided" (CP5.407, 1878). But now arises an obvious question: What guarantees a particular outcome? Peirce's reply is easy to reconstruct: in "The Fixation of Belief," the precursor in this series of articles to "How to Make Our Ideas Clear," he had distinguished four major methods for forming beliefs. Now, in the present discussion, he relies on his earlier distinctions, recognizing how the inferior methods provoking the disputations of the past have been superseded by the method of science (CP5.406, 1878). Thus the exposition of truth would have been more completely and more explicitly developed by adding a clause: "The opinion which is fated to be ultimately agreed to by all who investigate, *following the method of scientific inquiry*, is what we mean by the truth." Greater explicitness only raises further questions, however. What exactly is the method of scientific inquiry? Why is it privileged?

Peirce takes the former question seriously—and pays less attention to the latter. It is not hard to see why. For there is an obvious threat of circularity. The methods of science would have epistemic priority, it would seem, just in case they were more reliable than others. But what constitutes reliability here? The most obvious suggestion would be that they are more likely than rival methods to lead inquirers to . . . the truth. Can Peirce avoid this Peircean circle?

His official view would take the methods of the sciences to be privileged in terms of their capacity for settling doubt. Yet this appears to introduce a worrying subjectivity: when a scientific inquiry ends, those who have pursued it are soothed and can rest contented. Their relaxed contentment can't, however, be warranted if, from this point on, they sleepily ignore potential challenges. Behind the idea of settling doubt is the thought of an objective success. The further course of experience will not "boil over" in ways that dissolve what has emerged from inquiry. James articulates this thought in his own characterization of truth, thereby explaining more adequately the privilege enjoyed by methods of scientific inquiry. By pursuing investigations in the ways scientists do, inquirers maximize the probability of arriving at beliefs that will survive the future challenges of experience. The conclusions emerging from scientific inquiries will enable those who accept them to address the practical problems confronting them, so that they can attain their goals.

A Peircean version of this approach might emphasize specific aims. Scientific communities have particular ends. Science, he might say, aims at prediction and control—perhaps at understanding as well. The methods adopted by scientific communities prove their worth in supplying techniques of prediction and control (maybe explanations too) that continue to prove successful in the further march of collective experience.

As far as I know, Peirce never developed his account of the privilege of science in this Jamesian way. He was far more interested in understanding, and improving, the methods of science. "How to Make Our Ideas Clear" concludes with an apologetic passage,[7] in which he promises his readers that the next article in the series will "return to the easily intelligible, and not wander from it again" (CP5.410, 1878). That article considers "the doctrine of chances" as "the science of logic quantitatively treated" (CP2.647, 1878). It is an early instance of a large corpus of methodological essays that establish Peirce as one of the most important logicians and philosophers of science of the nineteenth century.

The turn to methodology reflects a pragmatist appraisal of the significance of the question of privilege. His early appraisal of "the spirit of Cartesianism" advised his readers not to "pretend to doubt in philosophy what we do not doubt in our hearts" (CP5.265, 1868). Since he does not doubt the superiority of the method of science to its rivals, the issue of privilege appears idle. The serious task is to formulate the canons of good scientific inquiry as clearly as possible, to refine and improve them, and to apply the results as widely as possible.

Inquiry is initiated by doubt—*serious* doubt—and pursued by using the methods of science we can identify as proving their worth in the past. The community of scientists rightly accepts the results of inquiry, takes them to be true, and puts them to work. To be sure, practicing scientists recognize what contemporary philosophers call the "pessimistic induction on the history of science"—they know that beliefs confidently hailed as true in the past have been abandoned. Yet, with equal confidence they regard their practice as justified. For, in the past, holding the results of scientific inquiry to be true, and putting them to work, has had beneficial consequences. Subjecting what has emerged from scientific inquiry to the trial of further experience has sometimes (perhaps infrequently?) left the beliefs of the community unchanged. Those beliefs have survived triumphantly and become further entrenched. Yet, when the beliefs have been discarded, the scientific practice has also been successful. For by taking the results of inquiry to be true, and consequently putting them to work, the community has been led to *better* beliefs, capable of being deployed successfully across a larger range of contexts. Either way, the practice Peirce recommends is pragmatically justified. Heads, it wins; tails, it wins.

So emerges Peirce's "belief–doubt" model of scientific inquiry. Respond only to genuine doubt. Start inquiry when genuine doubt arises. Pursue inquiry by following the method of science. Close inquiry when doubt has been settled. Accept the results. Take them to be true—but don't be too "cock-sure" about them. Continue in this way. In the indefinite limit, you will arrive at the truth. It is "fated" to emerge from this process.

9.

Neither James nor Dewey would quarrel with this characterization of scientific inquiry. Indeed, it is implicit in James's—scientific—study of religious experience (James 1985) and explicit in Dewey's mature account of logic as the theory of inquiry (Dewey 1986). If commitment to the exposition of truth and the belief–doubt model is taken as the core of pragmatism, then we appear to have found a single movement uniting the three designated classical pragmatists. Since Peirce supplied the model, he is correctly viewed as the founder of that movement.

Not quite. For the agreement turns on the inclusion or exclusion of a qualifying adjective. James and Dewey would sign on to the belief–doubt model, as I have characterized it, if that model were regarded as characterizing *scientific* inquiry. Peirce regards science as supplying the pattern for *all* proper inquiry. Hence he takes the model to direct the form of all well-pursued inquiry—period. Here, James and Dewey would demur. For differing reasons.

One of the great Peircean insights lies in the appreciation of systematic inquiry as a collective business. Peirce breaks with Cartesian epistemology not only in rejecting artificial doubt and disavowing the search for foundations, but also in abandoning Descartes's simplifying assumption of setting aside the ways in which people learn from others. (Peirce is the first thinker to recognize the importance of social methodology, and to attempt to formalize it [CP7.139–157, 1879; CP5.158–161, 1902]). James, by contrast, focuses on the inquiries carried forward by individuals with goals that may be entirely separate from those pursued by community enterprises. His epistemology emphasizes features Peirce does not consider. As a result, he cannot accept the belief–doubt model in the form in which Peirce derives from the practices of the sciences.

"The Will to Believe," probably the most influential essay written by any American philosopher, starts from a Peircean point. The options among which people decide, James tells us, may be "living or dead," "forced or avoidable," or "momentous or trivial" (James 1979, 14). Here, he is moving toward a refinement of his friend's recommendation against launching inquiry when there is no genuine doubt. Investigations properly begin when the options are real possibilities for us, when we cannot sidestep decision-making, and when they *matter*. The last qualification adds a new dimension to Peirce's account. For we cannot assume that what matters is the same for all individuals, in the way that the goals attributed to science—prediction, control, and (maybe) understanding—serve as the touchstone for what scientific questions are worth pursuing. Recognizing this dimension prompts James to distinguish cases that the vision of a homogeneous community bound together by shared goals for inquiry would overlook.

He does so by recognizing "two ways of looking at our duty in the matter of opinion"—the imperative to "believe truth" overrides when people need information in order to attempt to reach their goals; the command to "shun error" takes precedence when accepting something false would ruin their hopes (James 1979, 24). Momentousness may arise in different ways, sometimes urging us to decide as soon as possible, on other occasions demanding caution. On James's account, then, the values assigned to outcomes—surely differing for different individuals—dictate how much evidence inquiry should generate to warrant acceptance. There's no uniform standard for settling doubt, independent of the importance of the consequences. The apparent unity behind accepting the outcomes of inquiry as true dissolves.

Famously, James deploys his distinctions to ward off a late-nineteenth-century skepticism shared by intellectuals who, like Peirce, are devotees of the thought that all inquiry should be conducted after the pattern exemplified by science—his targets are T.H. Huxley, John Tyndall, and W.K. Clifford ("that delicious *enfant terrible*" [James 1979, 17]). Just as we found a gap opening up between James and Peirce because of the former's opposition to the imperialism of the physical sciences, so too here—an apparently shared picture of inquiry turns out to mask major differences. Peirce, we might say, recognizes a monolithic method, characterizing not only the sciences but also all proper inquiry. James pleads for pluralism.

So also does Dewey, albeit on very different grounds. His early essay on Darwin's influence on philosophy recognizes that different branches of inquiry need to develop their own methods of investigation. Before Darwin, "the impact of the new scientific method upon life, mind and politics, had been arrested" (Dewey 1977a, 7) because methods of investigating the organic world had been unavailable. Through his *creative* work in developing an example of such methods, Darwin "freed the new logic for application to mind and morals and life" (Dewey 1977a, 7–8). Dewey's own account of that logic, elaborated most extensively in Dewey (1986), presents a general—nonformal—framework, within which particular domains of inquiry, those of the various sciences, as well as areas of human and social concern (ethics, politics, law, education, and many others), are to develop their own distinctive canons for proper pursuit of the investigations on which they focus. Dewey is not interested in the Peircean project of offering a formal account of method modeled on the physical sciences. He is deeply concerned with the transition envisaged in the Darwin essay: working out ways to pursue human questions more intelligently.

Moreover, he regards the various forms of inquiry as entangled. Physics cannot identify the kinds of questions to which it should devote itself until the ways in which various endeavors might contribute to the progress of human lives and of human societies have been analyzed and considered. Ultimately, the methods of any science must be judged in light of contributions to human goals—and those goals themselves assessed in light of what is genuinely valuable. So, at any historical stage, the judgment of the methods of the physical sciences awaits scrutiny of their advancement of what is worth pursuing, and that, in turn, can only be assessed in light of the best interrogation of human values the age can contrive. Peirce's bold idea of the truth as emerging from a collective endeavor, in which investigators fathom the structure of a fixed nature according to rules that logicians and methodologists can present formally, gives way to a radically different vision. Nature has no agenda to present to inquirers. Nor does it have a privileged language. The questions inquirers pose are those that matter to members of our species. The terms in which they are posed are those that prove helpful as people attempt to achieve their goals. And those goals themselves evolve in light of historically situated estimations of what is valuable.

Moreover, that vision has further consequences, conclusions from which Peirce would wish to distinguish himself. In his *Principles of Psychology*, James contends that the worlds different species inhabit are different. Because of variation in biological makeup, "how different must be the worlds in the consciousness of ant, cuttlefish, or crab!" (James 1981, 277; cf. also 274–278). Dewey adds to this thought the idea of the human experiential world as continually reconstructed in light of our evolving culture (Dewey 1981, 40). The world of our daily experience is an *ordered* world, one in which processes have beginnings and endings, things have spatiotemporal boundaries, entities are divided into kinds. Realists (like Peirce) suppose that, in the proper march of inquiry, these divisions will match the intrinsic structure of a reality awaiting human discovery. Dewey and James view that as an unnecessary metaphysical hypothesis. Applying the pragmatic maxim—the "principle of Peirce"!—they see the question of how much humans contribute to the ordering and how much is "really there" as idle. Inquiry into "nature" focuses on the world we experience, constantly remade in accordance with our changing purposes. So Dewey's epistemology thoroughly rejects the picture of human spectators responding to a static "reality" (Dewey 1984, *passim*), and James triumphantly declares that "truth happens to an idea" (James 1975b, 3).

10.

If conceived as a single movement, classical pragmatism is a scatter of themes, loosely connected to one another, some emphasized heavily and others firmly rejected, with different choices made by the three major figures who are usually associated with it. Perhaps Peirce was right to call pragmatism "a house at war against itself concerning not inconsiderable questions" (CN3:234, 1905). Peirce is plainly the author of some of the most striking ideas and theses, and both James and Dewey owe debts to him in these respects. Hence if you are a taxonomic lumper, you will view Peirce as the architect of a major philosophical movement. You might defend your lumping tendencies by noting that the three pragmatists have about as much in common as the three seventeenth-century rationalists.

A comparison with the British empiricists, however, might incline you to split the taxon. Perhaps there are radical empiricists, and humanists, and instrumentalists, and naturalists, and pragmaticists—with some authors straddling different groups. There was no single movement in the late nineteenth century, and even less in the revival of "pragmatism" in the early twenty-first. For the differences among contemporary neo-pragmatists—Richard Bernstein, Robert Brandom, Kate Elgin, Peter Godfrey-Smith, Susan Haack, Cheryl Misak, Sami Pihlström, Huw Price, Hilary Putnam, Ruth Anna Putnam, Richard Rorty, and others—are even more striking than those I have tried to expose. Even if you are inclined to think of a single classical pragmatism, accepting *one* neo-pragmatist movement might give you pause.

Too much lumping blinds commentators to nuances and begets simplifications of complex issues. It is easy to forget that philosophers emerge from distinct intellectual trajectories and have distinctive filiations to traditions and figures who precede them. I want to close with a brief reminder of the backgrounds from which Peirce, James, and Dewey emerged—and at the potential influence of a figure who loomed large in the cultural milieu in which they came of age.

11.

American education in the mid-nineteenth century tended to link philosophy to two areas of study regarded as adjacent to it: psychology and religion. The traces of those educational connections are evident in two of James's major works. He benefited from the exceptionally rich version of psychologically informed, religiously tinged philosophy available to undergraduates in the Harvard of his youth. Dewey received a lower-budget version of the orthodox way of fitting philosophy into the curriculum. At the University of Vermont, part of philosophy's mission was to develop a richer conception of Protestant Christianity. Psychology came later, in the graduate training he received at Johns Hopkins.

Peirce began very differently. He read Kant before he was in his teens, but the dominant mode of his education, before and after his career at Harvard, was in mathematics and in the physical sciences (particularly chemistry). Turning to philosophy, after advanced training in the sciences (and work for the geodetic survey), he side-stepped the post-Kantian developments of the standard American philosophy curriculum (in which both James and Dewey had been trained). He came to his mature reading of philosophers on his own terms, terms largely set by his experiences in the laboratory: he tells readers that "he himself may almost be said to have inhabited a laboratory from the age of six until long past maturity" (CP5.411, 1905).

But he also relates that he was "born and reared in the neighborhood of Concord—I mean in Cambridge—at the time when Emerson, Hedge, and their friends were disseminating the ideas that they had caught from Schelling, and Schelling from Plotinus, from Boehm, or from God knows what minds stricken with the monstrous mysticism of the East" (CP6.102, 1892). Peirce is confident that he has not "contracted any of that virus" (CP6.102, 1892). Perhaps, though, some "benignant form of the disease" has been "implanted" in him, prompting him to take up metaphysical topics

(CP6.102, 1892). Fortunately, though it has been modified by his mathematical and physical investigations.

Emerson was, of course, godfather to William James, a presence in the home of James's childhood. And, as Anuk Arudpragasam has shown, James's mature philosophy was pervaded by Emersonian influences, not only in the obvious places—the conceptions of religion in *Varieties of Religious Experience* and "The Will to Believe"—but also in James's approach to values (Arudpragasam, 2019). So too for Dewey. The moral psychology of *Human Nature and Conduct* is heavily indebted to themes in Emerson's writings. Moreover, in "Emerson—The Philosopher of Democracy," Dewey engages with critics (maybe like Peirce?) who deny that Emerson is a philosopher (Dewey 1977b, 184–192). He replies that Emerson *is* a philosopher, but not merely a philosopher—he works "by art, not by metaphysics" and is, throughout his varied writings, "a poet" (Dewey 1977b, 185).

The moral of these scraps of potted history should be evident: we should *expect* the kinds of divergences I have attempted to describe to occur among three philosophers whose connections to the previous generation of American culture are so diverse. Treating pragmatism as a single movement founded by Peirce easily extends to a faulty myth. American philosophy truly began when Peirce strode boldly onto the stage and founded an important philosophical movement. Peirce's contributions to the history of philosophy are enormous, but, without attention to the longer evolution of American thought, we are likely to misunderstand him and his alleged fellow pragmatists. Our appreciation for the three great "classical pragmatists" can be enriched if, from time to time, we suspend application of the label and consider their thoughts from a larger perspective, one that sensitive intellectual historians have thoroughly and illuminatingly given us (Kuklick 1976, 1985, 2001; Richardson 1995).[8]

Notes

1. References to Peirce's writings will be given by citing volume and paragraph number of the *Collected Papers*, edited by Charles Hartshorne and Paul Weiss; I refer to the edition published by Harvard University Press in the late 1950s and 1960s, where the parts of the original edition are rebound in four volumes, each containing two parts.
2. So far as I am aware, there is no direct evidence for my conjecture. However, since Peirce and James were regularly in touch during the 1890s, it seems unlikely that James would have introduced Peirce's "bantling" to the philosophical world without consulting his old friend in advance.
3. As Cornelis de Waal reminded me, James had once been quite concerned with how the movement should be named, preferring 'practicalism' to 'pragmatism.' However, by the late 1890s, he seems to have overcome his reservations about the latter title.
4. The treatment of 'hardness' seems particularly close to James's own illustrations of the practice of pragmatism. Peirce seems to have regretted its nominalistic tendencies, as his own predilections for realism about universals grew more pronounced. Perhaps, in

consequence, he came later to see the example that inspired James as setting James's pragmatism on a different path from the one he had chosen?
5. With some reason. Then, as now, physics and psychology differed in prestige. Moreover, as a scientist, James diverges from Peirce's image of the patient toiler in the laboratory, carefully gathering data and analyzing it.
6. Although, as Bruce Kuklick pointed out to me, this may be to assimilate Peirce too closely to his more recent admirers. Given his Kantian sympathies, Peirce might have been more sympathetic to the idea of a grand synthesis with an overarching architectonic than contemporary analytic philosophers tend to be.
7. I am grateful to Cornelis de Waal for the information that this passage may have been inspired by comments of the editor of *Popular Science* who had complained that Peirce's articles were wandering too far into metaphysics.
8. I am deeply grateful to Cornelis de Waal and to Bruce Kuklick for their generous and constructive comments on an earlier draft.

REFERENCES

Arudpragasam, Anuk. 2019. *Faith and Habit: Emersonian Themes in the Ethics of James and Dewey*, Doctoral dissertation, Columbia University.
Dewey, John. 1977a. "The Influence of Darwin on Philosophy," in *The Middle Works* Volume 4, Carbondale, University of Southern Illinois Press, 3–14.
Dewey, John. 1977b. "Emerson—The Philosopher of Democracy," in *The Middle Works* Volume 3, Carbondale, University of Southern Illinois Press, 184–192.
Dewey, John. 1980. *Democracy and Education*, The Middle Works Volume 9, Carbondale, University of Southern Illinois Press.
Dewey, John. 1981. *Experience and Nature*, The Later Works Volume 1, Carbondale, University of Southern Illinois Press.
Dewey, John. 1982. *Reconstruction in Philosophy*, The Middle Works Volume 12, Carbondale, University of Southern Illinois Press.
Dewey, John. 1984. *The Quest for Certainty*, The Later Works Volume 4, Carbondale, University of Southern Illinois Press.
Dewey, John. 1986. *Logic: The Theory of Inquiry*, The Later Works Volume 12, Carbondale, University of Southern Illinois Press.
Hookway, Christopher. 2012. *The Pragmatic Maxim*, Oxford: Oxford University Press.
Kuklick, Bruce. 1976. *The Rise of American Philosophy*, New Haven, CT: Yale University Press.
Kuklick, Bruce. 1985. *Churchmen and Philosophers*, New Haven, CT: Yale University Press.
Kuklick, Bruce. 2001. *A History of Philosophy in America, 1720–2000*; Oxford: Oxford University Press.
James, William. 1975a. *Pragmatism*, Cambridge, MA: Harvard University Press.
James, William. 1975b. *The Meaning of Truth*, Cambridge, MA: Harvard University Press.
James, William. 1978. *Essays in Philosophy*, Cambridge, MA: Harvard University Press.
James, William. 1979. *The Will to Believe, and Other Essays in Popular Philosophy*, Cambridge, MA: Harvard University Press.
James, William. 1981. *The Principles of Psychology*, Volume I, Cambridge, MA: Harvard University Press.

James, William. 1985. *The Varieties of Religious Experience*, Cambridge, MA: Harvard University Press.

Peirce, Charles S. 1931–1958. *The Collected Papers of Charles Sanders Peirce*. 8 vols. Vols. 1–6 edited by Charles Hartshorne and Paul Weiss, vols. 7–8 edited by Arthur W. Burks. Cambridge, MA, Harvard University Press. (Cited as CP.)

Peirce, Charles S. 1975–1987. *Charles Sanders Peirce: Contributions to* The Nation. 4 vols. Edited by Kenneth L. Ketner and James E. Cook. Lubbock: Texas Tech University Press. (Cited as CN.)

Richardson, Robert. 1995. *Emerson: The Mind on Fire*, Berkeley: University of California Press.

CHAPTER 19

WHY PHILOSOPHERS MUST BE PRAGMATISTS

Taking Cues from Peirce

CORNELIS DE WAAL

It is likely that the term pragmatism was coined in jest in the Metaphysical Club, an informal group of friends who met in Cambridge, Massachusetts, in the early 1870s. After all, pragmatism meant "busy impertinence" and a pragmatist was a busybody (CD:4667).[1] We know that the name of the club itself was meant in jest. As Peirce later testified, "we called ourselves, half-ironically and half-defiantly 'The Metaphysical Club,'—for agnosticism was riding its high horse, and was frowning severely upon all metaphysics" (EP2:399, 1907). Hence, it is not unreasonable to suspect that the club's youthful members saw themselves as 'meddling impertinently' with metaphysics—a discipline that Peirce decades later still considered "a *puny, rickety,* and scrofulous *science*" (EP2:375, 1906). It is further safe to say that this meddling went far beyond metaphysics and that over time the word pragmatism lost much of its negative connotation, even among philosophers.

Whatever the nature of its origin, the philosophic term makes its first public appearance in an 1898 lecture by William James. In this lecture, James attributes the term to Peirce, specifically referring to Peirce's 1878 "How to Make Our Ideas Clear," more precisely to the third way of making our ideas clear, which is now known as the pragmatic maxim (ILS:90).[2] This paper, which also has its roots in the Metaphysical Club, was part of a series of papers, published in *Popular Science Monthly*, in which Peirce sought to explain both the motives and the means for conducting scientific inquiry. It is only after James made the term public, and credited Peirce not only for coining it but also for the idea it represented, that Peirce began to call himself a pragmatist—albeit later, due to disagreements with other self-proclaimed pragmatists, he switched to pragmaticist instead (EP2:335, 1905). In this chapter, I examine what this pragmatism comes down to, how it features within inquiry, and what its limits are—all with the aim of showing that philosophers should be pragmatists. To do so, I first discuss what Peirce meant by philosophy and how it relates to science and inquiry more generally.

1. Logic, Philosophy, and Scientific Inquiry

Peirce, himself an experienced scientist, firmly situated philosophy in what he called "the sciences of discovery," which he distinguished from "the practical sciences" (or, as we now call them, the applied sciences) and "the sciences of review." The latter seek to put the discoveries of the various sciences in some framework (CD:5397). Though acknowledging other roles for philosophers (R787:5, c. 1895), Peirce's interest is squarely in the sciences of discovery and the role philosophy plays within them.[3] The purpose of these sciences of discovery is to find things out *and nothing else*. What we want is to have our questions answered no matter what those answers might be or what they might bring us.

Importantly, when Peirce speaks of science, he is thinking of something much broader than what the term has come to mean in the twentieth century, especially within the Anglo-Saxon tradition. It encompasses *any inquiry* aimed at finding something out, at establishing some fact, where fact is to be understood as what makes a proposition true or false (CD:2112). To put it differently, a fact is "an element of truth expressible as a proposition" (R418:06, 1893). This means that Peirce takes the sciences of discovery to encompass *any* inquiry aimed at true propositions. By taking such a broad notion of science, Peirce rejects the view that only the methods of the natural and physical sciences generate true propositions about the world. In fact, Peirce rejects that there is a specific methodology—oft referred to as "the scientific method"—that distinguishes scientific from other inquiries.[4] For Peirce, the only restriction put upon inquiry is that it is engaged with the desire to have one's questions answered. In other words, determining what methods to use belongs to inquiry itself and is not something to be externally imposed upon it. Science is thus defined in terms of inquiry, where inquiry is defined in terms of its purpose, which is to have our questions answered and where the answers express in propositions certain aspects of the world of lived experience.

Within the sciences of discovery, Peirce further distinguished between the positive sciences and mathematics. With the positive sciences, Peirce meant those that seek to draw facts from experience, where experience is "that which is quite irresistibly forced in upon us in the course of life" (R1336:01, n.d.). The situation is very different with mathematics. Though "some truths are forced in upon the mathematician in the study of his hypotheses," Peirce denies that such truths are "forced in upon him *in the course of life*"; for, as Peirce explains, the mathematician's hypotheses are "quite voluntary, and as it were, arbitrarily set up" (R1336:01, emphasis added). In brief, mathematics does not concern itself with the world of experience, but studies arbitrarily construed worlds of hypotheses.

Philosophy, in contrast, *is* a positive science. As Peirce puts it forcefully, "to decide what our sentiments ought to be toward things in general *without* taking any account of human experience of life, would be most foolish" (R1336:01, emphasis added). Peirce further separates philosophy from specialized positive sciences such as physics, psychology, or bacteriology. Such specialized sciences focus their attention on very narrow parts of our experience that are oft far removed from daily life and that tend to be inaccessible to the general public because they involve specialized equipment (such as thermocyclers or cyclotrons), travel (as in archeology), or domain-specific knowledge (for instance, to interpret the results of electrophoresis). In this way, philosophy is cast as an observational science, but one that is "based exclusively on such observations as *must be* open to every scientific intelligence" (R787:5, *c.* 1895). With the latter, Peirce has in mind everyone who wants to know how things are for its own sake; that is without any ulterior motive. The domain of philosophy consequently consists of the "facts of everyday life, such as present themselves to every adult and sane person, and for the most part in every day and hour of his waking life" (EP2:146, 1903).

In line with this, Peirce divided philosophy in the early 1890s into logic and metaphysics. The first concerns "the study of the most general intellectual relations" and the second "the study of the most general real characters of things" (R1337:06, n.d.). Well over a decade later, Peirce moved from this descriptive bifurcation to a threefold division with a decidedly normative slant. This division consists of phenomenology, which seeks to draw up "an inventory of appearances without going into any investigation of their truth" (CP2.120, *c.* 1902), the normative sciences (esthetics, ethics, and logic), and metaphysics. In this setup, the aim of the normative sciences is to connect the shifting phantasmagoria of our actual experience with a metaphysics that is meant to give us a general *Weltanschauung*, one that becomes the touchstone for the special sciences.[5] It is here that questions are asked such as, What is truth?, What makes something real?, What do we mean by "a thing"?, What are facts?, etc. Within metaphysics thus conceived, the fruits of philosophy are drawn together into a more or less comprehensive conception of the world that we find ourselves in and our relationship to it.

What about these normative sciences? In 1903, Peirce defined ethics, still within the context of the sciences of discovery, as "the theory of the self-control of conduct in order to realize a deliberatively adopted purpose" (R602:09, *c.* 1905), and he conceived of esthetics as the science that furnishes such purposes. Against this backdrop, the normative science of logic comes to constitute that branch of ethics that concerns the question of how we should conduct ourselves when our purpose is to correctly represent something, that is, when we want to do good in the realm of representation. As we will see, Peirce considered the pragmatic maxim as a rule of logic. Importantly, in this scenario, logic, like philosophy, emerges as one of the sciences of discovery. In other words, and in agreement with what we have seen so far, the rules of logic are products of scientific inquiry.[6]

There is another aspect of the sciences of discovery that needs to be brought out. When we seek to discover things, we rather quickly find that new discoveries come with the risk of undermining, or even negating, what we take to be true, including even our most firmly held beliefs. Consequently, though we can be quite certain that many of our beliefs are true—as otherwise we would not be able to conduct our lives, let alone engage in inquiry—we cannot extend this certainty to any particular belief. This includes not only the beliefs that we already have, but also any of our new beliefs, as we can be mistaken in our discoveries too. Peirce called this position fallibilism and anti-cocksurism. This puts us in the following predicament: proceeding from the faith that we can know things, our desire for knowing them must always come with a contrite fallibilism (CP1.14, c. 1897)—a fallibilism that, like original sin, is not merely the acceptance of an unavoidable aspect of life, but that comes with a constant desire for atonement.[7] Now, as there is no higher court of appeal, any such atonement must happen within the sciences of discovery themselves. In brief, because we are fallible, inquiry must be self-corrective. Put briefly, since the aim of the sciences of discovery is to find things out, we must be continually on the lookout for what we may be wrong about, work hard at preventing this from happening, and seek to correct any mistakes or false beliefs we may pick up on the way. This is precisely why ethics must precede metaphysics and logic must be considered a branch of ethics.

Returning to Peirce's distinction between philosophy and the special sciences, the challenge for philosophy is thus not that of procuring expensive equipment, travel grants, or expansive factual knowledge, but to develop the ability to critically rethink the things we take for granted, and to do so on a continual basis and in a productive manner. Having explicated what Peirce meant by philosophy, I next turn to the role of pragmatism within philosophy.

2. Pragmatism as a Rule of Logic

Reasoning comes naturally and at a very young age. We do not, however, naturally reason correctly. Quite the opposite. We are prone to let our emotions rule and are subject to all sorts of biases.[8] Especially in areas where experience does not set us straight, we are most capable of piling mistake upon mistake. In short, experience reveals that there is both good and bad reasoning and the aim of logic is to help us distinguish between the two. More specifically, within the context of the sciences of discovery logic aims to tell us how to reason when we have questions that we like to see answered.[9] But what is reasoning? According to the *Century Dictionary*, in a definition written by Peirce, reasoning is "an idea acting as a cause to create or confirm a belief, or to induce a voluntary action" (CD:4990). For instance, you see dark clouds at the horizon, you recall that this often leads to rain, so you conclude that rain is likely and that you'd better bring an umbrella. Elsewhere, Peirce describes reasoning as "such fixation of one belief by another as is reasonable, deliberate, self-controlled" (EP2:347, 1905). Let's take a brief look at these three terms.

First, what we consider reasonable typically refers to those connections between beliefs or ideas that have proven their worth in experience and that, subsequently, entered the fallible backdrop against which we ask our questions and seek to answer them. What counts as reasonable is thereby an experiential affair (EP2:60, 1901).[10] It also entails a historical component. For instance, estimates by nineteenth-century geodesists about the age of the earth were considered unreasonable because, given what was known about combustion, those estimates made the earth older than the sun. Only in the twentieth century, with the discovery of nuclear energy, could the sun be deemed old enough for such estimates to be reasonable. Similarly, whereas it was once reasonable to argue that one could cure just about any disease with bloodletting, it is no longer reasonable to maintain this.

Second, reasoning is deliberate. This means, Peirce observes, that it is consciously engaged in "with a view to making it conform to a purpose or ideal" (EP2:376, 1906). We call reasoning good when it is conducive to reaching that purpose or meeting that ideal. In this process, reasoning, so to speak, "approves of itself. It tells itself that the process by which its conclusion was reached was a trustworthy process. Had it *not* been so," Peirce perceptively continues, "a different proceeding would have been used" (R597:3, *c.* 1902). As Peirce puts it elsewhere, reasoning is self-corrective because "there is reasoning that reason itself condemns" (R832:2, n.d.). And it is in the end this self-correctiveness of reasoning that enables inquiry to be self-corrective.

This last point brings in the third term Peirce used, namely, that reasoning is self-controlled. Reasoning may be self-corrective, but it does not correct itself. The latter requires rational agents who constantly re-evaluate what they are doing and, where needed, use the result to readjust what they are doing. This need for self-control connects with our fallible nature, discussed earlier, as well as the absence of a court of higher appeal that we can shift our responsibility to.

Within the sciences of discovery, an inference can be said to be reasonable when individuals familiar with the art of reasoning who direct their attention to having their questions answered would assent to it on the ground that it is conducive to that purpose. In that sense, logic is not really different from carpentry. There, too, it is ultimately the experience of the seasoned but still fallible carpenter that provides the ground for calling a certain way of making wood joints good or bad.[11] And like logic, making wood joints is a self-controlled activity that involves deliberation, and like logic it must accommodate itself to a world that is already there—the world as it enters experience (R409:54–55, 1993).

The discovery that there is both good and bad reasoning, however, does not by itself entail that there are any rules that, by following them, guarantee that our reasoning is good. Consequently, Peirce writes, "the first thing to ask, is why we should suppose that there are any such rules, and in what sense they can have any authority" (R598:03, *c.* 1902). This is especially relevant for questions where experience does not give us timely feedback as, for instance, when we use reason to determine the age of the earth. For questions like this, such rules are pretty much all we have that could lend authority to the reasoning process, and hence to the conclusion.

In "Reason's Rules," Peirce looks at several possible sources for such authority: we can repeat rules that worked in the past, we can accept rules on the authority of others, and rules can derive their authority from sounding very convincing.[12] Importantly, as we saw, for the sciences of discovery such rules originate within and are sustained by the actual practice of inquiry. As Peirce puts it in "The Fixation of Belief," "each chief step in science has been a lesson in logic"—a view he illustrates with references to Antoine Lavoisier, Charles Darwin, and James Clerk Maxwell (ILS:48, 1877). Rules originate because any decision to proceed in a certain manner comes with the (tacit) realization that whenever the circumstances are as they are now, we should proceed in the same manner. In his 1903 Lowell Lectures, Peirce draws a direct connection between reasoning and how it steers not only current but also future conduct: "A person who draws a rational conclusion, not only thinks it to be true, but thinks that similar reasoning would be just in every analogous case. *If he fails to think this*, the inference is not to be called reasoning. It is merely an idea suggested to his mind and which he cannot resist thinking is true" (CP1.606, 1903; emphasis added). In brief, when deliberation guided by self-control results in a decision to act, the decision through which people tell themselves what they should do becomes normative; it tells them not only what they should do in the current situation, but also what they should do when they are facing relevantly similar situations in the future. This is true even when the issue is entirely theoretical. Again, to quote Peirce, "to say that conduct is deliberate implies that each action, or each important action, is reviewed by the actor and that his judgment is passed upon it, as to whether he wishes his future conduct to be like that or not" (EP2:377, 1905). What this comes down to is that what we call laws of logic are effectively practical rules for proper inquiry. Moreover, what rules to accept is an experiential affair; it is something we learn from the practice of inquiry.[13]

If we combine our fallible nature with reasoning being deliberate, self-corrective, and subject to self-control, we see that a continuously critical attitude is crucial to the development and maintenance of rules, and for ensuring that they remain living prescripts rather than rote prescriptions. In this manner, logic becomes a critic of rules. This may be in part why Peirce insists that what makes science good or bad, genuine or fake, is the attitude with which it is engaged in, not the methods that are being used. Without a living quest for truth animating the inquirer, any method or rule is at best a blunt instrument. This because mere rule followers are unequipped at adapting existing rules and methods to the subtleties of the situations to which they seek to apply them. One might describe this as the need for a *fingerspitzengefühl*—a great situational awareness combined with the ability to respond appropriately and tactfully (that is, reasonably).

One such rule of logic is Peirce's pragmatic maxim. This maxim prescribes, within certain parameters, how to assign meaning when we seek to represent something. Recall that Peirce took the sciences of discovery to encompass any inquiry aimed at establishing some fact, where the latter is to be understood as "an element of truth expressible as a proposition" (R418:06, 1893). In this way pragmatism can be understood as a critic of meaning.

3. Pragmatism as a Critic of Meaning

Even though, for Peirce, pragmatism applies broadly to the sciences of discovery, the remainder of this chapter focuses largely on philosophy conceived as the most basic of these sciences.[14] We saw that, for Peirce, philosophy is a positive science of discovery. From what James called the buzzing and blooming confusion that marks unconceptualized experience, it extracts a *Weltanschauung*, or metaphysics, and it does so by means of the normative sciences, insofar as they culminate in logic—the discipline that concerns the question of how to truthfully represent something. In the process, logic discovers rules, and it is suggested that the pragmatic maxim is one such rule.

"One of the greatest difficulties with philosophy," Peirce writes, "is that every beginner brings to the study a stock of confused ideas upon the subject. Consequently, there has to be for each question we attack a serious, preliminary business of rendering our ideas clear" (R953:10, n.d.). Especially for topics not easily checked by experience, an exact nomenclature for basic philosophical concepts is essential for philosophers with divergent views to have a fruitful discussion.

In "How to Make Our Ideas Clear," Peirce distinguishes three grades of clearness with respect to our ideas—that is, with respect to anything that comes before the mind in any way. An idea reaches the first grade, Peirce writes, when it "will be recognized whenever it is met with, and so that no other will be mistaken for it" (ILS:80, 1878). The pawnbroker's idea of gold is like this. All that is required for the pawnbroker is a familiarity with gold objects. Reaching this first grade need not be restricted to the narrowly empirical. One can obtain a clear idea of unicorns, the trinity, or truth by becoming familiar with how these concepts feature within our language and culture. Being conversant with an idea, however, often does not suffice when we leave familiar situations. In microbiology, for instance, the search for macromolecules is greatly facilitated by attaching some gold to them. This, because it makes them easier to find when using an electron microscope. Here the expertise of the pawnbroker will be of little help. Quite the opposite. What is more, the pawnbroker and the microscopist are likely to have very different ideas of gold if *all* we can go on is this first grade of clearness.

The second grade of clearness aims to accommodate for this. We attain the second grade, Peirce writes, when we provide "an abstract logical analysis of it into its ultimate elements, or as complete an analysis as we can compass" (CP6.481, 1908). The definition of gold as the chemical element with atomic number 79 is an example of this. Here the abstract definition tells us what counts as gold and what not. Whatever has atomic number 79 *has* to be gold, no matter what the pawnbroker, or the microbiologist, thinks or says it is, or experiences it to be. It is worth noting that such definitions need not be grounded in the first grade of clearness. Take, for instance, the various elements defined by Dmitri Mendeleev's periodic table that were only later discovered to exist. For a more philosophical example of an abstract definition, we can think of truth as it is commonsensically understood (its first grade of clearness) and how Aristotle famously defined it: "To say of what is that it is not, or of what is not that it is, is false, while to say of what is that it is, and of what is not that it is not."[15]

The drawback of abstract definitions is that they are disconnected from experience. What makes something gold, or what makes something true, is not determined by what we encounter in experience, but by whether it matches certain pre-set criteria. Peirce's third grade of clearness comes in here. It does so in the form of the following maxim:

> "Consider what effects, which might conceivably have practical bearings, we conceive the object of our conception to have. Then, our conception of these effects is the whole of our conception of the object" (ILS:90, 1878).[16]

Logic, we saw, aims to tell us how we should conduct ourselves when we are in the business of trying to represent something. The pragmatic maxim aims to tell us what is involved in having a conception of an object when we seek to represent something in thought. It tells us what conceptions we can accept (and why) and, by extension, what conceptions we must reject. According to the maxim, our (current) conception of an object cannot go beyond the effects that we conceive that object to have—not just in circumstances we expect to encounter, but in all circumstances we might conceive of. Moreover, these effects must be such that they might have some practical bearing, suggesting that what has no conceivable practical bearings cannot contribute to our conception of the object. With its reference to practical bearings instead of sensory impressions, the maxim differs substantially from traditional empiricism. In line with the description of logic as normative, meaning relates to action, to a particular kind of response, rather than to us passively undergoing an impression.[17] But I'm running ahead. Let's first look more carefully at the maxim.

Grammatically, the first sentence's parenthetical phrase could be read as a nonessential clause the removal of which would leave the maxim unaffected. Moreover, the interjection of "might" seems to make these practical bearings mighty optional as well. In later reflections, however, Peirce reveals that such reading is not what he intended. As he explains in 1903, pragmatism "is the doctrine that every conception is a conception of conceivable practical effects" (EP2:235), meaning that the parenthetical phrase should be read as a restriction on what kinds of effects count. They must be such that they might conceivably have practical effects, where the "might" indicates that we must look at every circumstance we can think of, no matter how far-fetched, and not just those we expect to actually encounter. It is further worth noting that the maxim is not written in the first person singular, but in the first person plural. It is not about what I may or may not consider but about what my community considers. For Peirce, inquiry is not an individual but a social affair.

The next thing to observe is that the maxim is not cast in terms of words, propositions, theories, or ideas (even though the paper itself is titled "How to Make Our Ideas Clear"), but hinges heavily on the related terms conceive and conception. In the *Century Dictionary* Peirce rendered conception as "that which is conceived in the mind" (CD:1162), where the verb to conceive means "to apprehend in the mind," to seize or grasp mentally (CD:1161). Conceptions, as generally understood, differ from mental states such as feelings or sensations. To feel or sense a toothache is not the same as to conceive of one. One point of difference is that the mere sensation of a toothache does not guide deliberate action, such as going to the dentist, whereas having conceived, or interpreted, a particular sensation as a toothache does. In this way, conceptions often come with possible plans of action. None of this is particularly controversial. It is just not clear that this is *always* the case and *all* that they are, as the pragmatic maxim contends. It may sound plausible for a word like toothache, but it is less clear whether it applies to all our mathematical, philosophical, scientific, and religious conceptions.

About sensations, we can further say that they are unique; they are how they present themselves. It is only through an act of the mind that one can judge two sensations similar or "the same." In philosophical parlance, sensations are particulars. Conceptions, in contrast, at least when taken as plans of action, are general, not particular. Rather, they cover a variety of feelings or sensations that are brought together by the circumstance that they suggest the same path of action—in our example earlier, seeking out a dentist. In this way conceptions convey more than any particular grouping of feelings, or sense impressions. Moreover, conceptions are open ended. For instance, the conception of a toothache always allows for new, yet unfelt sensations to count as a toothache.

The maxim further proclaims that conceptions have objects. They are about something. Next it states that what such an object can mean to us is determined by how we might conceive that object to affect us, and then Peirce further restricts this to conceivable *practical* effects. Why practical effects? Why not purely theoretical implications? To answer this question, it helps to recall the context. As we saw, the pragmatic maxim is a rule of logic, where the latter is situated within the positive sciences of discovery as the normative discipline that tells us how we should reason when we seek to answer the questions we are asking. Put differently, we are looking at conceptions only insofar as they function within the context of reasoning, that is, when we let our thoughts be determined in a manner that is reasonable, deliberate, and self-controlled. In addition, when we reason within the positive sciences (and we saw that for Peirce this includes philosophy) we are letting ourselves be guided by experience; or, as Peirce also put it, "by what has a conceivable bearing upon the conduct of life" (EP2:332, 1905). This, in contrast to mathematics, where, as we saw, we reason about hypothetical constructions of thought arbitrarily set up. Now, whatever can affect reasonable, deliberate, and self-controlled conduct, Peirce terms practical (CP8.322, 1906).

Importantly, however, Peirce does not restrict the practical to current problems that need fixing, whether something as mundane as a leaky faucet or as momentous as global warming—a move that would reduce the sciences of discovery to the practical sciences. Rather, by focusing on *conceivable* practical effects, the maxim "allows any flight of imagination, provided this imagination ultimately alights upon a possible practical effect" (EP2:235, 1903). The resulting notion of the practical thus also includes flights of imagination that practical scientists generally consider tiresome and counterproductive, as well as conceptions traditionally considered theoretical. In fact, even something as abstract as the principle of noncontradiction affects reasonable, deliberate, and self-controlled conduct by guiding us in accepting or rejecting certain propositions, theories, courses of action, etc.[18]

In light of all of this, we might modify the pragmatic maxim as follows:

> Consider what effects, which might conceivably affect reasonable, deliberate, and self-controlled conduct, we conceive the object of our conception to have. Then, our conception of these effects is the whole of our conception of the object.[19]

This still leaves us with at least two questions: First, is it really *the whole* of our conception of the object that is at stake here, as the maxim proclaims it to be? Second, must it apply to *all* conceptions that enter the sciences of discovery, including philosophy?

Let's begin with the second. We saw that Peirce distinguished three grades of clearness and that we reach the third by applying the pragmatic maxim. Do all our conceptions really need to reach this third grade? Peirce argues they do not, and reasonably so. The purpose of the maxim, he states, is not "to aid us in defining ordinary words so much as it is in aiding us to get clear ideas of the real significance of philosophical terms, such as *reality, necessity, belief, cause,* the *self,* in which there is great danger of our using words without attaching any significance at all to them" (LoF1:258, 1896). This is inspired in part by another principle of logic, that of the economy of research, and in part by the realization that we cannot question everything at once but can only pose questions against a background of which we are sufficiently confident. When we can define a concept "in terms of *sensible* relations, or relations of everyday *experience*," we typically do not need the pragmatic maxim. Rather, all we need is to bring them "down to ground where there is no fear of meaningless distinctions" (LoF1:258, 1896). In other words, the maxim is to be employed, not always, but whenever there is a reasonable chance that a term is used without meaning or when we run the risk of some meaning being inappropriately ascribed to it. Even within the sciences of discovery there can be legitimate inquiries where the pawnbroker's conception of gold is really all we need. However, if reasoning is to be deliberate and self-controlled, then we must ensure that the conceptions by which we seek to express our conclusions remain appropriate for the conclusions we draw. This includes preventing that their meaning is informed by preexisting, possibly outmoded philosophical or scientific frameworks. Briefly put, the idea is that whenever we depart from familiar, well-trodden paths that consistently served us well, we must continuously re-evaluate the conceptions on which our conclusions hinge and, where appropriate, apply the pragmatic maxim.

With this in mind, we can return to the first question. Must our conception of the object be strictly confined to effects that might conceivably affect reasonable, deliberate, and self-controlled conduct, or may it also include effects, or other aspects, that do not meet this requirement? As we saw, being a principle of logic, Peirce's pragmatic maxim is normative. It tells us what we should do, accept, demand, etc. So, in situations where the pragmatic maxim is being called for, we are asked to ensure that the object of our conception is cast entirely in terms of conceivable practical consequences, and nothing else. The reason for this, as we have also seen, is to avoid including elements that are meaningless.

One possible reason for proceeding this way is prudence—a better-safe-than-sorry approach. The drawback of this, however, is that we quickly run the risk of violating a third principle of logic, which is not to block the way of inquiry (CP1.135, 1898). A better-safe-than-sorry approach risks obstructing what initiated, and sustains, the inquiry, namely, our desire to learn, that is, to have our questions answered come what may.

A better reason for casting at least some conceptions wholly in terms of conceivable practical consequences comes to the fore when we connect it with why we are bringing in the maxim. We call on the maxim when we are asking questions that we believe that reasoning—which is deliberate and self-controlled—might be able to answer. We also saw that Peirce termed practical whatever might affect reasonable, deliberate, and self-controlled conduct. Thus conceived, *only* what is practical can affect reasoning. In other words, whatever may be left in the concept that has no conceivable practical bearings cannot further inquiry. It can, however, impede it, as our rationality is limited, and we are easily distracted by nonrational considerations. The latter happens especially where we have some vested interest in what the answer is going to be. Allowing our conceptions to mean more than what might conceivably affect reasonable, deliberate, and self-controlled conduct is a bit like preferring a dull and dirty knife above a sharp and clean one. What the pragmatic maxim thus tells us is that, wherever possible, we should always aim for clean and sharp knives rather than be content with dull and dirty ones.

4. Pragmatist Philosophy

The above considerations show that one cannot truly be engaged in philosophy without being a pragmatist. Philosophy, even when conceived more broadly than is done here, crucially involves reasoning. And, as the above discussion indicates, insofar as philosophers use reason—that is, insofar as they let themselves be guided in a way that is reasonable, deliberate, and self-controlled—they must be pragmatists.

That being said, the maxim is best looked upon as a prima facie prescription of logic. As we saw, there are other prescriptions as well—prescriptions it may have to compete with, such as those related to the economy of research and the prohibition against blocking the way of inquiry. Because of this, and because inquiry always takes place against a backdrop that is taken for granted—even if only for the purpose of the inquiry—being a pragmatist should not be taken to mean that whenever we engage in inquiry, we must employ Peirce's maxim to calibrate every single conception we plan on using. Being a pragmatist only requires applying the maxim to some conceptions.

So, then, who gets to decide what conceptions to apply the maxim to? Still going with Peirce, and in line with what was said above, that is a decision eventually to be made within the inquiry itself, where inquiry is to be taken as an open-ended communal affair: open-ended both in time and with respect to those involved. As Peirce explains in his Adirondack Summer School Lectures of 1905: "What I mean by a 'science,' both for the purpose of this classification & in general, is the life devoted to the pursuit of truth according to the best known methods on the part of a group of men who understand one another's ideas and works as no outsider can. It is not what they have already found out which makes their business a science; it is that they are pursuing a branch of truth according, I will not say, to the best methods, but according to the best methods that are known at the time" (R1334:11–13). In Peirce's view, the various sciences grow organically from the inquiries that are conducted, which, in turn, are products of the questions that are asked and what methods are considered appropriate for answering them. The latter then includes determining what conceptions to apply the pragmatic maxim to, and why. What is true here for science equally applies to philosophy. It is the kind of questions that are being asked, and how one goes about answering them, that makes someone a philosopher of biology, rather than a molecular biologist or an ethicist.

Part of why Peirce conceives of science, and by extension philosophy, as a communal affair is his conception of the self. Peirce dismisses the Cartesian notion of the self as an individual who enters the world fully formed at birth—a world that is powerless to affect her in any essential way. For Peirce, in contrast, the individual is not defined in terms of a predetermined "essence," but, quite the opposite, in terms of error and ignorance (W2:203, 1868). Briefly put, I differ from you because I'm wrong and ignorant about different things than you are. Because of this, science does not proceed along Cartesian lines—confirming or disproving our views in terms of the light of nature as it shines within us—but by us correcting each other. This community also determines, inspired by a contrite fallibilism, what counts as reasonable and what not. And it is within this process that we must see the use of the pragmatic maxim play out. As was noted earlier, there is no higher court of appeal, and as it turns out, there is no need for one either.[20]

Does all of this imply that there is no true meaning because the meaning of our terms continuously shifts depending on who is speaking? To this it can be answered that meaning is not dependent upon who speaks but is relative to the context with which it is integrated. The meaning of our conceptions is not static but grows with inquiry. Though Peirce's pragmatic conception of truth is a topic for another day, there seems to be a close connection between a pragmatic conception of truth and a pragmatic conception of meaning.[21] Roughly stated, Peirce's pragmatic conception of truth identifies truth as the opinion that would be reached in the long run, when inquiry has naturally come to a close, assuming that this inquiry was conducted by an open-ended community for a sufficiently large amount of time. The idea behind this is that there is at least an ideal point at which no rational disagreement about the answer is still possible. Pragmatically, Peirce argues, "truth" cannot mean more than this. Assuming the correctness of this, truth, as the final opinion, will appear in the form of a proposition. This suggests that at the end of inquiry there will also be a shared opinion, an opinion that can no longer be rationally improved upon, about the meaning of the conceptions that are being used. And there is no guarantee that the meanings of the conceptions through which this final opinion is expressed will exactly (or, at times, even remotely) agree with what we take those conceptions to mean today. And perhaps we can say that this would be their true meaning.

Notes

1. Though various scholars have noted that Peirce did not define pragmatism for the *Century Dictionary*, and though Peirce later wrote defensively about this omission as well, little is said about what the entries for pragmatist and pragmatism looked like. Both were lifted largely from the four-volume *Imperial Dictionary*, the copyright of which had been purchased by the Century Company, and which became the basis for the twenty-four-volume *Century Dictionary*. For Peirce's extensive involvement with the *Century Dictionary*, see, for example, Orin Hargraves, "The Century Dictionary Definitions of Charles Sanders Peirce," *Dictionaries: Journal of the Dictionary Society of North America* 40.2 (2019): 31–53.
2. Peirce first refers to it as a maxim in 1903 (EP2:133).
3. William James held that pragmatism should also, if not primarily so, be applied to questions that serve a practical purpose. This is in part why he closely connected his pragmatism with his will-to-believe argument. Their different takes on transubstantiation might be helpful to show the difference. Whereas Peirce takes our conception of transubstantiation as a prime example of a conception that is pragmatically meaningless, James takes it to be a clear case of a conception that is pragmatically meaningful. James does so on the ground that even though it may be *empirically*, or scientifically, meaningless, its meaning can still be cast in terms of the practical effects it has on those who do or do not believe in it. In that way, James contends, pragmatism effectively rescues our concept of transubstantiation from the rubbish bin of nonsense (see, e.g., de Waal 2022, 21–22). The current chapter is limited to pragmatism and philosophy as they feature within the sciences of discovery and, with Peirce, it considers the accompanying maxim as a rule for determining the meaning of our conceptions.
4. It is worth noting that when Peirce speaks of "the method of science," what he has in mind is not the use of some method that can be called scientific, but merely by letting our belief be fixed, not by what we already believe, "but by some external permanency—by something upon which our thinking has no effect" (ILS:66–67, 1877).
5. Importantly, the findings of the specialized sciences can also influence philosophy, including logic and metaphysics.
6. In addition to the positive science of logic, Peirce also distinguished mathematical logic—an area to which he contributed significantly. Broadly speaking, mathematical logic is a product of the application of the hypothetical science of mathematics to the positive science of logic, not unlike how mathematics is applied in physics or economics. For instance, Isaac Newton employed calculus to express his views on terrestrial and celestial motion, finding it superior to English or Latin. Peirce takes this same view toward logic. Logic too can use mathematics when developing views on proper and improper ways of representing something. What we have here is essentially a model-theoretic account of the role of mathematics in the positive sciences.
7. This also relates to another normative component of inquiry and answering questions, which is that "to assert a proposition is to make oneself responsible for its truth" (R597:43, c. 1902).
8. Psychologists are quite familiar with this. See, for example, Matt Warren and Miriam Frankel, *Are You Thinking Clearly? 29 Reasons You Aren't, and What To Do About It* (London: Coronet, 2022).

9. "How to Reason" is the title of what appears to be the only substantially completed logic book Peirce submitted for publication. See Cornelis de Waal, "The History of Peirce's 1894 Logic Book" *Peirce Project Newsletter* 3.2 (2000): 4–5.
10. The advantage of this phrase is that it can trade on two meanings of the word *experience*—having experience versus having an experience—while also acknowledging that having an experience amounts to more than a mere sensory affair.
11. This experience may be fortified by mathematical theories and by the views of others who possess relevant knowledge that falls outside the purview of the carpenter (such as the pros and cons of various adhesives).
12. This is a paraphrase of what Peirce argues in R598 (*c*. 1902) in a way that roughly aligns with the first three ways for fixing our belief in "The Fixation of Belief" (ILS:58–66, 1877).
13. It is important to keep Peirce's distinction between mathematics and positive science in mind here that is, to distinguish, for instance, between the law of excluded middle as belonging to mathematical logic (which is a hypothetical science) and as belonging to logic as the theory of right reasoning (which is a positive science).
14. Note that Peirce introduced the maxim when discussing the logic of science and that, with one exception, the examples that follow its introduction all come from science.
15. *Metaphysics* 1011b25.
16. Over the years Peirce gave different renderings of the maxim. For a helpful inventory, see Schmidt (2020).
17. Traditionally, this passivity is considered evidence that the impression is untainted by anything subjective.
18. A distinction is to be made between the principle of noncontradiction as a principle of logic and as a mathematical principle (the latter including mathematical, or formal, logic). See, for example, R409:54–55 (1893).
19. The closest Peirce comes to formulating the maxim this way is in a draft of a review of Herbert Nichols's *Treatise on Cosmology* (CP8.191, *c*. 1904).
20. For Descartes this higher court of appeal is God, who guarantees that what we clearly and distinctly perceive is also true. See his *Meditations Concerning First Philosophy*, esp. Meditation 3.
21. For Peirce's pragmatist conception of truth, see, for example, de Waal (2013, ch. 8) and Cornelis de Waal, "Eleven Challenges to the Pragmatic Theory of Truth," Transactions of the *Charles S. Peirce Society* 35.4 (1999): 748–766.

References

De Waal, Cornelis. 2013. *Charles S. Peirce: A Guide for the Perplexed*. London: Continuum Press.

De Waal, Cornelis. 2022. *Introducing Pragmatism: A Tool for Rethinking Philosophy*. New York, Routledge.

Peirce, Charles S. 1966–1970. Manuscripts held at the Houghton Library of Harvard University, as identified in Richard Robin. 1967. *Annotated Catalogue of the Papers of Charles S. Peirce*. Amherst, University of Massachusetts Press. And in Richard Robin. 1971. "The Peirce Papers: A Supplementary Catalogue." Transactions of the Charles S. Peirce Society 7, no. 1 (winter): 37–57. (Referred to as R.)

Peirce, Charles S. 1931–1958. *The Collected Papers of Charles Sanders Peirce*. 8 vols. Vols. 1–6 edited by Charles Hartshorne and Paul Weiss; vols. 7–8 edited by Arthur W. Burks. Cambridge, MA: Harvard University Press. (Referred to as CP with volume and paragraph number.)

Peirce, Charles S. 1992–1998. *The Essential Peirce: Selected Philosophical Writings.* 2 vols. Vol. 1 edited by Nathan Houser and Christian Kloesel, vol. 2 edited by the Peirce Edition Project. Bloomington: Indiana University Press. (Referred to as EP.)

Peirce, Charles S. 2014. *Illustrations of the Logic of Science.* Edited by Cornelis de Waal. Chicago: Open Court. (Referred to as ILS.)

Peirce, Charles S. 2019– . *Logic of the Future.* 3 vols. Edited by Ahti-Veikko Pietarinen. Berlin: De Gruyter Mouton. (Referred to as LoF.)

Schmidt, Jon Alan. 2020. "Peirce's Maxim of Pragmatism: 61 Formulations," *Transactions of the Charles S. Peirce Society* 56.4, 580–599.

Whitney, William Dwight (editor). 1889–1891. *The Century Dictionary: An Encyclopedic Lexicon of the English Language.* 24 vols. New York: Century Company. (Referred to as CD.)

CHAPTER 20

THEORY, PRACTICE, AND DELIBERATION

Peirce's Pragmatism Comprehensively Conceived

VINCENT COLAPIETRO

The *love of life is more than the love of sensuous life*: it is also the love of rational life.

—Charles S. Peirce (W2:122, 1867)

No philosophical distinction is more commonplace, controversial, or central than that between theory and practice (see, e.g., Lobkowicz 1967). Each of the classical pragmatists provided important insights into this crucial distinction, not least of all C. S. Peirce. His scattered remarks, however, have proven somewhat difficult to integrate into a coherent account. Given how sharply he distinguishes theory and practice, some expositors judge him to have betrayed his pragmatism. As Cheryl Misak, T. L. Short, Susan Haack, Mats Bergman, and others have shown, this is not the case.

Indeed, Peirce tends to draw a very sharp distinction between theory and practice (see, e.g., CP1.618, 642, 1898). Here we discern his apparently Kantian concern to identify the limits of rationality. He is not limiting reason to make room for faith (Kant 1965, 29), but appealing to faith, along with hope and love, to enlarge rationality (see especially EP1:150, 1878). That is, Peirce expanded the meaning of reason to include certain sentiments (EP1:150, 1878; Savan 1981, 331–333; cf. Dewey MW 14, 136).[1] In his judgment, the role of reason is severely limited with regard to practice, whereas it is much broader, though still somewhat restricted, with regard to theory. The distinction between practice and theory is drawn principally in terms of what limited role human reason plays.

1. THE TASK OF DISAMBIGUATION

As W. B. Gallie suggests, "the idea of practice . . . is shot through with ambiguities of philosophically crucial kinds" (1967–1968, 64) . He goes so far as to claim, "Peirce's formulations of his pragmatism display most if not all of the ambiguities in the idea of practice" identified by Gallie. If the idea of practice is "itself radically ambiguous," and if Peirce is enmeshed in these ambiguities, it would be helpful to sort out these distinct yet confused meanings. Any effort "to distinguish all of the ambiguities of the word 'practice' ... would be an impossibly complex and for the most part philosophically unrewarding task" (Gallie 1967–1968, 66). But, given the centrality of the distinction, failure to distinguish some of the main ambiguities in Peirce's writings would be a serious failure.

To cut to the capture, not merely the chase, to encompassing sense and a contrastive sense. In the encompassing sense, theory is itself a form of practice (put otherwise, practice is an extremely expansive concept, broad enough to encompass within itself the distinction between what Peirce himself means by *theory* and *practice*. In the contrastive sense, practice is defined in contrast to theory. Though it might seem paradoxical, the meaning of reason cuts across this divide: a unitary understanding of rationality is discoverable in the sharply contrasting realms of purely theoretical investigations and humanly vital affairs. Both theoretical and practical reason are instances of *phronesis*. The variable exercise of practical wisdom is no less discernible in the methodological deliberations of theoretical inquirers than the substantive deliberations of situated agents confronting existential choices of a typically urgent character. It would be, for example, unwise (see, e.g., EP2:32, 1898) to test certain hypotheses before other ones, just as it would be foolish or unwise to pursue a career in a field even though one lacked the most rudimentary aptitude for minimal competence in that given profession. The temporality of theoretical investigations is dramatically different from that of practical affairs. While a sense of *kairos* is demanded of theoretical inquirers no less than moral agents, "the long run" of open-ended inquiry and the fierce urgency of now entail a different orientation toward time. Science "has nothing at stake in any temporal venture but is in pursuit of eternal verities ... and looks upon this pursuit, not as the work of one man's life, but as that of generation after generation, indefinitely" (CP5.589, 1898; Misak 2004, 151). Practice in the sense in which it stands in contrast to theory (thus, to *science*) tends to force individuals to consider the fleeting opportunities of their onrushing lives.

2. Human Reason as a Deliberative Capacity

Since the distinction between practice and theory is framed by Peirce in terms of the contrasting role of reason in these domains of human engagement, the task of disambiguation encompasses a clarification of what *reason* means. The Peircean conception of reason is rooted in the classical vision of *Logos* (see Smith 1986, 284–286). This is evident in Peirce's conviction that reason enables us, without limit, to discover reality. Nothing in principle falls beyond the scope of our discovery. As appreciative as he was of human finitude (see, e.g., CP1.675, 1898), he unabashedly ascribed a limitless capacity to human rationality in its strictly theoretical pursuits. The range of our actual knowledge is indeed infinitesimally small.[2] The Peircean conception of rationality carried into late modernity the classical vision of *Logos* (Smith 1986, 284–286).

To appreciate its historical significance, we must note two other features. The first concerns the predominantly logical cast of that conception and the second the evolutionary context of human reason's origin, development, and self-transformations. "In its higher stages, evolution takes place more and more largely through self-control" (CP5.433, 1905). Deliberative agency is one of the offshoots of evolutionary processes and, with the emergence of such agents, nature becomes conscious of itself and evolution can in this or that instance become more than an altogether blind or random process. First, then, if we are to be faithful to Peirce's commitments, human reason in its defining struggle to acquire and enhance authoritative control over its exertions, endeavors, and even feelings must be formally conceived in normative terms, especially *logical* procedures, norms, and ideals. Human agents have self-consciously and -critically instituted self-corrective procedures for the sake of rendering their ideas both more secure and more fecund (EP2, see especially ch. 31). The Peircean conception of human rationality is interwoven with his normative account of objective inquiry. He is endeavoring to "re-think and re-establish logic at the most fundamental level" (Ransdell 2000, 342). Logic, reimagined as the normative science of such an inevitably historical or dramatic adventure is critical here, but, then, so are the other two normative sciences, esthetics and ethics. Deliberation must extend to an ongoing appraisal of our ultimate ideals (see, e.g., CP1.585–588, c. 1903; CP1.589–590, c. 1900; also CP1.591–615, 1903).

The evolutionary context of Peirce's concept needs to be appreciated as much as the normative cast of this conception. This context is invoked in his claim: "Whatever has vitality, whatever is to be called *good*, has been in process of development . . . and is still presumably to develop further" (EP2:466). The question to which we are, at every turn, driven is, "*How things grow*" (CP7.267n8, 1893). "Once you have embraced the principle of continuity," Peirce contends, "no kind of explanation of things will satisfy you except that they *grew*" (CP1.175, c. 1897). In his own mind, his synechism and evolutionism are of a piece. As much as he stressed continuity in most areas, however, he seems to have advocated a dichotomy between theory and practice.

3. THEORY VERSUS PRACTICE

The theoretical employment of reason is one thing, the practical employment another. Though it is the same capacity differently employed, it can seem that theoretical reason is virtually a different capacity than practical reason. For example, the degree of certainty allegedly attained by reason in its theoretical employment is much greater than that attained by reason in its concrete deliberations. From a classical perspective, the contingencies and vagaries confronting persons engaged in strictly moral deliberation allegedly preclude the degree of certainty and precision supposedly obtaining in our theoretical inquiries. From a Peircean perspective, our most certain theoretical claims are fallible. He does not recognize *theoria* as marking off an arena in which apodictic certainty is humanly attainable.

Though there have been influential attempts to explain away the love of truth for its own sake, Peirce found them unconvincing. He went so far as to identify reason with love, though the claim must be qualified. Reasonableness consists in bringing things together into self-luminous intelligibility, love in bringing them together in mutually enhancing harmony. "In the emotional sphere this tendency toward union appears as Love; so that the Law of love and the Law of Reason are quite at one" (Wiener 1965, 332).

The love of rational life might take myriad forms, including the passionate pursuit of purely theoretical discovery. The distinctive form of theoretical rationality is fundamentally different from that of either practical or productive rationality. Although he insists on the need to avoid confusing motive with ideal, the motive of the theoretical inquirer and the ideal of theoretical inquiry are, in practice, mutually supportive. "It has been a great, but frequent error of writers on ethics to confound an ideal of conduct with a motive to action" (CP1.574, 1906). While a motive might mean *any* "spring to action," it might more narrowly mean "an aim or end appearing ultimate to an agent" (CP1.585, c. 1903). In the narrower sense, the motive of an agent is the deliberately adopted ideal. Motive and ideal are qualifiedly identifiable: the ultimate ideal moves the deliberative agent to carry on; the operative motive is the deliberately adopted ideal in its inherent attractiveness.

The human face of human reason, even in the context of *theoria*, is the face of *phronesis*. It is a deliberative capacity. What distinguishes Peirce's view from that of Aristotle is that reason in its heuristic employment is one with reason in its deliberative exercise. Theoretical discovery and methodological deliberation are intrinsically conjoined.

This insistence does not erase distinction between theory and practice. It simply allows us to see human rationality in its most rudimentary guise. It is the capacity for deliberation, extending all the way to what deliberative agents come to envision as pursuitworthy ends. The attempt to reduce the process of deliberation to calculation is, for an Aristotelian, doomed to fail. Without question, calculations can serve deliberation; they can even be of incalculable value for communal deliberation! But they cannot replace deliberation.

More generally, Peirce appreciated the value of formalization. It is, however, telling that he did not identify himself as a formal logician, despite making significant contributions to the advancement of formal logic. His appreciation of the value of formalization was never separate from his appreciation of the limits of formalization. The latter is indicative of his commitment to the ideal of *phronesis*, even in the context of *theoria*. Though he considered himself mainly a logician, he deliberately refused to identify himself primarily as a formal logician.

The growth of knowledge depends on the continual proliferation of historical communities of experimental inquirers, ideally communities in which the open-ended pursuit of theoretical discovery for its own sake remains or eventually becomes embodied in historically evolving practices insulated from the corrupting influence of narrow practicality or, worse, vainglorious individuals. These communities are distinct arenas of communal deliberation wherein questions of method are at the heart of their deliberations. Nothing is more vital than the question, *How* ought we to attack this question? The first step in attacking any question, however, is taking the utmost pains to ensure that, given the state of inquiry, the question is properly formulated. What are we, as theoretical inquirers, trying to *do*? The *ethos* of theory demands "a code of honor" (Ransdell 2000), a strenuous ethic of heroic self-sacrifice.

The growth of knowledge drives toward the deliberate cultivation of the logical sentiments (above all, faith, hope, and love). These sentiments are constitutive of rationality, arguably theoretical rationality more than any other identifiable form. Like all virtues, they are obtainable only through passionate participation in communal practices.

Historical upheavals in the intellectual world have generated countless benefits but also disastrous effects. Not the least of these effects has been the deracination of reason. Human reason, especially in its characteristically *modern* deployment, has tended to uproot itself from local communities, historical inheritances, and indeed the natural world itself. Part of the wisdom of Peirce's philosophy is to appreciate the need for our reason to see itself rooted in nature and history, including quite local traditions and specific ecological locales. There is, at the heart of this wisdom, the disposition to recall what was central to the classical tradition of Western philosophy—and more than this tradition—the deep affinity between human intelligence and the boundless intelligibility of "the circumambient All."

Human reason is rooted in the natural world and the inescapable confluence of diverse histories. The modern tendency to define human rationality in stark opposition to the only world in which it could have arisen and evolved is the source of countless errors and the root of practical crises of global urgency. Reason so conceived is disembodied, unsituated, and deracinated. The humble yet audacious vision of *logos*, celebrated by Plato, Aristotle, and others, is championed by Peirce. As a logician, he foregrounded the normative and logical features of this ennobling vision. As a thoroughgoing evolutionist, he took account of both the context in which rationality emerged, evolved, and continues to evolve *and* this process of evolution itself.

He linked our capacity for radical deliberation and our capacity for theoretical discovery. When the different senses in which theory and practice are disambiguated, we are in a position to see how coherent, nuanced, and compelling is the Peircean account of human reason, in all of reason's deployments.

For Peirce, "'rational' means essentially self-criticizing, self-controlling, and self-controlled, and therefore open to incessant question" (CP7.77, n.d.). "Now control may itself be controlled, criticism itself subjected to criticism; and ideally there is no obvious limit to the sequence" (CP5.442, 1905). But, like explanation and justification, critique and our efforts to control our conduct, including the conduct of thinking itself, do come to an end.

From Peirce's perspective, "reason tends to correct itself, and the more so, the more wisely [i.e., the more deliberately] its plan is laid. Nay, it not only corrects its conclusions, it even corrects its premises" (CP5.575, 1898; cf. Sellars [1956] 2000, 250). As Wilfrid Sellars notes, "Empirical knowledge, like its sophisticated extension, science, is rational not because it has a *foundation*, but it is a self-corrective enterprise which can put *any* claim in jeopardy, though not *all* at once" (2000, 250).

"Reason is," Peirce asserts, "of its very essence egotistical" (CP1.361, c. 1890). It tends to wildly exaggerate its authority and efficacy. "In many matters," reason simply "acts the fly on the wheel" (CP1.631, 1898). "The machinery of logical self-control works as on the same plan as does moral self-control, in multiform detail" (CP5.440, 1905). Peirce is, however, quick to point out the "greatest difference" between these two forms of human autonomy: "moral self-control serves to inhibit mad puttings forth of energy," while logical self-control "most characteristically insures us against the quandary of Buridan's ass" (i.e., shows us the way beyond the impasses or aporias due to which the flow of reason becomes arrested). Though different in this and other respects, logical and moral self-control are, at bottom, two forms of the same capacity—deliberative agency.

His understanding of such agency is closer to that of Aristotle than the position of Kant (Fisch 1986, 239). "For one who had learned philosophy out of Kant, as the writer, along with nineteen out of twenty experimentalists who turned to philosophy, had done, and who still thought [in the late 1870s] in Kantian terms most readily," Peirce confessed, "*praktisch* and *pragmatisch* were poles apart" (CP5.412, 1905; Kant 1956, 84, including note). Practical reason (*practischen Vernunft*) was a pure—that is, a priori—capacity charged with discovering whatever universality and necessity might be characteristic of practical (or moral) reason. The pragmatic employment of human reason refers to what Kant identifies as "*counsels* of prudence." These are framed in terms of an end (thus, Peirce defines *pragmatisch* in Kant's sense as "relating to some definite human purpose" [CP5.412, 1905]).

However highly generalized a conception of duty we might frame, deontology ultimately falls back on teleology (put more simply, our duties only make sense in light of our purposes). At least for Peirce, "the word 'ought' has no meaning except relatively to an end" (CP5.594, 1903). The pragmatic (*pragmatisch*), in contrast to the a priori character of *practischen Vernunft*, concerns some "definite relation" to an identifiable purpose, even if we as agents are, in concrete circumstances or given endeavors, not altogether clear about our purposes. Our duties are intelligible only in reference to our ends (see, however, Short 2007, 346–347).

While *practical* can bear the meaning of purposive, deliberation designates, at least for Peirce, the process by which we identify inherently praiseworthy aims and the most effective means for their attainment. A qualification is needed. Mostly, we cannot but fix our ends in advance of their pursuit. The determination of one's end is the first order of any deliberative process. It turns out that these ends are rarely fixed, in any immutable manner: our identification of an end is usually of an evolved or emergent purpose. Of greater moment, our very pursuit of an end can contribute to the evolution of that end (see especially Short 1998). The radical implications of Peirce's "development teleology" are still not appreciated. Our ends themselves evolve in the very course of our endeavors. This is as true of science as anything else. The energetic, sustained, embodied pursuit of evolving purposes makes physical action indispensable.

"Pragmatism is [however] correct doctrine only insofar as it is recognized that material [or physical] action is the mere husk of ideas" (CP8.272, 1902). "The brute element [unquestionably] exists" and, accordingly, must be forthrightly acknowledged. "But the end of thought is action only in so far as the end of action [itself] is another thought" (CP8.272, 1902). He goes so far as to assert that the actualization of *thought* requires action ("the actualization of the thought without action remains unthought" [CP8.250, 1897]). This dependency, however, does not make thought subservient to action, but just the opposite. Human knowing entails physical exertion and the continual observation of the variable results of physical activity. Such action subserves such knowing, even when the latter is purely theoretical.

"Now just as Moral Conduct is Self-controlled conduct so Logical Thought is Moral, or Self-controlled, thought" (CP8.240, 1904). But self-control cannot be traced to an isolated act. It grows out of a protracted practice self-consciously espoused and cultivated (CP5.418–419, 1905; also CP5.440, 1905). It grows out of deliberation, making in Peirce's judgment self-controlled conduct the equivalent of deliberately controlled conduct (CP8.322, 1906; Holmes 1966).

In Peirce's lexicon, deliberate is a synonym for self-controlled. "The word 'deliberate' is," Peirce notes, "hardly completely defined by saying that it implies attention to memories of past experience [especially experience consequent upon action] to one's present purpose, together with self-control" (CP5.538, *c.* 1902). What else does *deliberate* signify? Tracing out the likely or foreseeable implications of imaginary lines of human conduct and, on the basis of such "forethought," shaping our *conduct* in light of those implications (CP5.538, *c.* 1902). This helps us to see why Peirce asserts, "The whole business of ratiocination, and all that makes us intellectual beings, is performed in imagination" (CP6.286, 1893; see Hull 2005).

"This act of stamping with approval, 'endorsing' as one's own, an imaginary line of conduct" (CP5.538, *c.* 1902–1903) is also part of deliberation. Unless we *resolve* to act in a certain way in certain circumstances, that is, unless our deliberation issues into a resolve or resolution, we are only playacting at deliberation. Imaginative rehearsal can have "real" or physical consequences. The resolution to act on the basis of such an exercise of imagination might be one formed by the theoretical inquirer, solely for the sake of theoretical discovery. It is "practical" in the sense it is apt to affect the conduct of the inquirer precisely as such an inquirer.

Peirce asserts: "By 'practical,' I mean apt to affect conduct; and by conduct, voluntary action that is self-controlled, i.e. controlled by adequate deliberation" (CP8.322, 1906). Please note: this might be the conduct of a purely theoretical inquirer, not necessarily that of a moral agent confronting choices imposed by vitally pressing situations. Peirce is explicit regarding this point: "Inquiry is only a particular kind of conduct" (R602:8, *c.* 1905; Bergman 2010, 24), that is, only a distinctive form of human practice. There is certainly no contradiction and, ordinarily, little ambiguity, in saying some theoretical inquirer possesses practical experience in that individual's chosen profession.

"It is," Peirce insists, "of the very essence of thought and purpose to be special, just as truly as it is of the essence of either to be general" (CP5.594, 1903). The drive toward specificity is evident in valuable ideas and purposes being fecund ("fruitful in special [or definite] applications"), whereas that toward generality is manifest in such ideas and purposes "always growing to wider and wider alliances" (CP5.594, 1903). Several distinctions need to be drawn. The applications of a theory might be to the very discipline in which the theory is formulated. They might pertain to domains far removed from this discipline. In the former case, the applications are *internal* to a practice, while in the later as *external* to that practice. Moreover, the applications as implied in this example might be intrinsically "theoretical."

Just as *practice* might be taken in an expansive or narrow sense, so too might *pragmatism*. In the finely focused sense in which Peirce introduced it in "How to Make Our Ideas Clear," pragmatism is simply a maxim,[3] devised by an expert inquirer for the sake of facilitating fruitful investigations. It is in itself not a theory of meaning but a procedure formally established for the purpose of clarifying a class of concepts (those on which "arguments concerning objective fact may hinge" [CP5.467, c. 1906]), presumed already to be meaningful.[4] His maxim makes explicit what is tacit in the theoretical inquiries of thoroughgoing experimentalists, for whom the conceivable "practical" effects are of greatest concern. This maxim only makes adequate sense in the larger contexts of its heuristic salience and in the still wider context of our shared practices. This wider sense of pragmatism is of course also a vaguer sense. It might be excessively vague without being utterly vacuous. Pragmatism can be taken in an expansive sense to designate all that is implied in the normative stance toward experimental investigation. Such a sense is hinted at in Peirce's own characterization of this stance as "an instinctive attraction for living facts" (EP2:158). The acknowledgment and endorsement of this attraction is a step toward methodological self-consciousness (the sort of consciousness more narrowly on display in the formulation of the pragmatic maxim). Pragmatism comprehensively envisioned is a distinctive orientation toward a delimited range of human practices (those concerned with "objective fact"). Habits of action, imagination (including conceptualization[5]), and feeling are made central to this account. In contrast, pragmatism narrowly conceived is a procedure designed to move us beyond the level of abstract definition to the level of the observable consequences of our deliberate and, as it turns out, even our unintended exertions.

In at least one place, Peirce identifies the esthetic ideal as "that which *we* all love and *adore*" (CP8.262, 1905; emphasis added to *adore*, not to *we*). The ultimate aim of a truly pursuitworthy character would be one worthy of adoration (that before which we bow our heads and bend our knees, assuming the posture of humble obedience to a sublime Power) (Peirce CP1.217, 1902; also EP2:55).

The human face of rational autonomy is deliberative agency. No agent is truly deliberative unless that individual engages in an ongoing critique of the inherited forms of human endeavor. But such individuals must acknowledge their deep rootedness in, and thus their incalculable debt to, their inheritances. Their critique extends to the cultivation of feelings for what is inherently attractive, admirable, or "adorable." The self-conscious participation is in a community of self-critical experimentalists, in which the cultivation, exercise, and refinement of an expansive array of moral dispositions (e.g., humility, patience, tolerance, and veracity), are of fundamental importance. The identification *in sentiment* with others is the form of solidarity at the root of the infinite community of experimental inquirers. "The course of life has," Peirce suggests, "developed certain compulsions of thought which we speak of collectively as Experience. Moreover, the inquirer more or less vaguely identifies himself in sentiment with a Community of which he is a member, and which includes ... besides his momentary self, his self of ten years hence; and he speaks of the resultant cognitive compulsions of the course of life of that community as Our Experience" (CP8.101, 1900; cf. CP5.402n.2, 1878; CP2.166, c. 1902).

It is easy to exaggerate the role that reason either actually plays or ideally ought to play in vital affairs. It is no less easy to denigrate the power or place of this capacity in this regard. Peirce's antirationalism inclined him to stress how disastrous reliance on rationality tends to be in guiding our conduct. His somewhat extravagant faith in our innate dispositions and historical inheritances blinded him from how deeply habituated we can be to systematic cruelty and degradation.

Part of wisdom is to appreciate the limits not only of our knowledge but also of the salutary effect of individual reason in offering trustworthy guidance. Our elders were often wiser than we appreciate, our traditions frequently more precious than we can discern (CP4.71, 1893; Colapietro 1997).

In the theoretical no less than the practical contexts of human endeavor, our *individual* rationality ultimately appeals to a set of identifiable sentiments (in the case of theory, reason appeals to faith, hope, and love). In doing so, it transcends itself, possibly even transforms itself, becoming more than a principally individual capacity.

Theoretical inquirers precisely as theoretical inquirers exercise, in the tightly circumscribed contexts of their communal pursuits, *phronesis*. At every turn, the question confronting them is, How shall we comport ourselves as inquirers? This is a question internal to the practice of inquiry. Moral, political, religious, and other questions about their comportment, as inquirers, might of course intrude themselves, but when they do these individuals have, however temporarily, ceased to be inquirers and become moral agents or human beings in some other distinctive role than that of an inquirer.

Peirce at once expands the role of *phronesis* by extending it to *theoria* and restricts that role by making it so dependent on instinct, tradition, and sentiment. He was an indefatigable champion of experimental reason who was extremely wary about using appeals to science to undermine traditional religion, traditional morality, and other inherited practices.

There is an ancient tradition, renewed in contemporary philosophy by Friedrich Nietzsche, Michel Foucault, Alexander Nehemas, Stanley Cavell, and many others, according to which philosophy principally concerns the conduct of life. Philosophy concerns such conduct in a direct and indeed urgent manner. There are rival traditions, one of the most important being that in which philosophical inquiry is a strictly theoretical pursuit, having little or nothing to do with "care for the self" or the cultivation of character. (This is not to dismiss the importance of such care, only to demur from identifying it with the practice of philosophy). While Peirce was allied with the intellectual tradition in which philosophical investigations are taken to be theoretical pursuits, he made the *conduct of inquiry* a focal concern of his own philosophical investigations. The nature of such conduct cannot be adequately comprehended except in contrast to other forms of human conduct, including the creative endeavors of artists and the practical engagements of women and men in either the informal circumstances of everyday life or the formal contexts of their avowed professions. The conduct of individuals, for whom nature is "a cosmos, so admirable, that to penetrate its ways seems to them the only thing that makes life worth living" (CP1.43, c. 1896), comes into sharpest focus when it is set into explicit contrast with artistic temperaments and practical persons. Whatever is discovered by such individuals is used as a means for pushing inquiry forward. This means that *science* designates not knowledge but inquiry, more specifically, "diligent inquiry into truth for truth's sake, without any sort of axe to grind, nor [even] for the sake of the delight in contemplating it, but [solely] from an impulse to penetrate into the reason of things" (CP1.44, c. 1896).

Peirce never doubted that a lifelong engagement in theoretical inquiry would have a profound influence on the inquirer's moral character, in the narrow, heuristic sense (cf. Bronowski 1990) but also likely in a broader ethical sense. He nonetheless resolutely refused to make this point of philosophy. A slow, indirect modification of a person's character is one thing; an "immediate," direct effort to change one's life is quite another.

Ultimately, theoretical reason is in no different position than practical reason. It is ultimately forced to appeal to sentiment for the justification of its own endeavor. Coercive demonstrations proffered by deductive reason are no less moonshine than the demonstrations of the metaphysicians (CP1.7, c. 1897). The best we can ever do is be guided by the sane or reasonable judgments having their ultimate basis in human sentiment.

In his historical context, reliance on "the cold light of reason" practically meant one of two things. It meant either devotion to "Americanism" in the most objectionable sense or somnambulism in a spiritual sense (cf. Emerson's "Experience"). "To pursue 'topics of vital importance' ... can lead only to one or other of two terminations—either on the one hand ... Americanism, the worship of business, the life in which the fertilizing stream of genial sentiment dries up or shrinks to a rill of comic tit-bits, or else on the other hand, to monasticism, sleepwalking in this world with no eye nor heart except for the other" (CP1.673, 1898). Peirce's exacting vision of the theoretical inquirer is unquestionably allied to a central imperative of traditional morality, for the theoretical inquirer no less than human beings as moral agents are enjoined to take, as their "highest business and duty," the acknowledgment that there is a higher business than one's own business (CP1.673, 1898).

The distinction between living and formal reason is not explicit in Peirce's writings (see, however, EP2:59; also in CP8.138, 1901). But John E. Smith's distinction captures something crucial about Peirce's approach to the topics explored in "A Neglected Argument." "Living reason needs," he claims, "to be recovered, for it is the form of reason required of all the concrete rational pursuits in which men [and women] are engaged—art, morality, politics, and religion" ([1968] 1995, 112). He draws the distinction principally in terms of "the relation of reason to the individual self" (112). He is quick to concede that there is a sense in which the rational self does participate in purely formal processes of logical reasoning. The coercive movement of purely formal thought makes the self feel as though formal reason is "an alien force." In contrast, the suasive promptings of living reason reveal to the individual self that this distinctive form of human rationality "is not a power alien to the self, a purely universal and abstract set of rules which is indifferent both to the individual self and to the differences between the various subject matters thought about" (113). The defining activities of living reason (e.g., musement, reflecting upon the meaning of our experience, including our experience with the sacred) are ones in which "the self seeks to trace out rational patterns in its own experience; the self recognizes and acknowledges its own nature as a rational being in that process" (113). The argument about God, as understood by Peirce, is one in which selves are implicated in the process of making sense of the disclosures of their experience. While the ideal of formal reason is that of "objective, formal, compelling proof" (115), that of living reason is a participatory mode of open-ended query in which deepened understanding, not demonstrative argumentation, is the abiding concern. At bottom, living reason is "a quest for intelligibility through dialectic or dialogue" (117). Those who find the claims of thinkers such as Peirce to be unwarranted are not to be dismissed, but the dialectic of faith and doubt in the lives of even the most skeptical thinkers needs to be identified.

A qualification is requisite. Even formal reason is, to some extent, a recognizable form of living reason, for it, at least insofar as it avoids being the mechanical execution of a mindless exercise, entails a degree of participating in the forms in and through which some *Sache* is being conceived and explored. What is dramatically true in the case of arguments about divinity is also true of, say, the forms of reasoning diagrammatically displayed in his existential graphs. The whole self is engaged more deeply in the one instance than in the other. The heroic self-restraint exercised by purely theoretical inquirers is a dramatic example of the exacting self-control demanded of them. The integrity and autonomy of *theoria* demands such restraint.

Peirce hardly abandons his commitment to pragmatism when he argues for the autonomy and integrity of theoretical inquiry as a vastly extended family of human endeavors. In a broad sense, theory is itself an instance of inquiry. In a narrower sense, it needs to be set in contrast to practice: *theoria* is not reducible to *praxis*, when *praxis* is taken to be pressing issues of vital importance (Misak 2004; Bergman 2010).

When Peirce insists on the difference between theoretical inquiry and practical affairs, he does so deliberately. His ethics of inquiry encompasses not only an inquiry into ethics but also a focused deliberation about the recurrent need to attain a yet clearer understanding of our actual endeavors. In this, his criticism of Plato can be leveled against himself: "It is a characteristic of the man that he sees more deeply into the nature of things than he does into the nature of his own philosophy, and it is a trait to which we cannot altogether refuse our esteem" (EP2:38).

From Peirce's perspective, what is manifestly observable in Plato's case is discoverable in other theorists. This is the point of his invocation of the line from Emerson's poem ("Of thine eye I am eyebeam"). Except in those circumstances in which some surface might serve as a mirror, the eyebeam sees what is other than itself. And even when our eyes are directed back at themselves, the eyebeam itself almost certainly eludes being seen. The seen eye ceases to be the seeing organ.

"We do not fully know," Justus Buchler asserts, "what we mean" (1961, 77). This is in truth a Peircean point (see, e.g., CP3.419, 1892). The meaning of our own utterances outstrips our comprehension of them. Hence the need for abstract definition and pragmatic clarification is recurrent. What is true of the meaning of our concepts and claims is all the truer of our undertakings and experiences. The task of philosophy is to fathom the depths of the *meaning* of not only our concepts and utterances but also our endeavors and experiences, our intergenerational practices and interwoven histories.

This is an immediately theoretical task but one having ultimately profound effects on the transfiguration of human character. The theoretical character of philosophical inquiry needs to be jealously guarded, but the slow, indirect impact of conscientious engagement in theoretical inquiry on the modification of the inquirer's character need not be denied. The crucial distinction between an "immediate," prompt impact and an indirect, slow "percolation gradually reaching the very core of one's being" (CP1.648, 1898) needs to be borne in mind here. The way for theoretical inquirers to care for their individual souls is by caring for the business of theory as their highest business. Such at least is Peirce's account of the matter. His position demonstrably avoids "vulgar pragmatism" (Haack 2004) while rigorously adhering to the pragmatic principles of his own theoretical commitments. In this as in some many other respects, one can readily discern the conscientious exercise of deliberative rationality. As Peirce sees it, such rationality extends to all forms of comportment, thus the distinctive comportment of theoretical inquirers. This makes *phronesis* a heuristic power *and* a normative capacity—the power by which discoveries are made but also the capacity by which alternative courses of conduct are distinctly identified and the most admirable course at least provisionally adopted. This maintains a sharp distinction between theory and practice while advancing an expansive understanding of *phronesis*. The pursuit of theoretical knowledge and the cultivation of practical wisdom can neither be identified with one another nor separated from each other. The practical wisdom required of the purely theoretical inquirer is not identical with that of moral agents, but it is manifestly the conscientious exercise of deliberative imagination.[6] "Reason's Conscience" is just that—a form of conscience, so much so that logic in Peirce's sense is aptly described as "the Ethics of the Intellect" (SS:112; letter to Victoria Welby, 1909, March 14).

Even if he was not as clear, consistent, or comprehensive as he might have been (or as some of us desire him to have been), Peirce's lifelong efforts bear witness to a nuanced comprehension of the complex relationship between theoretical knowledge and practical wisdom. In his writings, there is, despite rhetorical exaggeration (Short, 2001), no simple opposition between theory and practice. He was far too deliberate in thinking through the tangle of issues—including the host of ambiguities—linked to this contrast to make matters too simple or distinctions too absolute. This is so, despite appearances in some dramatic instances (most notably, his self-proclamation in 1898—"I stand before you, an Aristotelian and a scientific man, condemning with the whole strength of conviction the Hellenic tendency to mingle philosophy [or theory] and practice" [CP1.618, 1898]). In sum, the practical wisdom of this theoretical inquirer cannot be gainsaid. It is evident in both his devotion to the power of experimental (or deliberative) rationality and his appreciation of the limits of reason in this sense. Purely theoretical inquiry is itself a historically evolving practice or, more precisely, a widely extended family of such shared practices. In the context of such practices, reason reveals itself to be a disposition to engage in ceaseless questioning. The radical experimentalism definitive of theoretical inquiry might not have a place outside of purely theoretical contexts, especially those practical settings in which widely shared traditions ought *reasonably* to serve as a check on the destructive impulses of egotistically motivated reason (see Short 2001). A more conservative orientation might be more appropriate when dealing with the vital matters.[7] But, then, more resolutely ameliorative efforts are often called for (Bergman 2015: Dewey MW14, 114–116). In Peirce's own judgment, "continual amelioration of our own habits . . . is the only alternative to continual degeneration of them" (R674:1 [*c.* 1911]; Bergman 2010, 36). This extends to our habits of feeling, including "sentiments." Indeed, what Peirce calls "the regenerative metamorphosis of sentiment" (CP1.676, 1898), a process fostered by "poetry" (understood as art), is an integral part of the moral life. In a culture such as our own (one given to monetary calculations and purely individual), the "stream of genial sentiment" can dry up. Accordingly, it must be continually replenished; our most admirable sentiments must be regenerated. Arguably nothing is more vital to a culture than fostering habits of empathy, especially the capacity to be moved by the suffering of others.

When the lives of individuals are, in the name of individual freedom, systematically trammeled upon, sentimental conservatives might realize that the price of conserving their society is reforming or reconstructing it. The reign of reason can degenerate into a reign of terror. The tyranny of a minority can be a regime of terror. The amelioration of human suffering might in certain cases require a radical reform of traditional society. Dreading how reliance on reason can license a reign of terror ought not to blind us to how appeals to tradition can underwrite existing regimes of the most horrific terror. Practical wisdom demands critical attention to the actual conditions in which human beings live. The unavoidability of unintended consequences and the rather severe limits of human forethought cannot be gainsaid. Acknowledging both does not practically mean abandoning hope of amelioration. It does mean all such efforts in this regard ought to be undertaken in a spirit of humility, sensitivity, and above all fallibilism. In practice, the exercise of *phronesis* is often a difficult, delicate, and possibly even self-defeating task (in our efforts to be reasonable, we all too often prove ourselves to be prejudiced or blind, lacking in foresight or insight). This is far more the case regarding vital affairs than purely theoretical questions. For some philosophers, theoretical knowledge is one thing, practical wisdom quite another. While appreciative of this distinction, a theorist such as Peirce is one for whom the acquisition of theoretical knowledge depends on the exercise of practical wisdom (or *phronesis*). In order to conduct any promising investigation of a theoretical character, inquirers must deliberate about what methods to institute, which hypothesis to test first, and what experiments to devise. They must imagine an array of alternatives and select them as wisely as possible. From first to last, theoretical inquirers are at bottom deliberative agents.

Part of Peirce's genius can be, for however much he might have missed regarding the "nature of his own philosophy," seen here, for he did not miss this. His pragmatist portrait of experimental intelligence projected a compelling vision of deliberative agency. He deeply appreciated that, even with respect to mathematicians, thinking "in general terms is not enough. It is necessary that something should be DONE" (CP4.233, 1902). Apart from the relevant forms of human exertion, there is no possibility of acquiring knowledge or making discoveries, in mathematics or in any other field of inquiry. Apart from doing, there is no knowing. The inward exertions of deliberative imagination are hardly to be discounted here. The main point concerns the indispensability of *doing* something. This does not reduce knowing to doing, thought to action, or theory to practice. Rather it reveals one of the senses in which theory is itself a form of practice, in which knowing is always an instance of doing. Doing, knowing, and signifying (instituting, using, and modifying signs in the course of our doings) are distinct yet inseparable facets of an ongoing process. To judge that such an account of knowing is reductionist betrays an impoverished understanding of human doing. To see how intimately our theoretical pursuits and deliberative imagination are connected does not (con)fuse what ought to be kept separate. It rather captures something essential about the innermost character of theoretical inquirers—their deliberative agency. Part of Peirce's singular achievement is to have seen so clearly how discovery and deliberation are in practice linked. Properly understood, then, his commitment to insisting upon the autonomy of theory hardly entails betraying his pragmatism. It reveals how rich, nuanced, and encompassing that pragmatism is. In turn, this assists us in seeing how reasonable, commonsensical, and yet appropriately critical is his understanding of reason (or reasonableness) itself.[8] A life of intensely focused deliberations has indeed yielded a wealth of heuristically fruitful conceptions—to some extent, "a wild harvest" (CP1.12, *c.* 1897). This life not only reveals the struggle of a mind to claim possession of itself but also provides a distinctively philosophical account (though not a biographical narrative) of that heroic struggle. This practicing scientist was, partly on the solid basis of his intimate familiarity with communities of experimental inquirers, able to articulate an inclusive conception of practice and provide profound insights into "theory" (Dewey LW 11, 422–423; Gallie 1967–1968, 81–82).

Notes

1. Here is one of the places in which Peirce appears to fail in offering a coherent account of human reason in its diverse employments. On the one hand, he insists, "In theoretical matters I refuse to allow sentiment any weight whatever" (CP1.634, 1898). On the other hand, he identifies faith, hope, and love as "logical sentiments" (EP1:150, 1878), without which theoretical inquirers could not reasonably justify their arduous pursuits.

2. "However immense our science may become, we are only burrowing light into an infinitude of darkness. Once an infinitude, always an infinitude" (W1:8, 1860; see also CP1.117, c. 1896), while that of our possible knowledge is, without exaggeration, inherently boundless.
3. "Consider what effects, that might conceivably have practical bearings, we conceive the objects of our conceptions to have. Then, our conception of these effects is the whole of our conception of the object" (CP5.402, 1878; Hookway 2012).
4. We must turn to Peirce's semiotic, specifically, his theory of interpretants for his account of meaning. That account alone provides the context in which his pragmatism can be adequately understood.
5. Conceptualization is a species of imagination, concepts themselves being instruments of imaging (i.e., images, diagrams, or metaphors [see, e.g., CP2.277, c. 1902]). "A concept is," Peirce suggests in one place, "the living influence upon us of a diagram, or icon, with whose several parts are connected in thought an equal number of ideas or feelings" (CP7.467, 1893). In another place, he characterizes a concept "as a symbol present to the imagination" (R283:95, 1905). The manner in which a concept is so present needs to be itself conceived in terms of Peirce's nuanced conception of the iconic or hypoiconic (this, specifically, images, diagrams, and metaphors).
6. Dewey in effect puts forth a Peircean notion of the deliberative process when he writes, "Deliberation is a dramatic rehearsal (in imagination) of various competing possible lines of action" (MW14, 132; CP5.538, c. 1901; CP1.591–610, 1903).
7. T. L. Short is right to bemoan Peirce's "penchant for rhetorical overkill" (2001, 301), but he is selective in where he takes note of it.
8. The kind of critique undertaken by Kant might be a futile endeavor (see, e.g., Smith 1986, 282–286). While philosophy of course must be critical, the legitimate or viable or effective forms of critique are not necessarily Kantian in either the strict sense or even looser senses (see, e.g., Taylor 1995, ch. 2, on transcendental arguments).

BIBLIOGRAPHY

Atkins, Richard K. 2016. *Peirce and the Conduct of Life: Sentiment and Instinct in Ethics and Religion*. Cambridge: Cambridge University Press.
Ayim, Maryann. 1982. *Peirce's View of the Roles of Reason*. Meerut, India: Anu Prakashan.
Bergman, Mats. 2010. "Serving Two Masters: Peirce on Pure Science, Useless Things, and Practical Applications." In *Ideas in Action*, ed. Mats Bergman, Sami Paavola, Ahti-Veikko Pietarinen, and Henrik Rydenfelt (Helsinki: Nordic Pragmatism Network), 17–37.
Bergman, Mats. 2015. "Minimal Meliorism: Finding a Balance between Conservative and Progressive Pragmatism." In *Action, Belief and Inquiry: Pragmatist Perspectives on Science, Society and Religion*, ed. Ulf Zackariasson. Helsinki: Nordic Pragmatism Network, 2–28.
Bernstein, Richard J. 1971. *Praxis and Action*. Philadelphia: University of Pennsylvania Press.
Blanshard, Brand. 1962. *Reason and Analysis*. La Salle, IL: Open Court Press.
Bronowski, Jacob. 1990. *Science and Human Values*. New York: Harper.
Buchler, Justus. 1961. *The Concept of Method*. New York: Columbia University Press.
Burrell, David B. 1968. "Knowing as a Passionate and Personal Quest: C. S. Peirce." In *American Philosophy and the Future*, ed. Michael Novak (New York: Charles Scribner's Sons), 107–137.
Colapietro, Vincent M. 1987. "Toward a More Comprehensive Conception of Human Reason." *International Philosophical Quarterly* 27 no, 3: 281–298.

Colapietro, Vincent M. 1997. "Tradition: First Steps toward a Pragmatic Clarification." In *Philosophy in Experience,* ed. Richard Hart and Douglas R. Anderson (New York: Fordham University Press), 14–48.

Colapietro, Vincent M. 1999. "Peirce's Guess at the Riddle of Rationality." In *Classical American Pragmatism: Its Contemporary Vitality,* ed. Sandra B. Rosenthal, Carl R. Hausman, and Douglas R. Anderson (Urbana: University of Illinois Press), 15–30.

Colapietro, Vincent. 2009. "Habit, Competence, and Purpose." *Transactions of the Charles S. Peirce Society* 45, no. 3 (Summer): 348–377.

Dewey, John. 1922. *Human Nature and Conduct. The Middle Works of John Dewey,* vol. 14. Edited by Jo Ann Boydston. Carbondale: Southern Illinois University Press. (Referred to as MW14.)

Dewey, John. 1925. "The Development of American Pragmatism." *The Later Words of John Dewey,* vol. 2, 3–21. Edited by Jo Ann Boydston. Carbondale: Southern Illinois University Press. (Referred to as LW2.)

Dewey, John. [1929] 1984. *The Quest for Certainty. The Later Works of John Dewey,* vol. 4. Edited by Jo Ann Boydston. Carbondale: Southern Illinois University Press, 1984. (Referred to as LW4.)

Dewey, John. 1935. "Collected Papers of Charles Peirce" [Review in *The New Republic* of vols. 1–6 of CP]. *The Later Words of John Dewey,* vol. 11, 479–484. Edited by Jo Ann Boydston. Carbondale: Southern Illinois University Press. (Referred to as LW11.)

Dewey, John. 1935. "The Founder of Pragmatism" [Review in *The New Republic* of volume 5 of The Collected Papers]. *The Later Words of John Dewey,* vol. 11, 421–424. Edited by Jo Ann Boydston. Carbondale: Southern Illinois University Press. (Referred to as LW11.)

Fisch, Max H. 1986. *Peirce, Semeiotic, and Pragmatism.* Bloomington: Indiana University Press.

Foucault, Michel. 2005. *The Hermeneutics of the Subject,* trans. Graham Blechell. New York: Picador.

Gallie, W. B. 1967–1968. "The Idea of Practice." *Proceedings of the Aristotelian Society* [New Series] 68: 63–86.

Haack, Susan. 2004. *Manifesto of a Passionate Moderate: Unfashionable Essays.* Chicago: University of Chicago Press.

Holmes, Larry. 1966. "Peirce on Self-Control." *Transactions of the Charles S. Peirce Society* 2, no. 2: 113–130.

Hookway, Christopher. 2012. *The Pragmatic Maxim: Essays on Peirce and Pragmatism.* Oxford: Oxford University Press.

Hull, Kathleen. 2005. "The Inner Chambers of His Mind: Peirce's 'Neglected Argument' for God as Related to Mathematical Experience." *Transactions of the Charles S. Peirce Society* 41, no. 3 (Summer): 483–513.

Kant, Immanuel. 1956. *Groundwork of the Metaphysics of Morals,* trans. H. J. Paton. New York: Harper Torchbooks.

Kant, Immanuel. 1965. *Critique of Pure Reason,* trans. Norman Kemp Smith. New York: St. Martin's Press.

Lobkowicz, Nikolas. 1967. *Theory and Practice: History of a Concept from Aristotle to Marx.* Notre Dame, IN: University of Notre Dame Press.

Misak, Cheryl. 2004. "C. S. Peirce on Vital Matters." In *The Cambridge Companion to Peirce,* ed. Cheryl Misak (Cambridge: Cambridge University Press), 150–174.

Nehemas, Alexander. 1998. *The Art of Living: Socratic Reflections from Plato to Foucault.* Berkeley: University of California Press.

Niklas, Ursula. 1988. "On the Practical and the Theoretical in C. S. Peirce." *Versus* 49: 31–39.
Peirce, Charles S. 1931–1958. *The Collected Papers of Charles Sanders Peirce*. 8 vols. Vols. 1–6 edited by Charles Hartshorne and Paul Weiss; vols. 7–8 edited by Arthur W. Burks. Cambridge, MA: Harvard University Press. (Referred to as CP.)
Peirce, Charles S. 1977. *Semiotic and Significs: The Correspondence between Charles S. Peirce and Victoria Lady Welby*. Edited by Charles S. Hardwick. Bloomington: Indiana University Press. (Referred to as SS).
Peirce, Charles S. 1982–. *The Writings of Charles S. Peirce: A Chronological Edition*. 7 vols. to date. Edited by the Peirce Edition Project. Bloomington, IN: Indiana University Press. (Referred to as W.)
Peirce, Charles S. 1992–1998. *The Essential Peirce: Selected Philosophical Writings*. 2 vols. Vol. 1 edited by Nathan Houser and Christian Kloesel. Vol. 2 edited by the Peirce Edition Project. Bloomington, IN: Indiana University Press. (Referred to as EP.)
Pietarinen, Ahti-Veikko. 2005. "Cultivating Habits of Reason: Peirce & the *Logica Utens* and *Logica Docens* Distinction." *History of Philosophy Quarterly* 22, no. 4 (October): 357–372.
Ransdell, Joseph M. 2000. "Peirce and the Socratic Tradition." *The Transactions of the Charles S. Peirce Society* 36 no. 3 (Summer): 341–356.
Savan, David. 1981. "C. S. Peirce's Semiotic Theory of Emotion." In *Proceedings of the C. S. Peirce Bicentennial International Congress*, ed. Kenneth L. Ketner, Joseph M. Ransdell, Carolyn Eisele, Max H. Fisch, and Charles S. Hardwick. Lubbock: Texas Tech University Press, 319–333.
Sellars, Wilfrid. [1956] 2000. "Empiricism and the Philosophy of Mind." In *Knowledge, Mind, and the Given*, ed. Willem A. deVries and Timm Triplett (Indianapolis: Hackett), 205–276. Originally published in *Minnesota Studies in the Philosophy of Science*, vol. 1, 253–329.
Short, T. L. 1998. "The Discovery of Scientific Aims and Methods." *American Catholic Philosophical Quarterly* 72, no. 2: 293–312.
Short, T. L. 2001. "The Conservative Pragmatism of Charles Peirce." *Modern Age* 43, no. 4 (Fall): 295–303.
Short, T. L. 2007. *Peirce's Theory of Signs*. Cambridge: Cambridge University Press.
Smith, John E. [1968] 1995. *Experience and God*. New York: Fordham University Press.
Smith, John E. 1986. "Response [to Andrew Reck and Robert Neville]." *Transactions of the Charles S. Peirce Society* 22 no, 3 (Summer): 273–288.
Smith, John E. 1992. *America's Philosophical Vision*. Chicago: University of Chicago Press.
Taylor, Charles. 1995. *Philosophical Arguments*. Cambridge, MA: Harvard University Press.
Thayer, H. S. 1973. *Meaning and Action: A Study of American Pragmatism*. Indianapolis: Bobbs-Merrill.
Wallace, James D. 2009. *Norms and Practices*. Ithaca, NY: Cornell University Press.
Wiener, Philip P. 1965. *Evolution and the Founders of Pragmatism*. New York: Harper & Row.

CHAPTER 21

PRAGMATIC CLARIFICATION

Contexts and Purposes

MATS BERGMAN

MUCH ink has been spilled over the method C. S. Peirce designated "pragmatism." Indeed, the passage where he introduces pragmatism as a maxim of clarification is probably the most cited piece of text in his oeuvre. Yet, while many matters of the Peircean principle have been thoroughly interrogated over the years, it still presents us with a number of challenges of interpretation and application.

In this chapter, I turn my attention to a deceptively simple question: What purpose is Peirce's pragmatism meant to serve? At first blush, this query may feel almost willfully gratuitous. Surely, Peirce's aim is obvious: it is to "make our ideas clear." However, a closer look at Peirce's various articulations and uses of the maxim reveals a much more nuanced picture, with several objectives in play.

Here, I consciously adopt a narrow perspective on pragmatism as "pragmaticism," denoting a "special and limited form of pragmatism, in which the pragmatism is restricted to the determining of the meaning of concepts (particularly of philosophic concepts) by consideration of the experimental differences in the conduct of life which would conceivably result from the affirmation or denial of the meaning in question."[1] However, it should be acknowledged that this distinction between pragmatism and pragmaticism is not a hard and fast differentiation, not even within Peirce's own philosophy. While he sometimes underlines that pragmaticism is "only a method of thinking" (CP8.206, *c.* 1905) or "a mere rule of methodeutic"[2] (R322:12, 1907), there are also instances where he speaks of his pragmatism as involving "a whole system of philosophy" (CP8.191, 1904) or as "the master-key to all the doors of philosophy" (R328:5, *c.* 1905–1906). Although my entry point is pragmaticism in the delimited sense of a principle of clarification, attention to the motives behind the method exposes a richer field of questions than first impressions may suggest.

I will proceed as follows. First, I will briefly address the topic of the provenance of pragmatic elucidation in Peirce's thought and, on that basis, make the case for paying heed to the context of inquiry in clarifications. Next, I will turn to the elusive issue of what the method is supposed to clarify; and then, three aims of conceptual clarification, labeled *elimination*, *definition*, and *development*, will be identified. It should be noted that Peirce does not explicitly parse the matter like this. Nor should the purposes delineated be understood as mutually exclusive stages; rather, these aims occur concurrently in his writings. But as I suggest in the conclusion, the proposed differentiation elucidates pragmaticistic clarification in a way that can beneficially highlight some of its limits and prospects.

1. Contexts of Inquiry

Pragmatism, or rather the as-yet-unnamed principle, was introduced in print in the 1878 essay "How to Make Our Ideas Clear." According to Peirce's later reminiscences, it was not the first public appearance of the maxim; it had originally been presented at the legendary Metaphysical Club in the early 1870s. Incipient pragmatist ideas can certainly be detected in Peirce's abortive attempts to write a book on logic during the period in question. Peirce comes nearest to expressing the gist of the pragmatist principle in 1873, when he maintains that "the intellectual significance of all thought ultimately lies in its effect upon our actions" and emphasizes that the meaningful conduct is purposive (W3:108). A less obvious forerunner can be found in "Some Consequences of Four Incapacities" (1868), in which Peirce argues that the meaning of thought does not lie "in what is actually thought, but in what this thought may be connected with in representation by subsequent thoughts; so that the meaning of a thought is altogether something virtual" (W2:227).[3]

What we do not get in these embryonic articulations of pragmatism is a program for terminological clarification. A seed is arguably found in Peirce's 1871 Berkeley review, where he recommends avoiding the deceits of language by attending to its practical functions (W2:483); but this rule is thrown into the fray rather offhandedly, with little to suggest a systematic agenda or a venerable philosophical pedigree.[4]

In contrast, the published version of the method is framed as an improvement on the doctrine of "clear and distinct ideas" associated with René Descartes and Gottfried Leibniz. In the model delineated by Peirce, the old notion of the clear idea is recast as the first grade of clearness, construed as familiarity in use, while second-grade clarity or "distinctness" entails an idea in which no part is obscure. More concretely, the latter amounts to furnishing a formal analytic definition in abstract terms. Averring that these time-honored logical principles do not satisfactorily capture the realities of inquiry, Peirce then sets out to formulate the method for reaching a superior clearness of thought. The result is the renowned maxim, cited here once more for good measure: "The rule for attaining the third grade of clearness of apprehension is as follows:

Consider what effects, which might conceivably have practical bearings, we conceive the object of our conception to have. Then, our conception of these effects is the whole of our conception of the object" (ILS:90, 1878).

This is old hat for anyone well-acquainted with Peirce's philosophy. However, what is often overlooked is that he frames his principle as a response to the routine recycling of the clear-and-distinct doctrine in logical treatises "of the common sort." Although Peirce submits that their contributions are insignificant, I believe that his interest in clarification owes more to the belittled logics of science of his time than meets the eye. For not only do these intermediaries often advocate explication along the lines staked out in Peirce's two lower grades, but also, in some of the tracts, we additionally find references to something beyond simple clearness and analytic distinctness, typically identified in broadly Leibnizian terms as "adequacy" or "appropriateness."

Here, two examples may suffice. In *A Treatise on Logic*, Francis Bowen—Peirce's teacher—declares that the "three virtues of Clearness, Distinctness, and Adequacy constitute the perfection of Thought," in which the third "merit" comprises marks that are not only distinct but also pertinent attributes of the represented object.[5] In *Novum Organon Renovatum*, William Whewell—on whose theory of science Peirce lectures in the 1860s—maintains that the objective of explicating conceptions is to render ideas "distinct and appropriate," where "appropriateness" entails "modifications of that Fundamental Idea [. . .] by which phenomena can be really interpreted."[6] Additionally, Whewell contends that a discursive definition will not give us sufficiently clear conceptions. Although Peirce is highly critical of Whewell's approach, the two are in agreement about the insufficiency of analytic distinctness.

One practical lesson that Peirce extracts from these readings is the importance of separating a scientifically relevant issue from a mere question of words—a viewpoint that is arguably echoed in his subsequent delimitation of pragmatic clarification to "hard" concepts as well as in some of the eliminative objectives of his pragmaticistic program. It is also worth noting that Peirce later describes the third grade as imparting "Pragmatistic 'Adequacy'" (R649:2, 1910). Perhaps some germs of pragmatism are attributable to figures such as Bowen and Whewell.

Still, even if corroborated, such connections would not exhaust the impact of the logics of science on pragmatism. One influence is virtually hiding in plain sight. Some of the earliest manifestations of Peircean pragmatism are found in attempts to write a book on "practical logic," which gradually evolves into the series of "Illustrations of the Logic of Science" where "How to Make" is located. Thus, pragmatic clarification materializes as a vital constituent of Peirce's version of the informal logic of science—its very first lesson, no less.

So, one may inject, what difference does that make? To me, it raises two somewhat overlooked issues. First is the position of pragmatism in the scheme of investigation. The first two articles of "Illustrations" outline an elementary belief–doubt model, the nub of which is that we have certain belief-habits that guide our conduct, but which constantly encounter challenges that produce action-halting doubts of those beliefs; and the effort to reach or produce a new state of belief is inquiry. For our purposes, the most consequential upshot of the theory is that full-blown inquiry is something that requires genuine doubt, in contrast to what Peirce designates "paper doubt."

Hence, the question: Does pragmatic clarification amount to inquiry in the authentic Peircean sense? Turning to the sources does not provide us with a conclusive answer, for Peirce seems to waver between assigning pragmatic clarification a merely subsidiary role in inquiry and treating the pragmatic procedure as inquiry in its own right. This is partly because he never really works out the division of labor between the second and third grades of clearness; but it is also related to the varying goals set for the pragmatic method. I will return to these issues in the third section.

Second is the circumscription of pragmatic clarification by the context of inquiry. Is the application of the method to be limited to scientific investigation? And should the specific purpose of inquiry direct and delimit the actual process of clarification? To the latter question, Peirce gives somewhat divergent answers. On the one hand, he indicates that pragmaticistic clarification amounts to a pursuit of "total meaning" and is therefore not relative to any special circumstances, designs, or objectives (EP2:340, 1905);[7] but on the other hand, he also defines pragmaticism as the doctrine "that every concept (as distinguished from a generalized sensation, such as 'red') is equivalent to a conditional purpose, should one have certain desires and certain types of experience, to act in a certain general way" (RL107:5-6, 1904).[8] The obvious Peircean way out of this conflict would be to regard all clarifications as subservient to an overarching purpose—the "ultimate good" of furthering "the development of concrete reasonableness" (CP5.3, 1902). But attractive as such a comprehensive ideal can be in the abstract, it is of limited help in specific methodeutic pursuits; and if appealed to indiscriminately, it can even obscure some crucial features of pragmatic clarification "on the ground."

The challenges to which I allude can be illustrated with the case of "hardness," a perennial favorite of Peirce and Peirce scholars. Reflecting on the practical implications of the pragmatic principle, the young Peirce infamously argues that it is merely a matter of "the arrangement of our language" whether we call a particular diamond "hard" or "soft" if it is not actually put to the test (ILS:100, 1878). The later Peirce is one of the harshest critics of this "nominalist heresy." Hence, as he repeatedly stresses that pragmatism affirms the reality of habits as general "would-bes," the case of the hapless diamond gets relitigated time and again in the court of philosophy.

This turn toward the philosophical problem of nominalism/realism can be construed as a corrective informed by higher ideals of inquiry. But at the same time, we may lose sight of a key aspect of Peirce's original example—namely, that he is talking about "hardness" in a "strict mineralogical sense," which he clarifies as something that would "not be scratched by many other substances" (ILS:91, 1878; cf. EP2:401, 1907).[9] What Peirce almost certainly has in mind here is "scratch hardness" as operationalized by the Mohs scale. It is, at any rate, an experimental conception of hardness with which not only our self-professed laboratory inhabitant but also a key faction of his intended readership—that is, practicing scientists[10]—must have been familiar.

Thus, what Peirce is clarifying by conceivable experiments of scratching is a special conception of "hardness," set in a bounded purposive context of a certain line of inquiry.

Even if we put aside the trivial observation that "hard" has many varying uses, the clarification that Peirce proposes is in a pertinent respect relative to specific laboratory practices. It might be objected that the hardness clarified in "scratch hardness" functions as an explication of the common-sense idea of "hard things"; but that would not really hit the target. The wooden desk in front of me is "hard" by most lights; yet it would be scratched by many other substances.

The point that I am getting at is that the context of clarification matters. First, the aim of the inquiry will, to a significant extent, determine what kind and degree of clarification is deemed to be apt. Scratch hardness would constitute a fairly useless elucidation in most settings. This does not mean that such a clarification would not refer to a real would-be insofar as it hits its mark. My argument is simply that a clarification does not just occur in an all-embracing setting of generic inquiry; rather, it cannot be adequately apprehended without attention to what we might call its methodeutic context.

Second, the context significantly shapes our perception of the need for clarification. Practically anything could in principle be a target of elucidation; but we are rarely prompted to engage in such activity. I feel no urge to clarify the "hardness" that I attribute to my desk, although if pressed, I would have no problem in imputing a habitual reality to this object, imprecise as my idea of its hardness may be. However, it should be stressed that this context-dependency does not necessarily render all clarifications fullblown inquiries. Precise definitions are often called for by the protocols of scientific investigation. In such cases, the principal doubts and purposes motivating the activity are external to the clarifications as such, and second-grade clearness will normally suffice.

2. What Pragmaticism Clarifies

What, then, does pragmaticism clarify? In Peirce's early writings, the object of clarification is typically identified as "idea" or "thought." In the maxim cited above, this is restated in terms of "conception," indicating the conceptual side of ideas in contrast to their surface manifestations as terms or other sign vehicles. But as T. L. Short notes, this leaves it unclear whether clarification pertains to "apprehension of our conception of an object" or "our apprehension of the object itself."[11]

Since Peirce's maxim generally urges attention to the bearings of the object of *our* or *your* conception, I believe it is safe to say that the primary target of pragmatic clarification is internal—something that can be expounded in terms of his distinction between immediate and dynamical object. As Peirce puts the matter, "Collateral observation, aided by imagination and thought, will usually result in some idea, though this need not be particularly determinate.... Such an apprehension, approaching, however distantly, that of the Object strictly so called, ought to be, and usually is, termed the 'immediate object'" (EP2:409, 1907). In other words, we are dealing with the cognized idea-object as distinguished from "the Object in such relations as unlimited and final study would show it to be" (EP2:495, 1909). Yet, the meaning of the idea cannot be reduced to immediate conceptual content; on the contrary, it is doubly relational, involving reference to both a real or fictive object and potential interpretation. Put differently, intellectual concepts have "intrinsic significations beyond themselves" (EP2:401, 1907).

In the framework of Peircean semiotic, this puzzling intrinsic-outward meaning can be connected to the immediate interpretant. More tangibly, the "beyondness" can be associated with habitual bearings; for, as Peirce asserts, intellectual concepts "essentially carry some implication concerning the general behavior of some conscious being or of some inanimate object, and so convey [. . .] the *'would-acts'* of habitual behavior" (EP2:401–402, 1907). This provokes another question: Are we talking about the *habits of objects* or about *our habits*? The habits we ascribe to hard objects are obviously not identical to the habits of action that guide our conduct in relation to such things. Still, I believe that a fuller pragmatic clarification can well encompass both facets.

In an elaboration of the original pragmatist maxim, Peirce helpfully highlights this dual role of habit in pragmatic clarification: "Consider what effects that *might conceivably* have practical bearings,—especially in modifying habits or as implying capacities,—you conceive the object of your conception to have. Then your (interpretational) conception of those effects is the whole (meaning of) your conception of the object" (R322:11–12, 1907). If I consider my desk to be hard, then that conception implies both objective dispositions (inherent in the object) and potential habitual effects (on the interpreter). As noted earlier, I have presently no interest in this clarification; but if pursued sufficiently far, the two habitual aspects would cohere because the pragmatically significant capacities of the object are by definition such that they would make a difference to my conduct, given appropriate experiential conditions. Accordingly, Peirce identifies pragmatic signification with experimental effects on the conduct of life that would follow from affirming or denying the concept at hand.

But then, we encounter another problem. While Peirce mostly specifies the aim of pragmaticism as attainment of clear concepts, he also identifies several other objects of elucidation, for example, propositions, arguments, hypotheses, and theories. Most permissively, any sign (in the broad Peircean sense) might be pragmatically clarified; but this is typically qualified as symbols having meaning of a general kind. More narrowly, Peirce restricts the application of the method to "hard words and abstract concepts"—or, put differently, to such concepts "upon the structure of which arguments concerning objective fact may hinge" (EP2:400–401, 1907).

Thus, Peirce distinguishes his approach from the kind of pragmatism that would include generalized qualities of feeling, like "red" or "blue," among legitimate objects of clarification—his point being that such signs of sensation could be exchanged for each other without any implications for conditional conduct. Lacking intrinsic significations beyond themselves, the generalized sensations do not form concepts in the strict sense and are therefore not amenable to pragmaticistic analysis.

However, the delimitation of pragmaticism to concepts has not won the approval of all of Peirce's exponents. For example, Cheryl Misak argues that "the consequences with which pragmatism is concerned are predictions; we can predict that if H is true, then if you were to do A, B would result. Notice that we cannot, as Peirce seems to suggest, derive such conditionals from 'concepts' or from 'objects of conceptions.' We can only derive them from sentences or hypotheses."[12] Misak goes on to suggest that Peirce's way of talking about clarifying "hardness" is misleading, for the method proceeds by probing what we mean by saying that something is hard. Similarly, Christopher Hookway contends that "when Peirce clarifies a concept such as hard, he does so by describing the 'practical consequences' of some particular object being hard. We clarify hardness by clarifying propositions of the form 'That object is hard.'"[13]

Such arguments do find support in some of Peirce's writings. For example, in "What Pragmatism Is," the avowed aim is to show into what form a proposition ought to be translated in order to render its meaning clear (EP2:340, 1905); and in notes for a never-written book on "Calculations of Chances," Peirce states that the only proper method for analyzing an idea is to consider "what possible practical difference can be involved in the truth or falsity of a proposition involving that idea" (R211, 1896). More substantially, the propositional approach is propped up by the fact that Peirce maintains that terms merely name something. In contrast, propositions or "dicisigns" are precisely the kind of symbols that can be used in assertions and hence either true or false.

Indeed, it is difficult to say what the truth of a term or concept, to which Peirce surprisingly often appeals,[14] might entail. How could "hardness," as such, be true or false? However, judicious as the shift to propositions may seem, it is not altogether satisfactory, for the critics conflate the object of clarification with the means of clarification. True, specific propositions, such as "that diamond is soft" or "Putin's Russia is a democracy," are often the triggers for quests for illumination. But what we are ultimately seeking in applying the pragmatist principle to such cases is clarification of the conceptual part of the statements. That is, we are endeavoring to grasp that which other propositions predicating softness or the quality of democracy would have in common with the samples just mentioned.

The signs to be clarified are conceptual predicates, or, to use Peirce's technical terminology, *rhematic legisigns*.[15] This in no way conflicts with his assertion that "to be of any cognitive service," general concepts "must enter into propositions" (EP2:224, 1903). For the term "democracy," we can substitute the predicate-rhema "— is democracy." Its clarification is executed by virtual affirmation and assertion, which allows us to assess what the conceivable implications of a proposition like "it is true that Putin's Russia is a democracy" would be. But strictly speaking, in applying the pragmatist principle, it is the conceptual rhema that is being clarified—not any set of propositions. Yet, at the same time, the purposive context of inquiry, with its specific needs of assertion and interrogation, will—or at least should—determine what kind and level of clarification is called for.

3. Three Aims of Clarification

The purposive dimensions of pragmatism truly come to the fore in Peirce's mature writings. Not only does he note that the term "pragmatisch" implies a "relation to some definite human purpose"; he also maintains that the most outstanding feature of the theory is "its recognition of an inseparable connection between rational cognition and rational purpose" (EP2:333, 1905). Peirce even declares that of "the two implications of pragmatism that concepts are purposive, and that their meaning lies in their conceivable practical bearings, the former is the more fundamental" (CP8.322, 1906).

Peirce informs us that the rationale of the pragmatist method is "to consider what thought is *for*, and to take no step in reflection that is not required by that *purpose*" (R478, 1903). In "How to Make," the primary aim of thought is construed as the production of habits of action; later, this is qualified as habit formation in light of ultimate ends, of which the highest is contributing to the growth of concrete reasonableness. But how is a methodeutic maxim to serve such lofty purposes? I have already registered some reservations about the expediency of the Peircean *summum bonum* for specific pursuits of inquiry; but in the following, the question concerns what kinds of outcomes Peirce expects from putting his pragmatist principle to work.

My starting point here is that pragmaticism is principally a method for clarifying conceptual rhemas, as argued in the previous section. If we look at the concrete cases where Peirce applies his maxim, it is obviously abstract concepts like "reality," "force," and "time" that he considers in need of clarification. Some of these can be regarded as scientific terms; but many of the instances belong to what Peirce designates "ontological metaphysics." In relation to this domain, Peirce tends to characterize the goals of the pragmatist method negatively; but in addition to such eliminative objectives, pragmaticism is also portrayed as contributing to conceptual elucidation and habit development in a more positive sense.

3.1. Ontological Elimination

By "elimination," I here refer to pursuits that explicitly aim at halting or getting rid of something. In this strain, Peirce at times characterizes the task of pragmaticism as ending "those prolonged disputes of philosophers which no observations of facts could settle"—cases where "the disputants must be at cross-purposes," assigning divergent meanings to their words or using terms without any definite meaning (CP5.6, 1907). In this role, the pragmatic method is expected to dissolve disagreements that are merely verbal.

Although Peirce typically speaks of abolishing empty disputes in philosophy, his most conspicuous example homes in on a theological quarrel, that of transubstantiation. Targeting specifically the Catholic notion that the elements of the sacrament are literally flesh and blood, Peirce argues that "our action has exclusive reference to what affects the senses, our habit has the same bearing as our action, our belief the same as our habit, our conception the same as our belief; and we can consequently mean nothing by wine but what has certain effects direct or indirect, upon our senses" (ILS:89, 1878). Hence, he concludes that it is "senseless jargon" to assert that something possessing the sensible qualities of wine would in reality be blood. In this instance, at least, Peirce does not permit implications of religious habits to play any pragmatic role.

In this discussion, Peirce submits that our "idea" is pragmatically equivalent to conceivable sensible effects, which seems to approach outright verificationism. But even so, the gist of his argument is not that meaning would be reducible to sensory qualities per se, but rather that the significant habits involved relate to such effects. Still, somewhat ironically, Peirce's references to "sensations" are partly responsible for tendencies in the pragmatist tradition that he later finds problematic. In his early foray into pragmatist thinking, William James articulates a straightforward eliminative sensationalism. Explicitly referencing Peirce's method, James holds that achieving "sensational termini should be our aim with all our higher thought," because they "end discussion; they destroy the false conceit of knowledge; and without them we are all at sea with each other's meaning"; and he goes on to declare that "metaphysical discussions" are "like fighting with the air" on the basis that "they have no practical issue of a sensational kind."[16]

Although Peirce is critical of James's sensationalist tendencies, the two do seem to agree on some of the eliminative aims of pragmatism. According to Peirce, pragmaticism "will serve to show that almost every proposition of ontological metaphysics is either meaningless gibberish,—one word being defined by other words, and they by still others, without any real conception ever being reached,—or else is downright absurd; so that all such rubbish being swept away, what will remain of philosophy will be a series of problems capable of investigation by the observational methods of the true sciences" (EP2:338, 1905; cf. CP8.191, 1904). However, in spite of this "prope-positivism," Peirce does not advocate abolishing metaphysics altogether. Rather, his aim is to purge our thinking of unpragmatic elements—of obsolete and empty pseudo-concepts—employing the pragmatist maxim as a sharpened Ockham's razor to "give us an expeditious riddance of all ideas essentially unclear" (EP2:239, 1903).

The aim would then be not just to dismiss useless disputes, but also a more systematic cleansing of our conceptual vocabularies. This is qualified by the fact that Peirce mostly restricts such applications to philosophy and certain ontological remnants in scientific discourse. Moreover, notably few of Peirce's pragmaticistic analyses amount to terminological elimination. In one such case, Peirce sets out to clarify "matter," but what he targets is a professedly obsolete use of the word "to denote the homogeneous kind of substance within the surface of an atom, conceived as absolutely indivisible" (R290:38, 1905). Thus delimiting the scope of the clarification, Peirce concludes that "matter" means nothing, since all the relevant properties can be more effectively accounted for without reference to the conception in question.

This illustration is simultaneously enlightening and underwhelming. For while it nicely demonstrates the significance of the context of inquiry for clarification, the result is the "elimination" of a scientific conception deemed to be outdated ahead of the exercise. Still, this is perhaps what the sweeping away of "metaphysical rubbish" truly amounts to: removing leftovers of old ways of thinking by showing that they are of no conceivable use anymore in relevant contexts. So, while the eliminative objective is undeniably a motivator of Peirce's pragmaticist project, it plays a less significant role than some of his polemic proclamations suggest.

3.2. Elucidatory Definition

At least once, Peirce explicitly asserts that in addition to the eliminative office, his pragmatism targets "ideas essentially clear but more or less difficult of apprehension," with the aim of rendering them distinct (EP2:239, 1903). Thus, this objective seems to overlap with the second-grade pursuit of distinctness. However, barring grade collapse, the reasonable reading here is that the pragmatist method should provide us with a mode of distinctness that builds on that given by analytic definition. Modifying his youthful assessment that nothing "new can ever be learned by analyzing definitions" (ILS:83, 1878), the mature Peirce stresses that "pragmatistic adequacy" does not supplant abstract and precise definition (R649:2, 1910). From this angle, pragmaticism amounts to "a theory of logical analysis, or true definition" (CP6.490, 1908).

Since pragmatic clarification purportedly can give us an account of a conception by listing its conceivable practical bearings, it is easy to see how the aim of pragmaticism could be construed as higher-order definition. However, this raises the question whether such pursuits of clarification amount to a form of explication, that is, rendering explicit something that is already implicitly in the object under scrutiny. Evidently, pragmatic definition is meant to move beyond analytic definition, in which concepts are explicated in terms of other concepts; but both can be construed as steps toward bringing order to our confused ideas and beliefs.

In "Reason's Rules," Peirce distinguishes between heuretic reasonings that are "calculated to create beliefs" and explicatory elucidations that bring "into distincter apprehension the beliefs we already entertain" (R596:22–23, c. 1902–1903). The latter courses of thought constitute a form of "Socratic midwifery," which by raising awareness of our ideas can lead to doubt, but which are not products of doubts in themselves. Therefore, such handmaidens do not amount to ampliative inquiry; and as preparatory in this sense, the explications would arguably be exempt from the strict requirement of genuine doubt. This opens up a space for systematic clarification—analytic and pragmatic—the objective of which would be to render conceptions more precise, that is, to formulate "the definite ideas into which the vague notions of instinct, tradition, and uncontrolled intellection are to be translated" (R280:6, c. 1905). Thus, the aim of pragmatic analysis can now be construed as the sharpening of conceptions in order to bring out their respective meanings, but without thereby committing to a program of conceptual cleansing.

This implies that instead of being rival approaches to clearness, second- and third-grade clarifications can collaborate as explicatory tools of Peircean methodeutic. Unfortunately, Peirce never satisfactorily articulates the division of labor. Intriguingly, he suggests that the analytic grade of clearness should be subdivided into two and the pragmatic into three (ILS:193, 1909); but what this might entail is shrouded in mystery.

With some reservations, I propose that what Peirce designates the "phaneroscopic analysis" of concepts could be regarded as a subdivision of second-grade clearness. This reading is supported by his assertion that the first part of a theory of definition would amount to an account of "prebits" (that is, categories) (R646:13, 1910). However, the tools for this elementary clarification would be provided by the logic of relations, especially as articulated in the so-called existential graphs. It is well known that Peirce proposes to prove pragmaticism using these "moving pictures of thought" in his final years; but his turn to graphical logic also reveals the way in which phenomenological—or, as Peirce calls them, *phaneroscopic*—reflections can be said to prepare the canvas for pragmaticistic analysis proper. For what the graphs can make explicit are the formal relations of seemingly simple concepts. According to Peirce, traditional analytic definition proceeds by enumerating all the abstract predicates of a term and reaches its ideal culmination in simple ideas or "intuitions" such as "being," "substance," and "agency." This he deems insufficient, because such ostensibly basic conceptions are capable of further formal analysis into different modes of relationship. Interestingly, however, Peirce concludes that "the only alternative is to regard as the simplest the practically applied notions of familiar life" (EP2:239, 1903).

Therefore, my proposal is that pragmatic clarification takes over where phaneroscopic analysis reaches its limits. Whether this accords with Peirce's intentions or not is open for debate; as he sometimes declares that existential graphs can cover abduction and induction as well as deduction, he may have envisaged a more substantial role for his system. But as long as this claim is not substantiated, it remains rather moot. What graphical and other relational modes of analysis disclose are rhematic structures, the skeletons of conceptions, which in Peirce's ultimate analysis are either monadic, dyadic, or triadic. However, while a schematic graph of a concept "might be regarded as the passive object of a geometrical *intuitus*" (LI:352, 1906), the analysis also brings out the crucial capacity of rhemas to enter into relations. Insofar as this implies a form of action, it might be construed as the first step of pragmatic clarification. Yet, such a formal account inevitably falls short of fuller, experientially informed elucidation. In a sense, "— is hard" is a simple graph that exhibits how this predicate may be completed in thought and communication; but to attain a more robust account of its conceivable practical bearings, experiential factors must be brought in.

Whether "explication" is an apposite designation for the procedures sketched above is a good question. Strictly speaking, explicatory elucidation should leave the idea clarified unchanged. On the one hand, logical analysis can be construed as processing of extant information rather than as producing discoveries or originating knowledge. On the other hand, there is also something like observation and experimentation taking place in the internal arena where "true definitions" are generated. According to Peirce, pragmatic analysis entails performing purposive experiments on imaginary schemata, or conceptions understood as "composite photographs" of experience involving conditional resolutions bearing on conduct (R288:78, 1905). Furthermore, he characterizes pragmaticism as a form of "critical inquiry," by which we learn the meaning of abstract words, either (1) by attending to examples of their use that bring up conceptions virtually hidden in our minds or (2) by imagining ourselves as having certain habits of action (R327:2, *c.* 1906). For Peirce, the "instinctive" conceptions brought out in the former mode of analysis are evolutionarily grounded in practical purposes; but it is the latter that gives us the core pragmaticistic procedure.

3.3. Critical Development

If pragmatic analysis is a process of learning or inquiry, then it is at least partly ampliative and not merely explicative. In the context of clarification, this can be parsed in two different ways. First, it can entail acquiring knowledge about habits external to the knower, for example, what it would entail for something to be hard. But second, learning may also refer to a process whereby the habits of the knower are modified. In many of Peirce's late-period discussions of pragmaticism, these two facets in effect coalesce. The key is that it is always *our* conceptions that are at stake; therefore, in clarifying objects we ultimately relate their behavior to such practical bearings that we can conceive. The upshot is broadly speaking anthropomorphic, something that Peirce frequently and approvingly acknowledges.

This not only entails that the concept/conception is integrally associated with mental habit; pragmatic meaning also involves reference to the development of habit. Thus, Peirce argues that the veritable meaning—or the "ultimate logical interpretant"—of an intellectual sign cannot be a concept that "somewhat partakes of the nature of a verbal definition"; rather, it is a "living definition that grows up in the habit" and therefore "the most perfect account of a concept that words can convey will consist in a description of the habit which that concept is calculated to produce" (EP2:418, 1907; R318:76, 1907).

So portrayed, the "living definition" seems to amount to a higher kind of elucidation. But that is not all, for Peirce emphatically argues that the habit in question must be deliberately forged using powers of imagination. In other words, our conceptual analyses play a critical role in the development of the habits that constitute the ultimate meanings of our concepts. Accordingly, Peirce characterizes the ultimate logical interpretant as a "habit-change," by which he means "a modification of a person's tendencies toward action, resulting from previous experiences or from previous exertions of his will or acts, or from a complexus of both kinds of cause. It excludes natural dispositions, as the term 'habit' does, when it is accurately used; but it includes beside associations, what may be called 'transsociations,' or alterations of association, and even includes *dissociation*" (CP5.476, 1907). Consequently, the third—and perhaps ultimate—purpose of pragmatic clarification is the critical development of habits. It is an explicitly normative undertaking, relating to the regulation of our thought "by means of self-criticism [...] and the purposive formation of habit" (R655:24, 1910). Peirce qualifies this by stressing the limitations of such self-control. But that does not change the fact that pragmatic clarification can now be construed as an autonomous mode of inquiry. I would even venture to say that it is simultaneously normative and developmental, driven by the insight that the "continual amelioration of our own habits [...] is the only alternative to a continual deterioration of them" (R674:1, c. 1911).

Of course, this does not prove that the developmental-melioristic objective is viable. Much more should be added; but three supplementary observations will have to suffice here. First, to avoid repeating nominalist heresies, it should be underscored that the ultimate meaning is not constituted by any set of actual habit changes; rather, it relates to the capacity to modify habits in the three senses identified in the passage above. And this power is not blind but purposive. Sometimes, Peirce suggests that pragmatic meaning could be identified with purpose; however, in the end, he submits that "purpose is only the special character . . . of this or that self-controlled habit" (EP2:431, 1907). Perhaps it would be more apposite to say that they are two sides of the same coin.

Second, the primary arena of purposive habit development is internal, in the sense of taking place in a field of imaginary experimentation. Such inquiry can produce genuinely surprising results; but to perform abductions and inductions in the world of ideas, conceptual predicates must be embodied as images of rhemas. The procedure prescribed by Peirce could be characterized as mathematical in a broad sense, involving the experimental manipulation of iconic signs.[17] However, Peirce also likens the process to a kind of persuasive dialogue, where the inquirer addresses a future self, thereby imaginatively testing what conceivable consequences for action adopting a certain conception might have. This does not mean that the upshot would apply only to the inner world. On the contrary, Peirce stresses that habits acquired by imaginary reiterations "will have power to influence actual behavior in the outer world" (EP2:413, 1907).

But third, one might still feel that Peirce's procedure is gratuitously restrictive, as it seems to confine conceptual inquiry to the inner world. Given that he argues that thought should "be understood as covering all rational life, so that an experiment shall be an operation of thought" (EP2:337, 1905), the rationale for the delimitation is not apparent. However, in a largely ignored portion of the byzantine essay "Pragmatism," Peirce introduces a distinction between three logical interpretants corresponding to different phases of conceptual formation and development. Interestingly, the text in question associates ultimate meaning with the second logical interpretant, understood as "habits of internal or imaginary action, abstracted from all reference to the individual mind in which they happen to be implanted, and whose future actions they would guide" (R318:46, 1907). The third logical interpretant entails a turn from internal to external experience, prompting further deliberate habit changes. In other words, it amounts to experimentation in the exterior world—that is, putting concepts to the test outside of the theater of imagination. In another context, Peirce refers to "a third or evolutionarily pragmaticistic interpretation," which is aimed at producing "a reconciliation or interadjustment between reason and the facts of experience" (LI:392, 1908). This might be construed as the higher end-in-view of pragmatic clarification. Although Peirce does not explicitly say so, at this stage clarification becomes not only externally oriented, but also fully social—another criterion for genuine inquiry. At any rate, in the third logical interpretant, the work of the intellect purportedly reaches a state of provisional and partial consummation, which in Peirce's assessment is of highest logical import.

4. Some Limits and Possibilities of Pragmaticism

A couple of months before his death, Peirce somberly concluded that "the maxim of Pragmatism does not bestow a single smile upon beauty, upon moral virtue, or upon abstract truth" (EP2:465, 1913). The reason for this gloomy assessment is that he perceived of pragmaticism as providing merely security in reasoning, rather than anything of productive value. This is certainly true of the eliminative objectives of pragmatic clarification, and arguably also of those definitory pursuits that aim at explication in a narrow sense. It is less obvious to me that Peirce's judgment would accurately describe the contributions of pragmatic definition; and when it comes to what I have described as its developmental purposes, I actually find his appraisal rather misplaced.

Much hinges on how we understand the relationship between the pragmatic method and inquiry. In this chapter, I have attempted to lay the groundwork for a reading of Peircean pragmatism that would allow us to view it both as a methodeutic tool within scientific inquiry and as a mode of critical inquiry in its own right; and I have done so without appealing to many of the ideas that accompany pragmaticism. At the same time, I believe that the account I have been delineating suggests how even the narrow notion of pragmaticism can lead us to unexpected vistas. Of course, what I have provided is a skeletal outline at best; many gaps remain to be filled. So, I will conclude by noting three such issues pertaining to pragmatic inquiry.

The first relates to certain implications of treating pragmaticism as inquiry in the Peircean sense. As noted, clarification can be partly exempt from the strict demand of genuine doubt if it fulfills preparatory or subordinate objectives. But if it is regarded as a mode of inquiry, then pragmatic clarification should be instigated by genuine doubt—or, if this terminology feels too quaint, by some perceived problem affecting our practices. Especially if we allow a broad notion of inquiry, taking in much more than science in a narrow respect, such triggering factors do not need to be momentous; but they should involve some felt impediment to action. And this ought to guide our pursuits of clarification. In my view, the implication is a rejection of any comprehensive program of conceptual cleansing. Instead, clarification should proceed piecemeal and contextually, informed either by needs of inquiry or by concrete desires for clearness. Thus, although I believe that Peircean pragmatism can have much to contribute to agendas of conceptual ethics and conceptual amelioration, I feel less sanguine about the prospects of putting it to work within some of the conceptual engineering programs currently in vogue.

The second issue concerns the extent to which clarification can be reasonably pursued. In some instances, Peirce suggests that the ideal aim of clarification is to achieve perfect precision, that is, remove vagueness or "latitude of interpretation" from our concepts by means of explication or "preciding." But in more sober reflections, he points out that absolute definiteness in expression is never really attainable. Amusingly, Peirce even contends that his "fellow-pragmatists are so fond of clear thinking that they insist that every concept they entertain should be definite, though clearness and definiteness are quite different things" (R284:3–4, c. 1905; cf. SS:11, 1903). Along these lines, Peirce observes that there is often little to be gained from pushing clarification to its ultimate conclusion, and he sets the limit of judicious clearness at vague or "instinctive" beliefs related to the ordinary conduct of life. Faced with such "practical matters" as the hardness of my desk, it would simply be an idle exercise for me to seek an explicit clarification in terms of conceivable habits of conduct.

Here, we should note Peirce's claim that the realism of pragmaticism embraces not only real generals but also real possibles. The latter are equivalent to real, irreducible vagues. For as Peirce observes, in some cases "it is not because insufficient pains have been taken to precide the residuum, that it is vague: it is [. . .] vague intrinsically" (CP5.508, c. 1905). In a noteworthy passage, he goes so far as to discard his old view that if "the pendulum of opinion" would "continue to oscillate back and forth forever," there would be no real truth of the question at hand. Instead, he now contends that "the real truth would be of an indefinite nature" (LI:377, 1908).

To my knowledge, Peirce does not elaborate on what to expect from an attempt to clarify such a real vague. Would it all be in vain? Perhaps courting controversy, I submit that in relation to some concepts, like "democracy," interminable clarificatory endeavors can be pragmatically defensible. Debates relating to such "essentially contested concepts" could be construed as involving varying conceptions of a real vague object. Of course, there is no guarantee that a single conception would never hold sway; but the point is that even if reaching the terra firma of truth were impossible because of the nature of things, the conceptual development could still be pragmatically meaningful, engendering more or less viable habits of action.

If that is accepted, then the final issue I wish to bring up becomes even more important. For one thing that I have not properly dealt with in this chapter is the relationship of pragmatic clarification to higher ends and ideals. Again, I am not primarily thinking about the Peircean highest good, which I consider to be *too* vague to be of much pragmatic interest, apart from its all-purpose developmental spirit. Rather, instead of the top-down perspective that Peirce often advocates in his normative reflections, I believe the better Peircean approach is to consider ideals as organically generated by criticisms of criticism, with no definite upper limit to the procedure, yet at the same time recognizing pragmatic boundaries recommended by purposes of inquiry. In my brief discussion of the third logical interpretant, I drew attention to the fact that Peirce characterizes it as partial consummation. So, unless we are perfectly satisfied with our methods of clarification, the next reasonable step would be to subject those critical means to logical, ethical, and esthetic criticism, in effect employing and developing higher-order purposes—that is, ideals linked to habits—as we move along. And in the end, perhaps such a bottom-up approach, pursuing criticism in context, is what a pragmatic clarification of the "development of concrete reasonableness" really comes down to.

Notes

1. C. S. Peirce, "Pragmaticism," in Benjamin E. Smith, ed., *The Century Dictionary Supplement* (New York: Century Co., 1909–1910), 1050.
2. "Methodeutic" is Peirce's preferred mature-period name for the third, methodological branch of logic.
3. At R290:2–3, 1905, Peirce refers to the passage in question as approaching pragmaticism.
4. Later, Peirce identifies George Berkeley as a pivotal proto-pragmatist.
5. Francis Bowen, *A Treatise on Logic* (Cambridge, MA: Sever and Francis, 1864), 77, 82. Although Peirce is dismissive of his teacher's acumen, in later characterizations of "clearness" and "distinctness," he employs phrases that are strikingly reminiscent of Bowen's earlier account. The possible influence of Bowen on Peirce has not been widely noted in the literature; but see Cornelis de Waal's note in ILS102 and also the *Peirce Project Newsletter* 4, no. 1 (2001).
6. William Whewell, *Novum Organon Renovatum* (London: John W. Parker, 1858), 27, 30.
7. Cf. EP2:346, 1905; EP2:402, 1907.
8. See also CP5.548, 1907; R318:32, 1907.
9. Here, Peirce's original "will" has been changed to "would" in accordance with the realism of his later position.
10. I owe this observation regarding Peirce's scientific audience to Cornelis de Waal.
11. T. L. Short, "The 1903 Maxim," *Transactions of the Charles S. Peirce Society* 53 (2017): 349.
12. Cheryl Misak, *Truth and the End of Inquiry* (Oxford: Oxford University Press, 2004), 11.
13. Christopher Hookway, *The Pragmatic Maxim* (Oxford: Oxford University Press, 2012), 222.
14. See, for example, CP5.9, 1907; R321:12, 1907; EP2:448, 1908.
15. A legisign is "a sign which is of the nature of a general type, law, or habit" (R800:2, *c.* 1903). A rhema "is equivalent to a blank form such that if all its blanks are filled with proper names, it becomes a proposition, or symbol capable of assertion" (R491:3–4, *c.* 1903). Alternatively, a rhema can be characterized as "a sign whose proper interpretant ignores all difference between the sign and its object" (R800:5); it "is represented in its signified interpretant *as if it were* a character or mark" and as such it is neither true nor false (SS:34, 1904).
16. William James, "On the Function of Cognition," *Mind* 10 (1885), 43–44.
17. See, for example, R328:38–39, *c.* 1905–1906.

References

Peirce, Charles S. 1857–1914. Manuscripts held at the Houghton Library of Harvard University, as identified in Richard Robin. 1967. *Annotated Catalogue of the Papers of Charles S. Peirce.* Amherst: University of Massachusetts Press. And in Richard Robin. 1971. "The Peirce Papers: A Supplementary Catalogue." *Transactions of the Charles S. Peirce Society* 7, no. 1: 37–57. (Referred to as R; with RL for letters and RS for supplement.)

Peirce, Charles S. 1931–1958. *The Collected Papers of Charles Sanders Peirce.* 8 vols. Vols. 1–6 edited by Charles Hartshorne and Paul Weiss. Vols. 7–8 edited by Arthur W. Burks. Cambridge, MA: Harvard University Press. (Referred to as CP.)

Peirce, Charles S. 1977. *Semiotic and Significs: The Correspondence between Charles S. Peirce and Victoria Lady Welby*. Edited by Charles S. Hardwick. Bloomington: Indiana University Press. (Referred to as SS.)

Peirce, Charles S. 1982– . *The Writings of Charles S. Peirce: A Chronological Edition*. 7 vols. to date. Edited by the Peirce Edition Project. Bloomington: Indiana University Press. (Referred to as W.)

Peirce, Charles S. 1992–1998. *The Essential Peirce: Selected Philosophical Writings*. 2 vols. Vol. 1 edited by Nathan Houser and Christian Kloesel. Vol. 2 edited by the Peirce Edition Project. Bloomington: Indiana University Press. (Referred to as EP.)

Peirce, Charles S. 2009. *The Logic of Interdisciplinarity*. Edited by Elize Bisanz. Berlin: Akademie Verlag. (Referred to as LI.)

Peirce, Charles S. 2014. *Illustrations of the Logic of Science*. Edited by Cornelis de Waal. Chicago: Open Court. (Referred to as ILS.)

CHAPTER 22

PEIRCE, PERCEPTION, AND EMPIRICISM

AARON BRUCE WILSON

CHARLES S. Peirce's pragmatism subsumes a form of empiricism. It adds an element to the basic empiricist idea that, semantically and epistemically, our concepts and knowledge depend heavily on sense perception. The element that Peirce's pragmatism adds to empiricism is the idea that our concepts and knowledge also depend on *conduct* or *purposive action*. This point might not come across as clearly in his early works, including the 1868–1869 "cognition series" and the 1877–1878 series "Illustrations on the Logic of Science,"[1] as it does in his later works, especially his 1903 Harvard Lectures. Toward the end of the seventh and final lecture of that 1903 series, Peirce presents one of the best-known statements of his maxim of pragmatism: "The elements of every concept enter into logical thought at the gate of perception and make their exit at the gate of purposive action; and whatever cannot show its passports at both those two gates is to be arrested as unauthorized by reason" (EP2:241).

Thus, by 1903, Peirce realizes that, to explain his pragmatism, he must explain both sense perception and purposive action. In the Harvard Lectures, he explains the latter in relation to the normative sciences of logic, ethics, and esthetics, as all purposive action, according to him, is directed toward logical, ethical, or aesthetic ends. Regarding perception, Peirce remarks on it across the lectures, culminating with his three "cotary propositions" of pragmatism,[2] each of which is a substantial claim about perception that, he says, "put[s] the edge on the maxim of pragmatism" (EP2:226, 1903). Here we see his mature theory of perception begin to take shape, and it becomes the focus of a manuscript written shortly after the lectures that was intended to contribute to a debate over psychical research (R881, 1903). His theory of perception continues to develop after 1903, as he develops within in his semiotics or theory of signs distinctions which, I argue, elucidate the nature of perceptual representation.

Peirce's main concern with perception is its relationship with the *normative* sphere of reasoning and inquiry. The main significance of perception for reasoning and inquiry, on his view, is that our perceptual experience is *all we can* reason or inquire upon.

Our commitment to the general veracity of perception rests on the fact that we have no choice but to accept our perceptions if we are to reason or inquire at all. It does not rest on the idea that perception is an incorrigible or self-justifying source of knowledge, although he thinks we can have reason to doubt any given perception only in relation to a "theory of the facts" based on our wider perceptual experience.

However, Peirce's concern with the normative dimensions of perception invites other concerns, particularly metaphysical ones relating to exactly what types of propositions perception gives us no choice but to accept. On his view, we directly perceive the external world ("the doctrine of immediate perception") as well as generals or *thirds* ("the second cotary proposition of pragmatism"). But Peirce must explain how we can perceive the external world and its general and relational elements—that is, he must give an account of perceptual representation on which such things can be perceived. His account begins with a distinction between the "percept" and the "perceptual judgment," but it incorporates other distinctions, including the "pericipuum," or the percept *as it is* interpreted by the perceptual judgment, and "the third cotary proposition" that perception has an *abductive* structure. As I argue, his account must also be understood to incorporate distinctions from his general semiotic, such as the distinction between the "immediate object" and the "dynamical object" of a sign.

Thus, Peirce's mature theory of perception has three connected parts: *normative, metaphysical*, and *semiotic*.[3] In what follows, I will trace its development from the 1860s to 1906 while highlighting and explaining each of the above three parts of it. To ensure that I sufficiently cover its chronological development and each of its parts, and to avoid getting bogged down in technical disagreements and confusions, I will not attempt a complete survey of the secondary literature here. Some confusion and divergence in interpretation results from insufficient considerations of what Peirce says across his voluminous writings; although there are sufficient ambiguities, shifts in terminology, and seemingly conflicting statements in Peirce's writings about perception to have engendered disagreements worth exploring.[4] There is, however, broad agreement on many aspects of Peirce's account, such as that it adheres to the doctrine of immediate perception and that it avoids the Cartesian assumptions of earlier forms of empiricism.[5]

1. Peirce's Early Insights on Perception

Peirce's earliest written comments on perception concern the Scottish doctrine of "immediate perception," according to which "external reality itself constitutes the immediate and only object of perception."[6] While he adopts a form of this doctrine from at least 1871 onward, his earliest writings appear very critical of it. In 1864, he argues that this doctrine fails to be supported both by common sense and by "the pretended testimony of consciousness" (W1:194).

Peirce continues to reject any analysis of perception that rests on "the testimony of consciousness," as in his famous 1868 "anti-Cartesian" papers, he argues that we have neither an underived faculty of introspection nor an "intuitive faculty of distinguishing intuitive from mediate cognitions" (EP1:54). By "intuitive cognition" he means cognition that represents its object without being "determined by" other cognitions to do so.[7] In the first paper,[8] he does not quite argue that perception is not intuitive, but only that we have no intuitive ability to distinguish any cognition *as* intuitive—that is, he argues that perception is not *self-intuitive*. For Peirce, even if perception is intuitive, we could know this only through empirical research.[9] We cannot know the "first impressions" of perception simply from reflection on our own first-person case.

Peirce's remarks about perception in the 1868 papers are mostly psychological and physiological, and they are presented as evidence against "certain faculties claimed for man" rather than as elements of a positive theory. He cites how people commonly mistake something they inferred for something they immediately perceived. He also argues that sensory nerves are insufficient to present the continuous surfaces of the three-dimensional objects we commonly perceive, suggesting that the perception of continuous surfaces is the result of a mediated cognitive process.[10] He also mentions how its common among young children to suppose that they have always understood their native language, as they, like adults, apprehend the meaning of spoken words without any effort of thought, while adults know that our semantic cognition is largely acquired or dependent on "previous cognitions."[11]

Further, in the 1868 papers, Peirce denies that perception involves the creation of internal images or pictures, because not only are no pictures "painted on the nerves of the retina," but also the mind has no need to create internal pictures, as the amount of information we draw from perception is much less than what actual pictures afford. Images or pictures are fully determinate in their qualities, having *precise* shapes, *precise* dimensions, etc. However, Peirce argues, perceptions are *never* fully determinate or precise, and they cannot be, for otherwise we would be conscious of more information than we could handle: "But the conclusive argument against our having any images, or absolutely determinate representations in perception, is that in that case we have the materials in each such representation for an infinite amount of conscious cognition, which we yet never become aware of" (EP1:83). In addition, he takes this point, that perceptions are never fully determinate, to mean that perceptions are *general* so far as they are indeterminate (EP1:84). Peirce will again, in the 1903 Harvard Lectures, argue that perceptions are general, in that types, kinds, and other instances of thirdness are represented in perception, deeming it one of the three cotary propositions of his pragmatism.

It is evident from these early papers that Peirce rejects foundationalist forms of empiricism that take knowledge to rest upon sense perceptions, or reports thereof, assumed to be intuitive or to be irrefutable—from Lockean simple ideas to Carnapian protocol sentences. Peirce is a century ahead of his time with respect to empiricism in the philosophy of science.

However, from the 1868–1869 cognition series and onward, Peirce himself held some form of empiricism. For instance, he assumes some form of *meaning* or *concept empiricism* where he argues that we have "no conception of the absolutely incognizable" because "all our conceptions are obtained by abstractions and combinations of cognitions first occurring in judgments of experience" (EP1:60, 1868).[12] There is also evidence of an *epistemological empiricism* in Peirce's early work. Although he first declares that "all knowledge is based on experience" in 1883, "A Theory of Probable Inference," in his 1871 review of the works of George Berkeley (EP1.117–137),[13] he defends the hypothesis that inquiry into any meaningful question would, with sufficient *experience*, result in a "final opinion" on it (EP1:122).[14] While here he might include more than sense perception as "experience," it seems unlikely since he had, just three years earlier, argued against intuition and introspection as sources of knowledge.

An epistemological form of empiricism is more conspicuous in the 1877–1878 "Illustrations of the Logic of Science" series, with both Peirce's rejection of the "a priori method" of fixing belief and his defense of the "method of science." He describes the method of science as ascertaining how things really are by reasoning from how things affect our *senses* (EP1:151), implying that the scientific method of fixing belief, the only method he thinks would succeed in the long run, is particularly if not exclusively based on sense perception.

As Peirce espouses a form of empiricism yet rejects foundationalist forms of it, an articulation his own *non*foundationalist form of empiricism is wanting. The precise form it could take is complicated not only by his rejection of self-intuitive forms of experience but also by his seeming support for the doctrine of *innate ideas*. In the same 1883 article where he first declares all knowledge to be based on experience, he also argues that "all [animals] have from birth some notions, however crude and concrete, of force, matter, space, and time; and, in the next place, they have some notion of what sort of objects their fellow-beings are, and of how they will act on given occasions" (W4:520, 1883). So, Peirce needs to explain how all knowledge can be based on experience even though our notions of space, force, etc., are innate. I will suggest how he does so toward the end of the chapter.

It is important to note that Peirce objects to basing *logic* (which for him encompasses all epistemological concerns) on *psychology*. Objections appear in both early and later work.[15] While key arguments of the 1877–1878 series are psychological, particularly in "The Fixation of Belief," where the method of science is defended on sociopsychological grounds that the other methods are inherently unstable,[16] his objections mainly target attempts to base logic on the *introspective* type of psychology that was common during his time. In 1865, he remarked that "logic should be extricated once and forever from all the entanglements of introspection" (W1:350). In contrast, the sociopsychological claims of the 1877–1878 series are based, not on introspection, but on behavioral habits knowable through common experience. So, while Peirce's empiricism turns on some psychological arguments, it does not, or is not supposed to, turn on appeals to introspection.

However, not enough can be said about perception from a behavioral standpoint. Also, what was known about perception from neurobiology at that time was extremely limited. So, it is likely that Peirce avoided developing a positive account of perception because he was uncertain how to treat perception in a distinctly "logical" way that avoids introspective psychology. Peirce faced a problem: How do you explain the basis of knowledge in sense perception without treating perception as intuitive and self-certain, or without relying on introspective psychology?

2. Overview of Peirce's Mature Theory of Perception

At the dawn of the twentieth century, Peirce formulated an answer. One key is to distinguish between normative, semiotic, and psychological dimensions of knowledge—with the first two being the province of *logic* and the third being relevant only in limited ways to the first two. Another key is to examine the significance that perception has for the *normative* dimension of knowledge—that is, for the *self-controllable* activities related to knowledge, reasoning, and inquiry, which are subject to various norms. For Peirce, the significance that perception has for reasoning and inquiry is that *perceptual judgments*—or "the first judgment of a person as to what is before his senses" (EP2:191, 1903)—are the ultimate premises for all reasoning and inquiry, or for all knowledge resulting from any reasoning and inquiry (e.g., all scientific knowledge). Perceptual judgments comprise that class of judgments that we have no choice but to accept when we reason or inquire, and they constitute the observations or data upon which theories are accepted or rejected.

As I read Peirce,[17] a judgment must satisfy *three* conditions to count as a perceptual judgment. First, a perceptual judgment must arise, not directly from any deliberate thinking, but as an uncontrollable response to a *percept* or perceptual experience. We can control the external conditions under which our percepts occur, such as by closing our eyes or covering our ears, but as soon as we look or listen, we reflexively form some judgment about what we perceive. We also cannot dismiss a perceptual judgment in the presence of a percept. We can ignore it by turning our attention elsewhere, or we can look more carefully and perhaps form a different perceptual judgment; but, with any percept, we cannot help but perceive whatever the perceptual judgment tells us we perceive.

Second, despite occurring and persisting uncontrollably, perceptual judgments must still be available to the self-controllable levels of cognition. We must be able to reason deliberately with or upon our perceptual judgments. It is arguable that we form judgments uncontrollably in response to percepts that *remain* at an unconscious and hence uncontrollable level, so that we could never deliberately reason with them. While it is questionable whether Peirce would regard such "unconscious judgments" as genuine judgments, as he defines "judgment" as "the self-recognition of a belief" (CP8.337, 1904), if one could identify judgment-like mental states occurring entirely at an unconscious level, they would not, on his account, qualify as perceptual judgments. They must be available to our reasoning.

Peirce's distinction between self-controllable levels of cognition and un(self-)controllable levels of cognition corresponds roughly to the contemporary distinction between *personal* and *subpersonal* levels of cognition, which originates with Dennett (1969). This distinction has since been understood to distinguish between *normative* and *nonnormative* levels of cognition, or between a self-conscious responsiveness to reasons (the personal, self-controllable level) and an unconscious or subconscious automatic responsiveness to various stimuli (the subpersonal, uncontrollable level).[18] However, Peirce recognizes that there is no *sharp* boundary between these two levels of cognition and that our cognitive habits are self-controllable to varying degrees (e.g., CP7.647, 1903).[19] So, as he does not insist on perceptual judgments having some *precise degree* of uncontrollability, whether a given judgment is sufficiently uncontrollable to count as a perceptual judgment could partly depend on the context or situation (at least, this would be consistent with his account). For Peirce, if one can honestly say, "I cannot help but to see it this way," that would suffice for a perceptual judgment.

The third condition that, on Peirce's mature view, a judgment must satisfy to be a *perceptual* judgment is that the judgment must not only be an uncontrollable response to a percept, but also *describe something indexed by the percept that prompted it*. This is a controversial point that requires some explanation and argument, but one I have explained and argued elsewhere.[20]

Peirce tells us that the perceptual judgment represents the percept, but only as an *index* (CP7.628, 1903). An index is any sign that is in such a direct physical relation with its object that it can "direct the attention to [its object] by blind compulsion" (CP2.305–306, 1901). Indices "point" to their objects; so, perceptual judgments only point to their percepts. However, as a proposition, the perceptual judgment must also *describe* something. At some places, that seems to be the "perceptual fact" (e.g., EP2:155, 1903), but it is unclear how the perceptual fact stands in relation to the percept. I contend that the percept is itself an index that directs our awareness to the perceptual fact. Although at some places Peirce suggests that the percept is not a sign at all,[21] there are several reasons to regard the percept as an index. Not only does he directly say the percept is a sign, at least in one work (CP4.539, 1906), but also he writes of the percept as a "presentation" (e.g., CP7.631, 1903), where "presenting" counts as an indexical act. There are other reasons to regard the percept as an index, which I will cover later. The percept directs our awareness to something, although, by itself, that might be everything within our perceptual field. With the perceptual judgment, information is filtered out, and the percept directs our attention only to the fact that the judgment describes.

The condition that the facts we can perceive must be within our perceptual field, or that part of our environment to which percepts can direct our attention, eliminates many uncontrollable judgments as candidates for perceptual judgments. Suppose you return home and see your spouse's car keys on the table. You might uncontrollably judge "My spouse is home."[22] But this would not be a perceptual judgment because the subject, one's spouse, is not within the perceptual field, so the percept could not point to them. In contrast, "My spouse's keys are on the table" could be a perceptual judgment because the keys are within the perceptual field; the percept can directly point to them.

Per the normative part of Peirce's account, whatever we conclude about the semiotics of perception is itself based on perceptual judgments, including the conclusion that they could be *radically false*. He agrees that they *could be*, as the dream hypothesis seems consistent with our perceptual experience, but he does not think that any logically correct reasoning from perceptual judgments gives us reason to doubt them systemically. Against Descartes (and much of twentieth-century epistemology), Peirce denies that there is a standing justification requirement on sense perception. For him, a justification requirement could arise only during inquiry, or when *genuine* doubts arise concerning some matter (the "doubts" expressed by Descartes being "paper doubts"[23]). A justification requirement can also be part of a "method of inquiry," such as the method of science whereby we are required to test our hypotheses. However, it is not an automatic requirement of *all* inquiries; and as all inquiries rest on perceptual judgments, it is not a requirement on such judgments *as a whole class*. Any subset of perceptual judgments can be doubted and falsified, but only with respect to our wider perceptual experience. Philosophically, an account of how perceptual judgments are true is needed; and we should acknowledge the possibility of being radically wrong, but that commits us only to *fallibilism*, or to the claim that we *may not* know what we think we know.[24]

These points about Peirce's mature theory of perception slowly emerge in his writings from about 1900 to about 1908. They begin to emerge in his entry for "representationism" for Baldwin's 1901 dictionary. There he claims that both the "representationist," who holds that "percepts stand for something behind them," and the "presentationist," who upholds the doctrine of immediate perception, must admit that percepts "perform the function of conveying knowledge of something else" (CP 5.607, 1900). This is evidence that Peirce takes percepts to function as signs, although it is not immediately clear what *type* of sign the "representationist" and the "presentationist" each take the percept to be.

Peirce says more about perception in his January 1901 review of Karl Pearson's *The Grammar of Science*. After criticizing Pearson's views on the values and motives of science,[25] Peirce turns to Pearson's chapter, "Facts of Science," which defends a theory of cognition that, according to Peirce, "falls into the too common error of confounding psychology with logic" (EP2:60). Pearson claims that scientific knowledge is built up out of "sense-impressions," such that "each of us is like the operator at a central telephone office, shut out from the external world, of which he is informed only by sense-impressions" (EP2:61–62). In Peirce's response to this, we get our first glance at the normative part of his theory:

> But the starting point of all our reasoning is not in those sense-impressions, but in our percepts. When we first wake up to the fact that we are thinking beings and can exercise control over our reasonings, we have to set out upon our intellectual travels from the home where we already find ourselves. Now, this home is the parish of percepts. It is not inside our skulls, either, but out in the open. It is the external world that we directly observe. What passes within we only know as it is mirrored in external objects. (EP2:62)

Here Peirce describes percepts as observations of the external world, making them unlike "sense impressions" that close us off from it. He has yet to distinguish the perceptual judgment as such; so, here, its function seems assigned to the percept, as he suggests that percepts are the "ultimate premises" of all our reasonings. This makes the percept a *logical* distinction, albeit one with psychological attributes.

However, a little further on, and immediately after declaring percepts to be "our *logically* initial data," Peirce seems to psychologize percepts by claiming that they "are undoubtedly purely psychical, altogether of the nature of thought" (EP2:62). He then identifies three psychological elements of the percept: its "quality of feeling," its "reaction against the will," and its "associating element." Although he will continue to maintain that percepts have these elements, we are left wondering what their *logical* relevance is and how he could introduce the percept as a logical distinction, rejecting Pearson's account on the grounds that it is psychological, but then describe the percept in purely psychological terms. Peirce may have realized what he had done, as in the next paragraph he seems to dampen his criticism of Pearson's psychologism, remarking: "It might not be a very serious error to say that the facts of science are sense-impressions" (EP2:62).

A breakthrough seems to occur later in 1901 or in early 1902, in (what would have been) the first chapter of the *Minute Logic* (R425), with a distinction between the percept and the "perceptual fact." While arguing that thought is continuous and cannot be broken up into arguments, Peirce remarks: "The real thinking-process presumably begins at the very percepts. But a percept cannot be represented in words, and consequently, the first part of thinking cannot be represented by any logical form of argument. Our logical account of the matter has to start from a perceptual fact, or proposition resulting from thought about a percept" (CP2.27, c.1902). Peirce says more about the "perceptual fact" in the second chapter (R428), and it becomes clear that the "perceptual fact" is what, within one year, he will begin to call the "perceptual judgment":

> In place of the percept, which, although not the first impression of sense, is a construction with which my will has had nothing to do, and may, therefore, properly be called the "evidence of my senses," the only thing I carry away with me is the *perceptual facts*, or the intellect's description of the evidence of the senses, made by my endeavor. These perceptual facts are wholly unlike the percept, at best; and they may be downright untrue to the percept. But I have no means whatever of criticizing, correcting or recomparing them, except that I can collect new perceptual facts relating to new percepts, and on that basis may infer that there must have been some error in the former reports, or on the other hand I may in this way persuade myself that the former reports were true. The perceptual facts are a very imperfect report of the percepts; but I cannot go behind that record. As for going back to the first impressions of sense, as some logicians recommend me to do, that would be the most chimerical of undertakings. (CP2.141, c. 1902)

On Peirce's view, it would be "the most chimerical of undertakings" to appeal to "the first impressions of sense" because all we can take away from our perceptions are what *they strike us to be*, and that will always be some proposition or description. The moment we turn our attention to something within our perceptual field, we recognize something of some description, and that description is all that could ever serve as evidence for knowledge. Even if there were empirical evidence of the existence of "first impressions of sense," it would be *that evidence*, and not the "first impressions" themselves, that justifies knowledge claims.[26]

3. The 1903 Harvard Lectures

The 1903 Harvard Lectures were arranged by William James in strong consideration of Peirce's poor economic condition, and after Peirce had been denied funding from the newly formed Carnegie Institute for a proposed project comprising "three dozen memoirs" on the "logic" of science.[27] But having already completed substantial work on the project, and having been incentivized to return to his pragmatism by James's 1898 Berkeley lecture, he was well prepared to deliver seven lectures relating to pragmatism (although only six lectures were originally planned). Many scholars consider them to be the most systematic presentation of his mature thought. In her introduction to the lectures, Patricia Ann Turrisi comments: "The deeply systematic character of Peirce's 1903 Harvard lectures, like many of his other works, utterly refuted the lie that he had produced only a number of 'desultory' if ingenious 'suggestions' in the areas of logic and philosophy but had erected no finished construction" (1997, 11).

But despite their systematic character, these lectures are not easy to understand. James had warned Peirce against making them too inaccessible, anticipating that they would be well received only after Peirce was dead. In a letter to Peirce, James remarks: "As things stand, it is only highly skilled technicians and professionals who will sniff the rare perfume of your thought and, after you are dead, trace things back to your genius. You ought to gain a bigger audience *when living*" (Turrisi 1997, 17). The first lecture reintroduces the maxim of pragmatism and offers a more technical and narrow formulation of it.[28] It also offers a very technical application of the maxim that was likely the source of displeasure among James and others.

The lectures become more accessible as Peirce attempts to ground his pragmatism in the normative sciences and on the universal categories. In the second lecture, while explaining the category of *secondness*, he makes his first major claims about perception. He makes the phenomenological claim that perception involves a "double-consciousness" of two objects, an ego and a "non-ego" (i.e., the perceived object), which he says exemplifies the phenomenon of secondness by "the fact that in perception two objects really do so react upon one another" (EP2:155). More significantly, in the second lecture, Peirce distinguishes between perceptual *facts* and perceptual *judgments*. He remarks that "the whole question is what the *perceptual facts* are, as given in direct perceptual judgments" (EP2:155). Recall that, in the *Minute Logic*, the "perceptual fact" was not distinguished from the judgment. Now, in the 1903 Harvard Lectures, perceptual facts are what are "given in" perceptual judgments—that is, they are what perceptual judgments represent or describe. He also says that the perceptual judgment "asserts in propositional form what the character of a percept directly present to the mind is" (EP2.155). Here, one might take him to mean that the perceptual judgment asserts that the percept has a certain phenomenal quality, but we must avoid interpreting Peirce as a sort of phenomenalist.

Peirce goes on to argue that, because the processes by which perceptual judgments occur are uncontrollable, those processes cannot be evaluated as "good or bad." He remarks that "to pronounce an involuntary operation of the mind good or bad, has no more sense than to pronounce the proportion of weights in which hydrogen and chlorine combine . . . to be good or bad" (EP2:155). One will counter that uncontrollable facts can be good or bad in relation to our desires, ideals, etc. (e.g., the sun exploding today would be bad, despite being uncontrollable). However, Peirce's view is that such evaluations (such as of the sun exploding) would be *pragmatically* meaningless. Pragmatically, evaluations are implicit *prescriptions*. If, on the pragmatic maxim, the meaning of "theoretical propositions" lies in "practical maxims," as he says in the first lecture, then presumably the meaning of *evaluative* propositions would also lie in practical maxims. The meaning of "X is good" would be the maxim *Do X*; but then, if X is uncontrollable, "Do X" would violate the ought-implies-can principle and be, for that reason, nonsense.[29]

After defending the universal categories in the third lecture, Peirce returns to discussing perception in the fourth. There he defines the perceptual judgment as "the first judgment of a person as to what is before his senses" (EP1.191). Notice that the perceptual judgment is the first judgment of *a person*, highlighting that the perceptual judgment, despite being formed by subpersonal processes, must be available to deliberate reasoning at the personal level. We are free to reason with or about them, but we are not free to make them what we want. He then argues: "It follows, then, that our perceptual judgments are the first premisses of all our reasonings and that they cannot be called in question. All our other judgments are so many theories whose only justification is that they have been and will be borne out by perceptual judgments" (EP1.191).

At last, Peirce has articulated a nonfoundationalist form of empiricism—or, as I have explained elsewhere,[30] it *is* foundationalist, but with the caveat that the "foundations" (perceptual judgments) are neither incorrigible nor self-justifying, and that they are neither epistemically nor semiotically basic. As he explains later in the lectures, perceptual judgments are the results of *interpretative* processes that can be modeled as *abductive* inferences, whose only justification, he says, "is that if we are ever to understand things at all, it must be in that way" (EP2:205). Perceptual judgments are "foundations" only in the sense that they are the "inputs" of all our deliberate reasoning, scientific or otherwise. So far as doubts as to the veracity of any given perceptual judgment can be allayed or vindicated through reasoning, those doubts can be allayed or vindicated only through reasoning from *other* perceptual judgments.

In the fifth lecture, Peirce introduces and begins to defend the claim that we perceive generals or *thirds* (which, recall, is implied by his 1868 argument that we perceive indeterminate properties). But in this lecture, he argues that if "you admit the principle that logic stops where self-control stops, you will find yourself obliged to admit that a perceptual fact, a logical origin, may involve generality," because "generality, Thirdness, pours in upon us in our very perceptual judgments, all reasoning, so far as it depends on necessary reasoning, ... turns upon *the perception of generality and continuity* at every step" (EP2:207; my emphasis). I understand the argument here as follows: Reasoning requires general terms, or terms that repeat in a chain of reasoning. So, if reasoning can set out only from perceptual judgments, as Peirce maintains, then such judgments must themselves involve general terms. This part might not be so controversial. The controversial part is that, for Peirce, this means that the perceptual fact, or what is described by the perceptual judgment, itself has general elements.

One will argue that the fact that perceptual judgments involve general terms does not mean that we perceive things that are general in themselves, such as *kinds*. For example, one may argue that the kind, *dog*, is not perceived when one perceives a dog and judges "that is a dog." However, Peirce would argue to the contrary: if that kind, *dog*, is not part of the perceptual fact, then our perceptual judgment does not tell us what we perceive so much as it *projects* something onto what we perceive. Our judgment "that is a dog" is that the creature before us is of that kind, *dog*, and if it is not a *perceived fact* that the creature is of that kind, then, it seems, our perceptual judgment merely projects that onto the individual creature. This is psychology—or, rather, it is a certain metaphysics (i.e., *nominalism*) telling psychology what must happen in perception. At face value, the perceptual judgment is that the creature is of that kind, *dog*. We do not perceive the kind separately from the fact, but the kind is still an element of the fact that we perceive. While Peirce generally describes "fact" as an example of secondness (as in "facticity"), the "perceived fact" is the perceived *reality*, and reality, for him, always involves thirdness or generality (e.g., EP2:197).

In response, a nominalist might insist that the judgment, despite containing general terms or concepts, does not represent anything general in itself, and that the perceptual fact, *that is a dog*, is a simple or "unanalyzable" individual. But Peirce would regard such assertions of "unanalyzability" as instances of "blocking the way of inquiry" (CP1.170, c. 1897).[31] He makes additional arguments in the lectures that we perceive generality or thirdness, including toward the end of the seventh lecture, where he argues that those who claim that thirdness, "though not perceived in experiment, is justified by experiment" (EP2:240) will completely "sunder the real from perception; and the puzzle for him will be why perception should be allowed such authority in regard to what is real" (EP2:240). That is, as an essential element of reality, generality must be directly perceived, otherwise reality is not. With regard to those who simply deny that generality is real (i.e., nominalists), he remarks that they "ought to admit no general law as really operative," a position which he says "can practically not be maintained" (EP2:240).

In the sixth lecture, after elaborating on the justification of induction and abduction, Peirce returns to the maxim of pragmatism and begins explicating it in semiotic terms— terms that he further developed over the next several years. Toward the end of this lecture, he returns to a form of *meaning empiricism*, arguing that all general concepts derive from perception (EP2:223). He does not mean that all concepts originate, fully formed, from perceptual judgments. He means that the generals that are represented by perceptual judgments are the elements from which we form the rest of our general concepts (by abduction, with "small doses" of induction). Further, recall that, in 1883, he had claimed that some concepts are *innate*. One way to reconcile these two claims, that some concepts are innate, but that all concepts originate with perceptual judgments, is the further claim *that we are innately disposed to form certain concepts in response to percepts*. While all concepts derive from general phenomena first *occurring* in perception, with certain generals, we are innately disposed to perceptually represent them upon their first appearance. We are innately *sensitive* to them. So, our concepts of certain generals are innate because we are predisposed, without any prior learning, to form concepts of them *upon* their first appearing to us in perception, but we do not possess those concepts *prior* to perception.

So far in the lectures, Peirce has made two significant claims about perception: (1) that all our knowledge derives from perceptual judgments and (2) that we directly perceive general phenomena or thirdness. At the end of the sixth lecture, Peirce presents these two claims as "cotary propositions of pragmatism"—which, recall, he says "put[s] the edge on the maxim of pragmatism." He then introduces a *third* cotary proposition of pragmatism, relating perception with *abduction*.

> I do not think it is possible fully to comprehend the problem of the merits of pragmatism without recognizing these three truths: *first*, that there are no conceptions which are not given to us in perceptual judgments so that we may say that all our ideas are perceptual ideas.... *Second*, that perceptual judgments contain elements of generality, so that Thirdness is directly perceived; and finally, I think it of great importance to recognize, *third*, that the abductive faculty, whereby we divine the secrets of nature, is, as we may say, a shading off, a gradation of that which in its highest perfection we call perception. (EP2:223–224)

The sixth lecture was supposed to be the last. However, the cotary propositions, especially the third one, required further elaboration. Thus, on May 14, 1903, Peirce delivered his seventh and final lecture of the series. There, the third claim is split into *two parts*: The first part is that "abductive inference shades into perceptual judgment without any sharp line of demarcation between them." The second part is that "if we were to subject this subconscious process [through which the perceptual judgment occurs] to logical analysis we should find that it terminated in what that analysis would represent as an abductive inference resting on the result of a similar process." Atkins (2017) has called the second part the "fourth cotary proposition" because it seems distinct enough from the first part (I invite readers to see it either way).

The "abductive faculty" that Peirce claims to be continuous with perception is the capacity to generate ideas or hypotheses beyond what is afforded by necessary reasoning. Unlike perception, we have some direct self-control over this abductive "faculty," such as we do in brainstorming or "free association" endeavors—although, as Peirce says, when the abductive suggestion comes, it "comes to us like a flash." We have no direct self-control over the movement from the premises to the abductive conclusion; we can only put the premises before our minds and "let it happen."

Peirce identifies abduction and perception as being of the same cognitive kind because he thinks it helps ground the first two cotary propositions (EP2:229–231), and also because perception would have to involve operations that, if performed voluntarily, would be classified as abductive, rather than as deductive or inductive. Perception must involve more than the deductive transformations of symbols. It also cannot be inductive because, as Peirce understands it, induction is the experimental confirmation of a theory that leads us to accept it.[32] While induction is often represented as an act of *generalization* (e.g., swan 1 is white, swan 2 is white, etc., therefore, all swans are white—what Peirce calls "crude induction"), in induction the instances are understood to *support* the generalization, not *introduce* it. The act of generalizing is abductive, while the support of a generalization by particular instances is inductive. Further, it is well confirmed in the early twenty-first century that perception consists, in large part, in *pattern recognition*,[33] and pattern recognition would fall under abduction rather than induction, because pattern recognition is either the recognition of a pattern (generalization) or the fitting of an instance into a pattern, such as "x has p, S's have p, so x is an instance of S"—the classical form of an abductive inference.

The connection between abduction and pragmatism is that the maxim of pragmatism "cuts off" abductions that either make no recommendation for practical conduct or make the same recommendations as another abduction or hypothesis. The three cotary propositions establish an *empirical* condition for science or inquiry, which is that all legitimate inquiry is *empirical* inquiry, while the maxim of pragmatism further narrows the range of hypotheses to those that make distinct recommendations for scientific conduct.

4. The Semiotics of Perception

Peirce's manuscript on telepathy (R881) was written either after the 1903 Harvard Lectures or concurrent with the last two lectures, given that Peirce opens the manuscript with a reference to the April 1903 exchange in *The Nation* between James and John Trowbridge on the topic of psychical research (the seventh and final Harvard lecture was delivered May 14). Trowbridge was an ardent skeptic, believing that there is no science in the subject of telepathy, while James believed research in this area can be scientific. Perhaps grateful for James's recent support in organizing the lectures at Harvard, Peirce was careful not to side too decisively with Trowbridge. While Peirce agreed with Trowbridge that the hypothesis of telepathy has no scientific merit, he also criticized Trowbridge for his materialism and nominalism. But with the topic of perception fresh on his mind, Peirce took this opportunity to develop his mature theory further, and the manuscript contains his most sustained discussion of perception.

Many of the key points about the percept and the perceptual judgment made in the Harvard Lectures and in earlier works are also explained in R881, but in slightly different terms or with further qualifications. For instance, in R881, the percept and the perceptual judgment are described as "irrational" or "unreasonable" (CP7.628, 1903)— not because they are *contrary* to reason, but because we are compelled to accept them *regardless* of reason (an idea perhaps better expressed by "nonreasonable"). Further, it is in this manuscript that Peirce explains that the perceptual judgment represents the percept only as an *index* or "symptom" of it, which "means only that in some unaccountable manner we find ourselves impotent to refuse our assent to [the perceptual judgment] in the presence of the percept" (CP7.628, 1903). So, the percept cannot be the perceived object or fact itself, because the perceptual judgment, being a judgment as to "what is before [our] senses" (CP5.115, 1903), *describes* the perceived fact, but it only *indexes* the percept. So, if the perceptual judgment does not describe the percept, then the percept cannot itself be the perceived object or fact.[34]

In a 1906 paper "Prolegomena to Apology for Pragmaticism,"[35] we finally see, unambiguously, that the percept *is* a type of sign, although determining what type of sign it is requires connecting some dots. He says there that the percept is a *seme*, and he defines a "seme" as "anything which serves for any purpose as a substitute for an object of which it is, in some sense, a representative or Sign" (CP4.538, 1906). This makes "seme" seem just like another word for "sign." However, elsewhere, Peirce identifies a seme as an *index*: "An Index or Seme ({séma}) is a Representamen whose Representative character consists in its being an individual second" (CP2.283, *c*. 1902). Identifying the percept as an index, as opposed to a symbol or an icon, makes the best sense of percepts as signs, for at least three reasons.

First, indices represent their objects though physical connections with them, and it seems clear that the percept compels us to acknowledge the world through its physical connections to it (via our senses). Second, the percept cannot be a symbol because, as Peirce says, it is nothing like a proposition (EP2.155). He says it is more like an image or picture, although not in the sense of something "painted" over the "mind's eye," but in the sense that it is a presentation or appearance. It *has* sensory qualities, or sensory qualia, but it is not the qualia themselves that it presents. The idea that the percept presents only sensory qualia leads to the suggestion that it could function as an *icon*. However, and third, his commitment to "the doctrine of immediate perception" means that the percept cannot represent its object as an icon either, as icons represent their objects by bearing *likenesses* to them and we could only infer that our percepts bear likenesses to external objects. If percepts were either symbols or icons, then our perception of the external world would not be direct (contrary to the overwhelming evidence that Peirce believes it to be direct). In being intrusive or "forceful," the percept presents the world by compulsively directing us toward some part of it. That is how perception is "direct" on Peirce's account.

However, as I mentioned, the percept itself indexes whatever is physically connected to the information conveyed by a particular sense at a particular time. As Peirce says in R881, the percept presents its object "whole and undivided" (CP7.625, 1903)—that is, it presents the whole perceptual field. The process resulting in the perceptual judgment filters out further information to describe a particular fact (or conjunction of facts) within the perceptual field. As perception is continuous with our abductive abilities, perception results in one particular "explanation" of what we perceive over others that might be equally correct (because they explain different parts of the perceptual field, etc.). And, as he insists both in the lectures and in R881, perception is interpretive in that we perceive "what we are adjusted for interpreting" (EP2:229). We select something within the perceptual field and recognize it as a certain fact, based on our experience (and on our values, interests, etc.).

This interpretive and abductive character of perception indicates the perceptual judgment can be false, even though it "cannot be called into question" so far it does not conflict with other perceptual judgments. That is, the particular fact that a perceptual judgment describes might not be a *real* fact (as described). Yet, the judgment still indexes the percept and the real facts that the percept itself indexes via its physical connections. If the judgment is true, then it correctly describes some of those facts; if it is not true, then it does not correctly describe any of them.

Now, to function as an index of the fact described by the judgment, the percept only needs to bear a direct physical connection to the *subject* of the judgment. Its *predicate* may refer to a property that does not directly affect our senses—such as a property that traditionally has been thought to be "abstract." Such is the case where we perceptually judge the meaning of spoken or written words. We "hear meanings" in the sense that we immediately and uncontrollably judge sounds as linguistic signs of certain things or meanings. For example, if I perceptually judge that a voice said, "you should leave," the percept is physically connected only to the voice referred to in the subject term. But if the judgment is true, then I perceive the fact that those vocalized sounds have that meaning. So long as there is *some* direct physical connection to the subject of a judgment through which the indexical requirement can be satisfied, and so long as what the judgment says about that subject is true, then one perceives the fact that the judgment describes. Recall, Peirce says that it is the perceptual judgment that tells us what we perceive; the percept only directs us to it; and, to do so, the percept requires a physical connection only to the subject of the perceived fact.[36]

Thus, on Peirce's account, we perceive more than what physically acts on our senses at a given moment. We also perceive what we *expect* to act on our senses. In R881, Peirce argues that perception is continuous with *memory* and *expectation*: we perceive what we expect to perceive based on past experience or memory (CP7.648, 1903). If you have a coffee mug before you, you take yourself to perceive a *whole* mug and not just one side of it, because you expect that, if you were to turn the mug around, its other side would be intact. The expectation is part of the perception: we perceptually judge there to be a whole mug in front us, not just one side of mug. As contemporary researchers will say, the expectation "penetrates" the perception.[37] The mug could be missing its other side, as part of some prank; in that case, the perceptual judgment is *false* and there is *mis*perception. Nonetheless, the judgment still indexes the actual reality that the percept itself indexes.

We see that Peirce has an avenue for explaining the nature of *misperception* or perceptual error. Perceptual error involves a false perceptual judgment. However, it also involves a false *appearance*. In perception, we do not just judge things incorrectly; things *appear* incorrectly—such as, for example, in mirages. Explaining that part of perceptual error requires more in Peirce's account than what I have so far covered. It requires the "percipuum," which Peirce's introduces in R881. It also requires his distinction between the *immediate object* and the *dynamical object* of a sign, which appears in writings beginning in 1904.

Peirce offers two definitions of the "percipuum." First, he says he "invent[s] the term percipuum to include both percept and perceptual judgment" (CP7.629, 1903); however, later in the manuscript he says the percipuum is "the percept *as it is immediately interpreted in* the perceptual judgment" (CP7.643, 1903; my emphasis). As I have argued elsewhere, the correct understanding of the percipuum can be inferred from his claim, in R881, that the percept contains only elements of *firstness* and *secondness* (CP7.630, 1903). As the categories are supposed to be universal, a perceptual experience must also have *thirdness*. The solution is to take the perceptual judgment to give the experience a conceptual structure, a thirdness, and to take that conceptually structured experience to be the *percipuum*. The percipuum is the perceptual experience, the percept, but *as it is affected by the perceptual judgment*: what, in the early twenty-first century, is called cognitive penetration or "top-down processing." While nothing is distinct in the percept, the judgment renders objects and relations distinct, so that what appears is not a "booming, buzzing confusion" but a structured reality. Thus, whatever the perceptual judgment *says* is how the percipuum *appears*. And we always only experience the percipuum, never the uninterpreted percept. The percept is distinguishable but inseparable from the percipuum.

However, the percipuum could be an illusion, mirage, hallucination, or dream. These generally involve a false perceptual judgment, although not always, as we could perceptually judge the objects to be unreal. In either case, there are *two* objects: the unreal objects that appear to us and the real objects that are indexed by (and are physically connected to) the percept and the perceptual judgment. By 1904, Peirce has distinguished between the *immediate object* of a sign and its *dynamical object*.[38] I have defended my reading of this distinction elsewhere,[39] so I will not do so here. That said, Peirce says that the immediate object of a sign is the object "as the sign itself represents it" (CP4.536, 1906). However, on his semiotics, a sign cannot represent an object independent of an interpretant. So, the immediate object must be what a sign represents on a certain interpretant. Since he does not tie the immediate object to a particular type of interpretant, then it seems to be whatever a sign represents on any *given* interpretant. In perception, the immediate object is whatever is described by the judgment or whatever appears in the percipuum. This might be something *unreal*, as it is in dreams, hallucinations, etc. However, the *dynamical object*, or what a sign represents on its "final interpretant" (EP2:495), is the *reality* connected with the percept or percipuum. With dreams, the dynamical object would be the real fact that it is a dream. The perceptual judgment is false, so it does not describe its dynamical object, only its immediate object.

But, again, even a false perceptual judgment is an index of the reality, the dynamical object—the dream *as a* dream.

5. Nativism and Empiricism

I mentioned that Peirce's nativism about *some* concepts can be reconciled with the empiricism of his 1903 Harvard Lectures by recognizing that we can be innately disposed to form certain concepts *but only* in response to percepts. This way, it remains true that these concepts first *occur* in perception, or in perceptual judgments, even though their first occurrence in perception may be largely due to innate habits of mind. That is, it remains true that "all our ideas are perceptual ideas" and that "the elements of every concept enter into logical thought at the gate of perception," as he says in the Harvard Lectures, despite that the gate is opened only through inherited dispositions. Peirce suggests this approach by an example in a short 1906 paper, "Mr. Peterson's Proposed Discussion,"[40] where he describes a young man who was raised on an island colony of men, never having seen a woman, but who finally meets a young woman from another island. Peirce suggests that the young man's perception of the woman would be "colored by his instincts": he is innately disposed to perceive her as "attractive" (assuming he is heterosexual) although the notion of such attractiveness *first occurs* to him in his perception of the woman (CP5.612, 1906).

However, Peirce's nativism about *beliefs* is more difficult to reconcile with his empiricism. This form of nativism appears in "The Doctrine of Necessity Examined" (1892), where he suggests that we have "natural beliefs" that are "adaptations of nature," of which the "principle of causation" may be an example. A clearer commitment to nativism about beliefs appears in his 1905 papers on *critical common-sensism*, of which one was published, "Issues of Pragmaticism."[41] There, Peirce extends his analysis of the boundaries of logical normativity to include, besides perceptual judgments, "original beliefs," which "are of the general nature instincts" and which also serve as ultimate first premises of reasoning (EP2.348–349), contradicting what he had said or strongly implied in the 1903 Harvard Lectures (that perceptual judgments are not the *only* first premises of all our reasoning). While original beliefs are as uncontrollable as perceptual judgments, they cannot be included as perceptual judgments because they are not responses to percepts. Original beliefs are a separate class.

Peirce gives few examples of original beliefs, although *moral* beliefs seem to be his primary ones. He takes the universal taboo of parent–child and sibling–sibling incest as evidence that our belief in the wrongness of such incest is inherited and is, thus, an original belief. However, he stresses that original beliefs are very vague or imprecise, and that precise articulation of them is likely to expose their limited "jurisdiction" to "affairs that resemble those of a primitive mode of life" (EP2.349). Like perceptual judgments, original beliefs lie at the boundary of the personal and the subpersonal levels of cognition: they are available to voluntary reasoning and control, but only with sufficient effort (as with many of our biases, original beliefs are implicit). The critical common-sensist acknowledges that his original beliefs may be proved false with sufficient inquiry, so they are not empirically indefeasible or unfalsifiable. They are neither universal nor necessary truths. They do not constitute a priori knowledge, as their epistemic status depends on the course of experience. They are simply cognitive habits functioning as propositional signs that we seem to inherit but can still "shake off" with sufficient experience or learning.

Thus, Peirce's 1905 nativism about beliefs does not entirely abandon his 1903 empiricism, although it does change it from an empiricism on which all our knowledge *derives* from perception to an empiricism on which all knowledge *depends* on perception. Original beliefs can still be falsified through our perceptual experience. His nativism constitutes the recognition that we must be disposed toward holding certain beliefs over others in consequence of natural selection—a recognition that is abduced from experience (i.e., evolutionary science). Since he had distinguished "natural beliefs" in 1892 and had argued in 1898 that moral beliefs are sentimental instincts,[42] the 1903 Harvard Lectures should have mentioned natural or original beliefs, at least in relation to ethics. However, Peirce's interest there in showing pragmatism to be a form of empiricism, in developing a theory of perception to go with it, seems to have compelled him to push aside some of his earlier theoretical commitments.

Notes

1. Originally published in *Popular Science Monthly*. The series includes "The Fixation of Belief" (1877), "How to Make Our Ideas Clear" (1878), and "The Doctrine of Chances" (1878). The series was republished as *Illustrations of the Logic of Science*, edited by Cornelis de Waal (Chicago: Open Court, 2014).
2. "Cotary" derives from the Latin noun *cotis*, which refers to whetstones or stones used for sharpening blades.
3. To these three parts of Peirce's account of perception, one might add a *phenomenological* part, which includes such claims as that perception involves a "double consciousness" (e.g., EP5.154). However, the concern here is the epistemology and metaphysics of perception, so I will mention the phenomenology only so far as it informs the former two.
4. Articles on Peirce's theory of perception include Bernstein (1964), Almeder (1970), Hausman (1990), Haack (1994), Rosenthal (2004), Bergmann (2007), Atkins (2017), and Vargas (2017). Also, sections of major books on Peirce devote considerable space to his account of perception, including Murphy (1961, 301–400) and Hookway (1985, 151–180).
5. For instance, Rosenthal (1969) defends a reading on Peirce uses "perceptual judgment" to refer to an infallible "seeming" or "appearing" statement, but to refer to a fallible claim about objective reality.
6. Peirce was responding mostly to Sir William Hamilton (1788–1856), an influential figure in the Scottish common-sense tradition who was still active while Peirce first entered Harvard. Hamilton expounds this doctrine in his 1830 essay "Philosophy of Perception," printed in *Discussions on Philosophy and Literature, Education and University Reform* (Edinburgh: MacLachlan and Stewart, 1853). Peirce was likely introduced to the work of Reid and Hamilton through lectures delivered by Francis Bowen (1811–1890), one of his teachers at Harvard.

7. As Hausman (1993) points out, by "determined by previous cognition" Peirce means *mediated* by previous cognition, which could be a logical mediation, such as an inference, or it could be a causal sort of mediation. Either one, or another, would suffice for Peirce's purposes.
8. Peirce, Charles. "Questions Concerning Certain Faculties Claimed for Man," *Journal of Speculative Philosophy* 2 (1868): 103–114.
9. In the second paper of that series, "Consequences of Four Incapacities," Peirce makes the stronger claim that there are no intuitive cognitions at all (EP1.66).
10. Peirce mentions the blind spot on the retina and the fact that most people are unaware of it (EP1.151).
11. Peirce writes: "A child has, as far as we know, all the perceptive powers of a man. Yet question him a little as to how he knows what he does. In many cases, he will tell you that he never learned his mother-tongue; he always knew it, or he knew it as soon as he came to have sense. It appears, then, that he does not possess the faculty of distinguishing, by simple contemplation, between an intuition and a cognition determined by others" (EP1.151).
12. What would a conception of the incognizable possibly be? Haack (1996) suggests that Peirce means that "it is impossible to make sense of any question to which we could not, however long inquiry continued, determine the answer" (310).
13. Originally published in *North American Review* 113 (October 1871): 449–472.
14. Peirce writes: "There is, then, to every question a true answer, a final conclusion, to which the opinion of every man is constantly gravitating. He may for a time recede from it, but give him more experience and time for consideration, and he will finally approach it" (EP1.122–123).
15. Among his early work, it appears most notably in his 1865 lecture "Unpsychological View of Logic" (W1.344–360).
16. For example, Peirce argues against the "a priori method" on the ground that "it makes of inquiry something similar to the development of taste; but taste, unfortunately, is always more or less a matter of fashion, and accordingly metaphysicians have never come to any fixed agreement" (EP1.150). Even Peirce, in later writings, seems to admit that his 1877–1878 papers are based much on psychological reasonings. See Kasser (1999, 501–507), for useful commentary on these remarks.
17. See Wilson (2012; 2016, 187–233; and 2017a).
18. See Drayson (2012, 15).
19. One would expect this upon the methodological version of his principle of *synechism*. Peirce says that the "tendency to regard continuity, in the sense in which I shall define it, as an idea of prime importance in philosophy may conveniently be termed synechism" (CP6.103, 1892).
20. Wilson (2016, 190–204).
21. Particularly CP7.619, from R881 (the 1903 manuscript on telepathy). In this passage, it is easy to misunderstand Peirce as saying that the percept is the perceived object itself (e.g., the chair) and that, as perceived object itself, the percept is no type of sign at all. Peirce writes: "Let us say that, as I sit here writing, I see on the other side of my table, a yellow chair with a green cushion. That will be what psychologists term a 'percept' (*res percepta*). They also frequently call it an 'image.' With this term I shall pick no quarrel. Only one must be on one's guard against a false impression that it might insinuate. Namely, an 'image' usually means something intended to represent,—virtually professing to represent,—something

else, real or ideal. So understood, the word 'image' would be a misnomer for a percept. The chair I appear to see makes no professions of any kind, essentially embodies no intentions of any kind, does not stand for anything. It obtrudes itself upon my gaze; but not as a deputy for anything else, not 'as' anything. It simply knocks at the portal of my soul and stands there in the doorway." Based on this passage, Hausman attributes, to Peirce, an "injunction against the idea that percepts are themselves signs" (1990, 281). But one must be careful not to interpret this passage independently of what Peirce argues elsewhere. Bergman (2007) argues there are difficulties that arise with denying or with accepting the percept as a type of sign.

22. This comes from an example from van Cleve (2004) in context of Thomas Reid's theory of perception, which is supposed to be a counterexample Reid's own claim that a perceptual judgment is one that is immediate and uncontrollable.

23. See CP2.192, 1902; CP5.444, 1905; and CP5.514, 1905.

24. For instance, see CP1.148–149 (c. 1897).

25. The review of Pearson begins with counterpoints on the values and motives of science. Peirce does not disagree with Pearson that scientific research *has* ethical motives. However, Peirce objects to the claim, which he attributes to Pearson, that "the sole reason for scientific research is the good of society" on the grounds that it would encourage the public to see those in *applied* science, as opposed to theoreticians, as the "true men of science" (EP2:61). In the review, Peirce remarks: "The only ethically sound motive is the most general one; and the motive that actually inspires the man of science, if not quite that, is very near to it,—nearer, I venture to believe, than that of any other equally common type of humanity" (EP2:60). Here we see Peirce taking a great interest in ethics. Peirce had defended a form of sentimentalism about two years earlier, in his 1898 Cambridge conference lectures, and he makes reference to Josiah Royce, whose 1885 *Religious Aspect of Philosophy* helped to turn Peirce's interest more toward ethics.

26. One could say that Peirce is assuming (what in the early twenty-first century is called) evidentialism, although in that case Pearson also assumes evidentialism, and arguably any account of *scientific* knowledge, with which Peirce is most concerned, is evidentialist, so far as evidence is indispensable to science.

27. See Turrisi (1997, introduction) for a fuller account of the circumstances that led Peirce to deliver the series of lectures on pragmatism at Harvard in 1903.

28. "Pragmatism is the principle that every theoretical judgment expressible in a sentence in the indicative mood is a confused form of thought whose only meaning, if it has any, lies in its tendency to enforce a corresponding practical maxim having its apodosis in the imperative mood" (EP2.134–135). I consider this formulation to be narrower than the original because it applies only to "theoretical judgments."

29. In correspondence, Cornelis de Waal raised a case about perceptual judgments caused by abnormal psychological conditions that are treatable. Such judgments might be "bad" if they contribute to the harm, and if the conditions causing them are treatable, then describing those judgments as bad will have pragmatic meaning. Indeed, these judgments can be (pragmatically) described as "bad" so far as the process of their formation is controllable, such as by treating the underlying abnormal conditions. Of course, with sufficient advancement in biotechnology, all parts of the process resulting in perceptual judgments would be controllable. So, it is plausible to say that all evaluations of the perceptual process have *some* pragmatic meaning.

30. Wilson (2016, 216).

31. Peirce generally criticizes nominalists for blocking the way of inquiry. He remarks: "It is one of the peculiarities of nominalism that it is continually supposing things to be absolutely inexplicable. That blocks the road of inquiry" (CP1.170, c. 1897).
32. See EP2.215–216.
33. Large swaths of the contemporary cognitive psychological literature assume some model of pattern recognition for a given perceptual modality. Facial recognition in visual perception is a common example, but so is speech recognition in auditory perception. "Matching" is a form of pattern recognition that would be abductive, on Peirce's account.
34. Some scholars have taken the percept to be the object of perception, much due to the confusing passage at CP7.619 (see note 20). Bergman (2007, 68) is, at least, not careful to distinguish the perceptual judgment as an indexical sign of the percept and as a symbolic sign of what the percept itself indexes.
35. Originally published in *The Monist* 16:492–546.
36. See Wilson (2017a). The claim that we directly perceive the meaning of spoken or written language is defended independent of Peirce in, for instance, Brogaard (2018).
37. On the contemporary debate over the cognitive penetrability of perception, see Newen and Vetter (2014).
38. In R463, dated 1904, which is a draft of a letter to Lady Welby, Peirce writes that a sign "has two objects, the object as it really is independently of being signified or represented, and the object as it is represented to be."
39. See Wilson (2017b).
40. *The Monist* 16:147–151.
41. *The Monist* 15:481–199.
42. "Philosophy and the Conduct of Life," the first of the 1898 Cambridge lectures on "Reasoning and the Logic of Things." See Atkins (2016) for an extensive analysis of Peirce's sentimentalism there.

Works Cited

Almeder, Robert. 1970. "Peirce's Theory of Perception." *Transactions of the Charles S. Peirce Society* 6, no. 2 (Spring): 99–110.

Atkins, Richard. 2016. *Peirce and the Conduct of Life: Sentiment and Instinct in Ethics and Religion*. New York: Cambridge University Press.

Atkins, Richard. 2017. "Inferential Modeling of Percept Formation: Peirce's Fourth Cotary Proposition." In *Peirce on Perception and Reasoning: From Icons to Logic*, edited by Kathleen Hull and Richard Kenneth Atkins, 25–39. New York: Routledge.

Bergmann, Mats. 2007. "Representationism and Presentationism." *Transactions of the Charles S. Peirce Society* 43, no. 1 (Winter): 53–89.

Bernstein, Richard. 1964. "Peirce's Theory of Perception." In *Studies in the Philosophy of Charles Sanders Peirce: Second Series*, edited by E. C. Moore and R. S. Robin, 165–189. Amherst: University of Massachusetts Press.

Brogaard, Berit. 2018. "In Defense of Hearing Meanings." *Synthese* 195.7: 2967–2983.

Dennett, Daniel. 1969. *Content and Consciousness*. New York: Routledge & Kegan Paul.

Drayson, Zoe. 2012. "The Uses and Abuses of the Personal/Subpersonal Distinction." *Philosophical Perspectives* 26: 1–18.

Haack, Susan. 1994. "How the Critical Common-sensist Sees Things." *Histoire Épistémologie Langage* 16, no.1: 9–34.

Haack, Susan. 1996. "Reflections on Relativism: From Momentous Tautology to Seductive Contradiction." *Philosophical Perspectives* 10: 297–315.

Hausman, Carl. 1990. "In and Out of Peirce's Percepts." *Transactions of the Charles S. Peirce Society* 26, no. 3 (Summer): 271–308.

Hausman, Carl R. 1993. *Charles S. Peirce's Evolutionary Philosophy*. Cambridge: Cambridge University Press.

Hookway, Christopher. 1985. *Peirce*. London: Routledge & Kegan Paul.

Kasser, Jeffrey. 1999. "Peirce's Supposed Psychologism." *Transactions of the Charles S. Peirce Society* 35, no. 3 (Summer): 501–526.

Murphy, Murrey G. 1961. *The Development of Peirce's Philosophy*. Cambridge, MA: Harvard University Press.

Newen, Albert, and Vetter, Petra. "The Varieties of Cognitive Penetration in Visual Perception." *Consciousness and Cognition* 27: 62–75.

Peirce, Charles S. 1857–1914. Manuscripts held at the Houghton Library of Harvard University, as identified in Richard Robin. 1967. *Annotated Catalogue of the Papers of Charles S. Peirce*. Amherst: University of Massachusetts Press. And in Richard Robin. 1971. "The Peirce Papers: A Supplementary Catalogue." *Transactions of the Charles S. Peirce Society* 7, no. 1 (Winter): 37–57. (Referred to as R[catalogue#]:[sheet#].)

Peirce, Charles S. 1931–1958. *The Collected Papers of Charles Sanders Peirce*. 8 vols. Vols. 1–6 edited by Charles Hartshorne and Paul Weiss. Vols. 7–8 edited by Arthur W. Burks. Cambridge, MA: Harvard University Press. (Referred to as CP.)

Peirce, Charles S. 1982–2010. *The Writings of Charles S. Peirce: A Chronological Edition*. 7 vols. to date. Edited by the Peirce Edition Project. Bloomington: Indiana University Press. (Referred to as W.)

Peirce, Charles S. 1992–1998. *The Essential Peirce: Selected Philosophical Writings*. 2 vols. Vol. 1 edited by Nathan Houser and Christian Kloesel. Vol. 2 edited by the Peirce Edition Project. Bloomington: Indiana University Press. (Referred to as EP.)

Rosenthal, Sandra. 1969. "Peirce's Theory of the Perceptual Judgment: An Ambiguity." *Journal of the History of Philosophy* 7, no. 3 (Summer): 303–314.

Rosenthal, Sandra. 2004. "Peirce's Pragmatic Account of Perception: Issues and Implications." In *The Cambridge Companion to Peirce*, edited by Cheryl Misak, 193–213. Cambridge: Cambridge University Press.

Turrisi, Patricia A. 1997. *Pragmatism as a Principle and Method of Right Thinking: The 1903 Harvard Lectures on Pragmatism*. Albany: State University of New York Press.

van Cleve, James. 2004. "Reid's Theory of Perception." In *The Cambridge Companion to Reid*, edited by Terence Cuneo and Rene van Woudenberg, 101–133. Cambridge: Cambridge University Press.

Vargas, Evelyn. 2017. "Perception as Inference." In *Peirce on Perception and Reasoning: From Icons to Logic*, edited by Kathleen Hull and Richard Kenneth Atkins, 14–24. New York: Routledge.

Wilson, Aaron B. 2012. "The Perception of Generals." *Transactions of the Charles S. Peirce Society* 48, no. 2 (Spring): 169–190.

Wilson, Aaron B. 2016. *Peirce's Empiricism: Its Roots and Its Originality*. Lanham, MD: Lexington Books.

Wilson, Aaron B. 2017a. "What Do We Perceive? How Peirce 'Expands Our Perception.'" In *Peirce on Perception and Reasoning: From Icons to Logic*, edited by Kathleen Hull and Richard Kenneth Atkins, 1–13. New York: Routledge.

Wilson, Aaron B. 2017b. "The Peircean Solution to Non-Existence Problems: Immediate and Dynamical Objects." *Transactions of the Charles S. Peirce Society* 53, no. 4 (Fall): 528–552.

PART V
METAPHYSICS

CHAPTER 23

PEIRCE ON REALITY AND EXISTENCE

ROBERT LANE

1. The Real, the External, the Internal, and the Fictional

CHARLES Peirce was a realist in the simplest, most basic sense: he believed in reality. That is, he believed that there is a real world consisting of real things.[1] But what *is* reality, according to Peirce? On his view, what does it mean to say that there is a real world and that there are real things?

Peirce accepted the following verbal definition of the word "real": something is real exactly when its "characters are independent of how any representation represents it to be. Independent, therefore, of how any number of men think it to be" (W2:439, 1870).[2] In other words, something is real exactly when it has the characteristics that it has whether or not anyone represents it as having them, be that representation in thought or otherwise. The pencil on my desk is real, in that it has its properties—its specific size, shape, weight, position in space, etc.—whether or not I or anyone else thinks of it as having those properties, describes it has having them, or otherwise represents it as having them. Perhaps the earliest appearance of this understanding of reality in Peirce's extant works was in an early manuscript that he apparently intended as the first chapter of a book on logic: "The essential difference between a reality and a nonreality, is that the former has an existence entirely independent of what you or I or any number of men think about it" (W2:104, 1867). He stated or implicitly relied upon this definition of "real" again and again, in works published during his lifetime and in still-unpublished manuscripts, up until the last years of his life.[3] Some of his statements of this definition emphasize representation, for example: "*reality* . . . is of such a nature as to be independent of representations of it, so that, taking any individual sign or any individual collection of signs (such, for example, as all the ideas that ever enter into a given man's head) there is some character which that thing possesses, whether that sign or any of the signs of that collection represents the thing as possessing that character or not" (CP1.578, 1902–1903). It should be no surprise that Peirce, a pioneer of modern semiotics, would welcome a definition of reality in terms of representations or signs. And even his statements of the definition of "real" that do not explicitly mention representation still mention *aboutness*: the real is independent of what anyone says or thinks *about it*.[4] Here "thinks" has a very broad sense: "We call that *real* concerning which whatever is true will forever have been true, no matter what may at any time in any way be thought about it, using the word thought in the widest sense" (LoF1:146, *c*. 1910).

The concept of reality is similar to that of *externality*—so similar, Peirce wrote, that they were confused for each other by "some of the greatest Analysts of Thought that ever lived" (R642:18–19, 1909). The difference between the two ideas is subtle: "'the external' means simply that which is independent of what phenomenon is immediately present, that is of how we may think or feel; just as 'the real' means that which is independent of how we may think or feel *about it*; it must be granted that there are many objects of true science which are external, because there are many objects of thought which, if they are independent of that thinking whereby they are thought (that is, if they are real), are indisputably independent of all *other* thoughts and feelings" (W2:470, 1871).[5] While something is real exactly when its characteristics do not depend on what anyone thinks *about it*, something is external exactly when its characteristics do not depend on what anyone thinks *about anything*, whether about it or something else. These definitions imply that everything external is real: if something is independent of what anyone thinks, it is also independent of what anyone thinks about it (CP8.191, *c*. 1904). The real pencil on my desk is external, since its properties do not depend on anyone's thoughts, whether those thoughts are about the pencil or something else. Of course, the pencil is an artifact, and its design and creation were the outcomes of someone's thoughts. But they were not the *direct* outcomes: the pencil did not spring into being, either ex nihilo or from already existing wood and lead, due immediately to someone's thoughts. Those thoughts preceded and brought about actions that eventuated in the creation of the pencil. So we should understand Peirce's definition of "external" to mean that the external is that which is not *directly* affected by anyone's thinking: "Externality [is] irrelativity of all *direct* action of personal Cognition" (SWS:276, 1909, emphasis added).

On the one hand, in addition to reals[6] that are external, there are reals that are *internal* and that, unlike the external, *do* depend on someone's thinking: "The internal is that whose real existence depends on what I (or you or somebody) think of something" (W3:49, 1872).[7] Something internal is inside the mind of someone or other, but that does not imply that it is unreal. Any internal state or event the properties of which do not depend on someone thinking that that state or event has those properties is real. The pain I feel when I stub my toe is internal to my mind, and unfortunately for me it is very real; a dream is a real occurrence in the mind, and it really did have the content that it had, even if that content has been forgotten or misremembered by the dreamer.

On the other hand, that content—the things and events depicted in the dream—is not real. It is *imaginary, fictional*, or, as Peirce sometimes said, *fictive*. "It is true that when the

Arabian romancer tells us that there was a lady named Scheherazade, he does not mean to be understood as speaking of the world of outward realities, and there is a great deal of fiction in what he is talking about. For the *fictive* is that whose characters depend upon what characters somebody attributes to it; and the story is, of course, the mere creation of the poet's thought" (EP2:209, 1903).[8] Fictional characters, places, and events are not real, since they have their characteristics only because they were imagined by their creators as having them. But those creators *really did* imagine those characters, places, and events as having those characteristics, and the works of fiction that depict those characters are themselves real. Peirce sometimes explained the distinction between the real and the fictive using the examples of mental states like opinions and dreams: "The opinions of Malebranche were *real* opinions, since he opined as he did, whatever we may think he opined. The substance of a dream is not real, because whatever is true of it is so in that so the dreamer dreamed; and dreaming is only a particular kind of thinking. But the fact of the dream, if it actually took place, is a real fact, because it will always remain true that so and so was dreamed, whether the dreamer remembers it or not" (LoF1:146, *c.* 1910). When I daydream about walking on the beach in Tahiti, the event I am contemplating is imaginary—it is unreal, in that it is the way it is only because I am thinking of it as being that way. But the mental event that is the occurrence of the daydream is itself both internal and real. Peirce's definitions of "fictive" and "internal" imply that anything fictive is internal: if a thing has the traits that it has only because someone thinks of it as having those traits, then it has those traits only because of someone's thinking. So the Tahitian beach in my daydream is, like any other imaginary place, internal.

Real physical objects are external—they are independent of what anyone thinks. But on Peirce's view, the physical does not exhaust the external. There are also what he called *generals*—including kinds, laws, and relations—that are not only real but also external. The "external world" is not limited to individual physical things; "its most important reals have the mode of being of what the nominalist calls 'mere' words, that is, general types and would-bes" (CP8.191, *c.* 1904). Here Peirce was articulating his *scholastic realism*, that is, his realism about generals, so called because it was defended by certain medieval schoolmen.[9] While a nominalist maintains that only words possess generality and that everything else that is real is individual, the scholastic realist insists not only on the reality of general kinds, laws, and relations—and thus on their independence from every representation of them—but also on their externality. If a given law of nature were not external, that is, external to every individual mind, it would, given Peirce's definitions, be internal, that is, internal to the mind of someone or other. But real laws and other generals don't depend on any individual's thoughts.

2. Reality, Truth, and Pragmatism

Perhaps Peirce's best-known idea is his pragmatic maxim, a rule for attaining a deeper level of understanding of a given idea than is provided by a mere confident feeling of familiarity with it or that is evidenced by one's ability to provide a verbal definition of it—those are, respectively, merely the first and second levels or "grades" of clearness of an idea (e.g., W3:271, 1878; CP7.284, c. 1895; CP3.457, 1897; CP8.214, 218, 1910).[10] His first published statement of the pragmatic maxim (although he did not call it by that name at the time) was in 1878's "How to Make Our Ideas Clear" (HTM): "Consider what effects, which might conceivably have practical bearings, we conceive the object of our conception to have. Then, our conception of these effects is the whole of our conception of the object" (W3:266).[11] Peirce's own applications of the maxim, including to various ideas of the physical sciences—for example, *hardness*, *weight*, and *force*—suggest what he had in mind: we can attain the third grade of clearness with regard to an idea by considering how the things to which the idea applies might be connected to our actions and the experiential consequences of those actions. For instance, one's concept of *hardness* is pragmatically clear, that is, one has attained a third grade of clearness with regard to that concept, when they know, for example, that a hard thing "will not be scratched by many other substances" (W3:266, 1878)—that is, if you try to scratch it, it will resist being scratched.

In HTM, Peirce applied his maxim to just one philosophical idea: *reality*. Anyone who is sufficiently familiar with that idea to confidently sort things according to whether or not they are real has an idea of reality that possesses the first grade of clearness. One's concept of reality has a second grade of clearness if they can provide a verbal definition of "real," such as Peirce's own: "that whose characters are independent of what anybody may think them to be" (W3:271, 1878). But we can reach an even deeper, pragmatic level of clearness with regard to the concept of *reality* by applying the maxim, one stated in terms of the "practical bearings" of real things: "The opinion which is fated to be ultimately agreed to by all who investigate, is what we mean by the truth, and the object represented in this opinion is the real" (W3:273, 1878). To understand this clarification of the idea of reality, we need to consider Peirce's views of investigation and truth, especially as those views were articulated in the prequel to HTM, 1877's "The Fixation of Belief" (FOB).

In FOB, Peirce described four methods of dispelling doubt about a given issue and replacing it with belief. The first three methods (see W3:248–253) are *tenacity* (choosing a belief that you like and sticking to it no matter what, avoiding anything that might cause you to change your mind), *authority* (in which one person or group decides what everyone will believe and imposes that belief, via coercion and violence if need be), and the a priori method (which in its more developed form involves like-minded individuals sharing their ideas with one another, after which each individual settles on beliefs that strike them as most "reasonable"). The fourth method is *investigation*, which Peirce also called "the method of science" (W3:254). It works as follows: each inquirer has their own unique experiences, and then members of the whole community of inquirers reason together in order to figure out how the real world must be in order to give each of them their respective experiences. Peirce argued that investigation is better than the other methods at permanently settling belief because it is the method most likely to establish beliefs that are *public*—the same for everyone—and this is so because the beliefs it establishes "are caused by nothing human" but instead by the *external*—and therefore *real*—world: an "external permanency... something upon which our thinking has no effect" (W3:253).

Investigation thus assumes that there is a real world. That assumption is, in fact, part of "its fundamental hypothesis": "There are Real things, whose characters are entirely independent of our opinions about them; those realities affect our senses according to regular laws, and, though our sensations are as different as our relations to the objects, yet, by taking advantage of the laws of perception, we can ascertain by reasoning how things really are, and any man, if he have sufficient experience and reason enough about it, will be led to the one true conclusion" (W3:254).[12] Here we see two aspects of Peirce's concept of truth: a true belief is both a belief that represents the world as being how it really is *and* one that sufficient investigation—experience of the real world and reasoning about that experience—would permanently establish in the minds of inquirers. While the other three methods of fixing belief have their advantages, and while "[a] man should consider well of them[,] ... he should [also] consider that ... he wishes his opinions to coincide with the fact, and that there is no reason why the results of these three methods should do so. To bring about this effect is the prerogative of the method of science," that is, of investigation (W3:256, 1878).[13] Each of these aspects of Peirce's account of truth—the representationalist aspect, according to which a true belief is one that represents reality, and the investigative aspect, according to which a true belief is one that would be fixed by sufficient investigation—recurs throughout his later writings.[14]

So what is the pragmatic meaning of the claim that something is real? Again, to attain the third grade of clearness of a concept, we need to consider how it is connected to our actions and to their experiential consequences. When it comes to the concept of reality, the relevant action is investigation, and the relevant experience is the elimination of doubt and the establishment of belief. If something is real, then it will be represented in a belief that "is fated to be ultimately agreed to by all who investigate," that is, by a true belief. Thus, Peirce's pragmatic clarification of the idea of reality is dependent on the investigative aspect of his account of truth. He eventually called this pragmatic clarification of the idea of reality *conditional idealism* (EP2:419, c. 1907; R322:20–21, 1907). Why "idealism"? In a still-unpublished manuscript of 1872, Peirce wrote that "the main position of idealism ... is that being an object of thought—actual or possible—is an essential part of existence" (R935:3, 1872), that is, if a thing is real, then it can be represented in thought. This form of idealism, which is consistent with the view that there are real things, is implied by his pragmatic clarification of the idea of reality: pragmatically clarified, the claim that *x* is real means that if investigation were pushed so far as to permanently settle belief, then inquirers would have beliefs about *x*.

Decades after he wrote FOB and HTM, Peirce came to think of the investigative aspect of his account of truth as a pragmatic clarification of the idea of truth, although he had not presented it that way in that early pair of articles:

> The next application I shall make of pragmaticism[15] is to support a principle which might very well be regarded on the contrary, as a support of pragmaticism, and was

in fact originally so treated by me, being proved independently in my article of Nov. 1877 [viz., FOB].... The principle is that whatever is true would be logically inferred from sufficient experience by sufficient thought. (LI303, *c.* 1905)

In some other works, he seems to have viewed the representationalist aspect of his account of truth as providing a verbal definition of the word "true," for example, "That truth is the correspondence of a representation with its object is ... merely the nominal definition of it" (EP2:379, 1906). Combining these later views, we can say the following. A true proposition is, by definition of the word "true," one that is connected to reality via representation. What practical difference does this make for us? It is this: such a proposition is the content of a belief that would be permanently fixed were we to dispel our doubts by investigating.

That Peirce saw a tight connection between truth and reality is reflected in his claim that "reality belongs primarily to facts, and attaches to *things* only as elements of facts" (CP8.115, *c.* 1900). A fact, on Peirce's understanding, "is so much of the reality as is represented in a single *proposition*. If a proposition is true, that which it represents is a *fact*" (CP6.67, 1898; see also EP2:378, 1906). All true propositions are capable of being cognized; were this not the case, there would be some aspects of reality that would be forever beyond our understanding, and that possibly is ruled out by the pragmatic clarification of the idea of reality. If something is real, it must be an element of a fact, which can be represented by a true proposition. It is a fact that there is a pencil on my desk, and both the real pencil and the real desk are elements of that fact.

3. EXISTENCE

In addition to distinguishing among the real, the fictional, the external, and the internal, Peirce also distinguished reality from *existence*: "the Real is the proper contrary of Illusion, Delusion, or Figment, while to exist means, by virtue of the *ex* in *existere*, to act upon, to react against, the other things that exist in the psycho-physical universe" (ILS:258, 1909). An existing thing—an existent—is something that can react to, act upon, or react against something else. My pencil, which is real and external, is also an existent, since it can react to or against other things: I throw my pencil down on the desk in frustration, and it reacts by bouncing off the desk. Physical things—pencils, billiard balls, mountains, and planets—are, in addition to being external and therefore real, also existents. So while the concepts of reality and existence are very different—"*reality* means a certain kind of non-dependence upon thought, and is thus a character concerned with cognition, while *existence* means reaction with the environment, and is thus a dynamic character; and accordingly ... the two meanings are not the same" (R288:182, 1905)[16]—the extensions of the concepts overlap. Existence is the mode of being that characterizes individual things (like my pencil), as opposed to qualities (like the color that characterizes the pencil) and laws (like the law that determines that the pencil will fall to the floor if not supported by my desk, my hand, or some other existing thing). Unlike qualities and laws, "only existing individuals can react against one another" (CP2.84, 1902). What's more, only existents maintain their individual identities through time. On Peirce's view, existence just "is numerical identity, which is a dyadic relation of a subject to itself of which nothing but an existent individual is capable" (CP1.461, c. 1896). Some of my pencil's traits will change over time as it becomes worn down by use, but as an existent, it will maintain its identity—it will continue to exist as one and the same *thing*—throughout those changes.

Peirce's concept of existence gradually emerged from his concept of reality beginning in the 1880s, and tracking that emergence is tricky due to his shifting and inconsistent use of the relevant terminology. Initially, he used "existence" and its cognates as synonyms for "reality" and its cognates, for example, "the essential difference between a reality and a nonreality, is that the former has an existence entirely independent of what you or I or any number of men may think about it" (W2:104, 1867). He began using "existence" in his more specific sense in the mid-1890s, but even then he also continued to use it in a broader sense, although not to mean the same thing as "reality": "As for existence, it may be used in a wider or a narrower sense. In its wider sense it is synonym of Actual, and is such Being as is both Definite and in all respects Determinate; while in its narrower sense it is a Substance, or substratum which acts on, and is acted on by, the Universe of Substance" (ILS:257n, 1909).[17] Despite those difficulties, it is possible to trace the development of his thinking about existence and how it interlocks with some of his other metaphysical concepts.

First, notice that his definition of "real" implies that a real thing is characterized by a kind of resistance, namely, resistance to change caused solely by how that thing is represented. I might imagine the pencil on my desk sprouting wings and flying out the window, or type the words "The pencil on my desk just grew wings and flew away!" but being real, the pencil will fail to accord with any such representations of it. Granted, this is resistance in an attenuated sense; the pencil is not resisting by exerting force against any possible effects of my thoughts or words. Still, it resists my representations in that it is unmoved by them.

In the mid-1880s, Peirce began to connect reality to a more robust sort of resistance. This occurred as he was recording ideas that would become part of his evolutionary cosmology, his "guess at the riddle" of the origin of the universe. His cosmological "hypothesis" was "constructed from three elementary conceptions . . . the ideas of First, Second, Third" (W5:294). These conceptions correspond to Peirce's widely discussed "universal categories": firstness, secondness, and thirdness.[18] Here, in part, is how he described them in his earliest cosmological writings: "By the First . . . I mean simply what presents itself as first, fresh, immediate, free, spontaneous. An object at first blush, unreflectively taken. . . . The Second, last or term or end is in the fact of otherness, relation, force (not in the abstract, but as it feels when one gets hit), effect, dependence, occurrence, reality, upshot. The Third is the medium, or that which mediates between the absolute first and absolute last. Continuity. Process. Flow of time. . . . Sign, representative" (W5:294–295, 1886; see also W5:299, 1886). What's most relevant for present purposes is Peirce's connecting reality with secondness—which he also describes in terms of force, effect, and occurrence. This might be taken to suggest that firstness and thirdness are *not* real. But that would be a very strange view for him to have taken, since it would imply that two of the "elementary conceptions" that compose the universe are fictional or imaginary. Fortunately, nothing else that Peirce wrote in this context suggests that that is what he had in mind. In another draft of this material, he explained "the Second" in part as follows: "The Real, the stubborn fact, is that which is as it is, whatever I may opine about it, and which I must accordingly conceive as beside my thought, as a second or object over against me as subject or first. In the living feeling, the idea of first is prominent; in the hard fact of distinguishing assertion, that of second" (W5:300, 1886). This suggests not that "stubborn facts" are the only real things, but rather that *the concept of reality* is the concept of something that is "over against me," a second to my first. Peirce continued to connect the concepts of reality and secondness in subsequent iterations of these ideas (e.g., W6:171, 1887–1888; W6:209, 1887–1888). Through the first half of the 1890s, he connected the concept of reality with concepts like *irresistibleness* and *resistance* (W8:353, 1892), *dynamical reaction* (CP6.612, 1893), *compulsive power* and *insistence* (R680:5, 1893), *persistent force* (CP1.175, 1893), and *acting* and *being acted upon* (EP2:4, 1894). But it wasn't until "The Logic of Mathematics: An Attempt to Develop My Categories from Within" (CP1.417–520, c. 1896) that Peirce explicitly distinguished existence and reality as two different "modes of being":

> Existence is that mode of being which lies in opposition to another. To say that a table exists is to say that it is hard, heavy, opaque, resonant, that is, produces immediate effects upon the senses, and also that it produces purely physical effects, attracts the earth (that is, is heavy), dynamically reacts against other things (that is, has inertia), resists pressure (that is, is elastic), has a definite capacity for heat, etc. . . . Just . . . as a logical individual subject reappears in metaphysics as a thing, an *ens* having *existence* as its mode of being, so the logical reason, or premiss, reappears in metaphysics as a reason, an *ens* having a *reality*, consisting in a ruling both of the outward and of the inward world, as its mode of being. (CP1.457, 515)

Peirce held that the individual existence of a given existing thing is unintelligible. This isn't to say that the *concept* of existence is unintelligible. Nor is it to say that we cannot cognize existent things; after all, physical things, like my pencil, are external and therefore real, and given Peirce's pragmatic clarification of the idea of reality, everything real is a possible object of cognition. Still, there is something about a given existent object that we cannot cognize, namely, its own individual existence, that which distinguishes it from every other existent: "the existence of a thing consists in its reacting against the other things in the universe; and action and reaction is something which takes place at a given place in a given time and has no generality in it, and consequently no intelligibility, but is mere brute force" (HPPLS:1124, c. 1899). There are any number of generals that my pencil exemplifies and by which I can cognize it, but I cannot have a concept of *this* pencil's own specific existence, since its existence—its numerical identity and continued reaction to other things—is completely nongeneral and thus unthinkable. And of course, generals themselves are not existents; while some generals are real, they cannot react against other things, not even against other generals. We can *experience* an existent and its reactions, but we cannot *think* them *as* existents and *as* reactions: "a reaction may be experienced, but it cannot be conceived in its character of a reaction; for that element evaporates from every general idea" (CP3.613, 1901).[19]

Peirce's distinction between reality and existence is relevant also to his treatment of the topic of God. His view was that God does not exist—God is not an individual thing reacting against other things—but is nevertheless real:

> I myself always use *exist* in its strict philosophical sense of "react with the other like things in the environment." Of course, in that sense, it would be fetichism to say that God "exists." ... I define the *real* as that which holds its characters on such a tenure that it makes not the slightest difference what any man or men may have *thought* them to be, or ever will have *thought* them to be, here using thought to include, imagining, opining, and willing (as long as forcible *means* are not used); but the real thing's characters will remain absolutely untouched.
>
> Of any kind of figment, this is not true. So, then, the question being whether I believe in the reality of God, I answer, Yes. (CP6.495–496, c. 1906)[20]

At one point, he even suggested that God is the only thing that is *completely* real: "I do not believe that anything (unless it be God) quite fulfills the idea of the real" (CP2.532, 1893).

4. Reality as Gradational

But what would it be for something to be real but not *completely* so? The commonsense view of reality is that it is all or nothing: Paris, France is real—not real only to some degree but completely real—while the Emerald City is fictional—not merely *somewhat* fictional but *thoroughly* so. But as we have seen, Peirce defined "real" and "fictional" in terms of a kind of independence and a corresponding kind of dependence: the real is independent of how anyone represents it to be, while the fictional depends on how someone or other represents it to be. If those relations—the independence of a thing from, and the dependence of a thing on, representations of it—can be gradational, then so can reality and fictionality. The same holds for the relation of resistance, in terms of which Peirce understood reality during the years leading up to his eventual distinction between reality and existence. Given that resistance is a matter of degree, and given that a thing's reality amounts to its resistance (either resistance to change based only on how someone represents it to be or some other sort of resistance), then whether a given thing is real might turn out to be a matter of degree.

This is a deeply counterintuitive idea, but by the early 1890s Peirce had begun to take it seriously. The idea emerged in the context of his aforementioned evolutionary cosmology, according to which the universe—reality itself—evolved from a state of chaos into a state of greater regularity and lawfulness.

> Once you have embraced the principle of continuity no kind of explanation of things will satisfy you except that they grew. . . . If all things are continuous, the universe must be undergoing a continuous growth from non-existence to existence [i.e., from nonreality to reality[21]]. There is no difficulty in conceiving existence [i.e., reality] as a matter of degree. The reality of things consists in their persistent forcing themselves upon our recognition. If a thing has no such persistence, it is a mere dream. Reality, then, is persistence, is regularity. In the original chaos, where there was no regularity, there was no existence [i.e., reality]. It was all a confused dream. This we may suppose was in the infinitely distant past. But as things are getting more regular, more persistent, they are getting less dreamy and more real. (CP1.175, 1893)

The principle of continuity to which Peirce referred in that passage is what he called *synechism*, "the doctrine that all that exists is continuous" (CP1.172, 1893).[22] That principle "declar[es] that being is a matter of more or less, so as to merge insensibly into nothing" and thus rejects Parmenides's claim that "being is, and not-being is nothing" (EP2:2, 1893).[23]

The idea that reality is gradational also appears in Peirce's thought outside of the context of his evolutionary cosmology. For a time during the 1900s, he took seriously the idea that the reality of a given physical thing "is not absolute. For though I cannot open my window by mere 'willing' it to be open without willing the appropriate means, yet perhaps I cannot even change a character in a story I may be writing without using appropriate means. If I do use appropriate means I can influence bodies by willing; and that appears to me to detract from their absolute reality" (R939:27, 1905). Nevertheless, physical things "are, in the main, mighty real" (R939:27, 1905). He also seemed to take seriously the idea that a given thing might have some traits regardless of whether anyone represents it as having them and other traits only because someone represents it as having them. That thing would not be *thoroughly* real but instead real only to some less-than-maximum degree: "The real is that whose characters belong to it whether you or I think that they do or not. For 'whose characters' we read 'all whose characters' if we mean thorough reality" (R288:167, 1905).[24]

While Peirce took seriously the possibility that reality is gradational, he also thought that the idea signified a flaw in his philosophical views: " I am obliged, for the present, to admit degrees of reality. These seem to me to mark imperfections, crudities, unfinished parts, of the doctrine of pragmatism; but not any from which any ultimate danger to the doctrine is to be anticipated" (R1041:15, 1905). But if it was a flaw, it was one from which we might nonetheless learn something:

> No doubt there are grades of reality, meaning that objects of signs may yield with more or less resistance to opinion or other representation. According to the definition [of "real"] absolute resistance is essential to reality. But an approach to reality, something that is not in the slightest of the nature of pretense[,] is found wherever

an object of thought is sufficiently obstinate to enable us to say, it has *not* these characters, but it *does* have these. There is already a lesson in logic. Namely that one may lay down the very best of definitions, going to the very heart of things; & yet there will be, as it were, a little living mouse of a quasi exception which will find or make a hole to get in when all seemed hermetically closed. This mouse will not be a mere pest to be got rid of and forgotten. It will be a fellow being to be remembered and to be appraised. (R498:32–33, c. 1906)

Unfortunately, Peirce did not pursue the idea that reality is a matter of degree any further, and it seems that he eventually abandoned it: "one who knows the proper meaning of Reality will perceive that it is not subject to degrees" (R642:10, 1909).[25]

Notes

1. I call this view *basic realism*. See Lane (2018).
2. Peirce wrote that this meaning of the word "real" "did not become at all common [in philosophy] until Duns Scotus, in the latter part of the thirteenth century[,] began to use it freely" (CP6.495, c. 1906).
3. A few examples are found in W3:254, 1877; W5:288, 1886; CP6.610, 1893; EP2:342, 1905; ILS257n, 1909; R683:32, 1913.
4. Aboutness is commonly called *intentionality*, derived from Franz Brentano's phrase "intentional inexistence." Peirce did not use the word "intentionality" in this sense; see Short (2007, 6). But Peirce did author the *Century Dictionary* entry for the word "intentional," which includes the following: "In *metaph.*, pertaining to an appearance, phenomenon, or representation in the mind; phenomenal; representational; apparent" (CD3136, 1889–1891).
5. Peirce contrasts the real and the external in this way in various works. See, for example: W3:271, 1878; CP8.191, c. 1904; CP5.525, 1905; R498:32, c. 1906; CP6.327–328, 1908; ILS257n, 1909.
6. The plural noun "reals" is Peirce's coinage. See, for example, CP8.191, c. 1904; EP2:354, 1905; CP8.216, ILS273, 1910.
7. For similar characterizations of the internal, see W3:78, 1873; ILS257n, 1909.
8. For like descriptions of the imaginary, fictional, or fictive, see W3:46, 1872; W3:49, 1872; CP5.405, W3:271, 1878.
9. For more on Peirce's scholastic realism, see Haack (1992); Mayorga (2007); Lane (2018, chs. 5 and 6); and "A Science Like Any Other: A Peircean Philosophy of Sex?" by Shannon Dea in this volume. On the question how, on Peirce's view, we perceive generals, see Wilson (2012); and Short (2015).
10. For more on the Pragmatic Maxim, see "Pragmatic Clarification: Contexts and Purposes" by Mats Bergman in this volume.
11. Peirce provided several different statements of the pragmatic maxim over subsequent decades; see Schmidt (2020). For an account of how Peirce's expanding empiricism influenced his thinking about the Maxim, see Short (2015).
12. Peirce later revised this passage to read: "There are Real things, whose characters are entirely independent of our opinions about them; those Reals affect our senses according to regular laws, and, though our sensations are as different as are our relations to the objects,

yet, by taking advantage of the laws of perception, we can ascertain by reasoning how things really and truly are; and any man, if he have sufficient experience and he reason enough about it, will be led to the one True conclusion" (CP5.384).

13. Peirce later revised this passage to read: "there is no reason why the results of those three first methods should do so" (CP5.387).
14. For more on Peirce's theory of truth, see "Peirce on Truth" by Andrew Howat in this volume. For an account that emphasizes the representationalist and investigative aspects of Peirce's theory, see chapter 1 of Lane (2018).
15. By 1905, Peirce had begun referring to his specific version of pragmatism as *pragmaticism*, in order to distance it from the varieties of pragmatism defended by William James, F. C. S. Schiller, and others. See EP2:334–335, 1905.
16. This page in R288, which is a notebook, is unnumbered by Peirce, but it is the verso that immediately precedes the numbered recto 183.
17. In an unpublished manuscript of the previous year, Peirce distinguished between these two uses of "existence" as follows: "By existence in any particular one of the three Universes of experience, I mean merely actual being in that universe; but I often use exist and existence absolutely meaning the actual Being of a physical thing" (R204:A8, 1908); "By existence in any particular one of the three Universes of experience, I mean merely actual occurrence in the mode of Being common and peculiar to that universe. Yet I often use exist and existence ... without qualification; and then I mean the actual Being of a physical thing" (R204:8 variant, 1908).
18. One of Peirce's more general descriptions of his three universal categories is as follows: "Firstness is the mode of being of that which is such as it is, positively and without reference to anything else. Secondness is the mode of being of that which is such as it is, with respect to a second but regardless of any third. Thirdness is the mode of being of that which is such as it is, in bringing a second and third into relation to each other" (CP8.328, 1904). For more on the categories, see "Peirce's Formal and Material Categories in Phenomenology" by Richard Kenneth Atkins in this volume.
19. Peirce adopted Duns Scotus's term "haecceity" to refer to this aspect of an individual existent and began using it to express his own views in "A Guess at the Riddle" (W6:187; W6:205, 1887–1888); he also credited Scotus with "first elucidat[ing] individual existence" (CP1.458, c. 1896). According to Short (2007, 48–51), Peirce was motivated to recognize haecceity by his new conception of indexical signs.
20. For more on Peirce's religious philosophy, see "Peirce and Religion" by Gary Slater in this volume.
21. In this 1893 lecture, Peirce was still using "existence" synonymously with "reality."
22. Peirce sometimes presented synechism, not as a doctrine of metaphysics, but as a principle of philosophical methodology: "The tendency to regard continuity ... as an idea of prime importance in philosophy may conveniently be termed *synechism*" (W8:136, 1892).
23. Peirce also maintained that the internal—that which is internal to someone's mind—is continuous with the external—that which is outside of their mind (CP7.438, c. 1893; CP8.191, c. 1904). For an analysis of this view, see Lane (2018, 89–92).
24. This is similar to the approach Susan Haack takes in analyzing imaginative works that are set in fictionalized versions of real places and that involve fictionalized versions of real people and events. Such places, characters, and events "are partly fictional, but also partly real" ("The Real, the Fictional and the Fake," *Spazio Filosofico* 8 (2013): 209–217; quotation at 214). To accommodate this view, Haack shifts from Peirce's categorical definition

of "real" to a gradualist one: "*x is more fully* real, the more independent it is of what you or I or anyone believes about it" (2016, 45). She cites King Arthur as an example of a partly real, partly fictional person, and there are many others, for example, the fictionalized versions of Alan Turing in the movie *The Imitation Game* and in Neal Stephenson's novel *Cryptonomicon* and the fictionalized versions of Fred Hampton in the movies *Judas and the Black Messiah* and *The Trial of the Chicago 7*.

25. Peirce took seriously not only the idea that reality is gradational but also that it is indeterminate in the following way: there are real things for which it is neither the case that they do, nor that they do not, have a given real property. See Lane (2018, ch. 7).

References

Haack, Susan. 1992. "Extreme Scholastic Realism: Its Relevance to Philosophy of Science Today." *Transactions of the Charles S. Peirce Society* 28, no. 1 (Winter): 19–50.

Haack, Susan. 2013. "The Real, the Fictional, and the Fake." *Spazio Filosofico* 8: 209–217.

Haack, Susan. 2016. "The World According to Innocent Realism: The One and the Many, the Real and the Imaginary, the Natural and the Social." In *Susan Haack: Reintegrating Philosophy*, edited by Julia F. Göhner and Eva-Maria Jung, 33–55. Cham, Switzerland: Springer.

Lane, Robert. 2018. *Peirce on Realism and Idealism*. Cambridge: Cambridge University Press.

Mayorga, Rosa Maria. 2007. *From Realism to "Realicism": The Metaphysics of Charles Sanders Peirce*. Lanham, MD: Lexington Books.

Peirce, Charles S. 1857–1914. Manuscripts held at the Houghton Library of Harvard University, as identified in Richard Robin. 1967. *Annotated Catalogue of the Papers of Charles S. Peirce*. Amherst: University of Massachusetts Press. And in Richard Robin. 1971. "The Peirce Papers: A Supplementary Catalogue." *Transactions of the Charles S. Peirce Society* 7, no. 1 (Winter): 37–57. (Referred to as R[catalogue#]:[sheet#]; with RL for letters and RS for supplement.)

Peirce, Charles S. 1889–1891. Contributions to *The Century Dictionary: An Encyclopedic Lexicon of the English Language*, edited by W. D. Whitney. New York: Century. (Referred to as CD.)

Peirce, Charles S. 1931–1958. *The Collected Papers of Charles Sanders Peirce*. 8 vols. Vols. 1–6 edited by Charles Hartshorne and Paul Weiss. Vols. 7–8 edited by Arthur W. Burks. Cambridge, MA: Harvard University Press. (Referred to as CP.)

Peirce, Charles S. 1985. *Historical Perspectives on Peirce's Logic of Science*. 2 vols. Edited by Carolyn Eisele. The Hague: Mouton. (Referred to as HPPLS.)

Peirce, Charles S. 1982– . *The Writings of Charles S. Peirce: A Chronological Edition*. 7 vols. to date. Edited by the Peirce Edition Project. Bloomington: Indiana University Press. (Referred to as W.)

Peirce, Charles S. 1992–1998. *The Essential Peirce: Selected Philosophical Writings*. 2 vols. Vol. 1 edited by Nathan Houser and Christian Kloesel. Vol. 2 edited by the Peirce Edition Project. Bloomington: Indiana University Press. (Referred to as EP.)

Peirce, Charles S. 2009. *The Logic of Interdisciplinarity: The Monist Series*. Edited by Elize Bisanz. Berlin: De Gruyter. (Referred to as LI.)

Peirce, Charles S. 2014. *Illustrations of the Logic of Science*. Edited by Cornelis de Waal. Chicago: Open Court. (Referred to as ILS.)

Peirce, Charles S. 2019– . *Logic of the Future. Writings on Existential Graphs*. 3 vols in 4. Edited by A.-V. Pietarinen. Berlin: De Gruyter. (Referred to as LoF.)

Peirce, Charles S. 2020. *Selected Writings on Semiotics, 1894–1912*. Edited by Francesco Bellucci. Berlin: De Gruyter. (Referred to as SWS.)

Schmidt, Jon Alan. 2020. "Peirce's Maxim of Pragmatism: 61 Formulations." *Transactions of the Charles S. Peirce Society* 56, no. 4 (Fall): 580–599.

Short, T. L. 2007. *Peirce's Theory of Signs*. New York: Cambridge University Press.

Short, T. L. 2015. "Empiricism Expanded." *Transactions of the Charles S. Peirce Society* 51, no. 1 (Winter): 1–33.

Wilson, Aaron. 2012. "The Perception of Generals." *Transactions of the Charles S. Peirce Society* 48 no. 2 (Spring): 169–190.

CHAPTER 24

SCIENTIFIC PRIDE AND METAPHYSICAL PREJUDICE
Ens Quantum Ens, *Quantum Theory,* and Peirce

ROSA MAYORGA

If all men by nature desire to know, then they desire most of all the greatest knowledge or science.

—John Duns Scotus[1]

It makes no difference how imperfect a man's knowledge may be, how mixed with error and prejudice; from the moment that he engages in an inquiry in the [scientific] spirit [...] that which occupies him is science.

—Charles Peirce[2]

We each begin probably with a little bias and upon that bias build every circumstance in favor of it.

—Jane Austen[3]

Nature is richer than our metaphysical prejudices.

—Carlo Rovelli[4]

THE relationship between metaphysics and physics is an ancient and complex one. As in all relationships, there are both common and diverse interests; different ways of doing things, but with a general disposition to contribute toward a shared goal; along the way, disagreements, disputes, a drifting apart, and sometimes, happily, a reconciliation. Metaphysicians and physicists both share the proud[5] desire to understand the world and the things in it, the nature of reality. Almost one hundred years after it was first proposed, quantum theory has radically transformed the science of physics, inviting a conception of reality that is drastically at odds with our most rooted metaphysical convictions about it. Both a scientist and a metaphysician extraordinaire, Charles Peirce (1839–1914) was singularly poised to predict some of the "metaphysical prejudices" about the world and how we know it, which quantum theory, developed just over a couple of decades after Peirce, has revealed. Peirce scholars have noted how Peirce's tychism, his doctrine of absolute chance, anticipated quantum theory's declared indeterminism.[6] I propose to trace how Peirce's realism, inspired by the thirteenth-century Franciscan monk John Duns Scotus (c. 1266–1308), adapted for a reconceived scientific metaphysics, parallels some of the familiar enigmas posed by quantum physics.[7]

1. Metaphysics versus Science

As is familiar, the term "metaphysics," derived from classical Greek (*meta ta phusika*), means "after things of nature," a reference to the order in which Aristotle's (384–322 BC) writings on nature were compiled after his death.[8] Those topics, gathered under "physics," that dealt with observation, sense perception, and the natural world, were followed with the works that dealt with broader questions, such as causation, change, and "being as being" (*ens quantum ens* as expressed in Latin by his medieval commentators).[9] Metaphysics thus studies different kinds of beings that constitute what we call "reality"; not just physical objects such as apples, horses, and chairs (*res*, in Latin) accessible through the senses, but also nonphysical beings such as souls, as well as abstract kinds of things such as properties, events, and relations, not quite as directly accessible. This introduces questions of what makes something real, the nature of existence, and what kind of accessibility can lead to a claim of knowledge, if any.

Although both physics and metaphysics have a common goal of attaining knowledge of ultimate reality, their paths have diverged increasingly throughout the centuries, with physics and the rest of the applied sciences adding specialized instruments and processes to their methodology, while metaphysics continued to rely almost entirely on reasoning, intuition, and, in some cases, revelation. Charles Peirce, "a physicist and a chemist, and as such eager to push investigation in the direction of a better acquaintance with the minute anatomy and physiology of matter," explains that what led him to "metaphysical speculations, to which [he] had not before been inclined," was the fact that he was "mainly a student of the methods of science" (CP7.506, c. 1898). He asked himself, "How are we ever going to find out anything more than we now [know] about molecules and atoms [. . .] and [. . .] lay out a broad plan for any further grand advance?" (CP7.506, c. 1898). His answer was to "weld" metaphysics and science.

Peirce famously qualified the four methods we use in "fixing beliefs" as that of authority, tenacity, a priori, and the scientific method.[10] Peirce's concept of the scientific method, though, is much broader than that of working scientists'—it is any time an investigation using close observation (not necessarily with specialized instruments and equipment), experience, and reasoning, with an aim at getting at the truth, is utilized. This is the method that Peirce urges for revitalizing metaphysics, which he observed had been "in a deplorably backward condition" for some time (CP6.2, 1898),[11] deteriorating into a "puny, rickety, and scrofulous science," mostly due, he claimed, to its contamination with "seminary philosophy" (CP1.620, 1898).[12] While metaphysicians acquired the reputation of engaging in "ceaseless and trivial disputation" (CP6.5,1898), scientists proudly advanced knowledge in their respective areas by leaps and bounds. Armed with his pragmatic maxim, which serves to define concepts in terms of their experiential effects, Peirce proposes to rid metaphysics of "meaningless gibberish" and restore it to its original standing as a science, a scientific metaphysics, which makes it continuous with the special sciences—"so that all such rubbish being swept away, what will remain of philosophy will be a series of problems capable of investigation by the observational methods of the true sciences" (CP5.423, 1905).

A scientific metaphysics, then, is a true science, for it follows the scientific method of engaging with observable phenomena, without the need for specialized equipment, just "a comparison of the facts of everyday life such as present themselves to every adult and sane person," analyzed "with a more attentive scrutiny" by means of abductive, inductive, and deductive reasoning.[13] Now it's not the case that Peirce thought all was well with the special sciences of his day. He considered many erroneously subscribed to "necessitarianism" or determinism, "the common belief that every single fact in the universe is precisely determined by law" (CP6.36, 1891), and "explained familiar phenomena . . . by extending the operation of simple mechanical principles, which belongs to nominalism," as opposed to realism, the doctrine that he prescribed, and without which, he argued, science would not be possible (CP8.38, 1871).

Metaphysics provides the basic presuppositions upon which the rest of the sciences rest, but that still bear "industrious and solid investigation" such as "[. . . 1] Whether there be any strictly individual existence [. . . 2] any definite indeterminacy? [. . . 3] What [. . .] account can be given of the . . . apparent connection with determinations of mass, space, and time?" (CP6.6, *c.* 1903–1904).[14] Peirce approaches these metaphysical questions in light of his scholastic realism, couched in the terminology of his categories of firstness, secondness, and thirdness, and which are reflected in his cosmological theories of tychism, synechism, and agapism. But before we get to Peirce, let me return to the present and briefly highlight some of the metaphysical conundrums regarding individual existence, indeterminacy, and our "connection" with mass, space, and time posed by quantum theory, which I submit Peirce anticipated and tried to address.

2. Quantum Theory and *Res*

Quantum theory[15] requires that we must abandon what seems obvious and most natural to us—a metaphysical prejudice—the basic idea of a world made up of independently existent things that occupy space and are subject to time and certain laws. The years since it was first proposed have not diminished its shocking claims, and even those who have devoted themselves to its study find it bewildering still. But quantum mechanics is astonishingly successful—astrophysicists, engineers, biologists, and engineers use it daily; its products, computers, cell phones, microwave ovens, etc., are an integral part of our lives; and its predictions of new phenomena have turned out to be correct. It seemed, at one point in fairly recent history, that based on classic Newtonian-based physics, reality, as we conceived it, could be explained in simple terms—material objects unconditionally and predictably obey a few laws that could be expressed mathematically. With the advent of atomic theory and the claim that material objects are made of smaller particles composed of smaller subatomic particles, we were ever closer to a complete description of the things that surround us and the universal forces that guide them, which make up our vision of the real world. This vision of the world was shattered, though, at the beginning of the twentieth century with the work of Albert Einstein, Werner Heisenberg, Erwin Schrödinger, Louis de Broglie, Max Born, Niels Bohr, Pascual Jordan, Paul Dirac, Wolfgang Pauli, and many others since, who, through specialized observations, measurements, and mathematical calculations, found that once attention is focused on the subatomic level, the entire picture changes.[16]

While trying to explain how electrons move in orbits inside atoms, the basic building blocks of everything, Bohr discovers that they do so in certain precise ways, mysteriously "leaping" from one place to another while emitting precise amounts (photons) of light. Heisenberg decodes the pattern by replacing the usual variables (velocity, energy, position) with mathematical tables, or matrices, of probabilities instead, which enabled the correct computation of results and accurate predictions of the bizarre behavior observed in experiments.[17] Pauli, working together with Heisenberg, Born, and Jordan, completes the calculations, which are independently confirmed by Dirac.[18] The new theory not only confirms Bohr's strange findings about electron behavior, but also allows for calculation of the intensity of the emitted light, which matches those obtained through experimentation.[19]

Based on many experiments and analyses of the data gathered since, theoretical quantum physicists, such as Carlo Rovelli, have (generally) concluded that (1) there are no such things as *independently existing* elementary particles, no basic building blocks, but rather only wavelike patterns of (2) probable interconnections among things, which arise indeterminately without apparent cause and (3) behave in rather unexpected and extraordinary ways. These three conclusions, I find, line up with Peirce's questions summarized above regarding some of our metaphysical presuppositions (or prejudices), which he anticipated needed further scrutiny.

Let's begin with (1), the claim that once we dig deeper at the subatomic level, we find no one independently existing particle of matter, thing, or object (*res*), as we conceive of it, as having properties and occupying space.[20] The phenomenon observed in experiments with laser beams and refraction is called "quantum superposition," defined as "when two contradictory properties are, in a certain sense, present together"; for example, an object could be here but at the same time somewhere else. In a sense, it is in both places, in a "superposition" of positions.[21] The experiment goes something like this—a laser beam made up of a small number of photons is split by a prism into two parallel paths (A, B). The two paths are reintegrated again by another prism before being split again and ending up in two detectors (1, 2). If either the A or the B path is blocked (e.g., by a hand), half of the photons end up in detector 1, the other half in detector 2.

But if both paths are open, free of any blocks, all the photons end up in detector 2. This is peculiar; why does blocking one path have an effect on how the other (unblocked) path behaves? And why does not blocking any paths cause all the photons to go to just one detector, instead of half going to one and half to the other? The answer is "quantum interference"; there is interference with the wavelike photons in the A and B paths when they're both open. When one path is blocked, the photons behave differently. What we actually see, though, is not the superposition, but rather its consequence, "quantum interference."[22] This is the idea behind Heisenberg's description of the electron's position as a probability, and not as in one specific orbit or another. The electron is in a sense in all orbits, but if you search for it, it is only in one.

Heisenberg's uncertainty principle, as the postulate has come to be known, is often stated as the fact that one cannot know both the position and the speed of a subatomic object such as a photon or electron with perfect accuracy; the more we know its position, the less we know its speed, and vice versa. But this is not quite right; the claim is not that we cannot measure the position accurately and then the speed precisely; it can be done, but after measuring the speed, we will find the position changed. The point is that the two variables cannot be determined together; the situation can only be described as probabilistic. But Heisenberg's uncertainty principle is not just true in the subatomic world; quantum theory has been applied across all disciplines, predicting new phenomena never previously imagined, and to this day, the theory has not been proven wrong.[23] Its claims, then, apply to our everyday macroscopic world as well. This vision of a probabilistic indeterminate world is deeply disturbing metaphysically, however—it does not clarify how to conceptualize the everyday objects that we experience as humans and that science was supposed to explain.

Schrödinger tried to illustrate this enigma on a human scale with his famous thought experiment. A cat is enclosed in a box with a device that either will open a bottle of poisonous gas, which will result in the cat dying, or it will not open, and the cat will remain alive. If the cat is accurately described by quantum theory, it is in a quantum superposition, both "cat-dead" and "cat-alive" until we open the box and look inside; we will either see it alive or dead, but obviously not both. But to say that the cat is in quantum superposition while inside the box is different from saying that *we do not know* if the cat is alive or dead.[24] It is rather to say that it is indeterminate whether the cat is in one state or another. Just like there are interference effects between the two paths of the photons, there are interference effects between cat-alive and cat-dead (in the box) that change when the cat is observed. But the interference is too small for us to see the effects, and at our scale there are too many variables; this is why we are not aware of quantum mechanics in our daily lives. We cannot observe the quantum superposition between cat-alive and cat-dead, so we replace it with the fact that we do not know whether the cat is alive or not.[25] Since quantum interference and the minute fluctuations of probability are lost to us, we interpret the world as stable and determinate and facts as certain. However, this is just an approximation, as is revealed when we examine the subatomic world. Heisenberg's principle means that a quantum object never has perfectly determined variables, such as velocity and position; these are determined only in an interaction, when one or the other is indeterminate.[26] The claim, then, is that there is (2) a definite indeterminacy and, at the same time, an essential interconnection between the object and the observer.

The quantum phenomenon that embodies this interconnection of things is "entanglement." It is (3) a kind of strange connection sustained inexplicably between very distant objects—if they are entangled, they become "correlated," both displaying the same random features even when separated across great space–time distances. In an example of photons with a superposition of the colors red and blue, "each photon may reveal itself as either red or blue the moment it is observed, but if one is found to be blue, then the other—at a great distance away—[astonishingly] will also be blue."[27] And it is not the case that one photon signals the other to change to the other's color, nor is it the case that the color is predetermined before their separation; both these possible explanations have been excluded in countless experiments, and yet, the puzzling correlated results persist, no matter how far away the pair of photons is.[28] If we replace human "motive" with quanta " entanglement," Elizabeth Bennet's famous declaration in the novel *Pride and Prejudice* would still ring true—"The distance is nothing if one has motive [or entanglement]."[29]

One interpretation for these baffling quanta phenomena is known as the "relational" theory.[30] They are disconcerting, the claim goes, because quantum theory "does not describe the way quantum objects manifest themselves *to us*"; that is, to us they appear as isolated objects, or *res*, which is how we tend to divide up the world; but rather, quanta describe how every physical thing manifests itself to, or "acts on *any* other physical thing."[31] What we consider an individual existing object is really something that interacts with its surroundings; an object that does not interact or affect its surroundings in any way would be, for all practical purposes, nonexistent. Instead of describing the world as a collection of objects with definite properties in space and time, which is what we do from habit, quantum theory depicts the world as "a net of relations which determine the properties of objects as a result of their interactions with their surroundings."[32] What we call "reality," then, is a vast web of interacting entities that manifest themselves by interacting with each other, and we are a part of that web.[33]

The relational interpretation explains entanglement thus—to say that two objects are correlated is to say that both objects interact with a third object that observes; what seemed like a strange communication between two distant objects is explained by the existence of the third object that interacts with both. A correlation then is a property of the two objects when there is a third object that interacts with both.[34] But although quantum theory claims that properties exist only when there are interactions, and hence, are relative, at the same time, there is a certain consistency (subject to a real, but rare element of chance) when these interactions occur, which is what "grounds the objectivity of our communal vision of the world."[35]

In sum, quantum mechanics reverses classic mechanics theory and exposes our metaphysical prejudices about the nature of ultimate reality—the claim is that it's the whole that determines the properties and behavior of its parts, and not the other way around, as we had thought.[36] And in terms of its parts, quantum theorists further claim, the elementary particle "is not an independently existing, unanalyzable entity. It is, in essence, a set of relationships that reaches outward to other things."[37] Now the acknowledgment of relations as real, that relations are tripartite, and the claim that *singulars*, in a certain sense, do not exist[38] are familiar pronouncements to those acquainted with Peirce and the scholastic realism that he was "never able to think differently on" and that permeated his scientific metaphysics (CP1.20, 1903). Let us turn now to Duns Scotus, who "strongly influenced" Peirce and whose scholastic metaphysics, when "adapted to modern culture," Peirce was "convinced ... is best to harmonize with physical science" (CP1.6, 1897).

3. *QUANTUM ENS* AND SCOTUS

The term "quantum" is derived from Latin, meaning a particular amount, or unit, and was adopted as the name of the scientific theory at the turn of the twentieth century referencing the specific packets of energy detected when electrons leapt from one orbit to another.[39] But the Latin term *in quantum* also means "how" or "such as" and has described the primary focus of Aristotelian metaphysics, the study, or science of being as being, since the reintroduction of major parts of his corpus to western Europe mostly via Arab translations in the thirteenth century.[40]

Duns Scotus embraced Aristotle's way of understanding and explaining reality, as well as his theories of abstractive cognition and knowledge in lieu of the established Augustinian–Platonic model (more compatible with the medieval religious perspective) of divine illumination and innate ideas grounding the objectivity of all knowledge.[41] The main epistemological concern of the time centered on the possibility of any kind of knowledge of the world and the things in it.[42] A description of the constitution of the intellect and the process of cognition of particular things were primary foci. Reflecting upon the experience and conditions for human knowing "in this present life," Scotus achieves an affirmative answer to the epistemological question by elaborating on the Aristotelian approach to metaphysics and reframing it in Christian terms.[43] He does this in two significant ways: by asserting that "being" is a univocal term, and by expanding Aristotle's theory of cognition to include intuition, a separate intellective act from abstraction.[44] Scotus addresses these two aspects simultaneously when he answers his question, "What is the first object of the intellect?" in the *Ordinatio*—what first presents itself indistinctly to intellection at the most basic level is being (*ens*); being is what is most common to all that is and what initiates the abstractive and intuitive acts resulting in human knowledge.[45] The "greatest science," metaphysics, corresponds to "those things that are most knowable," which is being as being (*ens quantum ens*), since one can predicate being of everything that is.[46] The univocity of being grounds all human cognition and its relation to the world.[47] For Scotus, the world and the mind are in a relationship of mutual presence that results in our concepts, our knowledge of reality.

The mind, an immaterial substance, acquires knowledge of material objects by means of the immaterial essence or common nature (*quidditas*, or "whatness") inherent in them, through several stages in the process of abstraction. Abstraction begins with sense experience of an existing object, setting in motion the process of perception, which in turn gives rise to a perceptual sensible mental image (*phantasm*) in the imagination. This image forms the basis for the activity of intellection—the potential or possible (passive) part of the intellect receives the image, which the agent (active) part of the intellect turns into an intelligible likeness (*species intelligibilis*) or universal concept, which replaces the sensible image in the possible intellect. The final stage of this mediated process, which began with the material object, concludes with conceptual formulations in the possible intellect of the object, concepts (universals) that can then be called upon in the absence of the object itself. This is what Aristotle and Scotus called "scientific knowledge." But if all that the mind has access to are mental images that it manufactures into universal concepts through abstractions, in what sense are these abstract universals "real" and representative of true knowledge, and not mere fictions? Scotus tries to answer this in a couple of ways: with his theories of universal realism and intuitive cognition.

Scotus famously argues for the position of universal realism, the claim that universals are real, with William of Ockham representing the counterposition of nominalism, the claim that only material objects are real, while mental concepts are mere "names," lack existence, and are not real. Unlike Platonic universals that exist in the realm of the forms, Scotus's brand of "moderate" realism alleges that universals are real in spite of their lack of concrete existence per se. In other words, Scotus makes a distinction between existence and reality: everything that exists is real, but not all that is real exists. Universals are part of the conceptual order, the result of abstractive activity, but are still real because they are a product of the abstracted essence, the common nature, or *quidditas* in the object and makes it *what* it is. Once produced in the mind, a universal remains in the intellect, stored in the memory, and can be recalled and thought about without the presence of the perceptual object.

Scotus distinguishes three ways concepts are related to their perceptual objects: the *distinctio rationis* (conceptual distinction), where two different terms have the same referent in actuality, for example, Jane Austen and the author of *Pride and Prejudice*; the *distinctio realis* (real distinction), as in the two individuals Scotus and Peirce; and the *distinctio formalis* (formal distinction), based upon a real aspect of the object, but not existing independent of it, such as the common nature of humanity that Austen, Scotus, and Peirce share.[48]

The second way Scotus defends the claim of true knowledge of the world is by identifying a second act of cognition besides abstraction, namely, intuitive cognition. Like abstraction, intuitive cognition begins with sense experience, but unlike the latter, is immediate, not mediated via a representational image, but rather a direct awareness of the perceptual object as present and existing, an act of presence between the mind and the object without an intervening intelligible species created in the mind.[49] Self-evident propositions, such as "the whole is greater than its parts," are also known intuitively. The fact that God, as entailed by his divine essence, cognizes all possible finite things that remain in his thought for all eternity explains the "natural light" by which we recognize the truth of self-evident principles and anchors our human assent to this.[50] Intuition then provides certainty of the object's existence and presence, as well as self-evident propositions, while abstraction grasps the essence of the object, so with these two, we can claim to have scientific knowledge of the world.

But from our human perspective, our knowledge is limited; it is not knowledge of the singular object *qua* singular, in its singularity, its *haecceitas* ("thisness"), but only of its *quidditas*, which is what is abstracted; we can intuit the object as existing, but we don't grasp its singularity intellectually. We use the terms "particular," "individual," and "singular" synonymously, but they each point to a different feature of an existing thing. A particular is an instance, a "part," of a universal or general type; an individual cannot be divided further; and a singular, or singularity, is single, one, a unity, unique. Haecceity, or the ultimate individuating difference, as he preferred to call it, is the answer to Scotus's question of "what makes this this and not that, that is, why a nature is this [singular] and incommunicable to another."[51] Scotus argues that haecceity is not matter, form, accident, substance; nor is it "anything of which being can be quidditatively predicated" and hence it cannot be defined (at least by us, since our knowledge is quidditative).[52] It is not a thing, but yet it is not nothing (a *formalitas*)—a positive determining factor that accounts for the unique singular that completes the division of being, culminating in the perfection, or actualization, of the common nature.[53] Intuitive cognition does not pick out singularity—it just registers the external object as existing "here and now": "The intellect [. . .] intuitively knows that nature qua existing, and this cognition of an existent as existing suffices to make remembrance of it possible. . . . 'Here' and 'now' are singular properties which can pertain to a nature, not qua singular, although it is true that these properties can only pertain to something that is singular. . . . Nevertheless, they do not formally include, or essentially presuppose, singularity as the precise reason they are there" (*Ordinatio* IV, d.45, q.3, n.21).

It is an odd fact of our human existence that we are not privy, in our current state, to grasp haecceity. We encounter individuals and cognize them through their accidents or properties, but their singularity as such remains unintelligible to us. Scotus asks: "But what is this impediment? I respond: our intellect in this state is not apt to move or be moved immediately, unless it be moved by some imaginable or external sensible" (*Ord.* II, d.3, p.2, q.1, n.288).[54] Scotus speculates on possible reasons for our inability, at least in this life, to cognize individual differences as such. He mentions the possibility of Adam and Eve's sin, one of excessive pride in trying to attain God's knowledge by eating of the forbidden fruit, and the resulting punishment of a flawed nature (prone to errors and prejudices) inherited by their progeny, but he does not come to a definite conclusion.

But the fact that we cannot cognize singularity, either mediately or immediately in the intellect, poses a problem, Scotus believes, in explaining affective states, such as love, friendship, or faith, which are directed toward specific singulars that we need to distinguish. Scotus resolves this issue through his doctrine of the will, which, like the intellect, is a feature of the soul. Acts of love, friendship, and faith are volitional and provide the means for us to relate to individuals in their singularity this way, even though the singularity per se is out of intellectual reach. It is through his theories of cognition and his scholastic realism, though, that Scotus makes the case for claiming a limited kind of human knowing of the world. I turn now to Peirce.

4. Pride, Prejudice, and Peirce

Peirce tells us that he took satisfaction, or "pride in the entire absence of originality in all that [he] . . . ever sought to bring to the attention of logicians and metaphysicians" (CP8.213, c. 1905). Since there "is a residuum of error in every individual's opinions," he admired the scholastic philosopher's "complete absence of self-conceit . . . [whose] work is not designed to embody his ideas, but the universal truth" (CP8.11–12, 1871). This humble attitude is in contrast to "the tendency of men to conceited exaggeration of their reasoning powers" (CP1.662, 1898) and to "sham" reasoners, who in bad faith "learn to look forward and see what conclusions a given method will lead to before they give their adhesion to it" (CP1.57, c. 1896). Peirce's own notion of truth reflects the fact that although "an individual may not live to reach the truth . . . there is a definite opinion to which the mind of man is . . . tending" (CP1.57, c. 1896). And this final opinion "is independent, not indeed of thought in general, but of all that is arbitrary and individual in thought; is quite independent of how you, or I, or any number of men think" (CP1.57, c. 1896). Peirce's description of the real follows closely: "The real, then, is that which, sooner or later, information and reasoning would finally result in, and which is therefore independent of the vagaries of me and you" (CP1.57, c. 1896). This conception of reality also involves "the notion of a COMMUNITY, without definite limits, and capable of a definite increase of knowledge" (CP5.312, 1868).

Peirce acknowledges that his various ways of describing the real and reality are novel—"It is true that the question of realism was not originally stated this way" but rather, as "whether universals, such as the Horse . . . were *in re* or *in rerum natura*" (CP4.1, 1898). By way of these pragmatist revisions that highlight the role of common experience as well as reasoning in metaphysical inquiry, Peirce adapts scholastic realism "to modern culture," bringing "into prominence the kind of universals to which modern science pays most attention," namely, laws and regularities, which he prefers to call "generals," all the while keeping his epistemological, cognitive, and ontological claims Scotistic at heart (CP4.1, 1898). Early on, in his review of Fraser's edition of the works of George Berkeley, he rehearses Scotus's basic knowledge claim: "It is the very same nature which in the mind is universal and *in re* is singular; for if it were not, in knowing anything of a universal we should be knowing nothing of things, but only of our own thoughts" (CP8.18, 1871). And like Scotus, he believes that "all our conceptions are obtained by abstractions and combinations of cognitions first occurring in judgments of experience" (CP5.255, 1868). "Sensation and the power of abstraction or attention may be regarded as, in one sense, the sole constituents of all thought. . . . Attention is roused when the same phenomenon presents itself repeatedly on different occasions, or the same predicate in different subjects. We see that A has a certain character, that B has the same, C has the same; and this excites our attention, so that we say, 'These have this character.' Thus attention is an act of induction" (CP5.295, 1868).

Knowledge, or information, can be traced back to cognitions "which have been logically derived by induction and hypothesis from previous cognitions which are less general, less distinct," all the way back "to an ideal first, which is quite singular, and quite out of consciousness" (CP5.311, 1868). And then Peirce makes a rather shocking claim: "This ideal first is the particular thing-in-itself. It does not exist as such" (CP5.311, 1868). He is not denying existence of the world of things, though—"things ... doubtless are, apart from [their] relation" to the mind (CP5.311, 1868). What he means is that "there is no thing which is in-itself" in the sense of being absolutely incognizable, for "there can be no conception of the absolutely incognizable, since nothing of that sort occurs in experience" (CP5.311, 1868). But since "the meaning of a term is the conception which it conveys," a term like that "can have no such meaning": "If I think "white" ... what I think is of the nature of a cognition, and so of anything else which can be experienced. Consequently, the highest concept which can be reached by abstractions from judgments of experience—and therefore, the highest concept which can be reached at all—is the concept of something of the nature of a cognition" (CP5.257, 1868). This is, of course, reminiscent of Scotus's claims regarding haecceity, which Peirce admits is an "ultimate fact" of which, "in its isolated aggressive stubbornness and individual reality... it is not reasonable to expect an explanation" (CP1.405, c. 1890). "What Scotus calls the hæcceities of things, the hereness and nowness of them, are indeed ultimate.... Why IT, independently of its general characters, comes to have any definite place in the world, is not a question to be asked; it is simply an ultimate fact ... hæcceity is the *ultima ratio*, the brutal fact that will not be questioned" (CP1.405, c. 1890).

While Peirce is aware of the different historical uses of the terms "particular," "individual," and "singular," as well as their (sometimes problematic) meaning in the context of logic, mathematics and geometry,[55] he proposes the definition that "an individual is something which reacts ... is of such a nature that it might react, or have reacted, against my will" (CP3.613, 1901). This definition also reflects the notion that brute, or ultimate, facts are unintelligible, since "a reaction may be experienced, but it cannot be conceived in its character of a reaction; for that element evaporates from every general idea" (CP3.613, 1901). But again, Peirce is not denying "the truth that whatever exists is individual," just that existence in itself is unintelligible (CP3.613, 1901). However, "every fact of a general or orderly nature," that is, a general or universal, *does* call for an explanation; this is how we think, and the "sole immediate purpose of thinking ... is to render things intelligible" (CP1.405, c. 1890). Indeed, it is "the intellectual hope" implicit in science, or any type of inquiry, that there will be an explanation, perhaps not of all things, but "of any given thing whatever" (CP1.405, c. 1890). What allows Peirce to brand the explanation as knowledge is the claim that there are "real generals," in conjunction with the pragmatic revisions of the notions of truth and reality, his cognitive theory, and his cosmology. I should mention, in passing, that whereas Scotus also anchors knowledge claims on intuitive cognition, Peirce argues, "It is not self-evident that we possess this capacity" (CP5.246, 1868). However, Peirce does incorporate the notion of immediate presence (using the same "here and now" terminology) in his categories. I also see a parallel with Scotus's anchoring of intuitive content in God's thoughts, outside of the individual knower, with Peirce's emphasis on community and not the individual, as the ground of truth and reality; and Scotus's "natural light" with Peirce's "opinion to which the mind of man is... tending" (CP8.12, 1871). Again, this shows Peirce's rejection of nominalism, which he associated with excessive focus on the individual and material existence. Like Scotus, Peirce recognized that generals, such as laws, relations, and concepts, as well as individuals, are real; he also added potentiality to his categories.

Peirce considered that Aristotle's ten categories of being could be reduced to three, which he characterized in various ways depending on the context. Firstness, "pure nature, or quality, in itself without parts or features, and without embodiment," he described as potentiality, possibility, or chance (CP1.303, *c.* 1904). Secondness, "the element of struggle," is defined as actuality, reaction, or existence (CP1.322, *c.* 1904). Thirdness is "nothing but the character of an object which embodies Betweenness or Mediation," or regularity, generality, thought (CP5.104, 1903). Again, we can see the influence of Scotus—his concept of the "common nature-in itself" before it is contracted in the individual is reflected in the concept of firstness; the notion of the ultimate individual differentia or haecceity of the existent particular is seen in secondness; and thirdness is the universal, the mediated or abstracted common nature.

Peirce recognizes that Scotus proposes that something could be real, yet not existent, like universals. Peirce prefers the term "generals" and includes the laws of nature as thirds "will-be's"; he also claims that firsts, or "would be's" are real: "The *will be's*, the actually *is's*, and the have beens are not the sum of the reals. They only cover actuality. There are besides *would be's* and *can be's* that are real" (CP8.216, *c.* 1910).

However, Peirce does not share Scotus's explanation of what makes universals real, which, according to Scotus, is due to the connection with the existent singular. He thinks that this is a mistake: "Even Duns Scotus is too nominalistic when he says that universals are contracted to the mode of individuality in singulars [. . .] The pragmaticist cannot admit that" (CP8.208, *c.* 1905). To admit this is to reduce thirdness to secondness, rationality to existence.

Peirce believed that "three elements are active in the world: first, chance; second, law; and third, habit-taking," labeled tychism, synechism, and agapism, the basis for his cosmological theory (CP1.409, *c.* 1890). Tychism's claim is that there is an objective, real "element of pure chance" that remains in the world since its emergence out of an initial chaos. Tychism is Peirce's alternative to the deterministic, mechanical (and mistaken, he argues) picture of a "perfect clockwork" universe prevalent among the scientists of his day. Peirce scholars have noted the resemblance of tychism to quantum indeterminacy; Peirce likely developed this doctrine as a result of following the latest developments in molecular and atomic research.[56] "Since 1860 [. . .] physics has gained an optico-electrical theory, and radically new conceptions of molecular forces have been established; organic chemistry [. . .] has been enriched by the doctrine of the unsymmetrical carbon atom; in its inorganic division [. . .] the group of helium–argon elements has been added, and Mme. Curie has pronounced her magical 'Open, sesame!' " (CP8.196, 1905).

Synechism, "the tendency to regard everything as continuous" (CP7.565, *c.* 1892), is really a kind of generality (law)—"continuity is nothing but perfect generality of a law of relationship" (CP6.172, 1901). Peirce recognized that as humans, we are cognitively biased, or prejudiced—"We enormously exaggerate the part that law plays in the universe," since it is "by means of regularities that we understand what little we do understand of the world," in medieval terms, abstraction, "and thus there is a sort of mental perspective which brings regular phenomena to the foreground" (CP1.406, c. 1890). We then conclude, erroneously, "that every event is determined by causes according to law [. . .] that the events of the physical universe are merely motions of matter, and that these obey the laws of dynamics" (CP1.406, c. 1890). But this must not be regarded "as absolutely true"; it just "amounts to saying that among the countless systems of relationship existing among things we have found one that is universal and at the same time is subject to law [. . .] But we pay no attention to irregular relationships, as having no interest for us" (CP1.406, c. 1890). This does not mean, however, that these relationships do not exist, just that we are not necessarily in tune with them.

One "regularity" or "regular relationship" that we focus on is existence—"existence, or thing-ness, consists in regularities" (CP6.265, 1891). Peirce elaborates:

> The existence of things consists in their regular behavior. If an atom had no regular attractions and repulsions, if its mass was at one instant nothing, at another a ton, at another a negative quantity, if its motion instead of being continuous, consisted in a series of leaps from one place to another without passing through any intervening places, and if there were no definite relations between its different positions, velocities and directions of displacement, if it were at one time in one place and at another time in a dozen, such a disjointed plurality of phenomena would not make up any existing thing. Not only substances, but events, too, are constituted by regularities. The flow of time, for example, in itself is a regularity. (CP1.411, c. 1890)

Recall quantum theory's claim that properties exist when there are certain consistent interactions (subject to a real, but rare element of chance) and the fact that these interactions occur is what, as Rovelli claims, "grounds the objectivity of our communal vision of the world."[57]

Agapism, "the doctrine of evolutionary love," is Peirce's "guess" at describing how law, or regularity, came about; "Since law in general cannot be explained by any law in particular, the explanation must consist in showing how law is developed out of pure chance, irregularity, and indeterminacy" (CP1.407, c. 1890). The process is one of ever-increasing habit-taking, which began at some point in the infinitely distant past when undetermined possibilities began developing affinities, becoming habits after many repetitions, and eventually laws, which will "reign" completely in an infinitely distant future (CP1.409, c. 1890). Elsewhere, in a review of Josiah Royce's *The Religious Aspect of Philosophy*, Peirce speculates about conceiving of God's existence and omniscience and suggests it consists in "a tendency toward ends [that] is so necessary a constituent of the universe that the mere action of chance upon innumerable atoms has an inevitable teleological result. One of the ends so brought about is the development of intelligence and of knowledge; and therefore I should say that God's omniscience, humanly conceived, consists in the fact that knowledge in its development leaves no question unanswered" (CP8.44, c. 1885). This is reminiscent of Scotus's assertion that God's eternal cognition of all possible finite things grounds human intuition and knowledge, with an added

Peircean whiff of pragmaticism. I also see a distant connection (pun intended) between Peirce's hypothesis of how regularity developed, with quantum entanglement:

> The proposition that we can immediately perceive only what is present seems to me parallel to that other vulgar prejudice that "a thing cannot act where it is not." An opinion which can only defend itself by such a sounding phrase is pretty sure to be wrong. That a thing cannot act where it is not is plainly an induction from ordinary experience, which shows no forces except such as act through the resistance of materials, with the exception of gravity which, owing to its being the same for all bodies, does not appear in ordinary experience like a force. [...] A thing may be said to be wherever it acts; but the notion that a particle is absolutely present in one part of space and absolutely absent from all the rest of space is devoid of all foundation. (CP1.38, c. 1890)[58]

5. Conclusion

Peirce recognized the importance of restoring the ancient discipline of metaphysics to its original standing as a science, defined as "a living and growing body of truth," raising it from the rank of philosophical speculation to that of a scientific hypothesis using ordinary perception and abductive, inductive, and deductive reasoning to scrutinize everyday observable phenomena (CP6.428, 1893). There is no guarantee, though, that all questions will be answered, for we have any number of metaphysical prejudices, inherent or acquired, that have limited to some extent our understanding of the world.

Our ancestors evolved as hunters competing with others for survival in a hostile environment in this, our world of individual macro-objects.[59] Cognitive behavior that resulted in successful interactions and increased survival, such as ordering our experience in space and time, attentiveness to regularity, the ability to generalize and predict effectively, etc., prevailed. Until very recently in human history, we had no direct interactions with the micro world, and our established cognitive frameworks and theoretical constructions have not transferred well in our attempts to comprehend the subatomic world that quantum physics describes. This is where metaphysics and physics might once again be reconciled.

Peirce's scientific metaphysics, inspired by Scotus's realism, has yielded an "extraordinary harvest [...] of very fundamental truth of exceptional value" (CP1.128, c.1905). I've endeavored to show, that the metaphysical reflections of theoretical quantum physicists about individual existence, the element of chance, and the role of relations parallel those of Peirce and Scotus. Scotus denies direct epistemological access (in this life) to haecceity, the individual in-itself, which we know only mediately, through universals, or concepts, which are real. Peirce claims that existence in itself is unintelligible. We do not observe quantum superposition, only quantum interference, its effect; we experience as an individual a set of correlated interactions, quantum theorists claim. Peirce declares synechism, the element of chance, an active force in the universe, as a source of indeterminism. Quantum theorists postulate indeterminate variables and the world as probabilistic. Scotus claims that universals, or concepts, are real, but do not exist as such. Peirce's category of thirdness recognizes the reality and importance of laws and relations. Quantum theorists claim that the world is a web of interrelations. Scotus grounds the validity of human intuition in a beneficent God's eternal thought. Peirce proposes agapism, evolutionary love, as the mainspring of regularity. Quantum theorists pose entanglement as the source of correlated interactions.

It was Peirce's conviction that in order to raise his "Guess at the Riddle" of the universe from "the rank of philosophical speculation to that of a scientific hypothesis," it was necessary "to show that consequences can be deduced from it with more or less probability which can be compared with observation" (CP1.410, c. 1890). Peirce did not live to see the advent of the quantum revolution, but some of his philosophical speculations mirror the scientific hypotheses that have been compared with observation in the context of quantum theory. I think Peirce would have been proud.[60]

Notes

1. Duns Scotus (1997, 6).
2. CP7.54.
3. Austen (1998, 220).
4. Rovelli (2021, 135).
5. The notion of "pride" used here is the traditional one with the double meaning of justified self-worth, but when in excess, self-conceit.
6. See, for example, Reynolds (2002); Fernandez (2008); Short (2008); Hartshorne (1973).
7. My purpose in this paper is more constructive than critical. For more on the topic of Peirce's realism, see Boler (1963); Haack (1992); Mayorga (2007); and Lane (2018).
8. Boersema (2008).
9. In Latin, "*res*" is used for "thing" while "*ens*" usually indicates a "being."
10. See, for example, CP5.358.
11. The reason for its current backward state is not because of "any intrinsic difficulty of it." Metaphysics "really rests on observation," but this is not universally recognized because the kinds of phenomena on which it rests are those which "every man's experience is so saturated that he usually pays no particular attention to them" (CP6.2, 1898).
12. Peirce is here criticizing those who confuse theology with philosophy.
13. EP2:146.
14. I've rearranged the order in which Peirce lists them and numbered these few for my purposes in this chapter.
15. What follows is an attempt at a very general account of quantum theory by a nonphysicist.
16. The "heart of quantum theory," from which "everything else follows from it—from the quantum computer to the atomic bomb" can be expressed in one equation: $XP - PX = i \hbar$, where X indicates the position of the particle, P its speed multiplied by its mass, i is the mathematical symbol of the square root of −1, and $\hbar$ is Planck's constant. Rovelli (2021, 36).
17. Rovelli (2021, 12–13).

18. Ibid., 14. At the time, Born was in his forties, while Heisenberg, Jordan, Dirac, and Pauli were in their twenties. Ibid., 16.
19. Ibid., 15.
20. Schrödinger proposed that electrons are not particles, but waves, ψ. Born later revised this to say that "the value of the Schrödinger's wave ψ at a point in space is related to the *probability* of observing the electron at this point" (ibid., 27).
21. Ibid., 46.
22. Ibid., 45.
23. Ibid., 17–18. Among the list of new phenomena never previously imagined were nuclear warheads.
24. Ibid., 53.
25. Ibid., 210. There are other interpretations of quantum data, for example, the theories of many worlds, hidden variables, physical collapse, Q-bism, etc., but there is no room to discuss these here.
26. Ibid., 215.
27. Ibid., 90.
28. Ibid., 92.
29. Austen (1960, 33).
30. Rovelli argues for this possible interpretation as opposed to the many worlds, hidden variables, physical collapse, and Q-bism hypotheses. Although Rovelli mentions William James briefly, he does not seem acquainted with Peirce's work, with which I find he has many commonalities.
31. Rovelli (2021, 75).
32. Ibid., 79.
33. Ibid., 77.
34. Ibid., 97.
35. Ibid., 100.
36. Capra (1996, 31).
37. Ibid.
38. Note that "singulars," "particulars," and "individuals," although we use them synonymously most of the time, have different meanings (and Peirce was aware of this); more on this below.
39. I do enjoy the fact that the same term, "quantum," is used both in metaphysics and in physics.
40. Although the logical works were known since the sixth century, the corpus of more substantive texts was not available in the West until much later. See Ingham and Dreyer (2004, 2).
41. It was Scotus's difficult task to defend Aristotle's ideas during the time of the church's condemnations of 1270 and 1277, directed against Aristotelian positions that conflicted with Christian dogma (ibid., 6).
42. Not just knowledge of the world of finite or contingent beings, but also of God and other spiritual beings, such as angels.
43. As a Christian, Scotus believed that the human soul, the ground of the intellect and will, survives the death of the body in an afterlife.
44. In this way, God, angels, and souls are included as beings and are part of the epistemological project (Ingham and Dreyer 2004, 24).
45. Ibid.; John Duns Scotus, *Ordinatio* I, d.3, nn.137-39 (ed. Vat. 3:85–87).
46. Duns Scotus (1997, 8).

47. It also allows Scotus to declare that we can have knowledge of God.
48. The common-nature-in-itself is also a formality, since it is real, but does not exist separately from the existent singular.
49. This ability continues after death, when fortunate souls experience the beatific vision of God.
50. Pini (2020, 23).
51. Lazella (2019, 169).
52. Ibid., 166. Aristotle held that "perception is of particulars, knowledge is of universals" (*De Anima*, II.5 417b22–23). Scotus disagrees that the singular is unintelligible per se; it's just unintelligible to humans presently. Haecceities are intelligible to angels and God (and to those humans who achieve the beatific vision in the afterlife), since they have immediate, and not, like us, mediate knowledge through abstraction.
53. It is not existence, which is a modality, while actuality is a broader concept.
54. Lazella (2019, 184).
55. See, for example, CP3.611; CP5.299; CP5.540; CP5.450; CP3.65.
56. Reynolds (2022, 137).
57. Rovelli (2021, 100).
58. Also compare—"The existence of things consists in their regular behavior. If an atom had no regular attractions and repulsions, if its mass was at one instant nothing, at another a ton, at another a negative quantity, if its motion instead of being continuous, consisted in a series of leaps from one place to another without passing through any intervening places, and if there were no definite relations between its different positions, velocities and directions of displacement, if it were at one time in one place and at another time in a dozen, such a disjointed plurality of phenomena would not make up any existing thing. Not only substances, but events, too, are constituted by regularities. The flow of time, for example, in itself is a regularity. The original chaos, therefore, where there was no regularity, was in effect a state of mere indeterminacy, in which nothing existed or really happened" (CP1.411, 1890).
59. Of course, "macro" and "micro" are relative terms; our macro world of singular objects is on a different scale than the macro universe that the James Webb Space Telescope is currently exploring.
60. In the sense of "justified self-worth," of course. I wish to thank Cornelis de Waal for his helpful comments, as well as his expert skill and patience in putting this volume together.

Bibliography

Austen, Jane. 1960. *Pride and Prejudice*. New York: Washington Square Press.
Austen, Jane. 1998. *Persuasion*. London: Penguin Random House.
Becker, Adam. 2022. "The Origins of Space and Time." *Scientific American* 326, no. 2 (February): 26–33.
Boersema, David. 2008. "Metaphysics." In *American Philosophy: An Encyclopedia*, edited by John Lachs and Robert Talisse, 503. New York: Routledge.
Boler, John F. 1963. *Charles Peirce and Scholastic Realism*. Seattle: Washington University Press.
Capra, Fritjof. 1996. *The Web of Life: A New Scientific Understanding of Living Systems*. New York: Anchor Books.

Chwe, Michael Suk-Young. 2014. "Scientific Pride and Prejudice." *New York Times,* January 31, 2014. https://www.nytimes.com/2014/02/02/opinion/sunday/scientific-pride-and-prejudice.html

Cross, Richard. 2011. "Duns Scotus: Some Recent Research." *Journal of the History of Philosophy* 49, no. 3 (July): 271–295.

Duns Scotus, John. 1950–2013. *Ordinatio. Opera Omnia,* edited by Charles Balic. Vols. 1–14. Vatican City: Vatican Polyglot Press.

Duns Scotus, John. 1997. *Questions on the Metaphysics of Aristotle,* translated by Girard J. Etzkorn and Allan Wolter O.F.M. St. Bonaventure, NY: Franciscan Institute.

Fernandez, Eliseo. 2008. *Peirce in 21st Century Science and Philosophy: New Prospects.* https://arisbe.sitehost.iu.edu/menu/library/aboutcsp/fernandez/efpapers.htm.

Haack, Susan. 1992. "Extreme Scholastic Realism: Its Relevance to Philosophy of Science Today." *Transactions of the Charles S. Peirce Society* 28, no.1 (Winter): 19–50.

Haack, Susan. 2010. "The Differences That Make a Difference: William James on the Importance of Individuals." *European Journal of Pragmatism and American Philosophy* 2, no.1: 1–10.

Haack, Susan. 2020. "The World and How We Know It: Stumbling toward an Understanding." *Journal of Critical Realism* 19, no.1: 78–88.

Haack, Susan. 2021. "Scientistic Philosophy, No; Scientific Philosophy, Yes." *The Quarterly Journal of Philosophical Investigations* 15, no. 36 (Autumn 2021): 4–35.

Hartshorne, Charles. "Charles Peirce and Quantum Mechanics." *Transactions of the Charles S. Peirce Society.* Vol. 9, no. 4 (Fall 1973): 191–201.

Ingham, Mary Beth, and Mechthild Dreyer. 2004. *The Philosophical Theology of John Duns Scotus.* Washington, DC: Catholic University Press.

Kraaijeveld, Steven R. 2019. "Jane Austen and Cognitive Bias," May 19, 2019. https://stevenrkraaijeveld.com/blog/jane-austen-and-cognitive-bias.

Labatut, Benjamin. 2020. *When We Cease to Understand the World,* translated by Adrian Nathan West. New York: New York Review Books.

Lane, Robert. 2018. *Peirce on Realism and Idealism.* New York: Cambridge University Press.

Lazella, Andrew. 2019. *The Singular Voice of Being: John Duns Scotus and Ultimate Difference.* New York: Fordham University Press.

Mayorga, Rosa Maria Perez-Teran. 2007. *From Realism to Realicism: The Metaphysics of Charles Sanders Peirce.* Lanham, MD: Rowman & Littlefield.

Mayorga, Rosa Maria. 2020. "Metaphysics, Religion, and Death or We'll Always Have Paris." *Cosmos + Taxis Studies in Emergent Order and Organization* 8, no. 4-5: 49–59.

Mayorga, Rosa Maria. 2008. "Peirce's Moral Realicism." In *The Normative Thought of Charles Peirce,* edited by Cornelis de Waal and Krzysztof Piotr Skowronski, 101–124. New York: Fordham University Press.

Mayorga, Rosa Maria. 2008. "Realism: Scholastic." In American Philosophy: An Encyclopedia, edited by John Lachs and Robert Talisse, 651–652. New York: Routledge.

Peirce, Charles. 1931–1958. *The Collected Papers of Charles Sanders Peirce,* 8 vols., edited by Charles Hartshorne and Paul Weiss. Cambridge, MA: Harvard University Press. (Referred to as CP.)

Peirce, Charles. 1992–1998. *The Essential Peirce: Selected Philosophical Writings,* 2 vols. Vol. 1 edited by Nathan Houser and Christian Kloesel. Vol. 2 edited by the Peirce Edition Project. Bloomington: Indiana University Press. (Referred to as EP.)

Pini, Giorgio. 2020. "Duns Scotus on What Is in the Mind: A Roadmap." *Recherches de Théologie et Philosophie Médiévales.* 87, no. 2: 319–347.

Pini, Giorgio. 2008. "Scotus on the Objects of Cognitive Acts." *Franciscan Studies* 66: 281–315.
Pini, Giorgio. 2022. *Interpreting Duns Scotus*. Cambridge: Cambridge University Press.
Reynolds, Andrew. 2002. *Peirce's Scientific Metaphysics*. Nashville, TN: Vanderbilt University Press.
Rovelli, Carlo. 2021. *Helgoland: Making Sense of the Quantum Revolution*. New York: Riverhead Books.
Short, T. L. 2008. "Peirce on Science and Philosophy." *Philosophical Topics* 36, no. 1 (Spring): 259–277.
Short, T. L. 2010. "Did Peirce Have a Cosmology?" Transactions of the Charles S. Peirce Society 46, no. 4 (Fall): 521–543.

CHAPTER 25

PEIRCE ON KANT'S REFUTATION OF IDEALISM

GABRIELE GAVA

PEIRCE's relationship with Kant is perhaps one of the most controversial issues within Peirce scholarship. While some scholars, including myself, have argued that Peirce remained a "Kantian" throughout his entire career as a philosopher (for "Kantian" readings, see Apel [1981]; Hookway [1985]; Pihlström [2003]; Gava [2014a]; Gava and Stern [2016]; Chevalier [2016]), others have maintained that while the young Peirce was indeed strongly influenced by Kant, he later rejected Kant's approach in favor of a totally different line of inquiry (for "anti-Kantian" readings, see Short [2007]; Maddalena [2015]; Colapietro [2006]; Wilson [2016]). Despite this divergence of views, both camps agree that Kant was an important figure for Peirce, either as a continuous source of inspiration or, at least in his later years, as a target of radical criticism. Nonetheless, scholars have largely neglected two short texts from around 1890 where Peirce provides an antiskeptical argument inspired by Kant. The first text is a discussion of Kant's refutation of idealism (hereafter refutation),[1] while the second is a sketch of an argument against external world skepticism that clearly belongs to the same set of considerations.[2]

There are various reasons to explain why these texts have thus far been ignored. First, they are both very short and Peirce does not fully develop his argument in either of them. Second, even though Peirce directly refers to Kant's refutation in one of the two texts, he does not really engage in an analysis of Kant's argument. Rather, he sketches his own "refutation" that, in his view, presents a more direct route to achieving Kant's aim. Third, it is not at all clear whether Peirce's strategy could indeed be successful, that is, prove that the skeptic is wrong.

Even though these problems do exist, the texts are nonetheless interesting and worthy of close consideration. For starters, Peirce clearly expresses his appreciation for Kant's refutation, writing that it "betray[s] an elaborated and vigorous analysis, marred in the exposition by the attempt to state the argument more abstractly and demonstratively than the thought would warrant" (W8:80, c.1890). For Peirce, if there are problems with Kant's argument, they lie more in the exposition than in the reasoning itself. Kant's refutation is often described as problematic and unsuccessful; therefore, one should ask what aspect of it Peirce considered to be promising. It is important to keep in mind that the refutation is directed against what Kant calls "problematic idealism," which is the view that we can be immediately certain of our own existence and of the existence of our mental states, even though we can only infer the existence of outer objects from those states. Given that our inferences about the existence of external objects cannot be proven with certainty, their existence is doubtful (see B276–277; A366–367).[3] As early as the 1880s, Peirce famously held that we can directly refer to external objects through indices (see, for example, W5:163). In later writings, he connects this approach to the doctrine of "immediate perception," which maintains that we can directly perceive the existence of outer objects.

Peirce links the doctrine of immediate perception to a form of "dualism,"[4] which he attributes to Kant and Reid (EP2:155, 1903).[5] Indeed, Kant also uses the term "dualism" to describe a very similar approach. In the fourth paralogism in the first edition of the *Critique of Pure Reason*, Kant contrasts dualism (the view he endorses) with (problematic) idealism (the view he rejects) and writes: "That whose existence can be inferred only as a cause of given perceptions has only a *doubtful existence*: Now all outer appearances are of this kind: their existence cannot be immediately perceived, but can be inferred only as the cause of given perceptions: Thus the existence of all objects of outer sense is doubtful. This uncertainty I call the ideality of outer appearances, and the doctrine of this ideality is called *idealism*, in comparison with which the assertion of a possible certainty of objects of outer sense is called *dualism*" (A366–367). Therefore, according to Kant, dualism is the view that we can be immediately certain of the existence of external objects. Given this characterization, it is possible that Peirce's own use of the term was influenced by Kant. For our purposes, however, what is important to emphasize is that Peirce clearly valued Kant's refutation because he considered it an expression of a project he shared with Kant, namely, the attempt to demonstrate that we can directly perceive outer objects.

There might also be another reason why Peirce praised Kant's refutation. As we will see in Section 1, one important consequence of Kant's argument is that (if successful) it shows that the problematic idealist is wrong about the conditions that must obtain for successfully ordering our conscious states in time. Similarly, when devising his own "refutation," Peirce directly opposes a premise in the skeptic's argument, a premise that concerns how our consciousness is "in time." Peirce might have been sympathetic to Kant's attempt to challenge common but misleading assumptions regarding how time structures our consciousness.

Finally, upon closer scrutiny, it is also inaccurate to say that the two texts under consideration do not display *any* attention to Kant's original argument. In fact, Peirce directly refers to two passages of Kant's refutation: "Note 1," which is the first clarificatory annotation that Kant adds after the presentation of his argument, and the footnote to that note, where Kant presents a short argument that can be considered independent from the refutation (see W8:80).

At the very least, this is enough to show that Peirce's engagement with Kant's refutation of idealism is interesting and worthy of attention. In this chapter, my aim will be to reconstruct Peirce's anti-skeptical argument in the two texts under analysis to see how it relates to Kant's argument in his refutation. In Section 1, I will provide a reconstruction of Kant's refutation, singling out its main problems. In Section 2, I will present Peirce's account of the temporal structure of consciousness in "The Law of Mind," since this account forms the background of Peirce's anti-skeptical argument. Finally, in Section 3, I will provide a reconstruction of Peirce's argument, highlighting where it directly reelaborates points made by Kant.

1. Kant's Refutation of Idealism

In this section, I will provide a reconstruction of Kant's argument in the refutation, focusing in particular on its most controversial premises. Additionally, I will analyze the first clarificatory note that follows the argument and the footnote to it, since these are the two parts of the text to which Peirce explicitly refers.

Kant's argument runs as follows:

(1) "I am conscious of my existence as determined in time."
(2) "All time-determination presupposes something *persistent* [*Beharrliches*] in perception."
(3) "This persistent thing, however, cannot be something in me, since my own existence in time can first be determined only through this persistent thing."
(4) "Thus the perception of this persistent thing is possible only through a *thing* outside me and not through the mere *representation* of a thing outside me."
(5) "Consequently, the determination of my existence in time is possible only by means of the existence of actual things that I perceive outside myself." (B275–276)

In the B preface, Kant suggests substituting premise (3) with a clearer formulation:

(3′) "But this persisting element cannot be an intuition in me. For all the determining grounds of my existence that can be encountered in me are representations, and as such they themselves need something persisting distinct from them, in relation to which their change, and thus my existence in the time in which they change, can be determined." (Bxxxixn)

The argument begins with a premise about our consciousness that the skeptic will supposedly accept; it then attempts to show that what that premise claims is only possible if the very proposition doubted by the skeptic obtains.[6] There is a lot in the argument that needs unpacking. Let us consider each step in order.

In premise (1), it is not clear what "determined in time" means. This might simply mean that I am conscious of my existence in the present instant, or that I am conscious that there is a succession of mental states in my consciousness. Nonetheless, there is now decisive agreement among scholars that premise (1) actually asserts something more substantial: namely, it concerns our capacity to objectively order our mental states in time. This means that it asserts that we are able to order our mental states in a unique time that we share with other subjects.[7] One can here object that we can easily think of radical skeptics who would not accept this version of premise (1). For example, think of a memory skeptic who considers it possible that our recollections (and ordering) of past states are all fallacious (on this problem see Chignell [2010, 492]). However, this worry is unjustified, given that Kant explicitly says that his argument addresses a particular kind of skepticism (or idealism), which is based on the premise that there is a fundamental asymmetry between our consciousness of our mental states and our consciousness of external objects (see Bader [2017, 209]).

Premise (2) rests on Kant's argument in the first analogy. The A-version submits: "All appearances contain that which persists (substance) as the object itself, and that which can change as its mere determination, i.e., a way in which the object exists" (A182). The B-version asserts: "In all change of appearances substance persists, and its quantum is neither increased nor diminished in nature" (B224). The aim of the first analogy is to show that the category of substance is a necessary condition for determining objective relationships in time. It is first the "tool" we use to determine what is "persistent" in time. In turn, the ability to determine what is "absolutely" persistent in time is also necessary for determining objective relationships of succession and simultaneity. Kant's line of reasoning seems to be the following: relating objects and their states to time as the form of intuition is necessary for determining whether those objects and states are successive or simultaneous. Time, understood as such a form, "persists" and, furthermore, it is "within" it that change is possible. However, "time cannot be perceived by itself" (B225). This means that we cannot directly represent time as an object, as that "something" within which change happens. However, if we want to determine relations of succession and simultaneity that are "objective," that is, that are determined in relation to a unique time that we share with other subjects, we need a way to be sure that we are correctly tracking that unique time. This is the role played by "substance," as that "something" that persists through all change and that, as such, allows us to indirectly represent time: "Persistence gives general expression to time as the constant correlate of all existence of appearances, all change and all accompaniment. For change does not affect time itself, but only the appearances in time" (A183/B226).

Premise (3) and its alternative (3′) introduce the fundamental step in the argument. They establish that the persistent thing that is essential for determining objective time relationships among our mental states must be something external to consciousness. These premises are also the most controversial. It is not clear why the persistent thing that represents time must be something "outside" of the subject. Couldn't the conscious subject itself play the role of the persistent thing in reference to which we can determine objective time relationships (for this objection see, for example, Walker [1978, 114])? Couldn't the conscious subject be considered that "something" that "persists" through its changing mental states? Of course, Kant thinks that we cannot regard our selves as "substances" that persist,[8] but why should the external-world skeptic that Kant is refuting buy into his theory of the self at this point?

In order to avoid this problem, there have been attempts to make premises (3) and (3′) work without appealing to Kant's own theory of the self. In this respect, one strategy is to deviate from the letter of Kant's argument in the *Critique of Pure Reason* and appeal to some reflections where the emphasis is not on the need to refer to an outer persistent object, but rather on the need to refer to causal relationships between outer objects (see, for example, *Refl* 6313, 18:614).[9] The idea is that, in order to determine "objectively" the temporal order of my mental states, I need to be able to relate those states to objects or states that exist in space and stay in a causal relationship (proponents of this reading are, for example, Guyer [1987, ch. 13] and Dicker [2008]; for a criticism of this approach, see Chignell [2010]). Therefore, according to this strategy, the point of premises (3) and (3′) is better achieved when one focuses not (or at least not only) on a persistent thing that needs to be external, but rather on causal relationships between things or states that must be external.

One of the downsides of the latter strategy is that it partially departs from the argument published in the B-edition of the *Critique*. However, there are scholars who defend premises (3) and (3′) while maintaining the focus on the published text. For example, Dina Emundts has argued that the first analogy already shows that the "persistent thing" that we need for determining objective temporal relations must be spatial (Emundts 2010, 172–176). This is the case because the "absolute persistent" must be something that lasts through its changes. As such, this something must have "one magnitude that stays the same while it changes with respect to all its other determinations. This is only possible with respect to something that has not only an extension in time but also in space" (Emundts 2010, 176). By contrast, Ralf Bader has insisted on the fact that the persistence of the object we use for objective temporal determinations is something that needs to be proved. We need this proof for our application of the category of substance to be legitimate. But it is only for outer objects that this proof is possible: "The difference between the inner and the outer on which the Refutation relies is that one can prove permanence[10] for outer objects (for matter) and hence subsume them under the schematized category of substance, but that one cannot likewise prove permanence for inner objects (for the mind). This difference is due to the fact that any decrease in the intensive magnitude (reality) of outer objects goes together with a compensating adjustment elsewhere in space, such that if the intensive magnitude of some objects is diminished, then that of others is increased in a way that conserves the overall quantity of matter" (Bader 2017, 217). This relationship between the intensive and extensive magnitudes of matter allows us to grasp how substance "persists" while its states change. Obviously, we cannot establish a similar relationship between intensive and extensive magnitudes for the self and its states. I will here remain neutral on the issue whether and how premises (3) and (3′) can be made to work. What I hope is clear is that if we want to render them plausible, they need substantial interpretative work.

Steps (4) and (5) present the conclusions of the argument. Step (5) concludes that, given that we need to relate to an existing persistent in space in order to determine objective temporal relationships among our mental states, that determination is only possible if outer objects exist and I can perceive them. But since premise (1) assumed that we are able to determine objective temporal relationships in our consciousness, it follows that (some) outer objects must exist. As for step (4), it is not clear how it should directly follow from premise (3). However, it does follow from step (3′), since this version of the premise explicitly excludes that the persistent element used for time determination could be a representation. Of course, this does not mean that what Kant says in premise (3′) about excluding representations as candidates for the role of the persistent thing is convincing. In fact, it seems that the aim of the footnote to note 1 is to provide an independent argument for ruling out that we could only have representations of outer things. Let us move to our discussion of the note and the footnote.

Note 1 clarifies how Kant understood the argument of the refutation. Accordingly, he begins by claiming that "in the preceding proof the game that idealism plays has with greater justice been turned against it" (B276). Therefore, Kant took his argument to display an internal inconsistency in the position of the (problematic) idealist, such that one of the assumptions she makes implies that she cannot in fact doubt the existence of outer object, on pain of contradiction. The result of this "turning" of the idealist viewpoint against itself is that while the idealist took inner experience to be immediate and the outer to be inferred, it is in fact outer experience that is immediate, while inner experience "is consequently only mediate and possible only through outer experience" (B277). It is easy to see why Peirce was sympathetic to these claims.

It is in the footnote to note 1 that Kant introduces some new considerations. First, it emphasizes that the fact that we have an "*immediate* consciousness of the existence of outer things is not presupposed but proved in the preceding theorem" (B276n). Furthermore, it explicitly argues against the view that all our representations of outer objects could be solely the product of our imagination. Kant contends that in order for us to imagine outer objects, we must presuppose that we have an outer sense, that is, a way of immediately perceiving outer objects through our sensibility: "But it is clear that in order for us even to imagine something as external, i.e., to exhibit it to sense in intuition, we must already have an outer sense, and by this means immediately distinguish the mere receptivity of an outer intuition from the spontaneity that characterizes every imagining" (B276–277n). Kant's point seems to be that when we assert that all our representations of outer objects could be only the product of our imagination, we in fact render inconceivable what "imagining" outer objects could mean. We can only make sense of what this "imagining" could be if we hold fast to the distinction between what "imagining" outer objects and "perceiving" outer objects is. But to make this distinction, we must assume that at least some of our representations of outer objects are actual perceptions. This seems to be the idea behind Kant's remarks.[11] It is unlikely that the argument in the footnote can work against the problematic idealist. For our purposes, it is interesting because Peirce re-elaborates this idea in his own attempt at a refutation of external world skepticism.

2. The Temporal Structure of Consciousness in "The Law of Mind"

Before we move to our analysis of Peirce's own "refutation," it is useful to briefly present his account of the temporal structure of consciousness. Providing an account of time was very important for Peirce. The idea of continuity was central to his philosophy and he regarded time as "the continuum *par excellence*" (CP6.86; RLT:216, 1898). However, a comprehensive reconstruction of Peirce's views on time is still missing (some useful explorations are Helm [1983]; De Tienne [2015]; Colapietro [2017]; Schmidt [2022]). This is unsurprising given that his views are both very complex and scattered across different texts. In this section, my reconstruction will be limited in two ways: I will only focus on Peirce's views regarding the temporal structure of consciousness and the consciousness of time, avoiding any consideration of how these relate to his account of the nature of time as such. Additionally, since his views evolved considerably, I will only take into consideration his position around the time he composed the two texts inspired by Kant's refutation. In particular, I will focus on his position in "The Law of Mind," which was written only a couple of years after those texts.

But what does it mean to focus on the "temporal structure of consciousness" and the "consciousness of time"? These problems are closely related in the current debate over the consciousness of time. Roughly, when one speaks of the "temporal structure of consciousness," one is considering how our consciousness is temporally determined. Are episodes in our consciousness "instants" with no temporal extension, or do they occupy a span of time? If we answer positively to the first horn of this question, it becomes particularly apparent how the question of "the consciousness of time" can develop into a problem. If our consciousness were indeed constituted by instantaneous episodes, how could we be aware of temporally extended events and objects? Peirce's contribution to answering these questions is both interesting and elaborate. Moreover, it anticipates an approach that is still widely debated in the early twenty-first century (for an overview of the debate, see Dainton [2018]). Peirce defends an "extensionalist" position. He maintains that the "episodes" that form our consciousness are temporally extended. This makes it easier to understand how we could be aware of a temporal succession.

To clarify Peirce's view, let us begin by introducing a terminological distinction. He uses the term "instant" to mean "a point of time" and the term "moment" to mean "an infinitesimal duration" (W8:138). As a point of time, an instant has no temporal extension. Because time is fundamentally continuous, an instant should be understood as a "fiction" or an "*ens rationis*" (R295:102–103, quoted in Schmidt [2022, 238]). We can refer to it through a process of abstraction that begins with continuous time. However, it is not the case that our consciousness can really be "instantaneous." By contrast, saying that a moment has infinitesimal duration means that it is itself continuous. According to the theory of infinitesimals, infinitesimals are the ultimate "parts" of a continuum. They are quantities that are greater than zero but smaller than any assignable quantity. For our purposes, it is sufficient to keep in mind that "moments," as parts of a continuum that are themselves continuous, have a temporal extension.

But how does Peirce describe the "episodes" that form the parts of our consciousness? Clearly, they are "moments" with a temporal extension within which, by means of a process of abstraction, one can identify different "instants." Let us see how Peirce describes the structure of these moments and how they relate with one another: "In an infinitesimal interval we directly perceive the temporal sequence of its beginning, middle, and end,— not, of course, in the way of recognition, for recognition is only of the past, but in the way of immediate feeling. Now upon this interval follows another, whose beginning is the middle of the former, and whose middle is the end of the former. Here, we have an immediate perception of the temporal sequence of its beginning, middle, and end, or say of the second, third, and fourth instants" (W8:138, 1892). First, the passage makes clear that an "episode" of consciousness has a temporal extension with a complex structure, with its beginning, its middle point, and its end. These can be taken as three "instants" identifiable through a process of abstraction that starts from the "moment" encompassing them in an immediate episode of consciousness. Second, the passage illustrates how episodes of consciousness are not simply successive, but partially overlap with one another, so that the middle point and the end of the first episode are, respectively, the beginning and the middle point of the following episode and so on.[12] We can represent Peirce's model of the temporal structure of consciousness with the help of the following figure.

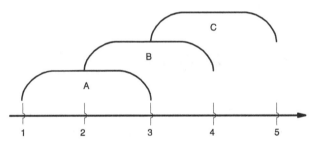

FIGURE 25.1 The temporal structure of consciousness according to Peirce

The arrow represents consciousness, as time passes. The numbers 1, 2, 3, etc., identify instants that we can abstract as "points" within that time. The letters A, B, C, etc., represent "moments" of consciousness that are temporally extended. The "episodes" of our consciousness are formed by such moments through which we are immediately conscious of a span of time. In Figure 25.1, instants 1, 2, and 3 constitute the beginning, middle, and end of moment A, whereas instants 2, 3, and 4 are the beginning middle and end of moment B. In this way, instant 2 is both the middle of A and the beginning of B and instant 3 is both the end of A and the middle of B (and the beginning of C).

Peirce argues that the "overlap" model explains how we can have a "mediate perception" of the temporal sequence within multiple moments. In his picture, we have an "immediate perception of the temporal sequence" (W8:138) contained in each moment, for example, in A and B. "From these two immediate perceptions, we gain a mediate, or inferential, perception of the relation of all four instants. This mediate perception is objectively, or as to the object represented, spread over the four instants; but subjectively, or as itself the subject of duration, it is completely embraced in the second moment" (W8:138).[13] We can be aware of past mental episodes because we can capture mediately the chain of these moments.

At this point, it is interesting to ask how we should characterize the "present" in this picture. Extensionalist models describe the present as "specious."[14] In general, "specious present" views maintain that we are directly aware of a temporal sequence in our "present" state of consciousness. Defending a particular version of this view, extensionalists maintain that we are able to have this awareness because the present state of consciousness is itself temporally extended (see Dainton 2018, sect. 5.1).[15] How does Peirce describe the present? I think Peirce has two ways of describing it. First, since a "moment" of our consciousness must be present at some point, he clearly believes that the present is "specious" and encompasses a temporal lapse. As a "specious" present, the present will have something in common with the immediate past and the immediate future. Taking moment B in Figure 25.1 as the "present moment," it will have something in common with the moment that just passed (that is, instant 2) and with the moment that is about to come (that is, instant 4). But the present could also be an "instant" that we abstract from the "specious" present. As such, it would be the "instant" in which past and present intersect. Again, taking B as the present "moment," instant 3 would constitute the "point" of this intersection.[16] As we will see, the nature of the "present" will play a central role in Peirce's own "refutation of idealism."

3. Peirce's Refutation of Idealism

As we saw above, Peirce considers Kant's refutation "an elaborated and vigorous analysis," even though the argument is stated "more abstractly and demonstratively than the thought would warrant" (W8:80, c.1890). In his "[Note on Kant's Refutation of Idealism]" he therefore sketches an argument that not only avoids the problems of exposition that he identifies in Kant's refutation, but also tries to achieve a similar conclusion by taking a different path. Peirce's idea is to attack the conception of the temporal structure of consciousness presupposed by the problematic idealist. According to him, this line of argument provides a more straightforward way to refute the idealist. Let us see how this strategy proceeds.

Peirce accepts Kant's claim in note 1 (B276) that the refutation "beats idealism at its own game" (W8:80). This suggests that his argument also starts with an assumption made by the idealist and shows how this assumption implies that the proposition questioned by the idealist must obtain. In Kant's argument, the idealist's assumption is that we are able to objectively order our mental states in time. The task of the refutation is to show that in order for that ordering to be possible, we must be able to perceive existing objects in space. But it does not seem that Peirce's argument proceeds in a similar way. Rather than showing that one assumption of the idealist implies the doubted proposition, Peirce's strategy is to reveal that there are problems with her fundamental assumption, namely, that we can only immediately know what is absolutely "present" to our consciousness (see W8:78, 80).

Let us first see how Peirce characterizes the idealist's argument such that the existence of outer objects is uncertain. Peirce writes: "The idealist says that all that we know immediately, that is, otherwise than inferentially, is what is *present* in the mind; and things out of the mind are not so present" (W8:80). Therefore, in Peirce's reconstruction, the problematic idealist assumes that we can only be certain of what is "present" to the mind. Since, however, we are not aware of the existence of outer objects in this way, and we rather infer their existence from what is "present," the belief that outer objects exist is problematic.

But what does Peirce mean when he speaks of the "present"? Does he mean the present "moment" of consciousness, which is an actual state of consciousness that is temporally extended, or the present "instant," which is only an abstraction and a "point" of consciousness with no temporal extension? Given that Peirce's first move against the idealist is to argue that her starting point renders us incapable of capturing the flow of time in our ideas, he clearly intends "present" to mean the present "instant."[17]

Here is Peirce's first "move" against the idealist: "The first move toward beating idealism at its own game is to remark that we apprehend our own ideas only as flowing in time, and since neither the future nor the past, however near they may be, is *present*, there is as much difficulty in conceiving our perception of what passes within us as in conceiving external perception" (W8:80). How should we read this first move? In our characterization of problematic idealism at the beginning of the chapter, we have seen that it rests on the assumption of a disparity between our consciousness of our own mental states and our awareness of outer objects. It is only the existence of outer objects that is inferred. Peirce and Kant agree on this general characterization. In Section 1, we added that, in Kant's view, the idealist assumes that we are able to objectively order our mental states in time. Peirce does not speak of a capacity to temporally *order* our mental states. Nonetheless, at least provisionally, Peirce's idealist accepts that our mental states follow one another in time. In Peirce's words, she accepts that "we apprehend our own ideas only as flowing in time." However, Peirce argues, when we assume that we are only conscious of what is "instantly" present, there is no guarantee that our belief in a temporal succession of ideas is correct. The existence of our prior mental states, as well as our future ones, would be as uncertain to us as is the existence of outer objects. Therefore, Peirce's first move shows that by following the idealist's assumptions, it is not only the existence of outer objects that should be questioned, but also some facts about the temporality of consciousness that the idealist, at least initially, is not so prone to doubt.

Peirce anticipates what could be the idealist's reaction to this objection: "If so, replies the idealist, instead of giving up idealism we must go still further to nihilism" (W8:80). The idealist could thus respond by endorsing a stronger version of skepticism that doubts not only the existence of outer objects, but also the existence of a flow of ideas in time. How can we reject this form of skepticism? It is here that Peirce appeals to Kant's footnote to note 1 in the refutation. As we saw in Section 1, in that context Kant argues that our representations of outer objects cannot all be products of our imagination because, if that were the case, we would in fact be unable to tell what "imagining" outer objects could mean. We can only make sense of what this "imagining" is if we hold fast to the distinction between what "imagining" outer objects and "perceiving" outer objects is. But this means that we must accept that at least some outer objects are "actually" perceived. Peirce takes inspiration from this line of reasoning and devises a version of it that applies to the idealist's doubt regarding the succession of ideas in time: "It is impossible we should so much as think we think in time unless we do think in time; or rather, dismissing blind impossibility, the mere imagination of time is a clear perception of the past" (W8:80). Peirce clearly tries to appropriate Kant's argument here, namely, that in order to make sense of the idea that we imagine outer objects, we must assume that we also perceive outer objects. Similarly, Peirce suggests, in order to make sense of the idea that we can think or imagine that we think in time, we must assume that we do think in time.

Does Peirce's countermove work? He does not provide any support for his claim. Moreover, if we consider the argument from which he draws inspiration, it does not seem very strong. Of course, in order to make sense of what "imagining to perceive" is, we must be able to distinguish between imagining and perceiving. However, this does not mean that what we regard as actual perception needs to be such. Rather, our idea that we can distinguish between imagining and perceiving can itself be an illusory product of the imagination. To put the thought differently: in order to explain our capacity to form the idea of what imagining to perceive is, it is necessary that we *take* some of our mental states as actual perceptions. But it does not seem to be necessary that they actually *are* such perceptions.

We can try to read Peirce's countermove differently: rather than focus on the relationship between perceiving and imagining to perceive *in general*, we might instead focus *specifically* on the characteristic way that we represent time. The idea could be that merely thinking or imagining that we think in time is impossible, since this thinking and imagining already presupposes a representation of time, where this representation must be temporally structured, thus implying the reality of time. However, the idea that a representation of time is itself temporally structured presupposes an extensionalist model of the consciousness of time and it is not clear, at this point in the argument, why the skeptic would have to accept that.

Perhaps this countermove is not so essential to Peirce's strategy. This becomes clear when we consider the conclusion of Peirce's "Note." "Hamilton stupidly objects to Reid's phrase 'immediate memory'; but an immediate, intuitive, consciousness of time clearly exists wherever time exists. But once grant immediate knowledge in time, and what becomes of the idealist theory that we immediately know only the *present*? For the present can contain no time" (W8:80). Any skeptical argument builds on the intuitive appeal of its starting point. This is also the case for the "idealist" targeted by Peirce. That we can only know immediately (and be certain of) what is "absolutely present" to our consciousness seems prima facie sound and in agreement with the phenomenology of our conscious states. However, if a consequence of this assumption is that we cannot know immediately (and be certain) that our consciousness is in time, the soundness of that assumption starts to waver. This occurs because the assumption that we are forced to give up—the immediate knowledge that our ideas flow in time—is at least as intuitively appealing as the assumption on which the idealist's argument builds, namely, that we only know immediately what is absolutely present. Indeed, Peirce's point is that it is even easier to give up the very assumption on which the whole idealist's argument rests.

Clearly, Peirce's argument presupposes that when the idealist claims that we know immediately only what is "present" to the mind, she endorses an "instantaneous" view of consciousness according to which an episode of consciousness is not temporally extended. At this point, one might wonder why the idealist should be depicted in this way. Why cannot she be an extensionalist? In her view, "present to the mind" could simply mean "immediately available to it," but this does not necessarily have to be related to a particular way of understanding the temporal structure of consciousness. After all, extensionalists also maintain that a span of time is immediately available to consciousness. Therefore, why couldn't she be open to an extensionalist model of consciousness?

I think there is a way of defending Peirce's assumption here. Obviously, the idealist cannot be ready to assume immediate knowledge of whatever one might want to describe as "immediately available" to us. Given that "immediate perception" accounts of outer experience claim that we directly perceive outer objects, she would have to be open to the idea that these objects could be "immediately available" to us, too; but, of course, this cannot be the case. Therefore, the idealist cannot remain neutral regarding what is "immediately available." In general, her strategy is to accept as actual knowledge only what is as secure as possible from a skeptical point of view. In this spirit, if we take her perspective, it seems reasonable to think that she would more easily assume that we have immediate knowledge of what is "instantly" present to consciousness than that we have immediate knowledge of a conscious time span.

4. Conclusion

In this chapter, I tried to make sense of Peirce's appreciation of Kant's refutation of idealism. I suggested that his positive evaluation of it was due to the fact that Peirce read the refutation as an argument supporting the immediate perception of outer objects. I also reconstructed the anti-skeptical argument that Peirce develops with inspiration from Kant's approach. In fact, the line of reasoning followed by Peirce is different from Kant's strategy in important respects. Kant attempted to show that an assumption made by the skeptic—that we can objectively order our mental states in time—implies the very proposition that she doubts, namely, that outer objects exist and that we can perceive them. Even though Peirce claims that his "refutation" similarly tries to "beat the idealist at her own game," his strategy contains important differences. He first shows that the assumption on which the idealist's argument rests—namely, that we can only immediately know (and be certain of) what is absolutely present to our consciousness—implies that we must give up another assumption we commonly make, namely, that we can immediately know (and be certain) that our consciousness is in time. In a second step, Peirce submits that the assumption that we can immediately know that our consciousness is in time is more fundamental than the assumption that we can only immediately know what is absolutely present to our consciousness. If this is the case, the idealist's argument fails because its most fundamental premise fails. Peirce's argument is more "modest" than Kant's in at least one respect: he does not aim to show that the proposition doubted by the skeptic must be accepted given her very premise. Rather, his strategy is to show that the starting point of the argument is not that obvious, after all. This strategy might sound disappointing to many, but it might have a greater chance of being successful.[18]

Notes

1. "[Note on Kant's refutation of idealism]" (W8:80). I will use the following abbreviations to cite Peirce's writings: CP for Peirce 1931–1952, followed by volume and paragraph number; EP for Peirce 1992–1998, followed by volume and page number; RLT for Peirce 1992; W for Peirce 1982–, followed by volume and page number; R for Peirce's unpublished manuscripts in Houghton Library at Harvard University, followed by manuscript number (according to Robin 1967).
2. "Notes on the Question of the Existence of an External World" (W8:78–79).
3. I refer to Kant (1781) and Kant (1787) with A and B, respectively. Translations are from Kant (1998).
4. In other contexts, as, for example, the discussion of Cartesian substance dualism (W8:18), Peirce describes himself as an anti-dualist, but he clearly uses another understanding of dualism.
5. For an analysis of Peirce's renewed appreciation of Kant when he began to argue that we need indices to directly refer to objects, see Gava (2014a, ch. 4; 2014b).
6. The structure of the argument has provided a model for much debate concerning the form of transcendental arguments (see Stern [2020]; Pereboom [2019]; Gava [2017, 2021]).
7. Even when we assume this stronger version of premise (1), there is space for disagreement. For example, some scholars have argued that the premise only concerns the capacity to order *past* mental states, given that it would be absurd to maintain that we cannot immediately distinguish between a present and a past mental state (see Bennett [1966, 205]; Dicker [2008, 85–86]). Moreover, while the majority of scholars claim that the premise asserts that we do actually determine the order of our mental states in time (or that we know how our states are objectively ordered), Bader reads it in a somewhat milder way, suggesting that it only asserts that objectively determining the order of our mental states is possible (Bader [2017, 210]).
8. There is a complication here, since the question whether the self is a substance can be asked both at the empirical and the transcendental level.
9. I refer to Kant (1900–) by indicating volume and page numbers. *Refl* refers to Kant's "*Reflexionen.*"
10. Note that Bader translates "beharrlich" with "permanent" and "Beharrlichkeit" with "permanence." I have followed Guyer and Wood's translation by using "persistent" and "persistence."

11. Ralf Bader (2017, 206n5) suggests that the argument in the footnote can be identified with a point Kant makes in the context of the A-paralogism, where he claims that we cannot only imagine outer objects because imagination is dependent on outer sense to receive materials it can work with (A373–375). I take the argument in the footnote to be different.
12. This has striking similarities with the "overlap model" among extensional accounts of temporal consciousness and the consciousness of time. In a similar way, this model regards episodes of consciousness as temporally extended and overlapping with one another (see Dainton [2000, ch. 7; 2018, sect. 5.4]).
13. Since the "mediate" perception of the complete sequence of the four instants is "subjectively" located in the second moment, Peirce seems to incorporate elements of a "retentionalist" account, too, where we attain consciousness of a sequence that spans through different moments thanks to the help of memory. The picture is complicated by the fact that since A and B are both infinitesimal durations, they can be taken together as forming a single infinitesimal duration that we immediately perceive (see W8:138). This might sound paradoxical, but it is due to the fact that these infinitesimal durations are parts of a continuum considered "in the small."
14. William James also defended a "specious" present view in his *Principles of Psychology* (see James [1890, ch. 15]).
15. An alternative specious present view is retentionalism (see Dainton [2018, sect. 6.2]). Hereafter, when I refer to the "specious" present, I mean the extentionalist specious present.
16. Helm (1983, 184) and Schmidt (2022, 243, n10) provide two opposite interpretations of the "present," but I think they are in fact compatible when we distinguish these two different ways of referring to it.
17. In "Notes on the Question of the Existence of an External World," Peirce explains that what is immediately present is "what we have in mind at the moment" (W8:78). Given that this "moment" is not extended in time, it cannot be the "moment" according to the technical definition given in "The Law of Mind."
18. I am grateful to Marcello Garibbo and Cornelis de Waal for some very useful comments on a previous version of this chapter.

References

Apel, Karl-Otto. 1981. *Charles S. Peirce: From Pragmatism to Pragmaticism*. Amherst: University of Massachusetts Press.
Bader, Ralf. 2017. "The Refutation of Idealism." In *Kant's Critique of Pure Reason: A Critical Guide*, edited by J. O'Shea, 205–222. Cambridge: Cambridge University Press.
Bennett, Jonathan. 1966. *Kant's Analytic*. Cambridge: Cambridge University Press.
Chevalier, Jean-Marie. 2016. "Peirce lecteur de Kant." *Philosophia Scientiæ*, 20: 143–163.
Chignell, Andrew. 2010. "Causal Refutations of Idealism." *The Philosophical Quarterly*, 60: 487–507.
Colapietro, Vincent. 2006. "Toward a Pragmatic Conception of Practical Identity." *Transactions of the Charles S. Peirce Society* 42: 173–205.
Colapietro, Vincent. 2017. "The Tones, Tints, and Textures of Temporality: Toward a Reconstruction of Peirce's Philosophy of Time." *Rivista di Storia della Filosofia*, 2017: 435–453.
Dainton, Barry. 2000. *Stream of Consciousness*. London: Routledge.

Dainton, Barry. 2018. "Temporal Consciousness." In *The Stanford Encyclopedia of Philosophy* (Winter 2018 edition), edited by Edward N. Zalta. <https://plato.stanford.edu/archives/win2018/entries/consciousness-temporal/>.

De Tienne, André. 2015. "The Flow of Time and the Flow of Signs: A Basis for Peirce's Cosmosemiotics." *American Journal of Semiotics*, 31: 29–53.

Dicker, Georges. 2008. "Kant's Refutation of Idealism," *Noûs*, 42: 80–108.

Emundts, Dina. 2010. "The Refutation of Idealism and the Distinction between Phenomena and Noumena." In *The Cambridge Companion to* Kant's Critique of Pure Reason, edited by Paul Guyer, 168–189. Cambridge: Cambridge University Press.

Gava, Gabriele. 2014a. *Peirce's Account of Purposefulness: A Kantian Perspective*. London: Routledge.

Gava, Gabriele. 2014b. "What Is Wrong with Intuitions? An Assessment of a Peircean Criticism of Kant." *Transactions of the Charles S. Peirce Society*, 50: 340–359.

Gava, Gabriele. 2017. "Transzendentale Argumente." In *Handbuch Metaphysik*, edited by Markus Schrenk, 410–416. Stuttgart: J. B. Metzler.

Gava, Gabriele. 2021. "Transcendental Arguments." In *Oxford Bibliographies in Philosophy*, edited by Duncan Pritchard. Oxford: Oxford University Press.

Gava, Gabriele, and Robert Stern, eds. 2016. *Pragmatism, Kant, and Transcendental Philosophy*. London: Routledge.

Guyer, Paul. 1987. *Kant and the Claims of Knowledge*. Cambridge: Cambridge University Press.

Helm, Bertrand. 1983. "The Nature and Modes of Time." In *The Relevance of Charles S. Peirce*, edited by Eugene Freeman, 178–188. La Salle, IL: Hegeler Institute.

Hookway, Christopher. 1985. *Peirce*. London: Routledge & Kegan Paul.

James, William. 1890. *The Principles of Psychology*, 2 vols. New York: Holt. Reprint, New York: Dover, 1950.

Kant, Immanuel. 1781. *Critik der reinen Vernunft*. Riga.

Kant, Immanuel. 1787. *Critik der reinen Vernunft*. 2nd ed. Riga.

Kant, Immanuel 1900– . *Kants gesammelte Schriften*. Berlin: De Gruyter, Reimer.

Kant, Immanuel. 1998. *Critique of Pure Reason*, translated by Paul Guyer and Allen W. Wood. Cambridge: Cambridge University Press.

Maddalena, Giovanni, 2015. *The Philosophy of Gesture: Completing Pragmatists' Incomplete Revolution*. Montreal: McGill–Queen's University Press.

Peirce, Charles Sanders. 1931–1952. *Collected Papers of Charles Sanders* Peirce, edited by C. Hartshorne and P. Weiss (volumes 1–6), and A. Burks (volumes 7–8). Cambridge, MA: Harvard University Press. (Referred to as CP.)

Peirce, Charles S. 1966–1970. *Charles S. Peirce Papers*. Microfilm, 39 reels. Cambridge, MA: Houghton Library, Harvard University. (Referred to as R.)

Peirce, Charles Sanders. 1982– . *Writings of Charles S. Peirce: A Chronological Edition*, 7 vols. to date, edited by the Peirce Edition Project. Bloomington: Indiana University Press. (Referred to as W.)

Peirce, Charles Sanders. 1992. *Reasoning and the Logic of Things*, edited by Kenneth L. Ketner. Cambridge, MA: Harvard University Press. (Referred to as RLT.)

Peirce, Charles Sanders. 1992–1998. *The Essential Peirce*, edited by the Peirce Edition Project, 2 vols. Bloomington: Indiana University Press. (Referred to as EP.)

Pereboom, Derk. 2019. "Kant's Transcendental Arguments." In *The Stanford Encyclopedia of Philosophy* (Spring 2019 Edition), edited by Edward N. Zalta. https://plato.stanford.edu/archives/spr2019/entries/kant-transcendental/.

Pihlström, Sami. 2003. *Naturalizing the Transcendental: A Pragmatic View*. Amherst, MA: Humanity Books.

Robin, Richard S. 1967. *Annotated Catalogue of the Papers of Charles S. Peirce*. Amherst: University of Massachusetts Press.

Schmidt, Jon A. 2022. "Temporal Synechism: A Peircean Philosophy of Time." *Axiomathes* 32: 233–269.

Short, Thomas, 2007. *Peirce's Theory of Signs*. Cambridge: Cambridge University Press.

Stern, Robert. 2020. "Transcendental Arguments." In *The Stanford Encyclopedia of Philosophy*, edited by Edward N. Zalta. https://plato.stanford.edu/archives/fall2020/entries/transcendental-arguments/.

Walker, Ralph. C. S. 1978. *Kant*. London: Routledge & Kegan Paul.

Wilson, Aaron B. 2016. *Peirce's Empiricism: Its Roots and Its Originality*. Lanham, MD: Lexington Books.

CHAPTER 26

PEIRCE ON TRUTH

ANDREW HOWAT

It is notoriously difficult to summarize Peirce's conception of truth (hereafter, PCT), for three main reasons. First, many scholars believe PCT is connected to Peirce's 'pragmatic maxim,' yet not only do we disagree over the correct interpretation of the maxim, but also Peirce himself modified it in various ways over the course of his career and never seemed entirely satisfied with it.[1] Second, these interpretive difficulties and the resulting methodological ambiguity tempt many nonspecialists to apply their own understanding of philosophical method to Peirce's remarks, yielding interpretations that Peirce himself would not have recognized. This is especially true of those who embrace nominalism (of which Peirce was a relentless critic) and of those treating his conception of truth as a reductive analysis. Third, even among specialists well acquainted with the historical and developmental subtleties of Peirce's remarks, there remains considerable diversity of opinion about both the content of PCT and its proper place in Peirce's philosophical system. This is in part because his writings are so technical, voluminous, and disorganized, but it also reflects what Peirce called his 'pedestrianism'—his tendency to modify his philosophical system gradually and constantly throughout his career.[2]

Almeder (1985) provides a particularly vivid illustration of the diversity of opinion about PCT, cataloging *thirteen* distinct interpretations of Peirce's view extant in the literature at that time. Thankfully, this diversity has diminished considerably in the wake of influential works such as Misak ([1991] 2004), Hookway (2002), and Lane (2018). Nevertheless, it is remarkable that it remains an open question whether it is best to understand Peirce's conception of truth as (1) an antirepresentationalist, antimetaphysical alternative to correspondence (e.g., Misak [1991] 2004), as (2) a distinctively pragmatist form *of* correspondence theory/representationalism deeply connected to Peirce's realism (e.g., Lane 2018), or even as (3) a unique and pioneering synthesis of *all* traditional conceptions of truth (e.g., Forster 2011).

What follows is an opinionated introduction to PCT. Section 1 highlights some key quotations and directs the reader to the most important primary sources. Section 2 summarizes three influential interpretations of PCT, starting with Misak ([1991] 2004).

Section 3 reviews three major lines of argument against PCT and briefly summarizes common replies. I conclude with a few remarks of my own concerning debate over the most defensible interpretation of Peirce's view, though it will of course be left to the community of inquiry and to the long run to determine which one is the truth.

1. Primary Sources for PCT

Peirce's most studied and quoted remarks about truth appear in his paper "How to Make Our Ideas Clear" (hereafter "Ideas") from 1878. However, given the interpretive challenges noted above, it is helpful to examine certain precursors and subsequent modifications. As Lane (2018) and others have shown, it is especially important to consider Peirce's change of heart concerning 'scholastic realism.' In this section I briefly present a few key ideas and quotations from various sources, to help the reader navigate Peirce's intimidating oeuvre.[3]

In 1868, in the course of critiquing Cartesianism, Peirce argues that "to make single individuals absolute judges of truth'—as Descartes's method of doubt arguably does—'is most pernicious" (W2:212). This idea explains the important role that the *community* of inquiry (or the opinion of that community in the long run) plays in PCT.

In several places in his early writings, Peirce also endorses a correspondence or representationalist definition of truth, something he continues to do throughout his career. In 1867, for example, he begins a passage, "Truth being, then, the agreement of a representation with its object . . ." (W2.99). In 1870 he writes, "Truth is the agreement of a meaning with a reality" (W2.439).[4] While some take these claims at face value and assume PCT is an effort to supplement, improve, or clarify such definitions in some way, others offer a more deflationary reading, one that sees Peirce as a pioneer of what we now call antirepresentationalism.[5] This is because Peirce also makes a number of seemingly 'anti-correspondence' remarks, which imply that such theories are metaphysical in a way pragmatists ought to consider objectionable.[6]

The two most important precursors to PCT's first detailed formulation in "Ideas" are Peirce's discussion of metaphysics in his 1871 review of Fraser's "The Works of George Berkeley" and his famous 1877 paper "The Fixation of Belief." In *The Berkeley Review*, Peirce offers some historical remarks on the medieval dispute between realism and nominalism, some of which clearly foreshadow PCT. In "Fixation," he gives what Lane (2018) has dubbed a 'genealogy of truth' intimately connected to his central arguments in "Ideas."[7]

Three claims about truth in *The Berkeley Review* deserve highlight. First, in describing the realist conception of reality (and contrasting it with the nominalist one), Peirce writes: "All human thought and opinion contains an arbitrary, accidental element, dependent on the limitations in circumstances, power, and bent of the individual; an element of error, in short. But human opinion universally tends in the long run to a definite form, which is the truth" (W2.468, 1871).

He then makes a claim about truth's knowability and provides a nuanced characterization of its 'mind-independence': "The individual may not live to reach the truth; there is a residuum of error in every individual's opinions. No matter; it remains that there is a definite opinion to which the mind of man is, on the whole and in the long run, tending. ... This final opinion, then, is independent, not indeed of thought in general, but of all that is arbitrary and individual in thought; is quite independent how you, or I, or any number of men think" (W2.469).

Finally, Peirce concludes by drawing an important conclusion about the metaphysical implications of these claims: "There is a general *drift* in the history of human thought which will lead it to one general agreement, one catholic consent. And any truth more perfect than this destined conclusion, any reality more absolute than what is taught in it, is a fiction of metaphysics. . . . This theory of reality is instantly fatal to the idea of a thing in itself,—a thing existing independent of all relation to the mind's conception of it" (W2.469). This metaphysical conclusion helps explain why Peirce often described his overall philosophy as Kantianism minus 'things in themselves.'[8]

In "Fixation," Peirce makes two kinds of remarks about truth. The first is broadly deflationary. After introducing his famous doubt–belief conception of inquiry, he writes:

> With the doubt, therefore, the struggle [of inquiry] begins, and with the cessation of doubt it ends. Hence, the sole object of inquiry is the settlement of opinion. We may fancy that this is not enough for us, and that we seek, not merely an opinion, but a true opinion. But put this fancy to the test, and it proves groundless; for as soon as a firm belief is reached we are entirely satisfied, whether the belief be true or false . . . we think each one of our beliefs to be true, and, indeed, it is mere tautology to say so. (W3.248, 1877)[9]

The second kind of remark concerns the relationship between truth and our methods of inquiry. Peirce contrasts four different methods for determining the truth of a belief: tenacity (refusing to consider contrary evidence), authority (deference to some outside power or expertise), the a priori method (seeking beliefs agreeable to reason through dialectic), and what Peirce calls the method of science (generating hypotheses, deducing the consequences of their truth, then testing for those consequences using experiments). He argues for the superiority of the method of science over all the others—that it alone has the potential to fix belief *permanently*, since it is the only method that seeks a belief determined solely by the facts and by nothing extraneous to the facts, such as or our own preferences, the opinions of experts, or what is intellectually fashionable (W3.253, 1877).

Most scholars assume that none of these precursors supplies us with a fully fledged theory or conception of truth (the exception is Lane [2018]). They assume this because prior to 1878's "Ideas," Peirce had not yet stated and argued for the pragmatic maxim—his methodological rule for the clarification of abstract intellectual concepts and arguably the core of his pragmatism. Many scholars assume that PCT is a product of Peirce applying the maxim to the concept of truth, and so they turn to "Ideas" for its definitive statement.

In "Ideas" Peirce examines what is involved in making clear an abstract concept such as reality, hardness, or force. He identifies three grades of clarity in our understanding of such intellectual concepts:

1. *Clearness:* basic familiarity, or the ability to apply that concept successfully in standard cases.
2. *Distinctness:* verbal definition, or the ability to give a precise definition of the concept in abstract terms.
3. *Pragmatic meaning:* expertise, or the ability to identify what habits a thing produces; knowledge of the practical consequences that follow from correct applications of the concept.[10]

Peirce's first formulation of the pragmatic maxim, his rule for discovering a concept's pragmatic meaning, is as follows: "Consider what effects, that might conceivably have practical bearings, we conceive the object of our conception to have. Then, our conception of these effects *is the whole of our conception of the object*" (W3.276, emphasis added).

Legg (2014) provides the following summary and illustration of the three grades of clarity:

> At the first grade, we can identify a concept's instances without necessarily being able to say how. At the second grade, we can give the concept a verbal or 'nominal' definition, as found in a dictionary. At the third grade, we can derive future expectations from hypotheses containing that concept. Thus, in Peirce's famous example, the first grade of clarity is to state, 'This table is hard,' the second grade is to state something like, 'Hardness is the ability to resist pressure,' and the third to predict, 'If I rest my lunch on this table, it will not fall through.' (205)

With this framework in place, we can now state the popular understanding of the nature and status of PCT: it is an attempt to provide a third-grade clarification of the concept of truth, or to state that concept's pragmatic meaning. We can also potentially explain the origin of Peirce's pro- and anti-correspondence remarks: perhaps Peirce regards 'correspondence of a representation with its object' as an adequate *definition* (second-grade clarification) of truth (pro-correspondence), but an inadequate 'pragmatic elucidation' (third-grade clarification) of truth (anti-correspondence).

After going on to illustrate the maxim by applying it to the concepts of weight and force, Peirce turns to the concept of reality.[11] He defines it by reference to the distinction "between reality and its opposite, fiction." This prompts him to distinguish between external and internal realities (W3.271, 1878). External realities are those "whose characters are independent of how you or I think," while internal realities, such as dreams, have characters that are dependent upon how we think, but not upon "what we think those characters to be." "Thus, a dream has a real existence as a mental phenomenon, if somebody has really dreamt it; that he dreamt so and so, does not depend on what anybody thinks was dreamt, but is completely independent of all opinion on the subject" (W3.271, 1878). It is worth noting that Peirce appears to be offering a distinctive definition of reality here—one that some philosophers might reject.[12]

Having defined reality, Peirce goes on to explain why making that concept clear at the third grade will require first clarifying the concept of truth, or the distinction between true and false belief: "Reality, like every other quality, consists in the peculiar sensible effects which things partaking of it produce. The only effect which real things have is to cause belief, for all the sensations which they excite emerge into consciousness in the form of beliefs. The question therefore is, how is true belief (or belief in the real) distinguished from false belief (or belief in fiction)" (W3.271, 1878). This is where Peirce refers back to the argument in "Fixation" mentioned above, wherein he contrasts the four methods of inquiry and argues for the superiority of the method of science over all the others (W3:253, 1877). The great virtue of this method, he reminds us, is that it ensures everyone inquiring concerning a particular hypothesis, no matter how diverse their approaches, will be carried "by a force outside of themselves to one and the same conclusion." He then makes his most famous remarks about truth:

> This activity of thought by which we are carried, not where we wish, but to a fore-ordained goal, is like the operation of destiny. No modification of the point of view taken, no selection of other facts for study, no natural bent of mind even, can enable a man to escape the predestinate opinion. This great hope is embodied in the conception of truth and reality. *The opinion which is fated to be ultimately agreed to by all who investigate, is what we mean by the truth, and the object represented in this opinion is the real. That is the way I would explain reality.* (W3.273, emphasis added)

A central point of contention among scholars is what Peirce is doing in this critical passage. Is he, as the popular understanding holds, providing a third-grade clarification of truth, stating its pragmatic meaning (Misak [1991] 2004)? Is he defining it at the second grade of clarity, that is, *defining* it, or perhaps giving a *criterion*, rather than a definition (Rescher 1973)?[13] Is he merely calling back to the 'genealogy of truth' we find in "Fixation" (Lane 2018)? Our answers to these questions will define not just our interpretation of PCT, but also the objections it is likely to face and what replies will seem either best or simply consistent with Peirce's views. Peirce himself did in fact supply an answer, when in 1905 he wrote: "The next application I shall make of pragmaticism is to support a principle which might very well be regarded on the contrary, as a support of pragmaticism, and was in fact originally so treated by me, being proved independently in my article of November 1877 [i.e., "Fixation"]" (R289, 13, 1905). After this passage, Peirce goes on to defend PCT. In other words, while Peirce evidently did not think of himself as applying the maxim ('pragmaticism,' a label he used later in his career to distinguish his view from that of William James) to the concept of truth when he wrote "Ideas," he did so subsequently.

Of the remarks Peirce made about truth after "Ideas," some of the most important appear in his entry for *Baldwin's Dictionary* (CP5.565, 1902). One novel aspect of these remarks is their strong emphasis on the idea that while truth may be a matter of accurate representation, all representation is to some extent indeterminate. Peirce writes:

> Truth is a character which attaches to an abstract proposition, such as a person might utter. It essentially depends upon that proposition's not professing to be exactly true. But we hope that in the progress of science its error will indefinitely diminish, just as the error of 3.14159, the value given for π, will indefinitely diminish as the calculation is carried to more and more places of decimals. What we call an ideal limit to which no numerical expression can be perfectly true.... Truth is that concordance of an abstract statement with the ideal limit towards which endless investigation would tend to bring scientific belief, which concordance the abstract statement may possess by virtue of the confession of its inaccuracy and one-sidedness, and this confession is an essential ingredient of truth. (CP5.565, 1902)[14]

Finally, as Atkins (2016) and many others rightly note, Peirce later qualifies his first statement of PCT in an important way when in 1911 (for example) he writes: "I call[ed] "truth" the predestinate opinion, by which I ought to have meant that which would ultimately prevail if investigation were carried sufficiently far in that particular direction'" (EP2:457).[15] These and other remarks later (e.g., CP5.549–554, 1906; CP5.555–564, c. 1906; CP5.565–573, 1902) see Peirce putting an ever greater emphasis on the subjunctive and/or counterfactual character of pragmatic clarifications of truth or reality—that they state what we expect *would* occur *if* certain conditions were met. The significance of this shift to the subjunctive will become clearer once we turn to challenges to PCT in Section 3.

2. Three Influential Interpretations of PCT

In this section I briefly outline three of the most influential recent interpretations of PCT, namely, those of Cheryl Misak, Christopher Hookway, and Robert Lane. My goal is to provide the reader with an introduction to contemporary debates about PCT, but in doing so I will occasionally express my own views about the strengths and weaknesses of these interpretations.

Those steeped in the literature on mainstream theories of truth in the analytic tradition tend to interpret PCT according to a specific methodological and metaphysical framework. This framework is a conjunction of four basic assumptions:

(1) There exists some property or feature F.
(2) F is had by all and only the true propositions.
(3) Truth is the property consisting in being F.
(4) F is necessary and sufficient for explaining why those propositions are true.[16]

Those who presuppose this framework interpret PCT as the claim that F is a property like the one Crispin Wright calls *superassertibilty*. "A proposition p is superassertible if and only if p is or can be, warranted to assert, and some warrant for the assertion of p would survive arbitrarily close scrutiny of its pedigree and arbitrarily extensive increments to or other forms of improvement of our information."[17]

Those who interpret PCT in this way are quick to point out that it faces a difficult objection, one Peirce himself anticipated. Although the details of this objection vary,[18] the central idea is generally as follows. Given assumption (4) above, a theory of truth will be considered satisfactory if and only if it explains all different types of true propositions—empirical, mathematical, legal, etc.[19] PCT seemingly fails this test, because it appears there are some true propositions—what Peirce called 'buried secrets' or 'lost facts'—that are not and cannot be warranted to assert at any stage of inquiry (W3:274, 1878). As Lynch (2009) puts it, "there are at least some truths—perhaps about the distant past, or far side of the universe, or the number of stars right now, for which no evidence will ever be available in principle" (43). Thus, to those familiar only with mainstream approaches, it often appears that truth cannot be superassertibility and PCT is therefore clearly false.[20]

In 1991, Cheryl Misak published *Truth and the End of Inquiry: A Peircean Account of Truth*, the first book-length treatment and defense of PCT. In the preface to the 2004 paperback edition, Misak rightly notes that the above understanding of PCT suffers from an extremely common defect. She writes: "It is still commonplace for philosophers to mischaracterize Peirce's account of truth as a definition and then scoff at what a poor definition it is. Even those who end up adopting something very close to Peirce's account of truth (for instance, Crispin Wright (1992) and Huw Price (2003)) make this mistake" (Misak [1994] 2004, viii).

Misak's most important and pioneering claim is that PCT is the outcome of applying the pragmatic maxim to the concept of truth and is thus a third-grade clarification or 'pragmatic elucidation' of that concept, *not* a definition one can easily refute by means of apparent counterexamples.[21] Misak offers a detailed and persuasive account of the difference between elucidation and definition, along with nuanced historical analysis of the relationship between this distinction and other related projects in the history of philosophy. She also anticipates and replies to numerous apparent objections. What follows is merely a brief sketch of her view.

In attempting to clarify the concept of truth, traditional philosophical theories typically assert a formal equivalence in the indicative mood, such as 'hypothesis H is true if and only if H corresponds with reality.' In contrast, Misak rightly notes that pragmatic elucidations, since they formalize the consequences or expectations of a concept's application, produce subjunctive conditionals of the form "if H is true, then we would expect that if you were to do x, y would result."[22] With this in mind, Misak argues that Peirce makes two basic claims.

> Peirce suggests that the following is a consequence of '*H* is true.' (T–I): if *H* is true, then, if inquiry were pursued as far as it could fruitfully go, *H* would be believed. And he argues that we had better not add anything to the notion of truth over and above

the specification of the relationship between truth and inquiry. That is, he adds another conditional. (I–T): if, if inquiry were pursued as far as it could fruitfully go, *H* would be believed, then *H* is true. For if we attempt to pack more than this into the notion of truth, our account will go beyond experience. (Misak 2004, 125)

It is natural to wonder why Misak keeps these two conditionals separate, rather than combining them into a single biconditional. There are several reasons, but the most important is that she argues that each has a slightly different status, something a material equivalence risks concealing.[23] Specifically, she argues that Peirce considers (T–I) to be a regulative assumption of inquiry—something we must hope or assume is true when we inquire concerning the truth of some hypothesis H. She denies that Peirce *asserts* (T–I), in much the same way Peirce seemingly declines to assert the law of excluded middle, when he writes: "Logic requires us, with reference to each question we have in hand, to hope some definite answer to it may be true. That *hope* with reference to *each* case as it comes up is, by a *saltus* [*a sudden leap or breach of continuity, AH*], stated by logicians as a law concerning all cases, namely the law of excluded middle" (*NE* iv, p. xiii, undated)[24] He does, she argues, assert (I–T) and is thus committed to the view that "truth is that feature belonging to all beliefs that are as good as they can be; beliefs that would be permanently settled upon or 'indefeasible'" (CP6.485, 1908).

Misak argues that together, (T–I) and (I–T) provide a 'pragmatically legitimate' conception of truth that illustrates the advantages of a pragmatist approach to conceptual clarification, while spurning pragmatically empty 'transcendental' or 'metaphysical' analyses of truth, such as correspondence theory. What makes such accounts empty is that they lack practical consequences, which means they provide only nominal or second-grade clarity. She writes: "Truth is the property of hypotheses that would be believed if inquiry were pursued as far as it could fruitfully go. To suggest that there is more to truth than that is to abandon the pragmatic methodology in favor of transcendental metaphysics."[25] Misak believes that if "we want our conception of truth to be pragmatically legitimate, we must see that there is nothing in the notion of truth over and above what can be squeezed out of the notion of inquiry."[26] This claim certainly reflects Peirce's 1878 insistence that third-grade clarifications *exhaust* our conception of the relevant object, as well as his implication (taken up with gusto by William James in his 1907 lectures) that any attempt to clarify a concept that does not appeal to the practical consequences of its correct application is effectively meaningless.

The primary difficulties facing Misak's view are arguably interpretive, rather than substantive.[27] First, there is the evidence quoted above that Peirce, at least in the 1870s, did not take himself to be clarifying the concept of truth at the third grade, but rather referring to the independently motivated 'genealogy of truth' that Lane (2018) sees in "Fixation." Second, there is an obvious tension between (I–T) and Peirce's apparent affirmations of correspondence theory, a tension not easily resolved. I will expand upon this point briefly before turning to Hookway's interpretation.

If, per Misak's (I–T), PCT says there can be literally *nothing more to* truth than its connection to beliefs and inquiry as spelled out in the two conditionals, this seemingly leaves no space for affirmations of correspondence definitions of truth. Misak resolves this tension by arguing that PCT is inherently 'set against' correspondence theory, supporting this claim by appeal to Peirce's apparently dismissive attitude toward definitions, or second-grade clarity.[28] This response is problematic because Peirce is much more equivocal about the relationship between the grades of clarity (particularly the second and third) than Misak's account might lead one to expect.

In "Ideas" Peirce initially concedes that "our existing beliefs can be set in order by this process" of making ideas clear and distinct, and that philosophers who advocate doing so "are right in making familiarity with a notion the first step toward clearness of apprehension, and the defining of it the second." In 1894 he adds that as we ascend from the lower to the higher grades of clarity "it is the lower order of clearness to which the higher is obliged to conform" (ILL:101). In 1910 he calls the second grade of clarity "indispensable to all Exact Reasoning." He also writes that "in regard to ["Ideas"], I ought to say that my three grades of clearness are not, as I seemed then to think, such that either the first or the second are superseded by the third."[29] These remarks clearly suggest the lower grades of clarity play an important, perhaps substantive, role in conceptual clarification, as does his introduction of a seemingly substantive account of the concept of reality in "Ideas" (one that, as noted above, many philosophers seemingly reject).

Yet Misak is undoubtedly right that Peirce sometimes evinces the opposite attitude. The phrase I italicized in his first statement of the maxim suggests he thinks that a concept's pragmatic meaning *exhausts* its content, and thus that the other grades of clarity, though perhaps useful heuristics, can nevertheless tell us nothing substantive about it. In "Ideas" Peirce writes that "nothing new can ever be learned by analyzing definitions" (W3.260, 1878). These remarks suggest a dismissive attitude toward the lower grades of clarity. This equivocal stance gives rise to many of the interpretive difficulties that still beset attempts to reconstruct PCT.[30]

Hookway (2002) is broadly sympathetic to Misak's reconstruction of PCT. His account differs slightly, however, in emphasizing the 'convergence' aspect of PCT (the beliefs of different inquirers converging on one proposition the longer their investigations continue), while also adding three additional elements. First, Hookway provides a novel way to resolve the tension just noted between (I–T) and correspondence. Second, this in turn generates a way of spelling out in clearer, more familiar philosophical terms the difference between PCT and other, more traditional theories of truth. Third, Hookway defends PCT in part on the grounds that it is 'metaphysically neutral.'

Hookway formulates PCT using Peirce's metaphor of convergence.[31] After considering several candidates, Hookway settles on the following characterization, noting (pace Misak) that some evidence suggests Peirce might have accepted this claim formulated as a biconditional: "*D5:* If it is true that *p*, then anyone who inquired into the question whether *p* long enough and well enough (using good methods of inquiry) would eventually reach a stable belief that *p* which would not be disturbed by further evidence or investigation."[32]

Hookway subsequently addresses the difficult question of how to reconcile such a claim with Peirce's many apparent endorsements of a correspondence definition of truth. He concedes that we might consider D5 to contain an 'echo' of correspondence definitions, since it might be taken to involve correspondence between a proposition and the 'final opinion' on which we converge.[33] Nevertheless, he argues against taking this echo too seriously, invoking a distinction between common-sense claims and philosophical theorizing: "It is common in philosophy to find phrases and formulations used in two very different ways, as plain, even common sense claims, and as claims which are to be understood in the context of systematic philosophical theorizing. For example we might take it that a phrase such as 'True propositions correspond to the facts' both as an unproblematic truism that carries little philosophical weight, and as the expression of a controversial philosophical theory of truth, which employs an ontology of *facts* and a relation of *copying*" (cf. William James's endorsement of the claim that true propositions agree with reality).[34]

Thus, Hookway can concede that Peirce frequently endorses correspondence as a definition of truth by reading those endorsements as "plain common sense claims."[35] When Peirce critiques correspondence or metaphysical conceptions of truth, by contrast, he is arguing against treating correspondence definition as anything *more* than common sense, for example, as some kind of philosophical theory. Doing so generates precisely the kind of metaphysical 'gibberish' or absurdity that Peirce and subsequent pragmatists famously oppose.[36] For Hookway, it is only when Peirce makes claims like D5 that he is offering us any kind of theory or philosophical substance.

Hookway also identifies three distinct projects one might attempt in seeking to clarify TRUTH (n.b. the labels are mine):

1. To provide an account of the meaning of the word 'true' and its cognates (p. 44, *semantics*).
2. To provide an account 'of the normative role of the concept of truth in assessing beliefs and assertions or keeping track of the progress of our investigations' (p. 44, *pragmatics*).
3. To provide a 'heavy-duty metaphysics' of TRUTH, i.e., "deep philosophical explanations of the relations between thought and reality" (p. 44, *metaphysics*).

Hookway defends the idea that PCT is a product of doing *pragmatics*, while eschewing (and perhaps exhibiting a deflationary attitude toward) *semantics* and remaining noncommittal or neutral regarding *metaphysics*. He argues that "pragmatic clarifications of concepts and propositions are best seen as accounts of the (experiential) commitments we incur when we assert or judge the proposition in question."[37] I label this 'pragmatics' because it focuses on certain acts we perform, centrally the speech-act of *assertion* and—what for Peirce is merely an internalization of that speech-act—private acts of judgment (CP5.29, 1903).

Thus, for Hookway, PCT says that when we assert or judge that something is true, we commit ourselves to it being indefeasible (such that we *would* believe it *if* inquiry concerning it were carried sufficiently far). But this normative commitment attaches to *actual uses* of the word or concept in real cases. It need not entail anything about merely hypothetical assertions, inquiries, or private acts of judgment, including—crucially—the kinds of putative counterexamples identified by critics concerned about buried secrets.

The crucial difference between PCT and definitions of truth, then, is that committing ourselves to a proposition's being indefeasible each time we judge or assert its truth neither entails nor requires that every truth is indefeasible. On Hookway's reading, Peirce can and does allow that some truths may lack that property—that there may be genuinely lost facts.[38] All that follows from PCT is that we *should not assert* a proposition we do not think is indefeasible in the relevant sense—it would be a violation of the normative commitment characteristic of assertion (the act of presenting a proposition *as true*).

Consider, finally, Hookway's argument that in addition to eschewing *semantics*, PCT is 'metaphysically neutral': "[PCT] can be held in conjunction with a realist or an anti-realist metaphysics. The most plausible view may be that some truths can be understood in a 'realist' manner, as dealing with a mind-independent reality, while others deal with matters whose character bears more marks of our interests, sentiments or constructive activities."[39]

Hookway foresees that both realists and anti-realists can endorse PCT, because they can offer differing explanations of why our opinions converge over time on different types of propositions. In the case of empirical propositions, convergence might be the product of the causal influence of a mind-independent reality, while in the case of mathematical propositions, it might be the result of certain rational structures, somehow built into our minds.

While Misak's and Hookway's characterizations of PCT are compatible, Lane (2018) diverges from both. Pace Misak, and as noted above, Lane argues that PCT predates Peirce's first presentation of and argument for the pragmatic maxim in "Ideas," being fully formed by the end of "Fixation."[40] Pace Hookway, Lane rejects the idea that PCT is metaphysically neutral, arguing instead that its appearance in "Ideas"—during Peirce's pragmatic elucidation of the concept of reality—shows that it is central to Peirce's broader metaphysical project of reconciling realism and idealism. This interpretation has the great virtue of taking seriously and literally Peirce's final remark, namely, "That is the way I would explain reality."

Lane characterizes PCT as a 'dual aspect' conception of truth, the two aspects being the *representationalist* (truth is correctly defined as correspondence between a proposition and the reality it represents) and the *investigative* (truth, at the third grade of clarity, means a belief that would be permanently settled in the minds of those who use the method of science to investigate that belief).[41] Lane argues that "the success of that method is due in part to the fact that it attempts to arrive at beliefs that represent how the world is apart from how it is believed to be, i.e. it attempts to arrive at beliefs that represent the real. When it succeeds—when it permanently dispels doubt and establishes belief—that belief represents reality."[42]

Given the tight relationship between truth and reality that Lane sees even in Peirce's earliest remarks and given Peirce's repeated endorsement of correspondence definitions, Lane sees nothing wrong with calling Peirce a 'correspondence theorist,' albeit of an unorthodox type. Misak continues to regard such a label as deeply misleading, calling PCT as Lane describes it "representationalist in name only" (2018, 425).

Overall, Lane's case for reading Peirce in this original way is detailed and meticulous. In my view it is currently the best supported by the textual evidence and makes the most sense of PCT's place within Peirce's overall system. However, the debate continues and remains lively and fruitful.

3. Three Objections to PCT

This section briefly outlines three common, widely discussed objections to PCT and popular replies to each: the problem of lost facts (Section 3.1), the threat of skepticism (Section 3.2), and the difficulty of separating PCT from deflationism (Section 3.2).

3.1. Lost Facts/Buried Secrets

If PCT says that it is a practical consequence of a hypothesis being true that it would be believed were inquiry carried sufficiently far, it is only natural to wonder whether there are counterexamples to this claim. The most obvious candidates are facts about the distant past or the far side of the universe that are seemingly impossible to discover. Misak's example is how many times Churchill sneezed in 1949—it is prima facie reasonable to think there is some proposition stating the truth of the matter, even though there may be no evidence available either now or in the future that would enable any amount of inquiry to converge upon it. Peirce himself anticipated such examples: "But I may be asked what I have to say to all the minute facts of history, forgotten never to be recovered, to the lost books of the ancients, to the buried secrets. . . . Do these things not really exist because they are hopelessly beyond the reach of our knowledge?" (W3.274, 1878). In response to this concern, Peirce writes: "it is unphilosophical to suppose that, with regard to any given question (which has any clear meaning), investigation would not bring forth a solution of it, if it were carried far enough. Who would have said, a few years ago, that we could ever know of what substances stars are made whose light may have been longer in reaching us than the human race has existed?" (W3.274, 1878).

This is the move that Misak reads as Peirce backing away from simply *asserting* the claim she calls (T–I) to the claim that it is merely a 'regulative assumption of inquiry.'[43] Hookway, as we saw above, sees it as Peirce sidestepping the problem in a slightly different way—by emphasizing what I called the *pragmatic* character of PCT, while distancing himself from a *semantic* characterization.[44]

Lane offers a fuller picture of Peirce's responses to the problem of lost facts, arguing he offered at least three different ones at various points in his career, some of them perhaps surprising and implausible (the labels that follow are mine).[45]

1. Extreme Epistemic Optimism: There simply are no *permanently* buried secrets. Every meaningful question, even if we cannot currently see how it could possibly be answered, *would* be answered, were we to investigate it for long enough.
2. Counterfactual Bravado: "Reality includes both what *would be* represented in the permanently settled beliefs of investigators and what *would have been* represented in those beliefs had investigation been pursued at a time before the relevant evidence disappeared."
3. Deficit Indeterminacy: Wherever there is a meaningful question that no amount of research can ever answer "there is a *lacuna* in the completeness of reality." (CP8.156, c. 1900)[46]

Legg (2014) argues that formulations of the problem of lost facts always involve one of three errors: a logical fallacy (quantifier scope ambiguity); use of hypotheses likely to become truth-apt in the course of inquiry; or a misguided commitment to 'enigmas' (propositions concerning entities essentially undetectable by us) that are meaningless according to the pragmatic maxim. De Waal (1999) also systematically rules out all counterexamples, after an exhaustive consideration of eleven different varieties.

One issue raised by all these responses is the extent to which the plausibility of PCT depends upon the plausibility of the pragmatic maxim, since one way to rule out apparent counterexamples (e.g., as Legg does with 'enigmas') is to claim they lack pragmatic meaning. I return to this issue in Section 3.3.

3.2. The Threat of Skepticism

The argument that PCT has skeptical implications runs roughly as follows. PCT seemingly entails that, practically speaking, knowing that *p* is true amounts to knowing that *p* is indefeasible (in Misak's sense) or that opinion regarding *p* would converge at the end of inquiry (as Hookway puts it). Yet Peirce, as a resolute fallibilist, seemingly concedes that it is not possible for anyone to determine whether such convergence would actually occur. In Misak's terms, we cannot know if or when we have reached the point when our belief has become indefeasible. Misak and Hookway, as we saw above, both interpret Peirce as saying merely that we must *assume* or *hope* that we can reach that point, or that we commit ourselves to this when we assert *p*. How is this compatible with the idea, central to Peirce's early anti-Cartesian works, that knowledge *is* possible and skepticism illegitimate?

Capps (2020) argues not only that Misak's reading of PCT entails skepticism, but also that Misak herself concedes as much: "Misak is explicit that while we can have true beliefs, we cannot know that we have true beliefs: 'we are never in a position to judge whether a belief is true or not' (2000, 57, emphasis added) and 'we cannot know when we have a true belief' (2000, 58). This is a problematic result... [it] goes against the grain of pragmatism, which generally treats skepticism as an almost self-evidently demented position, an attitude that extends as well to claims that directly entail such skepticism."[47]

Capps is correct that Misak ought not to have asserted these claims, for they undoubtedly entail skepticism. The argument is extremely simple:

1. PCT entails that it is not possible to know whether p is true.
2. By the equivalence schema, p is true iff p.
3. Hence, by substitution, PCT entails that it is not possible to know whether p.

Since this argument will work for any proposition p, PCT entails skepticism.

I think it is fair to assume, on Misak's behalf, that she did not mean to endorse skepticism here, or to attribute either a skeptical position or a skepticism-entailing position to Peirce. The context surrounding the passages that Capps quotes suggest that Misak is merely attempting to affirm Peirce's *fallibilism*. Peirce himself describes this as the view that "our knowledge is never absolute but always swims, as it were, in a continuum of uncertainty and of indeterminacy" and that it "only says that people cannot attain absolute certainty concerning questions of fact."[48] In other words, what Peirce and Misak both concede is that *certainty* (at least of a Cartesian sort) is impossible, not that knowledge itself is.

Thus, the real question facing advocates of PCT is whether its embrace of fallibilism—its acknowledgment that we can never be absolutely *certain* that our belief will never be overturned by future inquiry—leads to skepticism. Some argue that it does (e.g., Rorty 1991, 2000; Davidson 2005), while others (e.g., Hookway 2007) suggest that such arguments rely on the very Cartesian assumptions that Peirce was criticizing when he first developed pragmatism.

3.3. The Collapse into Deflationism

Since the turn of the twenty-first century, scholars have increasingly turned to exploring the relationship between PCT and other popular theories of truth, particularly correspondence theory (especially since Lane [2018]) and deflationism/minimalism (especially since Misak [2007]). While I have already briefly described debate over the relationship between correspondence and PCT, I conclude by examining some difficulties arising from the attempt to separate PCT from deflationism.

Some scholars argue that at least certain aspects of PCT, or certain statements of it, are deflationary (see, e.g., Wilson 2020). Many nonspecialists also find it difficult to understand how PCT adds anything over and above a deflationary or minimalist conception of truth. If Misak and Hookway are correct, then PCT eschews semantics, or metaphysics, or both and thus declines to make any substantive claim about either the meaning or the nature of truth, at least according to a traditional understanding of the term 'substantive.'[49] Instead, PCT appears to be a claim about our epistemic practices. For example, it may simply be the observation that when we inquire, we are forced to assume that doing so would produce indefeasible belief and/or convergence among rational inquirers, assuming we inquired long enough and well enough. While such a claim may be true and philosophically significant, it appears misleading at best to label it a 'conception of truth,' at least to those accustomed to the four-part framework mentioned in Section 2.

This line of objection reflects the fact that traditional theories of truth are typically sorted into one of two categories—deflationary/semantic accounts and substantive/metaphysical accounts. Legg (2014) argues that the distinctive methodology involved in PCT makes it impossible to classify in terms of this distinction.

> One might think that the truth theorist is forced to choose between ontological and semantic accounts. Ontological posits or no ontological posits—does this not partition logical space? But the practice-based nature of Peirce's theory of meaning, and its teleological explication of concepts, breaks up this dichotomy. If we hold a belief *p* to be true, Peirce can say more about what this means than merely: *p*, whilst not needing to say that something *exists*, the very existence of which entails *p*. Rather, our holding *p* to be true means that we expect that future inquiry will converge on *p*. (Legg 2014, 207)

The thought behind Legg's response is that for a pragmatist, to elucidate our epistemic practices *is* to elucidate the concepts employed in those practices—inquiry, truth, belief, doubt, etc. In other words, pragmatists reject the basic premise of the objection—the idea of a dichotomy between practices and the concepts implicated in those practices.

Given Misak, Hookway, and numerous others' extensive efforts to establish the distinctive status and methodology involved in PCT, this reply to the objection appears well motivated. Misak (2007) employs it to argue that the trouble with deflationism is that it does not adequately address truth's role as a norm of assertion.[50] However, this approach still poses a rhetorical problem for advocates of PCT, briefly noted at the end of Section 3.1. It suggests that PCT's plausibility depends upon the pragmatic maxim and perhaps too upon the understanding of meaning that underlies it (Peirce's *semiotic* or theory of signs). This makes PCT uniquely difficult to defend and perhaps even for nonspecialists to understand. It means pragmatists cannot sell PCT merely on its own merits, as it were. Rather, we must first convince our opponents to adopt a raft of other theoretical claims regarding the nature of concepts, meaning, practice, etc., before PCT can come to seem fully comprehensible, let alone appealing and correct.[51]

For those sympathetic to PCT, it would therefore be welcome if Peirce had offered some independent motivation for it, as it appears he took himself to be doing in the 1870s.[52] This is one major advantage of Lane's interpretation. First, it takes PCT to be already motivated, developed, and argued for before the maxim ever appeared. Second, it also emphasizes the continuities between PCT and correspondence theories, which might make it somewhat more comprehensible to and appealing for those who share the basic correspondence intuition. That said, Lane's approach still comes with a significant burden of proof, since PCT—even construed as a special type of correspondence theory—still comes with a raft of controversial commitments, in this case to what Peirce called his 'scholastic realism.' Since this too is entangled with his semiotic, it may simply be impossible to make a strong case for PCT without acknowledging that it is merely one aspect of Peirce's larger philosophical system, and thus its plausibility inevitably depends—either partly or wholly—on the plausibility of that system.

Notes

1. See, for example, Short (2017), Hookway (2012).
2. See Brent (1998). Given these difficulties, one cannot always trust summaries of Peirce's views as they appear in introductory and general texts on theories of truth. Blackburn and Simmons ((1999) and Burgess and Burgess (2011), for example, present Peirce's view through the lens of traditional theories, as though Peirce created a straightforward competitor to correspondence, coherence, or deflationary theories. Some texts, such as Kirkham (1992), Wrenn (2015), and Raatikainen (2021), at least mention the distinctive methodological character of Peirce's view, providing a short and broadly accessible summary, while prescinding from the more Byzantine aspects of Peirce's broader philosophical system. This chapter offers something in between an interpretation of PCT and a neutral literature review.
3. I focus here on precursors for Peirce's most widely studied views and remarks on truth from the late 1860s. See Chi-Chun (1995) for a thorough treatment of how Peirce understood truth in his first significant works from the early 1860s.
4. For a full selection of Peirce's apparent endorsements of correspondence, see Lane (2018, 21–22).
5. Legg (2014) writes, "Peirce's explication of truth does not contradict the Correspondence Theory but *goes further* in providing *expectations* from the hypothesis that a statement is true—for instance, that further inquiry will not overturn it" (205). Misak (2018), by contrast, writes: "It should be clear that pragmatism, of any stripe, will be set against versions of the correspondence theory of truth, on which a statement is true if it gets right or mirrors the human-independent world. For that concept of truth introduces an element that is unknowable by human inquirers and believers" (283).
6. See, for example, Almeder (1985, 81–83), who quotes, for example, the following: "If by truth and falsity you mean something not definable in terms of doubts and beliefs in any way, then you are talking of entities of whose existence you can know nothing, and which Ockham's razor would clean shave off" (CP5.416, 1905).
7. As I explain in Section 2, Lane argues that PCT is fully formed by the end of "Fixation," whereas other scholars argue it is only fully expressed in "Ideas."
8. See Burch (2021).
9. For critical discussion, see Wiggins (2004).
10. For more on why I use the label 'expertise' here, see Howat (2021). The label 'pragmatic meaning' does not appear in "Ideas" but is nevertheless the standard terminology employed by scholars and has precedent in remarks such as CP8.320 (1906).
11. I shall follow his lead in focusing solely on the second and third grades of clarity in what follows, on the assumption that the first does not really qualify as a philosophical achievement. Speaking of reality, Peirce writes, 'Every child uses it with perfect confidence, never dreaming that he does not understand it' (W3:271, 1878).
12. It is currently standard, when defining 'realism,' for example, to separate two dimensions: (a) existence—does the disputed entity or class of entities exist?, and (b) mind-independence—is the existence or character of the disputed entity/class independent of

the mind? The answers (a) yes, and (b) no are labeled 'anti-realism' about the relevant entity/class. Notice, however, that this is an unhappy label on Peirce's view, since for him internal realities are fully fledged *realities*—thus, we might say he is a realist about mental phenomena, even though most philosophers would label this same view anti-realist, since it affirms the mind-dependence of the relevant phenomena. Peirce's views on realism also have interesting and controversial consequences for the relationship between existence and reality. See Lane (2018).
13. See Haack (1976) for discussion and an argument against this approach.
14. As Lane (2018) notes, different Peirce scholars offer strikingly different readings of this passage (see 23n20).
15. Cited in Atkins (2016, 1187).
16. See Cory Wright (2012, 92).
17. Based on Crispin Wright (1992, 48).
18. Crispin Wright argues that superassertibility could only be a suitable truth-predicate for a limited range of discourses, namely, those in which the following claim holds: *if p is true, then p is knowable*. See Crispin Wright (1992, 58 75). Price (2010), by contrast, rejects Peirce's account because he thinks it falls into the trap of trying to define truth, which at best is a pointless endeavor and at worst simply leads to metaphysics and representationalism, both of which he rejects.
19. See Lynch (2009, 36 onward) and Howat (2014) for discussion.
20. I say more about this objection, often called 'the problem of lost facts,' in Section 3. For a very detailed discussion of possible counterexamples to PCT and a response to them, see de Waal (1999).
21. It is striking and almost incredible that Almeder (1985), who attempts to bring order to the chaotic debate between thirteen distinct extant interpretations of PCT, contains *no* mention of the grades of clarity and how these might be important to deciding between the interpretations. See especially Misak ([1991] 2004, ch. 1, sect. 7, titled "Definition, Pragmatism, and Truth.")
22. Misak ([1991] 2004, 42). Note that all citations to Misak's book are to the revised and expanded 2004 paperback edition. Peirce himself is explicit about the subjunctive form of the conditionals later in his career, even amending the pragmatic maxim to include reference to it; see, for example, EP2:241, 1903.
23. Ibid., 42–43.
24. Quoted in Misak, ibid., 157. 'NE' refers to Peirce's *The New Elements of Mathematics*.
25. Misak ([1991] 2004, 43).
26. ibid.
27. At times it sounds like Misak is primarily concerned with setting out the most defensible interpretation of PCT, not the one that most accurately captures Peirce's various and confusing remarks about it. In the interest of brevity, I set this concern to one side, but it would provide Misak with a way to sidestep the objections I'm about to raise.
28. Misak (2018, 283).
29. R647, 1910; and CP8.218, 1910.
30. See Wilson (2020) for discussion. For my part, I am inclined to take Peirce's later change of heart seriously, for reasons I set out in Howat (2021).
31. The idea that the opinions of different inquirers would converge upon a single answer the longer they inquired is clearly implied in his description of 'fated agreement.' His *explicit*

uses of the term 'convergence' and its cognates certainly support use of the metaphor in cases of inductive reasoning (CP7.210, 1901; CP2.775, 1902; CP7.110, 1903).
32. Hookway (2002, 49).
33. Though see de Waal (1999, 751), who argues that we should not read Peirce this way, but instead think of the truth and the final opinion as 'synonymous.'
34. Hookway (2007, 623).
35. Perhaps the best evidence of this, as Misak ([1991] 2004) notes on 38, is this passage from an unpublished manuscript: "So what is truth? Kant is sometimes accused of saying that it is correspondence of a predicate with its object. The great analyst was guilty of no such puerility. He calls it a nominal definition, that is to say, a suitable explanation to give to a person who has never before seen the word 'Wahrheit.'" (MS 283, 39, 'assorted pages,' 1905). See Howat (2023) for more in-depth discussion of Hookway's reading.
36. "Almost every proposition of ontological metaphysics is either meaningless gibberish— one word being defined by other words, and they by still others, without any real conception ever being reached—or else is downright absurd" (CP5.423, 1905).
37. Hookway (2012, 69). Misak seems to move in this direction herself in Misak (2007, 70).
38. Hookway (2002, 61).
39. Ibid., 77.
40. Peirce says as much explicitly in R289:13 (1905) when he writes: "The next application I shall make of pragmaticism is to support a principle which might very well be regarded on the contrary, as a support of pragmaticism, and was in fact originally so treated by me, being proved independently in my article of November 1877 [i.e., "Fixation"]."
41. Migotti (1998) also argues for a 'double aspect' interpretation of Peirce's view, though he differs on key points from Lane in his reading of "Fixation," for example. See Lane (2018, 24n22).
42. Lane (2018, 14).
43. I have argued elsewhere (Howat 2013) that there is a problem with this approach—namely, that Peirce rejected outright Kant's distinction between regulative and constitutive principles, which seems to be the very distinction on which Misak is relying: "Kant's distinction of regulative and constitutive principles is unsound" (CP3.215, 1880). I also argue, however, for an alternative reading of 'regulative' that draws upon what is now popularly called 'hinge epistemology' (see, e.g., Coliva 2015).
44. Atkins (2011) makes a similar move using slightly different terminology, emphasizing instead that propositions stating putatively lost facts would have to be *assertible* in order to count as genuine counterexamples.
45. More accurately, I chose them, but was inspired to do so by Misak (in the case of 'counterfactual bravado,' who in turn takes the phrase from Jardine [1986]) and Lane (in the case of 'deficit indeterminacy').
46. All citations from Lane (2018, 55–56).
47. Capps (2020, 477).
48. Quotations from CP1.171, 1893; and CP1.147, 1893; respectively.
49. The two most common ways to formulate deflationism about truth are (1) there is no property of truth or (2) property of truth is nonsubstantive. Most readings of PCT see it as consistent with one of these claims. But see Howat (2015) for discussion of how we should interpret 'substantive.'
50. I argue for something similar in Howat (2018).

51. Aikin and Talisse (2018) contains an extensive and very useful discussion of this problem, which they dub 'metaphilosophical creep.'
52. See Note 40.

Bibliography

Aikin, Scott, and Talisse, Robert. 2018. *Pragmatism, Pluralism, and the Nature of Philosophy.* New York: Routledge.

Almeder, Robert. 1985. "Peirce's Thirteen Theories of Truth." *Transactions of the Charles S. Peirce Society* 21, no. 1 (Winter): 77–94.

Atkins, Richard Kenneth. 2011. "This Proposition Is Not True: C. S. Peirce and the Liar Paradox." *Transactions of the Charles S. Peirce Society* 47, no. 4 (Fall): 421–444.

Atkins, Richard Kenneth. 2016. "Peirce on Facts and True Propositions." *British Journal for the History of Philosophy* 24, no. 6: 1176–1192.

100000Blackburn, Simon, and Simmons, Keith. 1999. *Truth.* Oxford: Oxford University Press.

Brent, Joseph. 1993. *Charles Sanders Peirce: A Life.* Bloomington and Indianapolis, IN: Indiana University Press.

Burch, Robert. 2022. "Charles Sanders Peirce." In *The Stanford Encyclopedia of Philosophy,* edited by Edward N. Zalta (Summer 2022) . https://plato.stanford.edu/archives/sum2022/entries/peirce/.

Burgess, Alexis, and Burgess, John. 2011 *"Truth."* Princeton, NJ: Princeton University Press, 4–5.

Capps, John. 2020. "A Common-Sense Pragmatic Theory of Truth." *Philosophia* 48, no. 2: 463–481.

Chi-Chun, Chiu. 1995. "The Notion of Truth in Peirce's Earliest System." *Transactions of the Charles S. Peirce Society,* 31, no. 2 (Spring): 394–414.

Coliva, Annalisa. 2015. *Extended Rationality: A Hinge Epistemology.* Palgrave–Macmillan.

Davidson, Donald. 2001. *Subjective, Intersubjective, Objective: Philosophical Essays Volume 3.* Oxford: Clarendon Press.

Davidson, Donald. 2005. *Truth, Language and History.* Oxford: Clarendon Press.

De Waal, Cornelis. 1999. "Eleven Challenges to the Pragmatic Theory of Truth." *Transactions of the Charles S. Peirce Society* 35, no. 4 (Fall): 748–766.

Forster, Paul. 2011. *Peirce and the Threat of Nominalism.* New York: Cambridge University Press.

Haack, Susan. 1976. "The Pragmatist Theory of Truth." *The British Journal for the Philosophy of Science* 27, no. 3: 231–249.

Hookway, Christopher. 2002. *Truth, Rationality, and Pragmatism: Themes from Peirce.* Cambridge: Cambridge University Press.

Hookway, Christopher. 2007. "The Inaugural Address: Fallibilism and the Aim of Inquiry." In *Aristotelian Society Supplementary Volume,* vol. 81: 1–22.

Hookway, Christopher. 2012. *The Pragmatic Maxim: Essays on Peirce and Pragmatism.* Oxford: Oxford University Press.

Howat, Andrew. 2013. "Regulative Assumptions, Hinge Propositions and the Peircean Conception of Truth." *Erkenntnis* 78 no. 2 (April): 451–468.

Howat, Andrew. 2014. "Prospects for Peircean Truth." *Canadian Journal of Philosophy* 44, no. 3–4: 365–387.

Howat, Andrew. 2015. "Hookway's Peirce on Assertion & Truth." *Transactions of the Charles S. Peirce Society* 51, no. 4 (Fall): 419.

Howat, Andrew. 2018. "Constituting Assertion: A Pragmatist Critique of Horwich's 'Truth.'" *Synthese* 195, no. 3: 935–954.
Howat, Andrew. 2021. "Pragmatism and Correspondence." *Philosophia* 49 no. 2 (April): 685–704.
Howat, A. 2023. "Hookway on Peirce on Truth" in *Pragmatic Reason: Christopher Hookway and the American Philosophical Tradition*, edited by Robert Talisse, Paniel Cárdenas, and Daniel Herbert, 42–54. New York: Taylor and Francis.
James, William. [1907] 2014. *Pragmatism*. Cambridge: Cambridge University Press.
Jardine, Nicholas. 1986. *The Fortunes of Inquiry*. Oxford: Oxford University Press.
Kirkham, Richard. 1992. *Theories of Truth: A Critical Introduction*. Cambridge, MA: MIT Press.
Lane, Robert. 2018. *Peirce on Realism and Idealism*. Cambridge: Cambridge University Press.
Legg, Catherine. 2014. "Charles Peirce's Limit Concept of Truth: Peirce's Limit Concept of Truth." *Philosophy Compass* 9 no. 3 (March): 204–213.
Lynch, Michael. 2009. *Truth as One and Many*. New York: Clarendon Press.
Migotti, Mark. 1998. "Peirce's Double-Aspect Theory of Truth." *Canadian Journal of Philosophy Supplementary Volume* 24: 75–108.
Misak, Cheryl. [1991] 2004. *Truth and the End of Inquiry: A Peircean Account of Truth*. Expanded pbk. ed. Oxford Philosophical Monographs. Oxford and New York: Clarendon Press and Oxford University Press.
Misak, Cheryl. 2007. "Pragmatism and Deflationism." In *New Pragmatists*, edited by Cheryl Misak, 68–90. Oxford: Oxford University Press.
Misak, Cheryl. 2018. "There Can Be No Difference Anywhere That Doesn't Make a Difference Elsewhere." *Transactions of the Charles S. Peirce Society* 54, no. 3 (Summer): 417–429.
Peirce, Charles Sanders. 1857–1914. Manuscripts held at the Houghton Library of Harvard University, as identified in Richard Robin. 1967. *Annotated Catalogue of the Papers of Charles S. Peirce*. Amherst: University of Massachusetts Press. And in Richard Robin. 1971. "The Peirce Papers: A Supplementary Catalogue." *Transactions of the Charles S. Peirce Society* 7, no. 1 (Winter): 37–57. (Referred to as R[catalogue#]:[sheet#]; with RL for letters and RS for supplement.)
Peirce, Charles Sanders. 1982– . *Writings of Charles S. Peirce: A Chronological Edition*. 7 vols. to date. Edited by The Peirce Edition Project. Bloomington, IN: Indiana University Press. (Referred to as W.)
Peirce, Charles Sanders. 1931–1958. *The Collected Papers of Charles Sanders Peirce*. 8 vols. Vols. 1–6 edited by Charles Hartshorne and Paul Weiss. Vols. 7–8 edited by Arthur W. Burks. Cambridge, MA: Harvard University Press. (Referred to as CP.)
Peirce, Charles Sanders. 1992–1998. *The Essential Peirce: Selected Philosophical Writings*, 2 vols. Vol. 1 edited by Nathan Houser and Christian Kloesel. Vol. 2 edited by the Peirce Edition Project. Bloomington: Indiana University Press. (Referred to as EP.)
Peirce, Charles Sanders. 2014. *Illustrations of the Logic of Science*. Edited by Cornelis de Waal. Chicago: Open Court. (Referred to as ILS.)
Peirce, Charles Sanders. 1976. *The New Elements of Mathematics*, 4 vols. in 5. Edited by Carolyn Eisele. The Hague: Mouton. (Referred to as NEM.)
Price, Huw. 2003. "Truth as Convenient Friction." *Journal of Philosophy* 100, no. 4:167–190.
Price, Huw. 2010. "Truth as Convenient Friction." In *Naturalism and Normativity*, edited by Mario de Caro and David Macarthur, 100: 167–190. New York: Columbia University Press.
Price, Huw. 2013. *Expressivism, Pragmatism, and Representationalism*. Cambridge University Press.

Raatikainen, Panu. 2021. "Truth and Theories of Truth". In *The Cambridge Handbook of the Philosophy of Language*, edited by Piotr Stalmaszczyk. Cambridge: Cambridge University Press.

Rescher, Nicholas. 1973. *The Coherence Theory of Truth*. Oxford: Oxford University Press.

Rorty, Richard. 1991. *Objectivity, Relativism, and Truth*. New York: Cambridge University Press.

Rorty, Richard. 2000. "Universality and Truth." In *Rorty and His Critics*, edited by Robert Brandom. Malden, MA: Blackwell, 1–30.

Short, T. L. 2017. "The 1903 Maxim." *Transactions of the Charles S. Peirce Society* 53, no. 3 (Summer): 345–373.

Wiggins, David. 2004. "Reflections on Inquiry and Truth Arising from Peirce's Method for the Fixation of Belief." In *The Cambridge Companion to Peirce*, edited by Cheryl Misak. Cambridge: Cambridge University Press, 87–126.

Wilson, Aaron Bruce. 2020. "Interpretation, Realism, and Truth: Is Peirce's Second Grade of Clearness Independent of the Third?" *Transactions of the Charles S. Peirce Society* 56, no. 3 (Summer): 349.

Wrenn, Chase. 2015. *Truth*. Cambridge, MA: Polity.

Wright, Cory. 2012. "Is Pluralism About Truth Inherently Unstable?" *Philosophical Studies* 159, no. 1: 89–105.

Wright, Crispin. 1992. *Truth and Objectivity*. Cambridge, MA: Harvard University Press.

CHAPTER 27

PEIRCE AND RELIGION

GARY SLATER

This chapter unfolds in three sections.[1] The first section engages Peirce's own life, in terms of both his own life of faith and his writings that are most relevant to religion. The second section traces the legacy of Peirce and religion, with particular interest in the emergence in the 1970s and 1980s of a coterie of thinkers who are distinctively Peircean even as they diverge from one another and have generated separate followings. This shift, whose leading figures are Robert C. Neville, Robert S. Corrington, Peter Ochs, and Michael Raposa, has left a lasting and permanent mark on the field. The third section looks at the current state of the field and speculates on emerging developments.

1. Peirce on Religion

Although Peirce was not primarily a religious writer, his work referred consistently to religion, a tendency that became more pronounced toward the last decades of his life. A few influences stand out when it comes to the formation of Peirce's own religious life.[2] An obvious influence, in spiritual matters as in so much else, was Peirce's father, Benjamin Peirce, whose conviction that the human mind was capable of knowing the world took on the character of an article of faith. Another influence was Peirce's first wife, Melusina ("Zina") Fay, who was responsible for Peirce's move to the Episcopal Church and away from the Unitarian Church of his youth. Fay was a convinced Trinitarian, having authored a feminist interpretation of the Trinity, and her Trinitarian convictions speak to Peirce's own long-standing obsession with triads. Still another influence was that of Harvard theology professor Frederic Dan Huntington, who employed a Pauline method to trace out the practical consequences of religious beliefs and thereby potentially repair errant practices. These influences, all of which date from Peirce's early years, manifested themselves across his life. This was the case in spite of—or perhaps because of—the personal, professional, and financial disruptions that befell Peirce in the 1880s and 1890s.

Disruptions aside, Peirce maintained a consistent, if not exactly orthodox, Christian faith throughout his life. His religious life was concerned less with doctrinal orthodoxy than with acting on the basis of a vague conservative sentiment. Relatedly, Peirce sharply distinguished religion from theology, actively disdaining the latter while consistently expressing support for the former. Peirce's objections to theology were intellectual as well as moral. Intellectually, Peirce found theology to be hidebound, dogmatic, and essentially unscientific. Writing of theologians, for example, Peirce claimed, "Nothing can be more unscientific than the attitude of minds who are trying to confirm themselves in early beliefs" (CP6.3, 1898).[3] The moral dimension of such dogmatism, in Peirce's view, is intolerance, such that "all the creeds that ever were made were made with a view of cutting somebody off from the church" (R865.3–7b, c. 1897). As for *religion* in contrast to theology: whether conceived in terms of moral sentiments or of historical communities, Peirce took a much more positive view. This view also happened to intersect with some of his most significant innovations, particularly during the final three decades of his life. Understanding this point requires some closer attention to a few of Peirce's most religiously significant compositions.

It is no longer an interesting question to ask whether Peirce's texts on religion are integral to Peirce's thought. Decades of scholarship from many quarters have established links to other areas of Peirce's thought, such that one sees in these writings innovations in logic, metaphysics, and even mathematics that both shed light on Peirce's other writings and can be used for engagement with religion and theology. From the 1890s onward, Peirce wrote increasingly about religion, with three groups of writings being especially important: the first *Monist* series of 1891–1893, the 1898 lectures in Cambridge, and the "Neglected Argument for the Reality of God" of 1908. Written at different moments for different contexts, and with different goals in each case, these texts are glimpses within an intellectual trajectory that was unfolding but continuous.[4]

Peirce's *Monist* series was published between 1891 and 1893, and it consisted of five articles: "The Architecture of Theories," "The Doctrine of Necessity Examined," "The Law of Mind," "Man's Glassy Essence," and "Evolutionary Love." A sixth article was intended, on a general sketch of a synechistic theory of the universe, but it was never finished. Although "Evolutionary Love" is the most overtly religious of the five essays, the entire series reflects a distinctively religious turn in Peirce's life and thought. Published at a difficult time for Peirce personally, these essays read as the words of a man imbued with a heightened sense of spiritual weight beyond every word. Featuring some of the most cosmically speculative material Peirce ever wrote, the *Monist* texts represent the application of Peirce's mathematics of continuity and statistics to cosmological, evolutionary, and religious ends. They also introduce his metaphysics of synechism, which asserts the principle of continuity as the very truth of life, thought, and reality. With debts to Friedrich Schelling, to Henry James Sr.'s writings on Emanuel Swedenborg, and to the Anglican Christian world in which Peirce spent his adult life, these texts hold that approaches to theories should be holistic, that is, architectonic and mutually supporting.

Notably, the cosmology of the 1891–1893 *Monist* series is explicitly evolutionary—and explicitly religious. As Peirce argued: "a genuine evolutionary philosophy, that is, one that makes the principle of growth a primordial element of the universe, is so far from being antagonistic to the idea of a personal creator that it is really inseparable from that idea" (W8:155, 1892). To the religious dimension of his evolutionism Peirce gave the name "evolutionary love," in which love, "recognizing germs of loveliness in the hateful, gradually warms it into life, and makes it lovely" (W8:186, 1893). The sort of evolution described here, which Peirce called *agapism*, entails that the chance variations by which biological organisms evolve are but one part of a universal tendency for new forms of regularity to emerge within cosmological development, such that in order for chance and actuality to interact in an identifiably developmental way, there must be a third principle of mediation that, across infinite time, infuses teleological purpose into the process.

Several years later, Peirce would write of some of the *Monist* series that it represented the "crudest of my struggles" with the notion of continuity, "regretted as soon as published" (CP6.182,1911). Some of Peirce's contemporaries saw these texts as evidence of mental and emotional instability. Several subsequent commentators on Peirce, however, have treated these texts more sympathetically, and Michael Raposa has convincingly argued that they form a critical part of the development of Peirce's work from its earlier innovations in the logic of relations to the insights that would come to fruition in his "Neglected Argument" in 1908.[5] Viewed from a contemporary standpoint, Peirce's *Monist* texts read as compelling, creative, and essential material for understanding the religious dimension of his thought. They do, however, lack a proper balance between their metaphysical and theological claims. As an example, Peirce holds that a genuine evolutionary philosophy implies a personal creator (W8:155, 1892), yet Peirce here was unable to clarify whether such a personal creator ought to be *grounded* in synechism or vice versa. To the extent that Peirce is suggesting the former, this is what Peter Ochs has called Peirce's "normative pragmatism," or his construal of his architectonic as an exclusive method for interpreting all claims, including those of theology.

Peirce's 1898 Cambridge Lectures comprise his second set of core texts on religion.[6] These lectures were organized by William James as a benefit to his friend; it says something about Peirce's toxic reputation at the time that even with James's support, Harvard University would not allow the lectures to be given on the university's campus. The lectures distinguish Peirce's views from James's, being in some sense Peirce's response to James's *Will to Believe*.[7] In this regard the first of these lectures, "Philosophy and the Conduct of Life," is of particular importance. In contrast with James's view that moral theories ought to inform public decision-making, here Peirce defends a version of conservative sentimentalism that refuses, at least for vitally important decisions, to base practical conduct upon abstract theory. For Peirce, conservative sentimentalism is "the doctrine that great respect should be paid to the natural judgments of the sensible heart" (CP6.292, 1893), emphasizing guidance to conduct via sentiment, as well as trust in the rightness of an outcome in the long run. There is a bit of the old Benjamin Peirce confidence at work here, not to mention a reflection of a lifelong conservative worldview.[8] Most of all, however, this stance reflects Peirce's sharp distinction between theology (abstract ideas formulated for the purpose of excluding people from the religious community) and religion (practical, grounded in sentiment and tradition, and concerned with cultivating moral virtues).[9]

That there should be a religious dimension to Peirce's lecture on the conduct of life is not surprising. What is interesting here, rather, is how Peirce's stance on conservative sentimentalism and religion connect with other areas of his thought. The 1898 lectures should not be understood as Peirce's final word on religion or on anything else, however. As Raposa has pointed out, the separation between theory and practice here was a marked departure from the close theory–practice affinities of "The Fixation of Belief" of twenty years prior; this is just another reflection of Peirce's tendency to revise his ideas.[10] Yet the links between religious thought and Peirce's other notions are no less valuable for being in flux. Of particular note is the link between the 1898 lectures and Peirce's views on vagueness and critical commonsensism. Regarding vagueness, Peirce believed that religious sentiments were meaningful but essentially vague. Far from being a problem, Peirce saw such vagueness as a salutary feature within religious language, since it could avoid getting bogged down in contradictions and absurdities while remaining a valuable guide for the conduct of life. As for critical commonsensism, one sees in Peirce's defense of sentimental conservatism an emerging commonsense position—with the belief in God included as a commonsense belief—that continued to characterize Peirce's thought after 1900.[11]

The final text that is crucial for understanding Peirce's religious thought is "A Neglected Argument for the Reality of God," which Peirce published in the *Hibbert* journal in 1908, along with some explanatory comments that were composed after publication—the Additament. The "Neglected Argument" is undoubtedly the text from Peirce that has received the most sustained attention from commentators.[12] Although the essay is justified as a major source of insight on Peircean religious thought, it is also rather confounding. One source of its difficulty is that, its title notwithstanding, the piece is not necessarily about the reality of God. As Richard Kenneth Atkins puts it, a "more a propos title might be the clunkier 'A Defense of the Rational Acceptability of Certain Lines of Thought That Lead to Belief in the Reality of God.'"[13] Atkins's suggested alternative title is well taken, yet both the structure of the text and its relationship with other areas of Peircean thought remain elusive. These issues bear exploring.

Regarding the structure of the "Neglected Argument," the first thing to note is that the essay refers not to a single argument, but rather to three distinct arguments: these are the humble argument (HA), neglected argument (NA), and scientific argument (SA). The three arguments are nested; that is, they work outward from one another in such a way that what comes later builds on what came before. Puzzling to the uninitiated, the structure here appears more elegant when considered in light of the broader movements of Peirce's thought. For example, Douglas Anderson has shown how the three arguments parallel the categories, with the HA relating to feeling (firstness), the NA to willing (secondness), and the SA to thinking (thirdness).[14] As with Peirce's other writings, the "Neglected Argument" relies heavily upon esoteric terminology. With respect to the HA, the first of the three arguments, the pivotal term here is "musement," which refers to a kind of musing, that is, a free play of mind. In Peirce's telling within the

HA, musement leads an inquirer gently and without force toward an aesthetically rich hypothesis as to the truth of God's reality. This may seem like a heavy result for such a light and frothy process, yet it is important to understand that, for Peirce, musement bears a strongly aesthetic dimension, and aesthetics is held to underpin both ethics and logic.[15] As to what makes the HA "humble," David Rohr notes that an unpublished manuscript (R905, 1908) alternatively labels the argument "Unpretentious," suggesting that the humility of the HA contrasts with the pretension that accompanies typical theological arguments; in Rohr's words, "Rather than *pretentiously* offering a human argumentation as an adequate basis for belief in God's reality, Peirce *humbly* invites readers to regularly and freely contemplate the universe, confident that meditation on God's great poem constitutes a 'postern entrance to the house of God'" (R905, 1908).[16] The upshot of the HA is that through one's musement one comes to wonder, with increasing expansiveness, how the beauty and diversity of the world's forms can be possible. In turn, this gives rise to the recognition that to have the experience of God's reality is the highest aesthetic good one can proclaim.

The second argument in the article is the NA, that is, the neglected argument proper. The NA holds that, having had the feeling of God's reality, one can then venture an act of abduction explaining the cause and sustainer of the world. Peirce argued that the logical structure by which the scientist—whose inquiries seek different objects and also play out in a much more controlled setting—and the muser experience their respective "Eureka!" moments is the same, namely, abductive. As Peirce put it: "Any normal man who considers the three Universes in the light of the hypothesis of God's Reality, and pursues that line of reflection in scientific singleness of heart, will come to be stirred to the depths of his nature by the beauty of the idea and by its august practicality" (CP6.467, 1908). Commentators from Christopher Hookway to Raposa have criticized Peirce's assumption that "any normal man" would come to the same conclusion as himself.[17] Yet as what John E. Smith has described as a "model in which both direct experience and argument are related in an intelligible and convincing way," the NA works.[18]

The third argument is the scientific argument, or SA, which looks at the consequences within one's life that follow from one's adoption of the belief in God's reality. The SA speaks to the pragmatic point that, upon arriving at a belief in God, one's actions will come to be shaped in such a way that helps to justify the goodness of that belief. In a critical assessment of Peirce's essay, J. Caleb Clanton arrives at the view that Peirce's three arguments ultimately do not make a convincing case as proof for the reality of God. As a consolation, Clanton allows the possibility that "Peirce, more modestly, means something like the following: if someone, after musing, is caused to believe that God is real, then that particular person is warranted in believing that God is real."[19] Clanton's remarks echo Atkins's suggestions about an alternative title that emphasizes the rational acceptability of certain lines of thought, rather than a formal proof of anything.

In order to appreciate the significance of Peirce's "Neglected Argument," it helps to consider the text alongside some of the fundamental preoccupations of Peirce's thought. For example, the essay speaks to Peirce's logic of abduction, or hypothesis. As Hookway has noted, Peirce's lifelong interest in the logic of abduction is evident both prior to the arrival of a God hypothesis, in the HA, and also in speculating as to the consequences of the belief.[20] Also evident are Peirce's continued interest in continuity and the pragmatic association between belief and the formation of habit. The "Neglected Argument" also resonates with new and emerging areas within his thought, specifically Peirce's turn toward pragmaticism and his existential graphs. Reflecting Peirce's latter-day turn toward pragmaticism, one does not in the "Neglected Argument" find an assumption that modes of inquiry must refer to a single architectonic; one instead finds a defense of analytical pluralism. One sees this change at work in the recognition that the hypothesis of God's reality does not arise out of pragmatic practice or reflection, but out in the world, in life, in the community—in a word, elsewhere.

As for the existential graphs (EGs), these can be understood as a backdrop to the mature semeiotic that is expressed in the "Neglected Argument." Not discussed directly within the "Neglected Argument," the EGs constitute an iconic logic of relations that was designed to capture the movement of thought in diagrammatic form. In explaining the EGs in manuscript 280, for example, which dates from 1905–1906, Peirce wrote of a dynamic interaction between "Graphist" and "interpreter" that directly prefigured the arguments of the "Neglected Argument." As Peirce put it in that manuscript, the EGs feature a "sheet of assertion" that is a "mirror of the interpreter's mind, and through that it is the sign of what the Graphist authorizes" (R280.29e, c. 1905). As for the universe, this is "simply the collective whole of all things to the assertion of whose existence the Graphist interposes no veto, or extends a positive permission" (R280.29e, c. 1905). As to how such claims bear on the "Neglected Argument," Kathleen Hull puts it well as follows: "Diagrams become significant dramatis personae since Peircean mathematics includes the conjuring up, in imagination, of mathematical objects in the form of diagrams, or signs. . . . Peirce maintained that diagrams have an effect on their interpreters."[21] The brilliance of the EGs as expressions of an iconic logic of relations is that they are able to bring thinking-as-object and thinking-as-process as close together as possible in such a way as to generate insights not only about thinking itself, but also about the objects to which thinking refers.[22] This is an innovation that bears fruit when one looks at how Peirce's thought supports the study of religion as a cultural object.

2. Trajectories of Religious Studies and Theology Derived from Peirce

With one important exception, the noteworthy discussions of Peirce and religion have taken place since his death, with the richest commentary emerging only within the past two generations. The exception was Josiah Royce. Royce had attended and been inspired by Peirce's 1898 lectures, which profoundly influenced several of Royce's best-known writings. Most prominent among the latter is Royce's 1913 masterwork, *The Problem of Christianity*, in which Royce employed a theological method based on "Peircean premises," including the interpretive nature of experience and the essentially social character of interpretation.[23] Atkins has drawn from Peirce's influence on this text a nonanthropocentric insight, in that, for Royce, "just as Peirce had maintained that the community of inquirers must be regarded as embracing all (not just human) rational life with whom we might come into mediate or immediate intellectual relation and must be regarded as extending beyond all bounds, so too the project of Christianity must be regarded as embracing not just humans but anyone loyal to the cause that Christianity endorses."[24] Atkins's contribution notwithstanding, it is fair to say that a sufficient study of the fruitfulness of the relationship between Peirce and Royce has not yet been undertaken.

In the decades following Peirce's death in 1914, his writings on religion were at first unavailable, and then they were unfashionable. It is not that they were ignored entirely—the *Collected Papers* do, after all, designate the second part of 1935's Book VI to Peirce's thoughts on religion. It is rather that, once they became more available, these writings were perceived as being separate from what was really worthwhile in Peirce's thought: his writings on logic, science, pragmatism. Charles Hartshorne, for example, wrote in 1941 of Peirce's religious writings that they were not only inconsistent, but also represented a failure to sufficiently break beyond traditional notions of God.[25] In 1951, Thomas Goudge argued that there were really "two Peirces," severing and essentially denigrating Peirce's religious writings and other speculative materials relative to the rest of his output.[26] A year later, W. B. Gallie described the intensely religious 1901–1903 *Monist* series in particular as the "black sheep or white elephant" within Peirce's thought.[27] Such views are indicative of the general lack of esteem in which Peirce's religious writings were held during the mid-twentieth century. To be sure, enduring commentaries did begin to emerge as the century progressed; these included valuable work in 1967 from Vincent Potter[28] and in 1984 from Donna M. Orange.[29] Yet valuable as these materials might be, there is a sense of them as being sporadic lights in the darkness, flashes of brilliance against Cimmerian darkness, to echo James.

The situation began to change in the 1970s, with credit belonging to the scholarship and teaching of John E. Smith. Smith taught in Yale University's philosophy department from 1952 to 1991, and over a long career as an essayist, scholar of American thought and religion, and teacher, he lived out his convictions that philosophy is a publicly relevant pursuit, that pragmatism is a sophisticated manifestation of this conviction, and that religion is an integral part of pragmatism. Smith's career overlapped with that of other prominent resuscitators of pragmatism as Cornel West, Richard Rorty, and Jeffrey Stout, although Smith took a more sustained interest in Peirce than did these other figures. More important for present purposes, Smith passed these convictions on to his students, some of whom would go on to become leading commentators on Peirce and religion.[30] In addition to his contribution to the revival of pragmatism's academic fortunes or the content of his scholarship, it is his cultivation of a community of inquiry across generations that represents a major bequest of Smith.

Peirce-influenced commentators on religion and theology have undoubtedly come to constitute a community; in fact, such commentators now encompass multiple communities. A signal moment within this shift was the 1989 Peirce Sesquicentennial Congress at Harvard, which featured contributions from a rich set of scholars including Wayne Proudfoot, Hermann Deuser, and John Deely. The congress also included contributions from the scholars who might be called the big four of Peirce and religion: Robert C. Neville, Peter Ochs, Robert S. Corrington, and Michael Raposa.

Neville, Ochs, Corrington, and Raposa are the most significant commentators on Peirce and religion since Peirce's death, and the shift toward self-consciously communal inquiry initiated by Smith has been made permanent thanks to them. Granted, there are strong differences between these figures, and their respective followers do not always engage significantly with one another. For example, Ochs identifies with postliberal theology, whereas the other three are, each in his own way, liberal.[31] Yet each has done significant work with what Doug Anderson has called the "strands of a system"[32] given in Peirce's writings and touted by the likes of Smith: ground Peirce's thoughts on religion in relation to his other key ideas (Raposa), find and apply rabbinic semiotics as a complementary tradition to Peircean pragmatism (Ochs), appropriate the fractured or discordant elements of Peirce within broader explorations of loss and division (Corrington), and draw selectively from Peirce toward the constructive articulation of a philosophical theological system whose scope and consistency Peirce himself could not attain (Neville). Yet even in these figures' divergences and those of their followers lies a basic and important point, which is that there are now several multigenerational networks that attest to the breadth and enduring relevance of Peirce to religion. Given this fact, even the differences between the four can be directed toward productive contrasts relative to the common backdrop that Peirce represents.[33]

Proceeding broadly from most to least "Peircean," the first figure to discuss is Michael Raposa. Perhaps Raposa's greatest single achievement has been to convince the wider community of Peirce scholars that Peirce's religious writings are continuous with and integral to the other areas of his thought. Yet Raposa's wider research agenda, which he labels theosemiotic, goes beyond Peirce. Theosemiotic explores Peirce's claim that all the world is perfused with signs and that, theologically speaking, it may be perceived as something like "God's great poem." In terms of Peirce's corpus, Raposa has argued that Peirce's metaphysics of continuity is closely bound up with his "Neglected Argument for the Reality of God" and that the relation of semiotic activity in its fully aesthetic, ethical, and logical dimensions refers to God's reality, and hence is theosemiotic. Theosemiotic manifests itself most notably in two places: the final chapter of Raposa's 1989 book and the eponymous 2020 book.[34] These two books are by turns expository and constructive. The 1989 book remains one of the most helpful guides to religiously relevant Peircean texts, from Peirce's youthful encounters in the 1850s with Friedrich Schiller and Immanuel Kant to his 1908 "Neglected Argument." In his 2020 book, Raposa sums up the promise of theosemiotic by claiming that it "expedites the task of understanding what makes a community worth caring about" and "facilitates comparative work in theology and religion studies."[35] Theosemiotic comes across as less independent from Peircean prerogatives than does Och's scriptural reasoning, Corrington's ecstatic naturalism, or Neville's philosophical theology. Nevertheless, it makes constructive contributions in its interest in trans-species ethics, its programmatic character, and its ecumenical attitude toward figures and movements from across tradition and time period, including liberation theology, scholastic thought, and the mysticism of Simone Weil.

Peter Ochs is a founding figure of scriptural reasoning, which he formed in 1996 along with David Ford and Daniel Hardy. As a form of interfaith dialogue, scriptural reasoning has had considerable success both within the academy and in the wider public.[36] Scriptural reasoning offers a space in which Jews, Christians, and Muslims can come together and interpret each other's sacred texts without imposing a single mode of interpretation, even as the possibility for shared understandings is retained. As to Ochs's take on Peirce, Ochs is unique in demonstrating Peircean logic of vagueness as applied to specific religious utterances or passages. Ochs is also unique in how he draws from the EGs, which for him represent a way to map patterns of inquiry. For Ochs, the prototypical "existential graph" is scripture; as he puts it, "Scripture is the prototype as well as the primary book of instruction in the practice of repair, which Peirce calls 'existential graphs' . . . meant to perform, as well as represent, their subject matter."[37] Ochs's application of Peirce's EGs indicates his preference for Peirce's late-period turn toward pragmaticism. For Ochs, the vagueness and performative instrumentality of Peircean pragmaticism, including the "Neglected Argument," call for complementary communal norms that take the form of a logic of scripture. Although Ochs himself is quite careful about the extent to which these practices can be applied beyond scriptural communities, as well as suspicious of overtly metaphysical readings of Peircean categories, the logical innovations his work employs—interrogating errant binarism, reparative reasoning, a continuum between diagnosis and repair—offer a set of materials that suggest rich applications. These applications include interfaith dialogue and, as attested in Ochs's 2019 book, *Religion without Violence*, religious peacebuilding.

Robert S. Corrington is the founder of a school of thought called ecstatic naturalism, which has been the subject of recurring conferences since 2011 and has inspired several protégés. One such protégé is Leon Niemoczynski, who describes Corrington's project as "a metaphysical hybrid of the pragmatic and Continental philosophical traditions," in which "nature's transcendent aspect can and does afford religious experience, but transcendence is fully natural, and so the possibility for transcendence is deeply embedded within nature."[38] Corrington presents his project as a metaphysical alternative to perspectives that are too dependent either upon a brute descriptive materialism or upon an honorific process cosmology. In the ecstatic naturalist vision, nature is the dynamic entirety, the vast reality that creates itself out of itself alone. Corrington calls the religious picture that extends from this metaphysical fore-structure of ecstatic naturalism deep pantheism. In deep pantheism, God or gods exist within an evolutionary process of emergence in nature with no transcendent reference whatsoever. The method of deep pantheism is what Corrington calls ordinal phenomenology, which "uses the ordinal concepts that are also pertinent to the metaphysics of ecstatic naturalism, the 'frame' within which deep pantheism thrives and functions."[39] Regarding appropriations of Peirce, Corrington draws from Peirce's three categories, his ontology of signs, and the "depth-field that is linked to the under-consciousness of nature" to argue that there are "sacred folds" between semiotic categories that serve as the location for a religious encounter.[40] The possibility of the sacred thus comes from nature rather than any human projects or purposes, which are provisional. Corrington's work emphasizes discontinuity and tragedy in a way that is distinctive. Concepts drawn from psychoanalysis make their way into Corrington's writings, as does a unique emphasis on aesthetics that is quite compelling. In the ambiguity of its poetry and the association of a deep naturalism with discontinuity and tragedy, ecstatic naturalism has tendencies that diverge from those typically associated with pragmatism. Indeed, Corrington's work is a rare example in the field in its providing a sense of what is *not* possible, or of the futility of so many plans and projects. Taken too far, it is defeating. Yet as a kind of philosophical theological palette cleanser or a corrective to facile optimism, it is bracing.

Robert C. Neville is among the most encompassing and ambitious system-builders writing in the early twenty-first century, not just in the field of Peirce and religion, but anywhere. Neville's public roles have included United Methodist pastor, dean of the School of Theology and professor in the Department of Philosophy at Boston University, and president of the Metaphysical Society of America, the American Academy of Religion, the International Society for Chinese Philosophy, and the Charles S. Peirce Society. A key contribution from pragmatism to Neville's system lies in offering what Hermann Deuser, Hans Joas, and Matthias Jung have called the "conceptual foundations of the theological guidance that is required to live one's life well in the face of the ultimate realities," doing so within a vision that connects "symbol theory, ontology, epistemology, existential philosophy, and practical theology on the basis of a Peircean approach to semiotics."[41] Peirce's influence is observable in Neville's understanding of interpretation, in the logic of vagueness, in the hypothetical nature of inquiry (including metaphysics), and in the benefits of framing one's ideas as a nonreductive system. Yet Neville's project neither begins nor ends in Peirce, and Peircean exposition or even application is a mere solar system in the galactic spaces of Neville's philosophical theology. Equally important to Neville's thought are Paul Tillich's existentialist theology, a variety of Chinese philosophers, Alfred North Whitehead's process cosmology, the task of comparative theology, and Neville's own innovative argument for creation ex nihilo. Neville's most important recent work is his *Philosophical Theology* trilogy, which harmonizes the threads developed in previous works across Neville's career. Altogether, Neville's project is the sort of ambitious architectonic that Peirce wished he could have created.

3. On the Present Situation in Peirce and Religion

With regard to Peirce's prospects for impacting scholarly work on religion or theology, the present situation is ambiguous. On the one hand, the variety of Peircean theologies or studies of religion in the early twenty-first century is the richest it has ever been, with committed and enduring communities of inquiry, as well as probably a higher volume of relevant output than at any previous time. On the other hand, there is a persistent impression among many theologians or religionists that Peirce is a cult figure, capable of inspiring a devoted following, perhaps, but too esoteric or parochial to contribute much to the discourse, much less drive it.

This is a problem, one that, even if not exactly new, is that much more unfortunate given the valuable work on Peirce and religion that has been produced. Not helping matters is the fact that the world of Peircean religious and theological studies is less coherent than it was a generation ago. The International Centennial Congress on Peirce in 2014, for example, had much less of an impact than did the 1989 Sesquicentennial Congress in that regard. And in spite of a few promising intermediaries like the Institute for American Religious and Philosophical Thought (IARPT; this has Raposa as president, Neville as an active member, and Corrington having participated in some meetings and collaborative publications) or Jacob Goodson (the editor of the *Journal of Scriptural Reasoning* who is also a member of IARPT), there have been few, if any, regular interactions among the respective communities engaging with Raposa, Corrington, Ochs, or Neville.

These problems should not be overstated, nor do they affect existing contemporary projects equally. There are certainly projects unimpaired by the lack of coherence among the wider world of Peirce and religion, and there are projects unimpaired by any wider impression of Peirce as an esoteric or inaccessible figure. Considered independently, for instance, each of the big four Peirce-influenced projects has been successful in earning interdisciplinary, interreligious, and international attention, which is to say building genuine communities of inquiry.[42] Provided one is already convinced of the religious relevance of Peirce, it is also not hard to find current projects that yield insights on the embeddedness of Peirce's religious writings within his wider body of work or on the biographical context of Peirce's religious life.[43]

Where one encounters problems are cases in which the aforementioned lack of coherence contributes to the perception that Peirce is an esoteric figure and/or in which the disciplinary commitments in question have the effect of isolating projects perceived as esoteric. Constructive theologies of a certain type and philosophy of religion are particularly susceptible to these problems. Some Peircean theologies—Rory Misiewisz's *The Analogy of Signs* (2021), for example—enlist Peirce's insights on behalf of long-standing theological problems such as that of analogical language about God, and these tend to avoid these problems. When Peirce's terms are used *as themselves* raw materials for theology, however—as in Andrew Robinson's *God and the World of Signs* (2010), which views Peirce's categories of firstness, secondness, and thirdness as, respectively, Father, Son, and Holy Spirit—problems arise. It is not that such projects necessarily lack creativity, intellectual acuity, or, Peirce's own aversion to theology notwithstanding, fidelity to the source materials. The central problem is rather that theology tends to entail some historical tradition and real-world community out of which and toward which the theologian speaks, and Peircean theologies lack such a constituency.

As for philosophy of religion, the problem here is simply that figures perceived as esoteric tend to be ignored, and so to the extent that Peirce is considered as such, Peircean philosophies of religion do not get the attention they deserve.[44] This could change, and exceptions do exist. Still, the neglect is both real and unfortunate, since Peirce's work on logic, semiotics, and metaphysics represents vital contributions to the field, certainly more so than what one finds in the epistemologically oriented treatments of the "Neglected Argument" that tend to be the primary point of engagement.[45]

It may seem that these problems recapitulate Peirce's own distinction between theology and religion, or at least that Peirce's mistrust of academic theology might explain the difficulties in mounting constructive theologies on Peircean foundations. It is true that, as already observed, such projects face significant problems; conversely, projects that employ Peircean resources to probe religious cultures as an object of analysis are among the richest within the contemporary landscape.[46] Yet the current situation cannot be summed up simply by saying that Peircean theologies fail where Peircean projects studying religion as a cultural object succeed. Ochs's scriptural reasoning, for example, is undoubtedly a Peirce-influenced theological project that is flourishing. Granted, scriptural reasoning does not use Peircean norms as its foundation, and unlike the constructive theologies mentioned previously, its constituencies in the Abrahamic traditions are far more extensive and obvious.[47] Still, that the success of scriptural reasoning complicates a simple theology/religion binary is clear.

One hypothesis—admittedly only a tentative one—regarding the prospects for contemporary Peircean projects in religion and theology concerns the degree to which a given project is transparent about the relationship between its governing logics (with specific reference to the logical resources drawn from Peirce), the norms by which its success is judged, and the community or communities toward which it is oriented. That is, the more a given project can be transparent in a way that clarifies this relationship, the more successful it is likely to be. This is not only because such transparency allows for clearer understandings of how a project functions, but also because it raises the possibility that its logics might be reappropriated by other projects that do not necessarily share the same norms. To return to the scriptural reasoning example, thanks to the transparency of this project in the manner just described, the logical resources of this project have been shown to be exportable even into contexts in which scripture is not necessarily the governing norm, for example, democratic discourse[48] or comparative religious ethics.[49] Within the context of supportive venues like the *American Journal of Theology and Philosophy*, IARPT, or perhaps the *Journal of Scriptural Reasoning*, it is possible that similar work might be done to build links between the four leading communities of Peircean religious and theological studies; in so doing, the perception that Peirce is a marginal or cult figure might be combatted.

Notes

1. Sincere thanks are owed to David Rohr and Brandon Daniel-Hughes for their assistance with this project. Their diligent and detailed feedback on an earlier version of the chapter was instrumental in its reaching its final form.

2. For a comprehensive study on Peirce's personal faith across his life, see Ward (2018).
3. In this chapter, Peirce's writings are cited parenthetically with reference to their placement within the volume in which they have been compiled, as well as their initial year. The compilation in question for a given citation is indicated with an abbreviation.
4. The Open Court Publishing Company played a particularly significant role in Peirce's late-period writings on religion, having published the *Monist* series of 1891–1893, among other texts. In addition to providing Peirce with an outlet for his maturing philosophy, the Open Court was also an important source of financial support during a particularly disruptive period in Peirce's life. Without diminishing Peirce's own personal motives for emphasizing the religious element in his philosophy in his Open Court publications, it also bears mentioning that the Open Court specifically sought to publish perspectives contributing to the reconciliation between science and religion. So it is not a surprise that Peirce's writings in this context would explore religious topics.
5. A good compilation of these texts is Peirce (2009). See also Esposito (1980) and Hausman (1997). Perhaps the definitive primary-text resource for these texts is volume 8 of the *Writings*, which is not only organized more carefully than the *Collected Papers*, but also includes various drafts and false starts alongside the published materials; these supplementary materials begin at W8:380.
6. For a compilation devoted specifically to these lectures, see Peirce (1992).
7. For support for this claim, see de Waal (2022, 97–102).
8. Within Peirce's own life, including his personal views on politics and race, Peirce's conservatism expressed itself in some indefensible ways. Atkins (2016) does a good job resuscitating the redeeming features of Peirce's conservative sentimentalism without glossing over or neglecting such elements, which included both racism and lukewarm support for democratic politics. As Daniel Campos has argued (Campos 2014), Peirce also displayed consistent animus toward persons of Hispanic descent. Atkins also provides a helpful literature review as to the scholarly consensus on "Philosophy and the Conduct of Life." On the critical side, one finds, for instance, Misak (2004) and de Waal (2012); on the positive side, one finds Migotti (2005).
9. This distinction was explored most explicitly and concisely in Peirce's writings for the Open Court Publishing Company.
10. Raposa (2018, 488).
11. Hookway (2002, 269).
12. For a sample from recent scholarship, see Clanton (2014), Daniel-Hughes (2015), Linde (2018), Rodrigues (2017), Rohr (2019), Shook (2011), Sims (2008).
13. Atkins (2016, 86).
14. Anderson (1990, 352).
15. Short (2015).
16. Rohr (2019, 449).
17. Raposa (2018, 489).
18. Smith (1981, 491).
19. Clanton (2014, 196).
20. Hookway (2002, 279).
21. Hull (2005, 490).
22. The graphs have received extended treatment in Ochs (1998), Raposa (1989), and Roberts (1973), who published a very helpful book-length commentary on them. Shin (2002) represents, along with Roberts's book and research from Kenneth Ketner, one of the only

full-length treatments available on the EGs. Gary Slater (2015) also finds inspiration in the EGs to develop a diagram for religious interpretation called the nested continua model. For helpful contemporary scholarship on the EGs, see Peirce (2019–).
23. Raposa (1991, 349).
24. Atkins (2020, 49).
25. Hartshorne (1941).
26. Goudge (1951).
27. Gallie (1952).
28. Potter (1967).
29. Orange (1984).
30. Smith is cited as an important influence by both Neville and Ochs, for example, and he was also at Yale while Michael Raposa completed his undergraduate and master's degrees there.
31. For helpful further context on the meaning of this distinction, see Knight (2012).
32. Anderson (1995).
33. Bilateral interactions can be found regarding Raposa and Ochs (in the theological ethics of Gary Slater, as well as chapter 8 of Ochs [1998]), Raposa and Corrington (in Ejsing [2007, 140], and Niemoczynski [2011, 14]), Raposa and Neville (Raposa 2019), Neville and Ochs (in Gary Slater [2015, ch. 4–5]), Neville and Corrington (Corrington 1999, Neville 1999), and Ochs and Corrington (Goodson 2021, 41–47). Nevertheless, to date, no study has commonly looked at all four of these figures with any degree of seriousness.
34. In addition to these two books, Raposa's project is also the subject of a special issue of the *American Journal of Theology and Philosophy* (43, no. 1–2), which includes essays on theosemiotic from such commentators on Peirce as Brandon Daniel-Hughes, Roger Ward, and Rory Misiewisz.
35. Raposa (2020, xi).
36. The influence of scriptural reasoning is observable in the *Journal of Scriptural Reasoning*, regular sessions at annual meetings of the American Academy of Religion, and the Cambridge Interfaith Programme.
37. Ochs 2011, 15–16.
38. Niemczynski (2011, 20–21).
39. Corrington (2015, xxiiii).
40. Corrington (2009, x).
41. Deuser et al. (2016, 14).
42. For example, see James and Rashkover (2021; for the interdisciplinary), Koshul (2007; for the interreligious), or Yong and Heltzel (2004; for the international).
43. Examples of the former include Linde (2018) and Rohr (2019); an example of the latter is Ward (2018).
44. For notable examples of Peirce's neglect within philosophy of religion, see Lewis (2015) and Schilbrack (2014), which make no mention of Peirce or mention him only in passing. Even in such overtly pragmatist perspectives as Michael Slater (2014), which devotes a chapter to Peirce, significant Peircean insights are minimized or ignored.
45. Arnold (2021) is a particularly expansive example of the possibilities embedded within Peircean philosophy of religion.
46. The field of anthropology has long been interested in employing Peirce to in the study of human religion. Most famously, Geertz (1973) found inspiration in Peirce in his semiotic conception of religion in culture. More recently, innovative Peircean anthropologies of religion can be found in Rappaport (1999) and Kohn (2013).

47. As a postliberal project, scriptural reasoning has its own tendencies toward insularity. Yet unlike the legacy of Wittgenstein in such postliberal projects as that of George Lindbeck, the Peircean legacy in Ochs militates against these.
48. Gary Slater (2017).
49. Gary Slater (2019). Another text that demonstrates a compatible approach is Daniel-Hughes (2018).

Bibliography

Anderson, Douglas R. 1990. "Three Appeals in Peirce's Neglected Argument," *Transactions of the Charles S. Peirce Society* 26, vol. 3 (Summer): 349–362.

Anderson, Douglas. 1995. *Strands of System*. West Lafayette, IN: Purdue University Press.

Arnold, Dan. 2021. "Pragmatism as Transcendental Philosophy, Pt. II: Peirce on God and Personality." *American Journal of Theology & Philosophy* 42, vol. 2 (May): 3–71.

Atkins, Richard Kenneth. 2016. *Peirce and the Conduct of Life: Sentiment and Instinct in Ethics and Religion*. Cambridge: Cambridge University Press.

Atkins, Richard Kenneth. 2020. "Royce's The Problem of Christianity and Peirce's Epistemology." *American Journal of Theology & Philosophy* 41, no. 2–3 (May–September): 39–55.

Campos, Daniel. 2014. "Peirce's Prejudices against Hispanics and the Ethical Scope of His Philosophy." *The Pluralist* 9, no. 2: 42–64.

Clanton, J. Caleb. 2014. "The Structure of C. S. Peirce's Neglected Argument for the Reality of God: A Critical Assessment." Transactions of the Charles S. Peirce Society 50, no. 2 (Spring): 175–200.

Corrington, Robert S. 1999. "Neville's 'Naturalism' and the Location of God." *Interpreting Neville*, edited by J. Harley Chapman and Nancy K. Frankenberry, 127–146. Albany: State University of New York Press.

Corrington, Robert S. 2009. *A Semiotic Theory of Theology and Philosophy*. Cambridge: Cambridge University Press.

Corrington, Robert S. 2015. *Deep Pantheism: Toward a New Transcendentalism*. Lanham, MD: Lexington Books.

Daniel-Hughes, Brandon. 2015. "The Neglected Arguments of Peirce's Neglected Argument: Beyond a Theological Dead-End." American Journal of Theology & Philosophy 36, no. 2 (May): 121–139.

Daniel-Hughes, Brandon. 2018. *Pragmatic Inquiry and Religious Communities: Charles Peirce, Signs, and Inhabited Experiments*. London: Palgrave Macmillan.

Deuser, Hermann, Hans Joas, Matthias Jung, and Magnus Schlette. 2016. "Introduction." In *The Varieties of Transcendence: Pragmatism and the Theory of Religion*, edited by Hermann Deuser, Hans Joas, Matthias Jung, and Magnus Schlette, 1–14. New York: Fordham University Press.

De Waal, Cornelis. 2012. "Who's Afraid of Charles Sanders Peirce? Knocking Some Critical Common Sense into Moral Philosophy." In *The Normative Thought of Charles S. Peirce*, edited by Cornelis de Waal and Krzysztof Piotr Skowronski. New York: Fordham University Press, 83–100.

De Waal, Cornelis. 2022. *Introducing Pragmatism: A Tool for Rethinking Philosophy*. New York: Routledge.

Ejsing, Anette. 2007. *Theology of Anticipation: A Constructive Study of C. S. Peirce*. Eugene, OR: Wipf & Stock.

Esposito, Joseph. 1980. *Evolutionary Metaphysics*. Athens, OH: Ohio University Press.
Gallie, W. B. 1952. *Peirce and Pragmatism*. Harmondsworth: Penguin Books.
Geertz, Clifford. 1973. *The Interpretation of Cultures*. New York: Basic Books.
Goodson, Jacob L. 2021. *The Philosopher's Playground: Understanding Scriptural Reasoning through Modern Philosophy*. Eugene, OR: Cascade Books.
Goudge, Thomas. 1951. *The Thought of C. S. Peirce*. New York: Dover.
Hartshorne, Charles. 1941. "A Critique of Peirce's Idea of God." *The Philosophical Review* 50, no. 5 (September): 516–523.
Hausman, Carl. 1997. *Charles S. Peirce's Evolutionary Philosophy*. Cambridge: Cambridge University Press.
Hookway, Christopher. 2002. *Truth, Rationality, and Pragmatism: Themes from Peirce*. Oxford: Oxford University Press.
Hull, Kathleen. 2005. "The Inner Chambers of His Mind: Peirce's 'Neglected Argument' for God as Related to Mathematical Experience." *Transactions of the Charles S. Peirce Society* 41, no. 3 (Summer): 483–513.
James, Mark Randall, and Randi Rashkover, eds. 2021. *Signs of Salvation: A Festschrift for Peter Ochs*. Eugene, OR: Cascade Books.
Knight, John Allen. 2012. *Liberalism versus Postliberalism: The Great Divide in Twentieth-Century Theology*. Oxford: Oxford University Press.
Kohn, Eduardo. 2013. *How Forests Think: Toward an Anthropology beyond the Human*. Berkeley: University of California Press.
Koshul, Basit Bilal. 2007. "Bridging the Reason/Revelation Divide: A Qur'anic-Peircean Perspective." *Journal of the Iqbal Academy Pakistan* 48, no. 2. http://www.allamaiqbal.com/publications/journals/review/apr07/1.htm.
Lewis, Thomas A. 2015. *Why Philosophy Matters for the Study of Religion—and Vice Versa*. Oxford: Oxford University Press.
Linde, Gesche. 2018. "The Semiotic Structure of Peirce's Humble Argument, with Brief Remarks on Different Kinds of Abducent Signs." *Transactions of the Charles S. Peirce Society* 54, no. 4 (Fall): 515–531.
Migotti, Mark. 2005. "The Key to Peirce's View of the Role of Belief in Scientific Inquiry." *Cognitio* 6, no. 1: 44–55.
Misak, Cheryl. 2004. "C. S. Peirce on Vital Matters." In *The Cambridge Companion to Peirce*, edited by Cheryl Misak, 150–174. Cambridge: Cambridge University Press.
Misiewisz, Rory. 2021. *The Analogy of Signs: Rethinking Theological Language with Charles S. Peirce*. Lanham, MD: Fortress Press.
Neville, Robert C. 1999. "Responding to My Critics." *Interpreting Neville*, edited by J. Harley Chapman and Nancy K. Frankenberry, 291–328. Albany: State University of New York Press.
Niemoczynski, Leon J. 2011. *Charles Sanders Peirce and a Religious Metaphysics of Nature*. Lanham, MD: Lexington Books.
Ochs, Peter. 1998. *Peirce, Pragmatism, and the Logic of Scripture*. Cambridge: Cambridge University Press.
Ochs, Peter. 2011. *Another Reformation: Post-liberal Christianity and the Jews*. Ida, MI: Baker Academic.
Ochs, Peter. 2019. *Religion without Violence*. Eugene, OR: Wipf & Stock.
Orange, Donna M. 1984. *Peirce's Conception of God: A Developmental Study*. Lubbock, TX: Institute for Studies in Pragmaticism.

Peirce, Charles S. 1857–1914. Manuscripts held at the Houghton Library of Harvard University, as identified in Richard Robin. 1967. *Annotated Catalogue of the Papers of Charles S. Peirce*. Amherst: University of Massachusetts Press. (Referred to as R.)

Peirce, Charles S. 1931–1958. *The Collected Papers of Charles Sanders Peirce*. 8 vols. Vols. 1–6 edited by Charles Hartshorne and Paul Weiss. Vols. 7–8 edited by Arthur W. Burks. Cambridge, MA: Harvard University Press. (Referred to as CP.)

Peirce, Charles S.1992. *Reasoning and the Logic of Things*, edited by Hilary Putnam and Kenneth Laine Ketner. Cambridge, MA: Harvard University Press. (Referred to as RLT.)

Peirce, Charles S. 2009. *The Logic of Interdisciplinarity: The Monist Series*, edited by Elize Bisanz. Berlin: Akademie Verlag. (Referred to as LI.)

Peirce, Charles S. 2019–. *Logic of the Future. Writings on Existential Graphs*. 3 vols in 4, edited by A. V. Pietarinen. Berlin: De Gruyter. (Referred to as LoF.)

Potter, Vincent. 1967. *Charles S. Peirce: On Norms and Ideals*. New York: Fordham University Press.

Rapaport, Roy A. 1999. *Ritual and Religion in the Making of Humanity*. Cambridge: Cambridge University Press.

Raposa, Michael. 1989. *Peirce's Philosophy of Religion*. Bloomington: Indiana University Press.

Raposa, Michael. 1991. "Peirce and Modern Religious Thought." *Transactions of the Charles S. Peirce Society* 27, no. 3 (Summer): 341–369.

Raposa, Michael. 2018. "On Reading God's Great Poem: A Delayed Response to Christopher Hookway." *Transactions of the Charles S. Peirce Society* 54, no. 4 (Fall): 485–495.

Raposa, Michael. 2019. "Praying the Ultimate: The Pragmatic Core of Neville's Philosophical Theology." *American Journal of Theology & Philosophy* 40, no. 3: 49–64.

Raposa, Michael. 2020. *Theosemiotic: Religion, Reading, and the Gift of Meaning*. New York: Fordham University Press.

Roberts, Don. 1973. *The Existential Graphs of Charles S. Peirce*. The Hague: Mouton.

Robinson, Andrew. 2010. *God and the World of Signs: Trinity, Evolution, and the Metaphysical Semiotics of C. S. Peirce*. Leiden: Brill.

Rodrigues, Cassiano Terra. 2017. "The Vagueness of the Muse—The Logic of Peirce's Humble Argument for the Reality of God." *SOPHIA* 56:163–182.

Rohr, David. 2019. "The Humble Argument Is Musement on God's Great Argument." *Transactions of the Charles S. Peirce Society* 55, no. 4 (Fall): 429–453.

Schilbrack, Kevin. 2014. *Philosophy and the Study of Religions: A Manifesto*. Hoboken, NJ: Wiley-Blackwell.

Shin, Sun-Joo. 2002. *The Iconic Logic of Peirce's Graphs*. Boston: MIT Press.

Shook, John. 2011. "Peirce's Pragmatic Theology and Stoic Religious Ethics." *Journal of Religious Ethics* 39, no. 2: 344–363.

Short, T. L. 2015. "Empiricism Expanded." *Transactions of the Charles S. Peirce Society* 51, no. 1 (Winter): 1–33.

Sims, Jeffrey H. 2008. "A Fallible Groom in the Religious Thought of C. S. Peirce—A Centenary Revisitation," *Sophia* 47:47–91.

Slater, Gary. 2015. *C. S. Peirce and the Nested Continua Model of Religious Interpretation*. Oxford: Oxford University Press.

Slater, Gary. 2017. "Scriptural Reasoning and the Ethics of Public Discourse." *American Journal of Theology and Philosophy* 38, no. 2: 123–137.

Slater, Gary. 2019. "Between Comparison and Normativity: Scriptural Reasoning and Religious Ethics." In *Scripture, Tradition, and Reason in Christian Ethics: Normative Dimensions*, edited by Bharat Ranganthan and Derek Woodard-Lehman, 45–66. Cham, Switzerland: Palgrave Macmillan.

Slater, Michael R. 2014. *Pragmatism and the Philosophy of Religion*. Cambridge: Cambridge University Press.

Smith, John E. 1981. "The Tension between Direct Experience and Argument in Religion." *Religious Studies* 17, no. 4 (December): 487–497.

Ward, Roger. 2018. *Peirce and Religion: Knowledge, Transformation, and the Reality of God*. Lanham, MD: Rowman & Littlefield.

Yong, Amos, and Peter Heltzel, eds. 2004. *Theology in Global Context: Essays in Honor of Robert Cummings Neville*. New York: T & T Clark.

PART VI
SCIENCE AND SEMIOTICS

CHAPTER 28

A SCIENCE LIKE ANY OTHER

A Peircean Philosophy of Sex?

SHANNON DEA

If you have spent any time on social media since 2018 or so, you may have noticed an uptick in references to the science of sex. This increase corresponds to a massive increase in the attention to and increasingly polarized debate about trans issues in recent years within media and social media. A common trope within those debates—especially on social media—is the rhetorical invocation of science by both sides. Science shows that there are only two sexes, claims one side, pointing to chromosomes and gametes. Science shows that sex is a continuum, claims the other, pointing to hermaphroditic nonhuman species and intersex human beings.[1]

To a considerable degree, these latter pleas to understand biological sex "beyond the binary" reflect an explosion of scholarship on the philosophy of sex since the 1990s.[2] In various ways, historians of medicine, feminist biologists, sociologists of science, and philosophers, among others working in this area, have challenged traditional accounts of biological sex. This literature has served as an important corrective to the binarism and gendered ideology inherent in those accounts. However, the anti-realism about biological sex taxonomies that is endemic within these critical studies arguably neglects biological evidence of similarity among members of a sex, evidence of differences between the sexes, and practical (including clinical) deployments of sex categories.

In this chapter, I survey five scholarly challenges to the "standard view" of biological sex, all of them in some sense anti-realist. I then argue that our science of sex can be appropriately critical without necessarily being anti-realist. In other branches of science, it is possible to acknowledge both the historical contingency of scientific practice and theory choice, and the rich complexity of data while retaining a broadly realist metaphysics.

Debating whether or not intersex conditions are appropriately termed "disorders of sex development" (DSD), Ellen Feder and Katrina Karkazis argue that as a clinical umbrella term, DSD has the merit of treating intersex as "disorders like any other" rather than "disorders like no other."[3] Both the DSD appellation and Feder and Karkazis's defense of it are controversial due to the pathologizing connotation of "disorder."[4] I here remain agnostic on that aspect of Feder and Karkazis's argument but adopt and adapt their view to argue that neither sex nor sex variation demands sui generis clinical or scientific treatment. Put simply: the science of sex ought to be *a science like any other*. Moreover, if it is a science like any other, then it must in principle be possible for well-informed, properly critical theorists to be realists about sex.

I propose that the scholastic realism of American pragmatist Charles Sanders Peirce can handle our best evidence about the complexity of sex in a way that is rigorous and useful, but that does not efface, exclude, or pathologize members of the population with nontypical sex traits. I sketch the beginnings of a Peircean philosophy of sex, attending in particular to Peirce's so-called scholastic realism—his view that reality comprises individuals, laws, and possibilia. I argue that scholastic realism as applied to sex helps us to understand sex as bimodal rather than binaristic. While Peirce himself was uncharacteristically (for him) binaristic about sex categories, I work to recover the nuanced view of sex that Peirce ought to have adopted had he extended his scholastic realism to reproductive biology. Ultimately, my Peircean account treats sex differences as real but continuous rather than discrete.

1. Binaristic Biology

In recent decades, the nature of gender and the relationship between gender and biological sex categories have both been problematized in important and useful ways. However, it is with sex—the biological category whereby we deploy various markers to distinguish between male and female organisms—that I am in particular concerned in this chapter. That is, I am here interested in the categorial demarcation made in biology on the basis of such features as sex chromosomes, hormonal production and reception, gonad type, and phenotypic features such as genitalia, mammary glands, and facial hair. What exactly is it to be biologically male or female? More fundamentally, do the categories *male* and *female* carve nature at the joints?

In general, scholars offer two broad classes of answers to these questions. The first of these is traditional reproductive biology, which is in general committed to the view that there really are just two sexes and that the binarism of sex categories simply reflects this fact rather than reflecting underlying biases.

Historically, this view is notoriously evident in Geddes and Thomson's still influential characterization of female metabolism as anabolic (conserving energy and hence passive) and male metabolism as catabolic (expending energy and hence active). Geddes and Thomson's cell biology grounds their biodeterminism, which is encapsulated in the most oft-quoted passage from their 1889 *The Evolution of Sex*: "We have seen that a deep difference in constitution expresses itself in the distinctions between male and female, whether these be physical or mental. The differences may be exaggerated or lessened, but to obliterate them it would be necessary to have all the evolution over again on a new basis. What was decided among the prehistoric Protozoa cannot be annulled by Act of Parliament."[5]

While contemporary reproductive biology typically avoids polemics like that of Geddes and Thomson, it largely retains their conviction that there are two heterogeneous sexes, a view that sometimes requires some shoehorning of the evidence.

Consider, for instance, the quickness with which sexual binarism is projected onto simultaneous hermaphroditic species—that is, species each member of which throughout its life cycle produces both male and female gametes—or, less tendentiously, two different types of gametes.[6] Here, for example, is a much-reproduced popular science description of the mating behavior of hermaphroditic flatworms: "During penis fencing, each flatworm tries to pierce the skin of the other using one of its penises. The first to succeed becomes the de facto male, delivering its sperm into the other, the de facto female. For the flatworms, this contest is serious business. Mating is a fight because the worm that assumes the female role then must expend considerable energy caring for the developing eggs."[7]

Notice that the account just quoted assumes that reproduction necessarily involves not just male and female organs and gametes but also male and female *organisms*—that even hermaphroditic organisms that simultaneously produce both sperm and ova take on de facto male or female roles. Only a bias in favor of sexual binarism could explain imposing such a description on a hermaphroditic species.

Some biologists resist this binarism. In the early 2000s, interdisciplinary biologist Joel Parker made waves in popular science publications with his research on genetic caste determination in harvester ants and his suggestion that some harvester ant species have more than two sexes. While the species have only two phenotypic sexes, Parker argues that, "from the perspective of the number of gametic types required to make individuals in the population (functional definition) and the number required to prevent demographic extinction (stability definition)," the species have more than two sexes.[8] While Parker argues that some harvester ant species have more than two sexes, he nonetheless maintains that "sexual systems appear to be a binary process at some fundamental level."[9] Parker characterized his harvester ant discovery as evidence of a "major evolutionary transition." However, his view seems not to have been widely taken up outside of popular science venues. Still, Parker's work was part of a new focus on genes and chromosomes in the biology of sex that emerged in the early 2000s with the completion of the Human Genome Project.

In her 2013 book, *Sex Itself*, Sarah Richardson documents the influence of gender biases on research on the biology of sex. On her account, these biases led, and still lead, biologists to take sex binarism for granted and have in recent years encouraged the view that genetics and genomics might reveal "sex itself"—that is, a rock-bottom fact of the matter about sex categories. Richardson characterizes the history of sex chromosome research as a "history of contestations" in which, in the face of partial empirical evidence, scientists fell prey to the influence of gender biases.[10] In particular, she argues, they assumed rather than discovered chromosomal sex binarism. She focuses on genetic and genomic research to offer a feminist critique of the science of sex and ultimately a careful, nuanced understanding of sex categories. As part of her positive project, Richardson develops a sophisticated account of the sexes as "dynamic dyadic kinds" (as opposed to species, which are individual kinds) while offering a caution about the risk of the future encroachment of gender biases into sex science, including via feminist sex-based biology.[11]

2. Critical Sex Studies

Where traditional reproductive biology, including the postgenomic biology Richardson documents, tends to be binaristic and uncritically realist, the trend within what we might term "critical sex studies" is to deny (or problematize) binarism and to adopt some variety of anti-realism about sex. It is worth spending a bit of time here attending to some of the ways in which this second broad approach to sex taxonomies has played out in sex and gender scholarship.

On the face of it, critical sex studies is a reaction to the binaristic sex science we considered in the previous section. However, it is similarly resistant to a too-tidy demarcation between sex and gender that emerged in mid-twentieth-century feminist scholarship in the wake of Simone de Beauvoir's provocative query, "Are there even women?"[12] That twentieth-century bifurcation between sex and gender holds that sex as a biological category is fixed and inevitable while gender is a more fluid psychosociocultural epiphenomenon. In various ways, critical sex scholars invert this picture. They argue that the construction of sex categories and the conduct of the science of sex are influenced by beliefs and norms about gender, and thus that sex supervenes on gender and is neither fixed nor inevitable.

For Suzanne Kessler, our historico-culturally situated beliefs about gender inescapably influence our interpretations of biological evidence.[13] A case in point: her 1990 study of neonatal gender (re)assignment[14] among infants with ambiguous genitalia revealed that the Freudian phallocentric biases of clinicians frequently led to gender (re)assignments being made based on the size of the phallus rather than, for instance, chromosomal character. For Kessler, our judgments about sex taxonomies are so deeply gendered, and gender is so complex, that it is not possible to demarcate between sex categories and gender categories.

Thomas Laqueur's *Making Sex: Body and Gender from the Greeks to Freud* (1990) surveys medical history to arrive at a very similar conclusion to Kessler's.[15] Laqueur deploys the seeing versus seeing-as distinction in a persuasive case that physicians and biologists in any historical period cannot help but interpret evidence of reproductive biology in light of prevailing biases. Under the sway of Aristotelian and Galenic accounts of reproduction, Laqueur tells us, medieval anatomists saw—literally *saw*—vaginas as internal, inverted penises. The Aristotelian model treated males and females as two tokens of the same reproductive type but regarded females as underdeveloped males. The view went that all males and females perform broadly the same reproductive functions, but males perform them better. This treatment of male and female reproductive biology as isomorphic eventuated in the medieval view that both men and women must achieve orgasm in order to conceive offspring. This, appallingly, led to the view that females who became pregnant because of a rape were in fact willing participants in the rape and hence blameworthy for it.

Laqueur argues that new epistemological and political developments in the Enlightenment led to a shift away from the Aristotelian–Galenic model, in which male and female bodies were seen as "hierarchically, vertically, ordered versions of one sex," to a new model in which they were seen as "horizontally ordered opposites, as incommensurable."[16] For Laqueur, this modern conception of sex difference, while more familiar than the medieval one, is historically contingent, just as its predecessor was. On Laqueur's view, biological science reflects and reproduces the historico-cultural context in which it is produced.

Anne Fausto-Sterling is perhaps the most influential contemporary theorist of sex taxonomy. In her famous "The Five Sexes: Why Male and Female Are Not Enough" (1993), Fausto-Sterling argues that the incidence of female pseudo-hermaphroditism, male pseudo-hermaphroditism, and true hermaphroditism entail that there are actually five rather than two human sexes.[17] While conservative critics read the article as evidence of a creeping queer feminist agenda, scholars like Kessler argued that Fausto-Sterling's five-sex model was oversimplified—that given the rich sexual variation among humans (and, in particular, given the wide array of varieties of intersex), there are many more than five sexes. Fausto-Sterling herself later described her 1993 article as intentionally provocative and tongue in cheek.[18] In later work, Fausto-Sterling cites the wide range of human sexual variation in support of a continuum account of sex. She writes: "Complete maleness and complete femaleness represent the extreme ends of a spectrum of possible body types. That these extreme ends are the most frequent has lent credence to the idea that they are not only natural (that is, produced by nature) but normal (that is, they represent both a statistical and social ideal). Knowledge of biological variation, however, allows us to conceptualize the less frequent middle spaces as natural, although statistically unusual."[19]

In her *Hermaphrodites and the Medical Invention of Sex* (2000), Alice Domurat Dreger traces the history of intersex people and argues that sex category criteria are always historically contingent.[20] She regards the period 1870–1915 as "the Age of Gonads"—a time when, in cases of ambiguous genitalia, physicians and jurists used gonadal tissue to decide the matter of subjects' sex. An intersex person with testes was regarded—medically and legally—as male; an intersex person with ovaries was regarded as female. With the twentieth century, however, scientific and technological advances and changes in social mores led to a shift in the treatment of intersex people. Microbiology made it possible to determine sex based on chromosomal character, and women's increasing participation in the workforce (and the development of the birth control pill) made reproduction more or less optional. The gonads thus came to be seen as less important in sex assignment, and chromosomes became the chief marker for sex.

In a little-known 2011 study, philosopher Jill Oliver argues in favor of adopting what she terms a "multi-dimensional" account of sex.[21] Inspired by Sandra Bem's (1974)[22] and Christopher Kilmartin's (2000)[23] account of gender, and in particular their characterization of masculinity and femininity as independent dimensions, Oliver's multi-dimensional model treats male and female as orthogonal to each other rather than as opposites. Thus, a single organism might possess both highly male and highly female traits. For Oliver, "sex" is an umbrella term for a number of distinct biological traits, such as chromosomal character, hormonal production and reception, and genital anatomy. On Oliver's account, these are independent traits, united by convention, not by any real mind-independent category. Oliver argues that "parts" are sexed—that vaginas are female, for instance, and XY chromosomes male—but she denies that people have sexes. She terms this the "parts not people" view. Biologically, she argues, we are all clusters of male and female parts. Some of us possess the parts of only one sex; others possess a mixture. Further, Oliver recognizes that some parts, for instance, ambiguous genitalia, may not be exclusively male or female. Thus, the "parts not people" view is primarily a critique of the sexing of whole bodies rather than an argument in favor of sexing parts of bodies. Moreover, Oliver argues that for many of us—including trans people, women who undergo hysterectomies, etc.—the cluster changes over the course of a lifetime.

3. Beyond Critical Sex Studies: A Peircean Philosophy of Sex

There is much that is no doubt right about the critical sex scholarship I have just sketched. It is surely true that scientists' and clinicians' historico-cultural biases affect their judgments about sex. Moreover, there is indeed wide variation in sex trait expression within and across species. This variation raises serious challenges to a binaristic account of sex.

However, it is not at all clear that nominalism about sex is the right scientific attitude. In other branches of science, it is possible to admit the historico-cultural contingency of scientific practice and to admit the rich complexity of the phenomena under examination without necessarily plumping for anti-realism. Conversely, it is possible to assert an anti-realist position without recourse to historicism or worries about complexity. In the philosophy of science, metaphysics and epistemology often come apart.

Moreover, it might be argued that the critical sex scholars whose views I have just described pay too much attention to sexual variation and theory change and too little attention to statistical commonalities and theory resilience. While our science of sex has no doubt evolved (or, on Laqueur's account, undergone revolutionary change), the broad sex categories have remained remarkably stable over time. Further, while we are in the early twenty-first century better at understanding the tails of the sexual bell curve, the fact remains that the majority of the human population clusters within the bell of the curve.

I think that critical sex studies' movement toward historicism and attention to outliers within the population is a useful corrective to the deeply ideological, uncritically binaristic work on sex that often goes on in the life sciences. However, it cannot be the whole story and ought not to become the new orthodoxy. At the end of the day, if the science of sex is to be good science, then it should arguably be a science like any other, not a science sui generis. Thus, it should be subject to broadly the same norms and values as other sciences. In particular, it should be as attentive to convergence and stability as it is to variation and change. I want to suggest that Peirce's scientific metaphysics gives us the tools we need to take the next step in sex science. In this section, I sketch the beginnings of a Peircean philosophy of sex.

Despite a growing interest in pragmatism among feminist and queer theorists, Charles Sanders Peirce's work is seldom deployed in the context of sex and gender studies. One reason for this may be Peirce's own uncharacteristic binarism about sex. Peirce regarded male and female as one of the few pairs of true opposites in the world. In an undated fragment, he wrote that "in the external world polar distinctions are few. That of past and future . . . , with the right and left sides of our bodies, and the two sexes, seems pretty much to exhaust the list of them."[24]

Admittedly, this remark was a one-off and not the expression of a well-developed view, but it is in some ways out of character for Peirce. As I note below, he elsewhere refused to draw a sharp distinction between life and death or between mind and matter due to his view—which he termed *synechism*—that all of reality is ultimately continuous. While his description of the two sexes might seem to suggest a nonsynechistic understanding of sex, it is worth pointing out that his other examples in the above quote show that Peirce regarded at least some polar distinctions as continuous rather than discrete. After all, the past is continuous with the future, and the right half of the body is continuous with the left half.[25] Possibly, therefore, he regarded male and female likewise as polar but continuous distinctions.

Peirce's fallibilism and his commitment to leaving paths of scientific inquiry unblocked by dogmatism prevented him from asserting synechism as an "ultimate and absolute metaphysical doctrine,"[26] but it was certainly a metaphysical working hypothesis for him and served as an important normative ideal for his metaphysical inquiries. Peirce's commitment to the principle that *natura non facet saltus* led him ultimately to reject the law of excluded middle and to develop an early three-valued logic, as well as undergirding his openness to non-Euclidean geometries. Synechism led Peirce to regard all persons as constituting a single communal person,[27] to treat mind and matter as different degrees of the same thing (EP2:2, 1893), and to entertain the possibility of an afterlife (EP2:1–3, 1893). Thus, the doctrine of synechism had important consequences not only for Peirce's metaphysics, but also for his ethics, philosophy of mind, and philosophy of religion. He predicted that synechism would one day "play a part in the onement of religion and science" (EP2:3, 1893).

Peirce's synechism was at the heart of his doctrine of scholastic realism, the metaphysical position that he claimed would "go far toward supplying the philosophy which is best to harmonize with physical science" (CP1.6, 1897). In brief, for Peirce, scholastic realism is the view that reality consists of three fundamental ontological categories—which he termed *firstness*, *secondness*, and *thirdness*—all of them real.

Among these, secondness is the easiest to grasp. It refers to individuality, definiteness, action, and reaction. By contrast, firstness is the category for possibility, chance, quality, and feeling. Where secondness picks out some particular thing in the universe, firstness is prior to any particular thing. It represents possibility not yet actualized. It is not a "this" but "some." It is vague in the sense that the unactualized possibility could turn into this or that. Finally, thirdness is Peirce's category for relation, law, habit, necessity, and mediation. Where secondness is definite and firstness is vague, thirdness is general: laws, habits, and relations all imply more than one instance. Secondness refers to *this*, firstness refers vaguely to *this or that*, and thirdness refers generally to *these*.

An example may help to make sense of Peirce's triadic system. Consider a black horse, Bucephalus. We experience the blackness of the horse qualitatively. This quality alone is insufficient to pick out the individual or the species. Some other horses and some other nonhorses are also black. Our sensation of blackness raises the possibility of Bucephalus and of horses, but also of other things, like frying pans and deep shadows. In this respect, it is vague. This is firstness. Bucephalus—this particular horse—occupies the category of secondness. Qua being this particular horse, Bucephalus is definite and determinate. Finally, the species *horse* falls under the category of thirdness. Peirce regards all three of these categories—firstness, secondness, and thirdness—as real. The qualities possessed by Bucephalus and the species to which Bucephalus belongs are, for Peirce, every bit as real as the individual horse, and not mere names or concepts that we contingently associate with the horse.

On Peirce's account, it is firstness and thirdness that make his system scholastic realist.[28] He regarded nominalism as overemphasizing secondness—individuals—such that commonalities between individuals are regarded as mere words and not real relations or laws. Peirce argued that science is concerned with thirdness since it seeks not just an enumeration of individuals and their features but the laws that guide the behavior of individuals and the general categories under which individuals are subsumed. More radically, a science that takes seriously possibility and chance is also concerned with firstness. On Peirce's view, developments in evolutionary theory, fluid dynamics, and statistical mechanics all integrally involve not just individuals and their covering laws, but also stochastic causation—objective chance. Thus, on his account, a metaphysics that supports modern science must itself attribute equal importance to—and indeed allow for the equal reality of—all three categories, as his scholastic realism does.

Applying scholastic realism to the science of sex offers an alternative to both the binarism of mainstream biology and the anti-realism of critical sex studies. A scholastic realist sex science would attend with equal care to individuals and the particular sex traits they possess (secondness), to variations within large populations (firstness), but also to commonalities within those populations (thirdness). Where traditional biological and clinical approaches have tended to pathologize deviations from the statistical norm in human sex trait expression and to regard nonbinaristic sex traits in nonhuman populations as reducible to binaristic categories, the scholastic realist about sex would embrace sex trait variation as firstness. On the other hand, where critical sex studies has tended to de-emphasize the considerable statistical convergences and theoretical stability that lurk behind binarism about sex, a scholastic realist account would attend to such convergences as thirdness. In reifying statistical norms as binary sex categories, traditional sex science has overemphasized thirdness and neglected firstness. As a corrective to this, critical sex scholarship has neglected thirdness and focused on firstness. A Peircean account would urge that these converse approaches each only tells us a part of the story of reproductive biology, that if we want the whole story, we need both firstness and thirdness.

Further, Peirce's triadic metaphysics describes the universe both synchronically and diachronically. For Peirce, the universe—the whole universe, not just its biological components—is evolving. It originated in firstness—pure chance—and as it slowly takes on habits (thirdness), those habits instantiate as secondness and generalize as thirdness. Ultimately, on Peirce's account, the telos of the universe is absolute secondness. For Peirce, the laws of nature themselves are likewise evolving: they are habits the evolving universe has taken on, and as habits they are "of partial, varying, approximate, and statistical regularity."[29]

Since the laws of nature are evolving along with the universe, we can only approximate them. Peirce thinks this is revealed in the historical rise of non-Euclidean geometries: "The absolute exactitude of the geometrical axioms is exploded; and the corresponding belief in the metaphysical axioms, considering the dependence of metaphysics on geometry, must surely follow it to the tomb of extinct creeds. The first to go must be the proposition that every event in the universe is precisely determined by causes according to inviolable law. We have no reason to think that this is absolutely exact. Experience shows that it is so to a wonderful degree of approximation, and that is all" (CP1.400, c. 1890).

In the philosophy of sex that Peirce's scientific metaphysics underwrites, male and female are norms, not types. They are useful terms to describe broad statistical patterns, but there is nothing particularly special, precise, or permanent about convergence with these patterns. The scholastic realist about sex does not ignore the fact that a large proportion of the human population sits in one of two statistical "bells"—one corresponding to the unambiguous expression of a variety of sex traits tagged female, the other corresponding to the unambiguous expression of a variety of sex traits tagged male. However, neither do they ignore or dismiss the fact that a statistically significant portion of the population sits on a tail of one or both of those bell curves. For the scholastic realist about sex, male and female are bimodal distributions, not bivalent terms. In application, then, scholastic realism about sex allows us to retain pragmatically (and perhaps clinically) useful general terms without reifying them as essences, idealizing them, or exaggerating their significance, and without regarding those terms as normative for members of the population whose expression of sex traits is nontypical.

While I have so far focused on Peirce's scholastic realism, his fallibilism and pragmatic ethics of inquiry offer further advantages to the study of sex categories. One of the main themes that comes through in the critical sex scholarship I discussed earlier is the historical contingency of sex science. The authors I surveyed agree that scientists' and clinicians' implicit historico-cultural biases affect their account of human sexual biology. Peirce's scientific thought is capable of addressing such biases because of his emphasis on what he terms the "first rule of reason": "Upon this first, and in one sense this sole, rule of reason, that in order to learn you must desire to learn, and in so desiring not be satisfied with what you already incline to think, there follows one corollary which itself deserves to be inscribed upon every wall of the city of philosophy: Do not block the way of inquiry" (CP1.135, c. 1899).

For Peirce, the ethics of inquiry enjoins us not to treat our current views as axioms. As scientists, we are no more entitled to assume as an axiom that an organism has a sex, or that sexes only come in twos, than we are to adopt as an axiom that light is a particle or that the sun orbits the earth. We may adopt any of these views as working hypotheses and may even believe them, but we must be prepared to put them to the test when they conflict with the available evidence. "The last philosophical obstacle to the advance of knowledge [writes Peirce] ... is the holding that this or that law or truth has found its last and perfect formulation—and especially that the ordinary and usual course of nature never can be broken through. 'Stones do not fall from heaven,' said Laplace, although they had been falling upon inhabited ground every day from the earliest times. But there is no kind of inference which can lend the slightest probability to any such absolute denial of an unusual phenomenon" (CP1.140, c. 1899). By Peirce's own lights, while the idea that male and female are polar opposites may seem to some to accord with the ordinary and usual course of nature, we must remain open to the possibility that the ordinary and usual course of nature can be broken through.

Further, on Peirce's view, scientific inquiry is fundamentally communal. When we inquire within a community, we are exposed to the views of others. Some of these views come into conflict with our own, thereby stimulating doubt and leading us to further inquiry and correction. When Peirce in his "first rule of reason" warns against dogmatism, his solution to dogmatism is not skepticism but community. Thus, while the science of sex at any moment may reflect its historico-cultural context, the antidote to such biases lies in ensuring that researchers are exposed to a range of perspectives. Fallibilism, then, consists not so much in adopting "I might be wrong" as a mantra as in adopting community as a method.[30]

4. Practical Consequences

My focus here has been on Peirce's scholastic realism but it is worth remembering his pragmatism, and in particular his view that the measure of a concept is its practical consequences. Accordingly, let me conclude by sketching some of the possible practical consequences of adopting a Peircean philosophy of sex—these consequences relating to the treatment of intersex people and the focus on preclinical sex differences in health research.

At the outset of this chapter, I described the way in which evidence about intersex people is often invoked in online debates about trans people. Some of this no doubt relates to confusion about the difference between intersex people and trans people and to the conflation of sex and gender categories. Much of the popular use of intersex people as exemplars of the "beyond the binary" view of gender is the result of twenty years of teaching and scholarship in women's and gender studies (broadly construed) that instrumentalizes intersex in the service of social constructivist theses about sex and gender.[31]

In 2002, Koyama and Weasel found that intersex existence is understood and presented by women's studies instructors "largely as a scholarly object to be studied in order to deconstruct the notion of binary sexes (and thus sexism and homophobia) rather than as a subject that has real-world implications for real people."[32] Chief among those real-world implications are the historical and, in many regions, ongoing clinical practice of "correcting" intersex conditions through medically unnecessary surgery and hormonal treatments and the selective termination of intersex fetuses.[33] Other real-world implications include regulations that discriminate against intersex athletes.[34]

Framed in Peircean scholastic realist terms, we can understand the ways in which intersex experiences are often appropriated and instrumentalized within gender studies in the service of "beyond the binary accounts" of gender as an overemphasis on firstness and medical and regulatory discrimination against intersex people as an overemphasis on thirdness. In the first instance, gender studies scholars seeking to resist exclusionary and binaristic accounts of sex and gender focus on intersex people as statistical outliers in order to destabilize sex and gender norms. In the second case, clinical standards and athletic regulations are geared to assert the statistical norm and eliminate outliers from it. On both sides, intersex people end up on the losing end. Adopting a Peircean scholastic realist metaphysics of sex would help us to remember to keep firstness, secondness, and thirdness in mind in the study of sex and would thereby help to avoid the harms—especially to intersex people—attendant upon overemphasizing firstness or thirdness.

Correspondingly, Peirce's ethics of inquiry reminds us that treating intersex people as "poster children" for social constructivism and eliminating intersex people through clinical or regulatory means, each in its own way, blocks the path of inquiry. Subsuming intersex to social constructivism blocks inquiry by closing off other modes of philosophical understanding of intersex, including modes favored by many intersex scholars themselves. More seriously, the elimination of intersex people either by prohibiting their full participation in society or by reducing the incidence of intersex by means of medical interventions, including selective pregnancy termination, blocks inquiry by excluding intersex people from the community of inquirers—sometimes violently.

We have seen how a Peircean philosophy of sex grounded in scholastic realism and guided by Peirce's ethics of inquiry could help to avoid reductionism—either constructivist or eliminativist—about intersex. Recent scholarship on the use of preclinical sex differences in health research provides just one example of the need for a nonreductionist account of sex well beyond intersex.

In recent years, North American and European health organizations have instituted policies requiring the use of both male and female tissues and other materials in preclinical studies. The intention is good—to bend the stick in the other direction after a long history in which female biological materials were often excluded from preclinical research, often to the detriment of women's healthcare outcomes. However, some feminist science scholars argue that these new policies place too much emphasis on patient sex in the study of health phenomena that are actually not affected (or not primarily affected) by sex markers (such as chromosomal complement or reproductive organs).

Richardson et al. point to research on zolpidem (Ambien) as an example.[35] Owing to higher rates of adverse drug events to zolpidem by women than men, the Food and Drug Administration in 2013 reduced the recommended dosage of zolpidem for women. However, research since then into the mechanism for women zolpidem users' higher rate of adverse drug events revealed that body weight, not sex, explains the differential reaction. Moreover, it turns out that study results into sex-based differences in zolpidem's effects were confounded by a gendered (as opposed to sex-based) difference: among male and female subjects whose brain waves register the same level of impairment, the males tend to rate themselves as less impaired.[36] That is, when men and women are equally impaired physiologically, the men are more likely to downplay their level of impairment—a behavior that is more likely due to socialization than to biology. By reducing men and women to males and females, Richardson et al. argue, the new health research policies neglect "the embodied interaction of human sex- and gender-related variables in sex differences."[37] Put differently, the new policies may make it harder for researchers to notice gendered phenomena because they are primed to notice sexed phenomena.

These two chapters in health research—first excluding female tissue and cell samples and then requiring them—are two successive examples of assumptions that block the path of inquiry. The assumption that female samples are irrelevant to health research blocked inquiry into some sex-based health differences, but the assumption that different gendered health outcomes reduce to "sex itself" at the level of genes, cells, or tissues blocks inquiry in a different way.

As the science of sex and health science at the intersection of sex and gender continue to rapidly develop, Peircean fallibilism and scholastic realism can help us both to keep the path of inquiry open and to take seriously both thirdness—the patterns across populations—and firstness—the deviation from these patterns.

I began this chapter by contrasting two broad approaches to sex: "binaristic biology" and "critical sex studies." In some ways, the metaphysical dispute between these two camps concerns which of sex and gender to treat as fundamental and which to treat as epiphenomenal. Binaristic biology treats sex as fundamental and gender as emerging from that fundament. Critical sex studies flips it and treats gender as the fundament upon which sex is constructed. A Peircean philosophy of sex settles this dispute by denying that either sex or gender—or the putative distinction between them—is fundamental. It thereby leaves the path of inquiry into sex and gender open for discoveries that we can yet barely imagine. In short, Peirce provides us with the tools we need for a nonreductionist philosophy of sex that treats the science of sex as a science like any other.

Acknowledgments

I acknowledge that I live and work on Treaty 4, on the territories of the nêhiyawak, Anihšināpēk, Dakota, Lakota, and Nakoda, and the homeland of the Métis/Michif Nation. My thanks to audience members at the University of Waterloo Philosophy Colloquium; at the Applying Peirce 2 workshop, held at the Tallinn University of Technology and University of Helsinki, and at the International Peirce Centennial Congress, held at UMass Lowell, for their helpful comments on earlier versions of this paper. Thank you to Morgan Holmes for her advice on scholarly engagements with intersex. Finally, I am grateful to Kees de Waal for his patience and support as I completed this chapter and for his astute suggestions on the penultimate draft.

Notes

1. But see Section 4 on such rhetorical uses of intersex people.
2. My own work is part of that explosion and deploys "beyond the binary framing." See Dea (2016).
3. Feder and Karkazis (2008, 35).
4. Morgan Holmes, "The Intersex Enchiridion: Naming and Knowledge." *Somatechnics* 1.2 (2011): 388–411.
5. Geddes and Thomson (1889, 267).
6. This by way of contrast with sequentially hermaphroditic species, in which the type of gamete an individual produces depends upon what stage in the life cycle it is at. Various fish and amphibian species are sequentially hermaphroditic.
7. Sea Studios Foundation, *The Shape of Life*, 2001. Video.
8. Parker (2004, 86).
9. Ibid., 84.
10. Richardson (2013, 15).
11. On which, see Section 4.
12. Simone de Beauvoir, *The Second Sex*, trans. Constance Borde and Sheila Malovany-Chevallier (New York: Vintage, 2011): 3.
13. See Kessler and McKenna (1985); and Kessler (1990). Kessler and McKenna do not distinguish between sex and gender because they regard the distinction as ill-founded and often muddled. They thus use "gender" for both social and biological demarcations.
14. "Gender assignment" is the term for the first declaration that is made of an infant's gender—the moment, for example, that the attending obstetrician says "It's a boy!" "Gender reassignment" is the term for a neonatal revision to that declaration that is sometimes made in the case of intersex infants.
15. Laqueur (1990).
16. Ibid., 10.

17. Anne Fausto-Sterling, "The Five Sexes: Why Male and Female Are Not Enough," *The Sciences* 33.2 (1993): 20–24.
18. Fausto-Sterling (2000).
19. Blackless et al. (2000, 76).
20. Alice Domurat Dreger, *Hermaphrodites and the Medical Invention of Sex* (Cambridge, MA: Harvard University Press, 2000).
21. Oliver (2011)
22. Sandra Bem, "The Measurement of Psychological Androgyny," *Journal of Consulting and Clinical Psychology* 31.4 (1974): 634–643.
23. Christopher Kilmartin, *The Masculine Self*, 2nd ed. (Boston: McGraw-Hill Higher Education, 2000).
24. CP (1.330), emphasis mine.
25. Thank you to Kees de Waal for pointing this out to me.
26. CP (6.173).
27. EP2:2.3, 2.338, 1998.
28. I discuss this more fully in Shannon Dea, "Peirce and Spinoza's Pragmaticist Metaphysics," *Cognitio* 15.1 (2014): 25–35.
29. Robert Burch, "Charles Sanders Peirce," in *The Stanford Encyclopedia of Philosophy* (Winter 2021 ed.), Edward N. Zalta (ed.). https://plato.stanford.edu/archives/win2021/entries/peirce/.
30. Thank you to Kees de Waal for pushing me on this point.
31. An International Day against Homophobia, Transphobia and Biphobia (IDAHOT) guide on "How to Be an Ally to the Intersex Community" cautions "Don't use intersex to prove a theory about sex and gender. Don't expect intersex people to dismantle a gender binary": https://gate.ngo/wp-content/uploads/2020/03/IDAHOT-018-English-Intersex.pdf.
32. Emi Koyama and Lisa Weasel, "From Social Construction to Social Justice: Transforming How We Teach About Intersexuality," *Women's Studies Quarterly* 30.3/4 (2002): 170.
33. Holmes (2008).
34. Rachel Savage, "False Start for Intersex Athletes Barred from Olympics," *Reuters Healthcare* (2021): https://www.reuters.com/article/olympics-2020-athletics-intersex-idUSL8N2OW50W.
35. Sarah S. Richardson et al., "Focus on Preclinical Sex Differences Will Not Address Women's and Men's Health Disparities," *Proceedings of the National Academy of Sciences* 112.44 (2015): 13419–13420.
36. Heather Shattuck Heidorn and Sarah Richardson, "Focusing on Differences between the Sexes Is Leading Medical Researchers Astray," *The Washington Post* (May 30, 2019): https://www.washingtonpost.com/outlook/2019/05/30/focusing-differences-between-sexes-is-leading-medical-researchers-astray/.
37. Richardson et al., "Focus on Preclinical Sex Differences."

Bibliography

Blackless, Melanie, Anthony Charuvastra, Amanda Derryck, Anne Fausto-Sterling, Karl Lauzanne, and Ellen Lee. 2000. "How Sexually Dimorphic Are We? Review and Synthesis." *American Journal of Human Biology* 12: 151–166.

Dea, Shannon. 2016. *Beyond the Binary: Thinking About Sex and Gender*. Peterborough, ON: Broadview Press.

Dreger, Alice Domurat. 2000. *Hermaphrodites and the Medical Invention of Sex.* Cambridge, MA: Harvard University Press.
Fausto-Sterling, Anne. 1993. "The Five Sexes: Why Male and Female Are Not Enough." *The Sciences* 33, no. 2 (March/April): 20–24.
Fausto-Sterling, Anne. 2000. "The Five Sexes Revisited." *The Sciences* 40, no. 4 (July/August): 17–23.
Feder, Ellen, and Katrina Karkazis. 2008. "What's in a Name? The Controversy over 'Disorders of Sex Development.'" *Hastings Center Report* 38, no. 5 (September–October): 33–36.
Geddes, Patrick, and John Arthur Thomson. 1889. *The Evolution of Sex.* London: W. Scott.
Holmes, Morgan. 2008. "Mind the Gaps: Intersex and (Re-productive) Spaces in Disability Studies and Bioethics." *Journal of Bioethical Inquiry* 5, no. 2–3: 169–181.
Kessler, Suzanne. 1990. "The Medical Construction of Gender: Case Management of Intersexed Infants." *Signs* 16, no. 1: 3–26.
Kessler, Suzanne, and Wendy McKenna. 1985. *Gender: An Ethnomethodological Approach.* Chicago: University of Chicago Press.
Laqueur, Thomas. 1990. *Making Sex: Body and Gender from the Greeks to Freud.* Cambridge, MA: Harvard University Press.
Oliver, Jill. 2011. "A Multidimensional Model of Biological Sex." PhD diss. University of Waterloo.
Parker, Joel. 2004. "A Major Evolutionary Transition to More Than Two Sexes?" *Trends in Ecology and Evolution* 19, no. 2: 83–86.
Peirce, Charles S. 1931–1958. *The Collected Papers of Charles Sanders Peirce.* 8 vols. Vols. 1–6 edited by Charles Hartshorne and Paul Weiss. Vols. 7–8 edited by Arthur W. Burks. Cambridge, MA: Harvard University Press. (Referred to as CP.)
Peirce, Charles S. 1998. *The Essential Peirce: Selected Philosophical Writings.* Vol. 2 edited by the Peirce Edition Project. Bloomington: Indiana University Press. (Referred to as EP2.)
Richardson, Sarah. 2013. *Sex Itself: The Search for Male and Female in the Human Genome.* Chicago: University of Chicago Press.

CHAPTER 29

CHARLES S. PEIRCE AND THE FEELING OF UNDERSTANDING

The Power and Limit of Science from a Pragmatist Perspective

HERMAN C. D. G. DE REGT

> We'll restore science to its rightful place.
>
> Barack Obama, *Inaugural Presidential Address* (2009)

1. INTRODUCTION

In two of Peirce's classic papers, "The Fixation of Belief" (1877) and "How to Make Our Ideas Clear" (1878), many elements can be found for his pragmatist stance toward science as the most reliable method of belief fixation and the best way to make our ideas clear. Indeed, the pragmatist philosophy of science rests heavily on Peirce's ideas about the nature of science in his *Illustrations of the Logic of Science*, the collection of papers published in *Popular Science Monthly* in 1877/78. In this chapter, I focus on an underexposed but important aspect in these two papers that connects Peirce's ideas to the present discussion on the feeling of understanding and what constitutes a scientific explanation. I will argue how Peircean pragmatist ideas take issue with much of what philosophers of science in the early twenty-first century say about science and understanding, undermining from a pragmatist view the rather standard but (I think) wrong-headed idea of understanding in science.

What if. What if Peirce lived today cherishing the same ideas he expressed in his two classical papers? Let's be honest, Peirce is not modest in his claims. He would still enthusiastically defend science as the exalted form of inquiry into black holes, climate change, virus pandemics, or the alleged secret political elite's behavior. He would still argue the pragmatist proposal how to grasp the meaning of concepts as such, would not have been surprised by the huge success of scientific research, and would joyfully be impressed by the best explanations of everyday life phenomena.

I want to point out that, following Peirce's early pragmatism, mathematically expressed natural laws do scientifically explain, but do not help us to get a feeling of understanding of the world that we inhabit. I suggest that this pragmatist idea runs against an overly optimistic view of what science is capable of regarding understanding the world in terms of underlying, unobservable structures, entities, or processes. I will try to show how Peirce's two classical papers pave the way for a more down-to-earth approach of what science is, what it can achieve, and what its limits are in relation to us, humans. These papers form a fruitful framework for thinking about science in the early twenty-first century and are relevant and urgent for a society marked by a speed-of-light flow of information and disinformation that struggles with almost apocalyptic issues like climate change.

Peirce offers us a way to argue that we (1) understand what scientific inquiry means, (2) need to take the results of the application of scientific inquiry seriously, and (3) must not despair when we notice that scientific inquiry does (in the end) not generate a veridical feeling of understanding why things happen the way they happen—they just do as a matter of fact and law. To illustrate these three points, I will briefly and positively contrast a Peircean pragmatist view of understanding with the recent contextual theory of scientific understanding in Henk de Regt's *Understanding Scientific Understanding* (2017)—a philosophy of science that is widely supported and applauded (and honored with the 2019 Lakatos Award).

First, I recapture the main idea in Peirce's paper on what he calls "the methods of belief fixation." Peirce argues from an evolutionary and psychological point of view. From that point of view, humans are (of course) biological exemplars of a unique species, carrying very specific psychological characteristics. If we stress this aspect of Peirce's 1877 paper, we get to a notion of a feeling of understanding that is relevant for today's understanding of scientific understanding, especially when we add to this (what I believe is) the core of Peirce's subsequent 1878 paper on the elucidation of concepts, namely, the "rule for attaining the third grade of clearness of apprehension" of concepts (later more commonly known as *the pragmatic maxim*). This opens a way for concluding that since science (as a method of belief fixation) is seeking out the sensible effects of our ideas par excellence, it will also offer the best explanation of any phenomenon we experience.

Next, I argue from new psychological insights that we generate a feeling of understanding (bringing our minds at ease in a soothing state of belief) whenever the scientific explanations spell out phenomena in terms of colliding things—a direct consequence, so it seems, of the fact that we, like all other organisms, adapted to the observable and sensible thing-like environmental world of experience. Psychological research suggests humans generate a natural feeling of understanding if they grasp what they see in terms of objects that push and pull, bump and bounce—*literally* touching each other.

However, if scientific explanations merely use *metaphors* of colliding things (or metaphorical collisions), the result is an illusory feeling of understanding, not a veridical feeling of understanding. If we are after the truth in science, we need to drop the metaphor, and what we are left with is what I call the Peircean idea of natural laws in terms of mathematics. These mathematical natural laws are pragmatically the best scientific explanations we (will ever) have. Let me try to unpack this in the following sections. (Section 2 is based on chapter 11 of De Regt et al. [2021].)

2. Science, Belief Fixation, and Concept Elucidation

Peirce fiercely objected to Cartesian philosophy. As a man of science, he noticed empirical data that contradicted Descartes's idea that man's intuition is infallible. This allowed Peirce to question Descartes's rule that an intuitively clear and distinct idea is true. Do people really have an intuitive power of distinguishing an intuition from another form of cognition? According to Peirce: "There is no evidence that we have this faculty, except that we seem to feel that we have it. But the weight of that testimony depends entirely on our being supposed to have the power of distinguishing in this feeling whether the feeling be the result of education, old associations, etc., or whether it is an intuitive cognition; or, in other words, it depends on presupposing the very matter testified to. Is this feeling infallible? And is this judgment concerning it infallible and so on, ad infinitum?" (EP1:12, 1868). Much of Peirce's work is therefore focused on the problem of how to make ideas clear if one cannot rest assured that intuition makes ideas perfectly clear. For instance, Peirce asks "Does the reader know of the blind spot on the retina?" (EP1:15, 1868). Peirce's solution is clearly to bring in science to make our ideas clear.

Distinguishing (Cartesian) paper doubt from a real and living doubt that actually feels uncomfortable ("Let us not pretend to doubt in philosophy what we do not doubt in our hearts" [EP1:29, 1868]), Peirce argues there is a very relevant difference between the feeling of belief and the feeling of doubt. To have a belief means that we are in a relatively steady state of thought at rest—a habit has developed that determines our behavior. In a state of doubt, however, we feel the need to search for a means to get rid of that doubt—and act accordingly. Peirce implies a particular anthropological view here: human beings experience doubt as an irritation and can do nothing but try to get rid of this irritation and struggle to find a soothing state of belief. This anthropology is derived (partly) from evolutionary ideas about natural organisms and the origins of human beings.

The transition from an irritating state of doubt into a reassuring state of belief is what Peirce calls 'inquiry.' Indeed, he claims that "the sole object of inquiry is the settlement of opinion" (EP1:115, 1877, cf. de Waal 2013, ch. 6). This view of belief leads him to the observation (in line with what he thinks we know from the sciences) that "as soon as a firm belief is reached, we are entirely satisfied, whether the belief is true or false" (EP1:115, 1877).

Peirce offers an inventory of the methods of belief fixation that we may "choose" from, concluding that only "the method of science" carries with it the promise that we end up with beliefs that run the lowest risk of being refuted by future data. The method tends to keep us away from living doubt and to move us in the direction of truth.

Inquiry into phenomena, under the assumption that there is an external permanency (EP1:120, 1877), that is, independent from what I personally believe about the world, is what characterizes this method of science. Indeed, science proposes a distinctive hypothesis: "There are real things, whose characters are entirely independent of our opinions about them; those realities affect our senses according to regular laws, and, though our sensations are as different as our relations to the objects, yet, by taking advantage of the laws of perception, we can ascertain by reasoning how things really are, and any man, if he have sufficient experience and reason enough about it will be led to the one true conclusion" (EP1:120, 1877). Reflection on the nature of our beliefs (which are of the same order as behavioral habits) drives us to the conclusion that they cannot be more than our currently best ideas about the world and ourselves. Science becomes hypothetical to the core. Peirce suggests that the method of science is like a "chosen bride" and that we must "strive to be the worthy knights and champions of her" since "scientific investigation has had the most wonderful triumphs in the way of settling opinion" (EP1:123, 1877).

Now, since we evade doubt and strive for sustainable belief (Peirce follows Alexander Bain's suggestion that belief involves the establishment in our nature of a rule of action, or a habit [EP1:129, 1878]), we will also strive for a maximum degree of clarity in the concepts we use (when called for under the circumstances). In "How to Make Our Ideas Clear" (1878), Peirce introduces his hypothesis of concept elucidation (a proposal for what we mean by meaning). It can be formulated concisely as follows: "our idea of anything *is* our idea of its sensible effects" (EP1:132, 1878; see Fisch [1954]). Or: "Consider what effects, which might conceivably have practical bearings, we conceive the object of our conception to have. Then, our conception of these effects is the whole of our conception of the object" (EP1:132, 1878). Peirce argues that the "whole function of thought is to produce habits of action" (EP1:132, 1878). To determine the meaning of our thoughts we must determine which habits it produces in us, "for what a thing means is simply what habits it involves" (EP1:131, 1878). A difference in meaning is therefore a difference in practice, a difference in action. When "different" ideas do not make a difference in action we must conclude that these ideas in fact express the same idea in different ways—they mean the same. What we do in science is to find out par excellence what the effects, which might conceivably have practical bearings, the object of our conception has.

According to the pragmatist, science can be described in a very general way only: science is inquiry under the assumption that there is an external permanency. The detailed scientific techniques of different disciplines (i.e., physics, psychology, economics, sociology, biology, etc.) can differ extremely, depending on the domain of investigation. Controlled experiments, statistical analyses, interviews, historical research, questionnaires, participant observation, *Verstehen*, etc.—every domain has its own combination of characteristic techniques of scientific inquiry. However, the pragmatist would hold that these are scientific techniques only if they assume that there is something to be learned within that domain that is independent of what the researcher may happen to personally think about it. In other words, these techniques, if scientific, operate under the premise of an external permanency.

Importantly, pragmatism also applies the pragmatic maxim to "philosophical" concepts themselves. What does it mean for something to be real? What is the meaning of the concepts of reality and truth? Peirce observes that what is real is that which has an effect on our beliefs, given our inquiry: real things cause belief. In addition, Peirce asks himself how true belief (or belief in the real) is distinguished from false belief (or belief in fiction), and he states: "[As] we have seen in the former paper ["Fixation of Belief"], the ideas of truth and falsehood, in their full development, appertain exclusively to the scientific method of settling opinion" (EP1:137, 1878). Using the scientific method, we will (ultimately) find out what is real. But what do we mean by the idea of reality? Peirce consequently applies the pragmatic maxim to the concept of reality itself: "The opinion which is fated to be ultimately agreed to by all who investigate is what we mean by the truth and the object represented in this opinion is the real" (EP1:139, 1878). Thus, Peirce tries to capture the practical bearings of the concepts of truth and reality. Remember that the scientific method of belief fixation is taken to be the best method we have of getting rid of the arbitrariness and contingency of our beliefs. It implies a self-corrective mechanism: as a matter of course, we will notice when we are wrong if we are doing scientific work to elucidate our concepts and fixate our beliefs. Importantly, "we" refers to the whole community of researchers. Scientists, inquirers committed to the method of science, correct each other, not just themselves. Of course, our path through history could be such that we will never get into all the situations necessary to change our minds about the world in the direction of belief in the real, rather than belief in fiction. But Peirce's pragmatism suggests that what we *mean* to say by claiming that some belief is true is that we now think there is nothing whatsoever that would make us change our belief. So, ipso facto, scientific belief becomes that to which everybody would ultimately agree, and that final opinion cannot fail to be the truth, and the whole truth, about the world (cf. Misak [2021, ch. 7]).

Please note that emphasizing that the early Peirce (1870s) clearly draws an evolutionary and psychological picture of humans does not entail a psychologism in the sense that "truth consists in a certain feeling," or that "logical laws are grounded on psychological research" (see Cristalli [2017]). It is indeed the case, as Peirce later argues, that "we cannot trust a feeling as such" (EP2:386, 1906). The evolutionary account of humans and psychology as a science of the human mind are constant factors in Peirce's basic pragmatist ideas, witnessing for instance his much later paper 'What Pragmatism Is' (EP2:331–345, 1905).

Having spelled out what I believe to be important and relevant aspects of Peirce's classical papers, I will now focus on "the feeling of understanding" and the idea of "scientific explanation" that one discovers in these papers. These notions show what is wrong in (at least) one leading view of science and how a Peircean pragmatic meaning of science helps us understand why humans believe what they believe, what science is, what understanding is, and what an explanation is. Given the societal challenge to convince people of what is, for all we know, the true representation of the world, it is important to understand science in the right way. Let me therefore introduce the very idea of the feeling of understanding and how it is connected to the Peircean idea of science.

3. THE FEELING OF UNDERSTANDING

To introduce the idea of a feeling of understanding, and its relation to available explanations, I briefly introduce a spectacular discovery of a nowadays well-studied ancient Greek artifact from (most probably) the second century BC (Carman 2017), the so-called *Antikythera mechanism*. In 1901, near the Greek Island of Antikythera, sponge divers lifted, among many other artifacts, what later turned out to be the fragments of an intricate bronze astronomical calculator, consisting of a complex set of connected gearwheels. These gearwheels were originally arranged in such a way that, with the Earth at the center of the cosmos, the constellations of the known cosmological bodies at a chosen date could simply be read from the pointers and dials of the portable box (Jones 2017). Freeth et al. (2021) conclude their extremely educated reconstructive guess at the original mechanism by saying that

> the Antikythera Mechanism was a computational instrument for mathematical astronomy. [...] It calculated the *ecliptic longitudes* of the Moon, Sun and planets; the *phase* of the Moon; the *Age of the Moon*; the *synodic phases* of the planets; the *excluded days* of the Metonic Calendar; *eclipses—possibilities, times, characteristics, years* and *seasons*; the *heliacal risings and settings* of prominent stars and constellations; and the *Olympiad cycle*—an ancient Greek astronomical compendium of staggering ambition. It is the first known device that mechanized the predictions of scientific theories, and it could have automated many of the calculations needed for its own design [...]—the first steps to the mechanization of mathematics and science. [The Antikythera mechanism] challenges all our preconceptions about the technological capabilities of the ancient Greeks. (12–13)

Clearly, this discovery and reconstruction of the Antikythera mechanism is indeed a major discovery about not only the technological capabilities of the ancient Greeks but also probably the worldview of the Greek elite; at least there is the possibility that there was already a sense of what Dijksterhuis (1961) called the mechanization of the world picture that was taking place from Pythagoras to Newton (and beyond). Let me now, admittedly through a thought experiment, illustrate what the feeling of understanding refers to, using the Antikythera mechanism.

Suppose in ancient Greece a new person is initiated to the "portable cosmos." An expert would demonstrate the device showing that it has colossal predictive and retrodictive power concerning astronomical phenomena. For all practical purposes, the box exclusively generates true data (of course, the Antikythera mechanism would ultimately deviate from the true position of the heavenly bodies as it does not, in the long run, track their true movements). Yet, the mechanism inside the box is not miraculous at all (although it is indeed a genius design). What the philosophical elite conclude from the device is that the Sun, the Moon, the planets, and the zodiac are all fixed on cosmological gearwheels, connected to one another as depicted in the structural mechanism of the box. They may want to take the mechanism to represent the true cosmological mechanism. As the student gets the mechanism explained we can imagine that a feeling of understanding is growing in the mind of the newly initiated. The student sees the teeth of the turning wheels and, given their number and the physical relation between the gearwheels, the student can literally see what is happening: he is witnessing the literal pushes and collisions and the movement of the clockwork. When asked whether he or she now understands the astronomical movements, the person would certainly affirm this understanding.

Now, what will happen to this feeling of understanding if this student is transported through time only to re-emerge in the eighteenth century with its fully corroborated Newtonian mechanics? I think it is fair to say that that feeling is completely gone. The Antikythera explanation of astronomical movements is not true: there are no cosmological cogs and wheels; the mechanism in the Antikythera device is completely wrong. The fact that during a limited historical time the device generated rather exact astronomical data was due to the ingenious design of rather ad hoc—like traps that corrected the circular movement of the pointers over the dials. But it is wrong in its core. Newton explained the movements using the mathematical law of universal gravitation. It implied "action at a distance," something Newton himself was not comfortable with. Cohen, in a classical analysis of Newton's work, said:

> [Newton] was free to explore the properties and effects of a mathematical attractive force even though he found the concept of a grasping force "acting at a distance" to be abhorrent and not admissible in the realm of good physics. Next, he compared the consequences of his mathematical construct with the observed principles and laws of the external world such as Kepler's law of areas and law of elliptical orbits. Where the mathematical construct fell short Newton modified it. This way of thinking, which I call the Newtonian style, is captured by the title of Newton's great work: *Mathematical Principles of Natural Philosophy*. (1985, 169)

And he continues: "Those who accepted the Newtonian style fleshed out the law of universal gravity, showed how it explains many other physical phenomena, and demanded that an explanation be sought of how such a force could be transmitted over vast distances through apparently empty space. The Newtonian style enabled Newton to study universal gravity without premature inhibitions that would have blocked his great discovery" (170). Indeed, the mathematical success of his mechanics seduced Newton to think that the attractive force truly exists, but since he was unable to explain such a force he decided to simply stick to the mathematics and "not feign hypotheses." Our ancient Greek student, after dismissing the Antikythera mechanism, does not generate a new feeling of understanding trying to grasp astronomical Newtonian mechanics. No one understands why the planets move the way they do; they simply do so as a matter of the mathematical Newtonian law. Now, suppose we pull the Greek into the era of Einstein's theory of relativity. The person is told that the movement of the planets is the sensible effect of the geometry of spacetime. The feeling of understanding in the student is still gone.

What I try to illustrate with this thought experiment is that a feeling of understanding is, most important, a psychological aspect of human nature: if the empirically adequate explanation refers to *metaphorical* collisions, the explanation still generates (as a matter of fact) a feeling of understanding, but there is no truth (the feeling is not veridical). The true explanation is an empirically adequate explanation in terms of mathematical relations between variables in a model that as such represents the world—something that is implied by a pragmatic elucidation of concepts. Such mathematical explanations do not seem to generate a feeling of understanding.

Theoretical physicist Sean Carroll is taking this point to its extreme. He presents what Wilczek (2015) dubbed the core theory and argues that for the observable (or sensible) realm in which humans live their lives, this core theory mathematically explains everything in terms of natural laws. In fact, he presents the core theory as one long mathematical formula:[1]

$$W = \int_{k<\Lambda} [Dg][DA][D\psi][D\Phi] \exp\left\{ i \int d^4 x \sqrt{-g} \left[\frac{m_p^2}{2} R - \frac{1}{4} F^a_{\mu\nu} F^{a\mu\nu} + i\bar{\psi}^i \gamma^\mu D_\mu \psi^i + \left(\bar{\psi}^i_L V_{ij} \Phi \psi^j_R + \text{h.c.} \right) - |D_\mu \Phi|^2 - V(\Phi) \right] \right\}$$

I focus on the level of reality described by quantum field theory, in what we might call the "everyday-life regime" (ELR)—the energies, densities, temperatures, and other quantities characterizing phenomena that a typical human will experience in their normal lives. [...] Modern physics has constructed an "effective" quantum field theory that purports to account for phenomena within this regime, a model that has been dubbed the "Core Theory" (Wilczek, 2015). It includes the Standard Model of Particle Physics, but also gravitation as described by general relativity in the weak-field limit. I will argue that we have good reason to believe that this model is both accurate and complete within the everyday-life regime; in other words, that the laws of physics underlying everyday life are, at one level of description, completely known. This is not to claim that physics is nearly finished and that we are close to obtaining a Theory of Everything, but just that one particular level in one limited regime is now understood. (Carroll 2022, 28)

In an earlier publication Carroll stated: "We can be confident that the Core Theory, accounting for the substances and processes we experience in our everyday life, is *correct*. [...] We can't be metaphysically certain of this; it's not something we can prove mathematically, since science never proves things. But in any good Bayesian accounting, it seems overwhelmingly likely to be true. The laws of physics underlying everyday life are completely known" (2017, 177). Physics has arrived at the point where we have the mathematics to explain what will happen next, but the feeling of understanding is gone. Carroll's own interpretation of some of the variables in this mathematical core theory illustrates this, when he says: "In quantum field theory, it doesn't take that much information to specify the properties of a particular field or, equivalently, the particle with which it is associated. Each particle has a mass, and it also has a 'spin.' We can think of the particles almost like little spinning tops, except elementary particles (which are really vibrations of quantum fields) don't actually have any size; their spin is an intrinsic property, not the revolution of their bodies around an axis" (2017, 436). Nothing in these terms refers to anything that generates a feeling of understanding, I would argue. Furthermore, let me, in a Peircean vein, try to show how this idea of a feeling of understanding is supported by current psychological research and how it has implications for our thinking about science.

4. The Feeling of Understanding and the Science of Psychology

Peirce was one of the first to combine epistemological questions with new scientific theories of evolution. In a general sense, humans use whatever means they can to keep their homeostatic balance (Schulkin, 2004), consciously or unconsciously, even in epistemic situations. Peirce importantly pointed out that "it is true that we do generally reason correctly by nature. But that is an accident. [...] Logicality in regard of practical matters is the most useful quality an animal can possess, and might, therefore, result from the action of natural selection; but outside of these it is probably of more advantage to the animal to have his mind filled with pleasing and encouraging visions, independently of their truth; and thus, upon unpractical subjects, natural selection might occasion a fallacious tendency of thought" (EP1:112). Nowadays, we witness that natural selection might indeed occasion a fallacious tendency of thought and that those thoughts, false as they are, might even harm the believer himself, others, and a larger environment, making this tendency relevant to practical subjects. This is basically the idea behind natural, old cognitive dispositions, tendencies, and habits, becoming cognitive biases in a modern world. Peirce is essentially describing how human beings might easily fall victim to the psychology of beliefs through ancient evolutionary, brain-ingrained mechanisms.

Now, why do people lack the feeling of understanding given the core theory? Well, the only explanations that seem to generate a feeling of understanding in humans are explanations in terms of collisions broadly construed: the literal pull and push of objects, the bouncing and bumping of things—and such a mechanism of collisions of things is simply lacking in the core theory. Try to understand the core theory without colliding objects, spinning tops, and vibrating fields and *the feeling of understanding dissipates*. It dissipates because humans are (so it seems) by nature unable to generate a feeling of understanding without referring to collisions of objects.

The feeling of understanding seems to be an old evolutionary feature of the human brain that normally helps us to anticipate what will happen in the phenomenal, mechanistic, manifest world we inhabit. It is evolution's shorthand to let us feel we are in control and can trust our empirical expectations—enhancing the chance of sustaining our lives and bringing forth a new generation. This feeling of understanding was (evidently) so important that it completely determined human imagination: only what can be explained in terms of mechanistic collisions is within the grasp of our understanding. Given what we know of our evolutionary history, this makes sense. Humans, ancestral and modern, are better off with a reliable sign that things in the manifest world of events are sufficiently under control. Usually, the feeling of understanding does that job for us.

This feeling of understanding is a pleasant feeling, and the anticipation of losing it is a painful, nagging, irritating feeling to be avoided at great cost. There is a close relation between the feeling of understanding and what Alison Gopnik once aptly called "explanation as orgasm" (Gopnik 1998, 2000). Of course, we need to further explore how the feeling of understanding is connected to the 'hedonistic hotspots' in the brain. The *nucleus accumbens* and the *ventral pallidum*, together with neurotransmitters like GABA, dopamine, and glutamate, responsible for stimulating, through pleasurable feelings, behavior that is conducive for survival and producing offspring might likewise be involved in generating a pleasurable feeling of understanding (see Linden 2012; Mizraji and Lin 2017).

Is seems that feelings of understanding are only reached through mechanistic explanations in terms of colliding bodies (think of our time-traveling ancient Greek student). Where such explanation in terms of collisions is lacking, the feeling of understanding is lacking. To nevertheless generate a pleasant feeling of understanding we seem to take recourse to metaphors. Let me elucidate.

One way in which we, modern humans, have solved the incomprehensibility of (scientific) explanations is by using linguistic *collision metaphors*. Here the pioneering work of Lakoff and Johnson (1980) and Davidson (1978) on metaphors is crucial (see also the work on Peirce's pragmatism and metaphors in Hausman [2011]). Although metaphors are of course important heuristic devices in understanding, metaphors are basically false depictions of the world (here we assume that "Julia is like the Sun" is an analogy and "Julia is the Sun" is a metaphor). A specific kind of metaphors, namely, those in terms of collisions, give us real but false feelings of understanding, since what is explained by means of such a metaphor cannot truly be explained in terms of literal collisions *according to science itself*—as a matter of brute fact and law, we are left with mathematical relations only.

The feeling of understanding seems evolution's quick and dirty way to let one know that one is in control and that it is probably safe to move around doing what needs to be done to sustain one's life (retaining or regaining a homeostatic state). Because it is an old evolutionary ingrained mechanism of the human brain, it becomes a fundamental bias in an environment in which *language* takes over and depicts everything that is of vital importance in terms of literal collisions or, if that is impossible, in terms of collision metaphors. Both generate the pleasant feeling of understanding—the first is veridical, the second is illusory.

Scientists and laypersons alike will always seek refuge to collision metaphors to generate that (evolutionary old) addictive feeling of understanding in themselves and in the public at large. Therefore, even in science we find many pseudoscientific beliefs, and the psychology of pseudoscience must extend to the working mind of scientists as well. The ideas of "orbiting particles," "bouncing molecules," "waves through vacuum," and "flowing electrons," etc., are, in a sense, pseudoscientific beliefs. Indeed, the moment we generate a feeling of understanding using metaphors, we fall victim to the feeling of understanding as a bias, even in science.

Bringing together the two insights propagated by Peirce in two of his classical papers (science as a method of belief fixation and the explication of sensible effects of concepts), the latest neuroscientific inquiry of beliefs shows that Peirce put us on the right track thinking that it is the psychology of humans that determines whether we have a feeling of understanding when we are presented with some account of some phenomenon in some context. Bromberg-Martin and Sharot summarize this research, saying that "whenever we must adjudicate between multiple, potentially conflicting beliefs and desires, there is an opportunity for our motivations to put their thumb on the scales and influence belief formation [...] belief formation is an active process: we seek out information that is relevant to our interests, goals, and desires" (2020, 562). Surprisingly, neuropsychological research suggests that holding beliefs can trigger intrinsic rewards in the brain, meaning that individuals may be motivated to seek information they expect will resolve uncertainty or produce positive beliefs, and that "the goal in seeking information is not merely to change the *external* world, but also to change *internal* belief states," *simply because it feels good* (Bromberg-Martin and Sharot 2020, 562–563; see also Bromberg-Martin and Hikosaka 2009):

> In monkeys, single neurons can integrate primary reward and information into a common currency. [...]. Specifically, neural systems for reward prediction errors (RPEs), including lateral habenula and midbrain dopamine neurons, are thought to encode the difference between the reward value of the current situation and the reward value it was predicted to have (roughly speaking, "actual reward versus predicted reward"). Remarkably, these neurons respond in similar ways to "more/less water than predicted" and "more/less information than predicted." This seems to be the case in humans as well, where information-related RPEs are present as blood-oxygen-level-dependent signals in dopamine-rich midbrain regions and their prominent reward-related projection targets. [...]. These signals are further modulated by how likely information is to be desirable. In both monkeys and humans, variations in neural information-related signals predict differences in information seeking behavior. This suggests that the brain employs the potent reinforcing and motivational effects of the RPE-driven valuation system to instruct actions to seek both primary reward and information. (Bromberg-Martin and Sharot 2020, 563)

There is much more to say about this neuropsychological research into why people believe what they believe in which circumstances, but it suffices to point out that this inquiry backs up the claims in Peirce's two papers and the idea of a psychological notion of a feeling of understanding, even in science. As human beings, we want to move from an irritating feeling of doubt to a soothing state of belief and we have learned that we can best do so through scientific inquiry. But even in science we tend to look for explanations in terms of colliding things, since these generate in us a pleasurable belief and a feeling of understanding.

When we try to pragmatically elucidate what we mean by an explanation, we end up realizing that we ultimately need to get rid of metaphors in scientific accounts of phenomena, but the only thing left then is (basically) the depiction of natural laws in their mathematical form. Unfortunately for us, humans, these explanatory accounts no longer generate in us a feeling of understanding, leaving us craving such a feeling—and that in itself is an uneasy feeling we want to get rid of. Unfortunately, even science cannot help us here.

Trout (2002, 2016) has in like fashion drawn attention to the psychological meaning of understanding and explanation in science. But this modern way of thinking about a theory of scientific understanding finds, so I claim, a strong supportive and broad framework in Peirce's pragmatism, showing how a psychological account of the feeling of understanding is important to grasp the idea of science. To illustrate how the pragmatist framework I sketched here contrasts with a more leading and recent view of scientific understanding, let me briefly turn to Henk de Regt's influential contextual theory of scientific understanding.

5. A Peircean Idea of Science: Its Power and Limit

Henk de Regt (2017) introduces a couple of definitions to help understand scientific understanding. Understanding a phenomenon is equated with having an adequate explanation of the phenomenon (relating the phenomenon to accepted items of knowledge). 'Understanding a theory' is identified with being able to use the theory. The basic idea in De Regt's approach is to connect the intelligibility of theories to the scientific understanding of phenomena. Indeed, De Regt wants to develop a contextual theory of understanding that "focuses on the way in which individual scientists achieve understanding" and "allows for the possibility that there is individual variation" (2017, 90). To do so he introduces the following principle: "A phenomenon P is understood scientifically if and only if there is an explanation of P that is based on an intelligible theory T and conforms to the basic epistemic values of empirical adequacy and internal consistency" (2017, 92). Now, according to De Regt, the intelligibility of a theory not only depends on the qualities of the theory, but also on the scientists involved, their skills and background knowledge (93): "A scientific theory T (in one or more of its representations) is intelligible for scientists (in context C) if they can recognize qualitatively characteristic consequences of T without performing exact calculations" (102). Things become clearer when De Regt applies his contextual theory of scientific understanding to a paradigm case in philosophy of science: the kinetic explanation of the combined gas law. In a nontechnical way, high school students are usually asked to imagine what happens to a gas when it is trapped in a closed cylinder and gets heated. Take the perspective of the gas molecules being bouncing and colliding balls or bullets resulting in a certain measurable pressure. Boltzmann, in his *Lectures on Gas Theory*, said that the pressure of the gas is interpreted as the action of these molecules against the wall of the container (1964, 32). The idea of kinetic energy here means that more kinetic energy of gas molecules means faster movement, and the other way around. So, add heat to the cylinder and observe how the pressure goes up. What is the explanation that generates understanding of this phenomenon?

De Regt gives the example of Richard Feynman's explanation (Feynman et al. 1963–1965, 1:1–2ff.) for the observed increase in pressure when the cylinder with the trapped gas is heated:

> On the basis of a simple, idealized picture of a gas in a container, Feynman derives some qualitative results concerning the relations between pressure, temperature, and volume. First of all, the molecular-kinetic picture gives a qualitative account of the fact that a gas exerts pressure on the walls of its container. If a gas molecule collides with a wall of the container, it gives it a little push. The total effect of the pushing of the molecules produces the pressure. In more formal terms: molecules exert forces on the wall and the total force of all molecules on a unit area equals the macroscopic pressure. Subsequently, the relation between pressure and temperature can be determined qualitatively, given the basic principle of the kinetic theory that heat is molecular motion. This principle implies that *adding heat to a gas in a container of constant volume will lead to an increase of the velocities of the molecules, so that they will hit the walls of the container more often and with greater force. Accordingly, the pressure of the gas will increase.* In a similar manner, Feynman argues that if one decreases the volume of the container slowly (i.e., under constant pressure), the temperature of the gas will increase. When these conclusions are combined, one obtains a qualitative expression of the ideal-gas law. This reasoning does not involve any calculations; it is based on general characteristics of the theoretical description of the gas. (De Regt 2017, 104–105, italics added)

Basically, what we see Feynman and Boltzmann do here is try to show how we can understand the phenomenon of increasing pressure of a heated gas in a closed container. The drawing from the educational website Let's Talk Science (2020) captures in a different representation the same understanding of the phenomenon that P_2 is greater than P_1, where the 'comet tails' represent a higher velocity of the gas molecules in the right container (which is heated by flames). This is what we learned at high school when Joseph Louis Gay-Lussac's gas law was explained.

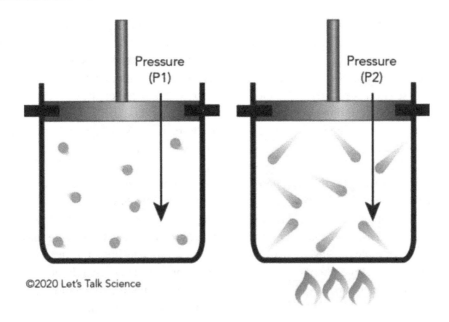

©2020 Let's Talk Science

De Regt now shows how the contextual theory of scientific understanding works:

> The ideal-gas model does not follow deductively from either the kinetic theory or the description of the phenomena but is constructed in a process that involves idealizations and approximations. Skills and judgment are needed to make the right steps, and it is the intelligibility of the kinetic theory (to scientists who possess these skills) that allows for the construction of a model that fits the phenomena (and thereby provides explanatory understanding). In a word, understanding is achieved only if [the thesis applies that understanding of phenomena requires intelligible theories]. That the kinetic theory is intelligible to scientists is indicated by the fact that they are able to reason with it in a qualitative way, recognizing characteristic consequences of it. (2017, 104)

De Regt thus concludes that "because qualitative insight into the consequences of a theory can be gained in many ways, [the contextual theory of scientific understanding] can accommodate the variety of ways in which understanding is achieved in practice" (108).

To be clear, there is of course much more to say about the contextual theory of scientific understanding, but if Peirce is right in his two classic papers—and given the development and results of physics and psychology, I think we can safely say he probably is—we need a completely different kind of theory of understanding since *the core theory in science itself shows there are no colliding gas molecules—it is just a metaphor we use to generate a pleasurable feeling of understanding. We only have the natural and mathematical laws as explanations.* The notion of understanding we need is one that incorporates the idea that humans are evolutionarily evolved creatures, that humans inquire to get rid of an irritating feeling of doubt, that humans want to fixate their beliefs, that there are different methods of belief fixation, and that science is the best method of belief fixation. The most promising theory of meaning is the pragmatic maxim, and science is the best way to make an inventory of sensible effects so that our concepts become more and more clear to us. The history of science, even in Peirce's time, is an illustration of the scientific image becoming so weird that we find ourselves in a state of not understanding that science. There is no feeling of understanding unless we take recourse to metaphors that generate a feeling of understanding in us due to the evolutionarily evolved characteristics we as a matter of fact have. Unfortunately, that feeling of understanding does only generate an illusory feeling of understanding: we know that the offered account is merely a metaphor and thus not true.

What we mean by *the feeling of understanding*, then, is to have available an account of some phenomenon in terms of colliding things. A veridical feeling of understanding is generated when these colliding things are part of the everyday life regime (basically, they are observable or sensible). A pleasurable but illusory feeling of understanding is generated when some phenomenon is accounted for in terms of merely *metaphorical* collisions of things. Take away the metaphor and the feeling of understanding is gone. If all we have is an (for all we know) empirically adequate mathematical description referring to the practical situation, *that* is our explanation—we think we have found a natural mathematical law. (This touches upon Peirce's realism, but I will not go into this here; see De Regt [1999, 2003].)

From an early Peircean perspective, given the history of science, the limit of science clearly emerges: science does not generate in humans a feeling of understanding when it merely talks of mathematical natural laws (core theory), but such laws are pragmatically our best explanations. We know more and more what the sensible effects are of the concepts we use. The laws are there (and are real) as they are the best explanations to understand why the model is empirically adequate. There is just no understanding as we cannot comprehend what happens in everyday life reality terms. Peirce's pragmatism is still a sound expression of the meaning of reality and truth, but his pragmatism also implies that what we in the long run end up with need not be a representation that generates in humans a feeling of understanding, although it is, again pragmatically, an explanation of the sensible world we live in.

6. Conclusion

What if. What if Peirce lived today cherishing the same ideas from his "The Fixation of Belief" and "How to Make Our Ideas Clear"? We have reason to believe that the 1877/78 Peirce would have applauded this conclusion from the latest neuropsychological inquiry into the nature of human beings:

> Whatever the evolutionary origin, understanding the process of motivated belief formation is an increasingly central necessity in our society. We each now have access

to an unprecedented and vast trove of information from which we can construct our beliefs. Some of this information is accurate, some is erroneous, and some is misinformation carefully tailored to appeal to our desires. We thus rely more than ever on our ability to seek out information, sift through it, and arrive at new beliefs that are beneficial for ourselves and for society. We hope that the emerging neuroscience of belief formation will inform the development of tools to help humans successfully navigate this information-rich era. (Bromberg-Martin and Sharot 2020, 564–565)

In the end, this is the compelling reason why these two classical papers by Peirce are still meaningful and relevant to us in the early twenty-first century. They help us to restore science to its rightful place in society, as the source of our best explanations of what happens in the world we sense, even if we have lost the feeling of understanding.

NOTE

1. Lewis Carroll, https://www.preposterousuniverse.com/blog/2013/01/04/the-world-of-everyday-experience-in-one-equation/

References

Boltzmann, Ludwig. 1964 *Lectures on Gas Theory*. Translated by Stephen G. Brush. Berkeley, CA: University of California Press.
Bromberg-Martin, Ethan S., and Okihide Hikosaka. 2009. "Midbrain Dopamine Neurons Signal Preference for Advance Information About Upcoming Rewards." *Neuron* 63, no. 1: 119–126.
Bromberg-Martin, Ethan S., and Tali Sharot. 2020. "The Value of Beliefs." *Neuron* 106, no. 4: 561–565.
Carman, Christián C. 2017. "The Final Date of the Antikythera Mechanism." *Journal for the History of Astronomy* 48, no. 3: 312–323.
Carroll, Sean M. 2017. *The Big Picture: On the Origins of Life, Meaning, and the Universe Itself*. New York: Penguin.
Carroll, Sean M. 2021. "The Quantum Field Theory on Which the Everyday World Supervenes." In S. Ioannidis, G. Vishne, M. Hemmo, and O. Schenker (eds.), *Levels of Reality in Science and Philosophy: Re-Examining the Multi-Level Structure of Reality*. Cham: Springer, 2022, 27–46.
Cohen, I. Bernard. 1985. *Revolution in Science*. Cambridge, MA: Harvard University Press.
Cristalli, Claudia. 2017. "Experimental Psychology and the Practice of Logic. Charles S. Peirce and the Charge of Psychologism, 1869–1885." *European Journal of Pragmatism and American Philosophy* 9, no. 1: 1–25.
Davidson, Donald. 1978. "What Metaphors Mean." *Critical Inquiry* 5, no. 1: 31–47.
de Regt, Herman C. D. G. 1999. "Peirce's Pragmatism, Scientific Realism, and the Problem of Underdetermination." *Transactions of the Charles S. Peirce Society* 35, no. 2 (Spring): 374–397.
de Regt, Herman C. D. G. 2003. "Restless Thought: A Pragmatist View on Belief and Scientific Realism." In Guy Debrock (ed.), *Process Pragmatism: Essays on a Quiet Philosophical Revolution*. Amsterdam: Rodopi, 103–120.

de Regt, Herman C. D. G., Hans Dooremalen, and Maurice Schouten. 2021. *Exploring Humans: Philosophy of Science for the Social Sciences. A Historical Introduction* (rev. ed.). Amsterdam: Boom Publishers.

de Regt, Henk W. 2017. *Understanding Scientific Understanding*. Oxford: Oxford University Press.

de Waal, Cornelis. 2013. *Peirce: A Guide for the Perplexed*. London: Bloomsbury.

Dijksterhuis, Eduard Jan. 1961. *The Mechanization of the World Picture*. Oxford: Oxford University Press.

Feynman, Richard P., Robert B. Leighton, and Matthew Sands. 1963-1965. *The Feynman Lectures on Physics*. Boston, MA: Addison-Wesley.

Fisch, Max H. 1954. "Alexander Bain and the Genealogy of Pragmatism." *Journal of the History of Ideas* 15, no. 3: 413-444.

Freeth, Tony, David Higgon, Aris Dacanalis, Lindsay MacDonald, Myrto Georgakopoulou, and Adam Wojcik. 2021. "A Model of the Cosmos in the Ancient Greek Antikythera Mechanism." *Scientific Reports* 11, no. 1: 1-15.

Gopnik, Alison. 1998. "Explanation as Orgasm." Minds and *Machines* 8, no. 1: 101-118.

Gopnik, Alison. 2000. "Explanation as Orgasm and the Drive for Causal Understanding: The Evolution, Function, and Phenomenology of the Theory-Formation System." In F. Keil and R. Wilson (Eds.), *Cognition and Explanation*. Cambridge, MA: MIT Press, 299-323.

Hausman, Carl R. 2011. "Peirce and the Interaction View of Metaphor." In V. Colapietro and Th. Olshewsky (eds.), *Peirce's Doctrine of Signs: Theory, Applications, and Connections*. Berlin: Mouton de Gruyter, 193-203.

Jones, Alexander. 2017. *A Portable Cosmos: Revealing the Antikythera Mechanism, Scientific Wonder of the Ancient World*. Oxford: Oxford University Press.

Lakoff, George, and Mark Johnson. 1980. *Metaphors We Live By*. Chicago: University of Chicago Press.

Linden, David J. 2012. *The Compass of Pleasure: How Our Brains Make Fatty Foods, Orgasm, Exercise, Marijuana, Generosity, Vodka, Learning, and Gambling Feel So Good*. New York: Penguin.

Misak, Cheryl. 2021. "Nothing Scoundrelous About Truth." In M. Schwartzberg and Ph. Kitcher (eds.), *Truth and Evidence*. New York: New York University Press, 176-194.

Mizraji, Eduardo, and Juan Lin. 2017. "The Feeling of Understanding: An Exploration with Neural Models." Cognitive *Neurodynamics* 11, no. 2: 135-146.

Peirce, Charles S. 1992-1998. *The Essential Peirce: Selected Philosophical Writings*. 2 vols. Vol. 1 edited by Nathan Houser and Christian Kloesel. Vol. 2 edited by the Peirce Edition Project. Bloomington: Indiana University Press. (Referred to as EP.)

Schulkin, Jay, ed. 2004. *Allostasis, Homeostasis, and the Costs of Physiological Adaptation*. Cambridge: Cambridge University Press.

Trout, Joseph D. 2002. "Scientific Explanation and the Sense of Understanding." *Philosophy of Science* 69, no. 2: 212-233.

Trout, Joseph D. 2016. *Wondrous Truths: The Improbable Triumph of Modern Science*. Oxford: Oxford University Press.

Wilczek, Frank. 2015. "Physics in 100 Years." *arXiv* preprint, arXiv:1503.07735.

CHAPTER 30

PEIRCE'S VIEWS ON EDUCATION AND LEARNING

TORJUS MIDTGARDEN

1. INTRODUCTION

CHARLES S. Peirce, the founding father of American pragmatism, did not systematically address education in his philosophy, apart from some short pieces he wrote and a lecture he gave on topics of higher education.[1] By contrast, his fellow pragmatist John Dewey persistently engaged the topics of learning and education throughout his career and has had a lasting effect on the philosophy of education and on theories of learning. Yet since the turn of the twenty-first century philosophers of education have turned to Peirce's work and explored its relevance. This new interest in Peirce has been sparked partly by reflections on convergences and commonalities between Peirce's, Dewey's, and William James's thinking. Some decades ago, Richard Bernstein (1991, 324) coined the term "the pragmatic *ethos*" by stressing Peirce's founding role for pragmatism but also the commonalities between his and the other pragmatists' thinking. Some philosophers of education followed Bernstein and took this pragmatic ethos as a starting point for exploring pragmatism's relevance (Garrison and Alvin 2003). More recently, other philosophers of education have directed their interest toward Peirce's pioneering contributions to a philosophical theory of signs—or semiotics. These contributions have provided opportunities to rethink processes of learning and education in terms of sign processes. The relevance of Peirce's semiotics has thus been explored through efforts to establish edusemiotics as an interdisciplinary theoretical field (Semetsky and Stables 2014; Stables and Semetsky 2015; Stables 2016; Deely and Semetsky 2017; Semetsky 2017). Attention has also been directed to Peirce's various sketches of distinct semiotic disciplines. More specifically, philosophers have considered the relevance of his mid-1890s outlines of a speculative grammar (Midtgarden 2010) and of his post-1900 definitions of and comments on a speculative rhetoric (Bergman 2013; Colapietro 2013; Liszka 2013; Strand 2013a, 2013b).

In this article, I revisit some of these recent efforts and consider how Peirce's semiotic work suggests perspectives on learning and education. I focus mostly on Peirce's mid-1890s speculative grammar,[2] although I also more briefly consider the earlier and later phases of his philosophical development. In his mid-1890s semiotic work[3] Peirce outlines and applies a philosophical method for analyzing various signs used in assertions. His analysis suggests how the uses of these signs serve as conditions for learning from experience. Qualifying these signs in terms of his symbol/index/icon typology, he analyzes how they serve as conditions for learning in everyday life and how they further prepare the learner for scientific education and specialization. Since this analysis is developed only in outline, I show how it may shed further light on learning processes in everyday life and in science through a comparison with Jürgen Habermas's theory of communicative action. Finally, I consider how Peirce's mid-1890s semiotic analysis can be complemented through perspectives on learning and education that have been developed from the recent considerations of his post-1900 speculative rhetoric and through the efforts to establish the interdisciplinary field of edusemiotics.

Yet Peirce's mid-1890s speculative grammar can only be understood more fully by first considering its broader intellectual context, as well as its background in Peirce's early philosophy. As for the former, I point out how Peirce's speculative grammar is part of a science classification through which Peirce proposes new roles for philosophical disciplines in facing the incessant specialization of the natural and social sciences. As for the latter, I show how Peirce's early anti-Cartesian epistemology provides a philosophical rationale for his method. I start by briefly considering Peirce's early epistemology through Bernstein's account of the pragmatic ethos (1991), before proceeding to Peirce's mid-1890s science classification and his speculative grammar.

2. Peirce's Early Epistemology and the Pragmatic Ethos

By drawing on the works of Peirce, James, and Dewey, Richard Bernstein (1991, 324) has collected and brought together themes under the label "the pragmatic ethos." The themes Bernstein draws from Peirce's early works include Peirce's rejection of Cartesian foundationalism, or the doctrine that our knowledge claims can be justified through certain basic beliefs that need no justification by other beliefs or that can be justified noninferentially through intuition.[4] In rejecting foundationalism Peirce developed the view that later became known (and debated) as his fallibilism.[5] This is the view that everything we hold as true may in fact prove to be false and that our ongoing inquiry may in the future correct (at least some of) our false beliefs. To these themes Bernstein adds Peirce's consideration of the social nature of knowledge development. The early Peirce held that any inquirer, philosopher, or specialized scientist would belong to a critical community of inquirers (CP5.319, 1868). Against the background of Peirce's early epistemology, Peirce's mid-1890s speculative grammar can be seen to develop several of the themes of Bernstein's pragmatic ethos. As I return to below, in outlining a philosophical method for semiotic analysis Peirce may be seen to apply both his fallibilism and his account of the social nature of knowledge development. To understand the broader intellectual context for his application of this philosophical method, however, we need to consider the role that his mid-1890s classification of the sciences assigns to philosophical disciplines generally and to speculative grammar in particular in relation to the specialized sciences.

3. A New Role for Philosophy

Through the 1890s, Peirce pondered how the roles and tasks of philosophy could be redefined given new developments in the empirical and the formal sciences. He contributed to some of these developments himself, above all, to the development of formal logic (Zeman 1986; Hintikka 1997), but he also made a pioneering contribution to experimental psychology (Cadwallader 1975). Since philosophical disciplines are more general than the ever more specialized natural or social sciences, he proposes that they should have roles different from the latter. Adopting aspects of Auguste Comte's (1855) influential classification of science, Peirce argues that the more general and abstract sciences should provide basic principles for the less general and more specialized sciences (CP3.427, 1896). At the heart of Peirce's own classification of the sciences from the mid-1890s are three philosophical and semiotic disciplines modeled on the medieval *trivium* (grammar, logic, rhetoric) (CP3.430, 1896). First, and as the most general philosophical discipline, Peirce places speculative grammar, which is to analyze assertions into their various sign elements.[6] A study of assertions provides a foundation for other sciences, Peirce argues, since logicians presuppose a notion of assertion in assigning truth values to propositions, and since all researchers in the natural and social sciences make assertions in raising truth claims about their objects of study. Second comes formal logic and, third, speculative rhetoric, which in his mid-1890s science classification is to study conditions and methods for development of scientific knowledge (CP2.229, c. 1895; R787:10–11, c. 1895). However, the role proposed for philosophical disciplines creates a methodological problem: philosophical disciplines cannot rely on methods and observations of the specialized sciences for which they are to provide a basis, on pain of vicious circularity (CP3.432, 1896). In particular, Peirce emphatically rejects the tendency of his day to base logic on psychology. His solution is to turn to everyday life experience, experience prior to observations made with the use of microscopes, telescopes, or any other research technology. Philosophy is concerned with "the universal phenomena of experience, and these are," he thinks, "sufficiently revealed in the ordinary observations of every-day life" (CP3.432, 1896). His most basic philosophical and semiotic discipline, speculative grammar, is thus to rest "upon observations of the rudest kind, open to the eye of every attentive person who is familiar with the use of language" and "able to converse at all with his fellows" (CP3.432, 1896). On Peirce's account, this domain of ordinary experience is to fulfill the methodological functions both as a source for developing semiotic distinctions and as evidence for testing these distinctions (CP2.233, c. 1895). Let us now consider how his method connects with his earlier epistemology as specified by the pragmatic ethos considered above.

4. Fallibilism and Philosophical Method

In outlining a method, Peirce appeals to our experience of ordinary language use by echoing his earlier rejection of Descartes's methodical or universal doubt (see W2:212, 1868). Contrary to the Cartesian method, Peirce wants to establish a method for addressing real doubt, not what he later called "paper-doubt" (CP5.445, 1905). "Proof does not consist in giving superfluous and superpossible certainty to that which nobody ever did or ever will doubt," he says, "but in removing doubts which do, or at least might at some time, arise" (CP3.432, 1896). In outlining a method, he draws on the classical rhetorical tradition by establishing experience of ordinary language use as "rhetorical evidence" (CP2.333, c. 1895) and he qualifies the latter as "observational sources from whence all true reasoning must be drawn" (CP2.333, c. 1895). More specifically, he appeals to a nonformal rhetorical standard of probability or likelihood for arguments.[7] This standard would allow theoretical input to his semiotic analysis to become only "more probable" through being tested against rhetorical evidence. By this standard, with its "undeniable formal imperfection" (CP2.333, c. 1895), tested results could be accepted only with reservations of fallibility. By assuming a standard of proof that only admits "removing doubts which do, or at least might at some time arise" (CP3.432, 1896), Peirce may thus be seen to implement his principle of fallibilism in his philosophical method (Midtgarden 2001, 90–91).

In drawing on the rhetorical tradition, Peirce applies yet another element in the pragmatic ethos considered above: his account of the social nature of knowledge development. In fact, by qualifying the source and the testing ground for his semiotic analysis as open to anybody who is "able to converse at all with his fellows" (CP3.432, 1896), Peirce suggests that his analysis of assertions would be doubly socially based. First, it would be enabled by the language community to which the student of speculative grammar belongs. Yet since speculative grammar "must analyse an assertion into its essential elements, independently of the structure of the language in which it may happen to be expressed" (CP3.430, 1896), its results should thus be acceptable for students and inquirers from any natural language community. Second, therefore, these students and inquirers would make up a community that itself becomes an enabling basis for knowledge development in speculative grammar.

Applying the method has further educational significance. Given Peirce's invocation of the medieval *trivium* and his classification of science more generally, speculative grammar is to prepare the student for studying formal logic and scientific methodologies and for specializing in any natural or social science. The application of the philosophical method itself presupposes an educational context of teacher and student and sets the stage for a reflexive learning process through which the student becomes aware of general conditions for scientific specialization (CP3.432, 1896). These conditions are general in that they need to be in place before appropriation of specialized methods, theories, and research technologies. But they are also general in the sense that they already enable learning in the prescientific lifeworld. For considering these general conditions Peirce further provides a conceptual starting point for his semiotic analysis of assertions: the concept of scientific intelligence.

5. Scientific Intelligence: Learning from Experience

Peirce defines his concept of scientific intelligence in terms of an intelligence that is capable of learning from experience and that needs to learn from experience (CP2.335, *c.* 1895; CP3.428, 1896; see also CP2.227, *c.* 1897; NEM4:ix–x, n.d.). Notably, Peirce abstains from a psychological definition of scientific intelligence, as well as of the terms 'learning' and 'experience.' He also avoids defining 'learning,' or 'experience,' in terms of specialized scientific methods or specialized scientific inquiry. Like his fellow pragmatists James and Dewey, he understands the term 'experience' in the prescientific sense of life experience or experience from "the course of life" (CP3.435, 1896; see also CP4.91,1893; CP2.784, 1901). In preparing its methodological role, Peirce applies the concept of scientific intelligence in reformulating his early definition of truth as the opinion ultimately agreed upon by all investigators (see W3:273, 1878). Assuming an intimate connection between the notions of assertion and truth, he now defines truth as the "definitive compulsion" of a scientific intelligence (CP2.333, *c.* 1895) or as "the compulsion of rational assent" (R787:13, *c.* 1895). Methodologically, he endeavors to employ this definition to "deduce" distinctions of basic sign elements in an assertion and then go on to test his semiotic distinctions against "rhetorical evidence" (CP2.333, *c.* 1895; CP2.335–2.336, *c.* 1895). Moreover, in this semiotic analysis, Peirce uses the concept of scientific intelligence in considering learning processes that originate in the prescientific lifeworld and that prepare scientific education and specialization. More specifically, by applying the concept, he aims to analyze signs that are used in our ordinary communicative practices and that prepare the appropriation and use of scientific methods and discourses. Through its methodological application the concept of scientific intelligence in turn becomes specified in terms of communicatively enabled and experientially constrained learning processes.

6. Icon, Index, Symbol: Conditions for Learning from Experience

In his semiotic analysis of assertions Peirce applies his typological distinction between icon, index, and symbol. An important part of his analysis concerns indexical signs since they prepare the learning of scientific discourses and their referential uses. Peirce stresses that indexical signs are needed in communication because we cannot refer to any real object or to the real world by merely using general descriptions: "The real world cannot be distinguished from a fictitious world by any description" (CP2.337, c. 1895). The indexical signs needed are omnipresent in everyday communication, for example, through paralinguistic signs such as tones of voice (intonation) (CP2.337, c. 1895) and gestures (CP2.338, c. 1895), as well as through personal and demonstrative pronouns used in ostensively referring acts (R787:20–21, c. 1895). Through our capacities to use them, these signs make us attuned to "the real world" (CP2.337, c. 1895). Indexical signs are further exemplified by natural language quantifiers (e.g., 'all,' 'some,' 'everything'). We learn to use quantifiers in referring to objects through "precepts" (CP2.336, c. 1895; R787:21, c. 1895). Precepts are practical instructions showing how a listener is to select a certain object or objects from the environment. Generally, indexical signs fulfill their referential function in communication through socially coordinated gestures and movements, practical instructions, or skilled use of technical devices (CP2.336, c. 1895; R787:21, c. 1895; see also CP2.330, 1903). On Peirce's account, our practical everyday use of natural language quantifiers prepares the use of quantifiers and quantified variables in formal logic; and our everyday use of quantifiers and demonstrative and personal pronouns prepares the referential uses of scientific discourses across fields of empirical research.

Peirce's analysis of assertions next turns to iconic signs. Iconic signs, he points out, can be defined as diagrams. In a diagram there needs to be "no sensuous resemblance between it and its object, but only an analogy between the relations of the parts of each," such as in the case of "a map" (CP2.279, c. 1895). Yet in analyzing iconic signs as integrated elements in assertions Peirce goes on to consider 'diagrammatic' or 'iconic' relationships between the expression and content level of a linguistic sign. These iconic relationships could be studied as what modern linguists call 'the iconicity of syntax' (see Haiman 1985; Simone 1995). More specifically, Peirce's analysis suggests that this iconicity could be studied at different levels of language and discourse: at the levels of constituent structure (phrase structure), syntactic and semantic argument structure, and information structure (see Midtgarden 2002, 232–238). Peirce's analysis further suggests that the iconicity of syntax supports language acquisition and comprehension. Moreover, for logicians and students of logic, one of the virtues of studying the iconicity of natural language syntax would be that it could aid the construction and re-interpretation of formalisms in logic (see Hintikka 1997, 23–24).

Peirce's semiotics recognizes that natural languages consist of conventional or symbolic signs. As he made clear after the turn of the century, symbolic signs can be analyzed as general "types" that are instantiated through concrete "tokens" in linguistic utterances (CP4.537, 1906; see also CP2.292, 1903; CP2.244–246, 1903). However, unlike Ferdinand de Saussure's concept of the linguistic sign ([1916] 1959, 66), Peirce does not analyze linguistic symbols only as two-sided units with an expression and a content side, but rather as having content or meaning through being interpreted as a representation (or as part of a representation) of an object. Already before the turn of the century, Peirce's concept of the symbolic sign thus involves a triadic relation between the sign, its object, and its interpretation (see W5:162–163, 1885; EP2:5, 1894; CP3.435, 1896). Peirce's stress on the sign object should be seen in the light of how his speculative grammar is to prepare the ground for studying formal logic, and thus for learning to use a formal language with propositional variables that are either true or false. Speculative grammar is further to prepare students for Peirce's speculative rhetoric, which concerns conditions and methods for the development of scientific knowledge. However, while Peirce's conception of the symbolic sign presupposes reference to objects or things, he emphasizes that a symbolic sign "does not, in itself, identify those things" (EP2:9, 1894). Peirce's speculative grammar, therefore, centers on propositional symbols or symbolic signs the syntax of which involves combinations with indexical signs that enable reference to and identification of objects. Moreover, since Peirce's analysis is informed and guided by the concept of scientific intelligence, an intelligence able and needing to learn from experience, his analysis considers certain specific conditions for language use. On the part of the speaker (or writer) this would require a capacity to use a syntactic construction for articulating an assertion experience has prompted and for conveying new information to the listener (or reader). This process of articulation and communication is aided by the iconicity of natural language syntax, and it requires the use of indexical signs enabling both parties to identify the same objects in their respective experience (CP3.435–3.436, 1896). The concept of scientific intelligence thus invites consideration on the capacities language users need to possess for using symbolic, iconic, and indexical signs in learning from experience. Yet, while these capacities are developed prior to scientific specialization they would be necessary for formulating a new scientific hypothesis—or what Peirce later called an "abduction" (see, for example, EP2:287, 1903; CP2.96, c. 1902)—and for developing, discussing, and testing it in a research community.

The analysis of the symbolic sign concludes Peirce's mid-1890s semiotic analysis of conditions and capacities for learning from experience. His analysis considers conditions and capacities that would enable learning in everyday contexts and prepare scientific education and specialization. To show how his analysis may shed further light on learning processes that originate in the lifeworld and that prepare for participation in scientific inquiry, I will make a comparison with Jürgen Habermas's theory of communicative action and his more recent elaborations.

7. Peirce and Habermas on Learning Processes Originating in Lifeworld Practices

In his earlier work, Habermas ([1968] 1972) draws extensively on Peirce's philosophy. Yet in Habermas's theory of communicative action ([1981] 1984, [1981] 1987) Peirce's philosophy is no longer in the foreground. Nevertheless, as Jørgen Dines Johansen has pointed out (1993, 289–308), there are significant parallels between Habermas's communication theory and Peirce's philosophy, in particular, Peirce's later and most elaborated semiotic work. Here, however, I will focus on those parallels between Habermas's theory and Peirce's analysis of assertion that shed light on learning processes that originate in the lifeworld and that prepare participation in scientific inquiry. These are parallels, we shall see, that come more clearly into view through Habermas's return to Peirce in his more recent work ([1999] 2003).

In ways resembling Peirce's analysis of assertions, Habermas develops a method for reconstructing our communicative capacities while making reservations of fallibility for the results of applying the method (1998, 45–46). In his communication theory he conceptualizes communicative action in terms of validity claims raised and responded to through speech acts. While Habermas distinguishes between different kinds of validity claims, his focus on the claims to truth and truthfulness, in addition to the claim to grammatical comprehensibility (1998, 22–25), may be seen as a parallel to Peirce's analysis. In the lifeworld, he observes, truth claims are often naively accepted and pass unchallenged due to shared background knowledge ([1981] 1987, 400–401; 1998, 242–246). Yet Habermas sets out to reconstruct certain ideal presuppositions or conditions for speech that involve an obligation to justify truth claims by reasons that could be acceptable to all interlocutors involved (1998, 86–87). In works originally developed in the 1970s he had elaborated these ideal conditions in terms of a consensus theory of truth inspired by Peirce's early notion of truth as the final agreement of a community of inquirers (see Habermas 1984, 2001).

In his more recent work, however, Habermas ([1999] 2003) has qualified the truth claims of assertive speech acts in a different way, one that draws his theory closer to Peirce's analysis of assertion and that is even directly inspired by Peirce's pragmatism.[8] In the lifeworld, Habermas now stresses, we are both communicative agents and engaged in various instrumental practices of coping and problem-solving. Through the latter we "rub up against constraints [the facticity of which] drives home the fact that objects offer resistance" (Habermas [1999] 2003, 27). We experience the constraints of recalcitrant objects through failed expectations, for example, when our use of tools and technologies proves ineffective or yields unforeseen consequences (15). Since our practices of coping and problem-solving are embedded in contexts of communicative action, however, these experiential constraints may lead us to suppose a "world of objects" (90) to which our truth-claims refer and about which our truth-claims sometimes need correction due to our failed expectations (39). Arguably, this supposition of objects anchors the truth-claims of assertive speech acts more firmly in lifeworld practices than do Habermas's ideal conditions of justification (see 90–91, 144). Moreover, through this supposition Habermas's communication theory may further suggest perspectives on learning processes that originate in lifeworld practices. This requires, however, that the supposition of objects is developed into an account of reference that in effect incorporates elements of Peirce's semiotic analysis of indexical signs.

Yet Habermas does not turn to Peirce's semiotics, but rather adopts Hilary Putnam's (1988, 30–37) account of the indexical reference of natural kind terms. Moreover, Habermas reframes Putnam's account of reference as concerned with extensive learning processes: "Hilary Putnam has dealt with the question of how it is possible for learning processes to traverse the bounds of different time periods and forms of life specifically in terms of the sameness of objective reference—a notion that is no less important in science than in everyday usage" ([1999] 2003, 35). The clue for addressing these questions concerning learning processes, Habermas argues, is an account of reference "that explains how we can refer to the *same* object (or objects of the same kind) under *different* theoretical descriptions" (10; see also 67). Habermas, however, does not pause to analyze the use of indexical signs but simply assumes that the indexical reference of assertive acts is anchored in an agent's instrumental coping and problem-solving practices (see [1999] 2003, 35). By contrast, Peirce assumes no categorial division between 'instrumental' and 'communicative action' but rather shows that the use of indexical signs in assertions itself involves interaction with objects in an environment. To bring out the relevance of Peirce's semiotic analysis, I first consider how one of his examples sheds light on individual learning processes.

For a student who embarks on the path of scientific specialization, and who receives teaching and instruction, the use of indexical signs serves to keep reference constant and thus enable appropriation of theoretical descriptions of the objects referred to. This is shown by Peirce's example of an operational definition of the element lithium intended as an alternative to standard textbook definitions (CP2.330, 1903). Instead of starting by providing a theoretical definition in terms of atomic weight, Peirce (who had academic training in chemistry[9]) instructs the student how to search for, select, and manipulate specimens of particular substances in a sequence of chemical operations. Finally, the student is to end up with a concrete product that can be referred to indexically by saying: "the material of *that* is a specimen of Lithium" (CP2.330, 1903). Hence the instructed action requires use of indexical signs (and concrete descriptions) in interaction with and manipulation of specimens of various substances as well as laboratory instruments. Moreover, by enabling the student to produce a specimen of lithium by following an established scientific practice, the instructed action provides experience that prepares the ground for appropriation of theoretical descriptions. Yet, as Peirce's analysis of assertions suggests, appropriation of scientific discourses and their referential use is prepared already through using indexical signs in everyday experience.

Habermas's adoption of Putnam's account of reference further hints at a perspective on collective learning processes within scientific communities over periods of time, involving revision, correction, or rejection of theories. Here, too, indexical reference established through shared scientific practices would play a significant role, and one could imagine relevant contexts for assessing indexical reference that would bear on learning. By drawing on Christopher Hookway's Peircean analysis of indexical reference (2000, 113–114), I distinguish three types of context. First, cooperating members of a subsection of a scientific community need to make sure that their experiments and measurements involve indexical reference to specimens of the same kinds at different times. As Peirce's operational definition of lithium already suggests, indexical reference would be established through the interactive use of indexical signs within an enduring laboratory environment with its artifacts.[10] Moreover, in a laboratory practice, reliable indexical reference would depend on agreed-upon standardizations of experimental setups and of procedures for purification or distillation of specimens of substances. Second, one further needs to assess whether research results obtained and communicated by members of other subsections of the community make reliable indexical references to specimens of the same kinds as one's own results. To use a contemporary example, within brain research, documentation in publication depends on (functional magnetic resonance imagining) scanning technologies for producing images that are used as indexical signs of substances involved in biochemical processes (see Gross 2008, 381–382). Here, too, indexical reference depends on standardizations at work in the use of these technologies in the community, and assessments of the reference must be made at both ends of the publication process. Third, after significant phases of research and publication, members need to assess and discuss whether the indexical references made and negotiated in the community have provided a sufficient empirical basis for correcting or rejecting theoretical descriptions of the objects and specimens referred to. These three types of context, then, would need to be considered when developing a perspective on collective scientific learning in the sense suggested by Habermas and which is now sketched in semiotic terms.

8. Peirce's Post-1900 Semiotics and Its Relevance for Philosophy of Education

While Peirce's mid-1890s speculative grammar provides perspectives on processes of learning, it is not his most elaborate semiotic contribution. It is rather from the first decade of the twentieth century that we find his most extensive and most often quoted semiotic work. In particular, his post-1900 semiotics provides more general and diversified considerations of different forms of signs and sign-processes, covering natural and nonlinguistic signs as well as linguistic and paralinguistic signs. Peirce's later sign typologies and sign classifications thus significantly expand his former symbol/index/icon typology.[11] This extended scope is theoretically grounded in a more comprehensive classification of the sciences, where Peirce's semiotic *trivium* is now preceded by a philosophical and phenomenological theory of three universal categories: firstness, secondness, thirdness (CP1.186, 1903; CP1.280, 1902; EP2:160–178, 1903), as well as by the normative sciences aesthetics and ethics (CP1.186, 1903; CP1.191, 1903; EP2:196–207, 1903; EP2:376–379, 1906). Like Peirce's former analysis of assertions, this phenomenological theory is methodologically based in everyday life experience. Yet he now uses the phenomenological categories to define his triadic sign concept and to provide a theoretical basis for his extensive sign typologies (see in particular EP2:289–294, 1903). While his phenomenological categories have arguably a more problematical methodological and theoretical status than his more modest analysis of assertions (see Midtgarden 2018, 112–116), his extensive and diversified considerations of signs have recently inspired philosophers of education to explore his semiotics. I will distinguish and comment on two tendencies in these recent explorations, focusing on how they complement the perspectives on learning processes presented above.

8.1. Engaging Peirce's Speculative Rhetoric

The first tendency concerns efforts to engage the third discipline of Peirce's semiotic trivium, his speculative rhetoric. In his sparse comments on this discipline after the turn of the twentieth century, he defines the subject matter of speculative rhetoric in terms of the relation of signs to their interpretations or "interpretants" (CP2.93, c. 1902; EP2:326, 1904). While his general definitions suggest opportunities for conceptualizing processes of education and learning as sign processes (or semiosis), philosophers of education have further considered Peirce's account of sign interpretation as habit-change (CP5.476–5.479, 1907) and explored ways of conceiving education and learning as semiotically conditioned processes of acquiring, nurturing, and transforming habits (Colapietro 2013; Bergman 2013; Strand 2013a, 2013b). Since Peirce now classifies his semiotic trivium as normative sciences (CP1.191, 1903; CP1.281, 1902), taking logical reasoning to be anchored in ethical self-control, his concept of habit is relevant for conceiving learning as a critical and self-reflective activity (Bergman 2013, 749–750; Colapietro 2013, 727–729). Peirce's speculative rhetoric further invites consideration of how habits are affected and shaped by signs of various sorts and through interaction with other sign-users. A Peirce-inspired and normative account of habits of learning could therefore be spelled out as what James Liszka has envisaged as virtues cultivated through interaction and dialogue in a community of inquirers (2013, 786). Drawing also on Peirce's early philosophy, Liszka focuses on virtues that would characterize community members as "honest, humble, keenly aware of their own ignorance," and that are shaped by social norms of inquiry, notably, norms demanding "a disavowal of authority as a means of establishing belief" and an "openness of mind and a sense of fallibilism that remedies error" (Liszka 2013, 786). This notion of virtue as situated and developing in a community of inquirers thus recalls Bernstein's pragmatic ethos (1991) and suggests a normative and social basis for Peirce's fallibilistic philosophical method considered above.

Since Peirce's remarks on his speculative rhetoric are general and sketchy, a further exploration of his relevance may turn to accounts he gave of his own teaching. As Liszka (2013) has emphasized, Peirce preferred a way of teaching and interacting with students that required and enabled them to learn through practical tasks and exercises. This could be seen through his courses in logic and Liszka (2013, 783) quotes from a description of a correspondence course in logic Peirce gave in 1887: "All education, broad or narrow, is intended to teach the student to *do* something" (W6:11). Other relevant examples are Peirce's attempts to write an elementary Arithmetic (NEM1:43–63, n.d.; 107–120, n.d.).[12] A source for his practical teaching method, however, can be found in his own educational background. As other interpreters have pointed out (de Waal 2013, 4–5; Ambrosio and Campbell 2017, 88–92), Peirce was intellectually influenced by his education and training in chemistry at the Lawrence Scientific School. The founder of the Lawrence Scientific School, Eben Horsford, had studied chemistry with Justus von Liebig in Germany, who offered his students "a very practical way of learning chemical analysis" (de Waal 2013, 5) and whose "idea of laboratory was a space where students and assistants could work side-by-side and learn by doing rather than by mere rote learning" (Ambrosio and Campbell 2017, 90). Since Horsford and Peirce's chemistry teacher, Josiah Parson Cooke, were both inspired by Liebig's teaching method, Peirce's view of education and learning could be seen to be indirectly influenced by Liebig's method. In fact, Peirce's example from chemistry considered above, his operational definition of lithium (CP2.330, 1903), may indicate an influence from Liebig and it may further be used to specify the educational relevance of his speculative rhetoric. As seen above, Peirce's operational definition instructs and guides the steps of the student's learning activity. If taken as a communicative act Peirce's instruction would invite and allow the student into a scientific practice and entrust her with responsibilities. The communicative act would in effect acknowledge the student as a fellow member of the scientific community and thus enable self-respect and self-esteem. Hence, this and other available sources on Peirce's teaching method[13] and educational background may offer ways to pin down the relevance of his speculative rhetoric through specifying educational, communicational, or rhetorical conditions for a Peircean community of inquirers and learners.

8.2. Peirce and Edusemiotics

A second tendency in the recent exploration of Peirce's semiotics comes with the efforts of establishing edusemiotics as an interdisciplinary branch of theoretical semiotics (see in particular Semetsky and Stables 2014; Stables and Semetsky 2015; Stables 2016; Semetsky 2017). Its two leading representatives, Andrew Stables and Inna Semetsky, have explored the more general and abstract aspects of Peirce's semiotics through philosophical lenses drawn from the process metaphysics of Alfred N. Whitehead (1978 [1929]), as well as Dewey's process philosophy (1929). Building on these various sources, edusemiotics sets out to provide a processual and semiotic account of learning by theorizing sign-processes as constitutive and relational aspects of experience (see Stables 2016). By following Dewey's philosophy in attacking ontological dualisms stemming from Descartes, and by enrolling Peirce's semiotics in this project, edusemiotics in effect extends and deepens the break with Cartesianism that follows from the pragmatic ethos considered above.

Through their rejection of dualisms and anthropocentrism in educational thinking, proponents of edusemiotics heighten awareness of the potential of Peirce's semiotics to dissolve received dichotomies, such as those of mind/body, society/nature, or human/nonhuman. We may see this tendency in his doctrine of synechism, which resists ontological dualisms and rather tends "to regard everything as continuous" (EP2:1, 1893), as well as when he later avoids using psychological or sociological terms in conceptualizing sign interpretation and rather uses the more general and formal term "interpretant" (CP1.541, 1903; CP2.92, 1903) or "quasi-mind" (CP4.536, 4.550–4.553, 1906). This tendency is due not only to his rejection of psychologism in logical theory, but also to a more systematic trait of his later hierarchical classifications of science. Since his semiotic disciplines are philosophical and considered as more general and basic than the specialized sciences, semiotic distinctions are defined logically prior to the division between natural and social sciences and cannot therefore be defined in terms of the latter. Yet due to their higher level of generality in the classification, philosophical and semiotic distinctions may guide and inform theory development in the specialized sciences and across the division of natural and social science (see CP1.246, 1.249–1.250, 1902). Against this background we may appreciate and elaborate on Stables's (2008) suggestion that Peirce's semiotics can provide resources for overcoming a vestige of dualistic thinking in Dewey's philosophy given by his signal/sign distinction. Briefly, on Dewey's account, only humans have minds and capacities for communication and for sharing each other's perspectives by using linguistic or other signs, whereas nonhuman animals' signaling acts are based on mere instinct and conditioned reflexes.[14] Peirce's diversified sign typologies may provide resources for mediating this distinction, and through its generality Peirce's semiotic distinctions could guide conceptualization in ways that would not so easily fall prey to a rigid human/nonhuman divide. In fact, in his own speculative attempts to conceptualize and classify human and nonhuman behavior at a level less general than that of semiotics, Peirce introduces typologies for classification that cut across the human/nonhuman divide. He starts out by introducing a general term, "system of performances," meant to cover both "animal and human performances, including organized associations," before distinguishing the two latter as "subfamilies" (CP7.378, 1902). Contrary to Dewey, Peirce's classification strategy, while speculative and sketchy, does not rule out from the outset that "instincts for communication" (CP7.379, 1902) are distributed across the human/nonhuman divide. Guided by his general and diversified sign typologies he rather explores the theoretical possibility that there is "some kind of language ... among nearly all animals" (CP7.379, 1902).

When thus seen to join or even complement Dewey's persistent attacks on ontological dichotomies, Peirce's semiotics could guide students and researchers in educational science and make them more critically aware of dichotomies that have influenced divisions between theories of learning, most notably those "grounded in cognitivism and behaviorism" (Stables 2016, 54). For research and education in adjacent fields, Peirce's semiotics could similarly guide a critique of rigid conceptual divisions or forms of reductionism. For example, one may follow Dewey (1946) and use Peirce's triadic sign concept in criticizing too-rigid divisions in semiotics and linguistics between syntactic, semantic, and pragmatic 'dimensions' of natural languages, or use the triadic sign concept to support a critique of reductivist 'dyadic' accounts of linguistic and social acts (see also Brock 1975, 126–127; Apel [1975] 1981, 125–130; Midtgarden 2018, 116–117). Yet as an interdisciplinary endeavor edusemiotics further brings to light that Peirce's semiotic trivium and science classification encourage not only theoretical mediation of dichotomies and divisions, but also what Peirce calls "dynamical relations between the different sciences" (CP7.52, n.d.). Taking a science to consist in "the very concrete life of a social group constituted by real facts of inter-relation," he observes how interaction and cooperation between sciences come about when "one group may stimulate another by demanding the solution of some problem" (CP7.52, n.d.). The encouragement of interdisciplinarity in the face of a shared problem would thus add another dimension to the Peircean community of inquirers considered above. Moreover, the encouragement of interdisciplinarity gains importance beyond circles of research and higher learning in so far as problems calling for an interdisciplinary approach tend to stem from a practical or social life context, such as education itself. Peirce himself notes that "the practical sciences incessantly egg on researches into theory" (CP7.52, n.d.). However, as Peircean philosophers edusemioticians would not engage in interdisciplinary work as specialists. They would rather engage by using their general capacities for critical inquiry and open discussion and by drawing on learning processes that originate in ordinary intercourse and life experience.

9. Conclusion

Although Peirce did not systematically address education as a topic in his philosophy, he highlighted the significance of learning processes outside of educational institutions and institutions of higher learning. Given the incessant specialization of the natural and social sciences, he saw a new role for philosophy in considering learning processes that evolve through everyday life experience and prepare scientific education and specialization. He reinvigorated the medieval trivium and proposed a set of general semiotic studies for enabling students to reflect on general capacities and conditions for appropriating specialized scientific methodologies and discourses. From a more general perspective, philosophy becomes a mediator between the prescientific lifeworld and the increasingly diversified and specialized sciences. Peirce knew firsthand that specialized sciences had become social lifeworlds of their own. "Bring together two men from widely different departments—say a bacteriologist and astronomer," he points out, "and they will hardly know what to say to one another; for neither has seen the world in which the other lives" (CP1.236, 1902). Through inviting reflection on shared capacities and on the prescientific lifeworld as a common frame of reference, philosophy in the Peircean vein is to facilitate mutual understanding across institutional divisions in higher learning. As part of the philosophical curriculum, semiotics would serve to mediate, criticize, or undermine ontological dualisms supporting institutional divisions, in particular those between the natural and social sciences. I will end by highlighting yet another role for philosophy and semiotics. While Peirce saw how practical problem-solving in the lifeworld requires interdisciplinary efforts (CP7.52, n.d.), he also realized the extent to which the lifeworld itself had become transformed through modern science and technology. "Modern science," he observed, "with its microscopes and telescopes, with its chemistry and electricity, and with its entirely new appliances of life, has put us into quite another world; almost as much so as if it had transported our race to another planet" (CP5.513, 1905). Although he took philosophy to be theoretical and not applied science, he saw the need for intervention on the part of its normative disciplines, including semiotics, to criticize and readapt inherited beliefs and values in relation to a technologically transformed world. When taking this suggestion of extending the role of philosophy, semioticians would not resort only to mediating or attacking dualisms and divisions within institutions of higher learning. In developing and updating this suggestion, students of Peirce's semiotics would go on to clarify and criticize ways in which inherited dualisms (such as mind/matter, body/mind, nonhuman/human) may have blinded us to the ways in which modern science and technology have transformed our lives and our relationships with nonhuman nature and thus undermined our capacities for responsible action.

Notes

1. See the following three texts: "Introductory Lecture on the Study of Logic" (W4:378–382, 1882); "University," (Peirce 1889–1891); "Review of *Clark University, 1889–1899, Decennial Celebration*" (Peirce 1900).
2. Interpretations and arguments in this article draw on and develop my earlier works on Peirce's speculative grammar: Midtgarden (2001, 2002, 2007, 2010). For other interpretations, see Brock (1975); Boyd (2016); Bellucci (2019); Brioschi (2021); Stjernfelt (2021).
3. Peirce's mid-1890s outlines of a speculative grammar are found in two texts. The first text has the title "That Categorial and Hypothetical Propositions Are One in Essence, with Some Connected Matters" and is cataloged as manuscript no. 787 in Robin (1967). While according to Robin the dating of the manuscript is somewhat uncertain, it is probably from 1895 (Robin 1967, 99). It is published in part in CP2.278–280, 332–356. (I refer to it as R787 when considering parts of the manuscript that are not published in CP.) The second text, titled "The Regenerated Logic," is from 1896 and is published in full in CP3.425–454.

4. See Peirce's two articles from 1868, "Questions Concerning Certain Faculties Claimed for Man" and "Some Consequences of Four Incapacities," in CP5.212-317.
5. For a critical discussion of both Peirce's and other pragmatists' versions of fallibilism, see Margolis (1998).
6. In his classification of the sciences after the turn of the century Peirce introduces phenomenology (phaneroscopy) as the most general philosophical discipline (see CP1.186, 1903; CP1.280, 1902), and he further classifies the normative and philosophical disciplines aesthetics and ethics as more general than his *trivium* (speculative grammar, formal logic, speculative rhetoric) (see CP1.186, 1903; CP1.191, 1903).
7. For an account of the notion of 'likely' or 'probable arguments' in classical Greek rhetoric, see Wardy (1996, 33-34).
8. See Habermas ([1999] 2003, 15, 26-27, 90-91, 154). While Habermas here makes no specific reference to any of Peirce's works, he may be seen to draw on his earlier interpretation of Peirce, in particular his account of Peirce's pragmatist method for clarification of meaning and his pragmatist theory of inquiry (see Habermas [1968] 1972, 113-130). For an interpretation of Habermas's recent use of Peirce's pragmatism, see Flynn (2014, 190-207).
9. In his biography, Joseph Brent describes Peirce's academic background in chemistry: "In 1863, [Peirce] received the first Bachelor of Science, *summa cum laude*, in chemistry from the Lawrence Scientific School, at the time the most important of the new experimentally oriented scientific schools being established in American colleges" (Brent 1998, 55).
10. Note in relation to this Putnam's comment (with his original emphasis): "*meaning is interactional. . . . The environment itself plays a role in determining what a speaker's words, or a community's words, refer to*" (Putnam 1988, 36).
11. See in particular Peirce's sign classification from 1903: "Nomenclature and Divisions of Triadic Relations, as Far as They Are Determined" (EP2:289-299).
12. I am grateful to Cornelis de Waal for pointing this out to me.
13. This example from chemistry could be further complemented by a testimony from Peirce's former student, the psychologist Joseph Jastrow: "It was Peirce who gave me my first training in the handling of a psychological problem, and at the same time stimulated my self-esteem by entrusting me, then fairly innocent of any laboratory habits, with a real bit of research. . . . The young men in my group who were admitted to his circle found him a most agreeable companion. The terms of equality upon which he met us were not in the way of flattery, for they were too spontaneous and sincere. We were members of his 'scientific' fraternity; greetings were brief, and we proceeded to the business that brought us together. . . . This type of cooperation and delegation of responsibility came as near to a pedagogical device as any method that he used" (Jastrow 1916, 724-725).
14. See Dewey (1929, 176-179, 272, 280). Note Steven Fesmire's critical interpretation of Dewey: "Analysis of Dewey's view of animals across his published work reveals residual traces of philosophies he elsewhere discredited, such as a vestige of Cartesianism in which animals are mindless automatons. . . . Dewey echoed the prejudice of his contemporaries that all nonhuman animals act out of blind habit" (Fesmire 2015, 71-72). As Fesmire makes clear, however, Dewey's distinction between human communication, on the one hand, and the signaling acts of nonhuman animals, on the other, is not rooted in an ontological division. The distinction is rather one of "descriptive categories" developed from generalizations of scientific results and it is therefore "fallible and provisional, to be revised in light of ongoing inquiry" (Fesmire 2015, 72). See also Dewey (1929, 272-273).

References

Ambrosio, Chiara, and Chris Campbell. 2017. "The Chemistry of Relations: Peirce, Perspicuous Representations, and Experiments with Diagrams." In *Peirce on Perception and Reasoning: From Icons to Logic*, edited by Kathleen A. Hull and Richard Kenneth Atkins, 86–106. New York: Routledge.

Apel, Karl-Otto. 1981. *Charles S. Peirce: From Pragmatism to Pragmaticism* (1975). Translated by John Michael Krois. Amherst: University of Massachusetts Press.

Bellucci, Francesco. 2019. "Peirce on Assertion and Other Speech Acts." *Semiotica* 228: 29–54.

Bergman, Mats. 2013. "Fields of Rhetoric: Inquiry, Communication, and Learning." *Educational Philosophy and Theory* 45, no. 7: 737–754.

Bernstein, Richard J. 1991. *The New Constellation: The Ethical-Political Horizons of Modernity/Postmodernity*. Cambridge, MA: Polity Press.

Boyd, Kenneth. 2016. "Peirce on Assertion, Speech Acts, and Taking Responsibility." *Transactions of the Charles S. Peirce Society* 52, no. 1 (Winter): 21–46.

Brent, Joseph. 1998. *Charles Sanders Peirce: A Life*. Revised and enlarged edition. Bloomington: Indiana University Press.

Brioschi, Maria Regina. 2021. "What If a Term Became an Assertion? Peirce on Rudimentary Assertions." *Transactions of the Charles S. Peirce Society* 57, no. 2 (Spring): 210–226.

Brock, Jarrett. 1975. "Peirce's Conception of Semiotic." *Semiotica* 14, no. 2: 124–141.

Cadwallader, Thomas C. 1975. "Peirce as an Experimental Psychologist." *Transactions of the Charles S. Peirce Society* 11, no. 3 (Summer): 167–186.

Colapietro, Vincent. 2013. "Neglected Facets of Peirce's 'Speculative' Rhetoric." *Educational Philosophy and Theory* 45, no. 7: 712–736.

Comte, Auguste. 1855. *The Positive Philosophy of Auguste Comte* (1830–1842). 2 vols. Translated by Harriet Martineau. New York: Blanchard.

Deely, John, and Inna Semetsky. 2017. "Semiotics, Edusemiotics and the Culture of Education." *Educational Philosophy and Theory* 49, no 3 (2017): 207–219.

de Saussure, Ferdinand. 1959. *Course in General Linguistics* (1916). Edited by Charles Bally and Albert Sechehaye, translated by Wade Baskin. New York: Philosophical Library.

De Waal, Cornelis. 2013. *Peirce: A Guide for the Perplexed*. London: Bloomsbury.

Dewey, John. 1929. *Experience and Nature*. Second edition. London: George Allen & Unwin.

Dewey, John. 1946. "Peirce's Theory of Linguistic Signs, Thought, and Meaning." *The Journal of Philosophy* 43, no. 4 (February): 85–95.

Dines Johansen, Jørgen. 1993. *Dialogical Semiosis: An Essay on Signs and Meanings*. Bloomington: Indiana University Press.

Fesmire, Steven. 2015. *Dewey*. London: Routledge.

Flynn, Jeffrey. 2014. "Truth, Objectivity, and Experience after the Pragmatic Turn: Bernstein on Habermas's 'Kantian Pragmatism.'" In *Richard J. Bernstein and the Pragmatist Turn in Contemporary Philosophy: Rekindling Pragmatism's Fire*, edited by Judith Green, 190–207. London: Palgrave Macmillan.

Garrison, Jim, and Alven Neiman. 2003. "Pragmatism and Education." In *The Blackwell Guide to the Philosophy of Education*, edited by Nigel Black, Paul Smeyers, Richard Smith, and Paul Standish, 21–37. Oxford: Blackwell.

Gross, Alan G. 2008. "The Brains in Brain: The Coevolution of Localization and Its Images." *Journal of the History of the Neurosciences: Basic and Clinical Perspectives* 17, no. 3: 380–392.

Habermas, Jürgen. 1972. *Knowledge and Human Interest* (1968). Translated by Jeremy J. Shapiro. Boston: Beacon Press.
Habermas, Jürgen. 1984. *Reason and the Rationalization of Society*, Vol. 1 of *The Theory of Communicative Action* (1981). Translated by Thomas McCarthy. Boston: Beacon Press.
Habermas, Jürgen. 1984."Wahrheitstheorien." In *Vorstudien und Ergänzungen zur Theorie kommunikativen Handelns*, 127–183. Frankfurt: Suhrkamp.
Habermas, Jürgen. 1987. *Lifeworld and System: A Critique of Functionalist Reason*, Vol. 2 of *The Theory of Communicative Action* (1981). Translated by Thomas McCarthy. Boston: Beacon Press.
Habermas, Jürgen. 1998. "What Is Universal Pragmatics?" In *On the Pragmatics of Communication*, edited by Maeve Cooke and translated by Thomas McCarthy, 21–103. Cambridge, MA: MIT Press.
Habermas, Jürgen. 2001. "Truth and Society: The Discursive Redemption of Factual Claims to Validity." In *On the Pragmatics of Social Interaction: Preliminary Studies in the Theory of Communicative Action*, translated by Barbara Fultner, 85–103. Cambridge, MA: MIT Press.
Habermas, Jürgen. 2003. *Truth and Justification* (1999). Edited and translated by Barbara Fultner. Cambridge, MA: MIT Press.
Haiman, John. 1985. *Iconicity in Syntax*. Philadelphia: John Benjamins.
Hintikka, Jaakko. 1997. "The Place of C. S. Peirce in the History of Logical Theory." In *The Rule of Reason: The Philosophy of Charles Sanders Peirce*, edited by Jacqueline Brunning and P. Forster, 13–33. Toronto: University of Toronto Press.
Hookway, Christopher. 2000. *Truth, Rationality, and Pragmatism: Themes from Peirce*. Oxford: Clarendon Press.
Jastrow, Joseph. 1916. "Charles S. Peirce as a Teacher." *The Journal of Philosophy, Psychology and Scientific Methods* 13, no. 26 (December): 723–726.
Liszka, James. 2013. "Charles Peirce's Rhetoric and the Pedagogy of Active Learning." *Educational Philosophy and Theory* 45, no. 7: 781–788.
Margolis, Joseph. 1998. "Peirce's Fallibilism." *Transactions of the Charles S. Peirce Society* 34, no. 3 (Summer): 535–569.
Midtgarden, Torjus. 2001. "Peirce's Speculative Grammar from 1895–1896: Its Exegetical Background and Significance." *Transactions of the Charles S. Peirce Society* 37, no. 1 (Winter): 81–96.
Midtgarden, Torjus. 2002. "Iconic Aspects of Language and Language Use: Peirce's Work on Iconicity Revisited." *Semiotica* 139 (March): 227–244.
Midtgarden, Torjus. 2007. "Peirce's Epistemology and Its Kantian Legacy: Exegetic and Systematic Considerations." *Journal of the History of Philosophy* 45, no. 4 (October): 577–601.
Midtgarden, Torjus. 2010. "Toward a Semiotic Theory of Learning." In *Semiotics Education Experience*, edited by Inna Semetsky, 71–82. Rotterdam: Sense Publishers.
Midtgarden, Torjus. 2018. "Categorical Analysis in Pragmatism: Specialization in Science and the Role of Philosophy." In *Mereologies, Ontologies, and Facets: The Categorial Structure of Reality*, edited by Paul M. W. Hackett, 107–133. Lanham, MD: Lexington Books.
Peirce, Charles S. 1857–1914. Manuscripts held at the Houghton Library of Harvard University, as identified in Richard Robin, 1967. *Annotated Catalogue of the Papers of Charles S. Peirce*. Amherst: University of Massachusetts Press. (Referred to as R.)
Peirce, Charles S. 1889–1891 "University." In *The Century Dictionary and Cyclopedia*, Vol. 6, Part 23, edited by William Dwight Whitney, 6623–6624. New York: Century. https://ia802702.us.archive.org/12/items/centurydictipt2300whituoft/centurydictipt2300whituoft.pdf.

Peirce, Charles S. 1900. "Review of *Clark University, 1889–1899, Decennial Celebration,*" *Science* 11, no. 277 (April): 620–622.

Peirce, Charles S. 1931–1958 *The Collected Papers of Charles Sanders Peirce*. 8 vols. Vols. 1–6 edited by Charles Hartshorne and Paul Weiss. Vols. 7–8 edited by Arthur W. Burks. Cambridge, MA: Harvard University Press. (Referred to as CP.)

Peirce, Charles S. 1976. *The New Elements of Mathematics*. 4 vols. in 5. Edited by Carolyn Eisele. The Hague: Mouton. (Referred to as NEM.)

Peirce, Charles S. 1982–2010. *The Writings of Charles S. Peirce: A Chronological Edition*. 7 vols. to date. Edited by the Peirce Edition Project. Bloomington: Indiana University Press. (Referred to as W.)

Peirce, Charles S. 1998. *The Essential Peirce: Selected Philosophical Writings*, Vol. 2. Edited by the Peirce Edition Project. Bloomington: Indiana University Press. (Referred to as EP.)

Putnam, Hilary. 1988. *Representation and Reality*. Cambridge, MA: MIT Press.

Robin, Richard. 1967. *Annotated Catalogue of the Papers of Charles S. Peirce*. Amherst: University of Massachusetts Press.

Semetsky, Inna (ed.). 2017. *Edusemiotics—A Handbook*. Singapore: Springer.

Semetsky, Inna, and Andrew Stables (eds.). 2014. *Pedagogy and Edusemiotics: Theoretical Challenges/Practical Opportunities*. Rotterdam, The Netherlands: Sense Publishers.

Simone, Raffaele. 1995. Iconic Aspects of Syntax: A Pragmatic Approach." In *Iconicity in Language*, edited by Raffele Simone, 153–169. Philadelphia: John Benjamins.

Stables, Andrew. 2008. "Semiosis, Dewey and Difference: Implications for Pragmatic Philosophy of Education." *Contemporary Pragmatism* 5, no.1 (June): 147–162.

Stables, Andrew. 2016. "Edusemiotics as Process Semiotics: Towards a New Model of Semiosis for Teaching and Learning." *Semiotica* 212 (September): 45–57.

Stables, Andrew, and Inna Semetsky. 2015. *Edusemiotics: Semiotic Philosophy as Educational Foundation*. London: Routledge.

Stjernfelt, Frederik. 2021. "Peirce's Theories of Assertion." *Transactions of the Charles S. Peirce Society* 57, no. 2 (Spring): 248–269.

Strand, Torill. 2013a. "Peirce's New Rhetoric: Prospects for Educational Theory and Research." *Educational Philosophy and Theory* 45, no. 7: 707–711.

Strand, Torill. 2013b."Peirce's Rhetorical Turn: Conceptualizing Education as Semiosis." *Educational Philosophy and Theory* 45, no. 7: 789–803.

Wardy, Robert. 1996. *The Birth of Rhetoric: Gorgias, Plato, and Their Successors*. London: Routledge & Kegan Paul.

Whitehead, Alfred North. [1929] 1978. *Process and Reality: An Essay in Cosmology*. Edited by David Ray Griffin and Donald W. Sherburne. New York: Free Press.

Zeman, J. 1986. "Peirce's Philosophy of Logic." *Transactions of the Charles S. Peirce Society* 22, no. 1 (Winter): 1–22.

CHAPTER 31

THE PHILOSOPHICAL RELEVANCE OF PEIRCE'S HISTORICAL STUDIES

TULLIO VIOLA

1. INTRODUCTION

SCATTERED through the many thousands of pages of Peirce's manuscripts are a considerable number of writings dealing with historical subjects. Devoted mostly to the history of science, these writings touch, however, on subjects as different as the history of philosophy, the history of art, the biography of political or military figures, and even historical linguistics or the history of measurement standards. This broad range of interests fits well into Peirce's polymathic profile. Yet to what extent were they relevant to the elaboration of his philosophy? The present chapter considers this question in such a way as to shed new light on Peirce's significance for ongoing discussions concerning the relationship between history and philosophy of science, the role of genealogical arguments in philosophy, or the epistemic status of historical explanations.

I will proceed in a loosely chronological fashion. Section 2 looks at Peirce's early work and describes the emergence of Peirce's interest in history as a component of his intellectual profile as a nineteenth-century polymath. His early preoccupation with logic and his indebtedness to the work of the British scholar William Whewell will play center stage. Section 3 focuses on the most momentous juncture in Peirce's career as a historian and philosopher of history, namely, the early 1890s. In that period, several different projects gravitated around a renewed consideration of the role of the history of science in a philosophical inquiry into the human mind and its evolutionary character. Section 4 traces the development of Peirce's most notable arguments for a dialogue between history and philosophy throughout the subsequent decade. It focuses, in particular, on history's relevance to logic. Finally, Section 5 wraps up the chapter by looking at the history–logic nexus from another perspective, namely, Peirce's attempt to develop a methodology of historical inquiry consistent with his ideas about logic.

2. A Polymath's Approach to History

According to a narrative most prominently offered by Max H. Fisch (1982, xx–xxiv), Peirce spent the first years of his intellectual career working out an interdisciplinary scientific profile based on a core interest in logic. His early interest in the history of science and philosophy is consistent with this profile. The three cycles of lectures delivered in Cambridge and Boston between 1865 and 1869 (W1:161–302; 357–504; W2:309–345) bear witness to his inclination to draw on history for a better understanding of philosophical issues such as the nature of logic, the theory of inference, and the definition of the sign.

Two main arguments support Peirce's early decision to take history seriously in the investigation of philosophical and scientific questions. Both arguments reached full maturity in the late 1860s, spurred by Peirce's polemic against the Cartesian conception of philosophy. They then acquired even greater force as a result of his simultaneous discovery of the writings of William Whewell, the British scientist and polymath who offered him a concrete model of interaction between philosophy and the history of science.

The first argument lies at the intersection of semiotics and metaphysics. It moves from a processualist conception of the mind to conclude that taking into account the historical development of ideas is essential for their proper understanding. Concepts or ideas, according to Peirce, are processual entities, the meaning of which cannot be disclosed in the "immediate present," but only if we factor in their past (W2:207, 1868). The same applies to "external symbols" (W2:241, 1868) such as the words of a language. Their meaning is the result of a long historical process that we ought not to ignore. We can observe, for example, that a "philosophical distinction emerges gradually into consciousness; there is no moment in history before which it is altogether unrecognized, and after which it is perfectly luminous" (W2:71, 1867). A historical analysis of this gradual process of generation of ideas is likely to bring some additional clarity to our own use of philosophical concepts.[1]

The second argument is more epistemologically oriented. It holds that history is one of the main remedies against closed-mindedness and unilateral thinking. It is rooted in Peirce's rejection of the Cartesian picture of solitary investigation and in his consequent development of a community-based model of scientific inquiry, a model profoundly influenced by his study of scholastic philosophy. Peirce read the works of medieval thinkers as based on the assumption that "what competent men disagree about is not certain" (W2:187, 1868). Their attitude can therefore teach us that the cultivation of historical awareness is a hallmark of intellectual thoroughness, as it allows us to take seriously different ways of thinking, thereby challenging our most ingrained beliefs.

In the Harvard Lectures of 1869, dealing principally with the study of logical ideas as "a branch of history," and most specifically with "the history of logical thought in the British Islands," Peirce opened with a programmatic statement about history that echoes the second argument just given. "The chief value of the study of historical philosophy is that it disciplines the mind to regard philosophy in a cold and scientific eye and not with passion as though philosophers were contestants." This does not mean that we should stop asking the normative, and essentially nonhistorical, question of whether the authors one deals with "were right or wrong." But it does mean that only a historical foundation will ensure that our normative judgment will pass the test of scientificity and rigor (W2:310). Peirce's approach to the dispute between realism and nominalism is an example of how he put these methodological recommendations into practice. To overcome disagreement among competent scholars, he contended, we must "let our decision rest on a historical basis, the only sound basis for any human institution—philosophy, natural science, government, church, or system of education" (W2:336).

It is important not to conflate this plea for history with a more generic defense of tradition. It is true that Peirce often praised the virtues of conservatism or traditionalism, especially as a tool against the "iconoclastic inventions" of Cartesian philosophy (CP4.71, 1893), as a sociopolitical attitude (Short 2001; Misak 2004), or as an aid to settle the "ethical" questions posed by the use of scientific terminology (SS:19, 1904). However, there is still a crucial difference between history and tradition. History is, in all intents and purposes, a scientific enterprise. As such, it is a manifestation of that critical and rational attitude of inquiry that Peirce himself considered to be the very corrective to traditionalism, conservatism, or common sense (see Haack 1994). In practice, this means that one can cultivate an attitude of conservative "reverence" for the past without knowing anything about "veracious history" and vice versa.[2]

Peirce's decisive encounter with the work of William Whewell (of which we have ample evidence from 1865 on: see Cowles [2016], Girel [2017]) helped him turn his two arguments in support of history into a much more precisely defined agenda for the integration of historical and philosophical studies. Peirce took Whewell to be the paradigm of a "most profound" (W1:211, 1865) and successful scholar, who nonetheless managed to stay clear of the dominant materialistic worldview of the nineteenth century. He also insisted on Whewell's work as "having all the characters of a scientific Induction from the History of Science": impartial, thoroughly empirical, and informing the details of his philosophical theorizing (W2:338, 1869). Moreover, Peirce was struck by Whewell's insistence on the importance of treating scientific discoveries themselves as historical entities. He noted that, for Whewell, a new empirical observation only becomes possible when scientists are equipped with suitable ideas (CP6.604, 1893). The consequences of this view are similar to the implications Peirce was keen to draw from his processualist view of concepts: they lead us to recognize that looking at scientific observations as atemporal entities can only obscure their meaning and make a sound evaluation of their actual purport more difficult.

Peirce would return to Whewell as a major source of inspiration in the early 1890s, when working on his first ambitious and comprehensive history of science, to be delivered as a second cycle of lectures at the Lowell Institute (see Section 3). But we can perhaps recognize the continuing influence of Whewell's scholarship in the 1870s and the 1880s as well. For in that period, Peirce's approach to history gradually became even more empirical, interdisciplinary, and inductive than it was in his earlier years.

A good case in point is Peirce's 1878 book-length report of the astronomical observations he conducted at the Harvard observatory, *Photometric Researches* (Peirce 1878). In that book, Peirce integrated his own data with data extrapolated from ancient scientific manuscripts, some of which he personally consulted in the course of his journeys to Europe (Viola 2020, 31; Eisele 1959). Again, during the years he spent lecturing at Johns Hopkins University, Peirce initiated a research project on the comparative biographies of "Great Men" that would accompany him throughout his life. Initially based on an extensive survey of biographical data (W5:25–105, 1883–1884), the project sought to give empirical grounding to a lively but highly speculative nineteenth-century debate that touched on the interplay between outstanding individuals and their environment, the existence of metahistorical laws of social change, and thornier social-political issues such as social Darwinism and eugenics.[3]

3. The Uses of History in the Early 1890s

The Lowell Lectures of 1892 (HPPLS:139–295) represent a crucial juncture in Peirce's career as a historian, as they provide a sweeping historical account of scientific progress from antiquity to modern time. However, if we take an all-round view of Peirce's scholarly activity in those years, we are led to recognize that those lectures were part of an even broader project, a project that sought to delineate a historically informed philosophy of evolution encompassing both the realm of nature and the realm of ideas (see Miller 1971; Pearce 2020, 221–225). The model was again William Whewell: Peirce's lectures on the history of science were supposed to lay the ground for his philosophy of evolution in the same way in which Whewell's *History of the Inductive Sciences* prepared his *Philosophy of the Inductive Sciences* (see HPPLS:143–144, 1892; Whewell 1837 and 1840).

Peirce developed the philosophical side of his ambitious project in the series of articles on metaphysics published in *The Monist* in the years 1891–1893 (W8:83–205). These articles take up the processualism we discussed in the previous section to turn it into a full-fledged evolutionary metaphysics. Evolutionary, yes, but not Darwinian: as becomes particularly clear in the article titled "Evolutionary Love" (W8:184–205, 1892), Peirce, without denying the local validity of evolutionary models based on random variation, like Darwin's, ended up endorsing a version of Lamarckism. A given physical or mental trait is first acquired thanks to the "striving" of an individual. It is then passed on to its offspring. What makes this transmission possible is a "bestowal of spontaneous energy by the parent upon the offspring" and a "disposition of the latter" to acquire that trait (W8:194, 1892).

Peirce believed that this evolutionary model applied not only to natural evolution but also to the evolution of human ideas. According to his view, individuals can feel an "immediate attraction" for an idea before they possess it. Such an attraction (or "love") for an idea, then, guides individuals in a teleological process of acquisition and further intellectual development (W8:196, 1892). In an attempt to buttress this view with empirical data, Peirce observed that the Lamarckian model of evolution is particularly suitable to describe those cases of social and cultural change that display a purposive and collective nature, like the development of large philosophical movements or the phenomenon of simultaneous scientific discoveries (W8:203–205, 1892). Darwinian evolution, on the contrary, gains credibility as a model of "backward" periods of history, which do not appear governed by any overarching principle (W8:198, 1892).

The Lowell Lectures on the history of science (which Peirce delivered in the same year in which "Evolutionary Love" came out) provide further empirical support to this general account of evolution. As I have anticipated, the lectures deal with the development of science from ancient history to modern Europe, with a special focus on the history of the physical sciences in the early modern period.[4] The question of the origin of science occupies a particularly important place in the lectures. Investigating this question increased Peirce's sensitivity for the necessity of a historicized conception of science and scientific truth. It also led him to investigate the different kinds of forces, both individual and collective, that shape the evolution of scientific ideas and its specific "law" or pattern of development (HPPLS:289, 1892).

As previously mentioned, the general framework holding together the Lowell Lectures on the history of science with the *Monist* series on evolutionary metaphysics was the model of historically grounded philosophy that Peirce adopted from Whewell. There are, however, three additional theoretical elements to be considered, which make the link between history and philosophy even tighter, if somewhat less straightforward. The remainder of this section will address them in turn. The first element is a series of remarks on why the history of science is intellectually "interesting," which Peirce embedded within the Lowell Lectures themselves. The second element is his conception of philosophy as an "architectonic" activity. The third is his classification of scientific disciplines.

Let me start with the first. In the Lowell Lectures, Peirce claims that "there are many ways in which the history of science is interesting." One of them, he says, is a "personal interest in how the truths we are familiar with got found out" (HPPLS:143, 1892). This "personal interest," however, is no matter of mere curiosity. Rather, it is related to something we have already discussed, namely, Peirce's inclination to cultivate a historical approach to our concepts and beliefs in order to have a better grasp of their veritable purport.[5] Another way in which the history of science is interesting, Peirce goes on, is "for the lessons it affords in regard to the investigation of new questions" (HPPLS:143, 1892) In other words, historians may provide scientists with guidance about the best way to carry out their research. Indeed, Peirce went as far as to compile a detailed list of "practical lessons" that scientists should draw from the history of their discipline (HPPLS:407–411, c. 1898; see Miller 1971). Finally, a third way in which the history of science is interesting is because it provides an "anatomy" of reasoning, thereby contributing to ascertaining its general pattern of evolution (HPPLS:143, 1892).

The latter point deserves a few additional remarks as it is the most ambiguous. In part, it can be understood as a direct reference to Peirce's development of his evolutionary philosophy in parallel with the history of science. As we saw, Peirce took history to be an empirical testbed for the elaboration of his evolutionary metaphysics.[6] But Peirce also hinted at something else, and important, about the history of science as an "anatomy of reasons." He claimed that this endeavor becomes particularly relevant once we accept a view of reasoning as irreducible to its deductive and mechanical component (HPPLS:143, 1892). Reasoning is a complex and eminently creative process, and a static logical system cannot offer an adequate map of this complexity. Only by integrating logic with the history of science can we achieve this goal. As we shall see in the next section, a similar intuition motivates Peirce's later arguments about history's relevance to logic at large. It also relates to the notion of history offering "practical lessons" for scientists. Because of their inherently open character, many questions related to the logic of discovery and knowledge acquisition can only be adequately answered once we factor in the historical development of scientific methods.[7]

The second element I would like to discuss is Peirce's "architectonic" conception of philosophy. This idea plays center stage in the first essay of the *Monist* series, titled "The Architecture of Theory" (W8:98–110, 1891), thereby posing as a sort of metaphilosophical introduction to the whole series. Peirce took the idea of philosophy as an "architectonic" enterprise from Kant, and both thinkers took this to mean, first and foremost, that philosophy has the systematic ambition of organizing the whole field of human cognition. Yet Peirce stressed the relation between the architectonic and the historical character of philosophy to a much greater degree than Kant would have allowed.[8]

Thinking of philosophy as an architectonic enterprise means recognizing the role of historical inquiry as a means to gather the construction materials that philosophical architects need in order to build a robust edifice. "My method of attacking all problems," says Peirce, "has ever been to begin with a historical and rational inquiry into the special method adapted to the special problem. This is the essence of my architectonical proceeding" (CP6.604, 1893). This implies that critical or philosophical thinking is not opposed to the painstaking study of the past. It only needs to be put to the right use within a rational system of cognitions. Moreover, Peirce suggested that thinking of philosophical systems as architectonic projects means recognizing their historical nature. Philosophical edifices can "outlast the vicissitudes of time" (W6:168, 1888), but they cannot last forever. The greatness of Aristotle as a philosophical architect consisted precisely of his ability to erect a system that could last for thousands of years. However, even Aristotle's philosophy must yield to the passing of time: the moment has come to proceed with deep renovations of his building (W6:168, 1888).

The third theoretical element I shall consider, the classification of scientific disciplines, is loosely related to the architectonic concept. Peirce started thinking seriously about this subject in the years 1890–1892 (see, e.g., W8:275, 1892). As Chiara Ambrosio (2016) has shown, moreover, he placed a classificatory scheme of the sciences at the beginning of his manuscripts for the 1892 Lowell Lectures, thereby suggesting—in the spirit of Whewell—that the system of scientific knowledge that people were acquainted with in the late nineteenth century was not an immutable construct, but rather the outcome of historical development (see HPPLS:239–240, 1892). At the same time, the decision to place a system of classification at the beginning of his lectures signals Peirce's intent to provide an abstract, systematic blueprint for his historical narrative regarding the progression of the sciences.

Despite this explicit intention to hold the two projects together, however, one might at first suspect that Peirce's system of classification is not easily reconciled with his interest in a rich dynamic interplay between historical and philosophical investigations. For in its general traits, Peirce's classification seems to follow the fairly rigid scheme of Auguste Comte: it allows for abstract and general sciences to influence the lower, empirical ones, but makes the opposite movement much harder to conceive.[9] In this sense, there would seem to be almost no space for history (a "descriptive" science, which lies at the bottom of the classificatory ladder) to have an influence on philosophy (which, by contrast, is placed quite high in the ladder, just below mathematics), aside from history perhaps "growing" into philosophy by means of progressive generalization (EP2:38–39, 1898). However, this would be an overly literal reading of Peirce's classification, not much consistent with the general drift of his thinking (see Esposito 1983, 161–162). As we shall better see in the next section, Peirce admitted the existence of many cases in which specific empirical observations can indeed affect general philosophical theories, without thereby having to reduce the qualitative difference between the two. One important reason behind his lifelong emphasis on the "outward clash" of empirical reality and the value of observation (see, e.g., W3:259, 1877; W5:225, 1885) is precisely his conviction that a dynamic exchange with the historical and empirical sciences is vital to the enrichment of philosophy.

Peirce's placing his classification of the sciences at the beginning of his Lowell Lectures also indirectly suggests something that could have otherwise easily gone unnoticed. Namely, it suggests that the classificatory inquiry *itself* is a historical kind of inquiry, although one of its own kind. It provides us with a portrait of what the sciences look like at a given historical time, and in doing so, it takes into account their historical development. This does not mean that the portrait of the sciences given by any classification is purely contingent on the historical period in which that classification is drafted. Instead, Peirce seems to suggest that the relation among scientific disciplines is a combination of invariant traits, independent of history (i.e., the fact that philosophy is always higher and more general than empirical disciplines) and traits that are historically variable. In this sense, compiling a classification of the sciences involves capturing the invariant traits that define the relationships among scientific disciplines by looking at those disciplines diachronically. This is a robustly historical kind of inquiry (see CP1.268, 1902), yet one that cannot be easily subsumed under the discipline of history as is depicted in the classification itself, because it has a more abstract and philosophical aim. That is, it aims to grasp the essential features of a given set of objects (here, the scientific disciplines) by looking at those objects historically.[10] Peirce called this kind of inquiry "genealogy," to emphasize that its aim is to "find out the true genesis of the objects classified" in order to operate a better, more objective classification (CP1.227, 1902).

4. Genealogy, Logic, and Natural History

Let's see more in detail, therefore, what "genealogy" means, as it constitutes one of the crucial concepts in which history and philosophy converge. Peirce discussed this concept in his writings from 1901 to 1903, particularly when dealing with the general question of how to carry out a study of a given domain of objects by delineating "natural classes." The "natural classification" of the sciences, which we analyzed in the previous section, is an example of this problem (CP1.203–237, 1902). But other examples are the natural classification of biological species or the classifications of artifacts carried out by archaeologists.[11]

Peirce's main point, as we saw already, is that we cannot correctly identify natural classes without resorting to a historical reconstruction of their genesis. Natural classes are ideal entities embodied in individuals. They are "families" of all those individuals that are the offspring of a single idea (CP1.222, c. 1902). The property of belonging to the same family, however, cannot be determined by means of "abstract definitions" (CP1.222, c. 1902) or analytical investigations. Why? Because nothing about the individuals themselves can assure us that the reason they share the same property is because they are members of the same family, rather than merely happening to be similar in certain respects. In the same sense, "no degree of resemblance between two men is proof positive that they are brothers" (EP2:126, 1902). In order to have that proof (and short of DNA testing), a genealogical reconstruction of their family tree is necessary.[12]

Peirce's definition of natural classes as ideas endowed with the power to generate individuals has heavy metaphysical presuppositions that I can only touch upon briefly in this context. It relies in particular on Peirce's teleology. Ideas are final causes: they have the power to bring about events in a different but no less real way than efficient causes. Thus, while attending to the variety of efficient causes that determine the development of a series of objects in time, genealogy also delineates the contours of the stabler ideal elements governing their production. While this strongly teleological metaphysics may seem untenable if applied to biological classification, it gains more plausibility in the field of culture. For in that case, we can translate Peirce's emphasis on final causation as a form of ideal genesis into the simpler language of human purposes. On this view, we can talk of a certain group of artifacts as belonging to the same natural class when they are produced according to a general purpose that is common to all of them. It does not matter whether they are tangible artifacts, such as tools or utensils, or abstract ones, like scientific disciplines.

At this point, we might be tempted to ask whether Peirce's argument about genealogy as being superior to "abstract definitions" in the field of natural classification can be applied to logical investigations as well. Is logic, in other words, something like a natural history or natural classification of thought? Should we use genealogical methods when classifying arguments or kinds of inferences, as we do when we classify scientific disciplines? In a debate with John Dewey, following the publication of the latter's *Studies in Logical Theory* (Dewey 1903), Peirce answered this question with a resounding "no." Logic, he argued, is a normative science, and this normative dimension is neglected in the Deweyan definition of logic as natural history (CP8.190, 1904). Peirce moreover remarked that logic does not classify "actualities" but ideal objects (CP8.190, 1904). In this sense, it should employ a diagrammatic method that is much closer to mathematics than to natural history (CP4.8, 1906).

Importantly, Peirce did *not* say that genealogical or historical considerations are always irrelevant to the study of logic. (If he had done so, he would have contradicted some of the arguments we encountered in the previous section.) Although Dewey's attempt to fully historicize logic was, in Peirce's opinion, fallacious, he did have the right to say that "for certain logical problems the entire development of cognition and along with it that of its object become pertinent, and therefore should be taken into account" (CP8.244, c. 1905). This means that certain logical problems are best understood under a genealogical or historicizing light. On other occasions, Peirce couched the same problem in terms more reminiscent of Whewell (CP2.74, 1902) by suggesting that there are cases in which the empirical observations provided by history do indeed have a bearing on logic.

What are those cases? They cannot have much to do with the normative aspect of logic, as we know, or with its deductive kernel. Rather, Peirce made cursory reference to the study of "probable" and other "special modes of reasoning" (CP2.213, 1902; CP2.74, 1902) as areas of logic that are likely to be enriched by history. Fragmentary as they are, his remarks point to the same argument we encountered in the 1892 Lowell Lectures: history is a tool to study the logic of discovery. That is, it contributes to those nondeductive parts of logic that deal with ampliative inferences and the concrete strategies of scientific research. In truth, Peirce's remarks in the Lowell Lectures were more generous than this, as they appeared to carve out a role for history even in the study of deductive logic, provided we took deductive logic to be a much broader domain than propositional or syllogistic logic. Here the scope of history seems instead more restricted. However, the underlying intuition is similar: history acquires a role whenever we confront a mode of reasoning that does not mechanically draw its conclusion from its premises but needs to take into account other circumstances as well.

One particularly noteworthy way in which the history of science plays a role in Peirce's logic of discovery is by providing grounds for a sort of "meta-abduction" about the validity of scientific abductions. By looking at the many illustrations of scientific progress supplied by the history of science, scientists and philosophers can legitimately advance the hypothesis that science is, on the whole, heading toward progress.[13]

Here it would actually seem that Peirce is running up against an all too obvious objection: Why should we assume that we can interpret the history of science under such an optimistic lens, as a sequence of successful abductions? Does not history show, quite to the contrary, that any scientific theory is eventually falsified? Should we not, therefore, conclude that today's science is, with all likelihood, as unsound as past science? Peirce was able to counter this skeptical objection thanks to the historicized conception of truth I mentioned before. Faithful to the lesson of Whewell, he considered the truth of a scientific doctrine to be dependent on context. A theory is true and scientifically sound insofar as it is the output of the best scientific criteria that were valid *at the time at which it was formulated*, and insofar as it contributed to pushing scientific inquiry forward in the right direction. The astronomical theories of Hipparchus or Ptolemy, for instance, were true when they were formulated because they constituted an ineludible step toward a progressively more accurate account of the solar system (HPPLS:354–355, 1898).

Finally, we can also approach Peirce's qualified rejection of the Deweyan conception of logic as a natural history of thinking from a slightly different perspective if we focus on his previously mentioned remark that logic does not deal with "actualities," and is therefore different from more empirical disciplines such as "Psychology, Linguistics, [. . .] History" (CP8.242, 1904). If we recall Peirce's decidedly antipsychologistic view of logic, it would seem once again that the observation of historical facts (like the observation of psychological or linguistic facts) can offer next to nothing to logic.

It should be reminded, however, that Peirce's antipsychologism is far from implying that empirical observations can never play a role in logical investigations (see Colapietro 2003; Cristalli 2017). If we take care not to expect from empirical or descriptive studies a degree of generality they cannot have, they may still be useful, for instance, in the clarification of certain concepts or as a heuristic device. A nice illustration of this approach is Peirce's invitation to delve deeper into the study of non-Indo-European linguistics precisely as a way to avoid illicit unconscious generalizations from the grammars of Greek or Latin to logical propositions (see, e.g., EP2:309, 1904). History's bearing on logic is thus not an exception to Peirce's general rejection of psychologism or what we might call "linguisticism." Rather, it illustrates his belief that we can appreciate empirical disciplines' contribution to philosophy without forfeiting the robust qualitative difference between the two.

5. "Abduction under Difficulties": The Logic of Historiography

We began the chapter by noting that Peirce's career as a polymath had logic as its natural center of gravity. Peirce carried out his interdisciplinary forays not only for their own sake but also with an eye to enriching his understanding of logical questions. We saw that his interest in history makes no exception. An additional but decisive piece of evidence of this attitude is the long text on the methodology of historical inquiry, titled "On the Logic of Drawing History from Ancient Documents, Especially from Testimonies" (HPPLS:705–800 and CP7.232–255), which Peirce wrote in 1901. This treatise is not only a long discussion of the logical and methodological issues posed by historiographical research. It is also one of Peirce's most comprehensive treatments of his logic of inquiry in its own right. Peirce was not just applying his logical knowledge top down to the specific case of historical inquiry. He was also proceeding, as it were, bottom up: he was taking seriously the methodological challenges posed by his extensive historical studies as an opportunity to offer a more general contribution to logic.

Peirce's decision to focus on how to draw history from *ancient* documents can in part be accounted for by his personal interest in that period of the history of science and philosophy (as we shall see, the three case studies he presented concern classical topics in the history of Greek philosophy). The most pertinent reason, however, seems to lie elsewhere, namely, in the specific epistemological problem posed by the reconstruction of a very distant past about which we seem to know so little. Even though the knowledge of events taking place in ancient times is necessarily fragmentary and uncertain, Peirce was adamant that this is no good reason to give in to skepticism about the very possibility of knowing the past.[14]

The rejection of skeptical attitudes in historiography is the reason behind Peirce's choice of his main polemical target, namely, the German school of historical criticism and the historian of philosophy Eduard Zeller.[15] Peirce's main objection to Zeller and his followers is their supposedly exaggerated reliance on subjectivism. He took issue with these scholars' tendency to assess the reliability of sources on the basis of the impression of likelihood they may leave on us, in a sort of subjectivist distortion of Hume's method for assessing testimonies (see Merrill 1991).

Moreover, Peirce charged German historians with the additional fallacy of combining this already problematic method with a second principle for the assessment of testimonies, which seems to go in the opposite direction as the first but turns in fact into an additional incentive to subjectivist historiography. Borrowed directly from philology (where it is normally called the principle of the *lectio difficilior*), this principle says that "in general, the more difficult reading [*of a source*] is to be preferred," on account of its being probably less tainted by subsequent trivializations (HPPLS:707, 1901). According to Peirce, the combination of these two principles gave German historians "freedom in manufacturing history to suit their subjective impressions" (HPPLS:707, 1901): If the content of a source was very unlikely, they could reject it because of the first principle (the balancing of likelihoods). If it was very likely, they could reject it on the basis of the second principle (the *lectio difficilior*).

Peirce argued on the contrary that a source should *never* be discarded, no matter its supposed reliability. For this reason, he suggested we operate a conceptual shift regarding our appraisal of historical sources. Especially when it comes to ancient history, we should look at sources as *monuments* before we consider their status as *documents* (HPPLS:760–761, 1901; HPPLS:997, 1910).[16] What does this mean? Peirce used the term "monument" not in the sense of commemorative statues or buildings, but in the less obvious sense of artifacts—including manuscripts—that convey information about the past, often in such a way as to transcend the original intention of its creators.[17] Before deciding whether the content of a certain document is reliable or not, as German higher criticism does, historians should take into account its *existence* as a monument and put forth a hypothesis about how they might have come about (HPPLS:761–762, 1901).

To do so, historians should operate yet another disciplinary shift, moving away from purely philological methods and embracing the contribution of archeology. It is the kind of material evidence studied by archeologists, in Peirce's view, that provides history with a much-needed antidote against subjectivism (HPPLS:705 and 719). More specifically, archeological evidence functions as an inductive test of historical hypotheses. As we know from the classification of the sciences, history is a branch of scientific inquiry. And notwithstanding some local differences, all empirical sciences follow a similar methodology, based on the use of the three forms of inferences as well as experiments and observations. Like all other scientists, scholars of ancient history should start with observing the evidence that they need to take into account (i.e., the "monuments") and formulate a hypothesis that best explains their existence. This hypothesis should then be inductively tested. Since, however, controlled experiments are not really possible in history, what performs inductive testing is primarily the operation of comparing our hypotheses with present and future archeological evidence. Overall, Peirce thus suggested a shift from the historical-critical analysis of documents, based primarily on philology, to a quasi-experimental account based primarily (although not exclusively) on archeology.

More implicitly, Peirce also offered a second argument against the principle of the *lectio difficilior* which is worth mentioning, as it seems based on a quintessential pragmatist understanding of creativity and human agency. The idea that we should always prefer the most difficult or unlikely reading of a source depends on postulating a qualitative difference between the author of a source and the people who subsequently copy or transmit it. Those people tend to be depicted as only able to carry out a noncreative, mechanical transmission of knowledge (see Pasquali [1934] 1952, ch. 2). Peirce, by contrast, seemed interested in deflating this difference. For better or worse, both authors and copyists are endowed with creativity and human biases. Aristotle's ancient editor Apellicon, for instance, was "stupid" (CP5.144, 1903) and corrupted the text of the master. But alleged stupidity is not the same as a lack of historical concreteness. Apellicon's work is hardly understandable without a historical investigation of him as a flesh-and-blood historical agent.

Peirce concluded his treatise on the logic of historiography with three case studies that were supposed to put his logical recommendations into practice. These case studies are the history of Aristotle's manuscripts (CP7.233–255, 1901), the reconstruction of the chronology of Plato's dialogues (HPPLS:763–791, 1901), and the biography of Pythagoras (HPPLS:791–800, 1901). Looking at the results Peirce reached in these specific investigations can be a sobering experience, especially if one contrasts such results with his fierce polemic against the historico-critical school and with his pretension to having finally set historiography on a scientific course. For these results do not appear to be much more solid than those reached by more traditional historiographic methods. His reconstruction of the history of Aristotle's writings, in particular, relies on rather unfounded speculations (see Liatsi [2006, 64–66] for details).

We can, however, cast this shortcoming into a better light if we take it as an opportunity to be reminded that Peirce's fight against skepticism and subjectivism is not tantamount to a return to a positivist conception of history as objective chronicle. It was not Peirce's intention to deprive history of its interpretive component, much less to limit historical narrative only to those facts of which we have almost absolute certainty. On the contrary, he was keen on advancing rather speculative conjectures, provided we do so with an eye to their logical accuracy, their predictive power, and their capacity to set our investigation on the course of steady progress in achieving historical truth.

We can better understand what is at stake here if we look at Peirce's remarks on his third case study, namely, the life of Pythagoras. Peirce's interest in Pythagoras is partly to be read in the context of his long-standing interest in biography as a specific kind of historical observation (see Section 2). But the life of Pythagoras also posed a crucial methodological challenge, due to the extremely limited number of things we can claim to know about him. Here, in other words, we have a limiting case of historical abductions performed "under difficulties" (HPPLS:1011, 1903), because it seems impossible to reach even the smallest degree of certainty about the facts we are investigating. But that does not mean we should relapse into skepticism or content ourselves with historical "verisimilitude." Rather, we should provide the most logically robust account on the basis of the sources we have, with the hope that this account will be improved in the future (HPPLS:791–792, 1901).

6. Conclusion

Peirce considered philosophy to be part and parcel of science, that is, the collective endeavor of people who are "devoured by a desire to find things out" (CP1.8, 1897). His remarks on history's relation to philosophy are best understood in light of this idea. History helps philosophers to find things out. It enriches their experience, and this allows them to break through the closed systems into which philosophy as an academic discipline occasionally locks itself up. Moving from this intuition, Peirce sought to steer a middle course between a fully ahistorical conception of philosophy, which would not have done justice to the interplay between experience and philosophical theorizing, and a reductionist form of historicism, which would have ended up denying the very existence of philosophy as an autonomous discipline.

If we were to attempt an overview, the plurality of arguments Peirce offered to justify the dialogue between history and philosophy throughout his career would appear to revolve around the same two axes that we first saw at work in his earlier writings. The first axis insists on the historical and evolutionary nature of reality. Both nature and the mind are best understood in processual terms. Therefore, if we want to grasp their functioning, a historical gaze is necessary. The second axis insists on history as an aid to avoid prejudices, enlarge the scope of our knowledge, and bring ourselves in touch with opinions that we would not have discovered otherwise. In this sense, history is first and foremost a tool to "cut the rope that ties us to the here and now" (W8:349, 1892).

Notes

1. Peirce's argument about the extended and processual character of meaning is related to his lifelong emphasis on the idea that symbols "grow," that is, tend to acquire a broader and more precise meaning over time (EP2:10, 1894; see Short 2007, 285–286; Haack 2009). This idea gives additional support to Peirce's inclination to subject philosophical and scientific concepts to historical analysis. By revealing the path of growth of a given concept, a historical or genealogical approach helps us become more aware of its range of applicability. But it also helps us adjudicate whether a concept that we may tend to take for granted deserves that "firmly established" status or not (in HPPLS:149, 1892, Peirce discusses, for instance, the concept of determinism and in CP7.54, c. 1902, the concept of science).
2. See HPPLS:314-315, c. 1898, and 439, 1894. These are remarks given while carrying out a comparison between ancient Egyptian and Babylonian civilizations. While Peirce praised Babylonians for being "great archaeologists" and for the "diligence with which some of them searched out their own history," he maintained that the Egyptians were a traditionalist people, but not good historians.
3. Later on, the empirical and inductive orientation of this project was to be undermined by Peirce's new conception of biographical inquiry as a *sui generis* historical genre, based on a qualitative kind of observation rather than on scientific induction. See HPPLS:873–874, c. 1902.
4. Peirce had suggested two possible topics for his lectures: "the history of science from Copernicus to Newton" or the "comparative biography of Great Men." And he added that he was not so much interested in Galton's "eminent men" as in describing men of a higher order—in presenting "a sort of scientific Plutarch" (HPPLS:141–142, 1891). See Section 2 of this chapter for a reference to Peirce's study of "Great Men" from the Johns Hopkins period on.
5. Cf. Peirce's claim, in HPPLS:761 (1901), that "one of the main purposes of studying history ought to be to free us from the tyranny of our preconceived notions."
6. Cf. HPPLS:202 (1892): "By far the most interesting aspect of the history of science, is that it shows how an important department of human thought has been developed from generation to generation, with a view of comparing this growth with the historical development of art, of religion, of politics, and of institutions generally, and not only with historical development, but also with the growth of the individual mind, and not only of mind, but of organisms both in their geological succession and in their individual development, and with the formation of worlds, and even with the gradual coming into being and crystallization of the fundamental laws of matter and mind,—from all of which facts taken together we are to expect in the future a grand cosmogony or philosophy of creation."
7. Cf. the closing lines of "How to Make Our Ideas Clear," W3:276 (1878): "How to give birth to those vital and procreative ideas which multiply into a thousand forms and diffuse themselves everywhere [. . .] is an art not yet reduced to rules, but of the secret of which the history of science affords some hints."

8. See also CP1.176–179 (*c.* 1896). On the relation to Kant, see Gava (2014, ch. 1).
9. For Peirce's debt to Comte, see Ambrosio (2016).
10. Peirce did ask himself what place in the classification should be occupied by the classificatory science itself, and his answer was that classification is a "science of review," not a "heuristic science" like philosophy, mathematics, or history. The internal articulation of the sciences of review remains, however, somewhat undertheorized. For some crucial remarks on the relation between history and sciences of review, see Topa (2019, 286–289).
11. Two of Peirce's paramount models in the field of natural classification are his teacher Louis Agassiz, a biologist, and the British archeologist Flinders Petrie. See CP1.209–210, 1902.
12. Peirce also discusses another, complementary reason why genealogy is crucial to classification: natural classes are not always sharply demarcated from one another (CP1.205–210, 1902), which makes a historical analysis an important integration to a purely morphological approach.
13. See Bellucci and Pietarinen (2020), who speak about history as a form of "ur-abduction." I prefer the term "meta-abduction," which goes back to Umberto Eco (1983), both because it's clearer and because I think that Peirce's argument can thereby be contrasted with the more famous "pessimistic meta-induction" developed by philosophers of science (see, e.g., Wray 2015). On Eco, see Bellucci (2018).
14. Max Fisch (1986:349) has noted Peirce's indebtedness to Richard Whately's Historic Doubts Relative to Napoleon Bonaparte (Whately 1819). Whately—whose logical writings Peirce had admired since his youth—caricatured skeptical arguments about the existence of the past by pretending to doubt the existence of Napoleon. Unlike Peirce, however, he did so with an eye to defending the truth of biblical revelation as against its historical-critical reading.
15. Peirce's polemic against Zeller's scholarship dates back to the 1892 Lowell Lectures. See HPPLS:169–170.
16. But see CP7.374 (1902) for a more nuanced account, in which Peirce advocates a division of labor between the criticism of documents and the analysis of monuments.
17. Regazzoni (2022) reconstructs a part of the early modern history of this use of the word "monument" and considers its relation to two ideas that play a crucial role in Peirce's historiography: the fight against historical skepticism and an emphasis on unintentional evidence. For the latter, see Viola (2020, 209–211). For the conceptual pair "document"/"monument," see Le Goff (1978).

REFERENCES

Ambrosio, Chiara. 2016. "The Historicity of Peirce's Classification of the Sciences." *European Journal of Pragmatism and American Philosophy* 8, no. 2. doi:10.4000/ejpap.625

Bellucci, Francesco. 2018. "Eco and Peirce on Abduction." *European Journal of Pragmatism and American Philosophy* 10, no. 1. doi.10.4000/ejpap.1122

Bellucci, Francesco, and Ahti-Veikko Pietarinen. 2020. "Peirce on the Justification of Abduction." *Studies in History and Philosophy of Science Part A* 84 (December): 12–19.

Colapietro, Vincent. 2003. "The Space of Signs: C. S. Peirce's Critique of Psychologism." In *Philosophy, Psychology, and Psychologism: Critical and Historical Readings of the Psychological Turn in Philosophy*, edited by Dale Jacquette, 157–179. Dordrecht: Kluwer Academic.

Cowles, Henry M. 2016. "The Age of Methods: William Whewell, Charles Peirce, and Scientific Kinds." *Isis* 107 no. 4: 722–737.

Cristalli, Claudia. 2017. "Experimental Psychology and the Practice of Logic." *European Journal of Pragmatism and American Philosophy* 9, no. 1.

Dewey, John, ed. 1903. *Studies in Logical Theory*. Chicago: University of Chicago Press.

Eco, Umberto. 1983. "Horns, Hooves, Insteps: Some Hypotheses on Three Types of Abduction." In *The Sign of Three*, edited by Umberto Eco and Thomas A. Sebeok, 198–220. Bloomington: Indiana University Press.

Eisele, Carolyn. 1959. "Charles S. Peirce. Nineteenth Century Man of Science." *Scripta Mathematica* 5: 304–324.

Esposito, Joseph L. 1983. "Peirce and the Philosophy of History." *Transactions of the Charles S. Peirce Society* 19, no. 2 (Spring): 155–166.

Fisch, Max Harold. 1982. "Introduction." In *Writings of Charles S. Peirce. A Chronological Edition*. Vol. 1, edited by Max H. Fisch and Christian J. W. Kloesel, xv–xxxv. Bloomington: Indiana University Press.

Fisch, Max Harold. 1986. *Peirce, Semeiotic, and Pragmatism: Essays*, edited by Kenneth Laine Ketner and Christian J. W. Kloesel. Bloomington: Indiana University Press.

Gava, Gabriele. 2014. *Peirce's Account of Purposefulness: A Kantian Perspective*. New York: Routledge.

Girel, Mathias. 2017. "«Éclaircir les conceptions»: Peirce et Whewell, 1869." *Cahiers philosophiques* 150: 35–44.

Haack, Susan. 1994. "How the Critical Common-Sensist Sees Things." *Histoire Épistémologie Langage* 16 no. 1: 9–34.

Haack, Susan. 2009. "The Growth of Meaning and the Limits of Formalism: In Science, in Law." *Análisis Filosófico* 29 no. 1: 5–29.

Le Goff, Jacques. 1978. "Documento/Monumento." In *Enciclopedia Einaudi*, edited by Ruggiero Romano, 5:38–48. Turin: Einaudi.

Liatsi, Maria. 2006. *Interpretation der Antike: die pragmatistische Methode historischer Forschung. Ein Kommentar zur Abhandlung von Charles Sanders Peirce "On the logic of drawing history from ancient documents, especially from testimonies."* Hildesheim: Olms.

Merrill, Kenneth R. 1991. "Hume's 'Of Miracles,' Peirce, and the Balancing of Likelihoods." *Journal of the History of Philosophy* 29, no. 1: 85–113.

Miller, Willard M. 1971. "Peirce on the Use of History." *Transactions of the Charles S. Peirce Society* 7, no. 2 (Spring): 105–126.

Misak, Cheryl. 2004. "Peirce on Vital Matters." In *The Cambridge Companion to Peirce*, edited by Cheryl Misak, 150–174. Cambridge: Cambridge University Press.

Pasquali, Giorgio. [1934] 1952. *Storia della tradizione e critica del testo*. Firenze: Le Monnier.

Pearce, Trevor. 2020. *Pragmatism's Evolution: Organism and Environment in American Philosophy*. Chicago: University of Chicago Press.

Peirce, Charles S. 1878. *Photometric Researches*. Leipzig: Engelmann.

Peirce, Charles S. 1931–1958. *The Collected Papers of Charles Sanders Peirce*. 8 vols. Vols. 1–6 edited by Charles Hartshorne and Paul Weiss. Vols. 7–8 edited by Arthur W. Burks. Cambridge, MA: Harvard University Press. (Referred to as CP.)

Peirce, Charles S. 1977. *Semiotic and Significs: The Correspondence between Charles S. Peirce and Victoria Lady Welby*, edited by Charles S. Hardwick. Bloomington: Indiana University Press. (Referred to as SS.)

Peirce, Charles S. 1982–2010. *The Writings of Charles S. Peirce: A Chronological Edition.* 7 vols. to date, edited by the Peirce Edition Project. Bloomington: Indiana University Press. (Referred to as W.)

Peirce, Charles S. 1985. *Historical Perspectives on Peirce's Logic of Science.* 2 vols, edited by. Carolyn Eisele. The Hague: Mouton. (Referred to as HPPLS.)

Peirce, Charles S. 1992–1998. *The Essential Peirce: Selected Philosophical Writings.* 2 vols. Vol. 1 edited by Nathan Houser and Christian Kloesel. Vol. 2 edited by the Peirce Edition Project. Bloomington: Indiana University Press. (Referred to as EP.)

Regazzoni, Lisa. 2022. "Unintentional Monuments, or the Materializing of an Open Past." *History and Theory* 61, no. 2: 242–268.

Short, T. L. 2001. "The Conservative Pragmatism of Charles Peirce." *Modern Age* 43, no. 4: 295–303.

Short, T. L. 2007. *Peirce's Theory of Signs.* Cambridge: Cambridge University Press.

Topa, Alessandro. 2019. "'In the Memory of These Concrete Living Gests': C. S. Peirce on Science of Review." *Transactions of the Charles S. Peirce Society* 55, no. 3 (Summer): 273–303.

Viola, Tullio. 2020. *Peirce on the Uses of History.* Berlin: De Gruyter.

Whately, Richard. 1819. *Historic Doubts Relative to Napoleon Bonaparte.* London: Hatchard.

Whewell, William. 1837. *History of the Inductive Sciences. From the Earliest to the Present Times.* 3 vols. London: John W. Parker.

Whewell, William. 1840. *The Philosophy of the Inductive Sciences, Founded upon Their History.* 2 vols. London: John W. Parker.

Wray, K. Brad. 2015. "Pessimistic Inductions: Four Varieties." *International Studies in the Philosophy of Science* 29, no. 1: 61–73.

CHAPTER 32

DIAGRAMS, SEMIOSIS, AND PEIRCE'S METAPHOR

TONY JAPPY

1. INTRODUCTION

IN 1903, in the syllabus intended to accompany a course of lectures, Peirce established a taxonomy of ten classes from three divisions of signs. One of these was the universally known icon–index–symbol trichotomy, the one most often employed in the analysis of verbal and pictorial signs not only within Peircean semiotics but also in competing theories of the sign. Within this division, the icon constitutes the sign's purely qualitative mode of representation whereby a sign might resemble its object, an important requirement in representational painting and portraiture, for example. Peirce further analyzed the icon into three more basic modes of qualitative representation, the hypoicons, thus enabling more penetrating structural analyses of signs, pictorial and otherwise. However, by 1908 his conception of signs had developed into a very different, six-stage process, namely, semiosis, from which the icon–index–symbol division, together with the hypoicons, was absent. Since, in view of the differing theoretical foundations distinguishing the three-division system of 1903 from the hexadic system of 1908, it might be thought that Peirce had introduced an unresolvable inconsistency into the two conceptions of the sign and a rejection of the analytical power of the hypoicons, the current chapter suggests ways for Peircean semiotics to accommodate both the potential for structural analysis offered by hypoiconicity and the intentionality of semiosis.

First, however, the precise form of the graphic representations of hypoiconicity to follow—a necessarily personal interpretation of the hypoicons—requires explanation. The schemata to be developed below derive from this definition of the sign from the syllabus of 1903: "A *Sign*, or *Representamen*, is a First which stands in such a genuine triadic relation to a Second, called its *Object*, as to be capable of determining a Third, called its *Interpretant*, to assume the same triadic relation to its Object in which it stands itself to the same Object" (EP2:272–273). Although Peirce was working with two objects and three interpretants in 1903 (EP2:275), he chose here only to use the sign and what in 1904 (SS:33–34) he identified as the dynamic object and the signified (final) interpretant in his construction of the three divisions yielding the ten classes: this is why there are only three correlates involved in the process represented in Figure 32.1. While the ten classes of signs derived in 1903 are atemporal and static, the sign itself operates in a three-correlate dynamic process, anticipating the semiosis of 1908. Summarizing the definition above, a sign is determined by its object to produce an effect upon an interpreter, and when the sign of 1903 functions as a sign, no less than that of 1908, it mediates in a determination "flow" from object to interpretant. Since the interpretant in any signifying process is mediately determined by the object, Figure 32.1 simply displays this determination flow implicit in the definition. Note, however, that it is not a schema ever introduced by Peirce.

Having defined the sign (also referred to at this time as a "representamen"), Peirce proceeds to introduce first two, then three divisions, by means of which he establishes the table of ten classes of signs. This is how the all-important relation holding between sign and object—the sign's mode of representation—is defined in the syllabus: "The first and most fundamental [division of signs] is that any Representamen is either an *Icon*, an *Index*, or a *Symbol*" (EP2:273), followed later by this definition of the icon: "An *Icon* is a sign which refers to the Object that it denotes merely by virtue of characters of its own, and which it possesses, just the same, whether any such Object actually exists or not. It is true that unless there really is such an Object, the Icon does not act /as/ a sign" (EP2:291): to function, the icon must involve all three correlates, hence the specification also of both object and interpretant in the figures given below. As a first, then, the icon—an iconic sinsign in the schemata—is, following the definition given above, the first correlate in a triadic relation; it is a sign, more precisely, a species of representamen determining a mental interpretant (EP2:273). In Figure 32.1, the three correlates display the determination process by which the sign is informed by its object. It is intended to represent the determination sequence from dynamic object to final interpretant, an earlier form of semiosis implicit in the 1903 definition of the sign. However, to illustrate structural differences distinguishing the three hypoicons, the schema on Figure 32.1 will henceforth be replaced by the "ellipses" on Figure 32.2.

FIGURE 32.1 The determination process in the "proto-semiosis" of 1903.

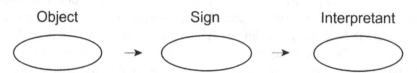

FIGURE 32.2 The action of the sign in 1903 represented as ellipses.

The trichotomization of the icon had already been mooted in one of the Harvard Lectures on pragmatism delivered in April that year: "Now the Icon may undoubtedly be divided according to the categories; but the mere completeness of the notion of the icon does not imperatively call for any such division" (EP2:163). This distinctly Peircean and highly innovative semiotic approach to iconic signs reappeared in the syllabus, where Peirce introduced the concept of hypoicon: "But a sign may be *iconic*, that is, may represent its object mainly by its similarity, no matter what its mode of being. If a substantive be wanted, an iconic [sign] may be termed a *hypoicon*. Any material image, as a painting, is largely conventional in its mode of representation; but in itself, without legend or label, it may be called a *hypoicon*" (EP2:273–274).

Thus, after having derived the icon subdivision through a form of categorial analysis, Peirce then proceeded to derive the three hypoicons by recursively applying these categorial distinctions to the icon itself, a process recorded in the statement establishing the three degrees of structural complexity, which are, in effect, the three grades or forms of resemblance presented by the hypoicons. The trichotomy resulting from this category-based process is the definition, describing image, diagram, and metaphor in order of increasing complexity: "Hypoicons may roughly [be] divided according to the mode of Firstness which they partake. Those which partake the simple qualities, or First Firstnesses, are *images*; those which represent the relations, mainly dyadic, or so regarded, of the parts of one thing by analogous relations in their own parts, are *diagrams*; those which represent the representative character of a representamen by representing a parallelism in something else, are *metaphors*" (EP2:274, 1903). Since this analysis of the icon yields image, diagram, and metaphor, and since Peirce later maintained that an index involved a sort of icon, and a symbol a sort of index (EP2:291–292, 1903), it follows by transitivity that indices and symbols can involve any or all of the three hypoicons. Finally, it should be noted that as with the structural complexity of icon, index, and interpretant (CP2.304, 1902), the increase in hypoiconic complexity in the definition follows what Peirce had earlier referred to as the logical categories of the monad, dyad, and polyad or higher set, which are "categories of the forms of experience" (CP1.452, 1896).

2. The Hypoiconic Structures Characterizing Image, Diagram, and Metaphor

The three fundamental ways in which the icon can resemble its object by virtue of Peirce's categorial distinctions are represented below as Figures 32.3, 32.4, and 32.5, rudimentary graphic representations of the structure of, respectively, Peirce's image, diagram, and metaphor, in which the arrows represent both the process of determination and the

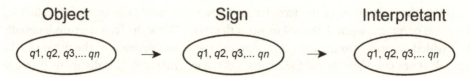

FIGURE 32.3 The generic structure of a sign with image hypoiconicity.

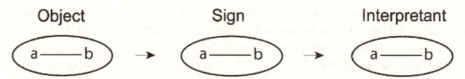

FIGURE 32.4 The generic structure of a sign with diagram hypoiconicity.

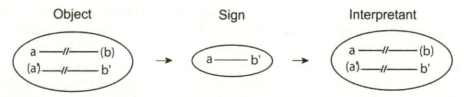

FIGURE 32.5 The structure of a sign with metaphor hypoiconicity.

passage of the process through an inescapably "sensible"—in other words, existential and perceivable—medium such as a piece of painted canvas, oils on a wood panel, the inked page of a book, the old-fashioned school chalk and blackboard, or the pixelated glass on a smartphone screen. Note that in all such cases the sign is necessarily a sinsign or the replica of a legisign, as it has to be perceivable—were it a legisign, it would be of the nature of thought or habit and would therefore be physically unperceivable. Note, too, that it is the sign alone that has hypoiconic structure since it is the "representing" correlate in the process.

Figure 32.3 is a very basic representation of some of the qualities (lines, shapes, colors) presumed to be inhering in features of the represented object that determine corresponding qualities, namely, the first firstnesses of the definition, in a portrait painting, for example, which is an iconic sinsign but also an *image* at its hypoiconic level.

Since the qualities—first firstnesses—represented are phenomenologically less complex than the secondness of the existential medium (the canvas and oils of a painting, for example), the intended representation of the qualities in the object is in no way inhibited by potential differences in complexity between the sign and its two correlates. In other words, since the qualities represented in this phenomenological conception of the process are less complex than the medium representing them, the intended representation of the qualities in the object is in no way inhibited.

Figure 32.4 represents the structure of a very basic diagram (most signs with diagrammatic structure would, of course, be far more complex than this), an icon composed essentially of the second firstnesses of the definition, namely, the dyadic relations mentioned there and simply represented as the single relation **a--b** between the two partial objects **a** and **b** in the entity, fact, or event represented by the sign, such relations being a step up the phenomenological scale from the necessarily vague, unstructured firstnesses composing the image: the latter are interpreted to conform to an object, the portrait-painter's model, for example, but there is no necessary correspondence between the image and the model. The diagram, by contrast, is an icon composed of lines and shapes organized by at least one dyadic relation inherited from the object that it represents (CP4.418, 1903) and, in more complex combinations of partial objects, informs not only the illustrations from geometry manuals and the graphic instructions on how to assemble furniture, but also all manner of informative exosomatic organs such as thermometers, barometers, speedometers, wind socks, and the complex form of sound spectrograms. In such cases, the diagrammatic complexity of the sinsign partakes of the secondness of the medium and the phenomenology explains how the representation of the structure of the object is similarly in no way inhibited by the medium through which it is communicated.

Finally, as indicated in Figure 32.5, metaphor is the hypoiconic structure presenting third firstness, a phenomenological complexity compatible with convention, synthesis, and mediation and, like the symbol, requires the experience of the interpreter in the interpreting process to construe the nature of the association or comparison being communicated concerning two (or more) generally disparate domains of experience, and in this metaphor is necessarily triadic. According to Peirce's concise definition given earlier, metaphor hypoiconicity informs a sign whose object—the "something else" of the definition—is structured by a two-tiered parallelism and is thus significantly more complex than the sign itself.

The schema of the sign correlate displayed above in Figure 32.4 contains a single "diagrammatic," that is, dyadic, relation, which is the formal structure, too, of some simple fact such as *This man is untrustworthy*, where **a** and **b** are, respectively, *This man* and the property *untrustworthy*. Metaphor, on the other hand, as defined by Peirce, presents at least two such relations in parallel in the object, as in Figure 32.5. Here we find counterpart mappings between elements in the relation (**man** —//— (**untr.**)), *This man is untrustworthy*, which constitutes the state of affairs that is being evaluated, and elements from the putative well-known fact (**fox** —//— (**cun.**)), *A fox is a cunning animal*, providing the evaluation. The two parallel relations can be identified, following the conceptual metaphor tradition, as the "target" and "base"' domains, respectively. The elements in the target domain are somehow controversial or contentious or not yet accepted, while the fact considered to be the basis of the judgment and hopefully self-evident to the addressee or interpreter is the idea that foxes are cunning, a culturally accepted and widely exploited negative judgment, even if anthropomorphic and therefore of dubious validity. In the very simple case in Figure 32.5, **man** maps to its counterpart in the base domain, **fox**, while the mapping from (**untr.**) to its counterpart in the base domain (**cun.**) (*untrustworthy* and *cunning animal*, respectively, on the schema) is absent from the sign. Owing to its vectorial, existential character, within Peirce's phenomenological framework the spoken sign with the copula expressing class membership *This man is a fox* is necessarily constrained in the amount of information that it can represent in the existential medium of air or a sheet of paper, and Figure 32.5 shows how certain participants in the original parallelism (displayed in parentheses) are bracketed by the unavoidable quantitative restriction caused by the sign's being an existent perceivable medium.

The structure of metaphor proposed in Figure 32.5 calls for three remarks. First, it should be noted that the repetition of the parallel structure of the object in the structure of the interpretant is a convention for showing that the intended meaning of the sign has been understood; in other words, it is a way of showing that the metaphor has been fully interpreted. Second, all three hypoicons are subclasses of a subdivision contributing to the identification of the ten classes of *signs*. By definition, a "Sign is a Representamen with a mental Interpretant" (EP2:273, 1903); these ten classes, therefore, necessarily determine a mental interpretant, hence the additional interest, in the case of metaphor, of including the structure of the interpretant in the schema. Should a child hear an adult state that a certain man is a fox (an example of the a'—a structure of the sign in Figure 32.5), as in the case of Peirce's own example of metaphor examined above, "Be very careful, this man is a fox!", the child might reply "But that's silly, a man can't be a fox, a fox is an animal." In such a case the structure of the interpretant has not realized the structure of the intended parallelism, and the utterance has been misunderstood. Any interpretation of metaphor is fully dependent, therefore, upon the experience of the interpreter, experience being that "cognitive resultant of our past lives" (CP2.84, 1902): it is in this, too, triadic. Third, although Peirce never used such schemata, what Figure 32.5 is intended to show, too, is that while the necessarily perceivable medium—the airwaves in a spoken utterance, any page on which the utterance is written, or the canvas and paint marks in the case of a painting—partakes necessarily of secondness within Peirce's theory of hypoiconicity, the parallelism in the structure of the object constitutes a third firstness and is therefore phenomenologically more complex than the audible, written, or pictorial sign representing it. In short, metaphoric form is more complex than the medium through which it must be communicated. This is why the elements enclosed in parentheses in the object and interpretant ellipses stand for participants that *cannot* figure in the sign.

We see that in Peirce's conception of metaphor in 1903—if the present analysis is accepted—the representation of the full structure of the object is inhibited, with the consequence that when viewed within Peircean semiotics all metaphorically informed signs are both *underspecified* (not all the elements of the original parallelism in the object find their way into the sign) and characteristically *incongruous*, as such signs perforce represent elements drawn from distinct and generally dissimilar domains reflecting to varying degrees the intensity of the judgments or commentary involved. Unfortunately, however, developments in Peirce's conception of signs and the process in which they function led to a radical modification of the theoretical status of the hypoicons.

3. Changing Versions of the Subclasses of Icons

Although described in detail in the syllabus, the trichotomization of the icon had already been suggested in the Harvard Lectures on pragmatism delivered earlier that year: "Now the Icon may undoubtedly be divided according to the categories; but the mere completeness of the notion of the icon does not imperatively call for any such division" (EP2:163). The following definition from the syllabus is the earliest of at least four different formulations of such a division of the icon into three subclasses, in which Peirce offers the *example* as the most complex subclass: "Icons may be distinguished, though only roughly, into those which are icons in respect to the qualities of sense, being *images*, those which are icons in respect to the dyadic relations of their parts to one another, being *diagrams* or dyadic analogues, and those which are icons in respect to their intellectual characters, being *examples*" (R478:209, 1903). This was followed by what is considered the standard definition of hypoicons, quoted in the introduction and schematized in Section 2, in which the three hypoicons are, in increasing phenomenological complexity, image, diagram, and metaphor. However, the subclasses of the icon subsequently underwent two radical redefinitions. The following extract is from the "Logic Notebook," dated October 12, 1905, where the *examples* and *metaphors* constituting the most complex subclasses of the icon from the syllabus have been reformulated as *diagrams*, with the phenomenologically less complex earlier *diagrams* redefined as *analogues* Peirce is reverting here to two terms, namely "likeness" and "analogue," which he had introduced in the 1860s: "A sign may represent its dynamical object simply by virtue of its own abstract quality. It thus represents whatever else has that quality. Such a sign is termed an Icon. Icons either represent unanalyzed qualities, when they are simple *likenesses* or they have structures like the structure of the object, when, [...] they are *analogues*, or if made for the purpose are *diagrams*" (R339:257r, 1905).

Similarly, in the following extract from manuscript R284, one of several draft attempts at a "Basis of Pragmaticism," the earlier *diagram* in the syllabus definitions is now simply described as bearing "brute Secundan relations of parts," whereas the *diagram*, here again the most complex of the three subclasses, "partakes of a symbolic flavor": "Icons are subdivided according to the nature of their significant likeness to their Objects which may be 1st in Priman characters or qualities of feeling; these alone have the iconic character in its purity; or 2nd in brute Secundan relations of parts; or 3rd in intellectual relations of parts. The last which are the most important may be called *Diagrams*. These partake of a symbolic flavor" (R284:61v-63, 1905). Such radical modifications suggest not only that Peirce was hesitating between redefining the subclasses now within the logic in the notebook and replacing the old phenomenological terminology framing the hypoicons by that of the newer phaneroscopy in R284, but also that he was founding the diagrammatic system of the graphs on a more "symbolcentric" conception of the logic itself.

Table 32.1 Four Versions of the Subclasses of the Icon

	Manuscript number and date			
	1903		1905	
	R478a	R478b	R339	R284
Discriminant:				
First firstness	Image	Image	Likeness	Priman: quality of feeling
Second firstness	Diagram	Diagram	Analogue	Secundan: relation of parts
Third firstness	Example	Metaphor	Diagram	[Tertian]: diagram

The redefinitions of the subclasses of the icon effected between the years 1903 and 1905 are displayed in Table 32.1.

Just why Peirce should have modified so fundamentally the subclasses of the icons is difficult to establish—as both 1905 versions were scrawled almost as afterthoughts in the manuscripts—but it was surely a consequence of the intense activity of the years 1905–1906. Between October 10, 1905, and August 31, 1906, he produced at least six ten-division typologies in his "Logic Notebook," published three papers on pragmatism in *The Monist*, and wrote numerous drafts for an intended "Basis of Pragmaticism," with work on the graphs culminating in the "Prolegomena" paper of 1906. This period also saw an extensive development of his conception of the sign and the process in which it functions. What seems to run through much of this work is a return to the symbolistic of Peirce's earliest years and the idea that the symbol is the prime, albeit not the sole, subclass of signs that founds his conception of logic. This was how he initially conceived "semiotic" as the science of representations:

> Logic is objective symbolistic.
> Symbolistic is the semiotic of symbols.
> Objective symbolistic is that branch of symbolistic which considers relations to objects.
> Semiotic is the science of representations. (W1:303, 1865)

Within this group, his own work clearly consisted in objective symbolistic, the field that studies the relation between signs and their objects, this being, in fact, the basis of his first division of signs, the one to which he returned many times over the years and the one that surely founded his theory of diagrammatic representation of thought. In the "Ethics of Terminology" prefacing the syllabus, he had already described the technical language appropriate to scientific research as being composed essentially of symbols, in spite of the problematic nature of their inevitable growth and the loss of precision of their original meaning: "The woof and warp of all thought and all research is symbols, and the life of thought and science is the life inherent in symbols" (EP2:263,

1903). Although he was clearly concerned with all types of signs, as a logician and a scientist he was principally interested in those connected with the communication of the ideas of science, in effect a relatively restricted scope of semiotics. A good example of this is to be found in the first of the three articles for *The Monist* in 1905 where he returns to the ethics of scientific terminology—a sort of editorial counterpart to the interpretive nature of pragmatism—in particular to the question of the symbol. To bring out the defining characteristics of his version of pragmatism he introduces a dialogue between himself and an imaginary questioner, in the course of which he admits to the application of pragmaticism being restricted to symbols when asked what the indexical expression "George Washington" meant (EP2:341–342, 1905). In short, pragmatism, like the practice of science in general, is principally concerned with the interpretation and employment of symbols and the generality of their scope.

Thus, the replacement of the *example* and *metaphor* of 1903 by the *diagram* as the most complex subclass of the icon shows that the graphs, too, are concerned principally with concepts, assertions, and the development of thought in the form of symbols. Thus, it not inconceivable that it was the prioritization of the symbol and the importance of the graphs that led to the radical revision of the three subclasses of the icon described above, and with it the apparent loss of the analytical power of his definition of metaphor.

4. Semiosis

4.1. Toward Semiosis

A further development comes with the manuscript "Pragmatism" of 1907 (R318). By this time, Peirce had defined the sign specifically as a medium, this medium seemingly becoming a sign as soon as it is "informed" by the immediate object: "I use the word '*Sign*' in the widest sense for any medium for the communication or extension of a Form (or feature). Being medium, it is determined by something, called its Object, and determines something, called its Interpretant" (SS:196, 1906). He had attributed specific values to the three interpretants, the intentional (immediate) and the effectual (dynamic), for example, being described, respectively, as a determination of the mind of the utterer and a determination of the mind of the interpreter (SS:196–197, 1906), and had introduced the concept of the quasi-mind, enabling him to describe the general context of the communication of meaning from one mind to another in R283, a version of the "Basis of Pragmaticism" (LI:280, 1905–1906).

Signs are the determination of the dynamic object, but for a logician like Peirce just how that dynamic object initiates a process of determination requires explanation. Although in this same draft he cites ordinary conversation as a perfect example of communication, he eschews any form of appeal to the fallible human element in such communication and adopts the far more abstract concept of two quasi-minds, between which, he suggests, the sign is the medium of communication (LI:278–280). This introduction of a theoretical context for the exchange of representations by signs anticipates the later concept of semiosis.

In "Pragmatism" Peirce defines semiotic and announces the need for future research into the identification in logic of all varieties, not simply of signs, but also of possible semiosis, thereby associating classes of signs with the types of semiosis producing them (R318:119, 1907). This new stage is also highly significant since it is in this text that we find the definition of semiosis. He describes the association of the three foundational constituents of semiosis as the "cooperation" of three "subjects," namely, a sign, its object, and its interpretant: "by 'semiosis' I mean [. . .] an action, or influence, which is, or involves, a coöperation of *three* subjects, such as a sign, its object, and its interpretant, this tri-relative influence not being in any way resolvable into actions between pairs" (EP2:411, 1907). By this time, too, the dynamic object was shown to be the locus of intentionality in the example of the "will" of an officer giving commands to soldiers (R318:373–379, 1907; see also EP2:493, 1909).

4.2. Category or Universe

Another significant development of Peirce's late conception of the sign and the way it functions occurs in 1908. True to his principle of supplying the theoretical framework to his classifications, as was the case with phenomenology in the syllabus (EP2:267–272) and the letter to Lady Welby of October 12, 1904 (SS:23–32), Peirce accompanies his description of semiosis with an introduction to the new theoretical background that underwrites it by presenting three modal universes:

> It is clearly indispensable to start with an accurate and broad analysis of the nature of a Sign. I define a Sign as anything which is so determined by something else, called its Object, and so determines an effect upon a person, which effect I call its Interpretant, that the latter is thereby mediately determined by the former. . . . I recognize three Universes, which are distinguished by three Modalities of Being.
>
> One of these Universes embraces whatever has its Being in itself alone . . . I denominate the objects of this Universe *Ideas*, or *Possibles*, although the latter designation does not imply capability of actualization . . .
>
> Another Universe is that of, 1st, Objects whose Being consists in their Brute reactions, and of, 2nd, the Facts. . . . I call the Objects, Things, or more unambiguously, *Existents*, and the facts about them I call Facts . . .
>
> The third Universe consists of the co-being of whatever is in its Nature *necessitant*, that is, is a Habit, a law, or something expressible in a universal proposition. Especially continua are of this nature. I call objects of this universe *Necessitants*. (SS:80–82, 1908)

Thus, by 1908, with the definition of the sign as a medium and semiosis as a "cooperation," the three universes supplied the system with "receptacles" of entities—possible, existent, and necessitant entities—that could function as signs, interpretants, and objects. If Peirce was maintaining his classification of the sciences, then logic was still dependent upon phaneroscopy. There is, therefore, a potentially traceable filiation from the categories to the universes, but the relation is tenuous—a category is purely phenomenal in scope; it is not a receptacle and has no "members" that can trigger the action of the sign, physically or otherwise. That these universes should have been derived from the categories, there is no doubt; they are nevertheless very different, being employed in a concrete communicative context. Making the distinction is important, as many nonspecialist readers of Peirce from other disciplines can easily be misled into thinking that the various classes of semiosis are based upon the phenomenology of 1903.

4.3. Semiosis Described

Finally, in a letter to Lady Welby dated December 23, 1908, he expanded the triadic "cooperation" involved in semiosis as defined in 1907 into a dynamic process involving the sign and its five correlates in the following formulation:

> It is evident that a possible can determine nothing but a Possible, it is equally so that a Necessitant can be determined by nothing but a Necessitant. Hence it follows from the Definition of a Sign that since the Dynamoid Object determines the Immediate Object,
> which determines the Sign itself,
> which determines the Destinate Interpretant,
> which determines the Effective Interpretant,
> which determines the Explicit Interpretant,
> the six trichotomies, instead of determining 729 classes of signs, as they would if they were independent, only yield 28 classes. (EP2:481, 1908)

This analytical description of the determination process itself can be represented more simply by the scheme in Figure 32.6, in which the interpretants have been standardized, respectively, from destinate, effective, and explicit to immediate, dynamic, and final. Note that some authors, for example, Savan (1988, 52), inverse this order, identifying the explicit as the immediate and the destinate as the final. Now, such an order would produce the illogical situation where the immediate interpretant finds itself at several removes from the sign in which it has always been defined to be "present." For Peirce, immediacy meant "presence in": "to say that A is immediate to B means that it is present in B" (R339:243Av, 1905).

$$Od \rightarrow Oi \rightarrow S \rightarrow Ii \rightarrow Id \rightarrow If$$

FIGURE 32.6 Semiosis as described in 1908.

Table 32.2 The Twenty-Eight Classes of Signs Set Out in Order of Semiosis

Subject (semiosis)	Od	Oi	S	Ii	Id	If
Universe: Necessitant	Collective	Copulant	Type	Relative	Usual	To produce self-control
Existant	Concretive	Designative	Token	Categorical	Percussive	To produce action
Possible	Abstractive	Descriptive	Mark	Hypothetical	Sympathetic	Gratific

Figure 32.6 displays in simple form the hexadic structure of semiosis as Peirce described it in 1908, in which the arrow (→) indicates the process of determination of the successive "stages" in the process in the sequence of the six divisions of the typology. The abbreviations Od, Oi, S, Ii, Id, and If in Figure 32.6 represent, respectively, the dynamic and immediate objects, the sign, followed by the immediate, dynamic, and final interpretants. Note, however, that Peirce never developed the twenty-eight-class system and that he never set out his numerous typologies in the horizontal format displayed in Figure 32.6 and Table 32.2.

Significantly, although the sign–object division is included in the ten divisions potentially yielding sixty-six classes of signs, these decadic systems all begin with the sign division, unlike the hexad, which is initiated by the dynamic object. The former are typologies of sign classes, not signifying processes, whereas the hexad is both. More relevantly, since the six divisions involve the correlates of semiosis, there is no provision for the relational icon–index–symbol division, and consequently there is no provision for the icon's three subclasses: iconicity is not incorporated in semiosis. However, for Peirce's theory of signs to be a viable scientific proposition we have to be able to account for every stage in the process of semiosis, and such an ability will require at some point that signs should be examined with respect to the nature of their immediate objects. Developing an idea mooted in Jappy (2019), the rest of the chapter, therefore, explores the stages in semiosis from the dynamic object to the sign via the immediate object, since any persuasive or influential activity requires the formal organization of its representation, and there can be no communication without representation, irrespective of the nature of the "agents," human or otherwise, involved. While not all representations are purpose-driven—those with an existent dynamic object are causal rather than intentional—this chapter presents one possible strategy for the preservation of iconicity in exploring the role of the immediate object in cases of conspicuous intentionality. What follows is based upon three principles.

First, conventionally, the effects of signs are to be found in an interpreter's reaction to a sign, in other terms, in the interpretants determined by the sign. However, as art historians have known for centuries, traces of the creative impulse determining the sign are also to be identified in the form of the sign, in the sign's composition. Second, the sign is taken in the process of semiosis to be a medium informed differentially in two successive stages by the objects of which it is a determination. Finally, the influence of the *intentionality* determining the sign, as described above in the six-stage sequence in the 1908 letter to Lady Welby, and as can be seen in Table 32.2, cannot be immediate. It follows, then, that in order to function, any intentionality triggering semiosis has to be in some way perceivable in some medium. To achieve the purpose of the agency it emanates from, this intentionality has to be mediatized, and the following sections hypothesize the way this mediatization is achieved and how this may accommodate iconicity. This involves examination of the function of the immediate object, the object "present in" the sign.

5. The Immediate Object

One way to determine the nature of the immediate object and to show how it communicates to the sign form from the dynamic object is by adopting the definition from 1906 mentioned earlier and treating the sign *strictly* as a medium—airwaves, a page in a book, a piece of canvas or an oak panel, a computer or cinema screen, even human skin . . . This is the strategy adopted here: *any sign determining its series of interpretants is the fusion of the form-communicating immediate object and a medium.* The semiotic nature of this "hint or its substance" constituting the immediate object mentioned in the epigraph can be exemplified in (1) the written version of a spoken utterance and (2) its phonemic transcription.

(1) What are those blue remembered hills
(2) [ˈwɒtəˈðəʊzˈbluːrɪˈmɛmbədˈhɪlz]

Utterances (1) and (2) constitute a simple case of diamesic variation: the same assertion expressed in two different media. In the case of the written utterance, it is the paper and the series of ink marks on it forming the written page that constitute the medium. In the second case, it is the air that transmits the utterance's particular form as the two and a half–second sequence of troughs and peaks of the airwaves conveying it. However, the utterance could just as easily be communicated in other media: a computer screen, for example, or a classroom blackboard and chalk, the particular distribution of the marks contributing to such media being the specific form of the immediate object. In each case, the intentionality of the dynamic object is the same, but the two distinct media in the examples will have been informed by equally distinct immediate objects.

Now, in the 1903 phenomenology-based system both utterances would be classified as replicas of a dicent symbol. The ten classes of this period are ahistorical, in which intentionality is not only untraceable but also theoretically irrelevant—Peirce provides no way of "accessing" the dynamic object, and consequently this correlate cannot participate as a division in the typology. The hexad of 1908, however, has both a dynamic and an immediate object, the latter communicating to the sign form inherited from the dynamic—in this case, a line of poetry—a property that makes Peircean semiosis a model of intention-based representation. With this in mind, we return to the hypoicons, to metaphor in particular in view of the instability of the icon subclasses, and examine the possibility of preserving iconicity in semiosis.

6. Preserving Iconicity

6.1. Mediatization

Consider, as an example, a photographic montage composing a politically motivated poster (Figure 32.7), Barbara Kruger's *Untitled (Your Body Is a Battleground)*, 1989, beginning with the text beneath the vertically divided image on the poster:

FIGURE 32.7 Barbara Kruger, *Untitled (Your Body Is a Battleground)*, 1989. Poster for March on Washington in support of legal abortion, birth control, and women's rights. Courtesy the artist and Sprüth Magers.

On April 26 the Supreme Court will hear a case which the Bush administration hopes will overturn the Roe vs. Wade decision, which established basic abortion rights. Join thousands of women and men in Washington D.C. on April 9. We will show that the majority of Americans support the woman's right to choose. In Washington: assemble at the Ellipse between the Washington Monument and the White House at 10 am; rally at the Capitol at 1:30 pm.

The poster was produced to support the Woman's March on Washington, a protest march against the Bush administration's attempt to overturn *Roe v. Wade*. This is a militant sign, as the text—itself obviously part of the mediatization process—clearly states: it was determined by one woman's intention to rally American citizens in defense of women's basic reproductive rights threatened by an all-male administration, and this intentionality is the sign's dynamic object as conceived within Peirce's 1908 sign-system. What follows is an analysis of the pictorial mediatization of that intentionality.

The medium is the duplicated ink and paper in poster form that was attached to walls and telephone poles at the time, while the form—the complex hypoiconic form to be analyzed below—is the dramatic, tabloid-style expression of this intentionality. The poster is typical of Kruger's artistic preferences at that time, and the characteristic combination of red, white, and black inks is evidence of her professional background as a fashion editor. The semiotic history of the poster begins, then, with the intention of rallying support through the process of conceiving the actual design that we see in it and culminates with the production of the poster. It incongruously features a partially exposed photograph of a woman's face appropriated from the 1950s, overlaid by a militant slogan and short informative statements in white on a red background. Both image and text are metaphoric in structure.

We "read" the two halves of the image conventionally from left to right, effectively from "now" to "what might follow." To the left there is the developed, autonomous generic woman and her right to choose, while, to the right, the threatened target risks devaluation to the undeveloped shadow of her former status if *Roe v. Wade* were overturned. Abstracting to the hypoicon (Figure 32.8), the base domain of the pictorial metaphor is composed of the positively exposed half of the face on the left, **a**, corresponding to the present fully developed status of women, **b**, while the target is composed of the negative exposure of the face on the right, **a′**, and woman's social status reduced to a simple potentiality, **b′**, if the original Supreme Court decision were to be overturned. Both **b** and **b′** are characteristically absent from the pictorial metaphor, Kruger thereby dramatically picturing the abstract concepts of status and empowerment by means of

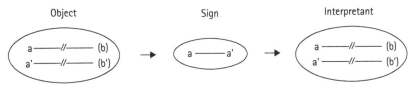

FIGURE 32.8 The metaphorical determination of Kruger's montage.

a manipulated photograph, rendered incongruous by the artist, who has intentionally manipulated the constraints of an existential two-dimensional medium.

Analysis of the verbal metaphor shows the base component of the metaphor to be the relation between a strategic position to be defended on a battlefield, while the target is women's control of their bodies and their reproductive rights to be defended in the political and ideological arena in the United States at the time. In Figure 32.7, the violence made explicit in the verbal metaphor is reinforced visually by the information tags streaked in red and white over the woman's face like war paint. Thus, the metaphorical structure of the slogan can be summarized verbally as follows, and schematically in Figure 32.9, where, as seen in the pictorial version, the bracketed elements—in this verbal example (a) and (b')—cannot, owing to the less complex structure of the linear medium, be reproduced in the sign:

Base: (strategic position to defend, **a**) on a battlefield, **b**

Target: women's control of their bodies, **a'**, to be defended in (the political and ideological arena, **b'**)

Clearly, in the determination process the immediate object is responsible for the organization of the poster in the course of the mediatization of the intentionality "behind" it. What the analyses above are meant to illustrate is the way the immediate object—the dynamic object as "hinted at" in the sign—plays a distinct role in semiosis and how the medium is only operational as a sign by displaying the form communicated when the immediate object functions as the relay of the influence of the object "outside" the sign. And, irrespective of whether Peirce identified the most complex subclass of the icon as metaphor or diagram, the form imparted to the medium by the immediate object can adopt any of the three formalisms represented by Figures 32.3, 32.4, and 32.5 above: if it can accommodate the most complex as in Figures 32.7, 32.8, and 32.9, it can necessarily accommodate the less. Thus, while hypoiconic analysis of the poster shows how metaphor *informs* in an older sense of the term both text and pictorial representation, the 1908 conception of semiosis allows us additionally to relate such structures to the intentionality determining the poster's social, political, and ideological significance, which no class from the three-division, ahistorical system of 1903 can account for.

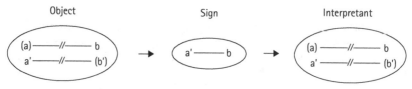

FIGURE 32.9 The metaphorical structure of the verbal statement "Your body is a battleground."

6.2. Discussion

There are two theoretical issues to be addressed regarding the analyses above; the first is specific to theoretical decisions adopted by Peirce, the second to decisions made in the chapter.

It was suggested earlier that Peirce probably renamed the most complex subclass of the icon as the diagram as a result of the development of pragmaticism and the graphs in the 1905–1906 period. These are incapable of identifying metaphorical utterances as a separate type of assertion, and consequently neither has a protocol for the analysis of metaphor in the conventional sense. Moreover, the change of name from metaphor to diagram has no drastic consequences for the original theory of the hypoicons for at least two reasons. First, the subsequent descriptions of the diagram in no way exclude a parallelism as a formal structure, since the original phenomenologically derived definitions were not invoked in 1905: the third thirdness of the original definition became irrelevant with the subclasses now being defined within the logic or with the newer terminology of phaneroscopy. Second, examination of Figures 32.4 to 32.9 shows that the representative of hypoiconic structure, namely, the sign, is always, owing to the constraints of necessarily existential media, diagrammatic in the 1903 definition of the term: context, namely, "made for the purpose," not definition, now determines degree of complexity.

The second problem concerns the schemata employed in this chapter to represent hypoiconicity. Figures 32.1 and 32.2 represented the determination flow as it would involve the correlates of the 1903 definition of the sign, identified in 1904 as the dynamic object and the final interpretant. By 1908 this triad had been expanded to a hexad, and the schemata for Figures 32.7, 32.8, and 32.9 were offered as the structures of the mediatization and interpretability of the intentionality originating in the dynamic object. In these cases, the object and interpretant indicated on the schemata must be immediate: the object and interpretant are "present in" the sign, with the immediate interpretant somehow mirroring the immediate object. What happens when an interpreter actually reacts to, say, a metaphorical sign, is irrelevant to the structure it has inherited from the dynamic object, and the particular nature of the reaction is a determination of the interpreter's personal experience.

With respect to this second point, Table 32.2 showed that while the sign with its diagrammatic structure mentioned earlier is necessarily existential in order to be perceived by potential interpreters, the two objects can both be necessitant. If the schemata system is theoretically valid, this is the most probable arrangement for complex mediatizations such as that displayed by Barbara Kruger's poster. The greater complexity of both dynamic and immediate objects exempts them from the existential constraints inhibiting the sign, necessarily a token, allowing the immediate object to communicate unconstrained the complex structure of a full parallelism in the case of metaphor—a parallelism also constituting a "Form (or feature)" extended to the medium in the 1906 definition of the sign—independent of the unavoidable underspecification to follow in the sign. Moreover, it is the structure of the parallelism that counts, not the label "metaphor," and there is no reason not to consider the parallelism as a diagram partaking of a "symbolic flavor."

7. Conclusion

This chapter has sought to show, first, that Peirce's remarkable definition of the hypoicons in 1903 is not in any way invalidated by redefinition of the icon's subclasses or their irrelevance to the process of semiosis, nor is iconicity in general; and, second, that by employing two distinct operational concepts, hypoiconicity and semiosis, the analysis of Figure 32.7 was enriched by insights from two theoretical backgrounds. The first is essentially an academic "laboratory" analysis from 1903, conducted by specialist researchers identifying atemporal sign classes but which enable fine-grained qualitative analysis of sign structure, while the second, drawing on the dynamic process of signification inscribed in time, identifies the placement of such structure in actual communicative processes.

Second, this chapter sought to show that since necessitant entities are not perceivable, with the nature of intentionality only inferable from the structure and contents imposed on the medium, potential universe disjunctions between objects and sign as displayed in Table 32.2 not only are consciously exploited by photographic artists such as Barbara Kruger, but also form the blueprint for lying and dissimulation, although the mediatizations of real-world intentionalities like the influencers and mavens on social media, for example, are obviously far more complex than the image in Figure 32.7. But the principle is the same—from their complex and sometimes devious mediatizations shall we know them.

References

Jappy, T. 2019, "Hypoiconicity, Semiosis and Peirce's Immediate Object," *Language and Semiotic Studies* 5, no. 2, 1–36.

Peirce, Charles S. 1931–1958. *The Collected Papers of Charles Sanders Peirce*, 8 vols. C. Hartshorne, P. Weiss, and A. W. Burks (Eds.), Cambridge, MA: Harvard University Press. (Referred to as CP.)

Peirce, Charles S. 1857–1914. Manuscripts held at the Houghton Library of Harvard University, as identified in Richard Robin, *Annotated Catalogue of the Papers of Charles S. Peirce*. Amherst: University of Massachusetts Press, 1967. (Referred to as R.)

Peirce, Charles S. 1998. *The Essential Peirce: Volume Two*, Peirce Edition Project (Ed.), Bloomington: Indiana University Press. (Referred to as EP2.)

Peirce, Charles S. 2009. *The Logic of Interdisciplinarity: The Monist-Series*, E. Bisanz (Ed.), Berlin: Akademie Verlag GmbH. (Referred to as LI.)

Peirce, Charles S., and Victoria Lady Welby 1977. *Semiotic and Significs: The Correspondence between C. S. Peirce and Victoria Lady Welby*, C. S. Hardwick (Ed.), Bloomington: Indiana University Press. (Referred to as SS.)

Savan, David 1988. An Introduction to C.S. Peirce's Full System of Semeiotic. Toronto: Toronto Semiotic Circle.

CHAPTER 33

PEIRCE ON BIOLOGY

A Critical Review

KALEVI KULL

> I am an ignoramus in biology.
> —Charles S. Peirce (CP1.229, 1902)

WHAT can a biologist learn from Charles Peirce? What is the current use of Peirce's ideas in biology? These are the questions to which we seek to find answers from the perspective of a biologist and biosemiotician.

The purpose of this chapter is to give a brief overview of the influence of Charles S. Peirce's work and ideas on biology. We will approach this by examining three aspects: (1) what Peirce himself wrote about biology—that is, a brief account of Peirce's own statements on biological issues, while also indicating some of the relevant criticisms; (2) the application of Peirce's views to biosemiotics—that is, an account of the usage of Peirce's ideas within semiotic biology, distinguishing in the process between the period before 1990 and the period after 1990; and (3) a critique of Peirce in biology and philosophy of biology—that is, a brief review of points that appeared within the biosemiotic literature that are critical of the application of some of Peirce's concepts in biosemiotics.

Thus, what we describe is not a Peirceology; it is rather a Peirceanism—to use a distinction that was drawn by Umberto Eco (1991) after he was criticized by Peirce specialists for treating Peirce's ideas imprecisely. What we are going to describe is thus not so much an attempt to reconstruct Peirce's thought (still we'll describe it in strictly biological terms within the first section), but mainly as it has been interpreted by various researchers who have applied it to biology.

Peirce certainly had a major influence on biosemiotics. He played a decisive role in the formation of the views of Jesper Hoffmeyer and Terrence Deacon and in the development of biosemiotics in the late 1990s and early 2000s. Given the acceptance of a semiotic basis to the development of theoretical biology, as well as biology as a whole, our topic turns out to be rather important. Until now, however, Peirce appears seldom in canonical surveys of the philosophy of biology (an exception being Hull [2008]), but that is probably because of the general absence of semiotic works in these surveys.

1. Peirce's Views on Biology

In this section, we restrict ourselves to what Peirce explicitly says of biology in his own writings and briefly discuss some of the commentary.

1.1. Biology in Peirce's Writings

In his classification of the sciences, Peirce makes biology a part of classificatory physics (CP1.194, 1903), that is, belonging to the physical sciences, or physiognosy, and not to the psychical sciences, or psychognosy (CP1.242, 1902). He writes: "Biology might be regarded (although, as a matter of fact, no such view is taken) as the chemistry of the album[in]oids and of the forms they assume. It is probable that all the differences of races, individuals, and tissues are chemical, at bottom. At any rate, the possible varieties of albuminoids are amply sufficient to account for all the diversity of organic forms" (CP1.195, 1903). "We may rationally conclude that all the variety of the biological world is due to the variety of the different kinds of chemical substances of this group [albuminoids], with their corresponding variety of properties and of natural figures" (CP1.261, 1902). Paradoxically this can be interpreted as an anticipation of the genocentric view in biology, which is based on molecular biology.

Interestingly, another part of biology, namely, the study of animal minds, belongs to psychognosy (CP7.386, 1903). Peirce makes a remarkable statement about the methodology of studying animal minds:

> I have no objection to admitting that zoölogy must perforce take some cognizance of the instincts of animals, just as on the other hand, it is quite evident that their minds can never be understood without taking some account of their anatomy and physiology. But for all that, if we are to admit that the study of animals' bodies is a study of efficiency, while the study of their minds is a study of finality, a distinction the truth and unescapableness [of which] will only be emphasized the more we study the different phases and facets of the subject, then we must acknowledge that those two studies of animals' minds and of animals' bodies are widely different, however much they may overlap. But in truth the overlapping is quite trifling. Very little psychology is needed by the biologist; and no very deep biology by the psychologist. (CP1.264, 1902)

It may seem that the latter part of this quotation contradicts with the statement that a description of anatomy and physiology is necessary for understanding animal minds, but obviously it does not.

For Peirce, biology served as one of the fields where the triad is at work: "In biology, the idea of arbitrary sporting is First, heredity is Second, the process whereby the accidental characters become fixed is Third" (CP6.32, 1891). Peirce devotes on this topic a whole chapter in his *A Guess at the Riddle*, "The Triad in Biological Development" (CP1.395–1.399, W6:199–202, 1888).

Peirce generally accepts Darwinism: "Whether the part played by natural selection and the survival of the fittest in the production of species be large or small, there remains little doubt that the Darwinian theory indicates a real cause, which tends to adapt animal and vegetable forms to their environment" (CP1.395, c. 1890). Both genocentrism (as mentioned above) and Darwinism became largely opposed by the contemporary biosemiotics as well as by the recent epigenetic biology. Thus, in this aspect it may look rather paradoxical why Peirce's views have gotten so much acceptance in recent biosemiotics. (One may, however, observe that the strongest proponents of Peirce in biosemiotics, like Sebeok, Hoffmeyer, and Deacon, tend to be slightly less critical of Darwin than some other biosemioticians who apply some of Peirce's concepts, including myself.)

Speaking about abduction, Peirce points out that there is an analogical mechanism at work within evolution as described by Darwin: "In the evolution of science, guessing plays the same part that variations in reproduction take in the evolution of biological forms, according to the Darwinian theory" (CP7.38, c. 1907). However, there is a difference. For Darwin, and particularly for Darwinism, the variability is seen as random. Indeed, Peirce acknowledged Darwin for his proposal to apply the statistical method to biology (CP5.364, 1877). But, for Peirce, paradoxically, biological variations are not random: "For just as, according to that [Darwinian] theory, the whole tremendous gulf, or ocean rather, between the moner and man has been spanned by a succession of infinitesimal fortuitous variations at birth, so the whole noble organism of science has been built up out of propositions which were originally simple guesses. For my part I refuse to believe that either the one or the other were fortuitous; and indeed I gravely doubt whether there be any tenable meaning in calling them so. As to the biological variations, I will spare the reader my reasons for not believing them fortuitous" (CP7.38, c. 1907). This is indeed a remarkable and rather fundamental disagreement with Darwinian theory. Thus, Peirce sees that natural selection is not enough: "Let us not, however, be cocksure that natural selection is the only factor of evolution; and until this momentous proposition has been much better proved than as yet it has been, let it not blind us to the force [of] very sound reasoning" (CP5.366n, 1877). Also, Peirce's evolutionism requires inexactness: "The adaptations of nature, beautiful and often marvelous as they verily are, are never found to be quite perfect" (CP6.50, 1892). Clearly of note is Peirce's classification of theories of evolution in his article "Evolutionary Love": "Three modes of evolution have thus been brought before us; evolution by fortuitous variation, evolution by mechanical necessity, and evolution by creative love. We may term them *tychastic* evolution, or *tychasm*, *anancastic* evolution, or *anancasm*, and *agapastic* evolution, or *agapasm*" (CP6.302, 1893). Here Darwinism is identified as tychasticism and Lamarckism as agapasticism (see also de Waal 2013, 144-148). This means that Darwinism is downgraded as describing the simplest type of evolution. On another occasion, Peirce positions the evolutionary view of Clarence King (American geologist, 1842–1901, who emphasized the 'survival of the plastic' as different from the 'survival of the fittest' as particularly apparent due to catastrophic events in the Earth's history) after Darwin's and Lamarck's (CP6.15–17, 1891).

Peirce also writes about the concept of natural classification: "All natural classification is then essentially [. . .] an attempt to find out the true genesis of the objects classified. But by genesis must be understood, not the efficient action which produces the whole by producing the parts, but the final action which produces the parts because they are needed to make the whole. Genesis is production from ideas. It may be difficult to understand how this is true in the biological world, though there is proof enough that it is so" (CP1.227, 1902). A critique of Darwinism is evident here, and more so when Peirce is supporting the views of Louis Agassiz, a notable anti-Darwinian, under whom Peirce studied the techniques of classification for some time during the early 1860s: "Those biologists whose views of classification are most opposite to those of Agassiz are saturated with metaphysics in its dangerous form—i.e. the unconscious form—to such an extent that what they say upon this subject is rather the expression of a traditionally absorbed fourteenth century metaphysics than of scientific observation" (CP1.229, 1902). An important aspect is that mind is a feature of seemingly all organisms:

> But to my apprehension [Eduard] Hartmann has proved conclusively that unconscious mind exists. What is meant by consciousness is really in itself nothing but feeling. [John] Gay and [David] Hartley were quite right about that; and though there may be, and probably is, something of the general nature of feeling almost everywhere, yet feeling in any ascertainable degree is a mere property of protoplasm, perhaps only of nerve matter. Now it so happens that biological organisms, and especially a nervous system are favorably conditioned for exhibiting the phenomena of mind also; and therefore it is not surprising that mind and feeling should be confounded. (CP7.364, 1902)

Peirce also admits that "the consciousness is a sort of public spirit among the nerve-cells" (CP1.354, c. 1890).

In "Man's Glassy Essence," Peirce turns to speak about protoplasm. The whole article is mainly about physical biochemistry and reflects problems widely discussed at the time.

> I have to elucidate [. . .] the relation between the psychical and physical aspects of a substance. The first step towards this ought, I think, to be the framing of a molecular theory of protoplasm. (CP6.238, 1892)

> It is [. . .] consonant with the facts of observation to suppose that assimilated protoplasm is formed at the instant of assimilation, under the influence of the protoplasm already present. (CP6.250, 1892)

> Closely connected with growth is reproduction; and though in higher forms this is a specialised function, it is universally true that wherever there is protoplasm, there is, will be, or has been a power of reproducing that same kind of protoplasm in a separated organism. [. . .] Another physical property of protoplasm is that of taking habits. [. . .] Very extraordinary, certainly, are all these properties of protoplasm [. . .].

But the one which has next to be mentioned, while equally undeniable, is infinitely more wonderful. It is that protoplasm feels. [...] It not only feels but exercises all the functions of mind. Such are the properties of protoplasm. The problem is to find a hypothesis of the molecular constitution of this compound which will account for these properties, one and all. (CP6.253–256, 1892)

Further down in the article, Peirce proposes a hypothetical mechanism of habit-taking in protoplasm, and concludes: "Since the phenomena of habit may thus result from a purely mechanical arrangement, it is unnecessary to suppose that habit taking is a primordial principle of the universe" (CP6.262, 1892). Moreover, he adds: "Protoplasm certainly does feel; and unless we are to accept a weak dualism, the property must be shown to arise from some peculiarity of the mechanical system" (CP6.264, 1892). It should not be left unsaid how Peirce continues; speaking about the origin of feeling, he writes: "Yet the attempt to deduce it from the three laws of mechanics, applied to never so ingenious a mechanical contrivance, would obviously be futile. It can never be explained, unless we admit that physical events are but degraded or undeveloped forms of psychical events" (CP6.264, 1892). Until this hypothesis in the last quote, Peirce's reasoning in this article looked like emergentism. He does show that habit-taking can arise under (or be a result of) the special molecular and physicochemical conditions of protoplasm. Yet with feelings he gives up. One may wonder whether Peirce's "never" in this last quote had been as strong as it was if he would have possessed the knowledge of complex systems mathematics that became available a hundred years later. (Related to this, there is another "never" that obviously influenced his philosophy: "Mechanical law can never produce diversification" [CP1.174, c. 1897]. Later, Ilya Prigogine's well-described mechanisms of bifurcation in nonlinear chemical dynamics disprove this claim.) There is also an alternative option, which is reading Peirce's statement as applicable to "[some] physical events" (as mostly used in biosemiotics accepting the emergentist nature of semiosis) instead of "[all] physical events" (i.e., in a panpsychist manner, as is often preferred by contemporary Peirce scholars).

Elsewhere Peirce says that "nothing but feeling is exclusively mental" (CP5.492, c. 1907). Remarkably, when defining the concept of sign, Peirce also provides a biological example of nonsign: "A *Sign* is a Representamen with a mental Interpretant. Possibly there may be Representamens that are not Signs. Thus, if a sunflower, in turning towards the sun, becomes by that very act fully capable, without further condition, of reproducing a sunflower which turns in precisely corresponding ways toward the sun, and of doing so with the same reproductive power, the sunflower would become a Representamen of the sun" (CP2.274, c. 1902). This sunflower example is quite often discussed in semiotic literature and is sometimes seen as a case of an index, which is something that Peirce certainly does not claim.

1.2. Discussions of Peirce's Views on Biology

While there exist a large number of biological works that use Peirce's general concepts or his philosophy, there are not many studies that review and analyze Peirce's explicit views on biological issues. Among the latter, Peter Skagestad (1979) provides an account of Peirce's views on biological evolution and Darwinism, pointing out his critique of Darwin. A rather detailed work is an article by Lucia Santaella Braga (1999a), in which she describes, in addition to Peirce's statements on both the place of biology among sciences and his views on life processes, the situation in biology at the time of Peirce's life. There are more works about Peirce's evolutionism (e.g., Goudge 1964; Wells 1964; Hausman 1993; Liszka 2014), while a detailed account of Peirce's views on evolution in the context of evolutionism of other pragmatists is presented in a book by Trevor Pearce (2020), and before him by Philip Wiener (1949). Peirce's thoughts on the features of protoplasm, together with description of their context in nineteenth-century biology, are reviewed in an article also by Trevor Pearce (2018).

2. The Reception of Peirce in Semiotic Biology

2.1. Before 1990

Works of Peirce have been referred to by biosemioticians from the beginning of explicitly semiotic biology, for instance, by Friedrich Rothschild (1963, 476), who had just introduced the term 'biosemiotic.' Thomas A. Sebeok (1972) and the zoologist Günter Tembrock (1977) refer to Peirce in relation with typology of signs in animal communication. Also, Giorgio Prodi ([1977] 2021) explicitly uses some of Peirce's terms. The entomologist and ethologist Rudolf Jander (1981, 230) compares his own concept of polysign with Peirce's icon.

Thomas Sebeok, when first introducing Jakob von Uexküll as a neglected semiotician, uses among his arguments the compatibility of Uexküll's views with Peirce's, particularly his concept of sign and its typology (Sebeok 1979). Also, Thure von Uexküll (1987, 173) finds it important to compare Jakob von Uexküll and Peirce: "It appears to me that the relation between Peirce's triadic and Uexküll's cyclic model becomes obvious if the former is conceived of as a synchronic system, the latter as a model for the discursive stream of sign processes." As pointed out later (Kull 2020b), Uexküll's model of *Funktionskreis* can be interpreted both as cycle and, alternatively, as circle. In the latter case, Uexküll's model is also synchronic and can be directly put into correspondence with semiosis (assuming that representamen, object, and interpretant appear simultaneously—in terms of subjective time—in the act of semiosis).

Peirce had some influence also on certain biologists who were not otherwise considered (or identified themselves) as biosemioticians, for example, probably on Konrad Lorenz in his distinction between signals and cues as two kinds of animal communication (see Huron 2015; cf. Kruse 1985). Another example of this kind is the ecologist Yrjö Haila (1986), who refers to Peirce in his reinterpretation of a model that describes the ecology of colonization of insular environments.

2.2. After 1990

A rather widespread turn in semiotics from the Saussurean to Peircean approaches took place in the 1980s. This turn's impact to biology was probably indirect. However, soon after, biosemiotics started to grow. An obvious reason for preferring Peirce to Saussure in biology was Peirce's richer vocabulary for describing the realm of prelinguistic sign processes and his more general concept of sign. Moreover, Peirce's philosophy looked promising in order to newly solve the teleological aspects of biological phenomena.

Probably the most important point that inspired some biologists to use Peircean semiotics as a basis for biological theory was the suggested identity of life and semiosis. This was the way biosemioticians came to read Peirce. Indeed, Peirce provides a direct reason for such interpretation: "The problem of how genuine triadic relationships first arose in the world is a better, because more definite, formulation of the problem of how life first came about; and no explanation has ever been offered except that of pure chance, which we must suspect to be no explanation" (CP6.322, 1909). Thus, beginning in the early 1990s Peirce becomes the major source for providing the general semiotic framework in biosemiotic works. From the side of semioticians, Thomas Sebeok and John Deely were among those who influenced biosemioticians to apply Peirce's semiotics. Sebeok's view was that semiosis and life are coextensive, but Deely argued that there exists also physiosemiosis, that is, semiosis before and outside of living beings (Deely 2001; see also his last article on this topic [Deely 2016]). Still, Deely did not accept pansemiotics. The philosopher Eliseo Fernández did much work to explain the further potentials of Peirce's work for biosemiotics (e.g., Fernández 2008b, 2014).

The Danish biologist Jesper Hoffmeyer (1996, 2008) was a main proponent of Peirce for biology. A reference to Peirce was included in almost every talk he gave on biosemiotics. The main concepts he took from Peirce were the triadic model of sign (Hoffmeyer 2008, 20ff.), the broad concept of final cause (40–41, 51ff.), understanding of habit and habit taking (62f.), indeterminacy (62), mind and law of mind (63–64), and realism (66).

Another leading biosemiotician, Terrence Deacon, turned to Peirce rather early in his studies, relating Peirce with cybernetics (Deacon 1976). In his influential *The Symbolic Species*, Deacon used Peircean sign typology for the description and explanation of the symbolic threshold at the origin of human language (Deacon 1997). In his further research, he applied a semiotic approach to the problems of origin of life. He also writes: "In contrast to the common tendency to interpret Peirce's sign types synchronically and independently, I propose to understand these hierarchical taxonomies as describing the constraints imposed on any constructive semiotic process by which more complex sign relations grow and emerge from more basic sign relations" (Deacon 2014, 95). A programmatic paper by a group of biosemioticians "who ground their work on a strongly Peircean framework" was published by Kull et al. (2009, 168). Donald Favareau included a chapter on Peirce in the *Essential Readings in Biosemiotics*, thus emphasizing Peirce's role (Favareau 2010).

In 2014, Vinicius Romanini and Eliseo Fernández edited an entire volume of papers entitled *Peirce and Biosemiotics: A Guess at the Riddle of Life* (Romanini and Fernández 2014), which includes eleven articles and an introductory paper by the editors. Among the contributors (Fernández 2014; Hulswit and Romanini 2014; Ibri 2014; Lane 2014; Nöth 2014; Queiroz, Stjernfelt, and El-Hani 2014; Romanini 2014; Silveira and Gonzalez 2014), however, there are no biologists. The book was reviewed by Donald Frohlich (2014) and Søren Brier (2016).

One of few monographs focusing on prelinguistic aspects of Peirce's theory is Frederik Stjernfelt's *Natural Propositions* (Stjernfelt 2014). If semiosis in any living being is primarily a decision, then it may have from the outset a propositional structure. Hence the connection with Peirce's theory—insofar as Peirce studies the proposition. How to use it for semiotic analysis of communication was less clear.

Claus Emmeche, João Queiroz, and Charbel El-Hani published a book (El-Hani et al. 2009) as well as a series of articles (El-Hani et al. 2010; Queiroz and El-Hani 2007; Queiroz and Ribeiro 2002; Queiroz, Emmeche, and El-Hani 2008; Queiroz et al. 2011; Queiroz, Stjernfelt, and El-Hani 2014) in which they apply Peirce's concepts using various biological examples—genetic information, mimicry, animal communication. Other remarkable works on Peircean semiotics and pragmatism in biology include Emmeche (1991), Salthe (1995), Santaella Braga (1999b), Pires (2000), Sharov (2001), Favareau (2007), Brier (2008), Hoffmeyer (2012, 2014), Hoffmeyer and Stjernfelt (2016), Cobley (2016), West and Anderson (2016), Cuccio and Gallese (2018), Pharoah (2020), Jappy (2023), etc.

The Danish biologist Mogens Kilstrup interprets the triadic sign as a systems property and emphasizes a two-staged structure of semiosis: "To understand and explain sign function, the process of sign utilization (semiosis) has to be divided into two temporally separated phases, a sign-establishment phase where a three-dimensional link ($\Psi(O, R, I)$) is formed between three sign elements, and a later sign-interpretation phase where the established linkage is used for inferring significance to a novel phenomenon, if this satisfies the criteria for being a Representamen for the sign" (Kilstrup 2015, 563). Biosemiotic inquiry became focused on the biological processes that enable semiosis. This has led to a discussion about the distinction between simple codes and semiosis (see Kull 2020a), which is related to finding a biological parallel to the divide between structuralist and poststructuralist approaches, as well as ways on how to integrate these models.

Contemporary discussions in evolutionary theory have proved the importance of the active role of the agent as a factor of evolution, which was not taken into account in neo-Darwinian theory. This theoretical development is close to Peirce's view. For instance, Menno Hulswit (1996) uses Peircean theory to criticize Ernst Mayr's neo-Darwinism. Akhtar et al. (2013, 203) "highlight the difference between Darwinian and Peircean understandings of natural evolution" and "show how cutting-edge work in molecular biology, symbiogenesis, epigenetics, and systems biology are moving in the direction of Peirce's ideas" (see more on Peirce's relationship to theories of evolution in Brioschi [2019]).

A topic of lively debate has been the proper correspondence of Peircean sign types to biological examples. Until now, only few works have used for this purpose more complex than threefold typology (e.g., Deacon 2011; Queiroz 2012; Stjernfelt 2014). For instance, cellular proteins were seen as iconic sinsigns (Faltýnek and Lacková 2021) when applying Peircean concepts on the level of protein folding (also Lacková and Zámečník 2020).

It is understandable and obvious that Peirce's ideas have been often used with insufficient precision. This aspect was pointed out, for instance, by Robert Lane (2014) concerning the interpretations of Peirce's concept of indeterminacy.

It should be noticed that a large part of the works that interpret Peirce's views as relevant to biology were written by nonbiologists whose understanding of life processes is a product of philosophical arguments rather than contemporary knowledge of biological mechanisms, so that it is not always useful or relevant to biology itself. Far more interesting is to observe the usage and application of various of Peirce's ideas by biologists (on the condition of their sufficient understanding of Peirce), who have proposed various combinations of his ideas with biological knowledge.

3. Critique of Peirce in Biology—or Just Updates

The biosemiotics that was developed after 1990 was dominated by Peircean approaches. However, since the 2010s, some critical notes about the Peircean model started to appear in biosemiotic writings. As remarked by Eliseo Fernández (2008a, 10–11), "In contrast to the situation we found in physics, the reception of Peirce's ideas in biology is marked by the direct influence of his writings. Far from passively adopting Peirce's ideas, biosemioticians have rigorously criticized them, while at the same time combining them with more recent notions which are in no way anticipated in those ideas." Thus, a section "(Re)interpretation of Peircean Semiotics" appeared in a state-of-the-art review of biosemiotics (Kull 2012, 13–16).

One of the principal statements of biosemiotics is the connectedness of semiosis with life, which in its radical form suggests that semiosis is coextensive with life and implies a lower threshold of semiosis. This directly contradicts universal synechism. Indeed, many biosemioticians suggest that semiosis is an emergent process (e.g., El-Hani et al. 2009; Rodríguez Higuera 2016). However, an emergentist reading of Peirce can be argued for as well (see Brioschi 2019), particularly one that is based on his concept of irreducibility of triadic sign.

At the end of the nineteenth century knowledge about the structure of protoplasm was very poor, in contrast to the understanding of the cell in the twenty-first century. Thus, the contemporary analysis of protoplasm looks immensely more complex. While not all systemic phenomena of cellular behavior are yet explained, the emergence of semiosis in certain complex cellular dynamics is rather probable, particularly if taking into account intercellular processes, including in neural tissues.

Biosemiotics is for the most part rather critical to Darwinism (and particularly to neo-Darwinism). Accordingly, it is understandable that the book review on *Peirce and Biosemiotics* (Romanini and Fernández 2014), which was written by Donald Frohlich (2014) from a neo-Darwinian and sociobiological perspective, is quite critical of the Peirce-based evolutionism found in most biosemiotic writings. As demonstrated by Akhtar et al. (2013, 203), "cutting-edge work in molecular biology, symbiogenesis, epigenetics, and systems biology are moving in the direction of Peirce's ideas."

The teleological and meaning-making behavior of living beings is based on the capacity to create an umwelt and make choices. Umwelt and semiosis are probably always related; one cannot exist without the other. This means that the approaches of Peirce and Jacob von Uexküll can (and should) be integrated (see, e.g., Clements 2018). It also implies that both theories become accepted in a restricted way, that is, based on a particular reading of Peirce and Uexküll.

Peirce does not draw a clear distinction between habit and physical law. The principle of fallibilism implies that all physical laws may have exceptions, which clearly contradicts with the concept of physical law in general physics. This was pointed out in our work (Kull 2014).

Attempts to identify Peircean sign typology with biological examples have led to modifications of Peircean theory. For instance, speaking about the sign typology, Hoffmeyer (2008, 285) writes: "Although a sign, according to Peirce, always consists in a triadic relation, the *interpretant* may often play a very limited role in the relation (as is the case with indices)—and that when also the object relation of the sign is close to disappearing, we get an icon." The latter was expressed in a more radical way in an article by Alexei Sharov and Tommi Vehkavaara (2015) when stating that signs in bacteria can exist without objects. Analyzing the close-to-semiosic processes in prokaryotic cells, they initiated a discussion about the possibility of "objectless semiosis" in which case Peirce's sign model does not entirely apply: "Thus, the traditional definition of sign as a representation of an object may not be universal" (Sharov and Vehkavaara 2015, 121). However, later this interpretation was slightly changed: "A specific feature of protosemiosis is that objects are only detected but not perceived by the agent" (Sharov and Tønnessen 2022)—that is, triadic sign with object is saved, while the particular kind of this link as it exists in bacteria was specified. It should be admitted that the article by Sharov and Vehkavaara was preceded by a work by Vehkavaara (2005), in which he analyzed the restrictions of Peirce's semiotics in biological applications.

Some biosemiotic critique on Peirce was described by Claudio Rodríguez Higuera (2019). Observing some recent deviations from a strictly Peircean approach in biosemiotics, he even speaks of the conceivability of a post-Peircean biosemiotics: "What I mean by a post-Peircean biosemiotics would then be a biosemiotics that is inclusive of the concepts brought forward by Peirce without a strong dependence on the limits of Peircean metaphysics, triadicity and the rigidity of his semiotics as logical forms" (Rodríguez Higuera 2019, 421).

4. Conclusion

Charles Peirce was not an expert in biology, in contrast to the other main precursor to biosemiotics, Jakob von Uexküll. It is through those who understood the work of both—such as Thomas Sebeok, Thure von Uexküll, Jesper Hoffmeyer, Claus Emmeche, a.o.—that biosemiotics was established. This is the biology wherein meaning-making through interpretation is seen as one of various rather universal processes of life and responsible for many aspects of life-specific phenomena. Such a biology was developed by a group of biologist-biosemioticians—Jesper Hoffmeyer, Claus Emmeche, Terrence Deacon, Donald Favareau, Søren Brier, Alexei Sharov, Franco Giorgi, and others, as well as groups in Tartu and Prague—together with specialists of other backgrounds, such as philosophers, linguists, physicists, and semioticians like Frederik Stjernfelt, the group in Olomouc, etc.

Understanding the meaning-making capacity of organisms required a model to advance in research. The triadic model was rather obvious for this, and Peirce further provided a whole philosophy that helped to link it with other difficult problems in philosophy of biology—intentionality, teleology, and typology of meanings. Until discoveries that would add appropriate distinctions from the side of physiology, this model can still be productive.

It should be stressed once again, however, that Peirce did not write much about biology, and it is further worth mentioning that his explicit writings on biological issues have barely been used in biosemiotics. Instead, Peirce's general framework and his central concept of sign became of major importance to biosemiotics beginning in the 1990s, albeit that Peirce's work had been already noticed and referred to in biosemiotics since the 1960s. However, it is worth remarking that those who were building biosemiotics were, as Eco put it, just Peirceans—they found part of their inspiration in Peirce; they were not specialists in Peirce studies—they weren't doing Peirceology. For the biosemioticians' reading of Peirce, the idea of the identity between the life process and semiosis was the central one.

As opposed to earlier studies in Peircean biology, we focused here on Peirce's explicit statements on the area of biology. When selecting just those pieces of Peirce's texts where he explicitly turns to biology, we saw that at least in some of his writings Peirce expresses emergentist views—which slightly deviates from the more canonical reading of Peirce. This means that Peirce's biosemiotics is generally more emergentist than was thought by many contemporary Peirce scholars.

Reading Peirce from the perspective of biology, particularly under the influence of empirical approaches, has its implications. The requirement to precisely identify how Peirce's concepts correspond to certain biological processes has drawn the attention to defining more exactly the necessary and sufficient conditions for minimal semiotic phenomena. More recently, this has led particularly to a certain critique of Peirce's model of semiosis in the context of attempts to integrate his model with other models of meaning-making as they are currently being worked out within semiotics and to relate his theory with the empirical findings in biology.

Acknowledgments

I thank Cornelis de Waal for his help in improving this chapter. The work was supported by Grant PRG314 from the Estonian Research Council.

References

Akhtar, Junaid; Awais, Mian M.; Koshul, Basit B. 2013. "Putting Peirce's Theory to the Test: Peircean Evolutionary Algorithms." *Transactions of the Charles S. Peirce Society* 49, no. 2 (Spring): 203–237.

Brier, Søren 2008. "The Paradigm of Peircean Biosemiotics." *Signs* 2: 30–81.

Brier, Søren 2016. "Biosemiotic Cosmogony of the Riddle of Life!" *Cybernetics & Human Knowing*, 23 no. 4: 85–91.

Brioschi, Maria Regina 2019. "Does Continuity Allow for Emergence? An Emergentist Reading of Peirce's Evolutionary Thought." *European Journal of Pragmatism and American Philosophy* 11, no. 2: 1–24.

Clements, Matthew 2018. "A World beside Itself: Jakob von Uexküll, Charles S. Peirce, and the Genesis of a Biosemiotic Hypothesis." PhD diss. Birkbeck, University of London.

Cobley, Paul 2016. *Cultural Implications of Biosemiotics*. (Biosemiotics 15.) Dordrecht, The Netherlands: Springer.

Cuccio, Valentina; Gallese, Vittorio 2018. "A Peircean Account of Concepts: Grounding Abstraction in Phylogeny through a Comparative Neuroscientific Perspective." *Philosophical Transactions of Royal Society* B 373:20170128.

Deacon, Terrence 1976. "Semiotics and Cybernetics: The Relevance of C. S. Peirce." In: System and Structure Study Group (eds.), *Sanity and Signification: Essays in Communication and Exchange*. Bellingham, WA: Fairhaven College Press.

Deacon, Terrence 1997. *The Symbolic Species: The Co-evolution of Language and the Brain*. New York: Norton.

Deacon, Terrence 2011. "The Symbol Concept." In: Gibson, Kathleen R.; Tallerman, Maggie (eds.), *The Oxford Handbook of Language Evolution*. Oxford: Oxford University Press, 393–405.

Deacon, Terrence 2014. "Semiosis: From Taxonomy to Process." In: Thellefsen, Torkild; Sørensen, Bent (eds.), *Charles Sanders Peirce in His Own Words: 100 Years of Semiotics, Communication and Cognition*. (Semiotics, Communication and Cognition 14.) Boston: De Gruyter Mouton, 95–104.

Deely, John 2001. "Physiosemiosis in the Semiotic Spiral: A Play of Musement." *Sign Systems Studies* 29, no. 1: 27–48.

Deely, John 2016. "Thirdness in Nature." *SCIO: Revista de Filosofia* 12: 75–80.

de Waal, Cornelis 2013. *Charles S. Peirce: A Guide for the Perplexed*. London: Bloomsbury.

Eco, Umberto 1991. Charles Sanders Pe(i)rsonal: Modelle künstlicher Interpretation. In: Burkhardt, Armin; Rohse, Eberhard (eds.), *Umberto Eco—Zwischen Literatur und Semiotik*. Braunschweig: Ars & Scientia, 3–28.

El-Hani, Charbel Niño; Queiroz, João; Emmeche, Claus 2009. *Genes, Information, and Semiosis*. (Tartu Semiotics Library 8.) Tartu, Estonia: Tartu University Press.

El-Hani, Charbel Niño; Queiroz, João; Stjernfelt, Frederik 2010. "Firefly Femmes Fatales: A Case Study in the Semiotics of Deception." *Biosemiotics* 3, no. 1: 33–55.

Emmeche, Claus 1991. "A Semiotical Reflection on Biology, Living Signs and Artificial Life." *Biology and Philosophy* 6: 325–340.

Faltýnek, Dan; Lacková, Ľudmila 2021. "In the Case of Protosemiosis: Indexicality vs. Iconicity of Proteins." *Biosemiotics* 14: 209–226.

Favareau, Donald 2007. "How to Make Peirce's Ideas Clear (First in an Inexhaustible Series)." In: Witzany, Günther (ed.), *Biosemiotics in Transdisciplinary Contexts: Proceedings of the Gathering in Biosemiotics 6, Salzburg 2006*. Salzburg, Austria: Umweb, 163–173.

Favareau, Donald 2010. "Introduction and Commentary: Charles Sanders Peirce." In: Favareau, Donald (ed.), *Essential Readings in Biosemiotics: Anthology and Commentary*. (Biosemiotics 3.) Berlin: Springer, 115–120.

Fernández, Eliseo 2008a. "Peirce en la ciencia y la filosofía del siglo XXI: nuevas oportunidades [Peirce in 21st Century Science and Philosophy: New Prospects]." In: Hynes, Catalina (ed.), *III Jornadas "Peirce en Argentina": GEP Argentina: 11–12.09.08*. Buenos Aires: Grupo de Estudios Peirceanos, 1–15. [https://www.unav.es/gep/IIIPeirceArgentinaEliseoFernandez.html. In English: https://www.lindahall.org/media/papers/fernandez/P_en_A_English.pdf.]

Fernández, Eliseo 2008b. "Biosemiotics and Self-Reference from Peirce to Rosen." In: *Eighth Annual International Gatherings in Biosemiotics*. University of the Aegean, Syros, Greece, June 23–28, 2008. https://www.lindahall.org/media/papers/fernandez/PRfinal.pdf

Fernández, Eliseo 2014. "Peircean Habits, Broken Symmetries, and Biosemiotics." In: Romanini, Vinícius; Fernández, Eliseo (eds.), *Peirce and Biosemiotics: A Guess at the Riddle of Life*. (Biosemiotics 11.) Heidelberg, Germany: Springer, 79–94.

Frohlich, Donald R. 2014. "Biology, Peirce, and Biosemiotics: Commentaires 'cénoscopic' d'un biologiste." *American Journal of Semiotics* 30, no. 1/2: 173–188. [Review of Romanini, Fernández 2014.]

Goudge, Thomas 1964. "Peirce's Evolutionism—after Half a Century." In: Edward C. Moore, and Richard S. Robin (eds.), *Studies in the Philosophy of Charles Sanders Peirce*. Amherst: University of Massachusetts Press, 323–341.

Haila, Yrjö 1986. "On the Semiotic Dimension of Ecological Theory: The Case of Island Biogeography." *Biology and Philosophy* 1, no. 4: 377–387.

Hausman, Carl R. 1993. *Charles S. Peirce's Evolutionary Philosophy*. Cambridge: Cambridge University Press.

Hoffmeyer, Jesper 1996. *Signs of Meaning in the Universe*. Bloomington: Indiana University Press.

Hoffmeyer, Jesper 2008. *Biosemiotics: An Examination into the Signs of Life and the Life of Signs*. Scranton, PA: Scranton University Press.

Hoffmeyer, Jesper 2012. "The Natural History of Intentionality: A Biosemiotic Approach." In: Schilhab, Theresa; Stjernfelt, Frederik; Deacon, Terrence (eds.), *The Symbolic Species Evolved*. Dordrecht, The Netherlands: Springer, 97–116.

Hoffmeyer, Jesper 2014. "Animals Use Signs, They Just Don't Know It." In: Thellefsen, Torkild; Sørensen, Bent (eds.), *Charles Sanders Peirce in His Own Words: 100 Years of Semiotics, Communication and Cognition*. (Semiotics, Communication and Cognition 14.) Boston: De Gruyter Mouton, 411–414.

Hoffmeyer, Jesper; Stjernfelt, Frederik 2016. "The Great Chain of Semiosis: Investigating the Steps in the Evolution of Semiotic Competence." *Biosemiotics* 9, no. 1: 7–29.

Hull, David L. 2008. "The History of the Philosophy of Biology." In: Ruse, Michael (ed.), *The Oxford Handbook of Philosophy of Biology*. Oxford: Oxford University Press, 11–33.

Hulswit, Menno 1996. "Teleology: A Peircean Critique of Ernst Mayr's Theory." *Transactions of the Charles S. Peirce Society* 32, no. 2 (Spring): 182–214.

Hulswit, Menno; Romanini, Vinicius 2014. "Semeiotic Causation and the Breath of Life." In: Romanini, Vinícius; Fernández, Eliseo (eds.), *Peirce and Biosemiotics: A Guess at the Riddle of Life*. (Biosemiotics 11.) Heidelberg, Germany: Springer, 95–126.

Huron, David 2015. "The Other Semiotic Legacy of Charles Sanders Peirce: Ethology and Music-Related Emotion." In: Maeder, Costantino; Reybrouck, Mark (eds.), *Music, Analysis, Experience: New Perspectives in Musical Semiotics*. Leuven, Belgium: Leuven University Press, 185–208.

Ibri, Ivo A. 2014. "The Continuity of Life: On Peirce's Objective Idealism." In: Romanini, Vinícius; Fernández, Eliseo (eds.), *Peirce and Biosemiotics: A Guess at the Riddle of Life*. (Biosemiotics 11.) Heidelberg, Germany: Springer, 33–49.

Jander, Rudolf 1981. "General Semiotics and Biosemiotics." In: De George, Richard D. (ed.), *Semiotic Themes*. Lawrence: Lawrence University of Kansas Publications, 225–250.

Jappy, Tony 2023. "Biosemiotics and Peirce." *Language and Semiotic Studies* 9, no. 2: 143–162.

Kilstrup, Mogens 2015. "Naturalizing Semiotics: The Triadic Sign of Charles Sanders Peirce as a Systems Property." *Progress in Biophysics and Molecular Biology* 119, no. 3: 563–575.

Kruse, Felicia E. 1985. "Konrad Lorenz: Cognitive Coevolution as Semiosis." In: Deely, John (ed.), *Semiotics 1984*. Lanham, MD: University Press of America, 589–599.

Kull, Kalevi 2012. "Advancements in Biosemiotics: Where We Are Now in Discovering the Basic Mechanisms of Meaning-Making." In: Rattasepp, Silver; Bennett, Tyler (eds.), *Gatherings in Biosemiotics*. (Tartu Semiotics Library 11.) Tartu, Estonia: University of Tartu Press, 11–24.

Kull, Kalevi 2014. "Physical Laws Are Not Habits, while Rules of Life Are." In: Thellefsen, Torkild; Sørensen, Bent (eds.), *Charles Sanders Peirce in His Own Words: 100 Years of Semiotics, Communication and Cognition*. (Semiotics, Communication and Cognition 14.) Boston: De Gruyter Mouton, 87–94.

Kull, Kalevi 2020a. "Codes: Necessary, but Not Sufficient for Meaning-Making." *Constructivist Foundations* 15, no. 2: 137–139.

Kull, Kalevi 2020b. "Jakob von Uexküll and the Study of Primary Meaning-Making." In: Michelini, Francesca; Köchy, Kristian (eds.), *Jakob von Uexküll and Philosophy: Life, Environments, Anthropology*. (History and Philosophy of Biology.) London: Routledge, 220–237.

Kull, Kalevi; Deacon, Terrence; Emmeche, Claus; Hoffmeyer, Jesper; Stjernfelt, Frederik 2009. "Theses on Biosemiotics: Prolegomena to a Theoretical Biology." *Biological Theory: Integrating Development, Evolution, and Cognition* 4, no. 2: 167–173.

Lacková, Ľudmila; Zámečník, Lukáš 2020. "Logical Principles of a Topological Explanation: Peirce's Iconic Logic." *Chinese Semiotic Studies* 16, no. 3: 493–514.

Lane, Robert 2014. "Peircean Semiotic Indeterminacy and Its Relevance for Biosemiotics." In: Romanini, Vinícius; Fernández, Eliseo (eds.), *Peirce and Biosemiotics: A Guess at the Riddle of Life*. (Biosemiotics 11.) Heidelberg, Germany: Springer, 51–78.

Liszka, James Jakób 2014. "Peirce's Evolutionary Thought." In: Thellefsen, Torkild; Sørensen, Bent (eds.), Charles *Sanders Peirce in His Own Words: 100 Years of Semiotics, Communication and Cognition*. (Semiotics, Communication and Cognition 14.) Boston: De Gruyter Mouton, 145–152.

Nöth, Winfried 2014. "The Life of Symbols and Other Legisigns: More Than a Mere Metaphor?" In: Romanini, Vinícius; Fernández, Eliseo (eds.), Peirce *and Biosemiotics: A Guess at the Riddle of Life*. (Biosemiotics 11.) Heidelberg, Germany: Springer, 171–181.

Pearce, Trevor 2018. "'Protoplasm Feels': The Role of Physiology in Charles Sanders Peirce's Evolutionary Metaphysics." *HOPOS: The Journal of the International Society for the History of Philosophy of Science* 8: 28–61.

Pearce, Trevor 2020. *Pragmatism's Evolution: Organism and Environment in American Philosophy*. Chicago: University of Chicago Press.

Peirce, Charles S. 1931–1958. *The Collected Papers of Charles Sanders Peirce*. 8 vols. (Vols. 1–6, Hartshorne, Charles; Weiss, Paul, eds.; vols. 7–8, Burks, Arthur W., ed.) Cambridge, MA: Harvard University Press. (Referred to as CP.)

Pharoah, Mark 2020. "Causation and Information: Where Is Biological Meaning to Be Found?" *Biosemiotics* 13: 309–326.

Pires, Jorge Luiz Vargas P. de Barros 2000. "Semiosis in the Biological World: An Approach Based on Charles S. Peirce's Philosophy." In: Tarasti Eero (ed.). *Commentationes in honorem Thomas A. Sebeok octogenarii A. D. MM editae*. Imatra, Finland: International Semiotics Institute, 50–62.

Prodi, Giorgio 2021 [1977]. *The Material Bases of Meaning*. (Tartu Semiotics Library 22.) Tartu, Estonia: University of Tartu Press.

Queiroz, João 2012. "Peirce's Ten Classes of Signs: Modeling Biosemiotic Processes and Systems." In: Maran, Timo; Lindström, Kati; Magnus, Riin; Tønnessen, Morten (eds.), *Semiotics in the Wild: Essays in Honour of Kalevi Kull on the Occasion of his 60th Birthday*. Tartu, Estonia: University of Tartu Press, 55–62.

Queiroz, João; El-Hani, Charbel Niño 2007. "On Peirce's Notion of Information: Remarks on De Tienne's Paper 'Information in Formation.'" *Cognitio* 8, no. 2: 289–298.

Queiroz, João; Emmeche, Claus; El-Hani, Charbel 2008. "A Peircean Approach to 'Information' and Its Relationship with Bateson's and Jablonka's Ideas." *The American Journal of Semiotics* 24, no. 1/3: 75–94.

Queiroz, João; Emmeche, Claus; Kull, Kalevi; El-Hani, Charbel 2011. "The Biosemiotic Approach in Biology: Theoretical Bases and Applied Models." In: Terzis, George; Arp, Robert (eds.), *Information and Living Systems: Philosophical and Scientific Perspectives*. Cambridge, MA: MIT Press, 91–129.

Queiroz, João; Ribeiro, Sidarta 2002. "The Biological Substrate of Icons, Indexes, and Symbols in Animal Communication: A Neurosemiotic Analysis of Vervet Monkey Alarm Calls." In: Shapiro, Michael (ed.), *The Peirce Seminar Papers* 5. Oxford: Berghahn, 69–78.

Queiroz, João; Stjernfelt, Frederik; El-Hani, Charbel Niño 2014. "Dicent Symbols and Proto-propositions in Biological Mimicry." In: Romanini, Vinícius; Fernández, Eliseo (eds.), *Peirce and Biosemiotics: A Guess at the Riddle of Life*. (Biosemiotics 11.) Heidelberg, Germany: Springer, 199–213.

Rodríguez Higuera, Claudio Julio 2016. "Just How Emergent Is the Emergence of Semiosis?" *Biosemiotics* 9, no. 2: 155–167.

Rodríguez Higuera, Claudio J. 2019. "Everything Seems So Settled Here: The Conceivability of Post-Peircean Biosemiotics." *Sign Systems Studies* 47, no. 3/4: 420–435.

Romanini, Vinicius 2014. "Semeiosis as a Living Process." In: Romanini, Vinícius; Fernández, Eliseo (eds.), Peirce *and Biosemiotics: A Guess at the Riddle of Life*. (Biosemiotics 11.) Heidelberg, Germany: Springer, 215–239.

Romanini, Vinicius; Fernández, Eliseo (eds.) 2014. *Peirce and Biosemiotics: A Guess at the Riddle of Life*. (Biosemiotics 11.) Berlin: Springer.

Rothschild, Friedrich S. 1963. "Posture and Psyche." In: Halpern, Lipman (ed.), *Problems of Dynamic Neurology: An International Volume: Studies on the Higher Functions of the Human Nervous System*. Jerusalem: Rothschild Hadassah University Hospital, 475–509.

Salthe, Stanley N. 1995. "A Peircean Semiotic Interpretation of Development." *Ludus Vitalis* 3, no. 4: 15–28.

Santaella Braga, Lucia 1999a. "Peirce and Biology." *Semiotica* 127, no. 1/4: 5–21.

Santaella Braga, Lucia 1999b. "A New Causality for the Understanding of the Living." *Semiotica* 127, no. 1/4: 497–519.

Sebeok, Thomas A. 1972. *Perspectives in Zoosemiotics*. The Hague: Mouton.

Sebeok, Thomas A. 1979. "Neglected Figures in the History of Semiotic Inquiry: Jakob von Uexküll." In: Sebeok, Thomas A., *The Sign & Its Masters*. Austin: University of Texas Press, 187–207.

Sharov, Alexei A. 2001. "Umwelt Theory and Pragmatism." *Semiotica* 134, no. 1/4: 211–228.

Sharov, Alexei A.; Tønnessen, Morten 2022. *Semiotic Agency: Science beyond Mechanism*. (Biosemiotics 25.) Cham, Switzerland: Springer.

Sharov, Alexei A.; Vehkavaara, Tommi 2015. "Protosemiosis: Agency with Reduced Representation Capacity." *Biosemiotics* 8, no. 1: 103–123.

Silveira, Lauro Frederico Barbosa da; Gonzalez, Maria Eunice Quilici 2014. "Instinct and Abduction in the Peircean Informational Perspective: Contributions to Biosemiotics." In: Romanini, Vinícius; Fernández, Eliseo (eds.), *Peirce and Biosemiotics: A Guess at the Riddle of Life*. (Biosemiotics 11.) Heidelberg, Germany: Springer, 151–169.

Skagestad, Peter 1979. "C. S. Peirce on Biological Evolution and Scientific Progress." *Synthese* 41, no. 1: 85–114.

Stjernfelt, Frederik 2014. *Natural Propositions: The Actuality of Peirce's Doctrine of Dicisigns*. Boston: Docent Press.

Tembrock, Günter 1977. *Tierstimmenforschung: Eine Einführung in die Bioakustik*. Wittenberg Lutherstadt, Germany: A Ziemsen Verlag.

Uexküll Thure von 1987. "The Sign Theory of Jakob von Uexküll". In: Krampen, Martin; Oehler, Klaus; Posner, Roland; Sebeok, Thomas A.; Uexküll, Thure von (eds.) 1987. *Classics of Semiotics*. New York: Plenum Press: 147–179.

Vehkavaara, Tommi 2005. "Limitations on Applying Peircean Semeiotic: Biosemiotics as Applied Objective Ethics and Esthetics rather Than Semeiotic." *Journal of Biosemiotics* 1, no. 2: 269–308.

Wells, Rulon W. 1964. "The True Nature of Peirce's Evolutionism." In: Moore, Edward C.; Robin, Richard S. (eds.), *Studies in the Philosophy of Charles Sanders Peirce*. Amherst: University of Massachusetts Press, 304–322.

West, Donna E.; Anderson, Myrdene (eds.) 2016. *Consensus on Peirce's Concept of Habit: Before and beyond Consciousness*. (Studies in Applied Philosophy, Epistemology and Rational Ethics.) Cham, Switzerland: Springer Nature.

Wiener, Philip P. 1949. *Evolution and the Founders of Pragmatism*. Cambridge, MA: Harvard University Press.

CHAPTER 34
....

PEIRCE'S UNIVERSAL GRAMMAR

Some Implications for Modern Linguistics

....

DANIEL L. EVERETT

1. INTRODUCTION

PEIRCE's ideas have frequently been borrowed piecemeal in linguistics and anthropology. One theory builds around his iconicity (Perniss, Thompson, and Vigliocco 2010). Another around indexes (Silverstein 2003). Another on his algebraic logic (Font and Jansana 1996). But this type of "inspiration by Peirce" as opposed to "engaging with Peircean theory" as a whole can create empirical and conceptual problems. Thus one of the goals here is to offer a brief discussion of some of the ways that overlooking Peirce has deprived modern linguistics and philosophy of a number of insights that seem beneficial empirically and theoretically to the objectives of that discipline, regardless of one's particular theoretical orientation, though the focus here is on formal linguistics (Tomalin 2006; cf. D. L. Everett [forthcoming] for a more detailed discussion of these and many other issues).

Even those superficially acquainted with C. S. Peirce's work will know that he was a brilliant polymath (D. L. Everett 2019). But many might be surprised to know that, according to Nöth (2000), "Although Peirce had 'no pretension to being a linguist' (CP 2.328, 1903), the Annotated Catalog of his publications and manuscripts lists no less than 127 papers classified as 'linguistic' and contains references to many other manuscripts dealing with language ... [in Robin, 1967, p133–142]."

The issues distinguishing Peirce's views from much of modern formal linguistics reject the following theoretical presuppositions of the latter in favor of Peirce's quite different approach: (i) taking form as the principal explanandum for linguistics; (ii) asserting that recursion in sentences is the core precondition for human language rather than recursion in interpretations; (iii) building models of language based strictly on unconnected sentences, rather than discourse; (iv) failure to recognize that three essential components of modern linguistics' methodology and values, namely, intuition, introspection, and compositionality, are each specific manifestations of the larger reasoning operation of inference; and (v) failure to recognize that the word "instinct" in earlier literature possesses several distinct senses, each with a variety of implications for our understanding of the sources of human language.

This chapter is organized into six sections: introduction to the issues to be addressed, Peirce's view of universal grammar, Peirce's linguistic depth of analysis, the semeiotics residue in modern linguistics, contributions of Peirce to current analytic issues in modern linguistics, and Peirce's role in the mathematical foundations of linguistic theory.[1]

2. Peirce on Universal Grammar

2.1. Terminology and Classification

Peirce first used the term universal grammar (UG) in 1865—the first usage of this term by anyone in the US so far as I can tell. He did not invent the term of course. This dates back to the thirteenth-century Modistae (Covington 1984; Rosier 1983). But his was the first in the US. Peirce being Peirce, the term did not satisfy him for long, however, and so he experimented with other terms, for example, "pure grammar" and "formal grammar," finally settling on "speculative grammar" (e.g., CP1.191, 1903; CP1.559, 1867; Bellucci 2018). This grammar was one of three branches of the study of logic/semiotics, the other two being logic proper (critic) and universal rhetoric.

In his classification of the sciences, Peirce, on the one hand, separated UG from linguistics. Whereas UG falls under Peirce's logic, linguistics as the study of individual human languages falls farther down in his list, in the classification of idioscopic sciences—those dedicated to making new observations (EP2:261, 1903). There linguistics is listed as a subtype of classificatory psychics (a classification that later linguistic anthropologists such as Franz Boas (2002) and Edward Sapir (1921) would have found congenial. As Nöth (2000) points out, Peirce wrote on both UG and individual languages.

For Noam Chomsky, on the other hand, UG refers to the *biological* capacity that underlies its direct offshoot, linguistics. Linguistics is part of biology, as is psychology, neither of them part of anthropology. This is part of the revolution that Chomsky instituted, differing from earlier figures in linguistics history such as Sapir and Saussure (and also Peirce). By classifying linguistics as a branch of biology, Chomsky removes any possibility that logic or culture exercises major ontogenetic effects on the "core grammar" of a language (Chomsky 1986).[2] And yet there is something to Chomsky's conception that, superficially at least, is reminiscent of Peirce. In the words of three prominent Chomskyan followers: "We decide to study the language faculty in its universal properties, rather than concentrating on the way it manifests itself differently in various languages. We study those aspects of language that may be thought of as 'structural,' as opposed to merely 'behavioral'" (Lasnik, Uriagereka, and Boeckx 2005, 1).

This statement echoes Peirce's distinction between UG and individual languages, at least superficially, in that it separates the study of UG from that of actual languages. Chomsky's latest research program, minimalism, is in one sense a theory of how propositions become linguistic objects. As Lasnik, Uriagereka, and Boeckx (2005) describe it, Chomsky's latest "theory/program" in linguistics is like Peirce's theory in this one respect (though they do not notice this). With this conceptualization of the role of UG in the study of human language, Chomsky, in a sense, is continuing Peirce's division of UG from linguistics proper, whether consciously or not is not clear, though see Section 4.3.1.

To restate this slightly, in Chomskyan theory, arguably the most widely known theory of UG, all of linguistics emerges from UG, which is the "biological capacity for language," while for Peirce UG is not biological. For Peirce, rather, UG is a set of semiotic (thus logical) constraints on grammars, defining, classifying, interpreting, and building signs into larger units.

Peirce's splitting of the responsibility between language (UG) and languages (linguistics) in this way has a variety of healthy empirical implications, for example, the evolution of human language from other animal forms of communication (D. L. Everett [2017] and Section 5.11). One implication of Peirce's theory that arguably broadens its interest is that *all plant* (Simard 2021, inter alia) *and animal communication* (Bradbury and Vehrencamp 2011) *must follow UG* in Peirce's sense.[3]

2.2. Animals and Universal Grammar—Two Approaches

2.2.1. *Symbols versus Indexes and Icons in Communication*

Pursuing this implication of Peirce's UG in more detail, animals, like all entities (even minerals), communicate via signs. The crucial Peircean difference between animal communication and human communication according to D. L. Everett (2017) is that nonhuman animals do not create symbols, or at least they do not create open-ended classes of symbols. I have argued (D. L. Everett 2017) that animals tend to use icons and indexes primarily, though much more research is needed to establish such a claim.

It is often overlooked that for Peirce a symbol "is a general sign, *i.e., a sign that represents a general object*" (Bellucci 2021, 169) This means that if we want to attribute symbol creation or recognition to animals, the object of each of their symbols must be shown to be a general concept, a type. But how can this be determined?

We can address this question following a methodology based on Pikean theory, drawing upon the important *etic* versus *emic* dichotomy. When we observe a behavior outside our own language or culture (e.g., in nonhuman communication), linguistic or otherwise, we observe it preanalytically from an etic perspective (Pike 1967).

If we think we are viewing a symbol, that is, a sign with a general object (at least according to Bellucci), then we must test our thinking by analysis. Our etic view, once analyzed, transforms from an outsider's preanalytic perspective into an insider's postanalytic perspective, or an emic perspective (these Pikean terms are drawn from "phonetic" and "phonemic," respectively).[4] Only by achieving this insider, postanalytic perspective, in conjunction with Peirce's semiotics, are we able to determine whether nonhumans use symbols.

If my understanding is correct, nonhumans of any species, plant or animal, are unlikely to possess symbols to the degree that they lack culture and the ability to generalize, which undergird all cultures, though their communication will nevertheless entail signs and be guided by Peirce's version of UG.

But again we must be careful that our analysis of nonhuman animal communication is based on a clear semiotic understanding of the extent of signs they use. A recent paper on symbol recognition in bees illustrates the need for a better understanding of Peirce's semiotics in science more generally. The article in question claims that bees can be taught symbols (Howard et al. 2019, 1):[5] "Here we show that honeybees are able to learn to match a sign to a numerosity, or a numerosity to a sign, and subsequently transfer this knowledge to novel numerosity stimuli changed in colour properties, shape and configuration. While honeybees learned the associations between two quantities (two; three) and two signs (N-shape; inverted T-shape), they failed at reversing their specific task of sign-to-numerosity matching to numerosity-to-sign matching and vice versa."

This article (as pointed out in D. L. Everett 2019) appears to confuse what are symbols for humans with what are almost certainly indexes (or indexical legisigns) for bees.[6] The paper shows that bees can recognize particular numerical symbols and correctly associate these human symbols with the correct quantities, for example, learning that the symbol '7' means *seven objects*. However, while the researchers have clearly trained bees that $x \to y; y \to x$—that is, if you see an x expect a y—they don't seem to have taught the bees anything other than indexes, which we already know that all animals recognize (as they use smells, footprints, broken branches, etc., to track other animals).

In other words, even if x and y are symbols to humans, they need not be for bees. There is no compelling reason to believe that members of Apoidea have learned anything other than an index for an object, as with Pavlov's dogs. Bees can learn that the appearance of one sign *indicates* the presence of a particular kind of object (whether that object is another sign or simply a natural object): that is, that the first sign is an index (not a symbol) of the latter. Symbols require culture but indexes do not.

Such (in my analysis) inaccurate understanding of symbols is also seen occasionally in computer science and elsewhere in the cognitive sciences (D. L. Everett forthcoming). This seems to underlie the difficulty pointed out by John Searle (1980) in his "Chinese room" thought-experiment about the Turing test. In this work he argued computers cannot understand symbols semantically when they perform automatic machine translation (thus even if their behavior would otherwise pass the Turing test, this is of little significance, according to Searle). In semiotic terms we can restate Searle's results more economically by seeing computers as able to interpret indexes, though perhaps not symbols in the particular translation case that concerned Searle (I am not making a global claim about artificial intelligence).

Searle's experiment, simply put, states that we can express what the computer is doing by imagining a human as the central processing unit (CPU). As Chinese comes in, the human CPU takes Chinese symbols and outputs, correctly and quickly, English symbols. The question that arises is "Does the human CPU understand Chinese?" And the answer, for Searle, is a resoundingly obvious "No." Though Searle did not use these terms, we can reinterpret Searle's "Chinese room" gedanken experiment semiotically. Thus the computer translator's input, say a squiggly line (unbeknown to him/her/they a Chinese character), serves as an index of another squiggle (English), which functions as the output. If this is characterization is correct, then the computer is not using symbolic meaning but only indexical reference, being programmed to treat one squiggly line as an index of another, like the bees in the experiment discussed earlier. So far as we know, only humans use the former (D. L. Everett 2017), but all animals use nonsymbolic signs. The computer is not interpreting signs as having general objects, but only linking one sign to another, that is, using one sign as an index of another. Thus semiotically, Searle's results and subsequent discussion make sense. Anyone arguing against Searle's conclusions needs to discuss the significance of the semeiotic interpretation of this experiment.

To take another example, if one could train their dog to fetch seven things when she sees the numeral '7,' it would be scientifically interesting if she could distinguish seven things *as* "seven things," but since there is no dog culture, there is no presymbolic 'agreement' between dogs that the sign '7' means seven *things*, which in this sense is an abstraction (see also D. L. Everett [2005] for a quite different explanation of why the Pirahã people lack numbers in their nominalistic culture (D. L. Everett forthcoming). The behavior simply shows a response to the stimulus of an index to a particular referent. It is learning, of course, but with no need to invoke symbols. However, even if my dog is understanding a symbol when I ask her to get a specific toy (which I doubt), she is not creating symbols (especially if we restrict these to general objects). But notice that in the case of nonhuman animals and computers, semiotics and therefore UG are crucial to any explanation of what they are doing in communication tasks.[7]

2.2.2. *Creating Symbols*

Let's explore these ideas a bit further. I think it is reasonable to investigate the hypothesis that some animals might be able to learn or create symbols. It is even possible that insects, for example, ants and bees, can learn or create symbols. But creation of open-ended symbol systems has not been shown for nonhumans. To put it another way, Pavlov's dog did not interpret the bell as a symbol of food, but as an index of food. When you see one, you see the other, or so it seems to have been learned. Pavlov's trick was to eventually take away the referent of the index from the immediate environment, while producing the same interpretant (salivation), much as Lucy does to Charlie Brown regularly in the *Peanuts* comic strip by Charles Schulz, when she urges him to kick the ball and then removes the ball just as he goes to kick it. She has removed the object, leaving only the form, her kneeling, and the interpretant, Charlie's kicking. But symbols are more abstract. They do not require an immediate connection between an object and a form for effective use and their objects are general. Only Peirce's semiotics captures this distinction. And so it is the most appropriate set of principles for testing claims about animal communication.

Icons and indexes also obey UG in Peirce's theory. Once again, it is significant that Peirce's UG accounts for all signs, the full range of signs (including animal legisigns where these are found) used by both nonhuman animals and humans.[8] The biological UG of Chomsky does not. This would of course not bother Chomsky, since he believes that there is little or nothing in common between animal and human communication. In his theory human linguistic communication is based on a recursive grammar, while animals lack recursive communication (though this is only a claim, to be tested empirically).[9] Thus there is nothing to compare. He has said (paraphrasing from public lectures) that claiming that animals have language "is like comparing bird flight with a man flapping his arms."

To drive this point home, consider the following quote from Samuels, Hauser, and Boeckx (2016), who address animal communication relative to Chomsky's version of UG:

> Do animals have Universal Grammar? The short answer must be "no." Otherwise, why do human children learn language with strikingly little conscious effort, while no other animal has even come close to approximating human language, even with extensive training or exposure to massive linguistic input? However, many of the cognitive capacities which clearly serve our linguistic ability—rich conceptual systems, vocal imitation, categorical perception, and so on—are shared with other species, including some of our closest living relatives. This suggests that the question is more complicated than it might first appear. In the present work, we use phonology as a case study to show what type of cross-species evidence may bear—now and in future work—on the issue of whether animals have various components of UG, which we construe here broadly as the systems that are recruited by language but need not be specific to it.

But their objections fail to consider the possibility that the crucial distinction between the genus *Homo* and other genuses rests not on a universal grammar of forms but on a universal grammar of signs. And this is a serious problem in understanding language evolution (as both Deacon [1997] and D. L. Everett [2017] make clear).

3. Peirce's Syntactic Depth of Analysis

3.1. Surfacey

From one perspective, Peirce's view of linguistics seems to be what modern linguists might refer to as "surfacey." Peirce tended to look at what speakers actually said, not what they might be implying covertly. For example, in a sentence like *John came in and sat down*, many linguists would propose that "sat down" has its own subject, but that the subject is covert; that is, it is syntactically and semantically present but phonologically absent. Peirce's view was different. Consider the following quote: "Proper nouns must exist in all languages; and so must such 'pronouns,' or indicative words as this, that, something, anything. But it is probably true that in the great majority of the tongues of men, distinctive common nouns either do not exist or are exceptional formations. In their meaning, as they stand in sentences, and in many comparatively wide-studied languages, common nouns are akin to participles, as being mere inflections of the verbs. If a language has a meaning 'is a man,' a noun 'man' becomes a superfluity" (CP3.459, 1897).

So for the sentence above a Peircean analysis would propose an underlying logical constraint on predicates requiring a subject, but not for an invisible or "covert" syntactic subject.[10] The subject is inferred in the interpretant of the construction as a whole, from verb forms and context. It need not be present in the phrase (neither syntactically nor phonologically present) in any form in order to be contextually inferred.

As an "inflection of a verb," a syntactically separate common noun (Peirce here seems to almost paraphrase the hypothesis that nearly a century later would come to be known as the "predicate argument hypothesis," the idea that the functions of noun can be manifested as verb affixes and need not actually manifest as independent words) is not necessary to grammar. For Peirce this would explain his observation that on the surface common nouns are less common than pronouns (which have indexical meanings) in sentences cross-linguistically. That is, he saw independent words as themselves inflections of verbs, along the lines of "pronominal arguments" found in many languages, for example, those of the Salish family (Chomsky 1994).

As Nöth (2000) puts it:

> Peirce defends the thesis that only proper nouns and not common nouns are universal categories of language (CP 2.328, 2.287 fn., 3.440, 3.459, 4.56, 4.151, 7.385 fn., 8.337). The reason for this assessment is the "impotence" (CP 3.419) of a mere common noun to evince reference by itself, without an indexical expression to specify it.... The word donation, e.g., "is indefinite as to who makes the gift, what he gives, and to whom he gives it" (CP 4.543). Hence, in contrast to proper nouns, which always have a specific referential object, common nouns are referentially open in the same way as verbs and adjectives are.

3.2. Deeper—Hypostatic Abstraction and Transformations

However, Peirce's understanding of language was not based on surface forms alone. For example, in his concept of hypostatic abstraction there is evidence that Peirce's view of UG entailed a concept similar to what modern linguists, following Chomsky, once labeled "deep" versus "surface" structures. Hypostatic abstraction is a formal operation that takes as input some predicate and outputs a relation. An example often given of this is the transformation of "Honey *is* sweet" into "Honey *has* sweetness." The original assertion of fact about a topic is turned into a property about that topic. This transformation is not merely (as in Harris's [1951] concept of transformation) a relationship between synonymous phrases with distinct discourse functions.[11] Nor is it claiming that one of these sentences is the syntactic base for the other (as in Chomsky's original theory where passive constructions are "transforms" of active constructions, e.g., *John saw Mary* [active] → *Mary was seen by John* [passive]). Rather Peirce is claiming that semantically/semiotically one implies the other. He does, however, leave open the possibility of a deeper analysis not unlike that of early transformational generative grammar (Chomsky 1957, 1965) when he claims that "thus, we transform the proposition, "honey is sweet," into "honey possesses sweetness" (CP4.235, 1902). But here the "transformation" is a logical one, not a syntactic derivation. For an enlightening discussion of the concept of "transformation" in the sciences, see Stjernfelt (2011).

Peirce claims that hypostatic abstraction is not only crucial to understanding propositions and signs, but also vital for rational thought: "Intuition is the regarding of the abstract in a concrete form, by the realistic hypostatization of relations; that is the one sole method of valuable thought" (CP1.383, 1890).[12]

The general properties of semiotic relationships thus constrain natural language forms in order to allow for the proper evaluation or selection of interpretants as well as to provide for an understanding of and restrictions upon reasoning, characterized by Peirce as a semiotic process. These general semiotic constraints, UG, are thus, as mentioned earlier, a separate domain of study for Peirce from the study of actual natural languages.

3.3. Language of Thought

Another point of similarity between Peirce and modern linguistics and philosophy of language is that, like Jerry Fodor (1980), Peirce's theory requires that there be a "language of thought." At the same time, unlike Fodor and others, Peirce's language of thought is more nuanced, and he argues that the language of thought should not rely exclusively on symbolic thought, because this can lead individuals astray in their reasoning. We must also think iconically and indexically (as animals appear to do, see below). As Peirce puts it, "It is not English grammar which forces these [illogical] words upon them, but it is the very grammar of thought—formal grammar—which forces the idea upon them. The idea of supposing that they can think of motion without an image of something moving" (CP4.127, 1893).

Peirce argues here that a purely symbolic language of thought is a problem leading our thinking astray at times. The problem can be corrected by supplementing symbolic reasoning with iconic thought/reasoning.

This is not only an important distinction for philosophers. Some artists have independently arrived at this conclusion. For example, Joan Didion (2021, 50ff.) recognizes this issue of thinking in images and symbols in her essay, "Why I Write:"

> Grammar is a piano I play by ear, since I seem to have been out of school the year the rules were mentioned. All I know about grammar is its infinite power. To shift the

structure of a sentence alters the meaning of that sentence, as definitely and inflexibly as the position of a camera alters the meaning of the object photographed. Many people know about camera angles now, but not so many know about sentences. The arrangement of the words matters, and the arrangement you want can be found in the picture in your mind. The picture dictates the arrangement. . . . The picture tells you how to arrange the words and the arrangement of the words tells you, or tells me, what's going on in the picture.

Fodor (1980) was of course not the first to propose a language of thought. But the point here is deeper than mere chronological priority. Peirce's language of thought is more detailed, more sophisticated, and more closely predicted by theory than any other version on offer.

Now let us turn to what I see as an ironic echo of Peirce's triadic semantics in the architecture of modern syntactic theories.

4. Semiotic Residue in the Architectonics of Modern Linguistics

4.1. The Overall Design of Modern Theories Is Semiotic

For example, Chomsky's tripartite division of the theory of grammar into logical form (interpretant), phonological form (representamen), and syntax (object) is a triadic semiotic (Peircean) conception of grammar. Take a sentence like *John ordered Bill to come in the room*. On the one hand, minimalism proposes that the atomic objects of this sentence (roughly the word tokens) are selected from the dictionary and then formed into syntactic objects by a recursive process of pairing units from the "bottom up." Thus we take "room" and pair it with "the" and take the result "the room" and pair it with "in" to derive "in the room," and so on until we finally pair the penultimate structure, the predicate, with "John," the subject, to form the sentence. This pairwise, recursive operation, which Chomsky calls merge, is the "basic operation" for the formation of linguistic signs.

The phonological form of a sentence, on the other hand, is the analysis of the spoken, signed, etc., physical form of a sentence, its representamen (which must also include accompanying hand gestures, intonation, and so on or the absence of speech sounds in sign languages, though these are ignored in Chomsky's "syntactocentric" theory [see Culicover and Jackendoff 2005]) for further exploration of syntactocentrism.

Chomskyan theories of linguistics thus all share the ternarity one would expect of semiotic systems, though not all theories recognize this ternarity explicitly. To see what is meant by ternarity in more detail, consider diagrams of the basic theories of

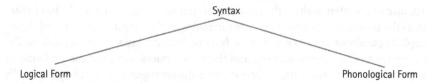

FIGURE 34.1 Ternary organization of Chomskyan theory.

tagmemics of Kenneth L. Pike and minimalism of Chomsky. Chomsky's theory is represented as in Figure 34.1:

Logical form in Figure 34.1 produces the semantic interpretant. Phonological form is the physical interpretant of the syntax, that is, the representamen of the sentence. The syntax is the linguistic object to be interpreted in the linguistic semiosis (real-world objects are brought in/linked through the logical form).

Tagmemics (Pike 1967; Pike and Pike 1976) – Table 34.1 below – is similar—three hierarchies are linked, with the phonological corresponding to representamens, the grammatical corresponding to objects, and the referential corresponding to overall meaning.

The ternarity in these models, therefore, however inadvertent, recognizes that language is a semiotic system, with a Peircean structure. Phonology is about the construction of representamens; logical form/referential hierarchy is about interpretants; grammar/syntax is about the production of propositions and linguistic objects (unfortunately omitting arguments/discourses in Peirce's theory). The extra step in linguistics is that the syntactic interpretations of "objects" of linguistic structures link them not only to extralinguistic objects but also to linguistic objects. In *John saw Mary* we interpret 'John' as referring to a person in logical form, but in the syntax as a subject, an agent, a topic, etc. In the phonology we interpret "John" as a unit composed of prosody (stress, intonation, length) and segments (ʤ, o, n), the representamen of the sign in logical form of a person named "John."

Table 34.1 Ternary Organization of Pikean Theory

Phonological hierarchy	<-->	Grammatical hierarchy	<-->	Referential hierarchy[a]
Ph. discourse		Discourse		Highest meaning unit
Ph. paragraph		Paragraph		
Breath group/contour		Sentence		
Ph. phrase		Phrase		
Phonological word		Word		
Phoneme		Morpheme		Lowest meaning unit

[a] Although Pike and Pike (1976) refer to a "referential hierarchy" as part of the triadic structure of linguistic theory—Pike saw most topics as triadic in structure, though he never, to my knowledge, cites Peirce as a source for this approach—it is not sufficiently worked out to include much detail here.

4.2. Peirce as Theoretician

As part of our investigation of the significance of Peirce for modern linguistics, it is important to note that overlooking Peirce or any other researcher does not diminish their contributions, only the scholarship of the person overlooking them. For example, consider the following statement by a British journalist on the relative inferiority of American as compared to European and British theoretical work: "Americans are not naturally given to grand theory. A glance across the social sciences and humanities for the 'great theorists' of the past century makes this abundantly clear, whether in philosophy (Wittgenstein, Heidegger, Derrida, Foucault, Habermas, Levinas), history (Bloch, Braudel, Hobsbawm, Needham, Elliott), sociology (Mosca, Pareto, Weber, Simmel, Mann), anthropology (Mauss, Lévi-Strauss, Dumont, Malinowski, Evans-Pritchard) or literary studies (Bakhtin, de Man, Barthes). All these foundational figures are European. The grand American exception is Chomsky" (Anderson 2016).

As a statement of about science and the arts, this quote is profoundly, laughably ignorant. It is both too strong and too weak. It is too weak when it claims that there is only one American exception to the rule, Chomsky. One could mention many American social scientists and humanists with broad theories—Leonard Bloomfield, Edward Sapir, Clifford Geertz, Marvin Harris, Napoleon Chagnon, Harold Bloom, and many more—all of whom are at least as important in theory construction as the European figures.

But the statement is also too strong when we consider (see below) how many times Chomsky has changed theories in substantial ways, leading one to question whether he ever had a grand theory (as Peirce did, one still going strong after more than 150 years) or simply a large group of followers and a succession of research ideas. By any standards, the leading American theoretician for the past 155 years is Charles Sanders Peirce, arguably surpassing all of the European and other American figures mentioned.[13]

No one creates theories ex nihilo, though. Modern linguistics and anthropology borrow ideas from varieties of traditions and theories within and outside of their disciplines, regularly incorporating these ideas and practices into new theories and methods. This is both sound intellectual husbandry and the useful curation of ideas to help with the resolution of current problems and concerns.

In well-designed theories all concepts are interrelated and each depends for its significance in part from how it is related to all other concepts of the containing theory. This is in essence the Duhem–Quine thesis (Harding 1976), where Pierre Duhem (1954) and Willard Van Orman Quine (1951) argued independently that scientific hypotheses cannot be tested in isolation, but that only theories can be tested, not their individual components.[14]

One of the most puzzling facts of modern linguistics is the near absence of any overt role for Peircean ideas in understanding the nature of human language. Major current theories such as Chomsky's minimalism (Chomsky 1995), Van Valin's role and reference grammar (Van Valin and LaPolla 1998), and the various versions of the popular theory of construction grammar (especially in the work of Princeton linguist Adele Goldberg [1995]), as well as Hans Kamp's discourse representation theory (Kamp and Reyle 1993), make no detailed references to Peirce. This is particularly ironic in the case of discourse representation theory and construction grammar, since discourse representation theory is "isomorphic" (Sowa 2013) to Peirce's EGs and construction grammar takes linguistics utterances to be "signs" (primarily in the Saussurean sense, but Peirce's ideas are clearly related).

Ultimately, evaluating modern linguistics against Peircean theory, the proof must be in the pudding. Comparisons between modern theories and Peirce therefore can be instructive. To take Chomsky's theory, for example, it arguably has few, if any, non-theory-internal discoveries, and even those are based on the passé idea that grammar is the center of language and that it stops/replicates once it reaches the sentence, with little concern for the causal role of meaning and culture, and paying little attention to the growing neurolinguistic evidence in favor of storage of symbols rather than grammar in the brain (Fedorenko and Thompson-Schill 2014; Fedorenko et al. 2020; Ivanova et al. 2021). Can such a theory survive and thrive empirically (theories long outlast their empirical utility due to professional pressures) over newer theories without such limitations? Time will tell.[15]

4.3. Misinterpretation of Peirce in Modern Linguistics

4.3.1. *Chomsky on Peirce*

Ironically, Chomsky does cite Peirce, especially with regard to the concept of abduction, also referring to Peirce as the philosopher to whom he felt the greatest affinity. So he says in his interviews with Mitsou Ronat (1976, 71) that, "in relation to the questions we have just been discussing [philosophy of language], the philosopher to whom I feel closest and whom I'm almost paraphrasing is Charles Sanders Peirce."

And yet Chomsky is not paraphrasing Peirce. He is caricaturing him. Just a small sample of how misunderstood Peirce can be comes from the following commentary by Chomsky.

> "QUESTION: I'm really intrigued by your concept of abduction. [Mitsou Ronat interview]
>
> Abduction? Well, Peirce had this one very stimulating essay, which I don't think he ever pursued further, called—when it was reprinted in the fifties, it was called—"The Logic of Abduction." I don't remember what he called it; I think that was the first time it ever appeared, actually—when the Peirce stuff started coming out in the fifties—but it was about the turn of the century. He began by saying that you can't—he's talking really about theory construction in the sciences, but the same would be true in any kind of learning whatever, and he made that clear—he said that you can't get anywhere by association, you can't get anywhere by induction; induction is not a method of acquiring any knowledge. He said that induction and confirmation, and so on, may be ways of checking out what you've discovered, and clarifying it and filling out the details, and so on, but there's something else going on. And the other thing that's going on is what he called abduction. He didn't tell you much about what

it was, which is not so surprising, but he said whatever it is, it's instinctive. He said it's on a par with a chicken pecking at grain, so there's some instinctive mechanism we have that is a kind of a theory construction module of the brain, to put it in contemporary terms. And that maps—that constructs—theoretical interpretation from scattered data. And we do it instinctively. And then we check it out by induction and methodology of science and all that kind of stuff [yes, the two other forms of inference]. And he said if you really understand what happens in science—or what happens in ordinary life when people gain a conception of the world—why, you have to understand this instinctive.... And I think that's exactly right."

Chomsky's interpretation misses/misunderstands key points of Peirce's concepts of abduction and instinct. When Chomsky claims that Peirce had only one essay on abduction and that he never pursued this further, he is profoundly incorrect (D. L. Everett forthcoming). Of course, Peirce's papers are in much better shape now (largely due to Harvard's Houghton Library and the Peirce Edition Project at Indiana University Indianapolis) than they were in the 1950s, but the *Collected Papers* were already available at that time (they were published in 1932—thanks to Hartshorne and Weiss), and they include many, many references to abduction.

When Chomsky claims that Peirce asserted that "you can't get anywhere by association, you can't get anywhere by induction," he is being very misleading, because for Peirce inference was key to human cognitive advancement, and abduction is but one of three components of/types of inference, the others being induction and deduction. The guesses of abduction needed to be tested by induction and deduction to have value. In this sense Chomsky's remarks miss the point almost entirely, because although he mentions these in the quote above, the vital significance of inference as a ternary operation is overlooked. For Peirce abduction is always a first step of ampliative inference, to be tested via iconic reasoning, induction, deduction, scientific method, etc. As for Peirce's concept of instinct, we return to this in Section 5.8. below.

4.3.2. *Jakobson on Peirce*

Roman Jakobson was one of the most important linguists of the twentieth century. Some of his most significant work occurred during his time in Prague in the late 1920s with the Prague Linguistics Circle and at Harvard, where his students included the late Morris Halle, who eventually would "discover" Noam Chomsky and recommend him for employment at MIT, where Halle was already established in a project directed by Victor Yngve (Yngve, pers. comm.). In Prague, Jakobson and Prince Nikolai Trubetskoy, among others, developed the concept of "oppositions" in phonological theory that led to the theory of "distinctive features." Although I have not been able to find any direct link between the work of the Prague Circle and Peirce, their influential ideas on binary oppositions were quite similar to Peirce's perspective on "secondness."

More direct influence might one day be found between Peirce and these early phonological theorists. But in the absence of evidence of direct influence of Peirce on the Prague Circle, we can point to one prominent member of that circle taking inspiration from Peirce, Roman Jakobson. In Jakobson (1985), an attempt was made to introduce

Peirce's "pathfinding" work to linguists, though arguably it failed. This is, in my view, because Jakobson, while claiming that Peirce's work was important, failed to consult the greater body of Peirce's work and so missed crucial points (see Shapiro 1983). Peirce has little overtly acknowledged influence in linguistics. In general Jakobson seems to have not understood Peirce's theory of signs well. However, it is likely that Chomsky heard of Peirce in part through Jakobson, since Jakobson exercised considerable influence over Chomsky directly and indirectly, through Halle.

5. Peirce and Current Linguistic Research Issues

5.1. Methodology: Intuition, Introspection, and Inference

5.1.1. *Intuition*

Peirce (CP5.213–263, 1868) argues at length that there is no such thing as intuition, a central component of cognitive research from Descartes to the present, and vital to many linguists (e.g., Chomsky). Defining intuition as a "cognition unlinked to a previous cognition," Peirce concludes that no such cognitions exist and that all cognition is part of a chain of inference with other cognitions.[16] He claims that the only evidence for intuition is that we think we have it: "A child has, as far as we know, all the perceptive powers of a man. Yet question him a little as to *how* he knows what he does. In many cases, he will tell you that he never learned his mother tongue; he always knew it, or he knew it as soon as he came to have sense. It appears, then, that he does not possess the faculty of distinguishing, by simple contemplation, between an intuition and a cognition determined by others [which would be an inference]" (CP5.218, 1868).

In spite of potential problems, intuitions nevertheless play a significant role in modern linguistic theory and are crucial to determining the grammaticality of utterances and thus in turn also crucial not only to the goals of linguistic theory, but also its methodology.[17] But intuition also figures into the very goals of linguistic theory.

Chomsky agrees that the goal of the linguist is epistemological, based on intuitions (which have direct access to grammatical knowledge): "The linguist . . . is trying to determine what constitutes knowledge of a language—to construct a correct grammar" (Chomsky 2006, 23).

And again:

> It seems reasonably clear, both in principle and in many specific cases, unconscious knowledge issues in conscious knowledge . . . it follows computations similar to straight deduction. (Chomsky 1986)

> We cognize the system of mentally represented rules from which [linguistic] facts follow. (Chomsky 1980, 9) (i.e., the facts expressed in intuitive judgments)

Thus at several levels, the linguist is involved in the construction of explanatory theories, and at each level, there is a clear psychological interpretation for his theoretical and descriptive work. At the level of a particular grammar, he is attempting to characterize knowledge of a language. (Chomsky 2006)

Similar remarks are not hard to find from other authors:

Our ability to make linguistic judgments clearly follows from our knowing the languages that we know. (Larson and Segal 1995, 10)

We can use intuitions to confirm grammars because grammars are internally represented and actually contribute to the etiology of the speaker/hearer's intuitive judgments. (Fodor 1981, 200–201)

But there are some who express reservations, for example, that "intuitions" might be forms of inference or at least not a direct connection to an internal grammar: "As Black, Stitch and others have stressed, it is not clear that the native speaker is right about anything when he accepts a sentence" (Levin 1983, 182).

Levin also says: "It is an empirical hypothesis that the grammarian's formal explanation has an empirical realization in speakers" (Levin 1983, 182). And, very tellingly: "The whole idea that grammars explain comes from smuggling into the idea of an empirically adequate grammar the quite separate assumption of its realization in human speakers" (Levin 1983, 182).

These quotes illustrate an immense divide among those who study natural languages regarding the object of inquiry. Is linguistics about epistemology or is it about language? Some theories (e.g., Pullum 2020) offer analyses of the data and try to understand the empirical implications of those data in relation to linguistic behavior, avoiding all talk of introspection or intuition.

But perhaps the most articulate critic of intuitions in linguistic theory, apart from Peirce, is Michael Devitt (2006b, 481): "Linguists take the intuitive judgments of speakers to be good evidence for a grammar. Why? The Chomskian answer is that they are derived by a rational process representation of linguistic rules in the language faculty. The paper takes a different view. It argues for a naturalistic and non-Cartesian view of intuitions in general. Intuitions are empirical central-processor responses to phenomena differing from other responses only in being immediate and fairly unreflective. Applying this to linguistic intuitions yields an explanation of their evidential role without any appeal to representation of rules."

Devitt's view is to be contrasted with what he calls the Chomskyan "Representational Thesis:" "A speaker of a language stands in an unconscious or tacit propositional attitude to the rules or principles of the language, which are represented in her language faculty" (Devitt 2006, 273).

Devitt goes on to argue that intuitions could only serve as evidence for grammatical rules if they "really were the voice of competence." "These linguists" (Chomskyans), Devitt claims, are "committed to the Cartesian view that intuitions are the voice of competence... [that these speakers] simply by virtue of being competent, have information about linguistic facts" (Devitt 2006, 97)Devitt rejects these ideas.

Peirce offered the best criticism of this type of research program, of any theory that relies on grammatical "intuitions" or "intuitive judgements." The problem with such theories from a Peircean perspective is that whenever a speaker offers a judgment, they are *inferring* the grammaticality of a given example based on their experience (unconsciously or consciously). The issue is that if, as Peirce would have it in "Questions Concerning Certain Capacities Claimed for Man" (CP5.213–263, 1868), an intuition is a "premiss which is not itself a conclusion," then we simply cannot be sure that no premise in a judgment/conclusion has not been previously a conclusion. That is, we have no special power to ensure that our judgments are "cognitions not determined by a previous cognition." Intuitions can thus never be proven to be intuitions in the sense of a special cognition, as opposed to inference.

All of our judgments and theories emerge from networks of knowledge and arguments and propositions and these are too complicated to sort through for any judgment of a single utterance of a given language to determine whether our acceptance of that utterance as grammatical is a direct deliverance of our grammatical competence (as Chomsky would have it) or inferring from our CPU, as Devitt argues. Given the fact that speakers' grammaticality judgments change in different circumstances, it seems most likely that Peirce's arguments against intuitions as special forms of cognitive evaluation are correct. Certainly no one has explained what intuitions are in any deep sense, other than to claim them as the source of native speaker judgments (see the papers in Schindler, Drożdżowicz, and Brøker [2020]) for more details.

What Peirce contributes in this regard to linguistic theory are strong arguments that intuitions are inference and reflect no special power or immediate connection to the "voice of competence."[18] And this holds true not only for intuitions, but also for compositionality and introspection and other questionable tools in the arsenal of modern linguistics.

One lesson to draw from this is that if intuitions, compositionality, and introspection are not privileged linguistic tools directly tied to our competence, then we can interpret these in more general inferential terms when talking about language (and other human behaviors). In other words, quantitative data and corpora are crucial to linguistic theory. Although the standard data of "intuitions" and "introspection" can be of value, we can only evaluate these inferentially and never take them as offering a "voice of competence." This is what many cognitive scientists have been arguing for some years now (see especially Gibson and Fedorenko 2013).

5.1.2. *Introspection*

Another crucial cognitive tool for modern linguistics that Peirce calls into question is the concept of introspection. Introspection about grammaticality judgments as windows into native speaker competence go hand in hand with intuitions in Chomskyan (and many other) theories. As Schwitzgebel (2010) puts it: "Introspection is a key concept in epistemology, since introspective knowledge is often thought to be particularly secure, maybe even immune to skeptical doubt. Introspective knowledge is also often held to be more immediate or direct than sensory knowledge. Both of these putative features of introspection have been cited in support of the idea that introspective knowledge can serve as a ground or foundation for other sorts of knowledge."

Moreover, as the author continues: "Introspection is generally regarded as a process by means of which we learn about our own currently ongoing, or very recently past, mental states or processes. Not all such processes are introspective, however: Few would say that you have introspected if you learn that you're angry by seeing your facial expression in the mirror. However, it's unclear and contentious exactly what more is required for a process to qualify as introspective."

However, the problem for introspection is the same as for intuition. If we think of these as just labels for types of inference, then there is no Peircean objection. We draw information in some way about our inner life and test our judgments about this following standard forms of induction, deduction, and abduction. But if we think of introspection as a special mental ability or special access to truth, knowledge, or inner states, and not a form of inference using data and standard scientific and logical argumentation, we delude ourselves. Once again, Peirce emphasizes that all knowledge is acquired by inferential reasoning, not by special powers (into which forms of spiritual revelation would also fall).

Since we have no way to understand the world within and around us other than by inference, it is crucial that modern linguistics develop more scientific methods for evaluating theories other than intuition and introspection. The quotes given at the beginning of this section claiming a special place for intuition and, by extension, introspection in linguistic theory are representative of the unscientific foundations of much of modern linguistics, which would almost certainly have appalled Peirce.

I now want to turn to consider another special form of inference, one that is considered a vital and special part of linguistic theory, yet distinct from inference in most work, namely, compositionality.

5.2. Compositionality

There are various related concepts of compositionality in linguistics and philosophy. It is an extremely important concept in modern linguistics. And it is usually assumed to have originated with Gottlob Frege, who writes that "it is enough if the sentence as whole has meaning; thereby also its parts obtain their meanings" (Frege 1884, section 60).

In more recent work, perhaps the most succinct definition of it is found in the following quote from Szabó (2000, 3): "*Principle of Compositionality*: the meaning of a complex expression is determined by meanings of its constituents and by its structure."

Another take on compositionality comes from Pietarinen (2005):

> Charles S. Peirce's pragmatist theory of logic teaches us to take the context of utterances as an indispensable logical notion without which there is no meaning.

This is not a spat against compositionality per se, since it is possible to posit extra arguments to the meaning function that composes complex meaning. However, that method would be inappropriate for a realistic notion of the meaning of assertions.

To accomplish a realistic notion of meaning (as opposed e.g. to algebraic meaning), Sperber and Wilson's Relevance Theory (RT) may be applied in the spirit of Peirce's Pragmatic Maxim (PM): the weighing of information depends on (i) the practical consequences of accommodating the chosen piece of information introduced in communication, and (ii) what will ensue in actually using that piece in further cycles of discourse. Peirce's unpublished papers suggest a relevance-like approach to meaning. Contextual features influenced his logic of Existential Graphs (EG). Arguments are presented pro and con the view in which EGs endorse noncompositionality of meaning.

But these versions of compositionality do not offer a solution for the temporal interpretations to be discussed in this section (see also D. L. Everett forthcoming). The question is how we achieve temporal interpretations for time words, affixes, and discourses in languages like the Amazonian isolate Pirahã, who do not use either precision time words or tense morphosyntax (D. L. Everett 1986). The concepts of compositionality given above do not work. The reason is that compositionality is a special form of inference and the entire resources of inference are required to arrive at appropriate semantic interpretations.

Consider the example from the Amazonian isolate Pirahã (my field notes):

(1) Kohóai   -xiigá.   Tíi gí ʔahoái -soog -abagaí
    eat   -continuative   I you talk   -want -frustrated initiation
    "(You) are eating. I want to talk to you."
    (Free translation: "When you finish eating, I want to talk to you.")

The interpretation of this example depends on the extralinguistic context, seeing someone eating or hearing someone quoting someone else. The interpretation also depends on the cultural understanding of **-abagaí**, which can also be an illocutionary force marker; that is, this is an indirect speech act (literally it is "I almost begin to want to talk to you," making it not quite a direct statement). So we only know the temporal meaning of this example by a combination of real-world knowledge and experience, with cultural values on how best to express ideas. Here are more examples:

(2) ti gáí   -sai.   asi   ti soʔóá ʔáab   -óp   -á   -p   -á.
    1 say   -old information assim 1   already turn -go   -up   -remote
    kapiiga -kakaí -sai   ʔoogiái hi   ʔigí - o
    paper   -mark -old information   Dan   3   with   -loc
    "I spoke. I just arrived. I want to study with/teach Dan."

These sentences *underdetermine* their semantics. Pirahãs (like all speakers everywhere) use inference to incorporate extralinguistic information and linguistic information into interpretations. Thus we see that in spite of the absence of tense morphemes and precise temporal lexical items (see D. L. Everett 1986, forthcoming), the speakers of Pirahã are nevertheless able to come up with precise temporal understandings, modulo culture (see below).[19] To accomplish this, they must *infer* from the context, the discourse, the words, expressions, gestures, and so on what time frame is implicated in the meaning of individual utterances.

    In fact, English presents similar cases:

(3) a. John reported that Mary has COVID-19/is happy.
     b. Yesterday, John reported that Mary has COVID-19/?is happy.
   *c. Almost a hundred years ago, scientists concluded that the ivory-billed woodpecker is pregnant/happy/flying. (modification of example from Barbara Partee, pers. comm.)
     d. Almost a hundred years ago, scientists concluded that the ivory-billed woodpecker is extinct. (example from Barbara Partee, pers. comm.)

(4) a. John claimed that Mary is pregnant.
     b. Yesterday, John claimed that Mary is pregnant.

(5) ?a. Twelve months ago, John claimed/reported that Mary has COVID-19.
   *b. Twelve months ago, John claimed/reported that Mary is pregnant.

(6) a. Twelve months ago, John reported that the elephant is pregnant.
   *b. Thirty six months ago, John reported that the elephant is pregnant.

(7) *a. Two years ago, John reported that his neighbor Tricia is happy.
   ?b. Two years ago, John reported that the Virgin Mary is happy.
   ?c. Today, John reported that his neighbor Mary is happy.
    d. Two thousand years ago, John reported that the Virgin Mary is happy.
    e. Zookeepers who examined Ellie the elephant in the Cincinnati zoo five months ago announced/published that she is pregnant. (example from Barbara Partee, pers. comm.)

(8) *a. One thousand years ago, John reported that Bill is his friend.
    b. One thousand years ago, John reported that Muhammed is God's prophet.
    c. Two thousand years ago, John reported that Jesus is alive.
   *d. Two thousand years ago, John reported that Bill is alive.
    e. The ancient Egyptians believed that the earth is flat. (example from Barbara Partee, pers. comm.)

People interpret and evaluate the grammaticality of the sentences above inferentially, via cultural and real-world knowledge, in conjunction with their knowledge of the words and structures of their languages. All of the conclusions relative to the grammaticality of these sentences rely exclusively on inferential reasoning (including memory, cultural associations, apperceptions, etc.; see D. Everett [2016]). Thus in (8c), Jesus, as an eternal being to some religions, can be alive after a thousand years, while Bill cannot be in a physical sense (though for some he is eternal in heaven). Each of the contrasts in (3)–(8) depend on inference in which the linguistic information is just one part of the final felicity/grammaticality of the example. One might of course argue that compositionality plays its role and then submits the result to pragmatics to determine if the constructed meaning fits the context. But there are a couple of problems with this suggestion. First, we must ask why this division is desirable or whether it only arises in order to artificially distinguish compositionality from the general inferential abilities independently known to be possessed by humans (indeed, all animals). Parsimony favors taking compositionality to be a special form of inference, continuous in fact with nonlinguistic inference.[20] Cooking by a recipe or solving crimes seem to be abilities that require a power and process of inference identical in operation to the construction of sentence meanings, within their own data-guided and data-specific domains.

The idea that there are only inferences in understanding our native tongues, not some other special capacity of the mind, obviously means that no speaker is able to make intuitive judgments about what is grammatical or not, because intuition doesn't exist. We only judge whether something is grammatical or not just as we only judge what something means in the first place—via inference, using one or more of the three "-ductions"—induction, abduction, or deduction. If I ask you if the following sentences are OK, what is the process by which you answer me?

(9) John is three years old and is CEO of a major company.

(10) John are the nicest guy I know.

(11) Talking about Mary, he is a smart woman.

(12) Who do you wonder whether saw John?

(13) Who do you wonder whether John saw?

According to Peirce, again, there is only one answer for any form of reasoning, inference. You (child or adult) know the answer to these questions because you *infer* (however tacitly and quickly) that it is ungrammatical or grammatical, as well as why it is based on its comparison to other sentences, using known signs to infer properties of unknown signs (as we have seen, Peirce demonstrates the vacuity of notions like "intuition" and "introspection," replacing them with inference).

But for Peirce the forms of inference are dependent on his theory of signs, his semiotic. Simply put, Peirce's semiotic system differs from all others in its strict triadicity. A sign must have three components (not merely the Saussurian dyadic of form + meaning). These are the object, interpretant, and representamen (the form of the sign). So "apple" has the phonemic form "apple" that varies by dialect and it has as object the red, sweet fruit that we make cider with. But the form and the object can only come together as a sign of some type if they have an interpretant—if they can be interpreted by other signs in the language. In "apple of my eye" the interpretant of apple will be different than in "apple in my eye" and so on. Semiotic inference uses knowledge of linguistic signs and their arrangement (the arrangement is also a sign) and other forms of knowledge in an inferential process built on cultural learning and semiotic principles, such as "closeness in function → closeness in syntax" (known by some as a form of iconicity). Also Peircean semiotics enables us to see compositionality/inference in the interpretation of iconic signs, such as street signs and so on, without concern for the fact that the signs mix symbols, icons, and indexes at different times.

This inference is distinct in beginning with words and structure and proceeding to context (or the other way around). As we saw, some meanings are thus produced holistically as well as being built up piecemeal by recursive processes, for example, merge.

But the examples above from Pirahã and English show us that native speakers cannot derive meanings from naive compositionality or structure-building alone, but also require inference, the ability to interpret context, drawing on reasoning, cultural knowledge, and so on.

5.3. Transitivity, Valency, and the Reduction Theorem

Consider the following examples from English:

It is raining. (monotransitive—no arguments)
I am running. (intransitive—one argument)
He sees you. (transitive—two arguments)
Sheila gave Mary a gift/Sheila gave a gift to Mary. (ditransitive—three arguments)
Peter bet Noam two dollars that it would rain. (tritransitive—four arguments)

There are linguists who believe that such verb–argument combinations represent semantically basic verb types. There is a problem, however. Consider that in tritransitives, an argument can be omitted, but not in the others:

*Running.
*He sees.
*Sheila gave a gift.
*Sheila gave Mary.
Peter bet Noam two dollars.
Peter bet Noam that it would rain.

What is interesting in these examples is that intransitives, transitives, and ditransitives require their full complement of arguments or the sentence is ungrammatical. However, this is not true for tritransitives. While there are linguists who believe that tritransitives do constitute a basic, nonderived semantic type of verb, there are no convincing answers to the paradigm above. If the fourth argument of a tritransitive were basic as the arguments of the other types are, it should not be able to be omitted.

Some linguists have long wondered why three arguments seem to be the maximum number allowed without semantic additions to the verb, for example, adpositions, causative morphology, and so on. Interestingly, this is exactly what Peirce's theory predicts. Three is the maximum number of basic arguments a verb can have in its lexical meaning, though extra arguments can be added or indicated by prepositions, affixation, or lexical processes (Van Valin 2007). Tritransitive verbs violate Peirce's reduction theorem for valency (the lexically basic semantics of a verb). Peirce introduced the concept of "valency" into linguistics from chemistry (CP3.470, 1897). This was natural for him, because he came into science through chemistry. The only way to produce a tritransitive verb is to superficially increase valency (what we would call in the early twenty-first century a transitivity alternation) in a deviation from the verb's basic semantics, one argument at a time.

Peirce's "reduction thesis" is stated by Atkins (2018, 58; see also Burch 2001) as follows: "There are three and only three basic propositional forms: the monadic form (firstness); the dyadic form (secondness); and the triadic form (thirdness). We need not posit any more than these three, and we cannot posit any fewer." Next, Atkins shows that Peirce came to this thesis through the EGs, which enabled him to maintain that:

> (1) All n-adic propositional forms where $n > 3$ are constructable from triadic propositional forms; (2) All n-adic propositional forms where $N > 3$ can be decomposed into triadic propositional forms; (3a) Triadic propositional forms cannot be constructed from monadic propositional forms alone; (3b) Dyadic propositional forms cannot be constructed from monadic propositional forms alone; and (4) All triadic propositional forms contain as abstractable logical ingredients both dyadic and monadic propositional forms. Hence, we may allow our most basic propositional forms to be monads, dyads, and triads and all other propositional forms to be constructable from or decomposable into these forms. (2018, 71)[21]

It is crucial, however, in evaluating Peirce's reduction thesis to draw a strict line between valency (this, appropriately, seems to mean "number of required lexical arguments" for most linguists) and transitivity (number of arguments of a verb in a sentence). This distinction can be overlooked in casual analyses of languages, by linguists, philosophers, and anthropologists. One superb study of the difference between transitivity and valency is Hopper and Thompson (1980).[22]

Thomason and Everett (1993) discuss transitivity and valency in Flathead/Montana Salish:

> Flathead, a Salishan language spoken in northwestern Montana, has a verbal system that seems at first glance to distinguish transitive constructions from intransitive ones in a quite straightforward way: transitive verbs have a transitive suffix and a characteristic set of subject and object markers, while intransitive verbs lack the transitive suffix and have a completely different set of subject markers. In addition, the two constructions differ systematically in their marking of adjunct (or argument) noun phrases. Initial appearances are deceiving, however. It turns out that morphologically intransitive verbs can take object noun phrases, and that certain transitive constructions, notably monotransitive continuatives, lack part of the transitive

morphology. The goal of this paper is to explore the morphosyntactic means by which different degrees of transitivity are signalled in Flathead, and to propose an analysis that pulls apparently disparate facts together in a unified way.

Transitivity (the number of syntactic arguments) can be reduced or expanded while valency (the number of lexical arguments) is held constant:

John saw Mary = transitive, bivalent

Mary was seen by John = intransitive, bivalent (see D. L. Everett [1996] for detailed discussion).

All serious theories of human linguistic capacity address the interrelationship between linguistic form and meaning. This is certainly built into Peircean (and Sausurrean) semiotics. But arguably only Peirce in the long history of the study of human language predicts this from the building blocks of his theory, UG.

5.4. Field Research

Peirce's phenomenology captures the task of linguistic field research well. Sakel and Everett (2011) offer a number of suggestions and guidelines for the conduct of linguistic field research. One of the things that we point out is that as the linguist moves from an etic perspective to an emic one, many sounds and structures and meanings in the language under study will go from vague impressions (tones) to clear oppositions (tokens) and finally will be related to particular emic analytical units (types). In Peircean terms we move from firstness to secondness to thirdness in field research. In terms of specific units we notice tones, analyze tokens, and construct types.

Kenneth Pike's (1967) ideas on proceeding from the unknown to the known, while he does not mention Peirce, mirror Peircean ideas. When we arrive in a new field situation, hearing a language for the first time that we do not speak or know anything about, we begin our work with phonetics (articulatory, acoustic, or auditory), which is the study of speech sounds from the perspective of a nonnative speaker, say, a physicist or linguist. But phonetics has already been preceded by vague and unclear perceptions we have of the language before we begin to transcribe or analyze. Once we complete our phonetic analyses and transcriptions, we are in a better position to analyze the phonemics, which is the study of the set of phonetic sounds that native speakers perceive as single sounds, that is, the sounds that are important from the perspective of a native speaker, an insider.[23] For example, English speakers all hear one sound, /p/ in the words [park], [spark], and [carp], when in fact there are at least three sounds, all written as 'p' in these words, namely, [p], [pʰ], and [p̚], respectively.[24] Native speakers thus know less *explicitly* about the sounds of their language than they tacitly know about them, since speakers in general never perceive the separate etic sounds but only the single emic sound that an etic sound is associated with. Yet they never confuse etic sounds in use. In just the same way, native speakers know how to use all the etic sounds of their language appropriately, for example, the three separate manifestations (technically, *allophones*) of /p/ in this example: "Use [p] in syllable-medial positions, [pʰ] in (some) syllable-initial positions, and [p˺] in phrase-final position."[25]

It is interesting that Peirce in effect predicts the order of field research in his phenomenological categories. However, to fully utilize his insights, linguists need to be aware not merely of his terms *type* and *token* but also of the etic, preanalytic category, *tones*, that are a crucial part of Peirce's model. And these correspond to Peirce's basic phenomenological categories of firstness (tones), secondness (tokens), and thirdness (types).

5.5. Recursion

In 2002, Marc Hauser, Noam Chomsky, and Tecumseh Fitch (HCF) offered a novel take on what they thought the core nature of language was: "We submit that a distinction should be made between the faculty of language in the broad sense (FLB) and in the narrow sense (FLN). FLB includes a sensory–motor system, a conceptual–intentional system, and the computational mechanisms for recursion, providing the capacity to generate an infinite range of expressions from a finite set of elements. We hypothesize that FLN only includes recursion and is the only uniquely human component of the faculty of language" (Hauser, Chomsky, and Fitch 2002, 1569).

They discussed their evidence for this claim, which was based on the idea that there is no longest sentence in any language: "There is no longest sentence (any candidate sentence can be trumped by, for example, embedding it in "Mary thinks that . . ."), and there is no nonarbitrary upper bound to sentence length. In these respects, language is directly analogous to the natural numbers (see below)" (HCF 2002, 1571).

When I later argued (D. L. Everett 2005) that the Pirahã language of the Brazilian Amazon lacked recursion in its sentential syntax and that it *did* have a longest sentence, this led to an eighteen-year (and counting) debate. I always claimed that the language did have recursion in its discourses, just not in its sentences. Recent work on the implications of my claim on discourse recursion has shown this idea to have interesting consequences (Maier 2021).[26]

Apart from discourse, however, had HCF and D. L. Everett (2005) adopted Peirce's perspective on recursion, universally overlooked in form-centered syntax and formal (math-based) syntax, much of this debate could have been avoided. The reason for this is that semiosis, which is as important to the Pirahãs as to English speakers, is inherently recursive. In other words, Peirce already claimed in effect that recursion is the heart of language (because it is the heart of semiosis) and thus that all languages must have recursion, just not necessarily in their sentence structures. In Peirce's system, recursion is found in the interpretant, not the object or representamen (as HCF would have it), that is, in the semantics, since each sign must be interpreted via another sign—a recursive process. There can be, if my work on Pirahã is correct (see Futrell et al. 2016; D. L. Everett and Gibson 2019, etc.), languages that have semiotic recursion and discourse recursion, but that lack sentential recursion.

We can think of the interpretation of signs recursively via the following interpretation rule:

SIGN → SIGN

One sign will always produce another sign as its interpretant. This cycle need not go on forever, just as even in Chomsky's systems there are no ten thousand–word sentences. We can account for this either by introducing an index to the right of the rule to stop the process at a physical connection to an object or by simply allowing the process to stop due to lack of interest, memory limitations, and so on. Logically it need not stop. But in terms of human capacity it will in natural languages.

If Chomsky simply wants to claim that recursion in language is the Narrow Faculty of Language or FLN, there is no problem. Peirce already explained this more than a century ago. But if Chomsky wants to claim that recursion in the syntactic form is what is crucial, that finds support neither in Peirce nor in the facts of natural languages.

One interesting proposal in more recent years within minimalism is found in Murphy (2015). Although he gives no reference to Peirce, the proposal introduces an element of semiotics into Chomsky's theory: "It is shown that the operation Label, not Merge, constitutes the evolutionary novelty which distinguishes human language from non-human computational systems; a proposal lending weight to a Weak Continuity Hypothesis and leading to the formation of what is termed Computational Ethology" (Murphy 2015, 1).

In other words, Murphy is claiming that syntax is not unique to humans but labeling of syntactic nodes is. Thus putting the words "hit" and "John" together in " . . . hit John" to form a verb phrase is less significant than the label "verb phrase." Other creatures put things together. Only humans label them (i.e., attach symbols to them). Murphy is absolutely correct, it seems to me. And absolutely Peircean in his insight, however unknowingly.[27]

5.6. Speech Acts and Peirce

Though a full discussion of Peirce's view of speech acts is beyond the scope of this chapter, it is worth noting not only that Peirce anticipated the theory of speech acts, but also that his "commitment view" of assertions prefigures Brandom's (1998) view of inference and responsibility.

> It is no pragmaticistic doctrine that responsibility attaches to a concept; but the argument is that the predication of a concept is capable of becoming the subject of responsibility, since it actually does become so in the act of asserting that predication. Thereupon it follows that the concept has a capability of having a bearing on conduct;

and this fact will lend it intellectual purport. For it cannot be denied that one, at least, of the functions of intelligence is to adopt conduct so as to subserve desire. If the argument is correct, this applies to any concept whatsoever, unless there be a concept that cannot be predicated. (CP 5.477–478)

C. S. Peirce held what John MacFarlane (2011) calls a "commitment view" of assertion. According to this type of view, assertion is a kind of act that is determined by its "normative effects": by asserting a proposition one undertakes certain commitments, typically to be able to provide reason to believe what one is asserting. Peirce's most explicit statement of his commitment view of assertion is that when one asserts a proposition one "takes responsibility" for its truth. (Boyd 2016, 21)

Brandom (1983, 641) discusses assertions in similar words: "This use suggests taking the commitment involved in asserting to be the undertaking of justificatory responsibility for what is claimed. In asserting a sentence, one not only licenses further assertions on the part of others, but commits oneself to justifying the original claim."

Unfortunately, Brandom does not cite Peirce in this article or in his later work (e.g., Brandom 1998). But though Brandom commits the common act of "discovering" a fact that Peirce had already discussed, Peirce's theory still holds the advantage, because Peirce's assertion theory is embedded in a logical theory of semiosis and therefore stands as part of a larger architectonic, its principals features derived rather than stipulated.

5.7 Peircean Discourse Analysis

The thesis of Longacre (1996, 1), *The Grammar of Discourse*, is: "Language is language only in context. For too long a time, linguistics has confined itself to the study of isolated sentences, either such sentences carefully selected from a corpus or, more often than not, artfully contrived so as to betray no need for further context."

Although much of modern linguistics ignored careful study of discourse until the 1950s (two of the foundational monographs from US scholars are Longacre [1996], but written much earlier and published under a different title, and Grimes [1975]), Peirce's pioneering work had already argued that arguments (a form of discourse) were "perfect symbols" that could be analyzed via his system of EGs. Interestingly, Chomsky has never acknowledged the important differences between discourse and sentences. Yet a failure to recognize discourses in his theory leaves him with no account of sentences as discourse constituents (which even his advisor Harris had done [Harris 1951]).

In more recent years, a new and widely respected theory of discourse has arisen in some areas of formal linguistics, developed by Hans Kamp and others (Kamp and Reyle 1993), which is, as Sowa (2013) puts it, "isomorphic" to EGs (CP4.347ff., 1902; see also Sowa [http://www.jfsowa.com/peirce/ms514.htm]). Modern theories of linguistics that focus on sentences seem to have done so via an implicit recognition that the proposition is, as Peirce claimed, essential to understanding speech acts. Sentences are primarily the realization of propositions in linguistic form. Unfortunately, they were never intended by Peirce or any other researcher, until Chomsky, to be the principal focus of linguistic theory to the exclusion of discourse. (Hilpinen [1982] offers an interesting analysis of the proposition in Peircean theory.)

Once again, however, we see that Peirce's theory is superior to modern formal linguistics in not only having a sophisticated theory of discourses, but also embedding the study of discourses and sentences into a larger, comprehensive theory of semiotics.

5.8. Peirce and Instinct

For Peirce, human "instincts" were derived from "feeding and breeding" (CP1.118, c. 1896).[28]

When Chomsky refers to abduction as "instinctive," he naturally interprets "instinct" as he uses it in his theory, which is an innate predisposition or knowledge. However, it is anachronistic to think that this is all Peirce could have meant by the term. Clearly Peirce did believe that innate knowledge in humans is plausible and likely. But in a survey of all occurrences of "instinct" in the *Collected Papers*, there are many references that are best interpreted as cultural or another form of acquired, not innate knowledge, along the lines of what I refer to as "dark matter of the mind" in D. L. Everett (2017). Here are a couple of Peircean quotes on instinct: "The study of animal and *vegetable* [emphasis mine] instinct (both of which, especially the latter throw much light on man's nature)" (CP1.266, 1902).

In discussing the role of instinct in understanding the temporal relationships implied by logical relationships (CP1.496, c. 1896), Peirce says that this "instinct may, therefore, be presumed to be an obscure perception that temporal succession is a mirror of, or framework for, logical sequence." But when Peirce here uses "obscure perception," he is not claiming that this ability is of necessity innate conceptual knowledge, but that we have an innate ability to perceive types of relations (similar to D. L. Everett's [2016] interpretation of instinct as "dark matter"). This is crucial because in Chomsky's theory instinct usually refers to innate conceptual knowledge (this is also the meaning of instinct/"core knowledge" that is found in Elizabeth Spelke's work [Spelke and Kinzler 2007]).

There is simply no unambiguous support in Peirce's work for the "instinct" that Chomsky uses and attributes to Peirce, or for Spelke's core knowledge (which goes against the definition of knowledge in pragmatism and Brandom [1998], among others, with no justification offered in Spelke's work). Moreover, Chomsky also misses the range of meanings associated with Peirce's use of the word "instinct," in his discussion reviewed earlier. Peirce nowhere made any statements that could be construed in modern terms as a "theory construction module of the brain."

What Peirce said is that our guessing is not random and that this could be guided by instinct of some form, which in his writings could be either biological or cultural. The most one can get out of this is that children have a type of solution space—either through biology or experience in language and culture—for making guesses that are "wrong most of the time [according to Peirce]." There is thus no support in Peirce for anything but the fact that children will somehow guess at what sentences mean and how they are structured. Which, of course, we all know. They learn by bits and pieces, not innate theories. (I believe this latter idea would have appalled Peirce.)

In his discussions of Peirce, Chomsky simply did not spend the time necessary to actually understand Peirce or Descartes or the Port Royal Grammarians, etc. In his "history of philosophy" work, he cherry-picks. And the result can be misleading, as it is above.

Examples of how "instinct" can be abused are found in often anachronistic expositions of other philosophers, for example, David Hume, who gave as an example of a "blind and powerful instinct of nature" that we see external objects and not images. But Jean Piaget argued that in the sensorimotor stage infants' major accomplishment is the recognition of the separateness and permanence of objects. Idealism has a problem with bumping into things. So it is not clear, superficially at least, what Hume means with this phrase. More to the point, what could Hume have meant by "instinct" in an age before genetics and theories of hereditability? He could have meant an unlearned categorization process. He could have meant unlearned conceptual knowledge (which is self-contradictory, contra Spelke). Or he could have meant tacit knowledge, regardless of the source (since "nature" can refer to experience as much as the a priori). My reading of Hume indicates that the word in his writings was vague and ambiguous in the ways just described and that it should not be appropriated qua term to support theories of nativism. It seems to have generally meant nothing more than tacit knowledge.

5.9. Linguistic Relativity and Peirce

Since Sapir and earlier, the idea that language influences our thinking has been explored and discussed heatedly by linguists (for a historical review of linguistic relativity and very careful, detailed discussion, see C. D. Everett [2016]).

Again, though, Peirce was there at the beginning. For Peirce, since language is a semiotic system and since all thinking is in signs, language could not be secondary to cognition, nor could words be secondary to, or otherwise independent from, the ideas that they express. As Peirce puts it, "it is wrong to say that a good language is important to good thought, merely; for it is the essence of it" (CP2.220, 1903).

5.10. Peirce, Language, and the Brain

Consider the following remarks by Fedorenko et al. (2020):

> To understand what you are reading now, your mind retrieves the meanings of words and constructions from a linguistic knowledge store (lexico-semantic processing) and identifies the relationships among them to construct a complex meaning (syntactic or combinatorial processing). Do these two sets of processes rely on distinct,

specialized mechanisms or, rather, share a common pool of resources? Linguistic theorizing, empirical evidence from language acquisition and processing, and computational modeling have jointly painted a picture whereby lexico-semantic and syntactic processing are deeply inter-connected and perhaps not separable. In contrast, many current proposals of the neural architecture of language continue to endorse a view whereby certain brain regions selectively support syntactic/combinatorial processing, although the locus of such "syntactic hub," and its nature, vary across proposals. Here, we searched for selectivity for syntactic over lexico-semantic processing using a powerful individual-subjects fMRI approach across three sentence comprehension paradigms that have been used in prior work to argue for such selectivity: responses to lexico-semantic vs. morpho-syntactic violations (Experiment 1); recovery from neural suppression across pairs of sentences differing in only lexical items vs. only syntactic structure (Experiment 2); and same/different meaning judgments on such sentence pairs (Experiment 3). Across experiments, both lexico-semantic and syntactic conditions elicited robust responses throughout the left fronto-temporal language network. Critically, however, no regions were more strongly engaged by syntactic than lexico-semantic processing, although some regions showed the opposite pattern. Thus, contra many current proposals of the neural architecture of language, syntactic/combinatorial processing is not separable from lexico-semantic processing at the level of brain regions—or even voxel subsets—within the language network, in line with strong integration between these two processes that has been consistently observed in behavioral and computational language research. The results further suggest that the language network may be generally more strongly concerned with meaning than syntactic form, in line with the primary function of language—to share meanings across minds.

What Evelina Fedorenko has been finding in her lab at the Massachusetts Institute of Technology's Brain and Cognitive Sciences Department over the years is that syntax seems secondary to meaning—to constructions and words. This makes perfect sense from a Peircean perspective because in Peirce's UG, the purpose of the grammar is not to produce syntactic structures per se but to support the interpretation of symbols (e.g., words and constructions). The neurolinguistics of language is thus offering preliminary support for the superiority of the predictions of a Peircean UG over a Chomskyan UG (or indeed almost any theory that takes lexical meaning as basic and syntax as derivative).

In other words, in my interpretation, Fedorenko's research shows that the brain network is a set of connections in which the principal functional nodes are symbols, not syntactic rules. This is worth exploring further from a semiotic perspective, but for now it is evidence that Peirce's theory appears to predict the findings of Fedorenko's lab about language and the brain.

5.11. Peirce, Chomsky, and Language Evolution

In D. L. Everett (2017), I argue that proposals on the evolution of human language often fail to see evidence for language in the archaeological record because they are looking for the wrong things. Thus most archaeologists are willing to count paintings, decorative ornaments, and so on as evidence for "symbolic thinking" because they fit popular understandings of the growth of culture and thought. But few studies make use of Peirce's semiotics in their analyses of the archaeological record.

Barham and Everett (2020, 1) argue that

> the origins of language can be detected one million years ago, if not earlier, in the archaeological record of *Homo erectus*. This controversial claim is based on a broad theoretical and evidential foundation with language defined as communication based on symbols rather than grammar. Peirce's theory of signs (semeiotics) underpins our analysis with its progression of signs (icon, index and symbol) used to identify artefact forms operating at the level of symbols. We draw on generalisations about the multiple social roles of technology in pre-industrial societies and on the contexts tool-use among non-human primates to argue for a deep evolutionary foundation for hominin symbol use. We conclude that symbol-based language is expressed materially in arbitrary social conventions that permeate the technologies of *Homo erectus* and its descendants, and in the extended planning involved in the caching of tools and in the early settlement of island Southeast Asia.

When we look exclusively for behavior reminiscent of modern *Homo sapiens* as evidence for the appearance of human language, rather than evidence for a full range of signs, especially symbols, we fail to understand the sophisticated behavior (boat-building, settlement divisions, tool refinement, and so on) characteristic of *Homo erectus* and dependent on the possession of language. D. L. Everett (2017) and Barham and Everett (2020) both argue that *Homo erectus* had language and that language, based on field studies of modern languages by D. L. Everett and others, need not conform to the grammar bias of the Chomskyan UG because language is fully expressive so long as it has symbols and a grammar just good enough to express them (a purely linear grammar suffices).

Moreover, because Peircean UG also applies to the signs used by nonhumans, the gap between human language and nonhuman communication is smaller than it is in the biological model of UG (which must produce a recursive grammar from nothing, via some sort of genetic saltation) and it is thus easier to comprehend that while other primates use icons and indexes (perhaps also the occasional symbol), humans (all members of the genus *Homo*) have fully expressive language as soon as they are able to create symbols (culturally) without a priori limits. Thus the Peircean view of UG, among its many advantages, also provides a richer potential explanation for the evolution of language.

6. Peirce and the Mathematical Foundations of Modern Linguistics

Tomalin (2006) provides an overview of the influence of the "formal sciences" (mathematics, logic, computer science, and the like) on the development of modern formal linguistics, an outgrowth of the pioneering work of Noam Chomsky and others. It is often and incorrectly assumed that formal theoretical research on human languages began with Chomsky. As Robert Lees erroneously states in his well-known 1957 review of Chomsky's first published book, *Syntactic Structures*: "Chomsky's book on syntactic structures is one of the first serious attempts on the part of a linguist to construct within the tradition of scientific theory-construction a comprehensive theory of language which may be understood in the same sense that a chemical, biological theory is ordinarily understood by experts in those fields" (Lees 1957, 377–378).[29]

Lees ignores Peirce's well-worked out and much more formal theory of words, propositions, and discourse (in his EGs), which together provide a comprehensive theory of language.

Tomalin's book, while well-written, knowledgeable, and highly informative, nonetheless commits major errors of omission regarding the history of the study of language, the history of the formal sciences, and the history of the classification and purposes of scientific theory. Peirce is a major, perhaps the most important, figure in the history of all of these ideas and is not mentioned by Tomalin.

The formal study of language began no later than Peirce's theory of signs (with honorable mention to Panini [Kumar 2017]), continued into his discussions of UG (1865), was developed in more detail in his speculative grammar (Bellucci 2018), and reached its pinnacle, never surpassed for most of the intervening 120 or so years, in Peirce's EGs.

Tomalin's review of the history of the formal sciences focuses on mathematics, explaining how it was foundational for formal linguistics. Yet there are surprising misses in his history. For example, he talks about Alfred North Whitehead, Bertrand Russell, Gottlob Frege, Guiseppe Peano, and Ernst Schröder, inter alia, but fails to catch the fact that behind all of these figures except Frege stood Peirce, who influenced them all profoundly. Thus, Tomalin attributes great significance to Whitehead and Russell's *Principia Mathematica* and its setting an agenda that came to influence formal sciences directly and formal linguistics indirectly. But this fails to account for Peirce's influence throughout *Principia Mathematica*. For example, although Russell and Whitehead give credit to Frege for the invention of formal logic, they use Peirce's ideas and notations (via Peirce directly as well as indirectly from Peano and Schröder [Putnam 1982]).

7. Summary: Signs, Form, Meaning, and Cognition

Semiotics studies the ways that meaning can be communicated (encoded and decoded). This interpretation of semiotics is not limited to human language since meanings are encoded and decoded throughout the universe, as Peirce argued. On the one hand, in this sense human languages are but one system in the universal communication of meaning and linguistics as a science is a branch of semiotics. On the other hand, many linguists would argue to the contrary that linguistics, far from being a subdiscipline of semiotics, is a completely independent entity, because it is governed by different principles and because language emerged from a different evolutionary trajectory than semiotics. To these researchers, semiotics connects with linguistics from time to time, but it is a distinct discipline.

Chomsky has argued for over sixty years that the best theory of language takes form to be the principal explanandum and that the explananda are independent of meaning. (Hence one sense of the label "formal linguistics," i.e., "centered on form," though most agree that the central definition of formal linguistics is "based on mathematical formalisms," a task that occupied much of Peirce's energy during his entire life). Additionally, there is, as of Chomsky's work in the twenty-first century, just one faculty that is crucial to having language, recursion. Not meaning. Not symbols. Not nouns. Not verbs. Just recursion. Therefore any discussion of the relationship between Peirce's work and modern formal linguistics must discuss the opposing theses about what is central to human language, symbols or grammar.

According to Tomalin (2006), Chomsky has been keenly interested in recursion's role in grammar at least since his interactions with Yehoshua Bar-Hillel in 1950. But Peircean recursion is much older, applicable throughout semiotics (not merely language), and, arguably, more rigorous in its theoretical development and presentation.

What follows are just a few of the points we have seen above in which Peirce's UG appears to enjoy advantages over Chomsky's:[30]

1. Data are selected and evaluated based on intuition, or what Michael Devitt (2006a and 2006b) refers to as the "Voice of Competence," for Chomsky. All interpretation and learning are inferential semiotics for Peirce. And inference generalizes more and fits cognitive science better than separate categories of intuition, which does not stand up to Peircean analysis.
2. Form, not meaning, is central to linguistic analysis and understanding for Chomsky.
3. Universal structural principles in Chomsky's theories are biological in nature, but logical in nature for Peirce. This extends the empirical reach of Peirce beyond human cognition and communication in necessary ways.
4. For Peirce, discourse, arguments, and propositions (sentences) can be recursive, but need not be. Since recursion is semiotic rather than syntactic, Peirce has ready analyses for languages like Pirahã, though there is no unproblematic analysis in Chomskyan theory.
5. Peirce predicts semiotic storage in the brain, whether specifically symbolic or potentially with images, and this is supported by Fedorenko's "language network" in the brain.
6. Peirce captures similarities between human and nonhuman communication, but most theories of linguistics, especially those that attribute linguistic principles to biology rather than logic or function, cannot.

8. Conclusion: Peirce and the Nature of Cognition

One thing that emerges from detailed examination of Peirce's work is that it underlies a good deal of work in modern linguistics and that the latter would profit from a deeper understanding of the ideas that it has used so widely, an understanding that requires a return to Peirce's own writings. Peirce's own work on evaluating theories is found in two important theses (Atkins 2018, 33):

Function Thesis: The function of conceptions is to reduce sense impressions to a unity.
Validity Thesis: A conception is valid just in case we cannot reduce the content of consciousness to unity without it.

The idea is that all humans are born with an innate UG. UG clearly satisfies the function thesis because its purpose is to unify many observations about humans' linguistic behavior under a single concept. But does UG satisfy the validity thesis? Is it crucial to understand humans' use and reducing all the observations about human language behavior to unity?

If the answer is yes, UG stands as a valid concept. If no, it does not. These theses apply to any concept, for example, linguistic rules, religious beliefs, electronic components, *Homo erectus* tools, and so on. The purpose of our reasoning is in part to deal with the phaneron—our conscious and unconscious experiences. Thus Peirce's phaneroscopy not only provides the best model for evaluating the simplicity of theories, focusing on the semantics rather than the syntax of theories, but also contributes to our understanding of individual inferential operations. A child learning their first language, for example, can be expected to regularly winnow their inferential conclusions, for example, rules of grammar learned, in light of the prerequisites of the function and validity theses. These theses do not fall exclusively within the domain of philosophers but are desirable for successful reason in science and daily life. Human reasoning must succeed by and large or we would go extinct.

By selecting its particular philosophies and objectives, any science's course of research is set for the future. This is what I call the "gyroscope issue." Two theories beginning with slightly different assumptions and goals will eventually be separated by large empirical and conceptual differences. And the wider the divergence in the initial settings of their gyroscopes, the greater the distance between the theories as time progresses. Their gyroscopes are leading them apart because they are set for different stars. We see this in the early twenty-first century in the contrast between Peirce's theory and Chomsky's, as representative of much of modern linguistics.

NOTES

1. These issues are all discussed in more detail in Everett (forthcoming).
2. Saussure (1959) divided the study of language into two parts, parole and langue, where the latter is a social concept/application of the mental component/knowledge of language. Sapir placed psychology and linguistics both in anthropology. As we will see, Peirce's view separates out the logical components of sign representations usually located in linguistics and moves them into logic. The study of actual languages and their variation he considers to be a separate field. However, languages are constrained by the logic of his UG, though his notion places these constraints outside of the nature–nurture debate.
3. Though UG has no such applications in Chomsky's theory, since from Chomsky's Cartesian perspective, nonhuman and human communication are unrelated in any significant way. But they *are* related in Peirce's theory because for Peirce nonhuman communication and human languages are all semiotic systems, subject to the logical constraints of UG (discussed in more detail in Everett [forthcoming]).
4. Pike's theory treats all human behavior, including language, as a kind of semiosis (though Pike does not use this term) in which watching a football game or speaking a sentence can both be broken down into "-emes" (e.g., phonemes and behavioremes), which include form, meaning, and referential link to object.
5. The next several paragraphs on bees paraphrase D. L. Everett (2019).
6. For an introduction to Peirce's semeiotics, see Short (2007).
7. My assertion that animals do not use symbols so far as we know might seem strange to some. So take a common example purportedly showing symbol use by animals in the wild, meerkat calls, that seem to fit the semiotic definition of indexes (but also show reasoning) (Townsend et al. 2012).
8. In D. L. Everett (forthcoming) I argue that the warning signs of many animals, for example, vervet monkeys, chimpanzees, meerkats, dolphins, and others, are indexical legisigns, rather than symbols. But even if it turned out that other animals could invent and use symbols, this would not alter the basic point that no animal other than those of the genus *Homo* invents open-ended symbols to apply to any new situation or interest.
9. S(ign) → S (one sign is interpreted by another).
10. This is quite different from the Chomskyan analytic strategy known as "pro-drop" (Chomsky 1981), in which a missing pronoun is only missing in the phonology, but present in the syntax. This is analyzed as a "parameter" in Chomsky's theory. For example, Portuguese has the pro-drop (pronominal dropping) parameter, while English does not:

    Está chovendo 'It is raining'
    It is raining vs. *Is raining

    The Portuguese example is fine, because it is pro-drop, so it does not require a subject. But the English example is ungrammatical because it does require subjects. Peirce might simply have said that the subject is known from the verb inflection in Portuguese, but cannot be so recovered from the much more impoverished verb conjugations of English. In any case, Peirce was aware of such examples and took them quite seriously.
11. Harris's transformations would simply state that the relationship between, say, *John saw Mary* and *Mary was seen by John* is a discourse relationship, where a proposition has more than one possible form to better fit discourse structure. In this case, if we want "John" as

the topic, we choose the active "transform" (or "allosentence" in some theories), and if we want "Mary" as topic, we choose the passive.
12. It should be noted that hypostatic abstraction in itself, however important as a mental operation, is not a major grammatical operation or device in most of the world's languages.
13. Moreover, Chomsky has never had a single theory last more than a few years. His most recent program, minimalism, he has been careful to call a program rather than a theory. One could respond that advocacy for a biological UG just is Chomsky's theory, but as the debate over recursion has shown, there is little if any substance (or science) to his UG. It is not recursion (D. L. Everett 2005, 2017; among many others), but that is what he claims it is, depending on how one construes his phrase "Narrow Faculty of Language."
14. It is also in harmony with Meillet (1903, 407) wrote "que chaque langue forme un systeme on tout se tient."
15. In the academic climate of Chomsky's early years as a junior fellow at Harvard (when he developed the basics of his transformational generative grammar), major concerns involved the proper analysis of propositions and sentences and how such analyses could be incorporated into computer science. His theory reflects these concerns and has never really moved beyond them. Peirce, however, always saw propositions as constituents of larger units, that is, arguments, including what we would call discourse in the early twenty-first century. For example, the shell structure hypothesis of Larson (2017) makes a series of valuable predictions within Chomsky's theory, but it is largely ignored outside of the literature of that theory. The reason is not because the other theories are inferior but rather that this kind of form-only analysis is less desirable for theories in which the principal causative power lies in meaning rather than form.
16. Peirce allows that indexes, by simply pointing out an object in the real or imagined world, may halt this recursive process or begin it. Infinite regress is thus avoided. In general, however, there is no need to restrict "infinite semiosis."
17. Peirce was a hard-working scientist who left copious documentation of his working methods, such as his analysis of Tagalog grammar; see D. L. Everett (forthcoming) for analysis.
18. Harman (1973) argues, as Peirce would, that inferences can be fast, instantaneous perhaps, and need not be conscious.
19. By the expression "modulo culture" I mean that cultures have different rankings of time values and their relevance (see D. L. Everett 2017). Thus their understandings of what a "long" time or a "distant" time is will vary, among other aspects of the mapping between temporal ontology and linguistic meaning.
20. Compositionality might seem to be un-inference-like to some, since it appears to be read off the structures of the sentences or other units it is assembling for semantic interpretation. However, all inference is sensitive to certain types of data. Compositionality can be thought of then as that form of inference that interprets signs as they are assembled by the grammar, but that is not necessarily monotonic—it can be overriden by new contextual information. So it infers from syntactic structures, but as a part of the more general forms of inference we have been discussing, since it can be overriden by contextual features, real-world knowledge, and so on. Calling the form-based inference "compositionality" and the contextual inference "pragmatics" obscures the fact that both are forms of inference that use the same processes of abduction, deduction, and induction, though their inputs might

begin differently (one with words and structure-building, the other with extralinguistic context, but both -ductions that are underlyingly the same process).

21. From this Atkins goes on (2018, 72ff.) to derive Peirce's phenomenology (phaneroscopy) of "firstness, secondness, and thirdness." Atkins (60ff.) argues that the reduction thesis is closely related to Peirce's EGs: "These discoveries were made possible by—and arguably only make sense in the context of—Peirce's Existential Graphs" (72).
22. This issue of tritransitives is further discussed competently in this piece written for a general audience: https://slate.com/human-interest/2014/04/does-english-have-any-tritransitive-verbs.html.
23. These are both idealizations. Our understanding of "phonetics" seen, for example, in something so erstwhile objective or etic as the international phonetic alphabet, is shaped by our emic perspectives and most etic categories are already idealized in cultural ways. So there is no truly objective vantage point, just ones less contaminated in ways we know of.
24. The standard convention in linguistics is that //s are used to enclose phonemic sounds and []s to enclose phonetic sounds.
25. For generative phonology, phonemics is not a theoretically recognized level of analysis. Nothing hangs on this debate here, however. So where I have written "phonemics," one can read "phonology" without any change in intended meaning.
26. Maier states:

"This paper explores the relation between the syntax of clausal embedding and the ability to represent what others are saying, thinking etc. I'm using the Pirahã controversy as a lens through which to study this relationship because, supposedly, the Pirahã language has no clausal embedding and hence no analogue of English indirect discourse ('Katy said/thought/dreamed that she was rich'). I first show how hearsay evidentiality and direct quotation, both of which are attested in Pirahã, differ semantically from each other and from indirect discourse. However, together, these two arguably embedding-free report strategies could cover two of the most common uses of indirect discourse in English, viz. efficient communication that keeps track of speaker's evidential sources through a not-at-issue information channel, and vivid description of speech and thought in narratives. I also argue that reporting in general is best understood as a discourse phenomenon, only optionally encoded in the grammar. Spelling this out in a formally explicit and independently motivated general model of discourse structure and coherence relations (including a non-veridical relation of Attribution) we actually derive Dan Everett's own diagnosis of the situation, viz. that "there can be recursive discourses in the absence of recursive sentences.""

27. We might call this "semiotic minimalism" in which, in accordance with Peirce, semiotics is basic, grammar is secondary, though I realize this is not at all what Murphy intends.
28. I would have preferred the alliterative "fucking and feeding," but that would have been even more offensive in Peirce's day.
29. Lees was Chomsky's PhD student. It is questionable whether publishing such a review is even in good taste, given the personal connection.
30. The principal developers of construction grammar were the late Charles Fillmore and his colleague at the University of California at Berkeley, Paul Kay. Currently, among the many names associated with this theory, perhaps the two most prominent are that of Adele Goldberg (Princeton) and William Croft (University of New Mexico).

References

Anderson, Benedict. 2016. "Frameworks of Comparison: Benedict Anderson Reflects on His Intellectual Formation." *London Review of Books* 38, no. 2 (January 21): 15–18.

Atkins, Richard Kenneth. 2018. *Charles S. Peirce's Phenomenology: Analysis and Consciousness*. Oxford: Oxford University Press.

Barham, Larry, and Daniel Everett. 2020. "Semeiotics and the Origin of Language in the Lower Paleolithic." *Journal of Archaeological Method and Theory* 28: 535–579.

Bellucci, Francesco. 2018. *Peirce's Speculative Grammar: Logic as Semeiotics*. New York: Routledge.

Bellucci, Francesco. 2021. "Peirce on Symbols." *Archiv für Geschichte der Philosophie* 103, no. 1: 169–188.

Boas, Franz, ed. 2002. *Handbook of American Indian languages*. Bristol, UK.: Thoemmes.

Boyd, Kenneth. 2016. "Peirce on Assertion, Speech Acts, and Taking Responsibility." *Transactions of the Charles S. Peirce Society* 52, no. 1 (Winter): 21–46.

Bradbury, Jack W., and Sandra L. Vehrencamp. 2011. *Principles of Animal Communication*. New York: Oxford University Press.

Brandom, Robert B. 1983. "Asserting." *Noûs* 17, no. 4: 637–650.

Brandom, Robert B. 1998. *Making It Explicit: Reasoning, Representing, and Discursive Commitment*. Cambridge, MA: Harvard University Press.

Burch, R. 2001. "Charles Sanders Peirce." In *Stanford Encyclopedia of Philosophy*, edited by Edward N. Zalta.

Chomsky, Noam. 1957. *Syntactic Structures*. The Hague: Mouton.

Chomsky, Noam. 1965. *Aspects of the Theory of Syntax*. Cambridge, MA.: MIT Press.

Chomsky, Noam. 1980. *Rules and Representations*. New York: Columbia University Press.

Chomsky, Noam. 1981. *Lectures on Government and Binding: The Pisa Lectures*. Dordrecht: Foris Publications.

Chomsky, Noam 1986. *Knowledge of Language: Its Nature, Origin and Use*. New York: Praeger.

Chomsky, Noam. 1994. "Interview with Noam Chomsky." In Michael C. Haley and Ronald F. Lunsford, eds. *Noam Chomsky*. New York: Twayne, 182–196.

Chomsky, Noam. 1995. *A Minimalist Program*. Cambridge, MA: MIT Press.

Chomsky, Noam. 2006. *Language and Mind*. New York: Cambridge University Press.

Covington, Michael A. 1984. *Syntactic Theory in the High Middle Ages*. Cambridge: Cambridge University Press.

Culicover, Peter W., and Ray Jackendoff. 2005. *Simpler Syntax*. New York: Oxford University Press.

Deacon, Terrence W. 1997. *The Symbolic Species: The Co-evolution of Language and the Brain*. New York: Norton.

Devitt, Michael. 2006a. *Ignorance of Language*. New York: Oxford University Press.

Devitt, Michael. 2006b. "Intuitions in Linguistics." *British Journal for the Philosophy of Science*. 57, 481–513.

Didion, Joan. 2021. *Let Me Tell You What I Mean*. New York: Knopf.

Duhem, Pierre. 1954. *The Aim and Structure of Physical Theory*. Princeton, NJ: Princeton University Press.

Everett, Caleb D. 2016. *Linguistic Relativity*. The Hague De Gruyter Mouton.

Everett, Daniel L. 1986. "Pirahã." In Desmond Derbyshire and Geoffrey Pullum, eds., *Handbook of Amazonian Languages*. Berlin: Mouton DeGruyter, I:200–326.

Everett, Daniel L. 1996. *Why There Are No Clitics*. Arlington, TX: SIL-UTA.

Everett, Daniel L. 2005. "Cultural Constraints on Grammar and Cognition in Pirahã: Another Look at the Design Features of Human Language." *Current Anthropology* 76, 621–646.

Everett, Daniel L. 2016. *Dark Matter of the Mind: The Culturally Articulated Unconscious*. Chicago: University of Chicago Press.

Everett, Daniel L. 2017. *How Language Began. The Story of Humanity's Greatest Invention*. New York: Liveright.

Everett, Daniel L. 2019. "The American Aristotle." *Aeon Magazine*. August 15. https://aeon.co/essays/charles-sanders-peirce-was-americas-greatest-thinker

Everett, Daniel L. Forthcoming. *Peircean Linguistics: A Chapter in the History of Realist Thought*. Oxford: Oxford University Press.

Everett, Daniel L., and Edward Gibson. 2019. "Review of *Recursion across Domains* by Luiz Amaral et al." *Language* 95, no. 4: 777–790.

Fedorenko, Evelina, Idan Asher Blank, Matthew Siegelman, and Zachary Mineroff. 2020. "Lack of Selectivity for Syntax Relative to Word Meanings throughout the Language Network." *Cognition* 203: 1–24.

Fedorenko, Evelina, and Sharon L. Thompson-Schill. 2014. "Reworking the Language Network. *Trends in Cognitive Science* 18 no. 3: 120–126.

Fodor, Jerry A. 1980. *The Language of Thought*. Cambridge, MA: Harvard University Press.

Fodor, Jerry A. 1981. *Representations: Philosophical Essays on the Foundations of Cognitive Science*. Cambridge, MA: MIT Press.

Font, Josep Maria, and Ramón Jansana. 1996. *A General Algebraic Semantics for Sentential Logics*. New York: Springer-Verlag.

Frege, Gottlob. 1884. *Die Grundlagen der Arithmetik*. Breslau, Germany: Verlag von Wilhelm Koebner.

Futrell, Richard, Laura Stearns, Steven T. Piantadosi, Daniel Everett, and Edward Gibson. 2016, March 2. "A Corpus Investigation of Syntactic Embedding in Pirahã." *PLoS ONE* 11(3): e0145289.

Gibson, Edward A. F., and Evelina Fedorenko. 2013. "The Need for Quantitative Methods in Syntax and Semantics Research." *Language and Cognitive Processes* 28: 88–124.

Goldberg, Adele. 1995. *Constructions: A Construction Grammar Approach to Argument Structure*. Chicago: University of Chicago Press.

Grimes, Joseph E. 1975. *The Thread of Discourse*. The Hague: Mouton.

Harding, Sandra G. (ed.). 1976. *Can Theories be Refuted? Essays on the Duhem–Quine Thesis*. New York: Reidel.

Harman, Gilbert. 1973. *Thought*. Princeton, NJ: Princeton University Press.

Harris, Zellig. 1951. *Methods in Structural Linguistics*. Chicago: University of Chicago Press.

Hauser, Mark, Noam Chomsky, and Tecumseh Fitch. 2002. "The faculty of language: What Is It, Who Has It, and How Did It Evolve?" *Science* 298 (5598): 1569–1579.

Hilpinen, Risto. 1982. "On C. S. Peirce's Theory of the Proposition: Peirce as a Precursor of Game-Theoretical Semantics." *The Monist* 65 no. 2: 182–188.

Hopper, Paul, and Sandra Thompson. 1980. "Transitivity in Grammar and Discourse." *Language*, 56, no. 2: 251–299.

Howard, S. R., A. Avarguès-Weber J. E. Garcia, A. D. Greentree, and A. G. Dyer. 2019. "Symbolic Representation of Numerosity by Honeybees (*Apis mellifera*): Matching Characters to Small Quantities." *Proceedings of the Royal Society B: Biological Sciences*, 286: 20190238.

Ivanova, A. A., Z. Mineroff, V. Zimmerer, N. Kanwisher, R. Varley, and E. Fedorenko. 2021. "The Language Network Is Recruited but Not Required for Nonverbal Event Semantics." *Neurobiology of Language* 2 no. 2: 176–201.

Jakobson, Roman. 1985. "A Few Remarks on Peirce, Pathfinder in the Science of Language." In Roman Jakobson, ed., *Selected Writings*. The Hague: Mouton, 7:248–253.

Kamp, Hans, and Uwe Reyle. 1993. *From Discourse to Logic: Introduction to Modeltheoretic Semantics of Natural Language, Formal Logic, and Discourse Representation Theory*. Boston: Springer.

Kumar, Vinod. 2017. *The Astadhyayi of Panini—A Treatise on Sanskrit Grammar*. Delhi: Parimal.

Larson, Richard. 2017. *On Shell Structure*. London: Routledge.

Larson, Richard, and Gabriel Segal. 1995. *Knowledge of Meaning: Introduction to Semantic Theory*. Cambridge, MA: MIT Press.

Lasnik, Howard, Juan Uriagereka, and Cedrik Boeckx. 2005. *A Course in Minimalist Syntax: Foundations and Prospects*. New York: Wiley.

Lees, Robert B. 1957. "*Syntactic Structures*" by Noam Chomsky. The Hague, Mouton.

Levin, Michael. 1983. "Explanation and Prediction in Grammar (and Semantics)." In Peter A. French, Theodore E. Uehling Jr., and Howard Wettstein, eds., *Contemporary Perspectives in the Philosophy of Language*. Minneapolis, MN: University of Minnesota Press, 179–188.

Longacre, Robert E. 1996. *The Grammar of Discourse*. New York, Plenum Press.

Maier, Ernst. 2021. "Reporting with Clausal Embedding and without: Another Look at the Pirahã Controversy." https://ling.auf.net/lingbuzz/006292.

Meillet, Antoine. 1903. *Introduction à l'étude comparative des langues indo-européennes*. Paris: Hachette.

Murphy, Elliot. 2015, June 3. "Labels, Cognomes, and Cyclic Computation: An Ethological Perspective." *Frontiers in Psychology* 6. Article 715.

Nöth, Winfried. 2000. "Charles Sanders Peirce, Pathfinder in Linguistics." In The Commens Encyclopedia: The Digital Encyclopedia of Peirce Studies. http://www.commens.org/encyclopedia.

Perniss, Pamela, Robin L. Thompson, and Gabriella Vigliocco. 2010. "Iconicity as a General Property of Language: Evidence from Spoken and Signed Languages." *Frontiers in Psychology* 1: Article 227.

Peirce, Charles S. 1931–1958. *The Collected Papers of Charles Sanders Peirce*. 8 vols. Vols. 1–6 edited by Charles Hartshorne and Paul Weiss. Vols. 7–8 edited by Arthur W. Burks. Cambridge, MA: Harvard University Press. (Referred to as CP.)

Peirce, Charles S. 1992–1998. *The Essential Peirce: Selected Philosophical Writings*. 2 vols. Vol. 1 edited by Nathan Houser and Christian Kloesel. Vol. 2 edited by the Peirce Edition Project. Bloomington: Indiana University Press. (Referred to as EP.)

Pietarinen, Ahti. 2005. "Compositionality, Relevance, and Peirce's Logic of Existential Graphs." *Axiomathes* 15: 513–540.

Pike, Kenneth L. 1967. *Language in Relation to a Unified Theory of the Structure of Human Behavior*. The Hague: Mouton.

Pike, Kenneth L., and Evelyn G. Pike. 1976. *Grammatical Analysis*. Dallas, TX: SIL International.

Pullum, Geoffrey Keith. 2020. "Theorizing About the Syntax of Human Language: A Radical Alternative to Generative Formalisms." *Cadernos de Linguística* 1, vol. 1: 1–33.

Putnam, Hilary. 1982. "Peirce the Logician." *Historia Mathematica* 9: 290–301.

Quine, W. V. O. 1951. "Two Dogmas of Empiricism." *Philosophical Review* 60, vol. 1: 20–43.

Ronat, Mitsou. 1976. "Grammaire et discours." In *Méthodes en grammaire française*, edited by Jean-Claude Chevalier and Maurice Gross. Paris: Klincksieck, 158–173.

Rosier, Irène. 1983. *La Grammaire Speculative des Modistes*. Lille: Presses Universitaires de Lille.

Sakel, Jeanette, and Daniel Everett. 2011. *Linguistic Field Work: A Student Guide*. Cambridge: Cambridge University Press.

Samuels Bridget, D., Marc Hauser, and Cedric Boeckx. 2016. "Looking for UG in Animals: A Case Study in Phonology." In Ian Roberts, ed., *The Oxford Handbook of Universal Grammar*. New York: Oxford University Press, 527–546.

Sapir, Edward. 1921. *Language*. New York: Harcourt, Brace, Jovanovich.

Saussure, Ferdinand de. 1959. *Course in General Linguistics*. Eds. Charles Bally and Albert Sechehaye. Trans. Wade Baskin. New York: Philosophical Society.

Schindler, Samuel, Anna Drożdżowicz, and Karen Brøker, eds. 2020. *Linguistic Intuitions*. New York: Oxford University Press.

Schwitzgebel, E. 2010. "Introspection." *Stanford Encyclopedia of Philosophy*, edited by Edward N. Zalta.

Searle, John. 1980. "Minds, Brains, and Programs." *Behavioral and Brain Sciences* 3 vol. 3: 417–457.

Shapiro, Michael. 1983. *A Sense of Grammar: Language as Semeiotic*. Bloomington: Indiana University Press.

Short, T. L. 2007. *Peirce's Theory of Signs*. New York: Cambridge University Press.

Silverstein, 2003. "Indexical Order and the Dialectics of Sociolinguistic Life." *Language & Communication* 23.3/4, 193–229.

Simard, Suzanne. 2021. *Finding the Mother Tree: Discovering the Wisdom of the Forest*. New York: Knopf.

Sowa, John. 2013. "From Existential Graphs to Conceptual Graphs." *International Journal of Conceptual Structures and Smart Applications* 1, 39–72.

Spelke, Elizabeth S., and Katherine D. Kinzler. 2007. "Core Knowledge." *Developmental Science* 10 vol. 1: 89–96.

Stjernfelt, Frederik. 2011. *Diagrammatology: An Investigation on the Borderlines of Phenomenology, Ontology, and Semeiotics*. New York: Springer.

Szabó, Zoltán Gendler. 2000. *Problems of Compositionality*. New York: Routledge.

Thomason, Sarah, and Everett, Daniel. 1993. "Transitivity in Flathead." In William Seaburg, ed., *Papers for the 28th International Conference on Salish and Neighboring Languages*, August 19–21, 1993. Seattle: University of Washington, 317–343.

Tomalin, Marcus. 2006. *Linguistics and the Formal Sciences: The Origins of Generative Grammar*. New York: Cambridge University Press.

Townsend, Simon W., Maria Rasmussen, Tim Clutton-Brock, and Marta B. Manser. 2012. "Flexible Alarm Calling in Meerkats: The Role of the Social Environment and Predation Urgency." *Behavioral Ecology* 23 no. 6: 1360–1364.

Van Valin, Robert D. 2007. "The Role and Reference Grammar Analysis of Three-Place Predicates." Unpublished MS. State University of New York. Buffalo.

Van Valin, Robert D., and Randy J. LaPolla. 1998. *Syntax: Structure, Meaning, and Function*. New York: Cambridge University Press.

Index

For the benefit of digital users, indexed terms that span two pages (e.g., 52–53) may, on occasion, appear on only one of those pages.

A

abduction, 169–70, 211, 377, 483, 587–88, 612–13
 discovery, 213–15
 in historiography, 559–62
 justification, 217–20
 hypothesis, 212–13, 396, 483, 537
 pursuit, 215–17
 See also deduction; induction; inference; perception
adequacy, pragmatistic, 369, 376
admirable, the, 101–2, 115–16, 124–25
adorable, 357–58
aesthetic goodness, 115–16
aesthetics, 100–1, 111–12, 142–43
 See also esthetics
agapasm, 150, 151, 587–88
agape, 148, 153
 cosmological power, 149, 150
 ethical-political power, 150–51
 See also *eros*; love
agapism, 131, 425, 434, 435–36, 480–81
Agassiz, Louis, 5, 6, 7–8, 9, 588
Alcott, Brandon, 6, 7
Alcott, Louisa May, 6, 7
Almeder, Robert, 458
Ambrosio, Chiara, 555–56
American Association for the Advancement of Science, 4
American Civil War, xviii
analytic philosophy, 236–37, 256
anancasm, 150, 587–88
Anderson, Douglas, 152–53, 155, 482–83
animal communication, 603
anti-Cartesianism, 470, 516
anti-cocksurism, 337–38
Antikythera mechanism, 519–21

anti-realism, 468, 499
anti-rationalism, 358
anti-representationalism, 459
apagoge, 211
Apel, Karl-Otto, 139
Apellicon, 561
Appleton, William Henry, xix, 31
Arago, François, 35
archeology, 561
Arengas, Gustavo, 301–3
argument, 84–85, 86, 168, 226, 227–28, 236
Arisbe, 12–14, 19, 22, 26–27, 38, 54, 308
 Preston Tuttle interviews, 17–18
Aristotle, 140–41, 156, 174, 429, 555
 abduction, 211
 categories, 65, 434
 induction, 208, 211
 intention, 135, 137
 metaphysics, 424, 429
 truth, 341–42
art, theory of, 113–14
Arudpragasam, Anuk, 332
assertion
 commitment view of, 626
 sheet of, 231–32, 249–50, 251, 306–7, 309
 theory of, 236, 536, 538
association, types of, 86–87
Atkins, Richard Kenneth, 482, 484–85

B

bacteriology, 594
Bader, Ralf, 446
Baeyer, Johann Jacob, 32, 33
Bain, Alexander, 28, 135
 on belief, 134–35, 517
Baldwin, James Mark, xxxii

Barbara syllogism, 208
Baumgarten, Alexander, 111–12
Bayes theorem, 218
Bayesian epistemology, 169–70
beautiful, the, 113–14
Beauvoir, Simone de, 502
belief, fixation of, 387, 412–13, 424–25, 460, 527–28
Bell, John L., 289, 290
Bentham, 61
Bergman, Mats, 142
Berkeley, George, 81
Bernstein, Richard, 84, 330–31, 531, 532–33
binarism, sexual, 501, 510–11
binary connectives, 304
biology, 585, 586
biosemiotics, 585, 587, 593
Biot, Jean-Baptiste, 34–35
Bohr, Niels, 426
Boltzmann, Ludwig, 525–26
Bond, William, 7–8
Boole, George, 193–94, 197–98, 235, 243–44
Boolean algebra, 49, 197, 249, 278–79
Bowen, Francis, 369
Brady, Geraldine, 307–8
Braga, Lucia Santaella, 589–90
Brandom, Robert, 140, 330–31, 625–16
Bratman, Michael, 135–36
British empiricists, 78–79, 81, 330–31
Bromberg-Martin, Ethan, 524
Brouwer fixed-point theorem, 295
Brunner, Émile, 35
Burch, Robert, 303–4, 307–8
buried secrets objection, 464, 469–70
Burks, Arthur, xxxi–xxxii

C

Campos, Daniel, 221
Cannon, Annie Jump, 7–8
Cantor, Georg, 305
Capps, John, 470–71
Carnegie Foundation, 12, 392
Carroll, Lewis, 279
Carroll, Sean, 521–22
Cartesianism, xix, 149, 327, 346, 459
Carus, Paul, xix, 13–14
categorics, xxi–xxii
categories, 61–62, 99, 376–77, 415–16, 434, 506
    formal *vs* material, 63, 72
    in phaneroscopy, 63, 72, 83–84
    See also Aristotle; firstness; Kant; secondness; thirdness
Cauchy, Augustin-Louis, 325
Cayley, Arthur, 51
cenoscopy, 61, 69, 98–99
    See also phaneroscopy
census theorem, 303
Century Club, 54
Century Company, xxxii
Century Dictionary (CD), 54, 78
chance, 149–50, 434, 435–37, 480–81, 506–7, 591
    See also tychasm
Chaney, Henry J., 36–37
Chinese room experiment, 604–5
Chomsky, Noam, 21, 602–3, 606, 609–10
Christianity, 154–55, 484–85
Cicero, 211
Clanton, J. Caleb, 483
classification, natural, 588
clearness, three grades of, 341–42, 344, 368–69, 376, 466
Cleveland, Grover, 53
Clifford, William Kingdom, 10–11, 28–29, 32, 45–46, 47, 263–64, 329
cocaine use, 50
cognition, theory of, 389, 390, 429
Colapietro, Vincent, 161
Colonna, B. A., 53
Colston, Edward, 158
Coltheart, Max, 215–16
combinatorics, 303–4
common sense, 131
communicative action, theory of, 538
compositionality, 617–18, 619–20
Comte, Auguste, 211, 533–34, 556
conditional, 200, 248–49
    material, 180–81, 246–47
    pragmatism, 136–37, 300, 370, 372–73
    quantified, 240–41
    subjunctive, 463, 464
    See also idealism
consciousness, 77, 121–22, 588
    stream of, 61–62
    temporal structure of, 448–49, 451

conservatism, 130–31
constructivism, 181
continuity, xviii–xix, 290, 305–6, 448
   See also infinitesimals; synechism
Conway, John, 289, 290, 305
Cooke, Josiah Parson, 542
copula, 226, 230
   functions of, 69
   relative, 248–50
Corrington, Robert S., 486–87
   See also ecstatic naturalism
corollarial reasoning, 198–99
cosmology
   evolutionary, 149, 415–16, 417–18, 434, 480–81
   religious, 480–81
Cristalli, Claudia, 264
critic, 130, 195–96, 340, 602
critical commonsense beliefs, 156–57
critical commonsensism, 157, 158, 400–1, 482
Cuddeback letter book, xxxv
Curd, Martin, 215
Curie, Marie, 434
curves, method of, 266, 268
cybernetics, 296, 304, 591
cyclosis, 303

D

Dancy, Jonathan, 204
Darwin, Charles, 80, 329, 340, 587–88, 589–90
Darwinism, 587–88, 594
   See also social Darwinism
Daston, Lorraine, 262–63, 265–66, 271–72
Davies, Martin, 215–16
Deacon, Terrence, 585–86, 591
de Belalcázar, Sebastián, 158
de Borda, Jean-Charles, 34–35
Dedekind, Richard, 174, 182
deduction, xvii–xviii, 198–99, 208, 209, 221–22, 253
   See also abduction; induction
Deely, John, 485–86, 591
deflationism. See truth
deliberation, 104, 194–95, 338, 339, 353, 355–56
   self-control, 340, 356
deliberative agency, 352

Delisle, Leopold, 35
De Morgan, August, 10–11, 28–29, 44–45, 193–94, 235
Dennett, Daniel, 63, 79–80, 89, 389
de Regt, Henk, 525–27
Descartes, René, 171–72, 178, 328, 368–69, 390, 459, 542–43, 614, 628
desire, 134
determinism, 425
Deuser, Hermann, 485–86, 488
development teleology, 355–56
Devitt, Michael, 615–16
de Waal, Cornelis ("Kees"), 56, 78–79, 132, 162–63n.12, 184, 403n.29, 470, 542, 587–88
Dewey, John, 8, 54–55, 142–43, 156, 322–23, 329, 332, 558
   aesthetics, 112–14
   education, 531, 542–44
   pragmatism, 322
   student of Peirce, 49
diagrammatic thinking, 261, 270–71
dialectical materialism, 150
dicisign, 228, 229–30
Dickinson, Emily, 6, 7–8
Didion, Joan, 608
DiLeo, Jeffrey, 196–97
Dirac, Paul 426
discourse analysis, 626–27
discourse ethics, 139
discourse representation theory, 611–12
discovery, logic of, 558
distinctio, 430
doubt-belief theory, 124, 321, 326–28, 369–70, 376, 460, 525
   See also belief; paper doubt
Douven, Igor, 220
Downard, Jeffrey, 304
Doyle, Arthur Conan, 214
Drake, Charles, 29
Dreger, Alice Domurat, 503
dualism, 80, 122, 443
Duhem, Pierre, 611
Duns Scotus, 78–79, 196–97, 423–24, 429–31
Dupin, C. Auguste, 214
dynamic object, 87

E

Eco, Umberto, 585
economy of research, 344
ecstatic naturalism, 486–88
Edmundts, Dina, 446
education, philosophy of, 531
edusemiotics, 531, 542–44
Eisele, Carolyn, xxxiii, 264–65
Eisele's law, 264–65
ekthesis, 198–99
Elgin, Kate, 330–31
El-Hani, Charbel, 592
Eliot, Charles, 9–10, 16, 44–45, 55
Ellis, Helen Huntington Peirce, 4
Emerson, Ralph Waldo, 6–7, 8–9, 331–32
   American Scholar, 43–44
   anticipates pragmatism, 8
Emmeche, Claus, 592
empathy, 159
empiricism, 78–79, 89, 342, 384–401
   radical, 91n.25, 315–16
Enderton, Herbert, 256
ens quantum ens, 424, 429
entia rationes, 89, 264
epagoge, 211
epigenetics, 592
eros, 112, 152–53
esthetics, 94–96, 99, 100–4, 115–16, 118, 337
Etchemendy, John, 244–45
ethics, 95–96, 98, 100, 104–5, 108–9, 113–16, 132–33, 337
   conceptual, 380
   experimental, 162–63n.12
   grammar of, 130, 133–36, 144
   melioristic, 142
   religious, 490
   of terminology, 78, 220–21, 574–75
   See also esthetics; inquiry; logic; science (normative)
Euclid, 198–99, 303–4
eudaimonia, 137, 160
eugenics, 553
Euler diagram, 180
European travels, xviii–xix, 10, 26, 44–45
evolution, 131–32, 554, 587–88, 589–90, 592, 594
   of language, 629–30
   by love, 150
   See also cosmology; love; metaphysics
excluded middle, law of, 291
   discontinuity, 293
existence, 81, 414–17, 435, 443
   unintelligible, 433–34
   See also reality
existential graphs. *See* graphs
experience, 78, 357–58
   categories of, 97
   lived, 87–88
experimentalism, 357–58
extension, 83, 227, 229–30
extensionalism, 448, 450, 452–53
externality, 410

F

fact, 336, 340
faith, 350
fallibilism, 131, 173, 183, 201–2, 221–22, 337–38, 470, 471, 532–33, 534–35, 594
   contrite, 337–38, 346
Fann, K. T., 213
Farquhar, Henry, 31
Fausto-Sterling, Anne, 19
Favareau, Donald, 591
Fay, Amy, 29, 32
Fay, Harriet Melusina ("Zina"), xix, 4, 10–11, 28–29, 32, 36, 479
   divorce, 45, 51
Faye, Hervé, 35
Feder, Ellen, 499–500
Fedorenko, Evelina, 628–29
feeling
   analysis of, CP4P31
   quality of, 112
Fernández, Eliseo, 591, 592, 593
Feynman, Richard, 526
fictional (fictive), 409–11, 415–16, 417
firstness, 66–67, 70–71, 83–84, 101, 112, 141, 177–78, 399, 434, 482–83, 506–7, 569–70, 572
   See also icon; secondness; thirdness
Fisch, Max H., xvii, 27, 200, 551
fixed point theorem, 304
Fodor, Jerry, 608
foundationalism, 386, 387, 393, 532–33

Frege, Gottlob, 21, 43, 174, 181, 199, 230, 236–37, 617, 631
   Begriffsschrift, 193–94, 227, 256
   normativity of logic (anti-psychologism), 203
   trees, 283–86
Frohlich, Donald, 594
Froissy, Juliette Annette. *See* Juliette Peirce
Fuller, Margaret, 6, 7

G

Gabbay, Dov, 216
Galileo Galilei, 219
Galison, Peter, 262–63, 271–72
Gallie, W. B., 350–51, 485
game-theoretic semantics, 255
game theory, 308
Gay, John, 588
Gay-Lussac Law, 526
Geddes, Patrick, 500–1
gender, nature of, 500
genealogy of the sciences, 557, 558
generals, 143, 385, 393–95, 411, 432–34
   reality of, 81, 88–89, 155, 318–19, 381, 411, 416–17
Gilman, Daniel Coit, 9–10, 12, 16, 46–47, 51–52, 55
god, 8–9, 359–60, 433–34, 435–36
   common-sense belief, 482
   reality of, 417, 482, 483, 486–87
Gödel, Kurt, 296
Gödel numbering, 296
Godfrey-Smith, Peter, 330–31
Goldfarb, Warren, 199
Goodman, Nelson, 169
Gopnik, Allison, 523
Goudge, Thomas, 485
grammar. *See* speculative grammar; universal grammar
graphist, 255, 484
graphs, 263–64
   entitative, 245–50, 251
   existential, 235–36, 248, 249–53, 261–62, 280–81, 294, 306–9, 376–77, 484, 487, 611–12
      alpha, 249, 280, 307–8
      beta, 65, 242, 252, 287–89, 306–8
      delta, 254
      gamma, 249, 254–55, 264–65, 301, 306–8
   tinctures, 254–55
   See also protographs
Gratry, Auguste Joseph Alphonse, 178–79
gravitation research, xviii–xix, 30–31, 33
Green, Nicholas St John, 28

H

Haack, Susan, 170, 201–2, 330–31, 361
Habermas, Jürgen, 139, 537–40
habit, 97, 103–4, 194–95, 372, 378–79, 506, 517, 541–42, 594
   in cosmology, 149–50, 151–52, 589, 594
   formation of, 107–8, 118, 149–50, 374, 434, 483–84
   See also doubt-belief theory
Hacking, Ian, 183
haecceitas, 431, 432–33
haecceitism, 196–97
Haila, Yrjö, 590
Hall, G. Stanley, 13–14, 47, 48
Hankins, Thomas, 263–64
Hanson, Norwood Russell, 213–14
Harman, Gilbert, 219
Hartshorne, Charles, xxxi–xxxii, 485
Hartley, David, 588
Hartmann, Eduard, 588
Harvard College Observatory, xviii
Harvard University, xviii, 9–10, 16, 43–44, 319
Hasse diagram, 300
Hausman, Carl, 82, 152
Havenel, Jérôme, 303
Hawthorne, Nathaniel, 6, 7
Hedge, Levi, 331–32
Hegel, Georg Wilhelm Friedrich, 49, 111–12, 150, 185
Hegeler, Edward C., 13
Heisenberg, Werner, 426
   uncertainty principle, 427–28
Hempel, Carl G., 209, 210, 218
Henle, James M., 289
Herron, Timothy, 305
Herschel, John, 263–64, 265–66
Heyting algebra, 292–93, 301–3
Higuera, Claudio Rodrîguez, 594

Hilbert-type logic, 306-7
Hintikka, Jaakko, 199, 215
Hipparchus, 559
historical-critical analysis, 561
historico-critical school, 561-62
historiography, 560
Hobbes, Thomas, 78-79, 141, 156
Hoffmeyer, Jesper, 585-86, 591
Holmes Jr., Oliver Wendell, 46
Holmes, Sherlock, 214
Holt, Edwin, 8
Hookway, Christopher, 196-97, 317, 372-73, 466-68, 483-84, 540
Horsford, Eben, 542
Hull, Kathleen, 484
Hulswit, Menno, 592
humanism, 315-16
human rights, 157
humble argument, 482-83
Hume, David, 78-79, 134, 169, 628
Huntington, Frederic Dan, 479
Husserl, Edmund, 21, 232-33
Hutcheson, Francis, 130
Huxley, Thomas Henry, 329
hypoicon, 567-68, 569, 583
   See also icon
hypostatic abstraction, 264-65, 608
hypothesis, 209

I

Ibáñez de Ibero, Carlos, 32
icon, 84-85, 229-30, 270-71, 397, 536, 568, 573, 590, 601, 606
   See also hypoicon; index; symbol
iconoscopy, 105
idealism, 450-51, 468, 628
   conditional, 412-13
   Kant's refutation of, 442-47
   Peirce's refutation of, 450-53
   problematic, 443, 447
   transcendental, 7, 9
ideals, 94, 101, 105-6, 107-8, 118, 155-56, 160, 381
idioscopy, 61, 99
il lume naturale. *See* natural light
illation, sign of, 278-80
imaginative rehearsal, 106

immediate perception, doctrine of, 397
indeterminacy, 134, 425, 434, 436-37, 470, 471, 593
index, 84-85, 229-30, 389, 397, 536, 606
   See also icon; index
individual, 433-34
induction, xvii-xviii, 208-151, 211, 212-13, 218, 221-22, 266, 396, 432, 552, 612-13
   crude, 396
   justification of, 394-95
   problem of, 169
   See also abduction; deduction; pessimistic meta-induction
inference
   to the best explanation, 43, 169, 219-22
   classification of, 208
   to an explanation, 209
inferentialism, 234
infinitesimals, 289, 290, 304
infinity, xxiv, 290, 294, 304
information, 227, 432-33
innate ideas, 387, 394-95
inquiry, 336, 370, 516-17
   community of, 139, 271-72, 325-26, 342, 346, 353-54, 357-58, 432, 459, 508, 542
   do not block (*see* reasoning, first rule of)
   doubt-belief model, 324, 327-28, 369-70
   end of, 346
   ethics of, 360, 508, 509-10
   theory of, 96
instinct, 627-28
Institute for Studies in Pragmaticism, xxxii-xxxiii
instrumentalism, 323
intelligence, scientific, 535, 537
intentionality, 578-79
interdisciplinarity, 544
internal, 410-11
internalism, moral, 134
interpretant, 85, 87, 541-42, 567-68, 572, 575, 609-10
   dynamic, 86
   final, 85, 399-400, 583
   immediate, 85, 233-34, 372, 577
   logical, 85, 378-79, 381
intersex people, 509-10
introspection, 387, 616-17

intuition, 430–31, 433–34, 516, 614, 615–16
    See also natural light
intuitionism, 181, 201–2, 308

J
Jakobson, Roman, 613–14
James, Henry, 8, 32–33, 45–46
James Sr., Henry, 6, 153, 480
James, William, xix, 5, 21, 28, 43, 49, 55–56, 83, 375
    consciousness, 77
    pragmatism, 84, 315–17, 319
    psychology, 123, 330
    See also will to believe
Jander, Rudolf, 590
Jastrow, Joseph, 48
Jevons, William Stanley, 10–11, 28–29, 44–45, 47, 218
Joas, Hans, 488
Johansen, Jørgen Dines, 538
Johns Hopkins University, xix, 9–10, 12, 16, 43
Jordan, Pascual, 426
Joyal-Street diagrams, 307–8
judgment, 106–7, 136–37, 265–66, 388–89, 616
    See also perceptual judgment
Jung, Matthias, 488

K
kairos, 351
kalon, to, 114, 115–16, 133, 140–41
Kamp, Hans, 611–12, 626–27
Kant, Immanuel, 6, 73, 78–79, 140, 156, 194, 331, 486–87, 555
    categorical imperative, 117
    categories, 64, 82–83, 196
    logic, 198–99, 208, 210, 216
    pragmatic, 136–37, 355
    refutation of idealism, 442–43, 444–47, 450
Kapitan, Tomas, 215
Karkazis, Katrina, 499
Kauffman, Louis, 304
Kelly, Maxwell, 307–8
Kennedy, John F., 12–13
Kent, Beverly, 142
Kepler, Johannes, 213–14, 219
Kessler, Suzanne, 502
Ketner, Kenneth Laine, 264–65
Keynes, John Maynard, 218

Kilstrup, Mogens, 592
King, Clarence, 587–88
Kirchheiss, Johannes, 56
Kitcher, Philip, 138
Kock, Anders, 305
Koyama, Emi, 509
Kruger, Barbara, 580, 581–82
Kuipers, Theo, 220
Kuratowski's ordered pairs, 303–4

L
Ladd-Franklin, Christine, 8, 48, 193–94, 197–98
Lamarckism, 553–54, 587–88
Lane, Robert, 200, 305, 459, 468–69, 593
Lange, Friedrich Albert, 180
Laqueur, Thomas, 502–3
Laudan, Larry, 215
Lavoisier, Antoine, 340
Lawrence Scientific School, xviii, 5–6, 542
laws of physics, 435–36, 507, 521–22, 594
    See also cosmology
Lawvere, William, 289, 307–8
Lawvere algebraic theory, 307–8
Lazzaroni, the, 4
LeConte, John, 5
lectio difficilior, 560, 561
Lees, Robert, 630–31
Legg, Cathy, 270–71, 461, 470, 472
Legisign, rhematic, 373
Leibniz, Gottfried Wilhelm, 289, 368–69
Leibniz's law, 210, 291
Lewis, Clarence Irving, 54–55, 307
Liebig, Justus von, 542
Liebig method, xvii, 542
limit, concept of, 289
linear associative algebra, xviii–xix, 4
linguisticism, 559
linguistics, 559, 601–2
    formal, 626–27
Lipton, Peter, 220, 221
Listing's census theorem, 303–4
Liszka, James, 541–42
Liszt, Franz, 32
Littrow, Karl L., 29
Locke, John, 7, 78, 81, 87, 141
    semiotics, 84
    simple ideas, 386

logic, 116, 168, 194–95, 202–3
  algebraic, 307–8, 601
  Aristotelian, 197–98
  diagrammatic, 199, 257, 264–65, 268, 270–71
  graphical, 257, 263–64, 307, 376–77
  grounded in ethics, 203, 337–38
  language or calculus, 199
  mathematical, xxxiii, 20–21, 172–73, 347n.6
  nonclassical, 292–93
  philosophy of, 183, 194, 226
  positive science, 195–96, 203
  of relations, 83–84, 196–97, 227, 303–4, 376–77, 481, 484
  of relatives, 32, 193–94, 240–41, 244, 245–46
  triadic, 200, 202, 305
  See also psychology; science (normative)
logical atom, 246
logical empiricists, 82, 213–14
logical sentiments, 354
logical positivism, 236–37
logica utens, 170
logicism, 181, 201–2
logos, 351–52
Longfellow, Henry Wadsworth, 5, 6, 7–8
Lorenz, Konrad, 590
love, 357, 431, 554
  ethical sentiment, 151–56
  evolutionary, 148–51, 435–36, 480–81, 553–54 (*see also* cosmology)
  law of, 353
  See also agape; agapism; agapism

M
MacColl, Hugh, 36–37
MacFarlane, John, 626
Maddalena, Giovanni, 305
Margolis, Joseph, 202
Marx, Karl, 80, 150
mathematics, xviii–xix, 54, 64, 98, 172–73, 181–83, 195–96, 201–2, 336–37
  diagrams, 199, 484
  observational science, 198–99
Maxwell, James Clerk, 11, 32, 45–46, 340
Mayr, Ernst, 592
Mcauliffe, William, 220–21
McCurdy, William James, 303–4
McKaughan, Daniel, 215

meaning empiricism, 394–95
meaning, inferentialist theory of, 234
medad, 246–47
  graphical, 247
Mendeleev, Dmitri, 62–63, 341–42
Mendenhall, Thomas Corwin, 14
meta-abduction, 558
metaphor, 523, 571–72
Metaphysical Club, 27–28, 46, 48, 335–36, 368
metaphysics, 195–96, 335, 337, 424
  evolutionary, 553–55
  scientific, 423–25, 436–37, 505, 507
methodeutic, 195–96, 367, 374
Mill, John Stuart, 156, 175
Minnameier, Gerhard, 220, 221
Minute Logic, 54, 167
Misak, Cheryl, 139–40, 330–31, 372–73, 464–66, 470–71
Misiewisz, Rory, 489
Mitchell, Oscar H., 197, 227, 242, 253
modal logic, 200, 307, 308
modernism, 301
Modistae, the, 602
molecular biology, 592
Moore, Matthew, 305
Morris, George Sylvester, 47, 48
Mouchez, Ernest, 34–35
Murphey, Murray, 196–97, 303
Murphy, Elliot, 625
musement, 482–83

N
Nagel, Thomas, 134
National Academy of Sciences, xvii, 4
naturalism, 78–79, 113, 487–88
natural light, 219, 430–31
  See also intuition
necessitarianism, 425
Neglected Argument, 359–60, 482–84
Nelson, Edward, 305
neo-Darwinism, 592, 594
neo-pragmatism, 114
neurolinguistics, 629
Neville, Robert Cummings, 486, 488
Newcomb, Simon, 9–10, 12, 14, 16, 51, 54
Newton, Isaac, 289, 520
Neyman-Pearson test, 220

Nickles, Thomas, 213–14
Nicod, Jean, 304
Niemoczynski, Leon, 487–88
nominalism, 81, 411, 425, 504, 506
   Daniel Dennett's, 80
   See also realism
nonstandard analysis, 305
normative sciences. *See* science
nouns, 606–7

O

object
   dynamic, 85–86, 233–34, 399, 567–68, 575–76, 578, 583
   immediate, 85–86, 233–34, 371–72, 399–400, 575, 579–80
objectivity, structural, 271–72
observation, collateral, 234–35, 371–72
Ochs, Peter, 486–87
Ockham, William of, 430
Ogden, Charles Kay, 55
Oliver, Jill, 504
ontological elimination, 374
Oostra, Arnold, 308
Open Court Publishing Company, xxxii
operational definition, 539
Oppolzer, Theodor von, 33
Orange, Donna, 485
Ostwald, Wilhelm, 319

P

Pacius, Julius, 211
Paine, Horatio, 111–12
Palmer, Edward H., 29
Palmer, George, 54
pansemiotics, 591
pantheism, 487–88
paper doubt, 181–82, 328, 369–70, 390, 516, 534
Parker, Joel, 501
Parker, Kelly, 143
Parmenides, 418
particularism, 78–79
Patterson, Carlile P., 31
Pauli, Wolfgang, 426
Pavlov's dog, 605–6
Peano, Guiseppe, 200, 631
Pearce, Trevor, 589–90

Pearson, Karl, 129–30, 141, 390–91
pedestrianism, 458
Peirce, Benjamin, xvii, 4, 5, 7–8, 9, 44, 46–47, 171–72, 479
   at the Coast Survey, xviii, 10, 30–31, 44
   death, 11, 35–36
   See also US Coast Survey
Peirce Sr., Benjamin, 4, 5
Peirce, Benjamin Mills, 4
Peirce, Charles Henry, xvii
Peirce, Helen Huntington. *See* Ellis, Helen Huntington Peirce
Peirce, Herbert Henry, 4
Peirce, James Mills ("Jem"), xvii–xviii, 4
Peirce, Juliette, CPP52, 12, 16, 18, 51–53
   at Arisbe, 12–13, 54
   marriage to, xix, 11, 36, 51
Peirce, Melusina ("Zina"). *See* Fay, Harriet Melusina
Peirce, Sarah Hunt Mills, 4
Peirce Edition Project, xxxii
Peirce pendulum, xviii–xix
Peirce's reduction thesis, 303–4
percept, 81–82, 270–71, 388, 391, 536
   type of sign, 397
perception, 62, 65, 78, 81–84, 290, 385–88, 452
   and abduction, 82, 211, 385, 395, 396, 398
   in esthetics, 102, 104, 118–19
   immediate, 442–43, 449–50
   laws of, 413, 517
   logic of, 86
   semiotics of, 86–87, 390, 396
   theory of, 270–71, 384–85
perceptual fact. *See* perceptual judgment
perceptual judgment, 81, 86–87, 270–71, 385, 389–90, 392–94, 397–400
   abduction, 82, 394–96
   semiosis, 86–87
percipuum, 82–83, 399–400
periodic table, 341–42
Perry, Ralph Barton, 8
persistence, 446
pessimistic meta-induction, 327, 564n.13
Peterson, James B., 77
phaneron, the, 61–62, 67, 83, 98–99
   classification of, 62

phaneroscopy, 61, 69, 98–99, 337, 376–77, 573, 623, 633
  See also phaneron, the
phenomenology. See phaneroscopy
philosophy, 337
  observational science, 337
  positive science, 38, 195, 337, 341
  task of, 195–96, 320–21, 323
Philström, Sami, 330–31
phonology, 610
Photometric Researches, xviii, 32–33, 38, 553
phronesis, 137–38, 351, 353, 358, 361
physicalism, 78–79
physical laws, 521–22, 594
physics, 47, 129–30, 317–18, 329–30, 337, 423–24, 425–26, 521, 586
  See also quantum physics
physiosemiosis, 591
Piaget, Jean, 628
Pickering, Edward C., 38
Pietarinen, Ahti-Veikko, 261–62, 264, 268–70, 308
Pike, Kenneth L., 603, 609–10, 623–24
Pikean theory, 603–4
Pinchot, Gifford, 12–13
Pinchot, James W, 12–13
Pinchot, Mary, 12–13
Pinchot, Nancy, 12–13
Plantamour, Émile, 32
Plato, 140–41, 156, 185, 360–61
Playfair, William, 263–64
pluralism, 483–84
Poe, Edgar Allan, 7, 214
poetic mood, 112–13
Popper, Karl, 213
Port Royal logic, 227, 628
possible-worlds semantics, 255
postmodernism, xix, 301
Potter, Vincent, 485
Pourtalai, Juliette Annette Froissy. See Peirce, Juliette
practical, 95–96, 114–15, 123–24, 134–35, 215, 340, 355–56
  effects, 151, 175–76, 316–17, 342, 343, 344–45, 378, 465, 508–9
  reasoning, 136–38
  wisdom, 361–63
  See also *phronesis*;pragmatic maxim; reason; science
practical theology, 488
practice vs theory, 351, 352–53, 360, 481–82
pragmatic ethos, 531
pragmaticism. See pragmatism
pragmatic maxim, 95, 135, 136–37, 175–76, 300–3, 317–19, 337, 342, 357, 368–69, 372–73, 384, 396, 461, 517–18
  applied to *reality*, 412, 413
  rule of logic, 337, 340
  See also practical
pragmatism, 84–85, 315–17, 335–36, 356, 367, 574–75
  in biology, 592
  critic of meaning, 340, 377–78
  normative, 481
  proof of, 85, 86, 301–3
  See also practical; pragmatic maxim
pragmatistic adequacy, 108
prebits, 376–77
precission, 83, 110n.11
predicate, adicity of, 65–66
predicate forms, three types of, 66
present, the, 450–51
Price, Huw, 330–31
Prigogine, Ilya, 589
probability, 48, 216, 218, 219–20, 326–27, 426–27, 534
  frequency theory of, 209
Prodi, Giorgio, 590
proposition, 194–95, 197–98, 226–29, 236, 246–47, 336
protasis, 198–99
protocol sentences, 386
protographs, 244–45, 247–48
protoplasm, 588–89, 593–94
protosemiosis, 594
Proudfoot, Wayne, 485–86
Psillos, Stathis, 219, 220
psychical research, 396
psychologism, 202–3, 543, 559
  See also psychology
psychology, 16, 28, 49, 65, 70, 132, 271–72, 320, 331, 522–25
  cognitive, 175
  and logic, 202–3, 262, 387, 390, 533–34

Ptolemy, 559
Ptolemy's star catalog, 32–33
Putnam, Hilary, 172, 330–31, 539
Putnam, Ruth-Anna, 330–31
Pythagoras, 561–62

Q

quantification, 240–41, 256–57, 306–7
quantificational dependencies, 245–46, 252–53
quantifiers, 197, 241–42, 252, 536
    Frege, 285–86
quantum entanglement, 428, 435–36, 437
quantum indeterminacy, 434
    See also Heisenberg; tychism
quantum physics, 303–4, 425–26, 435
quantum superposition, 426–27
quasi-mind, 543, 575–76
    See also interpretant
Queiroz, João, 592
quidditas, 429–30, 431
quincuncial world map, xviii–xix
Quine, William Van Orman, 78–79, 169, 173, 178, 181–82, 256–57, 307
    Duhem-Quine thesis, 611

R

racism, 158–59, 491n.8
radical empiricism, 315–16
Ramsey, Frank, 54–55
Raposa, Michael, 481, 486
rationality, 73–74, 354
    deliberative, 361–62
Rawls, John, 156
real, 138, 324, 409–11, 412, 414–15, 417, 432, 462, 518
    See also generals; realism; reality
realism, 370, 381, 425, 430, 459, 468, 552
    metaphysical, 80–81, 233, 305
    moral, 138
    propositional, 232–33
    scholastic, 254, 411, 425, 432, 459, 472–73, 500, 506–7, 509–10
    scientific, 211, 233
    Scotist, 233, 423–24
    See also anti-realism; nominalism
reality, 81–84, 99, 324, 409–10, 461–62, 518
    degrees of, 73–74

    gradational, 417–19
    See also existence; real; realism
reason, 351–52
    human, 354
    light of, 179
    living, 359–60
    practical, 136–37, 194, 203, 351, 352–53, 355, 359
    theoretical, 195, 203, 351, 352–53, 359
reason, first rule of, 56, 123–24, 194–95, 344–45, 508
reasonableness, 133–34, 339, 353
    concrete, 370, 381
    growth of, 103, 142–43
    ultimate end, 142
reasoning, 338–40
    diagrammatic, 228
    self-corrective, 339, 352, 354–55
    See also practical
Rechtsgefühl, 178
recursion, 624–25
reduction thesis, 621–22
Reichenbach, Hans, 213
Reid, Thomas, 130, 443
relational theory, 428
religion, 8–9, 323, 358, 479–84, 485–86, 488–89, 505
replica, 230
representamen. *See* sign
Repsold & Sohne, 31
research, economy of, 344, 345
rheme, 84–85, 228, 236, 377
Ribot, Théodule, 11, 34
Richardson, Sarah, 501–2
Riemann surface, 309
Roberts, Don, 242, 244, 254, 307, 308
Robin catalog, xxxii
Robin, Richard, xxxii–xxxiii
Robinson, Abraham, 289, 305
Robinson, Andrew, 489
Rock, Irvin, 81–82
Roe v. Wade, 581–82
Rohr, David, 482–83
Romanini, Vinicius, 592
Romanticism, Concordian, 8–9
Roosevelt, Theodore, 12–13
Rorty, Richard, 114, 330–31, 485

Rothschild, Friedrich, 590
Rovelli, Carlo, 426, 435
Royce, Josiah, xix, 8, 43, 48, 55, 435–36, 484–85
Russell, Bertrand, 20–21, 55, 232–33, 236–37, 631
Russell, Francis, xix, 55–56

S
Sachverhalt, 232–33
Santayana, George, 15
Sapir, Edward, 602–3, 628
Saussure, Ferdinand de, 591, 602–3
Schelling, Friedrich, 152, 331–32, 480
Schiller, Ferdinand Canning Scott, 315–16
Schiller, Friedrich, 111–12, 140, 144, 486–87
Schröder, Ernst, 43, 54, 200, 245–46, 631
Schrödinger, Erwin, 427–28
Schurz, Gerhard, 219
science, 336, 345–46
   of discovery (*see* science: heuretic)
   economy of, 265–66, 271–72
   heuretic, 97–99, 336, 376
   history of, 551, 554–55
   logic of, 264–66, 369
   normative, 84–85, 94–97, 99, 108, 114–16, 132, 133, 137–38, 160, 195, 337, 392–93
   positive, 38, 336–37, 343
   practical, 111, 114, 116–17, 336
   See also inquiry; scientific method
sciences, classification of, 194, 532–33, 543, 555–56
   natural, 557–58
scientific method, 28, 43, 329, 336, 387, 412–13, 424–25, 518, 613
scientific reform, 267–68
Searle, John, 604–5
Sebeok, Thomas A., 587, 590, 591
secondness, 28, 66, 83–84, 88, 99, 100, 115, 415–16, 434, 506–7, 572, 613
   degenerate, 69, 74
   in the phaneron, 71, 141, 202, 392–93
   See also categories; firstness; thirdness
self, the, 346, 358–60, 446
self-consciousness, 123
self-control, 94, 100, 103, 118, 133–34, 154–55, 159, 338, 339, 541–42
   See also deliberation

Sellars, Wilfrid, 79, 354–55
seme, 236, 397
Semetski, Inna, 542–43
semiosis, 86–87, 177–78, 541–42, 567, 575–76, 577, 590–91, 592
semiotics, 268, 537, 540–41, 543–44, 567, 591
   logic, 84–85, 94, 160, 234
   phaneroscopy/perception, 71–72, 390, 396–400, 540–41
   rabbinic, 486
   Saussurean, 591
   See also edusemiotics; pansemiotics
sensationalism, 375
sensations, 30, 65, 78, 121, 342–43, 375
sentiment, 123–24
   agape, 151
   moral, 130
sentimentalism, 130–31
   conservative, 481–82
set theory, 183, 299–300, 303–4, 305, 507
sex, philosophy of, 499, 505
Sextus Empiricus, 201
sexual binarism, 501
Shaler, Nathaniel Southgate, 56
sham reasoning, 67, 132, 432
Sharot, Tali, 524
Sharov, Alexei, 594
Short, T. L., 133, 139, 371
sign, 567–68, 589
   relation, 86
   vehicle, 235–36
   See also icon; index; semiosis; semiotics; symbol
signs, classification of, 86, 87, 227–28, 568, 594
sinsign, 227–28, 230, 568–71
Skagestad, Peter, 589–90
skepticism, 201, 444–45, 451–53, 470–71
slavery, 5
Smiley, Timothy, 173
Smith, John E., 483, 485
Smithsonian Institution, xvii
Smokler, Howard 218
social Darwinism, 130, 553
sociobiology, 594
somaesthetics, 116–19, 125
Sowa, John, 308, 626–27
speculative grammar, 195–96, 531–32, 534, 602

speculative rhetoric, 531, 534, 541–42
speech acts, 538–39, 625–27
Spencer-Brown, George, 282–83, 304
Spinoza, Baruch, 122
St. John, gospel of, 153–54
Stables, Andrew, 542–43
statistical deduction, 209
Stenning, Keith, 244–45
Stjernfelt, Frederik, 592
Stout, George F., 77
Stout, Jeffrey, 485
Studies in Logic, 48
subjectivism
    German, 181–82, 560–61
    moral, 137, 138
summum bonum, 108, 113–14, 137–38, 143
superassertibility, 464
supermultitudinous, 305
surreal numbers, 289, 290, 305
Swedenborg, Emmanuel, 480
Sylvester, James Joseph, 48, 50–51, 53, 55, 263–64
symbiogenesis, 592
symbol, 84–85, 220–21, 227–28, 300, 397, 537, 604
    See also icon; index; sign
synechism, 113–14, 123, 131, 142–43, 418, 434–35, 505–6
    See also continuity

T
tagmemics, 609–10
Tarski, Alfred, 308
teleology, 80, 148–51, 152, 160–61, 355–56, 557–58, 595
telepathy, 396
telos, 152
Tembrock, Günter, 590
terminology, ethics of. *See* ethics
Thagard, Paul, 220, 221
theology, 480, 484–88, 490
theorematic reasoning, 198
theosemiotic, 486–87
Thilly, Frank, 141
thing in itself, 460
thirdness, 99, 141, 150, 303–4, 394, 434, 506–7, 509
    degenerate, 67
    logical, 179, 181
    in phaneroscopy/perception, 66, 71–72, 74, 83–84, 88–89, 386, 393–94, 395, 399
    See also categories; firstness; secondness
Thomson, J. Arthur, 500–1
Thoreau, Henry David, 6
Throwbridge, John, 396
Tiercelin, Claudine, 203
Tillich, Paul, 488
Tomalin, Marcus, 630–31
tone-token-type distinction, 67, 80, 235–36, 623–24
topological logic, 307–8
topology, 291, 295, 303–4
transcendentalism, 202–3
    Emerson, 7, 8–9
    Kant, 137, 233
transubstantiation, 347n.3, 374
Trimble, Todd, 307–8
Trinitarianism, 479
Trout, Lara, 154, 158–59, 161
truth, 325, 458, 463
    consensus theory of, 538
    contextual, 559
    convergence theory, 138
    correspondence theory of, 324, 459, 466–67, 468
    deflationism, 460, 467, 471–72
    genealogy of, 459
    in the phaneron, 71–72
    pragmatic conception of, 346, 414
Turing test, 604–5
Turquette, Atwell, 200
tychasm, 149–50
tychism, 434
Tyndall, John, 329
type-token distinction. *See* tone-token-type distinction

U
Uexküll, Jacob von, 590, 594, 595
Uexküll, Thure von, 590
understanding
    contextual theory of, 525–26
    feeling of, 519–24
universal grammar, 602–3, 632

universal realism, 430
universals, 78–79, 180–81, 233, 430, 432, 434, 436–37
  See also generals
universe of signs, 576–77
US Coast Survey, xvii, 9–10, 12, 14, 16, 26, 30, 37, 44, 45, 50
  dismissal from xix, 9–10, 16–17, 47, 53–54
utilitarianism, 141

V
van Fraassen, Bas, 219, 220
van Heijenoort, Jean, 199
Vargas, Francisco, 305–6
Veblen, Thorstein, 49
VehKavaara, Tommi, 594
Venn diagram, 180
Venn, John, 49, 209
Victoria Lady Welby, xix, 54, 55, 85
Voevodsky homotopy, 301–3
von Foerster, Heinz, 296
von Liebig, Justus, xvii

W
Walton, Douglas, 220
Watt, James, 263–64
Weasel, Lisa, 509
Weierstrass, Karl, 171–72, 174
Weil, Simone, 486–87
Weiss, Edmund, 29
Weiss, Paul, xxxi–xxxii
Weltanschauung, 195–96, 337, 341
West, Cornel, 485
Whewell, William, 263–64, 265–66, 267, 369, 551, 552–53, 555–56
  on science, 559
Whipple, John, 7–8
Whitehead, Alfred North, 20–21, 488, 542–43, 631
Wiener, Philip, 589–90
Wiggins, David, 138
will to believe, 45–46, 328, 347n.3, 481–82
Wilson, John Cook, CP3P61
Wittgenstein, Ludwig, 55, 232–33, 236–37
Woods, John, 216
would-bes, 85, 254, 411, 434
Wright, Chauncey, 6, 28, 43, 46
Wright, Crispin, 464

Y
Yu, Shiyang, 220

Z
Zeller, Eduard, 560
Zellweger, Shea, 304
Zeman, Jay, 307, 308
Zenker, Frank, 220
Zermelo–Fraenkel set theory, 299–300, 305–6
zero, 293